Fodor's 96

USA

"When it comes to information on regional history, what to see and do, and shopping, these guides are exhaustive."

—*USAir Magazine*

"Usable, sophisticated restaurant coverage, with an emphasis on good value."

—Andy Birsh, *Gourmet Magazine* columnist

"Valuable because of their comprehensiveness."

—*Minneapolis Star-Tribune*

"Fodor's always delivers high quality...thoughtfully presented...thorough."

—*Houston Post*

"An excellent choice for those who want everything under one cover."

—*Washington Post*

Fodor's Travel Publications, Inc.
New York • Toronto • London • Sydney • Auckland

Fodor's USA

Editor: Jillian Stone

Editorial Contributors: David Allan, Steven K. Amsterdam, Christopher Billy, Jenner Bishop, Bob Blake, Andrew Collins, Fionn Davenport, Echo Garrett, Dawn Lawson, Bevin McLaughlin, Danny Mangin, Chelsea Mauldin, Rebecca Miller, Anastasia Mills, Kristen Perrault, Linda K. Schmidt, Melanie Sponholz, Mary Ellen Schultz, Nancy van Itallie, Stephen Wolf

Creative Director: Fabrizio LaRocca

Cartographer: David Lindroth

Cover Photograph: Nicholas Devore III/Photographers/Aspen

Text Design: Between the Covers

Copyright

ISBN 0-679-03078-6

Special Sales

Fodor's Travel Publications are available at special discounts for bulk purchases for sales promotions or premiums. Special editions, including personalized covers, excerpts of existing guides, and corporate imprints, can be created in large quantities for special needs. For more information, contact your local bookseller or write to Special Markets, Fodor's Travel Publications, 201 East 50th Street, New York, NY 10022. Inquiries from Canada should be directed to your local Canadian bookseller or sent to Random House of Canada, Ltd., Marketing Department, 1265 Aerowood Drive, Mississauga, Ontario L4W 1B9. Inquiries from the United Kingdom should be sent to Fodor's Travel Publications, 20 Vauxhall Bridge Road, London SW1V 2SA.

MANUFACTURED IN THE UNITED STATES OF AMERICA

10 9 8 7 6 5 4 3 2 1

CONTENTS

*Italic entries are maps.

ON THE ROAD WITH FODOR'S

WRITERS LAMENT the destruction of the American wilderness, yet it's good to remember how much of our landscape remains essentially unchanged from the days when the earliest explorers stepped ashore. Flowers continue to bloom each spring in the deserts of the Southwest, the oceans go on pounding the coasts of Oregon and Maine, and the Great Plains still stretch as far as the eye can see beneath endless arches of sky. From the Grand Canyon to the Hudson Highlands, from Yellowstone to the Smokies, you can still see much of what the early settlers saw, and with the same sense of wonder and awe.

A good travel guide is like a wonderful traveling companion. It's charming, it's brimming with sound recommendations and solid ideas, it pulls no punches in describing lodging and dining establishments, and it's consistently full of fascinating facts that make you view what you've traveled to see in a rich new light. In the creation of *USA '96,* we at Fodor's have gone to great lengths to provide you with the very best of all possible traveling companions—and to make your trip the best of all possible vacations.

WHAT'S NEW

A New Design

If this is not the first Fodor's guide you've purchased, you'll immediately notice our new look. More readable and easier to use than ever? We think so—and we hope you do, too.

Let Us Do Your Booking

Our writers have scoured the United States to come up with an extensive and well-balanced list of the best B&Bs, inns, resorts, and hotels, both small and large, new and old. But you don't have to beat the bushes to come up with a reservation. Now we've teamed up with an established hotel-booking service to make it easy for you to secure a room at the property of your choice. It's fast, it's free, and confirmation is guaranteed. If your first choice is booked, the operators can line up your second right away. Just call 800/FODORS-1 or 800/363-6771 (0800/89-1030 in Great Britain, 0014/800-12-8271 in Australia, 1800/55-9109 in Ireland).

Travel Updates

In addition, just before your trip, you may want to order a Fodor's Worldview Travel Update. From local publications all over the United States, the lively, cosmopolitan editors at Worldview gather information on concerts, plays, opera, dance performances, gallery and museum shows, sports competitions, and other special events that coincide with your visit. See the order blank at the back of this book, call 800/799-9609, or fax 800/799-9619.

And in the USA

In 1996 the United States greets travelers with world-class sporting events and new teams, government-mandated improvements in access for people with disabilities, new domestic airlines, and affordable dining and lodging options. What doesn't change is the country's delight in celebrating anniversaries, harvests, history, and itself.

For a glimpse of down-home all-American life, nothing beats the annual **state and county fairs,** farm shows, and special festivals that effervesce around the country each year. From the New York State Fair to the Iowa State Fair (which features a life-size cow sculpted entirely of butter) to the Georgia Apple Festival and Arts and Crafts Fair, attractions include exhibitions of livestock and local artists' works, pie baking and eating contests, and much more. State tourism boards can supply schedules of events.

The big news in sports is that Atlanta, Georgia, hosts the **1996 Olympic Games.** After spending several hundred million dollars, the city is fully prepared to be inundated by visitors this year (about 11 million tickets went on sale for the various events). Many of the new facilities built for the games—including the 85,000-seat Olympic Stadium, the Velodrome, and an aquatic center on the Georgia Tech campus—will become venues for sports events and other entertainment following the games.

The National Football League (NFL) and the National Basketball Association (NBA)—are expanding. Cities such as Jacksonville and Charlotte now have football teams to root for, and for the first time in basketball history, the NBA has awarded franchises to Canada, specifically to Toronto and Vancouver.

If you plan to travel by **car** in unfamiliar urban areas in 1996, you should be aware of a recent trend in crime—car-jacking. Use discretion, and when it seems prudent, keep your car doors locked. When leaving a freeway in a major city, be sure you know where the exit ramp leads; if possible, call ahead to your destination for clear, detailed directions from the highway.

On a more pleasant note, National Forest **Scenic Byways** are auto-touring routes that are often as appealing as your destination. Begun in 1988, when National Forest Service employees were invited to choose the roads they thought most beautiful, the Scenic Byways program has expanded from its original 50 selections to 122 roads that cover 7,002 miles in 34 states, and new routes continue to be designated. Regional Forest Service offices or the U.S. Forest Service Public Affairs office can provide listings.

With the current administration in Washington seemingly more attuned to environmental concerns than previous administrations, **ecotourism** within the country is growing. Local environmental groups are sponsoring service outings—cleanups, trail maintenance, tree planting—and nature preserves are welcoming visitors in order to educate them about the role that wilderness areas have in the greater environment and to inform them of the conflicts and problems that threaten local ecosystems. The Sierra Club (*see* Special-Interest Travel) and the Nature Conservancy (☎ 703/841–5300) are among the national organizations that arrange field trips and other activities.

Train travel in the United States took a revolutionary step on April 4, 1993, when **Amtrak** began the country's first regularly scheduled **transcontinental** passenger service, from Los Angeles to Miami. And in 1995, after a 14-year hiatus, Amtrak reinstated its Pacific Northwest line from Seattle to Vancouver, British Columbia. Financial problems, however, have led Amtrak to reduce train frequency on certain routes, and to eliminate some routes entirely. Faced with **Amtrak**'s threat to discontinue its *Montrealer* service in 1995 due to low ridership—which would leave Vermont with no passenger rail service—the state chose to subsidize the new *Vermonter,* which still skirts the state's eastern border before slicing over toward Burlington, but commences in Hartford, CT (instead of Washington, DC) and terminates in St. Alban's, VT (instead of Montréal).

Seven new domestic airlines have started up: Family, Kiwi, Morris, Reno, Skybus, UltrAir, and ValuJet. Except for UltrAir, they all offer various low-fare options based on one-class, high-density seating and/or high-volume or underserved routes. UltrAir targets business travelers by offering superior service and seating at prices comparable to full fares charged by the major airlines. Because airlines can go under as quickly as they start up, the challenge for these new operations will be to ride out the majors' fare cuts and frequent-flier lures.

The 1990 **Americans with Disabilities Act,** which established national access standards for public facilities, continues to be put into effect. Throughout the country you'll see lower public telephones, lower control panels with Braille indicators on elevators, fire alarms that flash as well as sound, ramps or elevators at restaurant and hotel entrances, more parking for people with disabilities, specially equipped hotel rooms and baths, and other much-needed changes.

Hotels in the United States are increasingly focusing on families and fitness-conscious travelers. Many are offering organized programs for children and teens and are expanding or installing health clubs and spas as well as providing parklands for "light adventure" and group activities such as bicycling, in-line skating, motocross, rodeos, and team sports. One Alaska chain (**Westmark**) even equips its properties with in-room fitness machines. Environmental concerns are not ignored either: The Hartford Air & Water Company has begun to install EverGreen Rooms, defined as "environmentally upgraded guest rooms." These include air-purification systems that remove dust, pollen, and mold spores from the air; a separate, filtered, drinking-water tap; and a filtered massage system for showers. Many hotels also offer special rates for families and a variety of packages that give you a choice of meal plans and sports and fitness activities. Booking your stay in advance is a cost-cutter at several hotel chains. Be sure to check your options when reserving.

The American Hotel and Motel Association has launched a campaign to make travelers conscious of **security** when they're away from home; peepholes and dead bolts on room doors are increasingly common, and in-hotel television channels highlight safety measures.

Restaurant owners in major U.S. cities have responded to the sluggish economy and to half-empty dining rooms by maintaining or, in many cases, lowering prices. In addition, a number of expensive restaurants, such as Le Bec-Fin in Philadelphia and Spiaggia in Chicago, have opened spin-off cafés and grills (often by converting a room of the existing restaurant) that have more casual decor and less-expensive fare. Taking this attitude of value for money one step further, many restaurants now serve portions that range from the hefty to the gargantuan. At such places as Carmine's in New York City, entrées are so large that diners commonly share a single order. U.S. visitors from rural and suburban areas will find dining in cities more affordable and relaxed than they may have expected; visitors from major European and Asian cities will find it a downright bargain.

FODOR'S CHOICE

No two people will agree on what makes a perfect vacation, but it's fun and helpful to know what others think. We hope you'll have a chance to experience some of Fodor's Choices yourself while traveling in the United States. For detailed information about each entry, refer to the appropriate chapters in this guidebook.

Historic Sites and Monuments

Northeast

Bunker Hill (Boston, MA)

Plimoth Plantation, (Plymouth, MA)

Ellis Island (New York, NY)

Statue of Liberty (New York, NY)

Mid-Atlantic

Independence National Historical Park (Philadelphia, PA)

Gettysburg National Military Park (Gettysburg, PA)

Washington Monument (Washington, DC)

Frederick Douglass National Historic Site (Washington, DC)

Vietnam Memorial (Washington, DC)

Harper's Ferry National Park (Harper's Ferry, WV)

Southeast

Civil Rights Memorial (Montgomery, AL)

Martin Luther King, Jr., National Historic District (Atlanta, GA)

Ft. Sumter National Monument (Charleston, SC)

Mississippi Valley

George Rogers Clark National Historical Park (Vincennes, IN)

Shaker Village of Pleasant Hill (Harrodsburg, KY)

Great Plains

George Washington Carver National Monument (MO)

Mt. Rushmore National Memorial (SD)

Southwest

Canyon de Chelly (Chinle, AZ)

Petroglyph National Monument (Albuquerque, NM)

Mission Ysleta (near El Paso, TX)

West Coast

Olvera Street (Los Angeles, CA)

Fort Clatsop National Memorial (Astoria, OR)

Pacific

The Pacific Ketchikan Totem Parks (AK)

Historic Buildings

Northeast

African Meeting House (Boston, MA)

Faneuil Hall (Boston, MA)

United Nations Building (New York, NY)

Mansions (Newport, RI)

Mid-Atlantic
B&O Railroad Museum (Baltimore, MD)

Monticello (Charlottesville, VA)

The White House (Washington, DC)

Southeast
Sixteenth Street Baptist Church (Birmingham, AL)

Mississippi Valley
The Old State House (Little Rock, AR)

Old Ursuline Convent (New Orleans, LA)

Rosalie (Natchez, MS)

Great Plains
Mark Twain (Samuel Clemens) Home (Hannibal, MO)

Southwest
Palace of the Governors (Santa Fe, NM)

West Coast
Hearst Castle (San Simeon, CA)

Sutter's Mill (Coloma, CA)

Pacific
Iolani Palace (Honolulu, HI)

Natural Wonders

Northeast
Niagara Falls (NY)

Mid-Atlantic
Delaware Water Gap (PA/NJ)

Natural Bridge (Natural Bridge, VA)

Southeast
Okefenokee (GA)

Mississippi Valley
Hot Springs (AR)

Mammoth Cave (KY)

Bayou Teche (Acadiana, LA)

Midwest
Pictured Rocks National Lakeshore (Munising, MI)

Boundary Waters (MN)

Apostle Islands National Lakeshore (WI)

Great Plains
Badlands (ND/SD)

Southwest
Grand Canyon (AZ)

Lake Tahoe (NV/CA)

Carlsbad Caverns (NM)

Palo Duro Canyon (TX)

Bryce Canyon (UT)

Zion Canyon (UT)

Rockies
Old Faithful Geyser (Yellowstone, WY)

West Coast
El Capitan and Half Dome (Yosemite National Park, CA)

Joshua Tree National Park (CA)

Muir Woods (Mill Valley, CA)

Crater Lake (OR)

Rain Forest (Olympic Peninsula, WA)

Pacific
Mt. McKinley (AK)

Kilauea Volcano (Hawaii, HI)

Viewpoints

Northeast
John Hancock Tower (Boston, MA)

World Trade Center Tower (New York, NY)

Mid-Atlantic
Top of the World–World Trade Center (Baltimore, MD)

Mississippi Valley
Sabine Wildlife Refuge Tower (LA)

Lookout Mountain (Chatanooga, TN)

Newfound Gap (near Gatlinburg, TN)

Midwest
Chicago from a boat on the river (IL)

Wyalusing State Park (Bagley, WI)

Great Plains
Mississippi River from Eagle Point Park (Dubuque, IA)

Theodore Roosevelt National Park from Painted Canyon Overlook (ND)

Southwest
Sandia Crest (Albuquerque, NM)

Dead Horse Point (near Moab, UT)

Rockies
Trail Ridge Road, Rocky Mountain National Park (CO)

West Coast
Golden Gate Bridge and San Francisco from Marin Headlands (CA)

Napa Valley from a hot-air balloon (CA)

Bixby Creek Bridge (Big Sur, CA)

Three Capes Scenic Loop (northern coast, OR)

Pacific
Calving tidewater glaciers from the deck of a cruise ship (AK)

Mt. Haleakala (Maui, HI)

Museums

Northeast
Museum of Fine Arts (Boston, MA)

Metropolitan Museum of Art (New York, NY)

Museum of Modern Art (New York, NY)

Frick Collection (New York, NY)

Mid-Atlantic
Winterthur (Wilmington, DE)

The Walters Art Gallery (Baltimore, MD)

The Chesapeake Bay Maritime Museum (St. Michaels, MD)

Smithsonian Institution (Washington, DC)

Phillips Collection (Washington, DC)

Midwest
Art Institute (Chicago, IL)

Museum of Science and Industry (Chicago, IL)

Walker Art Center (Minneapolis, MN)

Great Plains
Nelson-Atkins Museum of Art (Kansas City, MO)

Southwest
Navajo Nation Museum (Window Rock, AZ)

Museum of International Folk Art (Santa Fe, NM)

Kimbell Art Museum (Fort Worth, TX)

West Coast
San Francisco Museum of Modern Art (CA)

Los Angeles County Museum of Art (CA)

Los Angeles Museum of Contemporary Art (CA)

Seattle Art Museum (Seattle, WA)

Pacific
Alaska State Museum (Juneau, AK)

Towns

Northeast
Nantucket, MA

Hanover, NH

Middlebury, VT

Mid-Atlantic
Annapolis, MD

Solomons, MD

New Hope, PA

Middleburg, VA

Shepherdstown, WV

Southeast
Key West, FL

Savannah, GA

Charleston, SC

Mississippi Valley
Eureka Springs, AR

Oxford, MS

Midwest
Madison, IN

New Harmony, IN

Mackinac Island, MI

Lanesboro, MN

Great Plains
Amana Colonies, IA

Lindsborg, KS

Nebraska City, NE

Southwest
Acoma, NM

Jefferson, TX

Park City, UT

Rockies
Aspen, CO

Steamboat Springs, CO

West Coast
Mendocino, CA

Pacific
Homer/Halibut Cove, AK

Neighborhoods

Northeast
Beacon Hill (Boston, MA)

Greenwich Village (New York, NY)

Mid-Atlantic

Fells Point (Baltimore, MD)

Society Hill (Philadelphia, PA)

Georgetown (Washington, DC)

Southeast

Old Salem (Winston-Salem, NC)

Miss. Valley

Old Louisville (Louisville, KY)

French Quarter (New Orleans, LA)

Midwest

Summit Avenue/Ramsey Hill (St. Paul, MN)

German Village (Columbus, OH)

Southwest

Plaza (Santa Fe, NM)

Deep Ellum (Dallas, TX)

West Coast

North Beach (San Francisco, CA)

Rodeo Drive (Beverly Hills, CA)

Pioneer Square (Seattle, WA)

Parks and Gardens

Northeast

Central Park (New York, NY)

Mid-Atlantic

Winterthur Gardens (Winterthur, DE)

Sherwood Gardens (Baltimore, MD)

Longwood Gardens (Brandywine Valley, PA)

Dumbarton Oaks (Washington, DC)

Southeast

Bellingrath Gardens (Mobile, AL)

Town squares (Savannah, GA)

Biltmore Estate Gardens (Asheville, NC)

Magnolia Plantation (Charleston, SC)

Mississippi Valley

Tennessee Botanical Gardens at Cheekwood (Nashville, TN)

Great Plains

International Peace Garden (ND)

Southwest

Arizona–Sonora Desert Museum (Tucson, AZ)

Water Gardens Park (Fort Worth, TX)

West Coast

Golden Gate Park (San Francisco, CA)

Balboa Park (San Diego, CA)

Washington Park International Rose Test Garden and Japanese Gardens (Portland, OR)

Beaches

Northeast

Cape Cod National Seashore (MA)

Jones Beach (Long Island, NY)

Mid-Atlantic

Assateague Island (MD/VA)

Island Beach State Park (NJ)

Southeast

South Lido Park (Sarasota, FL)

Cumberland Island National Seashore (GA)

Hilton Head Island (SC)

Mississippi Valley

Gulf Islands National Seashore (Ocean Springs, MS)

Midwest

Indiana Dunes National Lakeshore (IN)

Great Plains

Lake McConaughy State Recreation Area (NE)

Southwest

Padre Island National Seashore (TX)

West Coast

Point Reyes National Seashore (CA)

Corona del Mar (CA)

Pismo Beach (CA)

Cannon Beach (OR)

Pacific

Kauanoa Beach (Hawaii, HI)

Wailea's five crescent beaches (Maui, HI)

Amusement and Theme Parks

Northeast

Coney Island (NY)

Mid-Atlantic

Adventure World (Mitchellville, MD)

Six Flags Great Adventure (Jackson, NJ)

Sesame Place (Langhorne, PA)

Southeast

Walt Disney World (Orlando, FL)

Mississippi Valley
Opryland USA (Nashville, TN)

Midwest
Six Flags Great America (Gurnee, IL)

Cedar Point Amusement Park (Sandusky, OH)

Great Plains
Silver Dollar City (Branson, MO)

Worlds of Fun (Kansas City, MO)

Southwest
Astroworld/Waterworld (Houston, TX)

West Coast
Disneyland (Anaheim, CA)

Universal Studios (Universal City, CA)

Pacific
Alaskaland Park (Fairbanks, AK)

Hotels

Northeast
Wyndham Copley Plaza (Boston, MA; $$$$)

The Mark (New York, NY; $$$$)

The Fitzpatrick (New York, NY; $$$)

Mid-Atlantic
Harbor Court (Baltimore, MD; $$$$)

The Homestead (Hot Springs, VA; $$$$)

Hay–Adams Hotel (Washington, DC; $$$$)

The Greenbrier (White Sulphur Springs, WV; $$$$)

Southeast
Casa Grande (Miami Beach, FL; $$$$)

Orlando Heritage Inn (Orlando, FL; $$)

Ritz-Carlton, Atlanta (Atlanta, GA; $$$$)

Mississippi Valley
The Seelbach (Louisville, KY; $$$)

Windsor Court Hotel (New Orleans, LA; $$$$)

Midwest
The Drake (Chicago, IL; $$$$)

Lafayette Hotel (Marietta, OH; $$)

Great Plains
Island Guest Ranch (Ames, OK; $$$)

Southwest
Hopi Cultural Center Motel (Second Mesa, AZ; $$)

Menger Hotel (San Antonio, TX; $$$)

Rockies
Oxford (Denver, CO; $$$)

Coeur d'Alene Resort (Coeur d'Alene, ID; $$$$)

Old Faithful Inn (Yellowstone, WY; $$)

West Coast
Huntington Hotel (San Francisco, CA; $$$$)

Ritz-Carlton Laguna Niguel (Dana Point, CA; $$$$)

Stephanie Inn (Cannon Beach, OR; $$$–$$$$)

Pacific
Camp Denali (Denali National Park, AK; $$$$)

Hotel Hana-Maui (Maui, HI; $$$)

Restaurants

Northeast
The Golden Lamb Buttery (Brooklyn, CT; $$$$)

Hurricane (Ogunquit, ME; $$–$$$)

Lespinasse (New York, NY; $$$$)

Boca Chica (New York, NY; $)

Mid-Atlantic
Tio Pepe (Baltimore, MD; $$$)

Le Bec-Fin (Philadelphia, PA; $$$$)

Jean-Louis at the Watergate Hotel (Washington, DC; $$$$)

Red Fox (Snowshoe, WV; $$$–$$$$)

Southeast
Louie's Back Yard (Key West, FL; $$$)

Le Coq au Vin (Orlando, FL; $$)

Elizabeth on 37th (Savannah, GA; $$$)

Mississippi Valley
Vincenzo's (Louisville, KY; $$$)

Commander's Palace (New Orleans, LA; $$$$)

Camellia Grill (New Orleans, LA; $)

Nick's (Jackson, MS; $$$)

Midwest
Charlie Trotter's (Chicago, IL; $$$$)

Lelli's Inn (Detroit, MI; $$)

Great Plains
Arthur Bryant's (Kansas City, MO; $)

Mandan Drug (Mandan, ND; $)

Cattlemen's Steak House (Oklahoma City, OK; $)

Southwest

Ristorante La Traviata (Santa Fe, NM; $$)

Calle Doce (Dallas, TX; $$)

Glitretind (Park City, UT; $$$$)

Rockies

Strings (Denver, CO; $$$)

West Coast

Chez Panisse (Berkeley, CA; $$$)

Stars (San Francisco, CA; $$$)

Granita (Malibu, CA; $$–$$$)

Pacific

The Double Musky (Anchorage, AK; $$–$$$)

Ka Ohelo Room (Hawaii Volcanoes National Park, Hawaii, HI; $)

Nightlife

Northeast

East Village, New York, NY (club of the moment)

Mid-Atlantic

Atlantic City, NJ (casinos and shows)

Georgetown, Washington, DC (political satire)

Southeast

Key West, FL (evening street performers)

Miami Beach, FL (dance clubs)

Mississippi Valley

Mountain View, AR (folk music)

New Orleans, LA (jazz, R&B, Cajun music)

Nashville, TN (country music)

Memphis, TN (blues)

Midwest

Chicago, IL (blues)

Great Plains

Branson, MO (country music)

Southwest

Dallas, TX (eclectic music in Deep Ellum neighborhood)

Las Vegas, NV (casinos, shows)

Rockies

Montana and Wyoming (cowboy bars)

Colorado (resorts' après-ski)

West Coast

Los Angeles, CA (comedy clubs)

South of Market, San Francisco, CA (dance clubs)

Pacific Northwest (brew pubs)

HOW TO USE THIS BOOK

Organization

Up front is the **Gold Guide,** comprising two sections on gold paper that are chock-full of information about traveling within your destination and traveling in general. Both are in alphabetical order by topic. **Important Contacts A to Z** gives addresses and telephone numbers of organizations and companies that offer destination-related services and detailed information or publications. Here's where you'll find information about how to get to the USA from wherever you are. **Smart Travel Tips A to Z,** the Gold Guide's second section, gives specific tips on how to get the most out of your travels, as well as information on how to accomplish what you need to in the USA.

The next chapter, "Special-Interest Travel," tells you the best places in the country to pursue your favorite hobby or sport. The 10 regional chapters that follow begin with the Northeast and zigzag across the country to the Pacific. Within each region, states are listed alphabetically; within each state are sections on the major cities, the most popular tourist areas, and worthwhile but less-known destinations grouped together under the heading "Elsewhere in the State." In the book's Appendix, you'll find state-name abbreviations; toll-free telephone numbers for airlines, train and bus companies, car rental companies, hotels and motels, and state tourist offices; and a chart giving mileages between major U.S. cities.

Stars

Stars in the margin are used to denote highly recommended sights, attractions, hotels, and restaurants.

Restaurant and Hotel Criteria and Price Categories

Restaurants and lodging places are chosen with a view to giving you the cream of the crop in each location and in each price range. Price categories are as follows:

For restaurants:

CHART 1 CATEGORY	(A) COST: MAJOR CITY OR RESORT	(B) COST: OTHER AREAS*
Very Expensive	over $50	
Expensive	$30–$50	over $25
Moderate	$15–$30	$10–$25
Inexpensive	under $15	under $10

**Rates are per person for a 3-course meal excluding drinks, tips, and taxes.*

For hotels:

CHART 2 CATEGORY	(A) COST: MAJOR CITY OR RESORT	(B) COST: OTHER AREAS*
Very Expensive	over $200	
Expensive	$125–$200	over $85
Moderate	$75–$125	$50–$85
Inexpensive	under $75	under $50

**Rates are for a standard double room for two, excluding tax and service charges.*

Hotel Facilities

Note that in general you incur charges when you use many hotel facilities. We wanted to let you know what facilities a hotel has to offer, but we don't always specify whether or not there's a charge, so when planning a vacation that entails a stay of several days, it's wise to ask what's included in the rate.

Dress Code in Restaurants

At very expensive restaurants in some cities, men may be required to wear a jacket and tie at dinner (we've noted such policies in our reviews in this book); otherwise, you can generally wear what you wish, as long as you are clean and neat.

Reservations Policy in Restaurants

We've noted restaurants that require reservations or that won't take any reservations at all, but except for the more inexpensive places, it's always a good idea to call ahead and reserve a table so you won't be disappointed.

Credit Cards

The following abbreviations are used: **AE,** American Express; **D,** Discover; **DC,** Diners Club; **MC,** MasterCard; and **V,** Visa.

PLEASE WRITE TO US

Everyone who has contributed to *USA '96* has worked hard to make the text accurate. All prices and opening times are based on information supplied to us at press time, and the publisher cannot accept responsibility for any errors that may have occurred. The passage of time will bring changes, so it's always a good idea to call ahead and confirm information when it matters—particularly if you're making a detour to visit specific sights or attractions. When making reservations at a hotel or inn, be sure to mention if you have a disability or are traveling with children, if you prefer a private bath or a certain type of bed, or if you have specific dietary needs or any other concerns.

Were the restaurants we recommended as described? Did our hotel picks exceed your expectations? Did you find a museum we recommended a waste of time? We would love your feedback, positive and negative. If you have complaints, we'll look into them and revise our entries when the facts warrant it. If you've happened upon a special place that we haven't included, we'll pass the information along to our writers so they can check it out. So please send us a letter or postcard (we're at 201 East 50th Street, New York, New York 10022). We'll look forward to hearing from you. And in the meantime, have a wonderful trip!

Karen Cure
Editorial Director

The United States

ONTARIO
CANADA
QUÉBEC
NEW BRUNSWICK
Fredericton
Québec
MAINE
Augusta
Montréal
Ottawa
Montpelier
VT.
Concord
N.H.
Boston
MASS.
R.I.
Providence
Albany
Hartford
CONN.
New York
N.J.
Trenton
Philadelphia
Dover
DEL.
MD
Annapolis
Baltimore
Washington, D.C.
Richmond
Norfolk
VIRGINIA
WEST VIRGINIA
Charleston
PENNSYLVANIA
Harrisburg
Pittsburgh
NEW YORK
Buffalo
Toronto
Lake Ontario
Lake Erie
Cleveland
Lake Huron
MICHIGAN
Lansing
Detroit
Lake Michigan
Lake Superior
MINNESOTA
Duluth
WISCONSIN
St. Paul
Minneapolis
Green Bay
Milwaukee
Madison
Chicago
IOWA
Des Moines
Omaha
ILLINOIS
Springfield
INDIANA
Indianapolis
OHIO
Columbus
Cincinnati
Frankfort
Louisville
KENTUCKY
Ohio R.
Mississippi R.
St. Louis
Topeka
Kansas City
Jefferson City
MISSOURI
Nashville
TENNESSEE
Tennessee R.
Memphis
Tulsa
ARKANSAS
Little Rock
NORTH CAROLINA
Raleigh
SOUTH CAROLINA
Columbia
Savannah R.
Atlanta
GEORGIA
Savannah
Birmingham
MISSISSIPPI
Jackson
ALABAMA
Montgomery
Mobile
Tallahassee
Jacksonville
FLORIDA
Orlando
Baton Rouge
New Orleans
LOUISIANA
Houston
ATLANTIC OCEAN
Gulf of Mexico
Bahama Islands
Nassau
Miami
N
0
200 miles
0
300 km

Amtrak Rail Passenger System

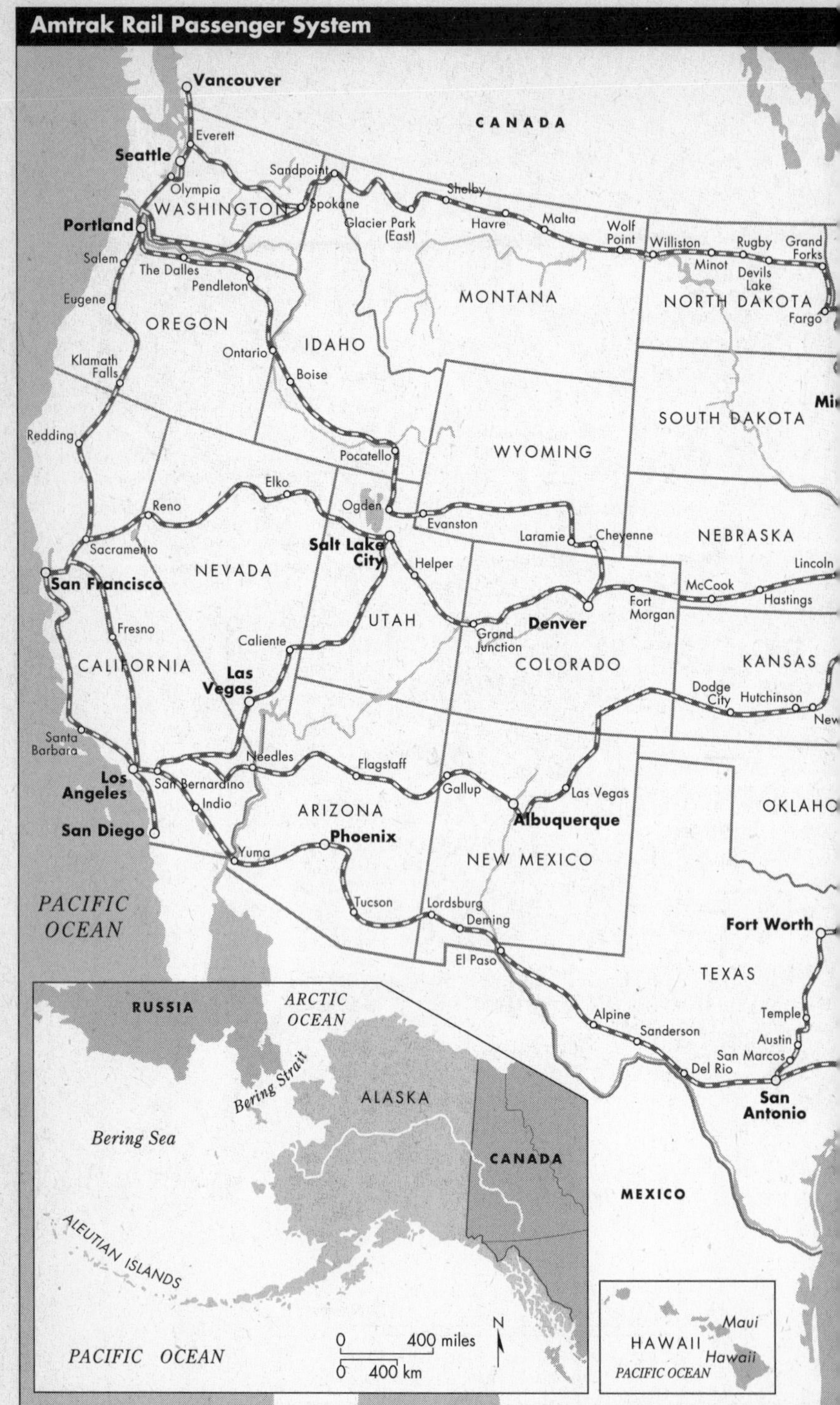

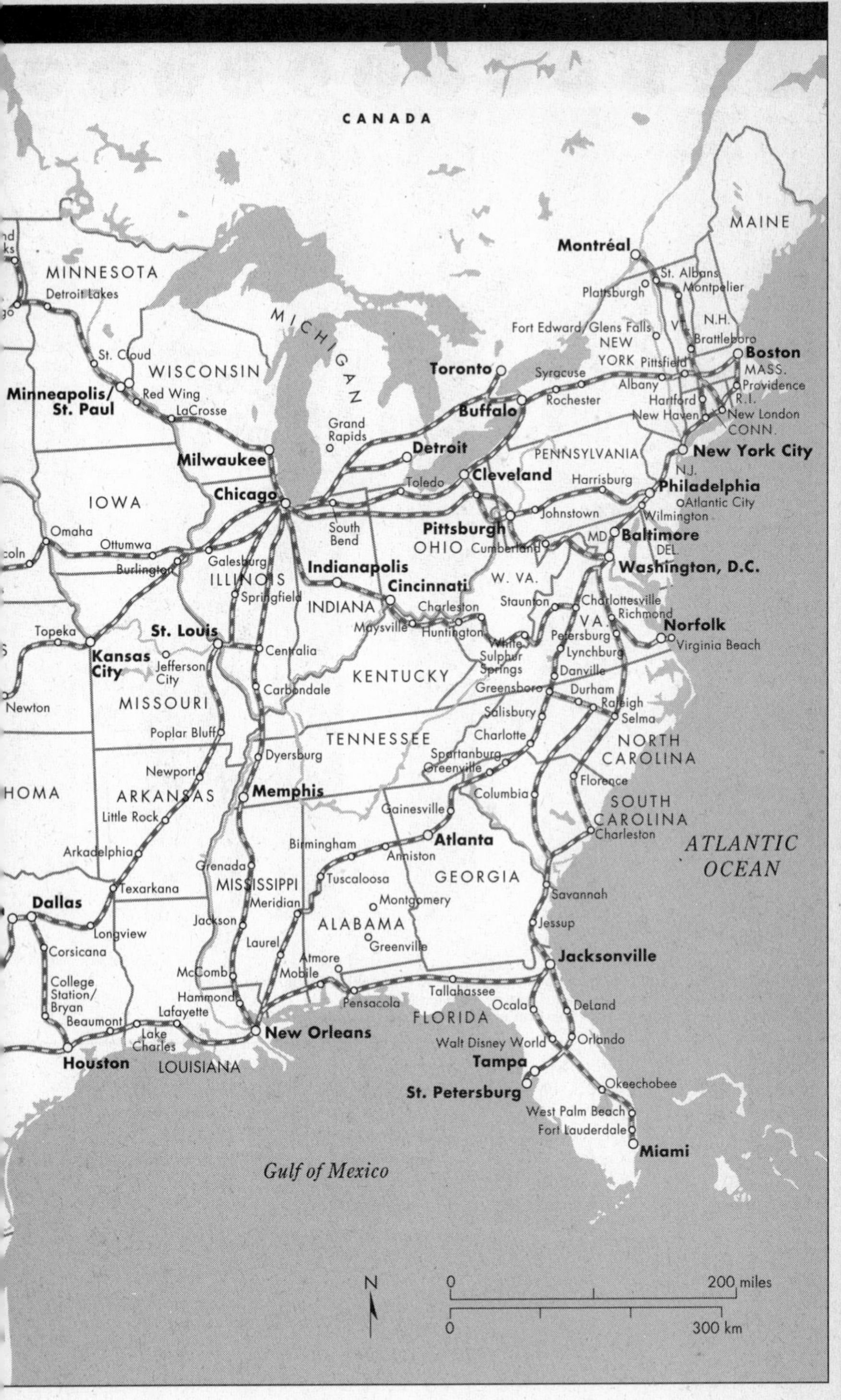
CANADA
MINNESOTA
Detroit Lakes
St. Cloud
WISCONSIN
Red Wing
Minneapolis/
St. Paul
LaCrosse
MICHIGAN
Grand
Rapids
Milwaukee
Detroit
Toronto
Buffalo
Montréal
MAINE
St. Albans
Plattsburgh
Montpelier
Fort Edward/Glens Falls
NEW
YORK
VT.
N.H.
Brattleboro
Boston
MASS.
Syracuse
Rochester
Albany
Pittsfield
Hartford
Providence
R.I.
New Haven
New London
CONN.
PENNSYLVANIA
New York City
N.J.
Philadelphia
Atlantic City
Harrisburg
Wilmington
Johnstown
Cleveland
Toledo
Chicago
IOWA
Omaha
Ottumwa
Burlington
Galesburg
ILLINOIS
Springfield
South
Bend
Pittsburgh
OHIO
Cumberland
MD.
Baltimore
DEL.
Washington, D.C.
Indianapolis
Cincinnati
W. VA.
INDIANA
Charleston
Staunton
Charlottesville
Richmond
VA.
Norfolk
Virginia Beach
Maysville
Huntington
Petersburg
Lynchburg
White
Sulphur
Springs
Danville
Topeka
St. Louis
Centralia
Kansas
City
Jefferson
City
KENTUCKY
Greensboro
Durham
Raleigh
Selma
Carbondale
MISSOURI
Newton
Salisbury
Poplar Bluff
TENNESSEE
Charlotte
NORTH
CAROLINA
Dyersburg
Spartanburg
Greenville
Newport
Florence
HOMA
ARKANSAS
Memphis
Columbia
SOUTH
CAROLINA
Little Rock
Gainesville
Charleston
ATLANTIC
OCEAN
Birmingham
Atlanta
Anniston
Arkadelphia
Grenada
Tuscaloosa
GEORGIA
MISSISSIPPI
Texarkana
Meridian
Savannah
Dallas
Montgomery
Jackson
ALABAMA
Jessup
Longview
Greenville
Corsicana
Laurel
Jacksonville
Atmore
McComb
Mobile
Tallahassee
College
Station/
Bryan
Hammond
Pensacola
Ocala
DeLand
Lafayette
FLORIDA
Beaumont
Lake
Charles
New Orleans
Walt Disney World
Orlando
Houston
LOUISIANA
Tampa
St. Petersburg
Okeechobee
West Palm Beach
Fort Lauderdale
Miami
Gulf of Mexico
N
0
200 miles
0
300 km

World Time Zones

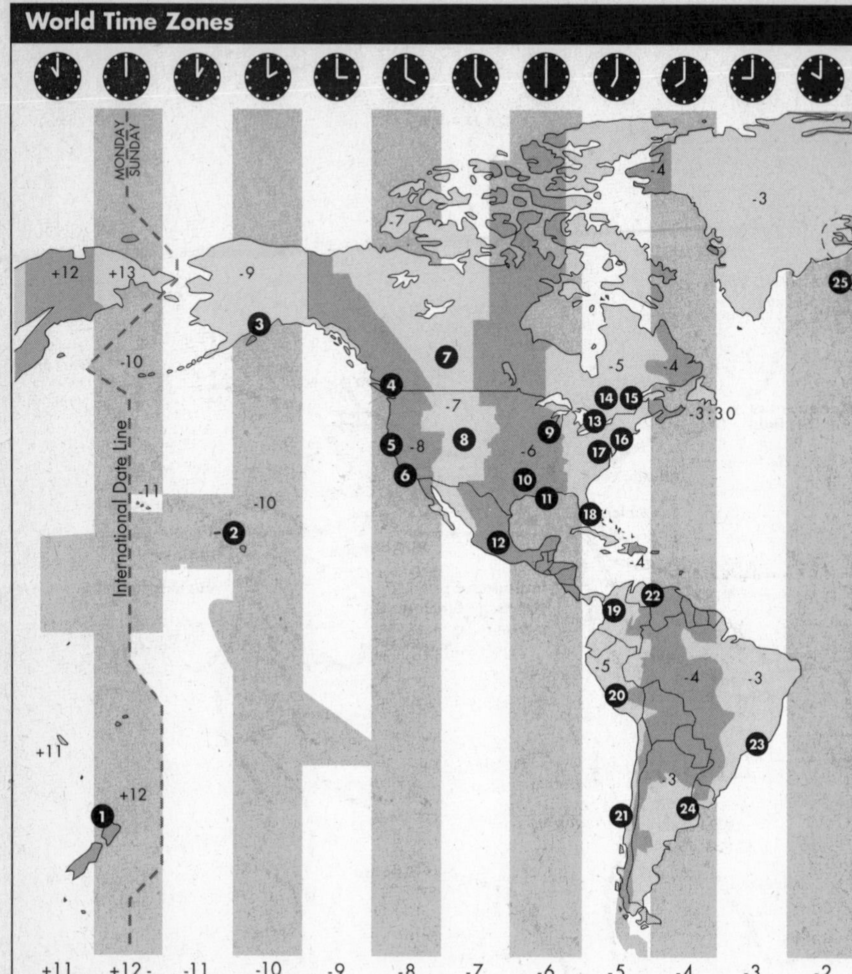

Numbers below vertical bands relate each zone to Greenwich Mean Time (0 hrs.). Local times frequently differ from these general indications, as indicated by light-face numbers on map.

Algiers, **29**
Anchorage, **3**
Athens, **41**
Auckland, **1**
Baghdad, **46**
Bangkok, **50**
Beijing, **54**
Berlin, **34**
Bogotá, **19**
Budapest, **37**
Buenos Aires, **24**
Caracas, **22**
Chicago, **9**
Copenhagen, **33**
Dallas, **10**
Delhi, **48**
Denver, **8**
Djakarta, **53**
Dublin, **26**
Edmonton, **7**
Hong Kong, **56**
Honolulu, **2**
Istanbul, **40**
Jerusalem, **42**
Johannesburg, **44**
Lima, **20**
Lisbon, **28**
London (Greenwich), **27**
Los Angeles, **6**
Madrid, **38**
Manila, **57**

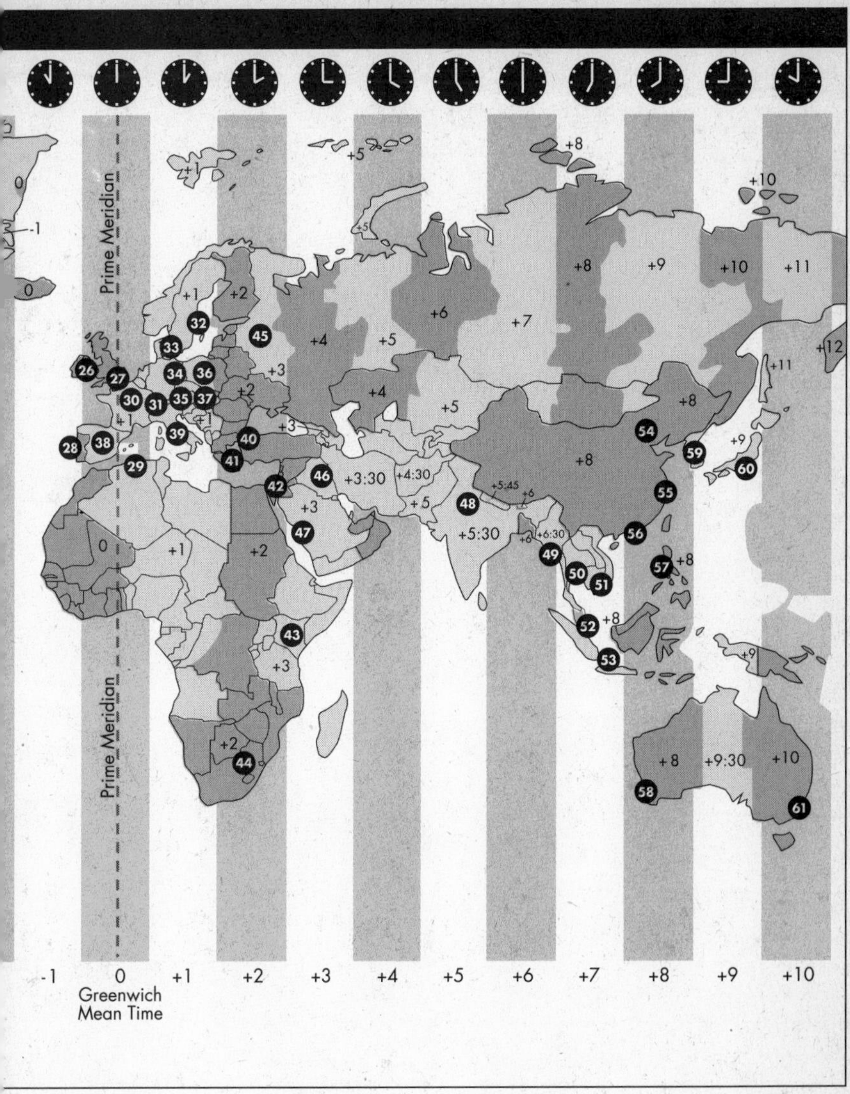

Mecca, **47**
Mexico City, **12**
Miami, **18**
Montréal, **15**
Moscow, **45**
Nairobi, **43**
New Orleans, **11**
New York City, **16**
Ottawa, **14**
Paris, **30**
Perth, **58**
Reykjavík, **25**
Rio de Janeiro, **23**
Rome, **39**
Saigon (Ho Chi Minh City), **51**
San Francisco, **5**
Santiago, **21**
Seoul, **59**
Shanghai, **55**
Singapore, **52**
Stockholm, **32**
Sydney, **61**
Tokyo, **60**
Toronto, **13**
Vancouver, **4**
Vienna, **35**
Warsaw, **36**
Washington, D.C., **17**
Yangon, **49**
Zürich, **31**

1 The Gold Guide

IMPORTANT CONTACTS A TO Z

An Alphabetical Listing of Publications, Organizations, and Companies That Will Help You Before, During, and After Your Trip

A

AIR TRAVEL

The major gateways to the USA include New York, Miami, Chicago, and Los Angeles. Flying time from London is 8 hours to New York; 8 hours, 40 minutes to Chicago; 9 hours, 45 minutes to Miami, and 11 hours to Los Angeles.

Flying time from Sydney is 21–22 hours to New York; and 13 hours, 25 minutes to Los Angeles on a direct flight. Flights from Melbourne add about 3 hours of flying time.

Flying time from Toronto is 1½ hours to New York, 4½ hours to Los Angeles. Flying time from Vancouver is 2½ hours to Los Angeles, 4 hours to Chicago.

CARRIERS

For a list of airlines and their toll-free telephone numbers, *see* Appendix.

FROM THE U.K.

The range of air services from Great Britain to the United States has improved remarkably over the past few years, with more destinations in the heart of the United States served directly from the United Kingdom. Airlines include **American Airlines** (☎ 0345/789789), **British Airways** (☎ 0181/897–4000 or 0345/222111), **Continental** (☎ 01293/776464), **Delta Airlines** (☎ 0800/414767), **Northwest** (☎ 01293/561000), **TWA** (☎ 0800/222222), **United Airlines** (☎ 0800/888555), and **Virgin Atlantic** (☎ 01293/747747). Most serve at least the New York area, plus their own U.S. hubs. British Airways serves the largest number of U.S. cities—an impressive 17 destinations.

FROM AUSTRALIA

Airlines flying from Australia include **Air New Zealand** (☎ 008/221–111), **Continental** (☎ 02/249–0111 in Sydney or 03/602–4899 in Melbourne), **Northwest** (☎ 008/221–714), **Qantas** (☎ 02/957–0111 in Sydney or 03/602–6111 in Melbourne), and **United** (☎ 008/230–322).

FROM CANADA

Every major U.S. airline flies between the United States and Canada, as does **Air Canada** (☎ 800/776–3000).

LOW-COST CARRIERS

For inexpensive, no-frills flights within the United States, contact **Branson Airlines** (☎ 800/422–4247), based in Riverside, California, which serves Kansas City, St. Louis, Nashville, and Dallas; Florida-based **Carnival Air Lines** (☎ 800/824–7386), which serves Ft. Lauderdale, Los Angeles, Miami, Nassau, New York, Puerto Rico, Tampa, and West Palm Beach; **Kiwi International** (☎ 800/538–5494), based in Newark and New York, serving Atlanta, Chicago, Orlando, San Juan, Tampa, and West Palm Beach; **MarkAir** (☎ 800/627–5247), based in Anchorage, Alaska, which serves Atlanta, Chicago, Cincinnati, Colorado, Dallas, Kansas City, Minneapolis, Newark, Phoenix, and Washington, DC; **Midwest Express** (☎ 800/452–2022), based in Milwaukee, which serves 45 U.S. cities; **Private Jet** (☎ 404/231–7571, 800/546–7571, or 800/949–9400), based in Atlanta, serving Cancún, Chicago, Cincinnati, Dallas, Las Vegas, Los Angeles, Miami, Orlando, St. Louis, St. Thomas, San Francisco, and Washington, DC; **Reno Air** (☎ 800/736–6247), which serves Las Vegas, Los Angeles, Phoenix, Portland, San Diego, San Jose, Seattle, and Tucson; **Southwest Airlines** (☎ 800/444–5660), based in Salt Lake City and serving Alabama, Arizona, Arkansas, California, Idaho, Illinois, Indiana, Kentucky, Louisiana, Maryland, Michigan, Missouri, Nevada, New Mexico, Ohio, Oklahoma, Oregon, Tennessee, Texas, Utah, and Washington; and **ValuJet** (☎ 404/994–8258 or 800/825–8538), also based in Atlanta and serving Chicago, Dallas, Ft. Myers, Indianapolis, Jacksonville, Louisville, Memphis, Nashville, New Orleans, Savannah, Tampa, Washington, DC, and West Palm Beach.

COMPLAINTS

To register complaints about charter and scheduled airlines, contact the U.S. Department of Transportation's **Office of Consumer Affairs** (400 7th St. NW, Washington, DC 20590, ☎ 202/366–2220 or 800/322–7873).

CONSOLIDATORS

Established consolidators selling to the public in the USA are **Euram Tours** (1522 K St. NW, Suite 430, Washington DC, 20005, ☎ 800/848–6789) and **TFI Tours International** (34 W. 32nd St., New York, NY 10001, ☎ 212/736–1140 or 800/745–8000).

PUBLICATIONS

For general information about charter carriers, ask for the Office of Consumer Affairs' brochure **"Plane Talk: Public Charter Flights."** The Department of Transportation also publishes a 58-page booklet, **"Fly Rights"** ($1.75; Consumer Information Center, Dept. 133-B, Pueblo, CO 81009).

For other tips and hints, consult the Consumers Union's monthly **"Consumer Reports Travel Letter"** ($39 a year; Box 53629, Boulder, CO 80322, ☎ 800/234–1970) and the newsletter **"Travel Smart"** ($37 a year; 40 Beechdale Rd., Dobbs Ferry, NY 10522, ☎ 800/327–3633); ***The Official Frequent Flyer Guidebook,*** by Randy Petersen ($14.99 plus $3 shipping; 4715-C Town Center Dr., Colorado Springs, CO 80916, ☎ 719/597–8899 or 800/487–8893); ***Airfare Secrets Exposed,*** by Sharon Tyler and Matthew Wonder (Universal Information Publishing; $16.95 plus $3.75 shipping from Sandcastle Publishing, Box 3070-A, South Pasadena, CA 91031, ☎ 213/255–3616 or 800/655–0053); and ***202 Tips Even the Best Business Travelers May Not Know,*** by Christopher McGinnis ($10 plus $3 shipping; Irwin Professional Publishing, 1333 Burr Ridge Pkwy., Burr Ridge, IL 60521, ☎ 708/789–4000 or 800/634–3966).

B

BETTER BUSINESS BUREAU

For local contacts, consult the **Council of Better Business Bureaus** (4200 Wilson Blvd., Arlington, VA 22203, ☎ 703/276–0100).

BUS TRAVEL

Contact **Greyhound Lines** (☎ 800/231–2222, TTY 800/752–4841).

DISCOUNT PASSES

The **International Ameripass** is available through your travel agent, or in New York City from **Greyhound International** (625 8th Ave., New York, NY 10018, ☎ 212/971–0492 or 800/246–8572); U.S. citizens can buy Greyhound's **Ameripass** (☎ 212/971–6300 or 800/231–2222).

C

CAR RENTAL

For a complete list of major car-rental companies in the U.S. and their toll-free telephone numbers, *see* Appendix.

CHILDREN AND TRAVEL

FLYING

Look into **"Flying With Baby"** ($5.95 plus $1 shipping; Third Street Press, Box 261250, Littleton, CO 80126, ☎ 303/595–5959), cowritten by a flight attendant. **"Kids and Teens in Flight,"** free from the U.S. Department of Transportation's Office of Consumer Affairs, offers tips for children flying alone. Every two years the February issue of ***Family Travel Times*** (*see* Know-How, *below*) details children's services on three dozen airlines.

KNOW-HOW

Family Travel Times, published 10 times a year by Travel with Your Children (TWYCH, 45 W. 18th St., New York, NY 10011, ☎ 212/206–0688; annual subscription $55), covers destinations, types of vacations, and modes of travel.

Also check ***Take Your Baby and Go! A Guide for Traveling with Babies, Toddlers and***

Young Children, by Sheri Andrews, Judy Bordeaux, and Vivian Vasquez ($5.95 plus $1.50 shipping; Bear Creek Publications, 2507 Minor Ave., Seattle, WA 98102, ☎ 206/322–7604 or 800/326–6566). ***100 Best Family Resorts in North America,*** by Jane Wilford with Janet Tice ($12.95), and the two-volume ***50 Great Family Vacations in North America*** ($12.95), both from Globe Pequot Press (add $3 shipping; Box 833, 6 Business Park Rd., Old Saybrook, CT 06475, ☎ 203/395–0440 or 800/243–0495, 800/962–0973 in CT) help plan your trip with children, from toddlers to teens. Travel with Your Children (*see above*) also publishes ***Skiing with Children*** ($29).

TOUR OPERATORS

Contact **Grandtravel** (6900 Wisconsin Ave., Suite 706, Chevy Chase, MD 20815, ☎ 301/986–0790 or 800/247–7651), which has tours for people traveling with grandchildren aged 7 to 17; or **Rascals in Paradise** (650 5th St., Suite 505, San Francisco, CA 94107, ☎ 415/978–9800 or 800/872–7225).

If your family is outdoorsy, look into the Conservation Summits, nature camps sponsored by the **National Wildlife Federation** (8925 Leesburg Pike, Vienna, VA 22184-0001, ☎ 703/790–4000 or 800/245–5484); **Ecology Tours** (c/o the Audubon Center of the North Woods, Box 530, Sandstone, MN 55072, ☎ 612/245–2648), which mix travel and nature study; Audubon Society family summer camps and **Ecology Workshops** (613 Riversville Rd., Greenwich, CT 06831, ☎ 203/869–2017), also from the Audubon Society; as well as programs from **American Wilderness Experience** (Box 1486, Boulder, CO 80306, ☎ 303/444–2622 or 800/444–0099), the **American Museum of Natural History** (79th St. and Central Park West, New York, NY 10024, ☎ 212/769–5700 or 800/462–8687), and **Wildland Adventures** (3516 N.E 155th St., Seattle, WA 98155, ☎ 206/365–0686 or 800/345–4453).

CUSTOMS

CANADIANS

Contact **Revenue Canada** (2265 St. Laurent Blvd. S, Ottawa, Ontario, K1G 4K3, ☎ 613/993–0534) for a copy of the free brochure **"I Declare/Je Déclare"** and for details on duties that exceed the standard duty-free limit.

U.K. CITIZENS

HM Customs and Excise (Dorset House, Stamford St., London SE1 9NG, ☎ 0171/202–4227) can answer questions about U.K. customs regulations and publishes **"A Guide for Travellers,"** detailing standard procedures and import rules.

D

FOR TRAVELERS WITH DISABILITIES

COMPLAINTS

To register complaints under the provisions of the Americans with Disabilities Act, contact the U.S. Department of Justice's **Public Access Section** (Box 66738, Washington, DC 20035, ☎ 202/514–0301, TTY 202/514–0383, FAX 202/307–1198).

ORGANIZATIONS

FOR TRAVELERS WITH HEARING IMPAIRMENTS➢ Contact the **American Academy of Otolaryngology** (1 Prince St., Alexandria, VA 22314, ☎ 703/836–4444, TTY 703/519–1585, FAX 703/683–5100).

FOR TRAVELERS WITH MOBILITY IMPAIRMENTS➢ Contact the **Information Center for Individuals with Disabilities** (Fort Point Pl., 27–43 Wormwood St., Boston, MA 02210, ☎ 617/727–5540, 800/462–5015 in MA, TTY 617/345–9743); **Mobility International USA** (Box 10767, Eugene, OR 97440, ☎ and TTY 503/343–1284; FAX 503/343–6812), the U.S. branch of an international organization based in Belgium (*see below*) that has affiliates in 30 countries; **MossRehab Hospital Travel Information Service** (1200 W. Tabor Rd., Philadelphia, PA 19141, ☎ 215/456–9603, TTY 215/456–9602); the **Society for the Advancement of Travel for the Handicapped** (SATH, 347 5th Ave., Suite 610, New

York, NY 10016, ☎ 212/447–7284, FAX 212/725–8253); the **Travel Industry and Disabled Exchange** (TIDE, 5435 Donna Ave., Tarzana, CA 91356, ☎ 818/344–3640, FAX 818/344–0078); and **Travelin' Talk** (Box 3534, Clarksville, TN 37043, ☎ 615/552–6670, FAX 615/552–1182).

FOR TRAVELERS WITH VISION IMPAIRMENTS➢ Contact the **American Council of the Blind** (1155 15th St. NW, Suite 720, Washington, DC 20005, ☎ 202/467–5081, FAX 202/467–5085) or the **American Foundation for the Blind** (15 W. 16th St., New York, NY 10011, ☎ 212/620–2000, TTY 212/620–2158).

IN THE U.K.

Contact the **Royal Association for Disability and Rehabilitation** (RADAR, 12 City Forum, 250 City Rd., London EC1V 8AF, ☎ 0171/250–3222) or **Mobility International** (Rue de Manchester 25, B1070 Brussels, Belgium, ☎ 00–322–410–6297), an international clearinghouse of travel information for people with disabilities.

PUBLICATIONS

Several free publications are available from the U.S. Information Center (Box 100, Pueblo, CO 81009, ☎ 719/948–3334): **"New Horizons for the Air Traveler with a Disability"** (address to Dept. 355A), describing legally mandated changes; the pocket-size **"Fly Smart"** (Dept. 575B), good on flight safety; and the Airport Operators Council's worldwide **"Access Travel: Airports"** (Dept. 575A). Some state tourism offices have special publications for travelers with disabilities; most have general accessibility ratings in their free vacation guides. However, the quality of this information varies.

Fodor's ***Great American Vacations for Travelers with Disabilities*** ($18; available in bookstores, or call 800/533–6478) details accessible attractions, restaurants, and hotels in 38 U.S. destinations. The 500-page ***Travelin' Talk Directory*** ($35; Box 3534, Clarksville, TN 37043, ☎ 615/552–6670) lists people and organizations who help travelers with disabilities. For specialist travel agents worldwide, consult the ***Directory of Travel Agencies for the Disabled*** ($19.95 plus $2 shipping; Twin Peaks Press, Box 129, Vancouver, WA 98666, ☎ 206/694–2462 or 800/637–2256). The Sierra Club publishes ***Easy Access to National Parks*** ($16 plus $3 shipping; 730 Polk St., San Francisco, CA 94109, ☎ 415/776–2211 or 800/935–1056).

TRAVEL AGENCIES AND TOUR OPERATORS

The Americans with Disabilities Act requires that travel firms serve the needs of all travelers. However, some agencies and operators specialize in making group and individual arrangements for travelers with disabilities, among them **Access Adventures** (206 Chestnut Ridge Rd., Rochester, NY 14624, ☎ 716/889–9096), run by a former physical-rehab counselor; **Tailored Tours** (Box 797687, Dallas, TX 75379, ☎ 214/612–1168 or 800/628–8542); and **Travel Trends** (2 Allan Plaza, 4922–51 Ave., Box 3581, Leduc, Alberta, T9E 6X2, ☎ 403/986–9000 or 800/661–2109 in Canada), which has group tours and is especially good for cruises. In addition, many general-interest operators and agencies (*see* Tour Operators, *below*) can also arrange vacations for travelers with disabilities.

FOR TRAVELERS WITH HEARING IMPAIRMENTS➢ One agency is **International Express** (7319-B Baltimore Ave., College Park, MD 20740, ☎ TTY 301/699–8836, FAX 301/699–8836), which arranges group and independent trips.

FOR TRAVELERS WITH MOBILITY IMPAIRMENTS➢ A number of operators specialize in working with travelers with mobility problems: **Accessible Journeys** (35 W. Sellers Ave., Ridley Park, PA 19078, ☎ 610/521–0339 or 800/846–4537, FAX 610/521–6959), a registered nursing service that arranges vacations; **Access Tours** (Box 2985, Jackson, WY 83001, ☎ 307/733–6664 in summer; 2440 S. Forest, Tucson, AZ 85713, ☎ 602/791–7977 winter–mid-May), which organizes national park tours; **Hinsdale Travel Service** (201 E. Ogden Ave., Suite 100, Hinsdale, IL 60521, ☎ 708/325–1335 or 800/303–5521), a travel agency that will give you access to the services of wheelchair-user Janice Perkins; **Over the Rainbow** (186 Mehani Circle, Kihei, HI 96753, ☎ 808/879–5521); and **Wheelchair Journeys** (16979 Redmond Way, Redmond, WA 98052, ☎ 206/885–2210), which can handle arrangements worldwide.

FOR TRAVELERS WITH DEVELOPMENTAL DISABILITIES➢ Contact the nonprofit **New Directions** (5276 Hollister Ave., Suite 207, Santa Barbara, CA 93111, ☎ 805/967–2841).

DISCOUNTS

Options include **Entertainment Travel Editions** (fee $28–$53, depending on destination; Box 1068, Trumbull, CT 06611, ☎ 800/445–4137), **Great American Traveler** ($49.95 annually; Box 27965, Salt Lake City, UT 84127, ☎ 800/548–2812), **Moment's Notice Discount Travel Club** ($25 annually, single or family; 163 Amsterdam Ave., Suite 137, New York, NY 10023, ☎ 212/486–0500), **Privilege Card** ($74.95 annually; 3391 Peachtree Rd. NE, Suite 110, Atlanta, GA 30326, ☎ 404/262–0222 or 800/236-9732), **Travelers Advantage** ($49 annually, single or family; CUC Travel Service, 49 Music Sq. W, Nashville, TN 37203, ☎ 800/548–1116 or 800/648–4037), and **Worldwide Discount Travel Club** ($50 annually for family, $40 single; 1674 Meridian Ave., Miami Beach, FL 33139, ☎ 305/534–2082).

DRIVING

AUTO CLUBS

The **American Automobile Association (AAA)** is a federation of state auto clubs that offers maps, route planning, and emergency road service to its members; members of Britain's Automobile Association (AA) are granted reciprocal privileges. To join AAA, check local phone directories under AAA for the nearest club, or contact the national organization (1000 AAA Dr., Heathrow, FL 32746–5063, ☎ 407/444–7000 or 800/222–4357).

G

GAY AND LESBIAN TRAVEL

ORGANIZATION

The **International Gay Travel Association** (Box 4974, Key West, FL 33041, ☎ 800/448–8550), a consortium of 800 businesses, can supply names of travel agents and tour operators.

PUBLICATIONS

The premier international travel magazine for gays and lesbians is **Our World** ($35 for 10 issues; 1104 N. Nova Rd., Suite 251, Daytona Beach, FL 32117, ☎ 904/441–5367). The 16-page monthly **"Out & About"** ($49 for 10 issues; ☎ 212/645–6922 or 800/929–2268), covers gay-friendly resorts, hotels, cruise lines, and airlines.

TOUR OPERATORS

Cruises and resort vacations are handled by **R.S.V.P. Travel Productions** (2800 University Ave. SE, Minneapolis, MN 55414, ☎ 800/328–RSVP) for gays, and **Olivia** (4400 Market St., Oakland, CA 94608, ☎ 800/631–6277) for lesbian travelers. For mixed gay and lesbian travel, contact **Atlantis Events** (8335 Sunset Blvd., West Hollywood, CA 90069, ☎ 800/628–5268). **Toto Tours** (1326 W. Albion, Suite 3W, Chicago, IL 60626, ☎ 312/274–8686 or 800/565–1241) has group tours worldwide.

TRAVEL AGENCIES

The largest agencies serving gay travelers are **Advance Travel** (10700 Northwest Freeway, Suite 160, Houston, TX 77092, ☎ 713/682–2002 or 800/695–0880), **Islanders/Kennedy Travel** (183 W. 10th St., New York, NY 10014, ☎ 212/242–3222 or 800/988–1181), **Now Voyager** (4406 18th St., San Francisco, CA 94114, ☎ 415/626–1169 or 800/255–6951), and **Yellowbrick Road** (1500 W. Balmoral Ave., Chicago, IL 60640, ☎ 312/561–1800 or 800/642–2488). **Skylink Women's Travel** (746 Ashland Ave., Santa Monica, CA 90405, ☎ 310/452–0506 or

800/225-5759) works with lesbians.

I

INSURANCE

Travel insurance covering baggage, health, and trip cancellation or interruptions is available from **Access America** (Box 90315, Richmond, VA 23286, ☎ 804/285–3300 or 800/284–8300), **Carefree Travel Insurance** (Box 9366, 100 Garden City Plaza, Garden City, NY 11530, ☎ 516/294–0220 or 800/323–3149), **Near Services** (Box 1339, Calumet City, IL 60409, ☎ 708/868–6700 or 800/654–6700), **Tele-Trip** (Mutual of Omaha Plaza, Box 31716, Omaha, NE 68131, ☎ 800/228–9792), **Travel Insured International** (Box 280568, East Hartford, CT 06128-0568, ☎ 203/528–7663 or 800/243–3174), **Travel Guard International** (1145 Clark St., Stevens Point, WI 54481, ☎ 715/345–0505 or 800/826–1300), and **Wallach & Company** (107 W. Federal St., Box 480, Middleburg, VA 22117, ☎ 703/687–3166 or 800/237–6615).

IN THE U.K.

The **Association of British Insurers** (51 Gresham St., London EC2V 7HQ, ☎ 0171/600–3333; 30 Gordon St., Glasgow G1 3PU, ☎ 0141/226–3905; Scottish Provident Bldg., Donegall Sq. W, Belfast BT1 6JE, ☎ 01232/249176; and other locations) gives advice by phone and publishes the free **"Holiday Insurance,"** which sets out typical policy provisions and costs.

L

LODGING

APARTMENT AND VILLA RENTALS

Among the companies to contact are **Hometours International** (Box 11503, Knoxville, TN 37939, ☎ 615/588–8722 or 800/367–4668), **Interhome** (124 Little Falls Rd., Fairfield, NJ 07004, ☎ 201/882–6864), **Property Rentals International** (1008 Mansfield Crossing Rd., Richmond, VA 23236, ☎ 804/378–6054 or 800/220–3332), **Rent-a-Home International** (7200 34th Ave. NW, Seattle, WA 98117, ☎ 206/789–9377 or 800/488–7368), **Vacation Home Rentals Worldwide** (235 Kensington Ave., Norwood, NJ 07648, ☎ 201/767–9393 or 800/633–3284), **Villas and Apartments Abroad** (420 Madison Ave., Suite 1105, New York, NY 10017, ☎ 212/759–1025 or 800/433–3020), and **Villas International** (605 Market St., Suite 510, San Francisco, CA 94105, ☎ 415/281–0910 or 800/221–2260). Members of the travel club **Hideaways International** ($99 annually; 767 Islington St., Portsmouth, NH 03801, ☎ 603/430–4433 or 800/843–4433) receive two annual guides plus quarterly newsletters, and arrange rentals among themselves.

CAMPING

For information on public and private parks contact the **National Association of RV Parks and Campgrounds** (ARVC, 8605 Westwood Center Dr., Suite 201, Vienna, VA 22182, ☎ 800/477–8669). When you call the toll-free number, you will receive a complimentary copy of the "Camping Vacation Planner," an invaluable publication that supplies addresses and phone numbers to which you may write or call for free directories of commercial campgrounds in any state of the Union.

For $17.95, you can purchase ***Woodall's 1995 North American Edition: Campground Directory*** at your local bookstore. All private parks in the United States and Canada are listed, quality inspected, and rated. Look for the annually updated directories published by the American Automobile Association for similar assessments. Fodor's publishes two guides, ***National Parks of the West*** and ***National Parks and Seashores of the East*** (both $17; available in bookstores, or call 800/533–6478), that provide in-depth coverage of campgrounds around the country.

HOME EXCHANGE

Principal clearinghouses include **HomeLink International/Vacation Exchange Club** ($60 annually; Box 650, Key West, FL 33041, ☎ 305/294–1448 or 800/638–3841), which gives members four annual directories, with a listing in one, plus updates; **Intervac International** ($65 annually; Box 590504, San Francisco, CA 94159, ☎ 415/435–3497), which has three annual directories; and **Loan-a-Home** ($35–$45 annually; 2 Park La., Apt. 6E, Mount Vernon, NY 10552-3443, ☎ 914/664–7640), which specializes in long-term exchanges.

M

MONEY MATTERS

ATMS

For specific **Cirrus** locations in the United States and Canada, call 800/424–7787. For U.S. **Plus** locations, call 800/843–7587 and enter the area code and first three digits of the number you're calling from (or of the calling area where you want an ATM).

CURRENCY EXCHANGE

In the U.S., contact **Thomas Cook Currency Services** (41 E. 42nd St., New York, NY 10017, or 511 Madison Ave., New York, NY 10022, ☎ 212/757–6915 or 800/223–7373 for locations) or **Ruesch International** (☎ 800/424–2923 for locations).

WIRING FUNDS

Funds can be wired via **American Express MoneyGram℠** (☎ 800/926–9400 from the U.S. and Canada for locations and information) or **Western Union** (☎ 800/325–6000 for agent locations or to send using MasterCard or Visa, 800/321–2923 in Canada).

N

NATIONAL PARKLANDS AND FORESTS

For information on the extensive U.S. system of national parks, battlefields, and recreational areas, write to the **National Park Service** (Department of the Interior, Washington, DC 20240) or call the regional offices: North Atlantic (☎ 617/223–5199); Mid-Atlantic (☎ 215/597–3679); National Capital Region (☎ 202/619–7222 or 202/619–7226); Southeast (☎ 404/331–4998); Midwest (☎ 402/221–3448); Rocky Mountains (☎ 303/969–2503); Southwest (☎ 505/988–6012); Western (☎ 415/744–3929); Pacific Northwest (☎ 206/220–4000); and Alaska (☎ 907/257–2696).

For information on recreational opportunities in national forests, write to the **U.S. Forest Service** (Department of Agriculture, 201 14th St. SW, Washington, DC 20250).

P

PASSPORTS AND VISAS

AUSTRALIAN CITIZENS

While in the United States, Australians may obtain information from the **Embassy of Australia** (1601 Massachusetts Ave. NW, Washington, DC 20036, ☎ 202/797–3000). Consulates are in Chicago, Honolulu, Los Angeles, and New York.

U.K. CITIZENS

For fees, documentation requirements, and to get an emergency passport, call the **London passport office** (☎ 0171/271–3000). For visa information, call the **U.S. Embassy Visa Information Line** (☎ 0891/200–290; calls cost 48p per minute or 36p per minute cheap rate) or write the **U.S. Embassy Visa Branch** (5 Upper Grosvenor St., London W1A 2JB). If you live in Northern Ireland, write the **U.S. Consulate General** (Queen's House, Queen St., Belfast BTI 6EQ). In Scotland, apply to the consulate at 3 Regent Terrace, Edinburgh EH7 5BW.

For additional information while visiting the United States, contact the **British Embassy** (3100 Massachusetts Ave. NW, Washington, DC 20008, ☎ 202/462–1340). Consulates are in Atlanta, Boston, Chicago, Cleveland, Houston, Los Angeles, Miami, New York, Orlando, San Francisco, and Seattle.

PHOTO HELP

The **Kodak Information Center** (☎ 800/242–2424) answers consumer questions about film and photography.

R

RAIL TRAVEL

Contact **Amtrak** (☎ 800/872–7245, TTY 800/523–6590).

FOR TRAVELERS WITH DISABILITIES

Contact Amtrak (National Railroad Corp., 60 Massachusetts Ave. NE, Washington, DC 20002) for a free copy of ***Access Amtrak,*** which outlines the services for riders with disabilities.

S

SENIOR CITIZENS

EDUCATIONAL TRAVEL

The nonprofit **Elderhostel** (75 Federal St., 3rd Floor, Boston, MA 02110, ☎ 617/426–7788), for people 60 and older, has offered inexpensive study programs since 1975. The nearly 2,000 courses cover everything from marine science to Greek myths and cowboy poetry. Fees for programs in the United States and Canada, which usually last one week, run about $300, not including transportation.

ORGANIZATIONS

Contact the **American Association of Retired Persons** (AARP, 601 E St. NW, Washington, DC 20049, ☎ 202/434–2277; $8 per person or couple annually). Its Purchase Privilege Program gets members discounts on lodging, car rentals, and sightseeing, and the AARP Motoring Plan furnishes domestic trip-routing information and emergency road-service aid for an annual fee of $39.95 per person or couple ($59.95 for a premium version).

For other discounts on lodgings, car rentals, and other travel products, along with magazines and newsletters, contact the **National Council of Senior Citizens** (membership $12 annually; 1331 F St. NW, Washington, DC 20004, ☎ 202/347–8800) and **Mature Outlook** (subscription $9.95 annually; 6001 N. Clark St., Chicago, IL 60660, ☎ 312/465–6466 or 800/336–6330).

PUBLICATIONS

The 50+ Traveler's Guidebook: Where to Go, Where to Stay, What to Do, by Anita Williams and Merrimac Dillon ($12.95; St. Martin's Press, 175 5th Ave., New York, NY 10010, ☎ 212/674–5151 or 800/288–2131), offers many useful tips. **"The Mature Traveler"** ($29.95; Box 50400, Reno, NV 89513, ☎ 702/786–7419), a monthly newsletter, covers travel deals.

STUDENTS

GROUPS

A major tour operator in the U.S. is **Contiki Holidays** (300 Plaza Alicante, Suite 900, Garden Grove, CA 92640, ☎ 714/740–0808 or 800/466–0610).

HOSTELING

Contact **Hostelling International–American Youth Hostels** (733 15th St. NW, Suite 840, Washington, DC 20005, ☎ 202/783–6161) in the United States, **Hostelling International–Canada** (205 Catherine St., Suite 400, Ottawa, Ontario K2P 1C3, ☎ 613/237–7884) in Canada, and the **Youth Hostel Association of England and Wales** (Trevelyan House, 8 St. Stephen's Hill, St. Albans, Hertfordshire AL1 2DY, ☎ 01727/855215 and 01727/845047) in the United Kingdom. Membership ($25 in the U.S., C$26.75 in Canada, and £9 in the U.K.) gets you access to 5,000 hostels worldwide that charge $7–$20 nightly per person.

YMCAs are another source of clean, respectable, low-cost accommodations. For information and reservations nationwide, contact **Y's Way** (224 E. 47th St., ☎ 212/308–2899).

I.D. CARDS

To be eligible for discounts on transportation and admissions, get the **International Student Identity Card** (ISIC) if you're a bona fide student or the **International Youth Card** (IYC) if you're under 26. In the United States, the ISIC and IYC cards cost $16 each and include basic travel-accident and illness coverage, plus a toll-free travel hot line. Apply through the Council on International Educational Exchange (*see* Organizations, *below*). Cards are available for $15 each in Canada from **Travel Cuts** (187 College St., Toronto, Ontario M5T 1P7, ☎ 416/979–2406 or 800/667–2887) and in the United Kingdom for £5 each at student unions and student travel companies.

ORGANIZATIONS

A major contact is the **Council on International Educational Exchange** (CIEE, 205 E. 42nd St., 16th Floor, New York, NY 10017, ☎ 212/661–1450) with locations in Boston (729 Boylston St., 02116, ☎ 617/266–1926), Miami (9100 S. Dadeland Blvd., 33156, ☎ 305/670–9261), Los Angeles (1093 Broxton Ave., 90024, ☎ 310/208–3551), 43 other college towns nationwide, and the United Kingdom (28A Poland St., London W1V 3DB, ☎ 0171/437–7767). Twice a year, it publishes *Student Travels* magazine. The CIEE's Council Travel Service offers domestic air passes for bargain travel within the United States and is the exclusive U.S. agent for several student-discount cards.

Campus Connections (325 Chestnut St., Suite 1101, Philadelphia, PA 19106, ☎ 215/625–8585 or 800/428–3235) specializes in discounted accommodations and airfares for students. The **Educational Travel Centre** (438 N. Frances St., Madison, WI 53703, ☎ 608/256–5551) offers rail passes and low-cost airline tickets, mostly for flights departing from Chicago.

In Canada, also contact **Travel Cuts** (*see above*).

PUBLICATIONS

See the Berkeley Guides to ***California, The Pacific Northwest and Alaska,*** and ***San Francisco*** ($17.50, $16.95, and $12.95, respectively; Fodor's Travel Publications, ☎ 800/533–6478 or from bookstores).

T

TOUR OPERATORS

Among the companies selling tours and packages to the U.S., the following have a proven reputation, are nationally known, and offer plenty of options.

GROUP TOURS

For deluxe escorted motorcoach tours of the U.S., contact **Maupintour** (Box 807, Lawrence, KS 66044, ☎ 800/255–4266 or 913/843–1211) and **Tauck Tours** (11 Wilton Rd., Westport, CT 06880, ☎ 800/468–2825 or 203/226–6911). Another operator falling between deluxe and first-class is **Globus** (5301 South Federal Circle, Littleton, CO 80123-2980, ☎ 800/221–0090 or 303/797–2800). In the first-class and tourist range, try **Collette Tours** (162 Middle Street, Pawtucket, RI 02860, ☎ 800/832–4656 or 401/728–3805), **Domenico Tours** (750 Broadway, Bayonne, NJ 07002, ☎ 800/554–8687 or 201/823–8687), and **Mayflower Tours** (1225 Warren Ave., Downers Grove, IL 60515, ☎ 708/960–3430 or 800/323–7604). For budget and tourist class programs, try **Cosmos** (*see* Globus, *above*)..

PACKAGES

Independent vacation packages to destinations throughout the U.S. are available from major tour operators and airlines. Contact **American Airlines Fly AAway Vacations** (☎ 800/321–2121), **Continental Airlines' Grand Destinations** (☎ 800/634–5555), **Delta Dream Vacations** (☎ 800/872–7786), **Globetrotters** (139 Main St., Cambridge, MA 02142, ☎ 800/999–9696 or 617/621–9911), **Kingdom Tours** (300 Market St., Kingston, PA 18704, ☎ 717/283–4241 or 800/872–8857), **United Vacations** (☎ 800/328–6877), and **USAir Vacations** (☎ 800/455–0123). **Funjet Vacations,** based in Milwaukee, Wisconsin, and **Gogo Tours,** based in Ramsey, New Jersey, sell packages to U.S. destinations only through travel agents.

FROM THE U.K.

Travel agencies that offer cheap fares to the USA include **Trailfinders** (42–50 Earl's Court Rd., London W8 6FT, ☎ 0171/937–5400), **Travel Cuts** (295a Regent St., London W1R 7YA, ☎ 0171/637–3161; *see* Students, *above*), and **Flightfile** (49 Tottenham Court Rd., London W1P 9RE, ☎ 0171/700–2722).

THEME TRIPS

For a complete list of operators, *see* Chapter 2, Special-Interest Travel.

ORGANIZATIONS

The **National Tour Association** (546 E. Main St., Lexington, KY 40508, ☎ 606/226–4444 or 800/682–8886) and **United States Tour Operators Association** (USTOA, 211 E. 51st St., Suite 12B, New York, NY 10022, ☎

212/750–7371) can provide lists of member operators and information on booking tours.

PUBLICATIONS

Consult the brochure **"Worldwide Tour & Vacation Package Finder"** from the National Tour Association (*see above*) and the Better Business Bureau's **"Tips on Travel Packages"** (publication No. 24-195, $2; 4200 Wilson Blvd., Arlington, VA 22203).

TRAVEL AGENCIES

For names of reputable agencies in your area, contact the **American Society of Travel Agents** (1101 King St., Suite 200, Alexandria, VA 22314, ☎ 703/739–2782).

V

VISITOR INFORMATION

State tourism offices, city tourist bureaus, and local chambers of commerce, which are usually the best sources of information about their communities, are listed throughout this book at the beginning of each state, city, or regional section; there's also a list of state tourism offices in the Appendix.

In the U.K., also contact the **United States Travel and Tourism Administration** (Box 1EN, London W1A 1EN, ☎ 0171/495–4466). For a free USA pack, write the USTTA at Box 170, Ashford, Kent TN24 0ZX. Enclose stamps worth £1.50.

Canadian travelers can contact **Travel USA** (☎ 905/890–5662 or 800/268–3482 in Ontario).

W

WEATHER

For current conditions and forecasts, plus the local time and helpful travel tips, call the **Weather Channel Connection** (☎ 900/932–8437; 95¢ per minute) from a touch-tone phone.

SMART TRAVEL TIPS A TO Z

Basic Information on Traveling in the USA and Savvy Tips to Make Your Trip a Breeze

The more you travel, the more you know about how to make trips run like clockwork. To help make your travels hassle-free, Fodor's editors have rounded up dozens of tips from our contributors and travel experts all over the world, as well as basic information on visiting the USA. For names of organizations to contact and publications that can give you more information, *see* Important Contacts A to Z, *above.*

A

AIR TRAVEL

The U.S. domestic air-route system is based on a pattern of hubs and spokes—each airline concentrates its services at certain hub cities and sends out spokes of connecting flights to other cities in the region. That's why, for example, many USAir flights are routed through Pittsburgh and Northwest flights through Minneapolis, even if those routes are not the most direct way to reach your final destination. Because of this system, it's wise to choose your airline according to which carrier has a hub closest to your destination. For major routes, however, such as New York–Los Angeles, you should have a range of options so you can shop around for the best available fare and the most convenient departure/arrival times.

If time is an issue, **always look for nonstop flights,** which require no change of plane. If possible, **avoid connecting flights,** which stop at least once and can involve a change of plane, although the flight number remains the same; if the first leg is late, the second waits.

If you want to book the flight yourself, call the airlines' toll-free reservation numbers. To qualify for an APEX fare, you may be asked to buy your ticket at a local ticket office or travel agent a certain number of days before departure. Otherwise, you can buy your ticket at the airport on the day of departure. In either case, try to arrive at the airport an hour before takeoff (the exception being hourly shuttle flights between neighboring major cities such as New York and Washington, DC). This will give you time to check your luggage, select your seat, and pass through the security metal-detectors. Flights usually begin boarding a half-hour or so before the scheduled departure time.

CUTTING COSTS

The Sunday travel section of most newspapers is a good source of deals. Generally, low season runs November 1–March 31, excluding the two weeks before Christmas. Shoulder seasons are April–May and October. Peak seasons are June–September and the pre-Christmas period.

MAJOR AIRLINES➤ The least expensive airfares from the major airlines are priced for round-trip travel and are subject to restrictions. You must usually **book in advance and buy the ticket within 24 hours** to get cheaper fares, and you may have to **stay over a Saturday night.** The lowest fare is subject to availability, and only a small percentage of the plane's total seats are sold at that price. It's good to **call a number of airlines, and when you are quoted a good price, book it on the spot**—the same fare on the same flight may not be available the next day. Airlines generally allow you to change your return date for a $25 to $50 fee, but most low-fare tickets are nonrefundable. However, if you don't use it, you can apply the cost toward the purchase price of a new ticket, again for a small charge.

On flights within the United States, most airlines offer non-U.S. residents discounted Visit USA fares, with savings of 25%–30%, provided the arrangements are made outside the United States. Many airlines, including **America West, American, Delta, Hawaiian, Northwest, TWA,** and **United,** also have air-pass programs that give you a fixed number of domestic flights for a flat fee (these also must be booked before you come to America). Check details with the airline or a travel agent.

CONSOLIDATORS➢ Consolidators, who buy tickets at reduced rates from scheduled airlines, sell them at prices below the lowest available from the airlines directly—usually without advance restrictions. Sometimes you can even get your money back if you need to return the ticket. Carefully read the fine print detailing penalties for changes and cancellations. If you doubt the reliability of a consolidator, **confirm your reservation with the airline.**

ALOFT

AIRLINE FOOD➢ If you hate airline food, **ask for special meals when booking.** These can be vegetarian, low-cholesterol, or kosher, for example; commonly prepared to order in smaller quantities than standard catered fare, they can be tastier.

JET LAG➢ To avoid this syndrome, which occurs when travel disrupts your body's natural cycles, try to maintain a normal routine. At night, **get some sleep.** By day, move about the cabin to **stretch your legs, eat light meals, and drink water—not alcohol.**

SMOKING➢ Smoking is banned on all flights within the U.S. of less than six hours' duration and on all Canadian flights; the ban also applies to domestic segments of international flights aboard U.S. and foreign carriers. Delta has banned smoking system-wide. On U.S. carriers flying abroad, a seat in a no-smoking section must be provided for every passenger who requests one, and the section must be enlarged to accommodate such passengers if necessary as long as they have complied with the airline's deadline for check-in and seat assignment. If smoking bothers you, request a seat far from the smoking section.

Foreign airlines are exempt from these rules but do provide no-smoking sections (British Airways has banned smoking, as has Virgin Atlantic on most international flights); some nations have banned smoking on all domestic flights, and others may ban smoking on some flights. Talks continue on the feasibility of broadening no-smoking policies.

B

BUS TRAVEL

Away from the two coasts and the major cities, long-distance buses (motor coaches) serve more of the United States than trains do. Various regional bus companies serve their areas of the country; the most extensive long-haul service is provided by Greyhound Lines. Generally no reservations are needed—**buy your tickets before boarding** (allow 15 minutes in advance in small towns, up to 45 minutes in larger cities). Usually you check in your baggage while boarding, and it is stowed in a large compartment at the bottom of the bus. Long-distance buses often feature reclining seats, individually controlled reading lights, rest rooms, and air-conditioning and heating.

BUS PASSES

Visitors from overseas receive as much as 50% savings on Greyhound by purchasing the International Ameripass through their travel agent prior to arriving in the United States. The cost is $124 for a 7-day pass, $175 for 15 days, and $225 for 30 days. In the United States, the pass can be obtained only in New York City, from Greyhound International; you must show a valid non-U.S. passport. U.S. citizens can also buy Greyhound's Ameripass for unlimited travel; the cost is $250 for 7 days, $350 for 15 days, and $450 for 30 days.

CHILDREN

On Greyhound buses, one child under age 2 travels free on an adult's lap, children 2–11 accompanied by an adult pay 50% of the adult fare. Again, call ahead for specifics, as special fares have restrictions.

SENIOR CITIZENS

Greyhound offers a 15% discount on regular fares for passengers 55 and older; there are restrictions, so be sure to call local numbers for specific information.

TRAVELERS WITH DISABILITIES

Greyhound offers no special fares or facilities for passengers with disabilities, but an attendant is entitled to ride for free. If you will be traveling alone and need special assistance, call Greyhound at least 48 hours before departure.

BUSINESS HOURS

Banks are generally open weekdays 9 AM–2 or 3 PM, post offices weekdays 8 AM–5 PM; many branches operate Saturday morning hours. Business hours tend to be weekdays 9–5, a little later on the East Coast and earlier the farther west you go. Many stores may not open until 10 or 11, but they remain open until 6 or 7; most carry on brisk business on Saturdays as well. Large suburban shopping malls, the focus of most Americans' shopping activity, are generally open seven days a week, with evening hours every day except Sunday. All across the country, so-called convenience stores sell food and sundries until about 11 PM. Along the highways and in major cities you can usually find all-night diners, supermarkets, drugstores, and convenience stores, as Americans gravitate toward a 24-hour society.

C

CAMERAS, CAMCORDERS, AND COMPUTERS

LAPTOPS

Before you depart, **check your portable computer's battery,** because you may be asked at security to turn on the computer to prove that it is what it appears to be. At the airport, you may prefer to **request a manual inspection,** although security X-rays do not harm hard-disk or floppy-disk storage.

PHOTOGRAPHY

If your camera is new or if you haven't used it for a while, **shoot and develop a few rolls of film** before you leave. Always **store film in a cool, dry place**—never in the car's glove compartment or on the shelf under the rear window.

Every pass through an X-ray machine increases the chances that your film might turn cloudy. To protect it, carry it in a clear plastic bag and **ask for hand inspection at security.** Such requests are virtually always honored at U.S. airports, and are usually accommodated abroad. Don't depend on a lead-lined bag to protect film in checked luggage—the airline may increase the radiation to see what's inside.

VIDEO

Before your trip, **test your camcorder, invest in a skylight filter to protect the lens, and charge the batteries.** (Airport security personnel may ask you to turn on the camcorder to prove that it's what it appears to be). The batteries of most newer camcorders can be recharged with a universal or worldwide AC adapter charger (or multivoltage converter), usable whether the voltage is 110 or 220. All that's needed is the appropriate plug.

Videotape is not damaged by X-rays, but it may be harmed by the magnetic field of a walk-through metal detector, so **ask that videotapes be hand-checked.**

CHILDREN AND TRAVEL

BABY-SITTING

For recommended local sitters, **check with your hotel desk.**

DRIVING

If you are renting a car, **arrange for a car seat when you reserve.** Sometimes they're free.

FLYING

Always **ask about discounted children's fares.** On flights within the United States, children under 2 not occupying a seat travel free, and older children currently travel on the lowest applicable adult fare.

BAGGAGE➢ In general, the adult baggage allowance applies for children paying half or more of the adult fare. Before departure, **ask about carry-on allowances** if you are traveling with an infant. In general, those paying 10% of the adult fare are allowed one carry-on bag, not to exceed

70 pounds or 45 inches (length + width + height) and a collapsible stroller; you may be allowed less if the flight is full.

SAFETY SEATS➢ According to the FAA, it's a good idea to **use safety seats aloft.** Airline policy varies. U.S. carriers allow FAA-approved models, but airlines usually require that you buy a ticket, even if your child would otherwise ride free, because the seats must be strapped into regular passenger seats. Carriers outside the United States may not allow infant seats, may charge the child's rather than the infant's fare for their use, or may require you to hold your baby during takeoff and landing, thus defeating the seat's purpose.

FACILITIES➢ When making your reservation, **ask for children's meals or a freestanding bassinet** if you need them; bassinets are available only to those with seats at the bulkhead, where there's enough legroom. If you don't need a bassinet, **think twice before requesting bulkhead seats**—the only storage for in-flight necessities is in the inconveniently distant overhead bins.

LODGING

Most hotels allow children under a certain age to stay in their parents' room at no extra charge, while others charge them as extra adults; be sure to **ask about the cut-off age.**

CUSTOMS AND DUTIES

IN THE USA

Entering the United States, a visitor 21 or older can bring 200 cigarettes, or 50 cigars, or 2 kilograms of tobacco; 1 liter of alcohol; and duty-free gifts, each to a value of $100. You may not bring in meat or meat products, seeds, plants, or fruit. Absolutely avoid carrying illegal drugs.

BACK HOME

IN CANADA➢ Once per calendar year, when you've been out of Canada for at least seven days, you may bring in C$300 worth of goods duty-free. If you've been away less than seven days but more than 48 hours, the duty-free exemption drops to C$100 but can be claimed any number of times (as can a C$20 duty-free exemption for absences of 24 hours or more). You cannot combine the yearly and 48-hour exemptions, use the C$300 exemption only partially (to save the balance for a later trip), or pool exemptions with family members. Goods claimed under the C$300 exemption may follow you by mail; those claimed under the lesser exemptions must accompany you.

Alcohol and tobacco products may be included in the yearly and 48-hour exemptions but not in the 24-hour exemption. If you meet the age requirements of the province through which you reenter Canada, you may bring in, duty-free, 1.14 liters (40 imperial ounces) of wine or liquor *or* 24 12-ounce cans or bottles of beer or ale. If you are 16 or older, you may bring in, duty-free, 200 cigarettes, 50 cigars or cigarillos, and 400 tobacco sticks or 400 grams of manufactured tobacco. Alcohol and tobacco must accompany you on your return.

An unlimited number of gifts valued up to C$60 each may be mailed to Canada duty-free. These do not count as part of your exemption. Label the package "Unsolicited Gift—Value Under $60." Alcohol and tobacco are excluded.

IN THE U.K.➢ From countries outside the EU, including the United States, you may import duty-free 200 cigarettes, 100 cigarillos, 50 cigars or 250 grams of tobacco; 1 liter of spirits or 2 liters of fortified or sparkling wine; 2 liters of still table wine; 60 milliliters of perfume; 250 milliliters of toilet water; plus £136 worth of other goods, including gifts and souvenirs.

D

DINING

Breakfast is served anywhere from 6 to 11 AM, lunch 11–2, dinner from 5 until late. Like business hours in general, mealtimes tend to become earlier when you leave the cities and as you go farther west.

FOR TRAVELERS WITH DISABILITIES

When discussing accessibility with an operator or reservationist, **ask hard questions.** Are there any stairs, inside *or* out? Are there grab bars next to the toilet *and* in the shower/tub? How wide is the doorway to the room? To the bathroom? For the most extensive facilities, meeting the latest legal specifications, **opt for newer accommodations,** which more often have been designed with access in mind. Older properties or ships must usually be retrofitted and may offer more limited facilities as a result. Be sure to **discuss your needs before booking.**

DRIVING

RULES OF THE ROAD

Highway speed limits are 55 miles per hour or 65 miles per hour. Watch for lower speed limits on smaller back roads. Except for limited-access roads, highways usually post a lower speed limit in towns, so slow down when houses and buildings start to appear. Most states require front-seat passengers to wear seat belts, and in all states children under age 4 must ride in approved child-safety seats.

In some communities, it is permissible to make a right turn at a red light once the car has come to a full stop and there is no oncoming traffic. When in doubt about local laws, however, wait for the green light. Beware of weekday rush-hour traffic—anywhere from 7 to 10 AM and 4 to 7 PM—around major cities. To encourage car-sharing, some crowded expressways may reserve an express lane for cars carrying more than one passenger. In downtown areas, watch signs carefully—there are lots of one-way streets, "no-left-turn" intersections, and blocks closed to car traffic, all in the name of easing congestion.

HIGHWAYS

The fastest routes are usually the interstate highways, each numbered with a prefix "I–". Even numbers (I–80, I–40, and so on) are east–west roads; odd numbers (I–91, I–55, and so on) run north–south. These are fully signposted, limited-access highways with at least two lanes in each direction. In some cases they are toll roads (the Pennsylvania Turnpike is I–76; the Massachusetts Turnpike is I–90). Near large cities, interstates usually intersect with a circumferential loop highway (I–295, and so on) that carries traffic around the city.

The next level of highway—not necessarily limited access, but well paved and usually multilane—is the U.S. highway (designated U.S. 1, and so on). State highways are also well paved and often have more than one lane in each direction. Large cities usually have a number of limited-access expressways, freeways, and parkways, referred to by names rather than numbers (the Merritt Parkway, the Kennedy Expressway, the Santa Monica Freeway).

E

EMERGENCIES

In most communities you **dial 911** in an emergency to reach the police, fire, or ambulance services. If your car breaks down on an interstate highway, try to pull over onto the shoulder of the road and either wait for the state police to find you or, if you have other passengers who can wait in the car, walk to the nearest emergency roadside phone and call the state police. If you are calling for help, note your location according to the small green mileage markers posted along the highway. Other highways are also patrolled but may not have emergency phones or mileage markers. If you are a member of the AAA auto club (*see* Auto Clubs, *above*), look in a local phone book for the AAA emergency road-service number.

F

FAX MACHINES

You can usually make hotel reservations via fax, and you can probably send a fax on the hotel's machine while staying there, especially if the hotel caters to business travelers. If your hotel isn't helpful or charges exorbitantly for this service, look for fax service at local photocopying stores;

the charge may be as much as $2 a page, more for overseas.

I
INSURANCE

Travel insurance can protect your investment, replace your luggage and its contents, or provide for medical coverage should you fall ill during your trip. Most tour operators, travel agents, and insurance agents sell specialized health-and-accident, flight, trip-cancellation, and luggage insurance as well as comprehensive policies with some or all of these features. Before you make any purchase, **review your existing health and homeowner's policies** to find out whether they cover expenses incurred while traveling.

BAGGAGE

Airline liability for your baggage is limited to $1,250 per person on domestic flights. On international flights, the airlines' liability is $9.07 per pound or $20 per kilogram for checked baggage (roughly $640 per 70-pound bag) and $400 per passenger for unchecked baggage. However, this excludes valuable items such as jewelry and cameras that are listed in your ticket's fine print. You can buy additional insurance from the airline at check-in, but first **see if your homeowner's policy covers lost luggage.**

FLIGHT

You should **think twice before buying flight insurance.** Often purchased as a last-minute impulse at the airport, it pays a lump sum when a plane crashes, either to a beneficiary if the insured dies or sometimes to a surviving passenger who loses eyesight or a limb. Supplementing the airlines' coverage described in the limits-of-liability paragraphs on your ticket, it's expensive and basically unnecessary. Charging an airline ticket to a major credit card often automatically entitles you to coverage and may also embrace travel by bus, train, and ship.

HEALTH

If your own health insurance policy does not cover you outside the U.S., **consider buying supplemental medical coverage.** It can pay from $1,000 to $150,000 worth of medical and/or dental expenses incurred as a result of an accident or illness during a trip. These policies also may include a personal-accident, or death-and-dismemberment, provision, which pays a lump sum ranging from $15,000 to $500,000 to your beneficiaries if you die or to you if you lose one or more limbs or your eyesight, and a medical-assistance provision, which may either reimburse you for the cost of referrals, evacuation, or repatriation and other services, or may automatically enroll you as a member of a particular medical-assistance company.

FOR U.K. TRAVELERS➢ According to the Association of British Insurers, a trade association representing 450 insurance companies, it's wise to **buy extra medical coverage when you visit the United States.** You can buy an annual travel-insurance policy valid for most vacations during the year in which it's purchased. If you go this route, make sure it covers you if you have a preexisting medical condition or are pregnant.

TRIP

Without insurance, you will lose all or most of your money if you must cancel your trip due to illness or any other reason. Especially if your airline ticket, cruise, or package tour is nonrefundable and cannot be changed, it's essential that you **buy trip-cancellation-and-interruption insurance.** When considering how much coverage you need, look for a policy that will cover the cost of your trip plus the nondiscounted price of a one-way airline ticket should you need to return home early. Read the fine print carefully, especially sections defining "family member" and "preexisting medical conditions." Also **consider default or bankruptcy insurance,** which protects you against a supplier's failure to deliver. However, such policies often do not cover default by a travel agency, tour operator, airline, or cruise line if you bought your tour and the coverage directly from the firm in question.

L

LIQUOR LAWS

Liquor laws vary from state to state, affecting such matters as bar and liquor store opening times and whether restaurants can sell liquor by the glass or only by the bottle. A few states—mostly in the South or Midwest—allow each county to choose its own policy, resulting in so-called dry counties, where no alcoholic beverages are sold, next to counties where the bars do a roaring business.

The drinking age is 21 in all states, and you should **be prepared to show identification** in order to be served. Restaurants must obtain a license to sell alcoholic beverages on the premises, so some inexpensive establishments, or places that have just recently opened, may not sell drinks at all, or may sell only beer or wine. In most of these restaurants, however, you can bring your own beer or wine in with you to drink with your meal. In this book, we note such a policy as BYOB (bring your own bottle).

Local laws against driving while intoxicated are growing stricter. Many bars now serve nonalcoholic drinks for the "designated driver" so at least one person in a group is sober enough to drive everyone else safely home.

LODGING

Motels are geared to motorists, with locations close to highways and convenient parking. Airport hotels, within a few minutes' drive of major airports, are geared to plane travelers in transit, with a strong business-travel clientele; noise may be a problem, although the best ones are excellently soundproofed. Convention hotels, in large cities near convention centers, have hundreds of guest rooms, warrens of meeting rooms (usually on separate floors), and big ballrooms used for exhibits and banquets; when a large convention is staying at one, other guests sometimes feel overwhelmed. Other downtown hotels cater more to individual guests and may offer more in the way of health facilities and à la carte restaurants. Some, however, may try to appeal to business travelers by emphasizing their extensive office services. Suburban hotels in many cities attract travelers who want to be close to the circumferential highway and to suburban office parks, shopping malls, or theme parks; they may be larger and more upscale than motels, offering more restaurants, health facilities, and other amenities. Resorts tend to be destinations in and of themselves—complete with golf courses, tennis courts, beaches, several restaurants, on-site entertainment, and so on. Sometimes a resort features one large hotel building surrounded by landscape; other times, a resort is designed with clusters of smaller buildings, down to individual cottages or huts. The setting usually emphasizes a particular outdoor activity, whether skiing, water sports, or golf. One variation on this is the dude ranch, where paying guests sample horseback riding, hiking, lake fishing, cookouts, and such Western-style activities as rodeos. Country inns and bed-and-breakfasts are generally charming older properties that, unlike European B&Bs, tend to be pricey and upscale. They may not have private bathrooms, an in-room phone, or TVs, and as they are frequently meticulously furnished with antiques, they may not be the best place to take young children. Breakfast is usually included in the room rate, but verify this when you make a reservation. For recommendations, see *Fodor's Best Bed & Breakfasts* books for various regions of the country. At the budget end of the scale, YMCAs and youth hostels offer somewhat more spartan accommodations, often dormitory-style, and limited amenities.

APARTMENT AND VILLA RENTALS

If you want a home base that's roomy enough for a family and comes with cooking facilities, **consider a furnished rental.** It's generally cost-wise, too, although not always—some rentals are luxury properties (economical only when your party is large). Home-exchange directories do list rentals—often second homes owned by prospective house swappers—and some services search for a house or apartment for you (even a castle if that's your fancy) and handle the paperwork. Some send an illustrated catalogue and others send photographs of specific properties, sometimes at a charge; up-front registration fees may apply.

CAMPGROUNDS

Some of the most reasonably priced campgrounds with the most compelling sites operate under the auspices of the National Park system (*see* National Parklands and Forests *in* Important Contacts A to Z). If, however, you opt for private commercial operations, your best source for nationwide information on both public and private parks is the National Association of RV Parks and Campgrounds (*see* Lodging *in* Important Contacts A to Z).

An overnight stay at a commercial campground can cost from $15 to $30, depending on three factors: 1) the amenities offered; 2) the location; and 3) the time of year. Tent camping, of course, is the least expensive form of accommodation; if you want water, electric, and sewage hook-ups, you move into the higher end of the price range.

Many private campgrounds are not open year-round, so it's important to **call ahead.** You can make reservations over the phone, and, customarily, a one-night deposit is required. The peak summer months of June, July, and August are very busy at the more desirable locations; the sooner you book, the more you can count on being awarded an attractive site.

HOME EXCHANGE

If you would like to find a house, an apartment, or other vacation property to exchange for your own while on vacation, **become a member of a home-exchange organization,** which will send you its annual directories listing available exchanges and will include your own listing in at least one of them. Arrangements for the actual exchange are made by the two parties to it, not by the organization.

HOTELS

Hotel chains dominate the lodging landscape in the United States. Some of the large chains, such as Holiday Inn, Hilton, Hyatt, Marriott, and Ramada, are even further subdivided into chains of budget properties, all-suite properties, downtown hotels, or luxury resorts, each with different names. While some chain hotels may have a standardized look to them, this "cookie-cutter" approach also means that you can rely on the same level of comfort and efficiency at all properties in a well-managed chain, and at a chain's premier properties—its so-called flagship hotels—decor and services may be outstanding.

Most hotels will hold your reservation until 6 PM; **call ahead if you plan to arrive late.** Hotels will be more willing to hold a late reservation for you if you reserve with a credit-card number.

When you call to make a reservation, **ask all the necessary questions up front.** If you are arriving with a car, ask if the hotel has a parking lot or covered garage, and whether there is an extra fee for parking. If you like to eat your meals in, ask if the hotel has a restaurant, or whether it has room service (most do, but not necessarily 24 hours a day—and be forewarned that it can be expensive). Most hotels have in-room telephones, but double-check this at inexpensive properties and bed-and-breakfasts. Most hotels and motels have in-room TVs, often with cable movies (usually pay-per-view), but verify this if you like to watch TV. If you want a crib for your child to stay in the room with you, there will probably be an additional charge.

M

MAIL

Every address in the United States belongs to a specific zip-code district, and each zip code has five digits. Some addresses include a second sequence of four numbers following the first five numbers, but while this speeds mail delivery for large organizations, it is not necessary to use it.

Each zip-code district has at least one post office, where you can buy stamps and aerogrammes, send parcels, or conduct other postal business. Occasionally you may find small stamp-dispensing machines in airports, train stations, bus terminals, large office buildings, drugstores, or grocery stores, but don't count on it. Most Americans go to the post office to buy their stamps, and the lines can be long.

Official mailboxes are either the stout royal-blue steel bins on city sidewalks or mail chutes on the walls of post offices or in large office buildings. A schedule posted on mailboxes and mail slots should indicate when the mail is picked up.

POSTAL RATES

First-class letters weighing up to 1 ounce can be sent anywhere within the United States with a 32¢ stamp; each additional ounce costs 23¢. Postcards need a 20¢ stamp. A half-ounce airmail letter overseas takes 50¢, an airmail postcard 40¢, and a surface-rate postcard 35¢. For Canada, you'll need a 40¢ stamp for a one-ounce letter, 30¢ for a postcard. For Mexico, you'll need 35¢ for a half-ounce letter, 30¢ for a postcard. For 45¢, you can buy an aerogramme—a single sheet of lightweight blue paper that folds into its own envelope, already stamped for overseas airmail delivery.

RECEIVING MAIL

If you wish to receive mail while traveling in the USA, **have it sent c/o General Delivery** at the city's main post office (be sure to use the right zip code). It should be held there for up to 30 days. You must pick it up in person, and bring identification with you. American Express offices in the United States do not hold mail.

MEDICAL ASSISTANCE

No one plans to get sick while traveling, but it happens, so **consider signing up with a medical assistance company.** These outfits provide referrals, emergency evacuation or repatriation, 24-hour telephone hot lines for medical consultation, dispatch of medical personnel, relay of medical records, cash for emergencies, and other personal and legal assistance.

MONEY AND EXPENSES

The basic unit of U.S. currency is the dollar, which is subdivided into 100 cents. Coins are the copper penny (1¢) and four silver coins: the nickel (5¢), the dime (10¢), the quarter (25¢), and the half-dollar (50¢). Silver $1 coins are rarely seen in circulation. Paper money comes in denominations of $1, $5, $10, $20, $50, and $100. All these bills are the same size and green color; they are distinguishable only by the dollar amount indicated on them and by different pictures of famous American men and monuments.

ATMS

Chances are that you can **use your bank card at ATMs** to withdraw money from an account and get cash advances on a credit-card account if your card has been programmed with a personal identification number, or PIN. Before leaving home, **check in on frequency limits** for withdrawals and cash advances. Also **ask whether your card's PIN must be reprogrammed** for use in the U.S.

Virtually all U.S. banks belong to a network of Automated Teller Machines (ATMs) that dispense cash 24 hours a day in cities throughout the country. These cash machines are usually found at bank branches along major local streets; in downtown areas, they are walk-up windows, but in suburban areas they may be drive-up windows. In many parts of the country, cash machines are also located in supermarkets and malls. You can usually find a couple at airports, train stations, and bus terminals as well. There are some eight major networks in the United States, the largest of which are Cirrus, owned by MasterCard, and Plus, which is affiliated with Visa. Some banks belong to more than one network.

On cash advances you are charged interest from the day you receive the money, whether from an ATM or a teller. Although transaction fees for ATM withdrawals outside your own country may be higher than fees for withdrawals at home, Cirrus and Plus exchange rates are excellent because they are based on wholesale rates only offered by major banks.

BANKS

In general, U.S. banks will not cash a personal check for you unless you have an account at that bank (it doesn't have to be at that branch). Only in major cities are large bank branches equipped to exchange foreign currencies. Therefore, it's best to rely on credit cards, cash machines, and traveler's checks to handle expenses while you're traveling.

CREDIT CARDS

MasterCard is the U.S. equivalent of the Access card in Britain, or the EuroCard in other European countries. Visa is the equivalent of the BarclayCard in Britain or the ChargeEx card in Canada. Charges incurred in the United States will appear on your regular monthly bill, converted to your own currency at the exchange rate applicable on the day the charge was entered.

EXCHANGING CURRENCY

In the United States, it is not as easy to find places to exchange currency as it is in European cities. In major international cities, such as New York and Los Angeles, currency may be exchanged at some bank branches, as well as at currency-exchange booths in airports and at foreign-currency offices such as American Express Travel Service and Thomas Cook (check local directories for addresses and phone numbers). The best strategy is to **buy traveler's checks in U.S. dollars** before you come to the United States; while the rates may not be as good abroad, the time saved by not having to search constantly for exchange facilities far outweighs any financial loss.

For the most favorable rates, **change money at banks.** You won't do as well at exchange booths in airports, rail, and bus stations, or in hotels, restaurants, and stores, although you may find their hours more convenient. To avoid lines at airport exchange booths, **get a small amount of currency before you leave home.**

At press time, the exchange rate was $1.32 to the pound sterling, $1.33 to the Canadian dollar, and $1.34 to the Australian dollar.

MONEY ORDERS, FUNDS TRANSFERS

Any U.S. bank is equipped to accept transfers of funds from foreign banks. It helps if you can plan specific dates to pick up money at specific bank branches. Your home bank can supply you with a list of its correspondent banks in the United States.

If you have more time, and you have a U.S. address where you can receive mail, you can have someone send you a certified check, which you can cash at any bank, or a postal money order (for as much as $700, obtained for a fee of up to $1 at any U.S. post office and redeemable at any other post office). From overseas, you can have someone go to a bank to send you an international money order (also called a bank draft), which will cost a $15–$20 commission plus airmail postage. Always bring two valid pieces of identification, preferably with photos, to claim your money.

TAXES

HOTEL➢ Many states and cities levy hotel taxes, usually as a percentage of the room rate. For example, in New York City, which already has an 8¼% sales tax, the progressive hotel tax can raise the tariff as much as 13% more, to 21¼%. When you make room reservations, **ask how much tax will be added to the basic rate.**

SALES➢ There is no U.S. value-added tax, but sales taxes are set by most individual states, and they can range anywhere from 3% to 8¼%. In some states, localities are permitted to add their own sales taxes as well. Exactly what is taxable, however, varies from place to place. In some areas, food and other essentials are not taxable, although you might pay tax for restaurant food. Luxury items such as cigarettes and alcohol are sometimes subject to an extra tax (known colloquially as a "sin tax"), as is gasoline, on the theory that car users should provide funds used to improve local roads.

TRAVELER'S CHECKS

Whether or not to buy traveler's checks depends on where you are headed; **take cash to rural areas and small towns, traveler's checks to cities.** The most widely recognized are American Express, Citicorp, Thomas Cook, and Visa, which are sold by major commercial banks for 1% to 3% of the checks' face value—it pays to **shop around.** Both American Express and Thomas Cook issue checks that can be counter-signed and used by you or your traveling companion. You can cash them in banks without paying a fee (which can be as much as 20%) and use them as readily as cash in many hotels, restaurants, and shops. Record the numbers of the checks, cross them off as you spend them, and keep this information separate from your checks.

WIRING MONEY

You don't have to be a cardholder to send or receive funds through MoneyGram[SM] from American Express. Just go to a MoneyGram agent, in retail and convenience stores and in American Express Travel Offices. Pay up to $1,000 with cash or a credit card, anything over that in cash. The money can be picked up within 10 minutes in the form of U.S. dollar traveler's checks or local currency at the nearest MoneyGram agent cash or check at the nearest MoneyGram agent or, abroad, the nearest American Express Travel Office. There's no limit, and the recipient need only present photo identification. The cost, which in the U.S. includes a free long-distance phone call, runs from 3% to 10%, depending on the amount sent, the destination, and how you pay.

You can also send money using Western Union. Money sent from the United States or Canada will be available for pickup at agent locations in 100 countries within 15 minutes. Once the money is in the system, it can be picked up at any one of 25,000 locations. Fees range from 4% to 10%, depending on the amount you send.

N

NATIONAL PARKLANDS AND FORESTS

Children 16 and younger are admitted free to all national parks and recreational areas.; U.S. residents age 62 or older can pick up a **Golden Age Passport,** a free lifetime pass to all national parks, at any park that charges admission. Non-U.S. citizens of all ages can buy a 12-month **Golden Eagle Pass,** which provides free admission to all national parks, for $25 at any national park facility.

P

PACKAGES AND TOURS

A package or tour to the USA can make your vacation less expensive and more convenient. Firms that sell tours and packages purchase airline seats, hotel rooms, and rental cars in bulk and pass some of the savings on to you. In addition, the best operators have local representatives to help you out at your destination.

A GOOD DEAL?

The more your package or tour includes, the better you can predict the ultimate cost of your vacation. Make sure you know exactly what is included, and **beware of hidden costs.** Are taxes, tips, and service charges included? Transfers and baggage handling? Entertainment and excursions? These can add up.

Most packages and tours are rated deluxe, first-class superior, first class, tourist, or budget. The key difference is usually accommodations. If the package or tour you are considering is priced lower than in your wildest dreams, **be skeptical.** Also, **make sure your travel agent knows the hotels** and other services. Ask about location, room size, beds, and whether the facility has a pool, room service, or programs for children, if you care about these. Has your agent been there or sent others you can contact?

BUYER BEWARE

Each year consumers are stranded or lose their money when operators go out of business—even very large ones with excellent reputations. If you can't afford a loss, take the time to **check out the operator**—find out how long the company has been in business, and ask several agents about its reputation. Next, **don't book unless the firm has a consumer-protection program.** Members of the United States Tour Operators Association and the National Tour Association are required to set aside funds exclusively to cover your payments and travel arrangements in case of default. Nonmember operators may instead carry insurance; look for the details in the operator's brochure—and the name of an underwriter with a solid reputation. Note: When it comes to tour operators, **don't trust escrow accounts.** Although there are laws governing those of charter-flight operators, no governmental body prevents tour operators from raiding the till.

Next, **contact your local Better Business Bureau and the attorney general's office** in both your own state and the operator's; have any complaints been filed? Last, **pay with a major credit card.** Then you can cancel payment, provided that you can document your complaint. Always **consider trip-cancellation insurance** (*see* Insurance, *above*).

BIG VS. SMALL➢ An operator that handles several hundred thousand travelers annually can use its purchasing power to give you a good price. Its high volume may also indicate financial stability. But some small companies provide more personalized service; because they tend to specialize, they may also be experts on an area.

USING AN AGENT

Travel agents are an excellent resource. In fact, large operators accept bookings only through travel agents. But it's good to **collect brochures from several agencies,** because some agents' suggestions may be skewed by promotional relationships with tour and package firms that reward them for volume sales. If you have a special interest, **find an agent with expertise in that area;** the American Society of Travel Agents can give you leads in the United States. (Don't rely solely on your agent, though; agents may be unaware of small-niche operators, and some special-interest travel companies only sell direct).

SINGLE TRAVELERS

Prices are usually quoted per person, based on two sharing a room. If traveling solo, you may be required to pay the full double occupancy rate. Some operators eliminate this surcharge if you agree to be matched up with a roommate of the same sex, even if one is not found by departure time.

PACKING FOR THE USA

The American lifestyle is generally casual: Women may wear slacks and men may go without a jacket and tie virtually anywhere, except expensive restaurants in larger cities. If you prefer to dress up for dinner or the theater, though, go right ahead. As a rule, people in the northeast dress more formally, while people in such places as Florida, Texas, and southern California are more informal. In beach towns, many hotels and restaurants post signs announcing that they will not serve customers who are shoeless, shirtless, or dressed in bathing suits or other skimpy attire, so tote along some shoes and cover-ups.

The United States is a big country, with a wide range of climates. When deciding what weather to dress for, read the "When to Go" section in this book's introductions to each region you'll be visiting. One caveat: Even in warm destinations, you may want an extra layer of clothing to compensate for overactive air-conditioning or to protect against brisk ocean breezes. Although you can count on all modern buildings being well heated in winter, historic inns and hunting lodges in rugged climates—New England, the Great Lakes states, the Rockies, or the Pacific Northwest—may be poorly insulated, drafty, or heated only by wood-burning fireplaces. It's charming, but you'll need warmer clothing.

If you'll be sightseeing in historic cities, you'll spend a lot of time walking, so bring sturdy, well-fitting, flat-heeled shoes. Don't forget deck shoes if you want to go sailing, and sandals for walking across the burning-hot sand of southern beaches. If you plan to hike in the country, pack shoes or boots with strong flexible soles, and wear long pants to protect your legs from brambles and insect bites.

Bring an extra pair of eyeglasses or contact lenses in your carry-on luggage, and if you have a health problem, **pack enough medication** to last the trip or have your doctor write a prescription using the drug's generic name, because brand names vary from country to country (you'll then need a prescription from an American doctor). **Don't put prescription drugs or valuables in luggage to be checked**, for it could go astray. To avoid problems with customs officials, carry medications in original packaging. Also don't forget the addresses of offices that handle refunds of lost traveler's checks.

Bring sunscreen lotion if you expect to be out in the sun, because prices may be high at beachside stores. These days, most upscale hotels provide a basket of toiletries—soaps, shampoo, conditioner, bath gel—but if you are picky about the brand you use, bring your own. Hand-held hair driers are sometimes provided, but don't rely on this. You can generally request an iron and ironing board from the front desk.

ELECTRICITY

Overseas visitors will need to bring adapters to convert their personal appliances to the U.S. standard: AC, 110 volts/60 cycles, with a plug of two flat pins set parallel to one another.

LUGGAGE

Free airline baggage allowances depend on the airline, the route, and the class of your ticket; ask in advance. In general, on flights within the United States and on international flights between the United States and foreign destinations, you are entitled to check two bags—neither exceeding 62 inches, or 158 centimeters (length + width + height), or weighing more than 70 pounds (32 kilograms). A third piece may be brought aboard; its total dimensions are generally limited to less than 45 inches (114 centimeters), so it will fit easily under the seat in front of you or in the overhead compartment. In the United States, the Federal Aviation Administration gives airlines broad latitude to limit carry-on allowances and tailor them to different aircraft and operational conditions. Charges for excess, oversize, or overweight pieces vary.

SAFEGUARDING YOUR LUGGAGE➢ Before leaving home, **itemize your bags' contents** and their worth, and label them with your name, address, and phone number. (If you use your home address, cover it so that potential thieves can't see it.) Inside your bag, **pack a copy of your itinerary.** At check-in, **make sure that your bag is correctly tagged** with the airport's three-letter destination code. If your bags arrive damaged or not at all, file a written report with the airline before leaving the airport.

PASSPORTS AND VISAS

While traveling, **keep one photocopy of the data page** of your passport separate from your wallet and leave another copy with someone at home. If you lose your passport, promptly call the nearest embassy or consulate, and the local police; having the data page can speed replacement.

AUSTRALIANS

Australian citizens are required to have a valid passport and visa to enter the United States. Passport applications are available at any post office or at passport offices located in every major city. In addition, details on applying for a passport are listed in public telephone books. A birth or citizenship certificate and photo ID are required. For information on obtaining a visa, contact the American Embassy or Consulate nearest you.

CANADIANS

No passport is necessary to enter the United States.

U.K. CITIZENS

British citizens need a valid passport. If you are staying fewer than 90 days and traveling on a vacation, with a return or onward ticket, you will probably not need a visa. However, you will need to fill out the Visa Waiver Form, 1-94W, supplied by the airline.

R

RAIL TRAVEL

Amtrak is the national passenger rail service. It runs a limited number of routes; the northeast coast from Boston down to Washington, DC, is generally well served. Chicago is a major rail terminus as well.

Some trains travel overnight, and you can sleep in your seat or book a roomette at additional cost. Most trains have diner cars with acceptable food, but you may prefer to bring your own. Excursion fares, when available, may save you nearly half the round-trip fare.

CHILDREN

Children under 2 ride for free (one child per adult) if they don't occupy a seat; children 2–15 accompanied by a fare-paying adult pay half-price (two children per adult); children 15 and over pay the full adult fare.

TRAVELERS WITH DISABILITIES

Amtrak requests 48 hours' advance notice to provide redcap service, special seats, or wheelchair assistance at stations equipped to provide these services.

Passengers with disabilities receive 25% off an adult one-way fare. A special fare for children under 15 with disabilities (38% off an adult one-way fare) is also available.

RAIL PASSES

The USA Railpass allows overseas visitors 15 or 30 days of unlimited travel for $318 or $399 (peak season, June 16–Aug. 20) and $218–$319 (Aug. 21–June 15), respectively; you can purchase this in the United States at any Amtrak station, but to qualify you must show a valid non-U.S. passport. U.S. citizens can buy All Aboard America tickets, which allow a coast-to-coast trip with as many as three stopovers in a 45-day period for $339 during peak season; off-peak, the cost is $259.

SENIOR CITIZENS

Senior citizens (over 62) are entitled to a 15% discount on the lowest available fares Monday–Thursday only.

RENTING A CAR

CUTTING COSTS

To get the best deal, **book through a travel agent and shop around.** When pricing cars, **ask where the rental lot is located.** Some off-airport locations offer lower rates—even though their lots are only minutes away from the terminal via complimentary shuttle. You may also want to **price local car-rental companies,** whose rates may be lower still, although service and maintenance standards may not be up to those of a national firm. Also **ask your travel agent about a company's customer-service record.** How has it responded to late plane arrivals and vehicle mishaps? Are there often lines at the rental counter, and, if you're traveling during a holiday period, does a confirmed reservation guarantee you a car?

INSURANCE

When you drive a rented car, you are generally responsible for any damage or personal injury that you cause as well as damage to the vehicle. Before you rent, **see what coverage you already have** under the terms of your personal auto-insurance policy and credit cards. For about $14 a day, rental companies sell insurance, known as a collision damage waiver (CDW), that eliminates your liability for damage to the car; it's always optional and should never be automatically added to your bill. California, New York, and Illinois have outlawed the sale of CDW altogether.

REQUIREMENTS

In the United States you must be 21 to rent a car; rates may be higher for those under 25. Extra costs cover child seats, compulsory for children under 5 (about $3 per day), and additional drivers (about $1.50 per day). To pick up your reserved car you will need the reservation voucher, a passport, a valid driver's license, and a travel policy covering each driver.

SURCHARGES

Before picking up the car in one city and leaving it in another, **ask about drop-off charges or one-way service fees,** which can be substantial. Note, too, that some rental agencies charge extra if you return the car before the time specified on your contract. To avoid a hefty refueling fee, **fill the tank just before you turn in the car.** Some companies make you pay extra for crossing state lines.

S

SENIOR-CITIZEN DISCOUNTS

To qualify for age-related discounts, **mention your senior-citizen status up front** when booking hotel reservations, not when checking out, and before you're seated in restaurants, not when paying your bill. Note that discounts may be limited to certain menus, days, or hours. When renting a car, **ask about promotional car-rental discounts**—they can net lower costs than your senior-citizen discount.

STUDENTS ON THE ROAD

To save money, **look into deals available through student-oriented travel agencies.** To qualify, you'll need to have a bona fide student I.D. card. Members of international student groups also are eligible. *See* Students *in* Important Contacts A to Z, *above.*

T

TELEPHONES

All U.S. telephone numbers consist of 10 digits—the three-digit area code, followed by a seven-digit local number. If you're calling a number from another area code region, dial "1" then all 10 digits. If you're calling from a distance but within the same area code, dial "1" then the last seven digits. For calls within the same local calling area, just dial the seven-digit number. A map of U.S. area codes is printed in the front of most local telephone directories; throughout this book, we have listed each phone number in full, including its area code.

Two special prefixes, "800" and "900," are not area codes but indicators of particular kinds of service. "800" numbers can be dialed free from anywhere in the country—usually they are prepaid commercial lines that make it easier for consumers to obtain information, products, or services. "900" numbers charge you for making the call and generally offer some kind of entertainment, such as horoscope readings, sports scores, or sexually suggestive conversations. These services can be very expensive, so **know what you're getting into before you dial a "900" number.**

CREDIT-CARD CALLS

U.S. telephone credit cards are not like the magnetic cards used in some European countries, which pay for calls in advance; they simply represent an account that lets you charge a call to your home or business phone. On any phone, you can make a credit-card call by punching in your individual account number, or by telling the operator that number. Certain specially marked pay phones (usually found in airports, hotel lobbies, and so on) can be used only for credit-card calls. To get a credit card, contact your long-distance telephone carrier, such as AT&T, MCI, or Sprint.

LONG-DISTANCE

International calls can be direct-dialed from most phones; dial 011, followed by the country code and then the local number (the front pages of many local telephone directories include a list of overseas country codes). To have an operator assist you, dial 0 and ask for the overseas operator. The long-distance services of AT&T, MCI, and Sprint make calling home relatively convenient and let you avoid hotel surcharges; typically, you dial an an 800 number in the United States.

OPERATOR ASSISTANCE

For assistance from an operator, dial 0. To find

out a telephone number, call directory assistance, 555–1212 in every locality. These calls are free even from a pay phone. If you want to charge a long-distance call to the person you're calling, you can call collect by dialing 0 instead of 1 before the 10-digit number, and an operator will come on the line to assist you (the party you're calling, however, has the right to refuse the call).

PUBLIC PHONES

Instructions for pay telephones should be posted on the phone, but generally you insert your coins—anywhere from 10¢ to 30¢ for a local call—in a slot and wait for the steady hum of a dial tone before dialing the number you wish to reach. If you dial a long-distance number, the operator will come on the line and tell you how much more money you must insert for your call to go through.

TIPPING

Tipping is a way of life in America, and some individuals may even be rude if you don't give them the size of tip they expect. At restaurants, a 15% tip is standard for waiters; up to 20% may be expected at more expensive establishments. The same goes for taxi drivers, bartenders, and hairdressers. Coat-check facilities usually expect $1; bellhops and porters should get about 50¢ per bag; hotel maids in upscale hotels should get about $1 per day of your stay. On package tours, conductors and drivers usually get $10 per day from the group as a whole; check whether this has already been figured into your cost. For local sightseeing tours, you may individually tip the driver-guide $1 if he or she has been helpful or informative. Ushers in theaters do not expect tips.

W

WHEN TO GO

Although there is no country-wide tourist "season," various regions may have high and low seasons that are reflected in airfares and hotel rates. Unless the weather is a real drawback (as in Alaska in the winter or Miami in August), **visit areas during their off-season to save money and avoid crowds.**

2 Special-Interest Travel

By Karen Cure

YOU CAN SEE THE UNITED STATES in many ways, but you'll have the most fun seeing it in the company of like-minded travelers, doing what you like to do best. The following pages suggest what's available; contact state tourism departments for other ideas.

Group Trips

Want a vacation-immersion in archeobotany? How about studying the natural history of New York's Finger Lakes, or whooping cranes, or bald eagles? Have you always wanted someone to teach you kayaking? Or yearned to ride-and-roll the white water down the Colorado? Whatever your interest, you'll find a program or an organization sponsoring group trips in the field.

How to Choose

First pick a destination, then gather names of outfitters or resorts in the area you want to visit and contact them. For trips, ask about group size and composition (singles, couples, families, and so on), daily schedules, required gear, and any specifics of the activity. When looking into resorts, consider size, facilities, activities, and style. For courses and workshops, also find out about lodging arrangements, instructors' qualifications, and diversions for nonparticipating traveling companions. In every case, inquire about costs—what's included (meals, equipment), what's extra, how you pay, and how you get a refund if necessary. Check references.

Sports and the Outdoors

Sightseeing isn't always the best way to see the sights. Americans themselves may provide your most memorable travel experience; the nation's deep forests, mighty waters, and wide-open spaces are some of its most distinctive sights. The best way to experience the people and the land is in the great outdoors, pursuing one of the nation's favorite sports.

Group Trips

Knowledgeable leaders make group trips the safest way to develop or add to your wilderness experience. Because you overnight in campgrounds or simple accommodations, costs are often modest. Some trips are sponsored for members by conservation-minded nonprofit groups, such as the **American Forestry Association** (1516 P St. NW, Washington, DC 20005, ☎ 202/667–3300 or 800/368–5748), the **Appalachian Mountain Club** (5 Joy St., Boston, MA 02108, ☎ 617/523–0636), and the **Sierra Club** (730 Polk St., San Francisco, CA 94109, ☎ 415/776–2211). On Sierra Club trips, members volunteer as leaders, participants do camp chores, and costs stay low. **American Youth Hostels** (AYH, Box 37613, Washington, DC 20013-7613, ☎ 202/783–6161), strong on biking, also offers other trips, all open to travelers of all ages.

Private firms offering outdoors-oriented trips include **American Wilderness Experience** (Box 1486, Boulder, CO 80306, ☎ 800/444–0099); adventure-travel pioneer **Mountain Travel Sobek** (6420 Fairmount Ave., El Cerrito, CA 94530-3606, ☎ 800/227–2384); and for the Southeast, **Nantahala Outdoor Center** (13077 Hwy. 19W, NC 28713, ☎ 704/488–6737).

Bookings and Information

Pat Dickerman, in business since 1949, matches travelers with congenial operators in her comprehensive books, ***Adventure Travel North***

America and *Farm, Ranch, and Country Vacations* ($19 and $17 respectively, plus postage, from Adventure Guides, Inc., or Farm & Ranch Vacations, Inc., 7550 E. McDonald Dr., Scottsdale, AZ 85250, ☎ 800/252–7899). Fodor's publishes **Great American Sports and Adventure Vacations** ($17; available in bookstores, or call 800/533–6478), covering 30 activities with details on more than 500 schools, workshops, and tours throughout the United States. The quarterly ***Specialty Travel Index*** (305 San Anselmo Ave., Suite 313, San Anselmo, CA 94960, ☎ 415/459–4900; $10 annually) has ads for everything from fishing and mountain-bike trips to gambling and shopping trips. Specialty magazines available on newsstands are full of ideas; the following sections suggest other resources.

Bicycling

Biking the nation's byways shows off its bewitching hodgepodge of farms and factories, antique mansions and trailer parks, forests and strip malls. The leisurely pace makes it easy to stop to inspect a cottage garden or get ice cream at a local stand.

DISTINCTIVELY AMERICAN CYCLING

Clapboard houses, salty seacoasts, and pine-and-hardwood forests beckon cyclists to **New England,** particularly the Maine coast, Vermont's green and bucolic Northeast Kingdom, the forests and farms along New Hampshire's Connecticut River banks, Massachusetts's beach-ringed Martha's Vineyard and moor-covered Nantucket Island, northwest Connecticut (hilly but not killingly so, and scattered with old houses and charming inns), and mansion-laden Newport, Rhode Island.

The flat to mildly rolling landscape yields a bounty of scenic nooks and crannies in corners of the **mid-Atlantic states,** such as Pennsylvania's Lancaster County, full of peaceful byroads and Amish farms; northern Virginia's manicured, emerald horse country; Maryland's Eastern Shore, with its long Atlantic beaches and marshy backwaters; and the woods-edged towpath of the old C&O Canal near Washington, D.C.

In the **Rockies,** cyclists are mad for rugged, fat-tired mountain bikes—common sights in the piney-rugged high country near Durango, Colorado, and on the sandstone-clifftop Slickrock Trail near Moab, Utah, where the landscape is the color of sunset.

In **California,** the pedaling is good on the roads through the vineyards of the Napa Valley and on the rock-bound Monterey Peninsula, while Hwy. 1, teetering on the clifftops above the Pacific, is the trip of a lifetime. Traveling by bike is also a great way to experience **Hawaii.**

Some 50,000 mi of **abandoned railroad beds nationwide** are slated to become bike trails; contact Rails to Trails Conservancy (1325 Massachusetts Ave. NW, Washington, DC 20005, ☎ 202/797–5400) for information on the 7,500 mi converted so far.

MOUNTAIN BIKING

Climbing steep inclines, fording streams, and darting over dirt trails are all part of the exhilaration of mountain biking, now a subculture all its own. Look for designated trail systems in city, county, and state parks; in addition, many ski resorts open their slopes, trails, and chairlifts to mountain bikers during the off-season. *See* Resources, *below,* for organized tours.

WITH A GROUP

Bicycle-tour operators package basic-to-sumptuous lodging with escorts, "sag wagons" to carry luggage and weary pedalers, optional rental bikes and helmets, and sometimes meals. They also supply maps that pinpoint easy-to-strenuous routes between overnights—you choose the one that suits you and pedal at your own pace. **Adventure Cycling** (Box 8308, Missoula, MT 59807, ☎ 406/721–1776), the country's largest non-profit recreational cycling organization, is as good a source as the **AYH** (*see* Sports and the Outdoors, Group Trips, *above*).

RESOURCES

Adventure Cycling (*see above*) has helpful trip-planning information for members ($25 annually). *Bicycling* magazine (☎ 212/697–2040) lists specialist operators such as the active **Backroads Bicycle Touring** (1516 5th St., Berkeley, CA 94710, ☎ 510/527–1555 or 800/462–2848); **Carolina Cycle Tours** (13077 Hwy. 19W, Bryson City, NC 28713, ☎ 704/488–6737), which specializes in the Southeast; **Country Cycling Tours** (140 W. 83rd St., New York, NY 10024, ☎ 212/874–5151), which roams up and down the East Coast and packages trips with transportation to and from Manhattan; **Timberline Bicycle Tours** (7975 E. Harvard St., #J, Denver, CO 80231, ☎ 303/759–3804), which concentrates on the West; and **Vermont Bicycle Touring** (Bristol, VT 05443, ☎ 802/453–4811), which has won many fans with its trips over country roads and overnight stops at local inns. For organized mountain-biking tours, contact **Backcountry Bicycle Tours** (Box 4029, Bozeman, MT 59772, ☎ 406/586–3556) for trips in the national parks of the West.

Canoeing and Kayaking

Paddling along the ocean's edge, across freshwater lakes, or down free-flowing streams gives a traveler a view of the wilderness that's hard to come by any other way. Moving almost soundlessly, canoes and kayaks seldom disturb wildlife feeding at the water's edge, and paddlers encounter birds and animals alike, practically eye to eye. The choice of craft is up to you: Canoes are more comfortable and give you more room to carry gear (and easier access to it); kayaks are more stable—important when you're maneuvering among boulders on white water.

DISTINCTIVELY AMERICAN CANOEING

You don't have to be an expert to tackle some of America's most beautiful paddling waters. Many are within the skills of even beginners—though that can be changed by wind, heavy rainfall, or spring runoff.

In the East, canoeists head for **Maine's wild Allagash River** and adjacent stream- and portage-connected lakes, or the island-flecked lakes in **New York's Adirondack Mountains,** where log lean-tos shelter campers on the mainland and on pristine islands. Lush hardwood forests edge white-water torrents in **West Virginia.** In the South, the still waters of **Florida's Everglades National Park** and **Georgia's Okefenokee National Wildlife Refuge** access water-based "prairies" and mangrove swamps. The water in parts of Okefenokee—stained black by leachings from vegetation—perfectly mirrors the verdant foliage overhead.

In the Midwest, Voyageurs National Park and the Superior National Forest and its Boundary Waters Canoe Area Wilderness showcase the mighty woods of **northern Minnesota,** crossed by rivers and streams and scattered with lakes; in some areas, no motorized vehicles are permitted, and you could explore for months without backtracking. **Missouri's Ozark National Scenic Riverways** and **Arkansas's Buffalo National River**—bluff-edged blends of rapids, fast water, and still pools—are just two of six National Rivers administered by the National Park Service (Box 37127, Washington, DC 20013-7127, ☎ 202/208–4747); the service also administers nine National Wild and Scenic Rivers.

RESOURCES

The century-old **American Canoe Association** (7432 Alban Station Blvd., Suite B226, Springfield, VA 22150, ☎ 703/451–0141) has lists of canoeing clubs, schools, books, and trips ($25 annually). Consult *Canoe* (☎ 206/827–6363) and *Paddler* (☎ 208/939–4500) magazines for other ideas.

River Rafting

The spray soaks your clothes and stings your face, the roar drowns out your screams, and every roll and drop leaves your heart somewhere back *there:* Nothing reveals nature's power like roller-coaster white water. By comparison, the quiet stretches are all the more peaceful, the campfires more glowing, the air fresher, the picnic lunches and steak-and-potatoes dinners more savory. It's no wonder river rafting is so popular.

DISTINCTIVELY AMERICAN RAFTING

Rafting the **Colorado** through the Grand Canyon may be the ultimate American river experience, with the hundred-odd devilishly named rapids and the glowing canyon scenery on both sides. However, it gets a run for its money from the river's demanding **Cataract Canyon** section, in Utah's Canyonlands National Park; Idaho's **Salmon** (both the Main Fork, the stream that Lewis and Clark called the River of No Return, and its Middle Fork, with 80 stretches of white water); and Idaho's sometimes-hellish **Selway.** Long, smooth stretches between rapids make Oregon's **Rogue,** a National Wild and Scenic River (*see* Canoeing and Kayaking, *above*), especially good for families.

In the East, the most famous white-water rafting stream may be Georgia's **Chattooga,** where *Deliverance* was filmed. But river rats know West Virginia as the country's most concentrated area of challenging and diverse white water. One case in point is the powerhouse **New River** (actually the oldest river on the continent), which roars through a gorge so deep it's known as the Grand Canyon of the East.

RAFT TRIPS

Commercial outfitters make even the rowdiest white water accessible to the inexperienced. They also supply gear, food, and appropriate permits—all you have to do is show up (and hold on!). Some outfitters use motorized rafts, some only oar power; some request paddling help, others prohibit it. Find out what's expected before you book.

RESOURCES

State tourism offices and **America Outdoors** (Box 1348, Knoxville, TN 37901, ☎ 615/524–4814) have names of outfitters. **OARS** (Outdoor Adventure River Specialists; Box 67, Angels Camp, CA 95222, ☎ 209/736–4677), established in 1972, and the nonprofit **American River Touring Association** (24000 Casa Loma Rd., Groveland, CA 95321, ☎ 209/962–7873 or 800/323–2782) have extensive programs, as does **Dvořák Kayak & Rafting Expeditions** (17921 U.S. 285, Nathrop, CO 81236, ☎ 719/539–6851 or 800/824–3795), the outfitter that introduced you-paddle trips. *Paddler* magazine (☎ 208/939–4500) covers guided trips and paddling schools.

Climbing and Mountaineering

Every year scores of hardy walkers visit the nation's highest peaks and leave invigorated by the view and exhilarated by their accomplishment. Rock-climbing skills put just that many more summits within reach on longer mountaineering expeditions.

DISTINCTIVELY AMERICAN CLIMBS

Routes on Colorado's 14,255-ft **Longs Peak,** Maine's 5,267-ft **Mt. Katahdin,** New Hampshire's 6,288-ft **Mt. Washington,** and New York's 5,344-ft **Mt. Marcy** are within the abilities of well-conditioned hikers. Many other peaks require rock-climbing skills—or expert guiding. In the West, the most famous of these may be 20,320-ft **Mt. McKinley,** "The Great One," in Alaska's Denali National Park; but the 13,770-ft hunk of granite known as the **Grand Teton,** in Wyoming's eponymous national park, and the granite walls and domes of California's **Yosemite** have comparable charisma. Easterners find challenges in New York's **Adirondacks** and **Shawangunks.**

SCHOOLS AND GUIDED ASCENTS

For extra excitement in national parks, try a day at the **Colorado Mountain School** (Box 2062, Estes Park, CO 80517, ☎ 303/586–5758) in Rocky Mountain National Park, **Exum Mountain Guides** (Box 56, Moose, WY 83012, ☎ 307/733–2297) in the Tetons, and **Yosemite Mountaineering School** (Yosemite National Park, Yosemite, CA 95389, ☎ 209/372–1244 or 209/372–1335 in summer). Offering a good mix of guided climbs and lessons at beginner-to-advanced levels are the **American Alpine Institute** (1515 12th St., Bellingham, WA 98225, ☎ 206/671–1505), **Fantasy Ridge Mountain Guides** (Box 1679, Telluride, CO 81435, ☎ 303/728–3546), **Sierra Wilderness Seminars** (Box 707, Arcata, CA 95521, ☎ 707/822–8066), and, in the East, **Adirondack Alpine Adventures** (Box 179, Keene, NY 12942, ☎ 518/576–9881), the southern Appalachians' **Nantahala Outdoor Center** (13077 Hwy. 19W, Bryson City, NC 28713, ☎ 704/488–6737), and the White Mountains' **Eastern Mountain Sports** (Main St., Box 514, North Conway, NH 03860, ☎ 603/356–5433).

RESOURCES

Contact the **American Alpine Club** (710 10th St., Suite 100, Golden, CO 80401, ☎ 303/384–0110) for more information on climbing schools.

Fishing

The challenge of filling up a stringer isn't the only reason angling is the country's single most popular sport. There's also the prospect of a fresh-fish dinner. And the quiet hours spent by the water are their own reward.

DISTINCTIVELY AMERICAN ANGLING

Surf-casting on Atlantic-pounded beaches and jetties yields good sport from Cape Cod to south Florida. **Deep-sea fishing** gives you a good dose of the local culture. You can charter anything from a creaky wooden boat to a state-of-the-art yacht, or join the often rough-and-ready crowd aboard party boats, where anglers pay by the head. Ocean City, Maryland, thinks of itself as the world's white-marlin capital, but marlin is prime quarry in Hawaii, too, where a whole fleet of boats leave Kona every morning. There are huge sportfishing fleets in the Florida panhandle at small towns such as Destin and Fort Walton Beach, and in the Florida Keys, particularly Islamorada, Marathon, and Key West, where you might catch a long, gleaming, needle-nosed tarpon. **Fishing for snook,** a wily, scrappy, bony fish, is great sport—the Florida west coast town of Naples is a hotbed—as is **casting for bonefish** in shallow saltwater flats.

In fresh water, **trout fishing** is a whole angling subculture on such celebrated streams as Vermont's Battenkill, New York's Beaverkill, Arkansas's White River, and many rivers in Michigan and the northern Rockies. In Missouri, **river fishing** is for bass in clear, slow, bluff-

and forest-edged streams; in Idaho, it's for steelhead and chinook in waters like the Salmon, Snake, and Clearwater; in Oregon, it's for steelhead, with huge runs in winter.

Other anglers prefer **lake fishing** and take motorboats or canoes in search of their quarry: lake trout and landlocked salmon in deep waters such as Maine's Moosehead and New Hampshire's Winnepesaukee; crappie and largemouth bass on such man-made lakes in the South and Midwest as Kentucky's Lake Barkley and Kentucky Lake, and South Carolina's Lakes Marion and Moultrie. Northern Minnesota woodlands are as famous for yielding creels of scrappy walleye and northern pike, and large- and smallmouth bass, as for canoeing.

In a class by itself, **fishing in Alaska** is legendary: in the southeast panhandle for salmon (including sockeye, humpback, calico, king, and coho), and in the interior and the south-central part of the state for grayling. Good fishing is often right beside a highway; but fly-in trips to remote lakes and streams are common.

To plan a trip, decide what kind of fishing you want to do, then pick a destination. A letter to appropriate state fish and wildlife departments and a follow-up phone call are the first steps to a good creel. (Or choose a fishing lodge in an area you want to visit, and let the pros find the fish.) Bait-and-tackle shops or sporting-goods stores, thriving wherever there are waters to fish, can tell what's biting where and sell necessary licenses (usually required only by states and necessary only for freshwater fishing).

SCHOOLS

To hone your skills, spend time at the **Joan and Lee Wulff Fishing Schools** (HCR1, Box 70, Lew Beach, NY 12758, ☎ 914/439–4060) or **Bud Lilly's Trout Shop** (Box 698, 39 Madison Ave., West Yellowstone, MT 59758, ☎ 406/646–7801), both founded by veteran anglers, or at **Orvis Fly Fishing Schools** (Rte. 7A, Manchester, VT 05254, ☎ 802/362–3622), sponsored by the noted equipment maker.

RESOURCES

Fishing lodges—establishments dedicated to the care and feeding of anglers—advertise in *Field & Stream* (☎ 212/779–5000), *Fishing World* (☎ 816/531–5730), and *Fly Fisherman* (☎ 717/657–9555).

Golf

Although most top courses are at private clubs, U.S. resorts offer challenges for itinerant players, not to mention the chance to enjoy some of the country's lushest scenery.

DISTINCTIVELY AMERICAN GOLFING

The Masters Tournament, held annually at the Augusta National Golf Club in Augusta, Georgia, has made the Southeast famous among golfers. Although that course is not open to the public, golfers can enjoy southern graciousness along with equally verdant, beautifully tended layouts at another American golf center—**Pinehurst, North Carolina,** home of the PGA Hall of Fame, the Pinehurst Hotel (Box 4000, Pinehurst, NC 28374, ☎ 800/487–4653), and no less than seven golf courses. Two old-line southeastern mountain resorts offer an equally sharp picture of golfing America: the **Homestead** (U.S. 220, Hot Springs, VA 24445, ☎ 703/839–5500) and the **Greenbrier Hotel** (White Sulphur Springs, WV 24986, ☎ 304/536–1110). On **Hilton Head Island, South Carolina,** the beach scene meets the golf culture, and the hybrid attracts golfers from all over the country.

The golf-loving Japanese bought the world-class **Pebble Beach Golf Links** (17-Mile Dr., Pebble Beach, CA 93953, ☎ 408/624–3811) with a view to making a virtually private enclave of this California institution flung along the ragged edge of the rocky Monterey Peninsula; but public outcry has ensured that it will continue to show off the best side of U.S. golfing to itinerant players. For sheer numbers, golf enthusiasts look south to **San Diego,** home of six dozen courses. Courses like the Gold at the posh **Wigwam Resort** (Box 278, 300 E. Indian School La., Litchfield Park, AZ 85340, ☎ 602/935–3811) have brought Arizona the fame once reserved for California. Meanwhile, elegant Hawaii resorts such as **Mauna Kea** (1 Mauna Kea Beach Dr., Kohala Coast, HI 96743, ☎ 808/882–7222), **Mauna Lani** (Box 4959, Kohala Coast, HI 96743, ☎ 808/885–6655), and **Princeville at Hanalei** (Box 3040, Princeville, HI 96722, ☎ 808/826–3040) mix challenges with verdant coastline scenery and attract a golf-loving crowd from all over the country.

GOLF CLINICS

Most resort pros also teach. Then there are golf clinics, where golfers spend whole vacations working on their swing: the ***Golf Digest* Instruction Schools** (5520 Park Ave., Box 395, Trumbull, CT 06611–0395, ☎ 203/373–7130 or 800/243–6121), with programs year-round at resorts nationwide, and the **Craft-Zavichas Golf School** (600 Dittmer Ave., Pueblo, CO 81005, ☎ 719/564–4449).

Hiking and Backpacking

The United States has forests and trails to wear out a lifetime of hiking boots. If you've graduated from short walks in local parks, you're ready to tackle the wide-open spaces of national parks and forests.

DISTINCTIVELY AMERICAN BACKPACKING

The Rockies showcase snowcapped mountains, high-country lakes, and mixed conifer-hardwood forests. Key destinations include national forests such as the huge, wild, and varied **Nez Perce** (Rte. 2, Box 475, Grangeville, ID 83530, ☎ 208/983–1950), and trail-crossed national parks such as Colorado's **Rocky Mountain National Park** (Estes Park, CO 80517, ☎ 303/586–2371), northern Wyoming's **Grand Teton National Park** (Drawer 170, Moose, WY 83012, ☎ 307/739–3300), and **Yellowstone National Park** (Box 168, Yellowstone National Park, WY 82190, ☎ 307/344–7381) to the north. For a unique experience in **Glacier National Park** (Belton Chalets, Box 188, West Glacier, MT 59936, ☎ 406/888–5511), book a night in one of its spartan pair of World War I–era chalets, accessible only by trail. The Sierras have an entirely different mountain landscape, with granite peaks, lichen-splotched granite boulders, and pine and fir forests; in **Yosemite National Park,** you don't even have to carry camping gear if you stay in one of the five High Sierra Camps ($78 per night, by reservation from Yosemite Park & Curry Co., 5410 E. Home Ave., Fresno, CA 93727, ☎ 209/252–4848).

In the East, backpackers tramp the Appalachians, ancient mountains with rounded summits, hardwood forests, and many a killer grade. In the Appalachians' bare, windswept **White Mountains' Presidential Range,** the Appalachian Mountain Club runs no-frills hikers' huts ($50 nightly by reservation through the AMC, Box 298, Gorham, NH 03581, ☎ 603/466–2727). The **Great Smoky Mountains National Park** (Gatlinburg, TN 37738, ☎ 615/436–1200), which preserves another range of the Appalachians and is crossed by some 800 mi of trails, shows off a gentler side of these old mountains, splendid in spring when the dogwood is in bloom and in fall when the foliage is at its peak.

Backpacking is less common in some areas in the middle of the country, except in Arkansas reserves such as the **Ouachita National Forest** (Box 1270, Hot Springs, AR 71902, ☎ 501/321–5202) and the **Ozark National Forest** (Box 1008, Russellville, AR 72811, ☎ 501/968–2354). For hikers in **northern Michigan and Minnesota,** the draw is often the superior fishing in waters that are accessible only on foot. **Isle Royale National Park** (800 E. Lakeshore Dr., Houghton, MI 49931, ☎ 906/482–0984) and **Superior National Forest** (Box 338, Duluth, MN 55801, ☎ 218/720–5324) are popular.

LONG TRAILS

Veteran hikers aspire to walk the length of the 2,147-mi, Maine-to-Georgia **Appalachian Trail** (Appalachian Trail Conference, Box 807, Harpers Ferry, WV 25425, ☎ 304/535–6331), Vermont's 265-mi **Long Trail** (Green Mountain Club, R.R. 1, Box 650, Waterbury Center, VT 05677, ☎ 802/244–7037), the 2,700-mi **Continental Divide Trail** (Box 30002, Bethesda, MD 20824, no ☎), and the 2,638-mi **Pacific Crest Trail** (1350 Castle Rock Rd., Walnut Creek, CA 94598, ☎ 510/939–6111).

OFFBEAT GUIDED TRIPS

If you don't have the experience to tackle a long backpacking trip on your own, go with a group. In the West you have the option of llama treks; **Shasta Llamas, Ltd.** (Box 1088, Mt. Shasta, CA 96067, ☎ 916/926–1146), the first in the nation to use these sturdy, gentle animals to carry gear, now has many imitators. In the East, inn-to-inn trips put country comfort at trail's end—and innkeepers transport your gear between stops. Contact **Country Inns Along the Trail** (R.D. 3, Box 3115, Brandon, VT 05733, ☎ 802/247–3300) or **Knapsack Tours** (5961 Zinn Dr., Oakland, CA 94611, ☎ 510/339–0160). **Vermont Walking Tours** (Box 31, Craftsbury Common, VT 05827, ☎ 802/586–7767) specializes in backroads walks in the Green Mountain State's unspoiled Northeast Kingdom.

RESOURCES

Fodor's Sports: Hiking ($12) covers other trips and trails. Magazines such as *Outside* (☎ 312/951–0990) and *Walking* (☎ 617/266–3322) list many group trips.

Horseback: Pack Trips and Dude Ranches

Seeing the country from the back of a horse has more than a few advantages—not the least of which is that you don't have to carry your gear and can cover more ground than you would on foot yet still penetrate deep into the wilderness.

PACK TRIPS

The horse fancier's version of guided backpacking trips, pack trips mix days of traveling between base camps and layover days filled with hiking, fishing, loafing, and eating. Western hospitality prevails, and experience is seldom required. Some outfitters schedule trips in advance, while others do custom trips; daily cost is $85–$175. When choosing, ask about the ratio of traveling to layover days, daily distances covered, and the extent of horse care you're expected to provide.

If this appeals to you, look into the American Forestry Association's **Trail Riders of the Wilderness** program (*see* Group Trips, *above*) or contact local specialists; for names, consult state tourism offices or Pat Dickerman's ***Adventure Travel*** (*see* Bookings and Information, *above*).

INN-TO-INN RIDES

Eastern horse lovers relish the inn-to-inn rides of **Kedron Valley Stables** (Box 368, South Woodstock, VT 05071, ☎ 802/457–2734) and **Vermont Icelandic Horse Farm** (R.R. 376-1, Waitsfield, VT 05673, ☎ 802/496–7141).

DUDE RANCHES

Some are spiffy, upscale resorts, such as **Rancho de los Caballeros** (1551 S. Vulture Mine Rd., Wickenburg, AZ 85390, ☎ 602/684–5484), where riding is combined with top-notch tennis and golf. Others, such as **Lone Mountain** (Box 69, Big Sky, MT 59716, ☎ 406/995–4644), also offer rafting trips, fishing excursions, and other outdoor activities. At working ranches like **C Bar M** (Box AE, Clyde Park, MT 59018, ☎ 406/686–4687), pitching in is part of the fun. All offer a healthy dose of horse-related activities, such as pack trips, breakfast cookout rides, and horseback picnics. Rates range from $500 to more than twice that weekly.

Pat Dickerman's ***Farm, Ranch & Country Vacations*** (*see* Bookings and Information, *above*) is a good source; for other listings, contact the **Colorado Dude and Guest Ranch Association** (Box 300, Tabernash, CO 80478, ☎ 303/887–3128), the **Dude Ranchers Association** (Box 471, LaPorte, CO 80535, ☎ 303/223–8440), and **Old West Dude Ranch Vacations** (c/o American Wilderness Experiences, Box 1486, Boulder, CO 80306, ☎ 800/444–3833), as well as state tourism offices.

Nature and Wildlife Education

Spotting moose and seals and focusing your binoculars on trumpeter swans are among the pleasures of outdoor activities. Specialized programs and tours help you understand what you see.

NATURE CAMPS

Naturalists on hikes, in classrooms, and around evening campfires offer insights into nature and its interdependencies at several summer programs. The half-century-old **Audubon Ecology Camps** (613 Riversville Rd., Greenwich, CT 06831, ☎ 203/869–2017) attract people of all ages to one- and two-week summer sessions held in Wyoming's Wind River Range, on a 300-acre Maine island, and at a Greenwich, Connecticut, nature sanctuary. Accommodations are simple but comfortable. These are almost as well known among outdoors lovers as the **Sierra Club Base Camps** (730 Polk St., San Francisco, CA 94109, ☎ 415/776–2211), wilderness camps in the Sierras, the Rockies, the Smokies, and other wild places where club members spend a week or two among similarly conservation-minded vacationers, day-hiking into the surrounding countryside, helping with camp tasks under staff supervision, and paying relatively modest fees. Also look into **National Wildlife Federation Conservation Summits** (1400 16th St. NW, Washington, DC 20036-2266, ☎ 703/790–4363), which mix nature, outdoor skills, and folk culture; and the **Chewonki Foundation** (R.R. 2, Box 1200, Wicasset, ME 04578, ☎ 207/882–7323), an environmentally oriented group with the twin objectives of nature education and personal growth that numbers naturalist Roger Tory Peterson among its alumni.

IN THE NATIONAL PARKS

Participants learn more about the environment through lectures, field courses, and photography and writing workshops at **Canyonlands Field Institute** (Box 68, Moab, UT 84532, ☎ 801/259–7750) in Canyonlands National Park; the **Glacier Institute** (Box 7457, Kalispell, MT 59904, ☎ 406/756–3911); the **Olympic Park Institute** (HC 62, Box 9T, Port Angeles, WA 98362, ☎ 206/928–3720); **Point Reyes Field Seminars** (Bear

Valley Rd., Point Reyes Station, CA 94956, ☎ 415/663–1200), at the Point Reyes National Seashore; and the **Yellowstone Institute** (Box 117, Yellowstone National Park, WY 82190, ☎ 307/344–2295).

NATURALIST-LED TOURS AND CRUISES

Guided by university professors, botanists, or zoologists, wildlife tours reveal dimensions of the American landscape that most vacationers never even suspect. Hiking and camping may be involved, but often accommodations are comfortable or even luxurious and travel is by small cruise boat or van. Whale-watching is often a feature. **Biological Journeys** (1696 Ocean Dr., McKinleyville, CA 95521, ☎ 707/839–0178) and **Nature Expeditions International** (474 Willamette Ave., Box 11496, Eugene, OR 97440, ☎ 503/484–6529) are typical.

WILDERNESS SKILLS PROGRAMS

Here you might learn winter camping, sea kayaking, rock-climbing, minimum-impact camping, or river rafting; but it's the personal growth that comes from mastering something new that attracts participants to the rigorous mental and physical challenges of **Outward Bound** (Rte. 9D, R2, Box 280, Garrison, NY 10524-9757, ☎ 914/424–4000 or 800/243–8520), the granddaddy of such programs, or the **National Outdoor Leadership School** (288 Main St., Lander, WY 82520, ☎ 307/332–6973), originally founded to train trip leaders.

Sailing

The mighty U.S. coastline ranks among the nation's most stirring sights, and while roads provide access to much of it, seeing it from the water gives an undeniably better view.

DISTINCTIVELY AMERICAN SAILING

Nothing says United States quite like **Maine's rocky coast,** known to sailors all over the world for its scenery, good moorings, and abundant facilities. But there's comparable variety among the islands, coves, and shoreside towns of the **Chesapeake Bay** and **Long Island Sound.** The waters off **Newport, Rhode Island,** home of the Museum of Yachting, are light-years away from landlubber gridlock; the crowd is well-heeled and tony. In the **Florida Keys,** the winds are good, the waters teeming with marine life, and the shoreside life casual and laid-back. In the Midwest, sailors relish the challenging **Great Lakes,** inland seas. **California** is sail-crazed; Sausalito, near San Francisco Bay, and Marina del Rey and Newport Beach, in the south, are boating centers. In northwest Washington State, the **San Juan Islands** offer their own barefoot life amid coves and beaches teeming with birds and animals. For the adventurous side of the sport, consider **Alaska**—extraordinary with its fjords, shoreline peaks and waterfalls, good fishing, and abundant wildlife.

CHARTERS

You can book craft either crewed (staffed to handle cooking and navigation) or bareboat (for experienced sailors only). Contact state tourism offices for lists of charter operators.

SCHOOLS

The pleasures of the sea mix with the satisfaction of acquiring a new skill at the nation's two principal sailing programs: the **Annapolis Sailing School** (Box 3334, Annapolis, MD 21403, ☎ 410/267–7205 or 800/638–9192), which has a branch in the U.S. Virgin Islands, and the **Offshore Sailing School** (16731 McGregor Blvd., Suite 110, Fort Myers, FL 33908, ☎ 813/454–1700 or 800/221–4326), founded by former Olympian Steve Colgate and now offering programs on Florida's Captiva Island, in Newport, Rhode Island, and in Port Washington, New York.

RESOURCES

Consult *Fodor's Sports: Sailing* ($12) for more on great sailing destinations. Ads and information on charter operators can be found in *Sail* (☎ 617/964–3030), *Cruising World* (☎ 401/847–1588), and *Yachting* (☎ 212/779–5300).

WINDJAMMER CRUISES

The beating of sails in the wind, good food, the smell of the sea, and the excitement of calling at scenic ports create unbeatable camaraderie on cruises aboard the nation's fleet of tall ships—restorations or reconstructions of 19th-century craft that accommodate fewer than 30 passengers. Per-person fares of $75–$100 a day, much lower than those for larger cruise ships, are a plus, and most people don't mind the spartan cabins and cold showers (or absence thereof), since it's easy to clean up at local marinas.

In the East, Rockland, Camden, and Rockport, Maine, are base for a dozen ships, mostly members of the **Maine Windjammer Association** (Box 317, Rockport, ME 04856, ☎ 800/624–6380). Also contact Maine's state tourism office. In the Midwest, look into the **Traverse Tall Ship Company** (13390 S.W. Bay Shore Dr., Traverse City, MI 49684, ☎ 616/941–2000).

Skiing

Ski areas can be found even in such unlikely states as Indiana, but the best skiing in the country—and some of the best in the world—is in the Rockies.

True, the typical ski area in the Alps has a greater vertical drop (as skiers call the altitude difference between lift base and the highest lift-served point). But no other ski areas have comparable snow quality. Not only is snowfall (usually) abundant, but it is also dry and featherlight, and snow quality is consistent from top to bottom—a fact that dazzles skiers from Europe, where this is seldom the case. To enjoy it all, you don't have to be a hotdog mogul skier or one of the manic daredevils dubbed "extreme skiers," who like to drop onto mountaintops from helicopters. U.S. mountains have slopes you can ski no matter what your ability.

DISTINCTIVELY AMERICAN SKIING

In the Rockies you'll find an affluent crowd in **Sun Valley,** Idaho; a certain former Colorado mining town known as **Aspen;** faux-Alpine **Vail** not far away; and perhaps **Deer Valley,** Utah—relentlessly tasteful right down to the marble in the base lodge rest rooms. For mellow western charm in addition to abundant facilities, it's hard to beat **Breckenridge, Copper Mountain, Keystone,** and **Steamboat,** Colorado, or even **Park City,** Utah, or friendly, low-key spots like **Big Mountain,** near Whitefish, Montana, practically unknown outside the West. The same can't be said of New Mexico's challenging **Taos;** Wyoming's one-of-a-kind **Jackson Hole;** Utah's cozy, rustic **Alta,** the sine qua non among powder skiers; and its mod cousin, **Snowbird.** But even then, by comparison to the big Colorado resorts, their fame is limited.

Elsewhere in the West, California's Sierras get massive amounts of snow, and skiers come by the thousands to the resorts around crystal-clear Lake Tahoe, including **Squaw, Heavenly, Northstar,** and **Kirkwood.**

In the East, narrow trails and icy conditions magnify the challenges, although slope grooming and snowmaking ease the sting at Vermont's **Stowe** and its Vermont cousins closer to the big cities: huge **Killington** and **Mt. Snow,** genteel **Stratton** and **Sugarbush.** New Hampshire resorts such as **Waterville Valley** are even more relaxed.

To choose, consider area personality, terrain, and convenience. Are there slopeside accommodations or do you need a car? Can you find the lodgings you want (motel, inn, B&B, dorm, resort) at a price you can afford? Are there programs for kids? Families appreciate areas with centralized lift layouts, which make it easy to rendezvous for lunch or at day's end.

SKI SCHOOLS AND PACKAGES

Most ski areas offer instruction and packages. Some offer deals on multiday lift tickets; others add lessons, lodging, meals, or other perks. The best deals are midweek, particularly in areas with heavy weekend traffic.

RESOURCES

Ski (☎ 212/779–5000), *Skiing* (☎ 212/779–5000), *Snow Country* (☎ 203/323–7038), and *Powder* (☎ 714/496–5922) magazines cover the field.

Ski Touring

Heavy snows that otherwise make the nation's meadows and forests inaccessible are no problem for those who can cross-country ski.

DISTINCTIVELY AMERICAN SKI TOURING

National and state park and forest trails are sometimes suitable for cross-country skiing, although rental equipment is not always available. At ski areas, valleys at the base and high ski-touring ridges and plateaus often offer excellent sport.

For a once-in-a-lifetime experience there's nothing like **Yellowstone National Park.** In winter, waterfalls freeze into bizarre sculptures; steam billowing from the thermal features turns trees into hoary ghosts; and icicles glitter everywhere. Lodging, equipment, and instruction are available.

Elsewhere in the West there's abundant ski touring at several areas in and around Wyoming's **Grand Teton National Park** and California's **Yosemite National Park.** Idaho's **Sun Valley** has hundreds of skiable acres, and you can even helicopter up to the high country. Communities of cross-country fanatics flourish in Colorado at **Steamboat Springs** and **Vail,** and the trail system in **Aspen** is one of the nation's most extensive. Minnesota's **Superior National Forest** enjoys abundant snowfall and hundreds of miles of trails.

In the East, prime areas include Massachusetts's **Berkshire Mountains,** full of parks, forests, and inns; New Hampshire's **Mt. Washington Valley;** and Vermont's **Stowe,** where dozens of miles of trails link restaurants, inns, and shops.

GROUP TRIPS

Rock-climbing schools (*see* Climbing and Mountaineering, *above*) often have cross-country skiing programs. For inn-to-inn tours, contact **Country Inns Along the Trail** (R.D. 3, Box 3115, Brandon, VT 05733, ☎ 802/247–3300). A bit more rugged, hut-to-hut tours of Colorado's spectacular Tenth Mountain Trail are offered by **Paragon Guides** (Box 130, Vail, CO 81658, ☎ 303/926–5299).

RESOURCES

The **USIA Cross-Country Ski Areas Association** (259 Bolton Rd., Winchester, NH 03470, ☎ 603/239–4341) publishes a book detailing more than 500 cross-country areas and can send a list of those sponsoring overnight cross-country trips. Also read *Cross Country Skier* magazine (☎ 612/377–0312).

Tennis

If you have nonplaying companions, consider a full-scale resort with a heavy tennis program; otherwise consider tennis camps or clinics, where tennis is the only activity. Rather than trying to remake your game, most build on what you have to send you home a better player.

CAMPS AND CLINICS

Staged year-round at resorts nationwide and at private schools in summer, these provide the most intense tennis experience, with up to five hours of play every day. Established in 1968, **Tennis Camps, Ltd.** (444 E. 82nd St., New York, NY 10028, ☎ 212/879–0225 or 800/223–2442) is a major player. **Nick Bollettieri Tennis Academy** (5500 34th St. W, Bradenton, FL 34210, ☎ 813/755–1000 or 800/872–6425) and **Harry Hopman/Saddlebrook International Tennis** (5700 Saddlebrook Way, Wesley Chapel, FL 33543, ☎ 813/973–1111 or 800/729–8383) are both famed for turning prodigies into pros. For off-court luxury the last word is **John Gardiner's**—both the exclusive California ranch (Box 228, Carmel Valley, CA 93924, ☎ 408/659–2207) and its even posher desert cousin (5700 E. McDonald Dr., Scottsdale, AZ 85253, ☎ 602/948–2100). Former top players mastermind the friendly **John Newcombe's Tennis Ranch** (Box 310–469, New Braunfels, TX 78131, ☎ 210/625–9105 or 800/444–6204), the **Van Der Meer Tennis Center Camps** (Box 5902, Hilton Head Island, SC 29938, ☎ 800/845–6138), and the high-tech **Vic Braden Tennis College** (23335 Avenida la Caza, Coto de Caza, CA 92679, ☎ 714/581–2990 or 800/422–6878).

RESORTS

Planned resort developments almost always have extensive facilities. At **Hilton Head Island, South Carolina,** two resorts alone offer more than five dozen courts—Sea Pines Plantation (Box 7000, Hilton Head Island, SC 29938, ☎ 800/845–6131) and Palmetto Dunes (Box 5606, Hilton Head Island, SC 29938, ☎ 803/785–7300 or 800/845–6130). Ski resorts usually have extensive tennis programs—among them Bolton Valley, Killington, Stratton, and Sugarbush. So do large resort hotels. A special case is the elegant Gulf Coast **Colony Beach & Tennis Resort** (1620 Gulf of Mexico Dr., Longboat Key, FL 34228, ☎ 813/383–6464 or 800/237–9443), devoted exclusively to tennis.

To choose, ask the pro shop about court fees, reservations procedures and availability, game-matching services, night play, guest tourneys, court-time limits, instruction, and the resort's court-to-room ratio (1 to 10 is fine; half that if there are many other activities).

RESOURCES

See *Tennis* magazine (☎ 212/789–3000) for listings of tennis resorts, camps, and clinics.

Spiritual and Physical Fitness Vacations

Providing meaningful recreation for both mind and body is the objective of hundreds of establishments across the United States. Far from being spas in the old, European sense—grand hotels that cosset those who come to sip the waters—American spas reflect current attitudes on diet and health: *Fodor's Healthy Escapes* ($15.50) lists 243 fitness-oriented camps, resorts, and programs starting at $35 a day, some all-inclusive packages and some à la carte.

Holistic Centers

The verdant Catskills' **New Age Health Spa** (Rte. 55, Neversink, NY 12765, ☎ 914/985–7601 or 800/682–4348) helps guests balance body, soul, and mind via programs ranging from astrological consultations and aerobics to Zen meditation. Flotation tanks and massages supplement nutrition and counseling at such old-timers as the **Omega Institute** (260 Lake Dr., Rhinebeck, NY 12572, ☎ 914/266–4301 or 800/944–1001).

Spas for Luxury and Pampering

To those who say "No pain, no gain," others reply, "No frills, no thrills," and seek out deluxe establishments for regimens of body wraps, saunas, Swiss showers, massages, manicures, and maybe a yoga class or two. On the cutting edge is **Canyon Ranch** (165 Kemble St., Lenox, MA 01240, ☎ 413/637–4100 or 800/326–7080; 8600 E. Rock Cliff Rd., Tucson, AZ 85715, ☎ 602/749–9000 or 800/742–9000), where up-to-the-minute treatments are combined with such outdoor activities as hiking, biking, and tennis, as well as sophisticated spa cuisine. One for-women-only establishment sets the standard: **The Greenhouse** (107th St., Box 1144, Arlington, TX 76004, ☎ 817/640–4000), a study in elegant Texan style. More typically, luxury spas take the more active approach of the serene **Golden Door** (Deer Springs Rd., Box 463077, Escondido, CA 92046, ☎ 619/744–5777), where individually planned programs include 6 AM hikes and exercise classes. **La Costa Hotel & Spa** (Costa del Mar Rd., Carlsbad, CA 92009, ☎ 619/438–9111 or 800/854–5000) is the megaresort of the breed. The **Doral Saturnia International Spa Resort** (8755 N.W. 36th St., Miami, FL 33178, ☎ 305/593–6030 or 800/331–7768), a vision of Tuscany with its red-tile roof, fuses a typically American program involving exercise and stress-management training with European treatments, such as warm mud packs for muscular problems.

Weight Management and Preventive Medicine Centers

Another group of American spas involves extensive medical supervision. Typifying these are the well-rounded **Duke University Diet and Fitness Center** (804 W. Trinity Ave., Durham, NC 27701, ☎ 919/684–6331); the **Aerobics Center** (12230 Preston Rd., Dallas, TX 75230, ☎ 214/386–4777 or 800/444–5192), inspired by aerobics pioneer Dr. Kenneth H. Cooper; and the **Pritikin Longevity Centers** (1910 Ocean Front Walk, Santa Monica, CA 90405, ☎ 310/450–5433 or 800/421–9911; 5875 Collins Ave., Miami Beach, FL 33140, ☎ 305/866–2237 or 800/327–4914), which focus on the late Nathan Pritikin's belief that diet can reverse atherosclerosis.

Volunteer Vacations

Although fees for the nation's hundreds of vacation volunteer programs may be partly tax-deductible, their allure has less to do with money than with the satisfaction that comes from giving something back to society, the excitement of an entirely new activity, the intensity of the group experience. Will you enjoy it? Yes, if you're flexible and independent, can take the initiative and cope with the unexpected, have a sense of humor, and like to be a team player.

When choosing a program, be sure to ask about insurance, the number of participants and staff, and the standards by which project and leader were chosen.

FIELD RESEARCH

How about tagging dolphins, mapping mammoth bones, or collecting subtropical plants? Scientists in need of enthusiastic, inexpensive labor for projects like these are happy to enlist help from vacationers, who pay a stipend to cover their own expenses and defray expedition costs. Matching up scientists and vacationers are such organizations as **Earthwatch** (680 Mt. Auburn St., Watertown, MA 02272, ☎ 617/926–8200), the oldest in the field; the **Foundation for Field Research** (FFR, Box 771, St. Georges, Grenada [West Indies], ☏ 809/440–8854); **Smithsonian Research Expeditions Program** (490 L'Enfant Plaza SW, Room 4210, Washington, DC 20560, ☏ 202/287–3210); and the **University Research Expeditions Program** (UREP, c/o University of California, Berkeley, CA 94720, ☏ 510/642–6586), with University of California scientists.

ARCHAEOLOGICAL RESEARCH

It's hot, dirty, and strenuous—but you don't have to be an archaeologist to catch the excitement. Earthwatch, FFR, and UREP (*see above*) often list digs among their fieldwork opportunities. For other ideas, consult the lists in the Archaeological Institute of America's *Fieldwork Opportunities Bulletin* ($13.50 from the Kendall Hunt Publishing Co., Order Dept., Box 1840, Dubuque, IA 52004-1840, ☏ 800/228–0810).

TRAIL BUILDING AND MAINTENANCE

Helping state and national parks and forests maintain old trails, build new ones, and clean up and replant campgrounds is the mission of several private groups that welcome volunteers—among them the active **Sierra Club** (*see* Sports and the Outdoors, Group Trips, *above*) and the **Appalachian Mountain Club** (Trails Conservation Corps, Box 298, Gorham, NH 03581, ☏ 603/466–2721). Many state parks or conservation departments use volunteers, as do the National Park Service, U.S. Fish and Wildlife Service, and U.S. Forest Service.

SOCIAL SERVICE

Building community centers, repairing churches, setting up youth programs, and serving in group homes are just a few activities of volunteer work camps. Contact clearinghouses such as the **Volunteers for Peace International Workcamps** (43 Tiffany Rd., Belmont, VT 05730, ☏ 802/259–2759) and **Council on International Educational Exchange** (205 E. 42nd St., New York, NY 10017, ☏ 212/661–1414).

RESOURCES

The **Points of Light Foundation** (1736 H St. NW, Washington, DC 20006, ☏ 202/223–9186) and **Volunteers for Peace** (*see* Social Service, *above*) have listings of other volunteer opportunities.

Education and Culture

All travel stretches the observant voyager's mind. A number of programs—university-sponsored tours and continuing-education courses, as well as workshops in the arts—institutionalize that process.

Academic Tours and Programs

Once upon a time, **Chautauqua** (Box 28, Chautauqua, NY 14722, ☏ 716/357–6200) was unique among travel destinations in offering language, history, crafts, hobbies, music, and other arts programs. Established in 1874, it now crams more than 170 courses into the nine-week July–August program on its lakeside campus.

VACATIONS ON COLLEGE CAMPUSES

At these you can expand your intellectual horizons in the company of university professors and other inquisitive spirits, in the spirit of Chautauqua, at summer colleges sponsored by continuing-education divisions at major colleges and universities. Typically, these programs require no tests, give no grades, admit nonalumni as well as alumni, keep costs low with simple dormitory lodging and cafeteria meals, and explore such themes as Victorian England or capitalism in China. They also fill up fast.

Summer schools for adults are currently offered in the East at **Cornell** (626 Thurston Ave., Ithaca, NY 14850, ☎ 607/255–6260); **Dartmouth** (308 Blunt Alumni Center, Hanover, NH 03755, ☎ 603/646–2454); **Johns Hopkins** (3211 N. Charles St., Baltimore, MD 21218, ☎ 410/516–0363), which has programs in Snowmass, Colorado, as well as on campus; and **Penn State** (409 Keller Conference Center, University Park, PA 16802, ☎ 814/863–1743). Comparable programs have recently been mounted in the South at the **University of North Carolina at Chapel Hill** (Vacation College Humanities Program, Campus Box 3425, Alumni House, Chapel Hill, NC 27599-3425, ☎ 919/962–1544) and at **Washington and Lee University** (Office of Special Programs, Lexington, VA 24450, ☎ 703/463–8723), and in the Midwest at **Indiana University** (Mini University, Indiana Memorial Union, Suite 400, Bloomington, IN 47405, ☎ 812/855–4670) and the **College of Wooster** (Alumni Relations, Wooster, OH 44691, ☎ 216/263–2263).

Programs come and go, however, so it's best to pick a university you'd like to attend, then call its alumni office or its continuing-education or adult-education department to inquire about what's being offered.

ACADEMIC AND OTHER CULTURAL TOURS

Major U.S. museums sponsor dozens of study tours every year, most escorted by museum personnel, university professors, and other experts. Another option is the programs of independent operators; for extensive listings, consult the *Guide to Academic Travel* ($19.95 postpaid from Shaw Guides Publishers, Box 1295, New York, NY 10023, ☎ 212/799–6464 or 800/247–6553).

HISTORY TOURS

American architecture, social history, and culture are emphasized on tours led by the **National Trust for Historic Preservation** (1785 Massachusetts Ave., Washington, DC 20036, ☎ 202/673–4000). Four- to seven-day trips have explored Virginia's grand houses and plantations, the heritage of the Maine coast, and Rte. 66.

Cooking Schools

Those who love to cook, eat well, and enjoy fine wines have few better travel options than to sign up for an intensive multiday cooking course at a hotel or cooking school. When choosing, be sure to find out about the demonstration-to-participation ratio.

INTENSIVE COURSES AT COOKING SCHOOLS

Two- to five-day programs are widely available. Some are through professional schools such as the **Culinary Institute of America** (433 Albany Post Rd., Hyde Park, NY 12538, ☎ 800/888–7850), the nation's major professional school; the **California Culinary Academy** (625 Polk St., San Francisco, CA 94102, ☎ 415/771–3536); and **Johnson and Wales University** (Abbot Park Pl., Providence, RI 02903, ☎ 401/456–1000 or 800/343–2565).

Well-known chefs and cookbook authors sponsor other programs, notably **Julie Sahni's Indian Cooking** (101 Clark St., Brooklyn Heights, NY 11201, ☎ 718/625–3958) and **Karen Lee Chinese Cooking Classes** (142 West End Ave., New York, NY 10023, ☎ 212/787–2227). Other options are at such vineyards as the **Robert Mondavi Winery** (Box 106, Oakville, CA 94562, ☎ 707/944–2866) and **Beringer Vineyards** (Box 111, St. Helena, CA 94574, ☎ 707/963–7115), where Madeleine Kamman runs the school for American chefs.

PROGRAMS AT HOTELS, INNS, AND RESORTS

If your traveling companions would rather play golf or tennis than slave over a hot stove, look into short programs at such inns as the Delmarva Peninsula's elegant **Channel Bass Inn** (6228 Church St., Chincoteague, VA 23336, ☎ 804/336–6148), or at such grand resorts as the **Greenbrier Hotel** (White Sulphur Springs, WV 24986, ☎ 304/536–1110 or 800/624–6070), where La Varenne's Anne Willan directs.

RESOURCES

For extensive listings of both short- and long-term programs, as well as information on gourmet and wine tours, consult the *Guide to Cooking Schools* ($22.95 postpaid from Shaw Guides Publishers, Box 1295, New York, NY 10023, ☎ 212/799–6464 or 800/247–6553).

Crafts Workshops

Short workshops in the crafts and fine arts are staged by major museums and at national parks such as Glacier, Yosemite, and Olympic. More extensive programs lasting from one to several weeks and focusing on a range of crafts—from metal, wood, and ceramics to indigenous regional and Native American crafts—are held at colleges, crafts centers, and individual studios.

INTERDISCIPLINARY CRAFTS CENTERS

Dozens of weekend and weeklong courses in basketry, bookmaking, ceramics, woodworking, and other topics draw pros as well as beginners and intermediates to such crafts centers as **Anderson Ranch Arts Center** (Box 5598, Snowmass Village, CO 81615, ☎ 303/923–3181), on a Rocky Mountains ranch near Aspen; the **Arrowmont School of Arts and Crafts** (Box 567, Gatlinburg, TN 37738, ☎ 615/436–5860), founded in 1945 on 70 acres a mile from the Great Smoky Mountains National Park; and the **Haystack Mountain School of Crafts** (Deer Isle, ME 04627-0518, ☎ 207/348–2306), occupying a shingled, Atlantic-view studio complex on a Maine island. Several focus on traditional folk crafts; the oldest and most active are the **John C. Campbell Folk School** (Rte. 1, Box 14A, Brasstown, NC 28902, ☎ 704/837–2775), whose campus is a National Historic District, and the **Penland School of Crafts** (Penland Rd., Penland, NC 28765, ☎ 704/765–2359), on 500 acres in the Blue Ridge Mountains.

SPECIALIZED PROGRAMS

You can study everything from basketry and wooden boatbuilding to papermaking, couture sewing, and weaving. For extensive listings of what's available, consult the *Guide to Art & Craft Workshops* ($19.95 postpaid from Shaw Guides Publishers, Box 1295, New York, NY 10023, ☎ 212/799–6464 or 800/247–6553).

Painting and Fine-Arts Workshops

Amateurs can get professional tutelage at intensive programs at inns, resorts, museums, fine-arts centers, and even crafts schools nationwide (*see* Crafts Workshops, *above*).

VARIED PROGRAMS

Diverse programs that embrace disciplines ranging from printmaking, watercolor, portraiture, and still life to landscape painting are available at such schools as the **Art Institute of Boston** (Continuing Education, 700 Beacon St., Boston, MA 02215, ☎ 617/262–1223) and **Dillman's Sand Lake Lodge** (Box 98, Lac du Flambeau, WI 54538, ☎ 715/588–3143), an old family summer resort in northern Wisconsin. Programs abound in Maine, among them the **Maine Coast Art Workshops** (c/o Merle Donovan, Box 236, Port Clyde, ME 04855, ☎ 207/372–8200).

SPECIALIZED PROGRAMS

Some workshops concentrate on a specific medium, such as pastels or watercolors, or a specific style or theme—realism, western motifs, or seascapes, for instance. A comprehensive listing is in the *Guide to Art & Craft Workshops* (*see* Crafts Workshops, *above*).

RESOURCES

American Artist (☎ 212/764–7300) magazine lists a wide array of summer programs such as those in its March issue.

Photography Workshops and Tours

Throughout the year amateurs and professionals sign up for workshops and tours designed to polish their techniques and take them to photogenic spots at the best possible times.

WORKSHOPS

Each workshop has a distinctive focus. Some cover theory and practice through fieldwork and seminars in black-and-white and color, looking at photography as both a fine and an applied art, in fields ranging from fashion to reportage. The active, well-established **Maine Photographic Workshops** (2 Central St., Rockport, ME 04856, ☎ 207/236–8581) explores most aspects of photography, as do the well-respected if less picturesquely situated **International Center of Photography** (1130 5th Ave., New York, NY 10128, ☎ 212/860–1776) and **Visual Studies Workshop** (31 Prince St., Rochester, NY 14607, ☎ 716/442–8676). The **Friends of Photography Workshops** (250 4th St., San Francisco, CA 94103, ☎ 415/495–7000) carry on the tradition of the venerable Ansel Adams Workshop, founded in 1940, which it now encompasses.

GUIDED TOURS

Specialist tours, accompanied by professional photographers and scheduled to catch photogenic spots at optimal times, are offered by many organizations, including **Close-Up Expeditions** (1031 Ardmore Ave., Oakland, CA 94610, ☎ 510/465–8955), the official Photographic Society of America tour operator; **Photo Adventure Tours** (2035 Park St., Atlantic Beach, NY 11509, ☎ 516/371–0067); and **Thru the Lens Tours** (5855 Green Valley Circle, Culver City, CA 90230, ☎ 310/645–8480 or 800/521–5367).

RESOURCES

American Photo (☎ 212/767–6273) and *Popular Photography* (☎ 212/767–6000) magazines advertise tours and workshops. The *Guide to Photography Workshops & Schools* ($19.95 postpaid from Shaw Guides Publishers, Box 1295, New York, NY 10023, ☎ 212/799–6464 or 800/247–6553) has extensive listings of programs.

3 The Northeast

THE TWO MAJOR METROPOLITAN AREAS of the Northeast—New York and Boston—offer the best and worst extremes of modern city life. As a financial and cultural capital, New York City belongs to the world as much as to the country. Boston, the country's oldest (and still leading) college town, has been trying to redefine itself as a hub of new service and high-tech industries. Both cities are struggling to come to terms with shifts in the economy and infrastructures badly in need of repair. Neither metropolis really defines the region, though: Captured in a single wide-angle lens, the six states of New England and the massive bulk of New York State are decidedly un-urban, offering more variety in terms of landscape and outdoor diversions per square mile than any other part of the country.

Beyond the hustle and bustle, glitz and grime of New York City, the Northeast fans out in waves of increasingly soothing vistas, from the placid charms of the Connecticut River valley through the forests of Vermont and New Hampshire's Green and White mountains to the pristine hinterland of Maine's remote Allagash Wilderness Waterway. Similarly, the "wilderness" of upstate New York begins within an hour's drive of the Bronx: The Hudson River valley lures frazzled urban dwellers northward past the Catskill resorts to vast Adirondack Park—at 6.2 million acres, almost three times as large as Yellowstone National Park. At the western end of the state, the hydroelectric wonder of Niagara Falls continues to attract droves of nature-loving, photo-snapping tourists and misty-eyed honeymooners.

The region was historically defined by the coastline, where the Pilgrims first established a toehold in the New World. Until it veers inland north of Yarmouth, Maine, I–95 skirts the inlets and harbors that sheltered the whaling and trading vessels of 17th- to 19th-century settlers—Mystic, Connecticut; Providence, Rhode Island; Cape Cod, Nantucket, and Plymouth in Massachusetts; and Portland, Maine. Beyond the interstate's exits, in between the living museums and tourist centers, is a region that offers a broad spectrum of diversions cerebral, spiritual, and athletic. Nowhere else in the country are the seasons as clearly defined, and each time of year brings with it its own recreations, such as fishing in New York and Vermont's Lake Champlain, skiing in the White Mountains, camping on the Appalachian Trail, biking along Maine's rocky coast, sailing Long Island Sound, applauding world-class musicians in the Berkshires, or watching whales cavort off Cape Cod.

Tour Groups

Many tour companies offer 3- to 7-day tours of this region. A few extend their tours to 15 days, adding French-speaking Canada. Most tours are in the autumn for the foliage, though the companies listed also organize tours in summer. The following are some of the leading companies: **Domenico Tours** (751 Broadway, Bayonne, NJ 07002, ☎ 201/823–8687 or 800/554–8687) offers a variety of 3-day tours to Boston, Cape Cod, the Catskills, coastal Maine, New York City, and Niagara Falls; a 5-day "New England Special"; and an 11-day tour of East Coast highlights. **Gadabout Tours** (700 E. Tahquitz Canyon Way, Palm Springs, CA 92262, ☎ 619/325–5556 or 800/952–5068) leads weeklong tours of New York City and the Hudson River valley, 11-day tours to New England and Cape Cod, and 18-day fall foliage tours. **Globus** (5301 S. Federal Circle, Littleton, CO 80123, ☎ 303/797–2800 or 800/221–0090, FAX 800/289–4646) offers weeklong fall foliage tours of New England from New York City, with stops in Stowe, Vermont; Kennebunkport, Maine; Newport, Rhode Island; and Boston, Massachusetts. An 8-day fall tour from Boston includes Arcadia National Park in Maine; Lake Placid, New York; and Killington, Vermont. Also check out Globus's budget-minded affiliate, **Cosmos Tourama** (same address). **Maupintour** (Box 807, Lawrence, KS 66044, ☎ 913/843–1211 or 800/255–4266) offers a 12-day tour of historic New England and French Canada and a 7-day tour of Cape Cod, Martha's Vineyard, and Nantucket. **Talmage Tours** (1223 Walnut St., Philadelphia, PA 19107, ☎ 215/923–7100) features 4- and 5-day tours of New England, Lake George, and Saratoga Springs. A weeklong excursion to Maine is also available. **Tauck Tours** (11 Wilton Rd., Box 5027, Westport, CT 06881, ☎ 203/226–6911 or 800/468–2825) offers a tour of 7–11 days highlighting New England's fall foliage, an 8-day tour of Cape Cod and the islands, and a 7-day summer tour of the region.

When to Go

Each of the four seasons in the Northeast is distinct, and each has its own beauty. Spring blooms start in April along the south-coastal regions, later the farther north you go. This tends to be the quietest period throughout the region because of rains and melting snows. Summer, which ranges from a hot 85°F in the southern region to a low 59°F in the north, attracts beach lovers to the islands and coastal regions, while those preferring cooler climes make for the lakes in New York State; the mountains of Massachusetts, Vermont, and New Hampshire; or the mists of Maine. Autumn, the end of September in the north to the end of October in the south, is a kaleidoscope of colors as trees change their leaves from green to burning gold. Temperatures will still be around 55°F. Winter brings snow and skiers to the mountain slopes in every state of the region, Vermont being the most popular, while the coastal areas hibernate.

Prices during an area's peak season climb accordingly—Newport hotels in the summer, for example, are nearly double the late-autumn prices. Festivals also raise prices, such as the outdoor music festival at Tanglewood in Massachusetts's Berkshire Mountains. Reservations for hotels during peak seasons should be made well in advance, and traveling during summer weekends, especially on the overburdened Route 6 to Cape Cod, is best avoided.

Festivals and Seasonal Events

Mid-Jan.: Stowe Winter Carnival, among the country's oldest such celebrations, features winter-sports competitions in **Vermont.** ☎ *802/253–7321.*

Late June–Aug.: Jacob's Pillow Dance Festival, at **Becket, Massachusetts,** in the Berkshires, hosts performers from various dance traditions. ☎ *413/243–0745.*

July–Aug.: Tanglewood Music Festival at **Lenox, Massachusetts,** the summer home of the Boston Symphony Orchestra, schedules other top performers as well. ☎ *413/637–1600 or 617/266–1492.*

Mid-July: Newport (RI) Music Festival brings together celebrated musicians for two weeks of morning, afternoon, and evening concerts in Newport mansions. ☎ *401/846–1133.*

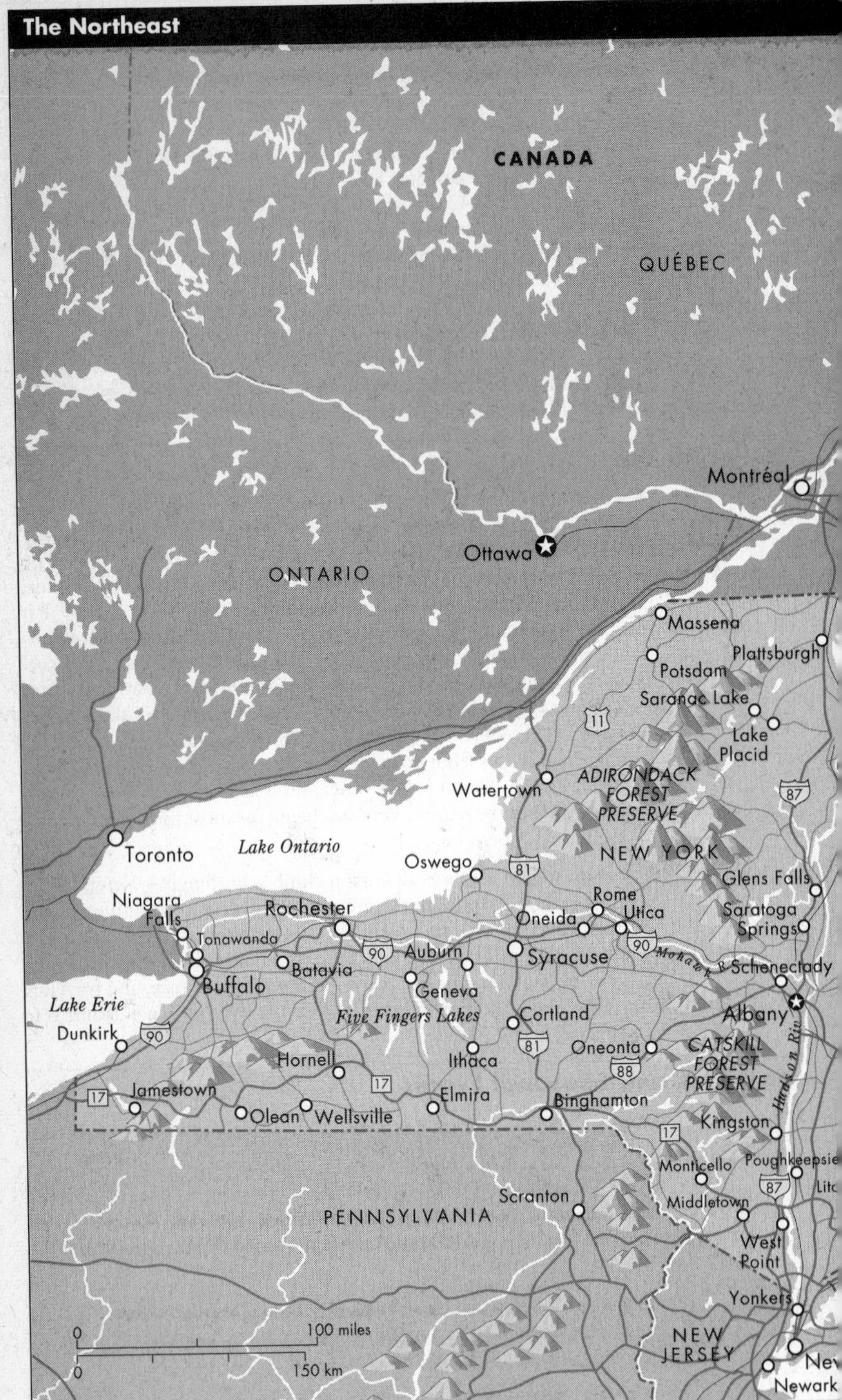
CANADA
QUÉBEC
ONTARIO
Ottawa
Montréal
Massena
Plattsburgh
Potsdam
Saranac Lake
Lake Placid
11
Watertown
ADIRONDACK FOREST PRESERVE
87
Toronto
Lake Ontario
Oswego
81
NEW YORK
Glens Falls
Niagara Falls
Rochester
Rome
Oneida
Utica
Saratoga Springs
Tonawanda
90
Auburn
Syracuse
Mohawk R.
Schenectady
Buffalo
Batavia
Geneva
Albany
Lake Erie
Five Fingers Lakes
Cortland
Dunkirk
Hornell
Ithaca
Oneonta
CATSKILL FOREST PRESERVE
88
Hudson Riv.
17
Jamestown
Olean
Wellsville
Elmira
Binghamton
Kingston
Monticello
Poughkeepsie
Middletown
Scranton
PENNSYLVANIA
West Point
Yonkers
NEW JERSEY
Newark
0
100 miles
150 km

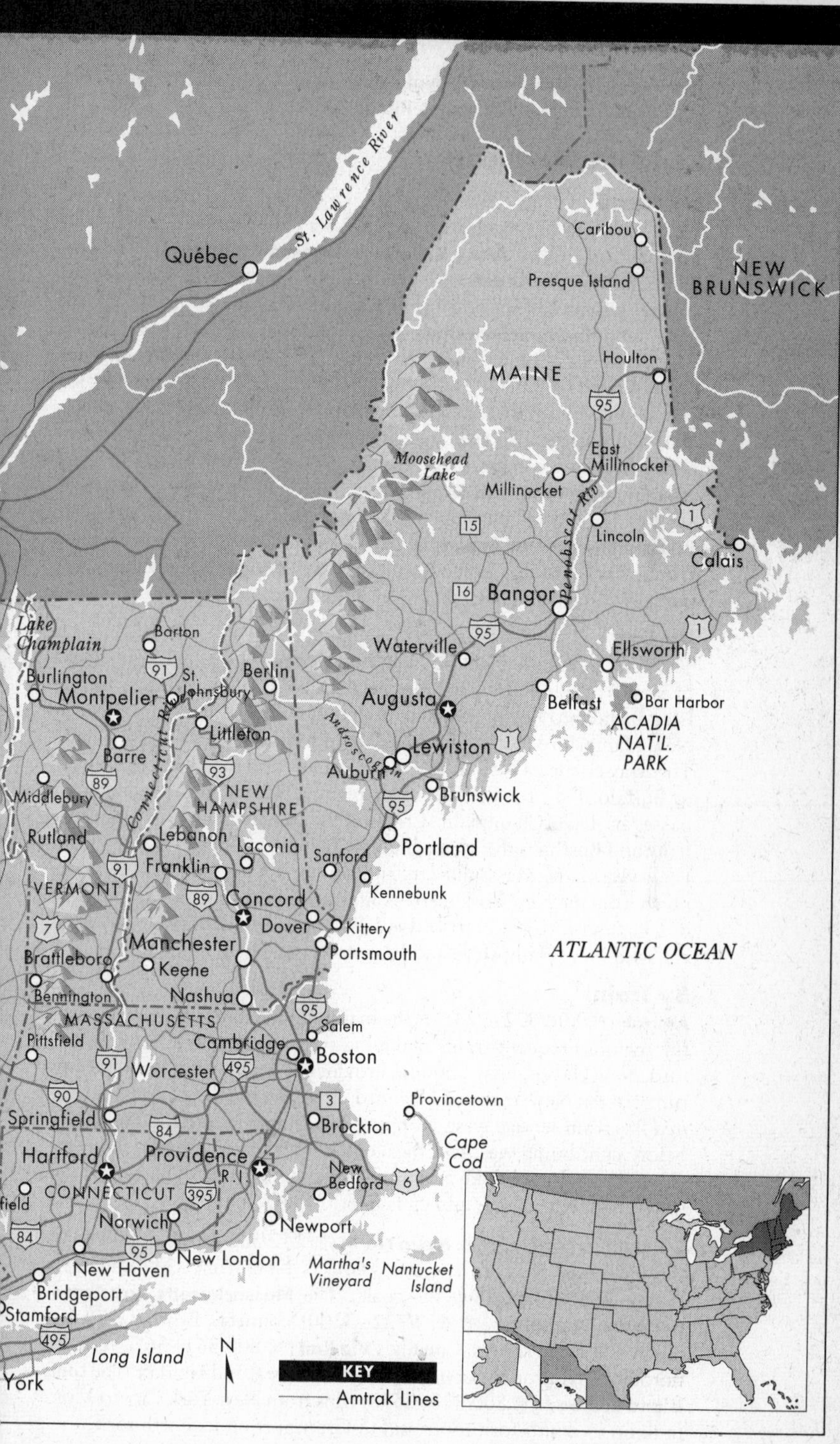

St. Lawrence River
Québec
Caribou
Presque Island
NEW BRUNSWICK
MAINE
Houlton
95
Moosehead Lake
East Millinocket
Millinocket
Penobscot Riv
15
1
Lincoln
Calais
16
Bangor
95
1
Waterville
Ellsworth
Lake Champlain
Barton
91
Berlin
Burlington
St. Johnsbury
Montpelier
Augusta
Belfast
Bar Harbor
ACADIA NAT'L. PARK
Connecticut River
Littleton
Androscoggin
Lewiston
1
Barre
93
Auburn
Brunswick
89
NEW HAMPSHIRE
95
Middlebury
Portland
Rutland
Lebanon
Laconia
Sanford
91
Franklin
Kennebunk
VERMONT
89
Concord
7
Dover
Kittery
Manchester
Portsmouth
ATLANTIC OCEAN
Brattleboro
Keene
Bennington
Nashua
95
MASSACHUSETTS
Salem
Pittsfield
Cambridge
Boston
91
Worcester
495
90
3
Provincetown
Springfield
Brockton
84
Cape Cod
Hartford
Providence
R.I.
New Bedford
6
CONNECTICUT
395
field
Norwich
Newport
84
95
New London
New Haven
Martha's Vineyard
Nantucket Island
Bridgeport
Stamford
495
Long Island
N
York
KEY
Amtrak Lines

Early Aug.: Maine Lobster Festival is a public feast held on the first weekend of the month in **Rockland.** ☏ *207/596–0376.*

Mid-Aug.: The JVC Jazz Festival brings renowned performers to Fort Adams State Park in **Newport, Rhode Island.** ☏ *401/847–3700.*

Getting Around the Northeast

By Plane

New York City has three major airports served by major domestic and international airlines: **John F. Kennedy International Airport** (☏ 718/244–4444), **La Guardia Airport** (☏ 718/533–3400), and **Newark Airport** (no general phone; call specific airline for information). Upper New York State has **Albany-Schenectady County Airport** (☏ 518/869–9611), which is served by most major airlines. Connecticut's **Bradley International Airport** (☏ 203/292–2000), in Hartford, is served by most major U.S. carriers. Massachusetts' **Logan International Airport** (☏ 617/561–1919), in Boston, is served by all major domestic airlines as well as several international carriers, such as British Airways. Vermont's main airport is **Burlington International Airport** (☏ 802/863–2874), served by six major airlines. For New Hampshire and southern Maine, the major airport is **Portland International Airport** (☏ 207/774–7301), served by several major U.S. airlines. Maine's other major airport is **Bangor International Airport** (☏ 207/947–0384), served by several major U.S. airlines.

By Car

The chief interstate through New England is I–95, which travels out of New York and along the Connecticut coast to Providence, Rhode Island, and into Boston, Massachusetts, before continuing up through New Hampshire and along the coast of Maine. The New York State Thruway connects New York City to Albany and then veers northwest to Buffalo. I–87 runs between Albany and Montréal in Canada and passes by Lake Champlain. Crossing the eastern region between Albany and Boston is the Massachusetts Turnpike (I–90). I–84 runs from Pennsylvania to Massachusetts and connects with I–684, which runs north from the New York metropolitan area, near the Connecticut border. Passing through Hartford is I–91, which links coastal Connecticut with New Hampshire and Eastern Vermont.

By Train

Amtrak (☏ 800/872–7245) is the major long-distance train service for the region. Frequent trains make the run between New York, Stamford, New Haven, New London, Providence, and Boston. Fewer trains run between New York and Hartford. From Boston the *Lakeshore Limited* has train service west, stopping in Springfield and the Berkshires before continuing west to Chicago. On summer weekends, the *Cape Codder* runs between Hyannis and Washington, D.C. The *Vermonter* starts in Hartford, CT, and ends in St. Albans, VT.

Local trains of the region: **Metro North** (☏ 212/532–4900 or 800/638–7646 outside New York City) connects New York City and New Haven with stops along the coast. The **Massachusetts Bay Transportation Authority** (☏ 617/722–3200) connects Boston with the north and south shores. Canada's **Via Rail** (☏ 800/361–3677) crosses northern Maine on its service between Montréal and Halifax. The **Long Island Railroad** (☏ 800/828–5540) runs from New York City to Montauk on its south-fork route and to Greenport on its north fork.

By Bus

The major bus lines are **Greyhound Lines** (☎ 800/231–2222) and **Bonanza** (☎ 800/556–3815). **Peter Pan** (☎ 413/781–3320) serves western Massachusetts and Connecticut.

By Boat

In Rhode Island, the **Block Island Ferry** (☎ 401/783–4613) has service from Providence, Newport, and Point Judith to Block Island. **Marine Atlantic** (☎ 800/341–7981) operates ferry service between Yarmouth, Nova Scotia, and Bar Harbor, Maine. **Prince of Fundy Cruises** (☎ 800/341–7540) operates ferry service between Yarmouth, Nova Scotia, and Portland, Maine (May–October only). **Casco Bay Lines** (☎ 207/774–7871) has ferries from Portland to the islands of Casco Bay. **Maine State Ferry Service** (☎ 207/596–2203) has ferry service from Rockland to Penobscot Bay. For information about ferry service to Martha's Vineyard and Nantucket, *see* Massachusetts. The **Bridgeport and Port Jefferson Steamboat Company** (☎ 203/367–3043 or 516/473–0286) has ferries connecting the north shore of New York's Long Island to Bridgeport, Connecticut. **Cross Sound Ferry** (☎ 203/443–5281) connects New London, Connecticut, with Orient Point, New York, in northeastern Long Island.

CONNECTICUT

Updated by Andrew Collins

Capital	Hartford
Population	3,277,980
Motto	He Who Transplanted Still Sustains
State Bird	American robin
State Flower	Mountain laurel

Visitor Information

Department of Tourism (865 Brook St., Rocky Hill 06067, ☎ 203/258–4355 or, for a brochure, ☎ 800/282–6863).

Scenic Drives

The narrow roads that wind through the **Litchfield Hills** in northwestern Connecticut offer scenic delights, especially in the spring and autumn. Each road bridge crossing the beautiful and historic **Merritt Parkway** (Rte. 15) between **Greenwich** and **Stratford** has its own architecturally significant design. Rtes. 57 to 53 to 107 to 302, connecting Exit 42 of the Merritt Parkway in **Westport** to Exit 10 of I–84 in **Newtown,** take you by Colonial homesteads, over steep ridges, and alongside the **Saugatuck Reservoir.** In northeastern Connecticut, Rte. 169 from **Norwich** to **North Woodstock** is one of the most outstanding scenic byways in the country.

National and State Parks

National Parks

The **Weir Farm National Historic Site** (735 Nod Hill Rd., off Rte. 33, Wilton 06897, ☎ 203/834–1896) is the first national park in the United States dedicated to the legacy of an American artist. Hikers and picnickers can take advantage of trails traversing the property's 60 wooded acres and tour J. Alden Weir's former studios.

State Parks

The largest of Connecticut's 91 state parks is the 4,100-acre **White Memorial Foundation** (Rte. 202, Litchfield 06759, ☎ 203/567–0857), with its nature center, wildlife sanctuary, and 35 mi of hiking and horseback-riding trails. For information on state parks, contact the **Department of Tourism** (*see* Visitor Information, *above*) or the **Bureau of Parks and Forests** (165 Capitol Ave., Hartford 06106, ☎ 203/566–2305).

COASTAL CONNECTICUT

The state's 253-mi coast comprises a series of bedroom communities serving New York City and smaller towns linked to Connecticut's major cities of Stamford, Bridgeport, New Haven, and New London. Along with its Colonial heritage and 20th-century urban sprawl, the region offers numerous nature centers and wilderness preserves for hiking and bird-watching, as well as restored 18th- and 19th-century townships and a wealth of marine and other museums dedicated to keeping Connecticut's past alive.

Tourist Information

Southeastern Connecticut: Connecticut's Mystic and More (27 Masonic St., Box 89, New London 06320, ☎ 203/444–2206 or **Southwestern Connecticut:** Coastal Fairfield County Tourism District (297 West Ave., The Gate Lodge–Matthews Park, Norwalk 06850, ☎ 203/854–7825 or 800/866–9255). **New Haven:** Greater New Haven Convention and Visitors District (1 Long Wharf Dr., Suite 7, New Haven 06511, ☎ 203/777–8550 or 800/332–7829).

Getting There

By Plane

The state's chief airport is **Bradley International Airport** (☎ 203/627–3000), 12 mi north of Hartford, with scheduled daily flights by most major U.S. airlines. Smaller airports along the coast are **Igor Sikorsky Memorial Airport** (☎ 203/576–7498), 4 mi south of Stratford, served by Delta, Northwest, and USAir; and **Tweed/New Haven Airport** (☎ 203/787–8283), 5 mi southeast of New Haven, served by USAir and Continental.

By Car

The Merritt Parkway and I–95 are the principal highways on the coast between New York and New Haven. I–95 continues beyond New Haven into Rhode Island. From Hartford, I–91 goes south to New Haven. Rte. 7 is the major state road to the Litchfield Hills and the northwest.

By Train

Amtrak (☎ 800/872–7245) stops at Greenwich, Stamford, Bridgeport, New Haven, Hartford, and New London. **Metro North** (☎ 212/532–4900 or 800/638–7646) runs between New York and New Haven, with stops at all towns along the coast.

By Bus

Greyhound Lines (☎ 800/231–2222) and **Bonanza Bus Lines** (☎ 800/556–3815) join Hartford, Middletown, New London, Stamford, Bridgeport, New Haven, and smaller towns with major cities of the eastern United States. **Connecticut Transit** (☎ 203/327–7433) provides bus service in the Stamford, Hartford, and New Haven areas. **Southeastern Area Rapid Transit** (☎ 203/886–2631) has local bus service between East Lyme and Stonington.

By Boat

The **Bridgeport and Port Jefferson Steamboat Company** (☎ 203/367–3043) has ferries connecting Bridgeport with the north shore of New York's Long Island. **Cross Sound Ferry** (☎ 203/443–5281) connects New London with northeastern Long Island's Orient Point.

Exploring Coastal Connecticut

Greenwich, which borders New York State, is the epitome of affluent Fairfield County, with gourmet restaurants and chic boutiques. The **Bruce Museum** (1 Museum Dr., ☎ 203/869–0376; donation suggested; closed Mon.) has wildlife dioramas, a worthwhile small collection of American Impressionist paintings, and many exhibits on the area. The small, barn-red **Putnam Cottage** (243 E. Putnam Ave., Rte. 1, ☎ 203/869–9697; admission charged; closed Mon.–Tues., Thurs., Sat.) was built in about 1690 and operated as Knapp's Tavern during the Revolutionary War. Inside are charts of battles, Colonial-era furnishings, and a huge stone fireplace. In the northern part of town the 485-acre **Audubon Cen-**

ter (613 Riversville Rd., ☎ 203/869–5272; donation suggested; closed Mon.) offers 8 mi of secluded hiking trails and exhibits on the local environment.

In **Cos Cob,** the **Bush-Holley House,** built in 1732, is now the headquarters of the Greenwich Historical Society. Exhibits include paintings by Hassam, Twachtman, and Elmer Livingston MacRae, sculpture by John Rogers, and pottery by Leon Volkmar. *39 Strickland Rd.,* ☎ *203/869–6899. Admission charged. Closed Mon., Sat., Jan.*

Stamford's shoreline may be given over primarily to industry and commerce, but to the north is the 118-acre **Stamford Museum and Nature Center** (39 Scofieldtown Rd., ☎ 203/322–1646; admission charged; closed Sun.), a 19th-century working farm and country store with exhibits of farm tools and local Native American life. Shows are offered at the center's observatory and planetarium. In the Champion International Corporation building, downtown, is the **Whitney Museum of American Art Champion.** Exhibits of primarily 20th-century American painting and photography change every 10–12 weeks, often featuring works from the Whitney's permanent collection in New York City. *Atlantic St. and Tresser Blvd.,* ☎ *203/358–7652. Closed Sun.–Mon.*

Beyond Stamford, I–95's Exit 15 leads to **South Norwalk,** dubbed affectionately SoNo. Just steps away from a restored avenue of art galleries, restaurants, and boutiques is the **Maritime Center,** with a huge aquarium, marine vessels such as the steam tender *Glory Days* and the oyster sloop *Hope,* and an IMAX theater. *10 N. Water St.,* ☎ *203/852–0700. Admission charged.*

A brief detour away from the coast, up Rte. 7 and Rte. 33, traverses the wooded countryside of **Wilton** and **Ridgefield,** two well-preserved communities with good antiques shopping. Wilton has Connecticut's first national park, the **Weir Farm National Historical Site** (*see* National and State Parks, *above*). Ridgefield, with its sweeping lawns and stately mansions, is home to the **Aldrich Museum of Contemporary Art** (258 Main St., ☎ 203/438–4519; admission charged; closed Mon.), which offers changing exhibits; one of the finest sculpture gardens in the Northeast; and lectures, concerts, and films.

East of Norwalk is **Westport,** long an artistic and literary community and now a trendy hub of shops and eateries. In summer, the **Westport Playhouse** (*see* The Arts and Nightlife, *below*) presents a series of first-rate plays—many of which make their way to Broadway. At the **Levitt Pavilion** (☎ 203/226–7600), folk, jazz, and classical artists perform under evening skies. Nearby **Sherwood Island State Park** (I–95 Exit 18, ☎ 203/226–6983) has the only beach accessible year-round between Greenwich and New Haven.

From Sherwood Island, drive east along Greens Farms Road, dubbed Connecticut's "Gold Coast," where grand mansions built in the days of conspicuous consumption are hidden behind high walls. The road leads into the exclusive Colonial village of **Southport,** on the Pequot River, and continues into **Fairfield,** where, in the northern part of town, the **Connecticut Audubon Society** (2325 Burr St., ☎ 203/259–6305; admission charged) maintains a 160-acre wildlife sanctuary.

Bridgeport, a city that has fallen on hard times lately, is unsafe at night and rather unappealing even during the day. Two attractions here, however, warrant visiting. The **Barnum Museum** (820 Main St., ☎ 203/331–1104; admission charged; closed Mon., Sept.–May), associated with onetime resident and mayor P. T. Barnum, has exhibits depicting the

Southwestern Connecticut

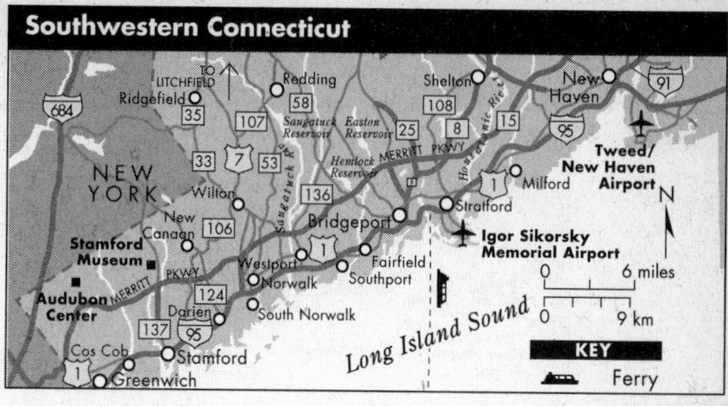

great showman's career and a scaled-down model of his famous creation, the three-ring circus. To the north, **Beardsley Park and Zoological Gardens** (Noble Ave., ☎ 203/576–8082; admission charged) is Connecticut's largest zoo. It shows off more than 350 species of animals, as well as an indoor walk-through South American rain forest.

New Haven is a city of extremes: Though the area around the common—encompassing the elite campus of **Yale University** and the numerous shops, museums, and restaurants of **Chapel Street**—prospers, ⅕ of the city's residents live below the poverty level. Stay near the campus and city common, especially at night, and get a good map of the city. Knowledgeable guides give free one-hour walking tours of the campus (344 College St., Phelps Gateway, ☎ 203/432–2300). The **Yale Art Gallery** (1111 Chapel St., ☎ 203/432–0600; closed Mon.), the country's oldest college art museum, contains Renaissance paintings; American, African, Near and Far Eastern art; and European art of the 20th century. Across the street, the **Yale Center for British Art** (1080 Chapel St., ☎ 203/432–2800; closed Mon.) has the most extensive collection of British paintings, drawings, prints, sculpture, and rare books outside the United Kingdom. The **Peabody Museum of Natural History** (170 Whitney Ave., ☎ 203/432–5050; admission charged) is the largest of its kind in New England. Along with exhibits of dinosaur fossils and meteorites, emphasis is placed on Connecticut's environment, including early Native American life and birds.

The urban buildup that characterizes the Connecticut coast west of New Haven dissipates as you drive east on I–95 toward New London. In **East Haven,** the **Shoreline Trolley Museum** houses more than 100 classic trolleys, among them the oldest rapid-transit car and the world's first electric freight locomotive. *17 River St., ☎ 203/467–6927. Admission charged. Closed Jan.–Mar.; weekdays Sept.–Oct., Dec.; Mon.–Sat. Apr., Nov.*

On the western side of the mouth of the Connecticut River is **Old Saybrook,** once a lively shipbuilding and fishing town. Today the bustle comes mostly from its many summer vacationers. On the other side of the river mouth is **Old Lyme.** Here the **Florence Griswold Museum** (96 Lyme St., ☎ 203/434–5542; admission charged), built in 1817, once housed an art colony that included Willard Metcalfe, Clark Voorhees, and Childe Hassam. Today the mansion displays many of these artists' works, along with early furnishings and decorative items. A few steps away is the **Lyme Academy of Fine Arts** (84 Lyme St., ☎ 203/434–5232; donation suggested). In a structure dating to 1817 that was formerly a private home, the gallery has works by contemporary artists.

New London is widely known as the home of the **U.S. Coast Guard Academy.** The 100-acre cluster of traditional redbrick buildings includes a museum and a visitors' pavilion with a gift shop. When the three-masted training bark the *Eagle* is in port, you may board from Friday to Sunday, noon–5 PM. *15 Mohegan Ave.,* ☎ *203/444–8270.*

Across the Thames River at **Groton** is the **U.S. submarine base** and, just outside the entrance, the **U.S. Nautilus/Submarine Force Library and Museum.** The world's first nuclear-powered submarine, the *Nautilus,* was launched from here in 1954 and is now permanently berthed and open to visitors. The adjacent library and museum contains submarine memorabilia, artifacts, and displays, including working periscopes and controls. *Rte. 12,* ☎ *203/449–3174 or 203/449–3558. Closed Tues.*

A few miles east is **Mystic,** the celebrated whaling seaport. **Mystic Seaport** (50 Greenmanville Ave., ☎ 203/572–0711; admission adults $15, children $7.50)—the nation's largest maritime museum, on 17 riverfront acres—features 19th-century sailing vessels you can board, a maritime village with historic homes, craftspeople who give demonstrations, steamboat cruises, and small-boat rentals. Just off I–95, on Mystic's Coogan Boulevard, is the **Mystic Marinelife Aquarium** (☎ 203/536–3323; admission charged). Here are more than 6,000 specimens and 50 live exhibits of sea life, as well as dolphin and sea lion shows every hour on the half hour.

Little **Stonington Village** is your final peek at Connecticut's coastline, and some say the most memorable. Poking out into Fishers Island Sound, this quiet fishing community clustered around white-spired churches remains far less commercial than neighboring Mystic. Past the historic buildings that surround the town green and border Water Street is the imposing **Old Lighthouse Museum** (7 Water St., ☎ 203/535–1440; admission charged; closed Mon. and Nov.–Apr.). Inside you'll find a wealth of shipping, whaling, and early village displays. Climb to the top of the granite tower for a spectacular view of the sound and the ocean.

What to See and Do with Children

Most nature centers (*see* Greenwich's **Audubon Center, Stamford Museum and Nature Center,** and Fairfield's **Connecticut Audubon Society** in Exploring Coastal Connecticut, *above*) feature special attractions for children, including hands-on exhibits. Other places with particular appeal (*see* Exploring Coastal Connecticut, *above*) are the **Maritime Center** in South Norwalk, the **Barnum Museum** in Bridgeport, the **Shoreline Trolley Museum** in East Haven, the **Peabody Museum of Natural History** in New Haven, **Mystic Seaport** and the **Mystic Marinelife**

Aquarium in Mystic, and the **Children's Museum of Southeastern Connecticut** (409 Main St., Niantic, ☎ 203/691–1255; closed Mon.–Wed.).

Shopping

Southwestern Connecticut

Rte. 7, which runs through **Wilton** and **Ridgefield,** has dozens of fine antiques sheds and boutiques. Of particular note is the **Cannon Crossing** (just off Rte. 7, Cannondale, ☎ 203/762–2233) shopping complex. **Washington Street** in South Norwalk (SoNo) has excellent galleries and crafts dealers. **Our World Gallery** (The Stone Studio, 82 Erskine Rd., Stamford, ☎ 203/322–7018) shows the work of international and local painters and sculptors. The area's three **Hay Day** markets (1050 E. Putnam Ave., Greenwich, ☎ 203/637–7600; 21 Governor St., Ridgefield, ☎ 203/431–4400; 1385 Post Rd. E, Westport, ☎ 203/254–1880) stock exotic produce and locally made delicacies. The nine-story **Stamford Town Center** (100 Greyrock Pl., ☎ 203/356–9700) houses 130 mostly upscale shops. **Main Street** in **Westport** is the outdoor equivalent, with J.Crew, the Gap, Ann Taylor, Eddie Bauer, and dozens more fashionable shops. Downtown **New Canaan, Darien,** and **Greenwich** are also renowned for their swank, brand-name stores and boutiques.

Southeastern Connecticut

The New Haven and New London areas have typical concentrations of shopping centers. Downtown Mystic has a more interesting collection of boutiques and galleries and factory-outlet stores. **Olde Mistick Village** (I–95 Exit 90, Mystic, ☎ 203/536–1641), a re-created Colonial village, has crafts and souvenir shops. The **Mystic Factory Outlets** (Coogan Blvd.) have nearly two dozen stores offering discounts on famous-name clothing and other merchandise. The **Tradewinds Gallery** (20 W. Main St., Mystic, ☎ 203/536–0119) has nautical prints, maps, and other rare artwork. **The Antiques Village** (985 Middlesex Tpk., ☎ 203/388–0689) in **Old Saybrook** has more than 80 dealers. **Branford Craft Village** (779 E. Main St., ☎ 203/488–4689), set on the 150-year-old, 85-acre Bittersweet Farm, has 25 crafts shops and studios in a village setting, a small play area, and a café serving refreshments. **Old Lyme, Guilford,** and **Stonington** are also strong on antiques.

Sports and the Outdoors

Fishing

Saltwater fishing is best from June through October; bass, bluefish, and flounder are popular catches. Boats are available from **Hel-Cat Dock** (Groton, ☎ 203/445–5991) and **Yacht Haven** (Stamford, ☎ 203/359–4500). For private charters, contact **Brewer Yacht Charters**(Essex, ☎ 203/767–7655), **Niantic Bay Marina** (Waterford, ☎ 203/444–1999), and **Norwalk Cove Marina** (☎ 203/838–2326).

Golf

Danbury's 18-hole **Richter Park Golf Course** (Aunt Hack Rd., ☎ 203/792–2550) is one of the top public courses in the country. Also try the 18-hole **H. Smith Richardson Golf Course** (Morehouse Hwy., Fairfield, ☎ 203/255–5016), the Robert Trent Jones–designed **Lyman Meadow Golf Club** (Rte. 147, Middlefield, ☎ 203/349–8055; 18 holes), and **Shennecosset Golf Course** (Plant St., Groton, ☎ 203/445–0262; 18 holes).

Water Sports

Action Sports (324 W. Main St., Branford, ☎ 203/481–5511) and **Rick's Surf City** (570 Boston Post Rd., Milford, ☎ 203/877–4257) rent sailboards and surfboards. **Dodson Boat Yard** (184 Water St., Stonington, ☎ 203/535–1507), **Longshore Sailing School** (Westport, ☎ 203/226–4646), and **Shaffer's Boat Livery** (Mason's Island Rd., Mystic, ☎ 203/536–8713) rent sailboats and motorboats.

Dining and Lodging

Connecticut has undergone a gastronomic revolution in recent years: Preparation and ingredients now reflect the healthy New American trends of nearby Manhattan and Boston. Though a few traditional favorites remain, expect to be bombarded by heads of radicchio, slabs of chèvre, and bulbs of fennel. The drawback of this shift in cuisine is that finding an under-$10 entrée is proving increasingly difficult.

Connecticut offers a variety of accommodations. The **Covered Bridge B&B Reservation Service** (☎ 203/542–5944) and **Nutmeg B&B Agency** (☎ 203/236–6698) are reliable statewide services for B&Bs and small inns; **B&B, Ltd.** (☎ 203/469–3260) is a service for small B&Bs and rooms rented in private homes. Rooms are costliest in summer and autumn. For safety's sake, do not stay in Bridgeport and avoid staying in New Haven, downtown Groton, and downtown New London. A 12% lodging tax is added to each bill.

For price ranges, see Charts 1 (B) and 2 (B) in On the Road with Fodor's.

Greenwich

DINING

★ **Bertrand.** The brick-vault interior of this former bank building provides the setting for a menu of classic and nouvelle French cuisine. Salmon in puff pastry and confit of duck with sorrel sauce are just two of Christian Bertrand's delightful creations. *253 Greenwich Ave., ☎ 203/661–4618. Jacket and tie required. AE, DC, MC, V. Closed Sun. No lunch weekends. $$$*

DINING AND LODGING

Homestead Inn. Each bedroom is decorated with attractive furniture and period reproductions. The La Grange restaurant serves outstanding classic French cuisine. *420 Field Point Rd., 06830, ☎ and FAX 203/869–7500. 17 rooms, 6 suites. Facilities: restaurant. AE, D, DC, MC, V. $$$*

LODGING

Stanton House Inn. This large, Federal-period mansion within walking distance of downtown underwent considerable redesign by architect Stanford White in 1899. It has been carefully refurbished and redecorated with a turn-of-the-century flavor, mixing antiques and tasteful reproductions. *76 Maple Ave., 06830, ☎ 203/869–2110, FAX 203/629–2116. 25 rooms, 2 share bath. AE, MC, V. $$*

Mystic

DINING AND LODGING

The Inn at Mystic. The Corinthian-columned main inn and the gate house have guest rooms furnished in traditional Colonial style, some with four-poster or canopy beds. The best views are in the main inn, but the individually decorated rooms in the motor lodge are a better value. The sunlit Floodtide Restaurant serves traditional, if uninteresting, New England fare, such as Yankee pot roast. *Junction U.S. 1 and Rte. 27, 06355, ☎ 203/536–9604 or 800/237–2415, FAX 203/572–1635. 68 rooms. Facilities: restaurant, private dock with canoes and sailboats, outdoor pool and whirlpool, tennis. AE, D, DC, MC, V. $$–$$$*

The Whaler's Inn and Motor Court. In the heart of downtown, this group of white clapboard buildings comprises the original Victorian guest house, the sprawling main building, and the motor court across the parking lot. Decor is modern with nautical touches; there are some canopy beds, but mostly it's department-store maple. *20 E. Main St., 06355, ☎ 203/536–1506; outside CT, 800/243–2588; FAX 203/572–1250. 41 rooms. Facilities: 3 restaurants. AE, D, DC, MC, V. $$–$$$*

New Haven

DINING

Azteca's. This restaurant offers an elegant presentation of Mexican and southwestern dishes. Among the favorites are the shellfish quesadilla and the tortilla filled with roasted chili, smoked turkey, and chèvre. *14 Mechanic St., ☎ 203/624–2454. Reservations advised. MC, V. Closed Sun. No lunch. $$–$$$*

★ **Leon's.** The Varipapa family has been running this outstanding traditional Italian restaurant since 1938. The menu is extensive, 10 varieties of veal and a number of specialties you won't find anywhere outside of Italy. Portions are enormous, too. *321 Washington St., ☎ 203/777–5366. AE, DC, MC, V. Closed Mon. No lunch Sat. $$–$$$*

Frank Pepe's. The big ovens on the back wall bake pizzas that are served by smart-mouthed waitresses. On weekend evenings the wait for a table can be more than an hour, but the pizza—the sole item on the menu—is worth it. *157 Wooster St., ☎ 203/865–5762. No reservations. No credit cards. Closed Tues. No lunch Mon., Wed., Thurs. $*

LODGING

★ **The Inn at Chapel West.** Though it borders a questionable neighborhood, this 1847 Victorian mansion is one of the most polished small inns in the state. Luxurious rooms are furnished in styles ranging from Victorian to country home to contemporary. The staff knows all the great eateries and points of interest in town, and the inn is steps away from Yale's campus and New Haven's theater district. *1201 Chapel St., 06511, ☎ 203/777–1201, FAX 203/776–7363. 10 rooms. AE, D, DC, MC, V. $$$*

Colony Inn. In the center of the Yale-area hotel district, this inn also offers sidewalk dining in the glass-enclosed Greenhouse Restaurant. The guest rooms have Colonial-reproduction furnishings and modern baths. Some rooms on the higher floors have excellent views of the campus. *1157 Chapel St., 06511, ☎ 203/776–1234; outside CT, 800/458–8810; FAX 203/772–3929. 80 rooms, 6 suites. Facilities: restaurant, lounge. AE, DC, MC, V. $$*

New London

LODGING

Lighthouse Inn. This is the quintessential grand seaside inn, with splendid views of Long Island Sound. Although rooms in the turn-of-the-century mansion are more expensive and have better views than the 24 rooms in the carriage house, the furnishings in both are similar and include canopy beds and wing-back armchairs. *6 Guthrie Pl., 06320, ☎ 203/443–8411, FAX 203/437–7027. 51 rooms. Facilities: restaurant, lounge. AE, MC, V. $$$–$$$$*

Noank

DINING

★ **Abbott's Lobster in the Rough.** If you want the best lobster, clams on the half shell, mussels, and crab in the state, pick up a bottle of wine (it's BYOB) and head for this unassuming seaside lobster shack in sleepy Noank. Seating, which is indoors or on the dock, can be hard to come by, but the water views and mouthwatering lobster rolls are worth the wait. *117 Pearl St., ☎ 203/536–7719. No reservations. MC, V. Closed*

Columbus Day–Memorial Day and on weekdays Labor Day–Columbus Day. $$

North Stonington

DINING AND LODGING

★ **Randall's Ordinary.** Famed for its open-hearth cooking of authentic Colonial dishes, the Ordinary offers three-course fixed-price meals, served by staff in period costume. Accommodations are available in the John Randall House, where rooms are furnished simply, with a smattering of antiques, or in the converted barn, whose rooms have fireplaces and whirlpools. *Rte. 2, Box 243, 06359, ☎ 203/599–4540. 14 rooms. Facilities: restaurant (reservations required). AE, MC, V. $$–$$$*

Norwalk

DINING AND LODGING

Silvermine Tavern. Parts of the lodgings date back to 1642, but the tavern is best known for its extraordinary restaurant. It's enormous, but a low ceiling, Colonial decor, glowing candles, and many windows make this landmark restaurant an intimate setting for traditional New England favorites. The cozy rooms have wide-plank floors, and many have hooked rugs. *194 Perry Ave. (on the Wilton/New Canaan border), 06850, ☎ 203/847–4558, FAX 203/847–9171. 10 rooms. Facilities: restaurant. AE, DC, MC, V. Closed Tues. $$*

Old Lyme

DINING AND LODGING

Bee & Thistle Inn. Innkeepers Bob and Penny Nelson have furnished this two-story 1756 Colonial on the Lieutenant River with period antiques and plenty of warm touches. Most rooms have canopy or four-poster beds. Outstanding American cuisine is served in one of the most romantic dining rooms around. *100 Lyme St., 06371, ☎ 203/434–1667; outside CT, 800/622–4946; FAX 203/434–3402. 11 rooms, 2 share bath. AE, DC, MC, V. Closed 1st half Jan. $$–$$$*

Stamford

DINING

Il Forno Ristorante. Within walking distance of the city's theaters is this dining room with a two-story ceiling and decor reminiscent of a Venetian piazza. The list of specials always seems more extensive than the menu itself. Choose from among dozens of seafood and veal dishes or the crisp-crusted, brick-oven gourmet pizzas. *45 Atlantic St., ☎ 203/357–8882. AE, MC, V. $$*

Westbrook

DINING

★ **Aleia's.** This is an elegant dining room, with dark wainscoting and bentwood chairs. It has a superb, eclectic menu with several nouvelle-inspired pasta, veal, and poultry dishes, such as grilled chicken with artichokes and roasted tomatoes over a bed of couscous. *1353 Boston Post Rd., ☎ 203/399–5050. AE, MC, V. Closed Mon. $$–$$$*

LODGING

Water's Edge Inn. With a spectacular setting on Long Island Sound, this traditional weathered gray-shingle compound is one of the Connecticut shore's premier resorts. Rooms in the main building, though not as large as the suites in surrounding outbuildings, have better views and nicer furnishings. *1525 Post Rd., 06498, ☎ 203/399–5901 or 800/222–5901, FAX 203/399–6172. 88 rooms, 12 suites. Facilities: restaurant, tennis, indoor and outdoor pools, Jacuzzi, volleyball, lounge, meeting rooms, beach. AE, D, DC, MC, V. $$$*

Westport

DINING

★ **Meeting Street Grill.** Here you'll find the jazzy eloquence and down-home zest of New Orleans's Garden District: About the only thing missing is the clang of the St. Charles Streetcar. And when you've tasted the crawfish-and-crab cakes (topped with lemon-and-fennel remoulade), pecan-Creole mustard chicken, and apple-blueberry cobbler, you'll think you've died and gone to Dixie heaven. *1563 Post Rd. E, ☏ 203/256–3309. AE, MC, V. Closed Mon. $$$*

DINING AND LODGING

★ **The Inn at National Hall.** The self-important name belies the whimsical, exotic interior of this towering redbrick Victorian on the downtown banks of the Saugatuck River. Each room is a study in innovative restoration, wall-stenciling, furniture-collecting, and decorative design. Outstanding Continental dishes are served in the lushly decorated Restaurant Zanghi. Game, such as venison and rabbit, is listed beside some relatively more affordable and accessible entrées. *2 Post Rd. W, 06880, ☏ 203/221–1351 or 800/628–4255, FAX 203/221–0276. 7 rooms, 8 suites. Facilities: meeting rooms, VCRs and refrigerators in all rooms, kitchenette and fireplace in one suite. AE, DC, MC, V. $$$*

Motels

Along U.S. 1, paralleling I–95 up the coast, there are motels galore—the safest and cleanest are in Stamford and Mystic—with **Holiday Inn, Days Inn,** and **Howard Johnson** dominant. There are also smaller, less expensive spots: **Comfort Inn** (50 Ledge Rd., Darien 06820, ☏ 203/655–8211), 99 rooms; *$$*. **Niantic Inn** (345 Main St., 06357, ☏ 203/739–5451 or 800/722–6582), 27 rooms; *$–$$*. **Stamford Super 8 Motel** (32 Grenhart Rd., 06902, ☏ 203/324–8887 or 800/843–1991), 92 rooms, coffee shop; *$*.

Campgrounds

Along Connecticut's shore, **Riverdale Farm Campsites** (111 River Rd., Clinton, ☏ 203/669–5338), open April 15–September, has 250 tent and RV sites and water, electricity, showers, toilets, and a river for swimming. **Seaport Campground** (Rte. 184, Old Mystic, ☏ 203/536–4044) has 130 tent and RV sites, water, electricity, toilets, hot showers, and a laundry. It is open late March–October.

The Arts and Nightlife

The Arts

The Connecticut coast's wealth of successful repertory and Broadway-style theaters include **The Eugene O'Neill Theatre Center** (Waterford, ☏ 203/443–5378), **Goodspeed Opera House** (East Haddam, ☏ 203/873–8668), **Long Wharf Theatre** (New Haven, ☏ 203/787–4282), **Shubert Performing Arts Center** (New Haven, ☏ 203/562–5666), **Stamford Center for the Arts** (☏ 203/323–2131), **Westport Playhouse** (☏ 203/227–4177), and **Yale Repertory Theatre** (New Haven, ☏ 203/432–1234).

Most towns along the coast have outdoor summer concerts and music festivals, and some have smaller regional theaters. Call area tourist offices for details (*see* Tourist Information, *above*).

Nightlife

Bars and clubs are sprinkled liberally throughout southern Connecticut. The best of them are concentrated in **Westport, South Norwalk, New Haven's Chapel West** area, and along **New London's Bank Street.**

In 1992, **Foxwoods** (☎ 203/885–3000), an enormous gambling and entertainment complex, opened on the Mashantucket Pequots Reservation near Ledyard (8 mi north of Groton). Here you can try your hand at poker, baccarat, slot machines, blackjack, and bingo.

ELSEWHERE IN THE STATE

Litchfield Hills

Getting There

The Litchfield Hills are at the western end of Connecticut, about 1½ hours from New York City and less than an hour from Hartford. Rtes. 8 and 4 and U.S. 7, 44, and 202 are the primary routes through the region.

What to See and Do

This is an area of rolling countryside, wooded hills, and charming Colonial towns renowned for antiquing. The **Litchfield Hills Travel Council** (Box 968, Litchfield 06759, ☎ 203/567–4506) can offer assistance and information.

The mountainous northern towns of **Sharon, Lakeville, Salisbury,** and **Norfolk** are crisscrossed by scenic winding roads. Auto-racing fans come in summer to **Lime Rock Park** (Rte. 112, Lakeville, ☎ 203/435–2571), home to the best road racing in the Northeast. This is also terrific hiking terrain, with **Haystack Mountain** (U.S. 44, Norfolk), **Dennis Hill** (Rte. 272, Norfolk), and the 684-acre **Northeast Audubon Center** (Rte. 4, Sharon, ☎ 203/364–0520) offering the region's best opportunities.

Everything seems to exist on a larger scale in **Litchfield** than in neighboring towns: Enormous white Colonials line broad streets shaded by majestic elms, and serene **Litchfield Green** is surrounded by lovely shops and restaurants. Near the green is the **Tapping Reeve House and Law School** (South St., ☎ 203/567–4501; admission charged; closed mid-Oct.–mid-Apr.), America's first law school, which was founded in 1773. Alumni include six U.S. cabinet members, 26 U.S. senators, more than 100 U.S. congressmen, and numerous other politicians, justices, and college presidents. The **Litchfield Historical Society Museum** (corner of Rtes. 63 and 118, ☎ 203/567–4501; admission charged; closed mid-Dec.–mid-Mar.) has several well-laid-out galleries, an extensive reference library, and information on the town's many historic buildings. **White Flower Farm** (Rte. 63, 3 mi south of the green, ☎ 800/888–7756; closed Nov.–Mar.), where much of America shops in person or by mail for perennials and bulbs, is a restful stop, whether to buy or to browse.

To the south, the quiet villages of **Washington, Roxbury,** and **Bridgewater** offer a gentler landscape, in which numerous actors and writers seek refuge from the din of Manhattan and Hollywood. Here you can buy the ingredients for a gourmet picnic lunch—try the **Pantry** (Titus Sq., Washington, ☎ 203/868–0258)—then laze on the shores of sparkling **Lake Waramaug** or enjoy a leisurely country drive along precipitous ridges, passing gracious farmsteads and meadows alive with wildflowers.

The best antiques and crafts shopping is along Rte. 6 in **Woodbury** and **Southbury,** Rte. 45 in **New Preston,** U.S. 7 in **Kent,** Rte. 128 in **West Cornwall,** and U.S. 202 in **Bantam.**

The Connecticut River and Hartford

Getting There

Bradley International Airport is the main airport; **Amtrak, Greyhound, Bonanza,** and **Connecticut Transit** provide service to the Hartford area (*see* Coastal Connecticut, *above*). By car, take I–91N from New Haven or I–84, which cuts diagonally southwest–northeast through the state. Head north along Rte. 9 from Old Saybrook for a scenic drive through this historic area.

What to See and Do

The Connecticut River valley meanders through rolling hills, offering a taste of Colonial history and sophisticated inns. The **Connecticut River Valley and Shoreline Visitors Council** (393 Main St., Middletown 06457, ☎ 203/347–0028 or 800/486–3346) and the **Greater Hartford Tourism District** (1 Civic Center Plaza, Hartford 06103, ☎ 203/520–4480 or 800/793–4480) can provide information.

Essex, on the west bank of the Connecticut River, is where the first submarine, the *Turtle,* was built; a full-size reproduction is at the **Connecticut River Museum** (Steamboat Dock, ☎ 203/767–8269). In **Hadlyme** is the region's leading oddity, **Gillette Castle State Park** (67 River Rd., off Rte. 82, ☎ 203/526–2336), a 24-room oak-and-granite hilltop castle built by the actor William Gillette between 1914 and 1919.

East Haddam is the home of the **Goodspeed Opera House** (Rte. 82, ☎ 203/873–8668). The upper floors of this elaborate 1876 structure have served as a venue for theatrical performances for more than a century. On Main Street you'll find the **schoolhouse** where Nathan Hale taught (Rte. 149, rear of St. Stephen's Church, ☎ 203/873–9547).

Hartford, known as the "Insurance Capital of America," is the state capital as well. Mark Twain made his home here, in the extravagant Victorian mansion at **Nook Farm** (351 Farmington Ave., ☎ 203/493–6411). The neighboring cottage, built in 1871, was the home of Harriet Beecher Stowe, the author of *Uncle Tom's Cabin.* Personal memorabilia and original furnishings of both writers are displayed at a joint visitor center. Hartford was also the home and birthplace of Noah Webster, author of the *American Dictionary.* His 18th-century farmhouse, now the **Noah Webster House and Museum** (227 S. Main St., ☎ 203/521–5362), contains Webster memorabilia and period furnishings, along with changing exhibits. Hartford's most noteworthy attraction is the **Wadsworth Atheneum** (600 Main St., ☎ 203/247–9111 or 203/278–2670), the country's first public art museum. Along with changing exhibits, its more than 40,000 works span 5,000 years of art, including paintings by the Hudson River School, the Impressionists, and 20th-century artists.

MAINE

By Ed and Roon Frost
Updated by Hilary M. Nangle

Capital	Augusta
Population	1,227,928
Motto	I Direct
State Bird	Chickadee
State Flower	White pinecone and tassel

Visitor Information

Maine Publicity Bureau (325B Water St., Box 2300, Hallowell 04347, ☎ 207/623–0363; outside ME, 800/533–9595; FAX 207/623–0388). **Maine Innkeepers Association** (305 Commercial St., Portland 04101, ☎ 207/773–7670).

Scenic Drives

Any road that offers views of Maine's dramatic **coastline** is usually worth exploring (*see* Exploring sections, *below,* for recommended coastal routes). For a leisurely inland excursion, try **Rtes. 37** and **35** from Bridgton north through the Waterfords to the charming resort village of Bethel, continuing north on **Rte. 26** past the Sunday River ski resort to Grafton Notch State Park and into northern New Hampshire.

National and State Parks

National Parks

Acadia National Park (Box 177, Bar Harbor 04609, ☎ 207/288–3338), with fine stretches of shoreline and the highest mountains along the East Coast, offers camping, hiking, biking, and boating.

State Parks

More than two dozen state parks offer outdoor recreation along the coast and in less-traveled interior sections. For more information, contact the **Bureau of Parks and Recreation** (State House Station 22, Augusta 04333, ☎ 207/287–3821).

THE COAST: FROM KITTERY TO PEMAQUID POINT

Maine's southern coast offers sandy beaches, historic towns, fine restaurants, and factory-outlet malls within an easy day trip from many points in New England. Maine's largest city, Portland, is small enough to be seen in a day or two. In easy striking distance of Portland are Freeport, a mecca for shoppers, and Boothbay Harbor, the state's boating capital.

Tourist Information

Boothbay Harbor Region: Chamber of Commerce (Box 356, Boothbay Harbor 04538, ☎ 207/633–2353). **Freeport:** Merchants Association (Box 452, 04032, ☎ 207/865–1212). **Kennebunk-Kennebunkport:** Chamber of Commerce (173 Port Rd., Kennebunk 04043, ☎ 207/967–0857). **Portland:** Greater Portland Chamber of Commerce (145 Middle St., Portland, ☎ 207/772–2811). Additional information is available at the **Maine Publicity Bureau, the Maine Information Center** (Rte. 1 [Exit 17 off I–95], Yarmouth, ☎ 207/846–0833).

Getting There

By Plane

Portland International Jetport (☏ 207/774–7301), 5 mi from Portland, has scheduled daily flights by major U.S. carriers.

By Car

From Boston take U.S. 1N to I–95N, passing through the short New Hampshire seacoast to Kittery, the first town in Maine. I–95 continues past Portland (I–295 gives access to the city) and Freeport (Exit 20 for the outlet stores). Pick up U.S. 1 in Brunswick to reach the coastal communities of Down East.

By Bus

Vermont Transit (☏ 207/772–6587), part of Greyhound Lines, links Portsmouth, New Hampshire, with Portland, Maine. **Concord Trailways** (☏ 800/639–3317) has daily year-round service between Boston and Bangor (via Portland), with a coastal route connecting towns between Brunswick and Searsport.

Exploring from Kittery to Pemaquid Point

Paralleling I–95, U.S. 1 runs past more than 100 outlet stores between Kittery and the Yorks. Rtes. 103 and 1A hug the coastline and offer maritime scenery.

Rte. 1A north (reached from I–95 Exit 4) passes through fashionable **York Harbor** and the midriff-to-elbow summer cottages of **York Beach. Ogunquit,** a few miles north, is famed for its long white-sand beach and attractive galleries, shops, restaurants, and homes.

Rte. 35 (Summer St.) takes you past the Victorian Wedding Cake House into **Kennebunkport. Dock Square,** the busy town center, is lined with shops and galleries. Ocean Avenue follows the Kennebunk River to the sea, then winds around Cape Arundel.

Return to I–95 for the short drive to **Portland.** On Congress Square, the distinguished **Portland Museum of Art** has a strong collection of seascapes and landscapes by such masters as Winslow Homer, John Marin, Andrew Wyeth, and Marsden Hartley. *7 Congress Sq.,* ☏ *207/775–6148 or 207/773–2787. Admission charged. Closed Mon.*

Portland's **Old Port Exchange,** built following the Great Fire of 1866, was revitalized in the 1960s by artists and craftspeople. Now it is the city's shopping and dining hub, with boutiques, cafés, restaurants, and easy access to the waterfront. Allow a couple of hours to stroll on Market, Exchange, Middle, and Fore streets.

Continue north on I–95 or U.S. 1 to **Freeport,** the home of **L.L. Bean** (open 24 hours a day), which attracts some 3.5 million shoppers a year. Nearby, like seedlings under a mighty spruce, some 100 other outlets have sprouted, offering designer clothes, shoes, housewares, and toys at marked-down prices (*see* Shopping, *below*).

Farther up the coast, in **Bath,** the **Maine Maritime Museum and Shipyard** (take the Bath Business District exit from U.S. 1, turn right on Washington St., and follow the signs) has a collection to stir the nautical dreams of old salts and young. You can watch apprentice boatbuilders wield their tools on classic Maine boats at the restored shipyard. *243 Washington St.,* ☏ *207/443–1316. Admission charged.*

Continue northeast on U.S. 1 and drop south on Rte. 27 to **Boothbay Harbor,** a town for wandering, shopping, or hopping on an excursion

Southern Maine Coast

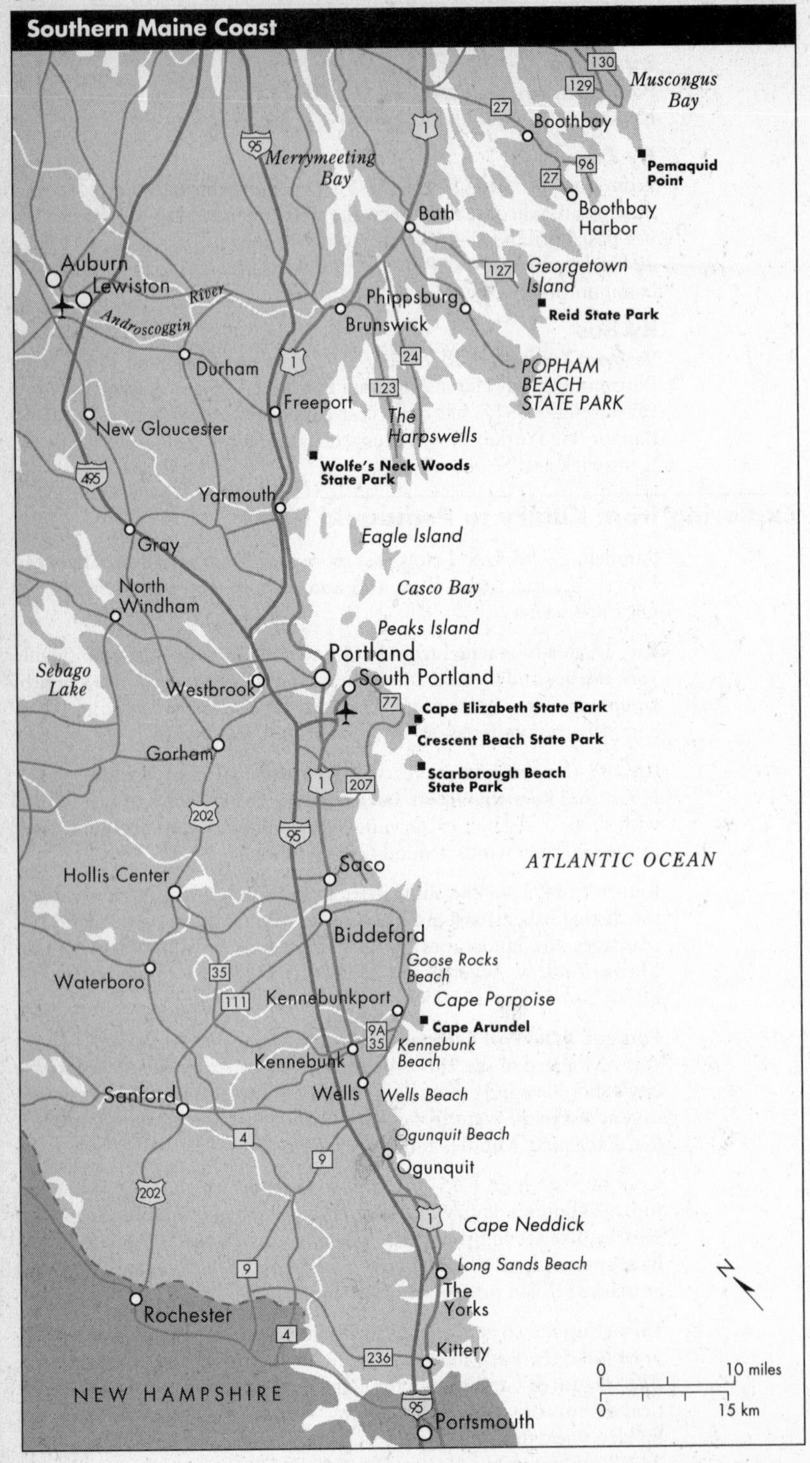

boat. Rte. 129/130 leads to **Bristol** and ends at **Pemaquid Point,** where a much-photographed lighthouse fronts the sea. About 5 mi south of Bristol on Rte. 130, look for the turnoff to the **Colonial Pemaquid Restoration** (☎ 207/677–2423; admission charged; closed Labor Day–Memorial Day), where excavations have turned up thousands of artifacts from an early 17th-century English fishing and trading settlement and from even earlier Native American settlements.

What to See and Do with Children

The old-fashioned pinball machines and hand-cranked moving pictures at the **Wells Auto Museum** (U.S. 1, Wells, ☎ 207/646–9064) fascinate kids of all ages. Trolley rides are the order of the day at the **Seashore Trolley Museum** (Log Cabin Rd., Kennebunkport, ☎ 207/967–2800). Touching is encouraged at the **Children's Museum of Maine** (142 Free St., Portland, ☎ 207/828–1234), where little ones can pretend they are lobstermen, shopkeepers, or computer experts.

Shopping

More than 100 **factory outlets** along U.S. 1 in Kittery offer clothing, shoes, glassware, and other products from top manufacturers. **Freeport**'s name is synonymous with shopping at **L.L. Bean** (☎ 800/341–4341) and 100 other factory outlets. The **Freeport Visitors Guide** (Freeport Merchants Association, Box 452, 04032, ☎ 207/865–1212) is a free complete listing. In Portland's **Old Port Exchange** (*see* Exploring from Kittery to Pemaquid Point, *above*) the better shops are concentrated along Fore and Exchange streets.

Sports and the Outdoors

Boat Trips

From Perkins Cove in Ogunquit, **Finestkind** (☎ 207/646–5227) runs boats to Nubble Light and lobstering trips. Boats offering whale-watching cruises and other excursions out of Kennebunkport include the ***Elizabeth II,*** the ***Nautilus*** (☎ 207/967–5595), and the ***Indian*** (☎ 207/967–5912).

In Portland, for tours of the harbor, Casco Bay, and the islands, try **Bay View Cruises** (☎ 207/761–0496), the ***Buccaneer*** (☎ 207/799–8188), or **Old Port Mariner Fleet** (☎ 207/775–0727). From Boothbay Harbor, choose between lobster boats and windjammers: The 66-ft ***Appledore*** (☎ 207/633–6598) runs trips to the outer islands, ***Balmy Days II*** (☎ 207/633–2284 or 800/298–2284) does day trips to Monhegan Island, ***Bay Lady*** (☎ 207/633–6990) offers two-hour sails, and **Argo Cruises** (☎ 207/633–2500) has a variety of offerings.

Canoeing

The **Maine Audubon Society** (☎ 207/781–2330) offers daily guided canoe trips in Scarborough Marsh (Rte. 9, Scarborough), the largest salt marsh in Maine.

Deep-Sea Fishing

Departing from Perkins Cove is the ***Ugly Anne*** (Perkins Cove, ☎ 207/646–7202). Half- and full-day fishing charters out of Portland include ***Anjin-San*** (☎ 207/772–7168) and ***Devils Den*** (☎ 207/761–4466). In Boothbay Harbor, try **Cap'n Fish's Deep Sea Fishing** (☎ 207/633–3244), **Lucky Star Charters** (☎ 207/633–4624), or the ***Bay Lady*** (☎ 207/633–6990).

Beaches

Kennebunk Beach consists of three beaches with cottages and old Victorian boardinghouses nearby; for parking permits, go to the Kennebunk Town Office (1 Summer St., ☎ 207/985–2102). **Goose Rocks,** north of Kennebunkport, is the largest area beach and a favorite with families with small children; the Kennebunkport Town Office (Elm St., ☎ 207/967–4244) sells parking permits.

Old Orchard Beach, with an amusement park reminiscent of Coney Island, is only a few miles north of Biddeford on Rte. 9.

At the end of Rte. 209 south of Bath, **Popham Beach State Park** (Phippsburg, ☎ 207/389–1335) has a good sand beach and picnic tables. **Reid State Park** (☎ 207/371–2303), on Georgetown Island, off Rte. 127, has three beaches, bathhouses, picnic tables, and a snack bar.

Dining and Lodging

For most visitors Maine means lobster, and lobster can be found on the menus of a majority of Maine restaurants. Aficionados prefer to eat them "in the rough" at classic lobster pounds, where you choose your lobster in a pool and enjoy it at a waterside picnic table. B&Bs and Victorian inns have joined the family-oriented motels of the coastal towns. For price ranges, see Charts 1 (B) and 2 (B) in On the Road with Fodor's.

Bath

DINING

Kristina's Restaurant & Bakery. This frame house turned restaurant, with a deck built around a huge maple tree, turns out some of the finest pies, pastries, and cakes on the coast. A satisfying dinner menu features new American cuisine. *160 Centre St., ☎ 207/442–8577. D, MC, V. Closed Mon. No dinner Sun. $$*

Boothbay Harbor

DINING

Black Orchid. Classic Italian fare is featured in a trattoria atmosphere. In summer, cocktails and a raw bar are served outdoors. *5 By-Way, ☎ 207/633–6659. AE, MC, V. No lunch. $$–$$$*

LODGING

Fisherman's Wharf Inn. All rooms overlook the water at this modern motel built 200 ft out over the harbor. The large dining room has floor-to-ceiling windows, and several day cruises leave from here. *42 Commercial St., 04538, ☎ 207/633–5090 or 800/628–6872. 54 rooms. AE, D, DC, MC, V. Closed late Oct.–May. $$$–$$$$*

Brunswick

DINING

Great Impasta. Whether it's lunch, tea, or dinner, this small storefront restaurant is determined to please. Try the seafood lasagna, or match your favorite pasta and sauce to create a new dish. *42 Maine St., ☎ 207/729–5858. No reservations. AE, D, DC, MC, V. $–$$*

LODGING

Captain Daniel Stone Inn. This Federal inn furnishes no two rooms identically, but many have whirlpool baths and pull-out sofas in addition to queen-size beds. *10 Water St., 04011, ☎ 207/725–9898. 28 rooms, 4 suites. Facilities: breakfast, restaurant. AE, DC, MC, V. $$$–$$$$*

Freeport

DINING

Harraseeket Lunch & Lobster Co. At this bare-bones lobster pound beside the town landing, fried-seafood baskets and lobster dinners are what it's all about. There are picnic tables outside and a dining room inside. *Main St., South Freeport,* ☎ *207/865–4888. No reservations. No credit cards. Closed Oct. 16–Apr. $*

DINING AND LODGING

Harraseeket Inn. Two white clapboard houses join a three-story building that looks like an old New England inn but is actually a steel-and-concrete structure with elevators and whirlpools. Antique furniture and fireplaces in the common rooms give the inn a countrified feel; guest rooms have reproductions of Federal-period canopy beds and bright, coordinated fabrics. In the formal dining room, waiters prepare fettuccine Alfredo and flaming desserts at your table. *162 Main St., 04032,* ☎ *207/865–9377 or 800/342–6423. 46 rooms, 6 suites. Facilities: restaurant, tavern. AE, D, DC, MC, V. $$$*

Kennebunkport

DINING

★ **White Barn Inn.** The rustic but elegant dining room of this inn serves regional New England cuisine. The menu changes weekly and may include steamed Maine lobster or grilled veal chop with baby carrots, wild rice cakes, sorrel, and lemongrass scented with curry sauce. *Beach St.,* ☎ *207/967–2321. Jacket required. AE, MC, V. $$$–$$$$*

LODGING

Captain Lord Mansion. A long and distinguished history, a three-story elliptical staircase, and a cupola with a widow's walk make the Captain Lord something more than the standard B&B. The guest rooms, named after old clipper ships, are large and stately, and the refined Gathering Room would look like a period room (Chippendale) in a museum but for the lounging guests. *Corner of Pleasant and Green Sts., Box 800, 04046,* ☎ *207/967–3141. 16 rooms, 11 with fireplace. Facilities: full breakfast. D, MC, V. $$$*

Ogunquit

DINING

★ **Hurricane.** Don't let the unpretentious, weather-beaten exterior mislead you—this small, comfortable seafood bar and grill has spectacular views of the crashing surf as well as first-rate cooking. *Perkins Cove,* ☎ *207/646–6348. AE, D, DC, MC, V. $$–$$$*

Portland

DINING

★ **Back Bay Grill.** Simply but elegantly restored, the grill is popular for its mellow jazz, the mural of Portland reflected by mirrors throughout, an impressive wine list, and carefully prepared food. *65 Portland St.,* ☎ *207/772–8833. AE, D, DC, MC, V. Closed Sun. $$$*

★ **Street and Co.** At what may be the best seafood restaurant in Maine, you enter through the kitchen, with all its wonderful aromas, and dine amid dried herbs and shelves of grocery staples. *33 Wharf St.,* ☎ *207/775–0887. AE, MC, V. No lunch. $$–$$$*

LODGING

Portland Regency Hotel. The only major hotel in the center of the Old Port Exchange, this luxurious renovation of a 19th-century armory has Victorian-style rooms, many complete with four-poster beds. *20 Milk St., 04101,* ☎ *207/774–4200 or 800/727–3436. 95 rooms, 8 suites.*

Facilities: restaurant, nightclub, health club, banquet rooms. AE, D, DC, MC, V. $$$

Scarborough

LODGING

Black Point Inn. At the tip of a peninsula 10 mi south of Portland stands one of Maine's great old-time resorts. The 115-year-old inn is decorated with Early American–Colonial and cherry-wood furniture, and the pastel colors of the rooms create a light and relaxed air throughout. The grounds offer beaches, hiking, a bird sanctuary, and sports. The dining room, with pale Renaissance-style wallpaper and water-stained pine paneling, offers a menu strong in seafood. *510 Black Point Rd., 04074, ☎ 207/883–4126 or 800/258–0003, FAX 207/883–9976. 80 rooms, 6 suites. Facilities: restaurant, bar, tennis, golf, salt- and freshwater pools. AE, MC, V. Closed Dec.–Apr. $$$$*

Spruce Head

DINING AND LODGING

Craignair Inn. The Craignair, built in the 1930s, commands a dramatic view of rocky shore and lobster boats. Accommodations are in either a country-cluttered gambrel-roofed house or a converted church dating from the 1890s. The waterside dining room serves such fare as bouillabaisse; lemon pepper seafood kebab; and those New England standards: shore dinner, prime rib, and scampi. *Clark Island Rd., HC 33, Box 533, 04859, ☎ 207/594–7644 or 800/760–7644, FAX 207/596–7124. 23 rooms, 8 with bath. Facilities: restaurant, canoe, hiking trails. AE, MC, V. Inn closed Feb., restaurant closed mid-Oct.–mid-May. $$–$$$*

The Yorks

DINING

★ **York Harbor Inn.** The dining room of this inn has country charm and great ocean views. Try the lobster-stuffed chicken breast with Boursin sauce or the angel hair pasta with shrimp and scallops. Just save room for the crème caramel or any of the other wonderful desserts. *Rte. 1A north, Box 573, York Harbor, ☎ 207/363–5119 or 800/343–3869. AE, DC, MC, V. No lunch off-season. $$–$$$*

DINING AND LODGING

Dockside Guest Quarters and Restaurant. On an 8-acre private island in the middle of York Harbor, the Dockside promises water views, seclusion, and quiet. Rooms in the Maine House, the oldest structure on the site, are furnished with Early American antiques, marine artifacts, and nautical paintings and prints. Four modern cottages tucked among the trees have less character but bigger windows on the water, and many have kitchenettes. Entrées in the esteemed dining room may include scallop-stuffed shrimp casino, broiled salmon, steak au poivre with brandied mushroom sauce, and roast stuffed duckling. There's also a children's menu. *York Harbor off Rte. 103, Box 205, York 03909, ☎ 207/363–2868. 22 rooms (20 with bath), 5 suites. Facilities: restaurant (☎ 207/363–2722; closed Mon.), private dock, motorboat, croquet, badminton, bicycles. MC, V. Closed late Oct.–Apr. $$–$$$$*

The Arts and Nightlife

The Arts

Ogunquit Playhouse (Rte. 1, ☎ 207/646–5511), one of America's oldest summer theaters, mounts plays and musicals from late June to Labor Day. **Portland Performing Arts Center** (25A Forest Ave., ☎ 207/744–0465) hosts music, dance, and theater. **Cumberland County**

Civic Center (1 Civic Center Sq., Portland, ☎ 207/775–3458) has concerts in a 9,000-seat auditorium.

Nightlife

Gritty McDuff's Brew Pub (396 Fore St., Portland, ☎ 207/772–2739) has been serving its fine ales—brewed on the premises—to Portland and her visitors for more than five years. **Three Dollar Dewey's** (446 Fore St., Portland, ☎ 207/772–3310) is an English-style alehouse, long a popular local nightspot.

THE COAST: PENOBSCOT BAY AND ACADIA

Purists hold that the Maine coast begins at Penobscot Bay, where water vistas are wider and bluer, the shore a jumble of broken granite boulders, cobblestones, and gravel. East of Penobscot Bay, Acadia is the informal name for Mount Desert (pronounced like *dessert*) Island and environs. Mount Desert, Maine's largest island, harbors most of Acadia National Park, the state's principal tourist attraction. Camden on Penobscot Bay and Bar Harbor on Mount Desert both offer a range of accommodations and restaurants.

Tourist Information

Bar Harbor: Chamber of Commerce (93 Cottage St., Box 158, 04609 ☎ 207/288–3393, 207/288–5103, or 800/288–5103). **Rockport-Camden-Lincolnville:** Chamber of Commerce (Public Landing, Box 919, Camden 04843, ☎ 207/236–4404).

Getting There

By Plane

Bangor International Airport (☎ 207/947–0384), 30 mi north of Penobscot Bay, has daily flights by major U.S. carriers. **Knox County Regional Airport** (☎ 207/594–4131), 3 mi south of Rockland, has frequent flights to Boston. **Hancock County Airport** (☎ 207/667–7329), 8 mi northwest of Bar Harbor, is served by Colgan Air.

By Car

U.S. 1 follows the west coast of Penobscot Bay, linking Rockland, Camden, and Ellsworth. From Ellsworth, Rte. 3 will take you onto Mount Desert Island.

Exploring Penobscot Bay and Acadia

An easy detour off U.S. 1 onto Rte. 131S brings you to **Tenants Harbor.** This is a quintessential Maine fishing town, its harbor dominated by squat, serviceable lobster boats, its shores rocky and slippery, its town a scattering of clapboard houses, a church, a general store. South of here is the fishing town of **Port Clyde,** point of departure for the mail boat that serves **Monhegan Island** (*see also* The Coast: From Kittery to Pemaquid Point, Sports and the Outdoors, *above*). The tiny, remote island, high cliffs fronting the open sea, was discovered by some of America's finest painters a century ago. Day-trippers now flock here for the scenery, the boat ride, and the artists' studios, which are occasionally open to visitors.

Return to U.S. 1 and proceed to **Rockland,** the coast's commercial hub, with fishing boats moored alongside a growing flotilla of cruise schooners. The **William A. Farnsworth Library and Art Museum** displays oil and watercolor landscapes of the coast you have just seen, among them N.C. Wyeth's *Eight Bells* and Andrew Wyeth's *Her Room. 532 Main St.,* ☎ *207/596–6457. Admission charged. Closed Mon. Oct.–May.*

From Rockland it's 8 mi north on U.S. 1 to **Camden,** where the mountains tower over the harbor and the fashionable waterfront. Camden is famous for the nation's largest windjammer fleet; such cruises are a superb way to explore the ports and islands of Penobscot Bay. The 5,500-acre **Camden Hills State Park** (☎ 207/236–3109), 2 mi north of town on U.S. 1, contains 20 mi of trails and a toll road up Mt. Battie.

Farther north on U.S. 1, **Searsport**—Maine's second-largest deepwater port—claims to be the antiques capital of Maine, with shops and a seasonal weekend flea market. Turn south onto Rtes. 175 and 166A, which terminate at **Castine.** Historic Castine, over which the French, the British, the Dutch, and the Americans fought, has two museums and the ruins of a British fort, but the finest thing about Castine is the town itself: the lively, welcoming town landing, the serene Federal and Greek Revival houses, and the town common.

Return to U.S. 1 and proceed to Ellsworth, where you pick up Rte. 3 to **Mount Desert Island.** Although most of **Bar Harbor's** grand mansions were destroyed in the fire of 1947, this busy resort town on the island's Frenchman Bay has retained its beauty. Shops, restaurants, and hotels are clustered along Main, Mount Desert, and Cottage streets.

The Hulls Cove approach to **Acadia National Park** (*see* National and State Parks, *above*) is northwest of Bar Harbor on Rte. 3. Though it is often clogged with traffic, the 27-mi Park Loop Road provides the best introduction to the park. The visitor center shows a free 15-minute film and has trail maps. The **Ocean Trail** is an easily accessible walk with some of Maine's most spectacular scenery. For a mountaintop experience without the effort of hiking, drive to the summit of Cadillac Mountain, the highest point on the eastern coast. The view from the bald summit is spectacular, especially at sunset.

What to See and Do with Children

Acadia Zoo (Rte. 3, Trenton, ☎ 207/667–3244; closed Dec.–Apr.) has wild and domestic animals.

Shopping

The best shopping streets are Main and Bayview in **Camden.** Antiques shops (abundant in **Searsport**) are scattered around the outskirts of villages; yard sales abound in summer. **Bar Harbor** is a good place to browse for gifts. For bargains, head for the outlets along Rte. 3 in **Ellsworth.**

Sports and the Outdoors

Biking

The carriage paths that wind through **Acadia National Park** are ideal for biking; pick up a map from the Hulls Cove visitor center. Bikes can be rented in Bar Harbor from **Acadia Bike & Canoe** (48 Cottage St., ☎ 207/288–9605) and **Bar Harbor Bicycle Shop** (141 Cottage St., ☎ 207/288–3886).

Boat Trips

From Bar Harbor, the ***Acadian Whale Watcher*** (☎ 207/288–9794) runs whale-watching cruises, the 65-ft ***Chippewa*** (☎ 207/288–4585) cruises past islands and lighthouses three times a day (including sunset) in summer, and the ***Natalie Todd*** (☎ 207/288–4585) offers weekend windjammer cruises. Camden is the East Coast windjammer headquarters (call or write Maine Windjammer Assoc., Box 317P, Rockport 04856, ☎ 800/624–6380); the local chamber of commerce also has current listings (*see* Tourist Information, *above*).

Hiking

Acadia National Park maintains nearly 200 mi of paths. Among the more rewarding hikes are the Precipice Trail to Champlain Mountain, the Great Head Loop, the Gorham Mountain Trail, and the path around Eagle Lake.

Sailing

In Bar Harbor, **Harbor Boat Rentals** (Harbor Pl., 1 West St., ☎ 207/288–3757) has Boston whalers and other powerboats. In Southwest Harbor, **Manset Yacht Service** (Shore Rd., ☎ 207/244–4040) rents sailboats.

Dining and Lodging

For price ranges, see Charts 1 (B) and 2 (B) in On the Road with Fodor's.

Bar Harbor

DINING

★ **George's.** Candles, flowers, and linens decorate the tables in four small dining rooms in a romantic old house. The menu shows a distinct Mediterranean influence. *7 Stephen's La., ☎ 207/288–4505. AE, D, DC, MC, V. Closed late Oct.–mid-June. No lunch. $$–$$$*

Jordan Pond House. Popovers and tea are a century-old tradition at this rustic restaurant in Acadia National Park, where you can sit on the terrace and admire the views. The dinner menu offers lobster stew, seafood thermidor, and fisherman's stew. *Park Loop Rd., ☎ 207/276–3316. AE, D, MC, V. Closed late Oct.–May. $$*

LODGING

★ **Inn at Canoe Point.** Seclusion and privacy are bywords of this snug, 100-year-old Tudor-style house on the water at Hulls Cove. The inn's large living room has huge windows on the water, a granite fireplace, and a waterfront deck where a full breakfast is served on summer mornings. *Rte. 3, Box 216, 04609, ☎ 207/288–9511. 3 rooms with bath, 2 suites. No credit cards. $$$$*

Wonder View Inn. While the rooms here are standard motel-style accommodations, this establishment is distinguished by its extensive grounds and lovely views of Frenchman Bay. *Rte. 3, Box 25, Bar Harbor 04609, ☎ 207/288–3358 or 800/341–1553, FAX 207/288–2005. 80 rooms with bath. Facilities: restaurant, pool. AE, D, MC, V. Closed late Oct.–mid-May. $$–$$$*

Camden

DINING

Waterfront Restaurant. Come for a ringside seat on Camden Harbor; the best view is from the outdoor deck, open in warm weather. The fare is primarily seafood. *Bay View St., ☎ 207/236–3747. No reservations. AE, MC, V. $$*

DINING AND LODGING

Whitehall Inn. Camden's best-known inn preserves memorabilia of the poet Edna St. Vincent Millay, who grew up in nearby Rockland. The inn, down to the faded Oriental rugs and old-fashioned phones, evokes an image of the past. The rooms are small and sparsely furnished, with dark-wood bedsteads and claw-foot bathtubs. The dining room, open to the public for dinner and breakfast, offers traditional and creative

American cuisine. *52 High St., Box 558, 04843, ☎ 207/236–3391, FAX 207/236–4427. 50 rooms, 8 share bath. Facilities: tennis, golf privileges. AE, MC, V. Closed mid-Oct.–late May. $$$*

LODGING

Norumbega. The public rooms in this elegant stone castle have oak and mahogany paneling and Empire furnishings. The guest rooms, named after various castles and palaces, are airy and spacious, with hardwood floors; many offer views of the water. *61 High St., 04843, ☎ 207/236–4646, FAX 207/236–0824. 12 rooms with bath. AE, MC, V. $$$*

Castine

DINING AND LODGING

Castine Inn. Upholstered easy chairs and fine prints and paintings are typical appointments in the light, airy guest rooms here. The third floor has the best views: the harbor over the handsome formal gardens on one side, the village on the other. The dining room features such New England staples as crab cakes with mustard sauce and chicken-and-leek pot pie. *Main St., Box 41, 04421, ☎ 207/326–4365. 20 rooms, 3 suites. MC, V. Closed Nov.–mid-Apr. $$–$$$*

Hancock

DINING

Le Domaine. On a rural stretch of U.S. 1, 9 mi east of Ellsworth, a French chef prepares *lapin pruneaux* (rabbit in a rich brown prune sauce), sweetbreads with lemon and capers, and *coquilles St. Jacques.* The elegant but unintimidating dining room has polished wood floors, hanging copper pots, and tables set with silver, crystal, and linen. *U.S. 1, ☎ 207/422–3395 or 800/554–8498. AE, D, MC, V. Closed Nov.–mid-May. No lunch. $$$*

Lincolnville

DINING

Chez Michel. This unassuming restaurant with windows overlooking the water across the street could ornament the Riviera as easily as Lincolnville Beach. Chef Michel Hetuin creates bouillabaisse as deftly as New England chowder. *Rte. 1, ☎ 207/789–5600. D, MC, V. Closed Nov.–mid-Apr. $–$$*

Northeast Harbor

DINING AND LODGING

Asticou Inn. At night, guests at this grand turn-of-the-century inn trade Topsiders and polo shirts for jackets and ties. The formal dining room is open to the public for a prix fixe dinner by reservation only. Guest rooms have a country feel, with bright fabrics, white lace curtains, and white painted furniture. Modern cottages are scattered on the grounds, and a Victorian-style lodge across the street also has rooms. *04662, ☎ 207/276–3344. 27 rooms, 23 suites, 6 cottages. Facilities: restaurant, tennis, heated pool. MC, V. Inn and restaurant closed mid-Sept.–mid-June; cottages and lodge closed Jan.–Mar. $$$*

Campgrounds

The two campgrounds in Acadia National Park—**Blackwoods** (☎ 800/365–2267) and **Seawall** (☎ 207/244–3600)—fill up quickly in summer. Nearby **Lamoine State Park** (☎ 207/667–4778) has a great location on Frenchman Bay.

The Arts

Bay Chamber Concerts (Rockport Opera House, ☎ 207/236–2823) offers chamber music every Thursday night and some Friday nights in July and August, plus monthly concerts September through May. **Arcady Music Festival** (☎ 207/288–3151) schedules concerts around Mount Desert Island from late July through August. **Bar Harbor Festival** (59 Cottage St., ☎ 207/288–5744) has concerts in summer.

WESTERN LAKES AND MOUNTAINS

Less than 20 mi northwest of Portland, the lakes and mountains of western Maine stretch along the New Hampshire border to Québec. The Sebago–Long Lake region has antiques stores and lake cruises on a 42-mi waterway. Kezar Lake, tucked away in a fold of the White Mountains, has long been a hideaway of the wealthy. Bethel, in the Androscoggin River valley, is a classic New England town, while the less-developed Rangeley Lakes area is a fishing paradise; both become ski country in winter.

Tourist Information

Bethel Area: Chamber of Commerce (Box 439, 04217, ☎ 207/824–2282). **Bridgton–Lakes Region:** Chamber of Commerce (Box 236, Bridgton 04009, ☎ 207/647–3472). **Rangeley Lakes Region:** Chamber of Commerce (Box 317, Rangeley 04970, ☎ 207/864–5571).

Getting There

By Car

U.S. 302 provides access to the region from I–95. U.S. 2, which runs east–west, links Bangor to Bethel.

Exploring the Western Lakes and Mountains

Sebago Lake State Park (☎ 207/693–6613 mid-June–Sept., 207/693–6231 Oct.–mid-June) offers opportunities for swimming, picnicking, camping, boating, and fishing. To the north is **Naples,** with cruises and boat rentals on Long Lake. **Bridgton,** near Highland Lake, has antiques shops in and around town. U.S. 302/Rte. 5 through **Lovell** or Rte. 37 through the **Waterfords** are scenic routes to **Bethel,** a town with white clapboard houses and a mountain vista at the end of every street.

The area from Bethel to **Rangeley Lake** is beautiful, particularly in the autumn. In **Grafton Notch State Park** (☎ 207/824–2912) you can hike to stunning gorges and waterfalls and into the Baldpate Mountains. For a century **Rangeley** has lured fishermen and hunters to its more than 40 lakes and ponds. The town has a rough, wilderness feel to it; the best parts are tucked away in the woods and around the lake. **Rangeley Lake State Park** (☎ 207/864–3858) offers superb scenery, swimming, picnicking, and boating. Campsites are set well apart in a spruce grove.

In the shadow of Sugarloaf Mountain, **Kingfield** is prime ski country. The picture-postcard town boasts a general store, historic inns, and a white clapboard church.

What to See and Do with Children

Sandy River & Rangeley Lakes Railroad (Phillips, ☎ 207/639–3352; open May–Oct., 1st and 3rd Sun. of month) offers rides through the woods on a century-old train.

Shopping

Bridgton and **Bethel** have lots of antiques and crafts shops.

Sports and the Outdoors

Canoeing

The **Saco River** and **Rangeley and Mooselookmeguntic lakes** are favorites. For rentals, try **Canal Bridge Canoes** (Rte. 302, Fryeburg Village, ☎ 207/935–2605), **Mooselookmeguntic House** (Haines Landing, Oquossoc, ☎ 207/864–2962), **Rangeley Region Sport Shop** (Main St., Rangeley, ☎ 207/864–5615), or **Saco River Canoe and Kayak** (Rte. 5, Fryeburg, ☎ 207/935–2369).

Fishing

Required fishing licenses can be obtained at many sporting-goods and hardware stores and at local town offices. The **Department of Inland Fisheries and Wildlife** (284 State St., Augusta 04333, ☎ 207/287–2871) has further information.

Skiing

Sugarloaf/USA (Kingfield 04947, ☎ 207/237–2000) has 91 downhill trails, a gondola, 12 lifts, a 2,837-ft vertical drop, and 53 mi of cross-country trails. **Sunday River** (Box 450, Bethel 04217, ☎ 207/824–3000) has 72 downhill trails, 12 lifts, and a 2,001-ft drop.

Water Sports

Sebago, Long, Rangeley, and Mooselookmeguntic are the most popular lakes for boating. Contact tourist offices for rentals.

Dining and Lodging

Bethel has the largest concentration of inns and B&Bs, and its chamber of commerce (*see* Tourist Information, *above*) has a lodging reservations service (☎ 207/824–3585). For price ranges, see Charts 1 (B) and 2 (B) in On the Road with Fodor's.

Bethel

DINING

★ **Four Seasons Inn.** The three small dining rooms of the region's front-running gourmet restaurant reveal tables draped with linens that brush the hardwood floors, and prim bouquets on the tables. The dinner menu is classic French: escargot, caviar, sautéed mushrooms, or onion soup to start; tournedos, beef Wellington, chateaubriand, veal Oscar, and bouillabaisse for entrées. *63 Upper Main St., ☎ 207/824–2755. AE, MC, V. Closed Mon. No lunch except Sun. brunch. $$$*

DINING AND LODGING

Bethel Inn and Country Club. Choice rooms in the old-fashioned hotel, sparsely furnished with colonial reproductions and George Washington bedspreads, have fireplaces and face the golf course and the mountains beyond. Condos on the fairway are clean and a bit sterile. The formal dining room serves roast duck and prime rib. *Village Common, Box 49, 04217, ☎ 207/824–2175 or 800/654–0125, FAX 207/824–2233. 57 rooms, 40 condo units. Facilities: restaurant, health club, tennis, golf, pool. AE, D, DC, MC, V. $$–$$$*

Kingfield

LODGING

Inn on Winter's Hill. Designed in 1895 by the Stanley brothers (of Stanley Steamer automobile fame), this Georgian mansion is renowned for rich Sunday brunches and New England dinners. The rooms of the renovated barn are simply and brightly furnished. *R.R. 1, Box 1272, 04947, ☎ 207/265–5421 or 800/233–9687. 20 rooms. Facilities: restaurant, tennis, pool, ice skating, cross-country skiing. AE, D, DC, MC, V. $$$–$$$$*

ELSEWHERE IN THE STATE

The North Woods

Getting There

Charter planes can be arranged from Bangor. Rte. 6 wends its way from I–95 to Greenville; Rte. 11 provides access from I–95 to Millinocket.

What to See and Do

Moosehead Lake, Maine's largest, offers rustic camps, restaurants, guides, and outfitters. Its 420 mi of shorefront are virtually uninhabited and mostly accessible only by floatplane or boat. Greenville is the largest town on the lake and the spot for canoe rentals, outfitters, and basic lodging. For information, contact **Moosehead Lake Region Chamber of Commerce** (Rtes. 6 and 15, Box 581, Greenville 04441, ☎ 207/695–2702).

Baxter State Park (64 Balsam Dr., Millinocket 04462, ☎ 207/723–5140) is a 200,000-acre wooded wilderness surrounding Katahdin, Maine's highest mountain and the northern terminus of the Appalachian Trail. There are 45 other mountains in the park, all accessible from a 150-mi trail network.

Even more remote is the **Allagash Wilderness Waterway,** a 92-mi corridor of lakes and rivers. **Ripogenus Dam,** 30 mi northwest of Millinocket on lumbering roads, is the most popular jumping-off point for Allagash trips. The **Maine Department of Conservation, Bureau of Parks and Recreation** (State House Station 22, Augusta 04333, ☎ 207/289–3821) has information on camping and canoeing.

MASSACHUSETTS

By Julia Lisella and Candice Gianetti

Updated by Jonathon Alsop, Jeanne Cooper, H. Constance Hill, Anne Merewood, and Kathryn Rhett

Capital	Boston
Population	6,016,425
Motto	By the Sword We Seek Peace, but Peace Only under Liberty
State Bird	Chickadee
State Flower	Mayflower

Visitor Information

Massachusetts Office of Travel and Tourism (100 Cambridge St., 13th Floor, Boston 02202, ☎ 617/727–3201 or 800/447–6277).

Scenic Drives

Much of Cape Cod's **Rte. 6A,** from Sandwich to Orleans, is a National Historic District preserving traditional New England seacoast towns. **Rtes. 133 and 1A** on the North Shore, from Gloucester to Newburyport, cover some of the earliest settlements in the United States, established in the 1630s. In the Berkshires, the **Mohawk Trail,** 63 mi of Rte. 2, between Greenfield and North Adams, is famous for its fall foliage, which peaks in late September and early October; and in the southwest, **Rte. 23** from Great Barrington to Westfield yields wooded hills and rural towns.

National and State Parks

National Parks

Cape Cod National Seashore (*see* Cape Cod and the Islands, *below*), a 40-mi stretch of dune-backed beach between Eastham and Provincetown, offers excellent swimming, bike riding, bird-watching, and nature walks.

State Parks

The **Department of Environmental Management** (Division of Forests and Parks, 100 Cambridge St., Boston 02202, ☎ 617/727–3159) has information on all state parks, including the Heritage State Parks, which feature exhibits on the state's industrial history.

Mt. Greylock State Reservation (Rockwell Rd., off Rte. 7, Lanesborough, ☎ 413/499–4262) and **Tolland State Forest** (Rte. 8, Otis, ☎ 413/269–6002) in the Berkshires have camping facilities and hiking trails. **Nickerson State Park** (Rte. 6A, Brewster, ☎ 508/896–3491) on Cape Cod has nearly 2,000 acres of forest, eight trout-stocked ponds, and camping.

BOSTON

New England's largest and most important city, and the cradle of American independence, Boston is just over 360 years old. Its most famous buildings are not merely civic landmarks but national icons; its greatest citizens—John Hancock, Paul Revere, and the Adamses—live at the crossroads of history and myth.

Boston is also New England's center of high finance and higher technology, a place of granite-and-glass towers rising along what were once rutted village lanes. Its enormous population of students, academics, artists, and young professionals makes the town a haven for the arts, foreign movies, late-night bookstores, alternative music, and unconventional politics.

Tourist Information

For general information and brochures, contact the **Greater Boston Convention and Visitors Bureau** (Box 490, Prudential Tower, Boston 02199, ☎ 617/536–4100 or 800/888–5515; open Mon.–Fri. 8:30–5) or the **Boston Welcome Center** (140 Tremont St., Boston 02111, ☎ 617/451–2227; outside MA, 800/765–4482; open daily 9–5). The latter has a second office at Park Street Station on the T-Line.

Boston magazine (on newsstands) and *Where: Boston* and *Panorama* (both free in hotels and visitor information offices) list arts and entertainment events.

Arriving and Departing

By Plane

Logan International Airport (☎ 617/567–5400) has scheduled flights by most major domestic and foreign carriers. Only 3 mi and Boston Harbor separate the airport from downtown, but traffic is heavy. Cab fare to downtown is about $15, including tip. For 24-hour information on parking; bicycle access; and bus, subway, and water shuttle transport, call Logan's **Ground Transportation Desk** (☎ 800/235–6426). The **Massachusetts Bay Transportation Authority (MBTA) Blue Line** subway from Airport Station (85¢) goes downtown; free shuttle buses connect the station with airline terminals and run every 8–12 minutes from 5:30 AM to 1 AM.

By Car

Boston is the traffic hub of New England: I–95 skirts the city along the coast, while I–90 heads west.

By Train

South Station (Summer St. at Atlantic Ave., ☎ 617/345–7451).

By Bus

Bonanza (145 Dartmouth St., ☎ 617/720–4110 or 800/556–3815). **Greyhound Lines** (at South Station, ☎ 800/231–2222). **Peter Pan Trailways** (555 Atlantic Ave., ☎ 800/237–8747). **Plymouth & Brockton** (at Peter Pan Terminal, ☎ 508/746–0378).

Getting Around Boston

Boston is meant for walking; its historic and architectural attractions are found in compact areas.

By Car

Avoid bringing a car into Boston if you can; streets are narrow and twisting, drivers rude and unpredictable. Major public parking lots are at Government Center and Quincy Market; beneath Boston Common (entrance on Charles St.); beneath Post Office Square; at the Prudential Center; at Copley Place; and off Clarendon Street near the John Hancock Tower. Rush hours are 6:30–9 AM and 3:30–6 PM; traffic becomes especially congested at the Callahan Tunnel and Tobin Bridge.

By Public Transportation

The **MBTA** (☎ 617/722–3200; TDD 617/722–5146), or T, operates subways, elevated trains, and trolleys along four connecting lines. Trains run from 5:30 AM to about 12:30 AM daily. Base fares are 85¢

adults, 40¢ children 5–11. Tourist passes are available for $9 for three days and $18 for seven days.

By Taxi

Cabs are not easily hailed; if you're in a hurry, try a hotel taxi stand or telephone for a cab. Fares are $1.60 per mile, with a pick-up fee of $1.50. Companies offering 24-hour service include **Checker** (☎ 617/536–7000), **Independent Taxi Operators Association** (☎ 617/426–8700), and **Cambridge Taxi** (☎ 617/547–3000).

Orientation Tours

By Bus and Trolley

Brush Hill/Gray Line (39 Dalton Ave., ☎ 617/236–2148) buses pick up passengers from several suburban and downtown hotels for a daily 9:30 AM departure of the 3½-hour "Boston Adventure" tour of Boston and Cambridge. They also offer tours to many popular destinations in the state.

Old Town Trolley (329 W. 2nd St., ☎ 617/269–7010) takes you on a 1½-hour narrated tour of Boston with 17 stops. You can catch it at major hotels, Boston Common, Copley Place, or in front of the New England Aquarium on Atlantic Avenue. The same company also offers an hour-long, four-stop tour of Cambridge, which leaves from Harvard Square.

By Boat

Boston Harbor Cruises (1 Long Wharf, ☎ 617/227–4320) has tours from mid-April through October.

By Boat and Bus

Boston Duck Tours (64 Long Wharf, ☎ 617/723–3825) uses a fleet of seven restored World War II amphibious landing vehicles (DUKWS) to take passengers on an 80-minute tour of the city that includes all the usual landmarks and a half-hour ride on the Charles River.

Walking Tours

The 2½-mi **Freedom Trail** tour is marked on the sidewalk by a red line that winds past 16 of Boston's most important historic sites, beginning at the Information Center at Boston Common. **Harborwalk** is a self-guided tour (beginning at the Old State House) that traces Boston's maritime history. Maps for both walks are available at the Boston Common Information Kiosk.

Exploring Boston

Boston Common and Beacon Hill

Boston Common is the oldest public park in the United States and undoubtedly the largest and most famous of the town commons around which all New England settlements were once arranged. The nearby Congregationalist **Park Street Church** (at Park and Tremont Sts., ☎ 617/523–3383) was built in 1809–10 and is where, in 1831, Samuel Smith's hymn "America" was first sung. Next to the church is the **Old Granary Burial Ground,** where the Revolutionary heroes Samuel Adams, John Hancock, and Paul Revere lie.

At the summit of Beacon Hill is the magnificent neoclassical **statehouse,** its dome sheathed in copper from Paul Revere's foundry. Tours are given weekdays. ☎ *617/727–3676. Closed weekends.*

With its brick row houses, most built between 1800 and 1850, the classic face of **Beacon Hill** is in a style never far from the early Federal norm.

Chestnut and **Mt. Vernon streets** are distinguished not only for their individual houses but for their general atmosphere and character as well. Mt. Vernon opens out on **Louisburg Square,** an 1840s model for town-house development.

On the north slope of Beacon Hill is the 1806 **African Meetinghouse** (8 Smith Ct.), the oldest standing African-American church building in the United States and where the New England Anti-Slavery Society was formed in 1832. Today the site marks the beginning of the **Black Heritage Trail,** a walking tour. Information is available at the **Museum of Afro-American History.** *46 Joy St., ☎ 617/742–1854. Admission charged.*

Across the Charles River, the **Museum of Science** has more than 400 exhibits covering astronomy, anthropology, medicine, computers, earth sciences, and more. The interactive exhibits are fun for both children and adults. The **Hayden Planetarium** and the **Mugar Omni Theater** are also here. *Science Park (Charles River Dam), ☎ 617/723–2500. Admission charged.*

The North End and Charlestown

In the 17th century the **North End** *was* Boston, as much of the rest of the peninsula was still under water. During most of this century the North End has been Italian Boston, full of Italian restaurants, groceries, bakeries, churches, social clubs, cafés, and festivals honoring saints and food.

Off Hanover Street, the North End's main thoroughfare, is North Square and the **Paul Revere House,** the oldest house in Boston, built nearly a century before its illustrious tenant's midnight ride. The restored rooms exemplify Colonial Boston dwellings. *19 North Sq., ☎ 617/523–1676. Admission charged. Closed Mon. Jan.–Mar.*

Past North Square on Hanover Street is **St. Stephen's,** the only one of Charles Bulfinch's churches still standing in Boston. Nearby on Tileston Street you can see the steeple of Christ Church, the **Old North Church** (193 Salem St., ☎ 617/523–6676), where the two lanterns were hung as a signal to Paul Revere on the night of April 18, 1775. The oldest church building in Boston, it was designed by William Price from a study of Christopher Wren's London churches.

Cross the Charlestown Bridge to reach the **USS *Constitution,*** nicknamed "Old Ironsides" for the strength of its oaken hull, not because of any iron plating. The oldest commissioned ship in the U.S. Navy, launched in 1797, it is moored at the **Charlestown Navy Yard.** During its service against the Barbary pirates and in the War of 1812, the ship never lost an engagement. *Constitution Wharf, ☎ 617/426–1812. Admission to* Constitution *free. Admission charged to the museum. The ship will be in dry dock through Mar. 1996 for repairs. During this time 2 decks will be open for tours (☎ 617/242–5670) daily 9:30–sunset; a film of the tour will be shown at the adjacent museum.*

The "Battle of Bunker Hill" is one of America's most famous misnomers. The battle was fought on Breed's Hill, and this is where Solomon Willard's **Bunker Hill Monument**—a 220-ft shaft of Quincy granite—stands. It rises from the spot where, on June 17, 1775, a citizens' militia—commanded not to fire "till you see the whites of their eyes"—inflicted more than 1,100 casualties on British regulars (who eventually did seize the hill). The views from the top are worth the 295-step ascent. *Main St. to Monument St., then straight uphill; ☎ 617/242–5641.*

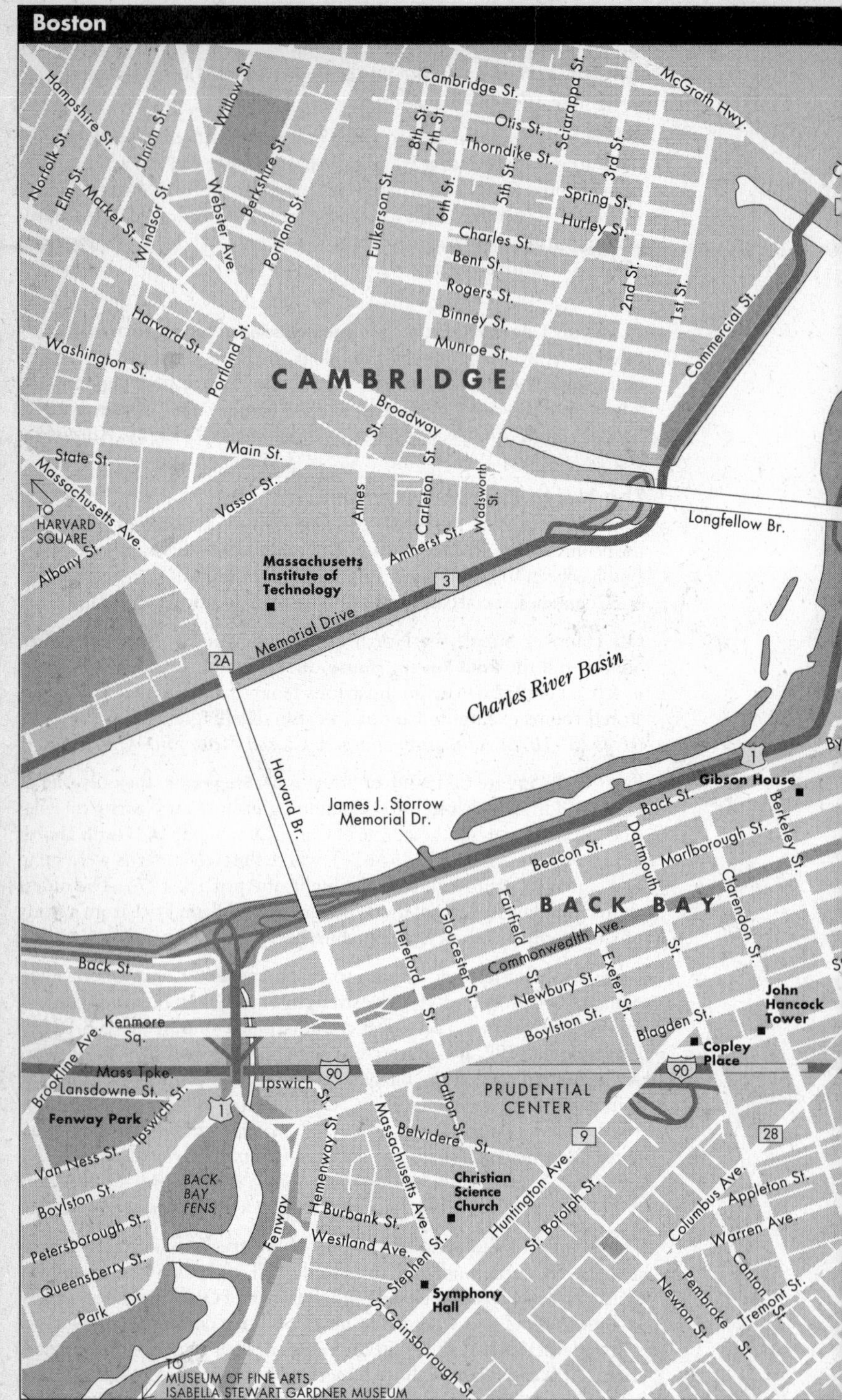
CAMBRIDGE
BACK BAY
Charles River Basin
Massachusetts Institute of Technology
Gibson House
John Hancock Tower
Copley Place
PRUDENTIAL CENTER
Christian Science Church
Symphony Hall
Fenway Park
BACK BAY FENS
TO HARVARD SQUARE
TO MUSEUM OF FINE ARTS, ISABELLA STEWART GARDNER MUSEUM
Longfellow Br.
Harvard Br.
James J. Storrow Memorial Dr.
Memorial Drive
Mass Tpke.
Kenmore Sq.
Cambridge St.
McGrath Hwy.
Otis St.
Thorndike St.
Spring St.
Hurley St.
Charles St.
Bent St.
Rogers St.
Binney St.
Munroe St.
Commercial St.
Broadway
Main St.
Vassar St.
Amherst St.
Massachusetts Ave.
Albany St.
State St.
Washington St.
Harvard St.
Hampshire St.
Norfolk St.
Elm St.
Market St.
Windsor St.
Union St.
Willow St.
Webster Ave.
Berkshire St.
Portland St.
Fulkerson St.
8th St.
7th St.
6th St.
5th St.
Sciarappa St.
3rd St.
2nd St.
1st St.
Ames St.
Carleton St.
Wadsworth St.
Back St.
Beacon St.
Marlborough St.
Commonwealth Ave.
Newbury St.
Boylston St.
Blagden St.
Berkeley St.
Clarendon St.
Dartmouth St.
Exeter St.
Fairfield St.
Gloucester St.
Hereford St.
Brookline Ave.
Lansdowne St.
Ipswich St.
Van Ness St.
Petersborough St.
Queensberry St.
Park Dr.
Fenway
Hemenway St.
Burbank St.
Westland Ave.
St. Stephen St.
Gainsborough St.
Dalton St.
Belvidere St.
Huntington Ave.
St. Botolph St.
Columbus Ave.
Appleton St.
Warren Ave.
Canton St.
Tremont St.
Pembroke St.
Newton St.
2A
3
1
90
9
28

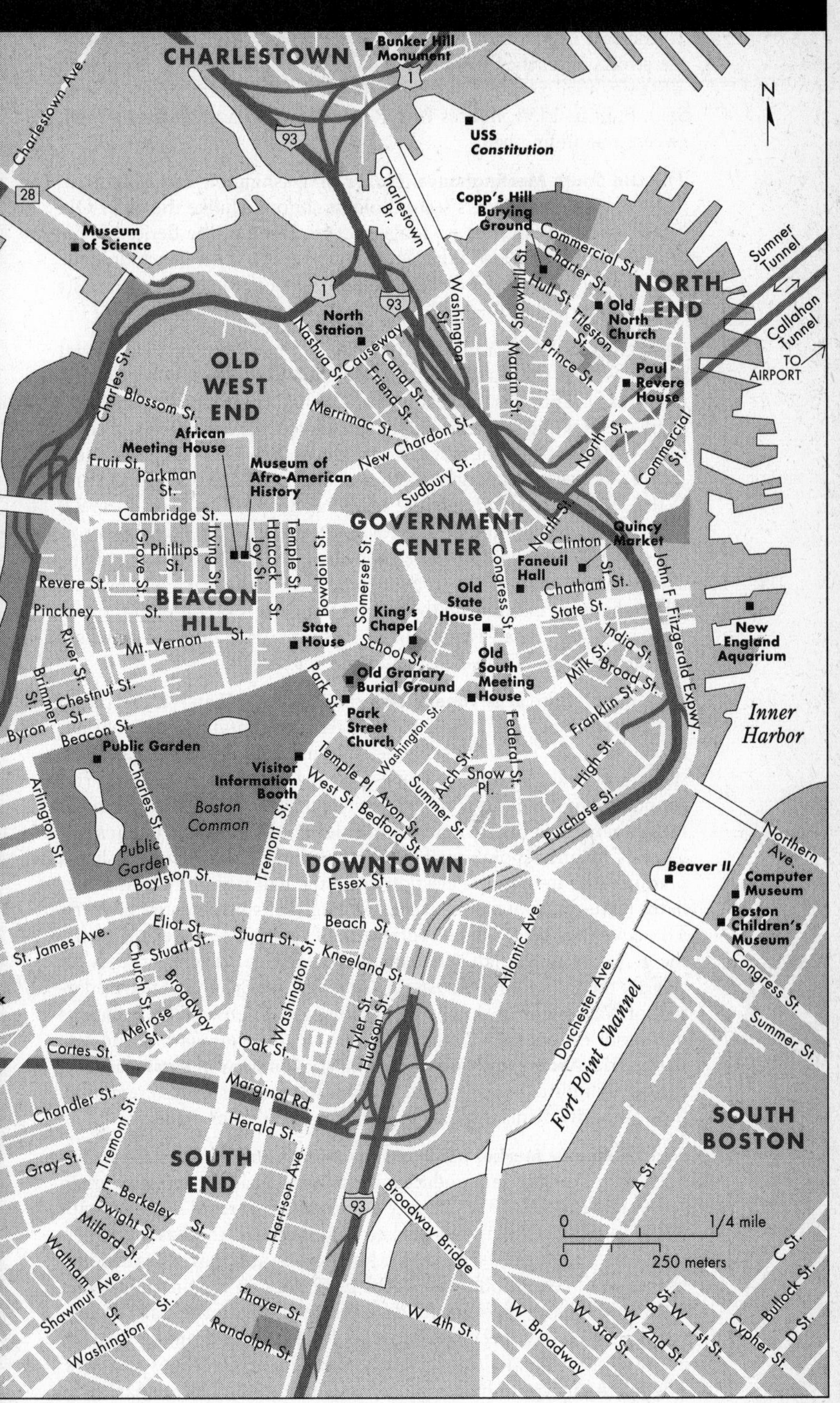

CHARLESTOWN
Bunker Hill Monument
USS Constitution
Charlestown Ave.
Museum of Science
Charlestown Br.
Copp's Hill Burying Ground
Commercial St.
Charter St.
Hull St.
Snowhill St.
Tileston St.
Old North Church
NORTH END
Sumner Tunnel
Callahan Tunnel
TO AIRPORT
North Station
Causeway
Canal St.
Friend St.
Nashua St.
Washington St.
Margin St.
Prince St.
Paul Revere House
OLD WEST END
Charles St.
Blossom St.
Merrimac St.
New Chardon St.
North St.
Commercial St.
African Meeting House
Museum of Afro-American History
Fruit St.
Parkman St.
Sudbury St.
Cambridge St.
GOVERNMENT CENTER
Quincy Market
Clinton St.
Faneuil Hall
Chatham St.
John F. Fitzgerald Expwy.
Grove St.
Phillips St.
Irving St.
Joy St.
Hancock St.
Temple St.
Bowdoin St.
Somerset St.
Congress St.
Revere St.
Pinckney St.
BEACON HILL
Old State House
State St.
New England Aquarium
King's Chapel
State House
School St.
India St.
Mt. Vernon St.
River St.
Brimmer St.
Chestnut St.
Old Granary Burial Ground
Old South Meeting House
Milk St.
Broad St.
Franklin St.
Inner Harbor
Byron St.
Beacon St.
Park St.
Park Street Church
Public Garden
Visitor Information Booth
Washington St.
Federal St.
Arch St.
Snow Pl.
High St.
Temple Pl.
West St.
Avon St.
Summer St.
Bedford St.
Purchase St.
Arlington St.
Charles St.
Boston Common
Public Garden
Tremont St.
DOWNTOWN
Northern Ave.
Beaver II
Computer Museum
Boston Children's Museum
Boylston St.
Essex St.
Beach St.
Eliot St.
St. James Ave.
Stuart St.
Kneeland St.
Atlantic Ave.
Congress St.
Church St.
Broadway
Melrose St.
Washington St.
Tyler St.
Hudson St.
Dorchester Ave.
Fort Point Channel
Summer St.
Cortes St.
Oak St.
Marginal Rd.
Chandler St.
Herald St.
SOUTH BOSTON
Gray St.
Tremont St.
SOUTH END
Harrison Ave.
E. Berkeley St.
Dwight St.
Milford St.
Broadway Bridge
A St.
0
1/4 mile
250 meters
Waltham St.
Shawmut Ave.
Washington St.
Thayer St.
Randolph St.
W. 4th St.
W. Broadway
W. 3rd St.
B St.
W. 2nd St.
W. 1st St.
Cypher St.
C St.
Bullock St.
D St.
N
1
93
28

Downtown Boston

To the east of Boston Common is **downtown.** There is little logic to the streets here; they were once village lanes but are now lined with 40-story office towers. The granite **King's Chapel** (Tremont and School Sts.), built in 1754, houses Paul Revere's largest and, in his opinion, sweetest-sounding bell.

The **Old South Meetinghouse** (corner of Washington and Milk Sts.), built in 1729, is Boston's second-oldest church. Unlike the older Old North, the Old South is no longer active. Some of the fieriest of the town meetings that led to the Revolution were held here, including the one Samuel Adams called concerning some dutiable tea that activists wanted returned to England.

A brightly colored lion and unicorn, symbols of British imperial power, adorn the facade of the **Old Statehouse** (Washington and Court Sts.). This was the seat of the Colonial government from 1713 until the Revolution, and thereafter served the independent commonwealth until the new statehouse on Beacon Hill was completed. John Hancock was inaugurated here as the state's first governor, and in the 1830s the Old Statehouse served as Boston City Hall. In 1992, after a two-year, $4 million federal preservation and renovation project, the Old Statehouse reopened and changed the focus of its exhibits. The permanent collection traces Boston's Revolutionary War history, while changing exhibits on the second floor address contemporary issues, such as "Urban Renewal and Boston's West End." *206 Washington St., ☎ 617/720–1713. Admission charged.*

On Congress Street is **Faneuil Hall** (pronounced "Fan'l"), erected in 1742 to serve as both a place for town meetings and a public market. It was here, in 1772, that Samuel Adams first suggested that Massachusetts and the other colonies organize a Committee of Correspondence to maintain semiclandestine lines of communication in the face of hardening British repression. In later years, Wendell Phillips and Charles Sumner spoke out for the abolition of slavery at the hall's podium, and in national election years the hall is usually host to debates featuring contenders in the Massachusetts presidential primary. Though it has been rebuilt, enlarged, and remodeled over the years, the great balconied hall is still made available to citizens' groups. Inside are the great mural *Webster's Reply to Hayne,* Gilbert Stuart's portrait of Washington at Dorchester Heights, and dozens of other paintings of famous Americans. On the top floors are the headquarters and museum of the **Ancient and Honorable Artillery Company of Massachusetts,** the oldest militia in the nation (1638). Its status is now ceremonial, but it proudly displays its arms, uniforms, and other artifacts.

Nearby **Quincy Market** has served as a retail and wholesale distribution center for meat and produce for 150 years. Thanks to creative urban renewal in the mid-1970s, it now houses a mix of retail shops, restaurants, and offices, all usually packed with shoppers, tourists, street performers, and locals. The central structure still has a traditional market-stall layout, but most of the businesses on the first floor offer international and specialty foods, interspersed with the stalls of provisioners who have been in the market for a century or more. Upstairs are restaurants, and along the arcades on either side, shops and bars. The north and south buildings, separated from the central market by pedestrian malls with trees and benches, house more substantial retail establishments, offices, and additional restaurants. Some people consider it all hopelessly trendy, but the 50,000 visitors who come here each day seem to enjoy it.

At the end of Quincy Market opposite Faneuil Hall, the newly constructed **Marketplace Center,** between the market buildings and the expressway, is filled with shops and boutiques. Beyond is Columbus Park, bordering on the harbor and on several of Boston's restored wharves. **Lewis Wharf** and **Commercial Wharf,** which long lay nearly derelict, had by the mid-1970s been transformed into condominiums, apartments, restaurants, and upscale shops. **Long Wharf's** Marriott hotel was designed to be compatible with the old seaside warehouses. Sailboats and power yachts are anchored here; Boston's workaday waterfront is now along the docks of South Boston, in East Boston (directly opposite Columbus Park), and in the huge containerized shipping facilities at the mouth of the Mystic River.

Central Wharf, immediately to the right of Long Wharf as you face the harbor, is the home of one of Boston's most popular attractions, the **New England Aquarium.** Here you'll find seals, penguins, a variety of sharks, and other sea creatures—more than 2,000 species in all, some of which make their home in the aquarium's four-story, 187,000-gallon observation tank. Ramps wind around the tank, allowing you to view the inhabitants from many vantage points. There are also dolphin and sea lion shows aboard *Discovery,* a floating marine-mammal pavilion.

Thanks to landfill, the exact site of the **Boston Tea Party** is marked by a plaque set into the wall of a commercial building on Atlantic Avenue at the foot of Pearl Street. When you cross Fort Point Channel on the Congress Street Bridge, you encounter the ***Beaver II,*** a faithful replica of one of the Tea Party ships that were forcibly boarded and unloaded on the night Boston Harbor became a teapot. ☏ *617/338–1773. Admission charged. Closed mid-Dec.–Feb.*

Back Bay and the South End

Southwest of Boston Common is **Back Bay,** once a tidal flat that formed the south bank of a distended Charles River until it was filled as far as the Fens in the 19th century.

Back Bay is a living museum of urban Victorian residential architecture. The **Gibson House** (1859) offers a representative look at how life was arranged in—and by—these tall, narrow, formal buildings. The house has been preserved with all its Victorian fixtures and furniture intact: A conservative Gibson family scion lived here until the 1950s and left things as they were. *137 Beacon St.,* ☏ *617/267–6338. Admission charged. Tours May–Oct., Wed.–Sun. at 1, 2, and 3; Nov.–Apr., weekends at 1, 2, and 3.*

Newbury Street is lined with sidewalk cafés and dozens of upscale specialty shops offering clothing, china, antiques, and art.

From the 60th-floor observatory of the tallest building in New England, the 62-story **John Hancock Tower,** you'll have one of the best vantage points in the city. *Trinity Pl. and St. James Ave.,* ☏ *617/247–1977. Admission charged.*

Copley Square is a civic space defined by three monumental buildings: the stately, bowfront **Copley Plaza Hotel; Trinity Church,** Henry Hobson Richardson's Romanesque Revival masterwork of 1877; and the **Boston Public Library** (☏ 617/536–5400), which, in 1895, confirmed the status of McKim, Mead, and White as apostles of the Renaissance Revival. With a modern, assertive presence, **Copley Place** comprises two major hotels (the Westin and the Marriott) and dozens of shops and restaurants, grouped on several levels around bright, open indoor spaces.

On Huntington Avenue is the headquarters of the **Christian Science Church** (175 Huntington Ave. at Massachusetts Ave., ☎ 617/450–3790). Mary Baker Eddy's original granite First Church of Christ, Scientist (1894) and the domed Renaissance basilica added to the site in 1906 are now surrounded by the offices of the *Christian Science Monitor* and by I.M. Pei's 1973 complex of church administration buildings. The best views of the precise, abstract geometry of the complex are from the **Prudential Center Skywalk** (800 Boylston St., ☎ 617/236–3318; admission charged), a 50th-floor observatory that overlooks Boston, Cambridge, and the suburbs to the west and south.

Symphony Hall (301 Massachusetts Ave., ☎ 617/266–1492), since 1900 the home of the Boston Symphony Orchestra, is another contribution of McKim, Mead, and White, though acoustics rather than exterior design make this a special place.

The **South End** was eclipsed by the Back Bay more than a century ago but is now back in fashion, with upscale galleries and restaurants that cater to young professionals. An anomaly of planning and architecture in Boston, the South End neither grew up haphazardly along cow paths and village lanes, like the old sections, nor followed a strict, uniform grid like that of the Back Bay. It is more a sum of random blocks and park-centered squares than of boulevards and long, clear vistas. The houses here continue the pattern established on Beacon Hill (in a uniformly bowfront style) but have more florid decoration.

There is a substantial black presence in the South End, particularly along Columbus Avenue and Massachusetts Avenue, which marks the beginning of the neighborhood of Roxbury. The early integration of the South End set the stage for its eventual transformation into a remarkable polyglot of ethnic groups. You are likely to hear Spanish spoken along Tremont Street, and there are Middle Eastern groceries along Shawmut Avenue. At the northeastern extreme of the South End, Harrison Avenue and Washington Street connect the area with **Chinatown,** and consequently there is a growing Asian influence. Still another minority presence among the neighborhood's ethnic groups, and sometimes belonging to one or more of them, is the largest concentration of Boston's gay population. To see elegant house restorations, go to **Rutland Square** (between Columbus Avenue and Tremont Street) or **Union Park** (between Tremont Street and Shawmut Avenue). These oases seem miles distant from the city around them.

The Fens

After all the work that had gone into filling in the bay, it would have been little extra trouble to march row houses straight through to Brookline. Instead, planners hired Frederick Law Olmsted to make the Fens into a park. Today's park consists of still, irregular reed-bound pools surrounded by broad meadows, trees, and flower gardens.

The **Museum of Fine Arts,** between Huntington Avenue and the Fenway, has holdings of American art that surpass those of all but two or three other U.S. museums; an extensive collection of Asian art; and European artwork from the 11th through the 20th century. Count on staying for a while if you have any hope of even beginning to see what is here. In the West Wing is a restaurant and a cafeteria. *465 Huntington Ave., ☎ 617/267–9300. Admission charged; free Wed. 4–9:45 PM, reduced price to West Wing Thurs. and Fri. 5–9:45 PM. Closed Mon.*

On the Fenway Park side of the museum, the **Tenshin Garden,** the "garden at the heart of heaven," is a landscape-as-a-work-of-art. A stone wall separates the formal garden from the nearby park, and a path of

Mexican river stones leads to a bench surrounded by white gravel. A combination of Japanese and American trees and shrubs fuses the concept of the Japanese garden with features of the New England landscape.

The Boston shrine known as **Fenway Park** is one of the smallest—and oldest—baseball parks in the major leagues. Built in 1912, it still has real grass on the field. **Kenmore Square** is home to fast-food parlors, new-wave rock clubs, an abundance of students from nearby Boston University, and the enormous, landmark neon Citgo Sign.

Cambridge

In 1636 the country's first college was established across the Charles River from Boston, in **Cambridge.** Named in 1638 for John Harvard, a young Charlestown clergyman who died that year, leaving the college his entire library and half his estate, **Harvard** remained the only college in the New World until 1693. The information office, in Holyoke Center (1350 Massachusetts Ave., ☏ 617/495–1573), offers area maps and a free hour-long walking tour of Harvard Yard most days. North of Cambridge Common is **Radcliffe College,** founded in 1897 "to furnish instruction and the opportunities of collegiate life to women and to promote their higher education"; since 1975 Radcliffe students have shared classes and degrees with Harvard students.

Harvard University has two celebrated art museums, each a treasure in itself. The more famous is the **Fogg Art Museum.** Founded in 1895, it now owns 80,000 works of art from every major period and from every corner of the world. Its focus is primarily on European, American, and East Asian works; it has notable collections of 19th-century French Impressionist and medieval Italian paintings. *32 Quincy St., ☏ 617/495–9400. Admission charged; free Sat. AM.*

Fogg admission also gets you into the **Arthur M. Sackler Museum** (☏ 617/495–9400) across the street, which concentrates on ancient Greek and Roman, Egyptian, Islamic, Chinese, and other Eastern art.

A ticket to the Fogg further gains you admission to Harvard's **Busch–Reisinger Museum** (☏ 617/495–9400), in the new Werner Otto Hall and entered through the Fogg. The collection specializes in Central and Northern European art.

The **Massachusetts Institute of Technology** sits on the banks of the Charles River south of Harvard Square. The West Campus, devoted to student leisure life, has buildings designed by Eero Saarinen and the Finnish architect Alvar Aalto. The Information Center (Bldg. 7, 77 Massachusetts Ave., ☏ 617/253–4795) offers free tours of the campus weekdays at 10 and 2.

Other Attractions

The world's first **Computer Museum** chronicles the spectacular development of machines that calculate and process information. Exhibits include "vintage" robots and computers. *300 Congress St., ☏ 617/426–2800. Admission charged. Closed Mon. except during school vacations and holidays.*

The **Harvard University Museums of Cultural and Natural History** are within a vast brick building that contains four distinct collections. The most famous exhibit is the display of glass flowers in the **Botanical Museum.** The **Peabody Museum of Archaeology and Ethnology** holds exhibits of Native American and Central and South American cultures. The **Museum of Comparative Zoology** traces the evolution of animals and humans. The **Mineralogical Museum** has a collection of exotic crystals and meteorites, and scale models of volcanoes and famous mountains.

26 Oxford St., Cambridge, ☎ *617/495–3045. Admission charged; free Sat.* AM.

The **Isabella Stewart Gardner Museum** is a monument to one woman's taste—and a trove of some 2,000 spectacular paintings, sculptures, furniture, and textiles, with an emphasis on Italian Renaissance and 17th-century Dutch masters. At the center of the building is a magnificent courtyard, enclosed beneath a glass roof. *280 The Fenway,* ☎ *617/566–1401. Admission charged. Closed Mon.*

Parks and Gardens

The **Back Bay Fens** mark the beginning of Boston's Emerald Necklace, a loosely connected chain of parks designed by Frederick Law Olmsted that extends along the Fenway, Riverway, and Jamaicaway to Jamaica Pond, the 265-acre **Arnold Arboretum** (125 Arborway, Jamaica Plain, ☎ 617/524–1718), and the **Zoo** at **Franklin Park** (Columbia Rd. and Blue Hill Ave., Dorchester, ☎ 617/442–2002).

The **Public Garden,** next to Boston Common, is the oldest botanical garden in the United States. Its pond has been famous since 1877 for its **swan boats,** which make leisurely cruises during the warm months of the year.

The **Dr. Paul Dudley White Bikeway,** approximately 18 mi long, runs along both sides of the Charles River. The river's banks are also popular with joggers.

Boston for Free—or Almost

The *Boston Travel Planner,* available from the Convention and Visitors Information Bureau (*see* Tourist Information, *above*), contains a calendar of events, sports and regional activities, and hotel weekend packages.

The **Hatch Memorial Shell,** on the esplanade along the Charles River, is the site of numerous free concerts in summer.

What to See and Do with Children

Boston Children's Museum contains a multitude of hands-on exhibits, many designed to help children understand cultural diversity, their bodies, and disabilities. *300 Congress St.,* ☎ *617/426–6500. Admission charged. Closed Mon. except during school vacations and holidays.*

The calendar of events in the ***Boston Parents Paper*** (☎ 617/522–1515), published monthly and distributed free throughout the city, is an excellent resource for parents and children.

Shopping

Most of Boston's stores are in the area bounded by Quincy Market, the Back Bay, downtown, and Copley Square. There are few outlet stores but plenty of bargains, particularly in Filene's Basement and Chinatown's fabric district. Boston's two daily newspapers, the *Globe* and the *Herald,* are the best places to learn about sales.

Shopping Districts

Copley Place, an indoor shopping mall connecting two hotels, has 87 stores, restaurants, and cinemas that blend the elegant, the glitzy, and the overpriced. **Downtown Crossing,** between Summer and Washington streets, is a pedestrian mall with outdoor food and merchandise kiosks, street performers, and benches for people-watchers. **Faneuil Hall Marketplace** has crowds, small shops, kiosks of every description, and one of the all-time great food experiences: **Quincy Market. Newbury Street** is where the trendy gives way to the chic and the expensive. **Charles Street** in Beacon Hill is a mecca for antiques lovers from all over the country.

Harvard Square in Cambridge has more than 150 stores within a few blocks; it is a book lover's paradise. **Cambridgeside Galleria,** between Kendall Square and the Museum of Science in Cambridge, has over 60 shops.

Department Stores

Filene's (426 Washington St.) is famous for its outstanding bilevel bargain basement, filled with an ever-changing array of high-quality overstock and irregulars from upstairs and other stores. Cambridge's **Harvard Coop Society** (1400 Massachusetts Ave., Harvard Sq.; 3 Cambridge Center), begun in 1882 as a service for students and faculty, is now a full-service department store known for its wide selection of records and books.

Food Markets

Every Friday and Saturday, **Haymarket** (near Faneuil Hall Marketplace) is a crowded jumble of outdoor produce, meat, and fish vendors.

Specialty Stores

CLOTHING

Louis, Boston (234 Berkeley St., ☎ 617/262–6100) is Boston's signature clothier, carrying elegantly tailored designs and subtly updated classics in everything from linen to tweeds.

JEWELRY

Shreve, Crump & Low (330 Boylston St., ☎ 617/267–9100) is an old, well-respected store that carries the finest in jewelry, china, crystal, and silver.

Spectator Sports

Baseball

Boston Red Sox (Fenway Park, ☎ 617/267–1700; Apr.–Oct.).

Basketball

Boston Celtics (FleetCenter, ☎ 617/523–3030 for information; ☎ 617/931–2000 for tickets; Nov.–Apr.).

Football

New England Patriots (Foxboro Stadium, Foxboro [45 min south of Boston], ☎ 800/543–1776; Aug.–Dec.).

Hockey

Boston Bruins (FleetCenter, ☎ 617/227–3200 for information; ☎ 617/931–2000 for tickets; Oct.–Apr.).

Dining

The choice of restaurants in Boston is wide and cosmopolitan, with nationally recognized spots featuring innovative young chefs as well as bastions of tradition. No matter what the style or cuisine, though, the main ingredient is still the bounty of the North Atlantic; the daily catch of fish and shellfish appears somewhere on virtually every menu. For price ranges, see Chart 1 (A) in On the Road with Fodor's.

$$$$ ★ **Jasper.** Jasper White has acquired a national reputation for his new American cuisine. Low-key decor, spacious seating, and good service complement a respectable wine list and innovative dishes, such as salad of grilled duck with cranberries and spiced nuts, as well as a traditional New England boiled dinner. *240 Commercial St. (North End), ☎ 617/523–1126. AE, D, DC, MC, V. Closed Sun.–Mon.*

$$$$ ★ **L'Espalier.** Owner-chef Frank McClelland serves contemporary French and American cuisines in three small but elegant dining rooms. All dinners are prix fixe; $62 for the regular menu and $76 for the seven-course tasting menu. Specialties include roast native partridge with chanterelles, salmon steak with mint and wild onion butter, and cappuccino chanterelle soup. *30 Gloucester St. (Back Bay), ☎ 617/262–3023. Reservations required. AE, D, MC, V. Closed Sun. No lunch.*

$$$ ★ **Hamersley's Bistro.** The restaurant has a full bar, a café area with 10 tables for walk-ins, and a larger dining room that's a little more formal and decorative than the bar and café, though nowhere near stuffy. Specialties include a garlic-and-seasonal-mushroom sandwich (served as an appetizer) and roast chicken. *553 Tremont St. (South End), ☎ 617/423–2700. D, MC, V.*

$$$ **The Harvest.** The restaurant continues to emphasize ingredients and game that are native to Massachusetts and New England. In summer, the less-expensive café section on the leafy patio (no reservations) is a good choice for an outdoor meal. *44 Brattle St., Cambridge, ☎ 617/492–1115. AE, D, DC, MC, V.*

$$$ **Seasons.** At this solariumlike restaurant in the Bostonian Hotel, overlooking Faneuil Hall, the cuisine of new chef Peter McCarthy is eclectic American with international influences. A summer menu might include steamed halibut with Oriental spices and apple paper. *North and Blackstone Sts., ☎ 617/523–3600. AE, DC, MC, V. No lunch Sat.*

$$–$$$ ★ **Biba.** Everything about Biba makes it Boston's overwhelmingly favorite place to see and be seen—from the vividness of the dining room's rambling mural to the huge street-level windows of the downstairs bar. Dishes are as simple as pan-fried oysters on semolina blinis or as elaborate as fried cauliflower in peppery olive oil on grilled sirloin with English Stilton. *272 Boylston St., ☎ 617/426–7878. D, DC, MC, V.*

$$–$$$ **East Coast Grill.** The specialty is new American and American (in particular, North Carolinian) barbecue, plus such ethnic dishes as whole rainbow trout with *hijiki* seaweed, grilled sweetbreads, or jerk chicken. The dining room is small, bright, and very busy. *1271 Cambridge St., Cambridge, ☎ 617/491–6568. D, MC, V. Reservations accepted for 5 or more; no reservations Fri. and Sat. No lunch.*

$$–$$$ ★ **Legal Sea Foods.** What began as a tiny adjunct to a fish market has grown to important status, with additional locations in Chestnut Hill, the Copley Place Mall, the Prudential, and Kendall Square in Cambridge. Whatever seafood is available each day is presented straightforwardly—raw, broiled, fried, steamed, or baked. *Boston Park Plaza Hotel, 35 Columbus Ave. (Back Bay), ☎ 617/426–4444. No reservations. AE, D, DC, MC, V.*

$$ **Daily Catch.** Like its original location in the North End, this Brookline storefront specializes in seafood and pasta prepared in the greatest Italian tradition. Especially delicious is the calamari and linguinie served in its own sauté pan. The wine list is short but sweet, featuring Italian favorites at modest prices. Try the Vernaccia with the calamari. *441 Harvard St., ☎ 617/734–5696. No reservations. No credit cards.*

$$ **Iruna.** This Spanish restaurant, popular with students for years, specializes in paellas and seafood and has exceptional salads. Dine outdoors on a private patio in warm weather. *56 John F. Kennedy St., Cambridge, ☎ 617/868–5633. AE, D, MC, V. Closed Sun.*

$$ **Ristorante Lucia.** Some aficionados consider Lucia's the best Italian restaurant in the North End. Its specialties from the Abruzzi region include batter-fried artichoke hearts as an appetizer and chicken *alla Lucia* (chicken breast sautéed with a spicy tomato sauce). *415 Hanover St., ☎ 617/523–9148. AE, MC, V. No lunch Mon.–Thurs.*

$$ **Union Oyster House.** At Boston's oldest restaurant, where Daniel Webster used to devour dozens of oysters in one sitting, the upstairs rooms are dark, low-ceilinged, and Ye-Olde-New-Englandy; the bar has a lighter feel. The food here tends to be broiled, fried, or heavy on the cream sauce, and topped with bread crumbs. *41 Union St. (near Faneuil Hall), ☎ 617/227–2750. AE, D, DC, MC, V. No lunch Sun.*

$–$$ ★ **Bombay Club.** Specializing in northern Indian cuisine with southern Indian dishes on Sunday, Bombay Club offers a beautiful view of Harvard Square. Dinner specials include kebabs of baby lamb chops, chicken *tikka masala* (boneless pieces of chicken marinated in a tomato sauce), and many homemade cheese dishes. *57 John F. Kennedy St., ☎ 617/661–8100. AE, DC, MC, V.*

$–$$ **Durgin–Park.** Opened in the 1830s, this simple upstairs hall seats diners family style, elbow to elbow. The floor is worn plank, the ceiling embossed tin, and red-checkered cloths cover the long tables. Traditional New England prime rib, pot roast, and baked beans are served in generous portions; the strawberry shortcake is mountainous. *340 Faneuil Hall Marketplace (North Market Bldg.), ☎ 617/227–2038. No reservations. AE, D, DC, MC, V.*

$–$$ ★ **Ho Yuen Ting.** A line forms nightly outside this hole-in-the-wall eatery in Chinatown. The house specialty is a sole-and-vegetable stir-fry served in a spectacular crisply fried whole fish. *13A Hudson St. (downtown), ☎ 617/426–2316. Reservations only for 7 or more. No credit cards.*

Lodging

Many of the city's most costly lodging places offer attractively priced weekend packages. Consult the *Boston Travel Planner* (*see* Boston for Free—or Almost, *above*) for current rates. At many hotels, children may stay free in their parents' room, or breakfast may be included in the rate.

Although Boston does not have a large number of B&Bs, there are several, with daily rates between $55 and $120 per room. Reservations may be made through **Bed and Breakfast Associates Bay Colony** (Box 57166, Babson Park Branch, Boston 02157, ☎ 617/449–5302 or 800/347–5088, FAX 617/449–5302).

For price ranges, see Chart 2 (A) in On the Road with Fodor's.

$$$$ **Boston Harbor Hotel at Rowes Wharf.** This luxury hotel provides a dramatic entryway to the city for travelers arriving from Logan Airport on the water shuttle that docks at the hotel. The guest rooms begin on the eighth floor and have city or water views; the lobby features lots of marble, and the furnishings tend toward mahogany armchairs and plush sofas. *70 Rowes Wharf, 02110, ☎ 617/439–7000 or 800/752–7077, FAX 617/330–9450. 204 rooms, 26 suites. Facilities: 2 restaurants, health club, marina, business center. AE, DC, MC, V.*

$$$$ ★ **The Copley Plaza—A Wyndham Hotel.** The stately, bowfront classic among Boston hotels was built in 1912 and refurbished in 1993. Guest rooms have carpeting from England, custom furniture from Italy, and new bathroom fixtures surrounded by marble tile. *138 St. James Ave., 02116, ☎ 617/267–5300 or 800/826–7539, FAX 617/247–6681. 319 rooms, 51 suites. Facilities: 2 restaurants, 2 bars. AE, DC, MC, V.*

$$$$ **Harborside Hyatt Conference Center and Hotel.** Although it is situated at Logan Airport, the city's newest hotel actually claims one of the most spectacular views of Boston's skyline. All rooms have a water view; half have a view of the city, while others look out over the harbor toward the sea. *101 Harborside Dr., 02128, ☎ 617/568–1234 or 800/233–1234, FAX 617/568–6080. 270 rooms. Facilities: health club, heated pool, business services. AE, D, DC, MC, V.*

$$$$ **Ritz-Carlton.** Since 1927 this has been one of the most luxurious and elegant hotels in Boston. The rooms are traditionally furnished; the suites in the older section have working fireplaces and views of the Public Garden. *15 Arlington St., 02117, ☎ 617/536–5700 or 800/241–3333, FAX 617/536–1335. 232 rooms, 48 suites. Facilities: restaurant, café, 2 bars, exercise room. AE, DC, MC, V.*

$$$ ★ **Lenox Hotel.** In recent years the Lenox was a comfortable, if uninspired, hotel popular with those on a budget, but extensive renovations transformed it into a first-class selection. Its wide corridors are now freshly carpeted and papered; the renovated, soundproofed guest rooms have spacious walk-in closets, color TV, AM/FM radio, and custom-made traditional furnishings. Structural renovations of the 1900 building have uncovered a number of handsome archways and elaborate moldings, particularly in the corner rooms, where there are even some working fireplaces. The lobby is ornate and handsome, trimmed in blues and golds and set off by a large, welcoming fireplace that gives the feel of a country inn. *710 Boylston St., 02116, ☎ 617/536–5300 or 800/225–7676, FAX 617/267–1237. 222 rooms. Facilities: 2 restaurants, valet service, valet parking (fee), baby-sitting service. AE, DC, MC, V.*

$$ **Cambridge House Bed and Breakfast.** This gracious old home on the National Register of Historic Places offers seven antiques-filled guest rooms and five more in its Carriage House. Convenient to the T and buses, it also serves as a reservations center for host homes in metropolitan Boston. *2218 Massachusetts Ave., Cambridge 02140, ☎ 617/491–6300 or 800/232–9989, FAX 617/868–2848. 12 rooms. AE, MC, V.*

$$ **Copley Square Hotel.** One of Boston's oldest hotels (1891), the Copley Square has recently undergone an extensive restoration. It is popular with Europeans and is European in flavor. The rooms, set off long, circuitous hallways, vary from very small to spacious. *47 Huntington Ave., 02116, ☎ 617/536–9000 or 800/225–7062, FAX 617/267–3547. 143 rooms. Facility: coffee shop. AE, DC, MC, V.*

$$ **Eliot Hotel.** Lots of marble gives this nine-floor, European-style, family-run hotel a certain elegance. The one- and two-bedroom suites have marble baths and period furnishings. *370 Commonwealth Ave., 02215, ☎ 617/267–1607, FAX 617/536–9114. 12 rooms, 82 suites. Facilities: bar, valet. AE, DC, MC, V.*

$ **Boston International Hostel.** At this youth-oriented hostel, guests sleep in three- to five-person dormitories and must provide their own linens or sleep sacks (sleeping bags are not permitted). The maximum stay is three nights in summer, seven nights off-season. Reservations are highly recommended. You must be an American Youth Hostel member to stay here; it is possible to join here. *12 Hemenway St., 02115, ☎ 617/536–9455. 190 beds in summer, 100 in winter. Facilities: 2 kitchens, 2 dining rooms. MC, V.*

$ **Susse Chalet Inn.** Typical of this chain, the inn is clean, economical, and sparse. It's a 10-minute drive from Harvard Square but within walking distance of the Red Line terminus, offering T access to Boston and Harvard Square. *211 Concord Tpke., Cambridge, 02140, ☎ 617/661–7800 or 800/258–1980, FAX 617/868–8153. 78 rooms. AE, DC, MC, V.*

Motels

Best Western (1650 Commonwealth Ave., 02135, ☎ 617/566–6260, FAX 617/731–3543), 73 rooms, parking, free Continental breakfast; *$*.
Harvard Manor House (110 Mt. Auburn St., Cambridge 02138, ☎ 617/864–5200 or 800/458–5886), 72 rooms, parking, cable TV; *$*.
Ramada Hotel (225 McClellan Hwy., East Boston 02128, ☎ 617/569–5250), 350 rooms, restaurant, outdoor pool, parking; *$*.

The Arts and Nightlife

Thursday's *Boston Globe* Calendar and the weekly *Boston Phoenix* provide comprehensive listings of events for the coming week.

The Arts

Bostix (Faneuil Hall Marketplace, ☎ 617/723–5181; closed Mon.) sells half-price tickets for same-day performances. **CONCERTCHARGE** (☎ 617/497–1118) and **TicketMaster** (☎ 617/931–2000) are ticket brokers for telephone purchases.

THEATER

First-rate Broadway tryout theaters are clustered in the theater district (near the intersection of Tremont and Stuart streets) and include the **Colonial** (☎ 617/426–9366), the **Shubert** (☎ 617/426–4520), and the **Wang Center for the Performing Arts** (☎ 617/482–9393). The **American Repertory Theatre** (Loeb Drama Center, 64 Brattle St., Cambridge, ☎ 617/495–2668) produces classic and experimental works. The **Huntington Theatre Company** (264 Huntington Ave., ☎ 617/266–0800) is affiliated with Boston University.

MUSIC

Boston's churches offer outstanding, often free music programs; check the Saturday listings in the *Globe*. **Symphony Hall** (301 Massachusetts Ave., ☎ 617/266–1492) is home to the Boston Symphony Orchestra and the Boston Pops.

DANCE

Dance Umbrella (☎ 617/492–7578) offers information on all dance performances. The **Boston Ballet** (19 Clarendon St., ☎ 617/695–6950) performs at the Wang Center.

FILM

The **Brattle Theater** (40 Brattle St., Cambridge, ☎ 617/876–6837) is a restored landmark cinema for classic-movie buffs. **Nickelodeon Cinema** (606 Commonwealth Ave., ☎ 617/424–1500) shows first-run independent and foreign films and revivals.

OPERA

Boston Lyric Opera Company (114 State St., ☎ 617/248–8660) presents three fully staged productions each season. They have performed operas of Massenet, Mozart, Strauss, and others, and they always include a 20th-century work in their repertoire.

Nightlife

Quincy Market, Copley Square, and **Kenmore Square** in Boston and **Harvard Square** in Cambridge are centers of nightlife.

CAFÉS

The **Blacksmith House** (56 Brattle St., Cambridge, ☎ 617/354–3036), the 18th-century house where Longfellow's blacksmith lived, is now operated by the Cambridge Center for Adult Education. It houses an excellent German bakery and has poetry readings, concerts, and plays. **Passim's** (47 Palmer St., Cambridge, ☎ 617/492–7679), by day a quiet basement café, is by night a renowned coffeehouse, offering folk or bluegrass music and poetry.

COMEDY

Catch a Rising Star (Upstairs at the Wursthaus, 4 John F. Kennedy St., Cambridge, ☎ 617/661–9887) has comedy seven nights a week. Nationally known acts appear Thursday–Saturday; new talents are showcased Sunday–Wednesday.

DISCO

Fast-paced **Avalon** (15 Lansdowne St., ☎ 617/262–2424) is one of Boston's largest clubs. Near Kenmore Square, it features high-energy disco and a giant dance floor. High energy and house music pervade at **Quest** (1270 Boylston St., ☎ 617/424–7747), a four-floor club, catering to a straight crowd on Thursday, Friday, and Sunday; a gay crowd on Monday, Wednesday (for retro music), and Saturday.

JAZZ

Some top names in jazz perform at **Regattabar** (Bennett and Eliot Sts., Cambridge, ☎ 617/864–1200), a spacious, elegant club in the Charles Hotel. The **Boston Jazz Line** (☎ 617/787–9700) reports jazz happenings.

ROCK

Paradise (967 Commonwealth Ave., ☎ 617/254–3939) is known for big-name rock, jazz, folk, blues, alternative pop/rock, and country shows.

Excursions from Boston

Lexington and Concord

The events of April 19, 1775—the first military encounters of the American War of Independence—are very much a part of present-day **Lexington** and **Concord.** These two quintessential New England towns are also rich in literary history: Concord, for example, is the site of Walden Pond, immortalized by Thoreau. Several historic houses have been preserved and can be visited; the **visitors center** in Lexington (1875 Massachusetts Ave., 02173, ☎ 617/862–1450) and the **Battle Road Visitors Center** (off Rte. 2A, ☎ 617/862–7753) can direct you.

GETTING THERE

To reach Lexington and Concord by car from Boston, take Rte. 2A (Massachusetts Ave.) west from Cambridge, or I–95/Rte. 128 north to the Lexington exit. Rte. 2A west will take you on to Concord. Both towns are about a half-hour drive from Metropolitan Boston. The MBTA (*see* Getting Around Boston, *above*) operates buses to Lexington.

The South Shore

Southeastern Massachusetts between Boston and the Cape is a region with strong historical associations. The great seafaring towns of **Fall River** and **New Bedford** offer marine museums and reminders of the area's industrial past. The **Plimoth Plantation** living-history museum (Rte. 3A Exit 4, ☎ 508/746–1622; closed Dec.–Mar.; admission $18.50 adults, $11 children 5–12) re-creates the Pilgrims' 1627 village. At the waterfront is the ***Mayflower II,*** an exact replica of the ship that brought the Pilgrims over from England, and nearby is **Plymouth Rock,** believed to be the very spot on which they first set foot in 1620 after unsuccessfully scouting the Provincetown area as a potential settlement.

GETTING THERE

The most direct way to Fall River and New Bedford (themselves connected by I–195) is via Rte. 24, about a 45-minute drive; I–93 and Rte. 3 connect Boston with Plymouth, which is about an hour's drive. From

Boston, **MBTA** buses (☎ 617/722–3200) serve both Quincy and Braintree, **American Eagle** (☎ 508/993–5040) serves New Bedford, and **Bonanza** (☎ 617/720–4110) serves Fall River; **Plymouth & Brockton Street Railway** (☎ 508/746–0378) calls at Plymouth en route to Cape Cod.

The North Shore

The North Shore extends from the northern suburbs to the Cape Ann region and beyond to the New Hampshire border. It takes in **Salem,** which thrives on a history of witches, millionaires, and maritime trade; **Rockport,** crammed with crafts shops and artists' studios; **Gloucester,** the oldest seaport in America; and **Newburyport,** with its redbrick center and rows of clapboard Federal mansions. For information, contact the **North of Boston Visitors and Convention Bureau** (248 Cabot St., Box 642, Beverly 01915, ☎ 508/745–2268).

GETTING THERE

Boston to Gloucester is about 40 mi. The primary link between Boston and the North Shore is I–93 north to Rte. 128 east, which then follows the line of the coast just inland as far north as Gloucester. The more scenic route is along coastal Rte. 1A (which leaves Boston via the Callahan Tunnel) to Rte. 127.

CAPE COD AND THE ISLANDS

Separated from the "mainland" by the 17.4-mi Cape Cod Canal, the Cape curves 70 mi from end to end. Its charming villages of weathered-shingle houses and white steepled churches, as well as its pinewoods, grassy marshes, and beaches backed by rolling dunes, attract crowds every summer. To the south, Martha's Vineyard and Nantucket are resort islands ringed with beautiful sandy beaches, and Nantucket preserves a near-pristine whaling-era town.

Tourist Information

Cape Cod: Chamber of Commerce (jct. Rtes. 6 and 132, Hyannis 02601, ☎ 508/362–3225. Information booths: Sagamore Bridge Rotary, ☎ 508/888–2438; Bourne Bridge on Rte. 28, ☎ 508/759–3814). **Martha's Vineyard:** Chamber of Commerce (Box 1698, Beach Rd., Vineyard Haven 02568, ☎ 508/693–0085). **Nantucket:** Chamber of Commerce (Pacific Club, Main St., Nantucket 02554, ☎ 508/228–1700).

Getting There

By Plane

Hyannis's **Barnstable Municipal Airport** is Cape Cod's air gateway, with flights from **Business Express/Delta Connection** (☎ 800/345–3400), **Cape Air** (☎ 800/352–0714), **Nantucket Airlines** (☎ 508/790–0300 or 800/635–8787), and **Northwest Airlink** (☎ 800/225–2525). **Provincetown Municipal Airport** is served by **Cape Air.**

By Car

From Boston take I–93 to Rte. 3 to the Sagamore Bridge. From New York take I–95 to Providence; change to I–195 and follow signs to the Cape.

By Train

Amtrak offers limited service in summer to Hyannis, with bus connections to Woods Hole.

By Bus

Plymouth & Brockton Street Railway (☎ 508/775–5524) has service from Boston and Logan Airport. **Bonanza** (☎ 508/548–7588 or 800/556–3815) connects Bourne, Falmouth, Woods Hole, and Hyannis with New York and points between.

By Boat

Ferries connect Martha's Vineyard and Nantucket to the mainland from New Bedford, Falmouth, Woods Hole, and Hyannis. The **Steamship Authority** (☎ 508/477–8600), **Hy-Line Cruises** (☎ 508/778–2600), and the ***Island Queen*** (☎ 508/548–4800) serve Martha's Vineyard; the Steamship *Authority* and Hy-Line serve Nantucket.

Exploring Cape Cod and the Islands

U.S. 6, the Mid-Cape Highway, traverses the relatively unpopulated center of the Cape. Paralleling U.S. 6 but following the north coast is Rte. 6A, the Old King's Highway, which passes through some of the Cape's best-preserved old New England towns. The south shore, traced by Rte. 28, is heavily populated and the major center for tourism, encompassing Falmouth, Hyannis, and Chatham. The sparse outer portion of the Cape, from Orleans to Provincetown, is edged with white-sand beaches and nature preserves. At the Cape's southwestern corner is **Woods Hole,** an international center for marine research. The **Marine Biological Laboratory** (☎ 508/548–3705, ext. 423) offers tours by reservation, or you can visit the **Woods Hole Oceanographic Institute Exhibit Center** (15 School St., ☎ 508/457–2000, ext. 2663). Before leaving Woods Hole, stop at **Nobska Light** for a splendid view of the Elizabeth Islands and the sea beyond.

Ferries connect Woods Hole with **Martha's Vineyard** year-round (in summer, boats also leave from Hyannis, Falmouth, and New Bedford). On the island, the town of **Oak Bluffs** has a warren of some 300 candy-colored Victorian cottages. The main port of **Vineyard Haven** has a street of shops and a back street preserved from whaling days. Tidy and polished **Edgartown** has upscale boutiques, elegant sea-captains' houses, flower gardens, and a ferry to **Chappaquiddick Island,** laced with nature preserves. Rural **West Tisbury** and **Chilmark** offer good biking past sheep, llama, and other farms. The dramatically striated red-clay **Gay Head Cliffs,** the major tourist site, lie in a Wampanoag Indian township on the island's western tip.

Back on Cape Cod, the village green in **Falmouth,** a military training field in the 18th century, is today flanked by Colonial homes, fine inns, and a Congregational church with a bell made by Paul Revere. The Falmouth Historical Society (Palmer Ave. at the Village Green, ☎ 508/548–4857) maintains two museums and conducts free walking tours of the town in season.

Quietly wealthy **Hyannis Port** is the site of the **Kennedy family compound.** In **Hyannis,** the Cape's year-round commercial hub, the first stage of a projected **John F. Kennedy Memorial Museum**—an exhibit of photographs from the presidential years focusing on John F. Kennedy's ties to the Cape—has been set up at the Old Town Hall on busy Main Street (☎ 508/775–2201).

From Hyannis, ferries travel year-round to **Nantucket,** 30 mi out in the open Atlantic Ocean. **Nantucket town,** an exquisitely preserved National Historic District, encapsulates the island's whaling past in more than a dozen historical museums along its cobblestone streets. The beach community of **Siasconset** began as an actors' colony and today offers a peaceful, unhurried lifestyle in beautiful surroundings including tiny rose-covered cottages and white-clamshell drives. Most of the 12- by 3-mi island is covered with moors, scented with bayberry, wild roses, and cranberries; ringing it are miles of clean, white-sand beaches.

At the southeast tip of Cape Cod, **Chatham** is a seaside town relatively free of the development and commercialism found elsewhere, though offering a downtown of traditional shops and fine inns. The view from **Chatham Lighthouse** is spectacular.

At the beginning of the Cape's north shore is **Sandwich,** founded in 1637. This picturesque town, centered by a pond with a waterwheel-powered gristmill, remains famous for the colored glass produced here in the 19th century. A large collection is exhibited at the **Sandwich Glass Museum** (129 Main St., ☎ 508/888–0251). Nearby is the **Hoxie House** (Rte. 130, ☎ 508/888–1173), a restored 1675 saltbox unique in that it was never modernized.

Off Rte. 130 is **Heritage Plantation,** a complex of museum buildings displaying classic and historic cars, antique military-related items, Currier & Ives prints, and other Americana—all set amid extensive gardens. *Grove and Pine Sts., Sandwich, ☎ 508/888–3300. Admission charged. Closed Nov.–mid-May.*

East on Rte. 6A, past fine views of meadows and the bay, is **Barnstable,** a lovely town of large old houses. In **Yarmouth, Hallet's Store,** a working drugstore and soda fountain, is preserved as it was 100 years ago. In **Dennis** is **Scargo Hill,** offering a spectacular view of Cape Cod Bay and Scargo Lake below.

Brewster has numerous mansions built for sea captains in the 1800s. The **Cape Cod Museum of Natural History** has environmental and marine exhibits and trails through 80 acres rich in wildlife. *Rte. 6A, Brewster, ☎ 508/896–3867. Admission charged.*

Nauset Beach in **Orleans** begins a virtually unbroken stretch of sand extending to Provincetown. The **Cape Cod National Seashore** preserves 30 mi of it, including superb beaches and lighthouses. Just past **Eastham** off U.S. 6, the national seashore's **Salt Pond Visitor Center** (☎ 508/255–3421; closed weekdays Jan.–mid-Feb.) offers displays, tours, lectures, and films.

Wellfleet was a Colonial whaling and codfishing port and is now home to fishermen, artists, and craftsmen. At the national seashore's **Pilgrim Heights Area,** trails take you through terrain the *Mayflower* crew explored before moving on to Plymouth.

The national seashore's **Province Lands** (visitor center, ☎ 508/487–1256; closed Dec.–mid-Apr.) embrace **Provincetown's** spectacular beaches and dunes, as well as walking, biking, and horse trails. In the town, which is filled with first-rate shops and galleries, Portuguese and American fishermen mix with painters, poets, writers, whale-watchers, and, especially in high season, a large gay and lesbian community. The **Pilgrim Monument and Provincetown Museum,** on a hill above the town center, commemorates the landing of the Pilgrims in 1620. From atop the 252-ft tower you have a panoramic view of the entire Cape. *High Pole Hill, ☎ 508/487–1310. Admission charged.*

What to See and Do with Children

ZooQuarium (Rte. 28, West Yarmouth, ☎ 508/775–8883; closed Dec.–mid-Feb.) offers sea-lion shows, a petting zoo, pony rides, and

Cape Cod

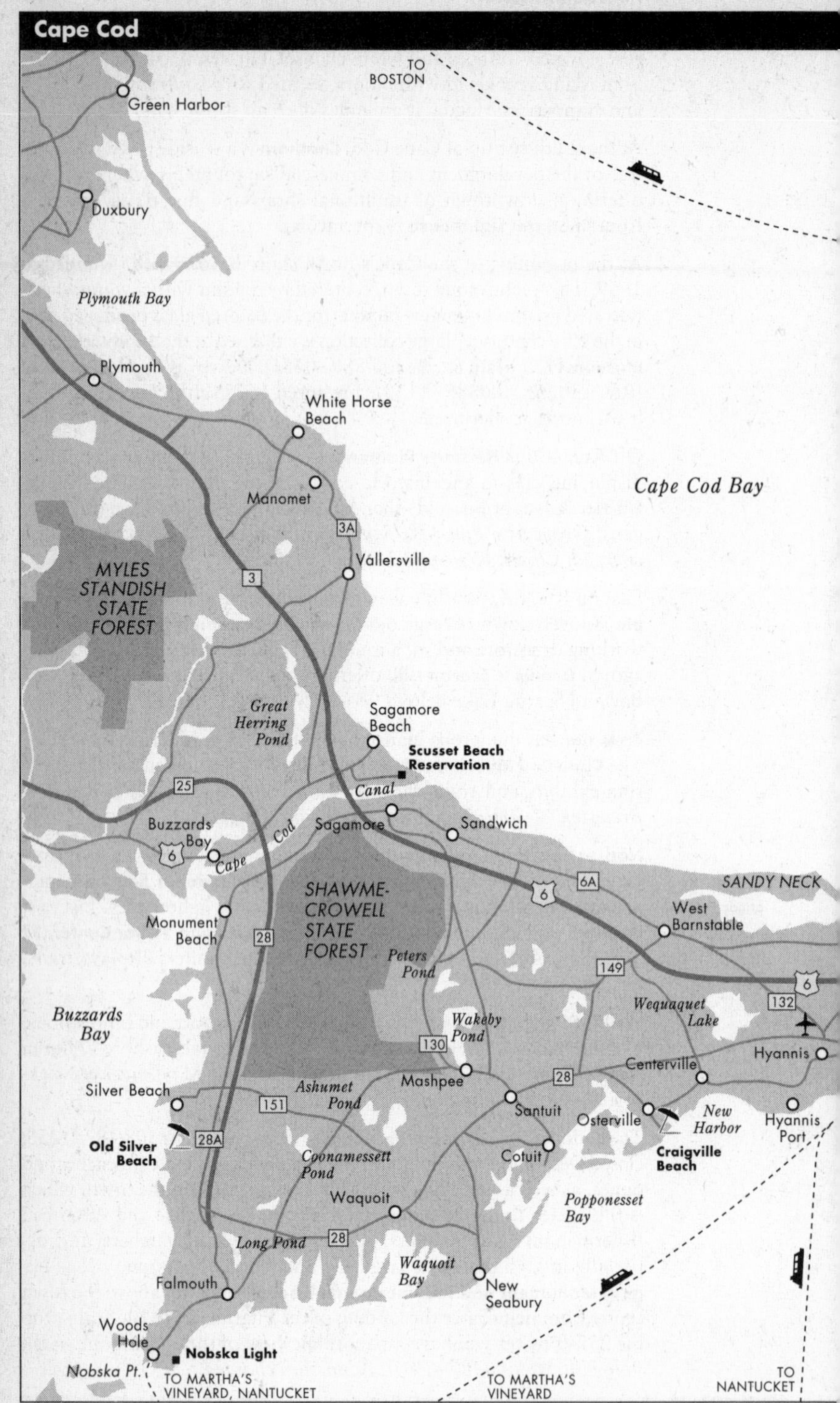

TO BOSTON
Green Harbor
Duxbury
Plymouth Bay
Plymouth
White Horse Beach
Manomet
3A
Vallersville
3
MYLES STANDISH STATE FOREST
Cape Cod Bay
Great Herring Pond
Sagamore Beach
Scusset Beach Reservation
Canal
25
Buzzards Bay
6
Cape Cod
Sagamore
Sandwich
6A
SANDY NECK
SHAWME-CROWELL STATE FOREST
Monument Beach
28
Peters Pond
West Barnstable
149
6
132
Wequaquet Lake
Buzzards Bay
Wakeby Pond
130
Hyannis
Centerville
Silver Beach
Ashumet Pond
Mashpee
28
151
Santuit
Osterville
New Harbor
Hyannis Port
Old Silver Beach
28A
Cotuit
Craigville Beach
Coonamessett Pond
Waquoit
Popponesset Bay
Long Pond
28
Waquoit Bay
New Seabury
Falmouth
Woods Hole
Nobska Light
Nobska Pt.
TO MARTHA'S VINEYARD, NANTUCKET
TO MARTHA'S VINEYARD
TO NANTUCKET

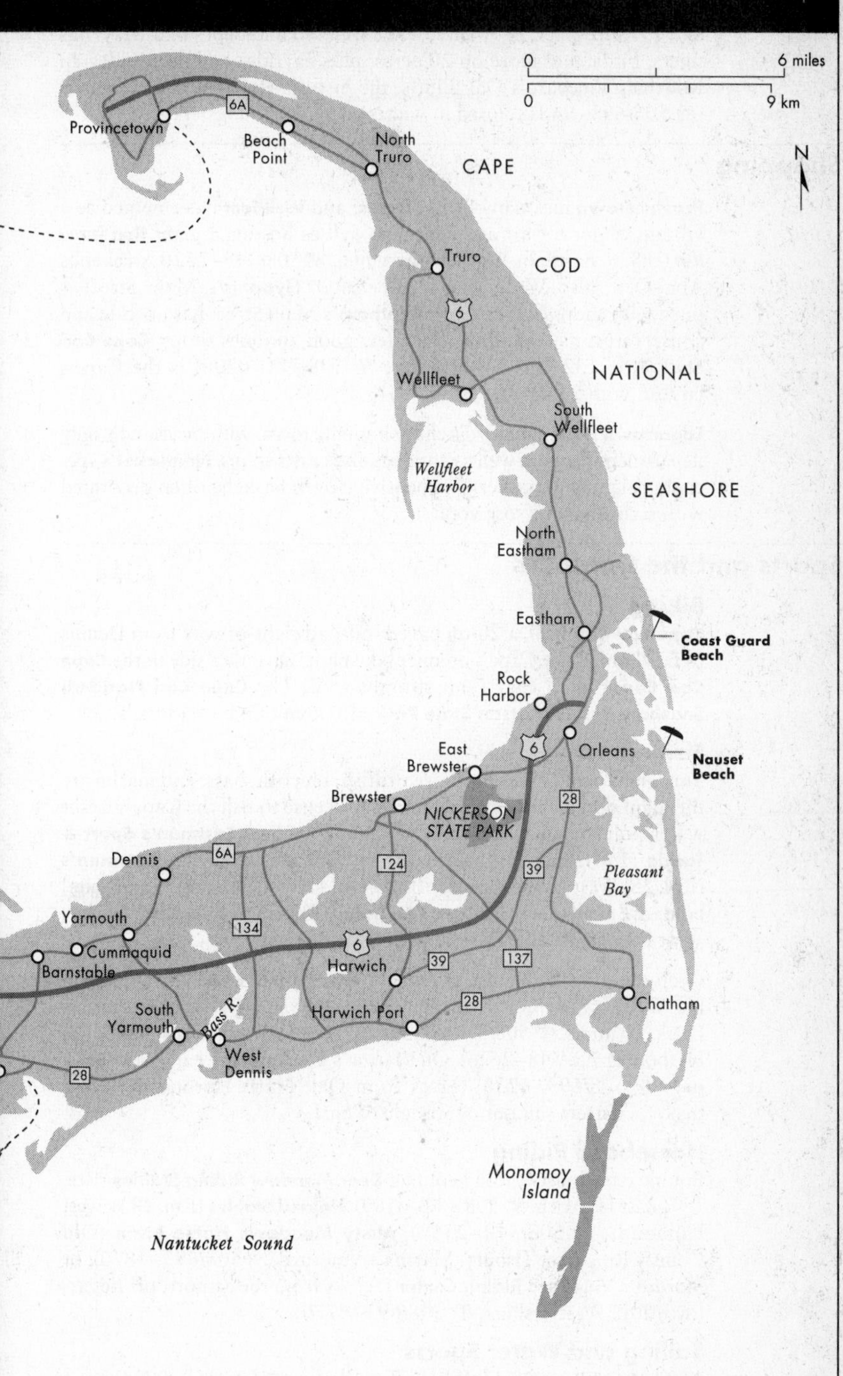

0
6 miles
0
9 km
N
Provincetown
6A
Beach Point
North Truro
CAPE
Truro
COD
6
Wellfleet
NATIONAL
South Wellfleet
Wellfleet Harbor
SEASHORE
North Eastham
Eastham
Coast Guard Beach
Rock Harbor
Orleans
Nauset Beach
East Brewster
Brewster
NICKERSON STATE PARK
28
Dennis
6A
124
39
Pleasant Bay
Yarmouth
134
Cummaquid
Barnstable
Harwich
39
137
South Yarmouth
Bass R.
West Dennis
Harwich Port
28
Chatham
28
Monomoy Island
Nantucket Sound

aquariums. **Bassett Wild Animal Farm** (Tubman Rd., between Rtes. 124 and 137, Brewster, ☎ 508/896–3224; closed mid-Sept.–mid-May) has tigers, birds, and more on 20 acres, plus hayrides and pony rides. In Martha's Vineyard's Oak Bluffs, the historic **Flying Horses Carousel** (☎ 508/693–9481; closed in winter) delights youngsters.

Shopping

Provincetown has many fine galleries, and **Wellfleet** has emerged as a vibrant center for art and crafts, as well as hosting a giant **flea market** (U.S. 6, Eastham-Wellfleet town line, ☎ 508/349–2520; weekends Apr.–Oct., also Wed.–Thurs. July–Aug.). **Hyannis's** Main Street is lined with shops of every sort. **Chatham's** Main Street has upscale and conservative merchandise, and a few good antiques shops. **Cape Cod Mall** (Rte. 132 and 28, Hyannis, ☎ 508/771–0200) is the Cape's largest, with 95 shops.

Edgartown is the Vineyard's chief shopping town, with the island's only department store, as well as antiques and crafts shops. **Nantucket's** specialty is lightship baskets—expensive woven baskets, often decorated with scrimshaw or rosewood.

Sports and the Outdoors

Biking

Cape Cod Rail Trail, a 20-mi paved railroad right-of-way from Dennis to Eastham, is the Cape's premier bike path. On either side of the **Cape Cod Canal** is an easy 7-mi straight trail. The **Cape Cod National Seashore** and **Nickerson State Park** also maintain bicycle trails.

Fishing

Tuna, mako and blue sharks, swordfish, bluefish, bass, and marlin are the main ocean catches. The necessary license to fish the Cape's freshwater ponds is available at tackle shops, such as **Eastman's Sport & Tackle** (150 Main St., Falmouth, ☎ 508/548–6900) and **Truman's** (Rte. 28, West Yarmouth, ☎ 508/771–3470), which rent gear. Rental boats are available from **Cape Cod Boats** (Rte. 28 at Bass River Bridge, West Dennis, ☎ 508/394–9268).

Deep-sea fishing trips are operated by **Cap'n Bill & Cee Jay** (MacMillan Wharf, Provincetown, ☎ 508/487–4330), **Hy-Line** (Ocean St. Dock, Hyannis, ☎ 508/778–2600), and **Patriot Party Boats** (Falmouth Harbor, ☎ 508/548–2626). On Martha's Vineyard, the party boat ***Skipper*** (☎ 508/693–1238) leaves from Oak Bluffs Harbor. On Nantucket, charters sail out of Straight Wharf.

Horseback Riding

Equine enthusiasts should contact **Deer Meadow Riding Stables** (Rte. 137, East Harwich, ☎ 508/432–6580), **Haland Stables** (Rte. 28A, West Falmouth, ☎ 508/540–2552), **Misty Meadows Horse Farm** (Old County Rd., West Tisbury, Martha's Vineyard, ☎ 508/693–1870), or **Martha's Vineyard Riding Center** (across from the airport, off Edgartown Rd., West Tisbury, ☎ 508/693–3770).

Sailing and Water Sports

Arey's Pond Boat Yard (off Rte. 28, Orleans, ☎ 508/255–0994) has a sailing school. **Cape Water Sports** (☎ 508/432–7079) has locations on several beaches for sailboat, canoe, and other rentals and lessons. Lessons and rentals are available at **Wind's Up!** (Beach Rd., Vineyard Haven, ☎ 508/693–4252) on Martha's Vineyard and at **Force 5** (Jetties Beach, ☎ 508/228–5358; 37 Main St., ☎ 508/228–0700) on Nantucket.

Beaches

Beaches fronting on **Cape Cod Bay** generally have cold water and gentle waves. South-side beaches, on **Nantucket Sound,** have rolling surf and are warmer. Open-ocean beaches on the **Cape Cod National Seashore** have serious surf, are contiguous, and have lifeguards and rest rooms. In summer, parking lots can be full by 10 AM.

Dining and Lodging

Hearty meat-and-potatoes fare is the cuisine of choice on the Cape, along with the ubiquitous New England clam chowder and fresh fish and seafood. Extraordinary gourmet restaurants can be found—on Rte. 6A in Brewster and on Nantucket especially—along with occasional ethnic specialties. On Martha's Vineyard only Edgartown and Oak Bluffs allow the sale of liquor.

For summer, lodgings should be booked as far in advance as possible. Assistance with last-minute reservations is available from the Cape Cod and island chambers of commerce (*see* Tourist Information, *above*). Off-season rates are much reduced, and service may be more personalized. The rates for many inns include full breakfast.

B&B reservations services include **House Guests Cape Cod and the Islands** (Box 1881, Orleans 02653, ☎ 800/666–4678) and **Bed and Breakfast Cape Cod** (Box 341, West Hyannis Port 02672, ☎ 508/775–2772). **Provincetown Reservations System** (293 Commercial St., Provincetown 02657, ☎ 508/487–2400 or 800/648–0364) makes reservations for accommodations and more. **Martha's Vineyard and Nantucket Reservations** (Box 1322, Lagoon Pond Rd., Vineyard Haven 02568, ☎ 508/693–7200) and **Accommodations Plus** (RFD 273, Edgartown 02539, ☎ 508/627–7374) book B&Bs, hotels, and cottages.

For price ranges, see Charts 1 (A) and 2 (A) in On the Road with Fodor's.

Brewster

DINING

★ **Chillingsworth.** The Cape's best restaurant, this elegant and elaborately decorated spot offers award-winning French and nouvelle cuisine and an outstanding wine cellar. The changing dinner menu features such entrées as venison with celery-root puree and fried pumpkin. *Rte. 6A, ☎ 508/896–3640. AE, DC, MC, V. Closed Thanksgiving–Memorial Day; also some weekdays (call). $$$$*

LODGING

Captain Freeman Inn. This 1866 Victorian has 12-ft ceilings and windows and a spacious wraparound veranda. Guest rooms feature antiques; suites include fireplaces and porches with private spas. A health club was added in '94. *15 Breakwater Rd., Brewster 02631, ☎ 508/896–7481 or 800/843–4664. 12 rooms, 3 share bath. Facilities: heated pool, health club. AE, MC, V. $$–$$$*

Chatham

LODGING

★ **Chatham Bars Inn.** An oceanfront resort in the old style (MAP available), this renovated Chatham landmark comprises the main building—with its grand lobby—and cottages on 20 landscaped acres. Many rooms have private porches, some with lovely ocean views. *Shore Rd., 02633, ☎ 508/945–0096 or 800/527–4884, FAX 508/945–5491. 152 rooms, 26 cottages. Facilities: 3 restaurants, private beach, tennis, pool, children's programs. AE, DC, MC, V. $$$$*

★ **Captain's House Inn.** This inn's tasteful Colonial decor and quiet comfort makes it one of the Cape's finest. Each room in the three buildings has its own distinct personality; the Hiram Harding Room has 200-year-old hand-hewn ceiling beams, a wall of raised walnut paneling, a working fireplace, and a rich red Oriental carpet. *371 Old Harbor Rd., 02633, ☎ 508/945–0127, FAX 508/945–0866. 14 rooms, 2 suites. AE, MC, V. Closed Jan.–mid-Feb. $$$–$$$$*

Falmouth

LODGING

Mostly Hall. Set in a landscaped yard, this imposing 1849 house has a wraparound porch and a cupola. Corner rooms have leafy views, reading areas, antique pieces, and reproduction canopy beds. Full breakfasts are complimentary and delicious. *27 Main St., 02540, ☎ 508/548–3786 or 800/682–0565. 6 rooms. AE, D, MC, V. Closed Jan.–mid-Feb. $$–$$$*

Hyannis

DINING

Penguins Sea Grill. This sophisticated, northern Italian restaurant focuses on seafood and homemade pastas. A signature dish is wood-grilled swordfish with either roasted pepper aïoli or lime caper butter. The newly redecorated interior has a bistro look with linen tablecloths and dark tones. *331 Main St., Hyannis, ☎ 508/775–2023. AE, DC, MC, V. No lunch. $$–$$$*

LODGING

Tara Hyannis Hotel & Resort. It's hard to beat the Tara's combination of landscaping, services, resort facilities, and location. Although the lobby is elegant, the rooms are bland, with pale colors and nondescript furnishings. All rooms have color TV and a private balcony or patio. *West End Circle, 02601, ☎ 508/775–7775 or 800/843–8272, FAX 508/790–4221. 224 rooms. Facilities: restaurant, 2 pools, tennis, health club, children's programs. AE, D, DC, MC, V. $$$*

Capt. Gosnold Village. An easy walk to the beach and town, this colony of motel rooms and cottages is ideal for families. The decor ranges from light and airy new to pine and Colonial reproductions. Units range from those with simple motel-style accommodations to those with three bedrooms, three baths, a kitchen, and a living room. All but the motel-style rooms have gas grills, phones, and decks. *230 Gosnold St., 02601, ☎ 508/775–9111. 40 units. Facilities: pool, playground. MC, V. Closed Nov.–mid-Apr. $$*

Martha's Vineyard

DINING

Black Dog Tavern. This island landmark serves basic chowders, pastas, fish, and steak, as well as more elaborate dishes. The glassed-in porch, lighted by ship's lanterns, looks onto the harbor. *Beach St. Ext., Vineyard Haven, ☎ 508/693–9223. No reservations. BYOB. AE, D, MC, V. $$–$$$*

LODGING

★ **Charlotte Inn.** The original 1865 house has grown into a complex of meticulously maintained accommodations and the excellent L'étoile restaurant. The inn is exquisitely furnished with English antiques, and artwork hangs in the hallways. Some rooms have fireplaces, some porches or verandas. *27 S. Summer St., 02539, ☎ 508/627–4751. 26 rooms. Facilities: restaurant, art gallery. AE, MC, V. $$$$*

Nantucket

DINING

★ **Chanticleer.** Within this rose-covered cottage is what may be the best restaurant on the island. The classic French fare includes such specialties as sautéed boneless loin of lamb with port-and-tarragon sauce, and grilled sea bass with roasted peppers and aïoli. The main dining room is formal; upstairs is more casual, and lunch in the rose garden is heavenly. *9 New St., Siasconset, ☎ 508/257–6231. Reservations required, well in advance for dinner. Jacket required at dinner. AE, MC, V. Closed Mon. and Columbus Day–Mother's Day. $$$$*

★ **Brotherhood of Thieves.** Long queues are a fixture outside this very Olde English pub-restaurant. Much of the seating is at long, tightly packed tables where you can dine on good chowder and soups, fried fish and seafood, and burgers. *23 Broad St., no ☎. No reservations. No credit cards. $$*

LODGING

★ **White Elephant.** This hotel is right on the harbor. Rooms in the Breakers, the hotel's ultraluxury arm, open onto private harbor-front decks. Main-inn rooms are done in English country style, with stenciled-pine armoires and florals. *Easton St., Box 359, Nantucket 02554, ☎ 508/228–2500 or 800/475–2637. 48 rooms, 32 cottages. Facilities: restaurant, lounge, heated outdoor pool, business services, boat slips. AE, D, DC, MC, V. Closed mid-Sept.–Memorial Day. $$$$*

Provincetown

DINING

★ **Ciro's.** After 30 years, this stage-set Italian restaurant—raffia-covered Chianti bottles hanging from the rafters, Italian opera in the air—is still a star. Veal and pasta dishes are specialties. *4 Kiley Ct., ☎ 508/487–0049. Reservations required in summer; Sat. dinner. MC, V. Closed Mon.–Thurs. Nov.–Memorial Day. $$–$$$*

LODGING

Hargood House. This apartment complex on the water a walk from the town center is a great option for longer stays and families. Most units have decks and large water-view windows; all have kitchens and modern baths. *493 Commercial St., 02657, ☎ 508/487–9133. 19 apartments. Facilities: private beach. AE, MC, V. $$$*

Campgrounds

Nickerson State Park (Rte. 6A, Brewster 02631, ☎ 508/896–3491), 420 sites, hot showers, convenience store, trails (walking, biking, jogging), fishing, boating, swimming, cross-country skiing (*see also* National and State Parks, *above*). **Shawme–Crowell State Forest** (Rte. 130, Sandwich, ☎ 508/888–0351), 260 campsites, showers, interpretive programs, walking trails, day use of nearby beach.

The Arts and Nightlife

The Arts

The Equity **Cape Playhouse** (Rte. 6A, Dennis, ☎ 508/385–3911) and the **Falmouth Playhouse** (off Rte. 151, North Falmouth, ☎ 508/563–5922) present summer stock. The **Vineyard Playhouse** (10 Church St., Vineyard Haven, ☎ 508/693–7333) offers Broadway-vintage works year-round and summer Shakespeare. **Actor's Theatre of Nantucket** (Methodist Church, Centre and Main Sts., ☎ 508/228–6325) presents several plays each summer, including children's matinees.

Nightlife

The Cape has all manner of nightlife, from the rowdiest college-crowd clubs to quiet folky coffeehouses, from Irish and country bars to ballrooms. Hyannis has the busiest, with many nightclubs and bars featuring live rock and jazz (Jazz Hot Line: ☎ 508/394–5277). Oak Bluffs is the center of Vineyard nightlife, with rowdy bars and a year-round dance club. Nantucket town offers rock clubs, as well as restaurants with sedate piano bars or rocking live bands. For listings of events, see local papers.

THE BERKSHIRES

Though only about a 2½-hour drive west from Boston or north from New York City, the Berkshires lives up to storybook images of rural New England, with wooded hills, narrow winding roads, and compact charming villages. Summer offers a variety of cultural events, not the least of which is the Tanglewood classical-music festival in Lenox. Fall brings a blaze of brilliant foliage. In winter, the Berkshires is a popular ski area. Springtime visitors can enjoy maple-sugaring. The region can be crowded any weekend.

Tourist Information

Mohawk Trail Association (Box 722, Charlemont 01339, ☎ 413/664–6256). **Berkshire Visitor's Bureau** (Berkshire Common Plaza, Pittsfield 01201, ☎ 413/443–9186 or 800/237–5747). **Lenox Chamber of Commerce** (Lenox Academy Bldg., 75 Main St., 01240, ☎ 413/637–3646).

Getting There

By Plane

The closest airports are in Boston (*see* Boston); Albany and New York City (*see* New York); and Hartford (*see* Connecticut). Small airports in Pittsfield and Great Barrington serve private planes.

By Car

The Massachusetts Turnpike (I–90) connects Boston with Lee and Stockbridge. The scenic Mohawk Trail (Rte. 2) parallels the northern border of Massachusetts. To reach the Berkshires from New York City, take either the New York Thruway (I–87) or the Taconic State Parkway. Within the Berkshires the main north–south road is Rte. 7.

By Bus

Peter Pan Bus Lines (☎ 413/442–4451 or 800/237–8747) serves Lee and Pittsfield from Boston and Albany. **Bonanza Bus Lines** (☎ 800/556–3815) connects the Berkshires with Albany, New York City, and Providence.

Exploring the Berkshires

Williamstown is the northernmost Berkshires town, at the junction of Rte. 2 and U.S. 7. Williams College opened here in 1793, and the town still revolves around it. Gracious campus buildings lining the wide main street are open to visitors.

Formerly a private collection, the **Sterling and Francine Clark Art Institute** is now an outstanding small museum, featuring paintings by Renoir, Monet, and Degas. *225 South St., Williamstown,* ☎ *413/458–9545. Closed Mon.*

For a fine scenic drive (especially in autumn), head east on the **Mohawk Trail,** a 63-mi stretch of Rte. 2 that follows a former Native American path from Williamstown. The first stop is **North Adams.** Once a railroad and industrial boomtown, North Adams is home to the **Western Gateway Heritage State Park** (☎ 413/663–6312), which exhibits photographs and artifacts of the town's industrial history in a restored freight yard and warehouse.

South of Williamstown off Rte. 7 is **Mt. Greylock,** at 3,491 ft the highest point in the state. **Pittsfield,** county seat and geographic center of the region, has a lively small-town atmosphere. In 1850, outside of town, Herman Melville purchased a house he named **Arrowhead** (780 Holmes Rd., ☎ 413/442–1793; admission charged). The house, including the writer's desk, personal effects, and whaling trinkets, is open on a limited basis. In town, at the **Berkshire Athenaeum** (Pittsfield Public Library, 1 Wendell Ave.), the **Herman Melville Memorial Room** (☎ 413/499–9486) houses memorabilia of the author of *Moby-Dick.*

Hancock Shaker Village, 5 mi west of Pittsfield on Rte. 20, was founded in the 1790s as the third Shaker community in America. The religious community closed in 1960, and the site, complete with living quarters, round stone barn, and working crafts shops, is now a museum. ☎ *413/443–0188. Admission charged. Closed Dec.–Mar.*

South of Pittsfield 5 mi on Rte. 7, the village of **Lenox** epitomizes the Berkshires for many visitors. In the thick of the "summer cottage" region, it's rich with old inns and majestic mansions, including **The Mount,** summer home of novelist Edith Wharton, and now the site of outdoor theater. *Plunkett St.,* ☎ *413/637–1899. Admission charged. Closed Nov.–late May.*

Outside the village is **Tanglewood,** summer headquarters of the Boston Symphony. Thousands flock to the 200-acre estate every summer weekend to picnic on the lawns as musicians perform on the open-air stage (*see* The Arts, *below*).

The archetypal New England small town of **Stockbridge** has a history of literary and artistic inhabitants, including the painter Norman Rockwell and the writers Norman Mailer and Robert Sherwood. The town's **Norman Rockwell Museum** (☎ 413/298–4100) boasts the world's largest collection of his original paintings. Nearby is **Chesterwood,** for 33 years the summer home of Daniel Chester French, best known for his statues of the Minute Man in Concord and of Abraham Lincoln at the Lincoln Memorial in Washington, D.C. *Williamsville Rd. (off Rte. 183),* ☎ *413/298–3579. Admission charged. Closed Nov.–Apr. except Veteran's Day weekend (special programs).*

Great Barrington is the largest town in the southern Berkshires and a mecca for antiques hunters.

What to See and Do with Children

The **Jiminy Peak** ski resort (Corey Rd., Hancock, ☎ 413/738–5500) offers an alpine slide and trout fishing in summer. The **Robbins-Zust Family Marionettes** (East Rd., Richmond, ☎ 413/698–2591) perform puppet shows in summer.

Shopping

Antiques

There are antiques stores throughout the Berkshires, but the greatest concentration is around Great Barrington, South Egremont, and

Sheffield. For a list of storekeepers who belong to the **Berkshire County Antiques Dealers Association** and guarantee the authenticity of their merchandise, send a self-addressed stamped envelope to R.D. 1, Box 1, Sheffield 01257.

Outlet Stores

Along Rte. 7 just north of Lenox are two factory-outlet malls, **Lenox House Country Shops** and **Brushwood Farms.** A number of outlet stores are concentrated at the **Buggy Whip Factory** (☎ 413/229–3576), some distance from the main tourist routes, on Rte. 272 in Southfield.

Sports and the Outdoors

Biking

The back roads of Berkshire County can be hilly, but the views and the countryside are incomparable. Bikes can be rented from **Plaine's Cycling Center** (55 W. Housatonic St., Pittsfield, ☎ 413/499–0294).

Boating and Canoeing

The **Housatonic River** flows south from Pittsfield between the Berkshire Hills and the Taconic Range toward Connecticut. Canoes and boats can be rented from the **Onota Boat Livery** (455 Pecks Rd., Pittsfield, ☎ 413/442–1724) on Onota Lake.

Fishing

The area's rivers, lakes, and streams abound with bass, pike, perch, and trout. **Points North Fishing and Hunting Outfitters** (Rte. 8, Adams, ☎ 413/743–4030) organizes summer fly-fishing schools.

Golf

Greenock Country Club (W. Park St., Lee, ☎ 413/243–3323) has a nine-hole course; **Pontoosuc Lake Country Club** (Kirkwood Dr., Pittsfield, ☎ 413/445–4217) and **Waubeeka Golf Links** (Rte. 7, Williamstown, ☎ 413/458–5869) have 18-hole courses.

Hiking

The **Appalachian Trail** goes through Berkshire County. Hiking is particularly rewarding in the higher elevations of **Mt. Greylock State Reservation** (*see* National and State Parks, *above*).

Ski Areas

Cross-Country

Brodie (Rte. 7, New Ashford 01237, ☎ 413/443–4752 or 413/443–6597) has 16 mi of trails. **Butternut Basin** (Rte. 23, Great Barrington 01230, ☎ 413/528–2000) has 4 mi of groomed trails.

Downhill

Berkshire East (Box 727, S. River Rd., Charlemont 01339, ☎ 413/339–6617) has a 1,200-ft vertical drop, 36 trails, four double chairlifts, and one surface lift. **Bousquet Ski Area** (Dan Fox Dr., Pittsfield 01201, ☎ 413/442–8316 or 413/442–2436) has a 750-ft drop, 21 trails, two double chairlifts, and two surface lifts. **Brodie** (*see* Cross-Country, *above*) has a 1,250-ft drop, 26 trails, four double chairlifts, and two surface lifts. **Butternut Basin** (*see* Cross-Country, *above*) has a 1,000-ft drop, 22 trails, one triple and five double chairlifts, and one surface lift. **Jiminy Peak** (*see* What to See and Do with Children, *above*) has a 1,140-ft drop, 26 trails, one triple and three double chairlifts, and one surface lift.

Dining and Lodging

Lodging rates may include full or Continental breakfast. For price ranges, see Charts 1 (B) and 2 (B) in On the Road with Fodor's.

Great Barrington

DINING

★ **Boiler Room Café.** In a turn-of-the-century clapboard house, three comfortable dining rooms are painted in warm colors accented by arches with white moldings and whimsical wood sculptures. The eclectic, sophisticated menu may include delicious, light New England seafood stew, mouthwatering grilled baby back ribs, or *osso buco Piedmontese* (unboned veal knuckle). Desserts range from straightforward cherry pie to complex pecan tart. *405 Stockbridge Rd.,* ☎ *413/528–4280. MC, V. Closed Mon.–Tues. $$$*

20 Railroad St. The exposed brick and subdued lighting lend atmosphere to this bustling restaurant, which features a 28-ft-long mahogany bar. Specialties include sausage pie, burgers, and sandwiches. *20 Railroad St.,* ☎ *413/528–9345. MC, V. $*

Lee

LODGING

Morgan House. Most guest rooms at this inn, which dates to 1817, are small, but rates reflect that. The furniture is Colonial style; some rooms have four-poster beds and stenciled walls. The lobby is papered with pages from old guest registers; among the signatures are those of George Bernard Shaw and Ulysses S. Grant. *31 Main St., 01238,* ☎ *413/243–0181. 14 rooms (12 share baths). Facilities: 3 dining rooms, bar. AE, D, DC, MC, V. $*

Lenox

DINING

Gateways Inn. Four dining rooms are hung with chandeliers and tapestries; working fireplaces soften the formal tone. Continental and American cuisine includes veal, pheasant, salmon, and rack of lamb. *71 Walker St.,* ☎ *413/637–2532. AE, D, DC, MC, V. Closed Sun. Nov.–May. $$$*

Church St. Cafe. In this popular restaurant, the walls are covered with original artwork, tables are surrounded by ficus trees, and classical music plays in the background. Specialties include roast duckling with thyme and Madeira sauce, and crab cakes. *69 Church St.,* ☎ *413/637–2745. MC, V. Closed Sun.–Mon. Nov.–Apr. $$*

LODGING

Blantyre. The castlelike Tudor architecture, vast public rooms, and 85 acres of beautiful grounds are impressive enough, but the guest rooms in the main house are also fabulous: huge and lavishly decorated. The stylishly prepared, five-course evening meal is wonderful. *16 Blantyre Rd. (off Rte. 7), 01240,* ☎ *413/637–3556 or 413/298–3806. 13 rooms, 10 suites. Facilities: restaurant, pool, tennis. AE, DC, MC, V. $$$$*

Eastover. This resort was opened by an ex-circus roustabout, and the tradition of noisy fun and informality continues. Guest rooms are functional and vary only slightly from dormitory to motel style. Nondescript but comfortable decor and furnishings temper the informality of the vast dining rooms. *East St. (off Rte. 7), Box 2160, 01240,* ☎ *413/637–0625. 165 rooms (45 share baths). Facilities: dining rooms (breakfast and dinner), tennis, 2 pools, exercise room, skiing, canoeing, horseback riding. AE, D, DC, MC, V. Closed weekdays Sept.–July. $$*

Pittsfield Area

DINING

Dakota. Moose and elk heads eye diners at this large restaurant with a rustic hunting-lodge atmosphere. A broiler stocked with Texas mesquite wood is used for swordfish, shrimp, sirloin, and chicken. *Rtes. 7 and 20, ☎ 413/499–7900. AE, DC, MC, V. No lunch Mon.–Sat. $$*

LODGING

Berkshire Hilton Inn. A spacious hall features wing chairs, glass, and brass. Guest rooms have reproduction furnishings and floral-print drapes; rooms on the top floors have the best views over the town and surrounding mountains. *Berkshire Common, South St., 01201, ☎ 413/499–2000 or 800/445–8667, FAX 413/442–0449. 175 rooms. Facilities: restaurant, pool, sauna, whirlpool. AE, DC, MC, V. $$$*

Dalton House. This B&B, built in the 1800s, has a sunny dining room with pine furniture and cheerful bedrooms with floral-print drapes and wallpaper. The carriage house has spacious deluxe rooms featuring period furnishings. *955 Main St., Dalton 01226, ☎ 413/684–3854. 9 rooms, 2 suites. Facilities: outdoor pool. AE, MC, V. $$–$$$*

Sheffield

DINING

Stagecoach Hill Inn. Constructed in the early 1800s as a stagecoach stop, the restaurant cultivates an English tone with such touches as pictures of the British royal family, hunting scenes, steak-and-kidney pie, roast beef and Yorkshire pudding, and British ale on tap. *Rte. 41, ☎ 413/229–8585. AE, D, DC, MC, V. $$$*

LODGING

Ivanhoe Country House. The Appalachian Trail runs across the property of this B&B, built in 1780; the antiques-furnished guest rooms are generally spacious. *254 South Undermountain Rd. (Rte. 41), 01257, ☎ 413/229–2143. 9 rooms, 2 suites with kitchen. Facilities: pool. No credit cards. $$$*

South Egremont

DINING AND LODGING

Egremont Inn. The public rooms in this 1780 inn are enormous; the main lounge alone, with its vast open fireplace, is worth a visit. Bedrooms are small, with wide-board floors, uneven ceilings, four-poster beds, and claw-foot baths. The sunny dining room serves Continental fare. *Old Sheffield Rd., Box 418, 01258, ☎ 413/528–2111. 22 rooms. Facilities: 3 dining rooms, lounge, pool, tennis. AE, MC, V. $$$*

Stockbridge Area

DINING AND LODGING

Red Lion Inn. An inn since 1773, and rebuilt after a fire in 1896, this landmark is now massive, with guest rooms in the main building and several annexes. Annex rooms are individually decorated and furnished with antiques. New England specialties are served in the elegant dining room. *Main St., 02162, ☎ 413/298–5545. 108 rooms (33 share bath), 10 suites. Facilities: dining room, pool, exercise room. AE, D, DC, MC, V. $$$*

★ **Merrell Tavern Inn.** Built between 1794 and 1800, this old New England inn on the National Register of Historic Places has some good-size bedrooms furnished with antiques and pencil-post beds. The breakfast room, with an open fireplace, contains the only complete "bird-cage" Colonial bar in America. *Rte. 102, South Lee 01260, ☎ 413/243–1794. 10 rooms. AE, MC, V. $$–$$$*

Williamstown

DINING

Four Acres. This restaurant has two dining rooms: One is decorated with street signs, paneling, and mirrors; the other features collegiate insignias and modern paintings. The American and Continental cuisine includes sautéed calves' liver with applejack glaze. *Rte. 2, ☎ 413/458–5436. AE, MC, V. Closed Sun. $$*

LODGING

River Bend Farm. Listed on the National Register of Historic Places, River Bend was constructed in 1770 by one of the founders of Williamstown. Some bedrooms have wide-plank walls, curtains of unbleached muslin, and four-poster beds with canopies; all are sprinkled with antique pieces. *643 Simonds Rd., 01267, ☎ 413/458–5504. 5 rooms share 2 baths. Facilities: lounge, river swimming. AE, D, MC, V. $$$*

The Arts and Nightlife

Listings appear daily in the *Berkshire Eagle* and weekly in the *Williamstown Advocate;* major concerts are listed in the Thursday *Boston Globe.* The quarterly *Berkshire Magazine* contains "The Berkshire Guide," covering events from theater to sports.

The Arts

DANCE

Jacob's Pillow Dance Festival, the oldest in the nation, mounts a 10-week summer program every year. *Rte. 20, Becket (Box 287, Lee 01238), ☎ 413/243–0745 (in season) or 413/637–1322.*

MUSIC

The best-known music festival in New England is at **Tanglewood** in Lenox (☎ 413/637–1940 June–Aug.; in the off-season, Boston Symphony Hall, Boston 02115, ☎ 617/266–1492), where the Boston Symphony Orchestra has its summer season (*see* Exploring the Berkshires, *above*). The **Berkshire Performing Arts Center** (40 Kemble St., Lenox, ☎ 413/637–4718) attracts top-name artists in jazz, folk, rock, and blues each summer.

THEATER

The **Berkshire Theatre Festival** (Rte. 102, Box 797, Stockbridge 01262, ☎ 413/298–5536) stages nightly performances in summer at a century-old theater. The **Williamstown Theatre Festival** (Adams Memorial Theatre, 1000 Main St., Box 517, Williamstown 01267, ☎ 413/597–3400) presents classics and contemporary works each summer.

Nightlife

The most popular local nightspot is the **Lion's Den** (☎ 413/298–5545), at the Red Lion Inn in Stockbridge (*see* Dining and Lodging, *above*), with nightly folk music and some contemporary local bands.

ELSEWHERE IN THE STATE

The Pioneer Valley

Getting There

I–91 runs north–south the entire length of the Pioneer Valley, from Greenfield to Springfield; I–90 links Springfield to Boston; and Rte. 2 connects Boston with Greenfield in the north. Amtrak stops in Springfield on routes from Boston and New York.

What to See and Do

The **Greater Springfield Convention and Visitors Bureau** (34 Boland Way, Springfield 01103, ☎ 413/787–1548) provides information about the Pioneer Valley area.

Home to a number of educational institutions, the valley is filled with cultural and historic attractions. **Historic Deerfield** (Rte. 5, ☎ 413/774–5581) in the north is a museum as well as the site of the prestigious Deerfield Academy. In **Amherst** are three of the valley's five major colleges—the University of Massachusetts, Amherst College, and Hampshire College—as well as the **Emily Dickinson Homestead** (280 Main St., ☎ 413/542–8161). **Northampton** is the site of Smith College, as well as the onetime home of the 30th U.S. president, Calvin Coolidge. The village of **South Hadley** is best known for Mount Holyoke, founded in 1837 as the country's first women's college.

East of the southern end of the valley is **Old Sturbridge Village,** a living, working model of an early 1800s New England town, with more than 40 buildings on a 200-acre site. *1 Old Sturbridge Village Rd., ☎ 508/347–3362. Admission charged.*

NEW HAMPSHIRE

By Ed and Roon Frost
Updated by Michelle Seaton

Capital	Concord
Population	1,109,252
Motto	Live Free or Die
State Bird	Purple finch
State Flower	Purple lilac

Visitor Information

New Hampshire Office of Travel and Tourism Development (Box 856, oncord 03302, ☎ 603/271–2343 or 800/944–1117). **Foliage hot line** (☎ 800/258–3608 or 800/262–6660).

Scenic Drives

The **Kancamagus Highway** (Rte. 112) rolls through 32 mi of the White Mountains between Lincoln and Conway. **Rte. 113** between Holderness and South Tamworth, also 32 mi, is full of hills and curves, and winds between mountains and plains with open views of both.

National and State Parks

National Forest

The **White Mountain National Forest** (Box 63, Laconia 03247, ☎ 603/528–8721) occupies 770,000 acres of northern New Hampshire (*see* The White Mountains, *below*).

State Parks

The **Division of Parks and Recreation** (Box 1856, Concord 03302, ☎ 603/271–3254) maintains 75 state parks, beaches, and historic sites. Surrounded by privately held forests, **Monadnock State Park** (Box 181, Jaffrey 03452, ☎ 603/532–8862) seems larger than its 5,000 acres. **Bearbrook State Park** (RFD 1, Box 507, Allenstown 03275, ☎ 603/485–9874) has 9,500 acres.

THE SEACOAST

The southern end of New Hampshire's 18-mi coastline is dominated by Hampton Beach—5 mi of sand, midriff-to-elbow sunbathers, motels, arcades, carryouts, and a boardwalk. At the northern end is Portsmouth, with its beautifully restored historic area, a slew of one-of-a-kind restaurants, and the state's only working port. In between are dunes, beaches, salt marshes, and state parks where you can picnic, hike, swim, boat, and fish.

Tourist Information

Seacoast Council on Tourism (235 West Rd. #10, Portsmouth 03801, ☎ 603/436–7678 or 800/221–5623). Greater Portsmouth: **Chamber of Commerce** (500 Market St., Portsmouth 03801, ☎ 603/436–1118). **Hampton Beach Area:** Chamber of Commerce (836 Lafayette Rd., Hampton 03842, ☎ 603/926–8717).

Getting There

By Plane

Pease Tradeport (Portsmouth, ☎ 603/334–6064) is served by Delta.

By Car

I-95 accesses the Hamptons (Exit 2), central Portsmouth (Exits 3–6), and Portsmouth harbor and historic district (Exit 7).

By Bus

Coast (Durham, ☎ 603/862–2328), **C&J** (☎ 603/742–5111), **Concord Trailways** (☎ 800/639–3317), **Peter Pan Trailways** (☎ 603/889–2121), and **Vermont Transit** (☎ 603/228–3300 or 800/451–3292) provide bus service among the area's cities and towns.

Exploring the Seacoast

From Rte. 1A, the Atlantic is rarely out of sight, and there are plenty of spots for pulling over. In **North Hampton,** enjoy the crashing surf on the rocky shore of **Little Boars Head Beach;** take a leisurely drive past the cottages of "Millionaire's Row"; or, in the summer, stop to see the 1,500 rosebushes at **Fuller Gardens** (10 Willow Ave., ☎ 603/964–5414; admission charged). From granite-bound **Rye Harbor** inlet, **New Hampshire Seacoast Cruises** (☎ 603/436–8084) takes whale-watchers near the Isles of Shoals, a Colonial fishing settlement. **Odiorne Point State Park** (Rte. 1A, Rye, ☎ 603/436–8043), site of the area's first English settlement, is now 230 acres of tidal pools and footpaths punctuated by the **Seacoast Science Center.**

Portsmouth is both a working port—full of huge freighters, little tugboats, and piles of scrap metal—and a walkable city beloved of Boston trendsetters. Showcasing its architectural diversity is **Strawbery Banke,** a 10-acre village-museum whose 40 buildings date from 1695 to 1820. The gardens are splendid. *Marcy St., ☎ 603/433–1100 or 603/433–1106. Admission charged. Closed Nov.–Apr.*

Prescott Park, across the street, has the **Sheafe Warehouse Museum** (☎ 603/431–8748), displaying decoys, ship models, and ship mastheads. The **Portsmouth Historical Society** (Middle and State Sts., ☎ 603/436–8420; admission charged) has a self-guided walking tour that includes six historic houses.

What to See and Do with Children

In Portsmouth, start with the lively, hands-on **Children's Museum** (280 Marcy St., ☎ 603/436–3853) or the **USS *Albacore*** (500 Market St., ☎ 603/436–3680), a vintage submarine.

Shopping

Portsmouth is chockablock with crafts shops, galleries, and clothing boutiques. Stop at the **North Hampton Factory Outlet Center** (Rte. 1, ☎ 603/964–9050) for bargains.

Sports and the Outdoors

Boating and Fishing

Rentals and charters are available from **Atlantic Fishing Fleet** in Rye Harbor (☎ 603/964–5220) or **Al Gauron** (☎ 603/926–2469) and **Smith & Gilmore** (☎ 603/926–3503) in Hampton Beach.

Beaches

New Hampshire's wide strands have hard white sand, moderate surf, and brisk but still swimmable waters; the more northerly have smaller crowds. The state runs **Hampton Beach, North Hampton Beach, Jen-**

ness Beach, and **Wallis Sands State Park,** the most northerly and a local favorite.

Dining and Lodging

Portsmouth shines in warm weather, when restaurants along Bow and Ceres streets open their decks for sea breezes and harbor views. Make lodging reservations well in advance for summer stays in the area. For price ranges, see Charts 1 (B) and 2 (B) in On the Road with Fodor's.

Hampton

DINING

Ron's Beach House. Imaginative fish dishes, such as sautéed scallops and shellfish gratinée, have made this restaurant popular year-round. *965 Ocean Blvd., ☎ 603/926–1870. AE, D, DC, MC, V. $$–$$$*

Hampton Beach

DINING AND LODGING

Ashworth by the Sea. At this centrally located favorite of generations of beachgoers, most rooms have decks. Go for one of the queen rooms, dominated by a four-poster bed and glowing cherry-wood furnishings. *295 Ocean Blvd., 03842, ☎ 603/926–6762 or 800/345–6736, FAX 603/926–2002. 105 rooms. Facilities: 3 restaurants, pool. AE, D, DC, MC, V. $$–$$$*

Portsmouth

DINING

★ **Porto Bello.** In this second-story dining room overlooking the harbor, enjoy daily antipasti specials like grilled portobello mushrooms and stuffed calamari; and pasta entrées such as spinach gnocchi and homemade ravioli filled with eggplant, walnuts, and Parmesan and Romano cheeses. *Veal carciofi*—a 4-oz center cut steak served with artichokes—is a specialty. The tastes are so simple and the ingredients so fresh, you won't have trouble finishing four courses. *67 Bow St., 2nd Floor, ☎ 603/431–2989. D, MC, V. Closed Sun.–Mon. $$*

Oar House and Deck. The river-view deck is fun for drinks and dinner in summer; the main building, a massively beamed old stone warehouse across the parking lot, delights year-round. Try the bouillabaisse. *55 Ceres St., ☎ 603/436–4025. AE, MC, V. $$–$$$*

LODGING

★ **Sise Inn.** This elegant Queen Anne town house, full of chintz and gleaming armoires, is convenient for waterfront strolls. No two rooms are alike; some have whirlpools. *40 Court St., 03801, ☎ and FAX 603/433–1200 or ☎ 800/267–0525. 34 rooms. AE, DC, MC, V. $$$*

The Arts and Nightlife

Summer concerts draw crowds at the **Hampton Beach Casino Ballroom** (Ocean Beach Blvd., ☎ 603/926–4541). Media folk catch sea chanties and Celtic ballads at the **Press Room** (77 Daniel St., Portsmouth, ☎ 603/431–5186).

THE LAKES REGION

The eastern half of central New Hampshire is scattered with beautifully preserved 18th- and 19th-century villages and sparkling lakes—Winnipesaukee ("Smiling Water") is the largest—that echo with squeals and splashes all summer long.

Tourist Information

Lakes Region Chamber of Commerce (11 Veterans Sq., Laconia 03246, ☎ 603/524–5531 or 800/531–2347). **Lakes Region Association** (Box 589, Center Harbor 03226, ☎ 603/253–8516).

Getting There

By Car

I–93 is the principal north–south artery. From the coast, Rte. 11 goes to southern Lake Winnipesaukee; en route to the White Mountains, north–south Rte. 16 accesses spurs to the lake.

By Bus

Concord Trailways (☎ 603/228–3300; in New England, 800/639–3317) serves Meredith, Center Harbor, Moultonborough, and West Ossipee.

Exploring the Lakes Region

Alton Bay, at Winnipesaukee's southernmost tip, has the lake's cruise-boat dock and a Victorian bandstand. In affluent Colonial **Gilford** there's a large state beach, as well as the **Gunstock Recreation Area** (Rte. 11A, ☎ 603/293–4341), with swimming, hiking, and camping. In honky-tonk **Weirs Beach,** fireworks light up summer nights; here you can board lake cruisers (☎ 603/366–2628) or the **Winnipesaukee Railroad** (☎ 603/279–5253) for shore tours.

Commercial **Meredith,** on the northern tip of the most westerly of three bays on the north shore, has restaurants and shops. Rte. 25 passes through **Center Harbor,** a modest version of Meredith at the end of the middle bay, en route to **Moultonborough,** at the tip of the easternmost bay, and the 5,000-acre **Castle in the Clouds** estate (☎ 603/476–2352 or 800/729–2468), anchored by an eccentric millionaire's former home.

Contrasting with the busy Winnipesaukee towns are pristine, historic **Center Sandwich; Tamworth,** whose birch-edged Chocorua Lake has been photographed so often that you may feel you've seen it before; and **Ossipee,** three lakeside villages with lots of antiquing. Scenic, lake-hugging Rte. 109 leads to **Wolfeboro,** an old-line resort. At **Canterbury Shaker Village** (Canterbury, ☎ 603/783–9511), southwest of Winnipesaukee, guided tours and crafts demonstrations depict 19th-century Shaker life.

What to See and Do with Children

Try Meredith's hands-on **Children's Museum and Shop** (28 Lang St., ☎ 603/279–1007); Holderness's **Science Center of New Hampshire** (Rte. 113, ☎ 603/968–7194); and, on Rte. 3 in Weirs Beach, the **Funspot** (☎ 603/366–4377), **Surf Coaster** (☎ 603/366–4991), and **Water Slide** (☎ 603/366–5161) amusement centers.

Shopping

Summer folk prowl area galleries and boutiques, such as those at the **Millworks Marketplace** (Rte. 3, Meredith, ☎ 603/279–4116) and at the **League of New Hampshire Craftsmen** shop in Meredith (Rte. 3, ☎ 603/279–7920). The **Old Country Store** in Moultonborough (Rte. 25, ☎ 603/476–5750) has been purveying pickles and penny candy since 1781. Look for **antiques** in Wolfeboro, the Ossipees, and Center Sandwich.

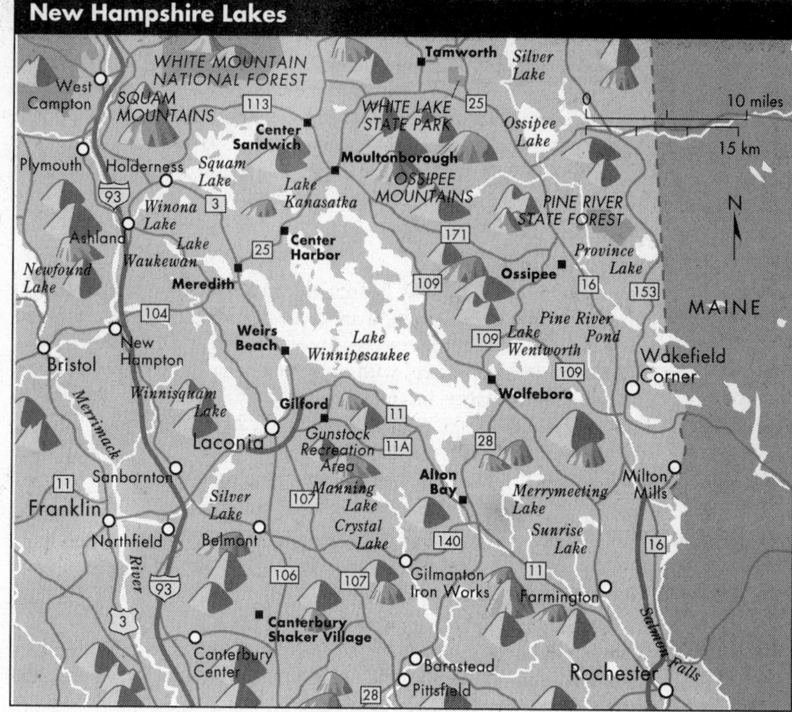

Sports and the Outdoors

Biking

Not too hilly, the Lakes Region is fun for even inexperienced bikers—though summer's heavy traffic can be a bit much. Lake's-edge roads make for good pedaling.

Boating

Rent at **Thurston's** in Weirs Beach (☎ 603/366–4811) or the **Meredith Marina and Boating Center** (☎ 603/279–7921).

Fishing

Local waters yield trout; Winnipesaukee also has salmon. Hardy anglers fish from "ice bob" huts in winter. The state fish and game department's local office (New Hampton, ☎ 603/744–5470) can tell you where the action is.

Beaches

Most are private, so it's good to know about **Ellacoya State Beach** (Gilford), a smallish man-made beach that's the area's major public strand. **Wentworth State Beach** is at Wolfeboro.

Dining and Lodging

This is steak-and-prime-rib country, though there are exceptions. Reserve ahead for both meals and rooms; summer and fall are crowded, and many businesses close in winter. For price ranges, see Charts 1 (B) and 2 (B) in On the Road with Fodor's.

Center Sandwich

DINING AND LODGING

Corner House Inn. This quaint Victorian inn with comfortable, old-fashioned guest rooms upstairs serves home-cooked meals in dining rooms cozy with local arts and crafts. Storytellers hold forth by the potbellied stove one night a week. *Junction of Rtes. 109 and 113, 03227, ☎ 603/284–6219. 3 rooms with bath. Facilities: restaurant (closed Nov.–mid-June Mon.–Tues.), beach permits. AE, MC, V. $$*

Tamworth

DINING AND LODGING

★ **Tamworth Inn.** This friendly B&B with romantic charm seems straight from an old movie. Guest rooms are decorated with 19th-century American pieces. The dining room serves American cuisine with a French twist, such as sautéed prime beef with mushrooms and artichokes, or roast duck with apricot sauce. In summer you can dine on the river-view porch. *Main St., Box 189, 03886, ☎ 603/323–7721 or 800/642–7352. 15 rooms. Facilities: breakfast, restaurant, pub, pool. MC, V. $$–$$$*

Wolfeboro

DINING AND LODGING

★ **Wolfeboro Inn.** This landmark waterfront resort, partly dating from the 19th century, is furnished with polished cherry and pine pieces and abloom with flowered chintz; armoires hide TVs. Old Wolfe's Tavern, anchored by a huge old fireplace, pours 45 brands of beer. *44 N. Main St., 03894, ☎ 603/569–3016 or 800/451–2389, FAX 603/569–5375. 38 rooms, 5 suites. Facilities: 2 restaurants, tavern, private beach, excursion boat. AE, D, MC, V. $$–$$$$*

Campgrounds

Gunstock (Laconia, ☎ 603/293–4344), **Yogi Bear's Jellystone Park** (Ashland, ☎ 603/968–3654), and **White Lake State Park** (Tamworth, ☎ 603/323–7350) have both tent and RV sites.

The Arts and Nightlife

The **Belknap Mill Society** (Mill Plaza, Laconia, ☎ 603/524–8813) has year-round concerts in an early 19th-century brick mill building. **Barnstormers** (Main St., Tamworth, ☎ 603/323–8500), New Hampshire's oldest professional theater, performs in July and August. The ***M/S Mount Washington*** (Weirs Beach, ☎ 603/366–2628) has moonlight cruises with dinner and dancing; it docks in Weirs Beach, Alton Bay, and Wolfeboro.

THE WHITE MOUNTAINS

Northern New Hampshire is the home of New England's highest mountains and the 750,000-acre White Mountain National Forest; the wilderness stretches to the Canadian border. Rivers are born here, gorges slash the forests, and hikers, climbers, and Sunday drivers marvel. Meanwhile, shoppers cheer for the bargain hunting in valley towns. Summers are busy, but foliage season draws the biggest crowds.

Tourist Information

Mt. Washington Valley: Visitors Bureau (Box 2300, North Conway 03860, ☎ 603/356–3171 or 800/367–3364).

Getting There

By Car

North–south routes include I–93 and Rte. 3 in the west, Rte. 16 in the east. Rte. 112, the Kancamagus Highway, is the main east–west thoroughfare.

By Bus

Concord Trailways (☎ 603/228–3300; in New England, 800/639–3317) serves Littleton, Colbrook, Berlin, Conway, Meredith, Plymouth, and other towns.

Exploring the White Mountains

One-street **North Conway** overflows with shops, restaurants, and inns. Trails from nearby **Echo Lake State Park** (off Rte. 302, North Conway, ☎ 603/356–2672 in summer) lead up to **White Horse** and **Cathedral ledges,** 1,000-ft cliffs overlooking the town in the west. The mountain lakes are good for swimming, and the park road for New England woodland scenery; the picnicking is great.

Mountain-rimmed **Jackson** is picture-perfect, with its clapboard inns and shops. Dramatic **Pinkham Notch** is the departure point for hikes to the top of the Northeast's highest mountain, 6,288-ft **Mt. Washington** (be sure to carry warm clothing in case of sudden, nasty storms). In summer and fall, you can corkscrew up via the **Mt. Washington Auto Road** (Glen House, ☎ 603/466–3988; admission charged) or, as sightseers have done since 1869, ride the steam-powered **Mt. Washington Cog Railway** (off Rte. 302, Bretton Woods, ☎ 603/846–5404 or 800/922–8825, ext. 7; admission charged; reserve ahead).

Crawford Notch State Park (Rte. 302 at Twin Mountain, ☎ 603/374–2272) is good for a picnic and a hike to a waterfall. The **Mount Washington Hotel** (Rte. 302, Bretton Woods, ☎ 603/278–1000) was the site of the 1944 International Monetary Fund Conference, which established the American dollar as the basic medium of international exchange. The view of the lawns and the mountains beyond makes the vast veranda a pleasant place to sojourn; you can also have a drink in the Princess Lounge (closed winter), a formal, intricately decorated club with a fireplace and live music. In **Franconia,** you can visit poet Robert Frost's home (Ridge Rd., ☎ 603/823–5510; admission charged). **Franconia Notch** is known for the **Old Man of the Mountains,** a rock formation that looks like a human profile, and the 800-ft-long natural chasm known as the **Flume** (☎ 603/823–5563).

The **Kancamagus Highway,** 32 mi of mountain scenery to the south (with bumper-to-bumper traffic during foliage season), starts in the resort town of **Lincoln** and passes campgrounds, picnic spots, scenic overlooks, and trailheads en route to Conway.

What to See and Do with Children

Youngsters love the antique steam- and diesel-powered **Conway Scenic Railroad** (Rtes. 16/302, North Conway, ☎ 603/356–5251 or 800/232–5251), the water slides at the **Whale's Tale** (Rte. 3, Lincoln, ☎ 603/745–8810), and two attractions on Rte. 16 in Glen: **Storyland** (☎ 603/383–4293), which has life-size nursery-rhyme characters and an African safari, and **Heritage New Hampshire** (☎ 603/383–9776), a simulated journey into New England history.

Shopping

More than 150 outlets and shops line **Rte. 16** north of Conway; **Lincoln** offers more of the same. Galleries throughout the region display local artisans' work.

Sports and the Outdoors

Fishing

Clear White Mountain streams yield trout and salmon; lakes and ponds have trout and bass. The state fish and game department's regional office (☎ 603/788–3164) has the latest.

Hiking

The White Mountains are crisscrossed with footpaths. The Maine-to-Georgia **Appalachian Trail** crosses the state; the **Appalachian Mountain Club** (Pinkham Notch, ☎ 603/466–2721) operates Spartan hikers' huts along the way. The club also provides information and suggests routes, as does the **White Mountains National Forest Office** (☎ 603/528–8721). **New England Hiking Holidays–White Mountains** (Box 1648, North Conway 03860, ☎ 603/356–9696) has guided inn-to-inn hikes.

Ski Areas

New Hampshire's best skiing is in the White Mountains. For the latest conditions statewide, call 800/262–6660 (cross-country) or 800/258–3608 (downhill).

Cross-Country

In **Jackson,** 100 mi of trails maintained by the **Jackson Ski Touring Foundation** (☎ 603/383–9355 for conditions or 603/383–9356 for lodging) string together inns, restaurants, and woodlands, and connect to another 40 mi of trails maintained by the Appalachian Mountain Club (*see* Hiking, *above*). There are 35 mi of trails at the grand **Balsams** hotel in Dixville Notch (*see* Dining and Lodging, *below*), 64 mi at **Bretton Woods** (Rte. 302, ☎ 603/278–1000), 30 mi at the **Franconia Inn** (Easton Rd., Franconia, ☎ 603/823–5542), and 45 mi at **Waterville Valley** (Rte. 49, Waterville Valley, ☎ 603/236–8311; 603/236–4144 for conditions).

Downhill

New Hampshire's biggest ski areas are pint-sized compared with those in neighboring Vermont; their charm is in their low-key atmosphere. **Waterville Valley** (*see* Cross-Country, *above*) has 53 trails, 13 lifts, and a 2,020-ft vertical drop. **Loon Mountain** (Kancamagus Hwy., Lincoln, ☎ 603/745–8111; 603/745–8100 for conditions) has 41 trails, 9 lifts, and a 2,100-ft drop.

In the **Mt. Washington Valley** are **Attitash** (Rte. 302, Bartlett, ☎ 603/374–2368; 603/374–0946 for conditions), with 28 trails, seven lifts, and a 1,750-ft vertical drop; **Mt. Cranmore** (Box 1640, North Conway, ☎ 603/356–5543; 800/786–6754 for conditions), with 33 trails, five lifts, and a 1,200-ft drop; and **Wildcat** (Rte. 16, Pinkham Notch, ☎ 603/466–3326 or 800/255–6439), with 30 trails, six lifts, and a 2,100-ft drop.

State-run **Cannon** (Franconia, ☎ 603/823–5563; 603/823–7771 for conditions) has 32 steep-and-narrow trails, six lifts, and a 2,146-ft vertical drop. **Balsams/Wilderness,** with 13 trails, four lifts, and a 1,000-ft drop, and **Bretton Woods,** with 30 trails, five lifts, and a 1,500-ft drop, are small areas at grand old resort hotels (*see* Cross-Country, *above*).

Dining and Lodging

Reservations are essential in fall and during winter vacations. For price ranges, see Charts 1 (B) and 2 (B) in On the Road with Fodor's.

Dixville Notch

DINING AND LODGING

The Balsams. This elegant turn-of-the-century resort hotel on 15,000 acres is a real Victorian, even today. Accommodations are spare, bright, and homey, with floral-print wallpaper and lace curtains, and the array of facilities gives you no reason to leave the grounds. At the famous formal brunch (jacket and tie advised), the huge dining room overflows with elegantly presented bounty. *Rte. 26, 03576, ☎ 603/255–3400 or 800/255–0600, FAX 603/255–4221. 232 rooms. Facilities: restaurant, pool, golf, tennis, winter sports, boating, children's program, dancing. AE, MC, V. Closed Apr.–mid-May, mid-Oct.–mid-Dec. $$$*

Franconia

DINING AND LODGING

Franconia Inn. Families like this resort: It's easy to get a baby-sitter, and the restaurant serves such fare as "Young Epicurean Cheeseburgers" to make mealtimes as pleasant for children as for parents. Guest rooms feature chintz and canopy beds; some have whirlpools or fireplaces. *Easton Rd., 03580, ☎ 603/823–5542 or 800/473–5299, FAX 603/823–8078. 34 rooms. Facilities: restaurant, pool, hot tub, tennis, horseback riding, soaring. AE, MC, V. Closed Apr.–mid-May. $$–$$$*

Jackson

DINING AND LODGING

Inn at Thorn Hill. Dark furniture and rose-motif wallpapers recall the inn's origins as a home designed by Stanford White in 1895. Yet the comforts are strictly up-to-date, and the food—New England fare with a Continental touch—is some of the area's best. Try the lobster loaf or the hazelnutty chicken breasts. Rates are MAP. *Thorn Hill Rd., 03846, ☎ 603/383–4242 or 800/289–8990, FAX 603/383–8062. 20 rooms. Facilities: restaurant, pub, pool, winter sports. AE, MC, V. Closed Apr. $$$*

Christmas Farm Inn. Despite its winter-inspired name, this 200-year-old village inn is an all-season retreat, popular with family vacations and romantic getaways alike. The restaurant's menu is mixed and varies with the seasons, but some standbys include vegetable-stuffed chicken and shrimp scampi. Rates are MAP. *Box CC, Rte. 16B, 03846, ☎ 603/383–4313 or 800/443–5837, FAX 603/383–6495. 38 rooms with bath. Facilities: restaurant, pub, game rooms, pool, putting green, sauna, volleyball. AE, MC, V. $$–$$$*

North Conway

DINING

Scottish Lion. This restaurant and pub serves more than Scotch, although you can choose from 50 varieties. The tartan-carpeted dining rooms serve scones and Devonshire cream for breakfast, game and steak-and-mushroom pies for lunch and dinner. The "Rumplethump" potatoes are famous locally, and hot oatcakes come with your meal. *Rte. 16, ☎ 603/356–6381. AE, D, DC, MC, V. $$*

The Arts and Nightlife

Look into the **Mt. Washington Valley Theater Company** (Main St., North Conway, ☎ 603/356–5776 or 603/356–5425). Catch some music at the **North Country Center for the Arts** (Mill at Loon Mtn., Lincoln, ☎

603/745–6032). Or sample the bars: the **Red Parka Pub** (Rte. 302, Glen, ☎ 603/383–4344) is favored by under-30s; the **Shannon Door Pub** (Rte. 16, Jackson, ☎ 603/383–4211) is the place to enjoy a Greek salad, Guinness on draft, and the area's best British and Scottish musicians. The **Wildcat Inn & Tavern** (Rte. 16A, Jackson, ☎ 603/383–4245) has live music and is popular with skiers.

WESTERN NEW HAMPSHIRE

The countryside east of the Connecticut River between the Massachusetts border and the White Mountains' foothills is a land of covered bridges and calendar-page villages, hardwood forests, jewellike lakes, and lonely mountains. Cultural centers enliven workaday urban centers such as Manchester, Nashua, and the capital, Concord.

Tourist Information

Lake Sunapee: Business Association (Box 400, Sunapee 03782, ☎ 603/763–2495; in New England, 800/258–3530). **Monadnock:** Travel Council (48 Central Sq., Keene 03431, ☎ 603/352–1303). **Concord:** Chamber of Commerce (244 N. Main St., 03301, ☎ 603/224–2508). **Hanover:** Chamber of Commerce (Box A–105, 03755, ☎ 603/643–3115). **Manchester:** Chamber of Commerce (889 Elm St., 03101, ☎ 603/666–6600). **Peterborough:** Chamber of Commerce (Box 401, 03458, ☎ 603/924–7234).

Getting There

By Car

I–89 cuts southeast–northwest into Vermont. North–south, I–93 provides often scenic travel while I–91 follows the river on its Vermont shore; in New Hampshire, Rtes. 12 and 12A are slow but beautiful. Rte. 4 winds between Lebanon and the coast.

By Bus

Concord Trailways (☎ 800/639–3317) operates within the state, **Advance Transit** (☎ 802/295–1824) within the area.

Exploring Western New Hampshire

Mountains and parks set off bright, clear **Lake Sunapee.** You can cruise it on the **MV *Mt. Sunapee II*** (Sunapee Harbor, ☎ 603/763–4030). Or you can rise above it on a chairlift, or picnic on a beach, at quiet, woodsy **Mt. Sunapee State Park** (Rte. 103, Newbury, ☎ 603/763–2356).

Dartmouth College, to the north in **Hanover,** is a picture of redbrick and white clapboard around a village green. On Wheelock Street, its **Hood Museum of Art** (☎ 603/646–2808) houses works from Africa, Asia, Europe, and America, while the modern **Hopkins Center** (☎ 603/646–2422) is a focal point for the local arts scene.

In modest **Cornish,** to the south via Rte. 12A, you can cross four covered bridges, including the longest in the country, and tour 19th-century sculptor Augustus Saint-Gaudens's studio complex. The **Saint-Gaudens National Historic Site** displays some of the artist's heroic, sensitive sculptures. *Off Rte. 12A, ☎ 603/675–2175. Admission charged. Closed late Oct.–late May.*

In **Charlestown** is the **Fort at No. 4** (Rte. 11, ☎ 603/826–5700; admission charged; closed Oct.–late May), a frontier outpost in Colonial times, where today costumed guides demonstrate crafts and occasionally stage militia musters. Eighteenth-century villages punctuate the riverbanks farther south. **Keene,** to the east, has fine old trees, a wide main street, and many stately 19th-century mill-owners' homes; the **Arts Center on Brickyard Pond** at Keene State College (229 Main St., ☎ 603/358–2168) has theaters, art and dance studios, and a gallery.

In **Monadnock State Park** (Rte. 124, Jaffrey, ☎ 603/532–8035), 20 trails ascend to the bald summit of 3,165-ft **Mt. Monadnock,** one of the world's most-climbed mountains. You can exit the park onto Rte. 101 near **Dublin,** where proper Bostonians summer and locals publish the *Old Farmer's Almanac.* **Peterborough,** the model for Thornton Wilder's *Our Town,* is now a computer-magazine publishing center.

Beautifully preserved **Fitzwilliam,** spreading from the edges of an oval common, warrants a detour. About 2 mi north, you can picnic in a pine grove at 294-acre **Rhododendron State Park** (Rhododendron Rd., ☎ 603/239–8153), washed with color in early July. The **Cathedral of the Pines** (off Rte. 119, Rindge, ☎ 603/899–3300), an outdoor place of worship, has a view of Mt. Monadnock; early afternoon organ meditations are held Tuesday through Thursday. **Amherst,** a bedroom community for Nashua, has a beautiful village green edged with antique houses on the National Register of Historic Places.

What to See and Do with Children

Reserve seats for shows at Concord's high-tech **Christa McAuliffe Planetarium** (3 Institute Dr., ☎ 603/271–7827).

Shopping

Look for church fairs and artisans' studios marked by neat state signs. Antiques dealers sell "by chance or by appointment"; keep an eye peeled along Rte. 119 west of Fitzwilliam and along Rte. 101 east of Marlborough. Keene has malls and **Colony Mill Marketplace** (222 West St., ☎ 603/357–1240) in a restored mill. You can buy outdoor gear at **Eastern Mountain Sports** (Vose Farm Rd., ☎ 603/924–7231).

Sports and the Outdoors

Biking

Try **Rte. 10** along the Ashuelot River south of Keene; spurs lead to covered bridges. Contact the **Granite State Wheelmen** (Salem, no ☎) for group rides, **Monadnock Bicycle Touring** (Harrisville, ☎ 603/827–3925) for inn-to-inn tours.

Boating

The Connecticut River, while usually safe after June 15, is not for beginners. Rent gear at **Northstar Canoe Livery** (Rte. 12A, Cornish, ☎ 603/542–5802).

Fishing

To find out where the action is on the area's 200 lakes and ponds, contact the **Department of Fish and Game's** regional office (☎ 603/352–9669).

Hiking

Networks of trails can be found in many state parks and forests, among them **Mt. Sunapee** (Newbury, ☎ 603/763–2356) and rugged **Pillsbury** (Washington, ☎ 603/863–2860) state parks, and **Fox State Forest** (Hillsboro, ☎ 603/464–3453).

Dining and Lodging

For price ranges, see Charts 1 (B) and 2 (B) in On the Road with Fodor's.

Bedford

LODGING

Bedford Village Inn. This former farm, minutes from Manchester, is now a luxury inn. Antique four-posters recrafted to hold king-size mattresses, and Italian marble in whirlpool baths bespeak the latest in elegance; some rooms have fireplaces. *2 Old Bedford Rd., 03110, ☎ 603/472–2602 or 800/852–1166. 12 rooms, 2 apartments. Facilities: restaurant. AE, DC, MC, V. $$$*

Concord

DINING

★ **Hermanos Cocina Mexicana.** Diners come from Boston for the Mexican fare served here; expect to queue. Don't eat too many nachos supreme on blue-corn chips; you'll want room for Miguel's Dream (chocolate, cinnamon, pecans, and honey in a warm tortilla). *6 Pleasant St. Ext., ☎ 603/224–5669. No reservations. MC, V. $–$$*

Hanover

DINING AND LODGING

★ **Hanover Inn.** Three stories of white-trimmed brick, this embodiment of American traditional architecture is the state's oldest operating business. Now owned by Dartmouth College, it's handsomely furnished with 19th-century antiques and reproductions. You can get classic New England fare in the Daniel Webster Room, lighter bites in the Ivy Grill. *Box 151, The Green, 03755, ☎ 603/643–4300 or 800/443–7024, FAX 603/646–3744. 92 rooms. AE, D, DC, MC, V. $$$–$$$$*

Peterborough

DINING

Boilerhouse Restaurant. Overlooking Noone Falls, this restoration of an old textile mill serves great gravlax of Norwegian salmon, and creatively sauced dishes like veal with forest mushrooms in a brandy-Madeira cream sauce. Weight watchers applaud the spa fare. *Rte. 202S, ☎ 603/924–9486. D, MC, V. $$–$$$*

The Arts and Nightlife

The Arts

In addition to the offerings of Keene's **Arts Center on Brickyard Pond** (Keene, ☎ 603/358–2168) and Hanover's **Hopkins Center** (*see* Exploring Western New Hampshire, *above*), the arts flourish at the **Claremont Opera House** (City Hall, Tremont Sq., ☎ 603/542–4433) and the **Palace Theatre** (80 Hanover St., Manchester, ☎ 603/668–5588), the state performing-arts center. **Monadnock Music** (Peterborough, ☎ 603/924–7610) has concerts in July and August. Milford is home to the state's largest professional theater, the **American Stage Festival** (Rte. 13N, ☎ 603/673–4005).

Nightlife

The **Folkway** (85 Grove St., Peterborough, ☎ 603/924–7484) is a regional tradition. **Del Rossi's Trattoria** (junction of Rtes. 137 and 101, Dublin, ☎ 603/563–7195) presents big names in jazz, bluegrass, folk, and blues. The **Colonial Theater** (95 Main St., Keene, ☎ 603/352–2033) has folk, rock, jazz, and movies.

NEW YORK

By David Laskin

Updated by Stephanie Dolgoff, Richard Kagan, David Low, Rathe Miller, Margaret Mittelbach, Marcy Pritchard, and Kate Sekules

Capital Albany
Population 17,990,455
Motto Excelsior
State Bird Bluebird
State Flower Rose

Visitor Information

New York State Division of Tourism (1 Commerce Plaza, Albany 12245, ☎ 518/474–4116 or 800/225–5697).

Scenic Drives

The **Taconic Parkway,** particularly the stretch from Hopewell Junction to East Chatham, passes through rolling hills, orchards, woods, and pastures reminiscent of the English countryside. To make a dramatic loop around the Adirondacks' **High Peaks** region, pick up Rte. 73 off the Northway at Exit 30, drive northwest through Lake Placid, proceed on Rte. 86 through Saranac Lake, then head southwest on Rte. 3 to Tupper Lake, due south on Rte. 30 to Long Lake, and east on Rte. 28N to North Hudson. For information on the dozen officially designated scenic drives, call 800/225–5697.

National and State Parks

National Parks

The **Gateway National Recreation Area** (Floyd Bennett Field, Bldg. 69, Brooklyn 11234, ☎ 718/338–3338) extends through Brooklyn, Queens, Staten Island, and New Jersey. It includes the **Jamaica Bay Wildlife Refuge,** where nature trails around ponds, marshes, and wooded uplands offer glimpses of migrating birds; **Jacob Riis Park,** where a boardwalk stretches along the surfy Atlantic; plus various beaches, parklands, and facilities for outdoor and indoor festivals. **Fire Island National Seashore** (120 Laurel St., Patchogue 11772, ☎ 516/289–4810) offers Atlantic surf and beaches on a popular summer resort island with a strong gay population.

State Parks

New York has 150 state parks, many offering outstanding recreational facilities. An **Empire State Passport,** permitting unlimited free entrance to the parks for a year (Apr.–Mar.), is available for $30 at most of the parks; you can also contact the **State Office of Parks and Recreation** (☎ 518/474–0456) or write for an application (Passport, State Parks, Albany 12238).

NEW YORK CITY

Whatever you're looking for in a big-city vacation, you'll find in New York. The city has a rich history, from early Dutch settlers and the swearing-in of George Washington as the first U.S. president to the arrival of millions of immigrants in the late 19th and early 20th centuries. The city today is known for its world-famous skyline, its world-class museums and performing-arts companies, and its status as the capital of finance, fashion, art, publishing, broadcasting, theater, and advertising. And, of course, New Yorkers themselves are world-famous, if not for their charm, at least for their panache, ethnic diversity, street smarts, and accents.

Beyond the laundry list of must-see sights, from the Statue of Liberty to Times Square, from the United Nations to Macy's, New York has an indefinable aura that exists nowhere else. It's a kind of energy level that has something to do with being in the big league, where everybody's watching and keeping score. Paraphrasing a slogan coined for the Plaza hotel, you get the feeling that "nothing unimportant ever happens in New York," and that gives an edge to everything that goes on here.

Tourist Information

New York: Convention and Visitors Bureau (2 Columbus Circle, at 58th St. and 8th Ave., 10019, ☎ 212/397–8222 or 212/484–1200, FAX 212/484–1280).

Arriving and Departing

By Plane

Virtually every major U.S. and foreign airline serves one or more of New York's three airports. **La Guardia** (☎ 718/533–3400) and **John F. Kennedy International** (☎ 718/244–4444) airports are in Queens. **Newark International Airport** (☎ 201/961–6000) is in New Jersey. Cab fare to midtown Manhattan runs $18–$23 plus tolls from La Guardia, $25–$30 plus tolls from JFK, and $28–$30 plus tolls from Newark. **Carey Airport Express** (☎ 718/632–0500, 800/456–1012, or 800/284–0909) runs buses to midtown every 20 minutes from La Guardia and every 30 minutes from JFK. The **Gray Line Air Shuttle Minibus** (☎ 212/315–3006) also connects both airports to Manhattan. **NJ Transit Airport Express** (☎ 201/762–5100) runs between Newark airport and Manhattan's Port Authority Terminal. By public transportation, the A subway line to Howard Beach connects with a free airport shuttle bus to JFK.

By Car

A complex network of bridges and tunnels provides access to Manhattan. I–95 enters upper Manhattan via the **George Washington Bridge,** and I–495 enters from Long Island via the **Midtown Tunnel.** From upstate New York, the city is accessible via the **New York (Dewey) Thruway** (I–87).

By Train

Pennsylvania Station (31st to 33rd Sts., between 7th and 8th Aves., ☎ 212/532–4900).

By Bus

The **Port Authority Terminal** (40th to 42nd Sts., between 8th and 9th Aves., ☎ 212/564–8484) handles all long-haul and commuter bus lines. Some of the individual bus lines serving New York include **Greyhound Lines** (☎ 800/231–2222), **Bonanza Bus Lines** (New England, ☎ 800/556–3815), **Martz Trailways** (northeastern Pennsylvania, ☎ 800/233–8604), and **New Jersey Transit** (New Jersey; ☎ 201/762–5100).

Getting Around New York

New York is a city of neighborhoods best explored at a leisurely pace, up close, and on foot. Extensive public transportation easily bridges gaps between areas of interest.

By Car

If you drive into Manhattan, don't plan to use your car much to get around. Driving in the city can be a nightmare of gridlocked streets and predatory fellow motorists. Free parking is almost nonexistent in midtown, and parking lots everywhere are exorbitant ($16 for three hours is not unusual in midtown).

By Public Transportation

The 714-mi **subway** system, the fastest and cheapest way to get around the city, serves Manhattan, Brooklyn, Queens, and the Bronx and operates 24 hours a day. Tokens cost $1.25 each, with reduced fares for the disabled and senior citizens, and are purchased in subway stations; transfers among subway lines are free at designated interchanges. Most **buses** follow easy-to-understand routes along the Manhattan grid, and some run 24 hours. Routes go up or down the north–south avenues, east and west on the major two-way crosstown streets: 96th, 86th, 79th, 59th, 42nd, 34th, 23rd, and 14th. Bus fare is $1.25 in change (no pennies or bills) or a subway token; for free transfer to a connecting bus line, ask for a transfer when paying the fare. For 24-hour bus and subway information, call 718/330–1234.

For subway or bus maps, ask at token booths or write to the New York City Transit Authority (Customer Service Department, 130 Livingston St., Room 9011D, Brooklyn 11201).

By Taxi

Taxis (officially licensed ones are yellow) are usually easy to hail on the street, in front of major hotels, and by bus and train stations. The fare is $1.50 for the first ⅕ mi, 25¢ for each ⅕ mi thereafter, and 25¢ for each 75 seconds not in motion. A 50¢ surcharge is added to rides begun between 8 PM and 6 AM. Bridge and tunnel tolls are extra, and drivers expect a 15% tip. Barring performance above and beyond the call of duty, don't feel obliged to give them more.

Orientation Tours

Bus Tours

Gray Line (1740 Broadway, ☎ 212/397–2620) offers a number of standard city bus tours, trolley tours, and day trips to Brooklyn and Atlantic City. **New York Doubledecker Tours** (Empire State Building, 350 5th Ave., Room 6104, ☎ 212/967–6008) covers the major attractions and allows you to hop on and off as often as you like.

Boat Tour

Circle Line (Pier 83, west end of 42nd St., ☎ 212/563–3200) offers a three-hour, 35-mi circumnavigation of Manhattan from March to December.

Walking Tours

Sidewalks of New York (☎ 212/517–0201) offers day and evening theme tours—Historic Churches, Ye Old Taverns, Celebrity Homes—on weekends. **New York City Cultural Walking Tours** (☎ 212/979–2388) focuses on the city's architecture, landmarks, memorials, outdoor art, and historic sites. The **Municipal Art Society** (☎ 212/935–3960) operates a series of bus and walking tours.

Exploring Manhattan

Midtown is the heart of New York City, so it makes sense to start your exploration there, then move on to the museum-rich Upper West and Upper East sides, then downtown to the funky neighborhoods of Greenwich Village, SoHo, Little Italy, and Chinatown, and finally to Lower Manhattan, the city's financial center.

Midtown

The heart of midtown is **Rockefeller Center,** a complex of 19 buildings occupying nearly 22 acres of prime real estate between 5th and 7th avenues and 47th and 52nd streets. The outdoor **ice rink,** on the Lower Plaza between 49th and 50th streets, is the center's trademark. Open from October through April, the ice rink becomes an open-air café the rest of the year. In December, the plaza is decorated with an enormous live Christmas tree. The **Channel Gardens** connecting the rink to 5th Avenue is a promenade with six pools surrounded by flower beds.

The backdrop for the Lower Plaza is Rockefeller Center's tallest tower, the 70-story **GE Building** (known as the RCA Building before GE acquired RCA in 1986). Across 50th Street from the GE Building is America's largest indoor theater, the 6,000-seat Art Deco **Radio City Music Hall** (☏ 212/247–4777). Home of the fabled Rockettes chorus line, Radio City was built as a movie theater with live shows; today it produces major concerts, Christmas and Easter extravaganzas, awards presentations, and other special events. Its interior and bathrooms are worth a look even without a show.

The stretch of 5th Avenue between Rockefeller Center and 59th Street glitters with world-famous shops, including **Saks Fifth Avenue, Gucci, Steuben Glass,** and **Tiffany & Co.** Also here is the Gothic-style **St. Patrick's,** the Roman Catholic cathedral of New York. Dedicated to the patron saint of the Irish—then and now one of New York's principal ethnic groups—the white-marble-and-stone structure was begun in 1858, consecrated in 1879, and completed in 1906.

On 53rd Street between 5th and 6th avenues is the **Museum of Modern Art** (MOMA), a bright and airy four-story structure built around a secluded sculpture garden. All the most famous modern artists, from van Gogh to Picasso, Matisse to Andy Warhol, are represented. Afternoon and evening film showings are free with the price of admission. *11 W. 53rd St., ☏ 212/708–9480. Admission charged. Closed Wed.*

A little farther west, the **American Craft Museum** shows the work of contemporary American and other craftspersons working in clay, glass, fiber, wood, metal, and paper. *40 W. 53rd St., ☏ 212/956–3535. Admission charged. Closed Mon.*

Southwest of here is **Times Square,** one of New York's principal energy centers. It's one of many New York City "squares" that are actually triangles formed by the angle of Broadway slashing across a major avenue—in this case, crossing 7th Avenue at 42nd Street. Known as the Crossroads of the World, the Great White Way, and the New Year's Eve Capital of America, it is perhaps best known as the Broadway Theater District. Most of the so-called Broadway theaters are actually on the streets west of Broadway, between 43rd and 52nd streets.

If you head east, between 40th and 42nd streets on 5th Avenue, you'll find two crouching marble lions guarding the entrance to the distinguished Beaux-Arts building that houses the **New York Public Library's** central research facility (☏ 212/930–0800). Farther east is **United Nations Headquarters** (☏ 212/963–7713), occupying a lushly landscaped riverside tract along 1st Avenue between 42nd and 48th streets. A line of flagpoles with banners representing the current roster of 159 member nations stands before the striking 550-ft-high slab of the Secretariat Building. Tours (admission charged) depart from the General Assembly lobby, where you can pick up free tickets to most sessions.

At the southern end of midtown is the **Empire State Building.** Though no longer the world's tallest building, it is certainly one of the world's best-loved skyscrapers. The Art Deco structure opened in 1931. Go to the concourse level to buy a ticket for the 86th- and 102nd-floor observation decks. *5th Ave. and 34th St., ☎ 212/736–3100. Admission charged.*

Upper West Side

Once one of New York's most rundown neighborhoods, the Upper West Side is now chic, with boutiques and cafés lining Columbus Avenue and renovated brownstones standing proudly on the side streets. **Lincoln Center** (Broadway, between 62nd and 66th Sts., ☎ 212/875–5351 for tour information), which spearheaded the area's revitalization, is today the West Side's cultural anchor. Flanking the central fountain are three major concert halls: **Avery Fisher Hall,** where the New York Philharmonic Orchestra performs; the glass-fronted **Metropolitan Opera House,** home of the Metropolitan Opera and the American Ballet Theatre; and the **New York State Theater,** home of the New York City Ballet and the New York City Opera.

The **American Museum of Natural History** (☎ 212/769–5100; admission charged) is set on a four-block tract bounded by Central Park West, Columbus Avenue, and 77th and 81st streets. Its collection of 30 million artifacts includes a stuffed 94-ft blue whale, the 563-carat Star of India sapphire, and lots of dinosaur skeletons. The adjacent **Hayden Planetarium** (on 81st St., ☎ 212/769–5920; admission charged) offers two stories of exhibits, plus several different Sky Shows projected on 22 wraparound screens.

Columbia University (founded in 1754) is a wealthy, private, coed institution that is New York City's only Ivy League school. Bounded by 114th and 121st streets, Broadway, and Amsterdam Avenue, the campus is so effectively walled off from the city by buildings that it's easy to believe you're in a more rustic setting. Enter at 116th Street for a look around.

Harlem

Harlem has been the mecca for African-American culture for nearly a century. In the 1920s, in an astonishing confluence of talent known as the Harlem Renaissance, black novelists, playwrights, musicians, and artists gathered here. By the 1960s, crowded housing, poverty, and crime had turned the neighborhood into a simmering ghetto. Today, Harlem is on the way to restoring itself. Mixed in with some seedy remains of the past are old jewels like the refurbished **Apollo Theatre** (253 W. 125th St., ☎ 212/749–5838), where such music greats as Ella Fitzgerald and Duke Ellington brought black musicians into the limelight, and the **Studio Museum** (144 W. 125th St., ☎ 212/864–4500), dedicated to collecting and exhibiting artwork of the African diaspora and black America in the form of paintings, sculpture, and photographs.

Upper East Side

The Upper East Side, east of Central Park between 60th and 96th streets, epitomizes the high-style, high-society way of life most people associate with the Big Apple. The neighborhood boasts singles bars and high-rise apartment buildings on 1st Avenue, sedate town houses in the east 60s, and an outstanding concentration of art museums and galleries. Along the **Madison Mile,** Madison Avenue between 59th and 79th streets, are patrician art galleries, unique specialty stores, and the boutiques of many of the world's major fashion designers. **Museum Mile** is a strip of cultural institutions, representing a broad spectrum of sub-

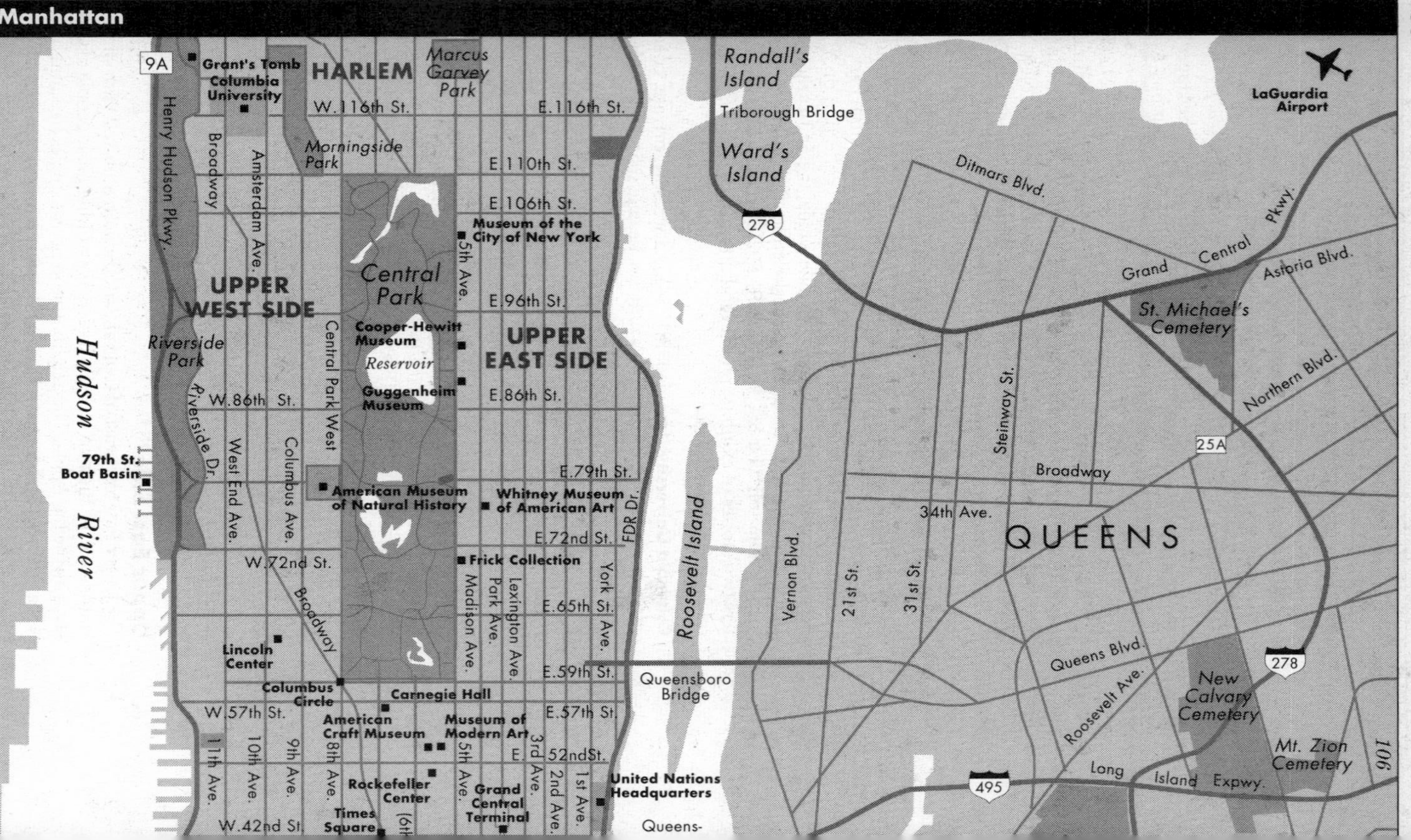
Manhattan
9A
Grant's Tomb
Columbia University
HARLEM
Marcus Garvey Park
W. 116th St.
E. 116th St.
Henry Hudson Pkwy.
Broadway
Amsterdam Ave.
Morningside Park
E. 110th St.
E. 106th St.
Museum of the City of New York
5th Ave.
Central Park
UPPER WEST SIDE
E. 96th St.
Cooper-Hewitt Museum
Reservoir
UPPER EAST SIDE
Riverside Park
Hudson
River
Riverside Dr.
W. 86th St.
Central Park West
Guggenheim Museum
E. 86th St.
79th St. Boat Basin
West End Ave.
Columbus Ave.
E. 79th St.
American Museum of Natural History
Whitney Museum of American Art
FDR Dr.
E. 72nd St.
W. 72nd St.
Frick Collection
Broadway
Madison Ave.
Park Ave.
Lexington Ave.
York Ave.
E. 65th St.
Lincoln Center
E. 59th St.
Columbus Circle
Carnegie Hall
W 57th St.
E. 57th St.
American Craft Museum
Museum of Modern Art
3rd Ave.
E. 52nd St.
11th Ave.
10th Ave.
9th Ave.
8th Ave.
5th Ave.
2nd Ave.
1st Ave.
Rockefeller Center
Grand Central Terminal
Times Square
(6th
W. 42nd St.
United Nations Headquarters
Queensboro Bridge
Queens-
Randall's Island
Triborough Bridge
Ward's Island
278
Roosevelt Island
Vernon Blvd.
21st St.
31st St.
Steinway St.
34th Ave.
Broadway
QUEENS
Ditmars Blvd.
Grand Central Pkwy.
Astoria Blvd.
St. Michael's Cemetery
Northern Blvd.
25A
LaGuardia Airport
Queens Blvd.
Roosevelt Ave.
New Calvary Cemetery
278
Mt. Zion Cemetery
Long Island Expwy.
495
106

Lincoln Tunnel
W. 42nd St.
Times Square
Terminal
Queens-Midtown Tunnel
Port Authority Bus Terminal
Public Library
E. 42nd St.
Newtown Cr
Calvary Cemetery
Javits Convention Center
W. 34th St.
MIDTOWN
(6th Ave.)
Lexington Ave.
2nd Ave.
Madison Square Garden/ Pennsylvania Station
Empire State Building
Ave. of the Americas
7th Ave.
Broadway
Madison Square
Gramercy Park
W. 23rd St.
E. 23rd St.
East River
Humboldt Ave.
Expwy.
Grand Ave.
CHELSEA
GRAMERCY
Union Square
W. 14th St.
E. 14th St.
GREENWICH VILLAGE
EAST VILLAGE
Washington Square
Sheridan Square
New York University
Lafayette St.
E. 4th St.
FDR Dr.
Brooklyn-Queens
Flushing Ave.
West Side Hwy.
Hudson St.
W. Houston St.
E. Houston St.
Williamsburg Bridge
NEW JERSEY
SOHO
LITTLE ITALY
Delancy St.
Bushwick Ave.
Holland Tunnel
Canal St.
Myrtle Ave.
Broadway
TRIBECA
CHINA-TOWN
Bowery
E. Broadway
Manhattan Bridge
Lafayette Ave.
Hudson River
West St.
Chambers St.
W. Broadway
Brooklyn Bridge
N
World Trade Center
Fulton St.
South Street Seaport
Bedford Ave.
Trinity Church
Wall St.
BROOKLYN
NY Stock Exchange
0 880 yards
0 800 meters
LOWER MANHATTAN
Flatbush Ave.
Battery Park
Staten Island Ferry Terminal
Fulton St.
Statue of Liberty
Brooklyn-Battery
Atlantic Ave.
107

jects and styles, located on or near 5th Avenue between 82nd and 104th streets. You may find the people in this neighborhood a bit snobbish compared with other New Yorkers, but take it in stride—they treat everybody that way.

The **Frick Collection,** housed in a Louis XVIII–style palace built by the Pittsburgh coke-and-steel baron Henry Clay Frick, is the city's finest small art museum. Specializing in European works from the late 13th to the late 19th century, it has masterpieces by Rembrandt, Fragonard, Bellini, and Vermeer, among others. *1 E. 70th St. at 5th Ave., ☎ 212/288–0700. Admission charged. Closed Mon.*

The **Whitney Museum of American Art,** a gray granite vault with cantilevering and startling trapezoidal windows that project out, is devoted exclusively to 20th-century American work, from naturalism and impressionism to pop art, abstractionism, and whatever comes next. *945 Madison Ave. at 75th St., ☎ 212/570–3676. Admission charged. Closed Mon.–Tues.*

Nearby is the **Metropolitan Museum of Art,** the largest art museum in the Western Hemisphere. Major displays cover prehistoric to modern times and all areas of the world, including impressive Greek and Egyptian collections and an entire wing devoted to tribal arts. The museum has the world's most comprehensive collection of American art, and its holdings of European art are unequaled outside Europe. Also here are the Temple of Dendur, an entire Roman-period temple (circa 15 BC), and galleries devoted to musical instruments and arms and armor. Walking tours and lectures are free with admission. *5th Ave. at 82nd St., ☎ 212/535–7710. Admission charged. Closed Mon.*

Frank Lloyd Wright's landmark **Guggenheim Museum,** expanded and restored in 1992, is a six-story spiral rotunda through which you wind down past mobiles, stabiles, and other exemplars of modern art. Displays alternate new artists and modern masters; the permanent collection includes more than 20 Picassos. *1071 5th Ave. at 88th St., ☎ 212/423–3500. Admission charged. Closed Thurs.*

A former residence of the industrialist and philanthropist Andrew Carnegie now houses the **Cooper-Hewitt Museum,** officially the Smithsonian Institution's National Museum of Design. The changing exhibitions, which focus on various aspects of contemporary or historical design, are invariably well researched, enlightening, and often amusing. Major holdings include drawings, prints, textiles, furniture, metalwork, ceramics, glass, woodwork, and wall coverings. *2 E. 91st St., ☎ 212/860–6868. Admission charged. Closed Mon.*

The **Museum of the City of New York** makes the history of the Big Apple—from its seafaring beginnings to yesterday's headlines—come to life with period rooms, dioramas, a video, and clever displays of memorabilia. *5th Ave. at 103rd St., ☎ 212/534–1672. Admission charged. Closed Mon.–Tues.*

Greenwich Village

With its narrow, tree-lined streets, brick town houses, tiny green parks, and hidden courtyards, Greenwich Village is the closest thing to a small town in Manhattan. The Village, as New Yorkers invariably call it, is ideal for strolling, window-shopping, and café-hopping.

The preferred haunt of generations of writers, artists, musicians, and bohemians, the Village is known for the scores of famous Americans who lived and worked here and the cultural movements they defined. Perhaps those most synonymous with Greenwich Village are the countercultural artists of this century, including abstract expressionist painters like Franz Kline and Mark Rothko, Beat writers such as Jack Kerouac and Allen Ginsberg, and folk musicians and poets, notably Bob Dylan and Peter, Paul, and Mary.

All kinds of history are encountered in a walk through the Village. Edna St. Vincent Millay and John Barrymore each lived at **75½ Bedford Street**—at 9½ ft wide, New York's narrowest house. Theodore Dreiser wrote *An American Tragedy* at **16 St. Luke's Place**, and Howdy Doody was designed in the basement of **12 Gay Street.** Two houses on **MacDougal Street (Nos. 127 and 129)** were built in 1829 for Aaron Burr, who held much of the land that is now Greenwich Village.

The best place to begin a walking tour is the gleaming white **Washington Arch** in **Washington Square,** at the foot of 5th Avenue. Designed by Stanford White, the arch was built in 1889 to commemorate the 100th anniversary of George Washington's presidential inauguration. Most of the buildings bordering the square belong to **New York University.** The surrounding area, around the intersection of Bleecker and MacDougal streets, attracts a young crowd to its offbeat shops, bars, jazz clubs, Off-Broadway theaters, cabarets, coffeehouses, pizza stands, fast-food stands, cafés, and unpretentious restaurants.

To the northwest, at **Sheridan Square,** is Christopher Street, the heart of New York's gay community and the location of many intriguing boutiques. West of 7th Avenue, the Village turns into a picture-book town of twisting, tree-lined streets, quaint houses, and tiny restaurants.

The gritty **East Village,** east of 4th (Lexington) Avenue, has over the centuries housed Jewish, Ukrainian, and Puerto Rican immigrants; beatniks; hippies; punk rockers; artists of various stripes; and, most recently, affluent young professionals. Soak up the eclectic atmosphere along St. Marks Place between 2nd and 3rd avenues, lined with vegetarian restaurants, jewelry stalls, cafés and offbeat shops.

SoHo, Little Italy, and Chinatown

SoHo (so named because it is the district *S*outh of *Ho*uston Street, bounded by Broadway, Canal Street, and 6th Avenue) is virtually synonymous with a certain postmodern chic—an amalgam of black-clad artists, hip young Wall Streeters, track-lit loft apartments, funky art galleries, and restaurants with a minimalist approach to both food and decor. It was a virtual wasteland 25 years ago, but now it's all very urban, very cool, very SoHo.

West Broadway (parallel to and four blocks west of Broadway) is SoHo's main drag, with many shops and galleries. On Saturday, the big day for gallery-hopping, it can be crowded, but still great for people-watching. Two fine examples of **cast-iron architecture**—SoHo has one of the world's greatest concentrations—can be found on Greene Street, at Nos. 72–76 and 28–30.

Walk one block east to Grand and Mulberry streets to enter **Little Italy,** an ever-shrinking enclave of the Italian way of life. **Mulberry Street,** lined with tenement buildings, has long been the heart of Little Italy; at this point it's virtually the entire body. Between Broome and Canal streets, Mulberry consists entirely of restaurants, cafés, bakeries, imported-food shops, and souvenir stores. Each September, the Feast of San Gennaro turns the streets of Little Italy into a bright and turbulent Italian kitchen.

In recent years, **Chinatown** has expanded beyond its traditional borders into Little Italy to the north and the formerly Jewish Lower East Side to the east. **Canal Street** abounds with crowded markets bursting with mounds of fresh seafood and strangely shaped vegetables in extraterrestrial shades of green. Food shops proudly display their wares, from almond cookies to roast ducks.

Mott Street is the principal business street of the neighborhood. Narrow and twisting; crammed with souvenir shops and restaurants in funky, pagoda-style buildings; crowded with pedestrians at all hours of the day or night—Mott Street looks the way you'd expect Chinatown to look. Within a few dense blocks, hundreds of restaurants serve every imaginable type of Chinese cuisine, from simple fast-food noodles or dumplings to sumptuous Hunan, Szechuan, Cantonese, Mandarin, and Shanghai feasts.

Lower Manhattan

Lower Manhattan is compact, but it is packed with attractions: narrow streets and immense skyscrapers, Colonial-era houses and the Brave New World complex of Battery Park City, Wall Street,and South Street Seaport. The city did not really expand beyond these precincts until the middle of the 19th century. Today Lower Manhattan is in many ways dominated by Wall Street, which is both an actual street and a shorthand name for the vast, powerful financial community that clusters around the New York and American stock exchanges.

Start your exploration outside the **Staten Island Ferry Terminal,** at the southernmost tip of Manhattan. To the west lies **Battery Park,** a verdant landfill loaded with monuments and sculpture, and the point of embarkation for visits to the Statue of Liberty and Ellis Island. Buy your ticket for either at **Castle Clinton,** inside the park, and be prepared to wait.

The popularity of the **Statue of Liberty** (☎ 212/363–3200) surged following its 100th-birthday restoration in 1986. Once on Liberty Island, you may have to wait three hours to take the elevator 10 stories to the top of the pedestal. The strong of heart and limb can climb another 12 stories to the crown.

Ellis Island (☎ 212/363–3200), which opened in 1990 after a $140-million restoration, was once a federal immigration facility. Between 1892 and 1954, 17 million men, women, and children—the ancestors of more than 40% of the Americans living today—were processed here.

The **World Trade Center,** a 16-acre complex, contains New York's two tallest buildings (1,350 ft high). Elevators to the observation deck on the 107th floor of 2 World Trade Center glide a quarter of a mile into the sky in only 58 seconds. The rock and soil excavated for the center begat **Battery Park City,** 100 new acres of Manhattan on the Hudson River. It includes office buildings, high-rise apartment houses, old-looking town houses, a modest selection of shops, and the **World Financial Center,** a mammoth granite-and-glass complex designed by Cesar Pelli.

Wall Street's principal facility is the **New York Stock Exchange** (☎ 212/656–5168; closed weekends), whose august Corinthian main entrance is around the corner on Broad Street. A self-guided tour, a multimedia presentation, and guides may help you interpret the chaos that seems to reign on the trading floor.

At Broad and Pearl streets is **Fraunces Tavern,** a combination restaurant, bar, and museum occupying a Colonial house built in 1719 and restored in 1907. Best remembered as the site of George Washington's farewell address to his officers celebrating the British evacuation of New York in 1783, it contains two fully furnished period rooms and other displays on 18th- and 19th-century American history. ☎ *212/425–1778. Admission charged. Closed Sun.*

Back on Wall Street, a regal **statue of George Washington** stands at the spot where he was sworn in as the first U.S. president in 1789. After the capital moved to Philadelphia in 1790, the original Federal Hall became New York's City Hall, but was demolished in 1812. The current **Federal Hall National Memorial** (26 Wall St., ☎ 212/264–8711; closed weekends, major holidays), built in 1842, is a stately period structure that contains exhibits on New York and Wall Street. Jet-black **Trinity Church** (Broadway and Wall St.) was New York's first Anglican parish (1646). The present structure (1846) ranked as the city's tallest building for most of the last half of the 19th century.

South Street Seaport is an 11-block historic district on the East River that encompasses a museum, shopping centers, historic ships, cruise boats, a multimedia presentation, art galleries, and innumerable places to eat and drink. You can view the historic ships from Pier 16, which is the departure point for the one-hour Seaport Liberty Cruise (☎ 212/630–8888).

Nearby is the **Brooklyn Bridge,** New York's oldest and best-known span. When it was completed in 1883, it was the world's longest suspension bridge and, like so many others in turn, the tallest structure in the city. Walking across the Brooklyn Bridge is a peak New York experience, but you'd do well to dress warmly when you do it, because the wind whips through the cables like a dervish.

Parks and Gardens

Central Park was designed by landscape architects Frederick Law Olmsted and Calvert Vaux for 843 acres of land acquired by the city in 1856. Bounded by 59th and 110th streets, 5th Avenue, and Central Park West, the park contains grassy meadows, wooded groves, and formal gardens; paths for jogging, strolling, horseback riding, and biking; playing fields; a small zoo; an ice-skating rink; a carousel; an outdoor theater; and numerous fountains and sculptures. **AAA Bikes in Central Park** (☎ 212/861–4137), beside the Loeb Boathouse parallel to 72nd Street, rents bikes.

The Bronx's **Bronx Park,** located along the Bronx River parkway and bisected by Fordham Road, contains the **Bronx Zoo** (*see* What to See and Do with Children, *below*) as well as the **New York Botanical Garden** (☎ 718/817–8705), a 250-acre botanical treasury around the dramatic gorge of the Bronx River, with a 40-acre forest, conservatory, museum, and specialty outdoor gardens.

New York for Free—or Almost

Most museums have free hours one night a week. Free concerts, recitals, and dance presentations are given in churches, college auditoriums, and public buildings all over town. During the summer, free outdoor concerts are held in Central Park and at the **Guggenheim Bandshell** at Lincoln Center. The best sources of information are the *Village Voice* and *New York* magazine. Also, art galleries all over town are free to the public; check local newspapers and magazines for locations and current exhibitions.

What to See and Do with Children

The **Bronx Zoo** (now officially known as the **International Wildlife Conservation Park**; Fordham Rd. and Bronx River Pkwy., the Bronx, ☎ 718/652–8400) is the nation's largest urban zoo, with more than 4,000 animals on 265 acres of woods, ponds, streams, and parkland.

New York's **Aquarium for Wildlife Conservation** (W. 8th St. and Surf Ave., Coney Island, Brooklyn, ☎ 718/265–3474), just off the Coney Island Boardwalk, has more than 20,000 creatures on display and performing in periodic exhibitions.

Shopping

You can buy almost anything you might want or need at almost any time of the day or night somewhere in New York City, but in general, major department stores and other shops are open every day and keep late hours on Thursday. Many of the upper-crust shops along upper 5th Avenue and the Madison Mile close on Sunday. Stores in such nightlife areas as SoHo and Columbus Avenue are usually open in the evenings. The bargain shops along Orchard Street on the Lower East Side are closed on Saturday, mobbed on Sunday.

Shopping Neighborhoods

Fifth Avenue from 49th to 58th Street and **57th Street** between 3rd and 6th avenues contain many of the most famous—and expensive—stores in the world. The area extending from **Herald Square** (6th Ave. and 34th St.) along 34th Street and up 5th Avenue to 40th Street includes several major department stores and a host of lower-price clothing stores. Fifth Avenue south of 23rd Street is home to some of New York's hippest shops. **Madison Mile,** the 20-block span along Madison Avenue between 59th and 79th streets, consists of mainly low-rise brownstones housing the exclusive boutiques of American and overseas designers. **SoHo**'s galleries, clothing boutiques, and avant-garde housewares shops are concentrated on West Broadway. **Columbus Avenue,** between 66th and 86th streets, features far-out European and down-home traditional fashions, some antiques and vintage stores, and outlets for adult toys. The **Lower East Side** is the place for clothing bargains.

Department Stores

Bergdorf Goodman (754 5th Ave. at 57th St., ☎ 212/753–7300) is where good taste reigns in an elegant and understated setting; the recently expanded men's store is across the street. **Bloomingdale's** (59th St. and Lexington Ave., ☎ 212/355–5900) is a New York institution, with a stupefying maze of cosmetic counters, mirrors, and black walls on the main floor. Selections are dazzling at all but the lowest price ranges. **Lord & Taylor** (424 5th Ave. at 38th St., ☎ 212/391–3344) is refined, well-stocked, and never overwhelming. **Macy's** (34th St. and Broadway, ☎ 212/695–4400), the country's largest retail store, has huge housewares and gourmet-foods departments, as well as high fashion. **Saks Fifth Avenue** (611 5th Ave. at 50th St., ☎ 212/753–4000) has an outstanding selection of women's and men's designer outfits.

Specialty Stores

ANTIQUES

America Hurrah (766 Madison Ave., between 65th and 66th Sts., 3rd Floor, ☎ 212/535–1930) is one of the country's premier dealers in Americana. At **Manhattan Art & Antiques Center** (1050 2nd Ave., between 55th and 56th Sts., ☎ 212/355–4400), more than 100 dealers stock three floors with antiques from around the world.

BOOKS

A browser's paradise, **Gotham Book Mart** (41 W. 47th St., ☎ 212/719–4448) emphasizes literature and the performing arts in books and magazines. Eight miles of shelves house more than 2 million volumes (including a rare-book collection) at the **Strand** (828 Broadway at 12th St., ☎ 212/473–1452), North America's largest used-book store.

CAMERAS, ELECTRONICS

Smart shoppers throng **47th Street Photo**'s no-frills stores (67 W. 47th St. and 115 W. 45th St., ☎ 212/921–1287) for great deals with a minimum of service.

MUSIC STORES

Bleecker Bob's Golden Oldies (118 W. 3rd St., ☎ 212/475–9677) is a Greenwich Village spot with all the good old rock. **HMV** (2081 Broadway at 72nd St., ☎ 212/721–5900; 1280 Lexington Ave. at 86th St., ☎ 212/348–0800; and 5th Ave. at 46th St., ☎ 212/681–6700) is a state-of-the-art music superstore that stocks hundreds of thousands of disks, tapes, and videos. **J&R Music World** (23 Park Row, ☎ 212/732–8600) offers a wide selection and good prices. **Tower Records** (692 Broadway at 4th St., ☎ 212/505–1500; 1961 Broadway at 66th St., ☎ 212/799–2500; 1535 3rd Ave. at 87th St., ☎ 212/369–2500; and 725 5th Ave., basement level of Trump Tower, ☎ 212/838–8110) has a huge selection of music and videos at competitive prices.

FOOD

From jams, cheeses, spices, and smoked fish to a superb selection of kitchen wares, **Zabar's** (2245 Broadway at 80th St., ☎ 212/787–2000) has long been a favorite with New York foodies. Those who never venture north of 14th Street head for **Dean & DeLuca** (560 Broadway at Prince St., ☎ 212/431–1691), the huge SoHo trendsetter with a splendidly bright white space and an encyclopedic selection.

JEWELRY

Every store is a jewelry shop in the **Diamond District** (47th St. between 5th and 6th Aves.); be ready to haggle. **Fortunoff** (681 5th Ave. at 54th St., ☎ 212/758–6660) draws crowds with its good prices on gold and silver jewelry, flatware, and hollow-ware. At venerable **Tiffany & Co.** (727 5th Ave. at 57th St., ☎ 212/755–8000), prices can be out-of-sight, but there's always a selection of inexpensive gift items.

Spectator Sports

Baseball

New York Mets (Shea Stadium, Roosevelt Ave. off Grand Central Pkwy., Flushing, Queens, ☎ 718/507–8499 or 718/307–6387; Apr.–Oct.). **New York Yankees** (Yankee Stadium, 161st St. and Jerome Ave., Bronx, ☎ 212/293–6000; Apr.–Oct.).

Basketball

New York Knicks (Madison Square Garden, 4 Penn Plaza, ☎ 212/465–6741; Knicks Hot Line, ☎ 212/465–5867; Nov.–Apr.).

Football

The **New York Giants** and the **New York Jets** both play at the Meadowlands Sports Complex (Rte. 3, East Rutherford, NJ, ☎ 201/935–8111 or 201/935–3900; Aug.–Dec.).

Hockey

New York Rangers (Madison Square Garden, ☎ 212/465–6741; Oct.–Apr.).

Tennis

The annual **U.S. Open,** one of the four grand-slam events of tennis, is held in late August and early September at the **USTA National Tennis Center** in Flushing Meadows–Corona Park, Queens (☎ 718/696–7284).

Dining

by J. Walman

J. Walman is a syndicated food and wine columnist.

New York restaurants are expensive, yet savvy diners know how to keep costs within reason. Go for lunch or brunch instead of dinner. Order prix fixe instead of à la carte. Or go ethnic: New York has restaurants specializing in almost any cuisine you can name. (Try Little India on 6th Street between 1st and 2nd avenues, Little Italy, or Chinatown, for starters.) Be sure to make reservations on weekends. For price ranges, see Chart 1 (A) in On the Road with Fodor's.

$$$$ **American Renaissance.** This is surely one of the most beatific restaurants to open in recent years: a dramatic staircase leads from the casual café on the first level (where you can sample the flavored vodkas) to the stunning dining room with its cascading waterfall, Beaux Arts ornamentation, and Ionic columns. Roasted Atlantic salmon glazed in vintage port with shaved asparagus and tahini-lime dressing might serve as prelude to the New York state organic fallow venison served with roasted wild chestnuts, gooseberry juice, and apple oil. Homemade citrus yogurt is the perfect finale. *260 West Broadway (at Erickson Place), ☎ 212/343–0049. AE, DC, MC, V. Closed Sun. No lunch Sat.*

$$$$ **Aquavit.** While the café upstairs costs less, the striking downstairs main dining room, with its atrium and waterfall, *is* Aquavit. The contemporary Swedish menu offers foie gras on honey-roasted cabbage with apple oil and Swedish blueberry soup with lemongrass ice. There's also New York's largest aquavit list. *13 W. 54th St., ☎ 212/307–7311. Reservations required. Jacket and tie required. AE, DC, MC, V. Closed Sun. No lunch Sat.*

$$$$ **Chanterelle.** Soft peach walls, luxuriously spaced tables, and flawless service set the stage for David Waltuck's inventions. Try the signature seafood sausage or saddle of lamb stuffed with *merguez* (a Moroccan sausage) in olive jus, and don't miss the chocolate *mille feuille*—all beautifully presented. Dinner is prix fixe. *2 Harrison St., ☎ 212/966–6960. Reservations required. AE, DC, MC, V. Closed Sun.–Mon.*

$$$$ **Gramercy Tavern.** A 91-ft mural of fruit and vegetables wraps around the bar of this newcomer to the Gramercy area. Although the dining area is reminiscent of an English tavern, the food is best classified as eclectic Mediterranean: Sevruga caviar on fingerling potato salad with crème fraîche and parsley vinaigrette and ragout of sea urchin, crab-and-potato puree, scented with curry. Fifteen beers from American micro-breweries, a stellar wine list, and smooth, benevolent service coupled with all the media hype at its opening makes this one of Manhattan's obligatory restaurant destinations. *42 E. 20th St., between Park Ave. S. and Broadway, ☎ 212/477–0777. AE, DC, MC, V. No lunch Sat. and Sun.*

$$$$ **Le Cirque.** The rich, the famous, and dentists from Des Moines all seek out this palace of international luxury not to eat, but for the experience—although the tuna tartare (with a hint of curry), scallops and truffles in pastry, and lobster-rosemary risotto are superb. Try the signature crème brûlée. *58 E. 65th St., ☎ 212/794–9292. Reservations required. Jacket and tie required. AE, DC, MC, V. Closed Sun.*

$$$$ ★ **Lespinasse.** The Louis XV decor of this St. Regis Sheraton dining room is an ideal backdrop for chef Gray Kunz's refined French cuisine with Asian touches. Note the complex salad of squash, chicken, foie gras, and taro root, and the chilled dessert soup with lemongrass and melon. *2 E. 55th St., ☎ 212/339–6719. Jacket required. AE, DC, MC, V. Closed Sun.*

$$$$ ★ **San Domenico.** Owner Tony May has raised American consciousness of Italian cuisine with his baby cuttlefish with vegetables, soft egg ravioli with truffle butter, and milk custard with balsamic vinegar. The set-

ting is like a modern villa, with terra-cotta floors and sumptuous leather chairs. The Italian wine list is encyclopedic. *240 Central Park S,* ☎ *212/265–5959. Reservations required. Jacket and tie required (except Sun.). AE, MC, DC, V. No lunch weekends.*

$$$ ★ **Four Seasons Grill Room.** This bastion of the power lunch offers one of Manhattan's top luxury dinner experiences at a realistic price. The concept delivers enthusiastic service, architect Philip Johnson's comfortable leather banquettes and rosewood walls, and such eclectic international fare as salmon-and-tuna tartar and shrimp and pork in rice paper. *99 E. 52nd St.,* ☎ *212/754–9494. Reservations required. Jacket required. AE, DC, MC, V. Closed Sun. No lunch Sat.*

$$$ ★ **Le Madri.** This Chelsea trattoria (whose name means "the mothers") serves up homey, robust dishes such as fried calamari with spicy roast pepper-tomato sauce and braised veal shank with portobello mushrooms and saffron risotto. The top-flight service and engaging Tuscan-style space add appeal. *168 W. 18th St.,* ☎ *212/727–8022. AE, DC, MC, V.*

$$$ **Smith & Wollensky.** The proliferation of steak houses in recent years has been shocking and this one, with its bold setting, gargantuan portions, and lofty list of wines is one of the best. Meat is dry-aged in-house and arrives cooked to a turn. The bustling, less-pricey Wollensky's Grill next door shares the main restaurant's carnivorous bias, but has pleasant sidewalk seating in summer. *201 E. 49th St.,* ☎ *212/753–1530 (Grill* ☎ *212/753–0444). AE, DC, MC, V. No lunch weekends in restaurant.*

$$$ **Zoë.** This colorful, high-ceilinged SoHo eatery with terra-cotta columns and floor is relatively noisy, but the open kitchen produces impressive food: crisp noodle-wrapped shrimp with soy and toasted peanut oil dressing, oak-smoked salmon with potato–goat cheese knishes, and drop-dead desserts—Mexican-chocolate pecan pie and butterscotch pot de creme with homemade ginger snaps. Zoë also offers a fine group of wines by the glass. There's brunch on weekends. *90 Prince St., between Broadway and Mercer,* ☎ *212/966–6722. AE, DC, MC, V.*

$$ **Arizona 206.** Stucco walls and blanched wood create a desert look here and in the less-expensive adjacent Arizona Café. But no Mojave truck stop serves dishes like green-chili corncakes with tequila-cured salmon and spicy grilled rabbit in cilantro oil. *206 E. 60th St.,* ☎ *212/838–0440. AE, DC, MC, V. No lunch Sun.*

$$ ★ **Dāwat.** One of the city's finest restaurants for Indian fare, it has smooth service and a menu full of consultant Madhur Jaffrey's subtle cuisine: shrimp in mustard seeds with curry leaves, lamb with white turnips, black-eyed peas and corn, and onion *kulcha*—an onion-stuffed bread flavored with fresh coriander. Don't miss dessert: try the *kheer* (rice pudding) with pistachios or the pudding-like carrot halva. *210 E. 58th St.,* ☎ *212/355–7555. AE, DC, MC, V. No lunch Sun.*

$$ **Kin Khao.** Hip downtowners have already discovered this inventive Thai restaurant in SoHo. It's jam-packed—and worth the wait. The good bar pours an intriguing ginger vodka, but the real payoff is the fabulous food. The masterful *gai tom kha,* traditional soup with chicken, coconut milk, mushrooms, and ginger, says it all. Sticky rice is heaven; for dessert, it comes with sesame seeds and fresh mango. *171 Spring St., between W. Broadway and Thompson,* ☎ *212/966–3939. Reservations only for 6 or more. AE, MC, V. No lunch.*

$$ **Markham.** This comfortable spot is very "in" and very understated with its creamy walls, green leather banquettes, and casual downstairs café. The food is simple, with a twist. Standouts are aged goat cheese and chicory salad with hot bacon vinaigrette, roasted red snapper on baked white beans, and a scrumptious butterscotch crème brûlée. *59 5th Ave., between 12th and 13th,* ☎ *212/647–9391. AE, MC, V. Closed Sun. No lunch Sat.*

$$ **98 Mott Street.** Like many of New York's Hong Kong-style Chinese restaurants, this one is a virtual palace, with its red and gold accents and attentive waiters in spiffy uniforms. Prices are low and the food is exciting. Try the minced scallops in the shell with mushrooms, the hard-shell crab with chili peppers (first deep fried, then baked in salt), or the thin noodles, stir-fried with dried squid. *98 Mott St., between Canal and Hester,* ☎ *212/226–6603. Reservations only for 4 or more. AE, MC, V.*

$$ ★ **Symphony Café.** At this sleek brasserie near Carnegie Hall, the food is first-rate and the presentation stylish: Grilled tuna and quail arrive on mini-hibachis, and consommé comes in a hollowed-out pumpkin. Or try the wood-grilled chicken with chanterelles. *950 8th Ave.,* ☎ *212/397–9595. AE, DC, MC, V.*

$ ★ **Boca Chica.** This raffish East Village restaurant has live music, dancing, and assertive food from several Latin American nations. Try the soupy Puerto Rican chicken-and-rice stew known as *asopao,* the Cuban sandwiches, or Bolivian corn topped with chicken. Try a potent Brazilian *caipirinha* cocktail, with lime and rum; and don't trip over the boa constrictor by the bar. *13 1st Ave.,* ☎ *212/473–0108. No reservations. AE, DC, MC, V.*

$ ★ **Carmine's.** Despite the mobs and low prices, it's worth lining up for this cavernous family-style eatery that serves up home-style meals. Dishes like rigatoni in broccoli, sausage, and white bean sauce are so gargantuan that you'll have enough for leftovers. *200 W. 44th St.,* ☎ *212/221–3800. AE.*

$ **Ludlow Street Café.** The food is beautifully prepared and excitingly spiced at this unadorned Lower East Side Cajun restaurant, filled with young people having a good time. So will you. Pickled shrimp with dill and balsamic vinegar whet your appetite. The red-bean soup and the fabulous gumbo prove how complex and exciting these robust dishes can be. *165 Ludlow St., between E. Houston and Stanton,* ☎ *212/353–0536. No reservations. AE. No lunch Wed.–Sat.*

$ ★ **Takahachi.** One of Manhattan's best small Japanese restaurants is neat and amazingly inexpensive, and offers unusual seared tuna with black pepper and mustard and grilled chicken stuffed with plum paste and shiso leaf. Wine and beer only. *85 Ave. A, between 5th and 6th Sts.,* ☎ *212/505–6524. No reservations. AE, MC, V. No lunch.*

Lodging

Once you've accepted that your New York hotel room is going to cost a lot of money, you'll have plenty of choices. The hotels usually compensate for small room size and lack of parking or landscaping with fastidious service, crackerjack maintenance, and restaurants that hold their own in a city of very knowledgeable diners.

Hundreds of B&B rooms are available in Manhattan and the outer boroughs, principally Brooklyn, and almost always cost well below $100 a night; some singles are available for under $50. Reservations may be made through **Bed and Breakfast Network of New York** (134 W. 32nd St., Suite 602, 10001, ☎ 212/645–8134), **City Lights Bed and Breakfast** (Box 20355, Cherokee Station, 10028, ☎ 212/737–7049), or **New World Bed and Breakfast** (150 5th Ave., Suite 711, 10011, ☎ 212/675–5600 or 800/443–3800). For price ranges, see Chart 2 (A) in On the Road with Fodor's.

$$$$ **The Carlyle.** Museum Mile and the tony boutiques of Madison Avenue are on the doorstep of New York's least hysterical grand hotel, where European tradition and Manhattan swank shake hands. The mood here

is English manor house. The Café Carlyle, where performers like Bobby Short entertain; Bemelman's Bar, with murals by Ludwig Bemelman, illustrator of the beloved *Madeline* children's books; and the formal Carlyle Restaurant are all eminently worth patronizing even if you're not staying here. *35 E. 76th St. at Madison Ave., 10021, ☎ 212/744–1600, FAX 212/717–4682. 190 rooms. Facilities: restaurant, café, bar, lounge, fitness center, VCRs, stereos, FAX machines, kitchenettes and pantries in larger units, meeting rooms. AE, DC, MC, V.*

$$$$ ★ **The Mark.** Find this friendliest of baby grand hotels one block north of the Carlyle and steps from Central Park. Guest-room extras such as double phone lines, VCRs, Belgian bed linens, and marble bathrooms with deep tubs make the Mark a serious contender among New York's elite hotels. *25 E. 77th St., 10021, ☎ 212/744–4300 or 800/843–6275, FAX 212/744–2749. 180 rooms. Facilities: restaurant, bar, café, meeting rooms. AE, DC, MC, V.*

$$$$ **The Pierre.** Since it opened, at the height of the Depression, the Pierre has symbolized dignified elegance. The Pierre's decor owes a lot to the Palace of Versailles, with chandeliers and handmade carpets in the lobby and much muted damask and mahogany in the rooms. *5th Ave. at 61st St., 10021, ☎ 212/838–8000 or 800/332–3442, FAX 212/940–8109. 204 rooms. Facilities: restaurant, bar, tearoom, meeting rooms. AE, DC, MC, V.*

$$$$ **The Plaza.** With its unsurpassed location opposite Central Park and F.A.O. Schwarz, the Plaza is probably the most high-profile of all New York hotels. Guest rooms are among the most spacious of the city's first-class hotels with color schemes in burgundy or teal blue. Even if it's your first time in New York, a quick nip at the Oak Bar or a stroll by the fin-de-siècle Palm Court will make you feel part of what makes the city tick. *5th Ave. at 59th St., 10019, ☎ 212/759–3000 or 800/228–3000, FAX 212/546–5324. 807 rooms. Facilities: 2 restaurants, café, 2 bars, art gallery, meeting rooms, disabled-accessible rooms, large concierge staff. AE, DC, MC, V.*

$$$$ **Waldorf-Astoria.** Along with the Plaza, this Art Deco masterpiece personifies New York at its most lavish and powerful. Hilton, its owner, spent a fortune refurbishing both public areas and guest rooms; the bloom has yet to fade, from the original murals and mosaics to the fine old-wood walls and doors. *301 Park Ave., 10022, ☎ 212/355–3000 or 800/445–8667, FAX 212/421–8103. 1,692 rooms. Facilities: 3 restaurants, coffee shop, tearoom, lounge, ballroom, fitness center, meeting rooms. AE, DC, MC, V.*

$$$ **The Algonquin.** While this landmark property's English-drawing-room atmosphere and burnished-wood lobby have been kept intact, its working parts (the plumbing, for instance) have been renovated. Bathrooms and sleeping quarters retain Victorian-style fixtures and furnishings, but now there are larger, firmer beds, VCRs, and Caswell-Massey toiletries. *59 W. 44th St., 10036, ☎ 212/840–6800 or 800/548–0345, FAX 212/944–1419. 165 rooms. Facilities: restaurant, 2 lounges, meeting rooms, free parking on weekends, business center. AE, DC, MC, V.*

$$$ ★ **The Fitzpatrick.** This cozy Irish "boutique" hotel—a real winner in terms of value and charm—is conveniently situated just south of Bloomingdale's and seconds away from anchor bus and subway routes. Nearly half of the 92 units are true suites that are priced well below the market average, even on weekdays. Though not especially large, bathrooms are modern and well equipped; most come with whirlpools. *687 Lexington Ave., 10022, ☎ 212/355–0100 or 800/367–7701, FAX 212/308–5166. 92 rooms. Facilities: restaurant, bar. AE, DC, MC, V.*

$$$ ★ **Manhattan Suites East.** Here's a group of good-value properties for the traveler who likes to combine full hotel service with independent pied-à-terre living. The four best are the **Beekman Tower** (3 Mitchell Pl.), near the United Nations; the **Dumont Plaza** (150 E. 34th St.), on a direct bus line to the Javits Center; the **Surrey Hotel** (20 E. 76th St.), near Madison Avenue art galleries and designer boutiques; and the **Southgate Tower** (371 7th Ave.), near Madison Square Garden and Penn Station. *Sales office: 500 W. 37th St., 10018, ☎ 212/465–3600 or 800/637–8483, FAX 212/465–3663. AE, DC, MC, V.*

$$$ **Renaissance.** The former Ramada Renaissance was redone to suit the business community, which provides about 70% of its patrons, though for the vacationer, off-season rates start low, and theaterland is on the doorstep. The decor is half hotel-chain, half deco splendor, with brass and mahogany where chrome and pine suffice elsewhere. There's a tiny gym and a Mediterranean restaurant called Windows on Broadway, with a great eye-level view of Times Square. *2 Times Sq., 10036, ☎ 212/765–7676, FAX 212/765–1962. 305 rooms. Facilities: restaurant, 2 bars, lounge, fitness rooms, meeting rooms. AE, D, DC, MC, V.*

$$$ ★ **Royalton.** As hip today as it was when it opened its steel-and-glass doors in the '80s, this is a second home to the world's media-, music-, and fashion-biz folk. French designer Philippe Starck transformed spaces of intimidating size into a paradise for poseurs, with vividly colored, geometrically challenged but comfy chairs and lots of catwalk-style gliding areas. Rooms, suffice it to say, are just as glamorously offbeat, some oddly shaped and none too big, but all are perfectly comfortable. *44 W. 44th St., 10036, ☎ 212/869–4400 or 800/635–9013, FAX 212/869–8965. 205 rooms. Facilities: restaurant with bar, meeting rooms, game and library areas, fitness center, VCRs, stereos. AE, DC, MC, V.*

$$ ★ **Hotel Beacon.** Once a Broadway residential building, this spiffy hotel has decent-size rooms with full kitchenettes—a real advantage, considering that some of New York's best gourmet stores, such as Zabar's and Fairway, are in the immediate area. The cherry-walnut furnishings are less institutional than expected, the baths are modern if not elegant, and your phone even comes with voice mail. The well-known nightspot, the China Club, is downstairs. *2130 Broadway at 75th St., 10023, ☎ 212/787–1100 or 800/572–4969, FAX 212/724–0839. 160 rooms. AE, DC, MC, V.*

$$ **Hotel Edison.** A popular budget stop for tour groups from here and abroad, this offbeat old hotel has had a face-lift. Guest rooms are brighter and fresher than the dark corridors seem to suggest. *228 W. 47th St., 10036, ☎ 212/840–5000, FAX 212/596–6850. 1,000 rooms. Facilities: restaurant, coffee shop, bar. AE, DC, MC, V.*

$ **Washington Square Hotel.** This cozy hotel has a true European feel, from the wrought-iron and brass in the small, elegant lobby to the personal attention given by the staff. Rooms and baths are simple but pleasant. Continental breakfast is included in the room rate. *103 Waverly Pl., 10011, ☎ 212/777–9515 or 800/222–0418, FAX 212/979–8373. 160 rooms. Facilities: restaurant, laundry service. AE, DC, MC, V.*

$ **International House.** This large nonprofit residence for graduate students from abroad, in a 10-story gray stone building near Columbia University, has simply furnished guest rooms and suites available for travelers year-round, as well as single student rooms from mid-May to late August. *500 Riverside Dr. at 123rd St., ☎ 212/316–6300, FAX 212/316–1827. 11 suites, 5 guest rooms, 10–100 student rooms with shared baths. Facilities: cafeteria, lounges, laundry, sports, cultural programs. MC, V.*

$ Vanderbilt YMCA. Of the various Manhattan Ys offering accommodations, this is the best as far as location and facilities are concerned. The rooms are little more than dormitory-style cells—even with only one or two beds to a room, you may feel crowded. The communal showers and toilets are clean. Guests are provided with such basics as towels and soap. The Turtle Bay neighborhood is safe, convenient, and interesting (the United Nations is a few short blocks away). *224 E. 47th St., 10017, ☎ 212/756–9600, FAX 212/752–0210. 430 rooms. Facilities: cafeteria, meeting rooms, self-service laundry, gift shop, luggage storage, 2 pools, fitness center. No credit cards.*

The Arts and Nightlife

Full listings of entertainment and cultural events appear in the weekly *New York* magazine; they include capsule summaries of plays and concerts, performance times, and ticket prices. The Arts & Leisure section of the Sunday *New York Times* lists and describes events but provides no service information. The Theater Directory in the daily *New York Times* advertises ticket information for Broadway and Off-Broadway shows. Listings of events also appear weekly in *The New Yorker* and *The Village Voice*.

The Arts

THEATER

New York boasts nearly 40 Broadway theaters, three dozen Off-Broadway theaters, and 200 Off-Off-Broadway houses. Broadway theaters are located in the Theater District, most of which lies between Broadway and 8th Avenue, from 43rd to 52nd streets. Off-and Off-Off-Broadway theaters are scattered all over town, including in Greenwich Village, on the Upper West Side, and along Theater Row, a strip of 42nd Street between 9th and 10th avenues.

New York's best-known discount source is the **TKTS booth** in Duffy Square (47th St. and Broadway, ☎ 212/768–1818) and in the Wall Street area (World Trade Center mezzanine, ☎ 212/768–1818). TKTS sells day-of-performance tickets for Broadway and some Off-Broadway plays at discounts that, depending on a show's popularity, often go as low as half price (plus $2.50 surcharge per ticket). The Broadway booth opens at 10 AM and the World Trade Center booth opens at 11 AM. TKTS accepts only cash or traveler's checks—no credit cards.

MUSIC

Much of New York's serious-music scene clusters around the magnificent concert halls and theaters of **Lincoln Center** (W. 62nd St. and Broadway, ☎ 212/875–5400). Its **Avery Fisher Hall** (☎ 212/875–5030) is home of the New York Philharmonic Orchestra, the American Philharmonic, the Mostly Mozart festival, and visiting orchestras and soloists. While Lincoln Center is only 30 years old, another famous classical music palace—**Carnegie Hall** (154 W. 57th St. at 7th Ave., ☎ 212/247–7800)—recently celebrated its 100th birthday. This is where Leonard Bernstein, standing in for New York Philharmonic conductor Bruno Walter, made his triumphant debut; where Jack Benny and Isaac Stern fiddled together; and where the Beatles played one of their first U.S. concerts.

OPERA

The **Metropolitan Opera House** (☎ 212/362–6000), at Lincoln Center, is a sublime setting for mostly classic operas performed by world-class stars. The **New York City Opera** (☎ 212/870–5570), at Lincoln

Center's State Theater, offers a diverse repertoire consisting of adventurous and rarely seen works as well as classic opera favorites.

DANCE

The **American Ballet Theatre** (☏ 212/362–6000) is the resident dance company of the Metropolitan Opera House in Lincoln Center. The center's New York State Theater is home to the **New York City Ballet** (☏ 212/870–5570), which reached world-class prominence under the direction of the late George Balanchine. **City Center** (131 W. 55th St., ☏ 212/581–7907) hosts innovative dance companies, such as the **Harlem Dance Theater** and **the Paul Taylor Dance Company.** The **Joyce Theater** (8th Ave. at 19th St., ☏ 212/242–0800) houses the avant-garde **Feld Ballet.**

FILM

On any day of the year, visitors to New York movie theaters will find all the major new releases, renowned classics, unusual foreign offerings, and experimental works. For information on schedules and theaters dial 212/777–FILM, the MovieFone sponsored by WQHT 97 FM, or check the local newspapers. *New York* and *The New Yorker* magazines publish programs and reviews. The vast majority of Manhattan theaters are first-run houses. Among the art-film and revival houses are the **Film Forum** (209 W. Houston St., ☏ 212/727–8110) in SoHo; the **Museum of Modern Art** (*see* Exploring New York City, *above*) also offers several film series every year.

Nightlife

CABARET

The very hip **Ballroom** (253 W. 28th St., ☏ 212/244–3005), in Chelsea, has a great tapas bar, top-name cabaret acts, and outrageous revues. At the intimate **Rainbow & Stars** (30 Rockefeller Plaza, ☏ 212/632–5000), singers such as Maureen McGovern and Rosemary Clooney entertain, backlighted by a view of the twinkling lights of the city.

COMEDY CLUB

Original Improvisation (433 W. 34th St., ☏ 212/279–3446), New York's original comedy showcase, is where all the big-name yucksters (Rodney Dangerfield, Richard Pryor, Robert Klein) got their first laughs.

DISCOS AND DANCE CLUBS

A native New Yorker hasn't set foot in the **Palladium** (126 E. 14th St., ☏ 212/473–7171) in years, but it's still a hoot with the suburban set. **Roseland** (239 W. 52nd St., ☏ 212/247–0200) is the place for "touch dancing" the way they used to do it. The **Rainbow Room** (30 Rockefeller Plaza, ☏ 212/632–5000) serves dinner, and dancing to the strains of a live orchestra takes place on a floor right out of an Astaire–Rodgers musical.

JAZZ CLUBS

The **Blue Note** (131 W. 3rd St., ☏ 212/475–8592) is a new incarnation of a legendary jazz club. **Michael's Pub** (211 E. 55th St., ☏ 212/758–2272) has mainstream jazz, top vocalists, jazz-based revues—and Woody Allen on the clarinet most Monday nights. The **Village Vanguard** (178 7th Ave. S, ☏ 212/255–4037) is a basement joint that has ridden the crest of every new wave in jazz for over 50 years.

POP, ROCK, BLUES, AND COUNTRY

The *Village Voice* carries the best listings of who's playing where on the pop and rock scenes. The **Bitter End** (147 Bleecker St., ☏ 212/673–7030) has been giving a break to folk, rock, jazz, comedy, and country acts for over 25 years. The **Bottom Line** (15 W. 4th St., off Mercer St., ☏ 212/228–

7880) features folk and rock headliners. **Dan Lynch's Blues Bar** (221 2nd Ave., ☎ 212/677–0911) is a divey blues bar in the East Village that bustles with jam sessions on Saturday and Sunday afternoons.

FOR SINGLES (UNDER 30)

At the **Ear Inn** (326 Spring St., near Greenwich St., ☎ 212/226–9060), it's the artsy crowd that makes the place: The regular poetry readings are called "lunch for the ear." Check out **Lucy's Retired Surfer's Bar** (503 Columbus Ave., ☎ 212/787–3009), a hit with Upper West Siders, and **Merc Bar** (151 Mercer St., ☎ 212/966–2727), which is at the heart of trendy SoHo.

FOR SINGLES (OVER 30)

Jim McMullen's (1341 3rd Ave., ☎ 212/861–4700) is a quintessential Upper East Side watering hole that has a busy bar decked out with bouquets of fresh flowers. **Pete's Tavern** (129 E. 18th St., ☎ 212/473–7676) is a crowded, friendly saloon famous as the place where O. Henry wrote "The Gift of the Magi." The **White Horse Tavern** (567 Hudson St. and 11th St., ☎ 212/243–9260) was patronized by Dylan Thomas.

GAY BARS

For advice on the bar scene, health issues, and other assorted quandaries of the gay community, call the **Gay and Lesbian Switchboard** (☎ 212/777–1800) or stop by the **Lesbian and Gay Community Services Center** (208 W. 13th St., ☎ 212/620–7310). Among the recommended bars are **1984** (formerly the Crowbar; 339 E. 10th St., ☎ 212/420–0670), where the tiny dance floor pulses and throbs every Friday to a fabulous array of new-wave syntho-garbage. Upstairs at **Monster** (80 Grove St., ☎ 212/924–3558), the tone-deaf gather and sing around the piano; downstairs, the rhythm-impaired gyrate in a campy pitch-black disco. At the **Spike** (120 11th Ave., ☎ 212/243–9688) you'll find the ultimate parade of black leather, chains, and Levi's; the bark here is always bigger than the bite. The staggering popularity of **Splash** (50 W. 17th St., ☎ 212/691–0073) is due as much to its size as to anything else. Most nights go-go dancers writhe in translucent shower cubicles. At the **Works** (428 Columbus Ave., ☎ 212/799–7365), whether it's Thursday's $1 margarita party or just a regular Upper West Side afternoon, the crowd is usually J. Crew–style or disco hangover. The crowd at **Crazy Nannys'** (21 7th Ave. S, ☎ 212/366–6312) is wide-ranging—from urban chic to shaved head—and tends toward the young and wild side. **Julie's** (204 E. 58th St., ☎ 212/688–1294) is popular with the sophisticated-lady, upper-crust crowd; this brownstone basement has a piano bar.

Excursions to the Other Boroughs

Brooklyn Heights

Brooklyn Heights—named for its enviable hilltop position—was New York's first suburb, linked to the city first by ferry and later by the Brooklyn Bridge. Some 600 buildings more than a century old remain intact today, making the Heights a kind of picture book of 19th-century American architecture. The mansard-roofed Federal-style residence at **24 Middagh Street** is the oldest home in the neighborhood; from a door in the wall on Willow Street around the corner you can see the cottage garden and carriage house in the rear.

The **Plymouth Church of the Pilgrims** (Orange St. between Henry and Hicks Sts.) was the vortex of abolitionist sentiment in the years before the Civil War, thanks to the oratory of the eminent theologian Henry Ward Beecher. The church was a major stop on the Underground Railroad, which smuggled slaves to freedom. Around the corner at **22 Willow Street** is the house where Beecher lived. **Willow Street,** between Clark and Pierrepont streets, is one of the Heights' prettiest and most architecturally varied blocks, with houses in the Queen Anne and Federal styles. Pierrepont ends at the **Brooklyn Heights Promenade,** a quiet sliver of park lined with benches facing the Manhattan skyline.

GETTING THERE

Walk across the Brooklyn Bridge from lower Manhattan near City Hall and return on the No. 2 or 3 subway from the Clark Street station, a few blocks southwest of the walkway terminus.

Queens

Astoria in Queens is one of New York's most vital ethnic neighborhoods; once German, then Italian, it is now heavily Greek and is filled with shops and restaurants reflecting the community. It is also the site of the **American Museum of the Moving Image** (35th Ave. at 36th St., ☎ 718/784–0077; admission charged; closed Mon.), where a theater features clips from the works of leading Hollywood cinematographers; galleries offer exhibits on the techniques of filmmaking, including hands-on displays; and the collection of movie memorabilia contains costumes worn by Rudolph Valentino and Bette Davis.

GETTING THERE

Take the No. 7 train from Manhattan (Grand Central) to Queensboro Plaza, then change for the N train and get off at Broadway.

The Bronx

The only New York borough attached to the mainland, the Bronx was first settled by Dutch, French, English, and Swedish country squires, who established manorial holdings there while fighting off the Native Americans. Little remains from the Colonial era, but the area dramatically illustrates another aspect of Bronx history: the influx of immigrant groups—first the Irish, then Germans, Italians, and Jews—from the 1840s on. Later waves included African-Americans, Hispanics, Albanians, and Cambodians.

Poe Park contains the **Edgar Allan Poe Cottage** (E. Kingsbridge Rd. and Grand Concourse, ☎ 212/881–8900), where Poe and his wife, Virginia, lived between 1846 and 1849. On Fordham Road is the 85-acre campus of **Fordham University,** begun as a Jesuit college in 1841. In **Bronx Park** are the **New York Botanical Garden** (*see* Parks and Gardens, *above*) and the **Bronx Zoo** (*see* What to See and Do with Children, *above*), two world-class attractions.

LONG ISLAND

At 1,682 sq mi, Long Island is not only the largest island on America's East Coast but the most varied. From west to east, Long Island has everything from suburban sprawl to the farmland of the North Fork and the world-famous resort villages of the Hamptons. It has arguably the nation's finest stretch of white-sand beach, as well as the notoriously congested Long Island Expressway (LIE).

Tourist Information

Long Island: Convention and Visitors Bureau (Eisenhower Park, 1899 Hempstead Turnpike, Suite 500, East Meadow 11554, ☎ 516/794–4222 or 800/441–4601). **Visitor centers:** at Eisenhower Park (parking field 6A, East Meadow), open year-round; on the Southern State Parkway (between Exits 13 and 14, Valley Stream); on the LIE (Dix Hills–Deer Park); and on Rte. 25 (Flanders), open late spring–early fall.

Getting There

By Plane

In addition to **John F. Kennedy International** and **La Guardia** airports in Queens (*see* New York City, Arriving and Departing, *above*), Long Island is served by **Long Island MacArthur Airport** in Islip (☎ 516/467–3210 for airline information).

By Car

The **Midtown Tunnel** (I–495) and the **Triborough Bridge** (I–278) connect Long Island with Manhattan. The **Throgs Neck Bridge** (I–295) and the **Whitestone Bridge** (I–678) provide access from the Bronx and New England.

By Train

The **Long Island Railroad** (☎ 516/822–5477) has frequent service from Penn Station in Manhattan to all major towns on Long Island.

By Bus

Hampton Jitney (☎ 516/283–4600; in New York City, 800/936–0440) links Manhattan and area airports with towns on the southeastern end of Long Island.

Exploring Long Island

The best way to get a feel for Long Island and explore its museums, stately mansions, nature preserves, and coastal villages is to avoid the traffic-choked LIE and take the more leisurely roads that parallel the coasts. On the North Shore, your best bet is Rte. 25A; on the South Shore, Rte. 27 (Sunrise Highway).

The stretch of wealthy suburbs just outside New York City on the North Shore is known as the Gold Coast. **Roslyn Harbor** is home to Long Island's largest art museum, the **Nassau County Museum of Art,** set amid 145 acres of formal gardens, outdoor art, and rolling fields, and housed in the former country home of Henry Clay Frick. The 10 galleries are hung with changing exhibits. *Rte. 25A, ☎ 516/484–9337. Admission charged. Closed Mon.*

Farther east, in the town of **Oyster Bay,** is the **Planting Fields Arboretum** (Planting Fields Rd., ☎ 516/922–9200; admission charged), 150 acres of immaculately landscaped grounds surrounding a Renaissance-style mansion. Nearby is **Sagamore Hill** (Cove Neck Rd., 1 mi north of Rte. 25A, ☎ 516/922–4447; admission charged), the Victorian summer White House of President Theodore Roosevelt.

The North Fork, the upper part of Long Island's eastern "tail," is beautiful farm country, with a thriving wine-growing business concentrated in **Cutchogue** and **Peconic. Hargrave Vineyard** (Rte. 48, Cutchogue, ☎ 516/734–5158; closed Jan.–Feb.), the pioneer winery in the region, offers tours and tastings.

Beautiful and historic **Shelter Island,** in Gardiners Bay, nestled between the North and South forks, was among the first parts of Long Island to be settled by the British and is now primarily a summer resort and boating center. You can use the island as a scenic stepping-stone between one fork and the other, taking the ferries that leave from **Greenport** on the North Fork (☎ 516/749–0139) and **North Haven** on the South Fork (☎ 516/749–1200).

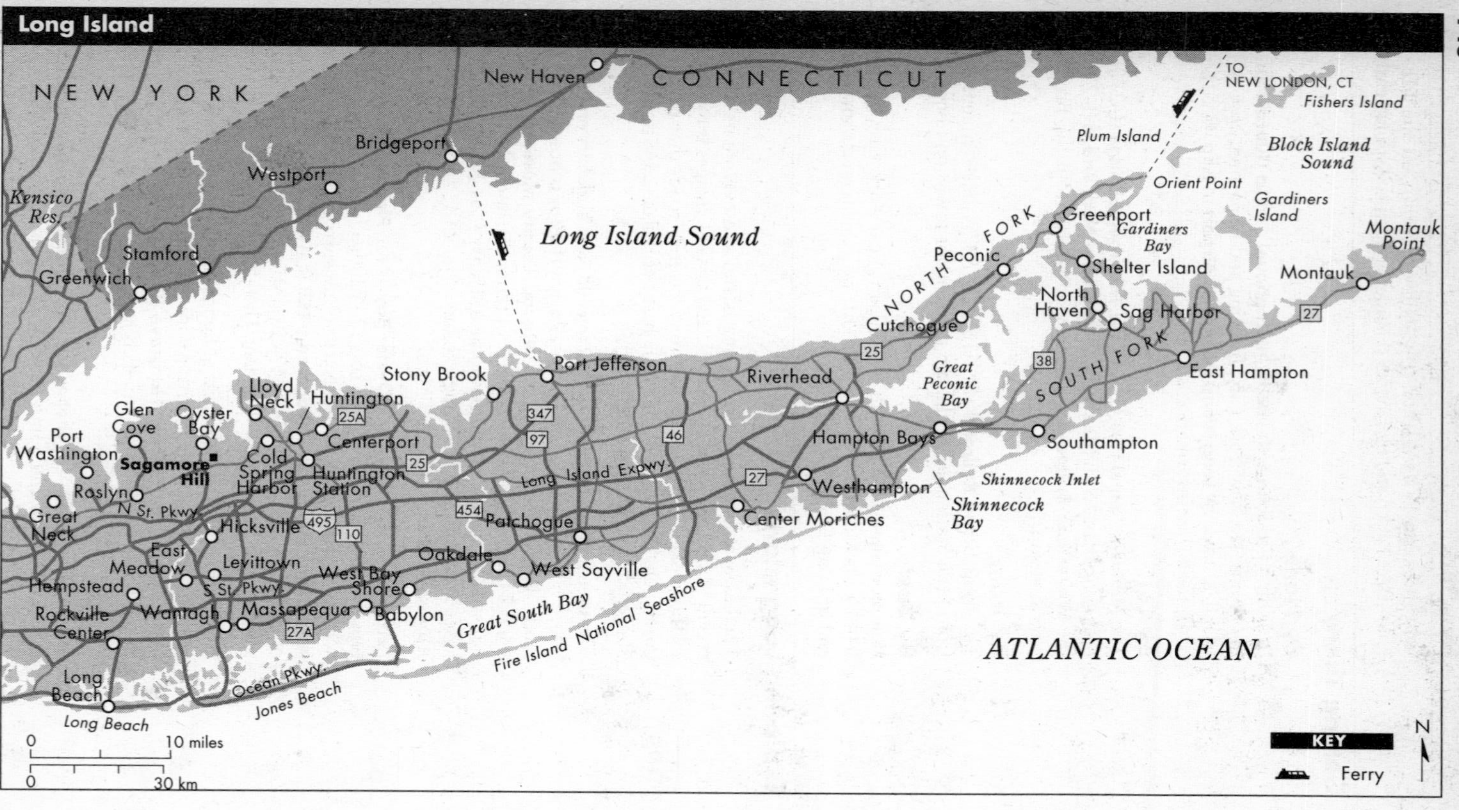
Long Island
NEW YORK
CONNECTICUT
New Haven
Bridgeport
Westport
Stamford
Greenwich
Kensico Res.
Long Island Sound
TO NEW LONDON, CT
Fishers Island
Plum Island
Block Island Sound
Orient Point
Gardiners Island
Greenport
Gardiners Bay
Montauk Point
Montauk
Peconic
NORTH FORK
Shelter Island
North Haven
Sag Harbor
Cutchogue
SOUTH FORK
East Hampton
Great Peconic Bay
Riverhead
Port Jefferson
Stony Brook
Lloyd Neck
Huntington
Glen Cove
Oyster Bay
Port Washington
Sagamore Hill
Cold Spring Harbor
Centerport
Huntington Station
Roslyn
Great Neck
N St. Pkwy.
Hicksville
East Meadow
Levittown
Hempstead
S St. Pkwy.
Rockville Center
Wantagh
Massapequa
West Bay Shore
Babylon
Oakdale
West Sayville
Patchogue
Long Island Expwy.
Center Moriches
Westhampton
Hampton Bays
Southampton
Shinnecock Inlet
Shinnecock Bay
Great South Bay
Fire Island National Seashore
ATLANTIC OCEAN
Ocean Pkwy.
Jones Beach
Long Beach
Long Beach
25A
25
347
97
46
454
495
110
27A
27
25
38
27
0
10 miles
0
30 km
KEY
Ferry
N

Sag Harbor, on the north shore of the South Fork, looks much as it did in the 1870s, when it was an important whaling center. The **Whaling Museum** displays logbooks, scrimshaw, and harpoons. *Garden and Main Sts., ☎ 516/725–0770. Admission charged. Closed Oct.–Memorial Day.*

The **Hamptons,** on the South Fork, are a string of seaside villages that the East Coast upper crust "discovered" in the late 19th century and transformed into elegant summer resorts. At the pinnacle of fashion and fame is **East Hampton,** which, despite the hordes of celebrities and tourists who descend each summer, retains the grace and dignity of its Colonial heritage. Main Street has the town's classic white Presbyterian Church (built in 1860) and stately old homes and inns, and the side streets are lined with Shingle-style mansions.

At Long Island's eastern tip, **Montauk** has the double allure of extremity and the sea. Though the village is rather touristy, the beaches are unsurpassed. **Hither Hills State Park** (Rte. 27, ☎ 516/668–2461) preserves miles of rolling moors and forests of pitch pine and scrub oak. From the 110-ft **Montauk Lighthouse** (Rte. 27, ☎ 516/668–2544) you can see all the way to Rhode Island.

What to See and Do with Children

Lewin Farms (Sound Ave., Wading River, ☎ 516/929–4327) is the island's largest pick-your-own farm, with apples, berries, and vegetables. **Long Island Game Farm** (Chapman Blvd., Manorville, ☎ 516/878–6644; closed mid-Oct.–mid-Apr.) has baby animals for children to bottle-feed, a wild-tiger show, and train rides.

Shopping

Long Island is known for its shopping malls, the largest of which is the **Roosevelt Field Mall** (☎ 516/742–8000) in Garden City, with more than 200 stores and more on the way. Branches of many New York City department stores are in Garden City (on Franklin Ave.). **Manhasset's "Miracle Mile,"** along Rte. 25A, has department stores and designer boutiques. If you're looking for bargains, visit the **Flea Market** at Roosevelt Raceway (Old Country Rd., Westbury, ☎ 516/222–1530) every Wednesday, Saturday, and Sunday.

Sports and the Outdoors

Boating

Captree Boatmen's Association (Captree State Park, Box 5372, Babylon 11707, ☎ 516/669–6464) has a fleet of 34 open and charter-fishing boats with courteous crews. **Oyster Bay Sailing School** (Box 447, West End Ave., Oyster Bay 11771, ☎ 516/624–7900) offers classes and three- to five-day vacation packages from April through October.

Spectator Sports

Hockey

New York Islanders (Nassau Coliseum, Hempstead Turnpike, Uniondale, ☎ 516/794–4100; Oct.–Apr.).

Horse Racing

Belmont Park (Hempstead Turnpike, Elmont, ☎ 718/641–4700; May–July, late Aug.–Oct.) is home to the third jewel in horse racing's triple crown, the Belmont Stakes, held in early June.

Beaches

Jones Beach State Park (Wantagh Pkwy., Wantagh, ☎ 516/785–1600), a wide, sandy stretch of ocean beach, is the most crowded but also the biggest and most fully equipped of Long Island beaches, with a restaurant, concession stands, changing rooms, a boardwalk, a theater, and sports facilities. Due east, **Robert Moses State Park** (Robert Moses Causeway, Babylon, ☎ 516/669–0449), on Fire Island, is a far less crowded, beautiful, sandy ocean beach.

Dining and Lodging

Long Island restaurants run the gamut from fast-food chains, pizzerias, and family-style eateries to ethnic restaurants and elegant country inns. Not surprisingly, the island draws on the bounty of the surrounding waters, especially on the east end, where commercial fishing remains a vital industry.

Recent years have brought all of the major motel chains to Long Island, as well as a resurgence in hotel construction. Resort hotels and country inns are concentrated in the Hamptons. For those who prefer the bed-and-breakfast route, most local chambers of commerce, particularly on the east end, have information on B&Bs in their towns. For price ranges, see Charts 1 (A) and 2 (A) in On the Road with Fodor's.

East Hampton

DINING

The Laundry. Locals and visitors alike flock nightly to this casual but elegant eatery that specializes in grilled seafood and shellfish. *31 Race La., ☎ 516/324–3199. No reservations. AE, DC, MC, V. No lunch. $$–$$$*

DINING AND LODGING

Huntting Inn. A powerful crowd of high-profile Upper East Siders come here on weekends to see and be seen, as much as to treat themselves to the lavish portions of steak and lobster for which the place is famous. Antiques fill the rooms of the historic 1699 inn. *94 Main St., 11937, ☎ 516/324–0411. 20 rooms. AE, DC, MC, V. No lunch. $$$$*

LODGING

★ **Maidstone Arms.** This charming inn, built in the 1830s, is the coziest and most comfortable in town. It also has one of the best locations—right across from a pond and a pristine park, surrounded by East Hampton's oldest streets and most beautiful homes. *207 Main St., 11937, ☎ 516/324–5006. 16 rooms, 3 cottages. Facilities: restaurant, bar. AE, MC, V. $$$*

Garden City

LODGING

★ **Garden City Hotel.** This hotel is more luxurious, more sophisticated, and even more expensive than the original. It is a world-class hotel, the most opulent on Long Island and the rival of the finest Manhattan has to offer. *45 7th St., 11530, ☎ 516/747–3000 or 800/547–0400. 273 rooms. Facilities: restaurant, bar, lounge, nightclub, health club, indoor pool, beauty salon, gift shop. AE, D, DC, MC, V. $$$$*

Greenport

DINING

Claudio's. Two large dining rooms, decorated with artifacts from the J-boats that raced in the America's Cup during the 1930s, face the harbor through large picture windows. Local seafood is the specialty. The clam bar offers alfresco dining at umbrella-shaded tables on a wharf overlooking Peconic Bay. *Foot of Main St., ☎ 516/477–0627. MC, V. Closed Jan.–mid-Apr. $$*

Jericho

DINING

Milleridge Inn. Basic, old-fashioned American food, including prime rib, is served in a Colonial mansion, complete with fireplaces and antiques. *Hicksville Rd., ☎ 516/931–2201. No reservations. AE, D, DC, MC, V. $$*

Montauk

DINING

Gosman's. This huge, classy fish restaurant, jam-packed in the summer, offers a spectacular location—at the entrance to Montauk Harbor—and the freshest possible fish, served indoors or out. You may have a long wait in peak season. *500 West Lake Dr., ☎ 516/668–5330. No reservations. MC, V. Closed mid-Oct.–Apr. $$*

Sag Harbor

LODGING

★ **Ram's Head Inn.** This 1929 center-hall Colonial-style island retreat makes for the perfect romantic getaway—far from the crowds of the Hamptons. The inn overlooks 800 ft of beachfront and has one of the best dining rooms in eastern Long Island. *108 Ram Island Dr., Shelter Island Heights 11965, ☎ 516/749–0811. 14 rooms. Facilities: restaurant, tennis, sailboats. AE, MC, V. $$–$$$*

Baron's Cove Inn. This renovated motel sits next to the water near the boats of an adjacent marina. The air-conditioned rooms have kitchenettes, and some have private patios or balconies with water views. *West Water St., 11963, ☎ 516/725–2100. 66 rooms. Facilities: pool, tennis, fishing, meeting rooms. AE, D, DC, MC, V. $$*

Motels

Best Western Hotel & Conference Center (80 Clinton St., Hempstead 11550, ☎ 516/486–4100 or 800/343–7950), 182 rooms, restaurant, lounge, exercise room, pool; *$$$*. **Ramada Inn East End** (Rte. 25, Riverhead 11901, ☎ 516/369–2200), 100 rooms, restaurant, bar, pool; *$$$*. **Drake Motor Inn** (16 Penny La., Hampton Bays 11946, ☎ 516/728–1592), 15 rooms, pool; *$$*. **Ramada Inn** (8030 Jericho Turnpike, Woodbury 11797, ☎ 516/921–8500), 102 rooms, pool, meeting rooms; *$$*.

Spa

★ **Gurney's Inn Resort and Spa.** Long popular for its fabulous location, on a bluff overlooking 1,000 ft of private ocean beach, Gurney's has become even more famous in recent years for its European-style health and beauty spa. The large, luxurious rooms all have ocean views. *Old Montauk Hwy., Montauk 11954, ☎ 516/668–2345 or 800/848–7639. 109 rooms. Facilities: restaurant, bar, health club, indoor saltwater pool, golf and tennis privileges, extensive spa facilities, beauty salon, recreation room, meeting rooms. AE, D, DC, MC, V. $$$$*

Campground

Hither Hills State Park (*see* Exploring Long Island, *above*) has both tent and RV sites.

The Arts and Nightlife

Check the Friday edition of *Newsday,* the Long Island newspaper, which has a weekend supplement containing an abundance of information about Long Island arts and entertainment, as well as the magazine *Long Island Monthly.*

The Arts

Jones Beach Marine Theatre (Jones Beach, Wantagh, ☎ 516/221–1000) hosts major outdoor concerts by contemporary pop artists May–September. **Nassau Coliseum** (Hempstead Turnpike, Uniondale, ☎ 516/794–9300) has major rock and pop concerts year-round. **Westbury Music Fair** (Brush Hollow Rd., Westbury, ☎ 516/334–0800) features live concerts, shows, and theater.

Nightlife

Long Island is a hot place for singles and young couples. Clubs feature the loudest in music and the fanciest in video displays, and there are big, glitzy discos. **Oak Beach Inn** (Ocean Pkwy., Oak Beach, ☎ 516/587–0097) has sing-along upstairs, top-40 downstairs, deli food, and live bands on weekends. The **Savoy** in the Huntington Hilton (598 Broad Hollow Rd., Melville, ☎ 516/845–1000) is one of the hottest clubs on the island from happy hour on. **Sonny's** (3603 Merrick Rd., Seaford, ☎ 516/826–0973) features live jazz nightly.

THE HUDSON VALLEY

The landscape along the Hudson River for the 140 mi from Westchester County to Albany, the state capital, is among the loveliest in America. Indeed, this natural beauty—dramatic palisades, pine forests, cool mountain lakes and streams—inspired an entire art movement, the Hudson River School, in the 19th century. Also a rich agricultural region, the valley has scores of orchards, vineyards, and farm markets along country roads. Proximity to Manhattan makes this a viable destination for day trips, but the numerous country inns, B&Bs, and resorts make more leisurely journeys especially attractive.

Tourist Information

Albany County: Convention and Visitors Bureau (52 S. Pearl St., Albany 12207, ☎ 518/434–1217 or 800/258–3582). **Columbia County:** Chamber of Commerce (527 Warren St., Hudson 12534, ☎ 518/828–4417). **Dutchess County:** Tourism Promotion Agency (3 Neptune Rd., Poughkeepsie 12601, ☎ 914/463–4000 or 800/445–3131). **Hudson River Valley:** Hudson Valley Tourism (Box 4471, Kingston 12471, ☎ 800/232–4782).

Getting There

By Plane

La Guardia, John F. Kennedy, and **Newark** airports (*see* New York City, *above*) are manageable distances from the Hudson Valley. In the area itself, **Stewart International Airport** (☎ 914/564–2100) in Newburgh and **Albany County Airport** (☎ 518/869–9611) in Colonie are served by major airlines.

By Car

From New York City, pick up the New York State Thruway (I–87), which parallels the west bank of the Hudson River, or the more scenic Taconic Parkway, which parallels the east bank. I–84 provides access to the region from southern New England.

By Train

Amtrak (☎ 800/872–7245) provides service to Hudson, Rhinecliff, Rensselaer (Albany), and points west and north of Poughkeepsie.

By Bus

Adirondack Trailways (☎ 800/225–6815) has daily service between New York's Port Authority Bus Terminal and New Paltz, Kingston, Albany, and other Hudson Valley towns.

Exploring the Hudson Valley

U.S. 9 hugs the east bank of the Hudson, passing through many picturesque towns, including Tarrytown, Hyde Park, Rhinebeck, and Hudson. Rte. 9W hugs the west bank from Newburgh to Catskill.

Sunnyside (W. Sunnyside La. off U.S. 9, Tarrytown, ☎ 914/591–8763; admission charged), just south of the Tappan Zee Bridge, was the romantic estate of Washington Irving, author of *The Legend of Sleepy Hollow* and *Rip Van Winkle.* The 17 rooms include Irving's library and many of his original furnishings.

Harriman and **Bear Mountain state parks** (off Palisades Pkwy., ☎ 914/786–2701) are the most famous parks of the vast Palisades Interstate system. Together they offer 54,000 acres and plenty of outdoor activity year-round, including boating, swimming, hiking, fishing, and cross-country skiing.

West Point (U.S. 9W, West Point, ☎ 914/938–2638 or 914/938–7049), America's oldest and most distinguished military academy, is on bluffs overlooking the Hudson River. The museum at Olmstead Hall houses one of the world's foremost military collections.

Across the river in Garrison stands **Boscobel** (Rte. 9D, ☎ 914/265–3638; admission charged), a fully restored early 19th-century mansion surrounded by beautiful gardens that afford a breathtaking view of the Hudson River. Nearby **Cold Spring-on-Hudson** is a small 19th-century village with quiet streets for strolling and shops full of antiques and crafts.

Farther up the river at **Hyde Park** are the **Franklin Delano Roosevelt National Historic Site** and nearby **Val-Kill,** the cottage where Eleanor Roosevelt lived from 1945 to 1962. The large Roosevelt family home contains original furnishings and a museum displaying manuscripts and personal documents. At Val-Kill, set on 172 wooded acres, the tour includes the film biography *First Lady of the World.* Two miles north of here, the elaborately decorated 54-room **Vanderbilt Mansion,** a former home of Frederick and Louise Vanderbilt, offers panoramic views of the Hudson. *All 3 sites: U.S. 9, ☎ 914/229–9115. Admission charged. Val-Kill closed Jan.–Mar., weekdays Nov.–Dec.; other sites closed Tues.–Wed. Nov.–Apr.*

A short distance away is the country's most respected cooking school, the **Culinary Institute of America** (U.S. 9, Hyde Park, ☎ 914/471–6608). Founded in 1946, the institute has 2,000 students enrolled in two 21-month culinary arts or baking and pastry arts programs. Facilities include 36 kitchens and bakeshops, plus eight instructional dining rooms, of which four are student-staffed restaurants open to the public (*see* Dining and Lodging, *below*).

The **Mohonk Mountain House** (☎ 914/255–1000; admission charged for day use of facilities; *see also* Dining and Lodging, *below*) in **Lake Mohonk,** west of New Paltz over the Walkill River, is a resort high above the Hudson River valley on several thousand unspoiled acres of the Shawangunk Mountains. The mountains are ideal for hiking, bird-watching, golf, ice-skating, horseback riding, and cross-country skiing.

Hudson Valley

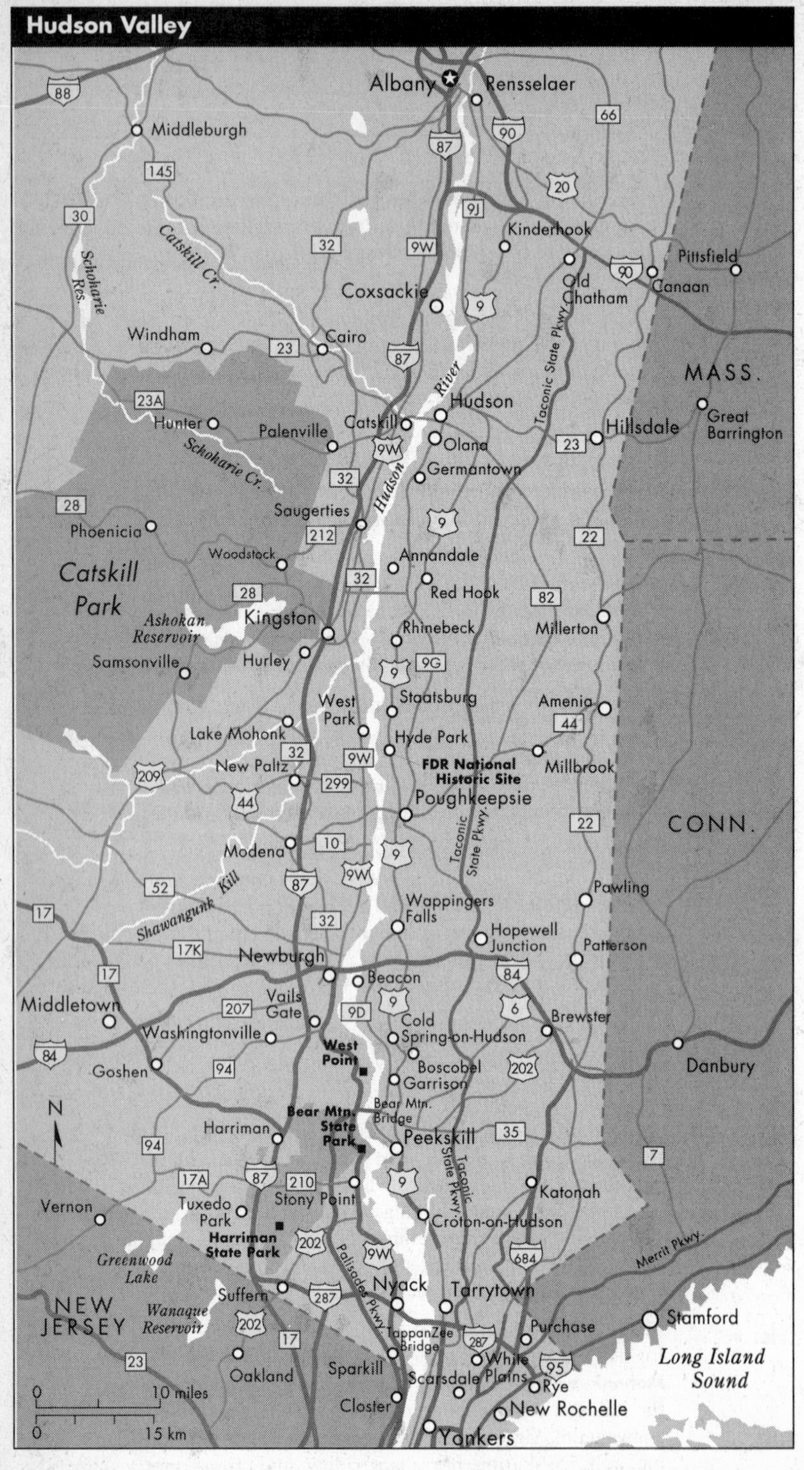

Woodstock became a rock-music legend after the 1969 concert (actually held 50 mi away, in Bethel). Today the town is an ideal place for walking, crafts shopping, and people-watching.

Frederic Church, the leading artist of the Hudson River School, built **Olana,** his 37-room Moorish-style castle, on a hilltop with panoramic vistas of the valley. *Rte. 9G, Hudson, ☎ 518/828–0135. Admission charged. Closed Nov.–mid-Apr.; Mon.*

In **Albany,** the **Albany Visitors Center** (25 Quackenbush Sq., corner of Broadway and Clinton Ave., ☎ 518/434–5132) has two permanent hands-on exhibits depicting Albany's past and present and offers guided and self-guided walking and driving tours. The **Henry Hudson Planetarium** here offers star shows on Saturday at 11:30 AM and 12:30 PM (admission charged) and a free orientation film about Albany on weekdays at 11:30 AM.

Albany's **Empire State Plaza** (☎ 518/474–2418) is a ¼-mi concourse with modern art and sculpture and a blend of government, business, and cultural buildings. The plaza includes the **Corning Tower,** with a free observation deck on the 42nd floor. Also on site is the **New York State Museum** (☎ 518/474–5877), where life-size exhibits depict the state's natural and cultural history. A new exhibit includes a reproduction of an Iroquois village with a full-size longhouse. Free guided tours of the adjacent **state capitol** (☎ 518/474–2418), including the Executive and Legislative Chambers, are conducted daily on the hour, except holidays.

What to See and Do with Children

Troy's **Junior Museum** (282 5th Ave., ☎ 518/235–2120) offers everything from constellation shows in a Sky Dome Theater to reproductions of log cabins. "Team Earth" is a new environmental exhibit featuring live animals.

Sports and the Outdoors

Fishing

The Hudson River estuary contains a remarkable variety of fish, most notably American shad, black bass, smallmouth and largemouth bass, and sturgeon. For information on licenses (required in fresh waters) and restrictions, as well as fishing hot spots and charts, contact the **New York State Department of Environmental Conservation** (21 S. Putt Corners Rd., New Paltz 12561, ☎ 914/256–3000; 50 Wolf Rd., Albany 12233, ☎ 518/457–3521; or Stony Kill Farm, Rte. 9D, Wappingers Falls 12590, ☎ 914/831–8780).

Golf

Beekman Country Club (11 Country Club Rd., Hopewell Junction, ☎ 914/226–7700) has 27 holes; **Dinsmore Golf Course** (Rte. 9, Staatsburg, ☎ 914/889–4751) and **James Baird State Park Golf Course** (Freedom Rd., Pleasant Valley, ☎ 914/452–1489) have 18.

Ski Areas

Cross-Country

Bear Mountain State Park (Bear Mountain 10911, ☎ 914/786–2701) has 5 mi of trails. **Clermont State Historic Site** (1 Clermont Ave., Germantown 12526, ☎ 518/537–4240) has 6 mi of trails. **Mills-Norrie State Park** (Old Post Rd., Staatsburg 12580, ☎ 914/889–4646 or 914/889–4111) has 6 mi of trails. **Olana State Historic Site** (RD 2, Hudson

12534, ☎ 518/828–0135) has 7 mi of trails. **Rockefeller State Park** (Rte. 117, North Tarrytown 10591, ☎ 914/631–1470) has 14 mi of trails.

Downhill

Catamount (Rte. 23, Hillsdale 12529, ☎ 518/325–3200) has a 1,000-ft vertical drop, five lifts, and 24 trails.

Dining and Lodging

For price ranges, see Charts 1 (B) and 2 (B) in On the Road with Fodor's.

Albany

DINING

★ **Ogden's.** On the ground floor of a 1903 brick-and-limestone building, Ogden's has two-story arched windows built into 30-ft-high ceilings. The menu focuses on Continental cuisine, including grilled Norwegian salmon, veal dishes, and pasta. *42 Howard St., ☎ 518/463–6605. AE, DC, MC, V. Closed Sun. No lunch Sat. $$$*

LODGING

Mansion Hill Inn. Albany's only downtown B&B is in an urban setting around the corner from the Executive Mansion. The three Civil War–era buildings have been completely renovated; the rooms are spacious, with cherry furniture and floral prints, and some have full kitchens and decks. *115 Philip St., 12202, ☎ 518/465–2038. 19 rooms. Facilities: restaurant. AE, D, DC, MC, V. $$$*

Bear Mountain

LODGING

Bear Mountain Inn. For more than 50 years, this chalet-style resort has been known for both its bucolic location (in Bear Mountain State Park on the shores of Hessian Lake) and its warm hospitality. There are rooms in the main inn and units in five lodges across the lake. *Rte. 9W, 10911, ☎ 914/786–2731. 60 rooms. Facilities: restaurant, lounge, outdoor pool, ice-skating, picnic grounds, hiking trails. AE, D, MC, V. $$*

Canaan

LODGING

Inn at Shaker Mill. This converted 1823 mill has a setting (woods, streams, and a waterfall outside your window), an interior (expert workmanship and Shaker antiques), and a host (Ingram Paperny—fascinating and friendly) that add up to an exceptional stop on your journey. *Cherry La., off Rte. 22, Canaan 12029, ☎ 518/794–9345, FAX 518/794–9344. 20 rooms. Facilities: swimming pond, sauna. MC, V. $$–$$$*

Cold Spring

LODGING

Olde Post Inn. This restored 1820 inn offers bed and breakfast in an Old World setting with such modern amenities as air-conditioning. Its stone tavern features jazz entertainment on weekends. *43 Main St., 10516, ☎ 914/265–2510. 5 rooms share 2 baths. Facilities: tavern, patio, garden. No credit cards. $$$*

Hopewell Junction

DINING AND LODGING

Le Chambord. Owner Roy Benich has brought his finely tuned sense of aesthetics and prodigious energies to every aspect of this 1863 Georgian mansion inn and restaurant. Nouvelle and classic French cuisine is served under antique Waterford crystal chandeliers or out on the flowered terrace. *2075 Rte. 52, 12533, ☎ 914/221–1941 or 800/274–1941. 25 rooms. AE, DC, MC, V. $$*

Hyde Park

DINING

Culinary Institute of America. The institute (*see* Exploring the Hudson Valley, *above*) has four public restaurants. **Escoffier** (*$$$*) features classic haute cuisine. **American Bounty** (*$$–$$$*) offers American regional fare. **Caterina de Medici** (*$$–$$$*) focuses on regional Italian cooking, both traditional and modern. **St. Andrew's Cafe** serves contemporary cuisine, from pizza to vegetarian dishes. *U.S. 9, ☎ 914/471–6608 (weekdays 9–5). Jacket advised in some rooms. AE, D, DC, MC, V. Closed school holidays and 1st 3 wks of July. $$*

Kingston

DINING

Skytop Steak and Seafood House. Panoramic views of the Hudson Valley are part of the attraction at this hilltop spot near the New York State Thruway. The menu features meats grilled over a charcoal pit and fresh lobster and seafood. *Rte. 28, ☎ 914/338–6161. AE, DC, MC, V. Dinner only except Sun. $$*

New Paltz

DINING AND LODGING

★ **Mohonk Mountain House.** On a lake amid 7,500 acres in the heart of the Shawangunk Mountains is this great resort with a stately Victorian feel. Room rates include three hearty American-style meals in the large, busy dining rooms and afternoon tea. Theme programs include mystery weekends (originated here in 1976), swing-dance weekends, and hikers' holidays. *Lake Mohonk 12561, ☎ 914/255–4500 or 800/772–6646. 276 rooms. Facilities: 3 dining rooms, fitness center, 6 tennis courts, golf course, beach, basketball court, croquet, lawn bowling, shuffleboard, softball, volleyball, horseback riding, carriage rides, 85 mi of hiking trails, nature preserve, cross-country skiing, ice-skating. AE, DC, MC, V. $$$*

Rhinebeck

DINING AND LODGING

★ **Beekman Arms.** This inn in the village center comprises 10 buildings, including smallish Colonial-style rooms in the original 1766 building and Victorian-style rooms in a mid-19th-century house a block away. All rooms have private baths and telephones; 22 have fireplaces. The inn's restaurant, the **Beekman 1766 Tavern,** serves American regional fare and incorporates the old taproom. *4 Mill St. (U.S. 9), 12572, ☎ 914/876–7077 (restaurant: ☎ 914/871–1766). 59 rooms. AE, DC, MC, V. $$*

West Point

LODGING

Hotel Thayer. On the grounds of the academy, this stately brick hotel steeped in history and tradition has been welcoming military and civilian guests for more than 60 years. Many guest rooms have views of the river and the West Point grounds. *U.S. 9W, 10996, ☎ 914/446–4731 or 800/247–5047. 197 rooms. Facilities: restaurant, lounge. AE, D, DC, MC, V. $$*

Woodstock

DINING

Artist's Grill. This charming restaurant 2½ mi from town is housed in a restored 150-year-old farmhouse. The menu emphasizes French country cuisine and fresh seafood. *Rte. 212, ☎ 914/679–5977. AE, DC, MC, V. Closed Mon.–Wed. Oct.–May. No lunch. $$*

Motels

Days Inn Colonie Mall (16 Wolf Rd., Albany 12205, ☎ 518/459–3600 or 800/325–2525), 165 rooms, health club, pool, Continental breakfast; *$$*. **Howard Johnson Lodge** (Rte. 9W, 416 Southern Blvd., Albany 12209, ☎ 518/462–6555 or 800/562–7253), 135 rooms, restaurant, lounge, exercise room, pool, sauna, indoor tennis courts, playground, laundry; *$$*. **Sheraton Civic Center Hotel** (40 Civic Center Plaza, 12601, ☎ 914/485–5300 or 800/325–3535), 213 rooms, restaurant, café, health club; *$$*. **Roosevelt Inn** (38 Albany Post Rd., Hyde Park 12538, ☎ 914/229–2443), 26 rooms, coffee shop (breakfast only), tennis, golf, cross-country skiing; *$–$$*.

The Arts and Nightlife

The **Empire Center at the Egg** (Madison Ave. and S. Swan St., Albany, ☎ 518/473–1845) and the **Palace Theater** (19 Clinton Ave., Albany, ☎ 518/465–4663) feature drama, dance, and musical events. Lively bars and clubs are found in some of the larger towns, including Nyack, New Paltz, Poughkeepsie, and Albany.

THE CATSKILLS

The Catskill Mountains have a beauty and variety disproportionate to their modest size. Just a two- or three-hour drive from New York City, the area offers streams for fly-fishing, paths for hiking, cliffs for rock-climbing, hills for skiing, and back roads for leisurely driving. Once known as the "borscht belt" for the resort complexes that catered to Jewish families from the city, the region now tends to attract wilderness lovers and craftspeople.

Tourist Information

Catskill: Association for Tourism Services (CATS; Box 449, Catskill 12414, ☎ 518/943–3223 or 800/355–2287). **Delaware County:** Chamber of Commerce (97 Main St., Delhi 13753, ☎ 800/642–4443). **Greene County:** Promotion Department (Box 527, Catskill 12414, ☎ 518/943–3223 or 800/355–2287). **Sullivan County:** Office of Public Information (100 North St., Box 5012, Monticello 12701, ☎ 914/794–3000, ext. 5010, or 800/882–2287).

Getting There

By Plane

Albany County Airport (*see* The Hudson Valley, *above*) is an hour's drive from the heart of the Catskills. **Oneonta Municipal Airport** (☎ 607/431–1076) is in the northwest corner of the region.

By Car

The northern Catskills can be reached off I–87 from Catskill (Rte. 23) and Kingston (Rte. 28). The resort region lies on both sides of Rte. 17 north from I–87 at Harriman or from I–84 at Middletown.

By Bus

Adirondack Trailways (☎ 800/858–8555) offers regular service to several Catskill communities, including Kingston, New Paltz, Phoenicia, Hunter, and Fleischmanns, from New York City and Albany. **Shortline** (☎ 800/631–8405) connects a half-dozen Sullivan County communities, including Bloomingburg, Monticello, and Wurtsboro, with New York City.

Exploring the Catskills

In the northeastern section of the Catskills is the actual village of **Catskill,** which has its share of museums and quaint buildings. Here the **Catskill Game Farm** is home to 2,000 birds and animals, including a large collection of rare hooved species, and has a petting zoo and a playground. *400 Game Farm Rd. (off Rte. 32),* ☎ *518/678–9595. Admission charged. Closed Nov.–Apr.*

In the area known as the High Peaks, Rte. 214 from **Phoenicia** north to the ski resort town of **Hunter** winds through **Stoney Clove,** a spectacular mountain cleft that has inspired countless tales of the supernatural. Another scenic route out of Phoenicia is across the Esopus River and south up lovely **Woodland Valley** to the well-marked trail to **Slide Mountain,** the highest peak in the Catskills.

Delaware County, newly discovered by big-city vacationers and second-home buyers, has gentler terrain than the High Peaks region. Fishermen prize the east and west branches of the Delaware River, and the county's more than 500 farms offer honey, eggs, cider, and maple syrup at numerous roadside stands. **Roxbury,** on Rte. 30, has a picture-perfect Main Street that Norman Rockwell would have loved.

What to See and Do with Children

Delaware & Ulster Rail Ride (Rte. 28, Arkville, ☎ 607/652–2821) runs a one-hour scenic route between Arkville and Fleischmanns. In Catskill, try **Peeling's Reptile Land** (Rte. 32, ☎ 518/678–3557), where children get to see snakes and lizards up close, or the **Ponderosa Ranch Fun Park** (Rte. 32, ☎ 518/678–9206), which has the region's largest go-kart track, as well as minigolf, batting cages, and game rooms.

Shopping

Shopping is a major diversion in the Catskills, with a scattering of auctions, flea markets, crafts fairs, antiques shops, and galleries. The Lower Catskills have a number of factory outlets and shopping villages. **Apollo Plaza** (E. Broadway, Rte. 17W, Monticello, ☎ 914/794–2010) is an enclosed mall with 30 outlet stores selling housewares, men's and women's apparel and jewelry, toys, gifts, and more at discounts of up to 70%.

Sports and the Outdoors

Canoeing

The 79-mi **Upper Delaware Scenic and Recreational River** is one of the finest streams for paddling in the region. For a list of trip planners and rental firms, contact the **Sullivan County Office of Public Information** (*see* Tourist Information, *above*).

Fishing

Trout are abundant in Catskill streams; smallmouth bass, walleye, and pickerel can be found in many lakes and in six reservoirs. For the "Catskill Fishing" brochure and map, write to **CATS** (*see* Tourist Information, *above*).

Golf

The region has nearly 50 golf courses, many of which are at the big resorts. For the "Golf Catskills" brochure, write to **CATS** (*see* Tourist Information, *above*).

Hiking

The New York State Department of Environmental Conservation (50 Wolf Rd., Albany 12233) puts out a brochure on the 200 mi of marked hiking trails through the **Catskill Forest Preserve.**

Tubing

Town Tinker (Bridge St., Phoenicia, ☎ 914/688–5553) rents tubes for beginner and advanced routes along the Esopus Creek between Shandaken and Mount Pleasant.

Spectator Sports

Horse Racing

Monticello Raceway (Rtes. 17 and 17B, Monticello, ☎ 914/794–4100), offers year-round harness racing.

Ski Areas

For information on area slopes and trails, contact **Ski the Catskills** (Box 135, Arkville 12406, ☎ 914/586–1944).

Cross-Country

Belleayre Mountain (*see* Downhill, *below*) has 5 mi of trails. **Mountain Trails at Hyer Meadows** in Tannersville (Box 198, Rte. 23A, 12485, ☎ 518/589–5361) has 20 mi.

Downhill

Downhill ski areas in the Catskills have snowmaking capabilities. **Belleayre Mountain** (Box 313, Highmount 12441, ☎ 914/254–5600), with 33 runs, eight lifts, and a 1,340-ft vertical drop, is the only state-run ski facility in the Catskills. **Hunter Mountain** (Box 295, Hunter 12442, ☎ 518/263–4223) has 48 runs, 14 lifts, and a 1,600-ft drop. **Ski Windham** (C.D. Lane Rd., Windham 12496, ☎ 518/734–4300) has 33 runs, seven lifts, and a 1,600-ft drop.

Dining and Lodging

While the region offers some outstanding food, the most inspiring aspect of its restaurants is often their setting. The Catskills are best known for mammoth resort hotels, but there are plenty of B&Bs and country inns that provide a personal touch, as well as ski-center condos and cabins in the woods. For price ranges, see Charts 1 (B) and 2 (B) in On the Road with Fodor's.

Big Indian

DINING

Jake Moon. The menu at this rustic country restaurant changes seasonally and features "Catskill Mountain cuisine"—fresh local produce, game, and fish. Large windows overlook the Big Indian valley. *Rte. 28, ☎ 914/254–5953. AE, D, DC, MC, V. $$*

Catskill

DINING

La Conca D'Oro. Twelve years ago chef-owner Alfonso Acampora brought his Italian culinary skills to the 19th-century town of Catskill. Fare includes elk, boar, and pheasant prepared with an Italian accent. *440 Main St., ☎ 518/943–3549. D, MC, V. Closed Tues. $$*

Elka Park

DINING AND LODGING

Redcoat's Return. The ambience of an English country inn is offered in the beautiful village of Platte Clove. Dinner, served in a room with a view of surrounding mountains or in the cozy library, might include Yorkshire pudding or steak-and-kidney pie. *Dale La., 12427, ☎ 518/589–6379. 14 rooms, 8 share bath. Facilities: breakfast, restaurant. AE, DC, MC, V. Inn closed Apr.–Memorial Day; restaurant closed Tues.–Thurs. Apr.–Memorial Day. $$–$$$*

Ellenville

DINING AND LODGING

★ **Nevele Hotel.** This legendary Catskills super-resort is set in five buildings on a woodsy, mountainous site with lakes and landscaping. The lobby is decorated in extravagant 1950s style with big bulky chairs, faux columns, and brass, but the rooms are strictly contemporary. The restaurant has a changing international menu to cater to convention guests, and big-name entertainers often perform here. *Nevele Rd., 12428, ☎ 914/647–6000 or 800/647–6000. 430 rooms. Facilities: restaurant, nightly entertainment, indoor and outdoor pools, golf course, 15 tennis courts, fitness center, ice rink, horseback riding, skiing, sledding, private lake, boating, fishing. AE, DC, MC, V. $$$*

Hunter

DINING AND LODGING

Scribner Hollow Lodge. There are 22 fireplaces in this ultramodern lodge, plus such theme rooms as Future World (sunken bath, waterfall, environmentally controlled bed chamber) and Hunting Lodge (Remington prints, sporty decor). The underground "grotto pool" has a cocktail bar and live entertainment on weekends. The restaurant overlooks the mountains; rates are MAP. *Rte. 23A, 12442, ☎ 518/263–4211 or 800/395–4683. 38 rooms. Facilities: restaurant, 2 pools, whirlpool, tennis court. AE, D, MC, V. $$$*

Kiamesha Lake

DINING AND LODGING

★ **Concord Resort Hotel.** One of the most enduring Catskill resorts, the Concord offers big-name entertainment, extensive sporting facilities, and nearby skiing. The hotel annually serves more than 2.5 million strictly kosher meals in dining rooms that can seat more than 3,000 people at a time (AP, EP, and MAP available). *Kiamesha Lake 12751, ☎ 914/794–4000 or 800/431–3850. 1,200 rooms. Facilities: 6 dining rooms, 3 nightclubs, health club, 2 pools, 3 golf courses, 40 indoor and outdoor tennis courts, horseback-riding trails, indoor-outdoor skating rink, volleyball, basketball, shuffleboard, toboggan run. AE, D, DC, MC, V. $$–$$$*

Kingston

DINING

Jake & Pepper's. The handsome chandeliered dining room with a burgundy-and-hunter-green color scheme specializes in aged beef. The lounge has a 40-ft oak-and-mahogany bar from the 1930s, and a raw bar with fresh oysters, clams, shrimp, and crab. *614 Broadway, ☎ 914/338–2600. AE, D, DC, MC, V. Closed Tues. $$*

Shandaken

DINING AND LODGING

L'Auberge. All the guest rooms in this French-style inn have been newly renovated and feature private baths and antiques. A former hunting lodge, the inn has a fireplace and a patio outside for drinks. The restaurant serves French bistro cuisine, with specialties from different provinces featured on weekends. Rates are MAP. *Rte. 42, 12480, ☎ 914/688–2223. 28 rooms with bath. AE, D, MC, V. $$*

Tannersville

DINING AND LODGING

Deer Mountain Inn. This circa-1900 mansion on a 15-acre wooded enclave is lushly packed with mountain ambience: moose heads, boar heads, bearskin rugs, paintings of European mountain villages, and heavy overstuffed furniture. The dining room, bracketed by two huge stone fireplaces, offers American fare—trout, veal, and seafood—with a European accent. *Rte. 25, 12485, ☎ 518/589–6268. 7 rooms. AE, MC, V. $$$*

Windham

DINING

★ **La Griglia.** Elegant country dining here features northern Italian cuisine. A house specialty is the *penne pepperata* (penne with sautéed sun-dried tomatoes, sweet red pepper, basil, and a whisper of light cream). The wine list may be one of the best in upstate New York. *Rte. 296, ☎ 518/734–4499. AE, DC. $$$*

DINING AND LODGING

★ **Thompson House.** Guests are remembered by their first names at this resort run by five generations of the same family for more than a century. Guest rooms, furnished with four-poster beds and antiques, are in the 1860s-era main house, the Victorian Spruce Cottage, and newer buildings. The restaurant serves Continental and American food from a changing menu. *Rte. 296, 12496, ☎ 518/734–4510. 100 rooms. Facilities: restaurant, heated pool, tennis, putting greens, golf adjacent. MC, V. Closed Nov. and Apr. $$*

Motels

Red Carpet Motor Inn (Rtes. 10 and 23, Stamford 12167, ☎ 607/652–7394 or 800/932–1090), 36 rooms, restaurant, lounge, pool, tennis court; *$$*. **Hunter Inn** (Rte. 23A, Hunter 12442, ☎ 518/263–3777) 42 rooms, exercise room, Continental breakfast; *$*.

The Arts and Nightlife

Several well-established regional organizations offer a full menu of performing and decorative arts year-round; in summer the cultural calendar is especially busy. The wide array of performances embraces music, theater, and dance, as well as film and literary series and changing art exhibits. Hunter has some lively nightspots during ski season and summer. The large resorts, such as the Concord and the Nevele (*see* Dining and Lodging, *above*), offer dancing and big-name acts.

SARATOGA SPRINGS AND THE NORTH COUNTRY

Saratoga Springs, about 30 mi north of Albany, is one of American high society's oldest summer playgrounds. The six-week Thoroughbred-racing season, starting in mid-July, is the high point of the year. Northwest of Saratoga, and in stark contrast, are the rugged mountains, immense forests, and abundant lakes and streams of the Adirondack Park, the largest park expanse in the United States outside Alaska. The North Country—anchored by the resort towns of Lake Placid and Lake George—hums with summer hikers and fall leaf-peepers, returning to life when the winter-sports enthusiasts descend.

Tourist Information

Greater Saratoga: Chamber of Commerce (494 Broadway, Saratoga Springs 12866, ☎ 518/584–3255). **Lake Placid:** Visitors Bureau

(Olympic Center, 12946, ☎ 518/523–2445 or 800/447–5224). **Saranac Lake:** Chamber of Commerce (30 Main St., 12983, ☎ 518/891–1990 or 800/347–1992).

Getting There

By Plane

The principal gateways are New York City (207 mi south of Lake George) and Montreal (177 mi north of Lake George). Other airports serving the region are in Albany, Syracuse, and Burlington, Vermont.

By Car

The primary route through the region is the Northway (I–87), which links Albany and Montreal.

By Train

Amtrak's (☎ 800/872–7245) *Adirondack* operates daily between New York and Montreal, with North Country stops in Saratoga Springs, Glens Falls, Whitehall, Fort Ticonderoga, Westport, and Plattsburgh.

By Bus

Adirondack Trailways (☎ 212/947–5300 or 800/225–6815) provides bus service to Saratoga Springs, Lake Placid, Lake George, Chestertown, Watertown, Bolton Landing (summer only), and many other towns throughout the region.

Exploring Saratoga Springs and the North Country

Saratoga Springs has been frequented for its medicinal springs since the late 18th century. In the late 19th century, it emerged as one of North America's principal resorts, both for the spa waters and for its gambling casino. It also became a horse-racing center in the 1890s, and August still brings crowds for the race meet and yearling sale.

Across from the **Saratoga Race Course** (*see* Spectator Sports, *below*), site of the renowned horse races (and listed on the National Register of Historic Places), is the **National Museum of Racing.** Its centerpiece is the Hall of Fame, which has video clips of races featuring the horses and jockeys enshrined here. *Union Ave., ☎ 518/584–0400. Admission charged.*

Also on Union Avenue is **Yaddo** (☎ 518/587–4886), a highly regarded retreat for artists and writers. The 400-acre grounds and rose garden are open to the public.

The **National Museum of Dance** features rotating exhibits on the history and development of the art form, as well as the Hall of Fame, honoring dance luminaries. The studios allow visitors to watch or participate in a dance class. *99 S. Broadway, ☎ 518/584–2225. Admission charged. Closed Labor Day–Memorial Day; Mon.*

Housed in **Canfield Casino**—the only building in downtown's Congress Park, off Broadway—is the **Historical Society of Saratoga Springs,** with a museum devoted to Saratoga's colorful history as a gambling center, a contemporary art gallery, and a museum store. *☎ 518/584–6920. Admission charged. Closed Jan.*

In the Adirondack Mountain range, the 6-million-acre **Adirondack Park** encompasses 1,000 mi of rivers and more than 2,500 lakes and ponds. The southern sections are more developed, while the High Peaks region in the north-central sector offers the greatest variety of wilderness activities. *Visitor Interpretive Centers: Paul Smiths (north of Saranac Lake),* ☎ *518/327–3000; Newcomb,* ☎ *518/582–2000.*

Lake George, 40 mi north of Saratoga, is a tourist town catering to families, with amusement parks, souvenir shops, and miniature golf. Cruises from the town dock are extremely popular from May through October; contact **Lake George Shoreline Cruises** (☎ 518/668–4644) and the **Lake George Steamboat Company** (☎ 518/668–5777). If you have an interest in the French and Indian War, you will want to visit **Ft. William Henry** (☎ 518/668–5471), reconstructed on the original 1755 site at the foot of Lake George.

Just south of town is **Great Escape Fun Park,** the North Country's largest amusement park. *U.S. 9,* ☎ *518/792–3500. Admission charged. Closed Sept.–May.*

Overlooking Blue Mountain Lake, the **Adirondack Museum** has a day's worth of exhibits on the history, culture, and crafts of the region. *Rte. 30,* ☎ *518/352–7311. Admission charged. Closed mid-Oct.–Memorial Day.*

Lake Placid, the hub of the northern Adirondacks, has a Main Street lined with shops and motels, two lakes in its backyard, and the **winter Olympics facilities** all around it. The Olympic Ice Arena and speed-skating oval are right in the center of town, the ski jump is 2 mi out, Whiteface Mountain (scene of the downhill competitions) is a 10-minute drive away on Rte. 86, and the bobsled run at Mt. Van Hoevenberg on Rte. 73 is 15 minutes away. All sites are open to the public.

In summer, you can ascend 4,876-ft **Whiteface Mountain** (☎ 800/462–6236; admission charged) either by chairlift or by car on Veterans Memorial Highway. A short walk to the summit provides a superb view: Lake Placid in one direction, Lake Champlain in another, and the High Peaks to the south. Go on a clear day if possible.

Self-guided tours can be made of the **John Brown Farm,** home and burial place of the famed abolitionist, who operated the farm for free blacks. *Off Rte. 73 past the Olympic ski jumps,* ☎ *518/523–3900. Closed late Oct.–late May.*

The serenity and mountain air of **Saranac Lake** (elevation: 1,600 ft) made it a famous health resort for the tubercular in the late 19th century. Ten miles west of Lake Placid, it is today the jumping-off point for canoe trips (*see* Sports and the Outdoors, *below*). Much of the lake is part of the **St. Regis Canoe Area,** which is off-limits to powerboats.

Cranberry Lake is the largest body of water in the relatively unexplored northwestern corner of the park. Several long and gentle hiking trails wind through the area around the lake, and the quick and easy hike to a lookout from Bear Mountain provides a sweeping view of the lake and the unspoiled countryside beyond.

There is much more to the region called the **Thousand Islands** than the island-studded area of the St. Lawrence River. The name usually refers to an area defined by the Adirondacks to the east, the St. Lawrence to the north, and Lake Ontario to the west. Most of the region is flat or rolling farmland, but the economy is heavily dependent on the St. Lawrence Seaway. The scenic **Seaway Trail,** a combination of Rtes. 37, 12, and 12E, follows the river and the Lake Ontario shore. In **Massena,** huge cargo vessels pass through the **Eisenhower Lock;** call ahead (☎ 315/769–2422) to find out what time a ship is scheduled to pass through.

What to See and Do with Children

The area has several amusement parks, the largest of which is **Great Escape Fun Park** (*see* Exploring Saratoga Springs and the North Country, *above*). Those not big on hiking can sample the beauty of the Adirondack region at **Ausable Chasm** (☎ 518/834–7454) on U.S. 9 just north of Keeseville; **High Falls Gorge** (☎ 518/946–2278) off Rte. 86 near Wilmington; and **Natural Stone Bridge and Caves** (☎ 518/494–2283) at Exit 26 off I–87 near Pottersville.

Shopping

The region's maple syrup and sharp Cheddar cheese make good gifts. The **ANCA Crafts Center** (Lake Placid Center for the Arts, Lake Placid, ☎ 518/523–2062) is a facility where year-round more than 275 local artisans show their wares. **Blue Mountain Lake** and **Lake Placid** are good bets for crafts hunting. Look for baskets and pottery with pinecones, unique to the area; you'll also find an array of jewelry, leather work, and quilting.

Sports and the Outdoors

Middle Earth Expeditions (Cascade Rd., Lake Placid 12946, ☎ 518/523–9572) leads tours and provides guides for individuals or groups in canoeing, white-water rafting, fishing, and backpacking. **All Seasons Outfitters** (168 Lake Flower Ave., Saranac Lake, ☎ 518/891–6159) sells and rents gear for canoeing, skiing, snowshoeing, and hiking.

Biking

Roadside signs mark several bike routes, most quite hilly, that wind through the North Country. For a map of routes in the Saranac Lake area, contact the **Saranac Lake Chamber of Commerce** (*see* Tourist Information, *above*).

Canoeing

The 170-mi **Raquette River** and the **St. Regis Canoe Area,** east of Saranac Lake, are among the best and most popular canoe routes in the North Country.

Fishing

Brook and lake trout are taken year-round on the lakes and streams of the North Country. Licenses can be obtained at town or county clerk offices, sporting-goods stores, and outfitters.

Golf

Among the more challenging courses are those at the **Whiteface Resort** (Whiteface Inn Rd., Lake Placid, ☎ 518/523–2551; 18 holes), the **Omni Sagamore Resort** (Lake Shore Dr., Bolton Landing, ☎ 518/644–9400; 18 holes), and the **Saranac Inn Golf Club** (Upper Saranac Lake, ☎ 518/891–1402; 18 holes).

Hiking

The most popular area for hiking is the High Peaks region, accessible from the Lake Placid area in the north, Keene and Keene Valley in the east, and Newcomb in the south. For more information, contact the **Adirondack Mountain Club** (ADK, Box 867, Lake Placid 12946, ☎ 518/523–3441; RR 3, Box 3055, Lake George 12845, ☎ 518/668–4447).

Rafting

Hudson River Rafting Co. (1 Main St., North Creek 12853, ☎ 800/888–7238) offers day trips on the Hudson, the Sacandaga, and the Black River from April to October.

Spectator Sports

For information on Lake Placid summer and winter athletic competitions, contact the **Olympic Regional Development Authority** (☎ 518/523–1655 or 800/462–6236). Events include concerts, ski jumping, and figure-skating shows.

Horse Racing

The six-week Thoroughbred-racing season starts in mid-July at **Saratoga Race Course** (Union Ave., Saratoga Springs, ☎ 518/584–6200). **Saratoga Harness** (Nelson Ave., Saratoga Springs, ☎ 518/584–2110) has harness- and Thoroughbred-racing March–November.

Ski Areas

Cross-Country

Mt. Van Hoevenberg on Rte. 73 has 50 km of groomed tracks, which connect with the **Jackrabbit Trail,** a 33-mi network of ski trails through the High Peaks region connecting Lake Placid, Saranac Lake, and Paul Smiths. For information and conditions, contact **Adirondack Ski Touring Council** (Box 843, Lake Placid 12946, ☎ 518/523–1365).

Downhill

Whiteface Mountain Ski Center (Wilmington 12997, 8 mi east of Lake Placid, ☎ 518/946–2223) has 65 runs, 10 lifts, a 3,216-ft vertical drop, and snowmaking.

Dining and Lodging

Saratoga is indisputably the North Country's culinary champion in quality and variety, with Lake Placid a distant second. Elsewhere expect large portions, home cooking, and a rustic atmosphere. Lodging runs the gamut from roadside motels to resorts. For information on B&Bs, contact the **Bed and Breakfast Association of Saratoga, Lake George, and Gore Mountain Region** (Box 99, Lake Luzerne 12846, ☎ 518/696–9912). For price ranges, see Charts 1 (B) and 2 (B) in On the Road with Fodor's.

Bolton Landing

DINING

★ **Omni Sagamore Resort.** Each of the four dining rooms at this island resort has its own atmosphere and cuisine, ranging from the formal, slightly nouvelle touches of the Trillium to the hearty burgers and steaks of Mr. Brown's Pub. *Lake Shore Dr., ☎ 518/644–9400. Reservations required at all but Mr. Brown's Pub. Jacket required at Trillium. AE, D, DC, MC, V. No lunch at Trillium. $$$*

Chestertown

DINING AND LODGING

★ **Friends Lake Inn.** Surrounded by forest, this traditional Adirondack lodge has a gourmet restaurant with an award-winning wine list. Many of the guest rooms have their own Jacuzzi, set in a window alcove overlooking the lake. *Friends Lake Rd., 12817, ☎ 518/494–4751. 13 rooms. MC, V. $$–$$$*

Lake Placid

DINING

Artist's Cafe. This popular spot has an enclosed lakeside deck and a cozy dining room and bar. Seafood, steaks, hearty soups, and imaginative sandwich combinations headline the menu. The paintings, by local artists, are for sale. *1 Main St.,* ☎ *518/523–9493. AE, D, DC, MC, V. $*

DINING AND LODGING

Lake Placid Lodge. Originally a rustic lodge built before the turn of the century, this intimate hotel has been renovated and has rooms and suites furnished with antiques and crafts by Adirondack artists. French cuisine is served in a dining room with a panoramic view of Lake Placid and Whiteface Mountain. *Whiteface Inn Rd., Box 550, 12946,* ☎ *518/523–2573. 22 rooms. Facilities: restaurant, lounge, beach, boating. AE, DC, MC, V. $$$–$$$$*

Saranac Lake

DINING

Red Fox. Locals heartily endorse this restaurant's consistently good American food and generous libations. Each of the four intimate rooms has a fireplace, wood paneling, and subdued lighting. *Rte. 3W, Tupper Lake Rd.,* ☎ *518/891–2127. MC, V. Closed Mon. and Tues. $$*

DINING AND LODGING

The Point. Onetime home of William Avery Rockefeller, this all-inclusive, elegantly rustic inn is the Adirondacks' most exclusive retreat. It is operated in the manner of a sophisticated private home with no commercial overtones, and guests are required to dress for dinner. *HCR 1, Box 65, 12983,* ☎ *518/891–5678 or 800/255–3530. 11 rooms. Facilities: restaurant, lounge, open bar, game room, swimming, sailing, cross-country skiing. AE. $$$$*

Saratoga Springs

DINING

★ **Eartha's Kitchen.** This small bistro is a local favorite, especially for the mesquite-grilled seafood dishes from the ever-changing, eclectic menu. The cinnamon-bread pudding with brandy-cream sauce is a house specialty. *60 Court St.,* ☎ *518/583–0602. Reservations required. AE, DC, MC, V. No lunch. $$*

LODGING

Adelphi Hotel. This downtown Saratoga showplace is opulent, extravagant, and fun. *365 Broadway, 12866,* ☎ *518/587–4688. 35 rooms. AE, MC, V. $$–$$$*

Warrensburg

LODGING

Bent Finial Manor. For three years, Patricia Scully searched for the perfect house in which to create a most elegant bed-and-breakfast. She found it in this 1904 Victorian mansion filled with rich woods, unique fireplaces, etched and stained-glass windows, and antiques. *194 Main St., 12885,* ☎ *518/623–3308. 5 rooms. No credit cards. $$*

Motels

Holiday Inn SunSpree Resort (1 Olympic Dr., Lake Placid 12946, ☎ 518/523–2556), 209 rooms, 2 restaurants, indoor pool, tennis, 9-hole putting green, health club, meeting facilities; *$$–$$$.* **Blue Spruce Motel** (Main St., Box 604, Old Forge 13420, ☎ 315/369–3817), 13 rooms; *$$.* **Days Inn of Lake George** (Rte. 9, Box 3202, Lake George 12845, ☎ 518/793–3196 or 800/325–2525), 91 rooms, restaurant, indoor pool, valet service; *$$.* **Alpine Country Motel** (HCR 2, Box 12F, Rte. 86, Wilmington [5 mi from Lake Placid] 12997, ☎ 518/946–2263), 15 rooms, restaurant, pool; *$.* **Empress Motel** (Rte. 29E, 177 Broadway, Schuylerville 12871, ☎ 518/695–3231 or 800/261–4101), 12 rooms; *$.*

Campgrounds

Adirondak Loj Wilderness Campground (Box 867, Lake Placid 12946, ☎ 518/523–3441) provides information about camping throughout the High Peaks region and operates a campground around Heart Lake with 34 tent sites and 13 lean-tos, water, no gas or electric, picnic table, seasonal showers, and toilets. **KOA Lake Placid–Whiteface Mountain** (HCR 2, Box 38, Fox Farm Rd., Wilmington 12997, ☎ 518/946–7878) has 90 tent sites and 144 RV sites, water and electric, hot showers, toilets, and laundry.

The Arts

Blue Mountain Lake (☎ 518/352–7715) and **Lake Placid** (☎ 518/523–2512) present concerts, dramas, films, and demonstrations of arts and crafts. The **Saratoga Performing Arts Center** (☎ 518/587–3330) hosts the New York City Opera, the New York City Ballet, the Philadelphia Orchestra, and Newport Jazz Festival–Saratoga, as well as big-name pop stars from June to September.

ELSEWHERE IN THE STATE

Leatherstocking Country and the Finger Lakes

Getting There

The Leatherstocking region is 200–300 mi from New York City via the New York State Thruway and Rte. 28 from Kingston. I–90 runs east–west through both Leatherstocking Country and the Finger Lakes, connecting Albany with Buffalo. I–88 runs northeast–southwest, leading to Binghamton.

What to See and Do

The early Yankees in their leather leggings gave the region its nickname; it is quintessential rural America, with gently rolling countryside, community chicken barbecues, and tree-shaded small towns. **Cooperstown** is home to the **National Baseball Hall of Fame,** where displays, paintings, and audiovisual presentations honor the heroes, recall great moments, and trace the history of the game. *Main St.,* ☎ *607/547–7200. Admission charged.*

Binghamton has the **Roberson Museum and Science Center** (30 Front St., ☎ 607/772–0660), a complex of museums, a planetarium, and a theater; and the wooded **Ross Park Zoo** (60 Morgan Rd. and 185 Park Ave., ☎ 607/724–5461), where animals (including tigers and a timber-wolf pack) live in natural environments. You can relive the old days of canal transport, including a ride in a horse-drawn canal boat, at **Erie Canal Village** (Rte. 49W, Rome, ☎ 315/337–3999), a reconstructed circa-1840 village.

The 11 **Finger Lakes,** from Conesus Lake south of Rochester to Otisco Lake near Syracuse, offer waterfalls, gorges, and diverse terrain. The region is studded with vineyards, and local wineries—the **Taylor Wine Co.** (Country Rd. 88, south of Hammondsport, ☎ 607/569–6111) is the area's largest—are open for tours and tastings, most from May to October, some year-round.

Rochester is the headquarters of the **Eastman Kodak Company.** The **George Eastman House,** onetime home of the company founder and photographic innovator, now houses the **International Museum of Photography,** the world's largest museum devoted to photographic art and technology. *900 East Ave., ☎ 716/271–3361. Admission charged. Closed Mon.*

Rochester was also home to **Susan B. Anthony,** whose **house** (17 Madison St., ☎ 716/235–6124) is furnished in the style of the mid-1800s. It was here that the 19th-century women's-rights advocate wrote *The History of Woman Suffrage.*

In **Corning,** the **Corning Museum of Glass** contains a world-class collection of glass, as well as a time-line exhibit describing 3,500 years of glass-making, a library covering everything ever written about glass, and a tour of the Steuben glass factory. *Off Rte. 17, ☎ 607/974–8229. Admission charged.*

Ithaca, at the tip of Cayuga Lake, is the home of **Cornell University** and the starting point for the **Cayuga Wine Trail.** The town is more spectacular than most in the Finger Lakes because of the deep gorges and more than 100 waterfalls that lace it.

About 5 mi west of the north end of Cayuga Lake is **Seneca Falls,** where, on July 18, 1848, 300 people attended America's first women's-rights convention, held at the **Wesleyan Methodist Chapel** (126 Falls St.).

For more information, contact the **Cooperstown Chamber of Commerce** (31 Chestnut St., 13326, ☎ 607/547–9983); **Leatherstocking Country, NY** (327 N. Main St., Herkimer 13350, ☎ 315/866–1500 or 800/233–8778); and the **Finger Lakes Association** (309 Lake St., Penn Yan 14527, ☎ 315/536–7488 or 800/548–4386).

Buffalo, Chautauqua, and Niagara Falls

Getting There

Access from the east, west, and south is primarily via I–90, the New York State Thruway.

What to See and Do

Buffalo is a city of Victorian elegance, with many churches and strongly ethnic neighborhoods. The **Albright–Knox Art Gallery** (1285 Elmwood Ave., ☎ 716/882–8700) has a superb collection of contemporary art.

The 50-mi drive from **Silver Creek** to **Ripley,** along the shores of Lake Erie, is known as the **Chautauqua Wine Trail,** and is sprinkled with five wineries and numerous farm stands and antiques shops.

Niagara Falls, the most accessible and famous waterfall in the world, is actually three cataracts: the American and Bridal Veil Falls, in New York, and the Horseshoe Falls, in Ontario, Canada. More than 750,000 gallons of water flow each second in the summer. For a good orientation to the falls, stop at the Niagara Visitor's Center in the **Niagara Reservation State Park** (Prospect Park, Niagara Falls 14303, ☎ 716/278–1701), the oldest state park in the nation. **Goat Island** provides the closest view of the American falls; cross to the Canadian side for the best view of Horseshoe Falls. The famous ***Maid of the Mist*** boat ride lets you view the falls from the water.

For more information, contact the **Greater Buffalo Convention and Visitors Bureau** (107 Delaware Ave., Buffalo 14202, ☎ 716/852–0511 or 800/283–3256), the **Chautauqua County Vacationland Association** (4 N. Erie St., Mayville 14757, ☎ 716/753–4304 or 800/242–4569), and the **Niagara Falls Official Information Center** (4th and Niagara Sts., 14301, ☎ 716/284–2000 or 800/338–7890).

Dining

For price ranges, see Chart 1 (B) On the Road with Fodor's.

Red Coach Inn. With a spectacular view of the upper rapids, this 1923 inn has an old-England atmosphere, plus wood-burning fireplaces and an outdoor patio for summer dining. Specialties include prime rib, Boston scrod, and seafood-sausage mornay. *2 Buffalo Ave., Niagara Falls, ☎ 716/282–1459. AE, D, DC, MC, V. $$–$$$*

Top of the Falls. If you like the feeling of being on top of the Falls, stop in here for the usual luncheon fare. *Goat Island, Niagara Falls, ☎ 716/285–3316. AE, D, DC, MC, V. Closed Nov.–Apr. No dinner. $$*

Lodging

For price ranges, see Chart 2 (B) in On the Road with Fodor's.

Days Inn Falls View. A longtime landmark, this bustling property recently underwent a much-needed renovation. The top floors, with views of the upper rapids, are best. *201 Rainbow Blvd., Niagara Falls 14303, ☎ 716/285–9321. 200 rooms. Facilities: dining room, cocktail lounge, games room, gift shop. AE, D, DC, MC, V. $$$*

Coachman Motel. Just three blocks from the Convention Center and the Falls, this motel represents one of the area's best values. *523 3rd St., Niagara Falls 14301, ☎ 716/285–2295. 18 rooms. AE, D, DC, MC, V. $*

RHODE ISLAND

Updated by Katherine Imbrie

Capital	Providence
Population	1,003,464
Motto	Hope
State Bird	Rhode Island Red
State Flower	Violet

Visitor Information

Rhode Island Department of Economic Development, Tourism Division (7 Jackson Walkway, Providence 02903, ☎ 401/277–2601 or 800/556–2484). **Greater Providence:** Convention and Visitors Bureau (30 Exchange Terr., 02903, ☎ 401/274–1636). **Newport County:** Convention and Visitors Bureau (23 America's Cup Ave., Newport 02840, ☎ 401/849–8048 or 800/326–6030). **South County:** Tourism Council (4808 Tower Hill Rd., Wakefield 02879, ☎ 401/789–4422 or 800/548–4662).

Scenic Drives

With 400 mi of shoreline, coastal scenes are Rhode Island's forte. The western coastline from Watch Hill to Narragansett along **Rtes. 1 and 1A** (with a detour down to Jerusalem and Galilee) takes you past state parks, forest areas, vast stretches of sandy beaches, and the marshes of Point Judith Pond. And nothing compares with the grand mansions along **Newport's Bellevue Avenue.**

National and State Parks

Rhode Island has no national parks, but it does have 37 state parks and recreational grounds, most of which are along the south coast between Westerly and Jamestown. **Burlingame State Park, Charlestown Breachway, Fishermen's Memorial State Park, George Washington Camping Area,** and the **Ninegret Conservation Area** allow camping. For information about the state parks, contact the Department of Economic Development (*see* Visitor Information, *above*).

AROUND RHODE ISLAND

Coastal Rhode Island is undervisited compared with other parts of New England, though not for lack of appeal: Some of its white-sand beaches rival Cape Cod's best, and a diversity of coastal environments makes for enjoyable drives (*see* Scenic Drives, *above*). Newport, with its grandiose mansions, is lively on both land and water. Providence, the state capital and an Ivy League college town, is rejuvenating its historic heritage.

Getting There

By Plane

The **Theodore Francis Green State Airport** (☎ 401/737–4000), 3 mi northeast of Warwick and 5 mi south of Providence, is served by major U.S. airlines and regional carriers. **Newport State Airport** (☎ 401/846–2200) is 3 mi northeast of Newport.

By Car

I–95 cuts diagonally across the state and is the fastest route to Providence from Boston, coastal Connecticut, and New York City. I–195 links Providence with New Bedford and Cape Cod. U.S. 1 follows the coast east from Connecticut before turning north to Providence.

By Train

Amtrak (☎ 800/872–7245) stops at Westerly, Kingston, and Providence's Union Station (100 Gaspee St.).

By Bus

Greyhound Lines (☎ 800/231–2222) and **Bonanza Bus Lines** (☎ 401/751–8800) link northeastern cities with the **Providence Bus Terminal** (Bonanza Way, off I–95 Exit 25). **Rhode Island Public Transit Authority** (☎ 401/781–9400 or 401/847–0209; in RI, 800/662–5088) provides local transportation in Providence and some service to other parts of the state.

By Ferry

Interstate Navigation Co. (☎ 401/783–4613) operates car ferries from Providence's India Street Pier to Newport and Block Island and from Point Judith's Galilee State Pier to Block Island. Reservations are required for cars, and service is irregular in the off-season.

Exploring Rhode Island

The South Coast

Watch Hill is a pretty Victorian-era resort town, with miles of beautiful beaches, a number of Native American settlements, and an active fishing port. On Bay Street is a **statue of Ninigret,** a 17th-century chief of the Rhode Island branch of the Niantic tribe. Nearby is the **Flying Horse Carousel,** built in about 1867 and the oldest merry-go-round in America. *Bay St., no ☎. Admission charged. Closed Labor Day–June 15.*

Ocean House (2 Bluff Ave., ☎ 401/348–8161) is one of several Victorian-era hotels in this part of Watch Hill. A walk to the end of Bay Street and a left into Fort Road will take you in the direction of the path (at the end of Fort Road) to **Napatree Point,** one of the best long beach walks in the state.

Charlestown is a resort filled with summer cottages and much history of the Narragansett Indians, native to the area. Its **Indian Church** is the last of three built in Rhode Island. The **Indian Burial Ground,** resting place of the Narragansett tribe, is on Narrow Lane, just north of U.S. 1.

U.S. 1 brings you to **South Kingstown,** an area made up of many small Colonial villages, full of crafts shops and galleries. It is also home to the **University of Rhode Island** and rowdy **Matunuck Beach.**

In the village of **Wakefield** is the old Washington County Jail, built in 1792, which now houses the **Pettaquamscutt Historical Society.** Here you can see jail cells and rooms from the Colonial period, a Colonial garden, and changing exhibits. *1348 Kingstown Rd., ☎ 401/783–1328. Closed Mon., Wed., Fri., Sun.; Nov.–Apr.*

Narragansett was a posh resort in the late 19th century. At Sprague Park is the **Narragansett Indian Monument.** The 23-ft monument is made from a single piece of wood, the trunk of a giant Douglas fir.

Galilee is one of the busiest fishing ports on the East Coast and where you catch the ferry to Block Island. The village has several excellent seafood restaurants. Nearby on Ocean Road are beaches and, at land's end, the **Point Judith Lighthouse** (☎ 401/789–0444), open during daylight hours. Drive north through the village of **Wickford** to the intersection of Rte. 1A and U.S. 1; take U.S. 1 north and turn right onto

Richard Smith Drive for **Smith's Castle,** built in 1678 and the site of many orations by Roger Williams, Rhode Island's most famous historical figure. ☎ *401/294–3521. Admission charged. Closed Mon.–Wed., Oct.–Apr.*

Newport

Bounded on three sides by water, **Newport** is one of the great sailing cities of the world. It is also host to world-class jazz, blues, folk, and classical music festivals, as well as international tennis tournaments.

Newport's first age of prosperity was in the late 1700s, and many homes and shops built in that era still stand in the Colonial section of the city. In the 19th century, Newport became a summer playground for America's wealthiest families.

A walk around **Colonial Newport**—the northwestern section of the city, clustered around the harbor—begins at the 1748 **Hunter House,** at 54 Washington Street. The carved pineapple over the doorway is a symbol of hospitality. ☎ *401/847–1000. Admission charged. Closed weekdays Apr. and Oct.*

Thames (pronounced "Thaymz") Street is the main street of Colonial Newport. Continue south on Thames to Washington Square. The **Brick Market,** built in 1760, was designed by Peter Harrison, who was also responsible for the city's Touro Synagogue and the Redwood Library. The building was first used as a theater, then as a town hall; today it's the center of a shopping area with some 40 stores.

Facing the market on Washington Square is the **Old Colony House.** Built in 1739, it was the headquarters of the Colonial and state governments, and from its balcony the Declaration of Independence was read to Newporters. ☎ *401/846–2980. Tours by appointment.*

Newport's oldest house, the **Wanton-Lyman-Hazard House,** displays a "two-room" plan typical of the time. As well as a Colonial garden, it offers demonstrations of 18th-century cooking. *17 Broadway,* ☎ *401/846–0813. Admission charged. Closed Sun.–Mon. Oct.–mid-June.*

On Marlborough Street is the **White Horse Tavern** (☎ 401/849–3600). In operation since 1687, the White Horse claims to be the oldest tavern in America, and its cozy yet elegant tables epitomize Newport's Colonial charm.

On the same corner stands the **Friends Meetinghouse,** built in 1699 and the oldest Quaker meeting house in America. *29 Farewell St.,* ☎ *401/846–0813. Tours by appointment.*

South, across Washington Square, on Touro Street, is the site of the oldest surviving synagogue in the country. **Touro Synagogue** (85 Touro St., ☎ 401/847–4794), dedicated in 1763, is very simple on the outside but elaborate within.

At 82 Touro Street is the headquarters of the **Newport Historical Society,** departure point for walking tours. Its museum features a large collection of Newport memorabilia, furniture, and maritime items. ☎ *401/846–0813. Closed Sat.–Mon.*

South of Washington Square, at the corner of Spring and Church streets, is **Trinity Church** (☎ 401/846–0660), built in 1724. The three-tier wineglass pulpit inside is the only one of its kind in America.

East along Church Street is the 1748 **Redwood Library,** the oldest library in continuous use in the United States. Although the building is made of wood, the original exterior paint was mixed with sand to make

Newport

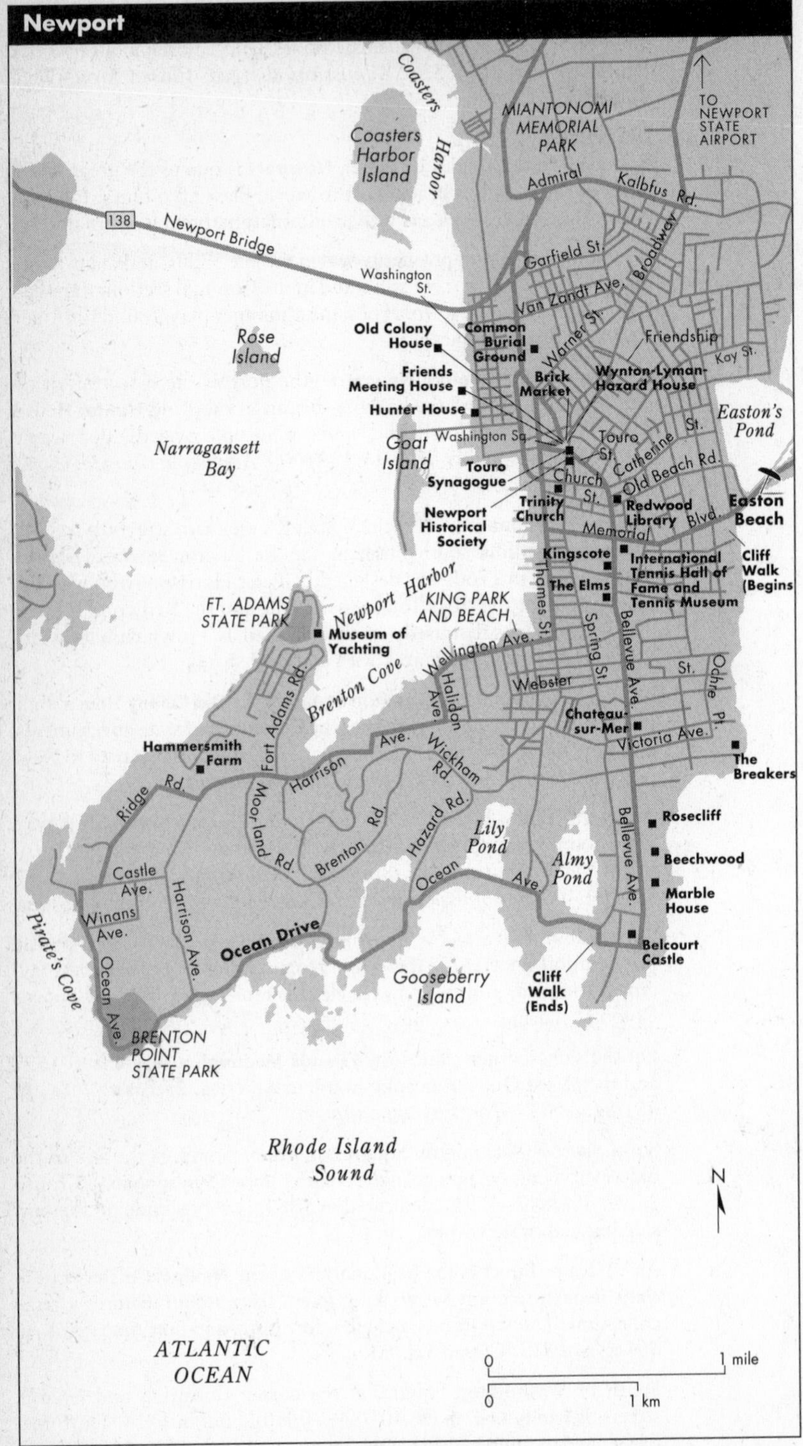
Coasters Harbor
Coasters Harbor Island
MIANTONOMI MEMORIAL PARK
TO NEWPORT STATE AIRPORT
Admiral
Kalbfus Rd.
138
Newport Bridge
Garfield St.
Broadway
Washington St.
Van Zandt Ave.
Rose Island
Old Colony House
Common Burial Ground
Warner St.
Friendship
Kay St.
Friends Meeting House
Brick Market
Wynton-Lyman-Hazard House
Hunter House
Easton's Pond
Narragansett Bay
Goat Island
Washington Sq.
Touro St.
Catherine St.
Old Beach Rd.
Touro Synagogue
Church St.
Trinity Church
Redwood Library
Easton Beach
Newport Historical Society
Memorial Blvd.
Kingscote
International Tennis Hall of Fame and Tennis Museum
Cliff Walk (Begins
The Elms
Thames St.
FT. ADAMS STATE PARK
Newport Harbor
KING PARK AND BEACH
Museum of Yachting
Spring St.
Bellevue Ave.
Wellington Ave.
Brenton Cove
Halidon Ave.
Webster St.
Ochre Pt.
Fort Adams Rd.
Chateau-sur-Mer
Victoria Ave.
Hammersmith Farm
Ave.
Wickham Rd.
The Breakers
Harrison
Ridge Rd.
Moor land Rd.
Brenton Rd.
Hazard Rd.
Lily Pond
Rosecliff
Beechwood
Almy Pond
Castle Ave.
Harrison Ave.
Ocean Ave.
Marble House
Winans Ave.
Ocean Drive
Belcourt Castle
Pirate's Cove
Gooseberry Island
Cliff Walk (Ends)
Ocean Ave.
BRENTON POINT STATE PARK
Rhode Island Sound
N
ATLANTIC OCEAN
0
1 mile
0
1 km

it resemble stone. The library houses a collection of paintings by early American artists. *50 Bellevue Ave., ☏ 401/847–0292. Closed Sun.*

South on Bellevue are the **Newport Art Museum and Art Association** (76 Bellevue Ave., ☏ 401/848–8200), with exhibits of Rhode Island art past and present, and the **International Tennis Hall of Fame and Tennis Museum** (194 Bellevue Ave., ☏ 401/849–3990), housed in a magnificent Stanford White building, the Newport Casino.

Six Newport mansions are maintained by the **Preservation Society of Newport County** (☏ 401/847–1000). A combination ticket gives you a discount on individual admission prices. Each mansion provides a guided tour that lasts about an hour.

Kingscote (closed Nov.–Mar.; weekdays Apr., Oct.), on Bowery Street, was built in 1839 for a plantation owner from Savannah, Georgia. It is furnished with antique furniture, glass, and Oriental art and has a number of Tiffany windows.

South on Bellevue Avenue is the **The Elms** (closed weekdays Nov.–Mar.), one of Newport's most graceful mansions. Classical in design, it was built for a coal baron at the turn of the century. A broad lawn, fountains, and formal gardens surround it.

Chateau-sur-Mer (closed weekdays Nov.–Mar.), the first of Bellevue Avenue's stone mansions, is modest compared with the opulence that came later. Built in 1852 and enlarged by Richard Morris Hunt for a China-trade tycoon, the mansion houses a toy collection; in December it is decorated on a Victorian Christmas theme.

On Ochre Point Avenue is **The Breakers** (closed weekdays Nov.–Mar.), built in 1893 for Cornelius Vanderbilt II and his small family. The 70-room showplace took more than 2,500 workmen two years to complete and required 40 servants to keep it running.

Return to Bellevue Avenue for **Rosecliff** (closed Nov.–Mar.), built in 1902. Modeled on the Grand Trianon at Versailles, this 40-room mansion includes a heart-shaped staircase designed by Stanford White. Rosecliff has appeared in several movies, including *The Great Gatsby.*

At **Beechwood,** built for the Astors, actors in period costume play the parts of family members including Mrs. Astor, the belle of New York and Newport society; servants; and household guests. *580 Bellevue Ave., ☏ 401/846–3772. Admission charged. Closed Mon.–Thurs. Feb.–Apr.*

The last of the Preservation Society's Bellevue Avenue properties is **Marble House** (closed Nov.–Dec.; weekdays Jan.–Mar.). With its extravagant gold ballroom, this palace in marble was the gift of William Vanderbilt to his wife, Alva, in 1892.

Belcourt Castle, just down the road, was designed by Richard Morris Hunt, based on Louis XIII's hunting lodge. The castle contains an enormous collection of European and Oriental treasures. *☏ 401/846–0669 or 401/849–1566. Admission charged. Closed weekdays Jan.*

Take Ocean Drive to **Hammersmith Farm,** the childhood summer home of Jacqueline Bouvier and the site of her wedding to John F. Kennedy. It is also the only working farm in Newport. The gardens were designed by Frederick Law Olmsted. *Near Fort Adams, ☏ 401/846–7346. Admission charged. Closed mid-Nov.–Feb., but with special openings during Christmastime.*

Out at **Fort Adams State Park** is a Revolutionary War–era fort (named after John Quincy Adams) where the annual Newport jazz and folk festivals are now held. Also on the park grounds is the **Museum of Yachting,** with four galleries of pictures: Mansions and Yachts, Small Craft, America's Cup, and the Hall of Fame for Single-handed Sailors. *Ocean Dr., ☎ 401/847–1018. Admission charged. Closed Nov.–Apr.*

Block Island

Newport (along with Galilee) is another jumping-off point for **Block Island,** 13 mi off the coast. Despite its popularity, the 11-sq-mi island's beauty and privacy are intact. Its freshwater ponds are a haven for migrating birds; its harbors are a sanctuary for sailors; and its narrow roads and walking trails are ideal for relaxed exploring. The **Block Island Chamber of Commerce** (Drawer D, Water St., 02807, ☎ 401/466–2982) can help with reservations at hotels and guest houses. Aside from the ferry service (*see* Getting There, *above*), **New England Airlines** (☎ 401/596–2460 or 800/243–2460) offers air service to the island from Westerly State Airport.

Providence

Thirty miles north of Newport is the state's capital, **Providence,** founded by Roger Williams in 1635 as a refuge for freethinkers and religious dissenters. Brown University, the Rhode Island School of Design (RISD), and the Trinity Square Repertory Company are major forces in New England's intellectual and cultural life. Historic walking-tour maps of the city are available at the tourist office (*see* Visitor Information, *above*).

Four Brown brothers had a major part in Providence's development in the 18th century. John Brown traded slaves, opened trade with China, and aided the American Revolution. Joseph Brown's architectural designs changed the face of the city. Moses Brown founded the Quaker School that bears his name. Nicholas Brown rescued the failing Rhode Island College—known today as Brown University.

The **Providence Athenaeum,** established in 1753, is one of the oldest lending libraries in the world. The library has a collection of Rhode Island art and artifacts, as well as an original set of the folio *Birds of America* prints by John J. Audubon. *251 Benefit St., ☎ 401/421–6970. Closed Sun.*

Down the street is the **Rhode Island School of Design Museum of Art.** This small but comprehensive museum exhibits textiles, Japanese prints, Paul Revere silver, 18th-century porcelain, French Impressionist paintings, and a mummy dating from circa 300 BC. *224 Benefit St., ☎ 401/454–6100. Admission charged (free Sat.). Closed Mon.*

Also on **Benefit Street**—known as the "Mile of History"—is a long row of small early Federal and 19th-century candy-colored houses crammed shoulder-to-shoulder on a steep hill overlooking downtown Providence.

Along South Water Street is **Market House** (Market Sq., S. Main St.), designed by Joseph Brown. Tea was burned here in March 1775, and the upper floors were used as a barracks during the Revolutionary War. North on South Water Street and west onto Westminster Mall is the **Arcade** (65 Weybosset St., ☎ 401/272–2340; closed Sun.), built in 1828 and America's first indoor shopping mall. Now a National Historic Landmark, the three-story Greek Revival Arcade still houses shops.

On Smith Street is the **state house,** built in 1900. Its dome—the first unsupported marble dome in America—is the world's second-largest after St. Peter's Basilica in Rome. On display is the original parchment charter granted by King Charles to the colony of Rhode Island in 1663. *82 Smith St., ☎ 401/277–2357. Admission charged. Closed weekends.*

South along Benefit Street is the **First Unitarian Church of Providence** (1 Benevolent St., ☏ 401/421–7970), built in 1816. The bell tower houses the largest bell ever cast in Paul Revere's foundry, a 2,500 pounder.

On Power Street is the **John Brown house,** designed by Joseph Brown for his brother in 1786. This three-story Georgian mansion is replete with elaborate woodwork and furniture, silver, pewter, glass, linens, Chinese porcelain from the late 18th and early 19th centuries, and an antique-doll collection. *52 Power St.,* ☏ *401/331–8575. Admission charged. Closed Mon.; Jan.–Feb. by appointment.*

Across the street, the **Ambrose Burnside mansion** (314 Benefit St.), a redbrick Victorian house with a turret, was built in 1850 for the Civil War general and later Rhode Island governor.

What to See and Do with Children

Norman Bird Sanctuary (583 3rd Beach Rd., Middletown, ☏ 401/846–2577) is a 450-acre sanctuary with nature trails, guided tours, and a small natural-history museum. In Newport, the **Children's Theatre** (☏ 401/848–0266) stages several major productions each year.

Shopping

Newport is a city for shoppers, though not for bargain hunters. Its specialties include antiques, traditional clothing, and marine supplies. Art and antiques shops, and boutiques with traditional clothing, line Thames Street. Spring and Franklin streets and the Brick Market area between Thames Street and America's Cup Avenue have some 50 shops with crafts, clothing, antiques, and toys. Bowen's and Bannister's wharves feature shops with a nautical theme.

Sports and the Outdoors

Biking

In Newport, **Ten Speed Spokes** (18 Elm St., ☏ 401/847–5609) has bikes, and **Fun Rentals** (Commercial Wharf and on Goat Island, ☏ 401/846–4374) has mopeds. For information on trails in Providence, call the **Department of Public Parks** (☏ 401/785–9450).

Boating

In Newport, **Old Port Marine Services** (Sayer's Wharf, ☏ 401/847–9109) offers harbor tours, yacht charters, and rides on a harbor ferry. **Sight Sailing of Newport** (Bowen's Wharf, ☏ 401/849–3333) organizes two-hour sailing tours of Newport Harbor in a six-passenger sailboat with a U.S. Coast Guard–licensed captain.

Beaches

The southern coast of Rhode Island boasts mile after mile of beautiful, mostly sandy ocean beaches with clear, clean water. The best are at **Westerly, Charleston, South Kingstown,** and **Narragansett.** Newport has several beaches: **Easton's Beach** (Memorial Blvd.), also known as First Beach, is popular for its miniature golf and children's carousel. **Fort Adams State Park** (Ocean Dr.) has a small beach with a picnic area, lifeguards, and beautiful views of Newport Harbor. **King Park** (Wellington Ave.), popular with scuba divers, also has lifeguards.

Dining and Lodging

Traditional Rhode Island fare includes johnnycake, a sort of corn cake cooked on a griddle, and quahogs (pronounced "KO-hawgs"), the local clams, served steamed, stuffed, fried, in chowder, or in a pie. Particularly popular are "shore dinners," which include clam chowder, steamers, clam cakes, baked sausage, corn on the cob, lobster, watermelon, and Indian pudding (a steamed pudding made with cornmeal and molasses).

While the big chain hotels are represented in Rhode Island, many visitors prefer to stay in smaller inns and B&Bs (**Bed and Breakfast of Rhode Island, Inc.,** Box 3291, Newport 02840, ☎ 401/849–1298). Entering Newport from the direction of Providence, you will find dozens of motels where room rates are considerably lower than those in downtown. Along the south shore there are many small motels along Rte. 1, especially on the outskirts of Westerly, and on the Post Road in North Kingston.

Low-season prices are reduced by as much as 50% from high-season rates. For price ranges, see Charts 1 (A) and 2 (A) in On the Road with Fodor's.

Newport

DINING

★ **Black Pearl.** Known to sailors throughout the world, this waterfront restaurant has a tavern for casual fare and drinks and a more formal (and more expensive) dining room for such appetizers as black and blue tuna with red-pepper sauce, and oysters warmed with truffles and cream. Entrées may include swordfish with Dutch-pepper butter or duck breast with green-peppercorn sauce. *Bannister's Wharf, ☎ 401/846–5264. Reservations required. Jacket required. AE, DC, MC, V. $$$$*

Brick Alley Pub. Low ceilings, small tables, plants, and American memorabilia give this place a friendly atmosphere. An extensive menu includes fresh fish, chowder, steaks, and homemade pasta. *140 Thames St., ☎ 401/849–6334. AE, D, DC, MC, V. $$*

★ **Puerini's.** The aroma of garlic and basil greets you as soon as you enter this friendly neighborhood restaurant with black-and-white photographs of Italy on the walls and lace curtains on the windows. The long and intriguing menu includes green noodles with chicken in marsala wine sauce, tortellini with seafood, and cavatelli in four cheeses. An expansion of the upstairs dining room has eased the summer wait for tables. Smoking is not allowed. *24 Memorial Blvd., ☎ 401/847–5506. No reservations. Closed Mon. in winter. No lunch. No credit cards. $$*

LODGING

★ **Francis Malbone House.** This stately 1760 house on Thames Street is beautifully restored and furnished with period reproductions. The large corner guest rooms face either the garden or the street and harbor beyond. Breakfast is served in the country kitchen. *392 Thames St., 02840, ☎ 401/846–0392. 8 rooms, 1 suite. Facilities: Continental breakfast, working fireplaces in 6 rooms. AE, MC, V. $$$$*

★ **Inn at Castle Hill.** Perched on an oceanside cliff 3 mi from Newport, this rambling inn was built as a summer home in 1874, and much of the original furniture remains. Some smaller unrefurbished rooms are much less expensive than those that have recently been renovated. The inn's Sunday brunches are famous—be sure to make reservations. *Ocean Dr., 02840, ☎ 401/849–3800. 10 rooms, 3 share bath. Facilities: Continental breakfast, restaurant (closed Nov.–Mar.), 3 private beaches. AE, MC, V. $$$$*

★ **Ivy Lodge.** The only bed-and-breakfast in the mansion district, this grand Victorian (small by Newport's standards but mansionesque anywhere else) bristles with gables and a Gothic turret. Even the brass four-poster beds, clawfoot tubs, window seats, and glorious antiques in the bedrooms pale beside the home's greatest feature: a 33-ft Gothic paneled oak entry with a three-story turned baluster staircase. A fire burns brightly on fall and winter afternoons in the huge brick fireplace shaped like a Moorish arch. *12 Clay St., 02840,* ☎ *401/849–6865. 10 rooms, 8 with bath. Facilities: parlor, parking, full breakfast included. AE, MC, V. $$$*

Providence

DINING

★ **Al Forno.** This restaurant cemented Providence's reputation as a culinary center in New England. The entrées, such as oven-roasted chicken cakes with applesauce, as well as sinful desserts like strawberry-and-rhubarb tart, are all made with fresh local ingredients. *577 S. Main St.,* ☎ *401/273–9760. No reservations. AE, MC, V. Closed Sun.–Mon. $$$*

★ **Casa Christine.** Family-run Christine's is a find on Federal Hill for its zesty pastas and other Italian entrées of chicken, veal, and seafood. Be sure to check the board for specials. *145 Spruce St.,* ☎ *401/453–6255. No credit cards. BYOB. Closed Sun.–Mon. $$*

Wes' Rib House. Sure, they serve vegetable kebabs for vegetarians, but this Providence institution is really for those who want to tear into sticky, meaty viands. Order wood-fire barbecued ribs by the piece, damn your cholesterol count, and dig in. *1 Robard Plaza,* ☎ *401/421–9090. Reservations accepted for 6 or more. D, MC, V. $$*

LODGING

★ **Omni Biltmore Hotel.** The Biltmore, completed in 1922, has a sleek Art Deco exterior, Old World charm, and an external glass elevator that offers attractive views of Providence at night. The attentiveness of the staff, the downtown location, and a recent face-lift make this an appealing perch from which to explore the city. *Kennedy Plaza, 02903,* ☎ *401/421–0700,* FAX *401/421–0210. 217 rooms, 21 suites. Facilities: restaurant, health club nearby, weekend packages. AE, DC, MC, V. $$$*

C.C. Ledbetter's. The somber green exterior of this Benefit Street home belies its vibrant interior—the place is filled with two English springer spaniels, lively art, books, photographs, handmade quilts, and a warm, homey blend of contemporary furnishings and antiques. Book early for Brown University's parents' and graduation weekends. *326 Benefit St., 02903,* ☎ *and* FAX *401/351–4699. 5 rooms, 4 share 2 baths. No credit cards. $$*

Holiday Inn. This high-rise motel is close to Exit 21 on I–95, near the Providence Civic Center. There is a comfortable piano bar off the lobby. *21 Atwells Ave., 02903,* ☎ *401/831–3900,* FAX *401/751–0007. 274 rooms. Facilities: restaurant, indoor pool, exercise room. AE, DC, MC, V. $$*

Motels

NEWPORT

Comfort Inn (936 W. Main Rd., 02840, ☎ 401/846–7600), 136 rooms, restaurant, pool; *$$$*. **Harbour Base Pineapple Inn** (372 Coddington Hwy., 02840, ☎ 401/847–2600), 48 rooms; *$*.

PROVIDENCE

Marriott (Charles and Orm Sts., 02904, ☎ 401/272–2400), 345 rooms, restaurant, health club, 2 pools; *$$$*. **Days Hotel on the Harbor** (220 India St., 02903, ☎ 401/272–5577), 136 rooms, restaurant, exercise room; *$$*.

SOUTH SHORE

Best Western (7075 Post Rd., 02852, ☎ 401/884–8000), 51 rooms, restaurant, outdoor pool; *$$*. **Wickford Motor Inn** (7650 Post Rd., 02852, ☎ 401/884–2230), 18 rooms, some with refrigerators; *$*.

Nightlife

The tourist offices (*see* Visitor Information, *above*) have listings of concerts, shows, and special events, as do the Newport and Providence newspapers.

Newport

To sample Newport's lively nightlife, you need only stroll down Thames Street after dark. For a classy bar, try the **Candy Star** in the Clark Cooke House restaurant (Bannister's Wharf, ☎ 401/849–2900). **Thames Street Station** (337 America's Cup Ave., ☎ 401/849–9480) plays high-energy dance music and videos and has live progressive rock bands Monday through Thursday in summer. **David's** (28 Prospect Hill St., ☎ 401/847–9698) is a mainly gay bar with a DJ daily in season and weekends in winter. **One Pelham East** (270 Thames St., ☎ 401/847–9460) draws a young crowd for progressive rock, reggae, and R&B.

Providence

Oliver's (83 Benevolent St., ☎ 401/272–8795), a hangout for Brown University types, has a pool table and good pub food. **Manhattan** (1 Throop Alley, ☎ 401/861–1996) offers mostly jazz and blues bands, Tuesday through Saturday nights. The **Hot Club** (575 S. Water St., ☎ 401/861–9007) is just that—a hip place with plants, a jukebox, and nice lighting.

VERMONT

Updated by Tara Hamilton

Capital	Montpelier
Population	563,000
Motto	Freedom and Unity
State Bird	Hermit thrush
State Flower	Red clover

Visitor Information

Vermont Travel Division (134 State St., Montpelier 05602, ☎ 802/828–3237). **Vermont Chamber of Commerce** (Box 37, Montpelier 05602, ☎ 802/223–3443).

Scenic Drives

Rte. 100, up the spiny backbone of the state, passes through a sampling of the faces of Vermont: small towns oriented to nearby ski areas, the eastern edge of Green Mountain National Forest, Mad River valley, Stowe, and on to Canada.

National and State Parks

National Park

The 300,000-acre **Green Mountain National Forest** (Rutland 05701; or Green Mountain Club, Rte. 100, Box 650, Waterbury Center 05677, ☎ 802/244–7037) runs through the center of the state, from Bristol south to the Massachusetts border.

State Parks

The 40 parks owned and maintained by the **Department of Forests, Parks and Recreation** (Waterbury 05676, ☎ 802/244–8711) offer nature and hiking trails, campsites, swimming, boating facilities, and fishing. Especially popular are the **Champlain Islands** sites: **Burton Island, Kill Kare** (*see* Northwestern Vermont, *below*), and **Sand Bar.**

SOUTHERN VERMONT

Southern Vermont is the cradle of the state's tradition of independence and rebellion. Many of the towns with village greens and white-spired churches were founded in the early 18th century as frontier outposts and later became trading centers. In the western region, the Green Mountain Boys fought off both the British and claims by land-hungry New Yorkers. The influx of new residents in the past 20 years means that the quaintness often comes with a patina of sophistication or funk; shoppers can find not only antiques but New Age crystals, Vermont-made salsa, and the highest-tech ski gear.

Tourist Information

Bennington: Chamber of Commerce (Veterans Memorial Dr., 05201, ☎ 802/447–3311). **Brattleboro:** Chamber of Commerce (180 Main St., 05301, ☎ 802/254–4565). **Manchester and the Mountains:** Chamber of Commerce (Adams Park Green, Box 928, 05255, ☎ 802/362–2100). **Rutland:** Chamber of Commerce, Convention and Visitors' Division (Box 67, 05702, ☎ 802/773–2747). **Woodstock:** Chamber of Commerce (4 Central St., 05091, ☎ 802/457–3555).

Getting There

By Car

I–91 runs north–south along the eastern edge of Vermont. U.S. 7 goes north–south through western Vermont, and Rte. 9 runs east–west across the state through Bennington and Brattleboro.

By Train

Amtrak (☎ 800/872–7245) stops at Brattleboro and Bellows Falls.

By Bus

The local **Greyhound Lines** subsidiary, **Vermont Transit** (☎ 802/864–6811 or 800/451–3292), links Bennington, Brattleboro, and smaller towns with nearby states and the rest of the country. **Bonanza Bus Lines** (☎ 802/442–4808) goes from Danbury, Connecticut, to Bennington.

Exploring Southern Vermont

It was at **Bennington** that Ethan Allen formed the Green Mountain Boys, who helped capture Fort Ticonderoga in 1775. The **Bennington Battle Monument** (15 Monument Ave., ☎ 802/447–0550; admission charged; closed Nov.–mid-Apr.), a 306-ft-tall stone obelisk, commemorates General John Stark's defeat of the British in their attempt to capture Bennington's stockpile of supplies. Piled higgledy-piggledy in cases at the **Bennington Museum** (W. Main St. [Rte. 9], ☎ 802/447–1571; admission charged; closed Nov.–mid-May) is a rich collection of Early American artifacts, including decorative arts, glassware, and the folk art of Grandma Moses.

Manchester has been a popular summer retreat since the mid-19th century (Mary Todd Lincoln visited here). Its tree-shaded marble sidewalks and stately old houses reflect the luxurious resort lifestyle of a century ago, while upscale factory-outlet stores appeal to the ski crowd. **Hildene** (Rte. 7A, 2 mi north of intersection with Rtes. 11 and 30, ☎ 802/362–1788), the 412-acre summer home of Abraham Lincoln's son Robert, features Georgian Revival symmetry and formal gardens.

The **Southern Vermont Art Center** (West Rd., ☎ 802/362–1405) offers a permanent painting collection and rotating exhibits. Its 375-acre Manchester site is dotted with contemporary sculpture, and concerts, dramatic performances, and films are presented here. The **American Museum of Fly Fishing** (Rte. 7A, ☎ 802/362–3300) displays the tackle of such noted anglers as Daniel Webster, Winslow Homer, and Bing Crosby. The steep 5.2-mi drive to the top of **Mt. Equinox** (Rte. 7A, ☎ 802/362–1114; admission charged; closed Nov.–Apr.) brings you to the Saddle, where the views are outstanding.

In **Rutland's Vermont Marble Exhibit** (off Rte. 3, ☎ 802/459–3311; admission charged), northwest of town, visitors can watch the transformation of the rough stone into slabs, blocks, and gift items. The **Chaffee Art Gallery** (16 Main St., ☎ 802/775–0356) houses the work of 250 Vermont artists.

On the eastern side of the state on U.S. 4, **Woodstock** is the quintessential quiet New England town. Exquisitely preserved Federal houses surround the tree-lined village green. The **Vermont Institute of Natural Science's Raptor Center** (Church Hill Rd., ☎ 802/457–2779; admission charged) features nature trails and 26 species of birds of prey. A half-mile north of town, the reconstructed farmhouse, school, general store, and workshop at the **Billings Farm and Museum** (Rte. 12, ☎ 802/457–2355; admission charged; closed Nov.–Apr.) demonstrate

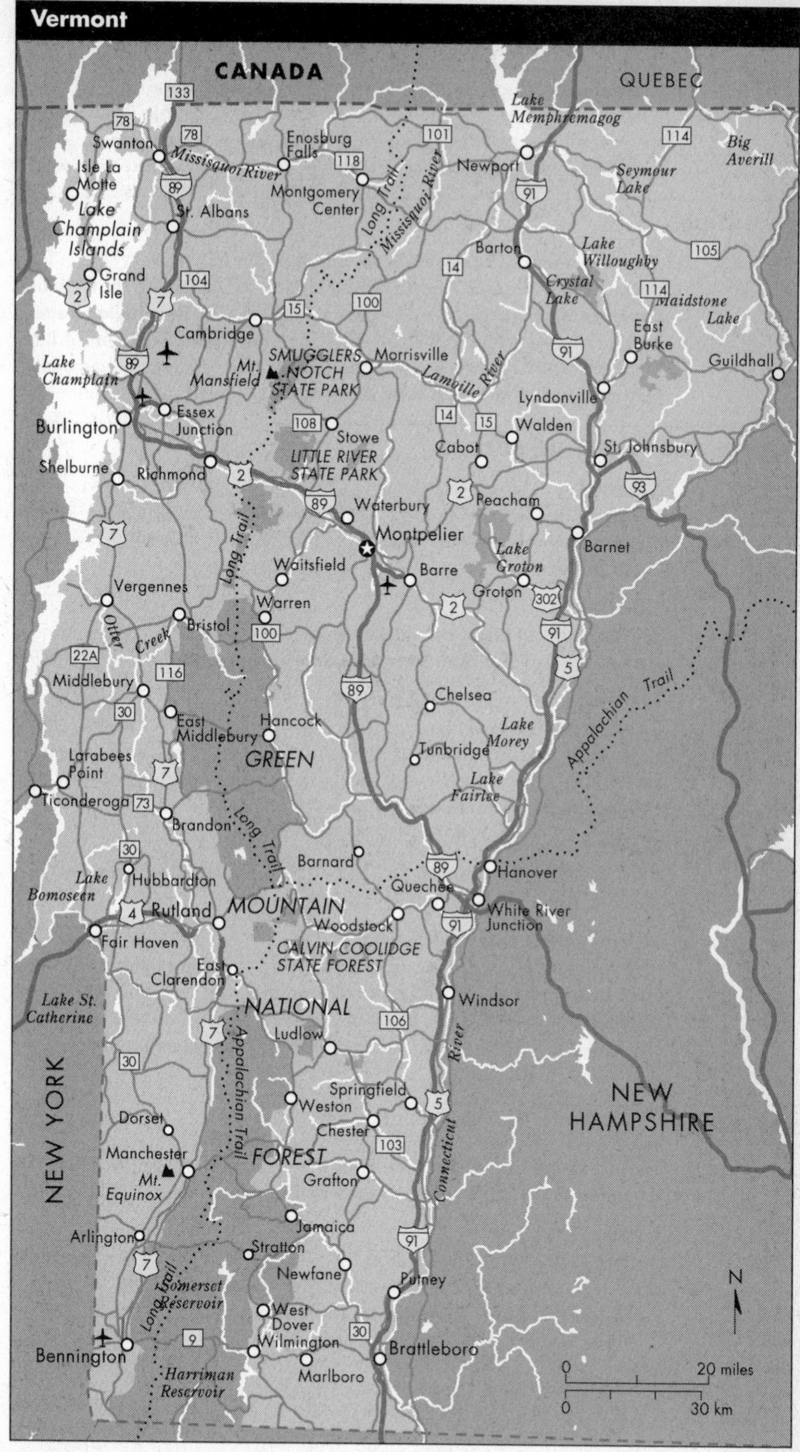
Vermont
CANADA
QUEBEC
Lake Memphremagog
Swanton
Isle La Motte
Lake Champlain Islands
Enosburg Falls
Montgomery Center
Missisquoi River
Long Trail
Newport
Seymour Lake
Big Averill
St. Albans
Barton
Lake Willoughby
Crystal Lake
Maidstone Lake
Grand Isle
Cambridge
East Burke
Guildhall
Lake Champlain
Mt. Mansfield
SMUGGLERS NOTCH STATE PARK
Morrisville
Lamoille River
Lyndonville
Burlington
Essex Junction
Stowe
Walden
LITTLE RIVER STATE PARK
Cabot
St. Johnsbury
Shelburne
Richmond
Waterbury
Peacham
Montpelier
Barnet
Lake Groton
Waitsfield
Barre
Groton
Vergennes
Warren
Otter Creek
Bristol
Middlebury
Chelsea
East Middlebury
Hancock
Lake Morey
GREEN
Tunbridge
Appalachian Trail
Larabees Point
Ticonderoga
Lake Fairlee
Brandon
Barnard
Lake Bomoseen
Hubbardton
Hanover
Quechee
Rutland
MOUNTAIN
White River Junction
Fair Haven
Woodstock
CALVIN COOLIDGE STATE FOREST
East Clarendon
Lake St. Catherine
NATIONAL
Windsor
Ludlow
Connecticut River
Springfield
Weston
NEW HAMPSHIRE
NEW YORK
Dorset
Chester
Manchester
FOREST
Mt. Equinox
Grafton
Jamaica
Arlington
Stratton
Newfane
Putney
Somerset Reservoir
West Dover
Wilmington
Bennington
Brattleboro
Marlboro
Harriman Reservoir
N
0
20 miles
0
30 km
133
78
101
114
118
89
91
105
104
14
15
100
7
2
108
93
302
22A
116
30
73
4
106
5
103
9

802/457–2355; admission charged; closed Nov.–Apr.) demonstrate the daily activities and skills of early Vermonters.

The mile-long **Quechee Gorge,** carved by a glacier and the Ottauquechee River, is visible from U.S. 4, but you can also scramble down one of the several descents. In the town of **Quechee,** at **Simon Pearce** (Main St., ☏ 802/295–2711), you can watch potters and glassblowers at work.

Shopping

Antiques and traditional and contemporary crafts are everywhere. Particularly good are **U.S. 7** north of Manchester to Danby and the **Antiques Center at Hartland** (U.S. 5, ☏ 802/436–2441). The **Bennington Potters Yard** (324 County St., ☏ 802/447–7531) has a huge selection of Bennington Pottery factory seconds. **Manchester,** with its designer names and factory outlets, has become to Vermont what Freeport is to Maine.

Sports and the Outdoors

Biking

Vermont Bicycle Touring (Box 711, Bristol 05443, ☏ 802/453–4811) and **Mad River Bike Shop** (Rte. 100, Waitsfield, ☏ 802/496–9500) operate guided tours.

Canoeing

The **Connecticut River** and the **Battenkill** offer easygoing canoe outings. Rentals are available from **Battenkill Canoe** (Arlington, ☏ 802/375–9559).

Fishing

The **Battenkill River** is famous for trout. The **Orvis Co.** (Rte. 7A, Manchester, ☏ 802/362–3900) runs an annual fly-fishing school. The necessary fishing license is easily available through tackle shops, or call the **Department of Fish and Wildlife** (☏ 802/244–7331).

Golf

In Manchester, **Equinox** (☏ 802/362–4700) and **Haystack Country Club** (☏ 802/464–8301) are public 18-hole courses.

Hiking and Backpacking

The southern half of the **Long Trail** is part of the **Appalachian Trail** and runs from just east of Rutland to the state's southern boundary. The **Green Mountain Club** (*see* National and State Parks, *above*) maintains the trail and staffs huts along it in summer, as well as mapping hiking elsewhere in Vermont.

Ski Areas

For up-to-date snow conditions in the state, call 802/229–0531. All downhill ski areas listed have snowmaking equipment.

Cross-Country

Bolton Valley (Box 300, Bolton 05477, ☏ 802/434–2131), 62 mi of trails. **Mt. Snow** (400 Mountain Rd., Mt. Snow 05356, ☏ 802/464–3333), 62 mi of trails. **Stratton** (Stratton Mountain 05155, ☏ 802/297–2200 or 800/843–6867), 20 mi of trails.

Downhill

Bromley (Box 1130, Manchester Center 05255, ☏ 802/824–5522), 35 runs, 10 lifts, 1,334-ft vertical drop. **Killington** (400 Killington Rd., Killington 05751, ☏ 802/773–1330), 107 runs, 19 lifts, 3,175-ft drop. **Mt. Snow** (*see* Cross-Country, *above*), 84 trails, 18 lifts, 1,700-ft drop. **Stratton** (*see* Cross-Country, *above*), 92 slopes, gondola, 11 lifts, 2,000-ft drop.

Dining and Lodging

For price ranges, see Charts 1 (B) and 2 (B) in On the Road with Fodor's.

Bennington

DINING

Main Street Café. A few minutes from downtown, this small storefront café draws locals with its northern Italian cuisine and a casual-chic atmosphere. *Rte. 67A, North Bennington,* ☎ *802/442–3210. AE, DC, MC, V. Closed Mon.–Tues. No lunch. $$$*

The Brasserie. The fare is hearty and creative, the decor as clean-lined as the Bennington pottery sold in the same complex. *324 County St.,* ☎ *802/447–7922. MC, V. Closed Tues. $$*

LODGING

South Shire Inn. Canopy beds in plushly carpeted rooms, ornate plaster molding on the ceilings, and the dark mahogany fireplace in the library add up to turn-of-the-century grandeur in a quiet residential neighborhood. *124 Elm St., 05201,* ☎ *802/447–3839. 9 rooms, 7 with fireplace. Facilities: full breakfast. AE, MC, V. $$–$$$*

DINING AND LODGING

★ **Molly Stark Inn.** This gem of a bed-and-breakfast gives the impression that you're staying with old friends. Tidy blue plaid wallpaper, gleaming hardwood floors, antique furnishings, and a woodstove in a brick alcove of the sitting room give a country charm to this 1860 Queen Anne Victorian. A full breakfast is included in the cost. *1067 E. Main St., 05201,* ☎ *802/442–9631. 6 rooms, 2 with bath. MC, V. $–$$*

Manchester

DINING

Garden Cafe. This sunny room has a terrific view of the spacious Southern Vermont Art Center grounds, an outdoor terrace, and such dishes as sautéed trout with almonds. *West Rd.,* ☎ *802/362–4220. No credit cards. Closed mid-Oct.–Memorial Day. $$*

Quality Restaurant. The model for Norman Rockwell's *War News* painting, this family-owned spot features sturdy New England standbys, such as hot open-faced roast beef or turkey sandwiches with gravy. *Main St.,* ☎ *802/362–9839. AE, MC, V. $$*

LODGING

★ **1811 House.** Staying here is like staying at an elegant English country house filled with antiques. The pub-style bar is decorated with horse brasses and equestrian paintings. *Rte. 7A, 05254,* ☎ *802/362–1811. 14 rooms. Facilities: full breakfast, lounge. No smoking. AE, MC, V. $$$*

Barnstead Innstead. This 1830s barn was transformed in 1968 into a handful of rooms that combine exposed beams and barn-board walls with modern plumbing and cheerful wallpaper. *Rte. 30, 05255,* ☎ *802/362–1619. 12 rooms. Facilities: cable TV, outdoor pool. MC, V. $$*

DINING AND LODGING

The Equinox. This white-columned resort was a landmark on Vermont's tourism scene even before Abraham Lincoln's family began summering here. The rooms, renovated in 1985, are furnished in Vermont pine. The front porch is perfect for watching the passing parade. The health center offers a medically supervised spa program. *Manchester Village 05254,* ☎ *802/362–4700 or 800/362–4747. 119 rooms, 18 suites, 9 3-bedroom town houses. Facilities: restaurant, tavern, tennis courts, golf course, 2 pools. AE, D, DC, MC, V. $$$*

Rutland

DINING

★ **Back Home Cafe.** Wooden booths, black-and-white linoleum tile, and exposed brick lend atmosphere at this second-story café where dinner might be baked stuffed fillet of sole with spinach, mushrooms, feta cheese, and tarragon sauce. *21 Center St., ☎ 802/775–2104. MC, V. $$*

LODGING

Comfort Inn. Rooms at this chain hotel are a cut above the standard, with an upholstered wing chair and blond-wood furnishings. *170 S. Main St., 05701, ☎ 802/775–2200. 103 rooms. Facilities: restaurant, fitness center, pool, tennis courts. AE, D, DC, MC, V. $$*

Inn at Rutland. In this renovated Victorian mansion, an ornate oak staircase leads to rooms with such turn-of-the-century touches as botanical prints, elaborate ceiling moldings, and frosted glass. *70 N. Main St., 05701, ☎ 802/773–0575. 12 rooms. Facilities: Continental breakfast. AE, D, MC, V. $$*

Woodstock

DINING

★ **The Prince and the Pauper.** In this romantically candlelit Colonial setting is served a prix fixe menu of nouvelle French with a Vermont accent. *24 Elm St., ☎ 802/457–1818. D, MC, V. Closed Sun.–Mon. late fall and early spring. No lunch. $$$*

Bentleys. Antique silk-fringed lamp shades, long lace curtains, and a life-size carving of a kneeling, winged knight lend a tongue-in-cheek Victorian air to burgers, chili, homemade soups, and entrées like duck in raspberry puree, almonds, and Chambord. *3 Elm St., ☎ 802/457–3232. AE, MC, V. $$*

DINING AND LODGING

★ **Kedron Valley Inn.** One of the state's oldest hotels, built in the 1840s, has rooms decorated with family quilts and antiques. The motel units in back feature exposed log walls. The dining room offers classic French technique and Vermont ingredients. *Rte. 106, 05071, ☎ 802/457–1473. 28 rooms. Facilities: full breakfast, restaurant, swimming/skating pond, lounge. D, MC, V. Closed Apr. $$$*

Woodstock Inn and Resort. This massive facility presides over the village green like a dowager duchess. The rooms' modern ash furnishings are enlivened by patchwork quilts and original Vermont landscape paintings. The menu in the dining room is nouvelle New England. *U.S. 4, 05091, ☎ 802/457–1100 or 800/448–7900. 146 rooms. Facilities: dining room (jacket required at dinner), pool, tennis, golf course, sports center, cross-country and downhill skiing. AE, MC, V. $$$*

Village Inn at Woodstock. The rooms in this renovated Victorian mansion are decorated simply with country antiques, chenille bedspreads, and dried flowers. *U.S. 4, 05091, ☎ 802/457–1255. 8 rooms (2 share bath). Facilities: restaurant, lounge. MC, V. Closed early Nov. $$*

Motels

Aspen Motel (Box 548, Manchester 05255, ☎ 802/362–2450), 24 rooms, cable TV, outdoor pool; *$$*. **Pond Ridge Motel** (U.S. 4, Woodstock 05091, ☎ 802/457–1667), 21 rooms, some with refrigerator and stove; *$$*. **Harwood Hill Motel** (Rte. 7A, Bennington 05201, ☎ 802/442–6278), 16 rooms; *$*.

Campgrounds

The campsites in the **Green Mountain National Forest** (*see* National and State Parks, *above*) operate on a first-come, first-served basis. The state park system runs nearly 40 campgrounds with more than 2,000 campsites; contact the Department of Forests, Parks and Recreation (*see* National and State Parks, *above*). The official state map lists private campgrounds.

The Arts and Nightlife

Like most things in Vermont, the arts and nightlife tend to be low-key. The summer **Marlboro Music Festival** (Marlboro Music Center, ☏ 802/257–4333) and the fall **New England Bach Festival** (Brattleboro Music Center, ☏ 802/257–4523) are among the best classical music festivals in the country. Most nightlife is concentrated at and around the ski resorts.

NORTHWESTERN VERMONT

More mountainous than the southern part of the state, northern Vermont is also less populated and contains the closest thing Vermont has to a seacoast—Lake Champlain—as well as the state capital. Its recorded history dates from 1609, when Samuel de Champlain explored the lake now named for him.

Tourist Information

Central Vermont: Chamber of Commerce (Box 336, Barre 05641, ☏ 802/229–5711). **Lake Champlain:** Regional Chamber of Commerce (209 Battery St., Box 453, Burlington 05402, ☏ 802/863–3489). **Smugglers' Notch:** Area Chamber of Commerce (Box 3264, Jeffersonville 05464, ☏ 802/644–2239). **Stowe:** Area Association (Main St., Box 1320, Stowe 05672, ☏ 802/253–7321).

Getting There

By Plane

Burlington Airport (South Burlington, ☏ 802/863–2874) is 4½ mi east of town off Rte. 2 and is served by major airlines. **E. F. Knapp Airport** (☏ 802/223–2060), served by regional airlines, lies between Barre and Montpelier.

By Car

I–89 runs from White River Junction to Vermont's northwest corner at the Canadian border.

By Train

Amtrak (☏ 800/872–7245) stops at Montpelier, Waterbury, Essex Junction, and St. Albans.

By Bus

Vermont Transit (☏ 802/864–6811 or 800/451–3292) connects Burlington, Stowe, Montpelier, Barre, St. Johnsbury, and Newport.

Exploring Northwestern Vermont

On the western edge of the region, **Middlebury** is Robert Frost country; Vermont's former poet laureate spent 23 summers at a farm near here. East of Middlebury on Rte. 125 is the **Robert Frost Wayside Trail,** which winds through quiet woodland with Frost quotations posted along the way.

The 100-acre **Shelburne Museum's** 35 buildings contain one of the largest Americana collections in the country. Exhibits include 18th- and 19th-century houses and furniture, fine and folk art, farm tools, carriages and sleighs, and an old side-wheel steamship. *U.S. 7, 5 mi south of Burlington, ☎ 802/985–3346. Admission charged.*

At the 1,000-acre **Shelburne Farms,** visitors can see a working dairy farm, attend nature lectures, or stroll the grounds along a stretch of Lake Champlain's waterfront. *Off U.S. 7, 3 mi south of Burlington, ☎ 802/985–8686. Admission charged.*

Burlington is enlivened by the 20,000 students at the **University of Vermont. Church Street Marketplace,** with its down-to-earth shops, chic boutiques, and an appealing menagerie of sidewalk cafés, food and crafts vendors, and street performers, is an animated downtown focal point. The ***Spirit of Ethan Allen*** (Perkins Pier, ☎ 802/862–9685), a replica of the paddle wheelers that once plied Lake Champlain, offers daily narrated cruises in summer.

A scenic summer alternative to I–89 east toward Stowe takes you through **Smugglers' Notch** (Rte. 15 to Jeffersonville, then south on narrow, twisting Rte. 108), the bouldered pass over Mt. Mansfield said to have given shelter to 18th-century outlaws. There are roadside picnic tables and a spectacular waterfall view.

Stowe is best known as a venerable ski center, but in summer you can take the 4½-mi toll road to the top of Vermont's highest peak, **Mt. Mansfield** (entrance on Mountain Rd., 7 mi from Rte. 100, ☎ 802/253–3000; admission charged; closed mid-Oct.–mid-May). At the road's end is a short and very scenic walk. Another way to ascend Mt. Mansfield is in the gondola that shuttles from the base of the ski area up 4,393 ft to the section known as "the Chin," where there are scenic views and a restaurant.

In the state capital of **Montpelier,** the interior of the **Vermont State House** (State St., ☎ 802/828–2228) is decorated with quotes about Vermont. The **Vermont Museum** (109 State St., ☎ 802/828–3391), on the ground floor of the Vermont Historical Society offices, can tell you why New England bridges are covered and what a "niddy-noddy" is.

What to See and Do with Children

The University of Vermont's **Morgan Horse Farm** (Rte. 23, 2.5 mi from Middlebury, ☎ 802/388–2011) offers tours of the stables and paddocks. Just south of Stowe is the Mecca, Nirvana, and Valhalla of ice-cream lovers, **Ben & Jerry's Ice Cream Factory** (Rte. 100, 1 mi north of I–89, ☎ 802/244–5641), which gives tours.

Shopping

The **Vermont State Craft Center at Frog Hollow** (Mill St., Middlebury, ☎ 802/388–3177; Church St., Burlington, ☎ 802/863–6458) is a display of the work of more than 250 juried Vermont artisans. Burlington's **Church Street Marketplace** is a pedestrian thoroughfare lined with boutiques.

Sports and the Outdoors

Biking

In addition to the numerous back roads along the Champlain Valley, Stowe has a recreational path, and Burlington has a 9-mi path along its waterfront. Several operators offer guided tours throughout the state (*see* Southern Vermont, *above*).

Fishing

Lake Champlain contains salmon, lake trout, bass, pike, and more. Marina services are offered by **Malletts Bay Marina** (228 Lakeshore Dr., Colchester, ☎ 802/862–4077) and **Point Bay Marina** (Thompson's Point, Charlotte, ☎ 802/425–2431).

Golf

Public courses include **Ralph Myhre's** 18 holes (Rte. 30, Middlebury, ☎ 802/388–3711) and 9 holes at **Montpelier Country Club** (U.S. 2, just south of U.S. 302, Montpelier, ☎ 802/223–7457).

Hiking and Backpacking

Aside from the Long Trail (*see* Southern Vermont, *above*), day hikes in northern Vermont include the **Little River** area in Mt. Mansfield State Forest near Stowe and **Stowe Pinnacle.**

Tennis

Stowe's **Grand Prix Tournament** is in early August (Stowe Area Association, ☎ 802/253–7321). Most resorts' courts are open only to guests. Tennis schools are offered at **Smugglers' Notch Tennis Camp** (Smugglers' Notch 05464, ☎ 802/644–8851) and **Sugarbush Tennis School** (Sugarbush Sports Center, R.R. 1, Box 350, Warren 05674, ☎ 802/583–2381).

Beaches

The center for water activities in Vermont is Lake Champlain. Marinas, rentals, and charters are available in or near Vergennes and Burlington. In Burlington, the **North Beaches** border the northern edge of town and are popular for swimming and sailboarding; **McKibben Sailing Vacations** (☎ 802/864–7733) has charter sailboats, **Burlington Rent All** (☎ 802/862–5793) rents rowboats and motorboats, and **Burlington Community Boathouse** (Burlington Harbor at College St., ☎ 802/865–3377) rents sailboats and sailboards. **North Hero State Park** (☎ 802/372–8727) has a children's play area nearby. **Kill Kare State Park** (off Rte. 36, south of St. Albans, ☎ 802/524–6021) has sailboard rentals and the ferry to Burton Island.

Ski Areas

For statewide snow conditions, ☎ 802/229–0531. All downhill areas listed have snowmaking.

Cross-Country

Burke Mountain (Box 247, East Burke 05832, ☎ 802/626–3305 or 800/541–5480) has 37 mi of trails and a ski school. Alpine resorts (*see* Downhill, *below*) that also have cross-country trails include **Jay Peak,** 25 mi; **Smugglers' Notch,** 23 mi; **Stowe,** 18 mi of groomed trails, 12 mi of back-country trails; and **Sugarbush,** 15 mi.

Downhill

Jay Peak (Rte. 242, Jay 05859, ☎ 802/988–2611 or 800/451–4449), 43 trails, 6 lifts, 2,153-ft vertical drop. **Mad River Glen** (Rte. 17, Waitsfield 05673, ☎ 802/496–3551), 33 runs, 3 lifts, 2,000-ft drop. **Smugglers' Notch** (Smugglers' Notch 05464, ☎ 802/644–8851 or 800/451–8752), 56 runs, 5 lifts, 2,610-ft drop. **Stowe** (5781 Mountain Rd., Stowe 05672, ☎ 802/253–3000), 45 trails, 9 lifts, 2,360-ft drop. **Sugarbush** (R.R. 1, Box 350, Warren 05674, ☎ 802/583–2381), 107 trails, 16 lifts, 2,600- and 2,400-ft drops.

Dining and Lodging

For price ranges, see Charts 1 (B) and 2 (B) in On the Road with Fodor's.

Burlington

DINING

★ **Isabel's.** This restaurant serving inspired American cuisine is notable for its artful presentation. The menu changes weekly and has included New Zealand lamb with walnut pesto as well as salmon stuffed with spinach and feta, wrapped in a phyllo pastry, and served with bechamel sauce. *112 Lake St., ☏ 802/865–2522. Reservations advised. No lunch weekends; no dinner Mon.–Wed. AE, DC, MC, V. $$*

★ **Sweet Tomatoes.** The wood-fire oven of this bright and boisterous trattoria sends off a mouthwatering aroma. With hand-painted ceramic pitchers; bottles of dark olive oil perched against a backdrop of exposed brick; and crusty, bull-headed bread that comes with a bowl of oil and garlic for dunking, this soulful eatery beckons you to Italy's countryside. The menu includes *caponata* (roasted eggplant with onions, capers, olives, parsley, celery, and tomatoes), *cavatappi* (pasta with roasted chicken and sautéed mushrooms, peas, and walnuts in a pecorino-Romano-carbonara sauce), and an extensive selection of pizzas. *83 Church St., ☏ 802/660–9533. Reservations accepted for large parties. MC, V. $–$$*

DINING AND LODGING

★ **Inn at Shelburne Farms.** Built at the turn of the century as the home of William Seward and Lila Vanderbilt Webb, the Tudor-style inn overlooks Lake Champlain, the distant Adirondacks, and the sea of pastures that make up this 1,000-acre working farm. Each guest room is different, from the wallpaper to the period antiques. The two dining rooms define elegance. A seasonal menu features home-grown products that might include loin of pork with an apple-cider-and-sun-dried-cranberry chutney, or rack of lamb with spinach-and-roasted-garlic pesto. *Harbor Rd., Shelburne 05482, ☏ 802/985–8498. 24 rooms, 17 with bath. Facilities: restaurant, tennis, game rooms, canoes, lake fishing and swimming. AE, DC, MC, V. Closed mid-Oct.–mid-May. $$–$$$$*

LODGING

Marriott Fairfield Inn. Clean, convenient, and entirely adequate, this hotel-cum-motel fills the niche for travelers in search of no-frills, yet dependable, accommodations. The spacious rooms, free local calls, and complimentary breakfast indicate a willingness to please, much more so than the average motel. *15 South Park Dr., Colchester 05446, ☏ 802/655–1400. 117 rooms with bath. Facilities: pool, Continental breakfast. AE, D, DC, MC, V. $*

Middlebury

DINING

★ **Woody's.** In addition to cool jazz, diner-deco light fixtures, and abstract paintings, Woody's offers a view of Otter Creek just below. The menu has nightly specials, and usually there's a Vermont lamb dish. *5 Bakery La., ☏ 802/388–4182. DC, MC, V. $$$*

DINING AND LODGING

Middlebury Inn. Fluted cream-and-rose columns and a green marble fireplace in the lobby speak of this 1827 inn's heritage. Rooms in the main building mix formal and country antiques; the 20 motel rooms have quilt hangings and floor-to-ceiling windows. The blue-and-white Colonial dining room offers an all-you-can-eat buffet. *Court House*

Sq., 05753-0798, ☎ 802/388–4961 or 800/842–4666. 75 rooms. Facilities: restaurant, lounge. AE, MC, V. $$$

Montpelier

DINING

Tubb's. The staff are all students at the New England Culinary Institute. A well-prepared, inventive menu changes daily but stays along the lines of swordfish with spinach and cherry tomatoes. The atmosphere is more formal than that of its sister operation down the block, the Elm Street Cafe. *24 Elm St., ☎ 802/229–9202. Reservations advised. MC, V. Closed Sun. $$$*

Horn of the Moon. The bowls of honey on the tables and the bulletin board of political notices hint at Vermont's prominent progressive contingent. This vegetarian restaurant's cuisine includes a little Mexican, a little Thai, a lot of flavor, and not too much tofu. *8 Langdon St., ☎ 802/223–2895. No credit cards. No dinner Sun.–Mon. $$*

DINING AND LODGING

★ **Inn at Montpelier.** This spacious early 1800s house has architectural detailing, antique four-posters, stately tapestry-upholstered wing chairs, and classical guitar on the stereo. *147 Main St., 05602, ☎ 802/223–2727, FAX 802/223–0722. 19 rooms. Facilities: restaurant, Continental breakfast. AE, MC, V. $$$*

Stowe

DINING

★ **Villa Tragara.** A farmhouse interior has been converted into a number of intimate dining nooks where romance reigns. Specialties include four-cheese ravioli with a tomato-cream sauce. *Rte. 100, 10 min south of Stowe, ☎ 802/244–5288. AE, MC, V. $$–$$$*

LODGING

★ **Inn at the Brass Lantern.** Homemade cookies in the afternoon, a freshly filled basket of logs by the fireplace, and stenciled hearts along the wainscoting all speak of the care taken in renovating this 18th-century farmhouse. A full breakfast is included in the room rate. *Rte. 100, 1 mi north of Stowe, 05672, ☎ 802/253–2229. 9 rooms, some with fireplace. AE, MC, V. $$*

DINING AND LODGING

10 Acres Lodge. Rooms in the main inn are smaller than those in the newer building high on the hill but all are carefully decorated. Contemporary pottery complements antique horse brasses over the living-room fireplace. *Luce Hill Rd., Box 3220, 05672, ☎ 802/253–7638 or 800/327–7357. 18 rooms, 2 cottages. Facilities: full breakfast, restaurant, lounge, pool. AE, MC, V. $$$*

Motels

Econo Lodge (101 Northfield St., Montpelier 05602, ☎ 802/223–5258), 54 rooms, restaurant; *$$*. **Greystone Motel** (U.S. 7, South Middlebury 05753, ☎ 802/388–4935), 10 rooms; *$$*.

Spa

For price range, see Chart 2 (A) in Chapter 1.

Topnotch at Stowe. The lobby of this resort, one of the state's poshest, features floor-to-ceiling windows, a freestanding circular stone fireplace, and cathedral ceilings. Rooms have thick rust carpet and a barn-board wall or an Italian print. *Mountain Rd., Stowe 05672, ☎ 802/253–8585 or 800/451–8686. 92 rooms, 8 suites. Facilities: restau-*

rant, lounge, 2 pools, 12 tennis courts, golf course, aerobics, health club. AE, DC, MC, V. $$$

Campgrounds

Camping on the Champlain Islands state parks can be arranged through the Department of Forests, Parks and Recreation (*see* National and State Parks, *above*).

The Arts and Nightlife

The Arts

Burlington has the **Vermont Mozart Festival** (☎ 802/862–7352) and the **Champlain Shakespeare Festival** (☎ 802/656–0090) in summer. Stowe has a summer **performing arts festival** (☎ 802/253–7321).

Nightlife

Burlington's nightlife caters to its college-age population, with pubs and a few dance spots. The **Vermont Pub and Brewery** (College and St. Paul Sts., Burlington, ☎ 802/865–0500) is the only pub in Vermont that makes its own beers. **Comedy Zone** (Radisson Hotel, 60 Battery St., Burlington, ☎ 802/658–6500) provides the laughs in town on weekends.

ELSEWHERE IN THE STATE

The Northeast Kingdom

Getting There

Drive up I–91 on the eastern side of the state.

What to See and Do

The greatest pleasure is driving through pastoral scenery and discovering charming small towns such as Peacham, Barton, and Craftsbury Common. The chief city is **St. Johnsbury,** where the **Fairbanks Museum and Planetarium** (Main and Prospect Sts., ☎ 802/748–2372) offers collections of plants and animals, Vermontiana, and a 50-seat planetarium. The **St. Johnsbury Athenaeum** (30 Main St., ☎ 802/748–8291), an architectural gem with dark paneling, polished Victorian woodwork, and ornate circular staircases that rise to the gallery, contains photographer Albert Bierstadt's *Domes of Yosemite.* **St. Johnsbury Chamber of Commerce** (30 Western Ave., 05819, ☎ 802/748–3678) has information on the region.

4 The Middle Atlantic States

By Conrad Paulus

IN THE CLOSING DECADES OF THE 18TH CENTURY, all the action in the New World was here, in the five original colonies. Washington's audacious crossing of the Delaware River made possible the colonists' victory in the Battle of Trenton; Virginia saw the war's final battles and surrender; Philadelphia saw the Constitution hammered out; Delaware ratified the Constitution and became the first state; and Maryland ceded land for the District of Columbia. Today, the people of these states remember the past, proudly tending their historic monuments and welcoming visitors.

The Middle Atlantic countryside of rolling farmland and woods, ancient, soft-edged mountains, broad rivers, and green valleys is a livable land in a manageable climate—a land much walked through and fought over. Besides the Revolution, the region suffered many of the battles of the Civil War and today commemorates their sites. On its eastern edge (part of the densely populated urban corridor that runs from Boston to Richmond), you'll find the cities and most of the history. The international, multiracial mix produces every possible cuisine, and you can buy anything on Earth in the upscale boutiques, department stores, and antiques shops.

Beyond the smog on the New Jersey Turnpike are long beaches, casino-filled Atlantic City, and Victorian Cape May to the east; horse country, ski resorts, and Philadelphia to the west. The Eastern Shore's Delaware and Maryland beaches are sedate or swinging; Virginia Beach is both. And the seafood anywhere near the Chesapeake Bay is superb. Baltimore combines historic buildings with new restaurants and shops; Annapolis and Oxford are ports for boaters gunkholing around the Chesapeake. Washington, D.C., seat of government, is a wonderful showplace for visitors, with myriad treasure houses among the cherry trees. Alexandria's historic district and Georgetown's splendid town houses recall the capital's early years. In Williamsburg, you'll hear echoes of the Revolution and sample 18th-century life.

West of the Tidewater, or coastal region, the towns are smaller and farther apart. Continuing on a circuit past Richmond, with its glorious capitol, you'll come to Charlottesville, Mr. Jefferson's hometown; farther west rise the Blue Ridge Mountains and West Virginia's Appalachians, sprinkled with palatial 19th-century resorts. At the stunning confluence of the Shenandoah and Potomac rivers sits Harpers Ferry, where John Brown met his fate; and back in Pennsylvania are Gettysburg and the Amish country. These are the habitats of the country auction, the wonderful local restaurant, and the farmhouse bed-and-breakfast—the secret places off the beaten track that you'll love to discover for yourself.

Tour Groups

Tours in the Middle Atlantic states highlight the region's natural and historic riches. Besides the operators listed in Chapter 1, the following firms offer tours of the region:

Gadabout Tours (700 E. Tahquitz Canyon Way, Palm Springs, CA 92262, ☎ 619/325–5556 or 800/952–5068) offers 11-day "West Virginia Country Roads" and 10-day "Blossom-Time in Washington, D.C." tours. **Globus** (5301 S. Federal Circle, Littleton, CO 80123, ☎ 303/797–2800 or 800/221–0090) has a "Historic East" tour that includes Washington, D.C., Monticello, Williamsburg, Gettysburg, Valley Forge, and

Philadelphia; Globus's budget-minded affiliate, **Cosmos Tourama** (same address), has a similar tour. **Maupintour** (Box 807, Lawrence, KS 66044, ☎ 913/843–1211 or 800/255–4266) arranges a week-long visit to the Baltimore area and 8- and 10-day "Colonial Cities" tours. **Talmage Tours** (1223 Walnut St., Philadelphia, PA 19107, ☎ 215/923–7100) offers four-day drives in Virginia and a paddle-wheeler cruise down the Ohio River through West Virginia and Pennsylvania. **Tauck Tours** (11 Wilton Rd., Box 5027, Westport, CT 06881, ☎ 203/226–6911 or 800/468–2825) takes an eight-day drive through Williamsburg, Washington, D.C., Gettysburg, Monticello, and Philadelphia.

When to Go

In the cool early **spring,** Washington's pink cherry blossoms bloom for a few spectacular days. The many equestrian events in Maryland and Virginia also herald the season. **Summer** is swampy in Washington, Baltimore, and Philadelphia, with temperatures in the 80s, yet thousands flock to all three for monuments or baseball. Ocean bathers head to the Jersey shore, Rehoboth, Ocean City, and Virginia Beach. The dazzling **autumn** foliage in Virginia's Shenandoah Valley draws hordes and also signals the opening of the orchestra, theater, and ballet seasons in the cities, most notably Philadelphia. In **winter,** when temperatures average in the 40s, workaday Washington grinds to a halt after just a sprinkling of snow, but Pennsylvania, Virginia, and West Virginia offer downhill and cross-country skiing, weather permitting.

Festivals and Seasonal Events

Jan. 1: The **Mummers Parade** in **Philadelphia** ushers in the year with some 30,000 sequined and feathered marchers between Broad Street and City Hall. ☎ *215/636–1666.*

Early Apr.: The **National Cherry Blossom Festival** takes place in **Washington, D.C.,** with a parade, a marathon, and a Japanese lantern-lighting ceremony. ☎ *202/737–2599.*

Mid-Apr.: The **Azalea Festival** in **Norfolk, Virginia,** features a parade, an air show, concerts, a ball, and the coronation of a queen from a NATO nation. ☎ *804/622–2312.*

Early May: Old Dover Days celebrates **Delaware**'s capital city with a parade, dancing, and tours of Colonial homes and gardens. ☎ *302/734–2655.*

Late May: The **Preakness,** held in **Baltimore,** is the second event of horse racing's Triple Crown, after the Kentucky Derby and before the Belmont Stakes. ☎ *410/542–9400.*

Early June: The **Blue and Grey Reunion** in **Philippi, West Virginia,** is four days of music, food, crafts, and a costumed reenactment of the Civil War's first land battle. ☎ *304/457–3700.*

Late June, early July: The **Festival of American Folklife,** held on the Mall in **Washington,** celebrates music, arts, crafts, and foods of regional cultures. ☎ *202/357–2700.*

Early July: The **Philadelphia Freedom Festival** features parades, hot-air balloon races, ceremonies at Independence Hall, a restaurant festival, and July 4 fireworks. ☎ *215/686–1776.*

Late July, early Aug.: The **Virginia Highlands Festival** in Abingdon offers crafts and farm animals on exhibit, antiques for sale, and country musicians in concert. ☎ *703/628–8141.*

The Middle Atlantic States

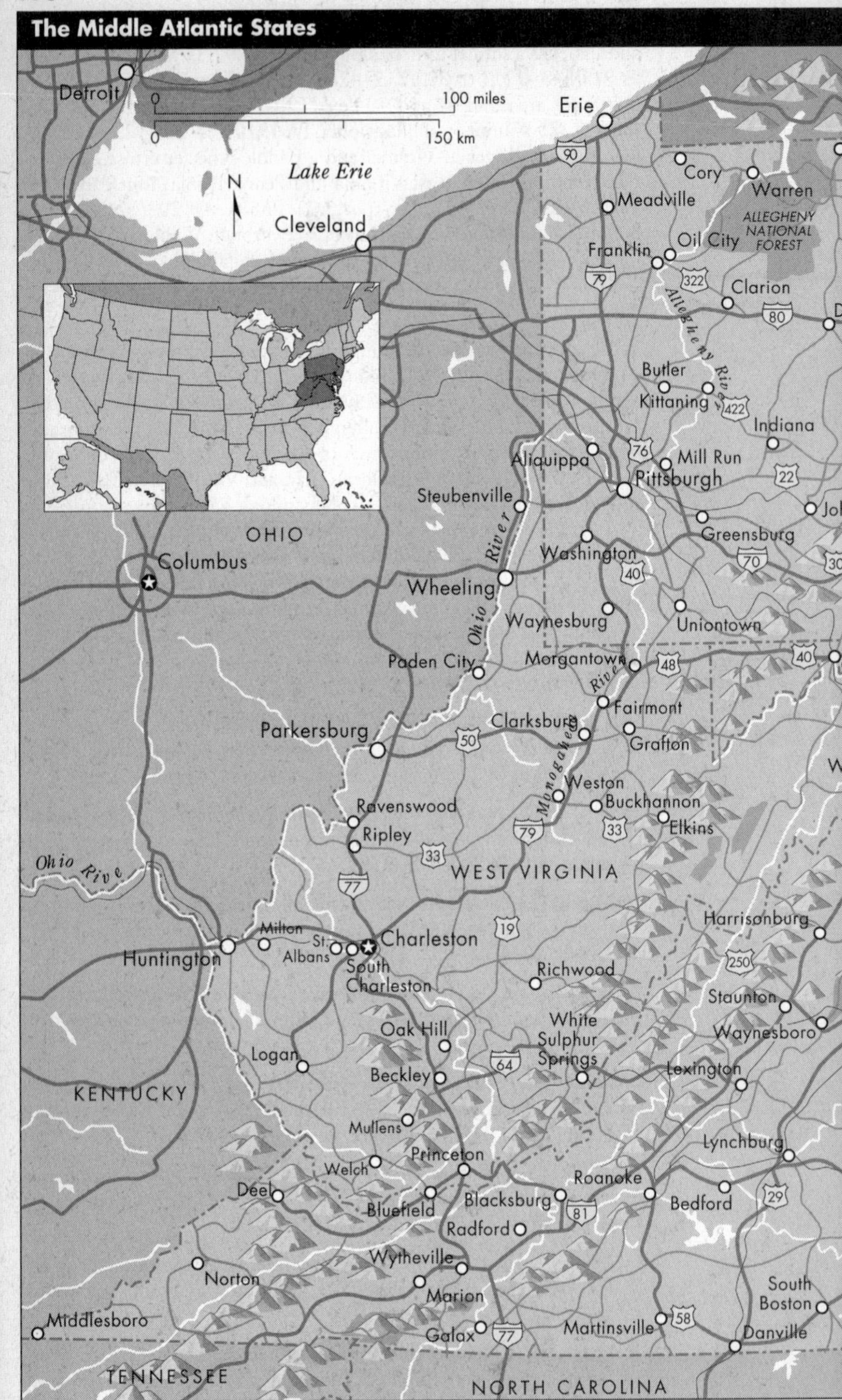

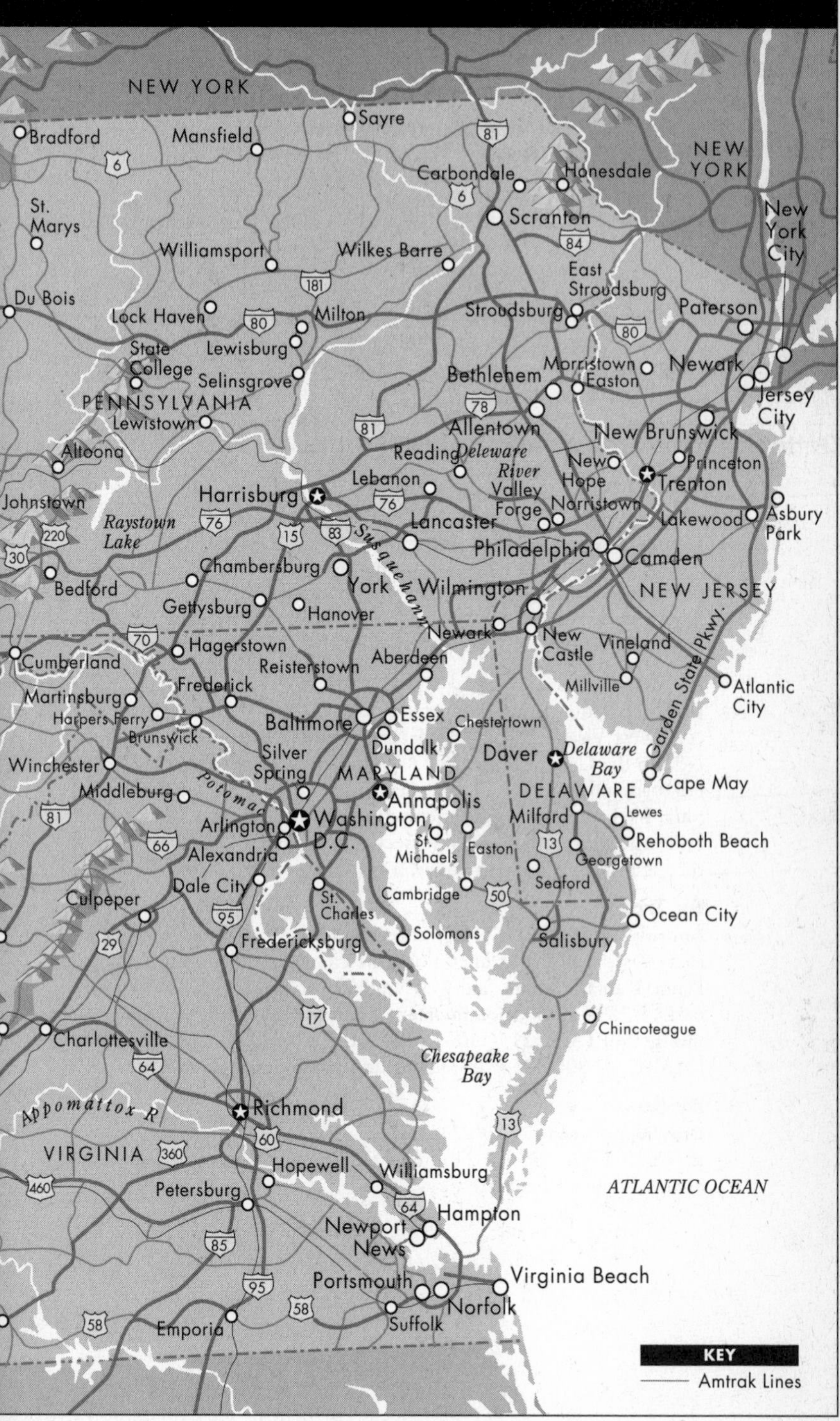
NEW YORK
Sayre
Bradford
Mansfield
Carbondale
Honesdale
NEW YORK
St. Marys
Scranton
New York City
Williamsport
Wilkes Barre
East Stroudsburg
Du Bois
Lock Haven
Milton
Stroudsburg
Paterson
State College
Lewisburg
Selinsgrove
Bethlehem
Morristown
Easton
Newark
PENNSYLVANIA
Lewistown
Allentown
Jersey City
New Brunswick
Altoona
Reading
Deleware River Valley
New Hope
Princeton
Trenton
Lebanon
Johnstown
Harrisburg
Forge
Norristown
Asbury Park
Raystown Lake
Lancaster
Lakewood
Susquehanna
Philadelphia
Camden
Chambersburg
Bedford
York
Wilmington
NEW JERSEY
Gettysburg
Hanover
Newark
New Castle
Vineland
Hagerstown
Cumberland
Reisterstown
Aberdeen
Garden State Pkwy.
Millville
Atlantic City
Martinsburg
Frederick
Harpers Ferry
Brunswick
Baltimore
Essex
Chestertown
Dundalk
Winchester
Silver Spring
Dover
Delaware Bay
MARYLAND
Cape May
Middleburg
Potomac
Annapolis
DELAWARE
Milford
Lewes
Arlington
Washington D.C.
St. Michaels
Easton
Rehoboth Beach
Alexandria
Georgetown
Dale City
Seaford
Culpeper
St. Charles
Cambridge
Ocean City
Fredericksburg
Solomons
Salisbury
Chincoteague
Charlottesville
Chesapeake Bay
Appomattox R
Richmond
VIRGINIA
Hopewell
Williamsburg
ATLANTIC OCEAN
Petersburg
Hampton
Newport News
Virginia Beach
Portsmouth
Norfolk
Suffolk
Emporia
KEY
Amtrak Lines

Early, mid-Oct.: United States Sailboat and Powerboat Shows, the world's largest events of their kind, take place in **Annapolis, Maryland.** ☎ *410/268–8828.*

Late Oct.: Sea Witch Weekend Festival, in **Rehoboth Beach, Delaware,** is a madcap Halloween spectacular that welcomes visitors with music, parades, hayrides, and the antics of masked marauders. ☎ *302/227–2233.*

Nov., Dec.: Yuletide at Winterthur is a Christmas-theme tour of the treasure-filled rooms at this vast museum near **Wilmington, Delaware.** ☎ *302/888–4600 or 800/448–3883.*

Early Dec.–Jan. 1: The **National Christmas Tree Lighting/Pageant of Peace** in **Washington, D.C.,** begins on the second Thursday in December, when the president lights the tree, and is followed by nightly choral performances at the Ellipse. ☎ *202/619–7222.*

Getting Around the Middle Atlantic States

By Plane

American, Continental, Delta, Northwest, TWA, United, and USAir, among others, serve **Philadelphia International Airport** (☎ 215/492–3181), **Greater Pittsburgh International Airport** (☎ 412/778–2601), **Baltimore-Washington International Airport** (☎ 410/859–7111), **Washington National Airport** (☎ 703/685–8003), and **Washington Dulles International Airport** (☎ 703/685–8000).

By Car

I–95, the major East Coast artery, runs through all of these states except West Virginia. The New Jersey Turnpike, a toll road, fills in for I–95 in the Garden State. The 470-mi Pennsylvania Turnpike, also a toll road, runs from the Ohio border to Valley Forge, just outside Philadelphia. I–64 runs east–west, intersecting I–95 at Richmond, Virginia. At Staunton, Virginia, I–64 intersects I–81, which runs north–south through the Shenandoah Valley, toward West Virginia and Tennessee.

By Train

Amtrak (☎ 800/872–7245) serves the region both north–south and east–west, with major lines along the coast and inland lines through Pennsylvania, Virginia, and West Virginia. **NJ Transit** (☎ 201/762–5100 or 215/569–3752), **Southeastern Pennsylvania Transportation Authority** (SEPTA; ☎ 215/580–7800), and **Maryland Area Rail Commuter** (MARC; ☎ 800/325–7245) provide service within their states.

By Bus

Greyhound Lines (☎ 800/231–2222) serves all these states. **NJ Transit** (☎ 201/762–5100 or 215/569–3752) provides bus service to many areas of the Garden State.

DELAWARE

By Marcia Andrews

Updated by Bob Willis

Capital	Dover
Population	673,000
Motto	Liberty and Independence
State Bird	Blue hen
State Flower	Peach blossom

Visitor Information

Delaware State Visitors Center (406 Federal St., Dover 19903, ☎ 302/739–4266). **Delaware Tourism Office** (99 Kings Hwy., Box 1401, Dover 19903, ☎ 302/739–4271 or 800/441–8846). **Information centers:** I–95, between Rtes. 896 and 273 (☎ 302/737–4059); at Delaware Memorial Bridge (☎ 302/571–6340); and north of Smyrna on Rte. 13 North (☎ 302/653–8910).

Scenic Drives

From Wilmington's west edge, a **30-mi loop** follows winding Rte. 100 past well-screened estates, a state park, and the meandering Brandywine Creek; a section of U.S. 1W in Pennsylvania past several historical attractions; and, back in Delaware, Rte. 52 (locally called "Château Country") to antiques-shop-lined villages, horse farms, and Winterthur, a major du Pont estate turned museum. A drive south along **Rte. 9** from New Castle to Dover slides past tidal marshes and across creeks on one-lane bridges; side roads veer into bird sanctuaries or out to points of land with a view of Delaware Bay.

National and State Parks

National Parks

Bombay Hook National Wildlife Refuge (Rte. 9, east of Smyrna; R.D. 1, Box 147, Smyrna 19977, ☎ 302/653–6872) is more than 15,000 acres of ponds and fields filled with resident and migrating waterfowl between April and November. **Prime Hook National Wildlife Refuge** (County Rd. 236, just off Rte. 16; R.D. 3, Box 195, Milton 19968, ☎ 302/684–8419) is a smaller, well-developed preserve with boat ramps, canoe trails, and a boardwalk trail through marshes.

State Parks

A dozen parks run by the **Delaware Division of Parks and Recreation** (89 Kings Hwy., Richardson and Robbins Bldg., Box 1401, Dover 19903, ☎ 302/739–4702) are set up for hiking, fishing, and picnicking. The chief inland parks, with freshwater ponds, add boat rentals to basic amenities. Parks are open year-round.

In spring and fall, **Brandywine Creek State Park** (intersection of Rtes. 92 and 100, Box 3782, Greenville 19807, ☎ 302/577–3534), about 5 mi from Wilmington, is probably the best park in the state for picnics. A nature center that specializes in environmental programs sits on 800-plus acres of both open fields and wooded grounds with 12 mi of hiking trails and perfect sledding slopes in winter. **Cape Henlopen** (42 Henlopen Dr., Lewes 19958, ☎ 302/645–8983; Seaside Nature Center, ☎ 302/654–6852), east of Lewes, has more than 150 campsites in pinelands. **Delaware Seashore** (850 Inlet, Rehoboth Beach 19971, ☎ 302/227–2800; marina, ☎ 302/227–3071) has both ocean surf and calm bay waters, and rustic and hookup campsites. **Lums Pond**

State Park (Rtes. 301 and 71, south of Newark; 1068 Howell School Rd., Bear 19701, ☎ 302/368–6989) has campsites. **Trap Pond** (off Rte. 24, east of Laurel; R.D. 2, Box 331, Laurel 19956, ☎ 302/875–5153) includes part of the Great Cypress Swamp and has rustic sites under a canopy of loblolly pines.

WILMINGTON

Surrounded by big, pressure-cooker cities, Wilmington is one of the quieter, less-stressed stops on the eastern corridor. It began as an early (1638) Swedish settlement and was quickly taken over successively by the Dutch and the English. More recently, it was populated by employees at DuPont company headquarters and nearby poultry ranches. Now the city's pro-business policies have enticed corporations whose towers of granite and glass reflect (literally) the Colonial stonework next door. The multinationals imported employees, and at some recent but unmarked instant, the city became home to more newcomers than natives.

Two nearby towns—Newark, home of the University of Delaware, and New Castle, the state's beautifully restored Colonial capital—are linked to Wilmington by a few miles of neighborhoods and strip malls and are important to the city's cultural, commercial, and social mix.

Tourist Information

Greater Wilmington: Convention and Visitors Bureau (1300 Market St., Suite 504, 19801, ☎ 302/652–4088 or 800/422–1181).

Arriving and Departing

By Plane

Philadelphia International Airport (☎ 215/492–3000) is about 30 mi north of downtown Wilmington and is served by all major U.S. and international airlines. Taxi fare is about $25 to Wilmington. Door-to-door shuttle buses to the center of the city—**Airport Shuttle Service** (☎ 302/655–8878) or **Delaware Express Shuttle** (☎ 302/454–7634 or 800/648–5466)—cost $19 or $20 and require reservations (24-hour advance notice is recommended).

By Car

Located between Baltimore and Philadelphia, Wilmington is bisected by I–95 north–south and linked to small-town Pennsylvania by U.S. 202 and Rtes. 52 and 41.

By Train

Wilmington Train Station (Martin Luther King Blvd. and French St.) has **Amtrak** (☎ 800/872–7245) service, as well as **SEPTA** (☎ 215/580–7800) commuter service to Philadelphia.

By Bus

Greyhound Lines (318 N. Market St., ☎ 800/231–2222).

Getting Around Wilmington

Downtown is compact enough to stroll, but visits to New Castle, Newark, or the museums and parks ringing Wilmington require a car. Downtown parking is midpriced in garages and hopeless on the streets in the jam-packed office district. Buses are geared to commuters, not explorers.

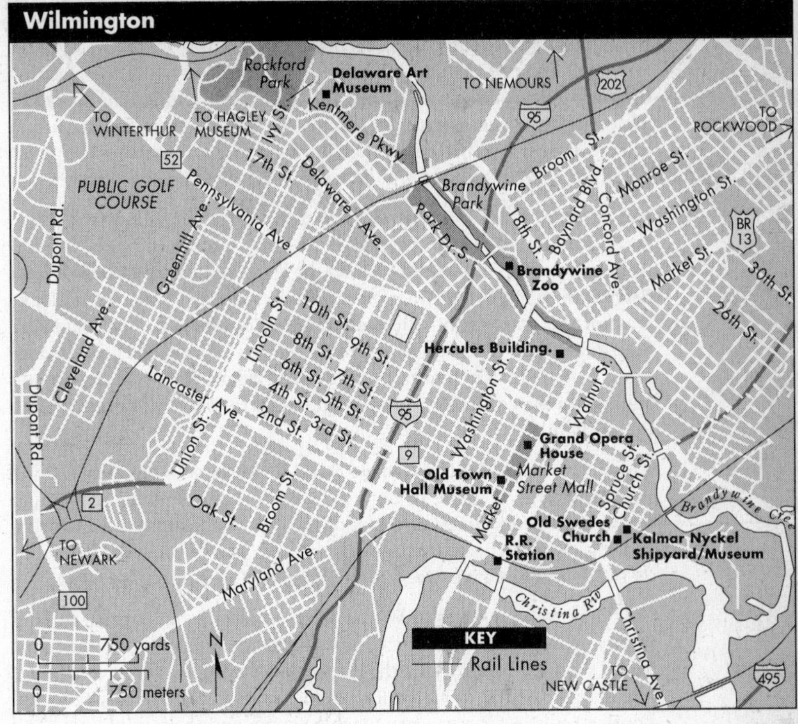

Exploring Wilmington

A tour of the city center starts on the four-block Market Street Mall. The **Grand Opera House** (818 Market St. Mall, ☎ 302/658–7897) is a working theater. Built by the Masonic Order in 1871 and restored in 1971, the four-story Grand's facade is cast iron painted white in French Second Empire style, to mimic the old Paris Opera.

Across the mall, the **Old Town Hall Museum** is a two-story Georgian-style building with meeting rooms, changing exhibits, and restored jail cells to tour. The hall and museum shop were restored as headquarters for the Historical Society of Delaware, which has its hands full of 18th- and early 19th-century buildings. *512 Market St. Mall, ☎ 302/655–7161. Closed Sun.–Mon.*

Five blocks north is the **Hercules Building** (1313 Market St.), built in the 1980s with ziggurat walls and a 20-foot-diameter clock. The core of the building is a 14-story atrium, with ground-level shops and a jungle of plants. Indoor and outdoor pools mirror sculptures and large marble globes rolling on columns of water.

About 10 blocks east of the mall (not an easy walk), a monument to the 1638 landing of a Swedish expedition marks the first permanent settlement in the Delaware Valley. At the **Kalmar Nyckel Shipyard/Museum** (1124 E. 7th St., ☎ 302/429–7447), volunteers are building a replica of that first Swedish vessel. Nearby stand **Old Swedes Church and Hendrickson House Museum** (606 Church St., ☎ 302/652–5629). The church, built in 1698, with its unchanged hipped roof and high wooden pulpit, is still regularly used for religious services. The farmhouse, built in 1690 by Swedish settlers, is furnished with period pieces.

In the Vicinity

Delaware Art Museum (2301 Kentmere Pkwy., ☎ 302/571–9590), a few miles west of the city center and I–95, houses a major collection of post-1840 American paintings and illustrations, including works by major figures such as Homer, Eakins, Hopper, Wyeth, Sloan, and illustrator Howard Pyle, as well as the foremost assemblage of English pre-Raphaelite paintings and decorative arts in the United States.

New Castle, 5 mi south of Wilmington on Rte. 9, is a barely commercialized gem rich in lovingly restored Colonial houses, cobblestone streets, and historic sites along the Delaware River. **William Penn's first landing** in North America is noted in Battery Park. Two blocks west of the waterfront, the **New Castle Courthouse** (211 Delaware St., ☎ 302/323–4453), Delaware's Colonial capitol, is a pristine museum of state history in three stolid brick wings. Its white cupola and spire were the compass point for the arc of the state's boundary with Pennsylvania.

Also in New Castle, the **George Read II House** was built in 1797 in Federal style by a signer of both the Declaration of Independence and the Constitution. Twelve rooms of the big brick house are open, including three furnished in period style. *42 The Strand, ☎ 302/322–8411. Admission charged. Closed Mon. and weekdays Jan.–Feb.*

On the northwest edges of Wilmington, along Rte. 52, former du Pont family properties have become impressive museums of the Brandywine Valley's industrial history. At the **Hagley Museum,** the DuPont company's beginnings in 1802 as an explosives manufacturer are recalled by gunpowder mills, a 19th-century machine shop, and the family home and gardens, all set on 230 acres. *Rte. 141, ☎ 302/658–2400. Admission charged.*

Winterthur Museum, Garden and Library focuses on Henry Francis du Pont's passion for collecting furniture and decorative arts made or used in America from 1640 to 1860. The nine-story, 196-room hillside stucco mansion and museum wing shelter a world-class collection in period settings. The naturalistic gardens showcase native and exotic plants. *Rte. 52, Winterthur, ☎ 302/888–4600 or 800/448–3883. Admission charged. Topical tours by reservation only.*

Nemours Mansion and Gardens shows another du Pont family's preference for fine automobiles, European antiques, Louis XVI–style architecture, and formal French gardens. *Rockland Rd., ☎ 302/651–6912 (reservations required). Admission charged. Closed Dec.–Apr.*

Odessa is a tiny, mostly residential village set on the banks of the Appoquinimink River, about 23 mi south of Wilmington off Rte. 13. Originally a grain-shipping port, it stopped growing in the mid-19th century when disease attacked its peach crops and the railroad passed it by. What you'll find today is an immaculate, quiet community of 303 people that is a bit of living history—until a few years ago, muskrat still topped the menu at the town's one-and-only restaurant. A newly installed branch of the **Winterthur Museum** includes four 18th- and 19th-century houses and the **Brick Hotel Gallery,** which houses rotating exhibits of American furniture and decorative arts. *☎ 302/378–4069. Admission charged.*

Parks and Gardens

In the center of town, in **Brandywine Park,** shady paths pass Colonial stone walls and a tiny brick church that was built in 1740 and used for British wounded during the Revolutionary War. Lush Brandywine Creek and a millrace attract fishermen and splashing children.

Rockwood Museum, a 19th-century country estate with a Gothic manor house, displays a collection of unusual specimen plants on 6 acres of cultivated grounds and 62 acres of woodlands. *610 Shipley Rd., ☎ 302/761–4340. Admission charged.*

What to See and Do with Children

Snow sledding in January or an outdoor picnic in June at **Brandywine Creek State Park** (*see* State Parks, *above*) are perfect for getting children outdoors; indoor activity is assured with the numerous children's environmental programs at the park's own nature center. Wilmington's **Brandywine Zoo** (North Park Dr., ☎ 302/571–7747; admission charged Apr.–Oct.; exotic-animal house closed Nov.–Mar.) tucks outdoor exhibits into cliffs along Brandywine Creek. Children who visit the **Delaware Museum of Natural History** (Rte. 52 N, ☎ 302/658–9111; admission charged), 5 mi northwest of Wilmington, can explore the mysteries of Australia's Great Barrier Reef, examine an African water hole and a 500-pound clam, and use all their senses in the numerous hands-on exhibits.

Shopping

Delaware's lack of a sales tax may lure out-of-staters for big-ticket items (cars), but outlet malls in Maryland and Pennsylvania are the magnets for many Delaware shoppers. The anchor stores at Newark's **Christiana Mall** (Rte. 7 at I–95 Exit 4S, ☎ 302/731–9815), which has 130 stores, are Macy's and Wanamaker's. Among the 87 stores at Wilmington's **Concord Mall** (4737 Concord Pike, ☎ 302/478–9271), Strawbridge & Clothier and Boscov's are the department-store biggies.

Dining

During the '80s boom, Wilmington's kitchens multiplied as new companies' globe-circling employees pushed for diversity. The most-established restaurants are Italian and Asian. It's safest to reserve on weekends, and jackets are preferred in the expensive places. For price ranges, see Chart 1 (B) in On the Road with Fodor's.

$$$ ★ **Green Room.** French cuisine, complete with elaborate sauces, is served in a dramatic, wood-paneled setting of 19th-century opulence with a 20th-century touch: original Andrew Wyeth paintings on the walls. *Hotel du Pont, 11th and Market Sts., ☎ 302/594–3154. Reservations required. Jacket advised. AE, D, DC, MC, V.*

$$$ **Positano.** The intimate room caters to small groups with discerning tastes in Italian cuisine—from fresh fish to intricate desserts. *The Devon, 2401 Pennsylvania Ave., ☎ 302/656–6788. AE, D, DC, MC, V.*

$$ ★ **Michele's.** Consistently busy without a dime spent on advertising, Michele's has made its name by word of mouth thanks to its fine French and northern Italian cuisine. Owners Sotir and Michele Sosangelis gutted and restored a town house in Wilmington's restaurant district: The upstairs is an elegant Victorian space with upholstered walls; in the more casual, contemporary downstairs dining area, you can order the same pasta, beef, veal, and lobster creations. *1828 W. 11th St., ☎ 302/655–8554. AE, MC, V.*

$$ **Caffè Bellissimo.** This casual Italian restaurant has won many awards for its generous portions of wood-fired pizza, grilled seafood, and fresh homemade pasta dishes. *3421 Kirkwood Hwy., ☎ 302/994–9200. AE, D, MC, V.*

$$ **Mirage.** In a colorful, contemporary space divided by arches into private dining pavilions, young servers (this is a university town) deliver such regional American specialties as poached salmon with vegetable broth and blue poppy seeds or sautéed veal with artichoke hearts, tomatoes, and leeks. The only fine-dining option in Newark, Mirage lures Wilmington visitors south with a low-priced menu—the most expensive entrée is under $20. *100 Elkton Rd., Newark, ☎ 302/453–1711. AE, D, MC, V.*

$ **Cellar Gourmet.** This environmentally conscious restaurant in the cellar of a historic New Castle edifice serves sandwiches, soups, and vegetarian and low-cholesterol dishes on recyclable paper plates. Freshly baked sweets and ice-cream treats are also served. Take-out items are ideal for a picnic on the town's nearby promenade bordering the Delaware River. *208 Delaware St., New Castle, ☎ 302/323–0999. No credit cards.*

$ **Coyote Cafe and Restaurant.** The room is colorful and quirky, with the signature animal in various forms. A few vegetarian and Caribbean dishes keep the updated Mexican menu interesting. *1801 Lancaster Ave., ☎ 302/652–1377. AE, MC, V.*

$ **Di Nardo's.** This crowded, casual tavern—more plastic than rustic, with Formica tables and unpadded chairs—specializes in seafood. The catch of the day is always fresh, and the spicy (or ask for plain, steamed) hard-shell crabs are famous. *405 N. Lincoln St., ☎ 302/656–3685. AE, D, DC, MC, V.*

$ ★ **India Palace.** The authentic Indian food served here includes spicy curry dishes and clay-oven specialties (tandoori). *101 Maryland Ave. (Rte. 4), ☎ 302/655–8772. No credit cards.*

Lodging

Most Wilmington-area hotels are designed for business travelers, with less emphasis on resort amenities and more on efficiency and value. For variety, there are restored Colonial inns (not modern adaptations) and a few B&Bs. Two reservation services—**Bed & Breakfast of Delaware, Inc.** (3650 Silverside Rd., Box 177, Wilmington 19810, ☎ 302/479–9500) and **Guesthouses, Inc.** (Box 2137, West Chester, PA 19380, ☎ 800/950–9130)—help locate moderately priced lodgings. For price ranges, see Chart 2 (B) in On the Road with Fodor's.

$$$ **Christiana Hilton Inn.** This modern high-rise southwest of Wilmington is convenient to I–95. The rooms are furnished traditionally, but the restaurant, Ashley's, is notable. *100 Continental Dr., Newark 19713, ☎ 302/454–1500, FAX 302/454–0233. 266 rooms. Facilities: 2 restaurants, bar, outdoor pool, free shuttle to downtown Wilmington. AE, D, DC, MC, V.*

$$$ ★ **Guest Quarters Suite Hotel Wilmington.** This former store, tucked into a nondescript downtown block, has dramatic contemporary architecture, suites with rich traditional furnishings, and a popular lounge. *707 King St., 19801, ☎ 302/656–9300 or 800/543–9106, FAX 302/656–2459. 49 suites. Facilities: restaurant, bar. AE, D, DC, MC, V.*

$$$ **Hotel du Pont.** This posh and popular downtown hotel has large rooms with living areas set off by mahogany dividers. The furnishings are 18th-century reproductions. *11th and Market Sts., 19801, ☎ 302/594–3100 or 800/441–9019, FAX 302/656–2145. 206 rooms, 10 suites. Facilities: 2 restaurants, bar, spa. AE, D, DC, MC, V.*

$$ **Radisson Hotel Wilmington.** In northwest Wilmington, this hotel has quiet, amply sized traditional rooms. *4727 Concord Mall, Rte. 202, 19803, ☎ 302/478–6000 or 800/333–3333, FAX 302/477–1492. 154 rooms. Facilities: restaurant, lounge, outdoor pool. AE, D, DC, MC, V.*

$$ **William Penn Guest House.** Irma and Dick Burwell have run this wonderful and affordable B&B in the heart of New Castle since 1956. Floorboards in their handsome Colonial are hewn from soft Delaware pine; an 18th-century chandelier lights the formal dining room; and a claw-foot tub in one bathroom provides perfect therapy for bone-weary cyclists. A Continental breakfast is included in the room rate. *208 Delaware St., New Castle 19720, ☎ 302/328–7736. 4 rooms. No credit cards.*

$ **Boulevard Bed & Breakfast.** This red-tile-roof B&B in the Triangle section of Wilmington is a citified and fancy—but reasonably priced—six-bedroom dwelling. Outside, notice the neo-Georgian elements in the facade and the eccentric, fluted columns; inside, don't miss the Mueller tiles around the library fireplace. Proprietors Charles and Judy Powell serve a full breakfast, the cost of which is included in the room rate. *1909 Baynard Blvd., 19802, ☎ 302/656–9700. 3 doubles with bath; 1 double and 1 single share a bath; 1 suite with whirlpool. AE, MC, V.*

$ **Fairfield Inn.** Close to the University of Delaware and about 9 mi west of Wilmington, this Marriott-owned inn is spartan but convenient. *65 Geoffrey Dr., Newark 19713, ☎ 302/292–1500. 135 rooms. AE, D, DC, MC, V.*

$ **Marriott Courtyard.** Centrally located in downtown Wilmington, this establishment guarantees very affordable rates in a Brandywine Valley ambience—lots of hunter green and cranberry colors with Wyeth reproductions to boot. A large number of businesspeople stay here, but the Courtyard also specializes in wedding parties and family reunions. One accessible unit is available. *1102 West St., 19801, ☎ 302/429–7600 or 800/321–2211, FAX 302/429–9167. 125 rooms. Facilities: 2 meeting rooms, fitness room. AE, D, DC, MC, V.*

$ **Rodeway Inn.** No-smoking rooms and proximity to historic New Castle are two advantages of this traditional motor inn. *111 S. DuPont Hwy., New Castle 19702, ☎ 302/328–6246 or 800/321–6246, FAX 302/328–9493. 40 rooms. AE, D, DC, MC, V.*

THE ATLANTIC COAST

As you drive Rtes. 9 and 1 south between farm fields and stands of 10-foot-high grasses, it's hard to believe the broad Delaware River and Delaware Bay are out there. Then, as you slide by a low spot in the marsh grass, the disembodied deck house of a boat comes into view, evidence of the small, mostly recreational fishing marinas along the shore. The water view opens up at Lewes and Cape Henlopen State Park; then sand dunes and wide, white Atlantic beaches mark the resort towns. The small inland towns house historic sites and dining and lodging alternatives.

Tourist Information

Bethany-Fenwick: Chamber of Commerce and Information Center (Rte. 1, N. Fenwick Island; Box 1450, Bethany Beach 19930, ☎ 302/539–2100 or 800/962–7873). **Lewes:** Chamber of Commerce and Visitors Bureau (Savannah Rd. and Kings Hwy., Box 1, 19958, ☎ 302/645–8073). **Milton:** Chamber of Commerce (101 Federal St., 19968, ☎ 302/684–1101). **Rehoboth Beach–Dewey Beach:** Chamber of Commerce (501 Rehoboth Ave., Box 216, Rehoboth Beach 19971, ☎ 302/227–2233 or 800/441–1329).

Delaware Today magazine (201 N. Walnut St., Suite 1204, Wilmington 19801, ☎ 302/656–1809 or 800/285–0400) publishes a monthly report on planned events and region-wide restaurant listings.

Getting There

By Car

From the north, exit I–95 to U.S. 13S at Wilmington. Take U.S. 113 at Dover and Rte. 1 at Milford. From the south, the scenic route to Delaware's northern shores crosses Chesapeake Bay at Annapolis and continues east via U.S. 301/50; follows U.S. 50 to Rte. 404 at Wye Mills, Maryland; then crosses Delaware on Rtes. 404/18 to Rte. 1 at Lewes.

By Bus

Greyhound Lines (☎ 800/231–2222) links Rehoboth Beach with Wilmington, New Castle, and Dover.

By Ferry

Cape May–Lewes Ferry (☎ 302/645–6346 or 302/645–6313 for recorded information) is a 70-minute ride from Cape May, New Jersey, to Lewes, Delaware.

Exploring the Atlantic Coast

It's wise to check current beach-pollution conditions with local tourism offices. Public access to the Atlantic surf and 23 mi of sand is ample, though crowds pour in from Washington, D.C., and points west on holidays. The Broadkill River, Rehoboth Bay, Indian River Bay, and Little Assawoman Bay offer sheltered waters.

Just west of the beaches are some of the state's historic villages and scenic bay-side parks (*see* National and State Parks, *above*). In **Milton,** once a major shipbuilding center at the head of the Broadkill River, the whole downtown area is a historic district of 18th- and 19th-century architecture, including old cypress-shingle houses. **Lewes,** a 1631 Dutch settlement at the mouth of Delaware Bay, cherishes its seafaring past with a marine museum and draws visitors with good restaurants, shops, and lodging that's away from the hectic beach resorts.

Coastal towns include **Rehoboth Beach,** the largest, with a busy boardwalk for noshing/strolling/shopping expeditions, and adjacent **Dewey Beach. Bethany Beach, South Bethany,** and **Fenwick Island** (founded as a church camp and known for its fishing), south of the Indian River inlet, are the quiet resorts, especially compared with Ocean City, Maryland, to the south.

Sports and the Outdoors

Fishing

Charter boats, for either deep-sea or bay (trout, bluefish) fishing, book day or half-day trips, including all the gear. Book through your hotel, or try **Fisherman's Wharf** (☎ 302/645–8862 or 302/645–8541) in Lewes or **Delaware Seashore State Park Marina** (☎ 302/422–8940) at the Indian River inlet.

Water Sports

Marinas on Rehoboth Bay and Delaware Bay (at Lewes) rent sailboards, sailboats, and motorboats. Catamarans are for rent at **Fenwick Island State Park** (½ mi north of Fenwick Island on Rte. 1, ☎ 302/539–9060) among others.

Shopping

On the Atlantic coast, bargain hunters scour the shops at **Ocean Outlets** (Hwy. 1, Rehoboth Beach, ☎ 302/227–6860), a manufacturers' outlet center touting 72 stores all with products sold at a 20% to 70% savings and, of course, no sales tax.

Dining and Lodging

Resort mavens from Washington, D.C., and Baltimore have sparked a growing variety of hotels and restaurants in the region. Seeking culinary thrills as far north as Milford, these weekenders support good chefs in off-beach towns. The resort strips, from Rehoboth Beach to Fenwick Island, are chockablock with two- and three-story balconied hotels and occasional high rises striving for ocean views. A few inns and B&Bs at Lewes and Milford are the quiet alternative. For price ranges, see Charts 1 (B) and 2 (B) in On the Road with Fodor's.

Bethany Beach

DINING

Sedona. Wild boar rubbed with a Thai mixture of ground cumin, spicy chilis, and garlic and served with a side dish of tumbleweed onions; West Texas crab cakes with Santa Fe salsa; and Southwestern pasta, a fresh homemade pasta accompanied by grilled fish and roasted corn, are a few of the showstoppers at this Southwestern establishment. While decidedly upscale in its culinary intentions, Sedona cultivates a relaxed, casual atmosphere with a decor more Santa Fe and Albuquerque than Bethany or Dewey Beach. *26 Pennsylvania Ave., ☎ 302/539–1200. AE, D, DC, MC, V. $$$*

Dewey Beach

DINING

Rusty Rudder. In this barnlike space with nautical decor overlooking Rehoboth Bay, the specialties are down-home service and local seafood, such as crab imperial. *Dickinson St., on the bay, ☎ 302/227–3888. AE, D, DC, MC, V. $$*

Lewes

DINING

★ **Kupchick's.** This is the best that Lewes has to offer. Expect American cuisine with some Continental specialties at both the grill and the formal Victorian dining room. Certified Angus beef, rack of lamb, and seafood characterize the menu here. Budget-minded guests enjoy the year-round 25% discount before 6 PM. *3 E. Bay Ave., ☎ 302/645–0420. Reservations advised on weekends. AE, D, DC, MC, V. $$$*

Rose & Crown. A dark, paneled, old-English pub, with British and American cooking, may stretch the imagination, but it works here—especially on fresh seafood and good steaks. A large selection of imported ale and beer is the main draw. *108 2nd St., ☎ 302/654–2373. AE, DC, MC, V. $$$*

LODGING

The Inn at Canal Square. Valued for its waterfront location and unusual accommodations, this inn has a full array of conventional rooms as well as *The Legend of Lewes,* a houseboat that floats peacefully at dockside and is equipped with a modern galley, two bedrooms, and two baths. (The houseboat is not recommended for landlubbers or families with children under 14.) A Continental breakfast is included in the room rate. *122 Market St., 19958, ☎ 302/645–8499 or 800/222–7902. 17 doubles, 1 suite, 1 houseboat. AE, D, DC, MC, V. $$$*

★ **The New Devon Inn.** Each room's antique furnishings and linens are unique and have a story, often documented by a local historian. The lobby and the parlor/breakfast room are treasuries of Early Americana. Ask about the biking inn-to-inn package. *2nd and Market Sts., Box*

516, 19958, ☎ *302/645–6466,* FAX *302/645–7196. 24 rooms, 2 suites. AE, D, DC, MC, V. $$$*

Milford

DINING AND LODGING

★ **Banking House Inn.** The country-French cooking in this restored Victorian bank building means less sauce and a lighter approach. Upstairs from the vivid Victoriana of the restaurant, the guest rooms—some with fireplaces—are traditionally decorated. *112 N.W. Front St., 19963,* ☎ *302/422–5708. 3 rooms. Facilities: restaurant. MC, V. $$*

LODGING

Traveler's Inn Motel. Rooms in this two-story, balconied motel are plain, with two double beds and minimal furnishings (a hanging rack, no closet). *1036 N. Walnut St., 19963,* ☎ *302/422–8089. 38 rooms. AE, MC, V. $*

Rehoboth Beach

DINING

Victoria's Restaurant. This elegant Victorian restaurant in the Boardwalk Plaza Hotel (*see* Lodging, *below*) gets a four-diamond rating from AAA for its regional American cuisine. Outdoor dining on the boardwalk is available in summer. *2 Olive Ave.,* ☎ *302/227–0615. AE, D, MC, V. $$$*

Sydney's Side Street Restaurant and Blues Place. The dining tables are on an enclosed porch; after dinner, the band plays near the bar, inside. Contemporary California-style cooking issues from the kitchen with such specialties as California shrimp-and-scallop stir-fry with spinach, pine nuts, and ginger over rice. The innovative "grazing menu" is great for light eaters or those who like to sample several choices. *25 Christian St.,* ☎ *302/227–1339. AE, D, DC, MC, V. $$*

Grotto Pizza. For years, come Labor Day weekend baby boomers who summered at the Delaware resorts have had to be weaned from this pizza they knew as mother's milk. It isn't a pretty sight. Grotto's has several beach locations. *36 Rehoboth Ave.,* ☎ *302/227–3451; The Boardwalk,* ☎ *302/227–3601; Rte. 1, Dewey,* ☎ *302/227–3407. No reservations. No credit cards. $*

Pierre's Pantry. Pierre's does a fast takeout business but has a few tables inside. The attractions are breakfasts, kosher items, and fresh seafood salads, plus some vegetarian entrées. *28 Wilmington Ave. (entrance on 1st St.),* ☎ *302/227–7537. No credit cards. $*

LODGING

Best Western Gold Leaf. The rooms at this hotel, a half block from the beach and across the street from the bay, are traditionally furnished and pleasant. Fourth-floor rooms have water views. *1400 Hwy. 1, 19971,* ☎ *302/226–1100 or 800/422–8566. 75 rooms. Facilities: outdoor pool. AE, D, MC, V. $$$*

Boardwalk Plaza Hotel. On the boardwalk, Rehoboth's only AAA four-diamond property has rooms, suites, and apartments with grand Victorian decor. Rooms for guests with disabilities are available. *2 Olive Ave., 19971,* ☎ *302/227–7169 or 800/332–3224. 27 rooms, 54 suites (including 3 with kitchens), 3 2-bedroom apts. Facilities: restaurant, pool, sundeck, exercise room, parking. AE, D, MC, V. $$$*

Brighton Suites. Each suite includes a traditionally furnished king-size bedroom and a living room with refrigerator and wet bar. *34 Wilmington Ave., 19971,* ☎ *302/227–5780 or 800/227–5788. 66 suites. Facilities: indoor pool, free parking. AE, D, DC, MC, V. $$$*

Atlantic Budget Inn. Rooms at this two-story brick inn are crowded, with double or king-size beds and side tables in motel-moderne style (hanging racks, no closets). *4353 Hwy. 1, 19971, ☎ 302/227–0401 or 800/245–2112. 74 rooms. AE, DC, MC, V. $*

ELSEWHERE IN THE STATE

Dover

Getting There

North and south approaches to Dover are on U.S. 13; Rte. 10 links it with Goldsboro, Maryland; Rte. 1 heads toward Dover from the Atlantic coast towns. **Blue Diamond Lines** (☎ 800/400–3800), a statewide public bus system, now serves Wilmington, Newark, Middletown, Dover, and the Atlantic beaches plus various intermediate points.

What to See and Do

An oasis of Colonial preservation in a bustling government center, the heart of the tree-shaded state capital is the **capitol complex** historic area, on a square laid out in 1722 to William Penn's 1683 plan. To view a slide presentation about Delaware's historic sites and attractions, stop in at the **Delaware State Visitors Center** (406 Federal St., ☎ 302/739–4266); the **Sewell C. Biggs Museum of American Decorative Arts** occupies the building's upper floors. Southeast of town is the **Dover Air Force Base** (☎ 302/677–3376 for tours) and its C-5 Galaxies (the largest aircraft in the world), visible from U.S. 13. The **John Dickinson Plantation** (R.D. 3, Box 257, 19901, ☎ 302/739–3277) offers visitors a glimpse of 18th-century plantation life in Kent County, Delaware.

A horse-drawn wagon, a crop duster, tractors, threshers, a corn house, and a privy are only a small portion of the fascinating collection of tools and structures exhibited at the **Delaware Agricultural Museum and Village,** an operation devoted to Delaware's rich agrarian past and present (agriculture is still the state's number-one industry). *866 N. DuPont Hwy., 19901, ☎ 302/734–1618. Admission charged.*

Had enough culture? Then head straight for **Dover Downs International Speedway** (north of Dover on Rte. 13, Box 843, 19903, ☎ 302/674–4600 or 800/441–7223) for stock-car and harness racing. The grandstands can handle up to 5,000 visitors.

MARYLAND

By Francis X. Rocca

Updated by Bob Willis

Capital	Annapolis
Population	4,965,000
Motto	Manly Deeds, Womanly Words
State Bird	Baltimore Oriole
State Flower	Black-eyed Susan

Visitor Information

The **Maryland Office of Tourism Development** (217 E. Redwood St., Baltimore 21202, ☏ 410/333–6611 or 800/543–1036) provides free publications and runs seven information centers.

Scenic Drives

U.S. 40 Alt., between Frederick and Hagerstown, rolls gently through farmlands and small picturesque towns. There are plenty of farm stands, with fresh fruit and produce in summer. The area is especially attractive in early autumn, when the leaves begin to change. **U.S. 50–301,** at the east end of Kent Island on Maryland's eastern shore, traverses a high-rise bridge that opened in 1991 and offers spectacular views of the inlet and the myriad fishing boats, pleasure craft, and sailboats below.

National and State Parks

National Parks

National Park Service attractions in Maryland include **Antietam National Battlefield Site** (☏ 301/432–5124), **Assateague Island National Seashore** (tel. 410/641–1441), **Blackwater National Wildlife Refuge** (☏ 410/228–2677), **Catoctin Mountain Park** (☏ 301/663–9330), **Chesapeake And Ohio Canal National Historic Park** (☏ 301/739–4200), **Fort McHenry National Monument and Historic Shrine** (☏ 410/962–4290), and **Fort Washington Park** (☏ 301/763–4600).

State Parks

Maryland has 47 parks and forests on more than 280,000 acres of land throughout the state. The **Department of Natural Resources** (☏ 410/974–3771) offers numerous programs, including guided canoe trips, hiking, backpacking, wildflower walks, forest walks, and guided mountain-bike trips. Many of the programs also offer instruction. In 1993, a litter-reduction program was set up, where visitors are provided with refuse bags on entry to the parks and are expected to carry their own trash out with them on departure. The Office of Tourism Development (*see* Visitor Information, *above*) has information about each of the parks.

BALTIMORE

Before 1980, it was a joke to speak of Baltimore as a tourist destination. Then Inner Harbor, a decaying downtown neighborhood refurbished in the 1970s, became a showcase of expensive hotels, shops, office buildings, and museums. Ever since, it has been drawing visitors to the city where Babe Ruth was born, where Edgar Allan Poe died, and where stalwart citizens under fire inspired the composition of the national anthem.

Tourist Information

Baltimore: Area Convention Visitors Association (☎ 410/837–4636 or 800/282–6632). Office of Promotion (200 W. Lombard St., 21201, ☎ 410/752–8632). International Visitors Center (World Trade Center, Suite 1353, 21202, ☎ 410/837–7150).

Arriving and Departing

By Plane

Baltimore Washington International Airport (☎ 410/859–7111), 10 mi south of town, is a destination for most major domestic and foreign carriers. Taxi fare to downtown is roughly $19. **Amtrak** and **Maryland Area Rail Commuter** (MARC; ☎ 800/325–7245) trains run between the airport station (10 minutes from the terminal via free shuttle bus) and Penn Station, about 20 minutes away. **Shuttle Express** (☎ 410/859–0800) has van service to downtown and to most suburban hotels.

By Car

Baltimore is on I–95, the major East Coast artery.

By Train

Amtrak serves Baltimore's Penn Station (Charles St. at Mt. Royal Ave., ☎ 800/872–7245). In addition, **Central Light Rail Line** (☎ 410/539–5000) provides service from Timonium, north of the city, through downtown, and south to Glen Burnie.

By Bus

Greyhound Lines (210 W. Fayette St., ☎ 800/231–2222).

Getting Around Baltimore

Most attractions are a walk or a short trolley ride (*see* Orientation Tours, *below*) from Inner Harbor. **Water Taxis** (☎ 410/563–3901) stop at Fells Point and at Inner Harbor locations. Beyond that a car is useful; the metro line is limited, and bus riding can mean lots of transfers (**Mass Transit Administration,** ☎ 410/539–5000).

Orientation Tours

From spring through fall, **Baltimore Trolley Tours** (☎ 410/752–2015) runs 90-minute narrated tours of Baltimore's downtown attractions. The tours also stop at all downtown hotels. Passengers may get on and off an unlimited number of times in one day for one price.

Exploring Baltimore

The city fans out northward from Inner Harbor, with newer attractions such as the National Aquarium and Oriole Park concentrated at the center and more historic neighborhoods and sites toward the edges. Running along the center, the major northbound artery is Charles Street; cross streets are "East" or "West" relative to it.

Charles Street

Head north on Charles Street from Baltimore Street toward the impossible-to-miss Washington Monument. Restaurants and art galleries lend an urbane tone to this neighborhood, a mix of 19th-century brownstones and modern office buildings. A block west of Charles is the **Basilica of the Assumption** (Mulberry St. at Cathedral St.), which was built in 1812 and is the oldest Catholic cathedral in the United States. In November 1994 Baltimore's archbishop, William Keeler, was elevated to the rank of cardinal, the third in Baltimore's history.

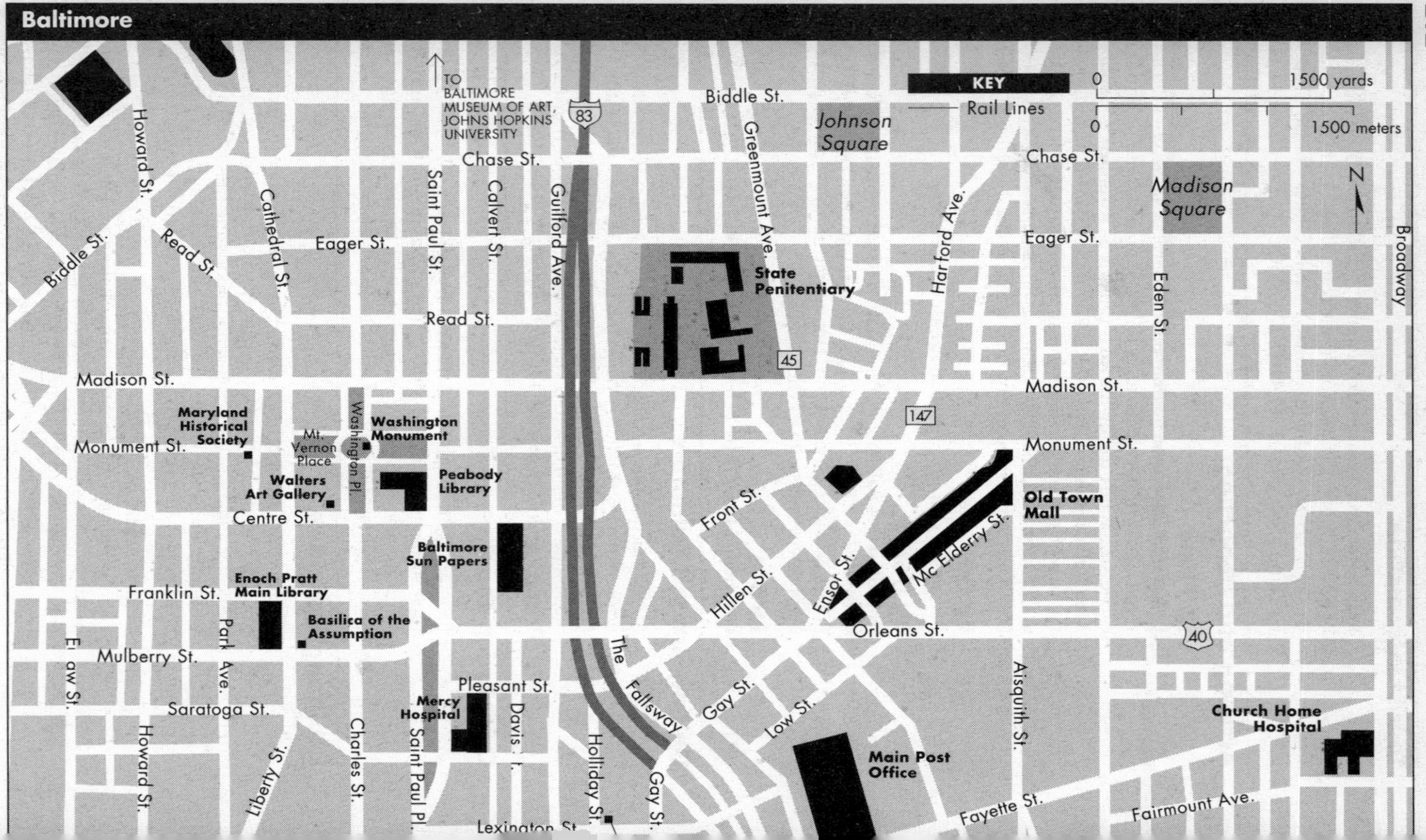
TO BALTIMORE MUSEUM OF ART, JOHNS HOPKINS UNIVERSITY
83
Biddle St.
Johnson Square
KEY
Rail Lines
0
1500 yards
0
1500 meters
Howard St.
Chase St.
Chase St.
Madison Square
N
Cathedral St.
Saint Paul St.
Calvert St.
Guilford Ave.
Greenmount Ave.
Harford Ave.
Broadway
Biddle St.
Read St.
Eager St.
Eager St.
State Penitentiary
Eden St.
Read St.
45
Madison St.
Madison St.
147
Maryland Historical Society
Washington Monument
Monument St.
Mt. Vernon Place
Washington Pl.
Monument St.
Walters Art Gallery
Peabody Library
Front St.
Old Town Mall
Centre St.
Mc Elderry St.
Baltimore Sun Papers
Hillen St.
Ensor St.
Enoch Pratt Main Library
Franklin St.
Basilica of the Assumption
Orleans St.
40
Park Ave.
Mulberry St.
The Fallsway
Pleasant St.
Aisquith St.
aw St.
Saratoga St.
Mercy Hospital
Gay St.
Low St.
Church Home Hospital
Howard St.
Liberty St.
Charles St.
Saint Paul Pl.
Davis
Holliday St.
Gay St.
Main Post Office
Fayette St.
Fairmount Ave.

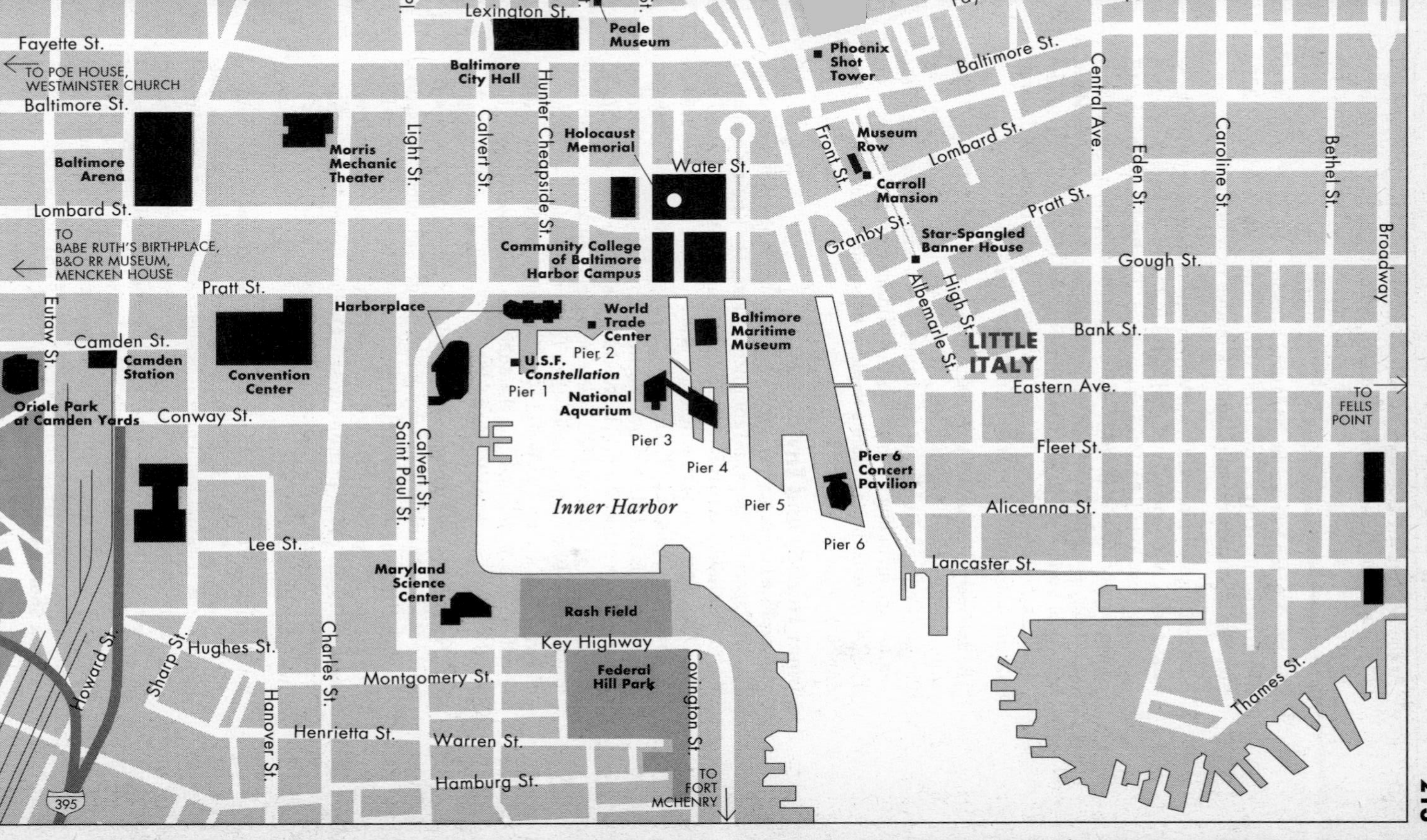

Lexington St.
Peale Museum
Fayette St.
TO POE HOUSE, WESTMINSTER CHURCH
Baltimore St.
Baltimore City Hall
Phoenix Shot Tower
Baltimore St.
Central Ave.
Caroline St.
Bethel St.
Broadway
Eden St.
Holocaust Memorial
Water St.
Front St.
Museum Row
Lombard St.
Carroll Mansion
Morris Mechanic Theater
Light St.
Calvert St.
Hunter Cheapside St.
Baltimore Arena
Lombard St.
TO BABE RUTH'S BIRTHPLACE, B&O RR MUSEUM, MENCKEN HOUSE
Community College of Baltimore Harbor Campus
Pratt St.
Granby St.
Star-Spangled Banner House
Gough St.
Pratt St.
Albemarle St.
High St.
Harborplace
World Trade Center
Baltimore Maritime Museum
LITTLE ITALY
Bank St.
Eutaw St.
Camden St.
Camden Station
Convention Center
Pier 2
U.S.F. Constellation
Pier 1
National Aquarium
Eastern Ave.
TO FELLS POINT
Oriole Park at Camden Yards
Conway St.
Saint Paul St.
Calvert St.
Pier 3
Pier 4
Fleet St.
Pier 6 Concert Pavilion
Inner Harbor
Pier 5
Aliceanna St.
Lee St.
Pier 6
Lancaster St.
Maryland Science Center
Rash Field
Key Highway
Howard St.
Sharp St.
Hughes St.
Charles St.
Montgomery St.
Federal Hill Park
Covington St.
Thames St.
Hanover St.
Henrietta St.
Warren St.
Hamburg St.
TO FORT MCHENRY
395

At the **Walters Art Gallery** (N. Charles and Centre Sts., ☏ 410/547–2787; admission charged), international art from antiquity through the 19th century is housed in an Italianate palace. The adjacent Hackerman House has a magnificent gallery of Asian art.

The **Washington Monument** (☏ 410/837–4636), built in 1829, is a 178-ft marble column topped by a 16-ft statue of the first president. A 228-step spiral staircase within leads to a unique view of the city.

Surrounding the monument is **Mt. Vernon Square,** flanked by four block-long parks. Note the bronze sculptures in the parks and the elegant brownstones along East Mt. Vernon Place. The **Peabody Library** (17 E. Mt. Vernon Pl., ☏ 410/659–8179) has a handsome reading room with a skylight in its five-story-high ceiling. At the nearby **Maryland Historical Society** (201 W. Monument St., ☏ 410/685–3750; admission charged), the eclectic display of state memorabilia includes the original manuscript of "The Star Spangled Banner."

The **Baltimore Museum of Art** (Charles and 31st Sts., ☏ 410/396–7101; admission charged), 1½ mi north, displays works by Rodin, Matisse, Picasso, Cézanne, Renoir, and Gauguin. A new wing containing 20th-century art, including 15 Andy Warhol paintings, opened in late 1994. The 140-acre campus of **Johns Hopkins University** is next door to the museum.

Inner Harbor and Environs

Harborplace comprises two glass-enclosed shopping malls with more than 100 specialty shops and gourmet markets. The Rouse Company's multilevel **Gallery** across Pratt Street offers upscale shopping and dining. Other waterfront attractions are nearby. At the **Maryland Science Center** (601 Light St., ☏ 410/685–5225; admission charged), the biggest draw is an IMAX movie theater with a five-story-high screen. There is also a planetarium. The **World Trade Center** (401 Pratt St., ☏ 410/837–4515) is the world's tallest pentagonal building (32 stories); its 27th-floor observation deck—the "Top of the World"—offers a terrific view of the city. The World War II submarine USS *Torsk* and the lightship *Chesapeake* make up the **Baltimore Maritime Museum** (Piers 3 and 4, Pratt St., ☏ 410/396–5528).

The **National Aquarium in Baltimore** (Pier 3, ☏ 410/576–3800) is home to more than 5,000 species of marine life, including sharks, dolphins, beluga whales, and puffins. Escalators whisk visitors from level to level past a tank with a huge coral reef, which you can later walk through, to the rooftop "rain forest." On Pier 4, the Marine Mammal Pavilion offers performances by Atlantic bottlenose dolphins and themed exhibit areas.

East of Inner Harbor is the **Star-Spangled Banner House** (Pratt and Albemarle Sts., ☏ 410/837–1793; admission charged), where the flag that inspired the national anthem was woven. Around Lombard Street courtyard between Front and Albemarle streets are the four institutions of **Museum Row** (Baltimore City Life Museums, ☏ 410/396–3523; admission charged). Highlights are a row house where actors perform short plays set in 1840; and the elegant town house of a signer of the Declaration of Independence. At East Fayette and Front streets is the **Phoenix Shot Tower,** used to make shot until the Civil War.

North of Inner Harbor on Holliday Street are the golden-domed **Baltimore City Hall,** built in 1875 and completely supported by ironwork, and the **Peale Museum** (225 N. Holliday St., ☏ 410/396–1149; admission charged), which shows paintings by Charles Willson Peale and his family and has been open since 1814, making it the oldest museum in the United States.

Other Attractions

A 10-minute trolley ride (or 12 minutes by water taxi) from Inner Harbor takes you to **Fells Point,** once a thriving shipbuilding center and now a neighborhood of cobblestone streets and historic redbrick houses, many of them shops, galleries, restaurants, and taverns. At Broadway and Thames Street is an operating tugboat pier.

West of Inner Harbor are the **H. L. Mencken House** (1524 Hollins St., ☎ 410/396–7997; admission charged), from which "the Sage of Baltimore" ruled American letters from the 1920s to the 1940s; the **Poe House** (203 N. Amity St., ☎ 410/396–7932; admission charged), where Edgar Allan Poe wrote his first horror story; and the **Westminster Church Grave** (W. Fayette and Greene Sts.), where Poe is buried.

The 50,000-seat **Oriole Park at Camden Yards** (Camden and Howard Sts., ☎ 410/685–9800), opened in 1992, has a 700-sq-ft video scoreboard, several restaurants, and a cocktail lounge. Its brick facade and asymmetric playing field evoke the big-league parks of the early 1900s. Built on the site of a former railroad depot, it is served by MARC trains from Washington, the Central Light Rail trains from the suburbs, and the local metro. Two blocks west is **Babe Ruth's birthplace** (216 Emory St., ☎ 410/727–1539), where the baseball legend was born in 1895.

Locomotives and railroad cars are on display at the **B&O Railroad Museum** (Pratt and Poppleton Sts., ☎ 410/752–2490; admission charged). One of the world's largest train museums, it sits on the site of the country's first railroad station.

At the end of the peninsula bounding the Patapsco River's northwest branch is **Fort McHenry,** a star-shaped brick building famous for its role in the national anthem. The "star-spangled banner" that Francis Scott Key saw "by the dawn's early light" on September 14, 1814, was the one flying above this fort. *Fort Ave. (off Key Hwy.),* ☎ *410/962–4290. Admission charged. Boat rides from Inner Harbor, Memorial Day–Labor Day.*

Parks and Gardens

Sherwood Gardens (Stratford Rd. and Greenway, 3 mi from Inner Harbor east of St. Paul St., ☎ 410/366–2572) is worth a special trip in late April and early May to see thousands of peaking tulips and azaleas. South of Inner Harbor is **Federal Hill Park** (Battery St. and Key Hwy.), with an excellent view of the downtown skyline and a jogging track in adjacent **Rash Field.**

What to See and Do with Children

Two attractions are especially popular with children: the **National Aquarium In Baltimore** and the **Maryland Science Center and IMAX Theatre,** both in Baltimore's Inner Harbor (*see* Exploring Baltimore, *above*).

The 150 acres of the **Baltimore Zoo** are a year-round child-pleaser. There are more than 1,200 animals, including polar bears, elephants, and penguins, that call the zoo home. *Druid Park Lake Dr., I–83 Exit 7,* ☎ *410/366–5466. Admission charged.*

Shopping

The city's most diverse and colorful shopping areas are the malls of **Harborplace** and the shops of **Fells Point** (*see* Exploring Baltimore, *above*).

There are more than three dozen first-rate shops on **Antique Row** (700 and 800 blocks, N. Howard St.; 200 block, W. Read St.). At **Kelmscott Bookshop** (32 W. 25th St., ☎ 410/235–6810) you can browse among the enormous stock of rare books in the coziness of a converted town house. The city of Baltimore owns and leases space to a number of indoor food markets; at least 100 years old are **Belair Market** (Gay and Fayette Sts.), **Broadway Market** (Broadway and Fleet Sts.), **Cross Street Market** (Light and Cross Sts.), **Hollins Market** (Hollins and Arlington Sts.), **Lexington Market** (Lexington and Eutaw Sts.), and **Northeast Market** (Monument and Chester Sts.).

Spectator Sports

Baseball

Orioles (Oriole Park at Camden Yards, Camden and Howard Sts., ☎ 410/685–9800; Apr.–Oct.).

Dining

Seafood, especially Chesapeake Bay blue crab (steamed in the shell, fried in a crab cake, or baked with a white-cream-and-wine sauce), is the specialty, but every major cuisine is available, including the ethnic offerings of the Greek and Italian neighborhoods. For price ranges, see Chart 1 (B) in On the Road with Fodor's.

$$$ **Citronelle.** The food, service, and preparation surpass even the spectacular view of Baltimore's "Cultural Corridor" you can enjoy while dining here, atop the Latham Hotel. Chef Karim Lakhani presides over the kitchen and makes certain guests are well served and imaginatively fed in the Franco-Californian style of Los Angeles chef Michel Richard. *612 Cathedral St., ☎ 410/837–3150. Jacket and tie. AE, D, DC, MC, V.*

$$$ ★ **Tio Pepe.** Paella à la Valenciana (chicken, sausage, shrimp, clams, mussels, and saffron rice) is served often in these candlelighted cellar dining rooms, as is the lesser-known Basque red snapper (with clams, mussels, asparagus, and boiled egg). *10 E. Franklin St., ☎ 410/539–4675. Reservations required. Jacket and tie required at dinner. AE, DC, MC, V.*

$$ ★ **Bertha's.** Mussels are the specialty here, served steamed (with a choice of eight butter-based sauces) or as a Turkish appetizer (stuffed with sweet-and-spicy rice). The decor is nautical. *734 S. Broadway, ☎ 410/327–5795. DC, MC, V.*

$$ **8 East.** This cozy, discreet restaurant serves such dishes as scallops sautéed with sun-dried tomatoes and chicken marsala with shallots and mushrooms. *Tremont Hotel, 8 E. Pleasant St., ☎ 410/576–1199. AE, D, DC, MC, V.*

$$ **Haussner's.** It has been said that if you have but one meal in Baltimore it should be at Haussner's, where the menu lists more than 100 entrées every day. German food is the specialty of the house, but there is fare—particularly the enormous desserts—to please everyone. The walls are adorned with hundreds of original paintings, including pieces by Gainsborough, Rembrandt, Bierstadt, Van Dyck, and Whistler. *3244 Eastern Ave., ☎ 410/327–8365. No reservations at dinner. AE, D, DC, MC, V. Closed Sun.–Mon.*

$$ **Raphael's.** On the southern edge of Little Italy and within walking distance of the Inner Harbor, this small restaurant pays close attention to the fine preparation of a variety of Italian dishes, including fettuccine Raphael (crab meat, shrimp, and scallops in a lobster-cream sauce) and veal DiFolco (scaloppine of veal with shrimp, artichoke hearts, and mushrooms in a lemon-wine sauce). Save room for dessert. *411 S. High St., ☎ 410/727–4235. AE, DC, MC, V.*

$ **Burke's Cafe.** Just a block from the Inner Harbor, convention center, and Baltimore Arena, Burke's has long been one of downtown's favorite casual dining spots. Its specialty is pub grub—frosty mugs, giant burgers, and platters of huge onion rings—and it has become popular with the "after the game" crowd, tourists, and conventioneers alike. *36 Light St., at Lombard St., ☎ 410/752–4189. AE, MC, V.*

$ **City Markets** (*see* Shopping, *above*). These are great for a stand-up or counter-side breakfast or lunch. Each features different local favorites including fresh Chesapeake Bay seafood, grilled wursts, homemade soups and salads, sushi, and Philadelphia cheese steaks.

$ **Donna's.** A good bet for both fresh-baked morning scones and after-theater espresso (open till 1 AM on Fri. and Sat.), this Italian coffee bar also serves a variety of pastas, salads, and innovative sandwiches from midday on. *1 Mt. Vernon Sq. (2 W. Madison St. at Charles St.), ☎ 410/385–0180. AE, MC, V.*

Lodging

Staying around Inner Harbor means ready access to the major attractions. Away from the water, as far north as Mt. Vernon, are reminders of an older Baltimore and some relative bargains in accommodations. For price ranges, see Chart 2 (A) in On the Road with Fodor's.

$$$$ ★ **Harbor Court.** Since 1986 this redbrick tower with an ersatz English-country-house interior (à la Ralph Lauren) has been Baltimore's most prestigious hotel. The priciest rooms have a harbor view. *550 Light St., 21202, ☎ 410/234–0550 or 800/824–0076, FAX 410/659–5925. 195 rooms, 8 suites. Facilities: 2 restaurants, bar, indoor pool, sauna, workout room. AE, D, DC, MC, V.*

$$$ **Latham Hotel.** The dark-wood-paneled lobby of the former Peabody Court hotel suggests a men's club, but the guest rooms are, for the most part, done in pastel color schemes, with horticultural prints on the wall. Rooms with views of Mt. Vernon Place and the Washington Monument are the most sought after. *612 Cathedral St., 21201, ☎ 410/727–7101 or 800/528–4261, FAX 410/789–3312. 104 rooms, 10 suites. Facilities: 2 restaurants. AE, DC, MC, V.*

$$$ **Sheraton Inner Harbor.** Just two blocks from Harborplace and Oriole Park, the Sheraton is the "official" hotel of the Baltimore Orioles. It's also within walking distance of most of the city's attractions and has the only Orthodox-Union-certified kosher hotel kitchen in town. *300 S. Charles St., 21201, ☎ 410/962–8300 or 800/325–3535, FAX 410/962–8211. 339 rooms, 20 suites. Facilities: restaurant, bar, indoor pool, sauna, workout room. AE, D, DC, MC, V.*

$$$ **Tremont Hotel.** This small hostelry on a quiet downtown block has a locally unsurpassed level of service: The concierge will arrange free local transportation, and the staff will do guests' personal shopping. All suites have kitchens. *8 E. Pleasant St., 21202, ☎ 410/576–1200 or 800/873–6668, FAX 410/244–1154. 60 suites. Facilities: restaurant, bar. AE, DC, MC, V.*

$$$ ★ **Tremont Plaza.** This plain, gray, 37-story tower has suites decorated in gentle earth tones. All units have kitchens, and those numbered 06 have the best views. *222 St. Paul Pl., 21202, ☎ 410/727–2222 or 800/873–6668, FAX 410/685–4215. 230 suites. Facilities: restaurant, deli, bar, outdoor pool, sauna, workout room. AE, DC, MC, V.*

Motels

Days Inn Inner Harbor (100 Hopkins Pl., 21201, ☎ and FAX 410/576–1000 or ☎ 800/325–2525), 250 rooms, 8 suites, restaurant, pool, bar; *$$*. **Hampton Inn Hunt Valley** (11200 York Rd., Hunt Valley

21031, ☎ 410/527–1500 or 800/426–7866, FAX 410/771–0819), 126 rooms; $.

The Arts and Nightlife

Events listings appear in the Friday *Baltimore Sun,* the Thursday *Evening Sun,* the monthly *Baltimore* magazine, and the *City Paper,* a free weekly distributed in shops and at street-corner machines.

The Arts

Center Stage (700 N. Calvert St., ☎ 410/332–0033) is the state theater of Maryland. Other venues include **Friedberg Hall** (Peabody Conservatory, E. Mt. Vernon Pl. and Charles St., ☎ 410/659–8124), **Lyric Opera House** (Mt. Royal Ave. and Cathedral St., ☎ 410/685–5086), **Meyerhoff Symphony Hall** (1212 Cathedral St., ☎ 410/783–8000), **Morris A. Mechanic Theater** (Baltimore and Charles Sts., ☎ 410/625–1400), and **Pier Six Concert Pavilion** (Pier 6 at Pratt St., ☎ 410/625–4230). There are also numerous dinner theaters in the Baltimore suburbs; check newspapers for details.

Nightlife

The harborside **Explorer's Club** (Harbor Court Hotel, ☎ 410/234–0550) offers jazz and remarkable views. **8x10** (8 E. Cross St., ☎ 410/625–2000) is the spot for blues and rock. Move to the latest dance mixes at the **Baja Beach Club** (55 Market Pl., ☎ 410/727–0468). Laughter is the sound heard at **Winchester's Comedy Club** (Light and Water Sts., ☎ 410/523–3837), while the talk is all sports at **Balls** (200 W. Pratt St., ☎ 410/659–5844) and the **Orioles Sports Bar** (Sheraton Inner Harbor Hotel, 300 S. Charles St., ☎ 410/962–8300).

The **Fells Point** area is Baltimore's answer to D.C.'s Georgetown. Nightclubs, restaurants, pubs, coffeehouses, and small theaters line cobblestone streets around the foot of Broadway.

MARYLAND'S CHESAPEAKE

Maryland encompasses the top half of the Chesapeake Bay, where the attractions are, naturally, quite water-oriented: Annapolis is a world yachting capital, the eastern shore is a major duck-hunting ground, and Ocean City is a bustling Atlantic resort. Yet bay-side towns are also rich in history, with many well-preserved 18th-century buildings.

Tourist Information

Annapolis and Anne Arundel County: Convention & Visitors Association (26 West St., Annapolis 21401, ☎ 410/268–8687). **Calvert County:** Department of Economic Development (County Courthouse, Prince Frederick 20678, ☎ 410/535–4583 or 800/331–9771). **Cecil County:** Economic Development (129 E. Main St., Elkton 21629, ☎ 410/479–0660). **Charles County:** Division of Tourism (Star Rte. 1, Box 1144, Port Tobacco 20677, ☎ 800/766–3386). **Dorchester County:** Office of Tourism (501 Court La., Cambridge 21613, ☎ 410/228–1000 or 800/522–8687). **Kent County:** Chamber of Commerce (118 N. Cross St., Chestertown 21620, ☎ 410/778–0416). **Ocean City:** Convention and Visitors Bureau (Box 116, Ocean City 21842, ☎ 410/289–2800 or 800/626–2326). **Queen Anne's County:** Visitors Service (102 E. Main St., Suite 103A, Stevensville 21666, ☎ 410/643–8908). **St. Mary's County:** Division of Tourism (Box 653, Leonardtown 20650, ☎ 301/475–4626 or 800/327–9023). **St. Michael's:** Talbot County Chamber of Commerce (805 Goldsborough St., Easton 21601, ☎

410/822–4606). **Somerset County:** Tourism Office (Box 243, Princess Anne 21853, ☎ 410/651–2968 or 800/521–9189). **Wicomico County:** Visitors Bureau (500 Glen Ave., Salisbury 21801, ☎ 410/548–4914). **Worcester County:** Tourism Office (Box 208, Snow Hill 21863, ☎ 410/632–3617).

Getting There

By Car

To Annapolis: From Baltimore, follow Rte. 3/97 to U.S. 50 (Rowe Blvd. exit). **To the western shore:** From Annapolis, take Rte. 2S, which becomes Rte. 4 in Calvert County. **To the eastern shore:** From Baltimore or Annapolis, cross the Bay Bridge (toll charged) northeast of Annapolis and stay on U.S. 50–301.

By Bus

Baltimore Mass Transit (☎ 410/539–5000) provides service—express on weekdays, local on weekends—between Annapolis and Baltimore. **Carolina Coach** (☎ 410/727–5014) links Annapolis to Ocean City and intermediate points on the eastern shore.

Exploring Maryland's Chesapeake

Annapolis

Start on the waterfront. Sailboats dock right at the edge of **Market Square,** where there is a visitor information booth. At **City Dock,** look for the sidewalk plaque commemorating the arrival of Kunta Kinte, the African slave immortalized in Alex Haley's *Roots.*

At the **Victualling Warehouse Museum** (77 Main St., ☎ 410/268–5576; admission charged) you can rent an audiocassette and let narrator Walter Cronkite be your guide on a walking tour of the Historic District.

On the riverside campus of the **United States Naval Academy** (known to West Pointers as the "country club on the Severn"), the most prominent structure is the bronze-domed **U.S. Naval Chapel,** burial place of the Revolutionary War hero John Paul ("I have not yet begun to fight!") Jones. Outdoors, full-dress parades of midshipmen are a stirring sight. ☎ *410/263–6933 or 410/267–3363.*

The **Hammond-Harwood House** (19 Maryland Ave., ☎ 410/269–1714), the **Chase-Lloyd House** (22 Maryland Ave., ☎ 410/263–2723), and the **William Paca House** (186 Prince George St., ☎ 410/263–5553) are all outstanding examples of redbrick Colonial architecture. **St. John's College** (College Ave., ☎ 410/263–2371) is the third-oldest college in the country and the home of a 600-year-old tree.

The **Maryland State House** (State Cir., ☎ 410/974–3400) is the oldest state capitol in continuous legislative use and the only one that has housed the U.S. Congress. Charles Willson Peale's painting, *Washington at the Battle of Yorktown,* hangs inside.

The Western Shore

Calvert County offers plenty of striking bay-side scenery, including the imposing **Calvert Cliffs** (some 100 ft high) and several miles of beaches, famous for the Miocene-period fossils that can be found along the water's edge. The forest primeval is open for inspection from an elevated boardwalk at the **Battle Creek Cypress Swamp Sanctuary** (Rte. 2/4 to Rte. 506, ☎ 410/535–5327), which boasts the northernmost naturally occurring stand of the ancient bald cypress tree in the United States. To see the cliffs and beaches, stop at **Calvert Cliffs State Park** (Rte. 2/4, Lusby, ☎ 301/856–8987). For a glimpse of the eastern shore on a clear day, try the observation deck at the **Calvert Cliffs Nuclear Power Plant** (☎ 410/586–4676) next door.

Down at the tip of the peninsula is **Solomons,** a still-tranquil but increasingly fashionable sailing town. At its **Calvert Marine Museum** (Rte. 2/4 at Solomons Island Rd., ☎ 410/326–2042), boats from various epochs and a 19th-century screw-pile lighthouse are on display.

Across the Patuxent in St. Mary's County is **Historic St. Mary's City** (Rte. 5, ☎ 301/862–0990), where the first colonists dispatched by Lord Baltimore, according to a grant of Charles I, settled in 1634. Until 1694 this was the capital of Maryland. Reconstructions of 17th-century buildings and of the ship that the settlers came on are to be seen at this less spectacular but more peaceful version of Virginia's Colonial Williamsburg. Plantation buffs may want to visit the **Sotterley Plantation** (Rte. 235, ☎ 301/373–2280) to the north.

The Eastern Shore

The William Preston Lane, Jr., Memorial Bridge links Annapolis to the eastern shore, passing along the way through **Kent Island,** the bay's largest island. This is the site of the first English settlement in Maryland—agents of Virginia's governor set up a trading post here in 1631. Rte. 50 continues south past historic towns near the bay and then leads east to the Atlantic.

In the town of **Wye Mills** (Rte. 662) is the state tree, the 400-year-old, 95-ft-tall **Wye Oak,** and a working 17th-century gristmill that once ground grain for Washington's troops at Valley Forge. The affluent town of **Easton** has a 17th-century Quaker meeting house and an 18th-century courthouse.

On the Miles River is **St. Michaels** (on Rte. 33), once a shipbuilding center and now a fashionable yachting destination. On display at its **Chesapeake Bay Maritime Museum** is everything from a Native American dugout canoe to a modern sailboat still under construction. Exhibitions of stuffed waterfowl, decoys, and guns are extensive. *Navy Point, ☎ 410/745–2916. Admission charged. Closed weekdays Jan.–Mar.*

The **Oxford-Bellevue Ferry** has been running since 1683, and today it takes cars and pedestrians across the Tred Avon River from a spot 7 mi south of St. Michaels to the 17th-century town of **Oxford.** Few of the surviving buildings in Oxford date to before the mid-1800s, but the bigger (and less charming) town of **Cambridge** 15 mi to the southeast has several from the 1700s. The area is well-suited to cycling; many roads have special bike lanes.

Southwest of Cambridge is the **Blackwater National Wildlife Refuge** (Rte. 335, ☎ 410/228–2677), 11,000 acres of marshland inhabited by Canada geese, ospreys, and bald eagles. Visitors can travel by car, bicycle, or on foot. The Blackwater Refuge is a favorite of serious nature photographers.

On the Atlantic side of the peninsula is **Ocean City,** with 10 mi of white-sand beach and a flashy 27-block boardwalk. Coastal Highway, with blocks of high-rise condos, runs down the center of town. More than 300,000 vacationers flock here every summer.

What to See and Do with Children

Vintage aircraft are parked outside the **Naval Air Test and Evaluation Museum** (Rte. 235 and Shangri-la Dr., Lexington Park [western shore], ☎ 301/863–7418). Indoors, failed contraptions on display include the improbable Goodyear Inflatoplane. The **Godiah Spray Plantation** (Rosecroft Rd., St. Mary's City 20686, ☎ 301/862–0990) offers authentic demonstrations of 17th-century plantation life, including planting, cooking, and building. **Trimper's Amusement Park** (Boardwalk and S. 1st St., Ocean City, ☎ 410/289–8617), with a huge roller coaster and other rides, celebrated its centennial in 1990.

Sports and the Outdoors

Biking

Viewtrail 100 is a 100-mi circuit in Worcester County, between Berlin and Pocomoke City. In **Ocean City,** the right-hand lanes of Coastal Highway are for buses and bikes. Many boardwalk shops rent bikes.

Fishing

The principal catches are black drum, channel bass, flounder, bluefish, white perch, weakfish, croaker, trout, and largemouth bass. One-week licenses are sold at many sporting-goods stores, one-year licenses from the **Department of Natural Resources** (Box 1869, Annapolis 21404, ☎ 410/974–3211). **Anglers** (435 Revel Hwy., Annapolis, ☎ 410/757–3442) sells and rents equipment. **Bunky's Charter Boats** (Solomons Island Rd., Solomons, ☎ 410/326–3241) and **Scheibels** (Wynne Rd., Ridge, south of Lexington Park, ☎ 301/872–5185) will arrange bay charters. The **Fishing Center** (Shantytown Rd., West Ocean City, ☎ 410/213–1121) runs private charters and daily deep-sea trips, and **Bahia Marina** (22nd St. and the bay, Ocean City, ☎ 410/289–7438) arranges deep-sea charters.

Golf

Eisenhower Golf Course (Generals Hwy., northwest of Annapolis, ☎ 410/222–7922) and the **Bay Club** (Rte. 818, west of Ocean City, ☎ 410/641–4081) have 18 holes. **Ocean City Golf and Yacht Club** (Rte. 611, ☎ 410/641–1779) has 36.

Sailing

Northeast Wind Yachts (222 Severn Ave., Annapolis, ☎ 410/267–6333) charters sailboats, with or without crews. **Annapolis Sailing School** (601 6th St., ☎ 410/267–7205 or 800/638–9192) offers outfitting and instruction. **Zanhiser's Sailing Center** (C St. at Back Creek, Solomons, ☎ 410/326–2166) arranges yacht charters. **Town Dock Marina** (305 Mulberry St., St. Michaels, ☎ 410/745–2400) and **Sailing, Etc.** (5305 Coastal Hwy., Ocean City, ☎ 410/723–1144) rent sailboats.

Beaches

Sandy Point State Park (Rte. 50, 12 mi east of Annapolis) is a good spot for fishing, swimming, or launching boats. Otherwise, western shore beaches are for strolling and looking. There are no Chesapeake Bay beaches of any consequence on the eastern shore. On the Atlantic, south of Ocean City, is the northern portion of **Assateague Island National Seashore** (*see* National and State Parks, *above*).

Dining and Lodging

Restaurants in Annapolis and the less-expensive western shore, though reliable for seafood, do not warrant a special trip. Across the bay are innovative kitchens and classic crab houses.

Lodging reservations are necessary as much as a year in advance of the Annapolis sailboat and powerboat shows in October, Naval

Academy commencement in May, and Easton's Waterfowl Festival in November.

For price ranges, see Charts 1 (B) and 2 (B) in On the Road with Fodor's.

Annapolis

DINING

The Corinthian. Cheerful waiters lend this oil-lamp-lighted dining room its sporty air. The distinctive crab cakes have an angel-hair-pasta binder, and the New York strip is three-week-aged. *Loews Annapolis Hotel, 126 West St., ☎ 410/263–7777. Jacket and tie required. AE, DC, MC, V. $$$*

★ **McGarvey's Saloon and Oyster Bar.** This casual bar and restaurant is a popular hangout with locals, tourists, and sailors. The kitchen serves up standard American fare—burgers, steaks, seafood, and fun finger foods—until 1 AM. *8 Market Space at NE corner of Market House, ☎ 410/263–5700. No reservations. AE, MC, V. $$*

LODGING

Annapolis Marriott Waterfront. Amenities such as bathroom phones typify the rooms, which face the water, the historic district, or—from private balconies—the bustle of City Dock. Juan Alfredo's Virgin Island Cafe is a casual first-level dining room overlooking Alfredo's Dock Spot Bar at the water's edge. *80 Compromise St., 21401, ☎ 410/268–7555, 800/336–0072, or 800/228–9290; FAX 410/269–5864. 150 rooms. Facilities: restaurant, 2 bars. AE, D, DC, MC, V. $$$*

Chez Amis Bed & Breakfast. Conveniently located within walking distance of major sites in Historic Annapolis, this charming B&B offers down comforters and terry robes to go with the comfortable king- and queen-size beds in each room. *85 East St., Annapolis, 21401, ☎ 410/263–6631 or 800/474–6631. 4 rooms, 2 with bath, 2 share 1 bath. Facilities: breakfast area, living room, roof deck. MC, V. $$*

Calvert County

DINING

Solomons Crabhouse. Inside this converted firehouse, diners smash hardshell crabs with wood mallets to the tune of country-and-western music from the stereo. *H&W Shopping Ct., Rte. 2/4, Solomons, ☎ 410/326–2800. AE, MC, V. No lunch weekdays. $$*

LODGING

Back Creek Inn. Rooms in this 19th-century wood-frame house feature brass beds with colorful quilts and views of the water, a garden, or a quiet street. *Calvert and A Sts., Solomons 20688, ☎ 410/326–2022. 4 rooms (3 share bath), 2 suites, cottage. Facilities: whirlpool. No credit cards. Closed mid-Dec.–mid-Feb. $$$*

Ocean City

DINING

The Hobbit. Murals and carved lamps portray J.R.R. Tolkien characters in this dining room with a two-angled view of Assawoman Bay. Veal with pistachios and sautéed catch of the day are menu highlights. *101 81st St., ☎ 410/524–8100. MC, V. $$$*

Lombardi's. Cozy wood booths, and tables and walls decorated with photos, provide the setting for outstanding thin-crust pizza. Cheese steaks and cold-cut sandwiches are the alternatives. *9203 Coastal Hwy., ☎ 410/524–1961. No reservations. MC, V. Closed Wed. $*

DINING AND LODGING

Hotels at Fager's Island. Ocean City's most prestigious guest address is actually two hotels linked by walkways over the street. The Lighthouse Club and the Coconut Mallory offer rooms with bedside Jacuzzis and balconies overlooking Assawoman Bay; some rooms also have fireplaces. Guests can dine in the hotels' restaurant, which boasts one of the state's most extensive wine lists. *56th St. in the Bay, Ocean City 21842, ☎ 410/723–6100 or 800/767–6060. 108 suites. Facilities: restaurant, 3 bars. AE, DC, MC, V. $$$*

St. Mary's County

DINING

Evans Seafood. Ask for a water view, then order lobster stuffed with crab imperial, or the spicy, secret-recipe hard-shell crab. *Rte. 249, Piney Point, ☎ 301/994–2299. No credit cards. No lunch weekdays. $$*

LODGING

Potomac View Farm. This 19th-century wood-frame farmhouse is furnished with simple oak furniture, quilts, and a life-size wooden cow in the living room. A mile away is an affiliated marina. Full breakfast is included. *Rte. 249, Tall Timbers 20690, ☎ 301/994–0418, FAX 301/994–2613. 7 rooms, 1 suite, 1 cottage. Facilities (at marina): restaurant, bar, outdoor pool, beach. AE, MC, V. $$*

St. Michaels

DINING

★ **208 Talbot.** An antiques-filled late-19th-century house is the setting for regional cuisine. Maryland's own rockfish is sautéed with wild mushrooms in an oyster-cream sauce. Fresh bay oysters are served with a champagne-cream sauce, prosciutto, and pistachio nuts. *208 N. Talbot St., ☎ 410/745–3838. MC, V. $$$*

Crab Claw. The bang-them-yourself steamed blue crabs are first-rate at this harborside eatery. The spicy deep-fried hard crab is worthwhile too, as is the vegetable crab soup. *Navy Point, ☎ 410/745–2900. No credit cards. Closed Dec.–Feb. $$*

DINING AND LODGING

★ **Inn at Perry Cabin.** This early 19th-century farmhouse has been made to resemble an English country house, with antiques and Laura Ashley in the bedrooms, a cozy library, spectacular gardens, and a formal dining room. Menu standouts are crab-and-lobster cake with black truffles, and rabbit with grilled squash and smoked bacon. *308 Watkins La., 21663, ☎ 410/745–2200 or 800/722–2949, FAX 410/745–3348. 27 rooms, 14 suites. Facilities: restaurant, bar, indoor pool. AE, DC, MC, V. $$$*

Motels

Dunes Motel (27th St. and Baltimore Ave., Ocean City 21842, ☎ 410/289–4414), 103 rooms, café, outdoor pool, wading pool; closed Dec.–mid-Feb.; *$$*. **Holiday Inn Conference Center and Marina** (155 Holiday Dr., Box 1099, Solomons 20688, ☎ 410/326–6311 or 800/356–2009, FAX 410/326–1069), 325 rooms, restaurant, 2 bars, outdoor pool, 2 tennis courts, Nautilus equipment, sauna; *$$*. **St. Michaels Motor Inn** (Rte. 33 and Peaneck Rd., St. Michaels 21663, ☎ 410/745–3333 or 800/974–9618, FAX 410/745–2906), 93 rooms, 1 suite, 2 pools; *$$*.

The Arts and Nightlife

The Arts

In summer, the **U.S. Naval Academy Band** performs at Annapolis's City Dock on Tuesday evenings, and the **Starlight Series** takes place on Sunday evenings. **Ocean City** (☎ 410/289–2800 or 800/626–2326) sponsors free boardwalk concerts. When the **Colonial Players** (108 East St.,

Annapolis, ☎ 410/268–7373) go on vacation, **Annapolis Summer Garden Theater** (Compromise and Main Sts., ☎ 410/268–0809) takes over.

Nightlife

Ocean City has plenty of places for dancing to rock—live or recorded; there is even an under-21 club, **Night Light** (Boardwalk at Worcester St., ☎ 410/289–6313), for those too young to drink. Bars in Annapolis, Solomons, and St. Michaels are favored by more subdued, and in many cases middle-aged, crowds.

ELSEWHERE IN THE STATE

Western Maryland

Getting There

From Baltimore, I–70 runs westward through Frederick and up to the state's narrowest point, pinched between West Virginia and Pennsylvania. U.S. 40 passes through the "Narrows" into the "Panhandle."

What to See and Do

In **Frederick,** the Visitor Center (19 E. Church St., 21701, ☎ 301/663–8687 or 800/999–3613) has information on several Civil War sites. These include the **Barbara Fritchie House** (154 W. Patrick St., ☎ 301/698–0630), where, according to legend and poetry, an old woman defied Stonewall Jackson by waving the Stars and Stripes.

Near Sharpsburg is **Antietam National Battlefield** (Rte. 65, ☎ 301/432–5124), where Union troops repelled Lee's invasion in 1862. This day of fighting was the bloodiest confrontation of the Civil War, fought on a road now known as Bloody Lane. **Hagerstown,** also in Washington County (Tourism Office, 1826 Dual Hwy., 21740, ☎ 301/791–3130), was a frontier town founded by Germans in the early 18th century; several buildings from that period have been preserved, including the frontier home-fortress of Jonathan Hager, the town's founder.

The mountain scenery grows rugged in aptly named **Allegany County** (Office of Tourism, Canal St., Cumberland 21502, ☎ 301/777–5905), where the Cumberland Gap provides an opening for U.S. 40, formerly the "National Road" taken by westward-bound settlers in the early years of the Republic. Here and in neighboring **Garrett County** (Promotion Council, 200 S. 3rd St., Oakland 21550, ☎ 301/334–1948) there are plenty of opportunities for outdoor recreation, including skiing.

NEW JERSEY

By Alexandra Roll Kenney

Updated by Andrea E. Lehman

Capital	Trenton
Population	7,760,487
Motto	Liberty and Prosperity
State Bird	Eastern goldfinch
State Flower	Purple violet

Visitor Information

New Jersey Department of Commerce and Economic Development (Division of Travel and Tourism, 20 W. State St., CN-826, Trenton 08625-0826, ☎ 609/292–2470 or 800/537–7397, FAX 609/633–7418). There are seven **tourist information centers** at major destinations around the state. For information on state parks, contact the **Department of Environmental Protection** (Division of Parks and Forestry, CN-404, Trenton 08625, ☎ 609/292–2797 or 800/843–6420).

Scenic Drives

For Hudson River views, take the **Palisades Interstate Parkway** north from the George Washington Bridge to the state line, or **River Road** from Weehawken north to Fort Lee. Both **Rte. 23** northwest from Newfoundland through High Point State Park and **Rte. 15** northwest from I–80 offer lakes, rural estates, and higher-elevation vistas. The back roads off **Rtes. 202 and 206** in central New Jersey pass by horse farms, antiques shops, and historic sites. Along the southern shore, **Ocean Drive** is a causeway that links barrier islands with a series of bridges.

National and State Parks

National Parks

Sandy Hook Unit of Gateway National Recreation Area (Box 530, Highlands 07732, ☎ 908/872–0115) preserves sandbar ecology and fortifications built to protect New York Harbor. On the Delaware River boundary between New Jersey and Pennsylvania is the **Delaware Water Gap National Recreation Area** (visitor center, Kittatinny Point, off I–80; mailing address, Bushkill, PA 18324; ☎ 908/496–4458; *see also* Pennsylvania), the largest national recreation area in the Northeast. The 40,000-acre **Edwin B. Forsythe National Wildlife Refuge's Brigantine Division** (Box 72, Great Creek Rd., Oceanville 08231, ☎ 609/652–1665) has an 8-mi wildlife drive, mainly through diverse coastal habitat, and two short nature trails especially popular during spring and fall bird migrations.

State Parks

New Jersey has the third-largest state-park system in the nation, with 36 parks, 11 forests, 4 recreation areas, 42 natural areas, 23 historic sites, 4 marinas, and 1 golf course. **Wharton State Forest** (R.D. 9, Hammonton 08037, ☎ 609/561–3262), New Jersey's largest, contains the **Batsto State Historic Site** (Rte. 542), a restored late-18th- and 19th-century Pinelands iron-working village, where traditional crafts are still demonstrated. **High Point State Park** is named after the state's tallest peak. Many of New Jersey's 19 lighthouses are preserved in state parks, including Barnegat Lighthouse, Cape May Point Lighthouse, and Sandy Hook Lighthouse (*see* The Jersey Shore, *below*).

THE JERSEY SHORE

The Jersey Shore is 127 mi of public beachfront, stretching like a pointing index finger along the Atlantic Ocean from the Sandy Hook Peninsula in the north to Cape May at the southern tip. There is no one description of what it's like "down the shore." Things change town by town, and sometimes season by season (winter storms have a habit of rearranging beaches and boardwalks). Busy seaside resorts crammed with amusements (and families) sit next to quiet, primarily residential communities with undeveloped waterfronts, which in turn might shoulder up to aging cities, restored Victorian districts, or anything in between. Unless you have "beachaphobia," though, there's probably a place on the shore that's right for you.

The shore offers saltwater fishing from pier, bridge, dock, or boat (licenses are not required); other water sports; bird-watching; and bicycling or strolling on the ubiquitous wood-plank or concrete boardwalks. In Atlantic City are the famed gambling casinos; in Cape May, Victorian bed-and-breakfasts.

Tourist Information

Atlantic City: Convention & Visitors Authority (2314 Pacific Ave., 08401, ☎ 609/348–7100 or 800/262–7395, FAX 609/345–3685). **Cape May:** Chamber of Commerce (Box 556, 08204, ☎ 609/884–5508). **Cape May County:** Chamber of Commerce (Cape May Court House, Box 74, 08210, ☎ 609/465–7181, FAX 609/465–5017). **Monmouth County:** Department of Promotion and Tourism (27 E. Main St., Freehold 07728, ☎ 908/431–7476 or 800/523–2587, FAX 908/866–3696). **Ocean County:** Tourism Advisory Council (Box 2191, Toms River 08754, ☎ 908/929–2138 or 800/365–6933, FAX 908/506–5000). **Wildwoods:** Information Center (Box 609, Wildwood 08260, ☎ 609/522–1407 or 800/992–9732).

Getting There

By Plane

Philadelphia International (*see* Pennsylvania), **Newark International** (☎ 201/961–6000), and the **New York City airports** (*see* New York) are closest to Atlantic City and shore points. **Atlantic City International** (☎ 609/645–7895) serves the southern shore.

By Car

The main road serving the Jersey Shore is the Garden State Parkway, a north–south toll road that ends in Cape May. From New York City, I–80 and the New Jersey Turnpike (toll) connect with the Garden State. From Philadelphia and southern New Jersey suburbs, take the Atlantic City Expressway (toll). From the south, take the Delaware Memorial Bridge and continue north on the New Jersey Turnpike. Toms River, Barnegat, and Tuckerton are linked by U.S. 9.

By Train

Amtrak (1 Atlantic City Expressway, near Kirkman Blvd., ☎ 800/872–7245) serves Atlantic City. **New Jersey Transit** (for northern NJ, ☎ 201/762–5100 or 800/772–2222 in NJ; for southern NJ, ☎ 215/569–3752 or 800/582–5946 in NJ) operates local commuter service to Atlantic City from Philadelphia and the shore towns of Monmouth and Ocean counties from New York City.

By Bus

New Jersey Transit (*see* By Train, *above*) offers bus service to most Jersey Shore towns. **Academy Lines** (☎ 908/291–1300) also runs buses between New York City and shore points. **Greyhound Lines** (☎ 609/345–6617 or 800/231–2222) serves Atlantic City. Ask Atlantic City casino hotels about direct service to their properties.

By Ferry

The **Cape May–Lewes Ferry** (☎ 609/886–9699 or 800/643–3779; in DE, 302/645–6346) is a year-round, 70-min car-ferry link (800 passengers, 100 cars per ferry) across Delaware Bay between Cape May and Lewes, Delaware.

Exploring the Jersey Shore

The **New Jersey Coastal Heritage Trail** (☎ 609/785–0676), being developed cooperatively by the National Park Service, State of New Jersey, and other organizations, will connect significant natural and cultural resources along the shore. Five theme routes are planned. The first, maritime history, has signs now in place; coastal habitat is under development; and others are scheduled for completion in the next several years.

At the shore's north end, the **Sandy Hook Unit of the Gateway National Recreation Area** (*see* National and State Parks, *above*) is 4 mi east of Atlantic Highlands on Rte. 36. Here on this peninsula of barrier beach you can glimpse the New York City skyline, 19 mi across the harbor from North Beach; splash in the usually gentle, shallow surf; and explore sleepy **Fort Hancock,** established in 1895.

Just south on Rte. 36, **Long Branch** was founded in the 18th century as one of America's first resorts; over the years it has hosted seven presidents, from Grant to Wilson.

A century ago **Asbury Park** was the shore's toniest resort, but efforts to revive that glory have so far been disappointing. Nowadays it is known for its place in rock history: The metal gate at 702 Cookman Avenue led to the second-floor **Upstage Club,** where the young Bruce Springsteen performed in the 1960s. By contrast, neighboring **Ocean Grove** has Victorian hotels and inns; relatively quiet beaches; a short, gameless boardwalk; and shops and cafés. The imposing **Great Auditorium** (Pilgrim Pathway, ☎ 908/775–0035; in NJ, 800/388–4768) presents a summer schedule of concerts, from big bands to country, jazz, '50s–'60s oldies, and current pop.

In **Belmar,** the **Municipal Marina** (Rte. 35, ☎ 908/681–2266), on the Shark River, has party and charter boats that head for the ocean daily in search of blackfish, blues, fluke, tuna, and shark. Neighboring **Spring Lake** has a totally uncommercialized boardwalk, three spring-fed lakes complete with swans, a small town center, and a handful of romantic B&Bs. The more family-oriented **Point Pleasant Beach** has **Jenkinson's Aquarium** (Ocean Ave., ☎ 908/899–1659; admission charged) on the boardwalk at the Broadway Beach area for rainy-day diversion.

On Barnegat Peninsula, the side-by-side resorts of **Seaside Heights** and **Seaside Park** have two major amusement piers plus a giant water-slide park on the boardwalk that runs between them. Just south but seemingly a world away is narrow **Island Beach State Park** (☎ 908/793–0506; admission charged), 10 mi of ocean and bay beaches with almost no evidence of human habitation.

Return inland over Barnegat Bay to **Toms River,** once a pirate and privateering port. The **Ocean County Museum** (26 Hadley Ave., ☎ 908/341–1880) contains Victorian artifacts and exhibits on the dirigibles that flew from the Lakehurst Naval Air Station, site of the 1937 *Hindenburg* tragedy.

Head south on U.S. 9 and east on Rte. 72 over Barnegat Bay to **Long Beach Island. Barnegat Lighthouse** (☎ 609/494–2016; admission charged), known locally as "Old Barney" and completed in 1858, is at the northern tip of the island. To the south is **Beach Haven,** the island's commercial center, with Victorian houses set around the town square. In one of these houses you'll find the **Long Beach Island Museum** (Engleside and Beach Aves., ☎ 609/492–0700; admission charged), which conducts walking tours of the historic district from late June to early September.

Back on the mainland, the Garden State Parkway and U.S. 9 lead to **Atlantic City.** It was originally popular for seaside holidays in fabulous stone hotels and for promenades on the **boardwalk,** the nation's first elevated wood walkway (1870), where saltwater taffy is still sold. Today more than 30 million people flood the town annually to gamble, dropping about $8 million daily in the **casinos.** (Be alert outside at night—the city has a high crime rate.) The dozen casino hotels are outrageous, from the Mardi Gras festivity of the Showboat and the onion-shaped domes of the whimsical Taj Mahal on the ocean-side boardwalk to the pair of quieter marina casinos on the bay.

Some of Atlantic City's famous ocean **amusement piers** can still be seen, but only the Moorish Revival Central Pier (St. James Pl./Tennessee Ave. and the boardwalk) retains its original 1884 appearance. The Garden Pier (New Jersey Ave. and the boardwalk) has been converted to an art center. The annual mid-September **Miss America Pageant** (☎ 609/345–7571) takes place in the **Convention Center** (2301 Boardwalk, ☎ 609/348–7100).

Heading south again, you'll find **Ocean City,** across Great Egg Harbor. Begun as a Methodist retreat (Billy Graham got his start here as a radio preacher in the 1940s), Ocean City is one of only two dry (that is, no alcohol sold) towns on the shore. Its **boardwalk** and boardwalk parades are family-oriented, and summer-evening concerts at the **Music Pier** (Moorlyn Terr.) are a tradition.

Savor a quiet walk on **Strathmere Beach** before heading on along Ocean Drive to the little boroughs known as the **Wildwoods.** The best-known, the loudest, the kitschiest, and the wildest is **Wildwood** itself. Its 2-mi **boardwalk** has the single greatest concentration of outdoor amusement rides on the shore, including seven amusement piers.

For a change of pace and scenery, travel to the southern tip of the shore and the re-created world of Victorian **Cape May.** Believed to be the state's oldest ocean resort, it was named for the Dutch captain who sighted it in 1620. Cape May today hosts myriad mostly-for-grownups bed-and-breakfasts, most in elaborately gingerbreaded Victorian houses. (Some B&Bs and restaurants close January through March.) In early October, **Victorian Week** (☎ 908/884–5404) combines madcap frivolity with serious lectures on period history and restoration (make reservations well in advance). The July 4 celebration is vintage Americana, while Christmastime has Dickensian flair, filled with plenty of tours of houses decked in Victorian finery.

The Cape May area also attracts flocks of birds and bird-watchers, especially during the spring and fall migrations. A favorite birding lo-

The Jersey Shore

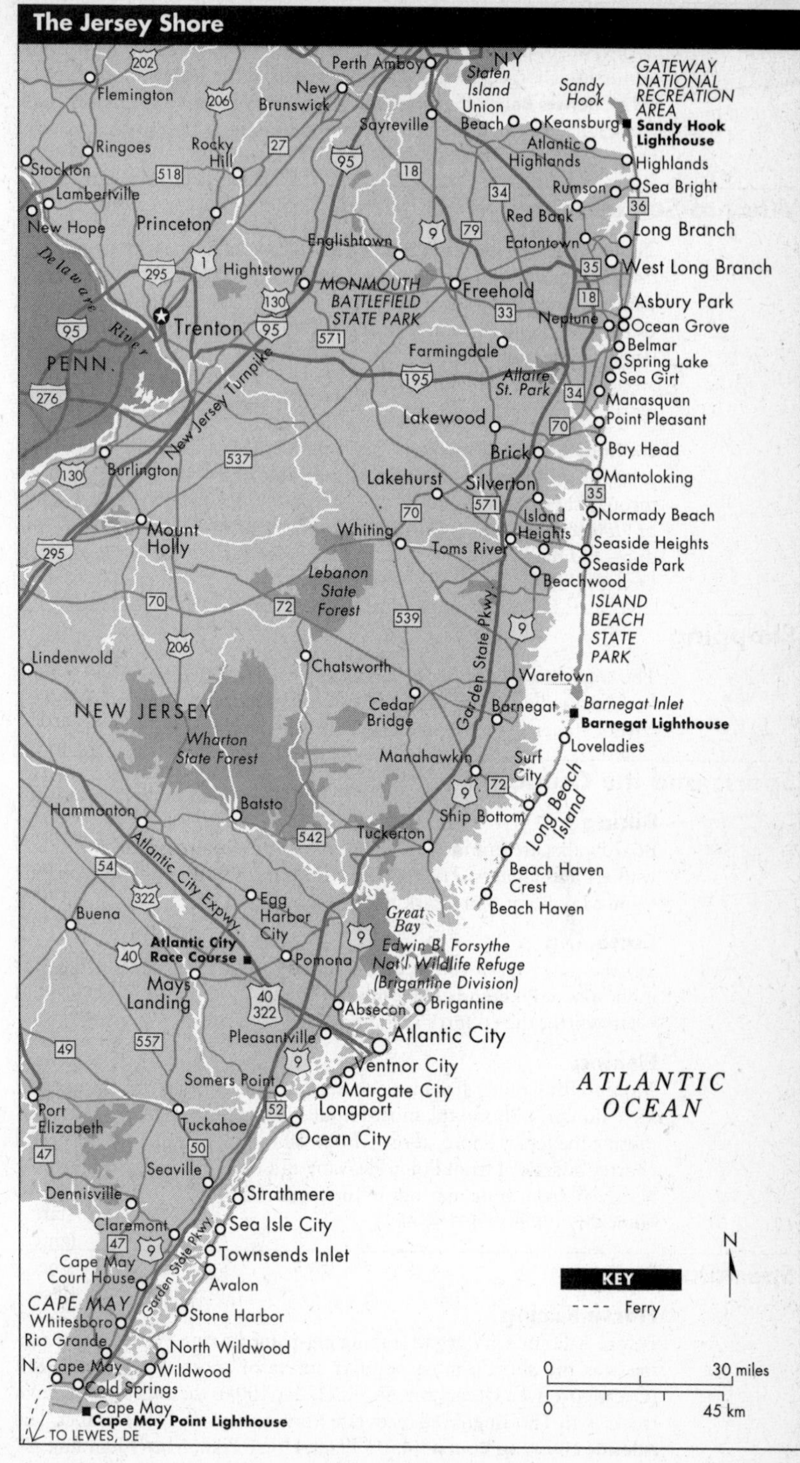

cale is **Cape May Point State Park** (Lighthouse Ave., ☎ 609/884–2159), site of the 1859 **Cape May Point Lighthouse** (☎ 609/884–5404; admission charged), which marks the end of the Jersey Shore. Not far away, **Sunset Beach** (Sunset Blvd., Cape May Point) is the place to collect Cape May diamonds, pebbles of pure quartz that wash up on the beach, and to watch the sun set over Delaware Bay.

What to See and Do with Children

The entire Jersey Shore is a children's playground, with its sandy beaches, usually gentle and shallow surf, and casual boardwalk snack bars. Towns with **amusement parks** or **rides** with child-appeal include Seaside Park, Ocean City, Point Pleasant Beach, and Wildwood. **Lucy the Elephant** (Atlantic and Decatur Aves., Margate, ☎ 609/823–6473; admission charged), an elephant-shaped building six stories high and a National Historic Landmark, has been drawing the curious of all ages since 1881.

Six Flags Great Adventure, a theme park bigger than Disneyland, comprises an amusement park with a multitude of rides, as well as a drive-through safari park. *Rte. 537, I–195 Exit 16, Jackson, ☎ 908/928–2000 or 908/928–1821 for recording. Admission $29.95 adults, $19.95 children, reduced rates for senior citizens and after 4* PM. *Closed late Oct.–mid-Apr.*

Shopping

The **Englishtown Auction** (90 Wilson Ave., ☎ 908/446–9644), a giant flea market held on weekends March–January plus selected holidays, covers 50 acres. Arrive at sunrise for the best buys.

Sports and the Outdoors

Biking

Boardwalks are grand for biking if you don't mind dodging weekend walkers and joggers. The road around Cape May Point takes you past Cape May Point State Park and its lighthouse.

Canoeing

Try the many freshwater creeks, streams, and tributaries in the 1.1-million-acre **Pinelands National Reserve** (☎ 609/894–9342) around Chatsworth, the country's first national reserve.

Fishing

Monmouth County has more charter and party boats than any other area along the shore; the most popular is the **Belmar Marina** (*see* Exploring the Jersey Shore, *above*). In Ocean County, numerous party and charter boats sail from Point Pleasant and Long Beach Island. Fishing boats sail from state marinas in **Leonardo** (☎ 908/291–1333) and **Atlantic City** (☎ 609/441–8482).

Spectator Sports

Horse Racing

Before Atlantic City began staging big-name boxing events, horse racing was the shore's most popular spectator sport. **Monmouth Park** (Oceanport Ave., Oceanport, ☎ 908/222–5100) is the area's best-known track, with Thoroughbred races late May through early September. The **Atlantic City Race Course** (4501 Black Horse Pike, May's Landing, ☎ 609/641–2190) has Thoroughbred racing June through early September. **Freehold Raceway** (U.S. 9 and Rte. 33, Freehold, ☎ 908/462–3800) offers harness racing mid-August through May.

Beaches

From Memorial Day to Labor Day the **Water Information Hotline** (☎ 800/648–7263) supplies information about the shore's water quality and beach conditions. **Island Beach State Park** (*see* Exploring the Jersey Shore, *above*) is the most scenic natural beach on the Jersey Shore. Shore beaches usually charge a fee from Memorial Day or mid-June to Labor Day for everyone 12 and older. Windsurfing is especially good in the calm waters of the open bays. Sailing, rowing, or powerboating is superb on sheltered Barnegat Bay in Ocean County.

Dining and Lodging

Though the restaurant fare ranges from cheap snacks to pricey haute cuisine, seafood is the Jersey Shore's biggest deal, with local catches featured on most menus. Ocean City and Ocean Grove do not allow the sale of liquor. For price ranges, see Chart 1 (A) in Chapter 1.

Lodgings should be booked far in advance in summer. Beachfront rooms are more expensive. Rooms in Atlantic City casino hotels are the most popular, the most costly, and the most difficult to reserve, especially on weekends from mid-June to Labor Day. Chambers of commerce (*see* Tourist Information, *above*) can provide assistance. **Bed & Breakfast Adventures** (2310 Central Ave., Suite 132, N. Wildwood 08260, ☎ 609/522–4000 or 800/992–2632, FAX 609/522–6125) handles inns and private homes statewide. For price ranges, see Chart 2 (A) in On the Road with Fodor's.

Atlantic City

DINING

★ **Le Palais.** Favorites such as the shellfish/vegetable mélange Olga, rack of lamb with rosemary and pine nuts, and individual dessert soufflés (order these at the start of the meal) are elegantly served in this lavish mirrored and art-hung dining room. *Merv Griffin's Resorts Casino Hotel, N. Carolina Ave. and Boardwalk, ☎ 609/344–6000 or 800/438–7424. Jacket requested. AE, D, DC, MC, V. Closed Mon.–Tues. $$$$*

Knife and Fork Inn. Established in 1912 in its Tudor-accented Flemish tavern and owned by the same family since 1927, this local institution serves straightforward seafood and steaks. *Albany and Atlantic Aves., ☎ 609/344–1133. Jacket required. AE, D, DC, MC, V. Closed Sun.–Mon. Nov.–Apr. $$$*

★ **Dock's Oyster House.** Owned and operated by the Dougherty family since 1897, the city's oldest restaurant serves seafood in a setting of wood and stained and engraved glass with nautical motifs. *2405 Atlantic Ave., ☎ 609/345–0092. AE, DC, MC, V. Closed Mon. $$–$$$*

Los Amigos. South of the border specialties, such as Mexican pizza, burritos, beer, and margaritas, served in the dimly lighted back room, are a good bet at this small bar and restaurant two blocks from the boardwalk casinos. *1926 Atlantic Ave., ☎ 609/344–2293. AE, DC, MC, V. $$*

★ **Angelo's Fairmount Tavern.** The locals flock here for lots of good Italian fare served up by the Mancuso family, the owners since 1935. *2300 Fairmount Ave., ☎ 609/344–2439. AE, MC, V. No lunch weekends. $*

White House Sub Shop. It claims to have sold more than 17 million overstuffed sandwiches since 1946. Photo walls proclaim its celebrity fans. *Mississippi and Arctic Aves., ☎ 609/345–1564 or 609/345–8599. No reservations. No credit cards. $*

LODGING

★ **Bally's Park Place Casino Hotel & Tower.** Guests can stay in the art deco–style rooms of the historic Dennis Hotel, built in 1860, or in the new 37-story tower, whose spacious, angular rooms have picture windows even in the marble-tiled bathrooms. *Park Place at Boardwalk, 08401, ☎ 609/340–2000 or 800/225–5977, FAX 609/340–1725. 1,255 rooms, 159 suites. Facilities: 8 restaurants, 1 lounge, 350-seat showroom, racquetball courts, basketball court, exercise room, 7 whirlpools, sauna, indoor pool, shops. AE, D, DC, MC, V. $$$–$$$$*

Trump Castle Casino Resort. Modern on the outside with medieval accents inside, the "Castle on the Bay" attracts a slightly more sophisticated crowd than the casino hotels on the boardwalk. *Huron Ave. and Brigantine Blvd., 08401, ☎ 609/441–2000 or 800/777–8477, FAX 609/441–8540. 563 rooms, 162 suites. Facilities: 7 restaurants, 3 lounges, boat docking, 4 tennis courts, health club, outdoor pool, exercise room, whirlpool, sauna, shops. AE, D, DC, MC, V. $$$–$$$$*

Flagship Resorts. This pleasant, modern, salmon-colored condo hotel is across from the boardwalk (facing Brigantine and the Absecon Inlet) and is quietly away from the casino action. Every room has a private terrace with a terrific view. *60 N. Main Ave., 08401, ☎ 609/343–7447 or 800/647–7890, FAX 609/343–6593. 440 suites. Facilities: restaurant, market/deli, bar, health club, pool, whirlpool, sauna. AE, D, DC, MC, V. $$$*

★ **Quality Inn Boardwalk.** One of Atlantic City's best values has a 17-story modern guest wing set atop a Federal-style base. Rooms are decorated with handsome Colonial-reproduction furnishings. Merv Griffin's casino is next door. *S. Carolina and Pacific Aves., 08401, ☎ 609/345–7070 or 800/356–6044, FAX 609/345–0633. 199 rooms, 4 suites. Facilities: restaurant, bar. AE, D, DC, MC, V. $$*

Cape May

DINING

★ **Mad Batter.** The fabulous and eclectic contemporary American cuisine—perhaps orange-and-almond French toast with strawberry dipping sauce for breakfast; a lunch of house-smoked maple chicken on a bed of mesculine greens; and, for dinner, crab Mappatello (crabmeat, spinach, ricotta, and onions in a puff pastry)—is served in the skylighted Victorian dining room or outdoors on the porch or garden terrace. *19 Jackson St., ☎ 609/884–5970. D, MC, V. Closed 1st 3 wks in Jan. $$–$$$*

LODGING

Queen Victoria. In the center of the historic district, the inn's three restored Victorian houses are blessed with a genteel air and are decorated with items that pay homage to the queen and the period named for her. Rooms are furnished with antiques but have modern touches unusual for a B&B, including minirefrigerators in every room, whirlpools in many, and TVs in the suites. *102 Ocean St., 08204, ☎ 609/884–8702. 17 rooms, 6 suites. Facilities: bicycles, free beach tags, parking. AE, MC, V. $$$–$$$$*

★ **The Mainstay.** This 1872 gambling and men's club, restored as a B&B, captures the feel of another era with 14-ft ceilings, stenciling and historic wallpapers, and harmoniously arranged antiques, while a recently restored building across the street contains suites filled with modern amenities. *635 Columbia Ave., 08204, ☎ 609/884–8690. 9 rooms, 7 suites. Facility: parking. No credit cards. $$$*

Chalfonte. This authentic Victorian summer hotel is definitely one of a kind. Despite very simple original furnishings, it attracts a loyal blue-blooded following. Interesting programs include evening entertainment; work weeks, during which students and other volunteers stay free at the hotel in return for help in upkeep; and a supervised children's dining room, where youngsters eat while parents dine on home-style, mostly Southern, cooking. *301 Howard St., 08204, ☎ 609/884–8409, FAX 609/884–4588. 78 rooms (67 share baths), 2 cottages. Facilities: restaurant, children's dining room, bar, meeting room, playground. MC, V. MAP. Closed Columbus Day–Memorial Day weekend. $$–$$$*

Manor House. On a quiet tree-lined street two blocks from the beach, this guest house mixes antiques, stained glass, art, such dashes of whimsy as an old-fashioned barber's chair, and a wisecracking innkeeper. *612 Hughs St., 08204, ☎ 609/884–4710. 8 rooms (2 share bath), 1 suite. Facilities: free beach tags, valet parking. D, MC, V. Closed Jan. $$–$$$*

Red Bank

LODGING

Oyster Point. This sleek, low rise on the Navesink River caters to business travelers but offers weekend packages and a marina for boaters. Contemporary-style rooms have such amenities as hair dryers, coffeemakers, and two TVs and phones; most suites have balconies. *146 Bodman Pl., 07701, ☎ 908/530–8200 or 800/345–3484, FAX 908/747–1875. 58 rooms, 6 suites. Facilities: restaurant, bar, conference center, exercise room. AE, D, DC, MC, V. $$*

Spring Lake

LODGING

The Breakers. Toward the northern end of the shore, this is one of the few remaining Victorian oceanfront hotels. However, siding and green outdoor carpeting are the first signs that the 19th-century mood has not been preserved. The interior is contemporary, with light colors and woods. It's nice to have a drink in the piano bar or watch the sun set from the veranda. *1507 Ocean Ave. (at Newark Ave.), 07762, ☎ 908/449–7700, FAX 908/449–0161. 64 rooms. Facilities: restaurant, bar, pool. AE, DC, MC, V. $$$–$$$$*

Hollycroft. Looking over Lake Como at the northern edge of town, this incongruous but beautiful B&B is a mountain lodge at the shore. A 16-ft ironstone fireplace; walls of knotty pine and, here and there, log or stone; and rooms decorated with collected treasures, stenciling, and good taste make this a charming getaway. *506 North Blvd., Box 448, 07762, ☎ 908/681–2254. 6 rooms, 1 suite. Facility: bicycles. AE. $$–$$$*

Toms River

DINING

Old Time Tavern. Italian dishes, steak, seafood, and sandwiches are the lures at this restaurant and tap room, and early-bird soup-to-dessert meals can be had at bargain prices. *N. Main St. (Rte. 166 off Rte. 37), ☎ 908/349–8778. AE, DC, MC, V. $$*

Motels

Ascot Motel (Iowa and Pacific Aves., Box 1824, Atlantic City 08404, ☎ 609/344–5163 or 800/225–1476), 80 rooms, outdoor pool; *$$*. **Best Western Bayside Resort at Golf & Tennis World** (8029 Black Horse Pike, W. Atlantic City 08232, ☎ 609/641–3546, FAX 609/641–4329), 110 rooms, restaurant, health club, 6 tennis courts, outdoor pools, casino shuttle; *$$*. **Midtown-Bala Motor Inn** (Indiana and Pacific Aves., Atlantic City 08401, ☎ 609/348–3031 or 800/932–0534, FAX 609/347–6043), 300 rooms, restaurant, bar, indoor and outdoor pools, free valet parking; *$$*. **Sandpiper** (Boulevard at 10th St., Ship Bottom 08008, ☎ 609/494–6909), 20 rooms, refrigerators, outdoor pool; closed Nov.–Apr.; *$–$$*.

The Arts and Nightlife

Garden State Arts Center (Garden State Pkwy. Exit 116, Holmdel, ☏ 908/442–9200) has a summer roster of performing-arts groups, star acts, and ethnic festivals. Nightlife is fierce at the **Atlantic City casino hotels,** between the gambling action and the nationally famous night-club acts; call the casino box offices for show reservations.

ELSEWHERE IN THE STATE

The Northwest Corner

Getting There

I–80 and, running northwest from it, Rtes. 23 and 15, provide easy access to this area from Manhattan.

What to See and Do

This sparsely developed region of small lakes and low mountains attracts skiers in winter, while the rest of the year brings outdoorsy types who come to enjoy water sports on the Delaware River and Lake Hopatcong, scenic roads, hiking on the Appalachian Trail, and historical sites from the 1700s and 1800s.

The state's highest elevation (1,803 ft) is in **High Point State Park** (*see* National and State Parks, *above*), 7 mi northwest of Sussex. Hugging the river from I–80 to the northern tip of the state is the **Delaware Water Gap National Recreation Area** (*see* National and State Parks, *above*). **Waterloo Village** (Waterloo Rd., Stanhope, ☏ 201/347–0900) is a restored Revolutionary War–era canal town. Its summer concert series attracts renowned jazz, classical, rock, and country performers.

The most popular ski areas, clustered around the nondescript town of **McAfee,** are fully outfitted with artificial snowmaking equipment, have both day and evening skiing, are family-oriented, and provide a good mix of all-ability ski terrain. **Vernon Valley/Great Gorge** (Rte. 94, Vernon, ☏ 201/827–2000; 14 chairlifts, 3 rope tows, 52 trails) is the largest, with slopes on three mountains. In summer, this one becomes **Action Park** (admission charged; closed Labor Day–Memorial Day), filled with water-park activities and other action rides (motorbikes, an alpine slide, race cars). **Hidden Valley** (Rte. 515, Vernon, ☏ 201/764–4200; 3 chairlifts, 12 trails) is a lively alternative. **Craigmeur Ski Area** (Rte. 513, Rockaway, ☏ 201/697–4500; 1 chairlift, 1 rope tow, 1 T-bar, 4 trails), small and friendly, is best for rank beginners or families with younger children.

Along the Delaware

Getting There

From Manhattan, the New Jersey Turnpike skirts the area, and U.S. 1 and I–195 are key access roads. From Philadelphia, I–95 runs up the Pennsylvania side of the river, crossing north of Trenton, while I–295 and the New Jersey Turnpike parallel it on the Jersey side.

What to See and Do

Forming New Jersey's "other shore" (its border with Pennsylvania), the Delaware slowly changes from a relatively small, often rock-studded river in the north to a mighty, navigable river as it flows past Philadelphia and empties into Delaware Bay. The towns that line it change as well. Part of the way down the state, quaint towns like **Milford, Frenchtown, Stockton,** and **Lambertville** hug the river below ridges and rolling hills beyond. The largest of these towns is Lambertville, across the bridge from the popular artsy town of **New Hope** in Bucks County (*see* Pennsylvania). Dotted with 18th-century buildings, galleries, antiques and crafts stores, excellent restaurants, and B&Bs and inns, the towns are often choked with weekend traffic. Inland a bit, **Flemington** is known for shopping of a different kind, thanks to a huge number of outlet stores. Its **Liberty Village** (Church St., ☎ 908/782–8550), for example, contains more than 60 factory and designer outlets.

Following the river south is an area where George Washington did actually sleep for 10 critical days in 1776–77. (In fact, Washington and the Continental Army spent about one-third of the war in New Jersey.) **Washington Crossing State Park** (Rte. 546, ☎ 609/737–0623) is the site of Washington's Christmas night 1776 crossing (reenacted each Christmas). Follow Washington's trail south to **Trenton,** where he surprised the sleeping Hessians in the **Old Barracks** (Barrack St., ☎ 609/396–1776; admission charged), now a museum. Previously a Colonial pottery and manufacturing center, the small city is today the state capital and is struggling with a quiet rebirth. One of its gems is **Chambersburg,** a.k.a. the "Burg," a residential neighborhood with dozens of superb Italian restaurants. Washington followed his victory in Trenton with one in **Princeton,** just to the north. The two battles were the first major victories for the Continental Army. Princeton is now a pretty university town with upscale shops and the governor's mansion, **Drumthwacket** (354 Stockton St., ☎ 609/683–0057).

South of Trenton, **Camden** is an aging industrial city that has Walt Whitman's home, Campbell Soup's national headquarters (and its museum of soup tureens), and the relatively new indoor and outdoor **Thomas H. Kean New Jersey State Aquarium** (1 Riverside Dr., ☎ 609/365–3300, admission charged). Though it doesn't dazzle with a lot of exotica, the aquarium nevertheless impresses with a 760,000-gallon open-ocean tank filled with 40 different species, including sharks and rays; a shipwreck; touch pools; seals; and displays of native New Jersey species. At this point the river is wide, and you can look out through the aquarium's wall of windows to see tugs pushing barges and the Philadelphia skyline in the background.

North Jersey

Getting There

From Manhattan, take either the Lincoln Tunnel or the George Washington Bridge, and you're in North Jersey. I–80, to the north, and I–78, through Jersey City and Newark, connect with the New Jersey Turnpike, Garden State Parkway, and I–287, which all run northeast–southwest through the region.

What to See and Do

For most people, visiting this part of the state has meant landing at Newark Airport on their way somewhere else or driving past the refineries along the New Jersey Turnpike with their car's air vents closed. But there's much more to this region than the urban and suburban areas that radiate out from New York City, though even they have treasures.

Jersey City and neighboring Hoboken offer superb views of the broad Hudson River and the Manhattan skyline. **Jersey City** is the site of **Liberty State Park** (New Jersey Turnpike Exit 14B, ☎ 201/915–3400), where boats leave for the **Statue of Liberty** and the century-old, restored **Ellis Island Immigration Museum** (*see* New York for both), less than 2,000 ft offshore. Within the park is the **Liberty Science Center** (251

Phillip St., ☎ 201/200–1000; admission charged), with three floors of hands-on and interactive exhibits plus the world's largest Omnimax theater (a domed screen 88 ft across and 125 ft high), as well as the restored, open-sided **Central Railroad of New Jersey Terminal,** built in 1889 and abandoned in 1967. You can explore its deserted ferry slips, train platforms, and terminal building, now used only for special events and exhibits. Or stroll along **Liberty Walk,** a promenade that extends along the waterfront.

Newark, the state's largest city, has a new arts center in the works that it hopes will become a major urban cultural venue. The **Newark Museum** (49 Washington St., ☎ 201/596–6550) has outstanding fine-arts, science, and industry collections.

To the west, outside suburban **Morristown,** is the **Morristown National Historical Park** (Washington Pl., ☎ 201/539–2085; admission charged), where George Washington and his Continental Army camped for the winter of 1779–80. The park includes the elegant Ford Mansion, once Washington's quarters, and the soldiers' log huts. From Morristown, follow U.S. 202 south past antiques shops and farm stands. This is chic horse country, with estates and meadows edged with wood fencing, especially around **Bedminster,** where many locals ride in hunts. Many horse farms are off U.S. 202 on Rte. 523. At the headquarters of the **U.S. Equestrian Team** (Rtes. 512 and 206, Gladstone, ☎ 908/234–1251), you can see the trophy room, displaying the team's Olympic medals, old photos, and other mementos. Competitions, including a major festival in June, are held throughout the year. **Far Hills** is the home of the U.S. Golf Association and its museum, **Golf House** (Rte. 512E off U.S. 202, ☎ 908/234–2300).

PENNSYLVANIA

By Rathe Miller

Capital	Harrisburg
Population	11,995,405
Motto	Virtue, Liberty, and Independence
State Bird	Ruffed grouse
State Flower	Mountain laurel

Visitor Information

Pennsylvania Department of Commerce, Office of Travel Marketing (453 Forum Bldg., Harrisburg 17120, ☎ 717/787–5453 or 800/847–4872). **Welcome centers:** on major highways around the state.

Scenic Drives

In Bucks County, **River Road** wends 40 mi along the Delaware River, offering views of 18th- and 19th-century stone farmhouses, tucked-away villages, and fall foliage along wooded hills. In the Poconos, **Rte. 209,** from Stroudsburg to Milford, passes untouched forests and natural waterfalls.

National and State Parks

National Park

The 500,000-acre **Allegheny National Forest** (Box 847, Warren 16365, ☎ 814/723–5150; visitor center, ☎ 814/726–1291 May–Sept.), in the northwestern part of the state, has hiking and cross-country-skiing trails, three rivers suitable for canoeing, and outstanding stream fishing.

State Parks

Pennsylvania's 114 state parks include more than 7,000 campsites. The **Bureau of State Parks** (Market Street State Bldg., Box, 8551, Harrisburg, 17105, ☎ 800/637–2757) provides information and campsite reservations. In the Poconos, the heavily wooded **Hickory Run State Park** (R.D. 1, Box 81, White Haven 18661, ☎ 717/443–0400) offers fishing, camping, and Boulder Field, an area covered in rock formations dating to the Ice Age. The 18,719-acre **Ohiopyle State Park** (Box 105, Ohiopyle 15470, ☎ 412/329–8591) has camping, swimming, cross-country skiing, and a 28-mi hiking and biking trail along the Youghiogheny River. **Presque Isle State Park** (Rte. 832, Erie 16505, ☎ 814/871–4251), a 3,202-acre sandy peninsula that extends 7 mi into Lake Erie, is popular for fishing, swimming and picnicking.

PHILADELPHIA

Almost a century after English Quaker William Penn founded Philadelphia in 1682, the city became the birthplace of the nation and the home of its first government. Today, for visitors and natives alike, Philadelphia is synonymous with Independence Hall, the Liberty Bell, cheese steak and hoagies, ethnic neighborhoods, theaters, buoyant classical music—and city streets teeming with life. With close to 1.6 million people, Penn's "City of Brotherly Love" is the fifth-largest city in the country, yet maintains the feel of a friendly small town.

Tourist Information

The **Philadelphia Visitors Center** (16th St. and John F. Kennedy Blvd., ☎ 215/636–1666 or 800/321–9563) is a good first stop for brochures, maps, discount coupons for tourist sites, plus hotel and restaurant information. There is also a gift shop that stocks Philly-kitsch items.

Arriving and Departing

By Plane

Philadelphia International Airport (☎ 215/492–3181), 8 mi southwest of downtown, has scheduled flights by most major domestic and foreign carriers. A **SEPTA** (*see* Getting Around Philadelphia, *below*) rail line connects the airport with center-city stations; the trip takes 25 minutes and costs $5. Airport shuttle services, such as **Airport-Limelight Limousine** (☎ 215/342–5557) and **Philadelphia Airport Shuttle, Inc.** (☎ 215/969–1818), charge about $10 per person. Taxis are plentiful; they cost about $20 plus tip.

By Car

The main north–south highway through Philadelphia is I–95; to reach center city, take the Vine Street exit off I–95S or the Broad Street exit off I–95N. From the west, the Schuylkill Expressway (I–76) has several exits to center city. From the east, the New Jersey Turnpike and I–295 provide access to either U.S. 30/I–676, which enters the city via the Benjamin Franklin Bridge, or New Jersey Rte. 42 and the Walt Whitman Bridge.

By Train

Amtrak serves **30th Street Station** (30th and Market Sts., ☎ 800/872–7245).

By Bus

Greyhound Lines (10th and Filbert Sts., ☎ 800/231–2222). **NJ Transit** (30th Street Station, ☎ 215/569–3752).

Getting Around Philadelphia

The traditional heart of the city is Broad and Market streets, where City Hall now stands. Market Street divides the city north and south. North–south streets are numbered, starting with Front (1st) Street, at the Delaware River, and increasing to the west. Most historical and cultural attractions are easy walks from the midtown area, which is safe during the day. After dark, ask hotel personnel about the safety of places you're interested in visiting, but in general, cabs are safer than walking.

By Car

These narrow streets were designed for Colonial traffic, and driving can be difficult. On-street parking is often forbidden during rush hours (parking facilities include those at 41 N. 6th St.; 16th and Arch Sts.; 10th and Locust Sts.). During rush hours, avoid the major arteries leading into and out of the city, particularly I–95, U.S. 1, and the Schuylkill Expressway.

By Public Transportation

SEPTA (☎ 215/580–7800; fare $1.60, transfers 40¢; exact change required) operates an extensive network of buses, trolleys, subways, and commuter trains. Certain lines run 24 hours a day. SEPTA's **Day Pass,** good for a day's unlimited riding, can be purchased at the visitors center (*see* Tourist Information, *above*) for $5. Bus route 76, called the **"Ben Frankline,"** connects the zoo in west Fairmount Park with Penn's

Landing at the Delaware River. The purple **Phlash** buses do the downtown loop.

By Taxi

Cabs are plentiful during the day—especially along Broad Street and near hotels and train stations. At night and outside center city, taxis are scarce, and you may have to call for service. Fares start at $1.80, and increase by $1.80 for every subsequent mile. The main companies are **Quaker City Cab** (☎ 215/728–8000), **United Cab** (☎ 215/238–9500), and **Yellow Cab** (☎ 215/922–8400).

Orientation Tours

Gray Line Tours (☎ 215/569–3666) offers a 5½-hour tour of historic and cultural areas. To combine lunch or dinner with a sightseeing cruise on the Delaware River, climb aboard the ***Spirit of Philadelphia*** (☎ 215/923–1419).

Carriage Tours

Philadelphia Carriage Co. (☎ 215/922–6840), **'76 Carriage Co.** (☎ 215/923–8516), and **Society Hill Carriage Co.** (☎ 215/627–6128) offer narrated tours of the historic area in antique horse-drawn carriages with costumed drivers.

Walking Tours

Audio Walk and Tour (Norman Rockwell Museum, 6th and Sansom Sts., ☎ 215/925–1234) offers a city historic tour with cassette player and map. **Centipede Tours** (☎ 215/735–3123; May–Oct.) offers guided candlelight strolls through Old Philadelphia. The **Foundation for Architecture** (☎ 215/569–3187) specializes in both theme and neighborhood tours.

Water Taxi

Philadelphia Water Taxi, Inc. (☎ 215/351–4170) stops at various waterfront entertainment spots, eating holes, and attractions, including Penn's Landing.

Exploring Philadelphia

Historic District

Most sites in "the most historic square mile in America" are part of **Independence National Historical Park** (☎ 215/597–8974). Except as noted, all have free admission and are open daily.

Start your tour at the **Visitor Center** (3rd and Chestnut Sts.), where park rangers staff the information desk, and the shop has books and gifts related to Colonial times and the Revolutionary War. Across 3rd Street you'll see the **First Bank of the United States,** the oldest bank building in the country. The redbrick path to the right of the bank leads to **Carpenter's Hall** (Carpenter's Ct.), where the first Continental Congress convened in 1774, the **Army–Navy Museum,** and the **Marine Corp National Memorial** (Chestnut St. between 3rd and 4th Sts.).

Follow the redbrick path another block across 5th Street to **Independence Square,** where, on July 8, 1776, the Declaration of Independence was first read out to the public.

Also on Independence Square is **Independence Hall** (Chestnut St. between 5th and 6th Sts., ☎ 215/597–8974), which was opened in 1732 as the State House for the colony of Pennsylvania. It was here that the Second Continental Congress convened on May 10, 1775; that the Declaration of Independence was adopted a year later; that the Articles of Confederation were signed in 1778; and that the Constitution was formally signed by its framers on September 17, 1787. The west wing is **Congress Hall,** formerly the Philadelphia County Courthouse, and the meeting place of the U.S. Congress from 1790 to 1800. The first floor was the House of Representatives; President John Adams was inaugurated here in 1797. In the second-floor Senate chamber, George Washington was inaugurated for his second term in 1793. Tours of Independence Hall are given year-round; from early May to Labor Day, expect a wait.

One block up the mall in front of Independence Square is the **Liberty Bell.** To keep it from falling into British hands during the Revolution, the bell was spirited 60 mi north by horse and wagon to Allentown. You can touch the 2,080-pound bell and read its biblical inscription: "Proclaim liberty throughout all the land unto all the inhabitants thereof."

Christ Church (2nd St. north of Market St., ☎ 215/922–1695) is where noted colonials, including 15 signers of the Declaration, worshiped. East of Second Street is **Elfreth's Alley,** the oldest continually occupied residential street in America, dating from 1702; **No. 126** (☎ 215/574–0560; closed weekdays Jan.–mid-Feb.) has been restored as a Colonial craftsman's home. The **Betsy Ross House** (239 Arch St., ☎ 215/627–5343; closed Mon.) is the burial site of the woman who is reputed to have sewn the first American flag.

The **United States Mint** (5th and Arch Sts., ☎ 215/597–7350), built in 1969, is the largest mint in the world and stands two blocks from the first U.S. mint, which opened in 1792. Tours and exhibits on coin-making are available.

The Waterfront and Society Hill

The spot where William Penn stepped ashore in 1682 is today a 37-acre park known as **Penn's Landing** (Delaware Riverfront from Lombard to Market Sts., ☎ 215/923–4992); docked here are the handsomely restored **USS *Olympia,*** Commodore George Dewey's flagship in the Spanish-American War, and the **USS *Becuna,*** a World War II submarine whose guides are submarine veterans. An ice rink is open during the winter, while the summer months bring open-air concerts and festivals. *Spruce St., ☎ 215/922–1898. Admission charged.*

Docked a block north when not at sea is the ***Gazela of Philadelphia.*** Built in 1883, it is the last of a Portuguese fleet of cod-fishing ships and the oldest wooden square-rigger still sailing. *Between Walnut and Spruce Sts., ☎ 215/923–9030. Closed Oct.–May.*

The **Bishop White House** (309 Walnut St.), built in 1786 as the home of the rector of Christ Church, has been restored to Colonial elegance. Nearby is the simply furnished **Todd House** (4th and Walnut Sts., ☎ 215/597–8974). Built in 1775, it has been restored to its appearance in the 1790s, when its best-known resident, Dolley Payne Todd (later Mrs. James Madison), lived here. The visitor center offers a free tour that includes both houses.

Head House Square (2nd and Pine Sts.) was once an open-air Colonial marketplace. Today, on summer weekends, it is the site of crafts fairs, festivals, and other activities.

City Hall and Environs

At the geographic center of Penn's original city stands **City Hall**—the largest city hall in the country and the tallest masonry-bearing building in the world. For a tour of the interior and a 360° view of the city from the Billy Penn statue, go to room 121 via the northeast corner of the courtyard, and ride the elevator to the top of the 548-ft tower. *Broad*

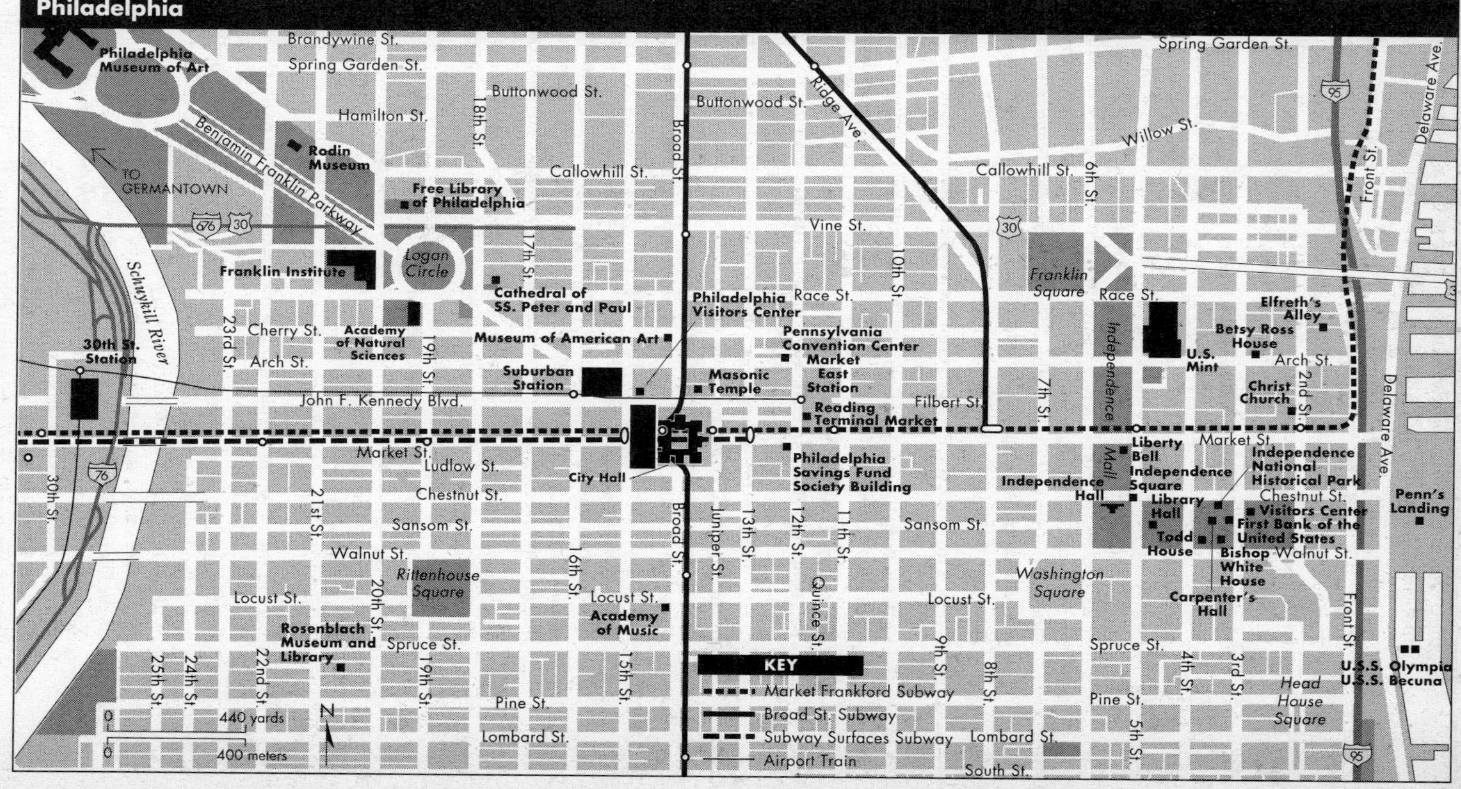

Philadelphia
Philadelphia Museum of Art
Brandywine St.
Spring Garden St.
Buttonwood St.
Hamilton St.
18th St.
Broad St.
Ridge Ave.
Willow St.
Front St.
Delaware Ave.
Benjamin Franklin Parkway
Rodin Museum
TO GERMANTOWN
Callowhill St.
6th St.
Free Library of Philadelphia
Vine St.
10th St.
Logan Circle
Franklin Institute
17th St.
Franklin Square
Race St.
Elfreth's Alley
Cathedral of SS. Peter and Paul
Philadelphia Visitors Center
Schuylkill River
23rd St.
Cherry St.
Academy of Natural Sciences
19th St.
Museum of American Art
Pennsylvania Convention Center
Independence
Betsy Ross House
Arch St.
U.S. Mint
30th St. Station
Market East Station
Suburban Station
Masonic Temple
Christ Church
2nd St.
John F. Kennedy Blvd.
Reading Terminal Market
Filbert St.
7th St.
Market St.
Liberty Bell
Independence Square
Mall
Independence National Historical Park
30th St.
Ludlow St.
City Hall
Philadelphia Savings Fund Society Building
Independence Hall
Chestnut St.
Library Hall
Visitors Center
First Bank of the United States
Penn's Landing
21st St.
Sansom St.
Juniper St.
13th St.
12th St.
11th St.
Todd House
Bishop White House
Walnut St.
Rittenhouse Square
16th St.
Quince St.
Washington Square
Carpenter's Hall
Locust St.
20th St.
Academy of Music
Rosenblach Museum and Library
Spruce St.
22nd St.
25th St.
24th St.
15th St.
KEY
Market Frankford Subway
Broad St. Subway
Subway Surfaces Subway
Airport Train
9th St.
8th St.
4th St.
3rd St.
Head House Square
U.S.S. Olympia
U.S.S. Becuna
Pine St.
0
440 yards
400 meters
Lombard St.
5th St.
South St.

the courtyard, and ride the elevator to the top of the 548-ft tower. *Broad and Market Sts., ☎ 215/686–2250. Closed weekends.*

Philadelphia is the mother city of American Masonry, and the **Masonic Temple** is home to the Grand Lodge of Free and Accepted Masons of Pennsylvania. The seven lodge halls, each decorated according to a different architectural theme, make for a fun 45-minute tour. *1 N. Broad St., ☎ 215/988–1917. Closed Sat. July–Aug.*

The city's classiest park, **Rittenhouse Square** (between 18th and 19th Sts. at Walnut St.) frequently hosts art festivals. The **Rosenbach Museum and Library** (2010 Delancey Pl., ☎ 215/732–1600) offers a one-hour tour of its sumptuous collection of antiques, paintings, rare books, and objets d'art. The **Academy of Music** (Broad and Locust Sts., ☎ 215/893–1900 or 215/893–1930 for tickets), modeled on Milan's La Scala opera house, is home to the Philadelphia Orchestra and the Opera Company of Philadelphia. The **Philadelphia Savings Fund Society Building** (12th and Market Sts., ☎ 215/928–2000), built in 1930, was one of the city's first skyscrapers.

Opened in 1993, the **Pennsylvania Convention Center** (12th and Arch Sts., ☎ 215/418–4700 or, for events, 215/418–4989), with 1.3 million sq ft, includes the restored Reading Train Shed. You can tour the $522-million complex on Tuesday and Thursday between 11:30 and 2:15.

Museum District

The **Benjamin Franklin Parkway** angles across the grid of city streets from City Hall to Fairmount Park. Lined with distinguished museums, hotels, and apartment buildings, this 250-ft-wide boulevard inspired by the Champs-Elysées was built in the 1920s. Off the parkway you'll find the **Free Library of Philadelphia** (19th St., ☎ 215/686–5322), with more than 2 million volumes; the **Academy of Natural Sciences** (19th St., ☎ 215/299–1020), America's first museum of natural history; the **Rodin Museum** (22nd St., ☎ 215/763–8100), which has the largest collection of Auguste Rodin's works outside France; and the **Franklin Institute** (20th St., ☎ 215/448–1200), a science museum with a planetarium and an Omniverse Theater showing science and nature documentaries.

The crown jewel of the parkway is the **Philadelphia Museum of Art.** Modeled on ancient Greek temples but on a larger scale, the 200 galleries house more than 300,000 works. The collection includes paintings by Renoir, Picasso, Matisse, and Marcel Duchamps; Early American furniture; Amish and Shaker crafts; and reconstructions, including a 12th-century French cloister and a 16th-century Indian temple. *26th St. and Benjamin Franklin Pkwy., ☎ 215/763–8100. Admission charged (free Sun. 10–1). Closed Mon.*

Behind the museum is **Fairmount Park** (accesses from Kelly Dr., West River Dr., and Belmont Ave., ☎ 215/685–0000). At 4,500 acres, it is among the largest city parks in the world and follows both banks of the Schuylkill River through woodlands, meadows, and rolling hills. Within the park's bounds are tennis courts, ball fields, playgrounds, trails, an exercise course, several celebrated cultural institutions (such as the **Ellen Phillips Samuel Memorial Sculpture Garden**), and some fine Early American country houses (**Laurel Hill, Strawberry Mansion,** and others). An excellent map of the park is available at most park sites for 25¢. **Boathouse Row,** 11 architecturally varied 19th-century buildings on the banks of the Schuylkill that are home to 13 rowing clubs, is best viewed from the West River Drive. In the northwest section of the park is the **Wissahickon,** a 5½-mi, forested gorge carved out by Wissahickon Creek. At **Valley Green Inn** (☎ 215/247–1730), a restaurant halfway up the valley, you can dine on the porch and watch the ducks swimming in the creek.

The **Museum of American Art** is the oldest art institution in the United States. Its collection ranges from Winslow Homer and Benjamin West to Andrew Wyeth and Red Grooms. *Broad and Cherry Sts., ☏ 215/972–7600. Admission charged (free Wed. 5–7).*

The Italian Renaissance–style **Cathedral of Saints Peter and Paul** (18th and Race Sts., ☏ 215/561–1313), built between 1846 and 1864, is the basilica of the Roman Catholic archdiocese of Philadelphia.

Germantown

In 1683, Francis Pastorius led 13 Mennonite families out of Germany to seek religious freedom in the New World; they settled 6 mi northwest of Philadelphia in what is now Germantown, and many became Quakers. **Cliveden** (6401 Germantown Ave., ☏ 215/848–1777), an elaborate country house built in 1763, was occupied by the British during the Revolution. On October 7, 1777, George Washington's attempt to dislodge them resulted in his defeat in the Battle of Germantown. During the yellow-fever plague of 1793–94, Washington lived in the **Deshler-Morris House** (5442 Germantown Ave., ☏ 215/596–1748) to avoid the unhealthy air of sea-level Philadelphia. Contact the **Germantown Historical Society** (5501 Germantown Ave., ☏ 215/844–0514) for information on all noteworthy sites in Germantown.

Museums

The **Barnes Foundation** (300 Latches La., Merion, ☏ 610/667–0290), with one of the world's great collections of French Impressionist paintings, is currently renovating its gallery but is scheduled to reopen in mid-October 1995. The **Museum of American Art** (*see* Exploring Philadelphia, *above*) is the oldest art institution in the United States. The **Mutter Museum** (19 S. 22nd St., ☏ 215/563–3737) is a medical museum with a plethora of anatomical and pathological specimens (a word of advice: this museum is best visited on an empty stomach!). The **University Museum** (33rd and Spruce Sts., ☏ 215/898–4000) is one of the finest archaeological-anthropological museums in the world.

Parks and Gardens

Fairmount Park (*see* Exploring Philadelphia, *above*) is the city's largest, encompassing varied terrains as well as many cultural sites. The University of Pennsylvania's **Morris Arboretum** (Hillcrest Ave. between Germantown and Stenton Ave., Chestnut Hill, ☏ 215/247–5777), is 166 acres of romantically landscaped seclusion. America's first zoo, the **Philadelphia Zoological Gardens** (34th St. and Girard Ave., ☏ 215/243–1100) is home to 1,600 animals on 42 acres.

Philadelphia for Free

Get a copy of the *Calendar of Events* at the visitors center (*see* Tourist Information, *above*) for listings of Philadelphia's myriad free events and attractions. Several museums schedule a period when admission is free to all.

What to See and Do with Children

The **Please Touch Museum** (210 N. 21st St., ☏ 215/963–0667), designed for children ages seven and younger, encourages hands-on participation. The **Annenberg Center Theater for Children** (37th and

Walnut Sts., ☎ 215/898–6791) schedules productions from October to May. **Sesame Place** (100 Sesame Rd., Langhorne, ☎ 215/757–1100), a 45-minute drive north of the city, is an amusement park for children ages 3 to 13 based on the popular public-television show.

Shopping

Pennsylvania's 6% (7% in Philadelphia) sales tax does not apply to clothing, medicine, or food bought in stores.

Shopping Districts

Walnut Street, between Broad Street and Rittenhouse Square, and the intersecting streets just north and south are filled with upscale boutiques and galleries. **Jewelers' Row,** centered on Sansom Street between 7th and 8th streets, is one of the world's oldest and largest markets of precious stones. Pine Street from 9th to 12th streets is **Antiques Row.** Along **South Street** are more than 180 unusual stores selling everything from New Age books and health food to avant-garde art. For local color, visit the outdoor stalls and indoor stores of the **Italian Market,** on 9th Street between Christian and Washington streets.

Department Stores

John Wanamaker (☎ 215/422–2200), Philadelphia's premier department store, occupies five floors of a building that embraces the entire block bounded by 13th, Juniper, Market, and Chestnut streets. **Strawbridge and Clothier** (☎ 215/629–6000), at 8th and Market streets, was founded in 1868.

Specialty Stores

Architectural Antiques Exchange (715 N. 2nd St., ☎ 215/922–3669) handles everything from embellishments from Victorian saloons and apothecary shops to stained and beveled glass. **Bauman Rare Books** (1215 Locust St., ☎ 215/546–6466) has volumes from the 19th century and earlier on law, science, English literature, and travel. **Wine Reserve** (205 S. 18th St., ☎ 215/560–4529) deals exclusively in fine wines and cognacs. **J. E. Caldwell** (Juniper and Chestnut Sts., ☎ 215/864–7800), a local landmark for jewelry since 1839, is adorned with antique hand-blown crystal chandeliers by Baccarat. Philadelphia-born **Urban Outfitters** (1801 Walnut St., 215/569–3131), now selling clothes, furnishings, and gifts to students in college towns across the country, opened its third store in this downtown Beaux Arts mansion.

Spectator Sports

Baseball

Philadelphia Phillies (Veterans Stadium, Broad St. and Pattison Ave., ☎ 215/463–1000; Apr.–Oct.).

Basketball

Philadelphia 76ers (Spectrum, Broad St. and Pattison Ave., ☎ 215/336–3600; Nov.–Apr.).

Football

Philadelphia Eagles (Veterans Stadium, ☎ 215/463–5500; Aug.–Dec.).

Hockey

Philadelphia Flyers (Spectrum, ☎ 215/336–3600; Oct.–Apr.).

Dining

Philadelphia has become a first-rate restaurant town. Here's a short list of a dozen, distinctly Philadelphian, sure bets. For price ranges, see Chart 1 (A) in On the Road with Fodor's.

$$$$ ★ **Le Bec-Fin.** This is the best restaurant in Philadelphia, and one of the best anywhere. An elegant chandelier, a mirrored mise-en-scène, the excellent (and rarely snooty) European service, and owner-chef Georges Perrier's obsessive perfectionism in creating the haute French menu all have their price, but at $97 a throw, it is most definitely worth it. *1523 Walnut St., ☎ 215/567–1000. Reservations required. Jacket and tie. AE, DC, MC, V. Closed Sun.*

$$$$ ★ **The Fountain.** Nestled in the lavish yet dignified lobby of the Four Seasons, the Fountain offers predominantly local and American entrées, such as roast Pennsylvania pheasant with bacon-flavored cabbage. *1 Logan Sq., ☎ 215/963–1500. Reservations required. AE, DC, MC, V.*

$$$ **Cafe Nola.** This establishment serves the best Cajun-Creole food in town, in two busy, upbeat, handsomely appointed rooms. House favorites include seafood jambalaya, coconut shrimp with orange sauce, Cajun popcorn, and spicy Jamaican jerk chicken. *328 South St., ☎ 215/627–2590. Reservations recommended. AE, D, DC, MC, V.*

$$$ ★ **Susanna Foo.** This is the most expensive—and arguably the best—Chinese restaurant in town. A million-dollar renovation has enlarged and beautified the already handsome room. Try the Eight Treasure quails and top it off with a chocolate-dipped fortune cookie. *1512 Walnut St., ☎ 215/545–2666. Reservations required. AE, DC, MC, V. Closed Sun.*

$$$ **Tiramisù.** Owner-chef Albert Delbella describes his fare as "nouvelle Jewish-Roman," but the only prerequisite neeeded to dine here is a love of garlic. It is found in almost everything, from the matzoh with olive oil to the veal scaloppine. The eponymous dessert (no garlic!) is delicious. *528 S. 5th St., ☎ 215/925–3335. AE, DC, MC, V.*

$$ **Restaurant School.** Managed and staffed entirely by students, this restaurant offers French haute cuisine and European service in the glass-enclosed atrium of a restored 1860 Victorian mansion—all for a mere $13.50. *4207 Walnut St., ☎ 215/222–4200. AE, DC, MC, V.*

$$ **Sansom Street Oyster House.** This Philadelphia favorite serves first-rate raw shellfish and grilled and blackened dishes. It's unpretentiously paneled in dark wood, with uncovered tables. *1516 Sansom St., ☎ 215/567–7683. Reservations only for parties of 5 or more. AE, D, DC, MC, V. Closed Sun.*

$$ ★ **Victor Cafe.** The northern Italian cuisine of the DiStefano family gets better all the time, but the big attraction here is the music: the wait-staff are all opera singers, and every few minutes one or more of them cuts loose with an aria. *1303 Dickinson St., ☎ 215/468–3040. Reservations required. AE, DC.*

$ **Joe's Peking Duck House.** Known for Peking duck and barbecued pork, Joe's is the best Chinese restaurant in Chinatown. *925 Race St., ☎ 215/922–3277. Reservations advised. No credit cards.*

$ **Famous Delicatessen.** This is the closest thing in Philadelphia to a classic New York deli. Boxes of tinfoil are kept handy to wrap up the left-over halves of the overstuffed sandwiches. *4th and Bainbridge Sts., ☎ 215/922–3274. AE.*

$ ★ **Reading Terminal Market.** A Philadelphia treasure, this potpourri of 80 stalls, shops, and lunch counters offers a smorgasbord of different cuisines, including Chinese, Greek, Mexican, Japanese, soul food, Middle Eastern, and Pennsylvania Dutch. *12th and Arch Sts., ☎ 215/922–2317. Closed Sun.*

Junk Food

"Philadelphia is the junk food capital of the world," says Mayor Ed Rendell. Indeed, no Philadelphia dining experience would be complete without tormenting your digestive system with at least one cheese steak or hoagie. **Pat's** (1237 E. Passyunk, ☎ 215/468–1546) serves up cheese steaks with traditional dollops of sauce and fried onions; **Lee's** (44 S. 17th St., ☎ 215/564–1264) is a hoagie heaven (be sure to ask for one with oil, not mayo); the **Reading Terminal Market** (*see* Dining, *above*) sells freshly baked soft pretzels with mustard—a Philly specialty. Stores all over town sell TastyKakes. **Philadelphia Favorites To Go** (☎ 800/808–8040) will vacuum-pack and send local treats anywhere in the United States.

Lodging

With the exception of the Army-Navy football game (around Thanksgiving) and when big conventions are in town, it is easy to find a hotel room. Most B&Bs operate under the auspices of booking agencies, such as **Bed and Breakfast, Center City** (1804 Pine St., 19103, ☎ 215/735–1137), or **Bed and Breakfast Connections** (Box 21, Devon 19333, ☎ 610/687–3565). For price ranges, see Chart 2 (A) in On the Road with Fodor's.

$$$$ ★ **Four Seasons.** Built in 1983, this eight-story hotel is Philadelphia's most expensive. Rooms are furnished in Federal style, and the best of them have romantic views overlooking the fountains in Logan Circle. *1 Logan Sq., 19103, ☎ 215/963–1500 or 800/332–3442, FAX 215/963–9506. 371 rooms. Facilities: restaurant, café, exercise room, indoor pool, concierge, no-smoking floors. AE, DC, MC, V.*

$$$ **Adam's Mark.** Guest rooms are small here, with an English-country motif; request one on an upper floor facing south toward Fairmount Park and the downtown skyline. The hotel's big attraction is the nighttime activity at its nightclub, sports bar, and fine restaurant, The Marker. *City Ave. and Monument Rd., 19131, ☎ 215/581–5000 or 800/444–2326, FAX 215/581–5089. 449 rooms, 66 suites. Facilities: 3 restaurants, bar, sports bar, exercise room, 2 pools. AE, D, DC, MC, V.*

$$$ **The Barclay.** The elegant lobby leads to a registration area sparkling with crystal chandeliers. Some rooms in this carefully renovated 1929-vintage hotel have four-poster beds; all have antique-style furniture. *Rittenhouse Sq. E, 19103, ☎ 215/545–0300 or 800/421–6662, FAX 215/545–2896. 235 rooms. Facilities: restaurant, lounge, concierge. AE, D, DC, MC, V.*

$$$ **Latham.** At this small, elegant hotel with a European accent and an emphasis on personal service, guest rooms have marble-top bureaus and French writing desks. *17th St. at Walnut St., 19103, ☎ 215/563–7474 or 800/528–4261, FAX 215/568–0110. 139 rooms. Facilities: restaurant, lounge. AE, D, DC, MC, V.*

$$$ **Philadelphia Marriott.** This 23-story, $200 million, full-service hotel opened in January 1995 next door to the Pennsylvania Convention Center. The spacious guest rooms have large windows and pastel colors. *1201 Market St., 19107, ☎ 215/972–6700 or 800/228–9290, FAX 215/625–6000. 1,145 rooms, 55 suites. Facilities: 2 restaurants, sports bar with billiard parlor, indoor pool, health club. AE, D, DC, MC, V.*

$$$ **The Warwick.** First opened in 1924, this 23-story hotel today attracts a theatrical clientele. The lobby, adorned with gilded mirrors and 18-ft Palladian windows, is always busy. Capriccio, a European-style café, serves desserts and espresso until late every night. *17th and Locusts Sts., 19103, ☎ 215/735–6000 or 800/523–4210, FAX 215/790–7766. 200 rooms. Facilities: 7 meeting rooms, garage. AE, DC, MC, V.*

$$ ★ **Ramada Suites-Convention Center.** Located in Chinatown, this 1890 building was once the Bentwood Rocker Factory. Every guest room is a suite, and many have exposed brick and wood beams. *1010 Race St., 19107, ☎ 215/922–1730 or 800/221–2222, FAX 215/922–6258. 92 suites. Facilities: Continental breakfast, parking. AE, D, DC, MC, V.*

$$ **Society Hill Hotel.** Rooms in this 1832 former longshoreman's house are furnished with brass beds and antiques. Continental breakfast is brought to your room with fresh-squeezed juice and fresh-baked goodies. *301 Chestnut St., 19106, ☎ 215/925–1394, FAX 215/925–3780. 6 rooms, 6 suites. Facilities: restaurant, outdoor café, piano bar. AE, DC, MC, V.*

$$ ★ **Thomas Bond House.** Spend the night in the heart of the Olde City, the way Philadelphians did more than two centuries ago. Built in 1769, this four-story house has rooms with marble fireplaces, whirlpool baths, and four-poster Thomasville beds. *129 S. 2nd St., 19106, ☎ 215/923–8523 or 800/845–2663, FAX 215/923–8504. 10 rooms, 2 suites. AE, D, DC, MC, V.*

$ **Bank Street Hostel.** On the cusp of Olde City and Society Hill, this clean, well-run establishment offers a dormitory arrangement that is a downtown Philly lodging bargain. *32 South Bank St., 19106, ☎ 215/922–0222 or 800/392–4678. 3 rooms with a total of 54 beds. Facilities: pool table, lounge area, 46" TV. No credit cards.*

$ **Chamounix Mansion.** This youth hostel is on a wooded bluff overlooking the Schuylkill River (and, unfortunately, the Schuylkill Expressway). The 1802 estate is loaded with character; the drawbacks are dorm-style living and shared baths. *Chamounix Dr., 19131, ☎ 215/878–3676 or 800/379–0017. 6 rooms with 48 beds. MC, V. Closed mid-Dec.–mid-Jan.*

The Arts and Nightlife

Philadelphia magazine (at newsstands), *Calendar of Events* and *Philadelphia Spotlite* (free at the visitor center), the *Welcomat* and the *City Paper* (weeklies available free from newsboxes in the city center), and the *Inquirer* and the *Daily News* (the city's daily papers) list arts and entertainment events. The **Donnelley Directory Philadelphia Events Hotline** (☎ 610/337–7777, ext. 2116) is an automated 24-hour service.

The Arts

THEATER

Performances by touring companies and pre-Broadway productions can be seen at the **Merriam Theater** (250 S. Broad St., ☎ 215/732–5446), the **Forrest Theater** (1114 Walnut St., ☎ 215/923–1515), and the **Walnut Street Theater** (9th and Walnut Sts., ☎ 215/574–3550). The **Philadelphia Drama Guild** performs at the Annenberg Center (3680 Walnut St., ☎ 215/898–6791). **Freedom Theater** (1346 N. Broad St., ☎ 215/765–2793) is the oldest and most active black theater in Philadelphia.

CONCERTS

The **Philadelphia Orchestra** performs at the Academy of Music (Broad and Locust Sts., ☎ 215/893–1900) in winter and at the Mann Music Center (W. Fairmount Park, ☎ 215/878–7707) in summer. The **Philly Pops** (☎ 215/735–7506), conducted by Peter Nero, performs at the Academy of Music.

OPERA

The **Opera Company of Philadelphia** (☎ 215/928–2100) performs at the Academy of Music from October to May.

DANCE
The classical **Pennsylvania Ballet** (☎ 215/551–7014) dances at the Academy of Music. The **Philadelphia Dance Company** (☎ 215/387–8200) performs modern dance in spring and fall.

Nightlife
South Street from Front to 7th streets still attracts nighttime crowds, but the big noise is the **Delaware Waterfront** entertainment boom, with more than a dozen clubs opening in the past few years. In the northwest part of the city, **Main Street** in **Manyunk** has joined **Germantown Avenue** in **Chestnut Hill** as an area in which to dine, shop, and stroll. On Wednesday night, downtown shops and some museums stay open late; outside, street bands entertain smiling crowds. On the **First Friday** of every month, 25 art galleries in Olde City stay open late. Call radio station WRTI's "Jazz Line" (☎ 215/204–5277) and "Concerts" (☎ 215/568–3222) for what's happening around town.

BARS, LOUNGES, AND CABARETS
Khyber Pass (56 S. 2nd St., ☎ 215/440–9683) has loud, live music, and more than 100 brands of beer. Nightly live music at **Katmandu** (Pier 25, Christopher Columbus Blvd., ☎ 215/629–1101), a large-capacity, outdoor island restaurant and disco, pleases crowds in their 20s, 30s, and 40s up until 2 AM from April 15 to early October. **Dirty Frank's** (347 S. 13th St., ☎ 215/732–5010) *is* dirty and attracts a motley crowd of writers, artists, students, and Philly characters. **Trocadero** (1003 Arch St., ☎ 215/922–0194), a rock-and-roll club, occupies a former burlesque house where W. C. Fields and Mae West performed. **Woody's** (202 S. 13th St., ☎ 215/545–1893) is the city's most popular gay bar; **Hepburn's** (254 S. 12th., ☎ 215/545–8088) is the city's premier lesbian bar. Head for **Zanzibar Blue** (301 S. 11th St., ☎ 215/829–1990) for late-night music and dancing on weekends.

COMEDY
Comedy Cabaret (126 Chestnut St., ☎ 215/625–5653) features top young comedians from both coasts.

MISCELLANEOUS
By day, **Painted Bride Art Center** (230 Vine St., ☎ 215/925–9914) is an art gallery. By night, it's a club featuring performance art, readings, dance, and theater. Since 1975, the **Cherry Tree Music Co-op** (3916 Locust Walk, ☎ 215/386–1640) has staged Sunday night folk-music concerts.

Excursion to Bucks County

Getting There
From Philadelphia, follow I–95N to the Yardley exit, then go north on Rte. 32 toward New Hope. The trip takes one hour.

What to See and Do
Bucks County is known for antiques, covered bridges, and country inns. **New Hope** is a hodgepodge of art galleries, old stone houses, and shops along crooked little streets. William Penn's reconstructed Georgian-style mansion, **Pennsbury Manor** (Tyburn Rd. E., off U.S. 13, Morrisville, ☎ 215/946–0400), and **Washington Crossing Historic Park** (Rtes. 532 and 32, ☎ 215/493–4076), where George Washington and his troops crossed the river on Christmas night 1776, are nearby. Contact the **Bucks County Tourist Commission** (Box 912, 152 Swamp Rd., Doylestown 18901, ☎ 215/345–4552) or the **New Hope Information Center** (1 W. Mechanic St., at Main St., 18938, ☎ 215/862–5880 or 215/862–5030) for more information.

Excursion to Valley Forge

Getting There

Take the Schuylkill Expressway (I–76) west from Philadelphia to Exit 25. Take Rte. 363 to North Gulph Road and follow the signs to Valley Forge National Historical Park, 18 mi from the city. **By bus,** take SEPTA Rte. 125 from 16th Street and John F. Kennedy Boulevard.

What to See and Do

The monuments, huts, and headquarters on the 3,500 acres of rolling hills of the **Valley Forge National Historical Park** (Rtes. 23 and 363, Valley Forge, ☎ 610/783–1077) preserve the moment in American history when George Washington's Continental Army endured the bitter winter of 1777–78. Nearby attractions include **Mill Grove** (Audubon and Paulings Rds., Audubon, ☎ 610/666–5593), the home of naturalist John James Audubon; the studio/residence of painter and woodcarver **Wharton Esherick** (Horseshoe Trail, Paoli, ☎ 610/644–5822); and **The Court and The Plaza** (Rte. 202 and N. Gulph Rd., King of Prussia, ☎ 610/265–5727), which claims to be the nation's second-largest shopping complex. For more information, contact the **Valley Forge Convention and Visitors Bureau** (600 W. Germantown Pk., Suite 130, Plymouth Meeting, 19462, ☎ 610/834–1550 or 800/441–3549).

Excursion to the Brandywine Valley

Getting There

Take U.S. 1S from Philadelphia about 25 mi to the valley.

What to See and Do

The Brandywine River valley has inspired generations of Wyeths and du Ponts—the Wyeths to capture its peaceful harmony on canvas, the du Ponts to recontour the landscape with grand gardens, mansions, and mills. The **Brandywine River Museum** (U.S. 1 and Rte. 100, Chadds Ford, ☎ 610/388–7601), in a preserved 19th-century gristmill, celebrates the Brandywine school of artists. **Longwood Gardens** (U.S. 1, Kennett Sq., ☎ 610/388–6741), Pierre-Samuel du Pont's 350 acres of ultimate estate gardens, has an international reputation. **Brandywine Battlefield State Park** (U.S. 1, Chadds Ford, ☎ 610/459–3342) is the site of one of the more dramatic turns in the American Revolution. The region is dotted with antiques shops and cozy inns. The **Tourist Information Center for the Brandywine Valley** (Box 910, U.S. 1, Kennett Sq., 19348, ☎ 610/388–2900 or 800/228–9933) has information.

PENNSYLVANIA DUTCH COUNTRY

First of all, the Pennsylvania Dutch aren't Dutch; the name comes from *Deutsch* (German). In the 18th century, this rolling farmland 65 mi west of Philadelphia became home to the Amish, the Mennonites, and other German and Swiss immigrants escaping religious persecution. Today their descendants continue to turn their backs on the modern world—and in doing so, attract the world's attention. In summer, busloads of tourists jam Rte. 30, the main thoroughfare. But there is still charm on the backroads, where you will discover Amish farms, hand-painted signs advertising quilts, fields worked with mules, and horse-drawn buggies.

Tourist Information

Pennsylvania Dutch Convention and Visitors Bureau (501 Greenfield Rd., Lancaster 17601, ☎ 717/299–8901). **Mennonite Information Center** (2209 Millstream Rd., Lancaster 17602, ☎ 717/299–0954).

Getting There

By Car

From Philadelphia (65 mi away), take the Schuylkill Expressway (I–76) west to the Pennsylvania Turnpike, leaving the pike at Exit 20, 21, or 22.

By Train

Amtrak (☎ 800/872-7245) has service from Philadelphia to Lancaster.

By Bus

Greyhound Lines (☎ 800/231–2222) has three runs daily from Philadelphia to Lancaster.

Exploring Pennsylvania Dutch Country

In **Lancaster,** several furnished farmhouses offer simulated, up-close looks at how the Amish live, including the **Amish Farm and House** (2395 Lincoln Hwy. E, ☎ 717/394–6185). Abe, of **Abe's Buggy Rides** (Rte. 340, Bird-in-Hand, no ☎), chats about the Amish during a 2-mi spin down country roads in an Amish family carriage.

The **Historic Lancaster Walking Tour** (☎ 717/392–1776), a two-hour stroll through the heart of this charming old Colonial city, is conducted by guides who impart lively anecdotes about local architecture and history. **Central Market** (Penn Sq., ☎ 717/291–4723) is one of the oldest covered markets in the country; this is where the locals shop for fresh produce, meats, and baked goods. The old city hall, reborn as the **Heritage Center of Lancaster County** (King and Queen St., ☎ 717/299–6440), shows the work of Lancaster County artisans and craftspeople.

Wheatland (1120 Marietta Ave. [Rte. 23], 1½ mi west of Lancaster, ☎ 717/392–8721), a restored 1828 Federal mansion, was the home of the only president from Pennsylvania, James Buchanan.

In **Strasburg,** the **Strasburg Railroad** (Rte. 741, ☎ 717/687–7522) is a scenic 9-mi excursion in a wooden coach pulled by a steam locomotive. The **Railroad Museum of Pennsylvania** (Rte. 741, ☎ 717/687–8628) features colossal engines, railcars, and memorabilia documenting railroading in the state.

In **Ephrata,** the 18th-century Protestants of the **Ephrata Cloister** (Rte. 272, ☎ 717/733–6600) led an ascetic life, living examples of William Penn's "Holy Experiment." Guides now give tours of the restored medieval-style German buildings.

Lititz, west of Ephrata, was founded by Moravians who settled in Pennsylvania to do missionary work among the Native Americans. It's a lovely town with a tree-shaded main street of 18th-century cottages and shops. Pick up a Historical Foundation walking-tour brochure at the General Sutter Inn (14 E. Main St.).

Shopping

Antiques

Antiques malls are on Rte. 272 between Adamstown and Denver, 2 mi east of Pennsylvania Turnpike Exit 21; **Barr's Auctions** (☎ 717/336–

2861), **Renninger's Antique and Collector's Market** (☎ 717/336–2177), and **Stoudt's Black Angus** (☎ 717/484–4385) all feature indoor and outdoor sales.

Crafts

Places to see fine local crafts include the **Weathervane Shop** at the Landis Valley Museum (2451 Kissel Hill Rd., Lancaster, ☎ 717/569–9312), the **Tin Bin** (Valley Rd. and Rte. 501, Neffsville, ☎ 717/569–6210), and the 30-shop **Kitchen Kettle Village** (Rte. 340, Intercourse, ☎ 717/768–8261). International crafts, ideal for Christmas gifts and stocking stuffers, can be found at the **Selfhelp Crafts Gift Shop and Tea Room** (240 N. Reading Rd., Ephrata, ☎ 717/738–1101), owned and operated by the Mennonite Central Committee.

Farmers Markets

In addition to Lancaster's **Central Market** (*see* Exploring Pennsylvania Dutch Country, *above*), the **Green Dragon Farmers Market and Auction** (R.D. 4 just off Rte. 272, Ephrata, ☎ 717/738–1117; open Fri. year-round) is an old, traditional agricultural market with a country-carnival atmosphere.

Sports and the Outdoors

Hot-Air Ballooning

Great Adventure Balloon Club (☎ 717/397–3623) offers a bird's-eye view of Pennsylvania Dutch Country.

Dining and Lodging

Like the German cuisine that influenced it, Pennsylvania Dutch cooking is hearty. To sample such regional fare as ham, buttered noodles, chowchow, and shoofly pie, eat at one of the bustling restaurants where diners sit with perhaps a dozen others and the food is passed around family style. A number of farm families open their homes to visitors and allow them to observe and even participate in day-to-day farm life. For information, contact the Convention and Visitors Bureau (*see* Tourist Information, *above*). For price ranges, see Charts 1 (B) and 2 (B) in On the Road with Fodor's.

Bird-in-Hand

DINING

Bird-in-Hand Family Restaurant. This family-owned spot specializes in hearty Pennsylvania Dutch home cooking. *Rte. 340, just west of N. Ronks Rd., ☎ 717/768–8266. MC, V. Closed Sun. $*

Churchtown

LODGING

★ **Churchtown Inn.** This restored 1735 fieldstone mansion overlooking an Amish farm has cozy bedrooms with pencil-post canopy, brass, and high-back Victorian beds. A five-course breakfast is served in the glass-enclosed garden room. *2100 Main St., Narvon 17555, ☎ 215/445–7794. 8 rooms (2 share bath), 1 suite. MC, V. $$–$$$*

Ephrata

DINING

★ **The Restaurant at Doneckers.** Classic and country-French cuisine is served downstairs amid Colonial antiques and upstairs in a country garden. *333 N. State St., ☎ 717/738–9501. Reservations advised. AE, DC, MC, V. Closed Wed. $$–$$$*

Lancaster

LODGING

Best Western Eden Resort Inn. Spacious contemporary rooms and attractive grounds contribute to the pleasant atmosphere here. The suites have kitchens and fireplaces. *222 Eden Rd. (U.S. 30 and Rte. 272), 17601, ☎ 717/569–6444, FAX 717/569–4208. 274 rooms, 40 suites. Facilities: 3 restaurants, disco, nightclub, indoor pool, whirlpool. AE, D, DC, MC, V. $$$*

Lititz

LODGING

★ **Swiss Woods.** This comfortable, friendly, European-style B&B on 30 acres looks like a Swiss chalet and offers contemporary country decor. *500 Blantz Rd., 17543, ☎ 717/627–3358 or 800/594–8018, FAX 717/627–3483. 6 rooms, 1 suite. Facilities: kitchenette, Jacuzzi. No smoking. D, MC, V. $$–$$$*

Mount Joy

DINING

Groff's Farm. Hearty Mennonite farm fare, including chicken, farm relishes, and cracker pudding, is served in a restored 1756 farmhouse decorated with country fabrics and fresh flowers. *650 Pinkerton Rd., ☎ 717/653–2048. Reservations required for dinner, advised for lunch. AE, D, DC, MC, V. Closed Sun.–Mon. $$$*

LODGING

Cameron Estate Inn. Rooms in this sprawling Federal redbrick mansion on 15 wooded acres have Oriental rugs, antique and reproduction furniture, and canopy beds; seven have working fireplaces. *1895 Donegal Springs Rd., 17552, ☎ 717/653–1773. 18 rooms, 2 share bath. Facilities: Continental breakfast, restaurant. AE, D, DC, MC, V. $$–$$$*

Strasburg

LODGING

★ **Limestone Inn.** This 1786 B&B is furnished with Colonial and primitive antiques and reproductions. A multicourse breakfast is served. The proprietors are happy to set you up for dinner at a local Amish home; reserve ahead. *33 E. Main St., 17579, ☎ 717/687–8392 or 800/278–8392. 6 rooms. AE. $$–$$$*

Campgrounds

The Convention and Visitors Bureau (*see* Tourist Information, *above*) has a list of area campgrounds. Two of the best are **Mill Bridge Village and Campresort** (½ mi south of U.S. 30 on S. Ronk's Rd.; Box 86, Strasburg 17579, ☎ 717/687–8181), attached to a restored 18th-century village, and **Spring Gulch Resort Campground** (Rte. 897; 475 Lynch Rd., New Holland 17557, ☎ 717/354–3100).

The Arts and Nightlife

Dutch Apple Dinner Theater (510 Centerville Rd., at U.S. 30, Lancaster, ☎ 717/898–1900) offers a buffet plus Broadway musicals and comedies. Plays and concerts, as well as performances by the **Lancaster Symphony Orchestra** and the **Lancaster Opera,** are presented at the **Fulton Opera House** (12 N. Prince St., Lancaster, ☎ 717/394–7133), a restored 19th-century Victorian theater and National Historic Landmark.

Excursion to Reading

Getting There

From Exit 22 off the Pennsylvania Turnpike, take I–276N to U.S. 422W into downtown Reading—it's about an hour from Lancaster.

What to See and Do

Reading, a 19th-century industrial city, today promotes itself as the "Outlet Capital of the World." If you're in the mood for a diversion after a shopping spree, **Skyline Drive** is a meandering road with miles of unspoiled vistas and an expansive view of the city. The **Daniel Boone Homestead** (☎ 610/582–4900) is a renovation of the frontiersman's home. For information contact **Berks County Visitors Bureau** (VF Factory Outlet Complex, Park Rd. and Hill Ave., Box 6677, Wyomissing 19610, ☎ 610/375–4085).

Excursion to Hershey

Getting There

Take I–76 to Exit 20 and follow the signs—it's about 45 minutes from Lancaster.

What to See and Do

The streets have names like Cocoa Avenue, and the streetlights look like Hershey's Kisses. A family-oriented amusement park called **Hersheypark** (U.S. 422, ☎ 717/534–3090) offers Pennsylvania Dutch, German, and English theme areas. At **Chocolate World** (Park Blvd., ☎ 717/534–4900), you can take a 12-minute ride through the process of chocolate-making. Contact the **Hershey Information Center** (Hershey 17033, ☎ 800/437–7439).

Excursion to Gettysburg

Getting There

From Lancaster, take U.S. 30E to Gettysburg (about 1½ hours).

What to See and Do

The battle of Gettysburg, in July 1863, was the turning point of the Civil War. At the **Gettysburg National Military Park** (Visitors Center, 97 Taneytown Rd., ☎ 717/334–1124), you can follow the course of the fighting along roads through the battleground and on a 750-sq-ft electronic map. The **Gettysburg Travel Council** (35 Carlisle St., 17325, ☎ 717/334–6274) provides information on the region.

PITTSBURGH

At the point where the Monongahela and Allegheny rivers meet to form the Ohio River is a natural fortress first named Ft. Pitt and later Pittsburgh. Prosperity in coal, iron, and steel made the city a giant in the industrial age—and earned it the nickname "Smoky City." Today the smoke has cleared, and Pittsburgh—recently rated one of the "nation's most livable cities"—has been recast into an artful blend of turn-of-the-century architectural masterpieces and modern skyscrapers.

Tourist Information

Greater Pittsburgh: Convention and Visitors Bureau (4 Gateway Center, 15222, ☎ 412/281–7711). **Visitor Information Centers:** Downtown (Gateway Center, ☎ 412/281–7711), Oakland (Forbes Ave., ☎ 412/624–4660), Mount Washington (Grandview Ave., ☎ 412/381–5134), Pittsburgh International Airport (☎ 412/778–2601). The

Greater Pittsburgh Convention and Visitors Bureau operates a 24-hour **Activities Line** (☎ 800/366–0093), which lets you in on the events of the week.

Arriving and Departing

By Plane

Greater Pittsburgh International Airport (☎ 412/472–3525), served by most major airlines, is 14 mi west of downtown, to which cab fare is about $28. **Airlines Transportation Co.** (☎ 412/471–8900) provides motor-coach or van service to the major downtown hotels for $12 one-way and $20 round-trip.

By Car

From the north or south, take I–79 to I–279, which leads into downtown. From the east or west, take the Pennsylvania Turnpike (I–76), then I–376 to the Grant Street exit.

By Train

Amtrak (Liberty and Grant Sts., ☎ 800/872–7245).

By Bus

Greyhound Lines (11th St. and Liberty Ave., ☎ 800/231–2222).

Getting Around Pittsburgh

Port Authority Transit (☎ 412/231–5707) operates daily bus and trolley service. Within the central business district, the subway, called the "T," is free at all times, and buses are free during the day. Two cable cars—the ***Duquesne Incline,*** from West Carson Street west on the Ohio River to the restaurant area of Grandview Avenue, and the ***Monongahela Incline,*** from Station Square on the Monongahela to Grandview Avenue—carry passengers from river level to the hilly south side of the city.

Exploring Pittsburgh

Downtown, an area framed by the three rivers called the "Golden Triangle," contains **Point State Park** (*see* Parks and Gardens, *below*) and major hotels, restaurants, and theaters. **PPG Place** (Stanwix St. and 4th Ave.), with its spires and towers evocative of a medieval castle, exemplifies the Pittsburgh renaissance, as do the beautifully restored or maintained commercial and public buildings from the early boom days. Chief among these are **Two Mellon Bank Center** (5th Ave. and Grant St.), Daniel Burnam's Union Station, now **The Pennsylvanian** (Grant St. and Liberty Ave.), the **Oliver Building** (6th Ave. and Smithfield St.), and H. H. Richardson's great **Allegheny County Courthouse and Jail** (5th Ave. and Grant St.). **Station Square** (☎ 412/471–5808), on the Monongahela across the Smithfield Bridge, is a restored turn-of-the-century rail station with boutiques, restaurants (*see* Dining, *below*), and nightclubs.

East of downtown, **Oakland** is the headquarters of many of the city's cultural, educational, and medical landmarks. **The Carnegie** is an opulent cultural center with the **Museum of Art,** the **Museum of Natural History,** the **Music Hall,** and the **Carnegie Library** all under one Beaux Arts roof. Don't miss the 19th-century French and American paintings; the Hall of Architecture, which re-creates in plaster some of the world's architectural masterpieces; the dinosaur collection; and the extravagant Music Hall lobby. *4400 Forbes Ave., ☎ 412/622–3131; tours, ☎ 412/622–3289.*

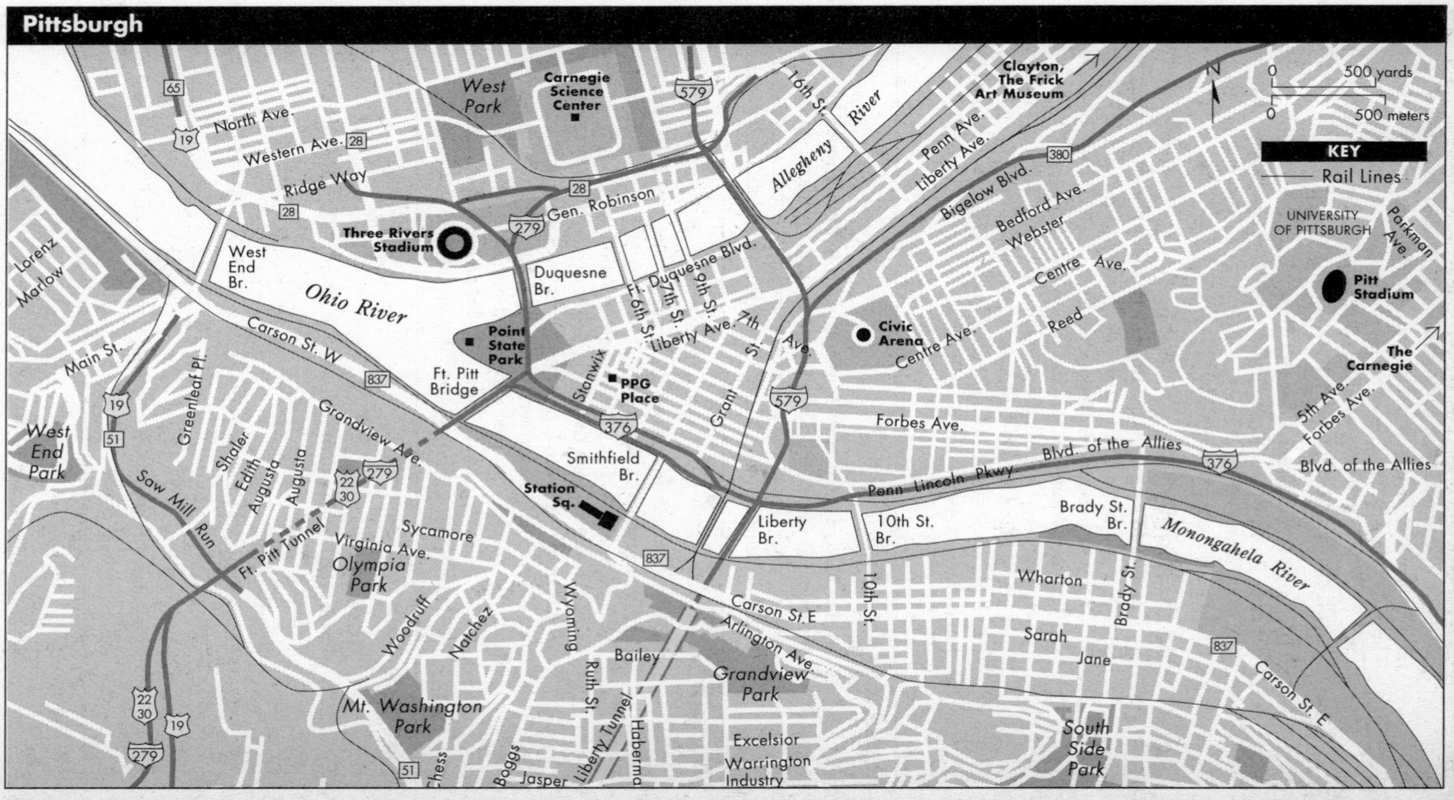
Pittsburgh
KEY
Rail Lines
0 500 yards
0 500 meters
N
Clayton, The Frick Art Museum
West Park
Carnegie Science Center
North Ave.
Western Ave.
Ridge Way
Gen. Robinson
Three Rivers Stadium
West End Br.
Ohio River
Duquesne Br.
Point State Park
Ft. Pitt Bridge
Allegheny River
16th St.
Penn Ave.
Liberty Ave.
Bigelow Blvd.
Bedford Ave.
Webster
Centre Ave.
Reed
UNIVERSITY OF PITTSBURGH
Parkman Ave.
Pitt Stadium
The Carnegie
5th Ave.
Forbes Ave.
Blvd. of the Allies
Ft. Duquesne Blvd.
6th St.
7th St.
9th St.
Liberty Ave.
7th Ave.
Grant St.
Stanwix
PPG Place
Civic Arena
Forbes Ave.
Smithfield Br.
Station Sq.
Penn Lincoln Pkwy.
Liberty Br.
10th St. Br.
Brady St. Br.
Monongahela River
10th St.
Brady St.
Wharton
Sarah
Jane
Carson St. E
Carson St. W
Grandview Ave.
Arlington Ave.
Grandview Park
Excelsior
Warrington
Industry
South Side Park
Lorenz
Marlow
Main St.
West End Park
Greenleaf Pl.
Shaler
Edith
Augusta
Saw Mill Run
Ft. Pitt Tunnel
Sycamore
Virginia Ave.
Olympia Park
Woodruff
Natchez
Wyoming
Bailey
Ruth St.
Liberty Tunnel
Haberma
Boggs
Jasper
Chess
Mt. Washington Park
65
19
28
279
579
380
376
837
22 30
51

The **Frick Art and Historical Center** (7227 Reynolds St., ☎ 412/371–0606 or 412/371–0600) consists of **Clayton,** the turn-of-the-century home of Henry Clay Frick that preserves the original furnishings and art, a carriage museum, and the **Frick Art Museum,** which possesses a small, choice collection of Old Master works.

The huge **Three Rivers Stadium** commands the north side of the Allegheny River. In the neighborhood, the **Carnegie Science Center** (Allegheny Center, ☎ 412/237–3300) has a planetarium, an aquarium, and hands-on science exhibits.

In the Vicinity

Northeast of Pittsburgh, the **Laurel Highlands** region has Revolutionary War–era forts and battlefields, restored inns and taverns, lush mountain scenery, and **Fallingwater** (Rte. 381, Mill Run, ☎ 412/329–8501; closed Mon. Apr. 1–Nov. 15 and all weekdays Nov. 15–Mar. 31; reservations required), the acclaimed stone, concrete, and glass house that Frank Lloyd Wright built over a waterfall. The Highlands are also noted for white-water rafting, hiking, and skiing. Contact **Laurel Highlands, Inc.** (Ligonier Town Hall, 120 E. Main St., Ligonier 15658, ☎ 412/238–5661).

Parks and Gardens

In the 36-acre **Point State Park** is the **Ft. Pitt Blockhouse** and **Ft. Pitt Museum** (☎ 412/281–9284). **Schenley Park** has a lake, trails, golf, and cross-country skiing. **Phipps Conservatory** (Schenley Park, ☎ 412/622–6914) is Henry Phipps's Victorian gardens—outdoors and under glass.

Shopping

Pittsburgh's best downtown department stores are **Saks Fifth Avenue** (513 Smithfield St.), **Lazarus** (200 Stanwix St.), and **Kaufmann's** (5th Ave. and Smithfield St.). Nearby are the shopping complexes **Fifth Avenue Place, 1 Oxford Centre** on Grant Street, and **PPG Place.** In the **Strip District** (betweeen Liberty and Penn Aves. and 16th and 22nd Sts.) are streets lined with farmers' market stalls and sellers of imported food and dry goods. Antiques shops and art galleries are along Carson Street East on the South Side. The **Shops at Station Square** (*see* Exploring Pittsburgh, *above*) has 70 shops and restaurants.

Spectator Sports

Baseball

Pittsburgh Pirates (Three Rivers Stadium, 400 Stadium Circle, ☎ 412/321–2827; Apr.–Oct.).

Football

Pittsburgh Steelers (Three Rivers Stadium, ☎ 412/323–1200; Aug.–Dec.).

Hockey

Pittsburgh Penguins (Civic Arena, Center Ave. and Auditorium Pl., ☎ 412/333–7328; Oct.–Apr.).

Dining

For price ranges, see Chart 1 (B) in On the Road with Fodor's.

$$$ **Common Plea.** This restaurant courts many of the city's lawyers and judges in its two dining rooms—one subdued in dark wood, the other flashy with glass and mirrors. Recommended are the fresh seafood and the veal dishes, including veal Romano (sautéed in an egg-and-Romano-cheese batter). *310 Ross St., ☎ 412/281–5140. Reservations advised. AE, DC, MC, V.*

$$$ ★ **The Grand Concourse/Gandy Dancer Saloon.** Set in a dazzling restored Beaux Arts railroad terminal, the restaurant features seafood, homemade pastas, and gracious service. In the Saloon, the emphasis is on raw-bar platters and lighter dishes. *1 Station Sq., Carson and Smithfield Sts., ☎ 412/261–1717. Reservations advised. AE, D, DC, MC, V.*

$$ **Georgetowne Inn.** Wraparound windows offer a majestic view from the Colonial-style dining rooms. The quality of the American food is exceptional; the low-key atmosphere makes this a good place for family dining. *1230 Grandview Ave., ☎ 412/481–4424. AE, D, DC, MC, V. No lunch Sun.*

$ **Gallagher's Pub.** In this relaxed neighborhood hangout, salads, burgers, and Irish stew are on the menu. *2 S. Market Sq., ☎ 412/261–5554. AE, DC, MC, V. Closed Sun.*

$ ★ **Richest's Restaurant.** Long, narrow, and evocative of the decade it opened, this kosher-style deli established in 1936 serves up classic deli fare in the heart of the cultural district. *140 6th St., ☎ 412/471–7799. AE, D, DC, MC, V. Closed Sun.*

Lodging

Choice hotels are limited in downtown Pittsburgh—and most are pricey. Nationally affiliated hotels are in Oakland and outlying suburban areas. For price ranges, see Chart 2 (B) in On the Road with Fodor's.

$$$ **Pittsburgh Vista Hotel.** The dramatically designed lobby leads to a 21-story tower housing rooms with contemporary decor. *1000 Penn Ave., 15222, ☎ 412/281–3700 or 800/445–8667, FAX 412/227–4500. 615 rooms, 47 suites. Facilities: restaurant, lounge, 18 meeting rooms, fitness center, pool. AE, D, DC, MC, V.*

$$$ ★ **Westin William Penn.** Pittsburgh's grand hotel has a sumptuous lobby with coffered ceiling, intricate plasterwork, and crystal chandeliers. It is always filled with people relaxing over drinks or afternoon tea. The guest rooms are light-filled, and many are large enough for a couch and wing chair. *530 William Penn Pl., Mellon Sq., 15230, ☎ 412/281–7100, FAX 412/553–5239. 595 rooms, 47 suites. Facilities: 2 restaurants, lounge, 39 meeting rooms, fitness room, beauty salon. AE, D, DC, MC, V.*

$$ ★ **The Priory.** This European-style hotel is furnished with antiques and reproductions. A hearty Continental breakfast is served. *614 Pressley St., 15212, ☎ 412/231–3338, FAX 412/231–4838. 21 rooms, 3 suites. Facilities: meeting room. AE, D, DC, MC, V.*

$$ **Ramada All-Suites Hotel.** In the Golden Triangle, across from the Civic Arena and adjacent to the Steel Plaza subway station, the Ramada is a convenient all-suite, midpriced hotel whose spacious rooms have conventional hotel furnishings. Full kitchens and kitchenettes are available. *One Bigelow Sq., 15219, ☎ 412/281–5800 or 800/225–5858, FAX 412/281–8467. 299 suites. Facilities: 5 meeting rooms, spa, restaurant, laundry, valet parking. AE, D, DC, MC, V.*

$ ★ **Clubhouse Inn Pittsburgh.** At this garden-style hotel 9 mi from the airport, guest rooms overlook a courtyard. The breakfast buffet is complimentary. *5311 Campbells Run Rd., 15205, ☎ 412/788–8400. 126 rooms, 26 suites. Facilities: pool, spa, free airport transportation. AE, D, DC, MC, V.*

$ **Howard Johnson Hotel University Center.** This modern nine-story hotel in the heart of Oakland provides easy access to the university and the museum district. *3401 Blvd. of the Allies, 15213, ☎ 412/683–6100* *or 800/245–4444. 119 rooms. Facilities: restaurant, lounge, pool. AE, D, DC, MC, V.*

The Arts and Nightlife

The Arts

The **Pittsburgh Symphony Orchestra** appears at the Heinz Hall for the Performing Arts (☎ 412/392–4800). The **Pittsburgh Opera** (☎ 412/281–0912) and the **Pittsburgh Ballet** (☎ 412/281–0360) are at the Benedum Center for the Performing Arts (☎ 412/471–6930). The **Point Park College Playhouse** (☎ 412/621–4445) presents dance and theater, including shows for children.

Nightlife

Station Square (Carson at Smithfield St.) has **Chauncy's** (☎ 412/232–0601) for dining and dancing, the **FunnyBone Comedy Club** (☎ 412/281–3130), and **Jellyrolls** (☎ 412/391–7464), a piano bar.

ELSEWHERE IN THE STATE

The Poconos

Getting There

I–80W leads to the Delaware Water Gap, I–84W to Milford. From the south, U.S. 611N skirts the Delaware River and takes you into Stroudsburg, which is 98 mi from Philadelphia, 135 mi from Harrisburg, and 318 mi from Pittsburgh.

What to See and Do

The Poconos, in the northeast corner of the state, encompass 2,400 sq mi of mountainous wilderness bordering the Delaware River, with lakes, streams, waterfalls, resorts, and enchanting country inns. A backroads drive will turn up quaint villages such as **Jim Thorpe** (Rte. 209), a late-Victorian mountain-resort town that has first-rate antiques shops and galleries. Winter brings downhill and cross-country skiing, skating, and snowmobiling; summer offers golf, boating, horseback riding, and hiking. **Pocono Mountains Vacation Bureau** (1004 Main St., Stroudsburg 18360, ☎ 717/424–6050 or 800/762–6667) provides information.

VIRGINIA

By Francis X. Rocca

Updated by M. D. Carnegie

Capital	Richmond
Population	6,187,358
Motto	Thus Always to Tyrants
State Bird	Cardinal
State Flower	Dogwood

Visitor Information

Virginia Division of Tourism (1021 E. Cary St., Richmond 23219, ☎ 804/786–2051 or 800/932–5827). Call **Visit Virginia** (☎ 800/847–4882) for a free state map. **Welcome centers:** in Bracey (on I–85), Bristol (I–81), Clearbrook (I–81), Covington (I–64), Fredericksburg (I–95), Lambsburg (I–77), Manassas (I–66), New Church (U.S. 13), Rocky Gap (I–77), and Skippers (I–95).

Scenic Drives

Skyline Drive, the **Blue Ridge Parkway,** and **Goshen Pass** offer spectacular mountain scenery (*see* Western Virginia, *below*). A 25-mi drive north along **Rte. 20** from Charlottesville to Orange takes you through gently rolling green countryside, past horse farms and vineyards. For a stirring panorama of the famous buildings and monuments of Washington, D.C., drive north from Alexandria on the **George Washington Memorial Parkway.** Between Virginia Beach and the Eastern Shore stretches the 17½-mi **Chesapeake Bay Bridge-Tunnel,** where you are surrounded by sea without leaving your car; there is an observation pier and a restaurant along the way.

National and State Parks

National Parks

Shenandoah National Park (Rte. 4, Box 348, Luray 22835, ☎ 703/999–2266)—195,000 acres with a vertical change in elevation of 3,500 ft—offers hiking, horseback riding, and fishing. Also in western Virginia are the 1.5-million-acre **George Washington National Forest** (Harrison Plaza, Box 233, Harrisonburg 22801, ☎ 703/564–8300) and the 700,000-acre **Jefferson National Forest** (210 Franklin Rd. SW, Roanoke 24001, ☎ 703/265–6054), which offer camping, boating, hiking, fishing, swimming, and horseback riding; and **Mt. Rogers National Recreation Area** (Rte. 1, Box 303, Marion 24354, ☎ 703/783–5196), with 116,000 acres, including the state's highest point—5,729 ft above sea level.

State Parks

The **Department of Conservation and Recreation** (203 Governor St., Richmond 23219, ☎ 804/786–1712) has information on Virginia's 35 state parks, which range in size from 500 to 4,500 acres. **Douthat State Park** (Rte. 1, Box 212, Millboro 24460, no ☎) and **Seashore State Park** (2500 Shore Dr., Virginia Beach 23451, no ☎) are the most popular.

WESTERN VIRGINIA

Residents of Charlottesville, in the Piedmont region of rolling plains, call it "Mr. Jefferson's Country." They speak of "The Sage of Monticello" as if he were still writing, building, and governing. Yet aware as it is of its past, Charlottesville is anything but backward. Home to the state university, and a fashionable retreat for tycoons and movie stars, it is one of America's most sophisticated small cities, often called the Santa Fe of the East.

In and along the Shenandoah Valley are small towns that were once frontier outposts; well-traveled driving routes with turnouts overlooking breathtaking scenery; many opportunities for outdoor recreation, on water and solid ground; and accommodations and restaurants to suit all tastes.

Tourist Information

Bath County: Chamber of Commerce (Rte. 220, Box 718, Hot Springs 24445, ☎ 703/839–5409). **Roanoke Valley:** Convention and Visitors Bureau (114 Market St., Box 1710, Roanoke 24008, ☎ 703/342–6025). **Shenandoah Valley:** Tourist Information Center (Box 1040, New Market 22844, ☎ 703/740–3132). **Charlottesville:** Thomas Jefferson Visitors Bureau and Center (Rte. 20, Box 161, 22902, ☎ 804/977–1783). **Lexington:** Visitor Center (102 E. Washington St., 24450, ☎ 703/463–3777). **Winchester:** Chamber of Commerce (1360 S. Pleasant Valley Rd., 22601, ☎ 703/662–4135 or 800/662–1360).

Getting There

By Plane

Charlottesville–Albemarle Airport (☎ 804/973–8341) is 8 mi north of town on Rte. 29. **Roanoke Regional Airport** (☎ 703/362–1999) is 6 mi north of town on Rte. 581.

By Car

Charlottesville is where U.S. 29 (north–south) meets I–64. I–81 and U.S. 11 run north–south the length of the Shenandoah Valley and continue south into Tennessee. I–66 meets I–81 and U.S. 11 at the northern end of the valley; I–64 connects the same highways with Charlottesville. Rte. 39 into Bath County connects with I–81 just north of Lexington.

By Train

Amtrak (☎ 800/872–7245) has service to Charlottesville's Union Station (810 W. Main St.), to Clifton Forge (for The Homestead resort in Bath County), and to Staunton.

By Bus

Greyhound Lines (☎ 800/231–2222) serves Charlottesville (310 W. Main St.), Lexington (Salerno's, 800 N. Main St.), Roanoke (26 Salem Ave.), and Staunton (1211 Richmond Rd.).

Exploring Western Virginia

Charlottesville

Jefferson built his beloved **Monticello** on a "little mountain" over a period of 40 years, 1769–1809. In details and overall conception, Monticello was a revolutionary structure, a neoclassical repudiation of the Colonial style with all its political connotations. Throughout the house are Jefferson's inventions, including a seven-day clock and a two-pen contraption for copying letters as he wrote them. It is impossible to see it all in one visit. *Rte. 53, ☎ 804/984–9800. Admission charged.*

Next door is a more modest presidential residence, James Monroe's **Ash Lawn.** The cozy rooms evoke the fifth president—our first to spring from the middle class. Outside, peacocks roam the grounds of this working plantation. *James Monroe Pkwy. (southwest of Rte. 53), ☎ 804/293–9539. Admission charged.*

The nearby **Historic Michie Tavern** is an 18th-century building moved here in the 1920s from a neighboring location. The period rooms are a bit too tidy but otherwise convincing. *Rte. 53, ☎ 804/977–1234. Admission charged.*

There is little to see in downtown Charlottesville besides a pedestrian shopping mall that takes up six brick-paved blocks of Main Street. At the west end of town is the **University of Virginia** (☎ 804/924–0311), founded and designed by Thomas Jefferson and still widely acclaimed as "the proudest achievement in American architecture." Pavilions flank the lawn as it flows down from the Rotunda, a half-scale replica of the Pantheon in Rome. Behind the pavilions, gardens and landscaping are laced with serpentine walls.

The Shenandoah Valley

At the top of the valley, and almost at the northernmost tip of the state, is **Winchester.** Because of its strategic location, the town has drawn more than its share of military action over the years. A young Colonel George Washington spent more than a year here during the French and Indian War; the log cabin he worked out of is now **George Washington's Office Museum** (Braddock and Cork Sts., ☎ 703/662–4412). Up the street is **Stonewall Jackson's Headquarters** (415 N. Braddock St., ☎ 703/667–3242), where the Confederate general planned the First Battle of Winchester (there were eventually three). The town is the site of happier activity, including parades and a beauty pageant, during the **Shenandoah Apple Blossom Festival** every May (☎ 703/740–3132). September is apple time at pick-your-own orchards throughout the surrounding countryside.

Belle Grove, just south of Middletown, is a grand 1790s house designed with the help of Thomas Jefferson. It served as headquarters for the victorious Union general Philip Sheridan during the Battle of Cedar Creek (1864) and is today a working farm. Call ahead if you plan to visit; it sometimes closes for part of the winter. *U.S. 11, ☎ 703/869–2028. Admission charged.*

Shenandoah National Park (*see* National and State Parks, *above*), encompassing some 60 peaks, runs more than 80 mi along the Blue Ridge, south from Front Royal to Waynesboro. Mountain meadows open up to gorgeous views of the range. Hiking, camping, fishing, and horseback riding are all available. For information on seasonal activities, pick up the free *Shenandoah Overlook* upon entering the park.

Skyline Drive winds 105 mi over the mountains of the park, affording panoramas of the valley to the west and the rolling country of the Piedmont to the east. On holidays and weekends in spring and fall, crowds slow down traffic to much less than the maximum of 35 mph. Many lodges, campsites, and eating places, and sometimes stretches of the drive itself, are closed from November through April.

Luray Caverns, the largest caves in the state, are just west of Skyline Drive. Water seepage over millions of years has created striking rock and mineral formations. Tours begin every 20 minutes. *Rte. 211, Luray, ☎ 703/743–6551. Admission charged.*

At **New Market,** the site of a costly Confederate victory late in the Civil War, the **New Market Battlefield Historical Park** has exhibits on the battle and the war. *I–81 Exit 67, ☎ 703/740–3102. Admission charged.*

In **Staunton** (pronounced "*Stan*-ton"), the **Woodrow Wilson House** (24 N. Coalter St., ☎ 703/885–0897; admission charged) has been restored to its appearance in 1856, when the 28th U.S. president was born here. Just outside town is the **Museum of American Frontier Culture** (230 Frontier Dr., ☎ 703/332–7850), an outdoor living museum that re-creates early American agrarian life on four genuine 18th-century farmsteads, right down to the animals and crops.

The 470-mi **Blue Ridge Parkway,** a continuation of Skyline Drive, runs south through the **George Washington National Forest** (*see* National and State Parks, *above*) to Great Smoky Mountains National Park in North Carolina and Tennessee. Less pristine than the drive, the parkway offers better, higher views—and free admission. **Peaks of Otter Recreation Area,** just off the parkway northeast of Roanoke, offers a 360-degree panorama.

In **Lexington,** the sixth-oldest college in the country, **Washington and Lee University,** is named for the first U.S. president (an early benefactor) and the Confederate commander Robert E. Lee, who served as college president after the Civil War. Among the campus's white-columned redbrick buildings is the **Lee Memorial Chapel and Museum** (☎ 703/463–8768), where a saintly statue of the recumbent general behind the altar marks his tomb.

Next door are the imposing neo-Gothic buildings of the all-male **Virginia Military Institute,** established in 1839. Here the **George C. Marshall Museum** (☎ 703/463–7103; admission charged) preserves the memory of the general, secretary of state, and Nobel Peace Prize winner. On display at the **Institute Museum** (☎ 703/464–7232) is Stonewall Jackson's horse, stuffed and mounted. Jackson's private life can be glimpsed nearby at the **Stonewall Jackson House** (8 E. Washington St., ☎ 703/463–2552; admission charged).

Between Lexington and **Bath County** (the site of thermal springs once used for medical treatments and still a popular resort area) runs **Goshen Pass,** a stunning 3-mi stretch of Rte. 39 that follows the Maury River as it winds its way through the Alleghenies. The countryside is lush with rhododendrons in May.

Natural Bridge, south of Lexington, is a 215-ft-high, 90-ft-long arch gradually carved out of limestone by the creek below it. It really *is* a bridge, supporting U.S. 11. *I–81 Exit 49 or 50, ☎ 703/291–2121. Admission charged.*

Roanoke is a quiet and cheerful railroad hub. A restored downtown warehouse called **Center in the Square** (Market Sq., ☎ 703/342–5760) houses a theater, a local historical museum, an art gallery, and a science museum with a planetarium. A stroll away is the **Virginia Museum of Transportation** (303 Norfolk Ave., ☎ 703/342–5670; admission charged), where dozens of original train cars and engines are on display.

A restored plantation southeast of Roanoke, **Booker T. Washington National Monument** is the birthplace of the great black educator and a living museum of life under slavery. *Rte. 122, ☎ 703/721–2094. Admission charged.*

About two hours east of Roanoke, and less than two hours south of Charlottesville, is the village of **Appomattox Court House,** restored to its appearance on April 9, 1865, when Lee surrendered to Grant in the parlor of the McLean house here. A slide show supplements a self-guided tour, and costumed interpreters answer questions in summer. *Rte. 24, ☎ 804/352–8987. Admission charged.*

What to See and Do with Children

At Charlottesville's **Virginia Discovery Museum** (400 Ackley La., ☎ 804/977–1025), children can step inside a giant kaleidoscope or an authentic log cabin; plays and concerts are also performed here. The **Science Museum of Western Virginia** in Roanoke (Market Sq., ☎ 703/342–5726) offers interactive exhibits, including computer games, that entertain youngsters while informing them on such topics as energy resources and natural history.

Shopping

Lewis Glaser Quill Pens (107 W. Main St., Charlottesville, ☎ 804/293–8531) sells feather pens and pewter inkwells of the kind it has made for the U.S. Supreme Court and the British royal family. **Paula Lewis** (4th and Jefferson Sts., Charlottesville, ☎ 804/295–6244) specializes in quilts by the Amish and Mennonite communities of Pennsylvania and Ohio.

Sports and the Outdoors

Canoeing

Front Royal Canoe (Rte. 340, ☎ 703/635–5440) and **Downriver Canoe** (Rte. 613, ☎ 703/635–5526) are both near Front Royal. **Shenandoah River Outfitters** (Rte. 3, ☎ 703/743–4159) is near Luray.

Fishing

To take advantage of the abundance of trout in some 50 streams of **Shenandoah National Park,** get a five-day Virginia fishing license, available in season (early Apr.–mid-Oct.) at concession stands along Skyline Drive.

Golf

Caverns Country Club Resort (Rte. 211, Luray, ☎ 703/743–6551). **Greene Hills Golf Club** (Rte. 619, Stanardsville, ☎ 804/985–7328). **The Homestead** (Rte. 220, Hot Springs, ☎ 703/839–5500 or 800/336–5771). **Wintergreen** (Rte. 664, Nellysford, ☎ 804/325–2200 or 800/325–2200).

Hiking

The stretch of the **Appalachian Trail** running through Shenandoah National Park takes hikers along the Blue Ridge skyline, offering stunning views of the Piedmont and the Shenandoah Valley in the distance; white-tailed deer often appear at arm's length. The main pathway's proximity to Skyline Drive and frequent parking lots make hike lengths flexible. For deep wilderness, 500 mi of marked side trails lead into the backcountry.

Skiing

The Homestead (*see* Golf, *above*) has cross-country, downhill, and night skiing. **Massanutten Village Ski Resort** (Rte. 33, McGaheysville, ☎ 703/289–9441) offers rentals and snowmaking. **Wintergreen** (*see* Golf, *above*) maintains 17 slopes and trails.

Tennis

Caverns Country Club Resort, The Homestead, and **Wintergreen** (*see* Golf, *above*) also offer tennis.

Spectator Sports

The **University of Virginia** (☎ 804/924–8821) is nationally or regionally ranked in several varsity sports. The *Cavalier Daily* has listings.

Equestrian Events

The **Virginia Horse Center** (Lexington, ☎ 703/463–2194) stages show jumping, hunter trials, and multibreed shows year-round.

Dining and Lodging

Bed-and-breakfast reservations in the region can be made through **Blue Ridge Bed & Breakfast** (Box 3895, Berryville 22611, ☎ 703/955–1246) and **Guesthouse Bed & Breakfast** (Box 5737, Charlottesville 22905, ☎ 804/979–7264).

For price ranges, see Charts 1 (B) and 2 (B) in On the Road with Fodor's.

Bath County

DINING AND LODGING

★ **The Homestead.** Famous for its mineral waters since 1766, this is today one of the country's most luxurious resorts. The spacious guest rooms have Victorian decor. The 15,000-acre property includes 100 mi of riding trails, four ski slopes, and 4 mi of streams stocked with rainbow trout. In the formal dining room a dance band plays every night Memorial Day–Labor Day. *Rte. 220, Hot Springs 24445, ☎ 703/839–5500 or 800/336–5771, FAX 703/839–7670. 518 rooms. Facilities: 7 restaurants, indoor pool, 2 outdoor pools, 3 golf courses, 19 tennis courts, bowling alley, movie theater, spa, horseback riding, skiing, fishing. AE, MC, V. $$$$*

Inn at Gristmill Square. These five buildings (gristmill, miller's house, country store, blacksmith's house, and hardware store) are a state historic landmark; a walk-in wine cellar is set among the gears of the original waterwheel. Entrées may include such dishes as breast of chicken stuffed with wild rice, sausage, apple, and pecans. The guest rooms are done in a rustic Colonial Virginia motif. *Rte. 645, Box 359, Warm Springs 24484, ☎ 703/839–2231. 9 rooms, 5 suites, 2 apartments. Facilities: restaurant, 3 tennis courts, outdoor pool, sauna. D, MC, V. $$$$*

Blue Ridge Parkway

LODGING

Doe Run Lodge. The location, on the crest of the Blue Ridge, means grand vistas of the Piedmont and proximity to golf, skiing, and hunting. Each chalet or villa has a fireplace and floor-to-ceiling windows. Book months in advance for the more-than-100-year-old log cabin. *Mile Post 189, Blue Ridge Pkwy., Hillsville 24343, ☎ 703/398–2212 or 800/325–6189, FAX 703/398–2833. 39 apartments, 3 villas, 3 specialty rentals. Facilities: restaurant, 3 tennis courts, outdoor pool, sauna, stocked fishing pond, hiking trails. AE, MC, V. $$$*

Wintergreen. From December through February, guests at this 11,000-acre resort may ski and golf on the same day; and there are plenty of sports options all year long. Accommodations range from studio apartments to six-bedroom houses, all wood buildings that blend in with the leafy surroundings. *Rte. 664, Box 706, Wintergreen 22958, ☎ 804/325–2200 or 800/325–2200, FAX 804/325–6760. 330 units. Facilities: 6 restaurants, bar, indoor pool, 5 outdoor pools, 25 tennis courts, lake, 2 golf courses, 17 ski slopes and trails, 25 mi of hiking trails, horseback riding, exercise room, sauna. AE, MC, V. $$$*

Rocky Knob Cabins. These log cabins, hidden away in the woods a short hike from spectacular Rock Castle Gorge, have kitchens but no bathtubs or phones. *Mile Post 174, Box 5, Meadows of Dan 24120, ☎ 703/593–3503. 7 cabins. DC, MC, V. Closed Labor Day–Memorial Day. $*

Charlottesville

DINING

C&O Restaurant. A boarded-up storefront hung with an illuminated Pepsi sign conceals a stark-white formal dining room. Try the *terrine de campagne* (pâté of veal, venison, and pork). If available, coquilles St. Jacques is a staple of the changing menu. The informal bistro downstairs serves light meals. *515 E. Water St., ☎ 804/971–7044. Reservations required upstairs; no reservations downstairs. MC, V. Closed Sun. $$$*

Eastern Standard. Specialties served in the casual but subdued upstairs dining room include rainbow trout stuffed with shiitake mushrooms, wild rice, and fontina cheese; and loin of lamb with mint pesto. The lively downstairs bistro serves pastas and light fare. *Downtown Mall, ☎ 804/295–8668. MC, V. Upstairs closed Sun.–Wed. No lunch. $$*

Crozet Pizza. There are up to 30 toppings to choose from, including snow peas and asparagus spears in season. The hardwood booths are always full, and takeout must be ordered hours in advance. *Rte. 240, Crozet, west of Charlottesville, ☎ 804/823–2132. No credit cards. Closed Sun.–Mon. $*

DINING AND LODGING

Boar's Head Inn. At this resort built around a restored early 19th-century gristmill set on two small lakes, the simple but elegant guest rooms are furnished chiefly with Victorian antiques. Some suites have fireplaces. *U.S. 250W, Box 5307, 22905, ☎ 804/296–2181 or 800/476–1988, FAX 804/977–1306. 173 rooms, 11 suites. Facilities: 3 restaurants, 3 pools, 17 tennis courts, 3 squash courts, sauna, biking, fishing, hot-air ballooning. AE, D, MC, V. $$$*

Silver Thatch Inn. The interior of this 18th-century farmhouse is decorated in Colonial Americana, each guest room unique. In the restaurant, provisioned by three organic farms, the fish is always fresh and the rabbits and chickens are locally raised. The wine cellar wins national awards. *3001 Hollymead Dr., 22901, ☎ 804/978–4686, FAX 804/973–6156. 7 rooms. Facilities: restaurant, outdoor pool, 2 tennis courts. DC, MC, V. $$$*

English Inn. This large-scale B&B has a Tudor-style dining room, but the guest rooms are in modern decor; suites have sitting rooms and reproduction antiques. *2000 Morton Dr., 22901, ☎ 804/971–9900, FAX 804/977–8008. 67 rooms, 21 suites. Facilities: Continental breakfast, indoor pool, sauna, exercise equipment. AE, DC, MC, V. $$*

Lexington

DINING AND LODGING

Maple Hall. In this mid-19th-century plantation house on 56 acres, guest rooms are furnished with period antiques and modern amenities. The main dining room has a large fireplace. Notable entrées include beef fillet with a green-peppercorn sauce. *Rte. 11, 11 N. Main St., 24450, ☎ 703/463–2044, FAX 703/463–7262. 21 rooms. Facilities: restaurant (no lunch), hiking trails, fishing pond, outdoor pool, tennis court. MC, V. $$$*

Roanoke

DINING

La Maison du Gourmet. The 12 dining rooms in this 1927 Georgian Colonial–style house range from grand to cozy. Filet mignon is flambéed at your table and served as steak Diane; the lamb is succulent and expertly grilled. *5732 Airport Rd., ☎ 703/366–2444. AE, D, DC, MC, V. No lunch weekends. $$$*

Texas Tavern. The sign says "We serve a thousand, ten at a time." The tavern is often packed, especially at night, so you may have to wait for one of the 10 stools; but the tough-looking guys behind the counter will fill your order quickly. Chili is the specialty. *114 Church Ave., ☎ 703/342–4825. No reservations. No credit cards. No liquor. $*

Staunton

DINING

Rowe's Family Restaurant. This bright dining room filled with booths has been operated by the same family since 1947. Specialties include Virginia ham, steak, chicken, and homemade pies (try the mincemeat). *I–81 Exit 222, ☎ 703/886–1833. D, MC, V. $$*

DINING AND LODGING

Belle Grae Inn. The dining rooms in this restored Victorian house are appointed with brass wall sconces and Oriental rugs; the menu is Continental. Guest rooms have rocking chairs and canopy or brass beds. *515 W. Frederick St., 24401, ☎ 703/886–5151, FAX 703/886–6641. 16 rooms. Facilities: full breakfast, restaurant. AE, MC, V. $$$*

LODGING

Frederick House. Three restored town houses dating from 1810 make up this inn in the center of the historic district. Guest rooms are decorated with antiques. *28 N. New St., 24401, ☎ 703/885–4220. 14 rooms. Facilities: full breakfast. No smoking. AE, D, DC, MC, V. $$*

Motels

Holiday Inn Civic Center (501 Orange Ave., Roanoke 24016, ☎ 703/342–8961 or 800/465–4329, FAX 703/342–8961 ext. 121), 153 rooms, restaurant, bar, outdoor pool, parking; *$$*. **Roseloe Motel** (Rte. 2, Box 590, Hot Springs 24445, ☎ 703/839–5373), 14 rooms, parking; *$*.

Campgrounds

In **Shenandoah National Park,** the **Big Meadows Campground** (☎ 703/999–2221) accepts reservations. Other campsites in the park are available on a first-come, first-served basis; for information, contact the park.

The Arts and Nightlife

The Arts

CHARLOTTESVILLE

For details on performances at the University of Virginia, check the *Cavalier Daily.* **McGuffey Art Center** (201 2nd St. NW, ☎ 804/295–7973), which houses the studios of painters and sculptors, also hosts concerts and plays.

SHENANDOAH VALLEY

Garth Newel Music Center (Hot Springs, ☎ 703/839–5018) hosts chamber-music concerts on summer weekends. **Lime Kiln Arts Theater** (Lexington, ☎ 703/463–3074) is an outdoor rock-wall pit—the ruins of a lime kiln—where plays and concerts (folk and classical) are performed throughout the summer. **Roanoke Ballet Theatre** (☎ 703/345–6099) performs in spring and fall. **Roanoke Valley Chamber Music Society** (☎ 703/774–2899) hosts visiting performers from October to May.

Nightlife

In Charlottesville, the large and comfortable **Miller's** (109 W. Main St., Downtown Mall, ☎ 804/971–8511) hosts folk and jazz musicians. In Roanoke, **Billy's Ritz** (102 Salem Ave., ☎ 703/342–3937) has rock bands and draws a young professional crowd. At **The Homestead** in Hot Springs (*see* Dining and Lodging, *above*), there's ballroom dancing to live music nightly in season.

NORTHERN VIRGINIA

The affluent and cosmopolitan residents of this region look more to neighboring Washington, D.C., than to the rest of the Commonwealth for direction. Yet they take pride in being Virginians and in protecting the historic treasures they hold in trust for the rest of the nation. Here is found some of America's most precious acreage, including Mount Vernon and the Civil War battlefield of Manassas (Bull Run). The enormous Potomac Mills Mall in Prince William is Virginia's most-visited site. The gracious Old South lives on in the fox hunting and steeplechases of Loudoun County. On the nearby Northern Neck, visitors can combine historic sightseeing with fishing and water sports.

Tourist Information

Fairfax County: Tourism and Convention Bureau (8300 Boone Blvd., Suite 450, Vienna 22182, ☎ 703/790–3329). **Loudoun County:** Visitor Center (108D South St. SE, Leesburg 22075, ☎ 703/777–0519). **Northern Neck:** Travel Council (Box 312, Reedville 22539, ☎ 800/453–6167). **Alexandria:** Convention and Visitor's Bureau (221 King St., 22314, ☎ 703/838–4200). **Fredericksburg:** Visitor Center (706 Caroline St., 22401, ☎ 703/373–1776).

Getting There

By Plane

Two major airports serve both northern Virginia and the Washington, D.C., area. The busy **Washington National Airport** (☎ 703/685–8000) in Arlington has scheduled daily flights by all major U.S. carriers. **Dulles International Airport** (☎ 703/661–2700) in Loudoun County, 26 mi west of Washington, is a modern facility served by the major U.S. airlines and many international carriers.

By Car

I–95 runs north–south along the eastern side of the region. I–66 runs east–west. Fredericksburg is 50 mi south of Washington, D.C., on I–95. Rte. 3 runs the length of the Northern Neck.

By Train

Amtrak (☎ 800/872–7245) stops in Alexandria (110 Callahan Dr.) and Fredericksburg (Caroline St. and Lafayette Blvd.); some travelers find it easiest to arrive at Washington, D.C.'s, Union Station (50 Massachusetts Ave. NE).

By Bus

Greyhound Lines (☎ 800/231–2222) serves Fairfax (4103 Rust St.), Fredericksburg (1400 Jefferson Davis Hwy.), and Springfield (6583 Backlick Rd.).

Exploring Northern Virginia

George Washington's **Mount Vernon** is the most-visited house museum in the country. The elegant, porticoed farmhouse, built from Washington's own plans starting in 1754, has been restored to its appearance during the years (1759–75, 1783–89, and 1797–99) the first president lived here. And here, in the land they loved, Washington and his wife, Martha, are buried. *Rte. 235, ☎ 703/780–2000. Admission charged.*

Washington's nephew Lawrence Lewis lived at nearby **Woodlawn** (U.S. 1, ☎ 703/780–4000; admission charged), designed by the architect of the Capitol and begun in 1800. The formal gardens include a large collection of rare old-fashioned roses. Also on the grounds is the small **Pope–Leighey House,** designed by Frank Lloyd Wright and built in 1940.

South of Mount Vernon is the relatively unvisited but meticulously restored **Gunston Hall** (Rte. 242, ☎ 703/550–9220; admission charged), the plantation home of George Mason, one of the framers of the Constitution.

North of Mount Vernon, on the Potomac, is **Alexandria,** a suburb of Washington, D.C., with an identity based on 2½ centuries of history. The Old Town is a neighborhood of 18th- and 19th-century town houses, most of them redbrick. Its major sights can be seen on foot within 20 blocks or so, and the area has scores of shops and restaurants. Parking is usually scarce, but the convention and visitor's bureau provides a one-day pass that allows free parking at two-hour meters.

The bureau—the best place to start a tour—is in the town's oldest structure, **Ramsay House** (221 King St., ☎ 703/838–4200), built in 1724 in Dumfries (25 mi south) and moved here in 1749. Like it, the **Old Presbyterian Meeting House** (321 S. Fairfax St., ☎ 703/549–6670) and the grand **Carlyle House** (121 N. Fairfax St., ☎ 703/549–2997) are 18th-century reminders of the town's Scottish heritage.

George Washington frequented the **Stabler–Leadbeater Apothecary Shop** (105–107 S. Fairfax St., ☎ 703/836–3713; admission charged), **Gadsby's Tavern** (134 N. Royal St., ☎ 703/838–4242; admission charged), and **Christ Church** (Washington and Cameron Sts., ☎ 703/549–1450). Another member of Christ Church was Robert E. Lee; the **Lee Boyhood Home** (607 Oronoco St., ☎ 703/548–8454; admission charged) is practically around the corner.

The homes of less-famous residents help to fill out a picture of 18th- and 19th-century life. The block of Prince Street between Fairfax and Lee, lined by imposing three-story houses, is called **Gentry Row,** and the cobblestone block of humbler residences between Lee and Union is **Captain's Row.**

Alexandria's cultural heritage is honored at the **Lyceum** (201 S. Washington St., ☎ 703/838–4994), with displays of decorative arts and exhibits on local history. Work by local artists is shown at the **Athaeneum** (201 Prince St., ☎ 703/548–0035). At the **Torpedo Factory Art Center** (105 N. Union St., ☎ 703/838–4565), a renovated waterfront building where torpedoes were made during both world wars, more than 180 artists and craftspeople make and sell their wares.

Possibly too far to walk to, but impossible to miss, is the 333-ft-high **George Washington National Masonic Memorial** (Shooter's Hill, ☎ 703/683–2007). Relics of the first president and exhibits on the Masonic Order are on display inside, and the top offers a spectacular view of Alexandria and nearby Washington.

For information on **Arlington National Cemetery** and the **Pentagon,** *see* Washington, D.C.

Fredericksburg, about an hour south, rivals Alexandria and Mount Vernon for associations with the Washington family. The future first president lived across the Rappahannock River at Ferry Farm from age 6 to 16. His sister Betty and her husband lived at **Kenmore** (1201 Washington Ave., ☎ 703/373–3381; admission charged), a house whose plain facade belies a lavish interior. The home of his brother Charles Washington later became the **Rising Sun Tavern** (1306 Caroline St., ☎

Northern Virginia

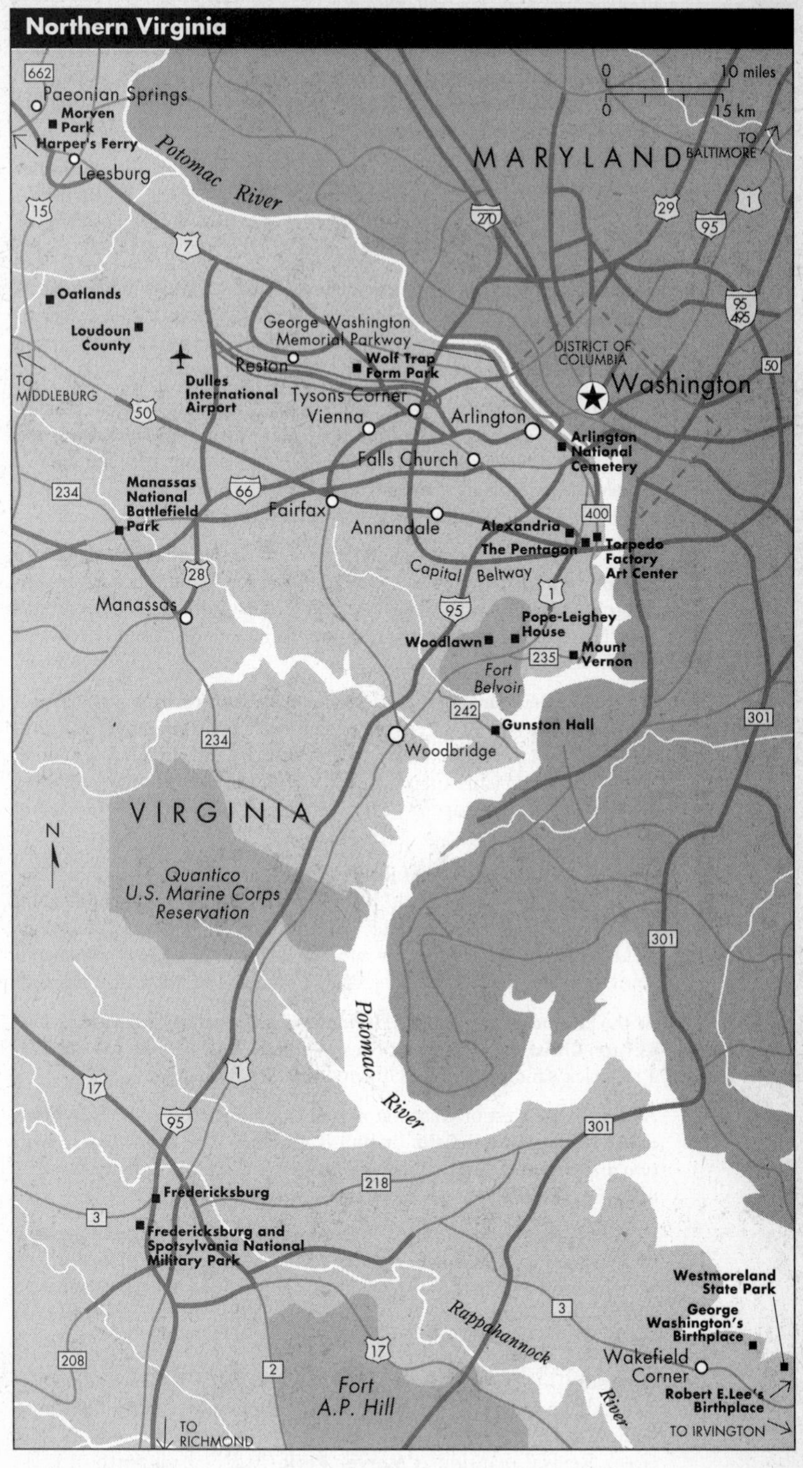

703/371–1494; admission charged), a watering hole for such revolutionaries as Patrick Henry and Thomas Jefferson. The **Home of Mary Washington** (Charles and Lewis Sts., ☎ 703/373–1569; admission charged) is a modest house George bought for his mother during her last years.

The future fifth president also lived in Fredericksburg, and the **James Monroe Museum and Memorial Library** (908 Charles St., ☎ 703/899–4559; admission charged) is in the tiny one-story building where he practiced law from 1787 to 1789.

At the **Hugh Mercer Apothecary Shop** (Caroline and Amelia Sts., ☎ 703/373–3362; admission charged), the guide's explicit descriptions of amputations, cataract operations, and tooth extractions can make latter-day visitors wince.

Four Civil War battlefields—Fredericksburg, Chancellorsville, the Wilderness, and the Spotsylvania Courthouse—make up the **Fredericksburg and Spotsylvania National Military Park.** All the sites are within 17 mi of Fredericksburg, where a **visitor center** (1013 Lafayette Blvd. [U.S. 1], ☎ 703/373–6122) has an introductory slide show and exhibits.

Rte. 3 east of Fredericksburg takes you into the **Northern Neck,** a strip of land bounded by the Potomac and the Rappahannock rivers. At the top of the Neck is Westmoreland County, which produced both the "father of our country" and one of the greatest tragic heroes of the Civil War.

George Washington's Birthplace National Monument, in Wakefield, preserves the memory of the first president with a working farm and a reproduction of the original early 18th-century plantation house (which burned down on Christmas day, 1779). Washington's family members are buried on the property. *Rte. 204, ☎ 804/224–1732. Admission charged.*

Stratford Hall, birthplace of Robert E. Lee, is an elegant original, built in the shape of an *H* in the 1730s, with brick and timber produced on the site. Farmers still cultivate 1,600 of the original acres, and their yield, a variety of cereals, is for sale. Lunch is served in a log cabin from April through October. *Rte. 214, ☎ 804/493–8038. Admission charged.*

At the far end of the Neck, in **Irvington,** is a jewel of Tidewater architecture: **Christ Church** (jct. of Rtes. 646 and 709, ☎ 804/438–6855), a redbrick sanctuary of cruciform design, built in 1732.

A 26-mi drive west of Washington is the monumentally important **Manassas National Battlefield,** or Bull Run, where the Confederacy won two major victories and Stonewall Jackson won his nickname. *Rte. 234 off I–66, ☎ 703/361–1339. Admission charged.*

Farther west is horse country. In **Loudoun County's** fashionable towns of **Leesburg** and **Middleburg,** the residents (many of them Yankee transplants) keep up the local traditions of fox hunts and steeplechases. The county visitor center in Leesburg (*see* Tourist Information, *above*) can suggest scenic drives.

Oatlands (U.S. 15, 6 mi south of Leesburg, ☎ 703/777–3174; admission charged) is a restored Greek Revival plantation house whose manicured fields host public and private equestrian events spring through fall. The Greek Revival mansion at **Morven Park** (Rte. 7, 1 mi north of Leesburg, ☎ 703/777–2414; admission charged), a White House look-alike, contains two museums: one of horse-drawn carriages, the other of hounds and hunting. And here in the midst of Thoroughbred country is the

American Workhorse Museum (Rte. 662, Paeonian Springs, ☎ 703/338–6290), a tribute to an unsung hero of this nation's economic history.

What to See and Do with Children

Wolf Trap Farm Park (*see* The Arts and Nightlife, *below*) hosts mime, puppet, and animal shows, as well as concerts, plays, and storytelling, mid-June–Labor Day. Events are often free. Emus, monkeys, a zebra, giant tortoises, and domestic farm animals inhabit **Reston Animal Park** (Rtes. 7 and 606, Hunter Mill Rd., Lake Fairfax, ☎ 703/759–3636 or 703/759–3637).

Shopping

Potomac Mills Mall (2700 Potomac Mills Circle, I–95, Prince William) is the state's most-visited attraction; Swedish furniture giant IKEA is one of 220 outlets. **Tysons Corner Center** (1961 Chain Bridge Rd., jct. Rtes. 7 and 123) houses 240 retailers, including Bloomingdale's and Nordstrom. Next door, the **Galleria at Tysons II** (2001 International Dr.) has 125 more, including Saks Fifth Avenue and Neiman Marcus. The first area branch of **Tiffany & Co.** (8045 Leesburg Pike, ☎ 703/893–7700) is a few minutes away.

The old towns of Alexandria and Fredericksburg are dense with **antiques** shops, many quite expensive, that are particularly strong in the Federal and Victorian periods. The town visitor centers (*see* Tourist Information, *above*) have maps and lists of the stores.

Sports and the Outdoors

Biking

The 19-mi **Mount Vernon Bicycle Trail** (☎ 703/285–2598) runs along the Potomac in George Washington Park and through Alexandria. The 4.7-mi **Burke Lake Park Bicycle Trail** (☎ 703/323–6600) in Fairfax County circles the lake. The Arlington Parks and Recreation Bureau (☎ 703/838–4343) offers a free map of the **county Bikeway System.**

Golf

Algonkian Park (600 Potomac View Rd., Sterling, ☎ 703/450–4655), **Burke Lake Park** (Fairfax Station, ☎ 703/323–1641), and **Shannon Green Resort** (Rte. 3, Fredericksburg, ☎ 703/786–8385) have public courses. The **Tides Inn** (☎ 804/438–5501; *see* Dining and Lodging, *below*) offers 18- and 9-hole courses.

Water Sports

The Northern Neck gives sailors, water-skiers, and windsurfers access to two rivers and the Chesapeake Bay. For information, contact the **Northern Neck Travel Council** (*see* Tourist Information, *above*).

Dining and Lodging

Old Town Alexandria's restaurants are many and varied, but they are also pricey and, on weekend nights, crowded. Arlington's Little Saigon, on and around Wilson Boulevard, has many excellent and affordable Vietnamese restaurants.

Lodging prices are high, but so are the standards of comfort and luxury. Bed-and-breakfasts tend to be more elegant here because many serve as romantic weekend hideaways for regular customers from Washington. For listings, try **Bed & Breakfast Ltd.** (Box 12011, Washington, D.C. 20005, ☎ 202/328–3510). **Princely Bed & Breakfast** (819 Prince St.,

Alexandria 22314, ☎ 703/683–2159) lists accommodations in historic Old Town homes.

For price ranges, see Charts 1 (A) and 2 (A) in On the Road with Fodor's.

Alexandria

DINING

Scotland Yard. The kilt-bedecked owner holds forth in the narrow, wood-paneled dining room while in the kitchen his children prepare such Caledonian favorites as venison game pie. Original recipes include lobster Drambuie and flaming whiskey steak. *728 King St., ☎ 703/683–1742. AE, MC, V. Closed Mon. No lunch. $$$*

Le Gaulois. At this quiet country bistro whose white walls are hung with scenes of southern France, the specialties include *pot-au-feu gaulois,* a beef-and-chicken stew with whole vegetables; and cassoulet, a rich bean casserole with sausage and beef. *1106 King St., ☎ 703/739–9494. AE, DC, MC, V. $$*

★ **Taverna Cretekou.** Surrounded by whitewashed stucco walls and brightly colored macramé tapestries, or outside in the canopied garden, diners enjoy such dishes as lamb *Exohikon* (baked in a pastry shell) and swordfish kebab. All the wines are Greek. *818 King St., ☎ 703/548–8688. AE, D, MC, V. Closed Mon. $$*

Hard Times Café. Recorded country-and-western music and framed photographs of Depression-era Oklahoma set the tone at this casual, always crowded hangout. Three kinds of chili are served—Texas (spicy), Cincinnati (mild), and vegetarian. *1404 King St., ☎ 703/683–5340. No reservations. AE, MC, V. $*

LODGING

Holiday Inn Old Town. The mahogany-paneled lobby and the hunting prints in the guest rooms suggest a men's club. Marble bathtubs, modem-ready phones, and extraordinary service (for example, exercise bikes are brought to your room upon request) make this an exceptional member of the chain. *480 King St., 22314, ☎ 703/549–6080 or 800/465–4327, FAX 703/684–6508. 227 rooms. Facilities: restaurant, lounge, indoor pool, sauna. AE, D, DC, MC, V. $$$*

★ **Morrison House.** Butlers unpack for guests in rooms furnished with four-posters, and tea is served every afternoon at this convincing Federal-style house (built in 1985). Most extraordinary of all, the employees never accept tips. *116 S. Alfred St., 22314, ☎ 703/838–8000, FAX 703/684–6283. 42 rooms, 3 suites. Facilities: 2 restaurants. AE, DC, MC, V. $$$*

Arlington

DINING

China Rose. Want to dine as the locals do? Check out this casual but elegant eatery tucked away in a nondescript shopping arcade. The owner is friendly, and the kitchen turns out superb versions of such Chinese classics as General Tso's chicken. *2250 Clarendon Blvd., ☎ 703/243–8181. MC, V. $*

LODGING

Marriott Crystal Gateway. Black marble, blond wood, and lots of greenery distinguish this hostelry for big-budget business travelers and tourists who want to be pampered. *1700 Jefferson Davis Hwy., 22202, ☎ 703/920–3230 or 800/228–9290, FAX 703/271–5212. 563 rooms, 131 suites. Facilities: 3 restaurants, lounge, nightclub, indoor and outdoor pools, whirlpool, sauna, exercise rooms. AE, D, DC, MC, V. $$$*

Ritz-Carlton Pentagon City. This soundproofed enclave of luxury five minutes from the airport features Persian carpets in the lobby and silk wallpaper in the reproduction Federal bedrooms. *1250 S. Hayes St., 22202, ☏ 703/415–5000 or 800/241–3333, FAX 703/415–5061. 304 rooms, 41 suites. Facilities: restaurant, bar, indoor pool, exercise room, sauna. AE, D, DC, MC, V. $$$*

Best Western Arlington. The attraction here is convenience: easy access to I–395 and a free shuttle to the airport. The rooms are done in unexceptional modern decor. *2480 S. Glebe Rd., 22206, ☏ 703/979–4400 or 800/528–1234, FAX 703/685–0051. 325 rooms. Facilities: restaurant, outdoor pool, exercise room, laundry and valet service. AE, D, DC, MC, V. $$*

Fairfax

LODGING

Bailiwick Inn. Each guest room in this 18th-century house is furnished with a feather bed and antiques or period reproductions. Some rooms have fireplaces, and the bridal suite has a four-poster bed and a Jacuzzi. *4023 Chain Bridge Rd., 22030, ☏ 703/691–2266, FAX 703/934–2112. 13 rooms, 1 suite. Facilities: full breakfast. AE, MC, V. $$$$*

Fredericksburg

DINING

Le Lafayette. The cuisine served in this pre-Revolutionary Georgian house could be called "Virginia French." The prix fixe menu may offer grilled breast of duck in red-currant sauce over braised red cabbage or poached salmon fillet in saffron broth with mussels, leeks, and tomatoes. *623 Caroline St., ☏ 703/373–6895. AE, D, DC, MC, V. Closed Mon. $$$$*

Ristorante Renato. At this unlikely candlelighted Italian restaurant in the midst of a Colonial town, the specialties include "Romeo and Juliet" (veal and chicken topped with mozzarella in white-wine sauce) and shrimp scampi Napoli with lemon-butter sauce. *Williams and Prince Edward Sts., ☏ 703/371–8228. Reservations advised weekends. AE, MC, V. $$*

LODGING

Richard Johnston Inn. This three-story row house across from the visitor center has parking in the rear under magnolia trees. Guest rooms are furnished with Empire-style and Chippendale antiques; the suites open onto a patio. *711 Caroline St., 22401, ☏ 703/899–7606. 7 rooms, 2 suites. Facilities: Continental breakfast. AE, MC, V. $$*

Best Western Fredericksburg. This generic, two-story, family-oriented hotel is five minutes from the battlefields. The most pleasant views are of the pool. *543 Warrenton Rd. (U.S. 17 and I–95), 22405, ☏ 703/371–5050 or 800/528–1234, FAX 703/373–3496. 87 rooms. Facilities: restaurant, outdoor pool, playground, nature trail. AE, D, DC, MC, V. $*

Great Falls

DINING

L'Auberge Chez François. White stucco, dark exposed beams, and a garden just outside create a country-inn ambience 20 minutes from Tysons Corner. The Alsatian cuisine includes salmon soufflé with salmon-and-scallop mousse and white-wine or lobster sauce. *332 Springvale Rd. (Rte. 674), ☏ 703/759–3800. Reservations required 2 wks in advance. Jacket required. AE, DC, MC, V. Closed Mon. No lunch. $$$$*

Northern Neck

LODGING

Tides Inn. At this 20-acre Colonial resort on a Rappahannock tributary, almost all the rooms have water views. For an even closer look, guests can take a dinner cruise on one of the inn's two yachts. *Rte. 200, Box 480, Irvington 22480, ☏ 804/438–5000 or 800/843–3746, FAX 804/438–5222. 92 rooms, 18 suites. Facilities: 4 restaurants, lounge,* *marina, 2 golf courses, outdoor pool, 4 tennis courts, sailboats, canoes, paddleboats, summer children's programs, privileges at nearby fitness center. AE, D, DC, MC, V. $$$$*

Tysons Corner

DINING

Clyde's. Quality is high, service attentive, and the tone always lively in these art-deco dining rooms. The long, eclectic menu includes fresh fish, often in such preparations as trout Parmesan. *8332 Leesburg Pike, ☎ 703/734–1900. AE, D, DC, MC, V. $$*

Motel

Hampton Inn (2310 Plank Rd., Fredericksburg 22401, ☎ 703/371–0330 or 800/426–7866, FAX 703/371–1753), 165 rooms, 1 suite, outdoor pool; $.

The Arts and Nightlife

The Arts

Fairfax County Council of the Arts (☎ 703/642–0862) acts as a clearinghouse for information about performances and exhibitions throughout northern Virginia. **Wolf Trap Farm Park** (I–495, Exit 10B to Rte. 7W, Vienna, ☎ 703/255–1860 or 703/938–2404), one of the major performing-arts venues in the greater Washington area, presents top musical and dance performers in a grand outdoor pavilion during the warmer months and in 18th-century farm buildings during other seasons.

Nightlife

Whitey's (2761 Washington Blvd., Arlington, ☎ 703/525–9825) often features live bluegrass. **Murphy's Grand Irish Pub** (713 King St., Alexandria, ☎ 703/548–1717) hosts Irish and folk performers. **Two Nineteen** (219 King St., Alexandria, ☎ 703/549–1141) has jazz upstairs and a sports bar in the basement. **Clyde's** (8332 Leesburg Pike, Tysons Corner, ☎ 703/734–1900) attracts unattached professionals.

RICHMOND AND TIDEWATER

Strictly speaking, Tidewater Virginia is the region east of the fall line of the rivers that flow into the Chesapeake Bay; but "Tidewater" has also come to stand for the genteel Old South. Richmond, on the fall line of the James, straddles the Tidewater region and the Piedmont region of rolling plains; so, too, it bridges Virginia past and present, with remnants of the Confederacy preserved amid the cultural and commercial bustle of a modern state capital. An hour southeast are two former capitals: Colonial Williamsburg, restored to its 18th-century splendor; and Jamestown, the very first, long deserted and all the more stirring. With Yorktown, where the Colonies won their independence, these pre-Revolutionary towns form the Historic Triangle.

Tourist Information

Metro Richmond: Visitor Center (1710 Robin Hood Rd. [Exit 78 off I–95 and I–64], 23220, ☎ 804/358–5511). **Petersburg:** Visitors Center (425 Cockade Alley, 23803, ☎ 804/733–2400). **Williamsburg:** Area Tourism and Conference Bureau (Drawer GB, 23187, ☎ 804/253–0192 or 800/368–6511). Colonial Williamsburg (Box C, 23187, ☎ 800/447–8679). **Yorktown:** Colonial National Historical Park (Box 210, 23690, ☎ 804/898–3400).

Getting There

By Plane

Richmond International Airport (☎ 804/226–3000) is served by six airlines. **Newport News–Williamsburg International Airport** (☎ 804/877–0924) in Newport News and **Norfolk International Airport** (☎ 804/857–3351) also serve the region.

By Car

Richmond is at the intersection of I–95 and I–64; U.S. 1 runs north–south by the city. Petersburg is 20 mi south of Richmond on I–95. Williamsburg is west of I–64 and 51 mi southeast of Richmond; the Colonial Parkway joins it with Jamestown and Yorktown.

By Train

Amtrak (☎ 800/872–7245) serves Richmond (7519 Staples Mill Rd.) and Williamsburg (468 N. Boundary St.).

By Bus

Greyhound Lines (☎ 800/231–2222) serves Richmond (2910 N. Boulevard) and Williamsburg (468 N. Boundary St.).

Exploring Richmond and Tidewater

Richmond

Most of **Richmond**'s historic attractions lie north of the James River, which bisects the city in a sweeping curve. West of downtown are such gracious residential neighborhoods as Monument Avenue, with its statues of Civil War heroes. Streets fan out southwesterly from Park Avenue to form the gaslighted **Fan District,** a hip neighborhood of restored turn-of-the-century town houses.

The heart of old Richmond is the **Court End** district, which contains seven National Historic Landmarks, three museums, and 11 more buildings on the National Register of Historic Places—all within eight blocks. At any museum you will receive a self-guided walking tour with the purchase of a discount block ticket, good for any admission fees. The museums include the **John Marshall House** (9th and Marshall Sts., ☎ 804/648–7998; admission charged), home of the early U.S. chief justice; and the **Museum and White House of the Confederacy** (1201 E. Clay St., ☎ 804/649–1861; admission charged), the official residence of President Jefferson Davis, with a newer building next door housing such relics as Robert E. Lee's sword.

The **Virginia State Capitol** (Capitol Sq., ☎ 804/786–4344), designed by Thomas Jefferson in 1785, contains a wealth of sculpture, including busts of the eight Virginia-born U.S. presidents and a life-size statue of George Washington. It was here that Lee accepted command of the Confederate forces.

Canal Walk, beginning at 12th and Main streets, follows the locks of the James River–Kanawha Canal proposed by George Washington. Plaques along the way note points of historic interest. The walk (less than 1 mi) continues over a footbridge to **Brown's Island,** the site of sculptures and outdoor concerts.

In the Church Hill Historic District, east of downtown, is **St. John's Episcopal Church.** It was here, on March 23, 1775, that Patrick Henry demanded of the Second Virginia Convention: "Give me liberty or give me death!" *25th and Broad Sts., ☎ 804/648–5015. Admission charged.*

The visitor center for **Richmond National Battlefield Park** (3215 E. Broad St., ☎ 804/226–1981) provides a movie and a slide show about the three campaigns fought here, as well as maps for a self-guided tour.

West of downtown one finds the **Science Museum of Virginia** housed in a massive, domed former train station. The planetarium doubles as a movie theater with a huge curved screen. *2500 W. Broad St., ☎ 804/367–1013. Admission charged.*

Aptly situated at the base of the artsy Fan District is the **Virginia Museum of Fine Arts,** whose collection includes paintings by Goya, Renoir, Monet, and van Gogh, as well as African masks, Roman statuary, Asian icons, and five Fabergé eggs. *The Boulevard and Grove Ave., ☎ 804/367–0844. Admission charged.*

Just west of the Fan District stands **Agecroft Hall,** a 15th-century English house reassembled here in 1925, surrounded by formal gardens, and extensively furnished with Tudor and early Stuart art and furniture. *4305 Sulgrave Rd., ☎ 804/353–4241. Admission charged.*

Petersburg

Twenty miles south of Richmond on I–95 lies Petersburg, the town that was the so-called last ditch of the Confederacy: Its fall in 1865 led to the fall of Richmond and the surrender at Appomattox. At **Petersburg National Battlefield** you can tread the ground where 60,000 soldiers died. The 1,500-acre park, laced with miles of earthworks, includes two forts. *Rte 36, ☎ 804/732–3531. Admission charged.*

In Old Town Petersburg the Civil War is examined from a local perspective at the **Siege Museum** (15 W. Bank St., ☎ 804/733–2402). Outstanding relics of antebellum Petersburg include the eccentric **Trapezium House** (244 N. Market St., ☎ 804/733–2404), built with no right angles; and the **Centre Hill Mansion** (Centre Hill Ct., ☎ 804/733–2401), remodeled in Victorian style at the turn of this century. The pre-Revolutionary **Old Blanford Church** (319 S. Crater Rd., ☎ 804/733–2396) is today a Confederate shrine, surrounded by the graves of 30,000 southern dead. The Memorial Day tradition is said to have begun in this cemetery.

The James River Plantations

Southeast of Richmond on Rte. 5, along the north bank of the James River, lie four historic plantations. **Shirley,** the oldest in Virginia, has belonged to the same family, the Carters, for 10 generations. Robert E. Lee's mother was born here. The 1723 house is filled with family silver, ancestral portraits, and rare books. The hall staircase rises three stories with no visible supports. *Rte. 608, ☎ 804/829–5121. Admission charged.*

Virginians say that the first Thanksgiving was celebrated not in Massachusetts but right here, at **Berkeley,** on December 4, 1619. Benjamin Harrison, a signer of the Declaration of Independence, and William Henry Harrison, the short-lived ninth president, were born here. The 1726 Georgian brick house has been restored and furnished with period antiques, and the boxwood gardens are well tended. There is a restaurant and outdoor tables for picnickers. *Rte. 5E, ☎ 804/829–6018. Admission charged.*

Westover was home to the flamboyant Colonel William Byrd II, member of the Colonial legislature and author of one of the region's first travel books (as well as a notorious secret diary). The 1735 house, celebrated for its moldings and carvings, is open only during April Garden Week, but the grounds and gardens can be visited all year. *Rte. 5,*

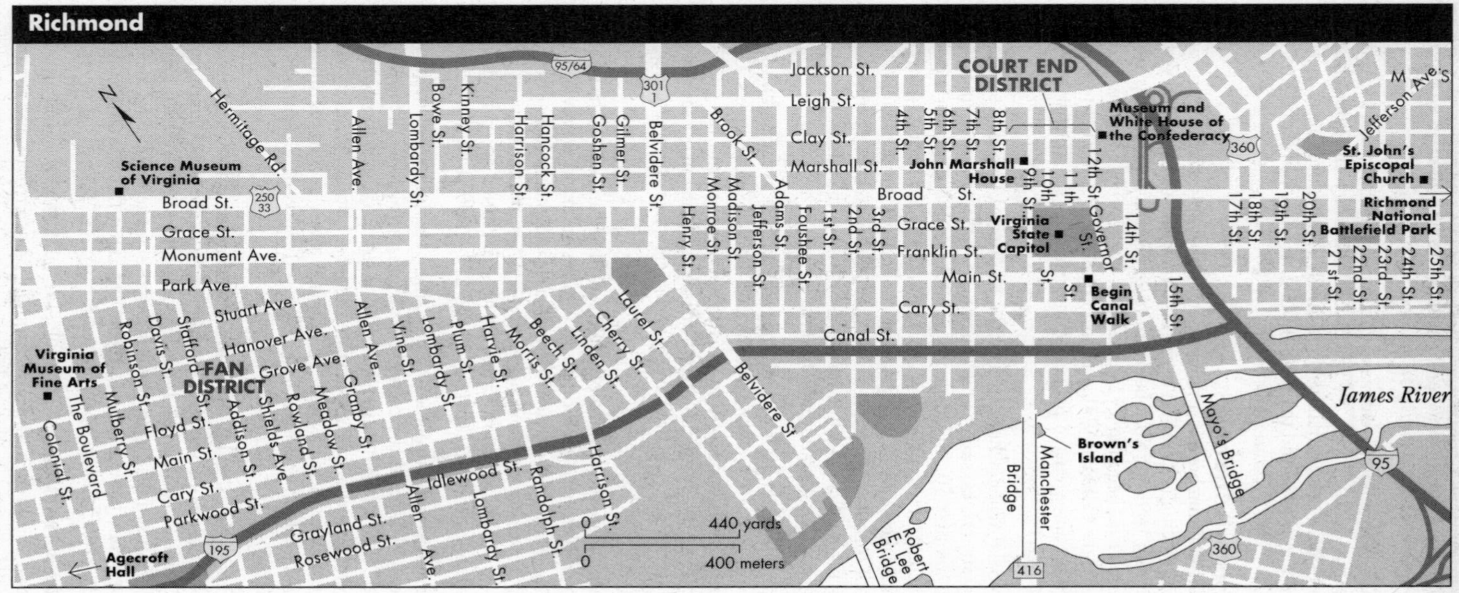

Richmond
COURT END DISTRICT
FAN DISTRICT
James River
Brown's Island
Museum and White House of the Confederacy
St. John's Episcopal Church
Richmond National Battlefield Park
John Marshall House
Virginia State Capitol
Begin Canal Walk
Science Museum of Virginia
Virginia Museum of Fine Arts
Agecroft Hall
Mayo's Bridge
Manchester Bridge
Robert E. Lee Bridge
Jackson St.
Leigh St.
Clay St.
Marshall St.
Broad St.
Grace St.
Franklin St.
Main St.
Cary St.
Canal St.
Monument Ave.
Park Ave.
Stuart Ave.
Hanover Ave.
Grove Ave.
Hermitage Rd.
W. Jefferson Ave. S.
Brook St.
25th St.
24th St.
23rd. St.
22nd St.
21st St.
20th St.
19th St.
18th St.
17th St.
15th St.
14th St.
12th St.
Governor St.
11th St.
10th St.
9th St.
8th St.
7th St.
6th St.
5th St.
4th St.
3rd St.
2nd St.
1st St.
Foushee St.
Adams St.
Jefferson St.
Madison St.
Monroe St.
Henry St.
Belvidere St.
Gilmer St.
Goshen St.
Hancock St.
Harrison St.
Kinney St.
Bowe St.
Lombardy St.
Allen Ave.
Laurel St.
Cherry St.
Linden St.
Beech St.
Morris St.
Harvie St.
Plum St.
Vine St.
Granby St.
Meadow St.
Rowland St.
Shields Ave.
Addison St.
Stafford St.
Davis St.
Robinson St.
Floyd St.
Mulberry St.
The Boulevard
Colonial St.
Cary St.
Parkwood St.
Idlewood St.
Randolph St.
Grayland St.
Rosewood St.
440 yards
400 meters
0
N
95
360
416
301
1
95/64
250
33
195

den Week, but the grounds and gardens can be visited all year. *Rte. 5, ☎ 804/829–2882. Admission charged.*

At 300 ft, **Sherwood Forest** may be the longest frame house in the country. Built in 1720, it was the retirement home of John Tyler, the 10th U.S. president, and remains in his family. The house, furnished with heirloom antiques, and the five outbuildings are open daily. *Rte. 5, ☎ 804/829–5377. Admission charged.*

The Historic Triangle

Colonial Williamsburg is a marvel: an improbably sanitary but otherwise convincing re-creation of the city that was the capital of Virginia in the years 1699–1780. The restoration project, financed by John D. Rockefeller Jr., began in 1926; the work of the archaeologists and historians of the Colonial Williamsburg Foundation continues to this day. (To obtain an extensive packet of information, *see* Tourist Information, *above.*)

On Colonial Williamsburg's 173 acres, 88 original 18th- and early 19th-century structures, such as the **courthouse,** have been meticulously restored; another 50, including the **capitol** and the **governor's palace,** were reconstructed on their original sites. In all, 225 period rooms have been furnished from the foundation's collection of more than 100,000 pieces of furniture, pottery, china, glass, silver, pewter, textiles, tools, and carpeting. Period authenticity also governs the landscaping of the 90 acres of gardens and public greens.

All year long, hundreds of costumed interpreters, wearing bonnets or three-cornered hats, rove and ride through the cobblestone streets. Dozens of costumed craftspeople, such as the bootmaker and the gunsmith, demonstrate and explain their trades inside their workshops; their wares are for sale nearby. Three taverns serve fare approximating that of 200 years ago.

One million people visit Colonial Williamsburg annually. The restored area must be toured on foot, as all vehicles are banned between 8 AM and 6 PM. Free shuttle buses run (available to ticket holders only) continually to and from the visitor center and around the edge of the restored area. Vehicles for visitors with disabilities are permitted by prior arrangement. *I–64 Exit 56, ☎ 804/229–1000. Admission charged.*

Jamestown Island, site of the first permanent English settlement in North America (1607) and the capital of Virginia until 1699, is now uninhabited. Foundation walls show the layout of the settlement, and push-button audio stations narrate the local history. The only standing structure is the ruin of a 1639 church tower. A 5-mi nature drive ringing the island is posted with historical markers. *Colonial Pkwy., ☎ 804/229–1733. Admission charged.*

Adjacent to the island is **Jamestown Settlement,** a living-history museum with a reconstructed fort manned by "colonists," and an "Indian Village" inhabited by buckskin-clad interpreters. At the pier are reproductions of the *Godspeed,* the *Discovery,* and the *Susan Constant,* the ships that brought the settlers. *Rte. 31 off Colonial Pkwy., ☎ 804/229–1607. Admission charged.*

At **Yorktown Battlefield** (Colonial Pkwy., tel. 804/898–3400) in 1781, American and French forces surrounded British troops and forced an end to the American War of Independence. Today the museum here displays George Washington's original field tent; dioramas, illuminated maps, and a short movie tell the story. After a look from the observation deck, you can rent the taped audio tour and explore the battlefield by car or join a free ranger-led walking tour.

The **Yorktown Victory Center** next door features a Continental army encampment, with tents, a covered wagon, and interpreters—costumed as soldiers or female auxiliaries—who speak to visitors in the regional dialects of the time. Also on site are a small working tobacco farm and a museum focusing on the experience of ordinary people during the Revolution. *Rte. 238 off Colonial Pkwy.,* ☎ *804/887–1776. Admission charged.*

Unlike Jamestown, **Yorktown** remains a living community, albeit a small one. Rte. 238 leads into **Main Street,** with an array of preserved 18th-century buildings on a bluff overlooking the York River. **Moore House,** where the terms of surrender were negotiated, and the elegant **Nelson House,** the residence of a Virginia governor and a signer of the Declaration of Independence, are open for tours in summer (☎ 804/898–3400). On adjacent Church Street, **Grace Church,** built in 1697, remains an active Episcopal congregation; its walls are made of marl (a mixture of clay, sand, and limestone containing fragments of seashells).

What to See and Do with Children

The 100-plus rides at **King's Dominion** (I–95, Doswell exit, ☎ 804/876–5000; closed Nov.–Mar.), north of Richmond, include simulated white-water rafting, two roller coasters, and a monorail through a game preserve. East of Williamsburg is **Busch Gardens, the Old Country** (U.S. 60, ☎ 804/253–3350; closed Nov.–Mar.). Rides include an especially fast and steep roller coaster, and nine re-creations of European hamlets offer the cuisine and entertainment of different countries.

Shopping

Fresh produce is for sale at Richmond's **Farmers Market** (17th and Main Sts.); art galleries, boutiques, and antiques shops are nearby. The **Colonial Williamsburg Crafts Houses** (Merchants Sq., ☎ 804/220–7747) sell approved reproductions of the antiques on display in the houses.

Sports and the Outdoors

Open to the public in Richmond—for free or at a nominal charge—are more than 150 tennis courts, 11 swimming pools, a golf driving range, and about 7 mi of fitness trails. The **Department of Recreation and Parks** (☎ 804/780–6091) has listings.

Biking

In Colonial Williamsburg, ticket holders can rent bicycles at the **lodge** on South England Street; others can try **Bikesmith** (York St., ☎ 804/229–9858).

Golf

The Crossings (jct. of I–95 and I–295, Glen Allen, ☎ 804/266–2254), north of Richmond, has an 18-hole course open to the public. **Colonial Williamsburg** (☎ 804/220–7696) operates three courses. **Kingsmill Resort** (☎ 804/253–3906), east of Williamsburg near Busch Gardens, has two courses.

Rafting

Richmond Raft (☎ 804/222–7238) offers guided white-water rafting through the heart of the city (class 3 and 4 rapids), float trips upriver, and overnight trips from April through October.

Tennis

Colonial Williamsburg (☎ 804/220–7794) has 8 tennis courts; **Kingsmill** (☎ 804/253–3945) has 15 courts open to the public; additional public courts in Williamsburg are at **Kiwanis Park** on Long Hill Road and **Quarterpath Park** on Pocahontas Street.

Dining and Lodging

The established upmarket dining rooms of Richmond are dependable, but keep an eye out for intriguing new bistros, often short-lived, in the Fan District. In Williamsburg, remember that dining rooms within walking distance of the restored area are often crowded, and reservations are advised.

Richmond's hotel rates are fair for its size, but standards of service lag behind those of many smaller communities. Williamsburg has a greater range of lodging choices for the money, but vacancies are scarce in summer.

For price ranges, see Charts 1 (B) and 2 (B) in On the Road with Fodor's.

Richmond

DINING

★ **Mr. Patrick Henry's.** Antiques and fireplaces create the Colonial ambience in the main room; there's also a basement pub and a garden café. Menu favorites include unusual crab cakes (crabmeat and spices in a puff pastry) and crisp roast duck with plum sauce. *2300 E. Broad St., ☎ 804/644–1322. Jacket and tie required. AE, DC, MC, V. No dinner Sun. $$$*

La Petite France. The emerald-green walls are hung with English landscapes and portraits. Tuxedoed waiters serve lobster baked in puff pastry with whiskey sauce and Dover sole amandine, among other specialties. *2108 Maywill St., ☎ 804/353–8729. AE, DC, MC, V. Closed Sun.–Mon. $$$*

Joe's Inn. The specialty at this Fan District hangout is Greek spaghetti, with feta and provolone baked on top; all the sandwiches are oversize. Regulars make newcomers feel right at home. *205 N. Shields Ave., ☎ 804/355–2282. AE, MC, V. $*

LODGING

★ **Jefferson Grand Heritage Hotel.** This 1895 National Historic Landmark has a grand lobby, with a tall staircase straight out of *Gone with the Wind*. The rather small guest rooms have reproduction 19th-century furnishings. *Franklin and Adams Sts., 23220, ☎ 804/788–8000 or 800/424–8014, FAX 804/225–0334. 274 rooms, 26 suites. Facilities: 2 restaurants, bar, spa privileges. AE, DC, MC, V. $$$$*

Omni Richmond. Guest rooms in this luxury hotel have a contemporary look, but the marble lobby, with its green velvet chairs, equestrian statues, and Romanesque vases, calls to mind a Venetian foyer. *100 S. 12th St., 23219, ☎ 804/344–7000 or 800/843–6664, FAX 804/648–6704. 364 rooms. Facilities: 3 restaurants, bar, indoor and outdoor pools, saunas. AE, D, DC, MC, V. $$$$*

Radisson Hotel. Triangular rooms at the point of this wedge-shape hotel have views of the skyline and the river. The three-story atrium lobby features a waterfall. *555 E. Canal St., 23219, ☎ 804/788–0900 or 800/333–3333, FAX 804/788–7087. 300 rooms. Facilities: restaurant, bar, indoor pool, health club, saunas. AE, D, DC, MC, V. $$$*

Massad House Hotel. This modest Tudor-style hotel is five blocks from the capitol in the business district, a quiet area after 6 PM. Guest rooms are small with stucco walls and are well maintained. *11 N. 4th St., 23219, ☎ 804/648–2893. 64 rooms. Facilities: restaurant. MC, V. $*

Williamsburg

DINING

★ **Regency Room.** Crystal chandeliers, Asian silkscreen prints, and full silver service set the tone. Rack of lamb is carved at the table; other specialties are lobster bisque and rich ice-cream desserts. *Williamsburg Inn, 136 E. Francis St., ☎ 804/229–1000. Jacket and tie required at dinner and Sun. brunch. AE, MC, V. $$$$*

The Cascades. Bare polished-wood tables are piled with all-American fare: baked crab imperial, Cheddar-cheese soup, sugar-cured ham, fried chicken, pecan pie. The daily Hunt Breakfast buffet includes fried chicken and oysters in season. *Visitor center area, ☎ 804/229–1000. AE, MC, V. $$*

The Trellis. Hardwood floors, ceramic tiles, and green plants evoke Napa Valley and set the mood for world-class American cuisine. Save room for Death by Chocolate: seven layers of chocolate topped with cream sauce. *Merchants Sq., ☎ 804/229–8610. AE, MC, V. $$*

Le Yaca. The country-French dining room is done in soft pastels with hardwood floors, candlelight, and a central open fireplace where leg of lamb roasts nightly on a spit. *1915 Pocahontas Trail, ☎ 804/220–3616. AE, DC, MC, V. Closed Sun., early Jan. $$*

LODGING

Embassy Suites. The former Quality Suites, built in 1987, became part of the Embassy Suites chain in February 1994. All units were renovated in 1994 and have a modern look. The quiet hotel is on 11 wooded acres. *152 Kingsgate Pkwy., 23185, ☎ 804/229–6800 or 800/333–0924, FAX 804/220–3486. 169 suites. Facilities: restaurant, indoor pool, whirlpool. AE, D, DC, MC, V. $$$$*

Williamsburg Hospitality House. This four-story redbrick building, constructed in 1973, faces the College of William and Mary. Guest rooms are furnished with Chippendale reproductions; some look onto a cobblestone courtyard with a fountain. *415 Richmond Rd., 23185, ☎ 804/229–4020 or 800/932–9192, FAX 804/220–1560. 309 rooms. Facilities: restaurant, bar, outdoor pool. AE, D, DC, MC, V. $$$$*

★ **Williamsburg Inn.** This is the local grand hotel, built in 1932 and decorated in English Regency style. The surrounding Colonial houses, equipped with modern kitchens and baths, are also part of the inn. *136 E. Francis St., 23185, ☎ 804/229–1000 or 800/447–8679, FAX 804/220–7096. 235 rooms. Facilities: restaurant, bar, outdoor pool, tennis, golf, health club. AE, MC, V. $$$*

Heritage Inn. Room furnishings include beds with two-poster headboards and an armoire concealing a TV. Some rooms open directly onto the parking lot, but this is an unusually quiet, leafy site, and the pool is set in a garden. *1324 Richmond Rd., 23185, ☎ 804/229–6220 or 800/782–3800, FAX 804/229–2774. 54 rooms. AE, DC, MC, V. $$*

War Hill Inn. Built in 1970 on a 32-acre operating cattle farm, the inn was designed to resemble an 18th-century brick-and-wood structure and has been furnished with appropriate antiques and reproductions. *4560 Long Hill Rd., 23188, ☎ 804/565–0248. 3 rooms, 1 suite, 1 cottage. AE, MC, V. $$*

Yorktown

DINING

Nick's Seafood Pavilion. Atlantic seafood with a distinctly Mediterranean flavor, including such house specialties as lobster pilaf and seafood shish kebab, are served in ample portions at this simply decorated riverside restaurant. *Water St., ☎ 804/887–5269. No reservations. AE, DC, MC, V. $$*

Motels

The Woodlands (Information Center Dr., Williamsburg 23187, ☎ 804/229–1000 or 800/447–8679, FAX 804/221–8942), 315 rooms, restaurant, 3 pools, miniature golf, putting green, tennis court, playground; *$$$.* **Days Inn North** (1600 Robin Hood Rd., Richmond 23220, ☎ 804/353–1287 or 800/325–2525, FAX 804/355–2659), 87 rooms, restaurant, bar, outdoor pool; *$$.* **Duke of York Motel** (508 Water St., Yorktown 23690, ☎ 804/898–3232), 57 rooms, restaurant, outdoor pool; *$$.* **Governor Spotswood Motel** (1508 Richmond Rd., Williamsburg 23185, ☎ 804/229–6444 or 800/368–1244), 78 rooms, outdoor pool, playground; *$.*

The Arts and Nightlife

The Arts

Barksdale Theatre (Hanover Tavern, Richmond, ☎ 804/537–5333), founded in 1953, was the first dinner theater in the country. **Swift Mill Creek Playhouse** (Richmond, ☎ 804/748–4411), another dinner theater, is housed in a 17th-century gristmill. **TheatreVirginia** (Richmond, ☎ 804/367–0831), an Equity theater maintained by the Virginia Museum of Fine Arts, has a strong repertory. The **Richmond Symphony** (☎ 804/788–1212) often features internationally known soloists. **Concert Ballet of Virginia** (Richmond, ☎ 804/780–1279) performs modern and experimental works. The **Richmond Ballet** (614 N. Lombardy St., ☎ 804/359–0906) is the city's classical-ballet company.

Nightlife

Bogart's (203 N. Lombardy St., Richmond, ☎ 804/353–9280) is a cozy jazz club. The **Flood Zone** (18th and Main Sts., Richmond, ☎ 804/643–6006) is a rock-and-roll dance club in a converted recording studio. **J.B.'s Lounge** at the Fort Magruder Inn near Williamsburg (☎ 804/220–2250) features Top 40, country, or rock most nights.

ELSEWHERE IN THE STATE

Hampton Roads, Virginia Beach, and the Eastern Shore

Getting There

Norfolk International and **Newport News–Williamsburg International airports** (*see* Richmond and Tidewater, *above*) are served by most major airlines. I–64 connects Richmond with Hampton Roads. U.S. 58 and Rte. 44 connect I–64 with Virginia Beach; U.S. 13 runs between Virginia Beach and the Eastern Shore via the Chesapeake Bay Bridge-Tunnel. **Greyhound Lines** (☎ 800/231–2222) serves Virginia Beach (1017 Laskin Rd.) and various locations along U.S. 13 on the Eastern Shore.

What to See and Do

The cities of Newport News and Hampton on the north and Norfolk on the south flank the enormous port of **Hampton Roads,** where the James empties into the Chesapeake. In **Newport News,** the **Mariner's Museum** (I–64 Exit 258A, ☎ 804/595–0368) displays tiny hand-carved models of ancient vessels and full-size specimens of more recent ones, including a gondola and a Japanese submarine. The very latest in transportation can be viewed in **Hampton** at the **Virginia Air and Space Museum** (600 Settlers Landing Rd., ☎ 804/727–0800), which opened in 1992; the exhibits include a lunar rock and an Apollo capsule. At Hampton's **Fort Monroe** (Rte. 258, ☎ 804/727–3391), the **Casemate Museum** tells the Civil War history of the moat-enclosed Union stronghold—object of the battle between the *Monitor* and the *Merrimac,* and President Jefferson Davis's prison after the Confederacy's defeat.

Norfolk is best known for the **U.S. Naval Base** (Hampton Blvd., ☎ 804/444–7955), home to more than 125 ships of the Atlantic and Mediterranean fleets, including the nuclear-powered USS *Theodore Roosevelt*—the world's second-largest warship. The sights are gentler at the **Norfolk Botanical Gardens** (I–64, airport exit, ☎ 804/441–5830), 175 acres supporting an abundance of azaleas, camellias, and roses—plus a lone palm tree. The arts are preserved at the **Hermitage Foundation Museum** (7637 North Shore Rd., ☎ 804/423–2052), a reconstructed Tudor mansion that houses a large collection of Oriental art; and at the **Chrysler Museum** (Olney Rd. and Mowbray Arch, ☎ 804/622–1211), whose collection ranges from Gainsborough to Roy Lichtenstein. Of historical interest are the elegant **Moses Myers House** (323 Freemason St., ☎ 804/622–1211), built in 1792 by Norfolk's first Jewish resident; and the **Douglas MacArthur Memorial** (Bank St. and City Hall Ave., ☎ 804/441–2965), burial place and museum of the controversial war hero.

The heart of **Virginia Beach,** 6 mi of crowded public beach and a raucous 40-block boardwalk, has been a popular summer gathering place for many years. One advantage of the commercialism is easy access to sailing, surfing, and scuba rentals. Almost 2 mi inland, at the southern end of Virginia Beach, is one of the state's most-visited museums, the **Virginia Marine Science Museum** (717 General Booth Blvd., ☎ 804/425–3474), where visitors can use computers to predict the weather, bird-watch in a salt marsh, and take a simulated journey to the bottom of the sea. Inland from the bay shore, and a throwback to much quieter times, is the 1680 **Adam Thoroughgood House** (1636 Parish Rd., ☎ 804/627–2737), said to be the oldest non-Spanish brick house in the country.

On the Eastern Shore, U.S. 13 takes you past historic 17th- to 19th-century towns, such as **Eastville,** with its 250-year-old courthouse. **Onancock** has a working general store established in 1842 and a wharf from which to catch that east-coast rarity: a sunset over the water (that is, the bay).

Assateague Island is a 37-mi-long wildlife refuge and recreational area that extends north into Maryland (*see* Maryland). Smaller and closer to shore is neighboring **Chincoteague Island,** where, despite invasive tourism and overdevelopment, at least one tradition survives from a simpler time: Every July the wild ponies from Assateague are driven across the channel and placed at auction here; the unsold swim back home. All year long, the fine beaches and natural beauty next door justify a visit to Chincoteague. On nearby **Wallops Island** is NASA's **Wallops Flight Facility** (Rte. 175, ☎ 804/824–2298), where a museum tells the story of the space program on the site of early rocket launchings.

For further information on the region, contact **Virginia Beach Visitors Center** (2100 Parks Ave., 23451, ☎ 804/437–4888 or 800/822–3224), **Chincoteague Chamber of Commerce** (Box 258, 23336, ☎ 804/336–6161), or **Eastern Shore of Virginia Chamber of Commerce** (Box R, Melfa 23410, ☎ 804/787–2460).

Lodging

Norfolk Waterside Marriott. Next door to the convention center and connected by a walkway to the Waterside mall, this hotel opened in late 1991. *235 E. Main St., 23510, ☎ 804/627–4200 or 800/228–9290, FAX 804/628–6466. 405 rooms. Facilities: 2 restaurants, lounge, health club, indoor pool. AE, D, DC, MC, V. $$$*

Omni International. Built in 1976 and renovated in 1993, this hotel offers views of the harbor from about half its rooms. The financial district is only a block away. *777 Waterside Dr., 23510, ☎ 804/622–6664 or 800/843–6664, FAX 804/625–4930. 442 rooms. Facilities: restaurant, lounge, health club, outdoor pool. AE, D, DC, MC, V. $$$*

WASHINGTON, D.C.

By John F. Kelly

Updated by Mary Case and Bruce Walker

Population	570,600
Official Bird	Wood thrush
Official Flower	American Beauty rose

Introduction

Washington, the District of Columbia, was founded in 1791 as the world's first planned national capital. It's a city of unforgettable memorials; a place where the striking image of the Washington Monument is never far from sight and the stirring memories of a young democratic republic are never far from mind.

The capital's attractions are more than just governmental, though; visitors will find world-class theaters, music, parks and gardens, and the many museums of the Smithsonian Institution. Washington is a showcase city and, like America itself, opens its arms to everyone.

Tourist Information

Washington, D.C., Convention and Visitors Association information center (1455 Pennsylvania Ave. NW, 20005 ☎ 202/789–7037; events recording: ☎ 202/737–8866). **Dial-A-Park** (☎ 202/619–7275) is a recording of events at National Park Service attractions. **White House Visitor Center** (1450 Pennsylvania Avenue NW, ☎ 202/208–1631).

Arriving and Departing

By Plane

National Airport (☎ 703/419–8000) in Virginia, 4 mi south of downtown Washington, has scheduled flights by most major domestic carriers. It is often cramped and crowded, but it's a convenient 20-minute subway ride from the center of Washington ($1.25, depending on the time of day). Cab fare downtown should average $9, including tip.

Many transcontinental and international flights arrive at **Dulles International Airport** (☎ 703/685–8000), a modern facility 26 mi west of Washington in Virginia. **Baltimore-Washington International (BWI) Airport** (☎ 410/859–7100) is in Maryland, about 25 mi northeast of Washington.

Bus service is provided to National and Dulles airports by **Washington Flyer** (☎ 703/685–1400) and to BWI by **The Airport Connection** (☎ 301/441–2345).

By Car

I–95 approaches Washington from the north and south, encircling the city in Maryland and Virginia as the Beltway. I–66 leads west through Virginia; I–270, northwest into Maryland.

By Train

Amtrak serves Union Station (50 Massachusetts Ave. NE, ☎ 800/872–7245).

By Bus

Greyhound Lines (1005 1st St. NE, ☎ 800/231–2222).

Getting Around Washington, D.C.

Washington's best-known sights are a short walk—or a short Metro ride—from one another.

By Car

A car can be a drawback in Washington. Traffic is horrendous, especially at rush hours (6:30–9:30 AM and 3:30–7 PM). Parking is also an adventure: Free spots are hard to find, private lots expensive. There is free, three-hour parking around the Mall on Jefferson Drive and Madison Drive, though these spots always seem to be filled. You can park free—in some spots all day—in parking areas south of the Lincoln Memorial on Ohio Drive and West Basin Drive in West Potomac Park.

By Public Transportation

The **Washington Metropolitan Area Transit Authority** (☎ 202/637–7000; TTY 202/638–3780) provides Metrorail and Metrobus service in the District and in the Maryland and Virginia suburbs. The base fare is $1; the actual price you pay depends on the time of day and the distance traveled (all bus rides within the District are $1). Children under five ride free when accompanied by a paying passenger. A $5 **Metro Tourist Pass** entitles you to one day of unlimited subway travel any weekend or holiday (except July 4).

By Taxi

Taxis in the District are not metered but operate on a curious zone system. Two major companies are **Capitol Cab** (☎ 202/546–2400) and **Diamond Cab** (☎ 202/387–6200). Maryland and Virginia taxis are metered but cannot take passengers between points within Washington.

Orientation Tours

Buses from **Tourmobile** (☎ 202/554–7950 or 202/554–5100) and **Old Town Trolley Tours** (☎ 301/985–3021) ply routes around the city's major attractions, allowing passengers to get on and off as often as they like. **Gray Line Tours** (☎ 301/386–8300) offers a four-hour motor-coach tour of Washington, Embassy Row, and Arlington National Cemetery; four-hour tours of Mount Vernon and Alexandria; and a combination of both.

Walking Tour

Not a specific walking route but a group of sites within historic neighborhoods, the **Black History National Recreation Trail** (brochure available from National Park Service, 1100 Ohio Dr. SW, 20242, ☎ 202/619–7222) illustrates aspects of African-American history in Washington, from slavery days to the New Deal.

Exploring Washington, D.C.

The Mall is the logical first stop for visitors to Washington. Ringing it are the major museums and galleries of the Smithsonian Institution. At the east end is the U.S. Capitol, to the west are the city's major monuments, and just a stone's throw away is the White House. Start your visit here to see Washington the capital, then venture farther afield to see Washington the city.

The Mall

The first museum built by the Smithsonian was architect James Renwick's Norman-style **Castle.** Today it's home to the **Smithsonian Information Center;** an orientation film inside provides an overview of the various Smithsonian offerings, and television monitors announce the day's special events. *1000 Jefferson Dr. SW. For all Smithsonian museums: ☏ 202/357–2700, TTY 202/357–1729.*

Walking counterclockwise around the Mall, you'll come to the Smithsonian's **Arts and Industries Building** (900 Jefferson Dr. SW), a treasure trove of Victoriana, then the striking **Hirshhorn Museum and Sculpture Garden** (7th St. and Independence Ave. SW), which has modern art.

Across the street is the most-visited museum in the world: the **National Air and Space Museum** (Jefferson Dr. at 6th St. SW). Twenty-three galleries tell the story of aviation, from humans' earliest attempts at flight to travels beyond our solar system. Breathtaking IMAX films are shown on the five-story screen of the museum's Langley Theater (admission charged), while images of celestial bodies are projected on a domed ceiling in the Albert Einstein Planetarium.

On the north side of the Mall are the two buildings of the **National Gallery of Art:** architect John Russell Pope's domed West Building and I. M. Pei's angular East Building. Modern works are generally shown in the East Building, while the West Building's more than 100 galleries provide a survey of Western art from the 13th to the 20th century. *Madison Dr. and 4th St. NW, ☏ 202/737–4215, TTY 202/842–6176.*

The **National Museum of Natural History** (Madison Dr. between 9th and 12th Sts. NW) is filled with bones, fossils, stuffed animals, and other natural delights, including the popular Dinosaur Hall, the Hope Diamond, and a sea-life display featuring a living coral reef.

The three floors of the **National Museum of American History** (Madison Ave. between 12th and 14th Sts. NW) trace the social, political, and technological history of the United States. Here you'll find a 280-ton steam locomotive, a collection of first ladies' inaugural gowns, and the Bunkers' living room furniture from the TV series *All in the Family.*

Across the Mall are three more Smithsonian museums: the **Freer Gallery of Art** (12th St. and Jefferson Dr. SW), a repository of Oriental art that's also known for James McNeill Whistler's stunning *Peacock Room;* the **Arthur M. Sackler Gallery** (1050 Independence Ave. SW), whose collection includes works from China, the Indian subcontinent, Persia, Thailand, and Indonesia; and the **National Museum of African Art** (950 Independence Ave. SW), dedicated to the collection, exhibition, and study of the traditional arts of sub-Saharan Africa.

The Monuments

Washington is a city of monuments. Those dedicated to the most famous Americans are west of the Mall on ground reclaimed from the marshy flats of the Potomac.

The tallest of them all is the **Washington Monument,** toward the Mall's western end. Construction of the 555-ft obelisk was started in 1848, interrupted by the Civil War (the reason for the color change about a third of the way up), and finally completed in 1884. An elevator takes those who wait out the sometimes long lines to the top of the monument, where the view is unequaled. *Constitution Ave. at 15th St. NW, ☏ 202/426–6840.*

On the south bank of the **Tidal Basin** is the **Jefferson Memorial,** honoring America's third president. One of the best views of the White House can be seen from the top steps of the memorial, John Russell Pope's reinterpretation of the Pantheon in Rome. *☏ 202/426–6821.*

Washington, D.C.

Washington Nat'l Cathedral
National Zoological Park
California St.
Massachusetts Ave.
Florida Ave.
New Hampshire Ave.
T St.
S St.
Decatur Pl.
R St.
Sheridan Circle
Phillips Collection
Q St.
DUPONT CIRCLE
Dupont Circle
Church St.
P St.
O St.
N St.
M St.
L St.
K St.
I St.
H St.
G St.
F St.
E St.
D St.
C St.
Corcoran St.
Rhode Island Ave.
Scott Circle
Thomas Circle
Connecticut Ave.
Rock Creek
GEORGE-TOWN
30th St.
29th St.
28th St.
27th St.
26th St.
25th St.
24th St.
23rd St.
22nd St.
21st St.
20th St.
19th St.
18th St.
17th St.
16th St.
15th St.
14th St.
Washington Circle
FOGGY BOTTOM
FARRAGUT NORTH
FARRAGUT WEST
Hay-Adams Hotel
St. John's Episcopal Church
McPHERSON SQUARE
National Museum of Women in the Arts
Pennsylvania Ave.
Decatur House
Lafayette Park
New York Ave.
Renwick Gallery
Blair House
Old Executive Office Building
Treasury
Octagon House
The White House
Willard
Corcoran Gallery of Art
Hotel Washington
Memorial Continental Hall (D.A.R. Museum)
The Ellipse
National Aquarium
FEDERAL TRIANGLE
Virginia Ave.
Constitution Ave.
Vietnam Veterans Memorial
National Museum of American History
Washington Monument
NW
SW
Arlington National Cemetery
Lincoln Memorial
Reflecting Pool
SMITHSONIAN
U.S. Holocaust Memorial Museum
Memorial Bridge
Independence Ave.
Kutz Bridge
Ohio Dr.
West Potomac Park
W. Basin Dr.
Tidal Basin
Outlet Bridge
Potomac River
Columbia Island
Jefferson Memorial
N
29
66
50
1
395

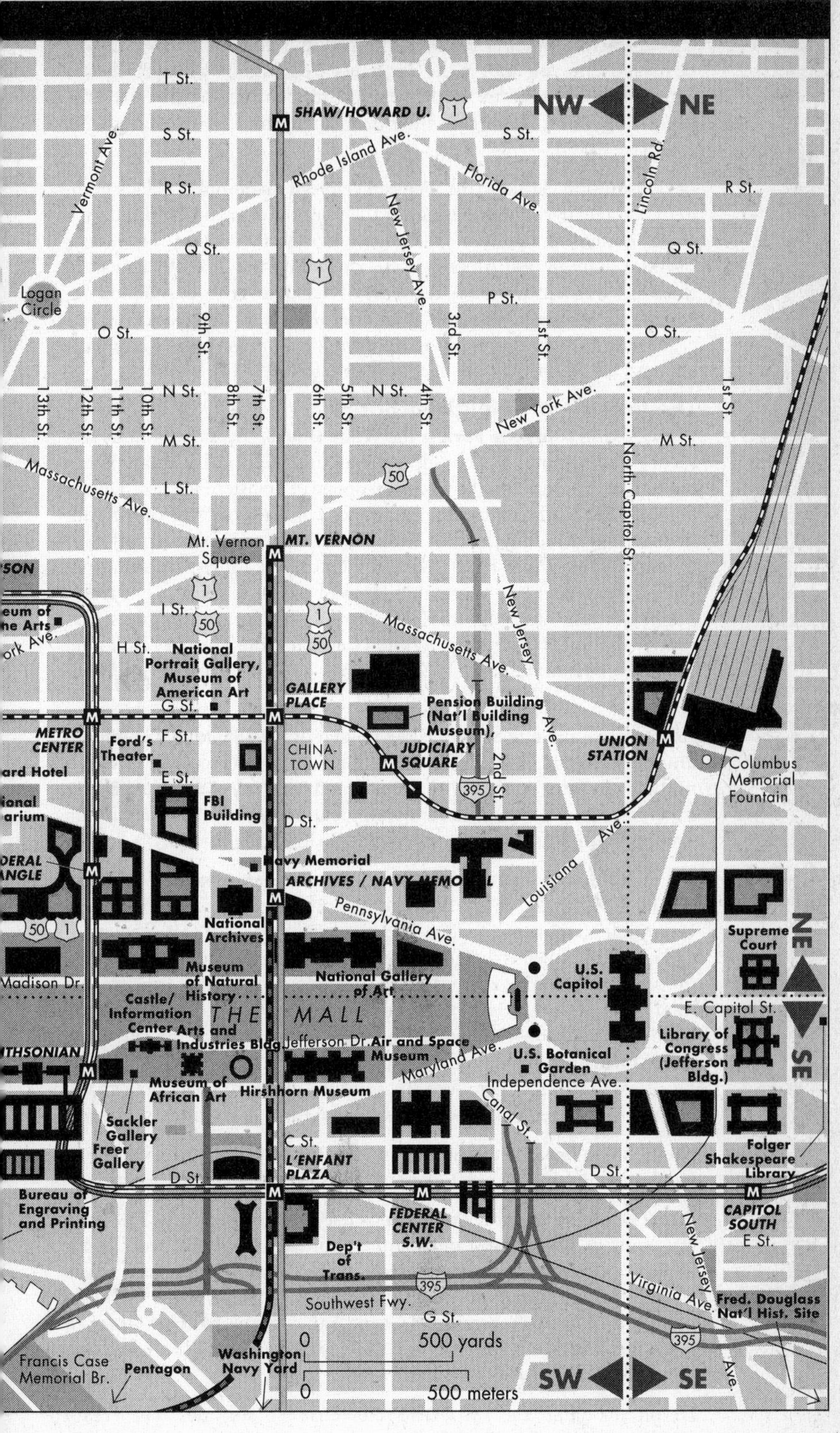
T St.
SHAW/HOWARD U.
NW
NE
S St.
Rhode Island Ave.
Florida Ave.
Vermont Ave.
R St.
New Jersey Ave.
Lincoln Rd.
Q St.
Logan Circle
P St.
O St.
9th St.
3rd St.
1st St.
13th St.
12th St.
11th St.
10th St.
N St.
8th St.
7th St.
6th St.
5th St.
4th St.
New York Ave.
M St.
Massachusetts Ave.
L St.
North Capitol St.
Mt. Vernon Square
MT. VERNON
I St.
H St.
Massachusetts Ave.
New Jersey Ave.
National Portrait Gallery, Museum of American Art
G St.
GALLERY PLACE
Pension Building (Nat'l Building Museum),
METRO CENTER
Ford's Theater
F St.
CHINA-TOWN
JUDICIARY SQUARE
2nd St.
UNION STATION
Columbus Memorial Fountain
E St.
FBI Building
D St.
Louisiana Ave.
Navy Memorial
ARCHIVES / NAVY MEMORIAL
Pennsylvania Ave.
National Archives
Supreme Court
Museum of Natural History
National Gallery of Art
U.S. Capitol
Madison Dr.
Castle/ Information Center
THE MALL
Arts and Industries Bldg.
Jefferson Dr.
Air and Space Museum
E. Capitol St.
Library of Congress (Jefferson Bldg.)
U.S. Botanical Garden
Maryland Ave.
Independence Ave.
Museum of African Art
Hirshhorn Museum
Canal St.
Sackler Gallery
Freer Gallery
C St.
L'ENFANT PLAZA
D St.
Folger Shakespeare Library
Bureau of Engraving and Printing
FEDERAL CENTER S.W.
CAPITOL SOUTH
E St.
Dep't of Trans.
Southwest Fwy.
G St.
Virginia Ave.
Fred. Douglass Nat'l Hist. Site
0
500 yards
500 meters
Francis Case Memorial Br.
Pentagon
Washington Navy Yard
SW
SE
395
50
1

Cherry trees ring the approach to the **Lincoln Memorial,** at the west end of the Mall. Henry Bacon's monument is considered by many to be the most moving spot in the city, a mood enhanced by Daniel Chester French's somber statue of the seated president gazing out over the **Reflecting Pool.** Visit this memorial at night for best effect. ☎ *202/426–6895.*

In Constitution Gardens, the **Vietnam Veterans Memorial**—a black granite *V* designed by Maya Ling and a sculptural group by Frederick Hart—is another landmark that encourages introspection. The names of more than 58,000 Americans are etched on the face of the wall in the order of their deaths. After years of debate over its design and necessity, the **Vietnam Women's Memorial** was finally dedicated on Veterans Day 1993 and sits southeast of the Vietnam Veterans Memorial. *23rd St. and Constitution Ave. NW,* ☎ *202/634–1568.*

The President's Neighborhood

Overlooking **Lafayette Park** is the **White House,** the most famous residence in Washington. The house was designed by Irishman James Hoban, who based it on the Georgian design of Leinster Hall near Dublin and of other Irish country houses. To get a glimpse of some of the public rooms—including the East Room and the State Dining Room—get a ticket at the White House Visitor Center (*see* Tourist Information, *above*) from March to September (arrive by 8 AM to be safe; one ticket per person); in other months, join the line that forms along East Executive Avenue, between the White House and the Treasury Building. *1600 Pennsylvania Ave. NW,* ☎ *202/456–7041 (recorded information) or 202/619–7222. Closed Sun.–Mon.*

Just across Lafayette Square is the golden-domed **St. John's Episcopal Church** (16th and H Sts. NW, ☎ 202/347–8766), the so-called Church of the Presidents. Across 16th Street stands the **Hay-Adams Hotel** (*see* Lodging, *below*), one of the most opulent hostelries in the city and a favorite with Washington insiders and visiting celebrities.

The first floor of the redbrick, Federal-style **Decatur House** (748 Jackson Pl. NW, ☎ 202/842–0920; admission charged) is decorated as it was when naval hero Stephen Decatur lived there in 1819. The green canopy at 1651 Pennsylvania Avenue marks the entrance to **Blair House,** the residence used by visiting heads of state. (When dignitaries are visiting the president, you'll often see their country's flag flying from the lampposts on Pennsylvania Avenue.) Across the street is the **Old Executive Office Building,** a French Empire–style structure. Dan Quayle had his office in here; Albert Gore, Jr., is a little closer to the action, in the West Wing of the White House, just down the hall from the president.

Facing the avenue is the Smithsonian's **Renwick Gallery** (Pennsylvania Ave. and 17th St. NW), devoted to American decorative arts.

A few blocks away is the **Corcoran Gallery of Art.** One of the few large museums in Washington outside the Smithsonian family, the Corcoran has a collection that ranges from works by early American artists to late-19th- and early-20th-century paintings from Europe. A highlight is the entire 18th-century Grand Salon of the Hôtel d'Orsay in Paris. *17th St. and New York Ave. NW,* ☎ *202/638–1439. Admission charged. Closed Tues.*

Despite its name, the 1801 **Octagon House** has six sides. The Treaty of Ghent, ending the War of 1812, was signed in an upstairs study. Exhibits relating to architecture, decorative arts, and Washington history are mounted here today. *1799 New York Ave. NW, ☎ 202/638–3105, TDD 202/638–1538. Admission charged. Closed Mon.*

On 17th Street is **Memorial Continental Hall,** headquarters of the Daughters of the American Revolution. The 50,000-item collection of the **DAR Museum** includes fine examples of Colonial and Federal silver, china, porcelain, stoneware, earthenware, and glass. *1776 D St. NW, ☎ 202/879–3240. Closed Sat.*

Across the Ellipse is the venerable **Hotel Washington** (515 15th St., ☎ 202/638–5900). The view from the rooftop Sky Top Lounge (open May–Oct.) is one of the best in the city. Across 14th Street is the huge Greek Revival **Treasury Building,** home to the Department of the Treasury.

Capitol Hill

Pierre L'Enfant, the French designer of Washington, called Capitol Hill (then known as Jenkins Hill) "a pedestal waiting for a monument." That monument is the **U.S. Capitol,** the gleaming white-domed building in which elected officials toil. George Washington laid the cornerstone on September 18, 1793, and in November 1800 Congress moved down from Philadelphia. The Capitol building has grown over the years and today contains some of the city's most beautiful art, from Constantino Brumidi's *Apotheosis of Washington,* the fresco at the center of the dome, to the splendid Statuary Hall. There are also live attractions: senators and representatives speechifying in their respective chambers. *East end of the Mall, ☎ 202/224–3121 or 202/225–6827.*

East of the Capitol are the three buildings of the **Library of Congress,** which contains 103 million items, of which only a quarter are books. The remainder includes manuscripts, prints, films, photographs, sheet music, and the largest collection of maps in the world. The green-domed **Jefferson Building** (1st St. and Independence Ave. SE, ☎ 202/707–8000), with its grand, octagonal Main Reading Room and mahogany reader's tables, is the centerpiece of the system.

Behind the Jefferson Building stands the **Folger Shakespeare Library.** Inside are a reproduction of an inn-yard theater and a gallery, designed in the manner of an Elizabethan Great Hall, that hosts rotating exhibits from the library's collection of works by and about the Bard. *201 E. Capitol St. SE, ☎ 202/544–4600. Closed Sun.*

After being shunted around several locations, including a spell in a tavern, the **Supreme Court** got its own building in 1935. The impressive, colonnaded white-marble temple was designed by Cass Gilbert. *1st and E. Capitol Sts. NE, ☎ 202/479–3000. Closed weekends.*

Union Station (50 Massachusetts Ave. NE) is now a shopping center as well as a train station. The Beaux Arts building's wonderful main waiting room is a perfect setting for the inaugural ball that's held here every four years.

Old Downtown and Federal Triangle

Before the glass office blocks around 16th and K streets NW became the business center of town, Washington's mercantile hub was farther east. The open-air markets are gone, but some of the 19th-century character of Washington's east end remains. More recent is Federal Triangle, a humongous complex built in the 1930s to accommodate the expanding federal bureaucracy.

The massive redbrick **Pension Building,** built in the 1880s to house workers who processed the pension claims of veterans and their survivors, is home to the **National Building Museum** (F St. between 4th and 5th Sts. NW, ☎ 202/272–2448), devoted to architecture and the building arts.

Judiciary Square is Washington's legal core, with local and district court buildings arrayed around it. At the center is the **National Law Enforcement Officers Memorial,** a 3-ft-high wall bearing the names of more than 15,000 American police officers killed in the line of duty since 1794. Not far away is Washington's compact **Chinatown,** bordered by G, E, 5th, and 8th streets NW.

Two more Smithsonian museums—the **National Portrait Gallery,** with its paintings and photographs of presidents and other notable Americans, and the **National Museum of American Art,** whose collection ranges from Colonial times to the present—are in the Greek Revival Old Patent Office Building (8th and G Sts. NW).

A few blocks away is **Ford's Theatre** (511 10th St. NW, ☎ 202/426–6924), where Abraham Lincoln was assassinated by John Wilkes Booth on April 14, 1865. A museum in the basement displays items connected with Lincoln's life and untimely death.

The Beaux Arts **Willard Hotel,** on the corner of 14th Street and Pennsylvania Avenue, is one of the most luxurious in Washington. The **Commerce Department Building** forms the base of **Federal Triangle.** Inside Commerce is the **National Aquarium,** the country's oldest public aquarium, featuring tropical and freshwater fish, moray eels, frogs, turtles, piranhas, even sharks. *14th St. and Pennsylvania Ave. NW, ☎ 202/482–2825. Admission charged.*

The tour of the hulking **J. Edgar Hoover Federal Bureau of Investigation Building** outlines the work of the FBI and ends with a live-ammo firearms demonstration. In high tourist season there may be up to an hour's wait to get inside. *10th St. and Pennsylvania Ave. NW (tour entrance on E St. NW), ☎ 202/324–3447. Tours weekdays.*

The Declaration of Independence, the Constitution, and the Bill of Rights are on display in the Rotunda of the **National Archives** (1 Constitution Ave. between 7th and 9th Sts. NW, ☎ 202/501–5000).

Across 7th Street is the **Navy Memorial,** a statue of a lone sailor staring out over the largest map in the world. In summer, the memorial's concert stage is the site of military-band performances (☎ 202/737–2300).

Georgetown

Georgetown, a former tobacco port, is Washington's poshest neighborhood, home to some of its wealthiest and best-known citizens. It's also the nucleus of Washington's nightlife scene, with dozens of bars and restaurants dotting Wisconsin Avenue and M Street, Georgetown's crossroads.

Starting in Georgetown and running parallel to the Potomac is the **Chesapeake & Ohio Canal,** a 19th-century waterway that once carried lumber, coal, iron, and flour into northwest Maryland. Joggers tread its scenic towpath, and in summer mule-drawn barges ply its placid waters (tickets available at the Foundry Mall, 1055 Thomas Jefferson St. NW, ☎ 202/653–5190).

Georgetown Park (3222 M St. NW), home to such high-ticket stores as F.A.O. Schwarz, Williams-Sonoma, and Polo/Ralph Lauren, is a multilevel shopping extravaganza that answers the question "If the Victorians had invented shopping malls, what would they look like?"

At the western edge of Georgetown is **Georgetown University,** the oldest Jesuit school in the country. When seen from the Potomac or from Washington's high ground, the Gothic spires of the university's older buildings give it an almost medieval look.

To the north is **Dumbarton Oaks,** an estate comprising two museums—one of Byzantine works, the other of pre-Columbian art—and 10 acres of stunning formal gardens designed by landscape architect Beatrix Farrand. *Art collections: 1703 32nd St. NW, ☎ 202/338–8278. Admission charged. Closed Mon. Gardens: 31st and R Sts. NW. Admission charged. Apr.–Oct.*

Other Attractions

The **Bureau of Engraving and Printing** is the birthplace of all paper currency in the United States. Despite the fact that there are no free samples, the 20-minute self-guided tour—which takes visitors past presses that turn out some $22.5 million a day—is one of the city's most popular. *14th and C Sts. SW, ☎ 202/847–3019. Closed weekends.*

Alongside the city's many museums celebrating the best of humanity's accomplishments is one that illustrates what humans at their worst are capable of. The **United States Holocaust Memorial Museum,** which opened in April 1993, tells in almost cinematic fashion the story of the 11 million Jews, Gypsies, Jehovah's Witnesses, homosexuals, political prisoners, and others killed by the Nazis between 1933 and 1945. Arrive early (by 9 AM to be safe) to get free, same-day, timed-entry tickets. *100 Raoul Wallenberg Pl. SW (14th St. and Independence Ave. SW), ☎ 202/653–9220.*

The **Phillips Collection** was the first permanent museum of modern art in the country. Holdings include works by Braque, Cézanne, Klee, Matisse, Renoir, and John Henry Twachtman. *1600–1612 21st St. NW, ☎ 202/387–2151. Admission charged.*

The **National Geographic Society's Explorers Hall** is the magazine come to life. Interactive exhibits encourage visitors to learn about the world. The centerpiece is a hand-painted globe, 11 ft in diameter, that floats and spins on a cushion of air, showing off different features of the planet. *17th and M Sts. NW, ☎ 202/857–7588.*

The 160-acre **National Zoological Park,** part of the Smithsonian Institution, is one of the foremost zoos in the world. Innovative compounds show animals in naturalistic settings, and the ambitious Amazonia recreates the complete ecosystem of a South American rain forest. *3001 Connecticut Ave. NW, ☎ 202/673–4717.*

The **Frederick Douglass National Historic Site** is at Cedar Hill, the Washington home of the noted abolitionist. The house displays mementos from Douglass's life and has a wonderful view of the Federal City, across the Anacostia River. *1411 W St. SE, ☎ 202/426–5961.*

The **National Museum of Women in the Arts** displays the works of prominent female artists from the Renaissance to the present, including Georgia O'Keeffe, Mary Cassatt, Elisabeth Vigée-Lebrun, and Judy Chicago. *1250 New York Ave. NW, ☎ 202/783–5000. Admission charged.*

The **Washington Navy Yard** is the Navy's oldest shore establishment. A former shipyard and ordnance facility, the yard today is home to the **Navy Museum** and the **Marine Corps Museum,** which outline the history of those two services from their inception to the present. *9th and M Sts. SE, ☎ 202/433–4882.*

It took 83 years to complete the Gothic-style **Washington National Cathedral,** the sixth-largest cathedral in the world. Besides flying buttresses, a nave, transepts, and rib vaults that were built stone by stone, it is adorned with fanciful gargoyles created by skilled stone carvers. *Wisconsin and Massachusetts Aves. NW, ☎ 202/537–6200. Suggested donation: $2 adults, $1 children.*

Arlington, Virginia

Though these attractions are across the Potomac, they're a part of any visit to the nation's capital. (For more suburban Virginia sites—including Mount Vernon and Old Town Alexandria—*see* Virginia.)

At **Arlington National Cemetery,** visitors can trace America's history through the aftermath of its battles. Dominating the cemetery is the Greek Revival **Arlington House,** onetime home of Robert E. Lee, which offers a breathtaking view across the Potomac to the Lincoln Memorial and the Mall. On a hillside below are the **Kennedy graves.** John F. Kennedy is buried under an eternal flame; Jacqueline Kennedy Onassis is next to him; and nearby, marked by a simple white cross, is the grave of his brother Robert. Also in the cemetery is the **Tomb of the Unknowns** (West end of Memorial Bridge, ☎ 703/692–0931).

Just north of the cemetery is the **United States Marine Corps War Memorial,** honoring Marines who have given their lives since the Corps was formed in 1775. The memorial statue, sculpted by Felix W. de Weldon, is based on Joe Rosenthal's Pulitzer Prize–winning photograph of six soldiers raising a flag atop Mt. Suribachi on Iwo Jima on February 19, 1945. (A word of caution: It is dangerous to visit the memorial after dark.)

The **Pentagon,** headquarters of the Department of Defense, is an exercise in immensity: 23,000 military and civilian employees work here; it is as wide as three Washington Monuments laid end to end; inside are 17½ mi of corridors, 7,754 windows, and 691 drinking fountains. Visitors can take a 75-minute tour. *Off I–395, ☎ 703/695–1776. Tours spring and summer, weekdays every ½ hr 9:30–3:30; fall and winter, weekdays every hr 9–3. Photo ID required. Closed on federal holidays.*

Parks and Gardens

The 444-acre **National Arboretum** blooms with all manner of plants, including clematis, peonies, rhododendrons, and azaleas. Also popular are the National Bonsai Collection, National Herb Garden, and an odd and striking hilltop construction of old marble columns from the U.S. Capitol. *3501 New York Ave. NE, ☎ 202/475–4815.*

Rock Creek Park (☎ 202/426–6829) is a cool tongue of green jutting down into the center of Washington. Its 1,800 acres include picnic sites and biking, hiking, and equestrian trails that wend through groves of dogwood, beech, oak, and cedar.

The **United States Botanic Garden,** just below the Capitol, is a peaceful, plant-filled conservatory that includes a cactus house, a fern house, and a subtropical house filled with orchids. *1st St. and Maryland Ave. SW, ☎ 202/225–8333.*

Shopping

Shopping Districts

Georgetown (centered on Wisconsin Ave. and M St. NW) is probably Washington's densest shopping area, with specialty shops selling everything from antiques to designer fashions. **Adams–Morgan** (around

18th St. and Columbia Rd. NW) is a bit funkier, with lots of used-book and clothing stores and a bohemian atmosphere.

The Shops at National Place (13th and F Sts. NW, ☎ 202/783–9090) is a glittering, three-story collection of stores, including Banana Republic, Victoria's Secret, and The Sharper Image. **Union Station** (50 Massachusetts Ave. NE, ☎ 202/371–9441) has trendy clothing boutiques like Cignal and Martinaro and neat special-interest shops like the Nature Company (decorative natural objects) and Political America (campaign buttons and memorabilia). **Mazza Gallerie** (5300 Wisconsin Ave. NW, ☎ 202/966–6114) is an upmarket mall straddling the Maryland border that's anchored by the ritzy Neiman Marcus and a Filene's Basement.

Department Stores

Washington's two main department stores are downtown, by the Metro Center subway stop. Both **Hecht's** (12th and G Sts. NW, ☎ 202/628–6661) and **Woodward & Lothrop** (11th and F Sts. NW, ☎ 202/347–5300) are bright and spacious, with a wide selection of items sensibly grouped.

Specialty Stores

Every museum in Washington has a gift shop; in each, the range of items reflects the museum's collection and extends far beyond the mere souvenir. The largest is probably in the **National Museum of American History** (*see* Exploring Washington, D.C., *above*).

Spectator Sports

Basketball

Bullets (Capital Centre, 1 Harry S. Truman Dr., Landover, MD, ☎ 202/432–7328 or 800/551–7328; Nov.–Apr.).

Football

All regular **Redskins** home games at RFK Stadium (E. Capitol and 22nd Sts. SE, ☎ 202/546–2222; Aug.–Dec.) are sold out to season-ticket holders. If you're willing to pay dearly, you can get tickets from brokers who advertise in the *Washington Post.*

Hockey

Capitals (Capital Centre, ☎ 202/432–7328 or 800/551–7328; Oct.–Apr.).

Dining

Washington's restaurants aren't exactly innovators, but neither are they blind to fashion. That means trends started elsewhere—nouvelle cuisine, New American, southwestern—quickly show up in the capital. Good ethnic meals can be found in Adams–Morgan (lots of Ethiopian), Georgetown (Afghani to Indonesian), and Chinatown. For price ranges, see Chart 1 (A) in On the Road with Fodor's.

$$$$ ★ **Jean-Louis at the Watergate Hotel.** This small restaurant is a showcase for the cooking of Jean-Louis Palladin. The contemporary French fare is based on regional American ingredients—crawfish from Louisiana, wild mushrooms from Oregon, game from Texas—combined in innovative ways. In 1993 Palladin opened a less-formal restaurant upstairs offering simpler, markedly less-expensive concoctions such as pot-au-feu, steak, sausage, and attractively presented salads. Palladin by Jean-Louis, as it's called, is open daily for breakfast, lunch, and dinner; reservations are required (☎ 202/298–4455). *2650 Virginia Ave. NW,* ☎ *202/298–4488. Reservations required. Jacket and tie. AE, DC, MC, V. Closed Sun. and last 2 wks in Aug. No lunch.*

$$$$ ★ **Le Lion d'Or.** The superior entrées at this French restaurant include lobster soufflé, ravioli with foie gras, and crepes with oysters and caviar. Don't forget to place an order for a dessert soufflé—it will leave you breathless. *1150 Connecticut Ave. NW, ☎ 202/296–7972. Reservations advised. Jacket and tie . AE, DC, MC, V. Closed Sun. No lunch Sat.*

$$$ **Occidental Grill.** Part of the stately Willard Hotel complex, this popular restaurant offers innovative dishes, attentive service, and lots of photos of politicians and other power brokers past and present. The menu changes frequently, but you can count on grilled poultry, fish, and steak, as well as salads and sandwiches. *1475 Pennsylvania Ave. NW, ☎ 202/783–1475. Reservations advised. AE, DC, MC, V.*

$$$ ★ **i Ricchi.** At this airy Tuscan restaurant, the spring/summer menu includes such offerings as rolled pork and rabbit roasted in wine and fresh herbs, while the fall/winter list brings grilled lamb chops and sautéed beef fillet. *1220 19th St. NW, ☎ 202/835–0459. Reservations advised. AE, DC, MC, V. Closed Sun. No lunch Sat.*

$$$ **Sam and Harry's.** Here is the quintessential steak house. The surroundings are understated and genteel, and the Evening Star jazz bar is a popular downtown gathering place. The main attractions are the porterhouse steak and the prime rib. *1200 19th St. NW, ☎ 202/296–4333. Reservations advised. AE, DC, MC, V. Closed Sun. No lunch Sat.*

$$ **Notte Luna.** Diners at this Italian restaurant sit in a dramatic black-and-fuchsia neon dining room while chefs work in an open kitchen around a wood-burning pizza oven. The ordinary here often has an unexpected twist; you can order your pizza topped with lamb sausage, your pasta with grilled salmon. *809 15th St. NW, ☎ 202/408–9500. AE, DC, MC, V. No lunch weekends.*

$$ **Old Glory.** Always teeming with visiting Texans, Georgetown students, and closet Elvis fans, Old Glory sticks to barbecue basics: sandwiches and platters of pulled and sliced pork, beef brisket, and smoked and pulled chicken, ribs, and sausage. The open pit will also roast vegetables, but they're an unusual choice here. *3139 M St. NW, ☎ 202/337–3406. Reservations for large groups only. AE, D, DC, MC, V.*

$ **American Café.** Healthy food—but not health food—served here includes roast beef on humongous croissants, fresh fish, seafood pie, and barbecued ribs. Weekend brunches offer such temptations as strawberry-banana-nut waffles and stuffed French toast. *The Shops at National Place, ☎ 202/626–0770. Also at 227 Massachusetts Ave. NE, ☎ 202/547–8500; 1200 19th St. NW, ☎ 202/223–2121; 5252 Wisconsin Ave. NW, ☎ 202/363–5400; 4238 Wilson Blvd., Arlington, VA, ☎ 703/522–2236; 8601 Westward Center Dr., Vienna, VA, ☎ 703/848–9488. Reservations accepted only for large parties. AE, MC, V.*

$ **Café Atlántico.** This lively spot in Adams–Morgan serves Caribbean specialties in a casual atmosphere. Appetizers include conch, cod, and yucca fritters, as well as shrimp and potato croquettes, all beautifully fried. Pork loin, jerk chicken, and lamb curry are among the main courses. *1819 Columbia Rd. NW, ☎ 202/328–5844. No reservations. AE, MC, V. No lunch.*

$ ★ **Meskerem.** Among Adams–Morgan's many Ethiopian restaurants, Meskerem is distinctive for a balcony where you can eat Ethiopian style: seated on the floor on leather cushions, with large woven baskets for tables. For a truly authentic experience, order the *injera* (spongy bread) made with *teff*, a grain grown only in Ethiopia and Idaho that imparts a distinctive sourness. *2434 18th St. NW, ☎ 202/462–4100. AE, DC, MC, V. No lunch Mon.–Thurs.*

Lodging

Many Washington hotels, particularly those downtown, offer special reduced rates and package deals on weekends, and some are available midweek; be sure to ask about them at the hotel of your choice. **Capitol Reservations** books rooms at more than 70 better hotels in good locations at rates 20%–40% off; call 202/452–1270 or 800/847–4832 from 9 to 6 weekdays; they also offer packages with tours and meals. **Washington D.C. Accommodations** will book rooms at any hotel in town, with discounts of 20%–40% available at about 40 locations; call 202/289–2220 or 800/554–2220 from 9 to 5 weekdays. To find reasonably priced accommodations in small guest houses and private homes, contact **Bed 'n' Breakfast Ltd. Accommodations of Washington, D.C.** (Box 12011, 20005, ☎ 202/328–3510) or **Bed and Breakfast League, Ltd.** (3639 Van Ness St. NW, 20008, ☎ 202/363–7767). For price ranges, see Chart 2 (A) in On the Road with Fodor's.

$$$$ ★ **Four Seasons Hotel.** This contemporary hotel, conveniently situated between Georgetown and Foggy Bottom, is a gathering place for Washington's elite. Guest rooms are traditionally furnished in light colors. The quieter rooms face the courtyard; others have a view of the C&O Canal. *2800 Pennsylvania Ave. NW, 20007, ☎ 202/342–0444 or 800/332–3442, FAX 202/944–2076. 167 rooms, 30 suites. Facilities: 2 restaurants, bar, health club, pool, nightclub.* AE, DC, MC, V.

$$$$ ★ **Hay-Adams Hotel.** Italian Renaissance in design, this hotel looks like a mansion in disguise. Seventeenth-century Medici tapestries adorn two lobby walls, while guest rooms are the most brightly colored in the city, decorated in 23 different English country-house schemes. *1 Lafayette Sq., 20006, ☎ 202/638–6600 or 800/424–5054, FAX 202/638–2716. 125 rooms, 18 suites. Facilities: restaurant, bar, laundry service, dry cleaning. AE, DC, MC, V.*

$$$$ ★ **Ritz-Carlton.** Exclusive and intimate, this Dupont Circle hotel has an English-hunt club theme, reflected in an extensive collection of 18th- and 19th-century English art heavy on horses and dogs. Rooms were renovated in late 1993. *2100 Massachusetts Ave. NW, 20008, ☎ 202/293–2100 or 800/241–3333, FAX 202/293–0641. 173 rooms, 33 suites. Facilities: restaurant, bar, exercise room, access to health club, concierge floor. AE, DC, MC, V.*

$$$ **Latham Hotel.** A Colonial-style hotel in the city's liveliest neighborhood, the redbrick Marbury is popular with Europeans, sports figures, and devotees of Georgetown. Some rooms are underground; others have views of the C&O Canal or busy M Street. *3000 M St. NW, 20007, ☎ 202/726–5000 or 800/368–5922, FAX 202/337–4250. 134 rooms, 9 suites. Facilities: 2 restaurants, 2 bars, room service 7* AM*–10:30* PM*, outdoor pool. AE, DC, MC, V.*

$$$ **Phoenix Park Hotel.** Just steps from Union Station and four blocks from the Capitol, this high-rise hotel has a wood-paneled and brass Irish men's-club theme and is the home of The Dubliner (*see* The Arts and Nightlife, *below*), one of Washington's best bars. Guest rooms, renovated in 1994, are bright, traditionally furnished, and quiet. A new wing was built in 1995, adding 61 new rooms and suites, three meeting rooms, and a ballroom. *520 N. Capitol St. NW, 20001, ☎ 202/638–6900 or 800/824–5419, FAX 202/393–3236. 136 rooms, 15 suites. Facilities: 2 restaurants. AE, DC, MC, V.*

$$$ ★ **Washington Hilton and Towers.** One of the city's busiest convention hotels, this high-rise also attracts travelers who like to be where the action is. The light-filled but compact guest rooms are furnished in hotel *moderne* and have marble bathrooms. *1919 Connecticut Ave. NW,*

20009, ☎ 202/483–3000 or 800/445–8667, FAX 202/265–8221. 1,062 rooms, 88 suites. Facilities: 3 restaurants, 2 bars, outdoor pool, health club, 3 tennis courts, parking (fee). AE, DC, MC, V.

$$ **Hotel Anthony.** A good value, this small hotel has a courteous staff, offers the basics in the midst of the K and L streets business district, and is close to the White House. Some rooms have a full kitchen, some a wet bar; king, queen, or extra-long double beds are available. Weekend rates are almost half-price. *1823 L St. NW, 20036, ☎ 202/223–4320 or 800/424–2970, FAX 202/223–8546. 99 rooms. Facilities: 2 restaurants, room service 7 AM–10 PM. AE, DC, MC, V.*

$$ **Hotel Tabard Inn.** Three Victorian town houses near Dupont Circle were linked in the 1920s to form an inn that is now the oldest continuously running hotel in Washington. Furnishings are broken-in Victorian and American Empire antiques, and a Victorian-inspired carpet cushions the labyrinthine hallways. *1739 N St. NW, 20036, ☎ 202/785–1277, FAX 202/785–6173. 40 rooms, 17 share bath. Facility: restaurant. MC, V.*

$ **Washington International Hostel.** Guests sleep in 4- to 14-person dormitories (some "couple" rooms are available, but reservations are required). Guests must bring their own linens or rent them from the hostel. The maximum stay is six days in summer, when reservations are highly recommended; off-season reservations are necessary only for groups. *1009 11th St. NW, 20001, ☎ 202/737–2333. 250 beds. MC, V.*

The Arts and Nightlife

Area arts and entertainment events are listed in the Weekend section in Friday's *Washington Post,* the free *City Paper, Washingtonian* magazine (on newsstands), and *Where: Washington* (free in hotels).

The Arts

TicketPlace (L St. between 15th and 16th Sts. NW, ☎ 202/842–5387; closed Sun.) sells half-price, day-of-performance tickets for selected shows. **TicketMaster** (☎ 202/432–7328 or 800/551–7328) takes phone charges for events around the city. All manner of cultural events, from ballet to classical music, are offered at the **John F. Kennedy Center for the Performing Arts** (New Hampshire Ave. and Rock Creek Pkwy. NW, ☎ 202/467–4600 or 800/444–1324).

THEATER

Arena Stage (6th St. and Maine Ave. SW, ☎ 202/488–3300) has three theaters and is the city's most respected resident company. The historic **Ford's Theatre** (511 10th St. NW, ☎ 202/347–4833) is host mainly to musicals. The **National Theatre** (1321 E St. NW, ☎ 202/628–6161) presents pre- and post-Broadway shows. Now in a new home, the **Shakespeare Theatre** (450 7th St. NW, ☎ 202/393–2700) presents classics by the Bard. Many scrappy smaller companies—including Source, Studio, and Woolly Mammoth—are clustered near 14th and P streets NW.

MUSIC

The **National Symphony Orchestra** (☎ 202/416–8100) performs at the Kennedy Center from September through June and during the summer at Wolf Trap Farm Park (☎ 703/938–2404) in Virginia.

The **Armed Forces Concert Series** offers free military-band performances from June through August, Sunday through Friday evenings, on the West Terrace of the Capitol and at the Sylvan Theater on the Washington Monument grounds. *Air Force, ☎ 202/767–5658; Army, ☎ 703/696–3718; Marines, ☎ 202/433–4011; Navy, ☎ 202/433–2525.*

OPERA

The **Washington Opera** (☏ 202/416–7800 or 800/876–7372) presents seven operas each season in the Kennedy Center's Opera House and Eisenhower Theater.

DANCE

Dance Place (3225 8th St. NE, ☏ 202/269–1600) hosts a wide assortment of modern and ethnic dance. The **Washington Ballet** (☏ 202/362–3606) performs mainly at the Kennedy Center and the Warner Theatre.

Nightlife

Georgetown, Adams-Morgan, Dupont Circle, and **Capitol Hill** are the main nightlife centers in Washington.

BARS

The **Brickskeller** (1523 22nd St. NW, ☏ 202/293–1885) sells more than 500 brands of beer—from Central American lagers to U.S. microbrewed ales. The **Dubliner** (Phoenix Park Hotel, 520 N. Capitol St. NW, ☏ 202/737–3773) features snug, paneled rooms, thick, tasty Guinness, and nightly live Irish entertainment.

CABARET

Two troupes offering political song and satire perform regularly in Georgetown clubs: the **Capitol Steps** (☏ 202/298–8222 or 703/683–8330) and **Gross National Product** (☏ 202/783–7212). The **Marquee Lounge** (Omni-Shoreham Hotel, 2500 Calvert St. NW, ☏ 202/745–1023) is home to funny lady Joan Cushing and occasional song and dance acts.

JAZZ

Blues Alley (rear 1073 Wisconsin Ave. NW, ☏ 202/337–4141) books some of the biggest names in jazz. **One Step Down** (2517 Pennsylvania Ave. NW, ☏ 202/331–8863) is an intimate, smoky space that's a favorite with hardcore devotees.

ROCK AND REGGAE

The **Bayou** (3135 K St. NW, ☏ 202/333–2897) in Georgetown features live rock. **Kilimanjaro** (1724 California St. NW, ☏ 202/328–3838) specializes in "international" music from the Caribbean and Africa. The **9:30 Club** (930 F St. NW, ☏ 202/393–0930) books an eclectic mix of local, national, and international artists, playing what used to be known as "new wave" music.

WEST VIRGINIA

By Dale Leatherman

Capital	Charleston
Population	1,800,000
Motto	Mountaineers Are Always Free
State Bird	Cardinal
State Flower	Rhododendron maximum

Visitor Information

West Virginia Division of Tourism and Parks (2101 Washington St. E, Charleston 25305, ☎ 304/348–2286 or 800/225–5982, FAX 304/558–0108).

Scenic Drives

In the eastern part of the state, the **Highland Scenic Highway** (Rte. 150 between Cranberry Glades and U.S. 219/Rte. 55 north of Edray) and the **Highland Trace** (Rte. 55 between the Virginia border and Elkins) wind through the Potomac Highlands, the state's high-mountain region. In the south, the historic **Midland Trail** (U.S. 60) runs east–west for 120 mi between White Sulphur Springs and Charleston, tracing the 200-year-old path through the Appalachians first used by buffalo and Native Americans.

National and State Parks

National Parks

The **Monongahela National Forest** (200 Sycamore St., Elkins 26241, ☎ 304/636–1800, FAX 304/636–1875) and **George Washington National Forest** (Lee Ranger District, Rte. 4, Box 515, Edinburg 22824, ☎ 703/984–4101, FAX 703/984–8989) encompass 900,000 and 100,000 acres, respectively, near the Virginia border.

State Parks

West Virginia is unique in that 8 of its 35 state parks have fine lodges with restaurants and resort amenities, such as downhill skiing or golf courses. Most have cabins and campsites with full hookups. **Cacapon Resort State Park** (Rte. 1, Box 304, Berkeley Springs 25411, ☎ 304/258–1022 or 800/225–5982) is noted for its Robert Trent Jones golf course; amenities include 30 cottages and a 49-room lodge with restaurant. At **Canaan Valley Resort State Park** (Rte. 1, Box 330, Davis 26260, ☎ 304/866–4121 or 800/225–5982), the 250-room lodge, restaurant, and lounge are bustling year-round; the park has an alpine-skiing area, an 18-hole golf course, and an indoor pool and fitness center. **Pipestem Resort State Park** (Box 150, Pipestem 25979, ☎ 304/466–1800 or 800/225–5982), southeast of Beckley, has two lodges (143 rooms) with restaurants, 25 deluxe cottages, and 82 campsites, as well as golf, indoor and outdoor pools, an aerial tramway, and cross-country skiing.

EASTERN WEST VIRGINIA

It's easy to slip into West Virginia from the east, through the time tunnel of Harpers Ferry, Charles Town, and Shepherdstown, where buildings predate the Revolutionary War and bear the scars of the Civil War. To the west, the scene changes to one of rugged splendor in a swath of mountain land blessed with Canadian weather patterns—and the ski industry to prove it. In the spring, the focus shifts to white-water rafting on some of the nation's most exciting rivers.

Tourist Information

Potomac Highlands: Jefferson County Visitor and Convention Bureau (Box A, Harpers Ferry 25425, ☎ 304/535–2627 or 800/848–8687); Martinsburg/Berkeley County Convention and Visitors Bureau (208 S. Queen St., Martinsburg 25401, ☎ 304/264–8801 or 800/498–2386); Potomac Highlands Travel Council (1200 Harrison Ave., Elkins 26241, ☎ 304/636–8400, FAX 304/636–9574). **Southern West Virginia:** Convention and Visitors Bureau (Box 1799, Beckley 25802, ☎ 304/252–2244 or 800/847–4898, FAX 304/252–2252); Travel Berkeley Springs (304 Fairfax St., Berkeley Springs 25411, ☎ 304/258–9147 or 800/447–8797).

Getting There

By Plane

The region is served by Beckley's **Raleigh County Memorial Airport** (☎ 304/255–0476), Bluefield/Princeton's **Mercer County Airport** (☎ 304/327–5308), Charleston's **Yeager Airport** (☎ 304/344–8033 or 800/241–6522), **Elkins/Randolph County Airport** (☎ 304/636–2726), Lewisburg's **Greenbrier Valley Airport** (☎ 304/645–3961), and Martinsburg's **Eastern West Virginia Regional Airport** (☎ 304/263–2106).

By Car

Three interstates traverse the region: I–64, between White Sulphur Springs and Beckley; I–77, Princeton to Charleston; and I–81, in the eastern panhandle. U.S. 340 enters Harpers Ferry from the east. From the west, U.S. 50, I–79, and I–64 provide the best access.

By Train

Amtrak (☎ 800/872–7245) has stations in Harpers Ferry, Martinsburg, Charleston, and White Sulphur Springs.

By Bus

Greyhound Lines (☎ 800/231–2222) has terminals in major towns.

Exploring Eastern West Virginia

Old and new mingle here in surprising harmony. In the eastern panhandle you can explore pre-Revolutionary-era buildings, shop for the latest in fashions, and relax in a Roman bath, all in the same day. To the west and south, the mountain roads are scenic but sometimes narrow and limited to 40 mph. Do your driving in the daytime—for safety's sake and to enjoy the many overlooks and small towns reminiscent of the 1950s.

On the state's eastern tip is **Harpers Ferry National Historic Park** (☎ 304/535–6298), where the Shenandoah and Potomac rivers join. Hand-carved stone steps lead to the overlook where Thomas Jefferson proclaimed the view "worth a trip across the Atlantic." The town grew around a U.S. armory built in 1740, and many buildings have been preserved.

Lining the cobblestone streets are shops and museums where park employees in period costume demonstrate Colonial skills. The **John Brown Wax Museum** depicts the abolitionist's raid on the town. ☎ *304/535–6342. Admission charged. Closed weekdays Dec.–Mar.*

In commerce-minded **Martinsburg** (*see* Shopping, *below*), two **pre–Civil War roundhouses** at the foot of Martin Street attract railroad buffs, though they're in poor condition. Downtown, pre–Civil War structures of Federal and Greek Revival style can be seen on John, Race, and North Spring streets.

From Martinsburg, Rte. 9 leads to **Berkeley Springs,** the nation's first spa, and George Washington's favorite. **Berkeley Springs State Park** (☏ 304/258–2711 or 800/225–5982) offers heated Roman baths and massages.

Driving south, U.S. 50 and Rte. 93 take you over the mountains to **Davis** and the **Canaan Valley,** home of the **Canaan Valley** and **Timberline ski areas** (*see* Ski Areas, *below*). The high, tundralike **Dolly Sods Wilderness Area** of the Monongahela National Forest (*see* National and State Parks, *above*) is used for hiking, cross-country skiing, and nature studies.

A southwesterly route leads through the **Potomac Highlands,** an area with boundless opportunities for outdoor recreation, to the **National Radio Astronomy Observatory** in Green Bank, where huge radio telescopes listen for life in outer space. The process is explained during a bus tour and slide presentation. *Rte. 28/92,* ☏ *304/456–2011. Closed weekdays Sept.–Oct. No tours Nov.–Memorial Day.*

Nearby is **Cass Scenic Railroad State Park,** where visitors ride up Cheat Mountain in open railcars drawn by steam locomotives that pulled lumber cars in the early 1900s. *Rte. 66, Cass,* ☏ *304/456–4300 or 800/225–5982. Admission: $13 adults, $7 children. Closed Nov.–May.*

Near Cass, the **Greenbrier River Trail State Park** (Star Rte., Caldwell, ☏ 800/336–7009), centered on a 76-mi former railroad bed, is now devoted to hikers (*see* Sports and the Outdoors, *below*), bikers, and cross-country skiers.

The towns of **Snowshoe** and **Slatyfork** mark the location of several downhill ski areas and miles of cross-country trails (*see* Ski Areas, *below*). **White Sulphur Springs** is the site of the **Greenbrier** (*see* Dining and Lodging, Spas, *below*), an elegant four-seasons resort visited by U.S. presidents and heads of state from around the world. The area's restorative springs have been an attraction for more than 200 years.

The **Lewisburg National Historic District** (☏ 304/645–1000) encompasses 236 acres and more than 60 18th-century buildings, many of native limestone or brick. At night, gas lamps flicker on quaint storefronts and signs, and no overhead power lines spoil the image of a bygone era.

To the south is **Winterplace ski resort** (*see* Ski Areas, *below*) and **Pipestem Resort State Park** (*see* National and State Parks, *above*). North is a land of raging waters that have played a major role in West Virginia tourism since the 1970s. Major white-water rafting areas (*see* Sports and the Outdoors, *below*) include the **New River Gorge National River Park** (☏ 304/465–0508) and the **Gauley River National Recreation Area** (☏ 304/872–3722).

What to See and Do with Children

With its wide range of outdoor sports, this area is one big natural amusement park for children. Rafting, on all rivers except the Gauley, is suitable for youngsters, as are the **Cass Scenic Railroad** and the **National Radio Astronomy Observatory** (*see* Exploring Eastern West Virginia, *above*).

Shopping

Fairs and festivals are plentiful, and perfect places to shop for mountain handicrafts; check with local tourist offices for schedules. **Martinsburg** has several outlet centers, including the **Blue Ridge Outlet Mall** (Stephen and Queen Sts., ☎ 304/263–7467 or 800/445–3993), which houses 60 major stores.

Sports and the Outdoors

Biking

Rentals, instruction, and tours are available from **Blackwater Bikes** (Davis, ☎ 304/259–5286), the **Elk River Touring Center** (Slatyfork, ☎ 304/572–3771), and **Snowshoe Mountain Biking Centers** (Snowshoe, ☎ 304/572–1000).

Canoeing

The **Greenbrier River** is one of the country's best paddling rivers. Area outfitters can put you on this and other waterways; for a list of operators, contact the Division of Tourism and Parks (*see* Visitor Information, *above*).

Fishing

Trout are abundant in faster streams and rivers, while bass, crappie, and walleye lurk in the lakes. Licenses are available at sporting and convenience stores. Most rafting companies also organize fishing trips.

Golf

Cacapon and **Canaan Valley resort state parks** (*see* State Parks, *above*) offer 18 holes each; the **Greenbrier** in White Sulphur Springs (*see* Dining and Lodging, Spas, *below*), 54 holes; **Locust Hill** in Charles Town (☎ 304/728–7300), 18 holes; **Pipestem Resort State Park** (*see* National and State Parks, *above*), 27 holes; **Stonebridge in Martinsburg** (☎ 304/263–4653), 18 holes; the Woods in Hedgesville (☎ 304/754–3358 or 800/248–2222), 27 holes.

Hiking and Backpacking

State and national parks have extensive trail systems. The **Appalachian Trail** (Harpers Ferry 25425, ☎ 304/535–6331), the **Big Blue Trail** (Potomac Appalachian Trail Club, 118 Park St. SE, Vienna, VA 22180, ☎ 703/242–0965), and the **Greenbrier River Trail** (Slatyfork 26291, ☎ 304/572–3771, or Watoga State Park, ☎ 304/799–4087) run through this region.

Rafting

The **New, Gauley,** and **Cheat** are West Virginia's most heavily traveled rivers, followed by the **Tygart** and **Shenandoah.** First-timers can tackle all but the Gauley. For information on nearly 50 outfitters that run white-water excursions, contact the Division of Tourism and Parks (*see* Visitor Information, *above*).

Riding

Horseback riding along trails is available in most state parks.

Ski Areas

Cross-Country

Elk River Touring Center (*see* Sports and the Outdoors, Biking, *above*) and the **White Grass Ski Touring Center** (Rte. 1, Box 299, Davis 26260, ☎ 304/866–4114) offer rentals, instruction, and tours.

Downhill

Call 800/225–5982 for snow conditions at these ski areas: **Canaan Valley Resort State Park** (Davis, 21 trails, 3 chairlifts, vertical drop 850 ft, 1¼-mi run), **Snowshoe/Silver Creek** (Snowshoe, 53 trails, 11 chairlifts, vertical drop 1,500 ft, 1½-mi run), **Timberline** (Davis, 35 trails, 3 chairlifts, vertical drop 1,000 ft, 2-mi run), and **Winterplace** (Flat Top, 25 trails, 4 chairlifts, vertical drop 603 ft, 1¼-mi run).

Dining and Lodging

Real West Virginia cooking is hearty, simple, and usually homemade from local ingredients—buckwheat cakes for breakfast, beef stew for lunch, brook trout or game for dinner—but more urbane fare is usually available. As for accommodations, you can find the "Ritz" in West Virginia, or motels where "the light's always left on for you," but local B&Bs afford access to the state's greatest treasure: its people (☎ 800/225–5982 for B&B listings and booklet). For price ranges, see Charts 1 (B) and 2 (B) in On the Road with Fodor's.

Berkeley Springs

DINING

The Country Inn. This restaurant's atmosphere suits its name—lots of natural wood and old prints. The best menu choices are crab cakes or lamb. *207 S. Washington St., ☎ 304/258–2210, FAX 304/258–3986. AE, D, DC, MC, V. $$*

LODGING

★ **Cacapon Resort State Park.** Locally crafted heavy oak pieces furnish the main lodge's rooms and woodsy dining room, which overlook the golf course or Cacapon ridge. Rustic cabins are tucked in the surrounding woods. *Off U.S. 522, Rte. 1, Box 304, 25411, ☎ 304/258–1022, FAX 304/258–5323. 49 lodge rooms, 30 cabins. Facilities: restaurant, tennis courts, lake, golf course. AE, MC, V. $ (winter)–$$ (summer).*

Davis

DINING

Blackwater Falls State Park. The stone-pillared dining room, furnished in handmade red oak, perches on the rim of the Blackwater Canyon. Diners' favorites are the breakfast bar, charbroiled chicken breast, and prime rib. *Rte. 32 to Blackwater Falls State Park Rd., ☎ 304/259–5216, FAX 304/259–5881. AE, MC, V. $$*

LODGING

Canaan Valley Resort State Park. The rooms here are motel-style but spacious, and the resort's wooded setting is superb. *Rte. 1, Box 330, 26260, ☎ 304/866–4121 or 800/622–4121, FAX 304/866–2172. 250 rooms, 23 cabins. Facilities: restaurant, lounge, indoor pool, golf course, downhill ski area. AE, D, DC, MC, V. $–$$*

Shepherdstown

DINING AND LODGING

★ **Bavarian Inn and Lodge.** In four alpine chalets overlooking the Potomac River, the rooms are luxurious, with canopy beds, fireplaces, and whirlpool tubs. The dining areas are decorated with antiques and fine china. The German and American cuisine includes wild pheasant, venison, and boar. *Rte. 1, Box 30, 25443, ☎ 304/876–2551, FAX 304/876–9355. 42 units. Facilities: restaurant ($$–$$$), pool, tennis courts, bike rentals. AE, DC, MC, V. $$$$*

Snowshoe/Slatyfork

DINING

★ **Red Fox Restaurant.** This restaurant offers an extensive menu and exceptional service. The chefs use local meats, fish, herbs, and cheeses for such specialties as wild game pâtés or roast highland quail cooked with apples, country ham, sausages, and applejack brandy. *Snowshoe Mountain Resort, off U.S. 219, ☎ 304/572–1111, FAX 304/572–2222. AE, D, MC, V. $$$–$$$$*

LODGING

Snowshoe/Silver Creek Mountain Resort. Accommodations vary from motel-style rooms to luxury condos. Snowshoe has an assortment of natural-wood structures in the forest fringing the ski slopes, and Silver Creek has lodgings in a high rise. *Off U.S. 219, 10 Snowshoe Rd., Snowshoe 26209, ☎ 304/572–1000, FAX 304/572–1000, ext. 268. 1,250 houses and condos, 302 lodge rooms. Facilities: 11 restaurants, 10 pubs, 4 indoor pools, exercise room, 2 downhill ski areas, golf course, tennis courts. AE, MC, V. $–$$$*

Motel

Sheraton Inn–Martinsburg (301 Foxcroft Ave., Martinsburg 25401, ☎ 304/267–5500, FAX 304/264–9157), 120 rooms, restaurant, coffee shop, lounge, indoor and outdoor pools and tennis courts, health club, parking; *$–$$.*

Spas

For price ranges, see Chart 2 (A) in On the Road with Fodor's.

★ **The Greenbrier.** One of the best hotels in the country, this 6,500-acre spa is done in grand turn-of-the-century style. Massive white columns rise six stories against a white facade, while inside, nine lobbies offer vast, chandeliered common areas. Every guest room is different, decorated in Dorothy Draper pastel prints. Restaurant menus feature such dishes as farm-raised striped bass and rack of lamb. *Off I–64, White Sulphur Springs 24986, ☎ 304/536–1110 or 800/624–6070, FAX 304/536–7854 or 304/536–7834. 700 units. Facilities: 4 dining rooms, lounge, health club, tennis, indoor/outdoor pool, 3 golf courses, horseback riding. AE, DC, MC, V. $$$$*

★ **Coolfont Resort.** Accommodations are in modern chalets, rustic cabins, or lodge rooms. Special programs for losing weight, reducing stress, and stopping smoking are offered. The soup/salad/bread bar is exceptional, as are the daily buffet and the fresh brook trout. *1777 Cold Run Valley Rd., Berkeley Springs 25411, ☎ 304/258–4500 or 800/888–8768, FAX 304/258–5499. 82 units. Facilities: restaurant ($$), lounge, indoor pool, lake, health club, tennis. AE, D, DC, MC, V. $–$$*

Campgrounds

State park camping facilities (*see* State Parks, *above*) and more than 100 commercial campgrounds are listed in a camping booklet (☎ 800/225–5982).

The Arts

West Virginians celebrate everything from potatoes and apple butter to the coming of spring with festivals and fairs (☎ 800/225–5982). Staged at Grandview State Park's **Theatre West Virginia** (☎ 304/256–6800 or 800/666–9142, FAX 304/256–6807) are the state's premier outdoor theatrical productions: *Honey in the Rock,* a Civil War story; *Hatfields and McCoys,* depicting the famous feud; and *Bye Bye Birdie.*

WESTERN WEST VIRGINIA

The Charleston/Huntington area is a center of commerce and culture quite different from the mountain wilderness to the east and the farmland to the north. Skilled craftspeople, such as those who supplied the Kennedy White House with glassware, make their homes in the mid–Ohio River valley. The northern panhandle suffers from steel-industry troubles, but its fine old mansions and Victorian architecture are reminders of better times. Wheeling's Oglebay Park is a cultural and environmental jewel.

Tourist Information

Charleston: Convention and Visitors Bureau (200 Civic Center Dr., 25301, ☎ 304/344–5075 or 800/733–5469, FAX 304/344–1241). **Huntington:** Cabell-Huntington Convention and Visitors Bureau (Box 347, Huntington 25708, ☎ 304/525–7333 or 800/635–6329). **Wheeling:** Convention and Visitors Bureau (1233 Main St., Suite 1000, 26003, ☎ 304/233–7709 or 800/828–3097, FAX 304/233–1320). **Northern West Virginia:** Convention and Visitors Bureau (709 Beechurst Ave., Morgantown 26505, ☎ 304/292–5081 or 800/458–7373, FAX 304/291–1354).

Getting There

By Plane

The region is served by Charleston's **Yeager Airport** (☎ 304/344–8033 or 800/241–6522), Huntington's **Tri-State Airport** (☎ 304/453–6165), Parkersburg's **Wood County Airport** (☎ 304/464–5113), Clarksburg/Fairmont's **Benedum Airport** (☎ 304/842–3400), and the **Morgantown Municipal Airport/Hart Field** (☎ 304/291–7461).

By Car

Major routes into the region are I–64, Charleston to Huntington; Clarksburg to I–77 north–south, Parkersburg to Charleston; I–79 north–south, Clarksburg to Charleston; and I–70, crossing the northern panhandle at Wheeling.

By Train

Amtrak (☎ 800/872–7245) provides service from White Sulphur Springs through Charleston to Huntington.

By Bus

Greyhound Lines (☎ 800/231–2222) has terminals in major towns.

Exploring Western West Virginia

Apart from the Mountain Lakes region, this area is heavily influenced by the Ohio River. Charleston, Parkersburg, and Huntington set an urban tone with museums, shopping malls, and cultural and entertainment centers, but the hustle is balanced by lazy days on the river. Moving north through valley farmland, you can watch glassblowers and other craftspeople at work. The boom and bust of the 1890s is reflected throughout the area in grand mansions and nicely preserved Victorian architecture.

In **Charleston,** the Italian Renaissance **capitol** merits a visit for its massive gilt dome and its 2-ton chandelier of Czechoslovakian crystal. *1900 Kanawha Blvd. E, ☎ 304/558–3809. Closed Sun. Labor Day–Memorial Day; no guided tours on weekends.*

Within the capitol complex is the **Cultural Center** (Greenbrier and Washington Sts., ☎ 304/558–0162), with its marble **Great Hall** and the **State Museum,** which traces West Virginian history.

Overlooking the capitol are the **Sunrise Museums,** two historic mansions that house art galleries, a children's museum, and a planetarium. Outside are gardens and wooded trails. *746 Myrtle Rd.,* ☎ *304/344–8035. Admission charged. Closed Mon.–Tues.*

Downtown are a large civic center and the pleasant **Town Center** shopping area. Eight styles of 19th-century architecture are represented in the **East End Historic District,** bordered by Bradford, Quarrier, and Michigan streets and Kanawha Boulevard.

Charleston takes pride in its waterfront, which bustles the week before Labor Day during the annual Sternwheeler Regatta. The paddle wheeler ***P.A. Denny*** (☎ 304/346–2465 or 304/348–6419) offers cruises year-round.

It takes an hour by I–64 to reach metropolitan **Huntington,** a river and rail town whose streets are lined with stately turn-of-the-century houses, particularly in the **9th Street West Historic District.** There the streets are brick, the houses Victorian frame bordered with wrought-iron fences. The **Huntington Museum of Art** (2033 McCay Rd., ☎ 304/529–2701; admission charged; closed Mon.), the state's largest museum, covers 52 acres and houses a Junior Art Museum, a celestial observatory, an auditorium, and an amphitheater.

Near Huntington, at **Milton,** is the **Blenko Glass Visitor Center and Factory Outlet,** one of more than a dozen handblown-glass factories between Huntington and Parkersburg, to the north. *Exit 28 off I–64 to U.S. 60,* ☎ *304/743–9081. No glassblowing weekends, some holidays.*

Another thriving Ohio River town, **Parkersburg** has many restored turn-of-the-century houses, but its main attraction is **Blennerhassett Island Historic Park and Mansion.** In 1800 Harman Blennerhassett's magnificent island estate was the talk of the Northwest Territory, but he was later arrested with Aaron Burr for treason. Besides the Palladian-style mansion, you can visit a crafts village and take horse-drawn-wagon tours of the island, which is reached aboard a sternwheeler. *Blennerhassett Museum, 2nd and Juliana Sts.,* ☎ *304/428–3000 or 800/225–5982. Admission charged. Museum and island closed Jan.–Apr. and Mon. year-round; island closed Mon.–Wed. Sept. 6–Oct. 30.*

In the heart of the state is the Mountain Lakes region, dotted with prime fishing areas (*see* Sports and the Outdoors, *below*) and a number of Civil War landmarks, such as **Carnifex Ferry Battlefield State Park.** The battle here dashed the South's hopes of controlling the Kanawha Valley. The **Patterson House,** which marked the line between Union and Confederate forces, has been restored as a museum and displays artifacts and a film on the battle. *Rte. 2, Summersville,* ☎ *304/872–0825. Museum closed Labor Day–Memorial Day.*

North of Clarksburg is **Morgantown,** home of **West Virginia University,** where the world's first fully automated transportation system carries students between campuses. There's all the bustle of a college town here, plus 1,700-acre **Cheat Lake,** which is served by three marinas (Blosser's, ☎ 304/594–2541; Edgewater, ☎ 304/594–2630; and Sunset Harbor, ☎ 304/594–1100).

In the northern panhandle, **Wheeling** was once the gateway to the West. Parks, museums, riverboat rides, and a wealth of restored Victorian houses (The Design Co./Eckhart House, ☎ 304/232–5439, and Victorian Wheeling Landmarks Foundation, ☎ 304/233–1600) are reminders of the old days. **Oglebay Park** (☎ 304/242–7272 or 800/624–6988) is a 1,500-acre municipal park/resort with a hotel

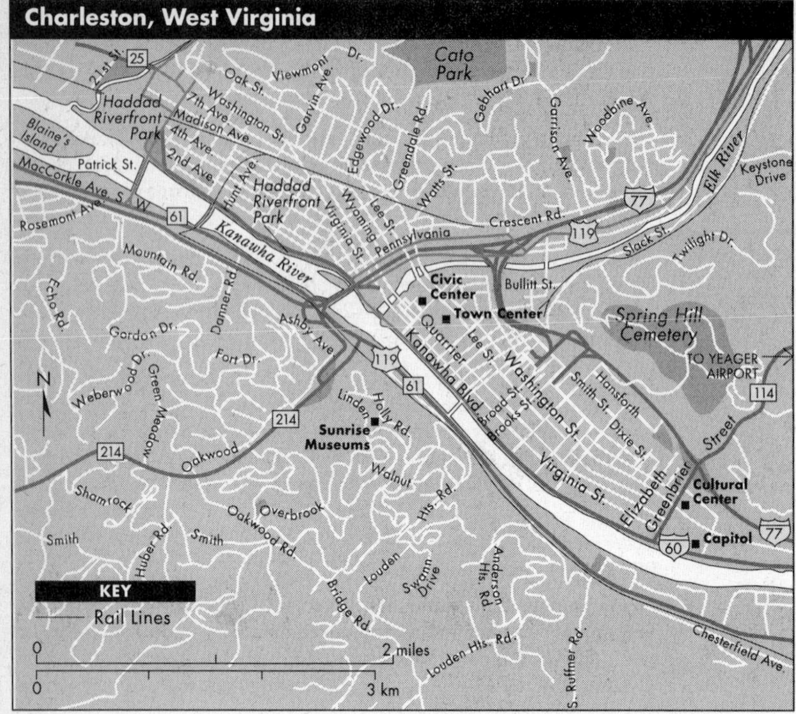

(*see* Dining and Lodging, *below*), a 65-acre zoo, a planetarium, a museum, a swimming pool, and a small ski area (3 lifts, snowmaking).

What to See and Do with Children

Riverboating, fishing, and canoeing are prime attractions in this region. Charleston's **Sunrise Museums** and Wheeling's **Oglebay Park** (*see* Exploring Western West Virginia, *above*) are geared for children.

Shopping

Antiques and native crafts, particularly handblown glass, are abundant in this region. Venues vary from roadside shops to outdoor fairs to sprawling glass-factory outlets (*see* Exploring Western West Virginia, *above*).

Sports and the Outdoors

Canoeing

The area's many lakes (contact the Army Corps of Engineers, ☎ 304/529–5211) are ideal for canoeing.

Fishing

Native trout are abundant in the faster streams and rivers, while bass, crappie, and walleye lurk in the lakes. Licenses are available at sporting and convenience stores. Rafting companies organize fishing trips. **Sutton Lake** (Sutton, ☎ 304/765–2705) and **Stonewall Jackson Lake** (Weston, ☎ 304/269–0523) are prime areas.

Golf

Coonskin Golf Course (Coonskin Dr., Charleston, ☎ 304/341–8000), 18 holes. **Lakeview Resort's Lakeview and Mountainview courses** (Morgantown, ☎ 304/594–1111 or 800/624–8300), 36 holes. **Ogle-**

bay Park's Crispin and Speidel courses (Wheeling, ☎ 304/243-4000 or 800/624-6988), 36 holes. **Twin Falls Resort State Park Golf Course** (Mullens, ☎ 304/294-4000 or 800/225-5982), 18 holes. **Worthington Golf Club** (3414 Roseland Ave., Parkersburg, ☎ 304/428-4297), 18 holes.

Hiking and Backpacking

The **Allegheny Trail** (633 West Virginia Ave., Morgantown 26505, ☎ 304/296-5158) and the **Kanawha Trace** (733 7th Ave., Huntington 25701, ☎ 304/523-3408) pass through state and national forests and wilderness areas with rocky overlooks and thickets of rhododendron and mountain laurel.

Rafting

The white waters of the **Cheat** and **Tygart** rivers flow through this region. More than 50 outfitters (☎ 800/225-5982 for brochures and list of licensed outfitters) guide trips.

Riding

Horseback riding along trails is available in most state parks.

Dining and Lodging

For price ranges, see Charts 1 (B) and 2 (B) in On the Road with Fodor's.

Charleston

DINING

★ **Chilton House.** In a charming Victorian house with seven gables, this restaurant overlooks the Coal River. Menu highlights include oysters Rockefeller, orange roughy with sesame sauce, and steak Diane flambé. *2 6th Ave., St. Albans, ☎ 304/722-2918. AE, D, MC, V. Closed Sun. $$*

Morgantown

DINING AND LODGING

★ **Lakeview Resort and Conference Center.** This country-club-turned-resort sits on a dramatic cliff overlooking Cheat Lake. Comfortable motel-style rooms are accessed by a warren of halls and stairways. Restaurants have lake or golf course views, and the popular lounge features live weekend entertainment. Two golf courses and a $2 million fitness center boost the convention trade. Prime rib and poached salmon are the main attractions in the Reflections on the Lake Restaurant. The Grill Restaurant serves a light healthy fare including soup of the day, chicken or steak salad, and an assortment of sandwiches. *Rte. 6, Box 88A, Morgantown 26505, ☎ 304/594-1111 or 800/624-8300, FAX 304/594-9472. 187 rooms. Facilities: 2 restaurants, lounge, 2 golf courses, 2 pools, lake, fitness and sports center with indoor tennis, racquetball, track. AE, D, DC, MC, V. $$*

Wheeling

LODGING

Oglebay Park. Connected to the rustic lodge, which has a huge, stone-floor lobby and a stone fireplace, are motel-style rooms and once-detached chalets. Nearby cabins sleeping 12 to 20 are rustic outside and ultramodern inside. (*See* Exploring Western West Virginia, *above.*) *Rte. 88N, 26003, ☎ 304/242-7272 or 800/624-6988, FAX 304/243-4070. 204 lodge rooms, 16 suites, 50 deluxe cabins. Facilities: dining room, golf, tennis, swimming, horseback riding, zoo, lake, museum, glass center, festivals. AE, D, DC, MC, V. $$-$$$*

DINING AND LODGING

★ **Stratford Springs.** This historic inn, composed of two turn-of-the-century houses, is secluded on 30 wooded acres. The rooms are Colonial style, with cherry-wood or Amish furniture. Among the restaurants, which cater mainly to nonguests, the formal Stratford Room (jacket and tie required) serves such dishes as stuffed strip steak or baby coho salmon. *355 Oglebay Dr., 26003, ☎ 304/233–5100 or 800/521–8435, FAX 304/232–6447. 3 rooms, 3 suites. Facilities: 4 restaurants, heated pool, athletic center, spa. AE, MC, V. $$–$$$*

Motel

Charleston Marriott (200 Lee St. E, Charleston 25301, ☎ 304/345–6500, FAX 304/353–3722), 354 rooms, restaurant, lounge, indoor pool, health club, tennis; $.

Campgrounds

The state tourism department (*see* Visitor Information, *above*) has listings of commercial campgrounds as well as facilities in more than a dozen state parks.

The Arts

Wheeling's **Capitol Music Hall** (1015 Main St., ☎ 800/624–5456), home of WWVA radio's "Jamboree USA," has live performances by country-music greats and two big-name jamborees in July and August.

5 The Southeast

By Conrad Paulus

FROM PINE TO PALM, lapped by the Atlantic Ocean and the Gulf of Mexico, stretch North and South Carolina, Georgia, Florida, and Alabama. While the world tends to think of southerners as dreaming life away on the veranda, julep in hand, among the magnolias and Spanish moss, still biting the black hand that feeds them, times have changed. Not too long ago nostalgia for times gone by and the Confederacy's lost cause shaped the region's point of view, but nowadays it is clearly dealing in the present, planning for tomorrow, and busily exploiting its plantation past in novels and as movie sets and B&Bs. Surprisingly, perhaps, the Southeast is also the most racially integrated part of the country, and one of the liveliest.

With the exception of Florida, all these states have both mountains (with resorts and sports) and the sea (with beaches and boating); Florida's watery edges are never more than 50 mi away. It's a good thing, too, because the region's temperatures and humidity are fierce, although air-conditioning has transformed the summers.

Post–Civil War poverty prevented much of the tearing down and rebuilding common in the rest of the East and forced people to make do with that outmoded old Chippendale and Sheraton furniture they had hoped to replace with the new machine-made Victorian marvels. Today dozens of Greek Revival mansions containing their original furnishings are open to visitors. The shabby white-columned houses have been restored, and travelers can often sleep in those tall mahogany and walnut beds.

Some of the cities are charmingly old-fashioned; in Savannah and Charleston, Edenton and Mobile, you can wander through houses on shady squares with brick courtyards and gardens of astonishing fecundity. There are modern cities, too—the dynamic Raleigh–Durham–Chapel Hill college triangle; the booming crossroads that is Atlanta; Birmingham, the former steel town that became a medical center; and Miami, now infused with Cuban culture—not to mention Disney World, already in the 21st century.

Food in the Southeast today bears little resemblance to the familiar greasy fare of yore. Having absorbed every cuisine that has come its way, the region is prepared to serve you fancy nouvelle, down-home soul, and spicy Cajun and Caribbean, along with the deep-fried classics. That adaptability is characteristic of a people who really do want to please: this is the basis of southern hospitality. Southerners are an easygoing bunch—talkative, courteous, and witty, with a talent for laughter and enjoying life.

Tour Groups

From the heights of the Blue Ridge Mountains to the Florida marshes, the South offers unparalleled scenic beauty, and the small towns and bustling cities across the region reveal the diverse lifestyles of southern America. Tours of this region are equally varied.

Domenico Tours (751 Broadway, Bayonne, NJ 07002, ☎ 201/823–8687 or 800/554–8687) offers a 10-day tour of Florida's highlights, a 6-day "Orlando Delight" tour, and an 8-day tour of the southeastern states, including Florida. **Gadabout Tours** (700 E. Tahquitz Canyon Way, Palm Springs, CA 92262, ☎ 619/325–5556 or 800/952–5068) takes a 9-day tour of Florida that includes a cruise to the Bahamas. It also offers a 15-day tour of the "Sentimental South," from New Orleans to Savannah and Charleston, and a three-week tour of "Mansions and

Magnolias" during the magnificent southern springtime. **Globus** (5301 S. Federal Circle, Littleton, CO 80123, ☎ 303/797–2800 or 800/221–0090) offers a week-long "Old South" excursion, including Charleston and Hilton Head Island in South Carolina; Savannah, Georgia; and Jacksonville, Florida. Or swing through the "Best of Florida" on a 10-day tour that includes St. Augustine, Miami, Key West, and Orlando and Disney World. For similar Florida tours at bargain prices, check out Globus's budget-minded affiliate, **Cosmos Tourama** (same address). **Maupintour** (Box 807, Lawrence KS 66044, ☎ 913/843–1211 or 800/255–4266) offers 8-day tours of the Carolinas and Georgia. **Talmage Tours** (1223 Walnut St., Philadelphia, PA 19107, ☎ 215/923–7100) has a 6-day tour to Myrtle Beach and Charleston, South Carolina, and a 5-day tour highlighting the sights of Key West, Florida. **Tauck Tours** (11 Wilton Rd., Box 5027, Westport, CT 06881, ☎ 203/226–6911 or 800/468–2825) heads north from Jacksonville, Florida, for an 8-day tour that includes Savannah, Georgia, and Hilton Head and Charleston, South Carolina. Week-long and 10-day tours of Florida resorts and attractions are also available.

When to Go

The best times to visit the South are **spring** and **fall,** when temperatures are in the 70s and 80s. That's when golf and tennis buffs converge on the region en masse. Spring also brings the magnificent azaleas, magnolias, and other flora of the region to life, and visitors come to ooh and aah their way through the gardens and historic homes that traditionally open to the public at this time of year. Fall, when colors reach their peak in the mountains of Alabama, Georgia, and the Carolinas, draws thousands of leaf worshipers. Autumn is a popular season for senior citizens to visit the region, taking advantage of smaller crowds and lower rates in beach and resort areas. **Winter** can be quite pleasant in the Southeast, especially in the more temperate, lower coastal regions of Georgia and Florida. In the higher elevations of western North Carolina and Georgia, temperatures often drop to freezing between mid-November and mid-March, producing ideal conditions for area ski resorts. **Summer** tends to be hot and muggy, with temperatures often soaring into the 90s, especially in Florida and at the lower elevations of Alabama, Georgia, and the Carolinas. That's when "flatlanders" (mountain slang for nonresidents) flock to the mountains to cool off.

Festivals and Seasonal Events

Festivals are a way of life in the Southeast. Even the smallest communities have planned celebrations around offbeat and often obscure themes, such as chitlins, hollering contests, and the woolly worm.

Mid-Jan.: Art Deco Weekend spotlights **Miami Beach**'s historic district with a street fair, a gala, and live entertainment. ☎ *305/539–3000.*

Late Jan.: Bamboleo Festival in **Tampa, Florida,** combines the old Gasparilla and Pirate Fest with a parade and other street festivities celebrating the city's Spanish heritage. ☎ *813/223–1111.*

Mid-Feb.: Mardi Gras in **Mobile, Alabama,** is an uproarious, pre-Lenten celebration similar to its more famous cousin in New Orleans. ☎ *334/434–7304 or 800/252–3862.*

Mid-Mar.: The Aiken (SC) Triple Crown, featuring Thoroughbred trials, harness races, and steeplechases, draws thousands of equestrian enthusiasts. ☎ *803/641–1111.*

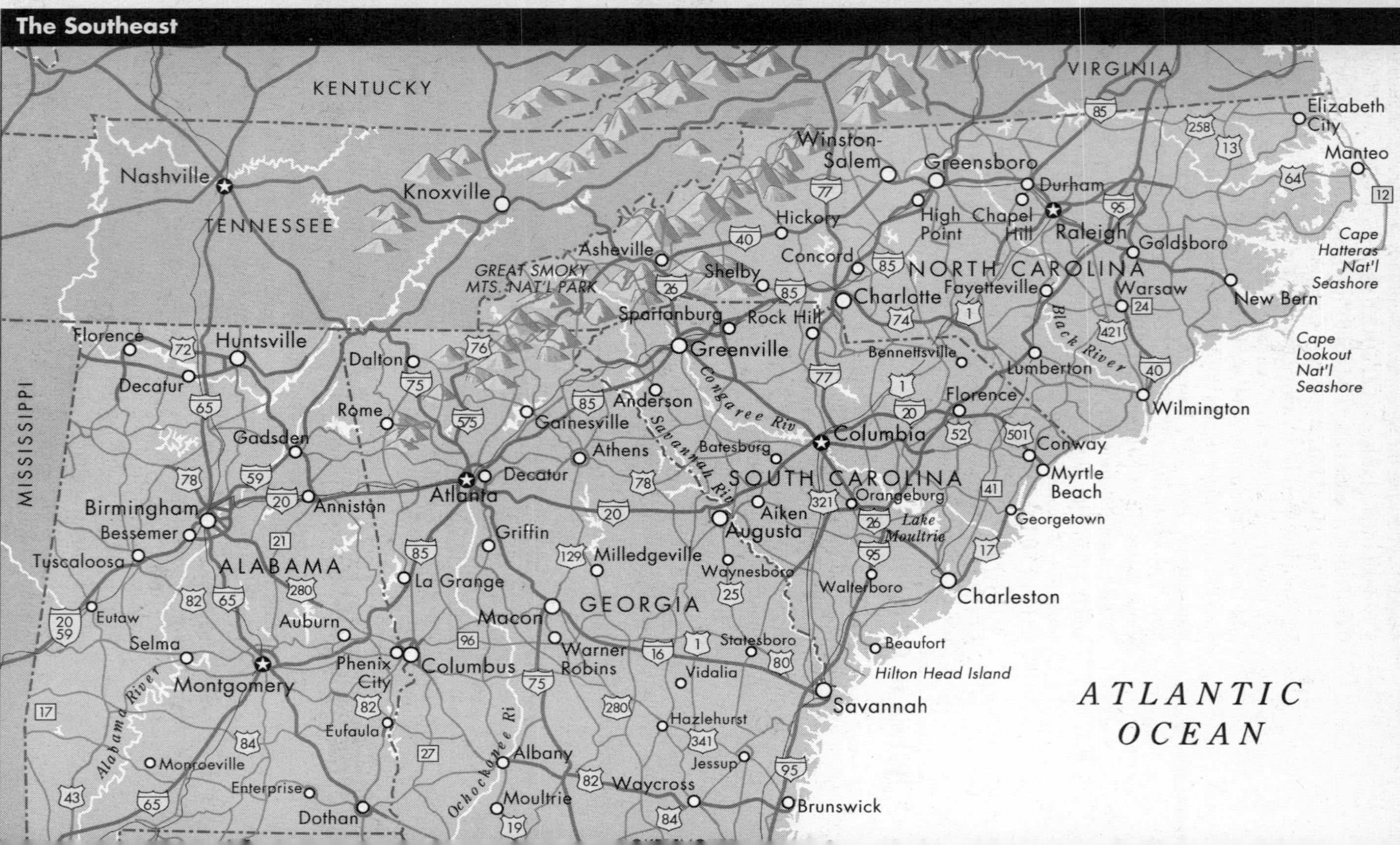
KENTUCKY
VIRGINIA
TENNESSEE
NORTH CAROLINA
SOUTH CAROLINA
GEORGIA
ALABAMA
MISSISSIPPI
ATLANTIC
OCEAN
Nashville
Knoxville
Winston-Salem
Greensboro
Durham
Elizabeth City
Manteo
High Point
Chapel Hill
Raleigh
Goldsboro
Hickory
Asheville
Concord
GREAT SMOKY MTS. NAT'L PARK
Shelby
Charlotte
Fayetteville
Warsaw
New Bern
Cape Hatteras Nat'l Seashore
Cape Lookout Nat'l Seashore
Spartanburg
Rock Hill
Black River
Florence
Huntsville
Dalton
Greenville
Bennettsville
Lumberton
Wilmington
Decatur
Anderson
Florence
Rome
Gainesville
Congaree Riv.
Columbia
Savannah Riv.
Gadsden
Athens
Batesburg
Conway
Myrtle Beach
Decatur
Atlanta
SOUTH CAROLINA
Birmingham
Anniston
Orangeburg
Aiken
Augusta
Lake Moultrie
Georgetown
Bessemer
Griffin
Tuscaloosa
Milledgeville
Waynesboro
Walterboro
Charleston
La Grange
Eutaw
Auburn
Macon
Statesboro
Beaufort
Selma
Warner Robins
Phenix City
Columbus
Vidalia
Hilton Head Island
Montgomery
Savannah
Alabama River
Eufaula
Hazlehurst
Ochlockonee Ri
Albany
Jessup
Monroeville
Enterprise
Waycross
Moultrie
Brunswick
Dothan
85
258
13
64
12
77
95
40
85
26
85
74
1
24
421
72
76
75
77
1
40
65
575
85
20
52
501
59
78
78
20
321
41
21
26
85
129
95
17
280
82
65
25
20
59
96
16
1
80
75
17
82
280
341
84
27
95
82
43
65
19
84

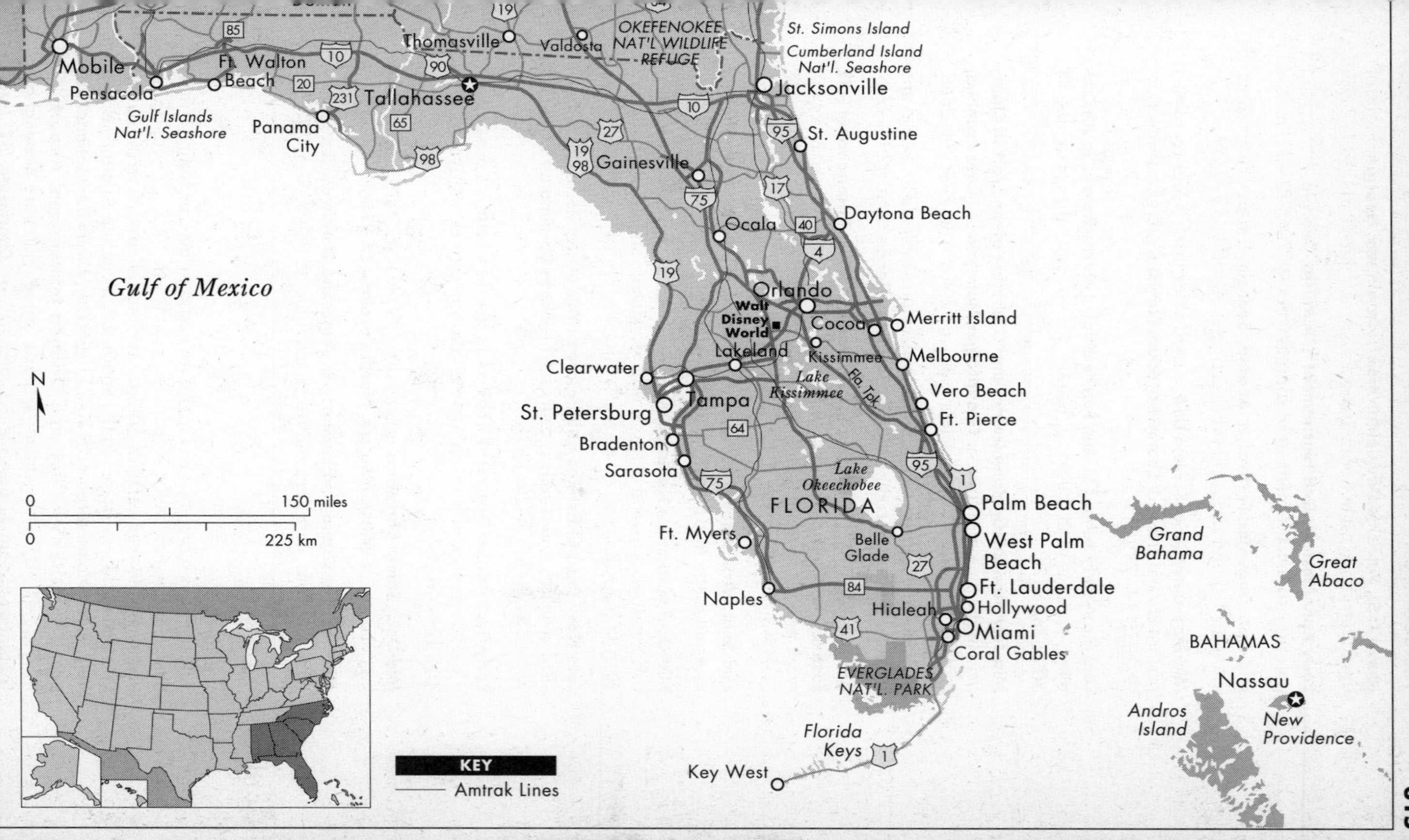
Mobile
Pensacola
Ft. Walton Beach
Gulf Islands Nat'l. Seashore
Panama City
Tallahassee
Thomasville
Valdosta
OKEFENOKEE NAT'L WILDLIFE REFUGE
St. Simons Island
Cumberland Island Nat'l. Seashore
Jacksonville
St. Augustine
Gainesville
Daytona Beach
Ocala
Gulf of Mexico
Orlando
Walt Disney World
Cocoa
Merritt Island
Lakeland
Kissimmee
Melbourne
Clearwater
Lake Kissimmee
Fla. Tpk.
Vero Beach
St. Petersburg
Tampa
Ft. Pierce
Bradenton
Sarasota
Lake Okeechobee
FLORIDA
Palm Beach
West Palm Beach
Ft. Myers
Belle Glade
Grand Bahama
Great Abaco
Ft. Lauderdale
Naples
Hollywood
Hialeah
Miami
Coral Gables
BAHAMAS
EVERGLADES NAT'L. PARK
Nassau
Andros Island
New Providence
Florida Keys
Key West
N
0
150 miles
0
225 km
KEY
Amtrak Lines
85
10
90
20
231
65
10
27
95
19 98
98
75
17
40
4
19
64
95
1
75
27
84
41
1

Mar. 17: St. Patrick's Day Celebration in **Savannah, Georgia,** is one of the country's largest honoring Ireland's patron saint. ☎ *800/444–2427.*

Early Apr.: Master's Golf Tournament in **Augusta, Georgia,** attracts top golf pros to this tournament of tournaments. ☎ *706/721–3276.*

Mid-Apr.: Dogwood Festival, in **Atlanta, Georgia,** features an art show, a hot-air balloon race, and other activities. ☎ *404/952–9151.*

Mid-May–early June: Spoleto USA, a festival featuring world-renowned performers and artists in **Charleston, South Carolina,** gets global attention. ☎ *803/724–7395.*

Late May–early June: The **Sun Fun Festival** in **Myrtle Beach, South Carolina,** features sand sculpting, beauty queens, and other activities. ☎ *803/626–8374.*

Mid-July: Annual Highland Games and Gathering of the Scottish Clans, held in the high meadows of **Grandfather Mountain in North Carolina,** is one of the largest Scottish celebrations in the world. ☎ *704/588–2660.*

Mid-July: The Hemingway Days Festival features look-alike contests and play and short-story competitions in **Key West, Florida.** ☎ *305/294–4265.*

Late July–early Aug.: Folkmoot USA: North Carolina International Folk Festival, held in **Haywood County** and surrounding areas over a two-week period, features dancers and singers from around the globe. ☎ *704/588–2660.*

Mid-Sept.: Arts Festival of Atlanta, held over nine days, is the largest arts and crafts festival in the Southeast. ☎ *404/885–1125.*

Mid-Oct.: Alabama's National Shrimp Festival, held in **Gulf Shores,** features seafood, arts and crafts, music, sky divers, and hot-air balloons. ☎ *800/745–7263.*

Late Nov.–Dec.: Christmas at Biltmore brings festive decorations, musical concerts, and candlelit tours to this **North Carolina** estate for six weeks. ☎ *800/543–2961.*

Early Dec.: Atlanta Festival of Trees celebrates the Christmas season with a parade and exhibit of elaborately decorated trees and wreaths. ☎ *404/325–6635.*

Mid-Dec.: Salem Christmas is celebrated in the restored Moravian village section of **Winston-Salem, North Carolina.** ☎ *910/721–7331.*

Mid-Dec.: The **Grand Illumination** in **St. Augustine, Florida,** features torch-lit processions, caroling, and other activities. ☎ *904/829–5681.*

Getting Around

By Plane

The region is served by most major domestic airlines, including American, Continental, Delta, Northwest, Southwest, TWA, United, USAir, and several foreign carriers. Some of the busiest airports in the nation and the world are located in the Southeast, including Atlanta's **Hartsfield International Airport** (☎ 404/530–6600), **Miami International Airport** (☎ 305/876–7000), and **Orlando International Airport** (☎ 407/825–2001). Other major airports in the region are **Birmingham (AL) International Airport** (☎ 205/595–0533), **Charleston (SC) International Airport** (☎ 803/767–1100), and **Charlotte–Douglas (NC) International Airport** (☎ 704/359–4000).

By Car

More than a dozen interstate highways, including I–10, I–16, I–20, I–26, I–40, I–59, I–65, I–75, I–77, I–85, and I–95, crisscross the Southeast, linking major cities and providing easy access to other parts of the country. In some cases, interstates and federal highways, such as U.S. 1 along the Florida Keys, link the region's many islands to the mainland. In other cases, ferries (*see* By Boat, *below*) are the only means of transport. Scenic highways include South Carolina's Foothills Parkway and the Blue Ridge Parkway, the latter traversing the Virginia and North Carolina mountains. Interstate and federal highways are usually well maintained; some secondary roads are narrow, a few unpaved, and in mountain sections often very curvy.

By Train

Amtrak (☎ 800/872–7245) provides service to major southern cities, including Charlotte, North Carolina; Charleston and Columbia, South Carolina; Atlanta and Savannah, Georgia; Miami and Orlando, Florida; and Birmingham and Mobile, Alabama.

By Bus

The major intercity carrier is **Greyhound Lines** (☎ 800/231–2222).

By Boat

Traveling by boat along the Southeast's extensive waterways and rivers is quite a popular (and, in some cases, essential) mode of transportation. The **Intracoastal Waterway,** which extends from New England around Florida to the Gulf of Mexico, is filled with north–south traffic, and many of the region's major rivers are navigable. Ferries connect major islands and the mainlands of Alabama, the Carolinas, Georgia, and Florida. For more information on waterways and ferry schedules, contact the highway departments of individual states.

ALABAMA

Updated by Dick Pivetz

Capital	Montgomery
Population	4,110,426
Motto	We Dare Defend Our Rights
State Bird	Yellowhammer
State Flower	Camellia

Visitor Information

Alabama Bureau of Tourism and Travel (401 Adams Ave., Box 4309, Montgomery 36103, ☎ 334/242–4169 or 800/252–2262). **Welcome centers:** I–59, at Valley Head and at Cuba; I–65, at Elkmont; I–10, at Robertsdale and at Grand Bay; I–20, at Heflin; I–85, at Valley; U.S. 231, at Slocomb.

Scenic Drives

Lookout Mountain Parkway is a 100-mi scenic stretch in northeast Alabama, encompassing Rtes. 117, 89, and 176; markers indicate routes for side trips to Little River Canyon, De Soto Falls, and Yellow Creek Falls. Maps are available at the welcome center off I–59 near the Georgia state line (☎ 205/635–6522). In and around Mobile, the well-marked **Azalea Trail** twines for 27 mi; the blooms are at their best in March and April.

State Parks

Alabama's 24 state parks include a wide variety of recreational activities and lodging accommodations. Visitors have the choice of resort lodges, hotels, campgrounds, chalets, and cabins, both modern and rustic. Several parks have marinas, golf courses, and tennis facilities. **Desoto State Park,** in northern Alabama, has the spectacular Little River Canyon and falls. Not far away is **Lake Guntersville State Park,** home of the annual Eagle Awareness programs. **Gulf State Park** near Gulf Shores has one of the most popular beach areas along the Alabama coast. Contact **Alabama State Parks** (64 N. Union St., Folsom Administrative Bldg., Suite 547, Montgomery 36130, ☎ 800/252–7275) for reservations or information on Alabama's state parks.

THE HIGHLANDS AND PLANTATION COUNTRY

This region encompasses the hilly Highlands around Birmingham, the state's largest city, and the antebellum history of the state capital, Montgomery, 90 mi south of Birmingham.

Tourist Information

Birmingham: Convention and Visitors Bureau (2200 9th Ave. N, 35203-1100, ☎ 205/252–9825 or 800/962–6453). **Montgomery:** Area Chamber of Commerce (41 Commerce St., 36104, ☎ 334/834–5200). Visitors Center (401 Madison Ave., 36104, ☎ 334/262–0013).

Getting There

By Plane

Major domestic airlines serve **Birmingham International Airport** (☎ 205/595–0533) and Montgomery's **Dannelly Field** (☎ 334/281–5040).

By Car

I–59 runs northeast from Birmingham into Georgia and Tennessee and southwest into Mississippi. I–20 runs east–west through the city. I–65 is the north–south route connecting Birmingham with Montgomery. I–85 leads southwest from Atlanta to Montgomery.

By Train

Amtrak (☎ 800/872–7245) serves Birmingham on the *Crescent* route and Mobile on the *Sunset Limited.*

By Bus

Greyhound Lines (619 N. 19th St., ☎ 800/231–2222 in Birmingham; 210 S. Court St., ☎ 800/231–2222 in Montgomery) serves major towns in the region.

Exploring the Highlands and Plantation Country

Birmingham blossomed with the rise of coal mines and the iron industry in the 19th century. Today its largest employer is the University of Alabama at Birmingham, home to one of the country's largest medical centers. The city has restored many of its 19th-century buildings and is a hospitable and beautiful metropolis.

The **Birmingham Museum of Art,** the Southeast's largest municipal museum, completed a $20 million renovation in 1993. The permanent collection has some 15,000 works, from Italian early Renaissance right up to Contemporary American. *8th Ave. and 20th St. N, ☎ 205/254–2565. Closed Mon.*

The **Alabama Sports Hall of Fame Museum** (corner of 22nd St. N and Civic Center Blvd., ☎ 205/323–6665), in the Civic Center, displays memorabilia of such Alabama athletic heroes as coach Bear Bryant, Jesse Owens, Willie Mays, and Hank Aaron. The Kelly Ingram Park area, southwest of the center, includes the **16th Street Baptist Church** (16th St. and 6th Ave. N, ☎ 205/251–9402), a civil rights landmark. Here numerous protests were staged during the 1960s, and four children lost their lives when a bomb exploded in 1963; a plaque in their memory was erected here. Across the street is the **Birmingham Civil Rights Institute** (6th Ave. and 16th St. N, ☎ 205/328–9696), which uses exhibits, multimedia presentations, music, and oral histories to document the civil rights movement from the 1920s to the present.

Two blocks away is the **Jazz Hall of Fame,** which has photos and memorabilia of the state's jazz greats, including Erskine Hawkins, Cleveland Eaton, and Dr. Frank Adams. *4th Ave. and 16th St. N, ☎ 205/254–2720. Admission charged. Closed Mon.*

Heading back east via 1st Avenue North, look for signs for **Sloss Furnaces.** The massive ironworks plant used ore dug from the hills around Birmingham between 1882 and 1971. Guided tours through this National Historic Landmark are given on Saturday. *1st Ave. N and 32nd St., ☎ 205/324–1911. Closed Mon.*

South on U.S. 31 is the **Red Mountain Museum** (1421 22nd St. S, ☎ 205/939–1176), which displays samples of the rocks, fossils, and minerals found in the area. South of the museum, sitting atop Red Mountain, is **Vulcan** (Valley Ave. at U.S. 31S, ☎ 205/328–6198; admission charged), the world's tallest cast-iron statue. From the enclosed observation deck at the base, you'll have a wonderful view of the city.

Forty miles from the city (head southeast on U.S. 280 to Childersburg, then east on Rte. 76) is **De Soto Caverns,** a network of onyx caves used as a Native American burial ground 2,000 years ago. Rediscovered by Spanish explorer Hernando de Soto in 1540, the caverns later served as a Confederate gunpowder mining center and a Prohibition speakeasy. Tours of the stalagmite and stalactite formations end with a sound, water, and laser-light show in the 12-story-high Great Onyx Cathedral. ☎ *205/378–7252 or 800/933–2283. Admission charged.*

Southwest of Childersburg, near Mountain Creek off U.S. 31, is **Confederate Memorial Park,** with a museum containing Civil War memorabilia and cemeteries where more than 300 Confederate veterans and their wives are buried. *437 County Rd. 63, Marbury 36051,* ☎ *205/755–1990.*

Montgomery, 90 mi south of Birmingham via I–65, is a city steeped in antebellum history. Today many of its old houses have been restored, and the city has become known as a cultural capital of the South. The **visitors center** (*see* Tourist Information, *above*) shows a brief slide presentation on the city; you can park your car here and visit many attractions on foot.

The handsome **State Capitol** (Bainbridge St. at Dexter Ave., ☎ 334/242–3184) reopened in 1993, following extensive restorations. Built in 1851, it served as the first capitol for the Confederate States of America. One block west is the **Dexter Avenue King Memorial Baptist Church** (☎ 334/263–3970), where Dr. Martin Luther King, Jr., began his career as a minister in 1955; a mural in the basement depicts people and events associated with the civil rights movement. At the corner of Washington Avenue and Union Street stands the first **White House of the Confederacy** (☎ 334/242–1861). Built in 1835, it contains many items that belonged to Jefferson Davis, the Confederate president, as well as Civil War artifacts.

At 400 Washington Avenue, in front of the Southern Poverty Law Center, is the **Civil Rights Memorial** (☎ 334/264–0286). Created by Maya Lin, designer of the Vietnam Veterans' Memorial in Washington, D.C., it features a plaza and a pool from which water flows over a 40-ft black granite wall. Inscribed on the wall are excerpts from Dr. Martin Luther King's "I have a dream . . ." speech. On the adjacent table are the names of many who gave their lives to the civil rights movement.

What to See and Do with Children

The **Birmingham Zoo** (2630 Cahaba Rd., ☎ 205/879–0408; admission charged) is one of the Southeast's largest zoos, with 800 animals. At **Discovery Place** (1421 22nd St. S, ☎ 205/939–1176; admission charged) children can try on firefighter's, police officer's, and ambulance driver's uniforms, "drive" a bus, and learn about science.

Shopping

Birmingham's **Riverchase Galleria** (☎ 205/985–3039), at the intersection of I–459 and U.S. 31S, is one of the largest shopping malls in the Southeast, with at least 200 stores. In **Boaz,** about 75 mi northwest of Birmingham, there are more than 140 outlet stores.

Dining and Lodging

Throughout Alabama, especially north of Mobile, Old South dishes—fried chicken, barbecue, roast beef, country-fried steak—prevail, though in recent years a number of upscale restaurants have opened in Birmingham and Montgomery. In Birmingham, hotels and motels offer weekend specials but are often crowded during football season; the same holds true in Montgomery when the state legislature is in session. For price ranges, see Charts 1 (B) and 2 (B) in On the Road with Fodor's.

Birmingham

DINING

★ **Highlands: A Bar and Grill.** Grand gourmet feasts prepared by owner-chef Frank Stitt are served in a sophisticated setting, accented with fine paintings and brass. Delicacies include fillet of sole with wine sauce; quail with raspberry sauce; and tomatoes stuffed with chunks of lobster, crab, shrimp, and corn. *2011 11th Ave. S, ☎ 205/939–1400. Reservations for dinner only. AE, MC, V. Closed Sun.–Mon. $$$*

Cobb Lane. This quaint restaurant dating from 1948 offers courtyard dining with cherry laurel trees and fountains. Walls are painted by French and local artists. Specialties include she-crab soup and chocolate roulade. There's also an antiques shop. *1 Cobb La., ☎ 205/933–0462. AE, D, MC, V. $$*

Ollie's Barbecue. Ollie's has been a Birmingham tradition since 1926 and is operated today by a fourth-generation member of the McClung family. The sauce is shipped worldwide. Save room for the homemade chocolate pie. *University Blvd., ☎ 205/324–9485. D, MC, V. $*

LODGING

★ **Tutwiler.** This National Historic Landmark was built in 1913 as luxury apartments and converted into a hotel in 1987. The elegant lobby has marble floors, chandeliers, antiques, and lots of flowers; guest rooms are furnished with antique reproductions. *Park Pl. at 21st St. N, 35203, ☎ 205/322–2100 or 800/845–1787, FAX 205/325–1183. 96 rooms, 53 suites. Facilities: restaurant, pub, reading room, use of nearby YMCA. AE, D, DC, MC, V. $$$*

Wynfrey Hotel. This deluxe hotel rises 15 stories above the Riverchase Galleria. The lobby is elegant, with an Italian marble floor, Chippendale furniture, an Oriental rug, an enormous floral arrangement, and a brass escalator. Rooms are furnished in English and French traditional styles. *1000 Riverchase Galleria (U.S. 31S), 35244, ☎ 205/987–1600 or 800/476–7006, FAX 205/987–9552. 329 rooms, 19 suites. Facilities: restaurant, café, lounge, health club, pool, whirlpool. AE, D, DC, MC, V. $$$*

Mountain Brook Inn. This eight-story glass-walled hotel at the foot of Red Mountain features a marble-floor lobby and bi-level suites with spiral staircases and Oriental decor. *2800 U.S. 280, 35223, ☎ 205/870–3100 or 800/523–7771, FAX 205/870–5938. 162 rooms, 8 suites. Facilities: restaurant, lounge, pool. AE, D, DC, MC, V. $$*

Montgomery

DINING

★ **Sahara Restaurant.** At Montgomery's finest restaurant, Joe and Mike Deep carry on a family tradition of friendly service. The snapper and scampi are broiled to taste, and the steaks are charbroiled. *511 E. Edgemont Ave., ☎ 334/262–1215. AE, D, DC, MC, V. Closed Sun. $$$*

Jubilee Seafood Company. In a small café setting you'll find some of the finest and freshest seafood in town. *1057 Woodley Rd., Cloverdale*

Plaza, ☎ 334/262–6224. No reservations. AE, DC, MC, V. Closed Sun.–Mon. $$

Chris' Dog Stand. A Montgomery tradition for more than 75 years, this small eatery is always busy at lunchtime. Mr. Chris's famous sauce contains chile peppers, onions, and a variety of herbs that give his hot dogs a one-of-a-kind flavor. *138 Dexter Ave., ☎ 334/265–6850. No reservations. No credit cards. Closed Sun. $*

LODGING

Madison Hotel. Elvis Presley slept here, but you're more likely to run into legislators and businessmen than rock stars at this downtown hotel. The six-story atrium lobby is filled with lush greenery and fountains. Rooms were remodeled in 1993 and 1994. *120 Madison Ave., 36104, ☎ 334/264–2231 or 800/228–5586, FAX 334/263–3179. 184 rooms, 6 suites. Facilities: 2 restaurants, 2 lounges, pool. AE, D, DC, MC, V. $$$*

Red Bluff Cottage. In this delightful cottage in the heart of downtown, guests can eat breakfast in the dining room or on a veranda overlooking the Alabama River. Rooms have ceiling fans and are furnished with antiques. There's a sitting room with fireplace and a music room/library where guests frequently congregate. *551 Clay St., 36104, ☎ 334/263–0056. 4 rooms. MC, V. $$*

Motels

Hampton Inn (1401 East Blvd., Montgomery 36117, ☎ 334/277–2400 or 800/426–7866), 105 rooms, 1 suite, pool; *$*. **Motel Birmingham** (7905 Crestwood Blvd., Birmingham 35210, ☎ 205/956–4440 or 800/338–9275, FAX 205/956–3011), 242 rooms, Continental breakfast, pool; *$*.

The Arts

In Montgomery, at the world-class **Alabama Shakespeare Festival** (Eastern By-Pass exit off I–85, ☎ 334/271–5353), Shakespearean plays, contemporary dramas and comedies, and musicals are performed on two stages.

MOBILE AND THE GULF COAST

In Mobile, a busy port and one of the oldest cities in Alabama, antebellum buildings survive as a bridge to the treasured past, and azaleas bloom in profusion each spring. The country's first Mardi Gras was created here, and today the city still glories in its pre-Lenten parades and merrymaking. South of Mobile, across the bay, the area around Gulf Shores encompasses 50 mi of white sandy beaches, including those on Pleasure and Dauphin islands. The eastern shore of Mobile Bay has the laid-back atmosphere of the past, with live oaks laced with Spanish moss and sprawling clapboard houses with wide porches overlooking the bay.

Tourist Information

Alabama Gulf Coast Area: Convention and Visitors Bureau (Hwy. 59, 3150 Gulf Shores Pkwy., Drawer 457, Gulf Shores 36542, ☎ 800/745–7263). **Mobile:** Department of Tourism (150 S. Royal St., 36602, ☎ 800/252–3862). **Orange Beach:** Chamber of Commerce (Hwy. 182, Drawer 399, 36561, ☎ 334/981–8000).

Getting There

By Plane

Mobile Regional Airport (☎ 334/633–0313) is served by most major domestic carriers, as is Florida's **Pensacola Regional Airport** (☎ 904/433–7800), 40 mi east of Gulf Shores.

By Car

I–10 leads west from Florida to Mobile and continues into Mississippi. I–65 leads south from Birmingham and Montgomery and ends at Mobile. Gulf Shores is connected with Mobile via I–10 and Rte. 59; Rtes. 180 and 182 are the main beach routes.

By Train

Amtrak (☎ 800/872–7245) connects Mobile with the east and west coasts on the *Sunset Limited.*

By Bus

Greyhound Lines (☎ 800/231–2222) has stations in Mobile (2545 Government Blvd.) and Pensacola, Florida (505 W. Burgess Rd.).

Exploring Mobile and the Gulf Coast

In 1711, Ft. Condé was the name the French gave to what would become **Mobile.** (Indeed, the city's French origins survive in its Creole cuisine.) **Ft. Condé,** too, survives, thanks to a $2.2 million restoration. One hundred fifty years after it was destroyed, remains of the fort were discovered during construction of the I–10 interchange. A reconstructed portion houses the city's **visitor center,** as well as a museum and several re-created rooms. Costumed guides conduct tours. *150 S. Royal St.,* ☎ *334/434–7304 or 800/252–3862.*

At the visitor center you can also get information on the major annual events hosted by Mobile, the biggest of which is **Mardi Gras,** featuring balls, parties, and parades. The **Azalea Trail Festival** is held March through April, depending upon when blooms peak. The **Historic Mobile Homes Tour** in March opens private homes for tours.

One and a half miles from Ft. Condé is **Oakleigh** (350 Oakleigh Pl., ☎ 334/432–1281; admission charged). The high-ceilinged, half-timbered mansion, built between 1833 and 1838, showcases fine period furniture, portraits, silver, jewelry, kitchen implements, toys, and more. Tickets include a tour of neighboring **Cox–Deasy House,** an 1850s cottage furnished with simple 19th-century pieces.

The battleship USS ***Alabama*** is anchored in Mobile Bay, east of the city. A tour gives a fascinating glimpse into the operation of the World War II vessel, which had a crew of 2,500. Anchored next to it is the USS *Drum,* a World War II submarine. Other exhibits in the 100-acre **Battleship Park** include the B–52 bomber *Calamity Jane* and a P–51 Mustang fighter plane. *Battleship Pkwy.,* ☎ *334/433–2703. Admission and parking fee charged.*

Southwest of here via I–10 lies **Bellingrath Gardens and Home,** site of one of the world's most magnificent azalea gardens. Here, amid a 905-acre semitropical landscape, 65 acres of gardens bloom in all seasons: 200 species of azaleas in spring, 3,000 rosebushes in summer, 60,000 chrysanthemum plants in autumn, and fields of poinsettias in winter. The one-time home of Coca-Cola bottling pioneer Walter D. Bellingrath, who started the gardens with his wife in 1917, offers one of the finest collections of antiques in the Southeast and also appears

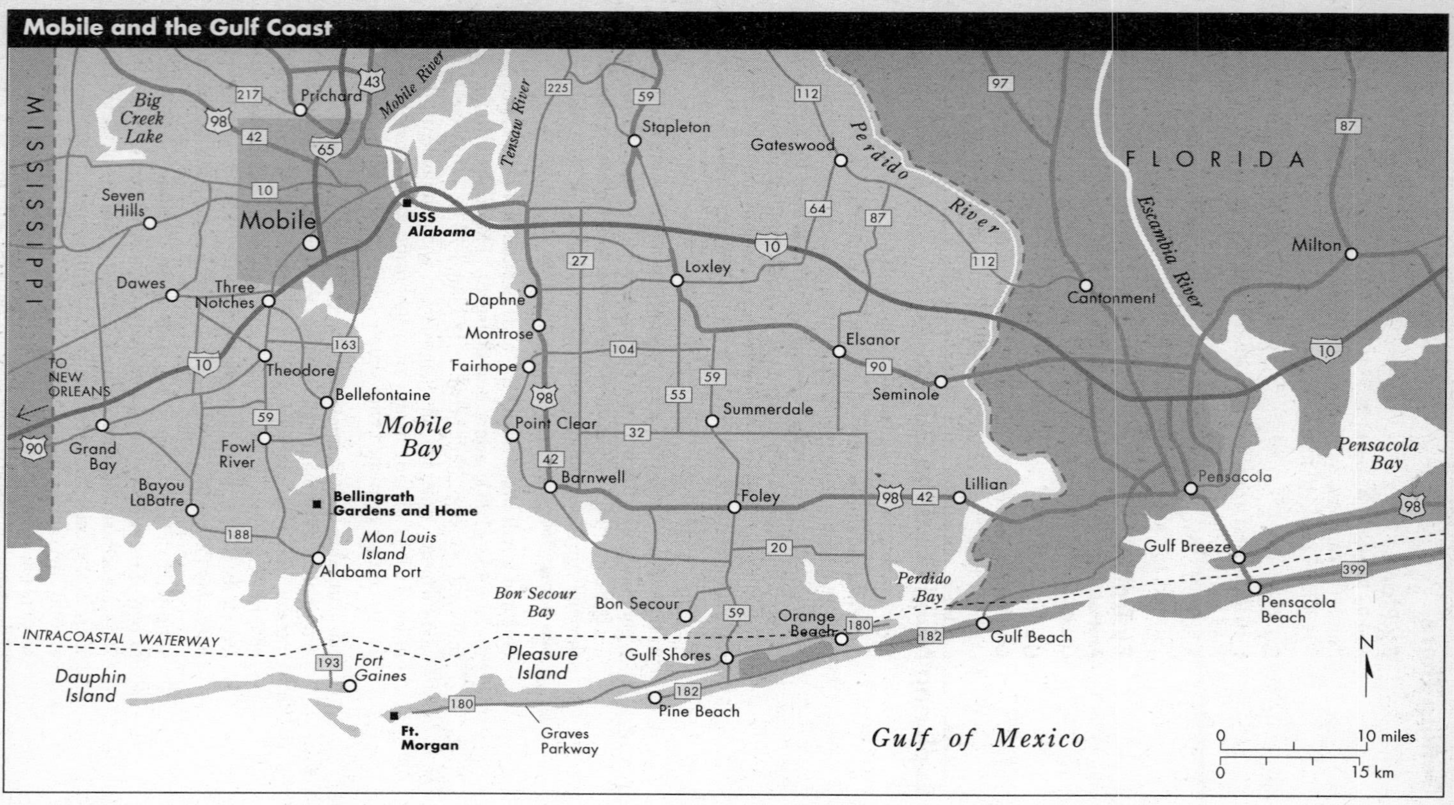
Mobile and the Gulf Coast
MISSISSIPPI
FLORIDA
Big Creek Lake
Prichard
Mobile River
Tensaw River
Stapleton
Gateswood
Perdido River
Escambia River
Milton
Seven Hills
Mobile
USS Alabama
Loxley
Cantonment
Dawes
Three Notches
Daphne
Montrose
Fairhope
Elsanor
Seminole
TO NEW ORLEANS
Theodore
Bellefontaine
Mobile Bay
Point Clear
Summerdale
Pensacola Bay
Grand Bay
Fowl River
Bayou LaBatre
Barnwell
Foley
Lillian
Pensacola
Bellingrath Gardens and Home
Mon Louis Island
Alabama Port
Gulf Breeze
Perdido Bay
Pensacola Beach
Bon Secour Bay
Bon Secour
Orange Beach
Gulf Beach
INTRACOASTAL WATERWAY
Fort Gaines
Pleasure Island
Gulf Shores
Dauphin Island
Pine Beach
Ft. Morgan
Graves Parkway
Gulf of Mexico
N
0 10 miles
0 15 km
217
98
42
43
65
10
225
59
112
97
87
64
27
163
104
90
55
32
20
182
180
193
188
399

on the National Register of Historic Places. *12401 Bellingrath Gardens Rd., Theodore, 36582,* ☎ *334/973–2217. Admission charged.*

From here you may continue south on Rte. 193 toward the Gulf or return to Mobile and take I–10 and Rte. 59S to **Gulf Shores,** a family-oriented beach area with hotels, restaurants, and attractions. There's ample free parking along the white-as-snow beach, though the traffic is bumper-to-bumper at peak times. At the western tip of **Pleasure Island,** 20 mi west of Gulf Shores at the end of Rte. 180, is **Ft. Morgan** (Mobile Point, ☎ 334/540–7125; admission charged), built in the early 1800s to guard the entrance to Mobile Bay. In 1864, Confederate torpedoes sank the ironclad *Tecumseh,* on which Admiral David Farragut commanded, "Damn the torpedoes! Full speed ahead!"

Sports and the Outdoors

Biking

Gulf State Park Resort (☎ 800/252–7275) in Gulf Shores rents bikes.

Canoeing

Sunshine Canoe Rentals (☎ 334/344–8664) runs canoe trips at Escatawpa River, 15 mi west of Mobile. The river has no rapids, so you travel at a leisurely pace past lots of white sandbars.

Fishing

Fishing here is excellent. In Gulf Shores, **Gulf State Park** (*see* State Parks, *above*) has fishing from an 825-ft pier; you can also rent flat-bottom boats for lake fishing. Deep-sea fishing from charter boats is very popular; Gulf Shores has the ***Moreno Queen*** (☎ 334/981–8499), which offers four- and six-hour fishing trips. Nearby **Orange Beach** has 90 charter boats from which to choose. You can obtain a fishing license from most bait shops. For more information, contact the **Department of Conservation and Natural Resources** (☎ 334/242–3829).

Water Sports

In Orange Beach, **Fun Marina** (☎ 334/981–8587) rents Jet Skis, pontoon boats, and 16-ft bay-fishing boats. In Gulf Shores, **Island Recreation Services** (☎ 334/948–7334) rents Jet Skis, bikes, mopeds, body boards, surf boats, and sailboats.

Dining and Lodging

In Mobile and throughout the Gulf area, the specialty is fresh seafood, often prepared Creole style, with peppery spices, crabmeat dressing, and sometimes a tomato-based sauce. The area's hotels and motels are comfortable and varied, offering the traveler the particular hospitality of the region alongside the comforts and amenities of the bigger, nationwide chain hotels. For price ranges, see Charts 1 (B) and 2 (B) in On the Road with Fodor's.

Gulf Shores

DINING

★ **Original Oyster House.** Dining at this plant-filled restaurant overlooking the bayou has become a local tradition. Oysters on the half-shell, plucked fresh from nearby Perdido Bay, are the specialty of the house. The Cajun-style gumbo—a concoction of crab claws, shrimp, amberjack, grouper, redfish, okra and other vegetables, and Cajun spices—has won 20 culinary awards. *Bayou Village Shopping Center, Hwy. 59,* ☎ *334/948–2445. No reservations. AE, D, DC, MC, V. $$–$$$*

LODGING

Gulf Shores Plantation. This 320-acre family resort, 8 mi east of Ft. Morgan on the Gulf, offers condominiums with fully equipped kitchens in high rises overlooking the beach. Abundant recreational activities are available. *Rte. 180W, Box 1299, 36547,* ☎ *334/540–2291 or 800/554–0344,* FAX *334/540–6050. 519 units. Facilities: 2 restaurants, lounge, indoor and outdoor pools, 8 tennis courts, 18-hole golf course, other sports facilities, gift shop. MC, V. $$–$$$*

Mobile

DINING

★ **La Louisiana.** At this antiques-filled old house on the outskirts of town the seafood is fresh. *2400 Airport Blvd.,* ☎ *334/476–8130. AE, D, DC, MC, V. Closed Sun. No lunch. $$$*

Roussos. Just across the street from Ft. Condé, this is one of the most popular seafood restaurants in the Mobile area. The outstanding service; the comfortable, family atmosphere; and the excellent seafood—served fried, broiled, or Greek style—make Roussos a fun place. *166 S. Royal St.,* ☎ *334/433–3322. AE, D, DC, MC, V. $$*

LODGING

Radisson Admiral Semmes Hotel. The hotel is popular with local politicians and party goers, the latter for its excellent location directly on the Mardi Gras parade route. Rooms are furnished in Queen Anne and Chippendale styles. *251 Government St., 36602,* ☎ *334/432–8000 or 800/333–3333,* FAX *432–8000, ext. 7111. 147 rooms, 22 suites. Facilities: restaurant, lounge, pool, whirlpool. AE, D, DC, MC, V. $$$*

Malaga Inn. A delightful, romantic getaway, the Malaga has a lobby furnished with 19th-century antiques and opening onto a tropically landscaped central courtyard with a fountain. The rooms are large, airy, and furnished with massive antiques. *359 Church St., 36602,* ☎ *334/438–4701 or 800/235–1586,* FAX *334/438–4701. 40 rooms. Facilities: restaurant, lounge, outdoor pool. AE, D, MC, V. $–$$*

Orange Beach

DINING

Dempsey's Restaurant. The tropical setting at this lakeside dining room is enhanced by a 20-ft waterfall. Cajun seafood specialties are temptingly arranged at the daily all-you-can-eat dinner buffet, which includes such dishes as stuffed jumbo shrimp. Blues is played nightly, and there's a small dance floor. *Rte. 182,* ☎ *334/981–6800. No reservations. AE, D, MC, V. $$*

★ **Hazel's Family Restaurant.** This plain family-style restaurant, with full menu, serves a good, hearty breakfast (the biscuits are famous), soup-and-salad lunches, and buffet dinners with such seafood dishes as flounder Florentine. There is also a self-service soft-ice-cream bar. *Gulf View Square Shopping Center, Rte. 182,* ☎ *334/981–4628. No reservations. AE, D, MC, V. $*

LODGING

★ **Original Romar House.** This unassuming beach cottage is full of surprises—from the Caribbean-style upstairs sitting area to the Purple Parrot Bar to the luxurious art deco–style guest rooms. In the evening, wine and cheese are served. *23500 Perdido Beach Blvd., Orange Beach 36561,* ☎ *334/981–6156 or 800/487–6627. 6 rooms. Facilities: full breakfast, hot tub, tandem bicycle, beach adjacent. MC, V. $$$*

Perdido Beach Resort. The eight- and nine-story towers of this Mediterranean-style hotel are stucco and red tile; the lobby is tiled in terra-cotta and decorated with mosaics by Venetian artists. Luxurious rooms have beach views and balconies. *Rte. 182E, Box 400, 36561, ☎ 334/981–9811 or 800/634–8001, FAX 334/981–5670. 329 rooms, 16 suites. Facilities: restaurant, café, heated indoor/outdoor pool, pool bar, exercise room overlooking beach, whirlpool, sauna, 4 lighted tennis courts. AE, D, DC, MC, V. $$$*

Point Clear

DINING AND LODGING

★ **Marriott's Grand Hotel.** Set within 550 acres of beautifully landscaped grounds on Mobile Bay, the "Grand" has been cherished since 1847. Extensively refurbished by Marriott, it is one of the South's premier resorts. Spacious rooms and cottages are traditionally furnished. Food is elegantly prepared and served in the restaurants, including the award-winning Magnolia Room. *U.S. Scenic 98, 36564, ☎ 334/928–9201 or 800/544–9933, FAX 334/928–1149. 282 rooms, 24 suites. Facilities: 3 restaurants, lounge, coffee shop, pool, 8 tennis courts, golf (36 holes), horseback riding, bicycle riding, marina with rental boats, sailing, charter fishing, children's day camp. AE, D, DC, MC, V. $$$*

ELSEWHERE IN THE STATE

U.S. Space and Rocket Center

Getting There

Huntsville is 100 mi north of Birmingham via I–65 and U.S. 72E.

What to See and Do

Home to the **U.S. Space Camp,** the center offers a bus tour of the NASA labs and shuttle test sites; hands-on exhibits in the museum; and an outdoor park filled with spacecraft. *1 Tranquillity Base, Huntsville, ☎ 205/837–3400 or 800/637–7223. Admission: $11.95 adults, $7.95 children.*

Ivy Green

Getting There

Tuscumbia is 120 mi northwest of Birmingham via I–65 and U.S. Alternate 72. Take exit 340 off I–65.

What to See and Do

Ivy Green is the birthplace of author and lecturer Helen Keller, who was left unable to hear or see at the age of 19 months. With the help of her teacher, Anne Sullivan, she graduated from Radcliffe with honors in 1904 and became a champion for all those with similar disabilities. Tours are year-round. *The Miracle Worker,* the play about Keller's childhood and her relationship with Sullivan, is performed outdoors from late June through late July. First staged in 1961, it is the state's official drama. *300 West North Commons, Tuscumbia, ☎ 205/383–4066. Admission: $3 adults, $1 children 6–11.*

FLORIDA

By Donna Singer

Capital	Tallahassee
Population	12,937,926
Motto	In God We Trust
State Bird	Mockingbird
State Flower	Orange blossom

Visitor Information

Florida Division of Tourism (126 Van Buren St., Tallahassee 32301, ☎ 904/487–1462 or 904/487–1463). **Information centers:** on U.S. 301 at Hilliard, U.S. 231 near Graceville, I–75 near Jennings, I–10 at Pensacola, I–95 near Yulee, and in the lobby of the capitol building in Tallahassee.

Scenic Drives

In **Everglades National Park,** the 38-mi drive from the Main Visitor Center to Flamingo reveals a patchwork of ecosystems, including mangrove and cypress forests, saw-grass marshes, and a variety of wildlife. Although traffic jams abound during the winter tourist season, the **Overseas Highway** (U.S. 1) from Key Largo to Key West offers spectacular vistas of the Atlantic, Florida Bay, the Gulf of Mexico, and the myriad islands of the keys.

Rte. 789 along the Gulf Coast south from Holmes Beach in Bradenton to Lido Beach in Sarasota, and from Casey Key south of Osprey to Nokomis Beach, passes over several picturesque barrier islands. Along the Atlantic coast, the **Buccaneer Trail** (Rte. A1A) from Mayport to the old seaport town of Fernandina Beach passes through marshlands and along pristine beaches. **U.S. 98** winds east from historic Pensacola through the lush coastal landscape of the Panhandle.

National and State Parks

National Parks

Everglades and Biscayne national parks (*see* Elsewhere in the State, *below*). In southwest Florida, **Big Cypress National Preserve** (20 mi east of Ochopee on U.S. 41; HCR 61, Box 110, Ochopee 33943, ☎ 813/695–2000 or 813/262–1066), noted for the bald and dwarf cypress that line its marshlands, is a sanctuary for alligators, bald eagles, and the endangered Florida panther.

Florida has three national forests. The 556,500-acre **Apalachicola National Forest** (Rte. 65; Edward Ball Wakulla Spring State Park, Wakulla Spring Rd., Wakulla 32305, ☎ 904/653–9419) is popular for canoeing and hiking, and has a recreational facility designed for the disabled. **Ocala National Forest** (Rte. 40 east of Ocala; Forest Visitor Center, 10863 E. Hwy. 40, Silver Springs 34488, ☎ 904/625–7470) has lakes, springs, hiking trails, campgrounds, and historic sites. **Osceola National Forest** (north of Lake City on I–10; Osceola Ranger District, Box 70, Olustee 32072, ☎ 904/752–2577) is dotted with cypress swamps and offers good fishing and hunting. In addition, the state has five national monuments, two national seashores, and eight national wildlife refuges.

State Parks

The state administers hundreds of parks, nature preserves, and historic sites. Among these are **Blackwater River State Park** (40 mi northeast of Pensacola on I–10; Rte. 1, Box 57C, Holt 32564, ☎ 904/623–2363), popular with canoeists; **Delnor-Wiggins Pass State Recreation Area** (North Naples; 1100 Gulfshore Dr. N, Naples 33963, ☎ 813/597–6196), with miles of beaches, picnic areas, and fishing spots; **Florida Caverns State Park** (Rte. 167, two hours north of Panama City; 3345 Caverns Rd., Mariana 32446, ☎ 904/482–9598), comprising 1,783 acres of caves and nature trails; **Fort Clinch State Park** (*see* Elsewhere in the State, *below*); and **St. Andrews State Recreation Area** (east end of Panama City Beach in the Panhandle; 4415 Thomas Dr., Panama City Beach 32408, ☎ 904/233–5140), encompassing 1,038 acres of beaches, pinewoods, and marshes for swimming, pier fishing, and dune hiking. For more information contact the **Florida Department of Natural Resources** (Marjory Stoneman Douglas Bldg., MS 525, 3900 Commonwealth Blvd., Tallahassee 32399-3000, ☎ 904/488–9872).

MIAMI

With more than half of its population Hispanic in origin, it's no wonder Miami is called the capital of Latin America. Indeed, Miami is a city of superlatives. This growing metropolis boasts one of the largest airports and *the* largest cruise-ship port in the world. More than 100 companies base their international operations in the city, and big-league sports are big news here. Undergirding all this energy and prosperity is a flourishing drug culture that fuels get-rich-quick lifestyles. Although Hurricane Andrew devastated south Miami in 1992, the storm did little damage to the areas that tourists visit most.

Tourist Information

Greater Miami: Convention and Visitors Bureau (701 Brickell Ave., Suite 2700, 33131, ☎ 305/539–3063 or 800/283–2707). **Miami Beach:** Chamber of Commerce (1920 Meridian Ave., 33139, ☎ 305/672–1270, FAX 305/538–4336). **South Dade County:** Visitors Information Center (160 U.S. 1, Florida City 33034, ☎ 305/245–9180 or 800/388–9669, FAX 305/247–4335).

Arriving and Departing

By Plane

Miami International Airport (☎ 305/876–7000) has scheduled service by most major domestic and Latin American airlines and many transatlantic carriers. It is 6 mi west of downtown via Rte. 836. Rental cars are available at the airport. Cab fare downtown is $15–$20; the flat fare to and from the Port of Miami, where cruise ships dock, is $15.75. **SuperShuttle** (☎ 305/871–2000) vans go from the airport to area hotels. Bus service (fare $1.25, exact change required; 25¢ transfer) is available across the lower-level lanes in the center of the airport.

By Car

I–95, which runs north–south along Florida's east coast, flows into the heart of Miami. From the northwest, I–75 leads to the city. Rte. 836 (also called East–West Expressway or Dolphin Expressway), connecting the airport to downtown (toll eastbound only, 25¢), continues across I–395 and the MacArthur Causeway to lower Miami Beach and the Art Deco District. Rte. 112 (Airport Expressway) connects the airport with midtown (toll eastbound only, 25¢) and continues across I–195 and the Julia Tuttle Causeway to mid–Miami Beach.

By Train

Amtrak (8303 N.W. 37th Ave., ☎ 305/835–1221 or 800/872–7245).

By Bus

Greyhound Lines (☎ 800/231–2222) stops at five terminals in Greater Miami.

Getting Around Miami

Greater Miami resembles Los Angeles in its urban sprawl and traffic congestion. You'll need a car to get from one area of the city to another. Metromover (*see* Metro–Dade Transit Agency *in* By Public Transportation, *below*), a light-rail mass-transit system, circles the heart of the city on twin elevated loops; use it to tour the downtown area. The Deco District in Miami Beach and the heart of Coconut Grove are best explored on foot.

By Car

Miami is laid out in quadrants: northwest, northeast, southwest, southeast. These meet at Miami Avenue, which separates east from west, and Flagler Street, which separates north from south. Avenues and courts run north–south; streets, terraces, and ways run east–west. Roads run diagonally, northwest–southeast. In Miami Beach, avenues run north–south; streets, east–west. Streets in Coral Gables have names, not numbers.

By Public Transportation

The **Metro–Dade Transit Agency** (☎ 305/638–6700) runs the Metrorail, Metromover, and Metrobus. **Metrorail** (fare $1.25) runs from downtown Miami north to Hialeah and south along U.S. 1 to Dadeland. **Metromover** (fare 25¢), a separate system, has two loops that circle downtown Miami, linking major hotels, office buildings, and shopping areas. **Metrobus** (fare $1.25) stops are marked by blue-and-green signs with a bus logo and route information. Frequency of service varies widely.

By Taxi

Be on your guard when traveling by cab in Miami. Some drivers are rude and unhelpful and may take advantage of visitors unfamiliar with their destinations. To avoid this, connect with a consortium of drivers who have banded together to provide good service: this nameless group can be reached through their dispatch service (☎ 305/888–4444). If you have to use another company, try to be familiar with your route and destination. Major cab companies include **Central Taxicab Service** (☎ 305/532–5555), **Diamond Cab Company** (☎ 305/545–5555), **Metro Taxicab Company** (☎ 305/888–8888), **Miami–Dade Yellow Cab** (☎ 305/633–0503), and **Yellow Cab Company** (☎ 305/444–4444). The fare is $1.75 per mile, 25¢ a minute waiting time, and there's no additional charge for extra passengers, luggage, or tolls.

Orientation Tours

Boat Tours

Island Queen, Island Lady, and ***Pink Lady*** (☎ 305/379–5119) offer 90-minute narrated water tours of the Port of Miami and Millionaires' Row from Bayside Marketplace.

Walking Tours

The **Miami Design Preservation League** (☎ 305/672–2014) runs a 90-minute tour of Miami Beach's Art Deco District at 10:30 AM Saturday, leaving from the Ocean Front Auditorium (1001 Ocean Dr., Miami Beach). Metro-Dade Community College history professor **Paul George** (☎ 305/858–6021) offers walking tours through downtown and other historic districts.

Exploring Miami

Downtown

Begin your tour of downtown Miami at the 3.3-acre **Metro-Dade Cultural Center** (101 W. Flagler St.), a Mediterranean expression of architect Philip Johnson's postmodern style. An elevated plaza provides a serene haven from the city's pulsations. Within the complex are several arts venues, including the **Center for the Fine Arts** (☎ 305/375–3000; admission charged). In the tradition of the European *Kunsthalle* (exhibition gallery), this art museum has no permanent collection (though a push toward forming one came with the arrival, in 1995, of a new director). Throughout the year CFA organizes and borrows temporary exhibitions on diverse themes. Also in the Cultural Center are the **Historical Museum of Southern Florida** (☎ 305/375–1492), with artifacts from prehistory to the present, such as Tequesta and Seminole Indian ceramics and a 1920 streetcar; and the **Main Public Library** (☎ 305/375–2665), with nearly 4 million holdings and art exhibits in its auditorium and second-floor lobby.

East of here, between Biscayne Boulevard and Biscayne Bay, is **Claude and Mildred Pepper Bayfront Park.** Japanese sculptor Isamu Noguchi redesigned the park just before his death in 1989; it now includes a memorial to the *Challenger* astronauts, an amphitheater, and a fountain honoring the late Florida congressman Claude Pepper and his wife.

Bayside Marketplace (☎ 305/577–3344), between Bayfront Park and the entrance to the Port of Miami, is a waterside entertainment and shopping center. Its 235,000 sq ft of retail space include 150 specialty shops, outdoor cafés, and an international food court. Street performers entertain throughout the day and evening, and free concerts, typically calypso, jazz, Latin rhythms, reggae, and rock, take place every day of the year.

Northeast of here on Biscayne Boulevard is the **Freedom Tower** (600 Biscayne Blvd.), where the Cuban Refugee Center processed more than 500,000 immigrating Cubans in the 1960s. Built in 1925 and renovated as office space in 1990, this imposing Spanish Baroque–style structure was inspired by the Giralda, an 800-year-old bell tower in Seville, Spain.

South of downtown proper, several architecturally interesting condominiums rise between Brickell Avenue and Biscayne Bay. Israeli artist Yacov Agram painted the rainbow-hued exterior of **Villa Regina** (1581 Brickell Ave.). Arquitectonica, a nationally prominant architectural firm based in Miami, designed three of these buildings: the **Palace** (1541 Brickell Ave.), the **Imperial** (1627 Brickell Ave.), and the **Atlantis** (2025 Brickell Ave.).

Miami Beach

Made up of 17 islands in Biscayne Bay, Miami Beach is officially a separate city from Miami. In recent years this "American Riviera" has revived its fortunes by renewing its mile-square Art Deco District, now on the National Register of Historic Places. Decorative, streamlined, modern facades dating from the Depression were repainted in lively pastels as residents reveled in their architectural heritage. Today the district is Florida's preeminent place for people-watching.

Start at the **Art Deco District Welcome Center** (1001 Ocean Dr., ☎ 305/531–3484), where the **Art Deco District** begins. Proceed north past pastel-hued deco hotels (outlined in brilliant neon at night) on your left and the palm-fringed beach on your right. The neighborhood's two main commercial streets are **Collins Avenue,** one block west of Ocean Drive, and, one block farther west, **Washington Avenue.** The latter is a colorful mix of Jewish, Cuban, Haitian, and more familiar American culture, containing delicatessens, avant-garde stores, produce markets, shops selling religious artifacts, and many of the best restaurants in the metropolis. West of Washington Avenue is the **Lincoln Road Mall,** a pedestrian shopping street that declined in popularity in the 1960s but is enjoying a comeback thanks to both an influx of artists and vendors and an ongoing $12 million facelift. The mall has become paired with Ocean Drive as part of "must-see" South Beach, especially on Saturday night, when art galleries schedule openings together.

North of Lincoln Road Mall and east on 17th Street is the **Miami Beach Convention Center** (1901 Convention Center Dr., ☎ 305/673–7311), Miami's largest convention space. Northwest of here, near Meridian Avenue, is the **Holocaust Memorial** (1933–1945 Meridian Ave., ☎ 305/538–1663 or 305/538–1673), a monumental sculpture and a graphic record in memory of the 6 million Jewish victims of the Holocaust. Just south of the convention center, at 17th Street and Washington Avenue, is the **Jackie Gleason Theater of the Performing Arts** (1700 Washington Ave., ☎ 305/673–7300) where Gleason's television show originated. North of here, the **Bass Museum of Art** (2121 Park Ave., ☎ 305/673–7530) has a diverse collection of European works. Return to Collins Avenue and drive north: The triumphal archway that looms ahead is a work of illusionary art by Richard Haas that depicts the **Fontainebleau Hilton Resort and Towers** (4441 Collins Ave., ☎ 305/538–2000), which actually sits behind it. The hotel is the largest in south Florida, with more than 1,200 rooms.

Little Havana

Some 35 years ago, the tidal wave of Cubans fleeing the Castro regime flooded an older neighborhood just west of downtown with refugees. The area became known as Little Havana, although today more than half a million Cubans live throughout Greater Miami. On the southwest corner of Flagler Street and Teddy Roosevelt Avenue is the **Plaza de la Cubanidad** (S.W. 17th Ave.), where redbrick sidewalks surround a fountain and monument inscribed with words from José Martí, a leader in Cuba's struggle for independence from Spain: LAS PALMAS SON NOVIAS QUE ESPERAN ("The palm trees are girlfriends who will wait").

South of here is **Calle Ocho** (S.W. 8th St.), the main commercial thoroughfare of Little Havana. Visit **Versailles** (3555 S.W. 8th St., ☎ 305/445–7614), a Cuban restaurant whose menu and decor will immerse you in Cuban-American popular culture. At Calle Ocho and Memorial Boulevard (S.W. 13th Ave.) stands the **Brigade 2506 Memorial,** which commemorates the victims of the unsuccessful 1961 Bay of Pigs invasion of Cuba by an exile force. The **Cuban Museum of Arts and Culture** (1300 S.W. 12th Ave., ☎ 305/858–8006; closed Mon.), created by Cuban exiles to preserve and interpret their heritage, now includes exhibits from the entire Hispanic art community.

Coral Gables, South Miami, Coconut Grove

Developed during the 1920s by visionary George Merrick, Coral Gables has remained remarkably true to his dream of a planned community, with broad boulevards, Spanish–Mediterranean architecture, and a busy commercial downtown. South Miami was a pioneer farming community that grew into a suburb while still managing to retain a small-town charm. Coconut Grove is the oldest section of Miami, begun during the 1870s and annexed to the city in 1925. Its earliest settlers included New England intellectuals, bohemians, Bahamians, and later, artists, writers, and scientists who established winter homes there. The Grove still reflects the pioneers' eclectic origins, with posh estates next to rustic cottages and starkly modern dwellings.

Coral Way runs east–west through **Coral Gables,** becoming **Miracle Mile** at Douglas Road (S.W. 37th Ave.). This is the heart of downtown Coral Gables, with more than 150 shops and a concentration of fine restaurants. Along Coral Way west of LeJeune Road (S.W. 42nd Ave.), the **Granada Golf Course** (2001 Granada Blvd., ☏ 305/460–5367) is one of two public courses amid Coral Gables' largest historic district. **Coral Gables Merrick House and Gardens** (907 Coral Way, ☏ 305/460–5361), George Merrick's boyhood home, has been restored to its 1920s appearance and contains family furnishings and artifacts.

South on Granada Boulevard is the **De Soto Plaza and Fountain,** a classical column on a pedestal with water flowing from the mouths of four sculpted faces. Northeast one block is the stunning **Venetian Pool** (2701 De Soto Blvd., ☏ 305/460–5356; admission charged), a municipal swimming pool created from a rock quarry. South of here is the 260-acre main campus of the **University of Miami,** with almost 14,000 students—the largest private research university in the Southeast. Its **Lowe Art Museum** (1301 Stanford Dr., ☏ 305/284–3535 or 305/284–3536; admission charged; closed Mon.) has a permanent collection of 8,000 works.

Fine old homes and mature trees line **Sunset Drive,** the city-designated "historic and scenic road" to and through downtown **South Miami.** Go south on Red Road to reach the grounds of the **Parrot Jungle,** one of Miami's oldest and most popular attractions. Many of the 1,100 parrots, macaws, cockatoos, and other exotic birds fly free, but they'll come to you for seeds, sold in old-fashioned gum-ball machines. You can watch a trained-bird show, stroll among exotic plants and trees, and see a cactus garden. *11000 S.W. 57th Ave., ☏ 305/666–7834. Admission: $10.95 adults, $7.95 children 3–12.*

Just south of here is the 83-acre **Fairchild Tropical Garden** (10901 Old Cutler Rd., ☏ 305/667–1651; admission charged), the largest tropical botanical garden in the continental United States. North of the garden, Old Cutler Road traverses Dade County's oldest and most scenic park, **Matheson Hammock Park** (9610 Old Cutler Rd., ☏ 305/667–3035), dating from the days of the Civilian Conservation Corps in the 1930s. The most popular feature is a bathing beach, where the tide flushes a saltwater "atoll" pool through four gates.

In **Coconut Grove,** northwest of South Miami, the **Plymouth Congregational Church** (3400 Devon Rd., ☏ 305/444–6521), a handsome coral-rock structure, dates from 1917. Also on the 11-acre grounds are natural sunken gardens; the first schoolhouse in Dade County (one room), which was moved to this property; and the site of the original Coconut Grove water- and electric works. Main Highway brings you to the historic **Village of Coconut Grove,** a trendy commercial district

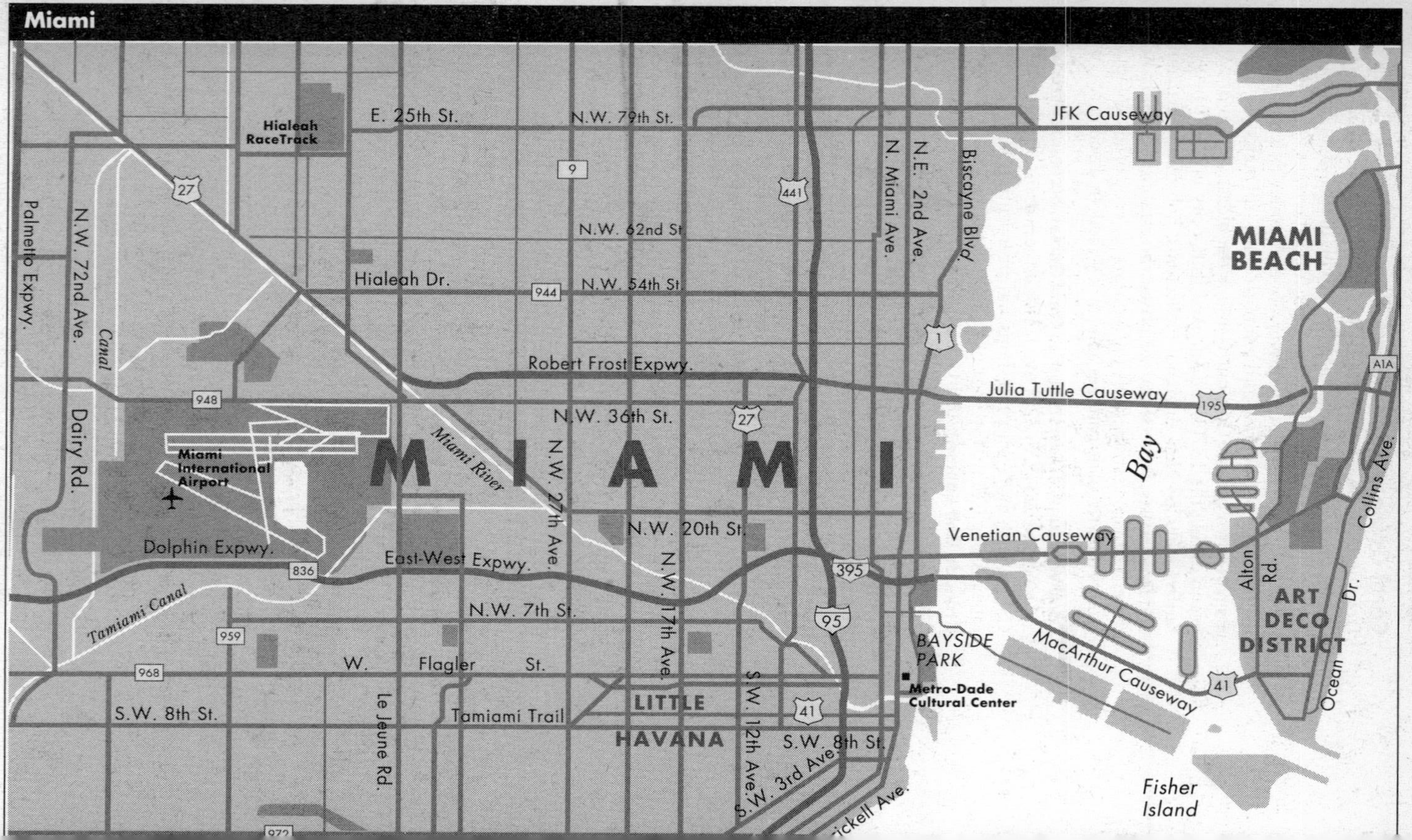
E. 25th St.
Hialeah RaceTrack
N.W. 79th St.
JFK Causeway
MIAMI BEACH
N. Miami Ave.
N.E. 2nd Ave.
Biscayne Blvd.
Palmetto Expwy.
N.W. 72nd Ave.
Canal
Dairy Rd.
N.W. 62nd St.
Hialeah Dr.
N.W. 54th St.
Robert Frost Expwy.
Julia Tuttle Causeway
N.W. 36th St.
Miami International Airport
MIAMI
Miami River
N.W. 27th Ave.
Bay
Collins Ave.
N.W. 20th St.
Venetian Causeway
Dolphin Expwy.
East-West Expwy.
N.W. 17th Ave.
Alton Rd.
ART DECO DISTRICT
Ocean Dr.
Tamiami Canal
N.W. 7th St.
BAYSIDE PARK
MacArthur Causeway
W. Flagler St.
Metro-Dade Cultural Center
S.W. 8th St.
Le Jeune Rd.
Tamiami Trail
LITTLE HAVANA
S.W. 12th Ave.
S.W. 8th St.
S.W. 3rd Ave.
Fisher Island
A1A
195
1
441
9
27
944
948
27
395
95
836
959
968
41
41

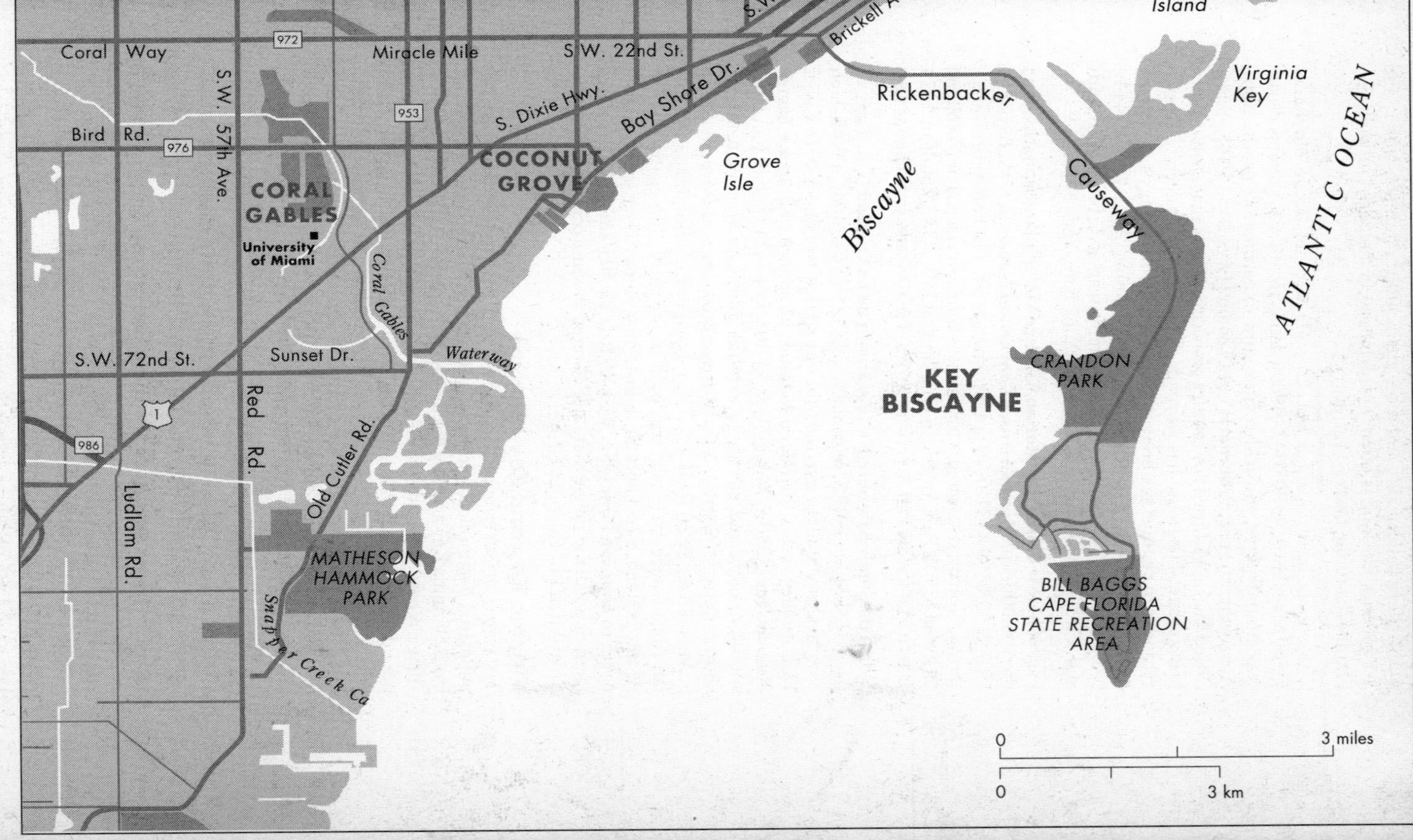

Island
Coral Way
972
Miracle Mile
S.W. 22nd St.
Brickell
Virginia Key
Rickenbacker
ATLANTIC OCEAN
S.W. 57th Ave.
953
S. Dixie Hwy.
Bay Shore Dr.
Bird Rd.
976
COCONUT GROVE
Grove Isle
Biscayne
Causeway
CORAL GABLES
University of Miami
Coral Gables
Waterway
S.W. 72nd St.
Sunset Dr.
Red Rd.
1
986
Old Cutler Rd.
KEY BISCAYNE
CRANDON PARK
Ludlam Rd.
MATHESON HAMMOCK PARK
Snapper Creek Ca
BILL BAGGS CAPE FLORIDA STATE RECREATION AREA
0
3 miles
0
3 km

with redbrick sidewalks and more than 300 restaurants, stores, and art galleries. Parking is often a problem, so be prepared to walk several blocks to the heart of the district.

The apricot-hued, Spanish Rococo–style **Coconut Grove Playhouse** (3500 Main Hwy., ☎ 305/442–4000), dating from 1926, presents Broadway-bound plays, musical revues, and experimental productions. Across the street is the **Barnacle** (3485 Main Hwy., ☎ 305/448–9445; closed Tues.–Wed.), a 19th-century pioneer residence that is now a state historic site. The house has a broad, sloping roof and deeply recessed verandas to channel sea breezes inside; many furnishings are original. In the village center is **CocoWalk** (3015 Grand Ave., ☎ 305/444–0777), a multilevel open mall of Mediterranean-style brick courtyards and terraces overflowing with restaurants, bars, and shops.

East of here is **Dinner Key Marina,** Greater Miami's largest marina, and the 105,000-sq-ft **Coconut Grove Convention Center** (2700 S. Bayshore Dr., ☎ 305/579–3310), site of antiques, boat, and home-furnishings shows. Nearby, decorated with nautical-motif Art Deco trim, is **Miami City Hall** (3500 Pan American Dr., ☎ 305/250–5357), built in 1934 as terminal for the Pan American Airways seaplane base at Dinner Key.

North on South Bayshore Drive is **Ermita de La Caridad** (Our Lady of Charity Shrine) (3609 S. Miami Ave., ☎ 305/854–2404), a 90-ft-high conical shrine built to overlook the bay so that worshipers face Cuba. Half a mile west is the **Miami Museum of Science and Space Transit Planetarium** (3280 S. Miami Ave., ☎ 305/854–4247), with hands-on sound, gravity, and electricity exhibits and laser-light planetarium shows. Across the street is the **Vizcaya Museum and Gardens** (3251 S. Miami Ave., ☎ 305/250–9133), a showplace of antiquities. The Italian Renaissance–style villa was built in the early 20th century as the winter residence of Chicago industrialist James Deering. Continue north to **Simpson Park** (55 S.W. 17th Rd., ☎ 305/856–6801), a fragment of the dense jungle that once covered the entire 5 mi from downtown Miami to Coconut Grove.

Virginia Key and Key Biscayne

The waters of Government Cut and the Port of Miami separate densely populated Miami Beach from two of Greater Miami's playground islands, Virginia Key and Key Biscayne—the latter no longer the laid-back village where Richard Nixon set up his presidential vacation compound. Parks and stretches of dense mangrove swamp occupy much of both keys. To reach the keys, take the **Rickenbacker Causeway** across Biscayne Bay at Brickell Avenue and S.W. 26th Road, about 2 mi south of downtown Miami. Across the high bridge is the 6,536-seat **Miami Marine Stadium** (3601 Rickenbacker Causeway, ☎ 305/361–3316), a former concert venue that has been closed indefinitely, and the **Miami Seaquarium** (4400 Rickenbacker Causeway, ☎ 305/361–5705; admission charged), featuring sea-lion, dolphin, and killer-whale performances and a 235,000-gallon tropical-reef aquarium.

Key Biscayne's commercial center is a mix of posh shops and stores catering to neighborhood needs. At the key's south end is the **Bill Baggs Cape Florida State Recreation Area** (1200 S. Crandon Blvd., ☎ 305/361–5811), with 1¼ mi of palm-topped white-sand beach.

The keys took a hit from Hurricane Andrew, and hotels suffered damage, as did the well-known public golf course. If you are planning a visit to Virginia Key and Key Biscayne, contact the Greater Miami Convention and Visitors Bureau (*see* Tourist Information, *above*) for an update on conditions.

Other Attractions

Southwest of Dade County's urban core is the 290-acre **Metrozoo** (12400 S.W. 152 St., ☎ 305/251–0400; admission charged), a favorite destination for area residents. Devastated by Hurricane Andrew, the zoo has reopened, though its monorail and Wings of Asia, a 1½-acre aviary that re-creates a rain-forest setting for hundreds of exotic birds, remain closed.

Next door is the **Gold Coast Railroad Museum** (12450 Coral Reef Dr., ☎ 305/253–0063), whose collection includes a 1949 Silver Crescent dome car and the *Ferdinand Magellan,* the only Pullman car ever constructed specifically for U.S. presidents. The museum was damaged in the hurricane, but most trains were expected back at the site before the end of 1995.

Shopping

Malls, an international free zone, and specialty shopping districts are the attractions in Miami. Many shopping areas have an ethnic flavor. Store hours vary.

Shopping Districts

More than 500 garment manufacturers sell their clothing in more than 30 factory outlets and discount fashion stores in the **Fashion District,** east of I–95 along 5th Avenue from 25th to 29th streets. Most stores in the district are open Monday through Saturday 9–5 and accept credit cards. The **Miami Free Zone** (2305 N.W. 107th Ave., ☎ 305/591–4300) is an international wholesale trade center—occupying 850,000 sq ft on three floors—where you can buy goods duty-free for export or pay duty on goods released for domestic use. More than 140 companies sell products from more than 100 countries, including clothing, computers, cosmetics, electronics, liquor, and perfumes. At **Cauley Square** (22400 Old Dixie Hwy., Goulds, ☎ 305/258–3543; closed most Sun.)—a complex of clapboard, coral-rock, and stucco buildings that housed railroad workers at the turn of the century—shops sell antiques, crafts, and clothing. To get there, turn right off U.S. 1 at S.W. 224th Street.

Sports and the Outdoors

Diving

Summer diving conditions in Greater Miami have been compared with those in the Caribbean. Winter can bring rough, cold waters. Fowey, Triumph, Long, and Emerald reefs are shallow 10- to 15-ft dives good for snorkelers and beginning divers. In 1994 a greatly expanded artificial-reef program was begun off the shores of Miami, and early reports confirm that fish life was quickly attracted to the new sites. **Divers Paradise of Key Biscayne** (4000 Crandon Blvd., Key Biscayne, ☎ 305/361–3483) offers dive charters, rentals, and instruction. The **Diving Locker** (223 Sunny Isles Blvd., North Miami Beach, ☎ 305/947–6025) is a 24-year-old dive shop that offers three-day and three-week certification courses, wreck and reef dives aboard the *Native Diver,* and full sales, service, and repairs. In Miami, **Bubbles Dive Center** (2671 S.W. 27th Ave., ☎ 305/856–0565) is an all-purpose dive shop. **Team Divers** (300 Alton Rd., ☎ 305/673–0101), in the Miami Beach marina, is the only dive shop in the South Beach area. All shops are PADI-affiliated.

Golf

Dade County has more than 30 private and public courses (☎ 305/857–6868 for county information, 305/575–5256 for Miami information, and 305/673–7730 for Miami Beach information).

Sailing

Dinner Key and the **Coconut Grove** waterfront remain the center of sailing in Greater Miami, although moorings and rentals are found elsewhere on the bay and up the Miami River. **Easy Sailing** (Dinner Key Marina, 3360 Pan American Dr., Coconut Grove, ☎ 305/858–4001) offers instruction and a fleet (19–127 ft) for rent by the hour or by the day.

Tennis

Greater Miami has more than 60 private and public tennis centers. All public courts charge nonresidents an hourly fee. **Biltmore Tennis Center** (1150 Anastasia Ave., Coral Gables, ☎ 305/460–5360) has 10 hard courts. **Flamingo Tennis Center** (1000 12th St., Miami Beach, ☎ 305/673–7761) has 19 clay courts. **Tennis Center at Crandon Park** (7300 Crandon Blvd., Key Biscayne, ☎ 305/361–8633), which hosts the annual Lipton Championships in March, provides 2 grass, 8 clay, and 17 hard courts.

Windsurfing

Sailboards Miami (Key Biscayne, ☎ 305/361–7245), on Hobie Island just past the tollbooth for the Rickenbacker Causeway to Key Biscayne, rents windsurfing equipment.

Spectator Sports

Baseball

Florida Marlins (Joe Robbie Stadium, 2269 N.W. 199th St., Miami, ☎ 305/626–7400 or 305/620–2578; Apr.–Oct.).

Basketball

Miami Heat (Miami Arena, 701 Arena Blvd., Miami, ☎ 305/577–4328; Nov.–Apr.).

Football

Miami Dolphins (Joe Robbie Stadium, 2269 N.W. 199th St., Miami, ☎ 305/620–2578; Aug.–Dec.).

Jai Alai

In this, the fastest game on earth, pelotas, the hard balls thrown from hand-held cowled baskets called cestas, travel at speeds of more than 170 mph. You can bet on a team to win or on the order in which teams will finish. **Miami Jai Alai** (3500 N.W. 37th Ave., Miami, ☎ 305/633–6400; Nov.–Apr. and mid-May–late Sept.) is the oldest fronton in America.

Beaches

Millions visit Dade County's beaches annually. The broadest is along **Miami Beach,** where a boardwalk runs from 23rd to 44th streets; along this stretch, various groups tend to congregate in specific areas. From 1st to 15th streets, senior citizens often gather early in the day. Lummus Park, the stretch of beach opposite the Art Deco District, between 5th and 15th streets, attracts a mix of perfect-bod types and those of all ages who can only ogle. Volleyball, in-line skating along the paved upland path, and a lot of posing go on here, and children's playgrounds make this a popular area for families. Along these beaches, city officials don't enforce the law against female bathers going topless, as long as everyone on the beach behaves with decorum. Gays frequent the beach between 11th and 13th streets. Sidewalk cafés parallel the entire beach area, which makes it easy to come ashore for everything from burgers to quiche. Families and anybody else who likes things quiet prefer North Beach, along Ocean Terrace between 72rd and 75th streets.

Two of metro Miami's best beaches are on Key Biscayne. Nearest the causeway is the 3½-mi county beach in **Crandon Park** (4000 Crandon Blvd., ☎ 305/361–5421), popular with young couples and families. Also in Key Biscayne is the **Bill Baggs Cape Florida State Recreation Area** (1200 S. Crandon Blvd., ☎ 305/361–5811).

Dining

Miami is gaining a world reputation for its fusion of tropical ingredients with the nouvelle-inspired remake of classical French cooking. Gourmet centers of the city are downtown Coral Gables and the Deco District of Miami Beach, with pockets of fine dining also in ethnic neighborhoods, such as Little Havana, and in popular nightlife districts, such as Coconut Grove and Bayside downtown. For price ranges, see Chart 1 (A) in On the Road with Fodor's.

$$$$ **Dominique's.** Woodwork and mirrors from a Vanderbilt home and other demolished New York mansions create an intimate setting in which to enjoy unique nouvelle cuisine. Specialties include the exotic sautéed alligator tail appetizer or the popular rack of lamb. *Alexander Hotel, 5225 Collins Ave., Miami Beach, ☎ 305/865–6500 or 800/327–6121. AE, DC, MC, V.*

$$$ ★ **Casa Rolandi.** Entirely refurbished in 1994, this restaurant combines rustic decor and northern Italian cuisine. The menu offers the expected antipasti and *caldi,* but on the way to the *gelati* and *dolci* you will happily tour through the risottos and pastas, or a few select veal, beef, and lamb entrées. *1930 Ponce de León Blvd., Coral Gables, ☎ 305/444–2187. Jacket advised. AE, DC, MC, V. Closed Sun.–Mon. No lunch Sat.*

$$$ **Chef Allen's.** In an art-deco setting of glass and neon, diners' gazes are drawn to the kitchen, visible through a large picture window, where chef Allen Susser creates new American masterpieces. Dishes such as honey-chilled roasted duck with stir-fried wild rice and green-apple chutney are *almost* too pretty to eat. *19088 N.E. 29th Ave., North Miami Beach, ☎ 305/935–2900. AE, DC, MC, V. No lunch.*

$$$ **Grand Cafe.** This upscale spot features a bilevel room with pink tablecloths and floral bouquets. International cuisine here means everything from pan-seared Florida crab cake to the baked macadamia-and-ginger-crusted salmon. *2669 S. Bay Shore Dr., Coconut Grove, ☎ 305/858–9600. Jacket advised. AE, DC, MC, V.*

$$$ ★ **Mark's Place.** At this popular restaurant, owner-chef Mark Militello excels with regional fare prepared in an oak-burning oven from Genoa. The menu changes nightly to take advantage of fresh local produce. *2286 N.E. 123rd St., North Miami, ☎ 305/893–6888. AE, DC, MC, V. Closed Thanksgiving, Christmas. No lunch weekends.*

$$$ ★ **Yuca.** This high-styled Cuban eatery, decorated with striking modern art prints and blond wood, attracts chic young Cubans and other fashionable types. Dazzling nouvelle tropical dishes include traditional corn tamale filled with conch and a spicy jalapeño and Creole cheese pesto, and plaintain-coated dolphin with a tamarind tartar sauce. *177 Giralda Ave., Coral Gables, ☎ 305/444–4448. Reservations required. AE, DC, MC, V. Closed Christmas, New Year's Day. No lunch Sun.*

$$ ★ **Didier's.** The three brothers Colongette have reestablished their corner of Provence in Coral Gables in the newly relocated Didier's, found in three large rooms done in a sunny French style. A starter like snails cooked in clay pots with garlic butter can be followed by a seafood entrée such as bouillabaisse or perhaps roasted rack of lamb with fine herbs and fava beans in a fresh mint sauce. All are wonderful and extraordinarily good values. *2530 Ponce de León Blvd., Coral Gables, ☎ 305/567–2444. AE, DC, MC, V. Closed Sun. No lunch Sat.*

$$ **Las Tapas.** *Tapas*—dishes of Spanish foods that come in appetizer-size portions—give you a variety of tastes during a single meal. Full-size meals are also served at this Bayside Marketplace restaurant, typically packed at all hours. *Bayside Marketplace, 401 Biscayne Blvd., Downtown Miami, ☎ 305/372–2737. Reservations required for large parties. AE, D, DC, MC, V.*

$$ **Los Ranchos.** There's nothing nouvelle at this beautiful, bayside Nicaraguan restaurant, where Argentine-style beef (lean, grass-fed tenderloin) is lovingly served to a loyal following. *Bayside Marketplace, 401 Biscayne Blvd., Downtown Miami, ☎ 305/375–8188 or 305/375–0666; 125 S.W. 107th Ave., Little Managua, ☎ 305/221–9367; Kendall Town & Country, 8505 Mills Dr., Kendall, ☎ 305/596–5353; Falls Shopping Center, 8888 S.W. 136 St., Suite 303, South Miami, ☎ 305/238–6867; 2728 Ponce de León Blvd., Coral Gables, ☎ 305/446–0050. AE, DC, MC, V. Closed Good Friday, Christmas Eve, New Year's Day.*

$$ ★ **Tony Chan's Water Club.** This beautiful dining room just off the lobby of the high-rise Grand Prix Hotel looks onto a bayside marina. The menu boasts more than 100 appetizers and entrées, including minced quail tossed with bamboo shoots and mushrooms wrapped in lettuce leaves, or pork chops sprinkled with green pepper in a black-bean-and-garlic sauce. *1717 N. Bayshore Dr., Downtown Miami, ☎ 305/374–8888. AE, MC, V. No lunch weekends.*

$$ ★ **Unicorn Village Restaurant & Marketplace.** This outstanding natural-foods restaurant, serving such dishes as spinach lasagna and vegetable spring rolls, has the added advantage of an outdoor setting among free-form ponds and fountains by a bayfront dock. If your meal inspires you, the 16,000-sq-ft market next door is an incomparable source of natural foods. *3565 N.E. 207th St., North Miami Beach, ☎ 305/933–8829. No reservations. AE, MC, V. No smoking.*

$ **Chez Moy.** This bustling restaurant with friendly staff is *the* choice in Little Haiti. Caribbean cuisine includes boiled spiced pork, conch with garlic and hot pepper, sugary fruit drinks, and sweet potato pie for dessert. *1 N.W. 54th St., Little Haiti, ☎ 305/757–5056. No credit cards. No smoking.*

$ ★ **Hy-Vong Vietnamese Cuisine.** This tiny restaurant seating 36 is popular with locals, who come for such Vietnamese dishes as barbecued pork with sesame seeds and fish sauce. Expect a wait if you come after 7 PM. *3458 S.W. 8th St., Little Havana, ☎ 305/446–3674. Reservations for 5 or more only. No credit cards. No smoking. Closed Mon., American and Chinese/Vietnamese New Year's, 2 weeks in Aug. No lunch.*

$ ★ **News Cafe.** This hip spot on Ocean Drive (open 24 hours) is always packed with people-watchers and those who enjoy such eclectic dishes as huge fresh-fruit bowls, burgers, bagels, pâtés, and chocolate fondue. A raw bar is the newest addition. *800 Ocean Dr., Miami Beach, ☎ 305/538–6397. No reservations. AE, DC, MC, V.*

$ ★ **Shorty's Bar-B-Q.** Miami's choice for barbecue and all the trimmings since the 1950s, Shorty's serves meals family style at long picnic tables. *9200 S. Dixie Hwy., ☎ 305/670–7732; 5989 S. University Dr., Davie, ☎ 305/680–9900. No reservations. MC, V at Davie location only. Closed Thanksgiving, Christmas.*

Lodging

Few urban areas can match Greater Miami's diversity of lodging options. The area has hundreds of hotels and motels in all price categories, from $8 a night for a hostel bed to $2,000 for a luxurious presidential suite. For B&B accommodations, contact **Bed & Breakfast Company,**

Tropical Florida (Box 262, Miami 33243, ☎ 305/661–3270). Lodgings are concentrated in Miami Beach and downtown Miami, around the airport, and in Coral Gables, Coconut Grove, and Key Biscayne. Winter is peak season; summer is also busy but rates are lower. For price ranges (which reflect high-season rates), see Chart 2 (A) in On the Road with Fodor's.

$$$$ ★ **Alexander Hotel.** Every room here is a large suite with two baths and a kitchen, ocean or bay view, and antique or reproduction furnishings. The hotel is renowned for service. *5225 Collins Ave., Miami Beach 33140, ☎ 305/865–6500 or 800/327–6121, FAX 305/864–8525. 160 suites. Facilities: restaurant, coffee shop, 2 outdoor pools, spa, beach, boating. AE, D, DC, MC, V.*

$$$$ ★ **Grand Bay Hotel.** This modern high-rise overlooking Biscayne Bay features a lobby enhanced by artwork and fresh flowers and guest rooms filled such superb touches as a canister of freshly sharpened pencils and an antique sideboard. The hotel's pyramid-like stepped profile gives each room facing the bay a private terrace. *2669 S. Bayshore Dr., Coconut Grove 33133, ☎ 305/858–9600 or 800/327–2788, FAX 305/858–1532. 132 rooms, 49 suites. Facilities: restaurant, lounge, bar, outdoor pool, beauty salon, health club, hot tub, saunas, massages. AE, DC, MC, V.*

$$$$ ★ **Omni Colonnade Hotel.** The twin 13-story towers of this $65 million swank hotel, office, and shopping complex dominate downtown Coral Gables. Oversize rooms feature sitting areas, built-in armoires, and traditional mahogany furnishings. *180 Aragon Ave., Coral Gables 33134, ☎ 305/441–2600 or 800/533–1337, FAX 305/445–3929. 157 rooms, 17 bilevel suites. Facilities: 2 restaurants, outdoor pool, 2 saunas, exercise room. AE, DC, MC, V.*

$$$$ ★ **Sonesta Beach Hotel & Tennis Club.** Public areas display museum-quality modern art by notable painters and sculptors, especially three drawings by Andy Warhol of rock star Mick Jagger in the hotel's disco bar, Desires. Some rooms are in villas with full kitchens and screened-in pools. *350 Ocean Dr., Key Biscayne 33149, ☎ 305/361–2021 or 800/766–3782, FAX 305/365–2096. 284 rooms, 14 suites, 2 villas. Facilities: 3 restaurants, bar, snack bar, health club, steam rooms, massage, outdoor pool, beach, 9 tennis courts (3 lighted), water sports, gift shop. AE, DC, MC, V.*

$$$$ ★ **Turnberry Isle Resort & Club.** Guests can choose from the new Mediterranean-style annex, the intimate Marina Hotel, the Yacht Club on the intracoastal waterway, or the Country Club Hotel beside the golf course at this 300-acre resort and condominium complex in North Dade. Oversize rooms feature light woods and earth tones. *19999 W. Country Club Dr., Aventura 33180, ☎ 305/932–6200 or 800/327–7028, FAX 305/933–6560. 300 rooms, 40 suites. Facilities: 6 restaurants, 5 lounges, 4 outdoor pools, saunas, spa, steam rooms, 24 tennis courts (18 lighted), 2 18-hole golf courses, health club, racquetball, water sports, boating, dive shop, helipad. AE, DC, MC, V.*

$$$–$$$$ **Park Central.** Across the street from a glorious stretch of beach, this seven-story Art Deco hotel is a favorite of visiting fashion models and other trendsetters. The stylish guest rooms have mahogany furnishings. There is an espresso bar on site, and the restaurant, Burt Reynold's Backstage, serves American food. *640 Ocean Dr., Miami Beach 33139, ☎ 305/538–1611 or 800/727–5236, FAX 305/534–7520. 121 rooms. Facilities: restaurant, bar, espresso bar, pool, exercise room. AE, DC, MC, V.*

$$$ **David William Hotel.** Easily the most affordable of the top Gables hotels, the DW stands 13 stories tall with a distinctive waffled facade. Rooms are very private, quiet, and large; south-facing rooms have balconies, many have kitchens, and all have marble baths. The desk staff

is excellent. Rooftop cabana guest rooms are the best bargains. *700 Biltmore Way, Coral Gables 33134, ☎ 305/445–7821; outside FL, 800/327–8770; FAX 305/445–5585. 70 rooms, 54 suites. Facilities: restaurant, bar, pool. AE, DC, MC, V.*

$$$ **Essex House.** Long one of the finest hotels in the Deco District, the Essex has undergone an outstanding restoration. Soundproof rooms are typically deco-small but supplied with designer linens and feather-and-down pillows. *1001 Collins Ave., Miami Beach 33139, ☎ 305/534–2700 or 800/553–7739, FAX 305/532–3827. 51 rooms, 9 suites. Facilities: breakfast room. AE, DC, MC, V.*

$$$ ★ **Hotel Place St. Michel.** This, the finest small hotel in metropolitan Miami, is an intimate jewel in the heart of downtown. Art Nouveau chandeliers are suspended from vaulted lobby ceilings, and the scent of fresh flowers is circulated through the public spaces by paddle fans. Rooms contain English, French, and Scottish antiques. *162 Alcazar Ave., Coral Gables 33134, ☎ 305/444–1666 or 800/247–8526, FAX 305/529–0074. 24 rooms, 3 suites. Facilities: restaurant, lounge. AE, DC, MC, V.*

$$–$$$ **Bay Harbor Inn.** Here's down-home hospitality in the county's most affluent area. The older building is furnished in antiques; all rooms in the newer building face Indian Creek and have midcentury decor. A complimentary Continental breakfast and the *Miami Herald* are provided for guests. *9660 E. Bay Harbor Dr., Bay Harbor Islands 33154, ☎ and FAX 305/868–4141. 25 rooms, 12 suites, penthouse. Facilities: 2 restaurants, lounge, outdoor pool. AE, DC, MC, V.*

$$ **Mermaid Guest House.** Part Caribbean hideaway, part Bohemian youth hostel, this place oozes the same kind of exuberance that early on sparked the birth of the Deco District. Vivid colors mark the decor, and beds are shrouded in mosquito netting despite the presence of air-conditioning. There are no ☎s or TVs. Frequent BYOB guest cookouts add to the family-style atmosphere. The youthful and young-at-heart clientele adores this place. *909 Collins Ave., Downtown Miami 33139, ☎ 305/538–5324. 10 units. MC, V.*

$$ ★ **Miami River Inn.** This hidden treasure is a 10-minute walk from the heart of downtown. The turn-of-the-century inn consists of five clapboard buildings on a grassy, palm-studded compound. Rooms are filled with antiques. *118 S.W. South River Dr., Downtown Miami 33130, ☎ 305/325–0045, FAX 305/325–9227. 40 rooms (2 share bath). Facilities: Continental breakfast, outdoor pool. AE, D, DC, MC, V.*

The Arts and Nightlife

The best sources for events are the widely distributed free weeklies *Miami Today* and *New Times;* the *Miami Herald* publishes a Weekend section on Friday and a Lively Arts section on Sunday. If you read Spanish, rely on *El Nuevo Herald* (a Spanish version of the *Miami Herald*).

The Arts

THEATER

The **Coconut Grove Playhouse** (3500 Main Hwy., ☎ 305/442–4000) stages Broadway-bound plays and musical revues, as well as experimental productions. **Colony Theater** (1040 Lincoln Rd., Miami Beach, ☎ 305/674–1026), once a movie theater, is now a 465-seat, city-owned performing-arts center featuring dance, drama, music, and experimental cinema. **Jackie Gleason Theater of the Performing Arts** (1700 Washington Ave., Miami Beach, ☎ 305/673–7300) is home of the Broadway Series (☎ 305/673–8300) and other stage events. **Teatro de Bellas Artes** (2173 S.W. 8th St., Miami, ☎ 305/325–0515), a 255-seat theater on Calle Ocho, presents eight Spanish plays and musicals year-round.

MUSIC

New World Symphony (541 Lincoln Rd., Miami Beach 33139, ☎ 305/673-3331), conducted by Michael Tilson Thomas, is a national orchestral academy for young musicians. **Concert Association of Florida** (555 Hank Meyer Blvd. [17th St.], Miami Beach 33139, ☎ 305/532-3491) is the South's largest presenter of classical artists.

OPERA

Florida Grand Opera (1200 Coral Way, Miami, ☎ 305/854-7890) presents five operas a year at the Dade County Auditorium.

BALLET

Miami City Ballet (905 Lincoln Rd., Miami Beach, ☎ 305/532-7713 or 305/532-4880) is an acclaimed troupe under the direction of Edward Villella.

Nightlife

The liveliest scenes are in SoBe (Miami Beach's Deco District) and Coconut Grove, but clubs can be found in the suburbs, downtown, Little Havana, and Little Haiti.

BARS WITH MUSIC

Tobacco Road (626 S. Miami Ave., Miami, ☎ 305/374-1198) is one of Miami's oldest bars, with excellent blues nightly. **Mac's Club Deuce** (222 14th St., Miami Beach, ☎ 305/673-9537) is a funky—some might say weird—SoBe spot where top international models come to shoot pool. **Bash** (655 Washington Ave., ☎ 305/538-2274) is a grottolike bar with dance floors that reverberate to different sounds—sometimes reggae, sometimes Latin, but mostly loud disco.

DANCE CLUB

The **Baja Beach Club** (CocoWalk, 3015 Grand Ave., Coconut Grove, ☎ 305/445-0278) is the place to be in Coconut Grove. Waiters and waitresses dress in beach attire, and the club overlooks the downtown strut.

NIGHTCLUBS

Some of the city's nightclubs offer a nostalgic look at the Miami of yore. **Les Violins Supper Club** (1751 Biscayne Blvd., Miami, ☎ 305/371-8668) offers a live dance band and a wood dance floor. The bands at **Club Tropigala at La Ronde** (Fontainebleau Hilton, 4441 Collins Ave., Miami Beach, ☎ 305/672-7469)—whose seven-level round room is decorated with orchids, banana leaves, and philodendrons to resemble a tropical jungle—play standards as well as Latin music for dancing.

DISNEY WORLD AND THE ORLANDO AREA

Cosmopolitan Orlando is a growing international business center and tourist mecca, largely due to the presence of Walt Disney World. Many other attractions, interesting shopping areas, and a varied nightlife make the area an exciting, if sometimes frenetic and crowded, vacation destination. Away from the tourist areas, hundreds of spring-fed lakes surrounded by graceful oak trees recall Orlando's slower-paced past. About an hour's drive from the city, on the Atlantic coast, are the Cocoa Beach area and the Kennedy Space Center, Spaceport USA.

Tourist Information

Kissimmee/St. Cloud: Convention and Visitor's Bureau (1925 E. Irlo Bronson Memorial Hwy., Kissimmee 32742, ☎ 407/363-5800, 407/847-5000, or 800/327-9159). **Orlando/Orange County:** Convention and Visitor's Bureau (8445 International Dr., Orlando 32819, ☎ 407/363–5871).

Getting There

By Plane

Orlando International Airport (6086 McCoy Rd., off the Bee Line Expressway, ☎ 407/825–2000) is served by major U.S. airlines, as well as many foreign airlines. **Delta Dream Vacations** (☎ 800/872–7786) offers travel packages to Disney World.

By Car

From Jacksonville, take I–95S, then I–4 from Port Orange. From Tampa/St. Petersburg, take I–4E. From Miami, take I–95N and connect with the northbound Florida Turnpike at White City. From Atlanta, take I–75S and connect with the Florida Turnpike.

By Train

Amtrak (☎ 800/872–7245) operates the *Silver Star* and the *Silver Meteor* to Florida. Both stop at Sanford, Winter Park, Orlando, and Kissimmee.

By Bus

Greyhound Lines (☎ 800/231–2222) provides service from major Florida cities and from outside the state.

Exploring Walt Disney World and the Orlando Area

Walt Disney World

The focal point of an Orlando vacation is **Walt Disney World** (Box 10040, Lake Buena Vista 32830, ☎ 407/824–4321), a collection of theme parks and attractions connected by extensive bus, monorail, motor-launch, and ferry systems (free if you stay at a Disney hotel/resort). Admission is not cheap: A one-day ticket to *either* the Magic Kingdom, the Epcot Center, or Disney-MGM is $37 for adults and $30 for children 3–9. Your best bet, even if you plan to stay only two or three days, may be to purchase a Four-Day Super Pass or a Five-Day Super Duper Pass; both admit you to all three parks, allow you to visit more than one on any given day, and include unlimited use of Disney transport.

THE MAGIC KINGDOM

Sprawling before you when you enter the Magic Kingdom is **Main Street U.S.A.**—a shop-filled boulevard with Victorian-style stores and dining spots. Stop at **City Hall** (on your left as you enter Town Square) for information or to snap a picture with the Disney characters who frequent the spot. Other Main Street attractions include a cinema that runs vintage Disney cartoons and the Penny Arcade, a historical version of today's electronic game rooms. Walk two blocks along Main Street and you'll enter Central Plaza, with **Cinderella Castle** rising directly in front of you. This is the hub of the Kingdom; all the "lands" radiate out from it.

A great way to get an overview of the Kingdom is to hop aboard the WDW Railroad and take a 21-minute, 1½-mi ride around the perimeter of the park. You can board at the Victorian-style station by Town Square. Other stations are in Frontierland and at Mickey's Starland on the border between Tomorrowland and Fantasyland.

The Magic Kingdom is divided into seven lands (of which Main Street U.S.A. is the first). Stories are told of tourists who spend an entire day in one land, thinking they have seen all the park; don't let that happen to you. The following are the highlights.

Adventureland is a mishmash of tropical and swashbuckling attractions that are among the most crowded in the Kingdom. Visit as late in the afternoon as possible or, better yet, in the evening. **Swiss Family Treehouse** (popular; all ages) is a good way to get some exercise and a panoramic view of the park. Visitors walk up the many-staired tree in single file, a trip that can take up to a half hour. **Jungle Cruise** (very popular; all ages) takes visitors along the Nile, the Mekong, the Congo, and the Amazon. The tour guide's narration is corny but nevertheless brings laughs. **Pirates of the Caribbean** (very popular; all ages) is a journey through a world of pirate strongholds and treasure-filled dungeons. The Audio-Animatronics pirates are first-rate.

Liberty Square is a journey back to Colonial America. The **Hall of Presidents** presents an electronic view of the history of the United States, while the **Mike Fink Keel Boats** and **Liberty Square Riverboat** cruise the Rivers of America. The star attraction here is Disney's special-effects extravaganza, the **Haunted Mansion.** Scary, but not terrifying, this ride on a "doom buggie" takes you past a plethora of dust, cobwebs, tombstones, and creepy characters.

Frontierland's big draw is **Big Thunder Mountain Railroad** (very popular; all ages), a scream-inducing roller coaster. Children must be at least 3′ 4″. Try to go in the evening when the mountain is lit up and lines are relatively short. **Splash Mountain** (very popular; all ages), an elaborate water-flume ride, is the newest attraction at the Magic Kingdom. Based on Disney's 1946 film "Song of the South," the ride includes characters from the movie as well as some of the songs. The eight-person hollowed-out log takes you on a half-mile journey that passes through Br'er Rabbit's habitat. The final plunge is down Chickapin Hill—the world's longest and sharpest flume drop—at speeds of up to 40 mph.

Fantasyland is, as the map says, "where storybook dreams come true." Fanciful gingerbread houses, gleaming gold turrets, and streams sparkling with shiny pennies dot the landscape, and its rides are based on Disney's animated movies. The first attraction on the left as you enter Fantasyland is **Legend of the Lion King.** Unlike many of the stage shows in the Magic Kingdom, this one showcases "humanimals," Disneyspeak for bigger-than-lifesize figures that are manipulated by human "animateers" hidden from audience view. (The adult Simba, for instance, is nearly 8 ft tall.) The preshow consists of the "Circle of Life" overture from the film. Other attractions include the rides **Dumbo, the Flying Elephant, Peter Pan's Flight,** and the **Mad Tea Party.** Kids of all ages love the antique **Cinderella's Golden Carrousel,** which encapsulates the entire Disney experience in its 90 prancing horses. Small children adore **It's a Small World,** a boat ride accompanied by its now-famous theme song of international brotherhood.

Mickey's Starland was built in 1988 to celebrate Mickey Mouse's 60th birthday. Here, in Duckburg, visitors can view Mickey's cartoons and films, visit Mickey's house, and have photos taken with Mickey in his Hollywood Theater dressing room. This is a good opportunity for weary parents to rest their feet while children explore a maze, pet young farm animals, or run around the playground.

Tomorrowland's top attraction is **Space Mountain** (very popular; children must be at least 3 years old, and children under 7 must be accompanied by an adult), a space-age roller coaster. It may never reach speeds of more than 28 mph, but the experience in the dark, with everyone screaming, is thrilling, even for hard-core roller-coaster fans.

To see the interior without taking the ride, hop aboard the WEDway PeopleMover. Also here is the CircleVision 360 **"American Journeys,"** which places you squarely in the middle of a circle of images—it will make you gasp.

EPCOT CENTER

Visitors familiar with the Magic Kingdom find something entirely different at Epcot Center. For one thing, Epcot is twice as large. For another, Epcot's attractions all have an educational dimension.

Future World features the **Spaceship Earth** geosphere—the giant, golf-ball-shaped Epcot icon whose ride explores the development of human communications—as well as seven corporate-sponsored pavilions covering energy, the Wonders of Life, technology, motion, the seas, the land, and imagination. With the exception of the Wonders of Life, the creatively educational exhibits include a self-contained ride and an occasional post-ride showcase.

World Showcase offers an adventure very different from what you will experience in either Epcot's world of the future or the Magic Kingdom's world of fairy tales. In 11 pavilions, an ideal image—a Disney version—of life in various countries is presented through native food, entertainment, and wares. Most of the nations have done an imaginative and painstaking job of re-creating scale models of their best-known monuments, such as the Eiffel Tower, a Mayan temple, and a majestic Japanese pagoda. During the day these structures are impressive enough, but at night, when the darkness inhibits one's ability to judge their size, you get the sense that you are seeing the real thing. It's a wonderful illusion, indeed.

Unlike Future World and the Magic Kingdom, the Showcase doesn't offer amusement-park-type rides (except in Mexico and Norway). Instead, it features breathtaking films, ethnic art, cultural entertainment, Audio-Animatronics presentations, and dozens of fine shops and restaurants featuring national specialties. The most enjoyable diversions in World Showcase are not inside the national pavilions but in front of them: Throughout the day, each pavilion offers some sort of live street show, featuring comedy, song, or dance routines and demonstrations of folk arts and crafts.

DISNEY-MGM STUDIOS THEME PARK

The **Backstage Studio Tour** and the **Animation Tour** are for those who want a close-up, behind-the-scenes look at a real studio. The backstage tour takes up to two hours, but half of it is on a tram that will take you through costuming, into a shop where scenery is made, down a back-lot "residential" street, into Catastrophe Canyon for a look at special effects, and for a quick glance at more back-lot props before the walking part of the guided tour begins. The walking portion—which includes following Roger Rabbit's pink paw prints through the Looney Bin—takes in a water-effects tank, special-effects workshops, soundstages, postproduction work, and a theater previewing new movies. The Animation Tour takes visitors step-by-step through the process by looking over the artists' shoulders from a raised, glass-enclosed walkway. **Star Tours** is one of Disney's more recent simulator thrill rides. Created under the direction of George Lucas, the five 40-seat theaters become spaceships, and you're off to the moon of Endor. Be warned: Lines are long, and the ride is rough.

The Making of *The Lion King* was originally produced for The Disney Channel and now runs for the masses at half-hour intervals. Narrated by Robert Guillaume (the voice of Rafiki, the film's psychic baboon),

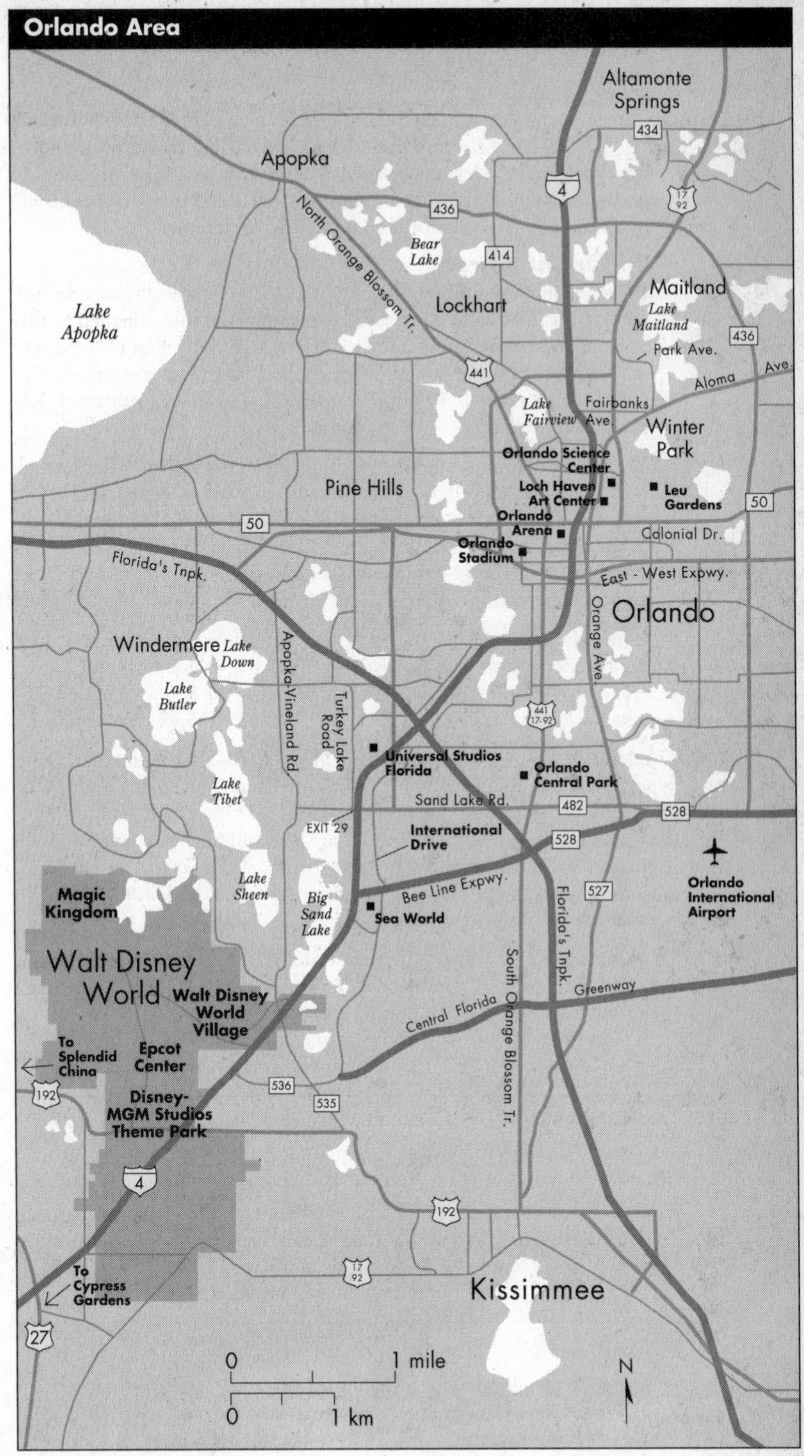
Orlando Area
Altamonte Springs
434
Apopka
4
17 92
436
Bear Lake
414
North Orange Blossom Tr.
Lockhart
Maitland
Lake Maitland
Lake Apopka
436
Park Ave.
441
Aloma
Ave.
Lake Fairview
Fairbanks Ave.
Winter Park
Orlando Science Center
Pine Hills
Loch Haven Art Center
Leu Gardens
Orlando Arena
50
50
Colonial Dr.
Orlando Stadium
Florida's Tnpk.
East - West Expwy.
Orlando
Windermere
Lake Down
Apopka-Vineland Rd.
Orange Ave.
Lake Butler
Turkey Lake Road
441 17-92
Universal Studios Florida
Orlando Central Park
Lake Tibet
Sand Lake Rd.
482
528
EXIT 29
International Drive
528
Lake Sheen
Bee Line Expwy.
527
Orlando International Airport
Magic Kingdom
Big Sand Lake
Sea World
Florida's Tnpk.
Walt Disney World
South Orange Blossom Tr.
Walt Disney World Village
Greenway
Central Florida
To Splendid China
Epcot Center
536
192
535
Disney-MGM Studios Theme Park
4
192
To Cypress Gardens
17 92
Kissimmee
27
0
1 mile
0
1 km
N

the film traces the creation of the animated classic from concept to final scenes.

OTHER ATTRACTIONS

Other Disney World attractions are the aquatic parks, **Typhoon Lagoon** (☎ 407/560–4142; admission $23 adults, $17.50 children) and **River Country** (Fort Wilderness Resort, ☎ 407/824–2760; admission $15 adults, $12 children), and the nature sanctuary **Discovery Island** (☎ 407/824–2875; admission $10 adults, $6 children).

The Orlando Area

Universal Studios Florida is the largest working film studio outside Hollywood. Visitors view live shows, participate in movie-themed attractions, and tour back-lot sets. The tour showcases the special-effects magic of creative consultant Steven Spielberg and the animation wizardry of Hanna–Barbera. *Exit 30B off I–4, ☎ 407/363–8000. Admission: $34 adults, $27 children.*

Performing dolphins and killer whales and a moving sidewalk through a shark tank capture your attention at **Sea World.** The park also has penguins, tropical fish, otter habitats, walrus-training exhibits, botanical gardens, and other educational diversions. *7007 Sea World Dr., Orlando, ☎ 407/351–3600 or 800/327–2424. Admission: $31.95 adults, $27.95 children.*

Beautiful **Cypress Gardens** offers walks through exotic gardens, bird and alligator shows, and the famous waterskiing-maidens show. *Off Rte. 540, east of Winter Haven, ☎ 813/324–2111 or 800/282–2123. Admission: $24.95 adults, $21.20 senior citizens, $16.45 children 3–9.*

Splendid China—12 mi southwest of Orlando—is a theme park with more than 60 scaled-down replicas of China's greatest landmarks. Among the painstakingly crafted models are the Great Wall, the Imperial Palace of Beijing's Forbidden City, and Suzhou Gardens, a re-creation of a 14th-century Chinese village. *300 Splendid China Blvd., Kissimmee, ☎ 407/397–8800. Admission: $23.55 adults, $13.90 children.*

In the **Cocoa Beach** area, 47 mi east of Orlando via Rte. 50 or the Bee Line Expressway, is the **Kennedy Space Center, Spaceport USA.** Here the wonders of space travel unfold through a superb film presentation and bus tours of spacecraft hangars and launch sites. *☎ 407/452–2121 or 800/432–2153. Admission charged. Closed Christmas.*

What to See and Do with Children

In addition to the Disney parks (*see* Exploring Walt Disney World, *above*), the Orlando area offers children the delights of **Gatorland Zoo** (U.S. 17/92 near Kissimmee, ☎ 407/855–5496 or 800/393–5297), with thousands of alligators, crocodiles, and other Florida wildlife, and **Fun'N Wheels** (6739 Sand Lake Rd. at International Dr., ☎ 407/351–5651), with go-carts, bumper cars and boats, and other rides.

Shopping

Unique native goods are available at the various country pavilions in the **World Showcase** at **Epcot Center. Altamonte Mall** (Rte. 436 in Altamonte Springs), the largest mall in central Florida, offers 165 specialty shops and five major department stores. The festive **Mercado Mediterranean Village** (8445 International Dr.) has specialty shops, an

International Food Pavilion, and free entertainment. **Flea World** (U.S. 17/92 between Orlando and Sanford) has more than 1,500 booths selling everything from citrus products to auto parts.

Sports and the Outdoors

Fishing

The area's plentiful freshwater lakes and rivers provide a year-round fisherman's paradise, with seasons for perch, catfish, and largemouth black bass. Contact the Orlando visitors bureau (*see* Tourist Information, *above*) for information. Fishing camps on **Lake Tohopekaliga,** a favorite destination for anglers, include **Red's Fish Camp** (4715 Kissimmee Park Rd., St. Cloud 34470, ☎ 407/892–8795) and **Richardson's Fish Camp** (1550 Scotty's Rd., Kissimmee 34744, ☎ 407/846–6540). Along the Atlantic coast, fishermen can troll for tuna, blue and white marlin, and sailfish; surf-cast for pompano and flounder; or deep-sea fish for grouper and red snapper. Deep-sea charters at Port Canaveral include **Cape Marina** (800 Scallop Dr., ☎ 407/783–8410).

Golf

Golf facilities open to the public include **Orange Lake Country Club** (8505 W. U.S. 192, Kissimmee, ☎ 407/239–0000), **Poinciana Golf & Racquet Club** (500 Cypress Pkwy., 18 mi southeast of Kissimmee, ☎ 407/933–5300), and **Timacuan Golf and Country Club** (550 Timacuan Blvd., Lake Mary, ☎ 407/321–0010). There are five championship courses within **Walt Disney World** (☎ 407/824–2270).

Horseback Riding

Fort Wilderness Campground (in Walt Disney World, ☎ 407/824–2832) and **Poinciana Riding Stables** (3705 Poinciana Blvd., Kissimmee, ☎ 407/847–4343) offer trail rides.

Tennis

Orlando Tennis Center (649 W. Livingston St., ☎ 407/246–2162) has 16 lighted courts. Many of the hotels and resorts within **Walt Disney World** also have courts.

Spectator Sports

Basketball

Orlando Magic (Orlando Arena, off I–4 at Amelia, ☎ 407/839–3900; Nov.–Apr.).

Dog Racing

Seminole Greyhound Park (2000 Seminola Blvd., Casselberry, ☎ 407/699–4510; May–Oct.) and **Sanford-Orlando Kennel Club** (301 Dog Track Rd., Longwood, ☎ 407/831–1600; Nov.–May) have dog racing Monday through Saturday nights.

Beaches and Water Sports

A plethora of water sports are available in the Orlando area. Marinas at resorts in **Walt Disney World** rent all types of boats, from canoes and catamarans to pedal boats. **Orange Lake Water Sports** (8505 W. Irlo Bronson Memorial Hwy., ☎ 407/239–4444) offers waterskiing and jet skiing. Just north of the Kennedy Space Center, the **Canaveral National Seashore** (Box 2583, Titusville 32780, ☎ 904/428–3384) has 25 mi of unspoiled, uncrowded beaches with facilities for swimming and boating.

Dining and Lodging

Dining is an adventure in the Orlando area, where international cuisines, fresh fish and seafood, and such exotic local dishes as grilled alligator tail tempt the hungry. Besides hotels in Walt Disney World, you'll find accommodations in Orlando; Kissimmee, just east of Disney World; and Lake Wales, south of Disney World near Cypress Gardens. Lodging options include luxury hotels and resorts, family resorts, and motel chains. For price ranges, see Charts 1 (B) and 2 (A) in On the Road with Fodor's.

Cocoa Beach

DINING

Mango Tree Restaurant. Candles, fresh flowers, paintings by local artists, and a garden aviary enhance the dining experience here. Broiled grouper topped with scallops, shrimp, and hollandaise is a menu favorite. *Cottage Row, 118 N. Atlantic Ave., ☎ 407/799–0513. AE, MC, V. $$$*

LODGING

Pelican Landing Resort on the Ocean. This family-oriented beachfront motel offers ocean views, a microwave in each room, picnic tables, and boardwalks to the beach. *1201 S. Atlantic Ave., 32931, ☎ 407/783–7197. 11 rooms. MC, V. $*

Kissimmee

DINING

Spaghetti House. This rather kitschy two-story restaurant lets you design your own Italian meal. Start with your favorite entrée (there are 31), then pick a sauce (primavera, bolognese, pesto) to go over your choice of pasta (available in spinach, whole wheat, and cholesterol-free versions). *4951 Sunward Dr., ☎ 407/351–3407. AE, D, DC, MC, V. $$*

LODGING

Casa Rosa Inn. This no-frills, Spanish-style motel offers clean, serviceable accommodations close to major Orlando attractions. *4600 W. Irlo Bronson Memorial Hwy. (U.S. 192), 32746, ☎ 407/396–2020 or 800/432–0665, FAX 407/396–6249. 54 rooms. Facilities: pool. AE, MC, V. $*

Lake Wales

DINING AND LODGING

★ **Chalet Suzanne.** This family-owned, Swiss-style country inn and restaurant nestled amid orange groves offers an intriguing mix of furnishings, reflecting its piecemeal expansion since the 1930s. The houses and cabins have balconies, thatched roofs, and old-fashioned tubs and basins. Dining is a memorable experience, with such specialties as shad roe, broiled grapefruit, and crepes Suzanne. *U.S. 27S, Drawer AC, 33859, ☎ 813/676–6011, FAX 813/676–1814. 30 rooms. Facilities: restaurant (jacket required; closed Mon. June–Aug.). AE, DC, MC, V. $$$*

Orlando

DINING

★ **Chatham's Place.** The office exterior belies what's inside—a small, unpretentious restaurant that is one of Orlando's finest. Enjoy such tantalizing entrées as black grouper with pecan butter and grilled duck breast. *7575 Dr. Phillips Blvd., ☎ 407/345–2992. MC, V. No lunch. $$–$$$*

Florida Bay Grill. Tasty, well-prepared, and fairly priced seafood is served in an atmosphere reminiscent of a Key West yacht club, with a turquoise-and-gray color scheme and cement floors. Try the grilled shrimp and mixed greens special. *8560 International Dr., ☎ 407/352–6655. AE, D, DC, MC, V. $$*

Planet Hollywood. Assembled by club owners Demi Moore, Bruce Willis, Arnold Schwarzenegger, Sylvester Stallone, and the biggest showman among the partners, restaurateur Robert Earl, Planet Hollywood houses movie memorabilia, like the bus that was used in the movie *Speed* and the leather jacket worn by Schwarzenegger in *The Terminator.* Memorabilia rotates between the Orlando Planet and its 17 sister restaurants around the country. The wait is about two hours most evenings. *Pleasure Island, Walt Disney World Village,* ☎ *407/363–7827. No reservations. AE, DC, MC, V. $$*

Hard Rock Cafe Orlando. At Universal Studios, this guitar-shaped eatery offers all-American burgers, fries, and shakes amid a rock music atmosphere conveyed by lots of memorabilia. *5401 S. Kirkman Rd.,* ☎ *407/363–7655. AE, MC, V. $*

LODGING

★ **Peabody Orlando.** The bland facade gives no hint of this 27-story hotel's beautifully decorated interior, with marble floors, fountains, and modern art. Many rooms have views of Walt Disney World. *9801 International Dr., 32819,* ☎ *407/352–4000 or 800/732–2639,* FAX *407/351–9177. 891 rooms. Facilities: 3 restaurants, health club, pool, 4 lighted tennis courts. AE, D, DC, MC, V. $$$–$$$$*

Best Western–Grosvenor Resort. This British Colonial–style hotel, with comfortable rooms, plentiful recreational facilities, and spacious public areas, is one of the best deals in the area. Rooms are average size but include refrigerator/bars and VCRs. *1850 Hotel Plaza Blvd., Lake Buena Vista 32830,* ☎ *407/828–4444 or 800/624–4109,* FAX *407/808–8120. 624 rooms, 6 suites. Facilities: 3 restaurants; 2 heated outdoor pools; 2 tennis courts; racquetball, volleyball, and basketball courts; children's playground; baby-sitting; game room. AE, D, DC, MC, V. $$$*

Walt Disney World

DINING

The **World Showcase** in **Epcot Center** offers some of the best dining in the Orlando area, with country specialties that will appeal to every taste. Phone reservations are open only to those staying at a Disney hotel (☎ 407/824–4000); otherwise, reservations, which are strongly advised, must be made in person at one of Epcot's WorldKey computer terminals. Reserve early in the day, before beginning your sightseeing.

L'Originale Alfredo di Roma Ristorante, in Italy of course, has pasta and such classic dishes as veal piccata, served by singing waiters (*$$$*). For a hearty portion of fish-and-chips with a Guinness stout, visit Britain's **Rose and Crown** pub on the shores of the lagoon (*$$*). For more exotic fare, try Moroccan couscous at **Restaurant Marrakesh** (*$$*).

LODGING

Although hotels and resorts on Disney property cost more than comparable facilities elsewhere, there are many perks to staying at one of them. For example, Disney guests get preference for golf tee-off times and restaurant reservations, and transportation to all parks is free. Book all Disney hotels—including the following—through the **Walt Disney World Central Reservations Office** (Box 10100, Suite 300, Lake Buena Vista 32830, ☎ 407/934–7639, FAX 407/354–1866).

★ **Grand Floridian Beach Resort.** With its brick chimneys, gabled roof, sweeping verandas, and stained-glass domes, this resort exudes Victorian charm yet has all the conveniences of a modern hotel. Water sports are a focal point at the marina. *900 rooms, 12 suites. Facilities: 6 restaurants, health club, pool, shops, child care. AE, MC, V. $$$$*

Caribbean Beach Resort. Set on a 42-acre tropical lake, this resort has several villages named after Caribbean islands, each with its own pool and beach. Facilities include a 500-seat food court, a 200-seat lounge, and an island in the lagoon with bike paths, trails, and play areas. *2,112 units. Facilities in each village: cafeteria-style food pavilion, pool, watercraft rentals, nature trails. AE, MC, V. $$*

Motels

U.S. 192 is crammed with motels that offer the basics at affordable prices, in a location near Disney World. Rates range from inexpensive to moderate, and most places have a pool, with few other extras. Among these are **Best Western, Comfort Inn,** and **EconoLodge** (*see* Toll-Free Numbers *in* Appendix).

Campgrounds

Fort Wilderness Campground Resort (Walt Disney World Central Reservations Office, *see* Lodging, *above*) is 730 acres of forests, streams, and small lakes within Disney World. You can rent a trailer or bring your own to campsites with electrical outlets, outdoor grills, running water, and waste disposal. Tent sites with water and electricity but no sewage are also available.

The Arts and Nightlife

The Arts

Carr Performing Arts Centre (401 Livingston St., Orlando, ☎ 407/849–2020) hosts dance, music, and theater performances. **Orange County Convention and Civic Center** (International Dr., Orlando, ☎ 407/345–9800) presents big-name performers.

Nightlife

Walt Disney World offers a variety of nightly entertainment, including the laser show **IllumiNations** at Epcot Center and the **Polynesian Revue** at the Polynesian Village Resort (☎ 407/934–7639). **Pleasure Island** (☎ 407/934–7781) is an entertainment complex offering theme nightclubs, a comedy club, movie theaters, and a teenage dance center. In Orlando, **Church Street Station** (129 W. Church St., ☎ 407/422–2434) is a popular entertainment complex in an authentic 19th-century setting. **Medieval Times** (4510 W. Irlo Bronson Memorial Hwy. [U.S. 192], Kissimmee, ☎ 407/239–0214 or 800/239–8300; in FL, 800/432–0768) is one of many exciting area dinner shows.

THE FLORIDA KEYS

The string of 31 islands—or keys—placed like a comma between the Atlantic Ocean and the Gulf of Mexico at the southern tip of Florida presents a paradox to the visitor. On the one hand, the Keys are natural wonders of lush vegetation, tropical birds, and wildlife, washed by waters teeming with more than 600 kinds of fish, where swimming, fishing, and boating are a way of life. But the Keys are also a highly commercialized tourist attraction that has brought a clutter of unsightly billboards, motels, and shopping malls to U.S. 1 (also known as the Overseas Highway) linking the islands to the mainland. Although the 110-mi drive from Key Largo to Key West is often clogged with traffic, it is still a mesmerizing journey into expanses of blue water and blue sky, especially where the road is the only thing separating the ocean from the Gulf.

Tourist Information

Florida Keys & Key West: Visitors Bureau (Box 1147, Key West 33041, ☎ 305/296–3811 or 800/352–5397). **Greater Key West:** Chamber of Commerce (402 Wall St., 33040, ☎ 305/294–2587 or 800/527–8539, FAX 305/294–7806). **Key Largo:** Chamber of Commerce (MM 106, BS, 105950 Overseas Hwy., 33037, ☎ 305/451–4747 or 800/822–1088).

Getting There

By Plane

Flights from Miami (American Eagle and USAir), Fort Lauderdale (Delta ComAir), Naples (Cape Air and Gulfstream International), **Orlando (USAir and Delta ComAir), and Tampa (USAir and Delta ComAir) arrive at Key West International Airport** (S. Roosevelt Blvd., ☎ 305/296–5439 for information, 305/296–7223 for administration).

Direct service between Miami and newly expanded **Marathon Airport** (MM 52, BS, 9000 Overseas Hwy., ☎ 305/743–2155) is provided by American Eagle and Gulfstream International. USAir Express connects Marathon with Tampa.

By Car

From Miami, take U.S. 1S to Florida City; just south of here U.S. 1 also becomes the Overseas Highway. To avoid Miami traffic, take the Homestead Extension of the Florida Turnpike (toll road) south until it links with U.S. 1.

Work on improving U.S. 1 from Card Sound to Key Largo, which includes widening at least a portion of the road to four lanes and replacing the Jewfish Creek bridge, began in 1994 and will continue through the decade.

By Bus

Greyhound Lines (☎ 800/231–2222) buses make eight scheduled stops between Miami and Key West, but you can flag down a bus anywhere along the route.

By Boat

You can travel to Key West via the Intracoastal Waterway through Florida Bay or along the Atlantic coast. Marinas abound in the Keys, but be sure to make docking reservations in advance. For more information, contact the **Florida Marine Patrol** (MM 49, OS, 2835 Overseas Hwy., Marathon, ☎ 305/289–2320).

Exploring the Florida Keys

The Keys are divided into the Upper Keys (from Key Largo to Long Key Channel), the Middle Keys (from Long Key Channel to Seven Mile Bridge), and the Lower Keys (from Seven Mile Bridge to Key West). Pause to explore the flora and fauna of the backcountry and the fragile reefs and aquatic life of the surrounding waters as you weave your way south to historically rich Key West. Addresses are listed by island or mile marker (MM) number. Residents use the abbreviation BS for the Bay Side of the Overseas Hwy. (U.S. 1) and OS for the Atlantic Ocean side of the highway.

The Upper Keys are dominated by **Key Largo,** with its wildlife refuges and nature parks. To view the elusive crocodile, drive through **Crocodile Lakes National Wildlife Refuge,** where between 300 and 500 of these shy, elusive reptiles can be found, on Card Sound Road in North Key Largo. **Key Largo Undersea Park** (51 Shoreland Dr., ☎ 305/451–

2353) includes an underwater archaeology exhibit that you have to snorkel or dive to; for groups of at least six there is an air-conditioned grotto theater with a multimedia slide show on the history of man and his relation to the sea. Through high-tech communications, audiences can interact with the divers in the 30-ft-deep lagoon where guides lead scuba and snorkel tours. A pilot submarine at the site gives three-hour tours for up to six people.

Farther south on the Overseas Highway, you'll find the **Maritime Museum of the Florida Keys** (MM 102.5, BS, Key Largo, ☎ 305/451–6444; admission charged). This small but earnest museum offers exhibits depicting the history of shipwrecks and salvage efforts along the Keys and including retrieved treasures, reconstructed wreck sites, and artifacts in various stages of preservation. Artifacts newly added in 1994 and 1995 have come from a fleet of treasure ships wrecked in 1715 by a hurricane 250 miles farther north along the Gulf Stream.

Continuing south on the Overseas Highway, you'll encounter three state parks that are accessible only by water. Take a glass-bottom dive and snorkel boat to **San Pedro Underwater Archaeological Preserve** (MM 79.5, OS, Islamorada, ☎ 305/664–2211), which features the 1733 wreck of a Spanish treasure ship. State-operated boat tours leave from the dock on Indian Fill Key (MM 78.5) to take you to **Indian Key State Historical Site,** commemorating the 1840 Indian massacre of a pioneer settlement, and **Lignumvitae Key State Botanical Site** (closed Tues.–Wed.), with a virgin hardwood forest and a house and gardens built by chemical magnate William Matheson in 1919. For information and reservations, contact **Long Key Recreation Area** (MM 67.5, OS, Box 776, Long Key 33001, ☎ 305/664–4815).

The bridge over **Long Key Channel** (one of 42 bridges on the drive) leads to **Conch Key,** a tiny fishing and retirement community that serves as a gateway to the Middle Keys. At the **Dolphin Research Center** (MM 59, BS, Marathon Shores, ☎ 305/289–0002; closed Mon.–Tues.) on **Grassy Key,** you can swim with dolphins.

At **Marathon** (MM 53–47), explore the **Museum of Natural History of the Florida Keys,** where dioramas and displays explain the Keys' geology, wildlife, and cultural history. Also here is the Florida Keys Children's Museum, a 1-mi indigenous loop trail, the remnants of a Bahamian village, and the restored George Adderly House, the oldest surviving example of Conch-style architecture outside Key West. From November to Easter, weekly docent-led hammock tours may be available; bring good walking shoes and bug repellent. During Pirates in Paradise, an annual four-day festival held on the first weekend in May, the museums sponsor a celebration of the region's history. *MM 50, BS, 5550 Overseas Hwy., Box 536, Marathon 33050, ☎ 305/743–9100. Admission (including tour): $5 adults, $4 senior citizens, $2 students 13 and older. ⏲ Mon.–Sat. 9–5, Sun. noon–5.*

After crossing **Seven Mile Bridge,** believed to be the world's longest segmented bridge, you'll enter the Lower Keys. The delicate Key deer can be viewed at **National Key Deer Refuge** (off Watson Blvd., ☎ 305/872–2239) on **Big Pine Key** (MM 32–30).

The journey ends at **Key West,** famous for its semitropical climate, laid-back lifestyle, colorful heritage, and 19th-century architecture. The town's rich ethnic past comes alive in the **Bahama Village** area (Thomas and Petronia Sts.), with the peach, yellow, and pink homes of early Bahamian settlers, and at the **San Carlos Institute** (516 Duval St., ☎ 305/294–

3887), the Cuban-American heritage center. History buffs head for **Fort Zachary Taylor State Historic Site** (Southard St., ☎ 305/292–6713), an important fort during the Civil and Spanish-American wars, and the **Lighthouse Museum** (938 Whitehead St., ☎ 305/294–0012), with its 92-ft lighthouse and 1847 keeper's cottage. Nature lovers will want to visit the **Audubon House and Gardens** (205 Whitehead St., ☎ 305/294–2116), with its tropical gardens and large collection of Audubon engravings. For literary types there is the **Hemingway House** (907 Whitehead St., ☎ 305/294–1575), a museum dedicated to the life and work of the author who wrote 70% of his works here, including *For Whom the Bell Tolls* and *The Old Man and the Sea.*

"Writers' Walk" is a guided tour past the residences of prominent authors who have lived in Key West (Elizabeth Bishop, Robert Frost, Ernest Hemingway, Wallace Stevens, and Tennessee Williams, among others). The self-guiding **Cuban Heritage Trail,** which comprises 36 sites related to Key West's historical involvement in the affairs of Cuba, is detailed in a free pamphlet and map available from the Historic Florida Keys Preservation Board.

What to See and Do with Children

Two outstanding attractions are **Key Largo Undersea Park** (*see* Exploring the Florida Keys, *above*) and **Theater of the Sea** (MM 84.5, OS, Islamorada, ☎ 305/664–2431), with dolphin and sea-lion shows, a touch tank, a pool where sharks are fed by a trainer,and a "living reef" aquarium.

Shopping

The Keys are a thriving artists' community, so art is in good supply here. **Rain Barrel** (MM 86.7, BS, 86700 Overseas Hwy., Islamorada, ☎ 305/852–3084) is a 3-acre crafts village with eight resident artists. A tearoom and a bakery are to be added by 1996. **Key West's** unique specialty shops, such as **Fast Buck Freddie's** (500 Duval St., ☎ 305/294–2007), selling banana-leaf-shaped furniture, have gained an international reputation. In a town with a gazillion T-shirt shops, **Boh-heem** (706 Duval St., ☎ 305/292–4035) is the one place you don't want to miss buying one, although **Last Flight Out** (710 Duval St., ☎ 305/294–8008) offers its classic namesake tees, which recall the pre-World War II heyday of tourist flights between Key West and Havana.

Sports and the Outdoors

Biking

A **bike path** parallels the Overseas Highway from Key Largo to Plantation Key (MM 106–86). Construction is expected to begin in mid-1995 on an additional 2-mi section on Lower Matecumbe Key. Trails crisscross the Marathon area; most popular is the 2-mi section of the **old Seven Mile Bridge** leading to Pigeon Key. Cycling is one of the best ways to explore Key West. For rentals, contact **Key Largo Bikes** (MM 99.4, BS, 105 Laguna Ave., ☎ 305/451–1910), **KCB Bike Shop** (MM 53, 11518 Overseas Hwy., Marathon, ☎ 305/289–1670), **Keys Moped & Scooter** (523 Truman Ave., Key West, ☎ 305/294–0399), or **Equipment Locker Sport & Cycle** (MM 53, BS, 11518 Overseas Hwy., ☎ 305/289–1670). The **Key West Nature Bike Tour** (Truman Ave. and Simonton St., ☎ 305/294–2882) departs from Moped Hospital on Sunday at 10:30 and Tuesday–Saturday at 9 and 3. The cost is $12 per person with your own bike, or you can rent a clunker for $3.

Diving and Snorkeling

The Keys are a diver's paradise, with miles of living coral reefs populated with 650 species of rainbow-hued tropical fish, as well as four centuries of shipwrecks, to explore. Outstanding diving areas include **John Pennekamp Coral Reef State Park** (MM 102.5, OS, Key Largo, ☎ 305/451–1202) and **Looe Key Reef,** 5 mi off Ramrod Key (MM 27.5). Dive shops include **Florida Keys Dive Center** (MM 90.5, OS, 90500 Overseas Hwy., Tavernier, ☎ 305/852–4599 or 800/433–8946) and **Looe Key Dive Center** (MM 27.5, OS, Ramrod Key, ☎ 305/872–2215 or 800/942–5397). A new administrative attempt to manage the natural resources of the Keys for private use (mainly fisheries and tourism), research, and preservation, the **Florida Keys National Marine Sanctuary** (Planning Office, 9499 Overseas Hwy., Marathon 33050, ☎ 305/743–2437) plan should be implemented sometime in 1996.

Fishing and Boating

Deep-sea fishing on the ocean or gulf and flat-water fishing in the back-country shallows are popular. Numerous marinas rent all types of boats and water-sports equipment. Particularly popular are the various glass-bottom-boat tours to the coral reefs. Check with local chambers of commerce for information on charter- and party-boat operators, or call **Adventure Charters** (6810 Front St., Key West 33040, ☎ 305/296–0362), **Back Country Eco-tours** (Rte. 2, Box 669-F, Summerland Key 33042, ☎ 305/745–2868), or **Everglades Safari Tours** (Box 3343, Key Largo 33037, ☎ 305/451–4540 or 800/959–0742).

Golf

Key Colony Beach Par 3 (MM 53.5, OS, 8th St., Key Colony Beach near Marathon, ☎ 305/289–1533; 9 holes) and **Key West Resort Golf Course** (6450 E. Junior College Rd., Key West, ☎ 305/294–5232; 18 holes) are open to the public.

Beaches

Since the natural shorelines of the Keys are a combination of marshes, rocky outcroppings, and grassy wetlands, most beaches for sunbathing and swimming are man-made from imported sand. **Bahia Honda State Park** (MM 36.5, OS, Bahia Honda Key, ☎ 305/872–2353) offers a sandy beach, plus a nature trail, campground (call for reservations up to 60 days in advance.), marina, and dive shop. Of the several Key West beaches, **Smathers Beach** (S. Roosevelt Blvd.) has 2 mi of sandy beach and good windsurfing, and **Higgs Memorial Beach** (White St.) is popular for sunbathing. Many hotels and motels also have their own small, shallow-water beach areas. Among those open to the public is **Plantation Yacht Harbor Resort & Marina** (MM 87, BS, Plantation Key, ☎ 305/852–2381); there's a delightful tiki bar just behind the crescent beach.

Dining and Lodging

The Keys have gained a reputation for fine cuisine. Many dishes have a Caribbean accent, mixing papaya, kiwi, and other tropical fruits, vegetables, and spices with local fish and citrus. Local specialties include conch chowder, Florida lobster, and Key lime pie. Accommodations, from historic hotels and guest houses to large resorts and run-of-the-mill motels, are more expensive here than elsewhere in southern Florida. For price ranges, see Charts 1 (B) and 2 (A) in On the Road with Fodor's.

Islamorada

DINING

★ **Squid Row.** This may look like just another cutely named, affordable food stop on the way to Key West, but this attitude-free roadside eatery is devoted to serving the freshest fish you haven't caught yourself. Seafood wholesalers own it, and they supply the kitchen with fresh daily specials. *MM 81.9, OS, ☎ 305/664–9865. AE, D, DC, MC, V. Closed Wed. $$*

LODGING

★ **Cheeca Lodge.** This 27-acre resort preserves its beautiful surroundings with a science camp for children and an extensive recycling program. One Cheeca policy, for example, combats natural-resource degradation by letting guests decide if they wish to reuse their sheets and towels, thereby helping reduce detergent waste. Guest rooms and suites feature periwinkle blue/strawberry, and green/hot orange color schemes; all have furniture of tightly woven wicker, cane, and bamboo. Each suite has a full kitchen and a screened balcony; fourth-floor rooms in the main lodge open onto bay- or ocean-view terraces. *MM 82, Upper Matecumbe Key, Box 527, Islamorada 33036, ☎ 305/664–4651 or 800/327–2888, FAX 305/664–2893. 139 rooms, 64 suites. Facilities: 2 restaurants, lounge, 9-hole golf course, 6 tennis courts, 3 pools, fishing pier, water-sports rentals, charter fishing fleet. AE, D, DC, MC, V. $$$$*

Key Largo

DINING

★ **Crack'd Conch.** Originally a fishing camp from the 1930s, this newly refurbished, unpretentious restaurant with a screened outdoor porch tempts hungry diners with conch chowder, conch fritters, fried alligator, and 115 kinds of beer. *MM 105, OS, 105045 Overseas Hwy., ☎ 305/451–0732. No reservations. AE, D, MC, V. Closed Wed. and holidays. $$*

★ **Mrs. Mac's Kitchen.** Popular with locals, this open-air restaurant offers nightly dinner specials and a tasty bowl of chili anytime in an informal room where beer cans, bottles, and license plates from around the world festoon the walls. *MM 99.4, OS, ☎ 305/451–3722. No credit cards. Closed Sun. $*

LODGING

★ **Marriott's Key Largo Bay Beach Resort.** At this 17-acre bayside resort, Marriott re-imagines Key Largo as if it hadn't become one more sense-dulling suburb of Miami. The facilities are as good as the guest rooms, which are joyfully styled and fully furnished for resort comfort with chintz, rattan, and straw; paddle fans; and sliding glass doors to balconies from which, at least in the better rooms, you can watch the sunset sweep across the bay. The resort creates its own virtual reality. You might even end up believing it's real. *MM 103.8, BS, 103800 Overseas Hwy., ☎ 305/453–0000 or 800/932–9332, FAX 305/453–0093. 122 rooms, 14 2-bedroom suites, 6 3-bedroom suites, 1 penthouse suite. Facilities: 3 restaurants (1 with nightly entertainment), tiki bar, freshwater pool, saltwater pool, beach, water-sports equipment rentals, marina, charter fishing boats, game room, boutiques. AE, D, DC, MC, V. $$$$*

★ **Largo Lodge.** A tropical garden surrounds the guest houses at this vintage-1950s resort, where every room is decorated differently. *MM 101.5, BS, 101740 Overseas Hwy., 33037, ☎ 305/451–0424 or 800/468–4378. 6 apartments with kitchen, 1 efficiency. Facilities: boat ramp and 3 slips. AE, MC, V. $$*

Bay Harbor Lodge. The rates and the waterfront setting make this place especially good. The resort offers a rustic wood lodge, tiki huts, and concrete block cottages; every room has either a small fridge or full kitchen. Laszlo Simoga and his wife, Sandra, are the kind of caring hosts who make mom-and-pop lodges such as this worth the visit. A pool is to be added by 1996. *MM 97.7, BS, 97702 Overseas Hwy., 33037, ☎ 305/852–5695. 16 rooms with bath. Facilities: weight equipment, 2 docks, paddleboats, rowboats, canoe, kayak, Jacuzzi, barbecue grills, boat-trailer parking. D, MC, V. $–$$*

Key West

DINING

★ **Louie's Backyard.** Key West paintings and pastels adorn the interior of this local institution, while outside you dine under the mahoe tree and feel the cool breeze off the sea. The ambience shares pride of place with chef Susan Ferry's culinary expertise. The loosely Spanish–Caribbean menu changes twice yearly but might include such house specials as loin of venison with port, wild mushrooms, and goat-cheese strudel, or pan-cooked grouper with Thai peanut sauce. Top off the meal with Louie's lime tart or an irresistible chocolate brownie brûlée. Lunch service, alas, can be out to lunch. *700 Waddell Ave., ☎ 305/294–1061. AE, DC, MC, V. $$$*

★ **Pier House Restaurant.** Steamships from Havana once docked at this pier jutting out into the Gulf of Mexico. Now it's a hotel (*see* Lodging, *below*) and an elegant place in which to dine, indoors or out, and to watch boats gliding by in the harbor. At night the restaurant shines lights into the water, attracting schools of brightly colored parrot fish. The menu emphasizes tropical fruits, spices, and fish and includes grilled sea scallops with black-bean cake and *pico de gallo* (tomato, shallots, cilantro, chopped chayote); lobster ravioli with a creamy pesto sauce and salmon caviar; and fresh catch prepared with tomatillo vinaigrette and saffron aïoli. *1 Duval St., ☎ 305/296–4600, ext. 555. AE, D, DC, MC, V. No lunch Mon.–Sat. Easter–mid-Dec. $$$*

★ **Antonia's.** Northern Italian cooking reaches new heights in a smart setting that was once the site of the Blue Boar Bar and the hippie coffeehouse Crazy Ophelia's. The bar opens to a darkly paneled and candlelit dining room with at most 30 tables. Co-chefs Antonia Berto and Phillip Smith turn out fluent renditions of Keys seafood and pasta and various salads. All pastas and focaccia are made in-house. Guests can order half-portions of pastas, and many Italian wines are offered by the glass. *615 Duval St., ☎ 305/294–6565. AE, DC, MC, V. Closed Thanksgiving. No lunch. $$*

Half Shell Raw Bar. Eat indoors or at outdoor picnic tables overlooking the deep-sea fishing fleet. Originally a fish market, this popular spot offers such daily specials as seafood linguine marinara. *Land's End Marina, ☎ 305/294–7496. No reservations. MC, V. $–$$*

El Siboney. This sprawling, family-style restaurant specializes in traditional Cuban dishes such as roast pork with black beans and rice. The atmosphere is relaxed and friendly. *900 Catherine St., ☎ 305/296–4184. No reservations. No credit cards. Closed major holidays, 2 wks in June. $*

LODGING

★ **Marquesa Hotel.** Adding on doesn't necessarily make a good thing better. A near doubling of size at this coolly elegant, restored 1884 home has traded an inspired intimacy for something more staged. Space, if no longer intimate, is hardly less private, and former guests needn't worry that the change will be jarring. Elegant rooms are detailed with eclectic antique and reproduction furnishings, dotted Swiss curtains, and botanical print fabrics. As ever, the lobby resembles a Victorian parlor, with antique furniture, Audubon prints, fresh flowers, and wonderful photos of early Key West, including one of Harry Truman driving by in a convertible. *600 Fleming St., 33040, ☎ 305/292–1919 or 800/869–4631, FAX 305/294–2121. 27 rooms. Facilities: restaurant, heated pool, free off-street parking. AE, DC, MC, V. $$$$*

Curry Mansion Inn. Wicker furniture and pastel colors characterize this modern guest house, which blends beautifully with the adjoining turn-of-the-century Curry Mansion (open for self-guided tours). *511 Caroline St., 33040, ☎ 305/294–5349, FAX 305/294–4093. 15 rooms, 8 suites. Facilities: Continental breakfast, happy hour, pool, privileges at Pier House Beach Club. AE, D, DC, MC, V. $$$–$$$$*

★ **La Concha Holiday Inn.** This seven-story Art Deco hotel in the heart of downtown is Key West's tallest building and dates from 1926. The lobby's polished floor of pink, mauve, and green marble and a conversation pit with comfortable chairs are among the details beloved by La Concha's guests. Large rooms are furnished with 1920s-era antiques, lace curtains, and big closets. The restorers kept the old building's original louvered room doors, light globes, and floral trim on the archways. *430 Duval St., 33040, ☎ 305/296–2991 or 800/745–2191, FAX 305/294–4093. 158 rooms, 2 suites. Facilities: 2 restaurants, pool, sundeck, whirlpool, fitness room, restaurant, 3 bars, bicycle and motor scooter rentals. AE, D, DC, MC, V. $$$–$$$$*

Pier House. Easily accessible to Key West attractions, yet offering the tranquillity of a tropical-island escape within its grounds, this hotel complex has a beach club, a fitness center, and an elegant restaurant (*see* Dining, *above*). The Caribbean Spa section has rooms and suites with hardwood floors and two-poster plantation-style beds. *1 Duval St., 33040, ☎ 305/296–4600 or 800/327–8340, FAX 305/296–7569. 109 rooms, 33 suites. Facilities: 5 restaurants, 5 bars, pool, fitness center, beach club. AE, D, DC, MC, V. $$$–$$$$*

Marathon

DINING

Ship's Pub and Galley. The 40-item salad bar with all-you-can-eat steamed shrimp and the mile-high shoofly mud pie are just two reasons to dine here. Photos of the Keys' railroad days adorn the walls. *MM 61, OS, ☎ 305/743–7000, ext. 3627. AE, DC, MC, V. $$*

LODGING

Sombrero Resort & Lighthouse Marina. This complex of one- to three-story buildings offers rooms with marina or pool views. Most suites have kitchens. *MM 50, OS, 19 Sombrero Blvd., 33050, ☎ 305/743–2250 or 800/433–8660, FAX 305/743–2998. 99 suites, 25 villa efficiencies. Facilities: restaurant, commissary, bar, pool, 54-slip marina with electric cable and phone hookups, boat ramp. AE, DC, MC, V. $$$*

Plantation Key

DINING

★ **Marker 88.** Savor the gorgeous Keys sunset as you sample such imaginative specialties as banana-blueberry bisque, sautéed conch, or alligator steak in this bayside restaurant. *MM 88, BS, Overseas Hwy., ☎ 305/852–9315. AE, DC, MC, V. Closed Mon. No lunch. $$*

The Arts and Nightlife

Key West is the Keys hub for artistic performances and nightlife. The city alone currently claims among its residents 55 full-time writers and 500 painters and craftspeople. The most popular entertainment is the nightly gathering of street vendors, performers, and visitors on **Mal-**

lory Square Dock to celebrate the sunset. The **Tennessee Williams Fine Arts Center** (Florida Keys Community College, 5901 W. Junior College Rd., Key West, ☎ 305/296–1520) offers dance, music, plays, and star performers. Among the many discos and clubs are two landmarks noted for their connection with Ernest Hemingway: **Capt. Tony's Saloon** (428 Greene St., ☎ 305/294–1838) and **Sloppy Joe's** (201 Duval St., ☎ 305/294–5717).

Four-hour, offshore casino gambling cruises depart from **Marathon** nightly on the ***Mr. Lucky*** (Marathon Marina, MM 47.5, ☎ 305/289–9700); day cruises run on weekends. There's also gourmet dinner service.

SOUTHWEST FLORIDA

Swimming, sunbathing, sailing, and shelling draw increasing numbers of visitors to the 200-mi coastal stretch between the Tampa Bay area and the Everglades. Venturing inland from the miles of sun-splashed beaches along the Gulf of Mexico, many visitors discover the culturally rich and ethnically diverse towns, interesting historical sites, and stellar attractions, such as Busch Gardens. Often this something-for-everyone mix is available at more affordable prices than elsewhere in Florida. The region is most accessible if divided into three areas: Tampa Bay (including Tampa, St. Petersburg, Clearwater, and Tarpon Springs), Sarasota (including Bradenton and Venice), and the Fort Myers/Naples area.

Getting There

By Plane

Most major U.S. airlines serve at least one of the region's airports. **Tampa International** (☎ 813/870–8700), 6 mi from downtown, is also served by international airlines. **Sarasota–Bradenton Airport** (☎ 813/359–5200) is just north of Sarasota off U.S. 41. **Southwest Florida Regional Airport** (☎ 813/768–1000) is about 12 mi south of Fort Myers and 25 mi north of Naples.

By Car

From the Georgia–Florida border, it's a three-hour drive via I–75S to Tampa, four hours to Sarasota, five to Fort Myers, and six to Naples. U.S. 41 (the Tamiami Trail) also traverses the region, but because it passes through many towns' business districts, traffic can be heavy. Naples is linked to Fort Lauderdale, on the eastern side of the state, via Alligator Alley (Rte. 84).

By Train

Amtrak connects most of the country with Tampa (601 N. Nebraska Ave., ☎ 813/221–7600 or 800/872–7245).

By Bus

Greyhound Lines (☎ 800/231–2222) provides statewide service, including stops at Tampa, St. Petersburg, Sarasota, and Fort Myers. For local bus service, contact **Hillsborough Area Regional Transit** (☎ 813/254–4278) for the Tampa area, **Sarasota County Area Transit** (☎ 813/951–5850) for Sarasota, and **Lee County Transit System** (☎ 813/939–1303) for the Fort Myers area.

The Tampa Bay Area

Tourist Information

Greater Tampa: Chamber of Commerce (Box 420, 33601, ☎ 813/228–7777). **St. Petersburg:** Chamber of Commerce (100 2nd Ave. N, 33701,

☎ 813/821–4069). **Tampa/Hillsborough:** Convention and Visitors Association (111 Madison St., Suite 1010, Tampa 33601-0519, ☎ 800/826–8358).

Exploring the Tampa Bay Area

Tampa is the commercial center of southwest Florida, with a bustling international port and the largest shrimp fleet in the state. It's also home to historic ethnic neighborhoods, such as Ybor City, where early Cuban immigrants established a cigar-making industry.

The city by the bay pays homage to its coastal setting with the **Florida Aquarium** (300 S. 13th St., ☎ 813/229–8861; admission charged), an $84 million complex at the intersection of Garrison and Ybor channels near downtown that opened in the spring of 1995. The 83-ft-high glass dome is already a landmark. Included are more than 4,300 specimens of fish, other animals, and plants representing 550 species native to Florida. In Tampa, reserve a day for a journey through the Dark Continent at **Busch Gardens** (3000 Busch Blvd., ☎ 813/987–5082; admission $27.95), a 300-acre African theme park with rides, live shows, and a fascinating monorail "safari." East of downtown is the **Seminole Indian Village** (5221 Orient Rd., Exit 5 off I–4, ☎ 813/620–3077), where alligator wrestling and demonstrations of traditional Seminole crafts are presented.

Ybor City (pronounced EE-bor), with its cobblestone streets and wrought-iron balconies, is Tampa's Cuban melting pot and thrived on cigar-making at the turn of the century. To get there, take I–4W to Exit 1 (22nd St.) and go south five blocks to 7th Avenue. Here you're in the heart of Ybor City, where the smell of cigars mingles with old-world architecture. Take a stroll past the ornately tiled Columbia Restaurant and the stores lining the street. **Ybor Square** (1901 13th St.) is a restored cigar factory that is now a mall with boutiques, offices, and restaurants.

On the Gulf about 25 mi north of Tampa is colorful **Tarpon Springs.** Famous for its sponge divers, the town reflects the heritage of its predominantly Greek population. A drive north from Tampa on U.S. 19, the area's major north–south artery, offers opportunities to view the endangered manatees, or sea cows, in springs and rivers. At **Weeki Wachee Spring** (45 mi north of Tampa on U.S. 19 and Rte. 50, Weeki Wachee, ☎ 904/596–2062; admission $14.95 adults, $10.95 children), "mermaids" present shows in an underwater theater.

About 15 mi farther north is **Homosassa Springs State Wildlife Park** (U.S. 19 to Rte. 490–A, ☎ 904/628–2311; admission charged), where you can watch manatees up close, visit reptile and alligator shows, cruise the Homosassa River, and view sea life in a floating observatory.

Heading south from Tampa, cross Old Tampa Bay on I–275 to get to the heart of neighboring **St. Petersburg.** Set on a peninsula bordered on three sides by bays and the Gulf of Mexico, the city offers beautiful beaches. **Great Explorations!** (1120 4th St. S, ☎ 813/821–8885; admission charged) is a hands-on museum divided into theme rooms such as the Body Shop, which explores health; the Think Tank, which features mind-stretching puzzles and games; Phenomenal Arts, which displays such items as a Moog music synthesizer (which you can play) and neon-filled tubes that glow in vivid colors when touched; and the Touch Tunnel, a 90-ft-long, pitch-black maze you crawl through.

South from St. Petersburg on U.S. 19 to I–275 takes you toward Sarasota via the **Sunshine Skyway** suspension bridge, with breathtaking views of Tampa Bay.

What to See and Do with Children

Adventure Island has water slides and man-made waves. *4545 Bougainvillea Ave., Tampa,* ☎ *813/987–6300. Admission: $16.95. Closed Dec.–Feb.*

Shopping

Seven blocks of fine shops and restaurants line Tampa's Swan Avenue in **Old Hyde Park Village** (☎ 813/251–3500). In Pinellas Park is **Wagonwheel** (7801 Park Blvd., ☎ 813/544–5319), a weekend flea market with about 2,000 vendors. For unique gifts, shop for natural sponges on Dodecanese Boulevard in **Tarpon Springs** or for Cuban cigars in **Ybor City** on Tampa's east side.

Dining

The ethnic diversity of the region makes for some adventurous dining, from honey-soaked Greek baklava to Cuban saffron-rice casserole. For price ranges, see Chart 1 (B) in On the Road with Fodor's.

★ **Bern's Steak House.** This renowned steak house boasts an extensive wine list, organically grown vegetables from the owner's farm, and scrumptious desserts served in upstairs rooms equipped with TV and radio. *1208 S. Howard Ave., Tampa,* ☎ *813/251–2421. AE, DC, MC, V. No lunch. $$$*

Columbia. An institution in Ybor City since 1905, this light and spacious Spanish restaurant serves excellent paella, with some flamenco dancing on the side. *2117 E. 7th Ave., Tampa,* ☎ *813/248–4961. AE, DC, MC, V. $$*

Louis Pappas' Riverside Restaurant. This waterfront landmark is always crowded with diners savoring the fine Greek fare, including the Greek salad made with feta cheese, onions, and olive oil. *10 W. Dodecanese Blvd., Tarpon Springs,* ☎ *813/937–5101. AE, DC, MC, V. $$*

Lodging

A generous mix of roadside motels, historic hotels, and sprawling resorts can be found here. For price ranges, see Chart 2 (A) in On the Road with Fodor's.

★ **Don CeSar Beach Resort.** Still echoing with the ghosts of Scott and Zelda, this sprawling beachfront "Pink Palace" has long been a Gulf Shore landmark. Turn-of-the-century elegance and spaciousness are everywhere, as is superb service. Recent improvements include the complete overhaul of the ground-floor Maritana Grille; a new beachside pool; and a beach spa, which offers thalassotherapy treatments and sea scrubs. *3400 Gulf Blvd., St. Petersburg Beach 33706,* ☎ *813/360–1881,* FAX *813/367–7597. 277 rooms. Facilities: 2 restaurants, lounge, 2 pools, beach, gym, 2 spas, tennis court, children's program. AE, DC, MC, V. $$$$*

Holiday Inn Busch Gardens. This well-maintained family-oriented motor lodge is just 1 mi west of Busch Gardens (transport provided). Rooms are bright and spacious; some look out on a central courtyard with garden and pool. *2701 E. Fowler Ave., Tampa 33612,* ☎ *813/971–4710,* FAX *813/977–0155. 392 rooms. Facilities: restaurant, lounge, exercise room, pool, sauna. AE, DC, MC, V. $$*

The Arts and Nightlife

The region between Tampa and Sarasota hums with cultural activities. Professional theater, dance, and music events are presented at **Tampa Bay Performing Arts Center** (1010 W.C. MacInnes Pl., Box 2877, Tampa, ☎ 813/221–1045 or 800/955–1045) and **Ruth Eckerd Hall** (1111

McMullen Booth Rd., Clearwater, ☎ 813/791–7400). The area's numerous discos and clubs include the **Comedy Works** (3447 W. Kennedy Blvd., Tampa, ☎ 813/875–9129).

The Sarasota Area

Tourist Information

Sarasota: Convention and Visitors Bureau (655 N. Tamiami Trail, 34236, ☎ 813/957–1877 or 800/522–9799).

Exploring the Sarasota Area

Known for its plentiful, clean beaches and profusion of golf courses, the Sarasota area, south of Tampa Bay via U.S. 41 or U.S. 301, is also a growing cultural center and winter home of the Ringling Brothers Barnum & Bailey Circus. At **De Soto National Memorial** (75th St. NW, Bradenton, ☎ 813/792–0458), costumed guides recount Spanish conquistador Hernando de Soto's 16th-century landing and expedition. Near Bradenton is **Gamble Plantation State Historical Site** (3708 Patten Ave., Ellenton, ☎ 813/723–4536), the only surviving pre–Civil War plantation house in south Florida.

U.S. 41S brings you to **Sarasota** and the **Ringling Museums** (U.S. 41, ☎ 813/355–5101; admission charged), which include the Venetian-style mansion of circus magnate John Ringling, his art museum with its world-renowned collection of Rubens paintings, and a circus museum. Farther south on U.S. 41 are the **Marie Selby Botanical Gardens** (800 S. Palm Ave., ☎ 813/366–5730), acclaimed for their orchid displays. There is also a small museum of botany and art in a gracious restored mansion on the grounds. For a good beach escape, head for the barrier islands of **Siesta Key** (*see* Beaches and Water Sports, *below*), **Longboat Key,** and **Lido Key.** Lido Key is reached via Rte. 789W; this same road leads north from Lido to Longboat Key. To reach Siesta Key, in southern Sarasota, take Rte. 41 south to Siesta Drive or Stickney Point Rd., which leads west to the island. In south Sarasota County, you can walk into a prehistoric Indian shell midden (an ancient refuse heap containing layers of archaeological relics) or try your hand at sizing oranges at the 19th-century citrus packing house at **Historic Spanish Point** (U.S. 41, Osprey, ☎ 813/966–5214).

What to See and Do with Children

Along with the **Ringling Circus Museum** (*see* Exploring the Sarasota Area, *above*), children enjoy the bird and reptile shows at **Sarasota Jungle Gardens** (3701 Bayshore Rd., ☎ 813/355–5305); also on site here are a petting zoo and a shell and butterfly museum.

Shopping

Art lovers can browse through the **art galleries** on Main Street and Palm Avenue in downtown Sarasota. A British telephone booth or an Australian boomerang is available for a price at the unique shops of Harding Circle on fashionable **St. Armand's Key,** west of downtown Sarasota across the Ringling Causeway.

Dining

The area boasts fine raw bars and seafood restaurants, many Continental restaurants, and several family-style places run by members of the large Amish community here. For price ranges, see Chart 1 (B) in On the Road with Fodor's.

★ **Cafe L'Europe.** One of the best restaurants along the Gulf Coast, the café specializes in fresh seafood and veal dishes graciously served in a plant- and art-filled room. *431 St. Armand's Circle, Sarasota, ☎ 813/388–4415. AE, DC, MC, V. $$$*

Crab Trap. Try the wild pig or seafood dishes at this rustic spot near Bradenton. *U.S. 19 at Terra Ceia Bridge, Palmetto, ☎ 813/722–6255. No reservations. D, MC, V. $$*

Ophelia's on the Bay. Sample mussel soup, eggplant crepes, chicken pot pie, seafood linguine, or cioppino, among other things, at this waterfront restaurant. *9105 Midnight Pass Rd., Siesta Key, ☎ 813/349–2212. AE, D, DC, MC, V. No lunch. $$*

Lodging

Tamiami Trail (U.S. 41), which traverses the region, is lined with inexpensive motels, while the islands have more expensive resort complexes and high-rise hotels. For price ranges, see Chart 2 (A) in On the Road with Fodor's.

Hyatt Sarasota. This contemporary hotel is ideally located, near city center and the major art and entertainment venues. Some rooms overlook Sarasota Bay. *1000 Blvd. of the Arts, Sarasota 34236, ☎ 813/366–9000, FAX 813/952–1987. 297 rooms. Facilities: restaurant, lounge, health club, sauna, pool, dock. AE, DC, MC, V. $$$*

Holiday Inn Riverfront. Suites overlook a courtyard at this Spanish-style motor lodge near the Manatee River. Rooms, with burgundy carpeting and mahogany furnishings, tend to be a bit dark. *100 Riverfront Dr. W, Bradenton 34205, ☎ 813/747–3727, FAX 813/746–4289. 77 rooms, 76 suites. Facilities: restaurant, lounge, pool, whirlpool. AE, DC, MC, V. $$*

The Arts and Nightlife

Sarasota is fast becoming one of Florida's cultural meccas. Broadway plays, concerts, dance, ice skating, and other shows are held at the **Van Wezel Performing Arts Hall** (777 N. Tamiami Trail, Sarasota, ☎ 813/953–3366). Other major venues in the city are the **Florida West Coast Symphony Center** (709 N. Tamiami Trail, ☎ 813/953–4252), the **Sarasota Opera** and the **Sarasota Ballet** (Opera House, 61 N. Pineapple Ave., ☎ 813/953–7030), and the **Asolo Center for the Performing Arts** (5555 N. Tamiami Trail, ☎ 813/351–8000).

The Fort Myers/Naples Area

Tourist Information

Lee County: Visitor and Convention Bureau (2180 W. 1st St., Fort Myers 33950, ☎ 813/338–3500 or 800/533–4753). **Naples Area:** Chamber of Commerce (3620 N. Tamiami Trail, 33940, ☎ 813/262–6141). **Sanibel–Captiva:** Chamber of Commerce (Causeway Rd., Sanibel 33957, ☎ 813/472–1080).

Exploring the Fort Myers/Naples Area

The bustle of commercially oriented Fort Myers gives way to the relaxed atmosphere of the Gulf communities in growing Lee County. Beach lovers head for the resort islands of Estero (popular with young singles), Captiva, and Sanibel, with its superb shelling and fine fishing. Most of the beautiful residences here are sheltered from view by tall Australian pines, but the beaches and tranquil Gulf waters are readily accessible. The sophisticated city of Naples has excellent beaches and golf courses and an upscale shopping district.

In **Fort Myers, McGregor Boulevard** is framed by hundreds of towering royal palms. Here you'll find **Thomas Edison's Winter Home,** a 14-acre estate that includes his laboratory and a museum with his inventions, and the adjoining **Mangoes,** automaker Henry Ford's home. *2350 McGregor Blvd., ☏ 813/334–3614. Admission charged. Closed major holidays.*

In the **Naples** area, return to Florida's unspoiled past at the **Corkscrew Swamp Sanctuary** (Rte. 846, east of I–75, ☏ 813/657–3771), an 11,000-acre tract set aside by the National Audubon Society to protect 500-year-old trees and endangered birds. Along Naples Bay, fishing shacks have been transformed into shops and artists' studios at **Old Marine Market Place at Tin City** (1200 5th Ave. S).

What to See and Do with Children

Babcock Wilderness Adventures (Rte. 31, east of Fort Myers, ☏ 813/656–6104, reservations required) offers 90-minute swamp-buggy excursions through a 90,000-acre swamp/woodland area to view wildlife. **Frannie's Teddy Bear Museum** (2511 Pine Ridge Rd. [Rte. 896], Naples, ☏ 813/598–2711) displays more than 1,500 bears.

Shopping

For an eye-popping display of shells, coral, and jewelry, visit the **Shell Factory** (2787 N. Tamiami Trail, North Fort Myers, ☏ 813/995–2141). For trendy boutiques selling resort wear, designer fashions, jewelry, and upscale gifts, try the **Royal Palm Square** area in **Fort Myers** (Colonial Blvd., between McGregor Blvd. and U.S. 41) and 3rd Street South and 5th Avenue South in **Naples.**

Dining

Stone-crab claw, available October 15 through May 15, is a favorite dish here. It's hard to find restaurants on Sanibel and Captiva islands that aren't expensive; for budget options, you'll have better luck in Fort Myers and Naples. For price ranges, see Chart 1 (B) in On the Road with Fodor's.

★ **Chef's Garden.** This elegant, award-winning restaurant offers Continental, traditional, and California cuisines, featuring such daily specials as Scottish smoked salmon with avocado and caviar or roast rack of lamb. The less formal Truffles bistro, upstairs, features creative sandwiches, pastas, and salads, plus tasty pastries to take out or eat in. *1300 3rd St. S, Naples, ☏ 813/262–5500. Jacket required during winter season. AE, D, DC, MC, V. $$$*

Snug Harbor. This harborfront restaurant offers absolutely fresh seafood—courtesy of the restaurant's private fishing fleet—in a casual, rustic atmosphere. *645 San Carlos Blvd., Fort Myers Beach, ☏ 813/463–4343. No reservations. AE, MC, V. $$*

Woody's Bar-B-Q. This no-frills barbecue pit serves generous portions of mouthwatering chicken, ribs, and beef at low prices. *13101 N. Cleveland Ave. (U.S. 41), North Fort Myers, ☏ 813/997–1424. AE, MC, V. $*

Lodging

In the Fort Myers/Naples area, take your choice of budget motels, all-inclusive resorts, historic hotels, or waterfront inns. Lodgings on the islands and those with waterfront views are most expensive. For price ranges, see Chart 2 (A) in On the Road with Fodor's.

★ **South Seas Plantation Resort and Yacht Harbor.** This busy 330-acre property has nine different types of accommodations, among them harborside villas, Gulf cottages, and private homes. Numerous activities here include waterskiing, tennis, golf, and shelling. Exotic vegetation covers the landscaped grounds, which invite strolling. *South Seas Plantation Rd., Captiva 33924,* ☎ *813/472–5111 or 800/237–1260,* FAX *813/472–7541. 600 rooms. Facilities: 4 restaurants, 2 lounges, pool, fishing, golf, tennis, waterskiing, windsurfing, sailing school, children's programs. AE, DC, MC, V. $$$$*

Sheraton Harbor Place. On the Caloosahatchee River in downtown Fort Myers, this modern pink high-rise has bright rooms with peach accents and lots of windows presenting panoramic views of the water and surrounding city. *2500 Edwards Dr., Fort Myers 33901,* ☎ *813/337–0300,* FAX *813/337–1530. 437 rooms. Facilities: exercise room, pool, tennis court, dock. AE, DC, MC, V. $$$*

Sandpiper Gulf Resort. This family-oriented motel just steps from the beach features large rooms with kitchens and private patios or balconies. *5550 Estero Blvd., Fort Myers Beach 33931,* ☎ *813/463–5721. 63 rooms. Facilities: 2 pools, whirlpool. MC, V. $$*

The Arts and Nightlife

Plays, concerts, and art exhibits are offered at the **Naples Philharmonic Center for the Arts** (5833 Pelican Bay Blvd., ☎ 813/597–1111). The **Naples Dinner Theatre** (Immokalee Rd., ☎ 813/597–6031) is famous for its professional productions and hearty buffet.

Sports and the Outdoors

Biking

Sanibel Island offers the best biking in the region, with extensive paths along the waterways and through wildlife refuges. Rent bikes at **Tarpon Bay Marina** (900 Tarpon Bay Rd., Sanibel, ☎ 813/472–8900).

Boating and Sailing

Sailing is popular on the calm bays and Gulf waters. Sailing schools include **O'Leary's Sarasota Sailing School** (U.S. 41, ☎ 813/953–7505) and **Fort Myers Yacht Charters** (Port Sanibel Yacht Club, South Fort Myers, ☎ 813/466–1800). For powerboat rentals contact **Boat House of Sanibel** (Sanibel Marina, ☎ 813/472–2531) or **Port-O-Call** (550 Port-O-Call Way, Naples, ☎ 813/774–0479).

Canoeing

Canoeists can explore many waterways here, including at **Myakka River State Park** (Rte. 72, 15 mi south of Sarasota, ☎ 813/361–6511) and **J.N. "Ding" Darling National Wildlife Refuge** (Sanibel, ☎ 813/472–1100; rentals available at Tarpon Bay Marina, *see* Biking, *above*). With several locations throughout Florida, **Canoe Outpost** offers canoe and camping trips on the **Little Manatee River** (18001 U.S. 301S, Wimauma, ☎ 813/634–2228) and the **Peace River** (Rte. 7, Arcadia, ☎ 813/494–1215).

Fishing

The Tampa Bay area and Fort Myers are major fishing centers. Speckled trout and kingfish are often caught in the Tampa Bay inlets. Deep-sea fishing enthusiasts can charter boats or join a party boat to catch tarpon, marlin, grouper, redfish, shark, and other species. Charter outfitters include **Florida Deep Sea Fishing** (4737 Gulf Blvd., St. Petersburg, ☎ 813/360–2082) and **Gulf Star Marina** (708 Fisherman's Wharf, Fort Myers Beach, ☎ 813/765–1500).

Golf

Championship and other courses abound here. Those open to the public include **Babe Zaharias Golf Course** (11412 Forest Hills Dr., Tampa, ☎ 813/932–4401), **Eastwood Golf Club** (4600 Bruce Herd La., Fort

Myers, ☎ 813/275–4898), **Lely Flamingo Island Golf Club** (8004 Lely Resort Blvd., Naples, ☎ 813/793–2223), **Longboat Key Club** (301 Gulf of Mexico Dr., Longboat Key, ☎ 813/383–8821), and **Pelican's Nest Golf Course** (Bonita Springs, ☎ 813/947–4600).

Spectator Sports

Baseball

For information on the 17 major-league teams that hold their spring training and exhibition games in southwest Florida, call the **Florida Sports Foundation** (☎ 904/488–0990).

Dog Racing

Derby Lane (10490 Gandy Blvd., St. Petersburg, ☎ 813/576–1361; Jan.–June). **Naples–Fort Myers Greyhound Track** (10601 Bonita Beach Rd., Bonita Springs, ☎ 813/992–2411; year-round). **Sarasota Kennel Club** (5400 Bradenton Rd., Sarasota, ☎ 813/355–7744; Dec.–June). **Tampa Greyhound Track** (8300 N. Nebraska Ave., Tampa, ☎ 813/932–4313; July–Dec.).

Football

Tampa Bay Buccaneers (Tampa Stadium, 4201 N. Dale Mabry Hwy., ☎ 813/461–2700 or 800/282–0683; Aug.–Dec.).

Horse Racing

Tampa Bay Downs (Race Track Rd., Oldsmar, ☎ 813/855–4401; Dec.–mid-Apr.) holds Thoroughbred races.

Beaches and Water Sports

The waters of the Gulf of Mexico tend to be cloudy, so snorkeling and diving are best done on the Atlantic side. The southwest beaches attract people who enjoy sunbathing on quiet stretches of sand, shelling, and watching spectacular sunsets.

In the Bradenton area, the popular **Manatee County Beach** on **Anna Maria Island** offers picnic facilities, showers, lifeguards, and rest rooms. **Fort Myers Beach** on **Estero Island,** 18 mi from downtown Fort Myers, attracts families and young singles; hotels, restaurants, and condominiums run its length. The island's shores slope gradually into the usually tranquil and warm Gulf waters. Along Gulf Shore Boulevard in Naples, **Lowdermilk Park** has 1,000 ft of beach, picnic tables, showers, rest rooms, and a pavilion with vending machines.

In the St. Petersburg area, the 900-acre **Fort DeSoto Park** encompasses five islands. Its miles of beaches include fishing piers, picnic sites, and a waterskiing-and-boating area. **Lighthouse Park** at the southern end of Sanibel Island attracts a mix of singles, families, and shellers. Beautiful **Siesta Beach** on Siesta Key near Sarasota features a concession stand, picnic areas, nature trails, and facilities for soccer, softball, volleyball, and tennis. South of here, **Caspersen Beach,** on Beach Drive in south Venice, is one of the country's largest parks. Beachcombers find lots of shells and sharks' teeth here.

THE GOLD AND TREASURE COASTS

The Gold Coast exudes wealth and opulence, but it's also steeped in natural beauty. Famous for years as spring-break heaven for the college crowd, Fort Lauderdale now attracts families by offering a variety of recreational, sports, cultural, and historical activities. Farther north is the international high-society resort of Palm Beach, with its elegant mansions and world-class shopping. Following downtown Fort Lauderdale's lead, West Palm Beach is trying to renew itself through a combination of governmental efforts and the arts and to become the hub of Palm Beach County and the Treasure Coast. Visitors can look for a number of new attractions: a children's park and museum, a town square, a park with a band shell, and a pedestrian mall. Inland about 50 mi is the 448,000-acre Lake Okeechobee, noted for catfish, bass, and perch fishing. Heading north from West Palm Beach to Sebastian Inlet, the Treasure Coast offers barrier islands, beaches, and sea-turtle havens to the east, and citrus groves and cattle ranches to the west.

Tourist Information

Greater Fort Lauderdale: Convention and Visitors Bureau (200 E. Las Olas Blvd., Suite 1500, 33301, ☎ 305/765–4466). **Palm Beach County:** Convention & Visitors Bureau (1555 Palm Beach Lakes Blvd., Suite 204, West Palm Beach 33401, ☎ 407/471–3995). Chamber of Commerce of the Palm Beaches (401 N. Flagler Dr., West Palm Beach 33401, ☎ 407/833–3711).

Getting There

By Plane

Major foreign and domestic carriers serve the **Fort Lauderdale–Hollywood International Airport** (4 mi south of downtown Fort Lauderdale off U.S. 1, ☎ 305/357–6100) and **Palm Beach International Airport** (Congress Ave. and Belvedere Rd., West Palm Beach, ☎ 407/471–7400).

By Car

Two major north–south routes, I–95 and U.S. 1, connect the region with Miami to the south and Jacksonville to the north. Alligator Alley (Rte. 84) runs east–west from Fort Lauderdale to Naples.

In 1995 a new nonstop four-lane route, Okeechobee Boulevard, began carrying traffic from west of downtown West Palm Beach, near the Amtrak station in the airport district, directly to the Flagler Memorial Bridge and into Palm Beach. Flagler Drive will be given over to pedestrian use by the end of the decade.

By Train

Amtrak (☎ 800/872–7245) provides daily service along the northeast coast to Fort Lauderdale, Hollywood, and Deerfield Beach in Broward County, and to West Palm Beach.

By Bus

Greyhound Lines (☎ 800/231–2222) stops in Fort Lauderdale, and **Broward County Mass Transit** (☎ 305/357–8400) serves the surrounding county. **CoTran** buses (☎ 407/233–1111 in Palm Beach, 407/272–6350 in Boca Raton–Delray Beach) ply the Greater Palm Beach area.

Exploring the Gold and Treasure Coasts

Fort Lauderdale and Palm Beach dazzle the visitor with their fabulous homes and pricey shops, shimmering beaches, plentiful sports activities, first-class museums, and cultural events. North of Fort Lauderdale are the Treasure Coast's 70 soothing miles of sand, sea, and nature refuges.

Fort Lauderdale's picturesque **Las Olas Boulevard** takes you through the **Isles,** where expensive homes line canals dotted with yachts. After this the boulevard becomes an upscale shopping street, with Spanish-colonial buildings housing boutiques and galleries. West of here, the **Museum of Art** (1 E. Las Olas Blvd., ☎ 305/525–5500; closed Mon.;

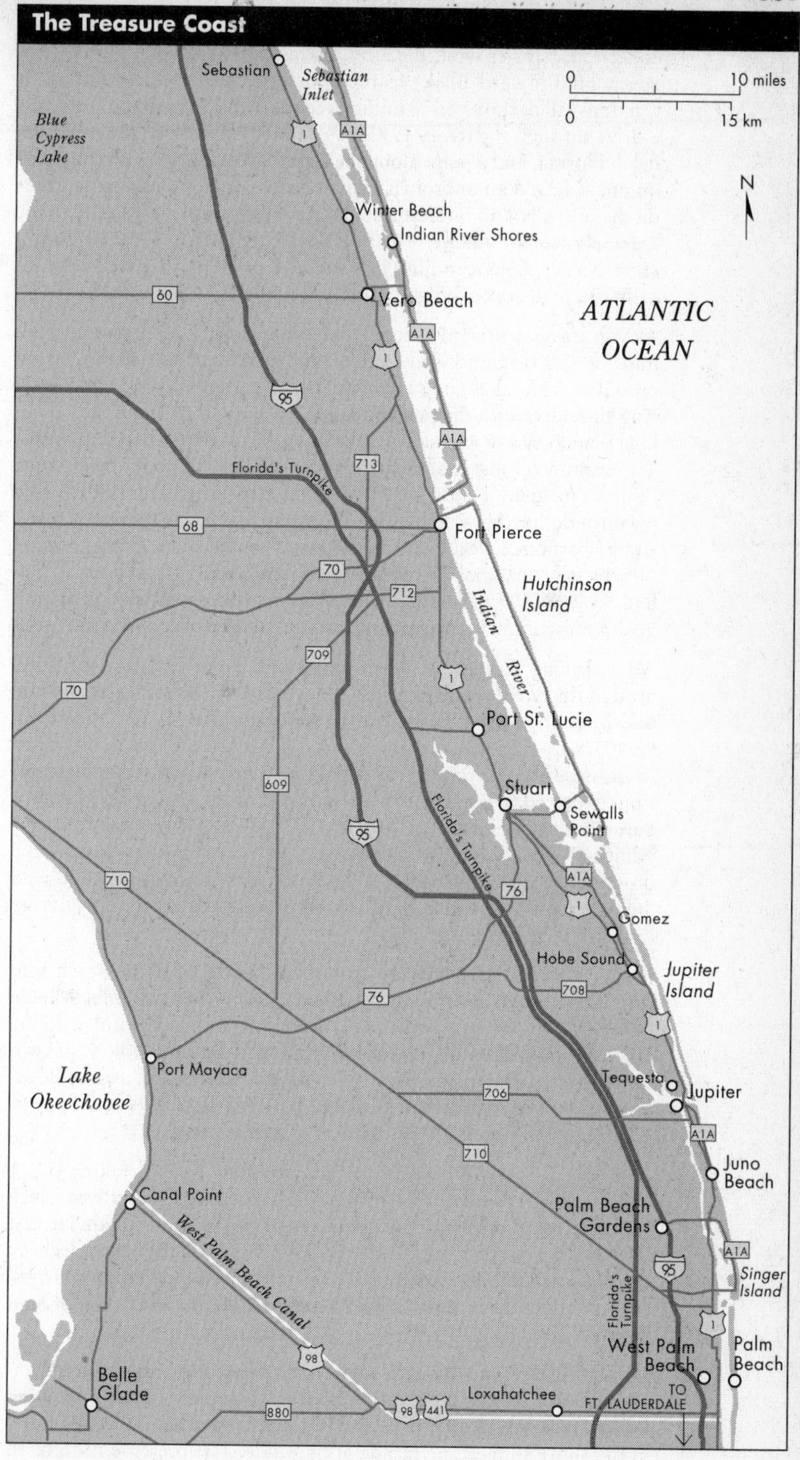
The Treasure Coast
Sebastian
Sebastian Inlet
Blue Cypress Lake
0 10 miles
0 15 km
N
Winter Beach
Indian River Shores
Vero Beach
ATLANTIC OCEAN
Florida's Turnpike
Fort Pierce
Hutchinson Island
Indian River
Port St. Lucie
Stuart
Sewalls Point
Gomez
Hobe Sound
Jupiter Island
Port Mayaca
Lake Okeechobee
Tequesta
Jupiter
Juno Beach
Palm Beach Gardens
Singer Island
Canal Point
West Palm Beach Canal
West Palm Beach
Palm Beach
Belle Glade
Loxahatchee
TO FT. LAUDERDALE

admission charged) has an extensive early 20th-century American art collection. Farther west, the 2-mi, palm-lined **Riverwalk** (along New River, off Broward Blvd.) features historic, scenic, and cultural attractions, all part of a $670 million redesign of downtown. Don't miss a drive through the **Henry E. Kinney Tunnel** (on U.S. 1), the only tunnel in Florida, and a jaunt along the **"strip"** (Rte. A1A), with the beach on one side and an unbroken string of motels, shops, and restaurants on the other. For an interesting side trip, head south a few miles to the **Seminole Native Village** (4150 N. Rte. 7, ☎ 305/961–3220) to observe Native American lifestyles and arts or to participate in the locally run high-stakes bingo parlor and low-stakes poker tables.

As you travel north from Fort Lauderdale along U.S. 1, pause to admire the 1920s Spanish-style architecture in affluent **Boca Raton.** A turn onto Rte. A1A takes you to the posh island community of **Palm Beach.** Rub shoulders with the rich and famous as you stroll along the 12-mi-long island's **Worth Avenue,** one of the world's premier shopping streets. To recapture the glitter and flamboyance of Florida's boom years, when railroad magnate Henry M. Flagler first established Palm Beach as a playground for the wealthy, visit his ornate hotel, the **Breakers,** a legendary bastion of wealth and privilege (*see* Dining and Lodging, *below*). Nearby is his palatial 73-room mansion, **Whitehall** (Cocoanut Whitehall Way, ☎ 407/655–2833; closed Sun.–Mon.; admission charged), now a museum, with original furnishings and an art collection.

After driving past the secluded mansions along County Road and around the northern tip of the island, cross Lake Worth to **West Palm Beach,** on the mainland. Its **Norton Gallery of Art** (1451 S. Olive St., ☎ 407/832–5194; closed Sun.–Mon.) has a fine collection of French Impressionists. Visitors in 1996 will find a new wing under construction, expected to open in 1997. Southwest of the city, at **Lion Country Safari** (Southern Blvd. [Rte. 80], ☎ 407/793–1084; admission $11.95 adults, $9.95 children), you can drive (with car windows closed) on 8 mi of paved roads through a 500-acre cageless zoo where 1,000 wild animals roam free. Lions, giraffes, zebras, ostriches, and elephants are among the animals in residence.

It's an abrupt shift from the man-made world of Palm Beach into primitive Florida at **Arthur R. Marshall Loxahatchee National Wildlife Refuge,** a wilderness of marshes, wetlands, and bountiful wildlife. Stroll the nature trails, fish for bass and panfish, or paddle your own canoe through the waterways. *South of West Palm Beach, west of Boynton Beach; headquarters at U.S. 441 between Rtes. 804 and 806,* ☎ *407/932–3684 or 407/734–8303. Admission charged.*

Explore the upper Treasure Coast at a leisurely pace by taking U.S. 1 and Rte. A1A north from West Palm Beach along the Indian River, which separates the barrier islands from the mainland. Of major interest from April to August are the sea turtles that nest on the beaches; check with local chambers of commerce for information on turtle watches, or learn about the turtles at **Loggerhead Park Marine Life Center of Juno Beach** (1200 U.S. 1, ☎ 407/627–8280; closed Sun.–Mon.).

Drive atop the sand dunes at **Jupiter** and pause to photograph the impressive 105-ft-tall **Jupiter Lighthouse.** At **Jupiter Island's Blowing Rocks Preserve** (☎ 407/575–2297), water sprays burst through holes in the shore's limestone facade at high tide. The preserve is home to large bird communities and a wealth of plants native to beachfront dune, marsh, and hammock. North of here is **Stuart,** where revival of the downtown is transforming this onetime fishing village of fewer than 15,000 into a magnet for people who want to live and work in a small-town atmosphere. The affluent community of **Vero Beach** has elegant houses, many dating from the 1920s. Continuing north, you will arrive at **Sebastian Inlet,** popular with fishermen and driftwood collectors. I–95 takes you back to Fort Lauderdale.

What to See and Do with Children

The Palm Beach area is not geared to family-oriented activities, but Fort Lauderdale and surrounding Broward County offer several child-pleasing attractions. The insect zoo is one of the hands-on exhibits at the **Museum of Discovery and Science** (401 S.W. 2nd St., ☎ 305/467–6637) along Fort Lauderdale's Riverwalk. **Ocean World** (1701 S.E. 17th St., Fort Lauderdale, ☎ 305/525–6611) offers close-up views of sea turtles, sharks, alligators, and river otters, as well as a chance to pet and feed a dolphin.

Shopping

Both Palm Beach and Fort Lauderdale have shopping districts that cater to a high-society clientele. In Fort Lauderdale, expensive boutiques are clustered along tree-lined **Las Olas Boulevard.** In Palm Beach, more than 250 specialty shops and pricey boutiques, with such famous names as **Gucci** (256 Worth Ave., ☎ 407/655–6955) and **Cartier** (214 Worth Ave., ☎ 407/655–5913), beckon to well-heeled shoppers along **Worth Avenue.** A few miles west of Fort Lauderdale proper is **Sawgrass Mills Mall** (intersection of Flamingo Rd. and Sunrise Blvd., ☎ 305/846–2350), reputedly the largest discount mall in America.

Sports and the Outdoors

Biking

The beautiful **Palm Beach Bicycle Trail** runs for 10 mi along the shoreline of Lake Worth; for rentals, try **Palm Beach Bicycle Trail Shop** (223 Sunrise Ave., ☎ 407/659–4583).

Diving

A popular place to dive is the 23-mi-long, 2-mi-wide **Fort Lauderdale Reef,** one of 80 dive sites in Broward County. Palm Beach County offers excellent drift-diving and anchor-diving off the Atlantic coast. Contact **Pro Dive** (Bahia Mar Resort & Yachting Center, Rte. A1A, Fort Lauderdale, ☎ 305/761–3413 or 800/772–3483) or **Force E** (2700 E. Atlantic Blvd., Pompano Beach, ☎ 305/943–3483; 2160 W. Oakland Blvd., Oakland Park, ☎ 305/735–6227).

Fishing

Anglers can deep-sea or freshwater fish year-round. Pompano, amberjack, and snapper are caught off the numerous piers and bridges, while Lake Okeechobee yields bass and perch. Sailfish are a popular catch on deep-sea charters, offered by such companies as **Bahia Mar Resort & Yachting Center** (*see* Diving, *above*) and **B-Love Fleet** (314 E. Ocean Ave., Lantana, ☎ 407/588–7612).

Golf

Among the 50-plus golf courses in Greater Fort Lauderdale are **Colony West Country Club** (6800 N.W. 88th St., Tamarac, ☎ 305/726–8430). Palm Beach County boasts 145 private, public, and semiprivate courses; those open to visitors include **Emerald Dunes Golf Club** (2100 Emerald Dunes Dr., West Palm Beach, ☎ 407/684–4653) and **Royal Palm Beach Country Club** (900 Royal Palm Beach Blvd., Royal Palm Beach, ☎ 407/798–6430).

Spectator Sports

Baseball

The Gold and Treasure coasts host spring training for several major-league teams: **New York Yankees** (Fort Lauderdale Stadium, 5301 N.W. 12th Ave., ☎ 305/776–1921); **Atlanta Braves** and **Montreal Expos** (West Palm Beach Municipal Stadium, 1610 Palm Beach Lakes Blvd., ☎ 407/683–6012); **Los Angeles Dodgers** (Holman Stadium, 4101 26th St., Vero Beach, ☎ 407/569–4900); and **New York Mets** (St. Lucie County Sport Complex, 525 N.W. Peacock Blvd., Port St. Lucie, ☎ 407/871–2115).

Dog Racing

Greyhounds race at **Palm Beach Kennel Club** (1111 N. Congress Ave., Palm Beach, ☎ 407/683–2222; year-round) and **Hollywood Greyhound Track** (831 N. Federal Hwy., Hallandale, ☎ 305/454–9400; Jan.–Apr.).

Horse Racing

Gulfstream Park Race Track (901 S. Federal Hwy., ☎ 305/454–7000; Jan.–mid-Mar.). **Pompano Harness Track** (1800 S.W. 3rd St., Pompano Beach, ☎ 305/972–2000; schedule varies, call ahead).

Polo

This sport of the wealthy has three major organizations in Palm Beach County, including the **Palm Beach Polo and Country Club** (13420 South Shore Blvd., West Palm Beach, ☎ 407/793–1440), which has games on Sunday, January–April.

Beaches

Crystal-clear, warm waters are the main draw of the miles of beaches along the Atlantic coast. Each coastal town has a public beach area; many, like **Pompano Beach,** have fishing piers. The area is popular with snorkelers and divers.

The **strip,** along Rte. A1A between Las Olas Boulevard and Sunrise Boulevard in Fort Lauderdale, is the most crowded beach in the region; shops, restaurants, and hotels line the road. South of here, in Dania, the **John U. Lloyd Beach State Recreation Area** (6503 N. Ocean Dr.), the locals' favorite, offers a fine beach; picnicking, fishing, and canoeing facilities; and 251 acres of mangroves to explore. **Bathtub Beach** on Hutchinson Island, north of Jupiter, has placid waters and a gentle sea slope, making it ideal for children.

Dining and Lodging

The Gold and Treasure coasts have a mix of American, European, and Caribbean cuisines, all featuring local fish and seafood. Accommodations are expensive in the Palm Beach area, but many inexpensive motels line U.S. 1 and the major exits of I–95 throughout the region. B&B accommodations are popular in Palm Beach County; contact **Open House Bed & Breakfast** (Box 3025, Palm Beach 33480, ☎ 407/842–5190). For price ranges, see Charts 1 (B) and 2 (A) in On the Road with Fodor's.

Boca Raton

DINING

★ **La Vieille Maison.** Closets transformed into private dining nooks are part of the charm of this 1920s home turned elegant French restaurant serving such dishes as pompano fillets with a pecan-chardonnay sauce. *770 E. Palmetto Park Rd., ☎ 407/391–6701. Jacket preferred. AE, D, DC, MC, V. Closed Labor Day, sometimes closed July 4. $$$–$$$$*

Tom's Place. It's worth the wait in line to relish the mouthwatering ribs or chicken in homemade barbecue sauce and the sweet-potato pie in this casual, family-run eatery. *7251 N. Federal Hwy., ☎ 407/997–0920. No reservations. MC, V. Closed Sept. No lunch Sun. and Mon. $*

Fort Lauderdale

DINING

Down Under. Under a bridge approach by the Intracoastal Waterway, this Aussie-run restaurant specializes in Florida blue-crab cakes, Florida lobster, and stone crab. *3000 E. Oakland Park Blvd., ☎ 305/563–4123. AE, D, DC, MC, V. $$$*

Shirttail Charlie's. After dining on crab balls or coconut shrimp with piña colada sauce on the outdoor deck or in the upstairs dining room of this 1920s-style restaurant, enjoy a free cruise on the New River (Sun.–Thurs. after dinner). *400 S.W. 3rd Ave., ☎ 305/463–3474. AE, D, MC, V. $$*

LODGING

★ **Riverside Hotel.** Amid the upscale shops on Las Olas Boulevard, this hotel boasts an attentive staff, murals by well-known artist Bob Jenny in some rooms and on the facade, and rooms with refrigerators and antique-oak furnishings. *620 E. Las Olas Blvd., 33301, ☎ 305/467–0671 or 800/325–3280, FAX 305/462–2471. 103 rooms, 7 suites. Facilities: 2 restaurants, pool, poolside bar, volleyball court, dock. AE, DC, MC, V. $$$*

Hutchinson Island

DINING AND LODGING

★ **Indian River Plantation.** This luxury resort on 192 island acres evokes a Victorian seaside ambience with its latticework trim, tin roofs, and cool verandas. Feast on steak Diane or fresh snapper at the Inlet, an intimate, elegant restaurant, or experience the Sunday champagne brunch at Scalawags. *555 N.E. Ocean Blvd., 34996, ☎ 407/225–6990 or 800/947–2148, FAX 407/225–0003. 200 rooms, 54 1- and 2-bedroom oceanfront apartments with kitchens. Facilities: 5 restaurants, 3 pools, 13 tennis courts, 7 lighted golf courses, outdoor spa, marina, water-sports rentals, beach club. AE, DC, MC, V. $$$$*

Lake Worth

DINING

John G's. Although short on decor, this beachfront breakfast and lunch eatery is long on crowd-pleasing dishes, such as stuffed sandwiches, eggs prepared in every conceivable way, and such seafood creations as Greek shrimp on linguine with feta cheese. *Off Rte. A1A, Lake Worth public beach, ☎ 407/585–9860. No reservations. No credit cards. No dinner. $*

Palm Beach

DINING

Ta-boo. Open 24 hours, this re-creation of a 1940s bistro offers such fare as gourmet pizzas and grilled chicken with arugula in three settings: a courtyard, a parlor with fireplace, and a gazebo. *221 Worth Ave., ☎ 407/835–3500. Jacket advised. AE, MC, V. $$*

DINING AND LODGING

★ **The Breakers.** Formality blends with a tropical-resort ambience at this historic oceanfront hotel that resembles an Italian Renaissance palace, with cool pink, green, floral, and white interiors and original 1920s furniture. Fresh from a $50 million, five-year renovation of its guest rooms, it has committed itself to another refurbishment scheme, this time costing $40 million and due to finish before the end of the century. Dine on rack of lamb Dijonnaise in the tapestry-filled Florentine Dining Room or the skylighted Circle Dining Room. *1 S. County Rd., 33480, ☎ 407/655–6611 or 800/833–3141, FAX 407/659–8403. 509 rooms, 53 suites. Facilities: 4 restaurants, lounge, health club, saunas, beach, heated pool, 20 tennis courts, 2 golf courses, croquet, shuffleboard, shopping arcade. AE, D, DC, MC, V. $$$$*

LODGING

Sea Lord Hotel. This newly refurbished, comfortable, off-the-beaten-track motel in a garden setting offers rooms that overlook the pool, the ocean, or Lake Worth. *2315 Ocean Blvd., 33480, ☎ and FAX 407/582–1461. 25 rooms, 15 efficiencies and suites. Facilities: restaurant, beach, pool. No credit cards. $$–$$$*

Spas

Fort Lauderdale

Bonaventure Resort and Spa. Part of a hotel and convention center complex, the resort's spacious rooms have tropical decor and balconies overlooking a lake or a golf course. The spa dining room is decorated in soft colors, with bamboo screens and mirrors. Menus follow the nutritional guidelines of the American Heart Association and the American Cancer Society. Complimentary caffeine-free herbal teas are offered in the morning and fresh fruit in the afternoon. *250 Racquet Club Rd., 33326, ☎ 305/389–3300 or 800/327–8090; in FL, 800/432–3063; FAX 305/384–0563. 493 rooms. Facilities: restaurant, indoor and outdoor pools, 23 tennis courts, 2 golf courses, 6 racquetball and squash courts, boating, horseback riding, exercise equipment, individualized fitness programs, massage, beauty treatments. AE, D, DC, MC, V. $$$$*

Palm-Aire Spa Resort. This 700-acre resort has both a luxurious resort hotel and a spa complex that promotes physical fitness and stress reduction. Large guest rooms have separate dressing rooms, and private terraces. *2601 Palm-Aire Dr. N, Pompano Beach 33069, ☎ 305/972–3300 or 800/272–5624. 192 rooms. Facilities: 2 restaurants, 2 pools, 37 tennis courts, 5 golf courses, racquetball, indoor squash court, exercise equipment, massage, beauty treatments. AE, DC, MC, V. $$$$*

Palm Beach

Hippocrates Health Institute. Personalized programs here are highly structured and emphasize holistic health and lifestyle management. Guests stay in a spacious hacienda or at private cottages on the 20-acre wooded estate. *1443 Palmdale Ct., West Palm Beach 33411, ☎ 407/471–8876, 407/471–8868, or 800/842–2125. 15 rooms. Facilities: outdoor pool, supervised exercise programs, massage. AE, MC, V. $$$$*

Spa at PGA National Resort. At this sybaritic getaway where golf and tennis pros exercise during tournaments, the spa facilities include the signature mineral pools with salts from around the world. Choose from large guest rooms with tropical decor or cottage units with two bedrooms and a kitchen. *400 Ave. of the Champions, Palm Beach Gardens 33418, ☎ 407/627–2000 or 800/633–9150. 336 rooms, 85 cottages. Facilities: 3 restaurants, 2 pools, 5 golf courses, 19 tennis courts, 26-acre sailing lake, exercise equipment and personalized programs, aerobics and dance studios, massage, beauty treatments. AE, DC, MC, V. $$$$*

The Arts and Nightlife

Fort Lauderdale and the Palm Beach area offer a full roster of performing arts events. Major venues include **Broward Center for the Performing Arts** (201 S.W. 5th Ave., Fort Lauderdale, ☎ 305/462–0222) and **Raymond F. Kravis Center for the Performing Arts** (701 Okeechobee Blvd., West Palm Beach, ☎ 407/832–7469). Vero Beach is the Treasure Coast's cultural center, with its resident Equity troupe at the **Riverside Theatre** (3250 Riverside Park Dr., ☎ 407/231–6990) and its **Center for the Arts** (3001 Riverside Park Dr., ☎ 407/231–0707). The **Jupiter Dinner Theatre** (formerly the Burt Reynolds Jupiter Theater, 1001 E. Indiantown Rd., Jupiter, ☎ 407/747–5566) is known for the Broadway and film stars who regularly perform in its productions. Fort Lauderdale has the liveliest nightlife, with comedy clubs, discos, and clubs featuring music for all ages and tastes; popular clubs include **Confetti** (2660 E. Commercial Blvd., ☎ 305/776–4080), the high-energy in spot for the 35- to 50-year-old crowd, and **Musicians Exchange** (729 W. Sunrise Blvd., ☎ 305/764–1912), featuring an eclectic mix of blues, jazz, and rock-and-roll. Events include a Monday blues jam.

ELSEWHERE IN THE STATE

Everglades and Biscayne National Parks

Getting There

Miami International Airport (*see* Miami, *above*) is about 35 mi from Homestead–Florida City, gateways to the national parks. Traveling south by car, take U.S. 1, the Homestead Extension of the Florida Turnpike, or Krome Avenue (Rte. 997) to the gateway towns.

What to See and Do

Everglades National Park (Box 279, Homestead 33030; Main Visitor Center, 40001 Rte. 9336, Florida City 33034-6733, ☎ 305/242–7700), the country's largest remaining subtropical wilderness, contains more than 1.4 million acres—half land, half water—that can be explored by boat, by bike, on foot, and partly by car. This slow-moving "river of grass" is a maze of sawgrass marshes, mangrove swamps, salt prairies, and pinelands that shelter a variety of plants and animals, even though increased pollution by pesticide runoff from local farms has reduced the number of birds and reduced the Florida panther to near extinction.

Biscayne National Park (Park Headquarters, N. Canal Dr.; Box 1639, Homestead 33090, ☎ 305/247–7275) is the nation's largest marine park and the largest national park in the continental United States with a living coral reef. It covers about 274 sq mi, mostly underwater, and has several ecosystems. Shallow Biscayne Bay is home to the manatee; the upper Florida Keys harbor moray eels and brilliantly colored parrot fish in a 150-mi-long coral reef; bald eagles and other large birds inhabit the mainland mangrove forests. A glass-bottom-boat tour, canoeing, snorkeling, and scuba diving are popular ways to experience the park.

The Panhandle: Northwest Florida

Getting There

Pensacola Regional Airport (☎ 904/435–1746) serves the region. I–10 and U.S. 90 are the main east–west highways across the top of the state, while U.S. 231, 331, and 29 and Rte. 85 traverse the Panhandle north–south.

What to See and Do

The Panhandle has been dubbed the Emerald Coast for its profusion of pine forests, magnolias, live oaks dripping with Spanish moss, lush bayous and swamps, and white-sand beaches lapped by blue-green waters. Historical and archaeological sites vie for attention with beautiful beaches, golf, hunting, hiking, water sports, and outstanding fishing.

Stroll through the historic districts of **Pensacola** and absorb some of the city's colorful Spanish, French, British, and Civil War past. East on coastal U.S. 98 is **Fort Walton Beach,** a family vacation playground famous for its beaches and spectacular sand dunes. Here you can tour **Eglin Air Force Base** (Rte. 85, ☎ 904/882–3931), the largest military base in the Western Hemisphere. Also here is the **Indian Temple Mound Museum** (139 Miracle Strip Pkwy. [U.S. 98], ☎ 904/243–6521), which details the lives of the peoples who lived in the region during the past 10,000 years.

Farther along this coastal route is the bustling fishing village of **Destin,** popular with anglers, sun worshipers, and gourmets. For simple relaxation, head for the snow-white beaches, miles of waterways, and amusement parks of **Panama City Beach,** a prime vacation area and the new in spot for students on spring break. The **Pensacola Convention and Visitors Information Center** (1401 E. Gregory St., 32501, ☎ 904/434–1234 or 800/874–1234) provides information on the region.

Northeast Florida

Getting There

Jacksonville International Airport (☎ 904/741–4902) serves the region. I–10 is the major east–west artery through the north, and I–4 from Tampa enters the region near Daytona Beach. The primary north–south routes are I–95 along the east coast and I–75 south from Valdosta, Georgia.

What to See and Do

Variety is the key word for northeast Florida, where you can see live-oak-framed roads and plantations that recall the Old South along the **St. Johns River**; Thoroughbred horse farms in **Ocala**; impressive savannas in **Gainesville**; the Civil War heritage of the state capital at **Tallahassee**; and the cosmopolitan city of **Jacksonville.** The beaches range from rocky shorelines to the glistening sand beaches of Jacksonville and the famous hard-packed, driveable beach at **Daytona.** The annual **Daytona 500** auto race is held at **Daytona International Speedway** (U.S. 92, ☎ 904/254–2700), and Jacksonville hosts collegiate football's **Gator Bowl** (☎ 904/396–1800).

St. Augustine, the oldest city in the United States, is a popular tourist destination (**Visitor Information Center,** 10 Castillo Dr., 32084, ☎ 904/825–1000). Explore the 300-year-old Spanish fortress of **Castillo de San Marcos National Monument** (1 Castillo Dr., ☎ 904/829–6506), guarding Matanzas Bay. Stroll down **St. George Street** through the restored Spanish-colonial village **San Agustin Antiguo** and glimpse life in the 1700s. Drink from the spring reputed to be the fountain of youth discovered by Ponce de León in 1513 at the **Fountain of Youth Archaeological Park** (155 Magnolia Ave., ☎ 904/829–3168).

Silver Springs (Rte. 40, 1 mi east of Ocala, ☎ 904/236–2121; admission $20 adults, $15 children), the state's oldest attraction and the world's largest formation of clear artesian springs, offers glass-bottom-boat tours and a jungle cruise. **Amelia Island (Amelia Island–Fernandina Beach Chamber of Commerce,** 102 Centre St., Fernandina Beach, 32034, ☎ 904/261–3248), just north of Jacksonville, contains the historic town of **Fernandina Beach,** with its 19th-century mansions, and **Fort Clinch State Park** (☎ 904/261–4212; admission charged), with its brick fort, nature trails, swimming, and living history reenactments.

For more information on the region, contact the **Jacksonville and Its Beaches Convention and Visitors Bureau** (6 E. Bay St., Suite 200, 32202, ☎ 904/353–9736) or the **Tallahassee Area Convention and Visitor Bureau** (200 E. College Ave., 32302, ☎ 904/681–9200 or 800/628–2866).

GEORGIA

By Mitzi Gammon

Updated by Echo and Kevin Garrett

Capital	Atlanta
Population	6,478,216
Motto	Wisdom, Justice, and Moderation
State Bird	Brown thrasher
State Flower	Cherokee rose

Visitor Information

Georgia Department of Industry, Trade and Tourism (Box 1776, Atlanta 30301, ☎ 404/656–3590 or 800/847–4842, FAX 404/656–3567). There are 11 **visitor centers** at various border points and local **welcome centers** in Atlanta, Savannah, and 20 other towns throughout the state.

Scenic Drives

Along the coast, Jekyll Island's **North Riverview Drive** offers scenery ranging from historic homes in Jekyll Island Club Historic District to vast expanses of marshland. **Rte. 157N** from Cloudland Canyon State Park to the Tennessee border at Lookout Mountain affords views of northwest Georgia's Cumberland Mountains. **U.S. 76E** from Dalton to the Chattooga River traverses the North Georgia Mountains and takes in the most beautiful sections of the Chattahoochee National Forest.

National and State Parks

National Parks

Andersonville National Historic Site (Rte. 1, Box 800, Andersonville 31711, ☎ 912/924–0343), which served as a Confederate prison camp, is the official site of the National Prisoners of War Museum for all POWs from the Civil War through Desert Storm. **Chattahoochee River National Recreation Area** (1978 Island Ford Pkwy., Dunwoody 30350, ☎ 404/952–4419) offers river swimming, hiking trails, and picnic areas. **Cumberland Island National Seashore** (*see* The Golden Isles, *below*). **Kennesaw Mountain National Battlefield** (900 Kennesaw Mountain Dr., Kennesaw 30144, ☎ 404/427–4686, FAX 404/427–1760), a 2,884-acre park outside Atlanta, commemorates one of the Civil War's most decisive battles and offers 17 mi of hiking trails and a spectacular view of the city. **Martin Luther King, Jr., National Historic District** (*see* Atlanta, *below*). **Okefenokee Swamp National Wildlife Refuge** (*see* Elsewhere in the State, *below*).

State Parks

Cloudland Canyon State Park (Rte. 2, Box 150, Rising Fawn 30738, ☎ 706/657–4050), on the west side of Lookout Mountain in the state's northwest corner, offers dramatic scenery and waterfalls. **Stephen C. Foster State Park** (*see* Elsewhere in the State, *below*). **Stone Mountain Park** (*see* Atlanta, *below*). **Vogel State Park** (7485 Vogel State Park Rd., Blairsville 30512, ☎ 706/745–2628), a 221-acre park surrounded by the Chattahoochee National Forest, includes a 17-acre lake with swimming and fishing.

ATLANTA

Atlanta is one of the fastest growing cities in the United States, its skyline constantly changing as new skyscrapers are erected along Peachtree Street and throughout the city. Initially founded as a railroad center, the city has blossomed into a major metropolis with over 3 million people. It is an important aviation hub and a regional leader in commerce and industry, perhaps some of the reasons why it was selected as host of the 1996 Summer Olympic Games. But for all its modernity, the city's winning character is still defined by the genteel charm of southern hospitality and by its near-picture-perfect residential neighborhoods.

Tourist Information

Chamber of Commerce (235 International Blvd., 30303, ☎ 404/880–9000). **Convention and Visitors Bureau information centers** (Peachtree Center Mall, 233 Peachtree St., Suite 2000, 30303, ☎ 404/222–6688; Underground Atlanta, 65 Upper Alabama St.; Georgia World Congress Center, 285 International Blvd.; Hartsfield International Airport, North Terminal at West Crossover; and Lenox Square Mall, 3393 Peachtree Rd.). **Atlanta Committee for the Olympic Games** (Box 1996, Atlanta, GA 30301, ☎ 404/224–1996).

Arriving and Departing

By Plane

Hartsfield International Airport (☎ 404/530–6830) has scheduled flights by most major domestic and foreign carriers. Traffic to downtown Atlanta, about 13 mi north of the airport via I–75N and I–85N, can be congested during rush hour. Cab fare is about $15 for one person, $8 each for two people, and $6 each for three. Cabs are found near the baggage-claim area. The **Metropolitan Atlanta Rapid Transit Authority** (MARTA, ☎ 404/848–4711; fare $1.25) rapid-rail subway train service is one of the quickest and easiest ways to reach the downtown, Midtown, and Lenox Square Mall districts.

By Car

Atlanta is commonly referred to as the "Crossroads of the South," and for good reason. Between South Carolina and Alabama, I–85 runs northeast–southwest through Atlanta and I–20 runs east–west; I–75 runs north–south from Tennessee to Florida. I–285 makes a 65-mi loop around the metropolitan area.

By Train

Amtrak (☎ 800/872–7245) serves **Brookwood Station** (1688 Peachtree St.).

By Bus

Greyhound Lines (81 International Blvd., ☎ 800/231–2222).

Getting Around Atlanta

Atlanta is a spread-out city, making a car a necessity, but it does contain a number of walkable neighborhoods and districts with interesting architecture and attractions.

By Car

Major public parking lots downtown are at the **CNN Center** (entrance off Techwood Dr.), the **Georgia World Congress Center** (off International Blvd.), **Peachtree Center, Macy's** (Carnegie Way, one block off Peachtree St.), and **Underground Atlanta.** In the Buckhead and Midtown areas, more on-street parking and lots are available. Rush hours are typically 6:30–9 AM and 4–6 PM on weekdays; traffic at these times is especially congested on Peachtree St., the interstate, and all major roads.

By Public Transportation

MARTA (☎ 404/848–4711) operates buses and a modern rapid-rail subway system. Fare for each is $1.25; exact change or a token is required. The rapid-rail trains operate from 5 AM to 1 AM; bus schedules depend upon the route.

By Taxi

You can hail a cab fairly easily at hotels in the downtown or Buckhead districts. **Buckhead Safety Cab** (☎ 404/233–1152), **Checker Cab** (☎ 404/351–1111), **Executive Limousine** (☎ 404/223–2000), and **Yellow Cabs** (☎ 404/521–0200) offer 24-hour service.

Orientation Tours

Van and Bus Tours

Atlanta Discovery Tours (☎ 404/667–1414) and **America Sightseeing Atlanta** (☎ 404/239–9140 or 800/572–3050) pick you up at area hotels for customized sightseeing or shopping tours. **Gray Line of Atlanta** (370 Lees Mill Rd., Forest Park 30050, ☎ 404/767–0594) offers tours of downtown, Midtown, and Buckhead; some tours include Stone Mountain and the King Center.

Walking Tours

The **Atlanta Preservation Center** (156 7th St., Suite 3, ☎ 404/876–2040 or 404/876–2041) offers 10 weekend guided tours of historic neighborhoods from February through November. A tour of the Fox Theatre is offered year-round, but only on selected days.

Exploring Atlanta

Beginning downtown, you can move north past an eclectic mix of Renaissance Revival towers and contemporary glass-and-steel skyscrapers; through Midtown's genteel, garden-filled neighborhoods punctuated by parks and museums; and into upscale Buckhead, lined with mansions and glitzy shopping centers bursting with designer-name boutiques and upscale department stores.

Downtown

Atlanta had its inauspicious beginning as a 19th-century cow crossing and later a railway depot; a few sites from the earliest days are preserved downtown. The three-level, six-block entertainment and shopping center called **Underground Atlanta** (Peachtree and Alabama Sts., ☎ 404/523–2311) encompasses some of the original city center's storefronts and streets. **Atlanta Heritage Row** (55 Upper Alabama St., ☎ 404/584–7879), within the complex, operated by the **Atlanta History Center** (*see also* Buckhead, *below*), offers a multimedia presentation about the city and other historical exhibits. Above the complex is the **Olympic Experience** (90 Upper Alabama St., Suite 290, ☎ 404/658–1996), a public information center with audio-visual exhibits and a gift shop dedicated to the games. Around the corner is the **World of Coca-Cola** (55 Martin Luther King Jr. Dr., ☎ 404/676–5151), with three floors of memorabilia from the century-old soft-drink company. Free samples are distributed; reservations are required for groups of 25 or more.

Four blocks from here, at the corner of Marietta Street and Techwood Drive, is the **CNN Center** (1 CNN Center, ☎ 404/827–2300 or 404/827–2400; admission charged), headquarters of media mogul Ted Turner's Cable News Network. Guided tours of the behind-the-scenes workings, including newscasters in action, are given daily.

Woodruff Park, at the corner of Peachtree Street and Park Place, is named for Robert W. Woodruff, the late Coca-Cola magnate. In warm weather, the park is a favorite alfresco lunch spot. Thrusting into the sky a block north of the park are the striking angles of the **red-marble tower that is the Georgia-Pacific Building** (Peachtree St. at John Wesley Dobbs Ave.). Built on the site of Loew's Grand Theatre, where *Gone with the Wind* premiered in 1939, the corporate flagship building houses the **High Museum of Art Folk Art and Photography Galleries** (30 John Wesley Dobbs Ave., ☎ 404/577–6940; *see also* Midtown, *below*).

Walking tours of the **Martin Luther King, Jr., National Historic District** start from the **King Center** (449 Auburn Ave., ☎ 404/524–1956), established by King's widow, Coretta Scott King. Inside the center are a museum, a library, and a gift shop; in front is King's tomb, where an eternal flame burns.

The Queen Anne–style bungalow that was **Dr. King's birthplace** (501 Auburn Ave., ☎ 404/331–5190) is open for tours. Three generations of the King family preached at the **Ebenezer Baptist Church** (407 Auburn Ave., ☎ 404/688–7263).

The **Georgia State Capitol**, several blocks southwest, houses government offices and a museum. Built in 1889, its dome is gilded with gold leaf from ore mined in nearby Dahlonega, the site of the nation's first gold rush. *206 Washington St., ☎ 404/656–2844. Free tours Mon.–Fri. 9:30 AM–11:30 AM and 1 PM–2 PM.*

North on **Peachtree Street,** the city's main thoroughfare, is **Peachtree Center** (☎ 404/614–5000), a climate-controlled complex filled with shops, restaurants, hotels, and offices. In the center's Mariott Marquis Two Tower is the **Atlanta International Museum of Art and Design** (285 Peachtree Center Ave., ☎ 404/688–2467; open Tues.–Sat. 11–5), specializing in international art, design, and crafts exhibitions.

Midtown

Midtown, just north of downtown and once the heart of Atlanta's hippie scene during the late 1960s and early '70s, is the city's primary art and theater district, and the home of a large segment of Atlanta's gay population. The area is popular with Atlantans who come to enjoy the bars, restaurants, and specialty shops. Like downtown, it has its own distinctive skyline, as many new office towers have been erected during the past decade.

The Moorish/Egyptian–style **Fox Theatre** (660 Peachtree St., ☎ 404/881–2100), the city's oldest movie palace, hosts splashy events ranging from Broadway plays to rock concerts; tours are offered year-round (*see* Orientation Tours, *above*). Across the street, the **Road to Tara Museum** (Georgian Terrace Bldg., 659 Peachtree St., ☎ 404/897–1939) has an impressive collection of *Gone With the Wind* memorabilia. Fifteen blocks north of here is the **High Museum of Art** (1280 Peachtree St., ☎ 404/733–4444; admission charged except Thurs. 1–5; closed Mon.), a glossy, white-enamel showplace designed by architect Richard Meir that houses a major collection of American contemporary and decorative art as well as sub-Saharan African art. Farther north is **Rhodes**

Hall (1516 Peachtree St., ☎ 404/881–9980), a Victorian mansion now headquarters for the **Georgia Trust for Historic Preservation.**

Buckhead

A large portion of Buckhead, 5 mi north of Midtown on Peachtree Street, is to Atlanta what Beverly Hills is to Los Angeles. This residential and shopping area is home to fine dining, designer boutiques, and expensive homes. To see the manicured lawns and mansions of Atlanta's elite, take a scenic drive along Tuxedo, Valley, and Habersham roads.

The white-columned **Georgia Governor's Mansion** (391 W. Paces Ferry Rd., ☎ 404/261–1858; closed Fri.–Mon.) is decorated with an impressive collection of Federal-period antiques; the neoclassical mansion is open for tours. On West Paces Ferry Road is the **Atlanta History Center** (130 W. Paces Ferry Rd., ☎ 404/814–4000), a 32-acre site that includes the new Atlanta History Museum, the Tullie Smith Farm 1845 plantation house, the symmetrical Palladian Swan House mansion, and McElreath Hall, where historical artifacts and the city's largest photo collection are displayed and lectures given in its auditorium.

Parks and Gardens

In Midtown between 10th and 14th streets is **Piedmont Park,** the city's premier urban green space, containing a children's playground, tennis courts, a swimming pool, and paved paths for biking, running, and roller skating. You can rent bikes, Rollerblades, and skates across the street at **Skate Escape** (1086 Piedmont Ave., ☎ 404/892–1292). The park was designed by Frederick Law Olmsted for the 1895 Cotton States and International Exposition.

Adjoining the park is the 30-acre **Atlanta Botanical Garden,** with landscaped gardens and the climate-controlled Fuqua Conservatory, containing tropical, desert, and endangered plants. *1345 Piedmont Ave., ½ mi north of 14th St., ☎ 404/876–5858. Admission charged. Closed Mon., major holidays.*

Stone Mountain Park (U.S. 78, ☎ 404/498–5690; admission charged), northeast of the city, features the world's largest sculpture memorial to Confederate war heroes Jefferson Davis, Robert E. Lee, and Stonewall Jackson (a cable car takes you 825 ft up the mountain face for a closer look). The 3,200-acre park also contains an antebellum plantation and historical museums and offers such recreational activities as a ride on a railroad or a cruise on a riverboat and nightly laser shows in summer. The 1996 Olympic archery, cycling, and tennis competitions will be held here.

Atlanta for Free

Performance stages in Piedmont and Chastain parks are the scene of free concerts in summer and early fall. The **Atlanta Symphony Orchestra** (*see* The Arts and Nightlife, *below*) performs six free Sunday evening concerts in summer at four locations: Lakewood Amphitheater, Cobb Galleria, and Piedmont and Grant parks. *Creative Loafing* (☎ 404/688–5623) is a free, comprehensive weekly newspaper listing free events around the city. It can be found at local restaurants, bookstores, and other businesses.

What to See and Do with Children

The *Atlanta Journal-Constitution*'s Saturday weekend guide has a "Kids" listing that highlights special happenings. **Fernbank Science Cen-**

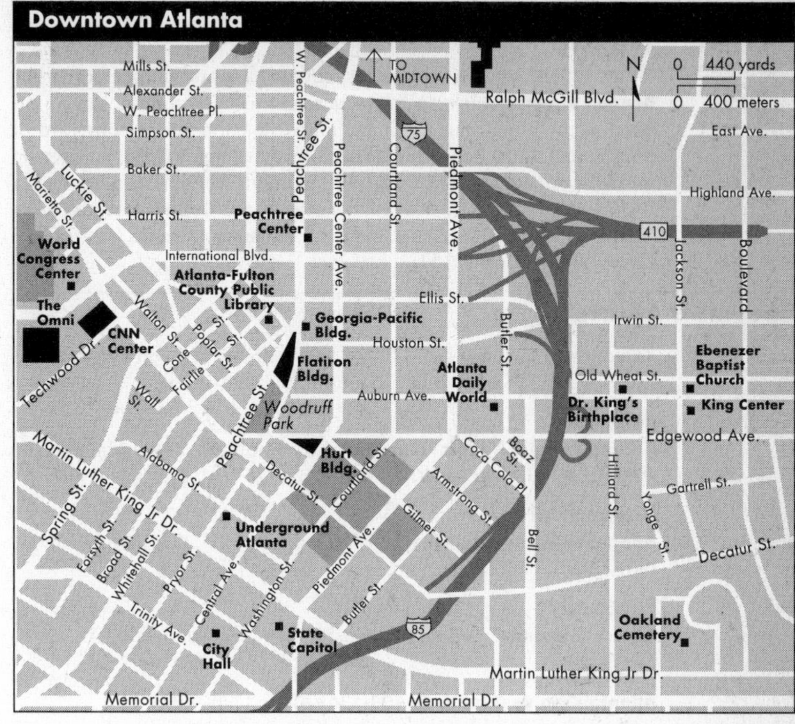

ter (156 Heaton Park Dr., ☎ 404/378–4311) features an authentic Apollo spacecraft and a planetarium. The **Center for Puppetry Arts Museum** (1404 Spring St., ☎ 404/873–3391; closed Sun.) displays puppets from around the world, holds puppet-making workshops, and stages original productions. **SciTrek** (395 Piedmont Ave., ☎ 404/522–5500), in Midtown, is among the top 10 science museums in the country, with hands-on exhibits and a special area for two- to seven-year-olds. **Zoo Atlanta** (800 Cherokee Ave., ☎ 404/624–5600) is in Grant Park, just south of downtown.

Six Flags over Georgia (I–20W at Six Flags Rd., ☎ 404/948–9290) is a major theme park offering dozens of rides (including heart-stopping roller coasters and refreshing water rides), musical revues, and concerts by top-name artists.

Shopping

Shopping Districts

Atlanta's shopping centers are generally open Monday through Saturday 10–6 and Sunday noon–5; many stay open until 9 or 9:30 several weeknights and most weekends. The primary downtown shopping area is **Underground Atlanta,** where specialty boutiques, chain stores, and pushcarts mix with restaurants and nightclubs. North of downtown in Buckhead, **Lenox Square** (3393 Peachtree St. NE) and the upscale **Phipps Plaza** (3500 Peachtree Rd NE) attract shoppers from throughout the Southeast. Lenox's new second level has expanded its size to 268 stores, while Phipps's new multistory wing, to be completed by July 1996, will more than double its size from 90 to 200 stores.

Specialty Stores

ANTIQUES

Shops selling antique pine pieces, collectibles, and unique crafts line **Bennett Street** in Buckhead. European furnishings and fine art are offered in the more than 25 shops lining the cobblestone courtyard of Buckhead's **2300 Peachtree Road** complex. **Miami Circle,** a street on the northern edge of Buckhead off Piedmont Road, is another mecca for lovers of antiques, with such stores as the **Gables Antiques** (711 Miami Circle, ☎ 404/231–0734) and **Williams Antiques** (631 Miami Circle, ☎ 404/264–1142).

Spectator Sports

Tickets for the teams listed below are available through **TicketMaster** (☎ 404/249–7630 or 800/326–4000).

Baseball

Atlanta Braves (Atlanta–Fulton County Stadium, 521 Capital Ave., ☎ 404/522–7630; Apr.–Oct.).

Basketball

Atlanta Hawks (Omni, 1 CNN Center, Suite 405, ☎ 404/827–3865; Nov.–Apr.).

Football

Atlanta Falcons (1 Georgia Dome, ☎ 404/223–8000; Aug.–Dec.).

Hockey

Atlanta Knights (Omni, ☎ 404/525–8900; Oct.–Apr.).

Dining

Atlanta prides itself on a wide selection of international restaurants. Italian, French, Moroccan, and Thai restaurants all command the attention of Atlanta's dining public, but not to be overlooked are the many offerings reflecting both the traditional and new-style cuisine of the Deep South. For price ranges, see Chart 1 (A) in On the Road with Fodor's.

$$$$ **Abruzzi Ristorante.** Some of the city's finest Italian cuisine is attentively served at this elegant, understated restaurant. Pasta is beautifully prepared here, especially the *papardelle* with game sauce, as are such regional specialties as quail over polenta. *2355 Peachtree Rd., ☎ 404/261–8186. Reservations advised. Jacket advised. AE, DC, MC, V. Closed Sun. No lunch Sat.*

$$$$ **City Grill.** The grand setting of this downtown restaurant in the historic Hurt Building includes high ceilings, bucolic murals, and romantic table lamps. The menu is American with a Southern flair. *50 Hurt Plaza, ☎ 404/524–2489. Reservations advised. Jacket and tie required. AE, D, DC, MC, V. Closed Sun. No lunch Sat.*

$$$$ ★ **Dining Room, in the Ritz-Carlton, Buckhead.** Chef Gunther Seeger has earned international acclaim for his imaginative haute cuisine, which incorporates such regional ingredients as Vidalia onions. The menu changes daily. *3434 Peachtree Rd., ☎ 404/237–2700. Reservations required. Jacket advised. AE, D, DC, MC, V. Closed Sun. No lunch.*

$$$ **Bacchanalia.** *Bon Appétit* voted it one of the country's 10 best new restaurants in 1993, and it has not disappointed. The influence is largely Mediterranean with touches of Asia; we recommend the $35 prix fixe menu. The entire restaurant is nonsmoking. *3125 Piedmont Rd., near Peachtree St., ☎ 404/365–0410. Reservations advised weekends. Jacket and tie required. AE, DC, MC, V. No lunch. Closed Sun.–Mon.*

$$$ **Ciboulette.** French-bistro food and atmosphere have Atlantans lining up for the variety of salmon specialties, the duck confit, and the roast squab. *1529 Piedmont Ave., ☎ 404/874–7600. No reservations. Jacket advised. AE, DC, MC, V. Closed Sun. No lunch.*

$$$ **Pricci.** The stamp of acclaimed designer Patrick Kuleto is apparent in the chic decor of this hot spot. Deceptively simple Italian fare is accompanied by Pricci's own breads. *500 Pharr Rd., ☎ 404/237–2941. Reservations advised. AE, D, DC, MC, V. No lunch Sun.*

$$ ★ **Buckhead Diner.** This ritzy establishment with a shimmering metallic exterior serves hearty American diner fare with an upscale twist, such as veal meat loaf, as well as dishes like crab spring rolls and asparagus. The diner is popular, so prepare to wait for a table when it is busy. *3073 Piedmont Rd., ☎ 404/262–3336. No reservations. AE, D, DC, MC, V.*

$$ ★ **South City Kitchen.** The cuisine at this bright, popular restaurant is traditional South Carolina coastal Low Country style; the catfish is superb and the desserts are delicious, albeit a calorie-counter's nightmare. *1144 Crescent Ave., ☎ 404/873–7358. AE, MC, V.*

$ ★ **Colonnade Restaurant.** For traditional southern cuisine, insiders know to avoid the tourist traps and head straight for the Colonnade, an Atlanta institution since 1927. *1879 Cheshire Bridge Rd., ☎ 404/874–5642. No credit cards.*

$ ★ **Luna Sí.** Funky meets uptown chic at this delightfully relaxed loft restaurant, where healthy cuisine in a healthy environment (smoking is strictly prohibited) is the order of every day. Butter and fat are nowhere to be seen here; fried dishes are done in virgin olive oil. The prix fixe menus are worth it. *1931 Peachtree St., ☎ 404/355–5993. AE, DC, MC, V. Closed Mon. No lunch Sun.*

Lodging

The city's booming convention business means hotel and motel options in all price ranges. The downtown, Buckhead, and north I–285 areas have the greatest concentration of accommodations. For price ranges, see Chart 2 (A) in On the Road with Fodor's.

$$$$ **Embassy Suites.** This Buckhead high-rise is just blocks from two of the city's top shopping centers, Phipps Plaza and Lenox Square. Suites range from basic bedroom and sitting room combinations to luxurious rooms with wet bars; a few standard rooms are available—all units have microwaves and refrigerators. *3285 Peachtree Rd., 30305, ☎ 404/261–7733 or 800/362–2779, FAX 404/261–6857. 313 suites, 15 rooms. Facilities: restaurant, lounge, fitness room, indoor and outdoor pools. AE, D, DC, MC, V.*

$$$$ **JW Marriott.** Connected to Lenox Square Mall and across from a MARTA subway station, this 25-story hotel's subdued style focuses on intimacy and comfort. Irregularly shaped rooms have oversize baths with separate shower stall and tub. *3300 Lenox Rd., 30326, ☎ 404/262–3344 or 800/328–9290, FAX 404/262–8689. 371 rooms, 30 suites. Facilities: restaurant, 2 lounges, health club, indoor pool. AE, D, DC, MC, V.*

$$$$ **Marriott Marquis.** The lobby of this popular convention hotel seems to stretch forever to the skylighted roof 50 stories above. Traditionally furnished guest rooms open onto this central atrium. *265 Peachtree Center Ave., 30303, ☎ 404/521–0000 or 800/328–9290, FAX 404/586–6299. 1,671 rooms, 71 suites. Facilities: 5 restaurants, 4 bars and lounges, health club, indoor and outdoor pools. AE, D, DC, MC, V.*

$$$$ ★ **Ritz-Carlton, Buckhead.** An elegant lobby featuring fine art, a fireplace, and comfortable, authentic antique furniture invites lingering over afternoon tea before returning to rooms containing luxury linens, marble baths, and reproduction furnishings. *3434 Peachtree Rd., 30326, ☎ 404/237–2700 or 800/241–3333, FAX 404/239–0078. 524 rooms, 29 suites. Facilities: 3 restaurants, lounge, health center, indoor pool. AE, D, DC, MC, V.*

$$$$ **Swissôtel.** An international clientele frequents this European-style luxury hotel, featuring a chic contemporary glass-and-white-enamel exterior and sophisticated Biedermeier-style interiors. *3391 Peachtree Rd., 30326, ☎ 404/365–0065 or 800/253–1397, FAX 404/365–8787. 362 rooms, 15 suites. Facilities: restaurant, lounge, health club, indoor pool. AE, D, DC, MC, V.*

$$$ ★ **Ansley Inn.** This Tudor mansion in the exclusive Midtown neighborhood of Ansley Park is decorated with Chinese porcelains and reproduction furnishings. Guest rooms are spacious; many overlook Piedmont Park. *253 15th St., 30309, ☎ 404/872–9000 or 800/446–5416, FAX 404/892–2318. 15 rooms. Facilities: pool, access to athletic club ($10 per visit). AE, D, DC, MC, V.*

$$ ★ **Quality Inn Habersham.** This small hotel on the north edge of downtown has large teal-and-mauve rooms that are pleasantly furnished with a desk, extra chairs, and a sofa. *330 Peachtree St., 30308, ☎ 404/577–1980 or 800/241–4288, FAX 404/688–3706. 91 rooms. Facilities: restaurant, coffee shop, exercise room. AE, D, DC, MC, V.*

$ **Barclay Hotel.** Renovated in 1994, this quiet, older hotel has a teal-carpeted lobby dominated by two chandeliers. All rooms have views of downtown; some have balconies. *89 Luckie St., 30303, ☎ 404/524–7991, FAX 404/525–0672. 73 rooms. Facilities: 2 restaurants, pool. AE, DC, MC, V.*

Motels

Holiday Inn Lenox (3377 Peachtree Rd., 30326, ☎ 404/264–1111 or 800/465–4329, FAX 404/233–7061), 297 rooms, 4 suites, restaurant, outdoor pool, access to Genesis Fitness Center (via shuttle; $5 fee); *$$.*

The Arts and Nightlife

Arts and nightlife events are listed in the *Atlanta Journal, Atlanta Constitution,* and *Creative Loafing* newspapers, available at newsstands, and in *Peachtree, Presenting the Season,* and *KNOW ATLANTA* magazines, available at visitor information centers and in hotels. The **Arts Hotline** (☎ 404/853–3278) also gives daily arts and nightlife information. Ticket brokers include **TicketMaster** (☎ 404/249–6400), the city's largest, and **Tic-X-Press** (☎ 404/231–5888).

The Arts

Most touring Broadway productions make their way to Atlanta's **Fox Theatre** (*see* Exploring Atlanta, Midtown, *above*), **Center Stage** (1374 W. Peachtree St., ☎ 404/874–1511), **Variety Playhouse** (1099 Euclid Ave., ☎ 404/524–7354), or **Civic Center** (395 Piedmont Ave., ☎ 404/523–6275). The **Alliance Theater Company** (1280 Peachtree St., ☎ 404/733–5000) is one of the city's leading theatrical groups. Woodruff Arts Center's **Symphony Hall** (1280 Peachtree St., ☎ 404/733–5000) is the home of the acclaimed **Atlanta Symphony Orchestra.** The **Atlanta Ballet Company** (☎ 404/873–5811) performs at various venues.

Nightlife

Underground Atlanta (*see* Shopping, *above*) and the **Buckhead, Virginia-Highland,** and **Little Five Points** neighborhoods are Atlanta's nightlife centers. Virginia-Highland's **Atkins Park Bar & Grill** (794 N. Highland Ave.,

☎ 404/876–7249), one of the city's oldest neighborhood bars, attracts a 30-something crowd. The upscale, high-energy, high-tech **Axys** (1150B Peachtree St., ☎ 404/607–0922) is Atlanta's new "in" dance club. A house orchestra plays popular dance numbers at **Ruperts** (Peachtree–Piedmont Crossing Shopping Center, 3330 Piedmont Rd., Buckhead, ☎ 404/266–9834). **Blind Willie's** (828 N. Highland Ave., ☎ 404/873–2583) offers New Orleans– and Chicago-style blues. **Eddie's Attic** (515B N. McDonough St., ☎ 404/377–4976; next to MARTA station), in nearby Decatur, is the best venue for local acoustic acts. For contemporary rock, try the **Cotton Club** (1021 Peachtree St., ☎ 404/874–9524) and the **Point** (420 Moreland Ave., ☎ 404/659–3522).

SAVANNAH

Four hours southeast of Atlanta, and a world away from the bustling, modern metropolis, lies Savannah, wrapped in a mantle of old-world grace. Established in 1733, the city preserves its heritage in a 2½-sq-mi historic district, the nation's largest urban landmark. Here 1,000 structures have been restored, and families still live in the 18th-century mansions and town houses. Known as the "City of Festivals," Savannah rarely lets a weekend pass without some sort of celebration, from a St. Patrick's Day bash to the Riverfront Seafood Festival in April, from the spring azalea and dogwood festivals to the house tours and concerts at Christmas. In the summer of 1996, Savannah will host the Olympic yachting events.

Tourist Information

Savannah: Convention and Visitors Bureau (222 W. Oglethorpe Ave., 31401, ☎ 912/944–0456 or 800/444–2427, FAX 912/944–0468). Visitors Center (301 Martin Luther King Jr. Blvd., 31499, ☎ 912/944–0455).

Arriving and Departing

By Plane

Savannah International Airport, served by major airlines, is 8 mi west of town on I–16. There is no bus service into town, but **McCall's Limousine Service** (☎ 912/966–5364 or 800/673–9365) runs a shuttle van between the airport and the city for $12 per person.

By Car

I–95, running north–south along the coast, and I–16, leading east from Macon, intersect west of Savannah; I–16 dead-ends downtown. The Coastal Highway (U.S. 17) runs north–south through town and U.S. 80 runs east–west.

By Train

The **Amtrak** station (2611 Seaboard Coastline Dr., ☎ 800/872–7245) is 4 mi southwest of downtown.

By Bus

Greyhound Lines (610 W. Oglethorpe Ave., ☎ 800/231–2222).

Getting Around Savannah

Savannah's historic district, though large, should be seen on foot to better observe the intricate architectural details. It's laid out in a grid pattern, and a number of strategically placed benches allow for frequent rests. If you bring a car, park it in one of the numerous metered and off-street pay lots here.

Exploring Savannah

A good way to start a tour is by picking up information at the **Savannah Visitors Center** (*see* Tourist Information, *above*), in the old Central Georgia railway station. Nearby is the restored **City Market,** a four-block area of shops, art galleries, restaurants, and jazz clubs.

Two blocks from City Market, narrow cobblestone streets wind from Bay Street down to Factors Walk and, below it, to River Street and the revitalized **River Front** district. A multimillion-dollar face-lift in 1977 transformed this once-musty warehouse district into a nine-block marketplace with boutiques, restaurants, and taverns. Also here is the **Ships of the Sea Museum** (503 E. River St., ☎ 912/232–1511), with memorabilia ranging from models of the earliest ships and nuclear submarines to nautical folk art.

Within easy walking distance of the River Front is the **Davenport House** (324 E. State St., ☎ 912/236–8097), one of the city's finest examples of Federal architecture, furnished with Chippendale, Hepplewhite, and Sheraton antiques. Within the graceful **Telfair Mansion** (121 Barnard St., ☎ 912/232–1177), designed by William Jay, is the South's oldest public art museum, displaying American, French, and German Impressionist paintings from the 18th and 19th centuries along with classical sculptures. The **Juliette Gordon Low Girl Scout National Center** (142 Bull St., ☎ 912/233–4501), in a Regency town house that was the city's first registered National Historic Landmark, displays memorabilia and original family furnishings of the founder of the Girl Scouts of America, who was born here.

East of here on McDonough Street is **Colonial Park Cemetery,** the burial ground for some of the city's earliest and most notable residents, such as Button Gwinnett, a signatory of the Declaration of Independence. Two blocks away is the French Gothic–style **Cathedral of St. John the Baptist** (222 E. Harris St., ☎ 912/233–4709; tours by appointment only), a late-19th-century structure containing Austrian stained-glass windows, an Italian marble altar, and German Stations of the Cross.

Across the street and through Lafayette Square is the 1848 **Andrew Low House** (329 Abercorn St., ☎ 912/233–6854), the childhood home of Juliette Gordon Low's husband, William. Some of the city's most impressive ironwork decorates the exterior; inside is a fine collection of 19th-century antiques. The **Green-Meldrim House** (14 W. Macon St., ☎ 912/233–3845), several blocks west, was built in 1850 for Low's business partner, cotton merchant Charles Green. Now a parish house for St. John's Episcopal Church, it is meticulously preserved and furnished with 16th-century antiques that reflect the original owner's luxurious tastes. The house is open for viewing Tuesday and Thursday through Saturday 10 AM–4 PM.

In the Vicinity

From Savannah, a 30-minute drive east on Victory Drive (U.S. 80/Tybee Rd.) leads across a bridge to **Tybee Island.** About 5 mi long and 2 mi wide, Tybee offers expansive white-sand beaches for shelling, crabbing, and swimming, as well as covered picnic facilities, a marina, and a wide variety of seafood restaurants, motels, and shops. The **Tybee Museum** (☎ 912/786–4077), which faces the **Tybee Lighthouse,** the state's oldest and tallest, traces the island's history from early Native American days.

Parks and Gardens

Integral to Savannah's design is its park system: 24 squares—large and small and each with a historic monument or a graceful fountain—dot the historic district. Near City Market is the earliest, **Johnson Square;** food carts are typically parked along its edges, so you can grab a snack while resting on a bench. Near the Green–Meldrim House on West Macon Street is **Forsyth Park,** where outdoor concerts are frequently held; at the center of its shady 20 acres, which include a jogging path and the Fragrant Garden for the Blind, is a graceful white fountain.

Shopping

Savannah's many specialty shops sell such merchandise as English antiques and Low Country handmade quilts. Stores in the historic district are housed in ground floors of mansions and town houses or in renovated warehouses along the waterfront. The **River Front** and **City Market** areas have a variety of shops (*see* Exploring Savannah, *above*).

Dining

Savannah offers an abundance of restaurants serving regional seafood; barbecue is also popular. If you want something fancier, the city has a number of fine Continental restaurants. For price ranges, see Chart 1 (B) in On the Road with Fodor's.

$$$ ★ **Elizabeth on 37th.** The restaurant has earned a regional reputation for the fine seafood and delicate sauces of owner-chef Elizabeth Terry. The cuisine is complemented by the renovated mansion's authentic Savannah decor. *105 E. 37th St., ☎ 912/236–5547. Reservations advised. AE, MC, V. Closed Sun. No lunch.*

$$ **Johnny Harris.** What started as a small roadside stand in 1924 is now one of the city's culinary mainstays. The menu includes steaks, fried chicken, seafood, and barbecued meats spiced with the restaurant's famous sauce. There's live piano or guitar music ranging from easy listening to mellow rock and popular standards on Friday nights, and dancing Saturday nights. *1651 E. Victory Dr., ☎ 912/354–7810. AE, MC, V. Closed Sun.*

$ **Mrs. Wilkes Dining Room.** Come to this unassuming basement restaurant for homey cooking served family-style. Patrons line up at breakfast and lunch for such quintessential southern dishes as biscuits, grits, collard greens, mashed potatoes, and fried chicken. *107 W. Jones St., ☎ 912/232–5997. No credit cards. Closed weekends. No dinner.*

$ ★ **Sea Shell House.** Forget the unprepossessing decor and dig into the combination platters of fresh steamed crab, shrimp, and oysters. Also on the menu is Low Country Boil, a regional dish of shrimp, sausages, and vegetables. *3111 Skidaway Rd., ☎ 912/352–8116. AE, MC, V.*

Lodging

For price ranges, see Chart 2 (B) in On the Road with Fodor's.

$$$ **Ballastone Inn & Townhouse.** At this handsome 1838 stucco inn, centrally located on the city's major thoroughfare, 18th- and 19th-century antiques decorate the double parlor. The old-world decor continues in the guest rooms, each with its own color scheme and some with working fireplaces. *14 E. Oglethorpe Ave., 31401, ☎ 912/236–1484 or 800/822–4553, FAX 912/236–4626. 20 rooms. AE, MC, V.*

Savannah and the Golden Isles

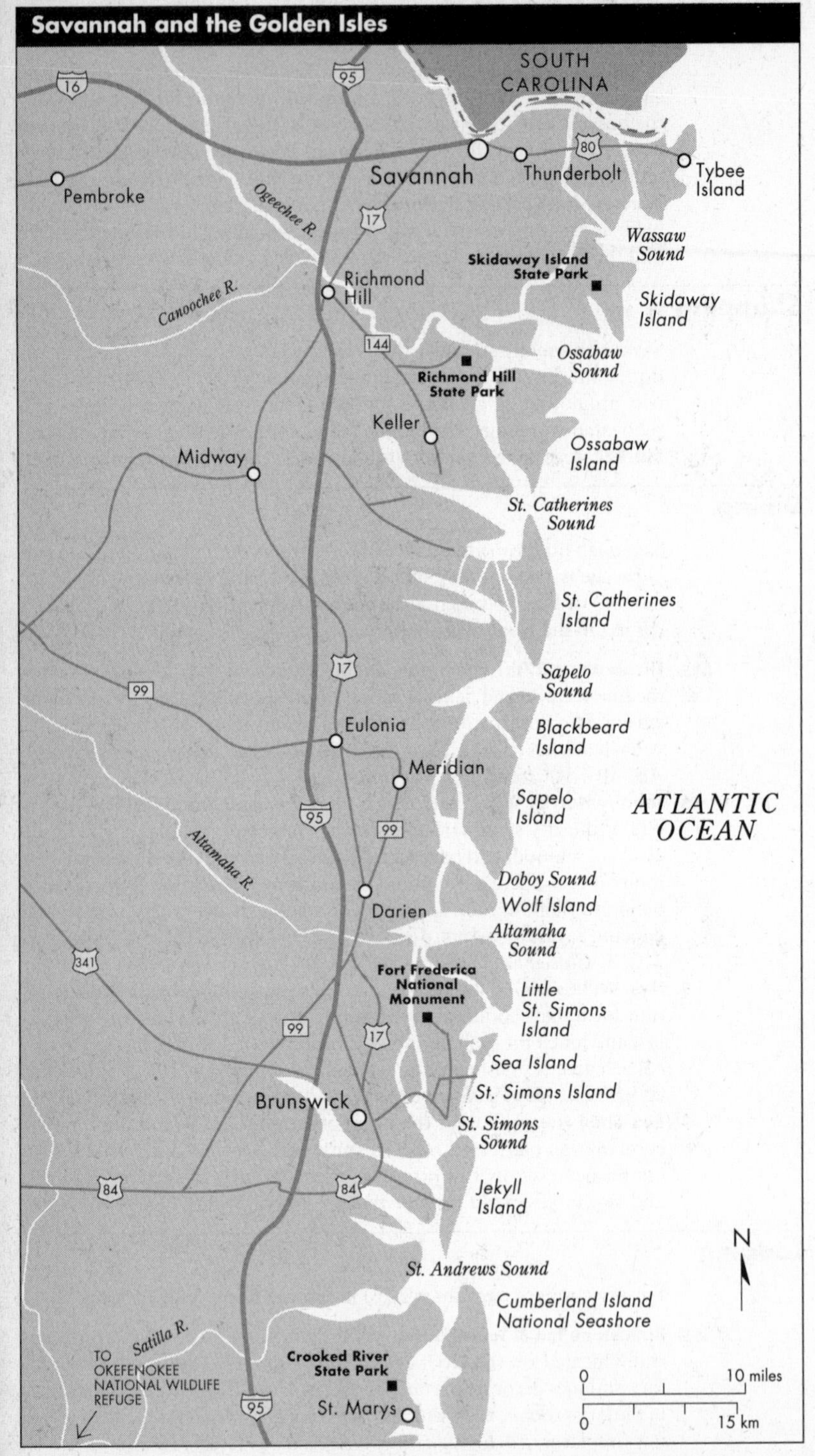

$$$ **DeSoto Hilton.** This popular convention hotel has comfortable guest rooms and an expansive lobby with discreet seating areas. Corner king rooms provide good views of the heart of the historic district. *15 E. Liberty St., 31401, ☎ 912/232–9000 or 800/426–8483, FAX 912/232–6018. 250 rooms, 9 suites. Facilities: restaurant, lounge, outdoor pool, golf and tennis privileges at area clubs. AE, DC, MC, V.*

$$$ ★ **The Gastonian.** The city's most deluxe accommodations are found at this 1868 inn two blocks from Forsyth Park. The two adjacent Regency Italianate mansions have been beautifully restored and maintained by live-in owners. Full breakfasts and tea are served in lushly appointed rooms filled with period antiques. *220 E. Gaston St., 31401, ☎ 912/232–2869 or 800/322–6603, FAX 912/234–0006. 13 rooms, 2 suites. Facilities: gas fireplaces in rooms, sundeck with hot tub. AE, MC, V.*

$$ **Magnolia Place Inn.** Striking two-story verandas overlooking lushly landscaped Forsyth Park wrap around this well-proportioned and ideally located Victorian house. Guest rooms are comfortable. *503 Whitaker St., 31401, ☎ 912/236–7674 or 800/238–7674. 7 rooms, 6 suites. AE, MC, V. Closed Jan.–mid-Feb.*

$ **Days Inn.** This older property's best asset is its location near the City Market and a block off River Street. Be prepared for typical motel-style modular furnishings and Spartan decor. *201 W. Bay St., 31401, ☎ 912/236–4440 or 800/325–2525, FAX 912/232–2527. 253 rooms. Facilities: restaurant, outdoor pool, free parking. AE, D, DC, MC, V.*

Nightlife

Savannah's nightlife is a reflection of the city's laid-back, easy-going personality. Some clubs feature live reggae, hard rock, and other contemporary music, but most stay with traditional blues, jazz, and piano bar vocalists. **Hard-Hearted Hannah's** (Pirate's House, 120 E. Brood St., ☎ 912/233–2225) is a rambunctious blues and rock club.

THE GOLDEN ISLES

An hour south of Savannah lie the Golden Isles, a chain of barrier islands stretching along Georgia's coast to the Florida state line. The three most developed—Jekyll Island, Sea Island, and St. Simons Island—are the only ones accessible by car; they are connected to the mainland near Brunswick by a network of causeways. A ferry from St. Marys connects Cumberland Island National Seashore with the mainland, and a launch transports visitors from St. Simons to Little St. Simons, a private vacation retreat. Spring, when temperatures are mild, is the ideal time for a visit; the superb beaches attract large crowds in summer.

Tourist Information

Cumberland Island: National Seashore (National Park Service, Box 806, St. Marys 31558, ☎ 912/882–4335). **Jekyll Island:** Convention and Visitors Bureau (901 Jekyll Island Causeway, 31527, ☎ 912/635–3636). **Little St. Simons Island** (Little St. Simons Island Retreat, ☎ 912/638–7472). **St. Simons Island:** Chamber of Commerce and Visitors Center (Neptune Park, 530B Beachview Dr., 31522, ☎ 912/638–9014). **Sea Island** (The Cloister resort, 31561, ☎ 912/638–3611 or 800/732–4752).

Getting There

By Plane

Glynco Jetport, on the mainland 6 mi outside Brunswick, is served by **Atlantic Southeast Airlines** (☎ 800/282–3424). International airports are an hour's drive north in Savannah and an hour's drive south in Jacksonville, Florida. Jekyll and St. Simons islands maintain small airstrips for private planes.

By Car

From Brunswick, take the **Jekyll Island Causeway** ($2 parking fee for all vehicles going to the islands) to Jekyll Island or the **F. J. Torras Causeway** (35¢) to St. Simons. From St. Simons you can reach Sea Island via the **Sea Island Causeway.** Only residents and park service personnel are allowed to drive cars on Cumberland Island.

By Boat

To reach Cumberland Island, you must reserve passage on the ***Cumberland Queen*** ferry, which leaves from St. Marys for the 45-minute journey. For a schedule or reservations, contact the Cumberland Island National Seashore (*see* Tourist Information, *above*).

By Bus

Greyhound Lines (☎ 800/231–2222) connects Brunswick with surrounding towns and cities, including Savannah and Jacksonville, Florida.

Exploring the Golden Isles

St. Simons Island

St. Simons, north of Jekyll and Cumberland islands, offers the contrasting beauties of white-sand beaches and salt marshes. As large as Manhattan, with more than 14,000 residents, it's the Golden Isles's most complete and commercial resort destination: Visitors here are well served with numerous hotels, beachfront cottages, and condominiums, as well as four golf-course developments.

At the island's south end, the **Village** is dotted with T-shirt and souvenir shops, boutiques, restaurants, and a public pier for fishing and crabbing. Adjacent to the village and overlooking the ocean is **Neptune Park,** with a playground, a miniature golf course, and picnic tables shaded by a canopy of live oaks. Also in the park is the **St. Simons Lighthouse,** built in 1872; climb to the top for a panoramic view of the beachfront, or visit the **Museum of Coastal History** (101 12th St., ☎ 912/638–4666) in the former lightkeeper's cottage.

At the other end of the island is **Fort Frederica National Monument,** which contains the foundation ruins of a fort and buildings inhabited by English soldiers and civilians in the mid-18th century. Tours begin at the **National Park Service Visitors Center** (Frederica Rd., ☎ 912/638–3639). On your way to and from the fort you will pass the Gothic-style, cruciform **Christ Church** (Frederica Rd., ☎ 912/638–8683). Three of the stained-glass windows tell the story of the church, which was rebuilt in 1886 after being destroyed by Union troops during the Civil War.

Little St. Simons Island

Accessible by private boat from St. Simons, Little St. Simons is a Robinson Crusoe–style getaway just 6 mi long and less than 3 mi wide. Owned and operated by one family since the early 1900s, the island's "retreat" (*see* Dining and Lodging, *below*) accommodates just 24 guests in rugged comfort. There's a 7-mi stretch of beach for swimming and water sports; other activities include horseback riding, nature walks, fishing, and shrimping and crabbing expeditions.

Sea Island

Across a marshy expanse from St. Simons is 5-mi-long Sea Island, whose main attraction is the **The Cloister,** a Spanish Mediterranean–style resort built in 1928 (*see* Dining and Lodging, *below*). This luxurious, low-key property encompasses a beach club with health spa, formal and casual restaurants, and such recreational activities as tennis, golf, horseback riding, sailing, and biking. The resort's roster of celebrity guests includes former president George Bush and Barbara Bush, who honeymooned here and returned in 1991 to celebrate their wedding anniversary. Outside the resort, beautiful mansions line Sea Island Drive.

Jekyll Island

Jekyll Island was once the favored retreat of the Vanderbilts, Rockefellers, Morgans, Pulitzers, and other American aristocrats. Many of these millionaires' elegant mansions (which they called cottages) are part of the **Jekyll Island Club Historic District** (Exit 6 off I–95, ☎ 800/841–6586; admission charged) and are open for tours. The lengthy system of bike paths crisscrossing the island and golf courses can be enjoyed year-round. Quiet beaches and an 11-acre water park, **Summer Waves** (210 Riverview Dr., ☎ 912/635–2074), rank as top summer attractions.

Cumberland Island National Seashore

Cumberland Island National Seashore, the largest and most remote of the Golden Isles, offers 18 mi of sandy beaches. You can tour the unspoiled terrain and the ruins of Thomas Carnegie's **Dungeness** estate on your own, or join history and nature walks led by park-service rangers (*see* Tourist Information, *above*). *Note:* You must bring whatever food, beverages, sunscreen, and insect repellent you may need with you; the island has no shops or markets.

Sports and the Outdoors

Biking

The flat terrain along the islands' coastlines is ideal for biking. Sea Island, Jekyll Island, and St. Simons have paved bike paths. You can rent bikes from the **The Cloister** on Sea Island (☎ 912/638–3611) or, on St. Simons, from **Barry's Beach Service** (1300 Ocean Blvd., ☎ 912/638–8053) and **Benjy's Bike Shop** (238 Retreat Village, ☎ 912/638–6766).

Fishing

The Intracoastal Waterway and the Atlantic Ocean are teeming with trout, barracuda, snapper, amberjack, and other fish. On St. Simons, **Island Charters** (☎ 912/261–0630 or 912/638–8799) and **Golden Isles Yachts** (☎ 912/638–5678) organize river and deep-sea fishing expeditions, and **Taylor Fish Camp** (☎ 912/638–7690) offers guided fishing trips through the marshes.

Golf

St. Simons Island has four courses: **Hampton Club** (100 Tabbystone Dr., ☎ 912/634–0255), **St. Simons Island Club** (100 Kings Way, ☎ 912/638–5131), **Sea Island Golf Club** (100 Retreat Ave., ☎ 912/638–5110), and **Sea Palms** (5445 Frederica Rd., ☎ 912/638–3351). Jekyll Island has several courses, including the **Oceanside 9-Hole Course** (Beachview Dr., ☎ 912/635–2170), constructed by the original millionaire residents in 1896, and the **Jekyll Island Golf Courses** (Indian Mound, Oleander, and Pine Lake, ☎ 912/635–2368).

Beaches

Wide expanses of clean sand beaches skirt all the islands. Choose the one where you'll spread your beach towel according to how you want to spend your afternoon. St. Simons's **East Beach** attracts large groups and families and offers sailboat rentals. The beaches rimming **Jekyll Island** are usually not too busy during the week but become crowded on weekends. On **Sea Island,** you can rent sailboats, sea kayaks, and boogie boards. The dunes and beaches of **Cumberland Island National Seashore** offer peaceful isolation.

Dining and Lodging

For price ranges, see Charts 1 (B) and 2 (A) in On the Road with Fodor's.

Cumberland Island

DINING AND LODGING

Greyfield Inn. Built by the Carnegie family, this turn-of-the-century house is the island's only lodging and stands by itself in the primitive landscape; its wide colonnaded porches beckon invitingly. The inn is furnished with its original Asian and English antiques; burnished hardwood floors are warmed by antique Persian rugs. Rates include all meals, which are delightful: hearty breakfasts, box lunches packed and left in the old-fashioned kitchen, and festive dinners. *Box 900, Fernandina Beach, FL 32035, ☎ 904/261–6408. 8 rooms share 3 baths (and outdoor shower house), 1 suite, 1 2-bedroom cottage. MC, V. $$$*

Jekyll Island

DINING AND LODGING

Jekyll Island Club Hotel. This renovated 1887 hotel is a turreted Victorian, complete with wraparound veranda and croquet lawn. Guest rooms are spacious and decorated to reflect the hotel's 19th-century origins. The Grand Dining Room serves gourmet cuisine; meal-plan rates are available. *371 Riverview Dr., 31527, ☎ 912/635–2600, FAX 912/635–2818. 118 rooms, 16 suites. Facilities: 2 restaurants, outdoor pool, tennis, biking. AE, D, DC, MC, V. $$$–$$$$*

Little St. Simons Island

DINING AND LODGING

Little St. Simons Island Retreat. Guests stay in spacious, airy rooms with private baths in one of four buildings: a two-bedroom cottage with screened porch and deck; the 1917 Hunting Lodge, with two antiques-filled guest rooms; or one of two houses with four guest rooms each. The buildings have screened porches and wraparound decks. Meals, which are included in the rate, are served family-style in the main dining room and include platters heaped with fresh fish, home-baked breads, and pies. *Box 1078, 31522, ☎ 912/638–7472, FAX 912/634–1811. 11 rooms. Facilities: horseback riding, canoeing, fishing, guided nature walks, pool. MC, V. Closed Dec.–Jan. Minimum 2-night stay. $$$$*

St. Simons Island

DINING

Crab Trap. Count on a crowd in high season at this spot popular for fresh seafood with side orders of hush puppies, coleslaw, corn on the cob, and batter-dipped fries. *1209 Ocean Blvd., ☎ 912/638–3552. MC, V. $*

LODGING

King and Prince Beach and Golf Resort. This beachfront hotel-and-condominium complex recently underwent a multimillion-dollar renovation that updated its spacious guest rooms and two- and three-bedroom villas. *201 Arnold Rd., 31522, ☎ 912/638–3631 or 800/342–0212, FAX 912/634–1720. 137 rooms, 47 villas. Facilities: restaurant, lounge, indoor and outdoor pools, tennis courts, access to golf course. AE, DC, MC, V. $$–$$$*

Days Inn of America. Opened in 1989, this chain motel offers sizable, clean rooms with microwaves and minifridges. *1701 Frederica Rd.,*

31522, ☎ 912/634–0660, FAX 912/638–7115. 101 rooms. Facilities: Continental breakfast, wine and cheese in lobby, pool, bike rentals. AE, MC, V. $–$$

Sea Island

DINING AND LODGING

★ **The Cloister.** At this classic resort, contemporary oceanside villas, condominiums, and rental homes have grown up around a 1920s Spanish Mediterranean–style hotel with large guest rooms. Formal dining, casual grill lunches, and seafood and breakfast buffets are included in the full American Plan. A new spa adjacent to the resort's beach club features a fully equipped fitness room, daily aerobics classes, facials, massages, and other beauty treatments. *101 1st St., Sea Island 31561, ☎ 912/638–3611 or 800/732–4752, FAX 912/638–5803. 262 rooms, 28 suites, 500 cottages, 44 condominiums. Facilities: 4 restaurants, 2 pools, tennis, golf, biking, skeet shooting, windsurfing, sailing, fishing, horseback riding, spa. No credit cards. $$$$*

Campgrounds

Cumberland Island National Seashore (*see* Tourist Information, *above*) maintains two tent campgrounds, one with rest rooms and showers, the other with cold-water spigots only.

ELSEWHERE IN THE STATE

Okefenokee Swamp National Wildlife Refuge

Getting There

The refuge is near the Georgia–Florida border, 40 minutes northwest of Jacksonville, Florida, and 40 minutes southwest of the Golden Isles. From Atlanta, take I–75S to U.S. 82 into Waycross. From the Golden Isles, take U.S. 84W to U.S. 301S.

What to See and Do

The **Okefenokee Swamp National Wildlife Refuge** (Folkston, ☎ 912/496–3331; admission charged)—a vast peat bog once part of the ocean floor and now 100 ft above sea level—covers more than 700 sq mi. Its thick vegetation is inhabited by at least 54 reptile species (including alligators), 49 mammal species, and 234 types of birds. The **Okefenokee Swamp Park** (8 mi south of Waycross, ☎ 912/283–0583; admission charged) is a major gateway to the refuge. Boardwalks lead to an observation tower; guided boat tours are offered, or you can rent a canoe ($9). There's an eastern entrance at the **Suwanee Canal** near Folkston (☎ 912/496–7156; admission charged) and an 11-mi waterway built more than a century ago. There's also a western entrance at **Stephen C. Foster State Park** (Rte. 1, Fargo, ☎ 912/637–5274; admission charged), an 80-acre park with boat rides through a swamp, a ½-mi nature trail, restored homesteads, and a large forest of cypress and black gum.

Paradise Garden

Getting There

Paradise Garden is a couple of blocks off U.S. 27 just north of Summerville, about midway between Atlanta and Chattanooga. From Atlanta, take I–75N to Exit 128, then Rte. 140W to U.S. 27N to Summerville.

What to See and Do

Best-known among Georgia's folk artists is the Rev. Howard Finster. His **Paradise Garden** (☎ 706/857–2926) is a complex of buildings, sculptures, and artwork. There's a church and a chapel, a two-story-tall sculpture created from old bicycles, and a shop where Finster's and his son's artwork is for sale. On the way you can stop at the **Adairsville Inn** (100 S. Main St., Adairsville, ☎ 404/773–2774), which serves excellent lunches (except Sat. and Mon.) and dinners (Fri. and Sat. only).

Callaway Gardens

Getting There

Callaway Gardens is on U.S. 27 in Pine Mountain, 70 mi southwest of Atlanta. From Atlanta, take I–85S to I–185S to U.S. 27S.

What to See and Do

Callaway Gardens (Box 2000, Pine Mountain, ☎ 800/282–8181; admission charged) is a 2,500-acre, year-round horticultural fantasyland and resort in the foothills of the Appalachian Mountains. The Callaway family began buying worn-out cotton fields and transforming them into impressive gardens more than 60 years ago, after discovering a rare, bright red azalea in the woods. Today the new **Cecil B. Day Butterfly Center** is the largest glass-enclosed tropical conservatory of living butterflies in North America, and the **John A. Sibley Horticultural Center** is one of the most advanced garden greenhouse complexes in the world. Walking trails and paved paths traverse the world's largest collection of hollies and more than 700 varieties of azaleas and wildflowers.

NORTH CAROLINA

By Carol Timblin

Updated by Susan Ladd

Capital	Raleigh
Population	7,070,000
Motto	To Be Rather Than to Seem
State Bird	Cardinal
State Flower	Dogwood

Visitor Information

North Carolina Division of Travel and Tourism (430 N. Salisbury St., Raleigh 27611, ☎ 919/733–4171 or 800/847–4862). **Welcome centers:** I–77S near Charlotte, I–77N near Dobson, I–85S near Kings Mountain, I–85N near Norlina, I–95S near Rowland, I–95N near Roanoke Rapids, I–26 near Columbus, and I–40W near Waynesville.

Scenic Drives

The **Blue Ridge Parkway** (*see also* Virginia) in the western part of the state extends from the Virginia state line to the Great Smoky Mountains National Park entrance near Cherokee—more than 250 mi of mountain views, nature exhibits, historic sites, parks, and hiking trails. **U.S. 441** from Cherokee to Gatlinburg, Tennessee, cuts through the middle of the national park for about 35 mi, climbing to a crest of 6,643 ft at Clingmans Dome, a short distance from Newfound Gap. Portions of **U.S. 64** travel through the Hickory Nut Gorge between Lake Lure and Chimney Rock and the Cullasaja Gorge between Lake Toxaway and Franklin, affording spectacular views of mountain peaks and cascading waterfalls. **N.C. 12,** connecting the Outer Banks, offers great views of the ocean and a landscape dotted with lighthouses and weathered beach cottages.

National and State Parks

The state tourism division's travel guide (*see* Visitor Information, *above*) includes a complete listing of state and national parks and recreation areas, as well as educational state forests.

National Parks

Cape Hatteras National Seashore (Rte. 1, Box 675, Manteo 27954, ☎ 919/473–2111) stretches 75 mi from Nags Head to Ocracoke and encompasses 30,318 acres of marshland and sandy beaches—a natural habitat for hundreds of species of birds, wild animals, and aquatic life.

Cape Lookout National Seashore (3601 Bridges St., Suite F, Morehead City 28557, ☎ 919/728–2250) extends 55 mi from Portsmouth Island to Shackleford Banks and includes 28,400 acres of uninhabited land and marsh, accessible only by boat or ferry. Portsmouth, a deserted village that was inhabited from 1753 until 1971, is being restored, and wild ponies roam the Shackleford Banks.

Great Smoky Mountains National Park (107 Park Headquarters Rd., Gatlinburg, TN 37738, ☎ 615/436–5615), with 8.5 million visitors a year, is the most visited national park in the country. Its 507,757 acres straddle the North Carolina–Tennessee border and offer camping, hiking, fishing, historic sites, and nature lore (*see also* Tennessee). To enter the park from North Carolina, take U.S. 441N from Cherokee.

State Parks

On the Intracoastal Waterway south of Wilmington, 1,773-acre **Carolina Beach State Park** (Box 475, Carolina Beach 28428, ☎ 910/458–8206, marina ☎ 910/458–7770) offers camping, fishing, swimming, boating, picnicking, and hiking. **Ft. Macon** (Box 127, Atlantic Beach 28512, ☎ 919/726–3775) centers on the fort built in 1834 to guard Beaufort Inlet. **Hanging Rock State Park** (Box 186, Danbury 27016, ☎ 910/593–8480) offers rock climbing and rappeling, hiking, camping, picnicking, and swimming. **Jockey's Ridge State Park** (Box 592, Nags Head 27959, ☎ 919/441–7132) offers hang-gliding instruction and flights from a 140-ft sand dune, the tallest in the East. **Kerr Lake State Recreation Area** (Rte. 3, Box 800, Henderson 27536, ☎ 919/438–7791) encompasses 106,860 acres and includes eight designated recreation sites around a huge man-made lake. **Merchant's Millpond** (Rte. 1, Box 141–A, Gatesville 27938, ☎ 919/357–1191) can be explored by canoe. **Mt. Mitchell** (Rte. 5, Box 700, Burnsville 28714, ☎ 704/675–4611) offers camping on the highest mountain in the East (6,684 ft).

THE PIEDMONT

The Piedmont is the heartland of North Carolina, a vast area of rolling hills that extends from where the coastal plain begins, east of the Triangle area (Raleigh, Durham, and Chapel Hill), to the foothills of the Blue Ridge Mountains, west of Charlotte and the Triad area (Greensboro, Winston-Salem, and High Point). Scattered along the major arteries of the region, including I–40, I–77, and I–85, are the state's largest towns, cities, and industries—banks, tobacco, textiles, and furniture. Here also are large rivers, man-made lakes, and woodlands; historic villages dating to the mid-1700s; crafts, antiques, and outlet shops; world-renowned colleges and universities; and one of the largest concentrations of golf courses in the world.

Tourist Information

Charlotte: Info Charlotte Visitor Information Center (330 S. Tryon St., 28202, ☎ 704/331–2700 or 800/231–4636). **Durham:** Convention & Visitors Bureau (101 E. Morgan St., 27701, ☎ 919/688–2855 or 800/772–2855). **Raleigh:** Capital Area Visitor Center (301 N. Blount St., 27611, ☎ 919/733–3456). Convention and Visitors Bureau (225 Hillsborough St., Suite 400, 27602, ☎ 919/834–5900 or 800/849–8499). **Winston-Salem:** Convention & Visitors Bureau (Box 1408, 27102, ☎ 910/725–2361 or 800/331–7018).

Getting There

By Plane

Major carriers serve **Charlotte-Douglas International Airport** (Charlotte, ☎ 704/359–4013), **Raleigh-Durham International Airport** (Raleigh, ☎ 919/840–2123), and **Piedmont Triad International Airport** (Greensboro, ☎ 910/665–5666). Taxi and limousine services are available at all airports.

By Car

I–40, U.S. 64, and U.S. 74 run east–west through the Piedmont; I–77 runs north from Charlotte; I–85 runs from Charlotte northeast through Greensboro and the Raleigh area.

By Train

Amtrak (☎ 800/872–7245) provides service to stations in 15 Piedmont cities, including Charlotte, Greensboro, and Raleigh. The *Carolinian* connects the three cities daily.

By Bus

Greyhound Lines (☎ 800/231–2222) provides service to Charlotte, Raleigh, Durham, Chapel Hill, Greensboro, and Winston-Salem.

Exploring the Piedmont

A reasonable starting point is **Charlotte,** the region's largest city. Its premier attraction is **Discovery Place,** an award-winning hands-on science museum. Here you can enjoy a touch tank, aquariums, an indoor rain forest, an Omnimax theater, and a planetarium, plus special exhibits. *301 N. Tryon St., ☎ 704/372–6261 or 800/935–0553. Admission charged.*

East of here, the **Hezekiah Alexander Homesite,** built in 1774, is the city's oldest dwelling. Named for the settler who built it, the site includes a log kitchen; costumed docents give guided tours. *3500 Shamrock Dr., ☎ 704/568–1774. Admission charged. Closed Mon.*

South of here via Eastway Drive, the **Mint Museum of Art,** built in 1837 as a U.S. mint, has served as a home for art since 1936. In recent years it has hosted internationally acclaimed exhibits. *2730 Randolph Rd., ☎ 704/337–2000. Admission charged. Closed Mon.*

It's a three-hour drive north on I–85 to **Durham,** a city once known for its tobacco production but today better known for **Duke University,** with its outstanding medical school. **Duke University Chapel** (☎ 919/681–1704), an ornate Gothic-style cathedral, serves as the focal point of the campus. It is open for tours and free organ concerts.

From Durham, drive for 30 minutes on I–40E to **Raleigh,** the state capital. You can walk to most of the government buildings and historical attractions downtown. The **State Capitol** (☎ 919/733–4994), built in 1840 and restored in 1976, commands the highest point in Capitol Square. Its appearance contrasts with the more contemporary legislative building, one block north, where sessions are currently held. Half a block north is the **North Carolina Museum of Natural Sciences** (102 N. Salisbury St., ☎ 919/733–7450), a favorite destination for children, who love its resident snakes and animal exhibits. Just next to the science museum on Bicentennial Plaza, the new **North Carolina Museum of History** (1 E. Edenton St., ☎ 919/715–0200) combines artifacts, audiovisual programs, and interactive exhibits to bring the state's history to life. The nearby **Executive Mansion** (200 N. Blount St., ☎ 919/733–3456), a turn-of-the-century Queen Anne–style structure in brick with gingerbread trim, is the governor's home.

Several miles from the state government complex, the **North Carolina Museum of Art** (2110 Blue Ridge Blvd., ☎ 919/833–1935) exhibits art ranging from ancient Egyptian to contemporary. The Museum Cafe is a favorite place for lunch or Friday night entertainment.

West of Raleigh on I–40 is **Winston-Salem.** In **Old Salem,** a restored 18th-century village, docents and craftsmen re-create the life and times of the Moravians, a Protestant sect that settled in the area in 1766. Also in the village is the **Museum of Early Southern Decorative Arts,** featuring period furnishings. *600 S. Main St., ☎ 910/721–7350. Admission charged.*

What to See and Do with Children

Enjoy thrilling rides at **Paramount's Carowinds** (15423 Carowinds Blvd., ☎ 704/588–2600 or 800/888–4386), a 91-acre theme amusement park straddling the North Carolina–South Carolina border near Charlotte. Thirty minutes south of Greensboro on U.S. 220, Asheboro's **North Carolina Zoological Park** (☎ 910/879–7000 or 800/488–0444) is home to more than 800 animals in their natural habitats. In Chapel Hill, 15 minutes south of Durham on U.S. 15/502, children can stargaze at the University of Carolina's **Morehead Planetarium** (☎ 919/962–1247). In Durham, the **North Carolina Museum of Life and Science** (433 Murray Ave., ☎ 919/220–5429) exhibits an eclectic assortment of life-size dinosaur models, NASA artifacts, and live animals.

Shopping

The Piedmont is a mecca for lovers of **antiques and crafts;** towns such as Waxhaw, Cameron, Pineville, and Matthews are devoted almost entirely to antiques. For directions and information, call Charlotte's visitor center (*see* Tourist Information, *above*). One of the country's largest antiques centers is **Metrolina Expo** (7100 Statesville Rd., ☎ 704/596–4643), near Charlotte.

The Seagrove area, between Greensboro and Pinehurst, offers nearly 60 shops that produce and sell handmade **pottery.** Burlington, between Greensboro and Durham, is a hub for **outlet stores.** Charlotte and Raleigh are major retail centers; the latter is home to one of the largest **farmers' markets** in the Southeast.

Sports and the Outdoors

Golf

The Sandhills area, in the southern part of the Piedmont, has more than three dozen courses, including Pinehurst's famous No. 2. For details, contact the **Pinehurst Area Convention and Visitors Bureau** (Box 2270, Southern Pines 28388, ☎ 910/692–3330 or 800/346–5362).

Spectator Sports

Basketball

Charlotte Hornets (Charlotte Coliseum, Tyvola Rd., off Billy Graham Pkwy., ☎ 704/357–0489; Nov.–Apr.) is the state's only NBA team.

The Piedmont is a college basketball fan's dream, with Atlantic Coast Conference rivals **Duke University** (☎ 919/681–2583) in Durham; **North Carolina State** (☎ 919/515–2106) in Raleigh; the **University of North Carolina** in Chapel Hill (☎ 919/962–2296); and **Wake Forest University** (☎ 910/759–5613) in Winston-Salem playing games November through March.

Football

The **Carolina Panthers** (Carolinas Stadium, 227 W. Trade St., ☎ 704/358–7800), one of the National Football League's expansion franchises, will kick off its first NFL season in August 1995.

NASCAR Racing

The Coca-Cola 600 and Mello Yello 500 races draw huge crowds to the **Charlotte Motor Speedway** (☎ 704/455–3200) off I–85 near Concord.

Dining and Lodging

The Piedmont has a growing number of upscale restaurants and ethnic eateries, as well as restaurants that specialize in the more traditional barbecue, fresh seafood, fried chicken, and country ham. Lodging is available at economy motels, upscale convention hotels, bed-and-breakfasts, and resorts. Breakfast may be included in the room rate, and children often stay free in their parents' room. Many city hotels offer weekend packages with discounted rates and extra amenities. For price ranges, see Charts 1 (B) and 2 (B) in On the Road with Fodor's.

Chapel Hill

DINING AND LODGING

★ **Fearrington House.** Set on an old farm, this elegant French-style country inn is a member of Relais & Châteaux. Rooms are decorated with chintz and antiques, and the cuisine is a deft blend of regional and French. *Fearrington Village Center, Pittsboro 27312, ☎ 919/542–2121, FAX 919/542–4202. 24 rooms. Facilities: 2 restaurants, pool, bicycles, shops. MC, V. $$$*

Charlotte

DINING

★ **Bravo!** The in place for special celebrations, this hotel restaurant is known not only for its authentic Italian cuisine but also for its singing wait staff. You might feel more comfortable in a jacket. *Adams Mark Hotel, 555 S. McDowell St., ☎ 704/372–5440. AE, D, MC, V. $$$*

Pizzarelli Trattoria. Wood-burning brick ovens are the key to delicious pizzas at this popular Italian restaurant. The owner is a former opera star who often sings for his patrons. *9101 Pineville–Matthews Rd., Pineville, ☎ 704/543–0647. No credit cards. $–$$*

DINING ANDLODGING

The Dunhill. Built in 1929, the hotel features reproduction 18th-century furnishings. The restaurant, Monticello's, gets rave reviews for beautifully presented California cuisine. *237 N. Tryon St., 28202, ☎ 704/332–4141 or 800/354–4141, FAX 704/376–4117. 59 rooms, 1 penthouse with whirlpool. Facilities: restaurant, lounge. AE, D, DC, MC, V. $$$*

Hyatt Charlotte at Southpark. Rooms ring a four-story atrium lobby at this modern hotel, popular with business travelers. The restaurant features northern Italian cuisine. *5501 Carnegie Blvd., 28209-3462, ☎ 704/554–1234 or 800/233–1234, FAX 704/554–8319. 262 rooms, including 4 suites. Facilities: restaurant, lounge, pool, health club. AE, D, DC, MC, V. $$$*

Morehead Inn. Though it caters to corporate clients, this Dilworth inn, built in the '20s as a private residence and restored in the '80s, has all the comforts of a luxurious home. Guests are served a complimentary Continental breakfast. *1122 E. Morehead St., 28204, ☎ 704/376–3357, FAX 704/335–1110. 11 rooms. Facilities: meeting rooms. AE, DC, MC, V. $$$*

Durham

DINING

Bullock's Bar-B-Cue. Patrons of this casual eatery queue up as early as four in the afternoon for the best Brunswick stew, barbecue, southern fried chicken, and hush puppies for miles around. *3330 Wortham St., ☎ 919/383–3211. No credit cards. Closed Sun. $$*

LODGING

★ **Washington Duke Hotel & Golf Club.** This luxurious inn on the campus of Duke University overlooks the Robert Trent Jones golf course. Duke family memorabilia are displayed in the public rooms; the bar is called the Bull Durham. *3001 Cameron Blvd., 27706,* ☎ *919/490–0999 or 800/443–3853,* FAX *919/688–0105. 171 rooms. Facilities: restaurant, lounge, outdoor pool, jogging trails, golf course. AE, DC, MC, V. $$$*

Raleigh

DINING

★ **Angus Barn, Ltd.** Housed in a huge rustic barn, this Raleigh fixture is known for its steaks, baby back ribs, prime rib, homemade desserts, and 35-page wine list. *U.S. 70W at Airport Rd.,* ☎ *919/781–2444. Reservations advised (no reservations Sat.). AE, DC, MC, V. $$$*

42nd St. Oyster Bar. This favorite gathering place for businesspeople and politicians serves fresh seafood daily. *West and Jones Sts.,* ☎ *919/831–2811. AE, DC, MC, V. $$–$$$*

LODGING

★ **Oakwood Inn.** This 1871 B&B in the Oakwood Historic District downtown is furnished with Victorian period pieces. *411 N. Bloodworth St., 27604,* ☎ *919/832–9712. 6 rooms. AE, D, DC, MC, V. $$$*

Velvet Cloak Inn. This elegant brick hotel with delicate wrought-iron decorations is a favorite spot for wedding receptions and political gatherings. Guest rooms have traditional, European-style decor. Afternoon tea is a tradition. *1505 Hillsborough St., 27605,* ☎ *919/828–0333 or 800/334–4372; in NC, 800/662–8829;* FAX *919/828–2656. 172 rooms, 4 suites. Facilities: restaurant, lounge, indoor pool, tropical garden. AE, DC, MC, V. $$–$$$*

Winston-Salem

DINING

Old Salem Tavern Dining Room. Moravian dishes, such as chicken pie and rack of lamb, are served by waiters in Moravian costume. In summer you can dine outside under the arbor. *736 S. Main St.,* ☎ *910/748–8585. AE, MC, V. $$*

LODGING

Brookstown Inn. Sleep under a handmade quilt before the fireplace, relax in the whirlpools that come in some rooms, and enjoy wine and cheese in the lobby or the complimentary Continental breakfast at this B&B, built in 1837 as a textile mill. *200 Brookstown Ave., 27101,* ☎ *910/725–1120 or 800/845–4262,* FAX *910/773–0147. 71 rooms. AE, DC, MC, V. $$$*

The Arts

In Winston-Salem, the **North Carolina School for the Arts** (☎ 910/721–1945) stages events and performances. The **Eastern Music Festival** (☎ 910/333–7450) brings six weeks of classical music concerts to Greensboro in summer. High Point's **North Carolina Shakespeare Festival** (☎ 910/841–6273) mounts several productions with nationally known actors August–October and *A Christmas Carol* in December. **North Carolina Blumenthal Center for the Performing Arts** (☎ 704/333–4686) in Charlotte hosts operas, concerts, plays, and other cultural events. The **North Carolina Symphony Orchestra** (☎ 919/733–2750) is based in Raleigh.

THE COAST

A chain of barrier islands flanks the bulk of the North Carolina coast. The Outer Banks stretch some 130 mi from the Virginia state line south to Cape Lookout; the southern coast, to the South Carolina line, includes the Cape Fear River region and Wilmington, the state's primary port. To these shores English settlers came more than 400 years ago to establish a colony on Roanoke Island, then mysteriously disappeared. Called the "Graveyard of the Atlantic" for the hundreds of ships that met their demise here, the Outer Banks proved a safe hiding place for notorious marauding pirates in the 1700s. For many years the region remained isolated, home only to a few fishermen and their families, but now, linked by bridges and ferries, the islands are a popular vacation spot. The Albemarle region, nearby, comprises charming towns full of early architecture. Hundreds of films have been shot in Wilmington, which boasts a restored historic district and waterfront. On the surrounding coast visitors can tour old plantation houses and azalea gardens, study sea life, and bask in the sun at nearby beaches.

Tourist Information

Cape Fear Coast: Convention and Visitors Bureau (24 N. 3rd St., Wilmington 28401, ☎ 910/341–4030 or 800/222–4757). **Carteret County:** Tourism Development Bureau (201 N. 17th St., Morehead City 28557, ☎ 919/240–7072 or 800/786–6962). **Craven County:** Convention and Visitors Bureau (Box 1413, New Bern 28563, ☎ 919/637–9400 or 800/437–5767). **Dare County:** Tourist Bureau (Box 399, Manteo 27954, ☎ 919/473–2138). **Historic Albemarle Tour, Inc.** (Box 759, Edenton 27932, ☎ 919/482–4747). **Ocracoke:** Visitor Center (☎ 919/928–4531).

Getting There

By Plane

The closest airports are **Raleigh-Durham International** (*see* The Piedmont, *above*), **New Hanover International Airport** in Wilmington (☎ 919/341–4333), and Virginia's **Norfolk International** (☎ 804/857–3340). **Southeast Airlines** (☎ 919/473–3222) provides charter service from **Dare County Regional Airport** (Airport Rd., ☎ 919/473–2600) at the north end of Roanoke Island.

By Car

Roads link the mainland to the Outer Banks at their northern end: U.S. 158 enters from the north near Kill Devil Hills, and U.S. 64/264 enters Manteo, on Roanoke Island, from the west. These connect with Rte. 12, the main route in the region, running south from Corolla to Ocracoke Island. Toll ferries (☎ 800/293–3779) connect Ocracoke with Cedar Island, to the south, and with Swan Quarter on the mainland; a free ferry travels from Hatteras Island to Ocracoke Island. From I–95 near Raleigh, U.S. 70 leads to Cedar Island via New Bern and Morehead City, and I–40 serves Wilmington.

By Bus

Greyhound Lines (☎ 800/231–2222) serves Elizabeth City, on the Albemarle Sound; Wilmington; and Norfolk, Virginia.

By Boat

There are more than 100 marinas along the Intracoastal Waterway, including **Manteo Waterfront Docks** (☎ 919/473–3320) and the **Park Service Docks** (☎ 919/928–5111) in Ocracoke. Beaufort is a popular stopover. The Wilmington area has public marinas at Carolina Beach State Park (☎ 910/458–7770) and Wrightsville Beach (☎ 910/256–6666). The ***North Carolina Coastal Boating Guide,*** compiled by the North Carolina Department of Transportation (☎ 919/733–2520), has a comprehensive list of marinas and other facilities for boaters; the appropriate county chamber of commerce can also provide boating information (*see* Tourist Information, *above*).

Exploring the Coast

Start your tour of the Outer Banks at Nags Head and Kill Devil Hills, where the Cape Hatteras National Seashore begins (*see* National and State Parks, *above*). You can drive from Nags Head to Ocracoke in a day, but be sure to allow plenty of time in summer, when ferries are crowded. During major storms and hurricanes, follow the evacuation signs to safety.

At **Kill Devil Hills,** the site of man's first flight, stands the **Wright Brothers National Memorial,** a tribute to Wilbur and Orville's feat of December 17, 1903. A replica of the *Flyer* is housed in the visitor center. *U.S. 158 Bypass,* ☎ *919/441–7430. Admission charged.*

Roanoke Island, accessible from U.S. 158 Bypass via U.S. 64/264, is the site of several attractions. The ***Lost Colony*** outdoor drama (☎ 919/473–3414 or 800/488–5012; admission charged; closed Sept.–mid-June) reenacts the story of the first colonists, who settled on Roanoke Island in 1587 and then disappeared. The **Elizabethan Gardens** (U.S. 64, Manteo, ☎ 919/473–3234; admission charged; closed weekends Dec.–Jan.) are a lush re-creation of a 16th-century English garden. **Fort Raleigh National Historic Site** (☎ 919/473–5772) is a reconstruction of what is thought to be the original fort. The ***Elizabeth II* State Historic Site** (☎ 919/473–1144; admission charged), a re-creation of a 16th-century vessel, is moored in Manteo Harbor.

Take a day trip to visit **Elizabeth City,** on the Albemarle Sound, and its **Museum of the Albemarle** (1116 U.S. 17S, ☎ 919/335–1453; closed Mon.). Then continue west to **Edenton,** the state capital from 1722 to 1743. In 1774, to protest English taxation, 51 local women staged the Edenton Tea Party. Be sure to see the Jacobean-style **Cupola House and Gardens,** built in about 1725; the 1767 **Chowan County Courthouse;** and **St. Paul's Church.**

Back on the Outer Banks, traveling south on Rte. 12, you'll cross the **Herbert C. Bonner Bridge,** which arches for 3 mi over Oregon Inlet to **Hatteras Island,** where the blue marlin reigns. The **Cape Hatteras Lighthouse** (☎ 919/995–4474), at 208 ft, is the tallest lighthouse in America. The visitor center has a small museum, and you can climb the lighthouse during the summer. At the south end of the island you can board the free ferry for the half-hour trip to **Ocracoke Island,** which was cut off from the rest of the world for so long that natives speak with a quasi-Elizabethan accent. The 1823 **Ocracoke Lighthouse** is the oldest operating lighthouse in the state.

From Ocracoke Island, take the Cedar Island ferry to the mainland and Rte. 12 and U.S. 70 to **Beaufort,** settled in 1710. The **Beaufort Historic Site** in the center of town comprises several restored buildings dating from 1767 to 1859, including the Carteret County Courthouse and the Apothecary Shop and Doctor's Office. Don't miss the Old Burying Grounds (1731). Here Otway Burns, a privateer in the War of 1812, is buried under his ship's cannon; a nine-year-old girl who died at sea is buried in a keg of rum; and an English soldier is buried upright in his

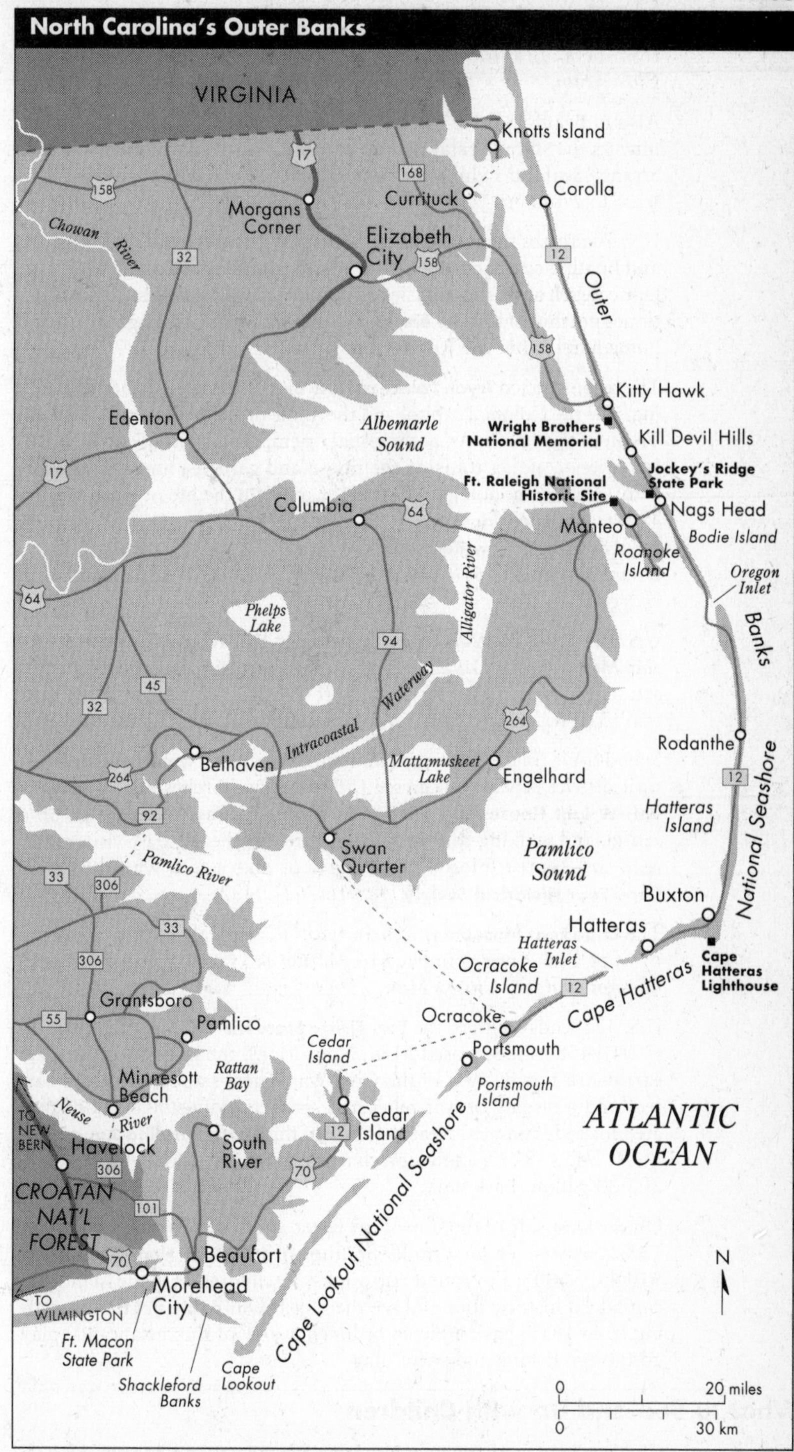
North Carolina's Outer Banks
VIRGINIA
Knotts Island
Corolla
Currituck
Morgans Corner
Elizabeth City
Chowan River
Outer Banks
Kitty Hawk
Wright Brothers National Memorial
Kill Devil Hills
Jockey's Ridge State Park
Ft. Raleigh National Historic Site
Nags Head
Bodie Island
Manteo
Roanoke Island
Oregon Inlet
Albemarle Sound
Edenton
Columbia
Alligator River
Phelps Lake
Intracoastal Waterway
Belhaven
Mattamuskeet Lake
Engelhard
Rodanthe
National Seashore
Hatteras Island
Swan Quarter
Pamlico Sound
Pamlico River
Buxton
Hatteras
Hatteras Inlet
Cape Hatteras Lighthouse
Ocracoke Island
Cape Hatteras
Ocracoke
Grantsboro
Pamlico
Cedar Island
Portsmouth
Rattan Bay
Portsmouth Island
Minnesott Beach
Neuse River
TO NEW BERN
Havelock
South River
ATLANTIC OCEAN
CROATAN NAT'L FOREST
Cape Lookout National Seashore
Beaufort
Morehead City
TO WILMINGTON
Ft. Macon State Park
Shackleford Banks
Cape Lookout
N
0 20 miles
0 30 km

grave, saluting the king. Tours on an English double-decker bus depart from here. *138 Turner St., ☎ 919/728–5225. Admission charged. Closed Sun.*

Also in Beaufort is the **North Carolina Maritime Museum,** which documents the state's seafaring and coastal history. Every August, at the Strange Seafood Exhibition, you get to eat the exhibits at a $15 buffet. *315 Front St., ☎ 919/728–7317.*

U.S. 70 crosses the Intracoastal Waterway to **Morehead City,** a fishing and boating center across Bogue Sound from Bogue Banks, where Atlantic Beach and Emerald Isle are popular family beaches. U.S. 70 continues northwest to **New Bern,** the state capital during English rule and immediately after the Revolution.

The reconstructed **Tryon Palace at New Bern,** an elegant Georgian building, was the Colonial capitol and the home of Royal Governor William Tryon in the 1770s. An audiovisual orientation is given, costumed interpreters conduct tours of the house and gardens, and (in summer) actors deliver monologues describing a day in the life of the governor. The stately **John Wright Stanly House** (ca. 1783), **Dixon-Stevenson House** (ca. 1826), and **New Bern Academy** (ca. 1809) are a part of the Tryon Palace Complex. *610 Pollock St., ☎ 919/638–1560. Admission charged.*

U.S. 17S leads to **Wilmington,** where the **USS *North Carolina* Battleship Memorial** (☎ 910/251–5797; admission charged), the city's major attraction, is permanently docked off U.S. 421. You can take the river taxi from Riverfront Park (in summer only) for a self-guided tour.

Spend some time exploring Wilmington's restored waterfront and historic district, where you can see 18th-century churches, the 1770 **Burgwin-Wright House,** and the 1852 **Zebulon Latimer House.** Pick up a self-guided walking-tour map from the Cape Fear Coast visitors bureau (*see* Tourist Information, *above*) or take a tour with the **Lower Cape Fear Historical Society** (☎ 910/762–0492).

The **Cape Fear Museum** traces the natural, cultural, and social history of Cape Fear River country. *814 Market St., ☎ 910/341–7413. Admission charged. Closed Mon.*

U.S. 421 leads south to the **Fort Fisher State Historic Site** (Kure Beach, ☎ 910/458–5538; closed Mon. Nov.–Mar.), the largest Confederate earthwork fortification of the Civil War. There's a reconstructed battery and a display of war relics and artifacts from sunken Confederate blockade runners. Nearby is one of the **North Carolina Aquariums** (☎ 910/458–8257; admission charged), complete with a freestanding, 20,000-gallon shark tank.

On the west side of the Cape Fear River, south of Wilmington on Rte. 133, a passenger ferry links Southport and **Bald Head Island** (☎ 910/457–5003; $15 round-trip adults, $8 children). On the island you can take a historic tour and see the 109-ft Old Baldy lighthouse, dating from 1817; have a picnic or lunch at one of the restaurants; play golf; or go fishing and swimming.

What to See and Do with Children

Children may enjoy flying a kite from the tallest sand dune in the East (about 140 ft) in **Jockey's Ridge State Park** (*see* National and State Parks, *above*). Three **North Carolina Aquariums** are open free of charge: on

Roanoke Island (☎ 919/473–3493); at Pine Knoll Shores on Bogue Banks (☎ 919/247–4004); and at Ft. Fisher (*see* Exploring the Coast, *above*).

Shopping

You can find **nautical items** at antiques shops and **hand-carved wooden ducks and birds** at local crafts shops in Duck, a few miles north of Nags Head, and in Wanchese, at the south end of Roanoke Island. **Kitty Hawk Kites** in Nags Head (☎ 919/441–4124 or 800/334–4777) offers every type of kite and windsock known to humanity. New Bern and Wilmington are centers for **antiques;** in Wilmington, many shops are at Chandler's Wharf, the Cotton Exchange, and Water Street Market on the waterfront.

Sports and the Outdoors

Boating

You can travel hundreds of miles over the sounds and inlets of this vast region along the Intracoastal Waterway. For marina and docking information, pick up a copy of the ***North Carolina Coastal Boating Guide*** (*see* Getting There by Boat, *above*), or contact the appropriate county chamber of commerce (*see* Tourist Information, *above*).

Fishing

The region teems with bass, billfish, flounder, mullet, spot, trout, and other fish. Fishing is permitted from piers all along the coast and from certain bridges and causeways. Charter boats for deep-sea fishing are available at the **Oregon Inlet Fishing Center** (☎ 919/441–6301) and **Tropico Charters** (☎ 910/791–8324) in Wilmington; ***Carolina Princess*** (☎ 919/726–5479) in Morehead City is available for charter. Licenses for freshwater fishing are available by calling the North Carolina Wildlife Commission (☎ 919/715–4091). No license is needed for saltwater fishing.

Golf

Among the public and semiprivate courses in the Greater Wilmington area is the breathtaking **Bald Head Island Golf Course** (☎ 910/457–7310), designed by George Cobb. Ocean Isle, near the South Carolina line, also has a number of outstanding courses. Contact the Cape Fear visitors bureau (*see* Tourist Information, *above*) or the South Brunswick Islands Chamber of Commerce (Box 1380, Shallotte 28459, ☎ 910/754–6644).

Scuba Diving

With more than 600 known shipwrecks off the coast of the Outer Banks, diving opportunities are legion. Dive shops include **Hatteras Divers** (☎ 919/986–2557), **Nags Head Pro Dive Shop** (☎ 919/441–7594), **Aquatic Safaris** (☎ 910/392–4386) in Wilmington, and **Olympus Dive Center** (☎ 919/726–9432) in Morehead City.

Surfing and Windsurfing

The region offers ideal conditions for these sports. **Kitty Hawk Kites** (*see* Hang Gliding, *above*) provides gear and instruction. Rentals are also available at shops in Wilmington, Wrightsville Beach, and Carolina Beach.

Beaches

Cape Hatteras and **Cape Lookout national seashores** offer more than 100 mi of beaches. Visitors also flock to **Atlantic Beach** and **Emerald Isle** on Bogue Banks near Morehead City, to **Wrightsville, Carolina,** and **Kure beaches** near Wilmington, and to **Ocean Isle** farther south.

Dining and Lodging

Fresh seafood is in abundant supply, prepared almost any way. Hearty southern cooking, with chicken, ham, and fresh vegetables, is also popular. Cottages, condominiums, motels, resorts, B&Bs, and country inns abound all along the coast. Most places offer lower rates from September through May. Condos and beach cottages may be rented through local realtors by the week or month. For price ranges, see Charts 1 (B) and 2 (B) in On the Road with Fodor's.

Beaufort

DINING

★ **Beaufort House Restaurant.** Fresh seafood (including such specials as seafood supreme and shrimp-and-crabmeat au gratin), steaks, and homemade desserts are the main agenda at this contemporary dockside eatery. *Boardwalk, ☎ 919/728–7541. D, MC, V. Closed Jan.–Feb. $$*

LODGING

★ **Langdon House.** Sleep with history surrounded by antiques, at this B&B built in 1733. Sumptuous southern breakfasts are created by host Jimm Prest. *135 Craven St., 28516, ☎ 919/728–5499. 4 rooms. No credit cards. $$$*

Duck

DINING AND LODGING

★ **Sanderling Inn Resort.** For special pampering, come to this remote beachside resort. Though the inn was built in 1985 and offers modern amenities, its stately, mellow look makes it appear older. The restaurant, housed in an old lifesaving station, offers such delicacies as crab cakes, roast Carolina duckling with black-cherry sauce, and fricassee of shrimp. *1461 Duck Rd., Box 319Y, 27949, ☎ and FAX 919/261–4111 or 800/701/4111. 60 rooms, 28 efficiencies. Facilities: restaurant, lounge, pool, tennis courts, health club, golf privileges, bicycles. AE, D, MC, V. $$$*

Kill Devil Hills

DINING

Etheridge Seafood Restaurant. The fish come straight from the boat to the kitchen at this family-owned restaurant decorated with fishing gear. *U.S. 158 Bypass, Milepost 9.5, ☎ 919/441–2645. MC, V. Closed Nov.–Feb. $$*

DINING AND LODGING

Ramada Inn. Guest rooms in this convention-style hotel have ocean views, and are equipped with refrigerators and microwave ovens. Peppercorns restaurant, overlooking the ocean, serves breakfast and dinner; lunch is available on the sun deck next to the pool. *U.S. 158, Milepost 9.5, Box 2716, 27948, ☎ 919/441–2151 or 800/635–1824, FAX 919/441–1830. 172 rooms. Facilities: restaurant, pool, Jacuzzi, meeting rooms. AE, D, DC, MC, V. $$–$$$*

Manteo

DINING

Weeping Radish Brewery and Restaurant. This Bavarian-style restaurant serves Hoplen beer, brewed on the premises, and German cuisine. Tours of the brewery are given upon request. *U.S. 64, ☎ 919/473–1157. Reservations advised. MC, V. $$*

DINING AND LODGING

Tranquil House Inn. This 19th-century-style waterfront B&B is only a few steps from shops and restaurants, and bikes are provided for adventures beyond. The restaurant, 1587, serves gourmet dinners. *Queen Elizabeth Ave., Box 2045, 27954,* ☎ *919/473–1404 or 800/458–7069. 25 rooms. AE, D, MC, V. $$$*

Morehead City

DINING

★ **Sanitary Fish Market and Restaurant.** In business for more than a half century, this basic, pine-paneled institution built out over the edge of Bogue Sound continues to please with heaping platters of fresh seafood—served fried, steamed, or broiled, with hush puppies, coleslaw, and french fries. *501 Evans St.,* ☎ *919/247–3111. D, MC, V. Closed Dec.–Jan. $$*

Nags Head

DINING

★ **Lance's Seafood Bar & Market.** You can contemplate the fishing and hunting memorabilia while you dine on steamed or raw seafood. Shells are disposed of through the hole in the table. *U.S. 158 Bypass, Milepost 14,* ☎ *919/441–7501. AE, MC, V. $$*

LODGING

First Colony Inn. Enjoy the view of the nearby ocean from the veranda of this historic B&B, which was built in 1932. Rooms have four-poster or canopy beds, armoires, and English antiques. *6720 Virginia Dare Trail, 27959,* ☎ *919/441–2343 or 800/368–9390,* FAX *919/441–9234. 26 rooms. Facilities: pool, afternoon tea. AE, D, MC, V. $$–$$$*

New Bern

DINING

★ **Harvey Mansion Restaurant and Lounge.** Swiss owner-chef Beat Zuttel excels in regional and international award-winning dishes. Original art decorates the walls of her restaurants, in a 1797 house near the confluence of the Trent and Neuse rivers. *221 Tryon Palace Dr.,* ☎ *919/638–3205. Reservations advised. AE, D, DC, MC, V. Closed Mon. $$–$$$*

LODGING

★ **Harmony House Inn.** At this historic B&B, convenient to all the attractions, you can sleep in spacious rooms, furnished with a mixture of antiques and reproductions, where Yankee soldiers stayed during the Civil War. The inn serves a hot breakfast buffet. *215 Pollock St., 28560,* ☎ *919/636–3810 or 800/636–3113. 9 rooms, 1 suite. AE, D, MC, V. $$$*

Ocracoke

DINING AND LODGING

Island Inn and Dining Room. This well-worn turn-of-the-century inn has third-floor rooms with cathedral ceilings and lovely views. The dining room is known for oyster omelets, crab cakes, and hush puppies. *Rte. 12, Box 9, 27960,* ☎ *919/928–4351 (inn) or 919/928–7821 (dining room). 35 rooms. Facilities: outdoor pool. MC, V. $–$$*

Southport

DINING AND LODGING

Bald Head Island. A self-contained, carless community complete with grocery store, restaurant, and golf course, reached by ferry from Southport, the island evokes images of Cape Cod with its modern, bleached-wood villas and shingled cottages. Guests travel the island on foot, bicycles, or in golf carts. *Bald Head Island 28461,* ☎ *919/457–5000 or 800/234–1666,* FAX *919/457–9232. 100 units. Facilities: restau-*

rant, pool, canoes, bicycles, golf, sailing, tennis, fishing, nature walks. AE, DC, MC, V. $$$

Wilmington

DINING

★ **Pilot House.** Resembling an elegant southern porch overlooking the Cape Fear River, with nautical prints, lanterns, and linen tablecloths, this Chandler's Wharf restaurant is known for its seafood, pastas, and vegetables, as well as for Sunday brunches. You can dine indoors or on a riverside deck. *2 Ann St., ☎ 910/343–0200. Reservations advised. AE, D, MC, V. $$*

LODGING

Blockade Runner Resort Hotel. This two-story, 1960s-vintage oceanside complex is widely known for both its food and its service. Guest rooms, which open off the exterior balcony, overlook either the inlet or the ocean. The Ocean Terrace Restaurant serves an especially popular Saturday seafood buffet and Sunday brunch. *275 Waynick Blvd., Wrightsville Beach 28480, ☎ 910/256–2251 or 800/541–1161, FAX 910/256–5502. 150 rooms. Facilities: restaurant (reservations advised), pool, health spa, meeting rooms, sailing center, bike rentals, golf privileges. AE, DC, MC, V. $$$*

★ **Inn at St. Thomas Court.** In the heart of the historic district, this trio of former commercial buildings (including a convent) has been transformed into luxurious suites decorated in turn-of-the-century style. *101 S. 2nd St., 28401, ☎ 910/343–1800 or 800/525–0909, FAX 910/251–1149. AE, DC, MC, V. $$$*

Campgrounds

Camping is permitted in designated areas of the **Cape Hatteras** and **Cape Lookout national seashores** from mid-April through mid-October and at most state parks (*see* National and State Parks, *above*). Private campgrounds are scattered all along the coast. For more information, contact the state's division of tourism (*see* Visitor Information, *above*).

The Arts and Nightlife

In Wilmington, plays and concerts take place in **Thalian Hall Center for the Performing Arts** (☎ 910/343–3664 or 800/523–2820), built in 1855–58 and recently restored. A favorite haunt on the waterfront is the **Ice House** (☎ 910/763–2084), an indoor-outdoor bar featuring live rhythm and blues.

ELSEWHERE IN THE STATE

Asheville

Getting There

You can get to Asheville via I–40E or I–40W. I–26 begins in Asheville and heads south, connecting with I–240, which circles the city. U.S. 23/19A runs through the city.

What to See and Do

I–40E to U.S. 25 leads to the astonishing **Biltmore Estate,** built as the home of George Vanderbilt in the 1890s. The 250-room French Renaissance–style château, designed by Richard Morris Hunt, is America's largest private residence, filled with priceless antiques and art treasures. The grounds, landscaped by Frederick Law Olmsted, include 17 acres of elaborate gardens and a state-of-the-art winery that occupies the former dairy. *Exit 50 off I–40E, ☎ 704/255–1700 or 800/543–*

2961. ☛ $24.95 adults, $18.75 children 10–15. Open daily 9–5. Festival of Flowers, early Apr.–late May; Christmas candlelight tours late Nov.–early Jan.

Forty-five miles west of Asheville, in the tiny town of Bryson City, the **Great Smoky Mountains Railway** takes passengers through tunnels and across high trestles as it winds through the mountain landscape. ☏ *704/586–8811 or 800/872–4681. Admission charged. Closed Jan.–Mar. and weekdays Apr.–May; call for Nov.–Dec. schedule.*

High Country

Getting There

The High Country—the Boone–Blowing Rock–Banner Elk area—is reached off I–40 via U.S. 321 at Hickory, Rte. 181 at Morganton, and U.S. 221 at Marion. U.S. 421 is a major east–west artery. The Blue Ridge Parkway bisects the region, traveling over mountain crests in the High Country.

What to See and Do

This once-remote region in the Blue Ridge Mountains now offers a wealth of sports and family activities. **Blowing Rock** refers to both a quiet mountain village and the nearby 4,000-ft rock for which it was named. Visitors to this looming outcrop enjoy views from its observation tower (☏ 704/295–7111) and its gardens of mountain laurel and other native plants.

About 10 mi south via the Blue Ridge Parkway, **Grandfather Mountain** soars 6,000 ft and affords sweeping views of the High Country from its Swinging Bridge. The **Natural History Museum** here features exhibits on native flora and fauna, and the **Environmental Habitat** is home to bald eagles, deer, cougars, and black bears. ☏ *704/733–4337. Admission charged. Closed in inclement weather.*

The High Country offers five alpine ski areas, plus many cross-country trails. Downhill skiing is available at **Appalachian Ski Mountain** at Blowing Rock (☏ 704/295–7828); **Hawksnest Golf & Ski Resort** (☏ 704/963–6561) at Seven Devils; **Ski Beech** at Beech Mountain (☏ 704/387–2011); and **Sugar Mountain** at Banner Elk (☏ 704/898–4521).

SOUTH CAROLINA

By Carol Timblin

Updated by Patricia Cheatham

Capital	Columbia
Population	3,643,000
Mottoes	While I Breathe, I Hope; Prepared in Mind and Resources
State Bird	Carolina wren
State Flower	Yellow jessamine

Visitor Information

South Carolina Division of Tourism (1205 Pendleton St., Box 71, Columbia 29202, ☎ 803/734–0235 or 800/346–3634). **Welcome centers:** U.S. 17, near Little River; I–95, near Dillon, Santee and Lake Marion, and Hardeeville; I–77, near Fort Mill; I–85, near Blacksburg and Fair Play; I–26, near Landrum; I–20, at North Augusta; and U.S. 301, near Allendale.

Scenic Drives

The **Cherokee Foothills Scenic Hwy.** (Rte. 11), passing small towns, peach orchards, and historical sites, traverses 130 mi of Blue Ridge foothills in the northwest corner of the state. The **Ashley River Road** (Rte. 61), which parallels the river for about 11 mi north of Charleston, leads to South Carolina's most famous plantations and gardens.

National and State Parks

National Parks

At **Cowpens National Battlefield** (Rte. 11, Box 308, Chesnee 29323, ☎ 803/461–2828), the American patriots soundly defeated the British in 1781; exhibits in the visitor center explain the battle. **Kings Mountain National Military Park** (I–85 near Blacksburg, Box 40, Kings Mountain, NC 28086, ☎ 803/936–7921), where the ragtag patriot forces whipped the redcoats in 1780, offers exhibits and dioramas depicting the famous battle. A paved self-guided trail leads through the battlefield. For white-water enthusiasts, the **Chattooga National Wild and Scenic River** (U.S. Forestry Service, 1835 Assembly St., Columbia 29201, ☎ 803/765–5222) forms the border between South Carolina and Georgia for 40 mi, dropping more than 493 ft on its journey from the Blue Ridge Mountains in North Carolina.

State Parks

Several of South Carolina's 48 state parks operate like resort communities, with everything from deluxe accommodations to golf. **Hickory Knob State Resort Park** (Rte. 1, Box 199-B, McCormick 29835, ☎ 803/391–2450), on Strom Thurmond Lake, offers fishing, golf, and skeet shooting. **Devil's Fork State Park** (161 Holcombe Circle, Salem 29676, ☎ 803/944–2639), which opened in 1991, has luxurious accommodations overlooking beautiful Lake Jocassee. **Calhoun Falls State Park** (Rte. 81, Calhoun Falls 29628, ☎ 803/447–8267), which opened in 1994, features a full-service marina, a campground, nature trails, and a picnic area.

The state's coastal parks—known for broad beaches, camping facilities, and nature preserves—draw the most visitors. They include **Huntington Beach State Park** (Murrells Inlet 29576, ☎ 803/237–4440), **Myrtle Beach State Park** (U.S. 17, Myrtle Beach 29577, ☎ 803/238–5325), and **Hunting Island State Park** (St. Helena Island 29920, ☎ 803/838–2011). For more information, contact the **South Carolina Division of State Parks** (1205 Pendleton St., Columbia 29201, ☎ 803/734–0159).

CHARLESTON

Charleston has withstood three centuries of epidemics, earthquakes, fires, and hurricanes to become one of the South's best-preserved and most beloved cities. Residents have rescued and restored block after block of old downtown homes and commercial buildings, as well as more than 180 historic churches. Each spring the city celebrates its heritage with symphony galas in stately drawing rooms, plantation oyster roasts, candlelight tours of historic homes and churches, and the renowned Spoleto Festival USA, a massive celebration of the arts staged in streets and performance halls throughout the city.

Tourist Information

Charleston: Area Visitor Information Center (Box 975, 375 Meeting St., 29402, ☎ 803/853–8000 or 800/868–8118).

Arriving and Departing

By Plane

Charleston International Airport (☎ 803/767–1100), 12 mi west of downtown Charleston along I–26, is served by several major domestic carriers. **Low Country Limousine Service** (☎ 803/767–7111 or 800/222–4771; advanced booking required) charges $9 per person to downtown. Some hotels also provide shuttle service from the airport.

By Car

I–26 traverses the state from northwest to southeast and terminates at Charleston. U.S. 17, a north–south coastal route, passes through the city.

By Train

Amtrak (4565 Gaynor Ave., N. Charleston, ☎ 800/872–7245).

By Bus

Greyhound Lines (3610 Dorchester Rd., N. Charleston, ☎ 800/231–2222).

By Boat

Boaters arriving at Charleston Harbor via the Intracoastal Waterway may dock at **City Marina** (Lockwood Blvd., ☎ 803/724–7357) or at the Isle of Palms' **Wild Dunes Yacht Harbor** (☎ 803/886–5100). Marinas sell detailed maps.

Getting Around Charleston

You can park your car and walk in the city's historic district, but you'll need a car to see attractions in outlying areas. **South Carolina Electric and Gas Company** (☎ 803/722–2226) provides bus service within the city and to North Charleston, and operates the trolley-style Downtown Area Shuttle buses, called **DASH** (☎ 803/747–0922). Fare on the latter is 75¢, or $1 for a one-day pass. Taxi companies include **Yellow Cab** (☎ 803/577–6565), **Safety Cab** (☎ 803/722–4066), and **Low Country Limousine** (*see* Arriving and Departing, *above*). A popular option is a horse-drawn-carriage tour. Guides are generally very knowledgeable and often provide unusual snippets of history and humor. Tours conducted by the **Old South Carriage Company** (☎ 803/723–9712), whose guides wear Confederate uniforms, depart from the corner of Anson and North Market streets; **Carolina Carriage Company** (☎

803/723–8687) tours leave from Market Square. **Charleston Carriage Company** (☎ 803/577–0042), the city's oldest, conducts one-hour tours of the historic district.

Exploring Charleston

You can get a quick orientation to the city by viewing ***Forever Charleston,*** a 24-minute multimedia presentation (admission charged) shown at the **Area Visitor Information Center** (Box 975, 375 Meeting St., ☎ 803/853–8000). Across from the center (where there's free two-hour parking) is the **Charleston Museum** (360 Meeting St., ☎ 803/722–2996; admission charged), founded in 1773 and the oldest city museum in the country. Now housed in a $6 million, contemporary complex, the collection includes Charleston silver, fashions, toys, and snuffboxes, as well as exhibits on natural history, archaeology, and ornithology.

Also part of the museum are three historic homes. The **Joseph Manigault House** (350 Meeting St.), just down the street, was designed in 1803 and is noted for its carved-wood mantels and elaborate plasterwork. Furnishings are British, French, and American antiques, including rare tricolor Wedgwood pieces. The **Aiken-Rhett Mansion** (48 Elizabeth St.), a few blocks north, was the Civil War headquarters of Confederate general P.G.T. Beauregard. Its ornate interior is furnished in a variety of 19th-century styles. Many blocks south, the **Heyward-Washington House** (87 Church St.) was the residence of President George Washington during his 1791 visit. The mansion is notable for fine period furnishings by local craftsmen and includes Charleston's only restored 18th-century kitchen open to visitors. You can purchase a combined ticket for admission to the museum and all three houses.

The heart of Charleston is the **Old City Market,** between Meeting and East Bay streets, with restaurants, shops, and open-air produce stands. Here you can buy vegetables, fruits, *benne*-seed (sesame-seed) wafers, sweet-grass baskets (*see* Shopping, *below*), and other local craft items.

South of the market, **Dock Street Theatre** (135 Church St., ☎ 803/723–5648) combines the reconstructed early Georgian playhouse that originally stood on the site with the 1809 Planter's Hotel. At the corner of Meeting and Broad streets is **St. Michael's Episcopal Church** (☎ 803/723–0603), modeled on London's St. Martin's-in-the-Fields. Completed in 1761, this beautiful structure is Charleston's oldest surviving church.

Fort Sumter National Monument, a man-made island in Charleston Harbor, is where the first shot of the Civil War was fired, on April 12, 1861. National Park Service rangers conduct free tours of the restored structure, which includes a historical museum with displays and dioramas. To get here, take a boat from Patriots Point (*see* What to See and Do with Children, *below*) or the Municipal Marina on Lockwood Boulevard. ☎ *803/722–1691. Charge for boat ride.*

Plantations, Parks, and Gardens

Charleston is famous for its public parks, magnificent plantations, and secret gardens that lie hidden behind the walls of private homes. **White Point Gardens,** on the point of the narrow Battery peninsula bounded by the Ashley and Cooper rivers, is the most popular gathering spot in the city. The new **Waterfront Park,** along Concord Street on the Cooper River, features a fishing pier, a picnic area, and landscaped gardens.

Drayton Hall (☎ 803/766–0188), built between 1738 and 1742, is 9 mi northwest of downtown via Ashley River Road (Rte. 61). Consid-

Charleston

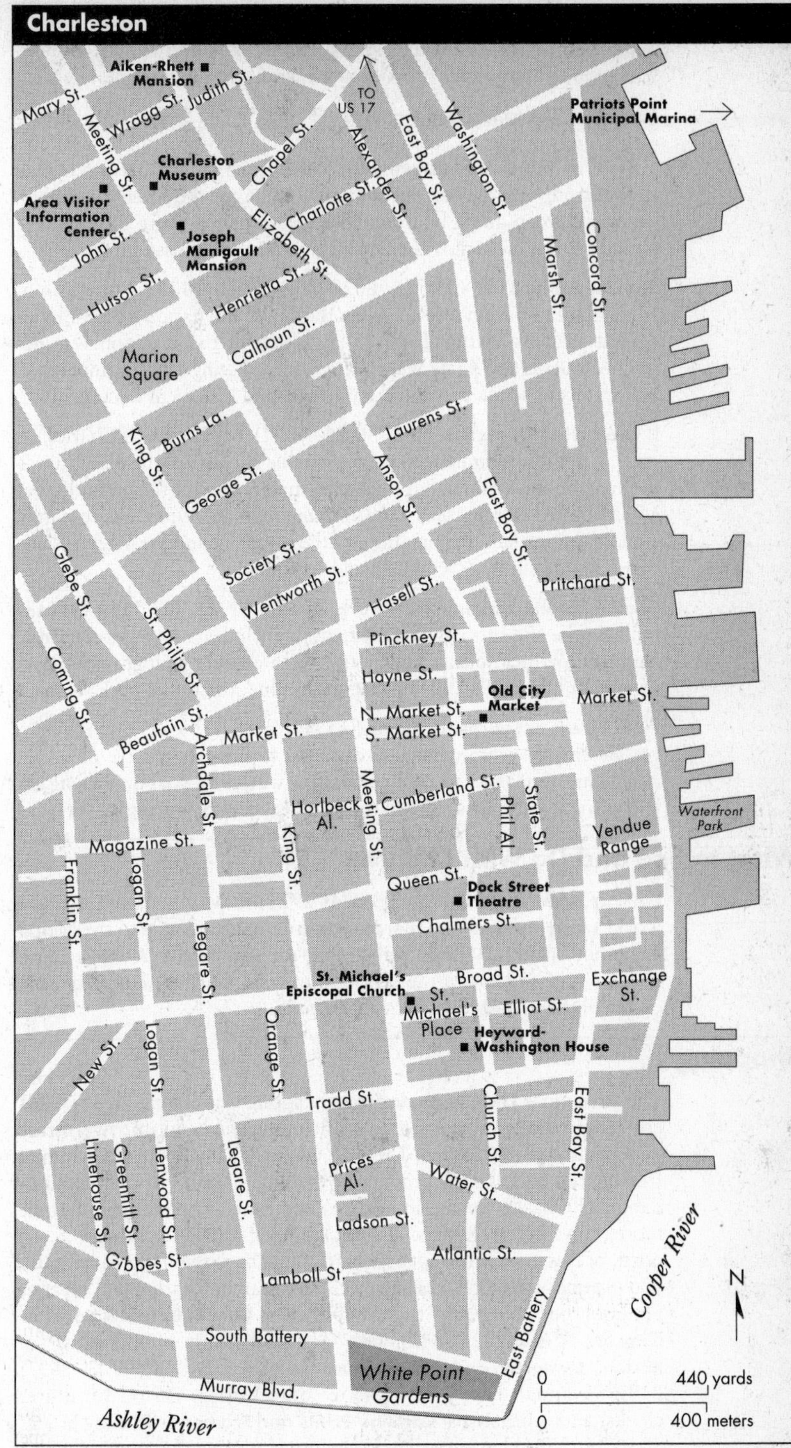
Aiken-Rhett Mansion
TO US 17
Patriots Point Municipal Marina
Mary St.
Wragg St.
Judith St.
Meeting St.
Chapel St.
Alexander St.
East Bay St.
Washington St.
Charleston Museum
Area Visitor Information Center
Charlotte St.
Elizabeth St.
Joseph Manigault Mansion
John St.
Hutson St.
Henrietta St.
Calhoun St.
Marsh St.
Concord St.
Marion Square
Burns La.
King St.
Laurens St.
George St.
Anson St.
East Bay St.
Society St.
Wentworth St.
Glebe St.
Hasell St.
Pritchard St.
St. Philip St.
Pinckney St.
Coming St.
Hayne St.
Old City Market
Market St.
N. Market St.
S. Market St.
Beaufain St.
Market St.
Archdale St.
Horlbeck Al.
Cumberland St.
Meeting St.
Phil Al.
State St.
Waterfront Park
Vendue Range
Magazine St.
King St.
Franklin St.
Logan St.
Queen St.
Dock Street Theatre
Chalmers St.
Legare St.
St. Michael's Episcopal Church
Broad St.
Exchange St.
St. Michael's Place
Elliot St.
Heyward-Washington House
New St.
Logan St.
Orange St.
Tradd St.
Church St.
East Bay St.
Limehouse St.
Greenhill St.
Lenwood St.
Legare St.
Prices Al.
Water St.
Ladson St.
Atlantic St.
Gibbes St.
Lamboll St.
Cooper River
South Battery
East Battery
N
White Point Gardens
Murray Blvd.
0
440 yards
0
400 meters
Ashley River

ered the nation's finest example of Georgian Palladian architecture, the plantation house is unfurnished to highlight the original plaster moldings, opulent hand-carved woodwork, and other ornamental details.

Magnolia Plantation and Gardens (☎ 803/571–1266) is 2 mi farther on Rte. 61. Begun in 1685, the gardens boast one of the largest collections of azaleas and camellias in North America. Nature lovers may canoe through the 125-acre Waterfowl Refuge, see the 60-acre Audubon Swamp Garden along boardwalks and bridges, explore 500 acres of wildlife trails, and enjoy the petting zoo and minihorse ranch.

Middleton Place (☎ 803/556–6020 or 800/782–3608), 4 mi north of Magnolia Plantation on Rte. 61, is the site of the nation's oldest landscaped gardens, dating from 1741. Much of the mansion was destroyed during the Civil War, but a restored wing houses impressive collections of silver, furniture, paintings, and historical documents.

If **Boone Hall Plantation** (☎ 803/884–4371), 8 mi north of Charleston on U.S. 17, looks familiar to you, it may be because of the plantation's avenue of oaks—said to have been the inspiration for the painting that MGM filmed to represent Tara in *Gone with the Wind.* Visitors may explore the gardens, the first floor of the mansion, and the original slave quarters. Lunch is served in the old cotton gin.

Charles Towne Landing State Park (Hwy. 171, ☎ 803/556–4450) is built on the site of a 1670 settlement. It includes a reconstructed village and fortifications, a replica of a 17th-century sailing vessel, gardens with bike trails and walking paths, and an animal park.

I–26N leads to **Cypress Gardens** (U.S. 52, ☎ 803/553–0515), a swamp garden created from what was once the freshwater reserve of a vast rice plantation. You can explore the inky waters by boat or walk along paths lined with moss-draped cypress trees and flowering bushes.

What to See and Do with Children

Patriots Point (U.S. 17, ☎ 803/884–2727) in Mount Pleasant is the world's largest naval and maritime museum, now home to the Medal of Honor Society. Berthed here are the aircraft carrier *Yorktown,* the nuclear ship *Savannah,* the World War II submarine *Clamagore,* the cutter *Ingham,* and the destroyer *Laffey.*

Shopping

The three-block **Old City Market** (*see* Exploring Charleston, *above*) yields colorful produce and varied gifts, including the beautiful sweetgrass baskets unique to this area. The craft was originally imported by slaves from Africa and is now practiced by only a handful of their descendants. The baskets come in all sizes and range in price from $10 to more than $100. (They are also sold at open-air stands along U.S. 17 north of town, near Mount Pleasant; if you have the heart to bargain, you *may* be able to get a better price here than in Charleston.) Elegant antiques shops line King Street, among them **Geo. C. Birlant & Co.** (191 King St., ☎ 803/722–3842), with 18th- and 19th-century English selections. **Livingston and Sons Antiques** (163 King St., ☎ 803/723–9697; 2137 Savannah Hwy., ☎ 803/556–3502) offers period furniture, clocks, and other items. **Carolina Prints and Frames** (188 King St., ☎ 803/723–2266) has superb reproductions. Among the town's chic art galleries are the **Birds I View Gallery** (119–A Church St., ☎ 803/723–1276), with bird paintings and prints by noted artists, and the **Virginia Fouche Bolton Art Gallery** (127 Meeting St., ☎ 803/577–9351), selling paintings and limited-edition lithographs of Charleston scenes. **Historic Charleston Reproductions** (105 Broad St., ☎ 803/723–8292) has superb replicas of Charleston furniture and accessories approved by the Historic Charleston Foundation.

Beaches

South Carolina's climate allows swimming from April through October. There are public beaches at **Beachwalker Park,** on Kiawah Island; **Folly Beach County Park** and **Folly Beach** on Folly Island; the **Isle of Palms;** and **Sullivan's Island.** Resorts with private beaches include **Fairfield Ocean Ridge** on Edisto Island; **Kiawah Island Resort** (*see* Lodging, *below*); **Seabrook Island;** and **Wild Dunes Resort** on the Isle of Palms. For more information, contact Charleston's visitors bureau (*see* Tourist Information, *above*).

Dining

Best known for its Low Country specialties—she-crab soup, sautéed shrimp, grits, and variations on pecan pie—Charleston is also a hotbed of a new American cuisine that blends down-home cooking with haute cuisine. For price ranges, see Chart 1 (B) in On the Road with Fodor's.

$$$ **82 Queen.** At this complex of pink stucco buildings dating from the mid-1880s, you can dine on such Low Country favorites as crab cakes served with sweet-red-pepper–cream sauce. Also on the menu are such delicacies as roast duck with blueberry Cointreau glaze and oysters stuffed with Daufuskie crab. *82 Queen St.,* ☎ *803/723–7591. AE, MC, V.*

$$ ★ **Gaulart and Maliclet French Cafe.** This chic, upbeat café serves ethnic and bistro French food. The menu of soups, salads, and sandwiches is enlivened by such evening specials as coq au vin and paella. *98 Broad St.,* ☎ *803/577–9797. AE, DC, MC, V.*

$$ ★ **Magnolias—Uptown/Down South.** Housed in an 1823 warehouse and decorated with a magnolia theme, the restaurant is prized for its Low Country fare, which includes grilled mahimahi fillet topped with creamed crabmeat and fresh herbs. *185 E. Bay St.,* ☎ *803/577–7771. Reservations advised. AE, MC, V.*

$$ **Shem Creek Bar & Grill.** This pleasant dockside spot is popular for its oyster bar and light fare, as well as a wide variety of seafood entrées. A menu highlight is the pot of steamed lobsters, clams, oysters, and sausages with melted lemon butter or hot cocktail sauce. *508 Mill St., Mount Pleasant,* ☎ *803/884–8102. No reservations. AE, D, MC, V.*

$ **Mike Calder's Deli & Pub.** Soups, salads, sandwiches, daily specials, and 12 different draft beers are offered in an antique setting, once a pharmacy in the historic district. *288 King St.,* ☎ *803/577–0123. No reservations. D, MC, V.*

$ **Slightly North of Broad.** This whimsically decorated eatery, which opened in December 1993, has several seats that overlook the action-packed kitchen. The Low Country cuisine is given trendy treatment here: Try the corn fritters with caviar and crème fraîche. *192 E. Bay St.,* ☎ *803/723–3424. No reservations. AE, D, MC, V.*

Lodging

Hotels and inns on the peninsula are generally more expensive than those in outlying areas of the city. Rates tend to increase during festivals, when reservations are essential. During Visitors' Appreciation Days (mid-Nov.–mid-Feb.), rates drop by as much as 50%. World-class resorts are located nearby, including Kiawah Island, Wild Dunes, and Seabrook Island resorts. For price ranges, see Chart 2 (A) in On the Road with Fodor's.

$$$$ ★ **John Rutledge House Inn.** The 1763 main house, built by a signatory of the U.S. Constitution, and two carriage houses (each with four rooms) opened in 1989 as a luxury B&B inn. Rooms feature high ceilings, plaster molding, and wood floors, and are decorated with antiques and four-poster beds. Complimentary wine and tea are served in the ballroom. *116 Broad St., 29401, ☎ 803/723–7999 or 800/476–9741, FAX 803/720–2615. 19 rooms. Facilities: Continental breakfast. AE, MC, V.*

$$$$ **Kiawah Island Resort.** This plush resort on 10,000 wooded acres offers accommodations in rooms, suites, or villas. All are decorated with light colors and have balconies with ocean or forest views. *21 mi from Charleston via U.S. 17S; Box 12357, Charleston 29422, ☎ 803/768–2121 or 800/654–2924, FAX 803/768–6099. 150 rooms, 48 suites, 300 villas. Facilities: 3 restaurants, lounge, golf, tennis, beaches, water sports. AE, DC, MC, V.*

$$$ **Hawthorn Suites Hotel at the Market.** This deluxe hotel features a restored entrance portico from an 1874 bank, a refurbished 1866 firehouse, and three lush gardens. The spacious suites, decorated with 18th-century reproductions and canopy beds, include full kitchens or wet bars. *181 Church St., 29401, ☎ 803/577–2644 or 800/527–1133, FAX 803/577–2697. 17 rooms, 164 suites. Facilities: full breakfast, afternoon refreshments, fitness center, pool. AE, D, DC, MC, V.*

$$$ **Mills House Hotel.** This luxurious property in the historic district is a reconstruction of a 19th-century hotel that once stood on the site. Antique furnishings and period decor lend charm to rooms and public areas. The Barbadoes Room serves some of the city's best seafood. *115 Meeting St., 29401, ☎ 803/577–2400 or 800/874–9600, FAX 803/722–2112. 214 rooms. Facilities: restaurant, 2 lounges, pool. AE, D, DC, MC, V.*

$$$ ★ **Omni Hotel at Charleston Place.** Rooms are furnished with period reproductions at this graceful low-rise in the historic district near upscale boutiques and specialty shops. Louis's Charleston Grill, with its mahogany-paneled walls and wrought-iron chandeliers, is an elegant backdrop for such dishes as pan-seared scallops with corn sauce and buttermilk tart with raspberries. *130 Market St., 29401, ☎ 803/722–4900 or 800/843–6664, FAX 803/722–6952. 394 rooms, 46 suites. Facilities: 2 restaurants, 2 lounges, fitness center, indoor pool, sauna, concierge floor. AE, D, DC, MC, V.*

$$–$$$ **Comfort Inn Riverview.** A little more than a mile from the historic district is this seven-story inn, whose yellow-brick exterior is in keeping with the historic character of the area. Inside, furnishings are contemporary, with a teal-and-mauve color scheme. *144 Bee St., 29401, ☎ 803/577–2224 or 800/221–2222, FAX 803/577–9001. 128 rooms. Facilities: Continental breakfast, pool. AE, D, DC, MC, V.*

$ **Hampton Inn–Historic District.** Opened in 1992, this downtown property features hardwood floors in the lobby, extra-large guest rooms furnished in period reproductions, a courtyard garden, and a pool. *345 Meeting St., 29403, ☎ 803/723–4000 or 800/426–7866, FAX 803/722–3725. 171 rooms. Facilities: Continental breakfast, pool. AE, D, DC, MC, V.*

Motels

Days Inn–Historic District (155 Meeting St., 29401, ☎ 803/722–8411 or 800/325–2525, FAX 803/723–5361), 124 rooms, restaurant, pool; *$$*. **Heart of Charleston Quality Inn** (125 Calhoun St., 29401, ☎ 803/722–3391 or 800/845–2504, FAX 803/577–0361), 126 rooms, restaurant, lounge, pool; *$$*.

The Arts and Nightlife

The Arts

Spoleto Festival USA (Box 157, 29402, ☎ 803/722–2764), a world-class annual celebration founded by maestro Gian Carlo Menotti in 1977, showcases opera, dance, theater, symphonic and chamber music performances, jazz, and the visual arts from late May through early June. The **Southeastern Wildlife Exposition** (☎ 800/221–5273), held each February, features art by renowned wildlife artists.

Nightlife

Top Charleston-area music clubs include **Windjammer** (☎ 803/886–8596), on the Isle of Palms, an oceanfront spot featuring live rock music. In the market area, try the **Jukebox** (☎ 803/723–3431) or **Louis's Jazz Lounge Grill** (☎ 803/722–4900), in the Omni Charleston. Another option is dining and dancing on the luxury yacht ***Spirit of Charleston*** (☎ 803/722–2628).

THE COAST

The South Carolina coast is a land of extremes. The Grand Strand, from the state's northeast border to historic Georgetown, is one of the East Coast's family-vacation megacenters and the state's top tourist area. It offers 60 mi of beaches, championship golf courses, campgrounds, seafood restaurants, giant shopping malls, factory outlets, and, at last count, nearly a dozen live entertainment theaters catering to families with everything from live country-western music and variety and magic acts to ice shows. The Low Country comprises the area between Georgetown and the state's southeast boundary, including Beaufort, as well as the barrier islands of Hilton Head, Edisto, and Fripp. Beaufort is a gracious antebellum town with a compact historic district of lavish 18th- and 19th-century homes. Hilton Head's exclusive resorts and genteel good life make it one of the coast's most popular vacation getaways.

Tourist Information

Beaufort: Chamber of Commerce (Box 910, 1006 Bay St., 29901-0910, ☎ 803/524–3163). **Georgetown:** Chamber of Commerce and Information Center (Front and Broad Sts., Box 1776, 29442, ☎ 803/546–8436 or 800/777–7705). **Hilton Head Island:** Chamber of Commerce (Box 5647, 29938, ☎ 803/785–3673). **Myrtle Beach:** Area Chamber of Commerce and Information Center (1301 N. Kings Hwy., Box 2115, 29578-2115, ☎ 803/626–7444; for brochures only, 800/356–3016 ext. 136).

Getting There

By Plane

The **Myrtle Beach Jetport** (☎ 800/282–3424) is served by USAir, American Eagle, and Delta's Atlantic Southeast Airlines. **Hilton Head Island Airport** is served by USAir Express. **Savannah International Airport** (*see* Georgia) is about an hour's drive from Hilton Head.

By Car

Major interstates connect with U.S. 17, the principal north–south coastal route.

By Train

Amtrak (☎ 800/872–7245) does not make stops in this area, although several of its stops are within driving distance: Florence is about 70 mi northwest of the Grand Strand; Yemassee, about 22 mi northwest of Beaufort; and Savannah, about 40 mi southwest of Hilton Head.

By Bus

Greyhound Lines (☎ 800/231–2222) serves Myrtle Beach, Beaufort, and Savannah.

By Boat

The South Carolina coast is accessible by boat via the Intracoastal Waterway. At Myrtle Beach, you may dock at **Hague Marina** (☎ 803/293–2141). Hilton Head has several marinas, including **Shelter Cove Marina** (☎ 803/842–7002), **Harbour Town Marina** (☎ 803/671–2704), and **Schilling Boathouse** (☎ 803/681–2628).

Exploring the Coast

With its high-rise beachfront hotels, nightlife, and amusement parks, **Myrtle Beach** is the hub of the Grand Strand. Downtown has a festive look, with its T-shirt shops, ice-cream and fudge parlors, and amusement parks, including the **Myrtle Beach Pavilion and Amusement Park** (9th Ave. N and Ocean Blvd., ☎ 803/448–6456), **Ripleys Believe It or Not Museum** (901 N. Ocean Blvd., ☎ 803/448–2331), and the **Myrtle Beach National Wax Museum** (1000 N. Ocean Blvd., ☎ 803/448–9921). Attractions are open daily from mid-March through early October, but the schedule varies the rest of the year; all charge admission.

From Myrtle Beach, U.S. 17 leads to **Murrells Inlet,** a picturesque fishing village where you'll find fishing charters as well as some of the most popular seafood restaurants on the Strand. **Brookgreen Gardens** (☎ 803/237–4218 or 800/849–1931; admission charged), a few miles farther south, are set on four former Colonial rice plantations. Begun in 1931, the gardens include more than 2,000 plant species, as well as more than 500 sculptures, including works by Anna Hyatt Huntington, Frederic Remington, and Daniel Chester French. Several miles farther on U.S. 17 is **Pawleys Island.** Four miles long and ½ mi wide, it's characterized by weathered old summer cottages nestled in the groves of oleander and oak. The famed Pawleys Island hammocks have been made by hand here since 1880.

On the shores of Winyah Bay at the end of the Grand Strand is **Georgetown.** Founded in 1729, it soon became the center of America's Colonial rice empire. Today tourists enjoy its quaint waterfront and historic homes and churches. The **Rice Museum** (Front and Screven Sts., ☎ 803/546–7423; admission charged) traces the history of rice cultivation through maps, tools, and dioramas. It is housed in the former market-meeting building, a graceful structure topped by an 1842 clock and tower.

About 18 mi east of U.S. 17 on U.S. 21 (about 70 mi southeast of Charleston) is the waterfront town of **Beaufort.** Established in 1710, it achieved prosperity at the end of the 18th century, when Sea Island cotton became a major cash crop. A few lavish houses built by wealthy landowners and merchants have been converted into bed-and-breakfast inns or house museums; others are open for tours part of the year. The **Beaufort Museum** (713 Craven St., ☎ 803/525–7077; closed Sun.), housed in a Gothic-style arsenal built in 1795 and remodeled in 1852, offers exhibits on prehistoric relics, Native American pottery, the Revolutionary and Civil wars, and decorative arts.

Hilton Head Island, a 42-sq-mi semitropical barrier island, was settled by cotton planters in the 1700s and developed as a resort destination in the 1960s and '70s. Oak and pine woods, lagoons, and a temperate climate provide an incomparable environment for tennis, water sports, and world-class golf. Choice stretches of the island are occupied by resorts, many of which have shops, restaurants, marinas, and recreational facilities that are open to the public.

Hilton Head is also blessed with vast nature preserves, including the **Sea Pines Forest Preserve,** a 605-acre wilderness tract within the resort of the same name (☎ 803/842–1449; admission charged for nonguests). The preserve's most interesting site is the 3,400-year-old Native American shell ring. Also inside the bounds of Sea Pines are the **Stoney–Baynard Ruins,** the site of a plantation dating from 1793 that is now being excavated.

What to See and Do with Children

Called the "Miniature Golf Capital of the World," Myrtle Beach has courses on such themes as dinosaurs, tropical islands, ghosts, and pirates, as well as **Hawaiian Rumble** (3210 Rte. 17S, ☎ 803/272–7812), with a volcano that really shakes. **Myrtle Waves Water Park** (U.S. 17 Bypass and 10th Ave. N, Myrtle Beach, ☎ 803/448–1026) is one of many area water parks.

Shopping

The Grand Strand is a great place to find bargains. **Waccamaw Pottery and Outlet Park** (U.S. 501 at the Waterway, Myrtle Beach, ☎ 803/236–0797 for information) is one of the nation's largest outlet centers. In North Myrtle Beach, shoppers head for the **Barefoot Landing** shopping center (U.S. 17, ☎ 803/272–8349). The **Hammock Shops at Pawleys Island** (U.S. 17, ☎ 803/237–8448) sell the famous handmade hammocks; there are about a dozen boutiques and restaurants, too. Hilton Head specialty shops include **Harbour Town Antiques** (☎ 803/671–5999), **Red Piano Art Gallery** (☎ 803/785–2318), and, for shell and sand-dollar jewelry, the **Bird's Nest** (☎ 803/785–3737).

Sports and the Outdoors

Biking

Pedaling is popular along the firmly packed beaches and pathways of Hilton Head Island. Rentals are available at most hotels and resorts, and at such shops as **Harbour Town Bicycles** (☎ 803/785–3546) and **South Beach Cycles** (☎ 803/671–2215).

Fishing

Because offshore waters along the South Carolina coast are warmed by the Gulf Stream, fishing is usually good from early spring through December. The Grand Strand has several piers and jetties, and fishing and sightseeing excursions depart from Murrells Inlet, North Myrtle Beach, Little River, and the Intracoastal Waterway at Rte. 544. Fishing tournaments are very popular. On Hilton Head, you can fish, pick oysters, dig for clams, or cast for shrimp. Licenses (required for fresh- and saltwater fishing from a private boat) can be purchased at local tackle shops.

Golf

The Grand Strand has nearly 80 public courses, many of championship quality. **Myrtle Beach Golf Holiday** (☎ 803/448–5942 or 800/845–4653) offers package plans throughout the year; most area hotels have golf packages, too. Some of Hilton Head's 22 courses are among the world's best; several are open to the public, including **Palmetto Dunes** (☎ 803/785–7300), **Sea Pines** (☎ 803/785–3333), and

Port Royal and Shipyard Golf and Racquet Clubs (☎ 803/689–5600). Sea Pines' **Harbour Town Golf Links** (☎ 803/842–1892) hosts the annual MCI Classic.

Horseback Riding

On Hilton Head, trails wind through woods and nature preserves; horses can be rented at Sea Pines' **Lawton Stables** (☎ 803/671–2586).

Tennis

There are more than 150 courts throughout the Strand, including free municipal courts in Myrtle Beach, North Myrtle Beach, and Surfside Beach. Hilton Head offers more than 300 courts; four resorts on the island—**Sea Pines, Shipyard Plantation, Palmetto Dunes,** and **Port Royal**—are rated among the top 50 tennis destinations in the United States. Each April, top women professionals participate in the Family Circle Magazine Cup Tennis Tournament at Sea Pines Racquet Club.

Water Sports

In Myrtle Beach, surfboards, Hobie Cats, Jet Skis, Windsurfers, and sailboats are for rent at **Downwind Sails** (Ocean Blvd. at 29th Ave. S, ☎ 803/448–7245). On Hilton Head you can take windsurfing lessons and rent equipment from **Windsurfing Hilton Head,** located at Sea Pines Resort's South Beach Marina (☎ 803/671–3577) or Shelter Cove Plaza (☎ 803/842–7001).

Beaches

Almost all Grand Strand beaches are open to the public. The widest expanses are in North Myrtle Beach. The ocean side of Hilton Head Island features wide stretches of gently sloping white sand, extending the island's 12-mi length. Although resort beaches on Hilton Head are reserved for guests and residents, there are about 35 public beach entrances from Folly Field to South Forest Beach near Sea Pines.

Dining and Lodging

Freshwater and ocean fish and shellfish reign supreme throughout the region, from family-style restaurants—where they're served with hush puppies and coleslaw—to elegant resorts and upscale restaurants featuring haute cuisine. You can have your choice of hotels, cottages, villas, and high-rise condominiums. Attractive package plans are available between Labor Day and spring break. For price ranges, see Charts 1 (B) and 2 (A) in On the Road with Fodor's.

Beaufort

DINING AND LODGING

Rhett House Inn. This stately 1820 Greek Revival mansion in the center of town is popular among visiting celebrities: Past guests have included Barbra Streisand, Jeff Bridges, and Robert Zemeckis. Completely refurbished by the owners, it is filled with antiques and original art. Continental breakfast and Low Country high tea in the afternoon are included in the tariff; the prix fixe dinner (by reservation only) is extra. *1009 Craven St., 29902,* ☎ *803/524–9030,* FAX *803/524–1310. 9 rooms, 1 suite. MC, V. $$$*

LODGING

Two Suns Inn. Overlooking the water, this 1917 Neoclassic–Revival B&B is run by the gregarious Kay family. Each room has its own theme—from Victorian to Asian—and your hosts offer everything from gourmet breakfasts to sightseeing advice to a full range of business facilities. *1705*

Bay St., 29202, ☎ and FAX 803/522–1122 or ☎ 800/532–4244. 5 rooms with bath. AE, MC, V. $$

Georgetown

LODGING

1790 House. Built in the center of town after the Revolution, at the peak of Georgetown's rice culture, this restored white Georgian house with a wraparound porch contains Colonial antique and reproduction furnishings. Guests are treated to hearty breakfasts, evening refreshments, and the use of bicycles. *630 Highmarket St., 29440, ☎ 803/546–4821. 6 rooms. AE, MC, V. $$–$$$*

Hilton Head Island

DINING

Harbourmaster's. With sweeping views of the harbor, this spacious, multilevel restaurant offers such dishes as chateaubriand and New Zealand rack of lamb with brandy demiglaze. After dining, guests can linger in Neptune's Lounge. *Shelter Cove Marina off U.S. 278, ☎ 803/785–3030. Reservations required. Jacket required at dinner. AE, DC, MC, V. Closed Sun., Jan. $$$*

Crazy Crab. This casual restaurant serves the freshest seafood on the island, prepared any way you like it. The steamed seafood pot and Crazy Crab boil are locally famous. *Harbour Town Yacht Basin, ☎ 803/363–2722. No reservations. AE, D, MC, V. No lunch. $*

LODGING

★ **Westin Resort, Hilton Head Island.** Among the island's most luxurious properties, this sprawling, horseshoe-shaped hotel enjoys a lushly landscaped oceanside setting. The expansive guest rooms have a pleasing mix of reproduction and contemporary furnishings. The Barony restaurant offers Low Country and Continental cuisine in an upscale French atmosphere. *Port Royal Plantation, 135 S. Port Royal Dr., 29928, ☎ 803/681–4000 or 800/228–3000, FAX 803/681–1087. 377 rooms, 38 suites. Facilities: 3 restaurants, 2 lounges, health club, pool, beach, water sports. AE, D, DC, MC, V. $$$$*

Palmetto Dunes Resort. This huge complex includes the Hyatt Regency Hilton Head, the island's largest resort hotel. Rooms are spacious and elegantly appointed, with light-color carpets, a king- or queen-size bed, and works by local artists. Each has a balcony, a coffeemaker, and an iron and ironing board. The complex also includes the Hilton Resort, formerly the Mariner's Inn. These spacious oceanfront rooms have kitchenettes and are colorfully decorated. *Hyatt: Box 6167, 29938, ☎ 803/785–1234, FAX 803/842–4695. 505 rooms. Hilton: 23 Ocean La., 29938, ☎ 803/842–8000, FAX 803/842–4988. 296 rooms, 28 suites. Facilities: restaurants, lounges, health clubs, pools, golf courses, tennis courts. AE, D, DC, MC, V. $$$*

Myrtle Beach

DINING

Rice Planter's Restaurant. Dine on fresh seafood, quail, or steak grilled to order in a homey, candlelight setting enhanced by Low Country antiques, plantation tools, and other artifacts. Shrimp Creole is the specialty of the house; the crab-finger appetizers are also delicious. *6707 N. Kings Hwy., ☎ 803/449–3456. AE, D, MC, V. $$*

★ **Sea Captain's House.** This picturesque restaurant with nautical decor and a fireplace has sweeping ocean views. Home-baked breads and desserts accompany Low Country fare. *3002 N. Ocean Blvd., ☎ 803/448–8082. AE, MC, V. Closed mid-Dec.–mid-Feb. $$*

LODGING

Kingston Plantation At Radisson Resort. Set amid 145 acres of oceanside woodlands, this 20-story glass-sheathed tower is part of the Kingston Plantation complex of shops, restaurants, hotels, and condominiums; it's easily the nicest resort in town. Guest rooms have bleached-wood furnishings and attractive art; some have kitchenettes. *9800 Lake Dr., 29572,* ☎ *803/449–0006 or 800/876–0010,* FAX *803/497–1110. 513 suites. Facilities: 2 restaurants, lounge, tennis, privileges at sports/fitness complex. AE, D, DC, MC, V. $$$$*

The Breakers Resort Hotel. Having undergone major renovations in 1993, the Breakers is one of the better values along the Grand Strand. There are 24 different types of room configurations—the suites with kitchenettes are ideal for families. All the major attractions are within walking distance. *2006 N. Ocean Blvd., Box 485, 29578,* ☎ *803/444–4444 or 800/845–0688,* FAX *803/626–5001. 247 rooms. Facilities: restaurant, 3 pools, 2 whirlpools, saunas, exercise room, lounge. AE, D, DC, MC, V. $$–$$$*

North Myrtle Beach

DINING

Oak Harbor Inn. Located on a quiet stretch of the beach and overlooking Vereen's Marina, this airy restaurant has become a local favorite since it opened in 1990. A house specialty is chicken Annie: boneless breast of chicken topped with ham and Swiss and blue cheeses in puff pastry, garnished with Parmesan and Mornay sauce. *U.S. 17N at 1300 Block, Vereen's Marina,* ☎ *803/249–4737. AE, DC, MC, V. $$–$$$*

Pawleys Island

DINING

Tyler's Cove. This restaurant specializes in such unusual Low Country fare as fried Carolina alligator in buttermilk batter, tossed with lettuce, cabbage, and jalapeño-honey dressing. *Hammock Shops, U.S. 17,* ☎ *803/237–4848. AE, MC, V. No dinner Sun. $$*

LODGING

Litchfield by the Sea Resort and Country Club. Contemporary gray-blue wood units are built on stilts within the 4,500-acre grounds, which include three golf clubs. The beach is a short walk away. *U.S. 17, 2 mi north of Pawleys Island, 29585,* ☎ *803/237–3000 or 800/845–1897,* FAX *803/237–4282. 97 suites. Facilities: restaurant, lounge, 2 pools, spa, racquetball court, tennis courts, golf. AE, MC, V. $$–$$$*

The Arts and Nightlife

The Arts

Area festivals include the **Canadian/American Days Festival** in March, the **Sun Fun Festival** in early July, and the **Atalaya Arts Festival** in fall. At **Art in the Park,** held in Myrtle Beach's Chapin Park three times each summer, you can buy handmade crafts and original artwork by local artists. Hilton Head's **Community Playhouse** (Arrow Rd., ☎ 803/785–4878) presents up to 10 musicals or dramas each year and offers a theater program for youth. During the warmer months, there are free outdoor concerts at **Harbour Town** and **Shelter Cove.**

Nightlife

Country-western shows are popular along the Grand Strand, which is fast emerging as the eastern focus of country-music culture. Music lovers have six shows to choose from: the 2,250-seat **Alabama Theater** (4750 U.S. 17, N. Myrtle Beach, ☎ 803/272–1111), opened in summer 1993; **Carolina Opry** (82nd Ave. N, Myrtle Beach, ☎ 803/238–8888 or 800/843–6779); **Dixie Jubilee** (701 Main St., N. Myrtle Beach, ☎ 803/249–4444 or 800/843–6779); Dolly Parton's **Dixie Stampede** (8901B U.S. 17 Bus., Myrtle Beach, ☎ 803/497–9700); **Myrtle Beach Opry** (1901 N. Kings Hwy., Myrtle Beach, ☎ 803/448–6779); and **Southern Country Nights** (301 U.S. 17 Bus., Surfside Beach, ☎ 803/238–8888 or 800/843–6779). Shagging (the state dance) is popular at **Studebaker's** (U.S. 17 at 21st Ave. N, Myrtle Beach, ☎ 803/626–3855 or 803/448–9747) and **Duck's** (229 Main St., N. Myrtle Beach, ☎ 803/249–3858). Hilton Head's hotels and resorts feature a variety of musical entertainment.

ELSEWHERE IN THE STATE

Columbia

Getting There

I–20 leads northeast from Georgia to Columbia. I–77 runs south to Columbia, where it terminates. I–26 runs north–south through town.

What to See and Do

Columbia, in the middle of the state, was founded in 1786 as the capital city. The Italian Renaissance–style **state capitol,** completed in 1855, contains marble and mahogany accents and a replica of Houdon's statue of George Washington. *Main and Gervais Sts., ☎ 803/734–2430. Guided tours every ½ hour. Closed weekends.*

The **South Carolina State Museum** (301 Gervais St., ☎ 803/737–4595; admission charged), set in a refurbished textile mill, interprets state history through exhibits on archaeology, fine arts, and scientific and technological accomplishments.

At **Riverbanks Zoological Park,** 2 mi from the capitol area via I–26, more than 450 species of birds and animals (some endangered) are cared for in their natural habitats. The park also offers a cage-free aviary, a reptile house, an aquarium, and facilities for breeding rare and fragile species. A new botanical garden is under construction at the zoo. *Junction of I–126 and Greystone Blvd., ☎ 803/779–8717. Admission charged. Closed Christmas.*

The **Greater Columbia Metropolitan Convention and Visitors Bureau** (1200 Main St., 9th Floor, 29202, ☎ 803/254–0479 or 800/264–4884) has brochures, maps, and advice for travelers; it also presents a short film on area history.

6 The Mississippi Valley

By Craig Seligman

STAND ON A SHORE of the Mississippi River and you're swept with large emotions: Here are the waters that have sweetened the delta and fed the imagination of the South. The five states that constitute the Mississippi Valley all sweat history; each has Civil War battlefields and citizens with long, long memories. You can find the New South here, of course, but the Old South—of Cotton Is King, of Christ Is Coming, of aristocracy and its flip side, poverty—is never far away.

The soil is rich: No sight in the world affects a southerner like the fields of cotton ready for harvest. The region isn't only farmland, though; Tennessee, Kentucky, and Arkansas are blessed with some of the most beautiful mountain scenery in America. The metropolises, from Louisville to Shreveport to Jackson, have their big-city grandeur and decay. Outside them you'll see the regal old plantation houses, but you'll also pass along godforsaken stretches of state road with tumbledown shanties that can look more desolate than any city slum.

Yet the folk culture that sprouted among the poor people of these states took root and spread its branches far out into the world. Nashville calls itself the capital of country music; Memphis will always mean blues; New Orleans is the cradle of jazz. And all three cities—all three musics—had a hand in delivering rock and roll. Graceland, the Memphis mansion where Elvis lived and died in tacky majesty, stands now as an unofficial monument to the best American art and the worst American taste.

The region gave us soul music, too—and soul food. A visitor can find ambrosial ribs in the barbecue palaces of Memphis or at hole-in-the-wall luncheonettes on Arkansas roadsides. Those lucky enough to have tasted fried chicken or fried catfish down here have been known to lose their taste for chicken and catfish anywhere else. Forget low-fat. Forget nouvelle. The scent of collard greens stewing in pork fat, of sweet potatoes glistening with sugar and butter, emanates from some deep place as central to the culture as the one that produced the Mississippi blues of Muddy Waters and the long, hypnotic periods of Faulkner.

Farther downriver, the spirit changes. The sauces become more complex; the music turns airier, and so does the mood. The fundamentalism of the Bible Belt loosens into a good-time Catholicism whose motto is *Laissez les bons temps rouler*—let the good times roll. Cajun festivals, for everything from gumbo to petroleum, are just about constant—any excuse for a party. The biggest excuse, of course, is Mardi Gras, the day before Lent begins, which is celebrated throughout southern Louisiana. By the time the Mississippi gets this close to the Gulf, its width is monumental, but the water is warm, unhurried. And so is New Orleans. It's as though the river chose this city as the place to deposit all the richness it has picked up on its long journey. You come here to slow down, relax, enjoy the good life, and dedicate your days to pleasure.

Tour Groups

If you're ready for a visit to Cajun country, the Ozarks, a cruise along the Mississippi, or an excursion through country-western capitals, the tours below offer just what you want.

Domenico Tours (751 Broadway, Bayonne, NJ 07002, ☎ 201/823–8687 or 800/554–8687) offers two 6-day tours of Tennessee, one of the

Smoky Mountains and the other of Opryland and Gatlinburg. **Gadabout Tours** (700 E. Tahquitz Canyon Way, Palm Springs, CA 92262, ☎ 619/325–5556 or 800/952–5068) travels Tennessee and Kentucky in depth for 12 days, as well as the Ozarks in 16 days. **Globus** (5301 S. Federal Circle, Littleton, CO 80123, ☎ 303/797–2800 or 800/221–0090) offers 8 days of "Country-Western U.S.A.," including the Smokies, Memphis, Nashville, and Opryland, as well as various tours of the New Orleans region. **Cosmos Tourama** (same address as Globus) offers budget country-western tours. **Maupintour** (Box 807, Lawrence, KS 66044, ☎ 913/843–1211 or 800/255–4266) covers the Ozarks, the Smokies, and Nashville, as well as New Orleans and Louisiana's plantation country. **Talmage Tours** (1223 Walnut St., Philadelphia, PA 19107, ☎ 215/923–7100) has a 7-day "Grand Ole Opry" tour of Tennessee and a 5-day tour of New Orleans. **Tauck Tours** (Box 5027, Westport, CT 06881, ☎ 203/226–6911 or 800/468–2825) views the Ozarks in 8 days, including Memphis; Hot Springs, Arkansas; Lake of the Ozarks and St. Louis, Missouri; and cruises on the Mississippi; it also offers a 9-day tour of New Orleans and Cajun Country.

When to Go

The best times to visit the Mississippi Valley states are April and October, when temperatures and humidity are comfortable: in Louisiana and Mississippi, the mid-70s; in the mountains of Arkansas, Kentucky, and Tennessee, the 60s, cooling off to the mid-40s at night. In **spring** everything is in glorious bloom, while in the **fall** the trees, especially in the mountains, are bright with turning leaves. You can tour magnificent historic mansions in spring and fall.

If you dislike crowds, avoid New Orleans during Mardi Gras (February or March, depending on the date of Easter) and Louisville during the Kentucky Derby (the first Saturday in May). Visits during these times require flight and hotel reservations long in advance; also, expect hotel prices to jump.

Festivals and Seasonal Events

Jan.–Feb.: The **Dixie National Rodeo/Western Festival/Livestock Show** in **Jackson, Mississippi,** offers rodeos and other events. ☎ *601/960–1891 or 800/354–7695.*

Feb. 18–28: Mardi Gras in **New Orleans, Louisiana,** is two weeks of madness—street festivals, parades with fantastic floats, marching bands, and eye-popping costumes. ☎ *504/566–5031.*

Mar.–Apr.: In **Mississippi, spring pilgrimages** to elegant antebellum mansions are held throughout the state, with **Natchez** (☎ 800/647–6724) claiming grande-dame status, followed by **Columbus** (☎ 800/327–2686) and **Vicksburg** (☎ 800/221–3536).

Apr.–May: The **Memphis in May International Festival** celebrates music on Beale Street, along with other events. ☎ *901/525–4611.*

Late Apr.: The **Annual Arkansas Folk Festival** in **Mountain View** salutes the folk culture of the Ozarks with music, dance, crafts, a parade, and a rodeo. ☎ *501/269–3851.*

Late Apr.–early May: The **New Orleans Jazz & Heritage Festival** draws thousands of musicians, fans, and artisans for a 10-day all-out jam session. ☎ *504/522–4786.*

May 4: In **Louisville,** the **Kentucky Derby,** one of horse racing's premier events, is preceded by a 10-day festival with parades, riverboat races, and many a mint julep. ☎ *502/584–6383.*

Mid-June: The **International Country Music Fan Fair** in **Nashville, Tennessee,** lets country music fans mix with their favorite stars in a weeklong celebration featuring live shows, exhibits, autograph sessions, and special concerts. ☎ *615/889–7503.*

Late Aug.: Louisville's **Kentucky State Fair** draws some half-million people with rooster-crowing contests, top-name concerts, a horse show, and an amusement park. ☎ *502/367–5000.*

Getting Around the Mississippi Valley

By Plane

New Orleans International Airport (☎ 504/464–0831), **Cincinnati/Northern Kentucky International Airport** (☎ 606/283–3151), **Nashville International Airport** (☎ 615/275–1600), and **Standiford Field** (Louisville, ☎ 502/367–4636) are served by most domestic carriers.

By Car

I–30 cuts diagonally across southern and central Arkansas. I–40 goes east–west through central Arkansas and central Tennessee. I–24 cuts diagonally across western Kentucky. I–64 runs east–west through Louisville. I–65 is a north–south route through Tennessee and central Kentucky. I–75 runs north–south through eastern Kentucky and Tennessee. I–55 runs from southern Louisiana north through Mississippi and Arkansas. I–10 runs east–west through southern Mississippi and New Orleans. I–20 is the major east–west road through northern Louisiana and Mississippi. There are bridges over the Mississippi River in New Orleans, Destrehan, Donaldsonville, and Baton Rouge, Louisiana, and in Vicksburg, in Natchez, and near Greenville, Mississippi. The river is bridged in Arkansas at Lake Village and Helena; in Tennessee at Memphis and east of Dyerburg; and in Kentucky at Hickman, Columbus, and Cairo.

By Train

Amtrak (☎ 800/872–7245) serves all states of the Mississippi Valley.

By Bus

Greyhound Lines (☎ 800/231–2222) provides service to cities and towns throughout the region.

By Boat

In Louisiana, ferries operate across the Mississippi River in New Orleans, Lutcher, Carville, and St. Francisville. In Tennessee, there are ferries across the Cumberland River near Nashville, Cumberland City, and at Dixon Springs; and across the Tennessee River at Dayton, Clifton, Saltillo, and near Decatur.

The **Delta Queen Steamboat Company** (Robin St. Wharf, New Orleans, LA 70130, ☎ 800/543–1949), the nation's only overnight riverboat, offers paddle-wheeler cruises on the Mississippi, Ohio, Tennessee, Arkansas, Atchafalaya, and Cumberland rivers as far east as Chattanooga; as far west as Tulsa, Oklahoma; and as far north as Minneapolis.

The Mississippi Valley

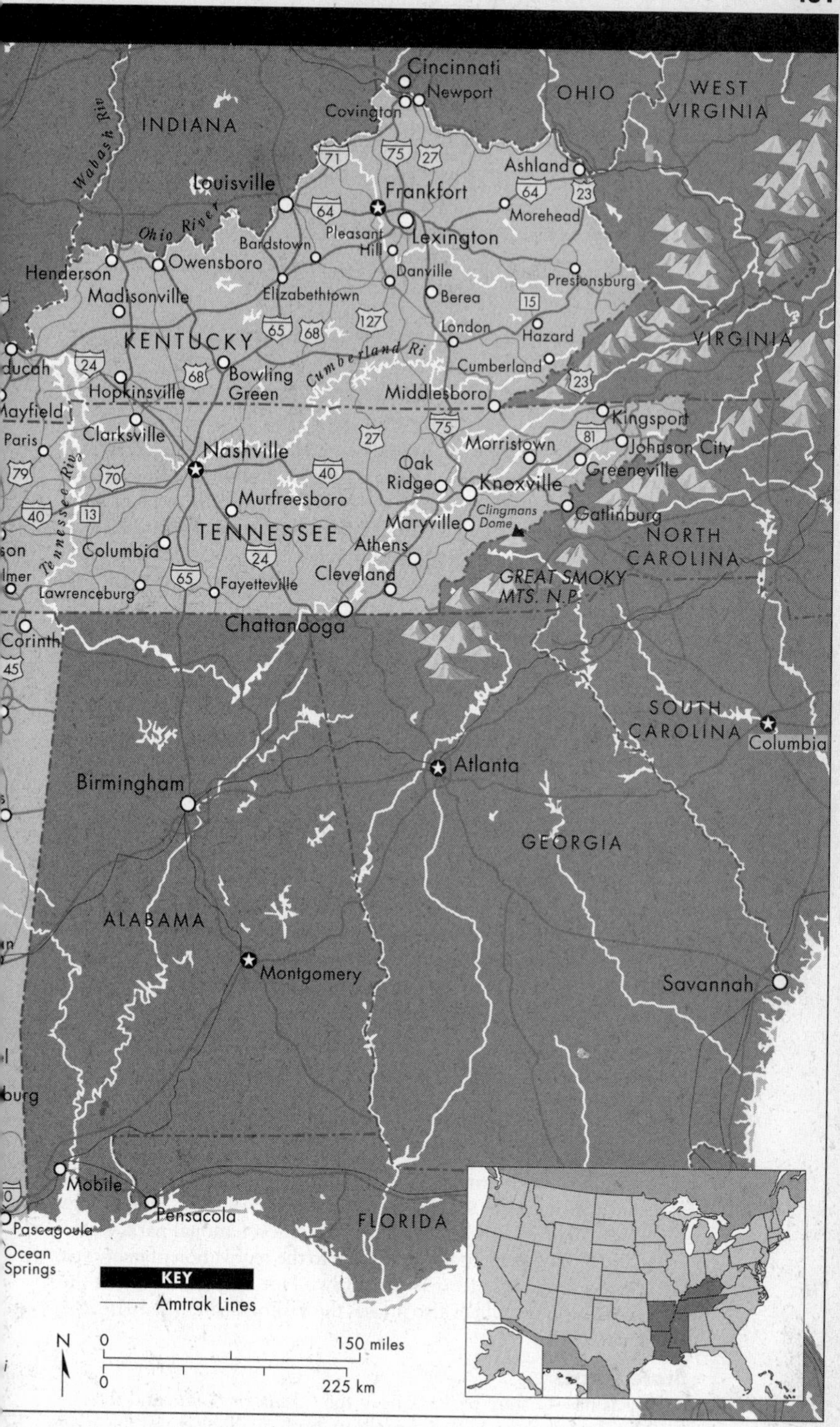

Cincinnati
Newport
Covington
OHIO
WEST VIRGINIA
INDIANA
Wabash Riv
Louisville
Frankfort
Ashland
Morehead
Lexington
Ohio River
Pleasant Hill
Bardstown
Owensboro
Henderson
Danville
Prestonsburg
Elizabethtown
Berea
Madisonville
London
Hazard
KENTUCKY
Cumberland Ri
VIRGINIA
Cumberland
Bowling Green
Hopkinsville
Middlesboro
Kingsport
Clarksville
Paris
Morristown
Johnson City
Nashville
Oak Ridge
Greeneville
Knoxville
Murfreesboro
Clingmans Dome
Gatlinburg
Maryville
Tennessee Riv
TENNESSEE
NORTH CAROLINA
Columbia
Athens
Cleveland
GREAT SMOKY MTS. N.P.
Lawrenceburg
Fayetteville
Chattanooga
Corinth
SOUTH CAROLINA
Columbia
Atlanta
Birmingham
GEORGIA
ALABAMA
Montgomery
Savannah
Mobile
Pensacola
Pascagoula
Ocean Springs
FLORIDA
KEY
Amtrak Lines
N
0
150 miles
0
225 km

ARKANSAS

By Delta Willis

Capital	Little Rock
Population	2.4 million
Motto	The People Rule
State Bird	Mockingbird
State Flower	Apple blossom

Visitor Information

Arkansas Department of Parks and Tourism (1 Capitol Mall, Little Rock 72201, ☎ 501/682–7777 or 800/628–8725).

Scenic Drives

Arkansas has 18 million acres of forests, and the Ozark Mountains rival New England for beautiful fall colors. The 70-mi stretch of Rte. 7 from **Harrison to Russellville** is one of the best foliage trails in the nation. **Rte. 7** to Hot Springs and Arkadelphia passes through the Ouachita National Forest. The **Talimena Scenic Drive** runs west on Rte. 88 for 55 mi from Mena, Arkansas, to Talihina, Oklahoma, and spans the Ouachita Mountains, the highest range between the Appalachians and the Rockies. The **Great River Road** (Rte. 1 from Helena to Lake Village) runs along the levees that border the Arkansas and Mississippi rivers. The elevated, graveled road is especially good for bird-watching, with egrets and herons year-round.

National and State Parks

National Parks

The **Buffalo National River** (Box 1173, Harrison 72602, ☎ 501/741–5443), in the northwestern part of the state, became the first national river in 1972. You can canoe, camp, hike, and fish along the 132-mi-long river's limestone bluffs year-round and go white-water rafting in early spring. Yellville and Marshall are gateway towns to the park. The 65,000-acre **Felsenthal National Wildlife Refuge** (Box 1157, Crossett 71635, ☎ 501/364–3167) is a mosaic of wetlands, with bayous, lakes, and two rivers, the Saline and the Ouachita.

The **Ouachita National Forest** (USFS Box 1270, Hot Springs 71902, ☎ 501/321–5202) extends from Pinnacle Mountain State Park, west of Little Rock, into Oklahoma, and includes 350 mi of walking trails. The **Ozark National Forest** (Box 1008, Russellville 72801, ☎ 501/968–2354) offers camping facilities, a view from the highest point in the state (Magazine Mountain, 2,753 ft), and caverns to explore near Blanchard Springs. **Hot Springs National Park** (Box 1860, Hot Springs 71902, ☎ 501/623–1433) is the nation's oldest national park, established in 1832. Federal funds have gone to the renovation of many spa facilities on Bathhouse Row in downtown Hot Springs, including the Fordyce Bathhouse, which also houses the Visitor Center (☎ 501/623–1433, ext. 640).

State Parks

Arkansas has 47 state parks. Check the *Camper's Guide* and the annual "Arkansas State Parks" brochure, both available from the state tourism office (*see* Visitor Information, *above*), for locations, lodge prices, camping fees, RV sites, and hookup fees. For information on fishing in Arkansas parks, contact the **Arkansas Game & Fish Commission** (☎ 501/223–6300).

Bull Shoals State Park (Rte. 178, Bull Shoals 72619, ☎ 501/431–5521) is in the Ozark Mountains below Bull Shoals Dam on the White River. **Crater of Diamonds State Park** (Rte. 1, Box 364, Murfreesboro 71958, ☎ 501/285–3113) is the only diamond deposit in the United States open to the public. **DeGray Lake Resort State Park** (Rte. 7, Bismark 71929-8194, ☎ 501/865–4501 or 501/865–2851) borders the northern shore of the 13,800-acre Lake DeGray. **Ozark Folk Center State Park** (Box 500, Mountain View 72560, ☎ 501/269–3851 or 800/264–3655), a unique park dedicated to preserving and perpetuating the Ozark Mountain way of life, offers traditional crafts demonstrations, music, and dancing, plus a gift shop, a lodge, and a restaurant in season. **Petit Jean State Park** (Morrilton 72110, ☎ 501/727–5441) is 3,471 acres on Petit Jean Mountain in the Ozarks, with waterfalls and hiking trails, a lodge, and cabins. **Toltec Mounds Archaeological State Park** (490 Toltec Mounds Rd., Scott 72142, ☎ 501/961–9442) is the site of the state's highest Native American burial mounds, which have yielded evidence of a sophisticated ceremonial and government settlement.

LITTLE ROCK

Like the state of Arkansas itself, Little Rock combines the sophisticated and the homespun. Though the skyline is dominated by shiny office towers and glittering hotels, residents continue to extend small-town hospitality.

With its sister city of North Little Rock, the capital is on the banks of the Arkansas River, which brought Northern European and Spanish explorers here in the 16th and 17th centuries. ("La Petite Roche," the small outcrop that served as a landmark for early river travelers, is now part of Riverfront Park, in the downtown area.) The capital moved here in 1821 from Arkansas Post, the first settlement in the lower Mississippi River Valley.

Little Rock is not only the governmental and financial center of the state but also its geographical center, with diverse terrain almost equally divided between forested highlands north and west of the city, and fertile agricultural lowlands to the south and east. The city is a major convention hub, with good restaurants and an exceptional arts center. Nevertheless, most visitors come to Arkansas to enjoy outdoor sports and the beautiful wild scenery, which begins within a few minutes' drive of the restored Victorian district downtown.

Tourist Information

Little Rock: Arkansas Department of Tourism (Box 3232, 72203, ☎ 501/376–4781 or 800/844–4781).

Arriving and Departing

By Plane

Most major airlines fly into **Adams Field** (☎ 501/372–3439), 5 mi east of downtown off I–440. There are daily scheduled flights between Little Rock and Fayetteville via **USAir Express** (☎ 800/428–4322). Some fishing lodges have private airstrips. Major Little Rock hotels provide airport shuttles. The cab fare from the airport to downtown is about $8. Call **Black & White Cabs** (☎ 501/374–0333) or **Capitol Cabs** (☎ 501/568–0462).

By Car

I–40 and I–30 lead to the city, as do U.S. 65 and U.S. 67. All major car-rental agencies have offices near the airport.

By Train

Amtrak (1400 W. Markham St., ☎ 800/872–7245).

Getting Around Little Rock

By Car

Little Rock traffic is civilized, there are plenty of parking facilities, and taxis are readily available.

By Bus

Central Arkansas Transit (☎ 501/375–1163) serves the Little Rock area.

Exploring Little Rock

Driving in the city is easy, but you can see a great deal by walking in the downtown area.

The **Quapaw Quarter** is a restored 19th-century neighborhood that includes homes, churches, and some of the city's oldest buildings. Free, self-guided walking tours are offered by the quarter's headquarters, an 1881 Italianate structure called the **Villa Marre.** Originally built by saloon keeper Angelo Marre, it now serves as a house-museum. The facade was featured in the TV series "Designing Women." *1321 Scott St., ☎ 501/374–9979. Admission charged. Closed Sat.*

On a hilltop west of the downtown area, the **state capitol** (Woodlawn and Capitol, ☎ 501/682–5080), built between 1899 and 1916 as a ¾-scale model of the U.S. Capitol, features a rotunda and massive staircases made of "Batesville marble," a local ivory-colored limestone.

The **Arkansas Territorial Restoration,** a group of 14 buildings from the early 1800s, includes a log cabin moved here from nearby Scott. Also here are an exhibit center and an excellent collection of Arkansas crafts for sale. *Scott and 3rd Sts., ☎ 501/324–9351. Admission charged.*

A fine example of Greek Revival architecture, the **Old State House** was built between 1833 and 1842 and served as the state capitol until 1911. It was also the site of President Bill Clinton's election-night celebration. It now contains a state museum, two restored legislative chambers and a governor's office from the 19th century, and a gift shop featuring Arkansas-related books. *300 W. Markham St., ☎ 501/324–9685. Donations accepted. Closed major holidays.*

The **Arkansas Museum of Science and History** has exhibits on geology and ornithology. The building, part of an arsenal built in 1838, was the birthplace of General Douglas MacArthur. *MacArthur Park, ☎ 501/324–9231. Admission charged.*

Adjacent to the museum, the **Arkansas Arts Center** houses six art galleries, a museum school, a children's theater, a gift shop, a restaurant, and various performing-arts organizations (*see* The Arts and Nightlife, *below*). The **Decorative Arts Museum,** set in an 1841 mansion near the arts center, features arts and crafts, including elaborate and colorful quilts. *7th and Rock Sts., ☎ 501/372–4000, ext. 358. Donation suggested.*

Parks and Gardens

Burns Park (☎ 501/758–2400), on 1,575 acres in North Little Rock, has hiking and jogging trails, a golf course, indoor and outdoor tennis and racquetball courts, and a crossbow range. The **Old Mill** (Lakeshore Dr. and Fairway, North Little Rock, ☎ 501/758–2400) is an authentic re-creation of a stone gristmill in a beautiful setting—it appeared in the opening scene of *Gone with the Wind.*

Pinnacle Mountain State Park (Hwy. 10, ☎ 501/868–5806), 15 mi west of Little Rock, comprises more than 1,800 acres, five trails, a picnic area, and the mountain for which it is named. Staff naturalists offer interpretive programs.

Riverfront Park edges both sides of the Arkansas River. Along the southern bank, at Little Rock's La Harpe Boulevard behind the State House Convention Center, is an amphitheater for bands, a history pavilion containing an open-air display of pictures and text on the early role of the city, and playgrounds, all with a view of passing river traffic. Docked on the north bank is the ***Spirit*** (☎ 501/376–4150), a paddle wheeler offering cruises from North Little Rock.

War Memorial Park (W. Markham St. and Fair Park Ave., ☎ 501/663–0854) features the Razorback football (☎ 501/663–0775) and Ray Wynder baseball (☎ 501/664–1555) stadiums, a public golf course, and an amusement park.

What to See and Do with Children

At the **Children's Museum** (1400 W. Markham St., ☎ 501/374–6655; admission charged), kids can play in a miniature version of a two-story Victorian house, shop at a farmers' market, and more.

The **Little Rock Zoo** (1 Jonesboro Dr., ☎ 501/663–4733; admission charged) is near the **amusement park** in War Memorial Park (*see* Parks and Gardens, *above*).

Shopping

Little Rock has major department stores at **Park Plaza Mall** (University Ave. and Markham St.) and **University Mall** (500 S. University Ave.). More interesting are shops selling traditional crafts, from quilts to wood carvings to jams and antiques, the best of which are at the **Arkansas Territorial Restoration** and the **state capitol** gift shop (*see* Exploring Little Rock, *above*).

Dining

Eating out in Little Rock is relatively inexpensive, and portions tend to be large. Outside the city, some counties are dry. For price ranges, see Chart 1 (B) in On the Road with Fodor's.

$$$ **Alouette's.** This first-class French restaurant serves such entrées as fresh duck in vinegar sauce with prunes. Dinner for two can be nearly $100. The wine list is excellent. *11401 Rodney Parham Rd., ☎ 501/225–4152. AE, DC, MC, V. Closed Sun.*

$$$ ★ **Ashley's.** In the Capital Hotel downtown is this romantic restaurant with fresh flowers and elegant china and silver. Lunch can be busy with local celebrities and executives. Especially recommended is the appetizer of goat cheese in pastry with spinach and red peppers. Fresh fish is a specialty. *111 W. Markham St., ☎ 501/374–7474. AE, DC, MC, V.*

$$ **André's.** At its two locations, one of Little Rock's best restaurants offers authentic French accents and service with a flourish. Soups and fish, including soft-shell crab and baked halibut, are excellent. *1121 Rodney Parham Rd., ☎ 501/224–7880 (closed Mon.); 605 N. Beechwood St., ☎ 501/666–9191. AE, DC, MC, V.*

$$ **Blue Mesa Grill.** This lively place with spicy dishes from the Southwest serves strong margaritas, grilled seafood, and wild game, including quail. Decorated with abstract prints and Sante Fe crafts, the restaurant also has a bar with a dance floor of black and white tiles. *1719 Merrill Dr., ☎ 501/221–7777. No reservations except for large groups. AE, D, DC, MC, V.*

$$ **Cajun's Wharf.** Set in an old warehouse near the Arkansas River, this seafood restaurant has a popular singles bar. Try the warm bread with honey butter, and shrimp or Cajun dishes. *2400 Cantrell Rd., ☎ 501/375–5351. AE, D, DC, MC, V. Closed Sun.*

$$ ★ **Juanita's.** This downtown hot spot is famous for its spinach enchiladas; the best live bands in town appear at the bar next door. *1300 S. Main St., ☎ 501/372–1228. No reservations. AE, DC, MC, V.*

$ **Franke's Cafeteria.** With two locations, family-owned Franke's has for decades been *the* practical place for eating lunch. Help yourself to simple, good food. *400 Broadway, ☎ 501/372–1919 and 300 S. University Ave., ☎ 501/663–4461. No reservations. No credit cards.*

Lodging

For price ranges, see Chart 2 (B) in On the Road with Fodor's.

$$$ **Capital Hotel.** Exquisitely decorated in antebellum style, the Capital has an atrium lobby topped by a stained-glass dome and a grand balcony where you expect to see Rhett Butler carrying Miss Scarlett off to one of the suites with four-poster beds. Ashley's, on the ground floor, is one of the city's best restaurants (*see* Dining, *above*). *111 W. Markham St., 72201, ☎ 501/374–7474 or 800/766–7666, FAX 501/370–7091. 123 rooms. Facilities: restaurant, lounge. AE, DC, MC, V.*

$$$ ★ **Carriage House Bed & Breakfast.** Within walking distance of the Governor's Mansion, this private Victorian home owned by a young couple has a renovated carriage house with two elegant bedrooms, two private baths, and a shared sitting room. Guests enjoy tea in the courtyard in summer and hot cider near the fireplace in winter. *1700 Louisiana St., 72201, ☎ 501/374–7032. 2 rooms. No credit cards.*

$$ **Guesthouse Inn.** This hotel on University Avenue near the Medical Center offers quiet suites with kitchenettes. A breakfast of coffee and doughnuts is included. *301 S. University Ave., 72205, ☎ 501/664–6800, FAX 501/663–7043. 71 rooms. Facilities: shuttle service to the airport and downtown. AE, D, DC, MC, V.*

$$ **Radisson Legacy Hotel.** Spacious and tastefully decorated rooms are offered by the Radisson chain. *625 W. Capitol Ave., 72201, ☎ and FAX 501/374–0100. 116 rooms with living areas, 9 suites, 3 penthouse suites. Facilities: restaurant, bar, pool. AE, DC, MC, V.*

Motels

Hampton Inn I-30 (6100 Mitchell Dr., 72209, ☎ 501/562–6667, FAX 501/568–6832), 122 rooms, pool; *$*. **Motel 6** (10524 W. Markham St., 72205, ☎ 501/225–7366), 150 rooms, restaurant, pool, meeting rooms; *$$*.

The Arts and Nightlife

The Arts

The free newspaper *Free Press* and the Friday issue of the *Arkansas Democrat–Gazette* list events. For a "What's Happening" report, call 501/372–3399.

Little Rock is also home to the **Arkansas Arts Center** (9th and Commerce Sts., ☎ 501/372–4000), the **Arkansas Repertory Theatre** (601

Main St., ☎ 501/378–0445), the **Arkansas Opera** (20919 Denning Rd., ☎ 501/821–7275), **Ballet Arkansas** (various locations, ☎ 501/664–9509), the **Arkansas Symphony Orchestra** (various locations, ☎ 501/376–4781), and **Wildwood Park for the Performing Arts** (20919 Denning Rd., ☎ 501/821–7275).

Broadway Theatre Series (1501 N. University Ave., ☎ 501/661–1500), the **Community Theatre of Little Rock** (13401 Chenal Pkwy., ☎ 501/663–9494), **Murrey's Dinner Theater** (6323 Asher Ave., ☎ 501/562–3131), **Robinson Center** (7 State House Plaza, ☎ 501/376–4781), and the **University of Arkansas Little Rock Fine Arts Galleries and Theater** (2801 S. University Ave., ☎ 501/569–3183) offer a variety of performing-arts productions.

Nightlife

There is good music and dancing in Little Rock, especially at restaurants like **Juanita's, Cajun's Wharf,** and the **Blue Mesa Grill** (*see* Dining, *above*).

NORTHWEST ARKANSAS

Whether your penchant is for forested mountains and deep blue lakes, breathtaking vistas, or comfortable camaraderie, northwest Arkansas has it. The region is booming, as it did in the 1800s when Eureka Springs's much-acclaimed curative waters began drawing travelers to the Ozarks. The Victorian village that developed around those vaunted springs is still a treasure trove of arts-and-crafts shops and other attractions; from mid-October to mid-November, you can watch crafts artisans at work during the annual crafts festival. Driving here is a treat in itself: The ride offers spectacular Ozark vistas, colorful fall foliage, historic Civil War battlefields at Pea Ridge and Prairie Grove, and beautiful lakes and rivers fringed with excellent fishing lodges.

Getting There

Though travel by car is the easiest way to get around, commercial flights to some destinations are available, and charter planes and buses can be booked from Little Rock. There is no passenger train service, except for short runs in the Ozarks.

By Plane

American Eagle, Northwest Airlines, and **USAir Express** offer regular service to Fayetteville.

By Car

To reach Fayetteville, Springdale, and Rogers from Little Rock, take I–40W to Rte. 71, currently being expanded to four lanes. From Rogers, Hwy. 62 will take you east to Eureka Springs.

By Bus

All Around Arkansas Tour (☎ 501/376–8033 or 800/648–8199) runs charters.

Eureka Springs

Tourist Information

Eureka Springs Chamber of Commerce (Box 551, 72632, ☎ 501/253–7333).

Exploring Eureka Springs

A Victorian village in the Ozark Mountains near the Missouri border, **Eureka Springs** has beautifully restored hotels and gingerbread-trimmed houses, which can be viewed by trolley car (for information, contact the Chamber of Commerce). **Thorncrown Chapel** (U.S. 62W, ☎ 501/253–7401), designed by architect Fay Jones, is a magnificent glass structure in the forest. The historic downtown area has several art and crafts galleries on Spring Street, and the **Hammond Museum of Bells** (2 Pine St., ☎ 501/253–7411). In May and October, the **War Eagle Craft Fair** features everything from sunbonnets to antiques (War Eagle Mill, ☎ 501/789–5343). From late June to mid-July, opera is performed at **Inspiration Point** (U.S. 62W, ☎ 501/253–8595). Lunch and dinner are served aboard the steam-powered **Eureka Springs & North Arkansas Railway** (☎ 501/253–9623), which makes short trips through the Ozarks daily.

Dining and Lodging

There are more than 40 restaurants in the area; the exceptional **Bean Palace Restaurant at War Eagle Mill** (Rte. 98, ☎ 501/789–5343) is worth the drive. **Dairy Hollow House** (515 Spring St., 72632, ☎ 501/253–7444 or 800/562–8650, FAX 501/253–7223) is a restaurant and a collection of separate, small farmhouses, each with a fireplace, sitting room, private bath, and minikitchen. There's also a hot tub in the woods.

There are more than 150 lodging facilities here, including several historic hotels. Convenient to shopping and slightly funky is the **Basin Park Hotel** (12 Spring St., 72632, ☎ 501/253–7837 or 800/643–4972, FAX 501/253–6985). The **Crescent Hotel** (75 Prospect St., 72632, ☎ 501/253–9766 or 800/342–9766, FAX 501/253–5296), on the mountaintop overlooking the city, is a National Historic Landmark. The **Bed and Breakfasts Association, Cabins and Cottages of Eureka Springs** (6 King's Hwy., 72632, ☎ 501/253–6767) has information on a wide range of lodgings.

Fayetteville

Tourist Information

Chamber of Commerce (Box 4216, 72702, ☎ 501/521–1710 or 800/766–4626).

Exploring Fayetteville

The **Arkansas Air Museum** (☎ 501/521–4947), housed in a historic wooden hangar at Drake Field, is a showcase of aviation history, airplane engines, and antique aircraft. **Headquarters House** (118 E. Dickson St., ☎ 501/521–2970), built in 1853 by Judge Jonas Tebbets, served as both Union and Confederate army headquarters at different times during the Civil War. President and Mrs. Clinton taught law at the **University of Arkansas,** where you can root for the Razorbacks, winners of the 1993 NCAA basketball championship. **Prairie Grove Battlefield Park** (☎ 501/846–2990), west of Fayetteville on Hwy. 62, preserves the site of a Civil War battle. **Walton Arts Center** (☎ 501/443–9216), the region's largest performing-arts facility, is home to two theaters and a music hall.

Springfest, held each April on colorful Dickson Street, ushers in the warm weather. June's **Music Festival of Arkansas** (☎ 501/521–4166) offers audiences the chance to hear internationally renowned artists and aspiring performers in classical, chamber, and light pops concerts. In October, **Autumnfest** celebrates fall-foliage season with the Harvest Ball, parades, and three days of special events.

Springdale

Tourist Information

Springdale: Chamber of Commerce (Box 166, 72765, ☎ 501/751–4694 or 800/972–7261).

Exploring Springdale

Shiloh Historic District and Museum (118 W. Johnson St., ☎ 501/750–8165) documents the history of local industry. **Tontitown,** just west on Highway 412, is a community settled in 1897 by Italian immigrants. **The Arts Center of the Ozarks** (☎ 501/751–5441) provides year-round theater, music, and dance performances. On weekends, the **Arkansas and Missouri Railroad** (☎ 501/751–5763) offers journeys back to Van Buren via restored turn-of-the-century railcars.

Rodeo of the Ozarks (☎ 501/751–4694 or 800/972–7261), held every July 1–4, is one of the largest outdoor rodeos in the nation. **Albert E. Brumley Sundown to Sunup Gospel Sing,** held the first week in August, draws music fans to hear southern gospel quartets.

Fishing Lodges

$$$ **Gaston's White River Resort.** This lodge attracts anglers from all over the nation; many fly their private planes onto the Gaston airstrip. Some cottages have fireplaces. *Rte. 1, Box 176NW, Lakeview 72642, ☎ 501/431–5202. 73 cottages. Facilities: restaurant, gift and tackle shop, fishing guides. MC, V.*

$ **Sportsman's Resort.** Guided fishing trips on the White River are available through this resort, which offers accommodations in air-conditioned cottages with cooking facilities. *Box 96, Flippin 72634, ☎ 501/453–2424 or 800/626–3474. 20 cottages. Facilities: pool, hot tub. D, MC, V.*

Numerous other facilities on the White River serve fishing enthusiasts. A sampling includes **Charlie's Riverfront Cabins** (☎ 501/253–9125) and **Riverview Resort** (☎ 501/253–8367). **Fletcher's Devil's Dive Resort** (☎ 417/271–3396) in Eagle Rock, Missouri, 10 mi north of Eureka, has fishing on White River and Table Rock Lake.

WESTERN ARKANSAS

The spectacular terrain of western Arkansas includes beautiful lakes and forested hills rich with the history of the frontier. Fort Smith, on the state's western border, celebrates that frontier heritage, preserving a hangin' judge's courtroom and gallows and such unusual sites as the only bordello on the National Register of Historic Places. The Ouachita (pronounced *Wauch*-it-taw) Mountains cradle Hot Springs, perhaps the best-known vacation destination in Arkansas. Nestled amid the five "diamond lakes," so named for their crystal-clear water and this diamond-bearing and quartz-rich region, the "Spa City" features naturally thermal waters, historic Bathhouse Row, and Oaklawn Park—a Thoroughbred horse-racing track. Hot Springs was the haunt of one former president (Harry Truman) and the boyhood home of our current one. Nearby Crater of Diamonds State Park is the only place in North America where you can dig for diamonds and keep any you find. Drive farther south to find Hope, President Clinton's birthplace, and Old Washington Historic State Park, site of Arkansas's Confederate capital. James Black, a local blacksmith, forged the famous Bowie knife here. The Ozark Highlands Trail, one of Arkansas's 242 hiking trails, begins just west of Little Rock and extends into Oklahoma; it's 168 mi long, with many short spurs.

Getting There

It is best to go by car. There is no passenger train service, although charter flights, buses, and limousines are available from Little Rock to Hot Springs.

BY PLANE

USAir Express runs charters.

BY CAR

To reach Hot Springs from Little Rock, take I–30 to U.S. 70 for 53 mi. Hot Springs can also be approached via scenic Rte. 7.

BY BUS

All Around Arkansas Tours (☎ 501/376–8033 or 800/648–8199) runs charters.

Hot Springs

Tourist Information

Hot Springs: Convention and Visitors Bureau (134 Convention Blvd., Hot Springs 71902, ☎ 501/321–2277 or 800/772–2489). The **Fordyce Bathhouse** (☎ 501/623–1433) houses a visitor center downtown.

Exploring Hot Springs

During the '20s this was a gambling town famous for its therapeutic bathhouses, which drew from the 47 thermal springs that explorer Hernando de Soto called Valley of the Vapors. Pure spring water has been bottled here for more than a century. Several spa hotels have been renovated; just north of Bathhouse Row is the **Arlington,** once the haunt of President Harry Truman.

Although there are facilities at the major hotels (*see* Lodging, *below*), you can enjoy a mineral bath and massage without even checking into any of them. The **Buckstaff Baths** (Bathhouse Row, ☎ 501/623–2308), a National Historic Landmark built in 1912, offers baths and massages for about $12 each (closed during lunch and on Sun.).

There is Thoroughbred horse racing at **Oaklawn Park** (☎ 501/623–4411 or 800/722–3652) from late January to late April. The downtown has many new art galleries (☎ 501/321–2277 or 800/772–2489 for gallery walks), and the city is surrounded by beautiful lakes. Local geologic formations have produced fantastic quartz crystals, sold at roadside stands and in shops.

The ***Belle of Hot Springs*** (Rte. 7S, ☎ 501/525–4438) is a 400-passenger riverboat that features lunch and dinner cruises.

At **Mountain Valley Spring Water** (13 mi north of the city, on Rte. 7N, ☎ 501/624–1635) visitors can sample the water and view the springs through a glass dome. Mountain Valley's headquarters (150 Central Ave., downtown Hot Springs, ☎ 501/623–6671) is a restored turn-of-the-century building with exhibits.

On U.S. 270W past Lake Ouachita is the town of **Mount Ida** (Chamber of Commerce, Box 6, 71957, ☎ 501/867–3541), with several crystal shops and the **Stanley Rock and Mineral Museum** (☎ 501/867–3556).

What to See and Do with Children

Mid-America Museum (off U.S. 270W at 400 Mid-America Blvd., ☎ 501/767–3461) is a hands-on museum of energy and science. **Alligator Farm** (847 Whittington Ave., ☎ 501/623–6172) has alligators large and small, plus a small zoo, including white-tail deer and mountain lions;

Hot Springs and the Ozarks

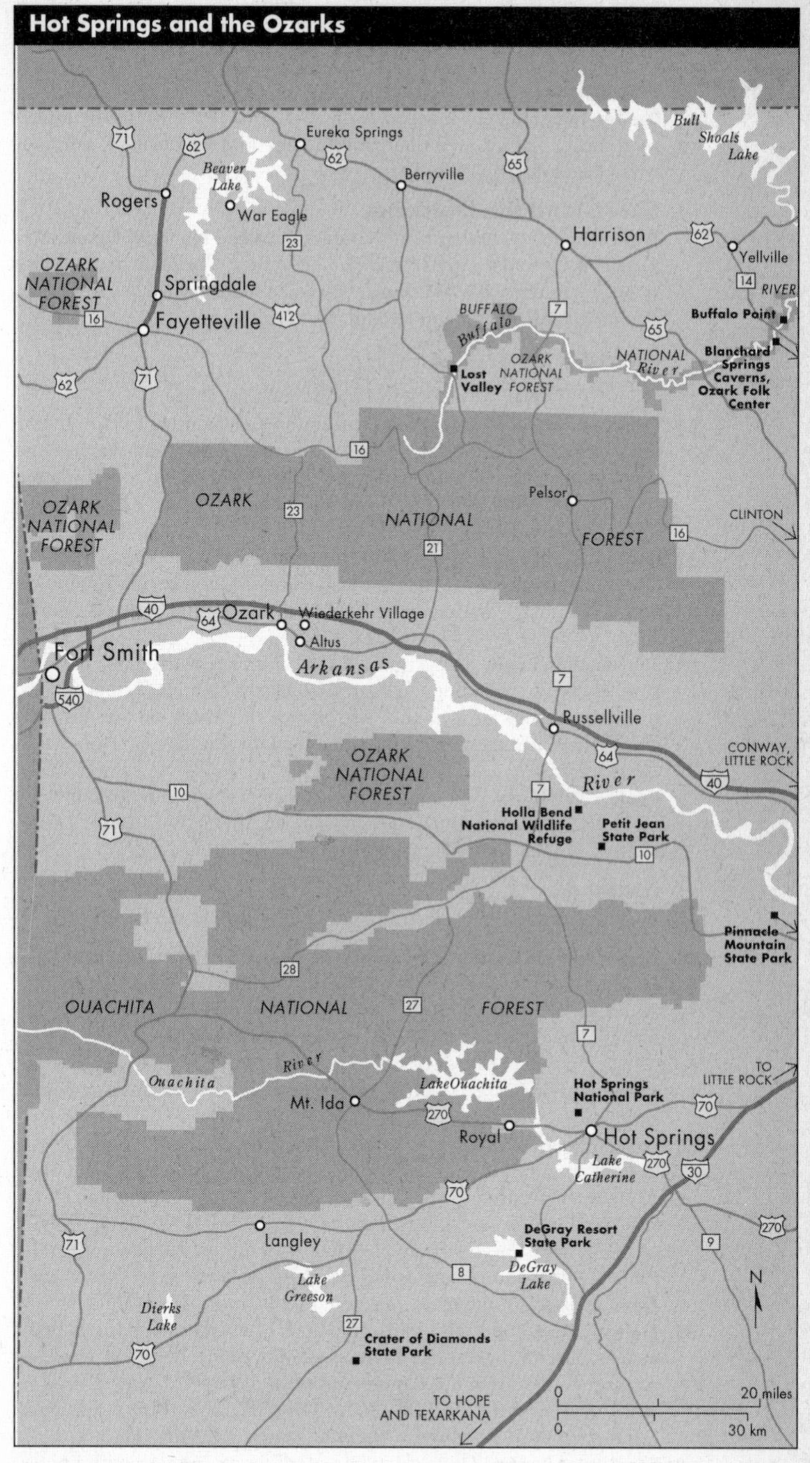

Eureka Springs
Beaver Lake
Rogers
War Eagle
Berryville
Bull Shoals Lake
Harrison
Yellville
OZARK NATIONAL FOREST
Springdale
Fayetteville
BUFFALO
Buffalo
Buffalo Point
RIVER
OZARK NATIONAL FOREST
NATIONAL River
Blanchard Springs Caverns, Ozark Folk Center
Lost Valley
OZARK
NATIONAL
FOREST
Pelsor
CLINTON
OZARK NATIONAL FOREST
Ozark
Wiederkehr Village
Altus
Fort Smith
Arkansas
Russellville
CONWAY, LITTLE ROCK
River
OZARK NATIONAL FOREST
Holla Bend National Wildlife Refuge
Petit Jean State Park
Pinnacle Mountain State Park
OUACHITA
NATIONAL
FOREST
River
Ouachita
Lake Ouachita
Mt. Ida
Hot Springs National Park
TO LITTLE ROCK
Royal
Hot Springs
Lake Catherine
Langley
DeGray Resort State Park
DeGray Lake
Lake Greeson
Dierks Lake
Crater of Diamonds State Park
TO HOPE AND TEXARKANA
0
20 miles
0
30 km
N

children can feed the animals. **National Park Aquarium** (209 Central Ave., ☎ 501/624–3474) has a large exhibit of fish and reptiles.

Shopping

Dream Catchers (239 Central Ave., ☎ 501/623–7778), in the lower-level shopping arcade of the Arlington (*see* Lodging, *below*), sells Native American jewelry and art.

Sports and the Outdoors

For a map of the **hiking** trails, contact **Ouachita National Forest** (Box 1270, Hot Springs 71902, ☎ 501/321–5202). The lakes around Hot Springs feature good bass **fishing,** with an annual tournament. (*See* Lodging, *below,* for fishing guides and boats.)

Dining

For price ranges, see Chart 1 (B) in On the Road with Fodor's.

$$ **Cajun Boilers.** Red-checkered tablecloths and a tin roof belie the exceptional crayfish, lobster, shrimp, and crabs, which come as hot and spicy as you can take them. Try the "Rajun Cajun" seafood platter. *3506 Albert Pike, ☎ 501/767–5695. No reservations. AE, DC, MC, V. Closed Sun.*

$$ **Grady's Grill.** The centerpiece of this restaurant in the Majestic Resort Spa (*see* Lodging, *below*) is the old-fashioned wood bar. The menu offers salads, pasta dishes, and grilled meats and fish. *Park and Central Aves., ☎ 501/623–5511. AE, D, MC, V.*

$$ **The Venetian Room.** This elegant setting, complete with chandeliers and candlelight, in the famous Arlington hotel (*see* Lodging, *below*), is best for elaborate buffet brunches with live piano music on Sunday. The cuisine is Continental. *Central and Fountain Sts., ☎ 501/623–7771. AE, D, MC, V.*

$ **Cookin' With Jazz.** This small, friendly place features gumbo dishes and po'boy sandwiches. *3907 Central Ave., ☎ 501/525–5629. No reservations. BYOB. AE, MC, V. Closed Mon.*

Lodging

For price ranges, see Chart 2 (B) in On the Road with Fodor's.

$$$ **Lake Hamilton Resort and Conference Center.** On a peninsula on Lake Hamilton, this luxurious all-suite resort built in 1984 is contemporary in design, with generous use of wood and stone. All rooms have balconies and lake views. *2803 Albert Pike, U.S. 270W, Box 2070, 71913, ☎ 501/767–5511 or 800/426–3184, FAX 501/767–8576. 114 suites. Facilities: restaurant, lounge, indoor pool, tennis court, boat rentals. AE, D, DC, MC, V.*

$$ **The Arlington.** This beautifully renovated spa hotel is decorated with opulent clusters of art-deco chandeliers and acres of chintz. Half- and full-day beauty programs are available, so you can glow alongside all the silver and brass. *Central and Fountain Sts., 71901, ☎ 501/623–7771 or 800/626–9768, FAX 501/623–6191. 486 rooms. Facilities: 3 restaurants, 2 pools, mountainside hot tub, bathhouse, tennis courts, conference facilities, shopping arcade, golf, hiking trails. AE, D, MC, V.*

$$ **Majestic Resort Spa.** This renovated hotel offers thermal mineral baths and wonderful massages administered by veteran hands. A weekend package for two is $180. *Park and Central Aves., 71901, ☎ 501/623–5511 or 800/643–1504, FAX 501/624–4737. 250 rooms. Facilities: restaurant, pool, conference facilities, shops. AE, MC, V.*

$ **Edgewater Resort.** These clean, air-conditioned cottages with knotty-pine interiors and kitchenettes are on the shore of Lake Hamilton. *200 Edgewater Circle, 71913, ☎ 501/767–3311 or 800/234–3687. 9 cottages. Facilities: boat dock and ramp. MC, V.*

Campgrounds

There are several public campsites on Lakes Ouachita, Catherine, and DeGray. For a recreation directory, contact **Ouachita National Forest** (*see* Sports and the Outdoors, *above*). **Hot Springs National Park** (800 McClendon Rd., Hot Springs 71901, ☎ 501/624–5912) has campsites with electricity, showers, pool, laundry, and RV hookups.

Fort Smith

Tourist Information

Fort Smith: Convention and Visitors Bureau (2 North B St., 72901, ☎ 501/783–8888 or 800/637–1477). The visitor center is housed in Miss Laura's Social Club, the only former bordello on the National Register of Historic Places.

Exploring Fort Smith

Fort Smith is where east met west in frontier days. The site of the original **fort** (3rd and Rogers Aves., ☎ 501/783–3961) is preserved as a National Historic Site commemorating events relating to the federal government's policy on Native Americans during the 1800s. Also preserved here is the historic courtroom from which Judge Isaac C. Parker dispensed frontier justice. The court, the famous "Hell on the Border" jail, and the old gallows have been restored. Nearby is the **Old Fort Museum** (320 Rogers Ave., ☎ 501/783–7841).

Hope

Tourist Information

Hope-Hempstead County: Chamber of Commerce (108 W. 3rd St., Hope 71801, ☎ 501/777–3640).

Exploring Hope

Hope's latest claim to fame is as the birthplace of President Bill Clinton. The city is also long renowned for champion watermelons. Melons weighing 150 to 200 pounds are common here, and they are celebrated each August with the **Hope Watermelon Festival.** The city itself offers a taste of small-town life in Arkansas. Nearby is **Old Washington Historic State Park** (Box 98, Hope 71862, ☎ 501/983–2684), an important resting stop on the rugged Southwest Trail and the Confederate capital of Arkansas following the capture of Little Rock. Within a short drive of Hope is the **Crater of Diamonds State Park** (Hwy. 301, ☎ 501/285–3113) near Murfreesboro. The park has the only public diamond mine in the world, and you can keep what you find.

ELSEWHERE IN THE STATE

Helena

Getting There

Helena is on the banks of the Mississippi River and can be reached by Rte. 49. The St. Francis National Park extends north to Marianna, and the White River National Wildlife Refuge is west toward Arkansas Post.

What to See and Do

The **Delta Cultural Visitors' Center** (Missouri and Natchez Sts., ☎ 501/338–8919), housed in a 1912 train depot, opened in late 1990 as the first phase of an $8.5 million project delving into local heritage. The museum documents area roots of Delta blues, the river life described by Mark Twain, and pioneer days when local farmers were defeated by floodwaters. There is also an excellent gift shop and an information desk that serves as a visitor center for the area.

In October the **King Biscuit Blues Festival** (☎ 501/338–9144) attracts musicians from all over the nation. The town also has the **Edwardian Inn** (317 Biscoe St., ☎ 501/338–8247), a restored 1904 Victorian mansion with 12 bedrooms. For further information, contact the **Phillips County Chamber of Commerce** (Box 447, Helena 72342-0447, ☎ 501/338–8327).

Texarkana

Getting There

Texarkana is on the Arkansas border with Texas and can be reached via I–30.

What to See and Do

The **Perot Theater** (221 Main St., ☎ 800/333–0927) hosts symphony orchestras, pop and country concerts, and ballet. The theater is named after Texarkana native H. Ross Perot, who financed the restoration of the 1924 structure. The **Texarkana Historical Museum** (219 State Line Ave., ☎ 903/793–4831) has artifacts of the Caddo Indians and turn-of-the-century furniture and farm implements. The **Ace of Clubs House** (420 Pine St., ☎ 903/793–7108) is a rare 1885 Victorian built from the winnings of a poker game. Each room is furnished in a different period.

There is a **Bluegrass Festival** in Fagan Park on both Memorial Day and Labor Day weekends. For more information, contact the **Texarkana Chamber of Commerce** (Box 1468, 75501, ☎ 903/792–7191).

KENTUCKY

By John Filiatreau

Capital	Frankfort
Population	3,685,296
Motto	United We Stand, Divided We Fall
State Bird	Cardinal
State Flower	Goldenrod

Visitor Information

Kentucky Department of Travel Development (2200 Capital Plaza Tower, Frankfort 40601, ☎ 502/564–4930 or 800/225–8747). **Welcome centers:** I–75S at Florence, I–65N at Franklin, I–64W at Grayson, I–24E at Paducah, I–75N at Williamsburg, and U.S. 68 at Maysville.

Scenic Drives

A loop drive of the rugged **Red River Gorge** in the eastern Kentucky mountains starts near Natural Bridge State Park on **Rte. 77** near Slade. **Forest Development Road 918** is a 9-mi National Scenic Byway in the Daniel Boone National Forest near Morehead. The 35-mi stretch of **Little Shepherd Trail** (U.S. 119) between Harlan and Whitesburg is breathtaking in fall. **Old Frankfort Pike** between Lexington and Frankfort passes through classic bluegrass countryside.

National and State Parks

National Parks

Daniel Boone National Forest (U.S. 27, Whitley City; 100 Vaught Rd., Winchester 40391, ☎ 606/745–3100) offers spectacular mountain scenery, especially in the Red River Gorge Geological Area, known for its natural arches, native plants, and 300-foot cliffs. **Land Between the Lakes** (100 Van Morgan Dr., Golden Pond 42211, ☎ 502/924–5602) is an uninhabited 40-mi-long peninsula between Kentucky and Barkley lakes, run as a demonstration project in environmental education and resource management. **Mammoth Cave National Park** (entrances on Rte. 70, 10 mi west of Cave City, and on Rte. 255, 8 mi northwest of Park City; Mammoth Cave 42259, ☎ 502/758–2328) is a 350-mi-long complex of twisting underground passages full of colorful mineral formations.

State Parks

Kentucky's 34 state parks reflect a nice balance between letting nature take its course and providing for visitors' amusement. Many are ideal for hiking or simply taking in the beauty of the countryside, but most also offer facilities for picnicking, camping, water sports, and horseback riding. Sixteen have rustic but comfortable lodges and/or cottages; 28 have tent and trailer sites (Apr.–Oct.); 13 have year-round campgrounds. For information contact **Kentucky Department of Parks** (Capital Plaza Tower, Frankfort 40601, ☎ 800/255–7275).

LOUISVILLE

Louisville (locally pronounced "LOO-uh-vul") was founded in 1778 by a Revolutionary War hero, Gen. George Rogers Clark, and named for King Louis XVI in gratitude for France's help during the war. The city's charter was signed in 1780 by Thomas Jefferson, then governor of Virginia, of which Kentucky was the westernmost district. Louisville's culture and history have been influenced greatly by its location, inside a bend in the mighty Ohio River, smack in the center of the eastern half of the nation. During the first half of the 19th century the city was a bustling river port. With the advent of the railroads, it became a hub of train traffic. Waves of European immigrants settled into colorful neighborhoods that retain much of their character today. Louisville attracts crowds of visitors every May for the nation's premier horse race: the Kentucky Derby.

Tourist Information

Louisville: Area Chamber of Commerce (1 Riverfront Plaza, 40202, ☎ 502/566–5000). Convention & Visitors Bureau (400 S. 1st St., 40202, ☎ 502/584–2121 or 800/626–2646; in KY, 800/633–3384). **Preservation Alliance of Louisville and Jefferson County** (716 W. Main St., Louisville 40202, ☎ 502/583–8622).

Arriving and Departing

By Plane

Standiford Field (☎ 502/367–4636) is 15 minutes south of downtown on I–65. It has a modern, spacious, comfortable terminal and is served by most major carriers. Cab fare from the airport to downtown Louisville runs about $15.

By Car

Louisville is well served by interstates. I–64 runs east–west, I–71 northeast, and I–65 north–south. I–264, also known as the Henry Watterson Expressway, rings the city. These converge downtown in a ramp-ridden area known as Spaghetti Junction; confusion here can result in a quick trip to Indiana.

By Bus

Greyhound Lines (720 W. Muhammad Ali Blvd., ☎ 800/231–2222).

Getting Around Louisville

The downtown area is defined north–south by Broadway and the Ohio, east–west by Preston and 18th streets. **Transit Authority of River City** (1000 W. Broadway, ☎ 502/585–1234) operates local buses (fare: $1 at peak times, 75¢ other times), as well as a free trolley along 4th Avenue between Broadway and the river. A car is needed for explorations beyond downtown.

Exploring Louisville

Downtown

The heart of Louisville is thick with historic sites and is best explored on foot. **West Main Street** has more examples of 19th-century cast-iron architecture than anyplace else in the country except New York City's SoHo. The **Hart Block** (728 W. Main St.), a five-story building designed in 1884 at the height of Louisville's Victorian era, has a facade that is a jigsaw puzzle of cast-iron pieces bolted together. Other historic attractions include the tiny **St. Charles Hotel** (634 W. Main St.), constructed before 1832, and the Roman Catholic **Cathedral of the Assumption** (443 S. 5th St.), a Gothic Revival structure built between 1849 and 1852 and restored between 1985 and 1994. The **Jefferson County Courthouse** (531 W. Jefferson St.), a Greek Revival landmark designed by Gideon Shyrock, was built in 1835 with the intent of luring the state government to Louisville.

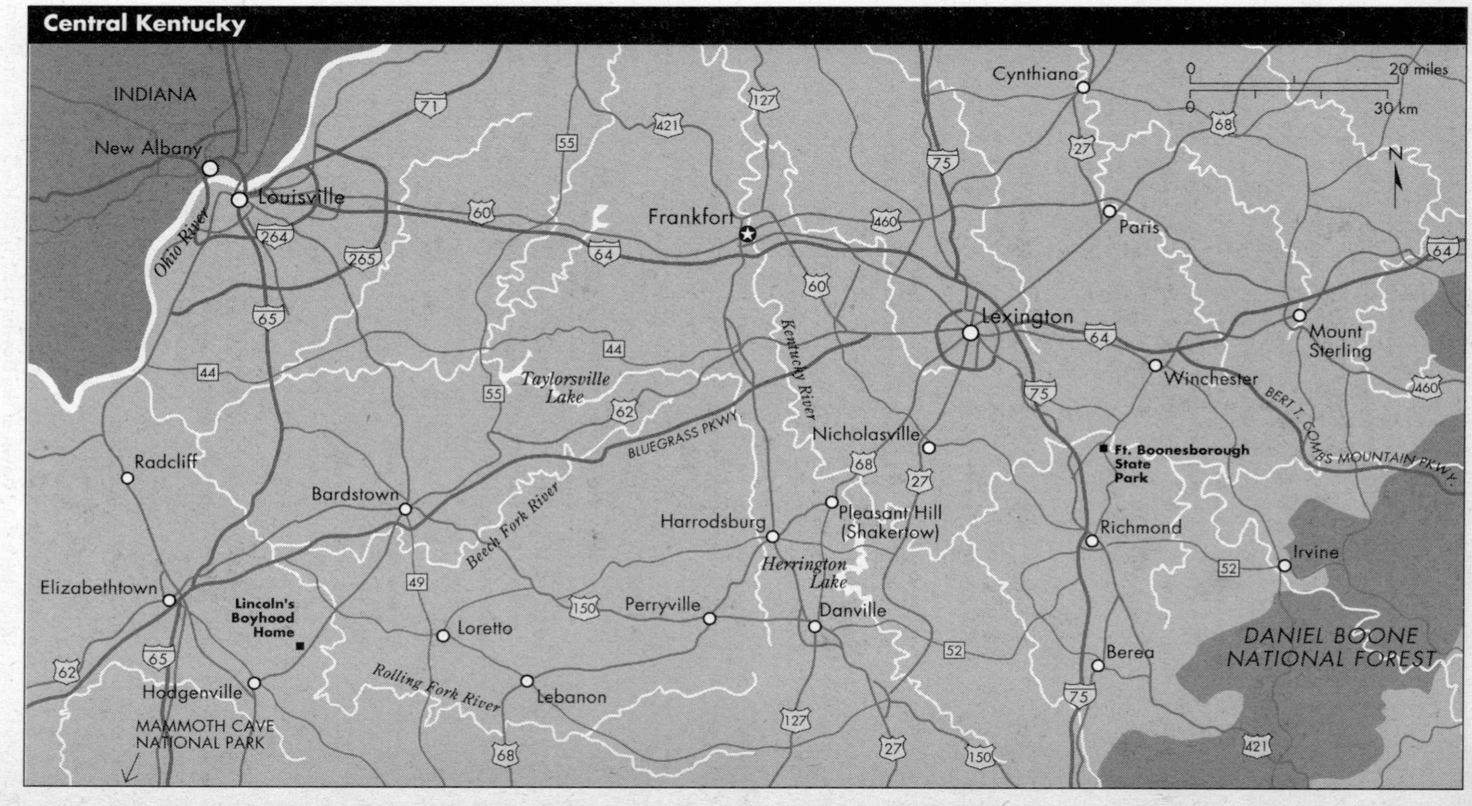
Central Kentucky
INDIANA
New Albany
Louisville
Ohio River
Frankfort
Cynthiana
Paris
Lexington
Mount Sterling
Winchester
BERT T. COMBS MOUNTAIN PKWY.
Taylorsville Lake
Kentucky River
BLUEGRASS PKWY.
Nicholasville
Ft. Boonesborough State Park
Radcliff
Bardstown
Beech Fork River
Harrodsburg
Pleasant Hill (Shakertow)
Richmond
Herrington Lake
Irvine
Elizabethtown
Lincoln's Boyhood Home
Loretto
Perryville
Danville
Berea
DANIEL BOONE NATIONAL FOREST
Rolling Fork River
Lebanon
Hodgenville
MAMMOTH CAVE NATIONAL PARK
0 20 miles
0 30 km
N

More contemporary sights include the grand, eclectic **Humana Building** (500 W. Main St.), designed by Michael Graves and finished in 1985. The **American Life and Accident Building** (3 Riverfront Plaza), designed by Mies van der Rohe and completed in 1973, is known as the "rusty building" for its covering of oxidized Cor-Ten steel. Just off the riverfront Belvedere, the 1988 **Louisville Falls Fountain** spews water in the form of a 375-foot-tall fleur-de-lis, the city's symbol.

The nearby **Kentucky Center for the Arts** (*see* The Arts and Nightlife, *below*), on Riverfront Plaza, is home to a distinguished collection of 20th-century sculpture by such artists as Alexander Calder, Tony Smith, and Jean Dubuffet. The **Louisville Science Center/IMAX Theatre** (727 W. Main St., ☎ 502/561–6103; admission charged), a 19th-century warehouse full of science arcades and demonstrations, includes an Egyptian mummy's tomb, a Foucault pendulum, and lots of hands-on exhibits.

While near the river, check out the ***Belle of Louisville*** (☎ 502/625–2355), usually moored at City Wharf at 4th and River streets with its calliope wailing. The gingerbread-trim steamboat, built in 1914, is the oldest Mississippi-style stern-wheeler still afloat. Should you grow tired, you can hire a horse-drawn carriage from **River City Horse Carriage** (☎ 502/895–7268) or **Louisville Horse Trams** (☎ 502/581–0100).

Nearby Attractions

Butchertown, east of downtown, was settled in the 1830s, largely by Germans who worked in meat-packing plants in the vicinity and lived in "shotgun" and "camelback" houses built in the shadow of the (still-in-business, often redolent) **Bourbon Stock Yards.** To the west is **Portland,** a community of French settlers that sprang up in 1814 where goods came ashore to be portaged past the falls of the Ohio. Today barges carry 5 million tons of cargo per month through the **McAlpine Locks and Dam** (27th St.).

The **Cherokee Triangle,** a few miles southeast of downtown, is a classic Victorian village of grand homes on broad tree-lined streets, built between 1870 and 1910. A few miles out Bardstown Road from the triangle is **Farmington** (☎ 502/452–9920; admission charged), a Federal-style mansion built in 1810 on a design by Thomas Jefferson, whose special touches include two octagonal rooms and an adventurously steep hidden staircase.

Old Louisville, just south of downtown, is the most elegant of Louisville's neighborhoods. Its architectural styles include Victorian Gothic, Richardsonian Romanesque, Queen Anne, Italianate, Châteauesque, and Beaux Arts; leaded- and stained-glass windows, turrets, and gargoyles are much in evidence. On the area's southern edge is the **University of Louisville** campus, where you'll find the **J.B. Speed Art Museum** (2035 S. 3rd St., ☎ 502/636–2893; closed Mon.), with masterworks by Rembrandt, Rubens, Picasso, Henry Moore, and many others, as well as frequent contemporary exhibits.

Just south of the university is **Churchill Downs** (700 Central Ave., ☎ 502/636–4400; admission charged; Apr.–June, Oct.–Nov.), world-famous as the home of the Kentucky Derby. Since the track's opening in 1875, scores of heroic three-year-old Thoroughbreds have thundered past its famous Twin Spires into legend. During the normal racing seasons, check out **"Dawn at the Downs"** (☎ 502/636–3351), a program in which fans may visit the track shortly after daybreak on Saturday, when the horses are out for exercise and the infield grass and flower beds are dew-bejeweled. It's magical. The **Kentucky Derby Museum** (☎

502/637–1111; separate admission charged) documents the careers of the champions. If you plan a trip to Louisville during the annual Kentucky Derby Festival—the two weeks leading up to and including Derby Day (the first Saturday in May)—be prepared to pay more for everything from lodging to transportation.

Just east of Louisville is pastoral **Locust Grove** (☎ 502/897–9845; admission charged), once the home of Louisville's founder. Three presidents—James Monroe, Andrew Jackson, and Zachary Taylor—slept here.

Outside the City

In the bourbon-whiskey country near Louisville is **Bernheim Forest** (on Rte. 245 just off I–65, about 25 mi south of the city, ☎ 502/543–2451). This 10,000-acre preserve features 1,800 species of plants, a nature center, a museum, picnic areas, hiking trails, and lakes; in spring it has the state's best show of rhododendrons and azaleas. A few miles southeast on scenic Rte. 245 is Clermont, site of the **Jim Beam American Outpost Museum** (☎ 502/543–9877), which has a collection of the famous Jim Beam bourbon decanters and a film about making bourbon.

Farther southeast on Rte. 245 is **Bardstown,** the bucolic, historic city best known as the site of **My Old Kentucky Home** (☎ 502/348–3502; closed Mon. Jan.–Feb.). This Georgian Colonial mansion was visited by Stephen Foster in 1852, shortly before he wrote the famous song that makes tears well up in the eyes of all Kentuckians when it's sung on Kentucky Derby Day. **Old Bardstown Village and Civil War Museum** (near 1st St. and Broadway, ☎ 502/348–5204 or 502/348–6501) has war displays and a fine 52-minute multimedia presentation about Kentucky's history and culture. Both Bardstown sites charge admission.

Southeast of Bardstown on Rte. 52, near Loretto, is **Maker's Mark Distillery** (☎ 502/865–2881; closed weekends Jan.–Feb.), a National Historic Landmark and a working distillery that you can tour for free. Southwest of Bardstown is the **Abraham Lincoln Birthplace National Historic Site** (3 mi south of Hodgenville on U.S. 31E/Rte. 61, ☎ 502/358–9474), where Lincoln was born on February 12, 1809. About 110 acres of the original Thomas Lincoln farm are included in the 116-acre park.

Parks and Gardens

In 1891, Louisville's Board of Parks hired Frederick Law Olmsted, designer of New York's Central Park, to design a system of public lands to be "free to all forever." Among the results were **Shawnee Park** in the west, a plain of river bottomland; **Cherokee Park** in the east, where Beargrass Creek wanders among woods and meadows; and **Iroquois Park** in the south, a tall, rugged escarpment offering vistas of the city. Sometimes overlooked by visitors and natives alike is little **Tyler Park** on Baxter Avenue, an Olmsted-designed jewel that serves as an envelope of solitude in the midst of city bustle.

What to See and Do with Children

The Louisville Zoo (1100 Trevilian Way, ☎ 502/459–2181) exhibits more than 1,300 animals in naturalistic environments. In summer, **Kentucky Kingdom Amusement Park** (Kentucky Fair and Exposition Center, ☎ 502/366–2231) has rides and games, including three roller coasters, a water park, and a playground for young children. **Stage One: The Louisville Children's Theatre** (425 W. Market St., ☎ 502/584–7777 or 800/283–7777) offers professional productions on weekends from October to May.

Shopping

Shopping Districts

The Galleria (4th Ave. between Liberty St. and Muhammad Ali Blvd., ☏ 502/584–7170), a glass-enclosed mall with 80 stores and 11 fast-food restaurants, is a city melting pot and the best place to shop downtown. **Bardstown Road,** southeast of downtown, is a 2-mi strip for strolling and browsing in antiques shops, bookstores, and boutiques. The **Jefferson Mall** (☏ 502/968–4101), 10 mi south of downtown on Outer Loop, is a huge enclosed mall, with more than 100 stores.

Department Stores

Lazarus (Jefferson Mall, ☏ 502/966–1800; Oxmoor Center, ☏ 502/423–3000) had been the city's leading department store for more than a decade when upscale **Jacobson's** (Oxmoor Center, ☏ 502/327–0200) came on the scene in 1994. Both will face competition when behemoth **Dillard's** opens two stores in the Louisville area in 1995. **Bigg's** "hypermarket" (12975 Shelbyville Rd., Middletown, ☏ 502/244–4760) is what its name suggests—big. It has everything from pastries to chain saws, at bargain prices.

Specialty Stores

The **Kentucky Art & Craft Gallery** (609 W. Main St., ☏ 502/589–0102) sells top-quality crafts. **Baer Fabrics** (515 E. Market St., ☏ 502/583–5521) has been amassing its world-renowned collection of buttons since 1905. **Joe Ley Antiques** (615 E. Market St., ☏ 502/583–4014) has an outstanding 2-acre litter of hardware, fixtures, and doodads.

Spectator Sports

Horse Racing

The Kentucky Derby at **Churchill Downs** (*see* Exploring Louisville, *above*) is a *very* tough ticket—unless you're willing to join tens of thousands of seatless young revelers in the infield, where you're unlikely even to get a glimpse of a horse.

Dining

Louisville has eating options to suit any taste or pocketbook. Dining alternatives range from sophisticated gourmet restaurants with adventurous menus and tuxedoed waiters to no-frills family-style eateries where a server might put a thumb through your sandwich. In general, a casual atmosphere prevails; you won't often encounter dress codes. For price ranges, see Chart 1 (B) in On the Road with Fodor's.

$$$ **Cafe Metro.** An ever-changing, ever-unusual menu offers such entrées as grilled salmon with a sauce of capers, cucumbers, and dill, served on a bed of spinach fettuccine. The ambience is street-smart and suggestive of Paris. *1700 Bardstown Rd., ☏ 502/458–4830. AE, MC, V. Closed Sun.*

$$$ ★ **Lilly's.** One of Louisville's most daring restaurants has a menu that changes frequently and always features dishes made with fresh, home-grown ingredients, such as pork tenderloin maintained and grilled in an apricot-sage beurre blanc, served with spinach, blue cheese tart, and baby vegetables. The glittery, vaguely art deco–style dining room, in green, black, and purple, is as bold as the cuisine. *1147 Bardstown Rd., ☏ 502/451–0447. AE, MC, V.*

$$$ ★ **Vincenzo's.** Deep leather chairs, 17th-century paintings, and crisp tablecloths provide the setting for just-so service. For the main course, consider *vitello alla Sinatra* (spinach-stuffed veal scaloppine with

wine sauce). *Humana Bldg., 150 S. 5th St., ☎ 502/580–1350. AE, D, DC, MC, V.*

$$ Asian Pearl. The walls are covered with color portraits of Asian meals. The floors sag under the weight of the "grand buffet," with more than 40 items; notable among them is Uncle Lin's chicken (lightly battered chunks sautéed with fresh zucchini and Chinese vegetables, with hot-and-spicy sauce). *2060 S. Hurstbourne Pkwy., ☎ 502/495–6800. AE, MC, V.*

$$ ★ Cafe Mimosa. This dark, quiet nook offers American and French fare but specializes in Vietnamese dishes. A good starter is *goi cuon* (delicate rice-paper cylinders surrounding shrimp, chicken, vermicelli, and vegetables, with sweet peanut sauce for dipping). *1216 Bardstown Rd., ☎ 502/458–2233. AE, MC, V. Closed Mon.*

$$ Jade Palace. The decor is suburban-shopping-center Mandarin, and service is variable, but the Friday–Sunday dim sum (a lavish buffet of Chinese appetizers and finger foods) is justly famous, and the dinner menu has just about everything your heart desires. If you're feeling adventurous, try *kwai may far chi* (sautéed squid with mushrooms, snow peas, onions, and Chinese vegetables with a 10-flavor hot sauce). *1109 Herr La., ☎ 502/425–9878. AE, MC, V.*

$$ ★ Mark's Feed Store. The atmosphere is decidedly no-frills, with concrete floors, rough-hewn wooden walls, and rolls of paper towels on the tables. What attracts the hordes of sauce-slathered diners are generous servings of tender, hickory-smoked, western Kentucky–style barbecue—slow-cooked, never refrigerated or reheated, and "pulled" rather than sliced. If you have the capacity, try Mark's homemade buttermilk pie for dessert. *11422 Shelbyville Rd., ☎ 502/244–0140. AE, MC, V.*

$ Check's Cafe. In this Germantown eatery the fare, like the atmosphere and the service, is decidedly down-home. Among menu favorites are chili, fish, and bratwurst sandwiches. *1101 E. Burnett Ave., ☎ 502/637–9515. No credit cards.*

$ Jessie's Family Restaurant. There's nothing fancy about Jessie's Formica tables and vinyl-covered booths. There's nothing fancy about the good food either: Plate-lunch favorites include pan-fried pork chops and pepper steak with rice. *9609 Dixie Hwy., ☎ 502/937–6332. No credit cards.*

$ The Rudyard Kipling. This diner in a renovated 19th-century house in Old Louisville has music and poetry most nights and becomes a dinner theater (separate admission; reservations advised) on Thursday, Friday, and Saturday. Try crepes Delbert (ham, black beans, and mushrooms in a sauce of cheese, mustard, and Chablis). *420 W. Oak St., ☎ 502/636–1311. AE, DC, MC, V. Closed Sun.*

Lodging

Like any port city, Louisville has a long tradition of hospitality to visitors. You can choose from lovingly restored, pricey downtown hotels to Roaring Twenties elegance, or opt for a budget room in a place that promises to leave the light on for you. B&B accommodations can be found through **Kentucky Homes B&B** (1431 St. James Ct., Louisville 40208, ☎ 502/635–7341). For price ranges, see Chart 2 (B) in On the Road with Fodor's.

$$$ The Brown. This 16-story historic hotel (built in 1923) has been fully restored, with old-English-style furnishings, artwork, atmosphere, and service. *4th St. and Broadway, 40202, ☎ 502/583–1234 or 800/866–7666, FAX 502/587–7006. 294 rooms. Facilities: restaurant, bar, exercise equipment. AE, D, DC, MC, V.*

$$$ **Hyatt Regency Louisville.** Hyatt's familiar plant-filled atrium and glass-and-brass lobby are the focus of this 18-story hotel. The rooms have been done in a back-to-nature theme, with redwood and soft pastels. *320 W. Jefferson St., 40202, ☎ 502/587–3434, FAX 502/581–0133. 388 rooms. Facilities: restaurant, bar, indoor pool, spa, tennis, supervised children's activities, concierge. AE, D, DC, MC, V.*

$$$ ★ **The Seelbach.** The refurbished guest rooms in this 11-story landmark (built in 1905), part of the Doubletree chain, have four-poster beds, armoires, and marble baths with gold fixtures. *500 4th Ave., 40202, ☎ 502/585–3200 or 800/626–2032, FAX 502/585–3200, ext. 292. 322 rooms. Facilities: restaurant, bar, concierge. AE, D, DC, MC, V.*

$$ **The Executive Inn.** The English Tudor style of this six-story hotel near the airport is carried through from the public areas to the rooms, which may look snug or gloomy, according to your taste. Some have private patios or balconies. *978 Phillips La. (off I–64), 40209, ☎ 502/367–6161 or 800/626–2706; in KY, 800/222–8284; FAX 502/367–6161. 465 rooms. Facilities: restaurant, bar, indoor and outdoor pools, exercise room. AE, D, DC, MC, V.*

$$ ★ **Galt House East.** Overlooking the river, this downtown hotel has an elaborately landscaped, modern 18-story atrium, but the room furnishings are of the grandpa's-overstuffed-chair variety, emphasizing old-time comfort. *141 N. 4th Ave., 40202, ☎ 502/589–3300 or 800/843–4258, FAX 502/585–4266. 600 rooms. Facilities: restaurant, bar, pool. AE, D, DC, MC, V.*

$$ **Old Louisville Inn Bed & Breakfast.** The guest rooms in this 1901 brick house have elaborately carved mahogany woodwork and are furnished with antiques. The atmosphere and service have a pleasant time-machine quality. *1359 S. 3rd St., 40208, ☎ 502/635–1574, FAX 502/637–5892. 11 rooms. MC, V.*

$ **Breckinridge Inn.** This two-story motor hotel is clean, plain, and comfortable. The predominant style in the guest rooms is art deco. *2800 Breckinridge La. (at I–264), 40220, ☎ 502/456–5050, FAX 502/451–1577. 123 rooms. Facilities: restaurant, bar, indoor pool, sauna, valet service, tennis. AE, D, DC, MC, V.*

$ ★ **Days Inn Downtown.** This conveniently located eight-story motor hotel has clean, spacious rooms decorated with muted colors in Early American style. *101 E. Jefferson St., 40202, ☎ 502/585–2200, FAX 502/585–2200, ext. 123. 177 rooms. Facilities: restaurant, bar, indoor pool, whirlpool, valet service. AE, D, DC, MC, V.*

$ **Wilson Inn.** Far from downtown and painted a horrid salmon color outside, this five-story motor hotel has a pleasant, tree-filled lobby. Milder pastels and earth tones predominate in the plain, contemporary rooms. *9802 Bunsen Pkwy. (I–64 at Hurstbourne La.), 40299, ☎ 502/499–0000 or 800/333–9457, FAX 502/499–0000, ext. 152. 44 rooms, 32 suites. Facilities: valet service. AE, D, DC, MC, V.*

The Arts and Nightlife

For news of arts and entertainment events, look for *Louisville* magazine on newsstands and for the Friday and Saturday editions of the *Courier-Journal* newspaper.

The Arts

Actors Theatre of Louisville (316 W. Main St., ☎ 502/585–1210) is a Tony Award–winning repertory theater in a bank building (circa 1837) designated a National Historic Landmark. **The Broadway Series** (611 W. Main St., ☎ 502/584–7469) hosts touring productions of Broadway's best. **Shakespeare in the Park** (Central Park at S. 4th St., ☎ 502/634–8237) transforms Louisville into the bard's town on summer weekends.

The three stages at the **Kentucky Center for the Arts** (5 Riverfront Plaza, ☎ 502/562–0100 or 800/283–7777) are alive with entertainment ranging from Broadway to Bach, bagpipes to bluegrass. The **Louisville Orchestra** (609 W. Main St., ☎ 502/584–7777 or 800/283–7777) has received international attention for its recordings of contemporary works.

Nightlife

The **Funny Farm Comedy Niteclub** (1250 Bardstown Rd. in the Mid-City Mall, ☎ 502/459–0022) and the **Legends Comedy Club** (9700 Bluegrass Pkwy. in the Hurstbourne Hotel & Conference Center, ☎ 502/459–0022) present circuit comics of the stand-up variety. **Coyote's** (116 W. Jefferson St., ☎ 502/589–3866; closed Mon.–Tues.) has live country music, a raucous but friendly clientele, and free instruction in two-step and line dancing. **LaBo's** (Lebanon Junction, about 30 minutes south of Louisville on I–65, ☎ 502/833–3954) is a down-home, good ol' country fun place for families that like country music and dancing. The **Clown House** (4028 S. 3rd St., ☎ 502/375–3870) showcases alternative rock, sometimes bordering on heavy metal. At the **Twice-Told Coffee House** (1604 Bardstown Rd., ☎ 502/456–0507) and **Highland Grounds** (919 Baxter Ave., ☎ 459–6478), the caffeine-powered entertainment could be anything from avant-garde theater to readings of epic poetry to Delta blues. **The Connection** (130 S. Floyd St., ☎ 502/585–5752) is a giant entertainment complex consisting of a restaurant, a bar with a Thursday-night talent show and the best and biggest dance floor in town, and a theater with female-impersonator revues on the weekends.

LEXINGTON AND THE BLUEGRASS

Lexington, the world capital of racehorse breeding and burley tobacco (a thin-bodied, air-cured variety), was named by patriotic hunters who camped here in 1775, shortly after hearing news of the first battle of the Revolutionary War, at Lexington, Massachusetts. A log structure built by a member of that historic hunting party is preserved to this day, on the campus of Transylvania University. The Bluegrass is a lush region of rolling hills, meandering streams, and manicured horse farms.

Tourist Information

Frankfort/Franklin County: Tourist and Convention Commission (100 Capital Ave., Frankfort 40601, ☎ 502/875–8687). **Lexington:** Greater Lexington Convention & Visitors Bureau (Suite 363, 430 W. Vine St., 40507, ☎ 606/233–1221 or 800/845–3959). **Richmond:** Tourism Commission (Box 250, City Hall, 40476, ☎ 606/623–1000).

Getting There

By Plane

Lexington Bluegrass Airport (4000 Versailles Rd., ☎ 606/254–9336), 4 mi west of downtown Lexington, is served by Delta, USAir, and regional lines.

By Car

The Lexington area and the Bluegrass are well served by I–64 east–west, I–75 north–south, and the state parkway system, a toll network that bisects the state east–west.

Exploring Lexington and the Bluegrass

Lexington

Downtown, take a hike—or a tour in a horse-drawn carriage from **Lexington Livery Co.** (☎ 606/259–0000; $25 for a 30-minute tour). In the **Gratz Park Historic District,** near 2nd Street and Broadway, are two fine houses from 1814: the lavish, privately owned **Gratz House** (231 N. Mill St.), built by a rich hemp manufacturer, and the **John Hunt Morgan House** (201 N. Mill St., ☎ 606/253–0362), the former home of a swashbuckling Confederate general and his great-grandson, Thomas Hunt Morgan, who won a Nobel Prize in 1933 for proving the existence of the gene. Check out the statue of General Morgan on the lawn of the **Fayette County Courthouse** (215 W. Main St.). When it was unveiled in 1911, it caused quite a stir because it portrays the Rebel raider astride a stallion though his best-known mount was a mare, Black Bess.

The Greek Revival campus of **Transylvania University** (300 N. Broadway, ☎ 606/233–8120), the first college west of the Alleghenies (established in 1780), has left its mark on two U.S. vice presidents, 50 senators, 34 ambassadors, and 36 Kentucky governors. The 1832 **Mary Todd Lincoln House** (578 W. Main St., ☎ 606/233–9999) belonged to the parents of Abraham Lincoln's wife and displays Lincoln and Todd family memorabilia. U.S. Senator Henry Clay, "The Great Compromiser," was a green 20-year-old lawyer when he came to Lexington in 1797 and opened his **law office** (176–178 N. Mill St.).

Two attractions at the **University of Kentucky** (Euclid Ave. and S. Limestone St.) are an **anthropology museum** (201 Lafferty Hall, ☎ 606/257–7112), with exhibits on evolution and Kentucky culture, and an **art museum** (121 Singletary Center for the Arts, ☎ 606/257–5716), which has an interesting permanent collection and frequent special exhibits.

A Lexington curiosity is the huge **castle** (just west of the city on Versailles Rd.), with eight turrets and 70-foot-tall corner towers. It was started by a Fayette County developer in 1969 as his private residence, but it was never finished. The **Headley-Whitney Museum** (Old Frankfort Pike, ☎ 502/255–6653; admission charged) is an eclectic, personal, three-building collection of Oriental porcelains, masks, paintings, shells, and jeweled bibelots.

The Bluegrass

Kentucky's Bluegrass area has more than 400 horse farms, some with Thoroughbred barns as elegant as French villas. Among the famous breeding farms is **Calumet** (just west of the city on Versailles Rd./U.S. 60), which has produced a record eight Kentucky Derby winners. The antebellum mansion at **Manchester** farm (nearby on Van Meter Rd.) is said to have been the inspiration for Tara in *Gone with the Wind.* **Spendthrift** (Ironworks Pike, ☎ 606/299–5271) is one of the few farms that routinely welcome visitors. Famous horses from the **C. V. Whitney** farm on Paris Pike have included Regret, the first filly to win the Kentucky Derby, and the appropriately named Upset, the only horse ever to finish in front of the legendary Man o' War. **Normandy** (a bit farther out on Paris Pike) has a famous L-shape barn that was built in 1927; it features a clock tower and roof ornaments in animal shapes. You'll note that the plank fencing these farms use to separate their paddocks is sometimes painted white, sometimes black. Some farm operators claim that the traditional white provides better visibility for the horses and is more attractive. Others note that black requires less frequent repainting—a serious economic factor for farms that must maintain miles of such fences, which cost about $18,000 per mile to install (painting's extra).

Southward on scenic U.S. 25 is **Fort Boonesborough State Park** (☎ 606/527–3131 or 800/255–7275; admission charged), a reconstruction of one of Daniel Boone's early forts, with a museum and demonstrations of pioneer crafts. In **Richmond,** visit **White Hall State Historic Site** (☎ 606/623–9178; admission charged), the home of the abolitionist Cassius Marcellus Clay, a cousin of Henry Clay and an ambassador to Russia. The elegant mansion combines two houses and two styles, Georgian and Italianate.

In **Berea,** where the Bluegrass meets the mountains, you'll find charming, tuition-free **Berea College** (☎ 606/986–9341), founded in 1855, whose 1,500 students—most of them from Appalachia—work for their education. On the campus is the **Appalachian Museum** (Jackson St., ☎ 606/986–9341, ext. 6078), which charts regional history through arts and crafts.

The **Shaker Village of Pleasant Hill** (Hwy. 68, ☎ 606/734–5411; admission charged), 25 mi southwest of Lexington, has 27 restored buildings of frame, brick, or stone, erected between 1805 and 1859 by members of a religious sect noted for industry, architecture, and furniture making. In nearby **Harrodsburg,** the first permanent settlement in Kentucky, **Old Fort Harrod State Park** (☎ 606/734–3314; admission charged) has a full-scale reproduction of the old fort, built on its original 1774 site.

About 15 mi south of Lexington, the beautiful, deep-blue-green **Kentucky River** flows gently but relentlessly through the Bluegrass. The combination of rolling river and rugged rock faces makes for dramatic landscapes. Take Jacks Creek Pike from Lexington through one of the most enchanting parts of Kentucky to **Raven Run Nature Sanctuary** (☎ 606/255–0835), a place of rugged, forested hills and untouched wildlife along the Kentucky River.

In lovely **Danville,** 30 mi southwest of Lexington, you can visit the **McDowell House and Apothecary Shop** (125 S. 2nd St., ☎ 606/236–2804; admission charged), the residence and shop of Dr. Ephraim McDowell (a noted surgeon of the early 19th century), refurnished with period pieces. West of Danville on U.S. 150 and north on U.S. 68 is **Perryville Battlefield** (☎ 606/332–8631), the site of Kentucky's most important (and bloodiest) Civil War battle, where 4,241 Union soldiers and 1,822 Confederates were killed or wounded.

Frankfort, between Louisville and Lexington on I–64, was chosen as the state capital in 1792 as a compromise between those cities' rival claims and has been caught in the middle ever since. The **state capitol** (☎ 502/564–3449), overlooking the Kentucky River at the south end of Capitol Avenue, is notable for its Ionic columns, high central dome, and lantern cupola; guided tours are given. Outside the capitol is the famous **Floral Clock,** a working outdoor timepiece whose face—made of thousands of plants—is swept by a 530-pound minute hand and a 420-pound hour hand.

In Frankfort Cemetery, on East Main Street, you can visit **Daniel Boone's Grave** (he died in Missouri, but his remains were returned to Kentucky in 1845). The restored, Georgian-style **Old Governor's Man-**

sion (420 High St., ☎ 502/564–3000), built in 1798, served as the residence of 33 governors until a new mansion was built in 1914. The later **Governor's Mansion** (☎ 502/564–3449) is styled on the Petit Trianon, Marie Antoinette's villa at Versailles (France, not Kentucky).

What to See and Do with Children

Kentucky Horse Park (4089 Iron Works Pike, off I–75, Lexington, ☎ 606/233–4303) is not just a Thoroughbred showcase; it offers films, a breeds show, and farm tours, as well as a museum, an art gallery, and campgrounds. The interactive exhibits at the **Lexington Children's Museum** (401 W. Main St., ☎ 606/258–3253) include an archaeology dig. **Lexington Children's Theatre** (☎ 606/254–4546) offers performances for young audiences.

Shopping

In Lexington, **Fayette Mall** (3473 Nicholasville Rd., ☎ 606/272–3493) has more than 100 stores and a dozen places to eat. For something out of the ordinary, try **Dudley Square** (380 S. Mill St.), in a restored 1881 school building; its shops feature antiques, prints, quilts, and the like. **Victorian Square** (401 W. Main St.) is an entire downtown block of renovated Victorian buildings that now contain tony retail and dining establishments. At nearby **Festival Market** (325 W. Main St., ☎ 606/254–9888) you can dine in an open-air café or take a spin on an old-time carousel. Lexington also has a plethora of **antiques shops;** the Convention & Visitors Bureau (*see* Tourist Information, *above*) maintains a list.

Sports and the Outdoors

Kentucky's lakes and streams are great for **fishing** for more than 200 species. You're seldom more than a 30-minute drive away from a public **golf** course. The state parks and national forests are full of **hiking** trails. Eastern Kentucky has several rivers that offer mild to moderate **white-water rafting** opportunities. For information, contact the parks department (*see* National and State Parks, *above*), the tourism offices (*see* Tourist Information, *above*), or the state **Department of Fish and Wildlife Resources** (1 Game Farm Rd., Frankfort 40601, ☎ 502/564–4336).

Spectator Sports

Horse Racing

Keeneland Race Course (4201 Versailles Rd., Lexington, ☎ 606/254–3412 or 800/456–3412; Apr., Oct.).

Dining and Lodging

While Lexington offers varied dining options, including Continental and ethnic cuisines, most restaurants outside the city are decidedly down-home. Menus tend to feature country-fried steak, country ham, and fried chicken. Many of the best places to dine are so out of the way and unimpressive-looking that you probably won't discover them on your own. Don't be bashful about asking the locals for guidance. For price ranges, see Chart 1 (B) in On the Road with Fodor's.

Most of the best places to lay one's weary head are restored historic properties, often modestly priced, that are short on amenities but long on charm. State park lodges and cottages are bargain-priced, rustic but comfortable. In many rural areas, you'll have to settle for bare-bones accommodations. In Lexington, **Dial Accommodations** (430 W. Vine St., ☎ 606/233–7299) can help with reservations. For price ranges, see Chart 2 (B) in On the Road with Fodor's.

Berea

DINING AND LODGING

★ **Boone Tavern.** This grand old Colonial-style hotel (1909) is operated by Berea College and outfitted with furniture handmade by students. The restaurant is famous for its spoon bread, chicken flakes in bird's nest, and Jefferson Davis pie. *Box 2345, Main and Prospect Sts., 40403, ☎ 606/986–9358 or 606/986–9359. 57 rooms. Facilities: restaurant (jacket required evenings, Sun.), drugstore. AE, D, DC, MC, V. $$*

Harrodsburg

DINING AND LODGING

Beaumont Inn. Guest rooms at this exemplar of southern hospitality are scattered among four timeworn (but polished) buildings furnished with antiques. The restaurant specializes in corn pudding and cured Kentucky country ham. *638 Beaumont Dr., 40330, ☎ 606/734–3381. 33 rooms. Facilities: restaurant, pool, tennis. AE, D, DC, MC, V. Closed mid-Dec.–mid-Mar. $$*

Inn at Pleasant Hill. Rooms in 27 restored buildings (circa 1800)—some with four floors and no elevators—are furnished with Shaker reproductions and hand-woven rugs and curtains. The restaurant, Trustees' House at Pleasant Hill, serves hearty family-style meals and specializes in a tangy Shaker lemon pie for which people have been known to drive 100 mi. *3500 Lexington Rd., 40330, ☎ 606/734–5411. 80 rooms. Facilities: restaurant (reservations required), riverboat cruises. No credit cards. Closed Dec. 24–25. $$*

Lexington

DINING

★ **The Mansion at Griffin Gate.** This historic, two-story restaurant is surrounded by a grove of stately trees more than 200 years old. Built in 1854 in the style of an Italian villa, the mansion is furnished with antiques, period paintings, and a dozen crystal chandeliers. The menu is similarly distinguished, offering the likes of Tournedos Helder, filet mignon and lobster tail covered with bordelaise and béarnaise sauces and served on a bed of diced tomatoes. *1720 Newton Pike, ☎ 606/231–5152. Jacket and tie preferred. AE, D, DC, MC, V. $$$*

A la Lucie. This chef-owned eatery has a cosmopolitan feel, with a tin roof, terrazzo floors, hot colors, green plants, and eclectic art. French, German, and American dishes appear on the menu, but the specialty is whatever seafood is at its seasonal best. *150 N. Limestone St., ☎ 606/252–5277. AE, DC, MC, V. Closed Sun. $$*

★ **Alfalfa Restaurant.** In this small, woody, old-fashioned restaurant, the fare is home-cooked international, organically grown vegetarian, and ethnic dishes. The menu, written on a chalkboard, may include ham-and-apple quiche; the house salad is lavish. *557 S. Limestone St., ☎ 606/253–0014. No credit cards. No dinner Mon. $$*

Dudley's Restaurant. Chic but unpretentious, this restaurant in a 100-year-old schoolhouse has a courtyard shaded by huge tulip poplar trees. A favorite on the Continental menu is pasta with chicken, sun-dried tomatoes, and vegetables. *380 S. Mill St., ☎ 606/252–1010. AE, MC, V. $$*

★ **Merrick Inn.** A spacious, comfortable, not-too-formal restaurant occupies a sprawling, white-columned, former horse-farm manor house (circa 1890) decorated in the Williamsburg style. The extensive menu offers steak, lamb, and a variety of pastas, but the Merrick's specialty is fresh seafood of the season (its signature dish is fried walleyed pike). *3380 Tates Creek Rd., ☎ 606/269–5417. AE, DC, MC, V. Closed Sun. $$*

A.P. Suggins Bar & Grill. This casual dining spot in Chevy Chase has a menu as long as your leg: Choose from beef, chicken, fish, Kentucky favorites, burgers, salads, soups, and Mexican food. *345 Romany Rd., ☎ 606/268–0709. AE, MC, V. $*

★ **Joe Bologna's.** This longtime college hangout occupies a church built in 1890; the original stained-glass windows are still in place. You can feast on small or large servings of an assortment of pastas, as well as pizza. *120 W. Maxwell St., ☎ 606/252–4933. MC, V. $*

LODGING

Gratz Park Inn. In an elegantly refurbished three-story medical building dating from 1887, the guest rooms are furnished with antiques. *120 2nd St., 40507, ☎ 606/231–6666 or 800/227–4362, FAX 606/233–7593. 44 rooms, 8 suites. Facilities: restaurant, bar, concierge. AE, D, DC, MC, V. $$$*

★ **Marriott's Griffin Gate Resort.** This gleaming, seven-story, contemporary resort hotel caters to a youngish crowd that likes physical activities and physical comforts. The rooms have private patios or balconies. *1800 Newtown Pike, 40511, ☎ 606/231–5100, FAX 606/231–5100, ext. 7580. 409 rooms. Facilities: restaurant, bar, health club, indoor pool, tennis, valet service. AE, D, DC, MC, V. $$$*

Campbell House Inn. Striving for a bed-and-breakfast ambience, this three-story motel has modern but homey rooms, with traditional furnishings. *1375 Harrodsburg Rd., 40504, ☎ 606/255–4281 or 800/354–9235; in KY, 800/432–9254; FAX 606/254–4368. 370 rooms. Facilities: restaurant, bar, pool, valet service, tennis. AE, D, DC, MC, V. $$*

Courtyard by Marriott. The trademark of this three-story motel is a sunny, gardenlike central courtyard. The green, brown, and mauve rooms are modern, with light woodwork and oversize desks. *775 Newtown Ct., 40511, ☎ 606/253–4646, FAX 606/253–9118. 146 rooms. Facilities: restaurant, bar, indoor pool, whirlpool, valet service, exercise equipment. AE, D, DC, MC, V. $$*

Wilson Inn. This five-story motor hotel resembles its Louisville counterpart: well away from downtown, contemporary in style, with a tree-filled lobby, and colored a horrid salmon outside with pleasant pastels and earth tones inside. *2400 Buena Vista Dr., 40505, ☎ 606/293–6113 or 800/333–9457, FAX 606/293–6113, ext. 157. 110 rooms. Facilities: Continental breakfast. AE, D, DC, MC, V. $*

The Arts and Nightlife

The Arts

Lexington's performing-arts scene is vigorous. For information on performances contact the **Actors' Guild** (☎ 606/233–0663), **Lexington Ballet** (☎ 606/233–3925), **Lexington Philharmonic** (☎ 606/233–4226), and **Opera of Central Kentucky** (☎ 606/245–2373). Concerts, plays, and lectures are also presented at **Transylvania University** and the **University of Kentucky.**

Nightlife

After-dark offerings in Lexington are pretty sparse and pretty tame. You might check out the **Brewery,** a friendly Texas-roadhouse-style bar where the tunes are classic rock and classic country, and **Sundance,** a country-western dance club (both at 509 W. Main St., ☎ 606/255–2822); **Comedy Off Broadway** (3199 Nicholasville Rd., ☎ 606/271–5653), where stand-up comics crack wise; and the **Wrocklage** (361 W. Shore St., ☎ 606/231–7655), the place for alternative, punkish rock.

LOUISIANA

By Honey Naylor

Capital	Baton Rouge
Population	4,419,723
Motto	Union, Justice, and Confidence
State Bird	Pelican
State Flower	Magnolia

Visitor Information

Louisiana Office of Tourism (Box 94291, Baton Rouge 70804-9291, ☎ 800/334–8626).

Scenic Drives

Rtes. 56 and 57 form a circular drive south of Houma, where shrimp boats dock along the bayous from May to December. Another circular drive is the **Creole Nature Trail** (Rte. 27) out of Lake Charles. **Rte. 82** runs through the coastal marshes and wildlife refuges along the Gulf of Mexico. The **Longleaf Trail Scenic Byway** south of Natchitoches is a 17-mi highway through the Kisatchie National Forest, linking Rtes. 117 and 119. **Rte. 182** runs for much of the way alongside Bayou Teche in southern Louisiana.

National and State Parks

National Parks

The **Jean Lafitte National Historical Park and Preserve** (U.S. Custom House, 423 Canal St., New Orleans 70130, ☎ 504/589–3882) preserves coastal wetlands south of New Orleans and offers nature trails and canoeing through exotic swampland. The 100,000-acre Kisatchie Ranger District of the **Kisatchie National Forest** (Box 2128, Natchitoches 71457, ☎ 318/473–7160) has hiking and equestrian trails through hardwood and pine forests.

State Parks

A prehistoric Native American site dating from ca. 1800 BC to 500 BC, the 400-acre **Poverty Point State Commemorative Area** (Rte. 577, HC-60, Box 208A, Epps 71237, ☎ 318/926–5492) is one of the country's most important excavations, with hiking trails and an interpretive center in addition to the ancient Native American mounds. The 600-acre **Louisiana State Arboretum** (Rte. 3, Box 494, Ville Platte 70586, ☎ 318/363–6289), lush with trees and plants native to the state, has 2½ mi of nature trails. Fishing, boating, and camping (cabins are available) are all possibilities in the 6,500-acre **Chicot State Park** (Rte. 3, Box 494, Ville Platte 70586, ☎ 318/363–2403) and at **Bayou Segnette** near New Orleans (7777 Westbank Expressway, Westwego 70094, ☎ 504/436–1107), **Lake Bistineau State Park** (Box 589, Doyline 71023, ☎ 318/745–3503), **Lake Fausse Point State Park** (Rte. 5, Box 5648, St. Martinville 70582, ☎ 318/229–4764), **North Toledo Bend State Park** (Box 56, Zwolle 71486, ☎ 318/645–4715), and **Sam Houston Jones State Park** (Rte. 4, Box 294, Lake Charles 70601, ☎ 318/855–2665).

NEW ORLEANS

Strategically located on the Mississippi River, New Orleans is Louisiana's largest and most important city. From its beginnings in 1718 the city has played a vital role in the nation's history. To wrest control of the port city from the French in 1803, President Thomas Jefferson paid Napoleon $15 million and got the entire Louisiana Territory in the bargain.

"The Big Easy" is the home of the splashiest festival in all of North America: Mardi Gras, which is held each February or March. New Orleans is a fun-loving city with an insouciant spirit reminiscent of the Caribbean. As Jelly Roll Morton said, New Orleans is "the place where the birth of jazz originated." And local chefs gave the world the exotic Creole cuisine. The French Quarter (also known as the Vieux Carré), with its honky-tonk Bourbon Street, is one of the nation's favorite partying places.

Tourist Information

New Orleans: Tourist Commission (1520 Sugar Bowl Dr., 70112, ☎ 504/566–5031, FAX 504/566–5046). Welcome Center (529 St. Ann St., in the French Quarter).

Arriving and Departing

By Plane

New Orleans International Airport (a.k.a. Moisant Field, ☎ 504/464–0831), 15 mi west of New Orleans, is served by most major domestic and some foreign carriers. Cab fare for the 20- to 30-minute trip downtown is $21 for one or two passengers, $8 for each additional passenger. The 24-hour **Airport Shuttle** (☎ 504/522–3500) drops passengers off at all hotels. Buses operated by **Louisiana Transit** (☎ 504/737–9611) run between the airport and the Central Business District; the fare is $1.10 (exact change in coins).

By Car

I–10 is the major east–west artery through the city; I–55, which runs north–south, connects with I–10 west of town. I–59 heads for the northeast. U.S. 61 and 90 also run through the city.

By Train and Bus

Union Passenger Terminal (1001 Loyola Ave., ☎ 504/528–1610).

Getting Around New Orleans

The French Quarter is best savored on leisurely strolls; the Central Business District (CBD) is also easily walkable.

By Car

Driving in New Orleans can be maddening. French Quarter streets are often clogged with traffic, street signs are indecipherable, and tow trucks operate with lightning speed. Leave your car in a secured garage until it's needed for excursions.

By Public Transportation

The **Regional Transit Authority,** or RTA (☎ 504/569–2700, TTY 504/569–2838), operates the bus and streetcar system and staffs a 24-hour information line.

Bus and **St. Charles Streetcar** fare is $1 (exact change); the **Riverfront Streetcar** ($1.25 exact change) links attractions along the Mississippi. The **Vieux Carré shuttle** runs through the French Quarter to the foot of Canal Street. VisiTour passes good on all RTA buses and streetcars cost $4 (one day) and $8 (three days).

By Taxi

Cabs cruise the French Quarter and the CBD, but not beyond. Reliable companies with 24-hour service are **United Cabs** (☎ 504/522–9771) and **Yellow-Checker Cabs** (☎ 504/943–2411). The fare is $1.70 at the flag drop, 20¢ for each additional ⅕ mi, and 50¢ for each additional passenger.

By Ferry

A ferry (Crescent City Connection, ☎ 504/364–8100; free outgoing, $1 returning) crosses the Mississippi from the Canal Street Wharf to Algiers, leaving the pier every 25 minutes.

Orientation Tours

Bus and Van Tours

Two- to three-hour city tours, as well as full- and half-day tours to plantation country, are available from **Gray Line** (☎ 504/587–0861), **New Orleans Tours** (☎ 504/592–0560, 504/592–1991, or 800/543–6332), and **Tours by Isabelle** (☎ 504/391–3544). Gray Line and New Orleans Tours also offer two-hour nightclub tours. **Le 'Ob's Tours** (☎ 504/288–3478) runs a daily black-heritage city tour.

Cruises

Riverboat sightseeing and dinner/jazz cruises are offered by the **New Orleans Steamboat Company** (☎ 504/586–8777) and **New Orleans Paddle Wheels** (☎ 594/524–0814). Bayou tours are offered by **Honey Island Swamp Tours** (☎ 504/641–1769) and **Cypress Swamp Tours** (☎ 504/581–4501).

Walking Tours

Friends of the Cabildo (☎ 504/523–3939) offers tours of the French Quarter. Rangers of the **Jean Lafitte National Historical Park and Preserve** (☎ 504/589–2636) conduct free tours of the Quarter and the Garden District. **Heritage Tours** (☎ 504/949–9805) offers literary tours of the Quarter. **Save Our Cemeteries** (☎ 504/588–9357) conducts tours of aboveground cemeteries. Free maps for self-guided walking tours are available at the New Orleans Welcome Center (*see* Tourist Information, *above*).

Exploring New Orleans

The French Quarter and the CBD

The French Quarter is the original colony founded in 1718 by French Creoles. A carefully preserved historic district as well as a residential district, the Quarter is also home to some famous French Creole restaurants and many a jazz club. An eclectic crowd ambles in and out of small two- and three-story frame, old-brick, and pastel-painted stucco buildings, most of which date from the mid-19th century. Baskets of splashy subtropical plants dangle from the eaves of buildings with filigreed galleries, dollops of gingerbread, and dormer windows. Secluded courtyards are awash in greenery and brilliant blossoms.

The heart of the Quarter is **Jackson Square,** a pretty green park surrounded by a flagstone pedestrian mall and centered by an equestrian statue of General Andrew Jackson. Originally known to the Creoles as Place d'Armes, the square was renamed in the mid-19th century for the man who defeated the British in the Battle of New Orleans. The mall is alive with sidewalk artists, food vendors, Dixieland bands, tap dancers, and clowns.

St. Louis Cathedral, soaring above the square, is a quiet reminder of the city's spiritual life. The present church dates from 1794 and was restored in 1849. Tours are conducted daily except during services.

The church is flanked by two 18th-century buildings of the **Louisiana State Museum.** As you face the church, the **Cabildo** is on the left, the **Presbytère** on the right. Transfer papers for the Louisiana Purchase of 1803 were signed on the second floor of the Cabildo. Damaged by fire in 1988, the building reopened in February 1994 after a meticulous $6.5 million restoration. New Orleans's rich multicultural history is explored through historic documents and artifacts, among which is a death mask of Napoleon—one of only three in the world. The Presbytère, originally built as a home for priests of the church, today houses changing exhibits. *For both: ☎ 504/568–6968. Admission charged. Closed Mon.*

Alongside the church are **Pirate's Alley** and **Père Antoine's Alley,** two ancient flagstone passageways redolent of bygone days. You can see what life was like for upscale 19th-century Creole apartment dwellers in the **1850s House,** also part of the state museum, which contains period furnishings, antique dolls, and a quaint kitchen. *525 St. Ann St., ☎ 504/568–6968. Admission charged. Closed Mon.*

The **Pontalba Buildings** that line Jackson Square on St. Ann and St. Peter streets are among the oldest apartment houses in the country. Built between 1849 and 1851, they boast some of the city's loveliest ironwork galleries.

The promenade of **Washington Artillery Park,** across Decatur Street, affords a splendid perspective on the square and Old Man River. Nearby is the **French Market**—a complex of shops, offices, and eating places in a row of renovated buildings that once housed markets during Spanish and French rule. Here, **Café du Monde** provides a 24-hour haven for café au lait and beignets (square doughnuts).

Downriver from the square, the **Old U.S. Mint** houses exhibits on jazz and Mardi Gras. This was the first branch of the U.S. Mint, in operation from 1838 until 1861. It's now part of the Louisiana State Museum. *400 Esplanade Ave., ☎ 504/568–6968. Admission charged. Closed Mon.*

The **Old Ursuline Convent,** erected in 1749 by order of Louis XV, is the only building remaining from the original colony. The Sisters of Ursula, who arrived in New Orleans in 1727, occupied the building from 1749 to 1824. Guided tours of the complex take in the splendid **Our Lady of Victory Chapel.** *1100 Chartres St., ☎ 504/529–3040. Admission charged. Closed Mon.*

The **Gallier House** was built in about 1857 by famed architect James Gallier, Jr., as his family home. This is one of the best-researched house-museums in the city and a fine example of how well-heeled Creoles lived. *1118–32 Royal St., ☎ 504/523–6722. Admission charged. Closed Sun.*

The tattered cottage at 941 Bourbon Street—dating from 1772 and typical of houses built by the earliest settlers—is **Lafitte's Blacksmith Shop,** a popular neighborhood bar. According to legend, the cottage was once a front for pirate Jean Lafitte's smuggling and slave trade. The **LaBranche House** (740 Royal St.), dating from about 1840, wraps around the corner of Royal and St. Peter streets. Its filigreed double galleries are the most photographed in the city.

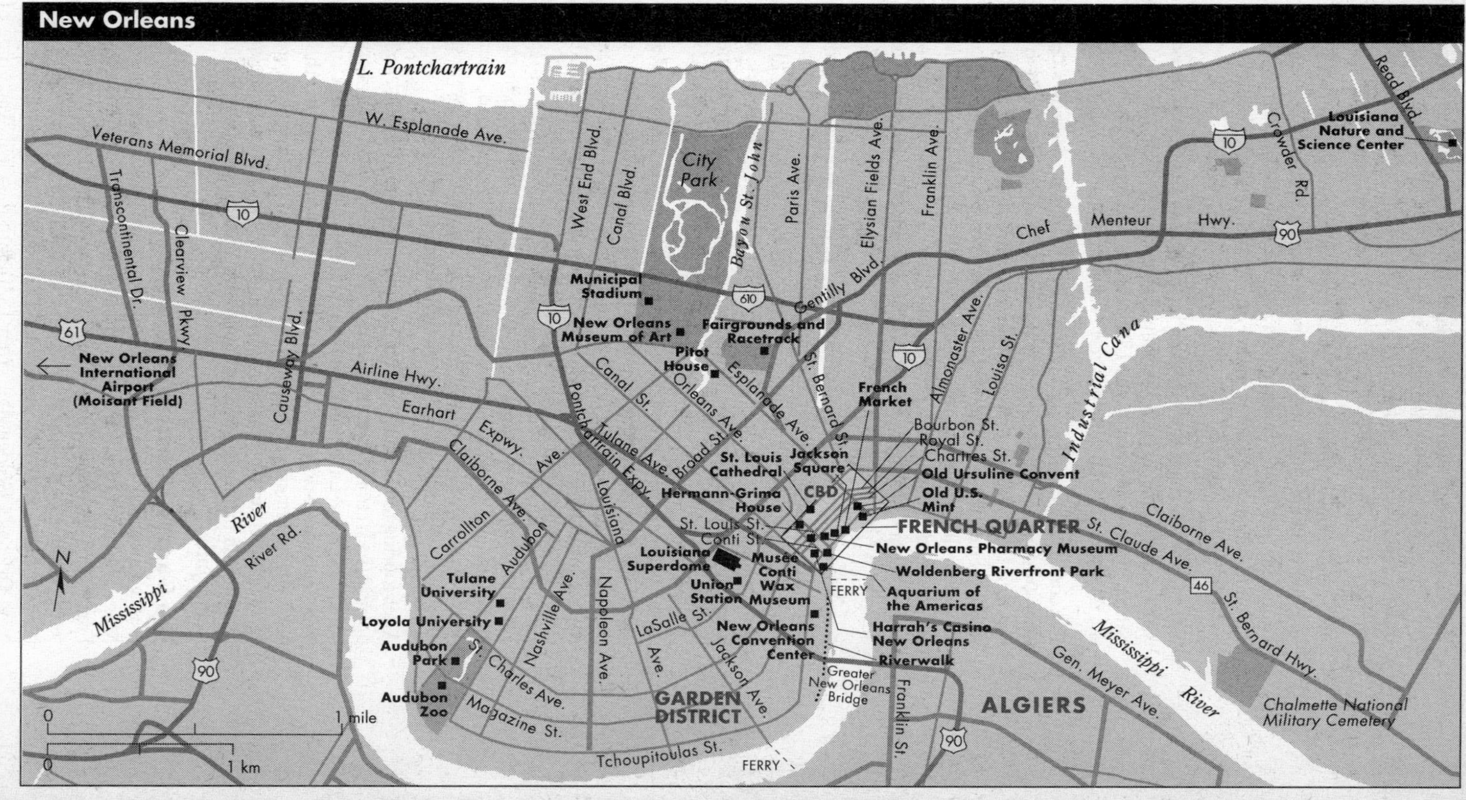
New Orleans
L. Pontchartrain
W. Esplanade Ave.
Veterans Memorial Blvd.
Transcontinental Dr.
Clearview Pkwy.
Causeway Blvd.
New Orleans International Airport (Moisant Field)
Airline Hwy.
Earhart Expwy.
Claiborne Ave.
West End Blvd.
Canal Blvd.
City Park
Bayou St. John
Paris Ave.
Elysian Fields Ave.
Franklin Ave.
Chef Menteur Hwy.
Crowder Rd.
Read Blvd.
Louisiana Nature and Science Center
Municipal Stadium
New Orleans Museum of Art
Fairgrounds and Racetrack
Gentilly Blvd.
Pitot House
Canal St.
Orleans Ave.
Esplanade Ave.
St. Bernard St.
French Market
Almonaster Ave.
Louisa St.
Industrial Canal
Bourbon St.
Royal St.
Chartres St.
Old Ursuline Convent
Old U.S. Mint
Pontchartrain Expy.
Tulane Ave.
Broad St.
St. Louis Cathedral
Jackson Square
CBD
Hermann-Grima House
St. Louis St.
Conti St.
FRENCH QUARTER
St. Claude Ave.
Claiborne Ave.
New Orleans Pharmacy Museum
Woldenberg Riverfront Park
Louisiana Superdome
Musee Conti Wax Museum
Union Station
FERRY
Aquarium of the Americas
Harrah's Casino New Orleans
Riverwalk
New Orleans Convention Center
Greater New Orleans Bridge
St. Bernard Hwy.
Mississippi River
Gen. Meyer Ave.
ALGIERS
Chalmette National Military Cemetery
Carrollton
Audubon
Louisiana
Tulane University
Loyola University
Nashville Ave.
Napoleon Ave.
LaSalle St.
Audubon Park
Audubon Zoo
St. Charles Ave.
Magazine St.
GARDEN DISTRICT
Jackson Ave.
Franklin St.
Tchoupitoulas St.
River Rd.
N
0
1 mile
1 km

The **New Orleans Pharmacy Museum** is a musty old place where the nation's first licensed pharmacist lived and worked. It's full of ancient and mysterious medicinal things. *514 Chartres St., ☎ 504/565–8027. Admission charged. Closed Mon.*

At the **Hermann–Grima House,** guides take you through the Georgian-style town house, built in 1831, and its picturesque outbuildings. On Thursdays in winter you can get a taste of Creole cuisine during cooking demonstrations. *820 St. Louis St., ☎ 504/525–5661. Admission charged. Closed Sun.*

Not to be missed are the tableaux in the **Musée Conti Wax Museum,** which wax lifelike on such Louisiana legends as Andrew Jackson, Jean Lafitte, and Marie Laveau, the 19th-century voodoo queen. *917 Conti St., ☎ 504/525–2605. Admission charged.*

The construction of the city's first land-based casino, **Harrah's Casino New Orleans,** is finally under way after more than two years of delays and legal wrangles. The Rivergate Exhibition Center at the foot of Canal Street has been demolished to make way for the 200,000-square-ft, $800 million facility, touted as the world's largest. The grand opening is scheduled for May 1996, but Harrah's opened a temporary casino in May 1995 in Armstrong Park's **Municipal Auditorium,** recently renovated for that purpose.

Canal Street, the upriver border of the Quarter, is a main thoroughfare of the CBD, as well as the dividing line between Uptown and Downtown. Nerve center of the nation's second-largest port, the CBD has the city's newest high-tech convention hotels, along with ritzy shopping malls, fast-food chains, stores, foreign agencies, and the mammoth Superdome.

At the foot of Canal Street, hard by the Mississippi River, is the **Aquarium of the Americas,** which offers close encounters with aquatic creatures in 60 displays in four major environments. The 16-acre Woldenberg Riverfront Park around the aquarium affords an excellent view of the river. *☎ 504/565–3033. Admission charged.*

The ferry landing is across from the aquarium, and adjacent to it is **Riverwalk.** This busy area comprises Spanish Plaza, a broad, open expanse of mosaic tile with a magnificent fountain; the Riverwalk shopping mall; and docks for various sightseeing riverboats.

After touring the French Quarter and the adjacent CBD, you can head upriver (west) to the Garden District and uptown. Mid-City, between the Quarter and Lake Pontchartrain, is home to lush **City Park** and the **Fair Grounds Race Track.** In December 1993 a fire destroyed the Fair Grounds buildings; at press time (summer 1995) the facilities were operating under tents. North of town, Lake Pontchartrain, popular for boating and fishing, is lined with marinas, picnic grounds, and seafood restaurants.

The Garden District and Uptown

Nestled between St. Charles, Louisiana, and Jackson avenues and Magazine Street, the Garden District is aptly named. Shunned by the French Creoles when they arrived in the early 19th century, American settlers built palatial estates upriver and surrounded them with lavish lawns. Many of the elegant Garden District houses were built during New Orleans's Golden Age, from 1830 until the Civil War. Some of these private homes are open to the public during Spring Fiesta tours.

"Uptown" is the area just upriver of the Garden District. **Tulane** and **Loyola** universities stand side by side on St. Charles Avenue, across from **Audubon Park** (*see* Parks and Gardens, *below*).

Mid-City

In **City Park** (*see* Parks and Gardens, *below*), the **New Orleans Museum of Art** displays Italian paintings from the 13th to the 18th century, 20th-century European and American paintings and sculptures, Chinese jades, and the Imperial Treasures by Peter Carl Fabergé. *Lelong Ave., ☎ 504/488–2631. Admission charged (free to LA residents on Thurs. mornings). Closed Mon.*

Across Bayou St. John from City Park, the **Pitot House** is a West Indies–style house built in the late 18th century. It is furnished with Louisiana and other American 19th-century antiques. *1440 Moss St., ☎ 504/482–0312. Admission charged. Closed Sun.–Tues.*

Parks and Gardens

City Park (City Park Ave., ☎ 504/482–4888), in Mid-City, is a 1,500-acre urban oasis shaded by majestic live oak trees. Its offerings include golf courses and tennis courts; lagoons for boating, canoeing, and fishing; botanical gardens; and a children's amusement park with puppet shows and storytelling, a carousel, and pony rides.

Smaller but no less lush, the 400-acre **Audubon Park** (6500–6800 blocks of St. Charles Ave.) features a 2-mi jogging trail with exercise stations, a riding stable, a swimming pool, tennis courts, a golf course, and a zoo.

The **Audubon Zoo** covers 58 acres of the park. Wooden walkways afford an up-close look at more than 1,800 animals in natural-habitat settings, including a Louisiana swamp and an African savanna. There's also a petting zoo and elephant and camel rides. *6500 Magazine St., ☎ 504/861–2537. Admission charged.*

New Orleans for Free—or Almost

Ferry rides (*see* Getting Around New Orleans, *above*) are inexpensive and scenic. **Street musicians** perform daily in Jackson Square and Woldenberg Riverfront Park and on Bourbon, Royal, and Chartres streets. **Free concerts** are given regularly in Dutch Alley and the French Market. The **New Orleans Museum of Art** is free to Louisiana residents each Thursday morning (*see* Exploring New Orleans, *above*). **Free walking tours** of the French Quarter and the Garden District are conducted by the Park Service (*see* Orientation Tours, *above*). **Mardi Gras,** featuring fabulous floats and eye-popping costumes, is called The Greatest Free Show on Earth.

What to See and Do with Children

The **Aquarium of the Americas** and the **Musée Conti Wax Museum** (*see* Exploring New Orleans, *above*), **City Park** and the **Audubon Zoo** (*see* Parks and Gardens, *above*), as well as the city's many **festivals and parades,** are always a hit with kids. The **Louisiana Children's Museum** (428 Julia St., ☎ 504/523–1357) features hands-on activities that are both educational and fun. **Le Petit Théâtre du Vieux Carré** (*see* The Arts and Nightlife, *below*) presents children's shows. **Louisiana Nature and Science Center** (11000 Lake Forest Blvd., ☎ 504/246–9381) has a planetarium and nature trails through forests and wetlands.

Shopping

Louisiana's **tax-free shopping** program grants shoppers from other countries a sales-tax rebate. Retailers who display the tax-free sign issue vouchers for the 9% sales tax, which can be redeemed on departure. Present the vouchers with your passport and international plane ticket at the tax-rebate office at New Orleans International Airport, and receive up to $500 in cash back. If the amount redeemable exceeds $500, a check for the difference will be mailed to your home address.

Store hours are generally 10 to 5:30 or 6 Monday through Saturday, noon to 5 on Sunday. Many stores in the French Quarter and in malls stay open till 9 PM. Sales are advertised in the daily *Times-Picayune.*

Shopping Districts

Most of the **French Quarter's** ritzy antiques stores, musty bazaars, art galleries, and boutiques are housed in quaint 19th-century structures. The sleek indoor malls of the **CBD** include **Riverwalk** (1 Poydras St.), with more than 200 specialty shops and restaurants; **Canal Place** (1 Canal Pl.), with more than 40 tony shops, a food court, and cinemas; and **New Orleans Centre** (600 Poydras St.), connected by a walkway to the Superdome and a hotel. The **Warehouse District** neighborhood of the CBD, especially Julia Street, off St. Charles Ave. is a major center for art galleries. Upriver from the CBD, **Magazine Street** has 6 mi of antiques stores and boutiques, many of them in once-grand Victorian houses, and **Riverbend** has specialty shops and restaurants, many of them cradled in small Creole cottages.

Department Stores

Maison Blanche (901 Canal St., CBD) is the local department store, with branches in suburban shopping centers. **Woolworth's** (737 Canal St., CBD) has budget shopping.

Specialty Stores

ANTIQUES

Royal Street in the Quarter is lined with elegant antiques stores; **Magazine Street** has everything from Depression glass to Persian rugs. The Royal Street Guild and the Magazine Street Merchants' Association publish pamphlets that are available free at the New Orleans Welcome Center (*see* Tourist Information, *above*).

FLEA MARKET

Locals as well as tourists turn out for the **French Market Flea Market** daily from 7 to 7.

FOOD

Bayou to Go (New Orleans International Airport, Concourse C, ☎ 504/468–8040) has packaged Louisiana food products. **Old Town Praline Shop** (627 Royal St., ☎ 504/525–1413) has the best pralines in town.

JAZZ RECORDS

For hard-to-find vintage items, go to **Record Ron's** (1129 Decatur St. and 407 Decatur St., ☎ 504/524–9444).

MASKS

Handmade Mardi Gras masks are available at **Little Shop of Fantasy** (523 Dumaine St. ☎ 504/529–4243) and **Rumors** (513 Royal St., ☎ 504/525–0292).

Spectator Sports

Baseball

The **New Orleans Zephyrs** (☎ 504/282–6777), a Class AAA minor-league team of the Milwaukee Brewers, play their home games in UNO's Privateer Park.

Football

New Orleans Saints (Superdome, 1 Sugar Bowl Dr., ☎ 504/522–2600; Aug.–Dec.). The annual **Sugar Bowl Classic** (☎ 504/525–8573) is played in the Dome on New Year's Day.

Horse Racing

There is Thoroughbred racing from Thanksgiving Day to April at the **Fair Grounds** (1751 Gentilly Blvd., ☎ 504/944–5515). Although a fire ripped through the Fair Grounds buildings in December 1993, facilities were up and running—albeit under tents—within three weeks. Permanent buildings, however, are expected to take several years to be completed.

Dining

New Orleans is renowned for Creole and Cajun cuisine. The essence of Creole is in sauces, herbs, and the prominent use of seafood. Cajun cooking, with lots of herbs and spices, tends to be red-hot. For price ranges, see Chart 1 (A) in On the Road with Fodor's.

$$$$ **Antoine's.** Established in 1840, Antoine's is the oldest restaurant in the United States under continuous family ownership. An elegant place, it originated oysters Rockefeller, pompano *en papillote,* and puffed-up soufflé potatoes. There is a moderately priced luncheon menu. *713 St. Louis St., French Quarter,* ☎ *504/581–4422. Reservations advised weekends. Jacket required for dinner. AE, DC, MC, V.*

$$$$ ★ **Commander's Palace.** Housed in a renovated Victorian mansion, this elegant restaurant offers the best sampling of old Creole cooking prepared with a combination of American and French touches. Entrées include veal chop Tchoupitoulas (hickory grilled with Creole seasoning—peppercorn, honey, and roasted peppers) and trout with roasted pecans. *1403 Washington Ave., Garden District,* ☎ *504/899–8221. Reservations required. Jacket required. AE, DC, MC, V.*

$$$$ ★ **Grill Room.** At this top-rated spot, New American cuisine with strong Continental overtones is served in an opulent setting highlighted by original artwork. As the name suggests, there is a grill, over which much good fish is prepared. *Windsor Court Hotel, 300 Gravier St., CBD,* ☎ *504/522–1992. Reservations advised. AE, DC, MC, V.*

$$$ ★ **Arnaud's.** Beveled glass, ceiling fans, and tile floors create an aura of traditional southern dining. The lively Sunday jazz brunch is a classic New Orleans experience. Pompano *en croûte* and veal Wohl (medallions of veal in a port wine sauce with crawfish tails) are good entrées; there is little on the menu that isn't excellent. *813 Bienville St., French Quarter,* ☎ *504/523–5433. Reservations required. Jacket required. AE, DC, MC, V.*

$$$ **K-Paul's Louisiana Kitchen.** National celebrity chef Paul Prudhomme's restaurant is a shrine to New Orleans Cajun cooking. Reservations are accepted for dinner only; long lines form for lunch, at which time strangers must often share a table. The food, however, is superb. *416 Chartres St., French Quarter,* ☎ *504/524–7394. Reservations advised for dinner. AE. Closed weekends.*

$$ ★ **Galatoire's.** Operated by the fourth generation, Galatoire's is a tradition in New Orleans. Every imaginable Creole dish is served in a large, brightly lighted room with mirrors on all sides. Avoid the long lines by arriving after 1:30 PM. *209 Bourbon St., French Quarter, ☎ 504/525–2021. No reservations. Jacket and tie after 5 PM and all day Sun. AE, MC, V. Closed Mon.*

$$ **Gautreau's.** This small café converted from an old pharmacy is one of the most popular restaurants in the Uptown area. The food is straightforward but imaginative and comfortably Creole. The dinner menu consists entirely of specials. *1728 Soniat St., Uptown, ☎ 504/899–7397. Reservations advised. AE, MC, V. No lunch; no dinner Sun.*

$$ **Palace Cafe.** A split-level restaurant with the ambience of a Parisian café, The Palace has a spiral staircase, a tile floor, wood paneling, and splashy murals. Specialties are seafood, game, and rotisseried chicken basted in garlic oil. Wait till you see the menu of chocolate desserts. *605 Canal St., CBD, ☎ 504/523–1661. Reservations advised. DC, MC, V.*

$ ★ **Camellia Grill.** This classy lunch counter with linen napkins and a maître d' serves the best omelets in town all day long, as well as great hamburgers, pecan pie, cheesecake, and banana-cream pie. Expect long lines on weekends for breakfast. *626 S. Carrollton Ave., Uptown, ☎ 504/866–9573. No reservations. No credit cards.*

$ **Napoleon House.** This ancient bar with peeling sepia walls and Napoleonic memorabilia has a limited menu, but the *muffuletta* (an Italian sandwich of meats, cheeses, and olive salad served on an oversize round roll) is one of the best in town. The taped classical music and mellow ambience make this a popular spot for chilling out. *500 Chartres St., French Quarter, ☎ 504/524–9752. AE, MC, V.*

$ **Praline Connection.** Down-home cooking in the southern-Creole style is the forte of these laid-back restaurants. The fried or stewed chicken, smothered pork chops, barbecued ribs, and collard greens are definitively done. *542 Frenchmen St., Faubourg Marigny, ☎ 504/943–3934; 901 St. Peters St., Warehouse District, ☎ 504/523–3973. No reservations. AE, MC, V.*

Lodging

When planning a stay in New Orleans, try to reserve well in advance, especially during Mardi Gras or other seasonal events. Frequently, hotels offer special packages at reduced rates, but never during Mardi Gras, when rates are much higher. For price ranges, see Chart 2 (A) in On the Road with Fodor's.

$$$$ **Fairmont Hotel.** The Fairmont, in the CBD, one of the oldest grand hotels in America, had a $22 million face-lift in 1993 in honor of its 100th birthday. Its lobby, where afternoon tea is served, is decked in red and gold Victorian splendor. Special touches in every room include four down pillows and electric shoe buffers. *University Pl., 70140, ☎ 504/529–7111 or 800/527–4727, FAX 504/529–4764. 685 rooms, 50 suites. Facilities: 4 restaurants with bars, 24-hr room service, heated outdoor pool, fitness center, 2 lighted tennis courts, business center, beauty salon, gift shop, newsstand, valet parking. AE, D, DC, MC, V.*

$$$$ ★ **Windsor Court Hotel.** Consistently rated one of the top luxury hotels in the country, this CBD gem features canopy and four-poster beds, wet bars, and high tea served daily in the plush lobby lounge. *300 Gravier St., 70130, ☎ 504/523–6000 or 800/262–2662, FAX 504/596–4513. 58 rooms, 266 suites. Facilities: 2 restaurants, lounge, entertainment, Olympic-size outdoor pool, health club, whirlpool, steam bath, sauna, valet. AE, DC, MC, V.*

$$$ Royal Orleans Hotel (Omni). An elegant white marble hotel in the French Quarter, the Royal O is reminiscent of a bygone era. Rooms, though not exceptionally large, are well appointed with marble baths (telephone in each) and marble-top dressers and tables. *621 St. Louis St., 70140, ☏ 504/529–5333, FAX 504/529–7089. 350 rooms, 16 suites. Facilities: 2 restaurants, 3 lounges, rooftop heated pool, exercise room, gift shop, beauty salon and barbershop, valet service, parking. AE, D, DC, MC, V.*

$$ Holiday Inn Château Le Moyne. The atmosphere and decor of this French Quarter inn are mostly Old World, with eight suites in restored Creole cottages that retain the original cedar ceilings and exposed beams. *301 Dauphine St., 70112, ☏ 504/581–1303, FAX 504/523–5709. 160 rooms, 11 suites. Facilities: restaurant, lounge, outdoor heated pool, valet parking. AE, D, DC, MC, V.*

$$ Josephine Guest House. European antiques fill the rooms of this restored Italianate mansion in the Garden District, built in 1870. The bathrooms are impressive in both size and decor. A complimentary Continental breakfast, served on Wedgwood china on a silver tray, can be brought to your room. *1450 Josephine St., 70130, ☏ 504/524–6361or 800/779–6361, FAX 504/523–6484. 6 rooms. AE, D, DC, MC, V.*

$$ ★ Le Richelieu. This small, friendly hotel in the French Quarter offers many amenities usually found in luxury high-rises. Some rooms have mirrored walls, walk-in closets, and refrigerators; all have hair dryers. Luxury suites are available. *1234 Chartres St., 70116, ☏ 504/529–2492 or 800/535–9653, FAX 504/524–8179. 69 rooms, 17 suites. Facilities: restaurant, lounge, outdoor pool, valet, free parking. AE, D, DC, MC, V.*

$$ ★ Pontchartrain Hotel. Maintaining the grand tradition is the hallmark of this quiet, elegant European-style hotel that has reigned in the Garden District for more than 60 years. Accommodations range from lavish sun-filled suites to small pension rooms with shower baths. *2031 St. Charles Ave., 70140, ☏ 504/524–0581 or 800/777–6193, FAX 504/529–1165. 60 rooms, 42 suites. Facilities: 2 restaurants, piano bar, 24-hr concierge, limousine, valet service, parking. AE, D, DC, MC, V.*

$ Rue Royal Inn. This circa 1850 home has balcony rooms overlooking a courtyard and Royal Street; one suite has a Jacuzzi. Each room has a coffeemaker and a small refrigerator. *1006 Royal St., 70116, ☏ 504/524–3900 or 800/776–2901, FAX 504/947–7454. 17 rooms, 2 with kitchenettes. AE, D, DC, MC, V.*

$ ★ St. Charles Guest House. Room sizes in this simple, family-run guest house in the Garden District vary from large to small "backpacker" rooms with shared baths and no air-conditioning. *1748 Prytania St., 70130, ☏ 504/523–6556. 26 rooms (4 share bath). Facilities: Continental breakfast, pool, lounge. AE, MC, V.*

The Arts and Nightlife

The Friday edition of the *Times-Picayune* and the weekly *Gambit* (free) carry comprehensive calendars of events in the arts and entertainment. *New Orleans* magazine (on newsstands), *This Week in New Orleans* and *Where: New Orleans* (both available free in hotels) also publish calendars of events. Credit-card purchases of tickets for events at the Saenger Performing Arts Center and UNO Lakefront Arena can be made through **TicketMaster** (☏ 504/888–8181).

The Arts

THEATER

The avant-garde and the satirical are among the offerings at **Contemporary Arts Center** (900 Camp St., ☏ 504/523–1216). **Le Petit Théâtre du Vieux Carré** (616 St. Peter St., ☏ 504/522–2081) presents more traditional fare, as well as children's theater. Touring Broadway shows and top-name talent appear at the **Saenger Performing Arts Center** (143 N. Rampart St., ☎ 504/524–2490). Nationally known artists perform at **Kiefer UNO Lakefront Arena** (6801 Franklin Ave., ☎ 504/286–7222).

CONCERTS

Free jazz concerts are held on weekends in **Dutch Alley** (French Market at St. Philip St., ☎ 504/522–2621).

Nightlife

New Orleans is a 24-hour town, meaning that there are no legal closing times and it ain't over till it's over. Bourbon Street in the French Quarter is lined with clubs; many local hangouts are Uptown.

JAZZ

Aboard the ***Creole Queen*** (Poydras St. Wharf, CBD, ☎ 504/529–4567) you'll cruise with jazz and a buffet. Live traditional jazz is also on land at the **Palm Court Jazz Cafe** (1204 Decatur St., French Quarter, ☎ 504/525–0200), **Pete Fountain's** (2 Poydras St., CBD, ☎ 504/523–4374), and **Preservation Hall** (726 St. Peter St., French Quarter, ☎ 504/523–8939).

R&B, CAJUN, ROCK, NEW WAVE

Top-notch local and nationally known musicians perform at **House of Blues** (225 Decatur St., French Quarter, ☎ 504/529–2583) and **Margaritaville Café** (1104 Decatur St., French Quarter, ☎ 504/592–2565). An institution, Professor Longhair's **Tipitina's** (501 Napoleon Ave., Uptown, ☎ 504/897–3943) is a laid-back place with a mixed bag of music. **Jimmy's Music Club** (8200 Willow St., Uptown, ☎ 504/861–8200) is popular with the college crowd. Industrial-strength rock rolls out of the sound system at the **Hard Rock Café** (440 N. Peters St., ☎ 504/529–8617). Two-step to a Cajun band at the **Maple Leaf Bar** (8316 Oak St., Uptown, ☎ 504/866–9359), **Mulate's** (201 Julia St., Warehouse District, ☎ 504/522–1492), and **Michaul's** (840 St. Charles Ave., CBD, ☎ 504/522–5517).

BARS

Pat O'Brien's (718 St. Peter St., French Quarter, ☎ 504/525–4823) has three lively bars. **Lafitte's Blacksmith Shop** (941 Bourbon St., French Quarter, ☎ 504/523–0066) and the **Napoleon House** (500 Chartres St., French Quarter, ☎ 504/524–9752) are longtime favorite hangouts.

CASINOS

Construction has begun on **Harrah's Casino New Orleans.** The $800 million, 200,000-square-ft facility—touted as the world's largest—is scheduled to open in May 1996. A temporary casino, housed in the renovated Municipal Auditorium in Armstrong Park and also operated by Harrah's, opened in May 1995. Meanwhile, the waterways in and around the city are aslosh with riverboat casinos. Some actually cruise, but others, contrary to state law, offer dockside gambling. At press time (summer 1995), legal action threatened to close the ***Star Casino***, the first riverboat casino to open in the area. New additions to the flotilla of riverboat casinos include the ***Flamingo*** (Riverwalk and the Hilton Hotel), the ***Boomtown Belle*** (Harvey Canal on the West bank), the ***Treasure Chest*** (Lake Pontchartrain in Kenner), and ***Circus Circus*** (Chalmette). At the River City development upriver of the Crescent City Connection, two additional riverboats were scheduled to open by March 1995.

Excursion to Plantation Country

Getting There

By car, take I–10W or U.S. 61 from New Orleans and follow the signs to the various plantations. Plantation Country maps are available at the New Orleans Welcome Center (*see* Tourist Information, *above*). Many local tour operators include visits to plantations in their itineraries (*see* Orientation Tours, *above*).

What to See and Do

Plantation Country lies upriver from New Orleans. You can see what went with the wind, and hear tales of Yankee invaders and ghosts, in some of the fine restored antebellum plantations sprinkled around the Great River Road between New Orleans and Baton Rouge, the state capital. The drive is marred by industrial plants, but elegant mansions such as **Nottoway** and **Houmas House** make the trip worthwhile.

CAJUN COUNTRY

Tourist Information

Southwest Louisiana: Convention & Visitors Bureau (1211 N. Lakeshore Dr., Lake Charles 70601, ☎ 318/436–9588 or 800/456–7952, FAX 318/494–7952). **Lafayette:** Convention & Visitors Commission (1400 N.W. Evangeline Thruway, Box 52066, ☎ 318/232–3808, 800/346–1958, or 800/543–5340 in Canada; FAX 318/232–0161).

Getting There

By Plane

Lafayette Regional Airport (☎ 318/232–2808) is served by American Eagle, Atlantic Southeast (Delta), Continental, and Northwest Airlink. **Lake Charles Regional Airport** (☎ 318/477–6051) is served by American Eagle and Continental.

By Car

The fastest route from New Orleans through Cajun Country is I–10W. U.S. 90 is a slower but more scenic drive. If you have time, take the back roads for exploring this area. Ferries across the Mississippi cost $1 per car; most bridges are free.

By Train

Amtrak (☎ 800/872–7245) serves Franklin, Schriever, Lafayette, New Iberia, and Thibodaux.

By Bus

Greyhound (☎ 800/231–2222) has frequent daily service to Lafayette, Lake Charles, and environs.

Exploring Cajun Country

Cajun Country, or Acadiana, comprises 22 parishes (counties) of southern Louisiana to the west of New Orleans. This is the cradle of the Cajun craze that swept the nation in the 1980s.

Cajuns are descendants of 17th-century French settlers who established a colony they called l'Acadie ("Cajun" is a corruption of "Acadian") in the present-day Canadian provinces of Nova Scotia and New Brunswick. After the British expelled the Acadians in the mid-18th century (their exile is described in Longfellow's epic poem *Evangeline*), they eventually found a home in southern Louisiana. They have been here since 1762, sharing their unique cuisine and culture with the nation and imbuing the region with a distinctive flavor summed up in the Cajun phrase, "Laissez les bons temps rouler!"

U.S. 90 dips down south of New Orleans into Terrebonne Parish, a major center for shrimp and oyster fisheries. (The blessing of the shrimp fleets in Chauvin and Dulac is a colorful April event.) A slew of swamp tours are based here, including **Annie Miller's Terrebonne Swamp & Marsh Tours** (☏ 504/879–3934). **Hammond's Cajun Air Tours** (☏ 504/876–0584) takes passengers up for a gull's-eye view of the alligators and other critters that inhabit the coastal wetlands.

Morgan City, on the Atchafalaya River, struck it rich when the first producing offshore oil well was completed on November 14, 1947, and the Kerr–McGee Rig No. 16 ushered in the "black gold rush." In 1917, the original *Tarzan of the Apes* was filmed in Morgan City; at the town **Information Center** (725 Myrtle St., ☏ 504/384–3343) a video of the film can be seen.

West of Morgan City, Rte. 182 branches off U.S. 90 and ambles northwest toward Lafayette. For much of the way the road travels along **Bayou Teche,** the largest of the state's many bayous. (*Teche* is an Indian word meaning "snake." According to an ancient legend, the death throes of a giant snake carved the bayou.) The road runs by rice paddies and canebrakes, and on the bayous you can see Cajun pirogues (canoelike boats) and cypress cabins built on stilts.

Traveling along Rte. 182, you'll come to **Franklin,** an official Main Street U.S.A. town (the title is bestowed by the National Trust for Historic Preservation). The street, lined with old-fashioned street lamps, rolls out beneath an arcade of live oaks. Six antebellum homes are open for tours in and around town. Franklin is nestled along a bend in Bayou Teche, and there is a splendid view of it from Parc sur le Teche.

Northwest of Franklin, **New Iberia**—the "Queen City of the Teche"—was founded in 1779 by Spanish settlers who named it for their homeland. **Shadows-on-the-Teche** (317 E. Main St., ☏ 318/369–6446; admission charged), one of the south's best-known plantation homes, was built in 1834 for sugar planter David Weeks. The big brick house is virtually enveloped in moss-draped live oak trees.

Red-hot Tabasco sauce was created in Louisiana in the 19th century; on **Avery Island** at **McIlhenny's Tabasco Company** (Rte. 329, ☏ 318/369–6243), southwest of New Iberia, you can tour the factory where it's still being manufactured by descendants of its creator. Here also are the 200-acre **Jungle Garden,** lush with tropical plants, and **Bird City,** a sanctuary with flurries of snow-white egrets.

Avery Island is actually a salt dome, capped by lush vegetation. So, too, is Jefferson Island, also called **Live Oak Gardens** (284 Rip Van Winkle Rd., off Rte. 14, ☏ 318/365–3332). The 19th-century American actor Joseph Jefferson, who toured the country portraying Rip Van Winkle, built a winter home here. His three-story house is surrounded by lovely formal and informal gardens.

Rte. 31 is a pretty country road that hugs the banks of the Teche between New Iberia and St. Martinville to the north. The little town of **St. Martinville** is awash with legends. Now a sleepy village, it was known in the 18th century as "Petit Paris," a refuge for aristocrats fleeing the French Revolution. It was also a major debarkation point for the exiled Acadians. Longfellow's poem was based on the true story of two young lovers who were separated for years during the Acadian exile.

The **Evangeline Oak** (Evangeline Blvd. at Bayou Teche) is said to have been the place where the ill-starred lovers met again—albeit briefly. On the town square is **St. Martin de Tours,** mother church of the Acadians, and the **Petit Paris Museum,** where there is a Mardi Gras collection. Be sure to visit the small cemetery behind the church, where a bronze statue depicts the real-life Evangeline.

The nearby hamlet of **Breaux Bridge** calls itself the Crawfish Capital of the World. The **Crawfish Festival,** held each May, draws upwards of 100,000 people. The town's other claim to fame is the Cajun food and music spot **Mulate's** (*see* Dining and Lodging, *below*).

Fifteen minutes west of Breaux Bridge, **Lafayette** proudly proclaims itself the capital of French Louisiana. In this part of the state, some 40% of the residents speak Cajun French, an antique, 17th-century dialect. As most Cajuns also speak standard French as well as English, this is a superb place to test your language skills. **Cajun Mardi Gras** rivals its sister celebration in New Orleans. Centrally located, Lafayette is a good base for exploring the region. The **Lafayette Natural History Museum** (637 Girard Park Dr., ☎ 318/268–5544; admission charged), within luxuriant Girard Park, offers workshops, movies, concerts, light shows, and a planetarium. It's also the venue for the annual September **Louisiana Native Crafts Festival.** The **Acadiana Park Nature Station** (E. Alexandre St., ☎ 318/235–6181) is a three-story cypress-pole structure with an interpretive center, discovery boxes for children, a nature trail, and guided tours (fee). The **Acadian Cultural Center** (501 Fisher Rd., ☎ 318/232–0789 or 318/232–0961), a unit of the **Jean Lafitte National Historical Park and Preserve,** traces the history of the Acadians through numerous audiovisual exhibits, including an excellent introductory film dramatizing the Acadian exile.

Small towns dot the flatlands west of Lafayette; residents are called Prairie Cajuns. **Eunice,** a tiny speck of a town, is home of the **"Rendez-Vous des Cajuns"** (*see* The Arts and Nightlife, *below*), the **Prairie Acadian Cultural Center** (corner of S. 3rd St. and Park Ave., ☎ 318/457–8499), and the **Eunice Museum** (220 S. C.C. Duson Dr., ☎ 318/457–6540; admission charged). In a former railroad depot, the museum contains displays on Cajun culture, including its music and Mardi Gras. Eunice and the surrounding villages of Mamou, Church Point, and Iota are the major stomping grounds for the annual **Courir du Mardi Gras,** which features a band of masked and costumed horseback riders on a mad dash through the countryside.

North of Lafayette, **Grand Coteau** is a religious and educational center, and the entire peaceful little village is on the National Register of Historic Places. Of particular note here is the **Church of St. Charles Borromeo,** a simple wooden structure with an ornate high-baroque interior. Nearby **Chretien Point Plantation** (about 4 mi from Sunset on the Bristol/Bosco Rd., ☎ 318/662–5876; admission charged), a splendid antebellum mansion, is a bed-and-breakfast. The staircase in Tara, Scarlett O'Hara's home in *Gone with the Wind,* was modeled on the one in this house.

A short drive up I–49 is **Opelousas,** the third-oldest town in the state. Founded by the French in 1720, the town was named for the Appalousa Indians, who lived in the area centuries before the French and Spanish arrived. For a brief period during the Civil War, Opelousas served as the state capital. At the intersection of I–49 and U.S. 190, the **Acadiana Tourist Commission** (☎ 318/948–6263) houses memorabilia of Jim Bowie, the Alamo hero who spent his boyhood here. The **Opelousas**

Museum and Interpretive Center (329 N. Main St., ☎ 318/948–2589) traces the history of this region.

Tucked away in the far southwestern corner of the state, **Lake Charles** is a straight shot (71 mi) from Lafayette on I–10. Called Charlie's Lake in the 1760s, the city has more than 50 mi of rivers, lakes, canals, and bayous. The **Imperial Calcasieu Museum** (204 W. Sallier St., ☎ 318/439–3797) has an extensive collection on Lake Charles and Imperial Calcasieu Parish, including an old-fashioned pharmacy, an Audubon collection, a Gay '90s barbershop, and a fine-arts gallery. The **Children's Museum** (925 Enterprise Blvd., ☎ 318/433–9420; admission charged) has innovative hands-on exhibits, including a miniature courtroom and grocery store, a brass rubbing center, and interactive computer games.

The **Creole Nature Trail** (*see* Scenic Drives, *above*) begins on Rte. 27 in Sulphur and continues on Rte. 82. Beautiful in the spring, this drive goes to the **Sabine Wildlife Refuge,** where a paved trail meanders into the wilds. There is an interpretive center and a tower at the end of the trail, which gives you an excellent view of the wilderness. (Take along some insect repellent!)

You can make a detour off the Creole Nature Trail and continue east on Rte. 82 (Hug-the-Coast Highway), which whips along the windswept coastal marshes through **Grand Chenier** to the **Rockefeller Wildlife Refuge.** At this 84,000-acre preserve thousands of ducks, geese, 'gators, wading birds, otters, and others while away the winter months.

Shopping

For Cajun food-to-go, try the **Cajun Country Store** (401 E. Cypress St., Lafayette, ☎ 318/233–7977) and **B.F. Trappey's & Sons** (900 E. Main St., New Iberia, ☎ 318/365–8281).

Antiques-seeking is a favorite pastime here. In Lafayette you can root around **Ruins & Relics** (802 Jefferson and Taft Sts., ☎ 318/233–9163) and **Travel Treasures Antique Mall** (Hwy. 93 and W. Congress St., ☎ 318/981–9414).

Sports and the Outdoors

Biking

These flatlands and lush parks make for easy riding. Bikes can be rented at **Pack & Paddle** (601 E. Pinhook Rd., Lafayette, ☎ 318/232–5854).

Canoeing

Paddling is almost a breeze on the easygoing Whisky Chitto Creek. Canoes can be rented at **Arrowhead Canoe Rentals** (9 mi west of Oberlin on Rte. 26, ☎ 318/639–2086 or 800/637–2086).

Fishing

Trips to fish, sightsee, bird-watch, or hunt can be arranged at **Cajun Fishing Tours** (1925 E. Main St., New Iberia, ☎ 318/364–7141). **Sportsman's Paradise** (☎ 504/594–2414) is a charter fishing facility 20 mi south of Houma. **Salt, Inc. Charter Fishing Service** (☎ 504/594–6626 or 504/594–7581), on Rte. 56 south of Houma at Coco Marina, offers fishing trips in the bays and barrier islands of lower Terrebonne Parish, as well as into the Gulf of Mexico. **Hackberry Rod & Gun** (☎ 318/762–3391) in Cameron (in the far southwest corner of the state) is a charter saltwater-fishing service.

Golf

City Park Golf Course (Mudd Ave. and 8th St., Lafayette, ☎ 318/268–5557), **Pine Shadows Golf Center** (750 Goodman Rd., Lake Charles, ☎ 318/433–8681), and **Vieux Chêne Golf Course** (Youngsville Hwy., Broussard, ☎ 318/837–1159) all have 18 holes.

Hiking and Nature Trails

The Old Stagecoach Road in Lake Charles's **Sam Houston Jones State Park** is a favorite for hikers who want to explore the park and the various tributaries of the Calcasieu River; the **Louisiana State Arboretum** in Ville Platte is a 600-acre facility with 4 mi of nature trails (for both, *see* National and State Parks, *above*). There are 7 mi of hiking trails in the **Port Hudson State Commemorative Area** near Baton Rouge (756 W. Plains-Port Hudson Rd. [Hwy. 61], Zachary, ☎ 504/654–3775). Near Natchitoches, backpackers and hikers explore the 8,700-acre **Kisatchie Hills Wilderness** with its Backbone Trail, part of the Kisatchie National Forest (*see* National and State Parks, *above*).

Horseback Riding

Trail rides, pony rides, and even hayrides are offered at **Broken Arrow Stables** (3505 Broken Arrow Rd., off Rte. 3013, New Iberia, ☎ 318/369–7669).

Spectator Sports

NBA exhibition and collegiate basketball, professional soccer exhibition games, wrestling, and other sports events take place at the **Cajundome** (444 Cajundome Blvd., Lafayette, ☎ 318/265–2100).

Thoroughbred racing can be seen April through Labor Day at **Evangeline Downs** (I–10 at I–49, Lafayette, ☎ 318/896–7266).

Dining and Lodging

With the state's wealth of waterways, it is no surprise that Louisiana tables are laden with seafood in every imaginable and innovative variety. In South Louisiana, sea creatures are prepared with a Cajun flair. Sleeping accommodations run from homey bed-and-breakfasts to chain motels to luxury hotels to elegant antebellum mansions open for overnighters. For price ranges, see Charts 1 (B) and 2 (B) in On the Road with Fodor's.

Breaux Bridge

DINING

★ **Mulate's.** This renowned roadhouse with tables covered in checkered plastic features Cajun seafood and dancing to live Cajun music noon and night. *325 Mills Ave.,* ☎ *800/422–2586; in LA, 800/634–9880. AE, MC, V. $$*

Carencro

DINING

★ **Prudhomme's Cajun Café.** In a suburb of Lafayette, celebrity chef Paul Prudhomme's sister Enola has a country-kitchen café with outstanding Cajun fare. *4676 N.E. Evangeline Thruway,* ☎ *318/896–7964. AE, MC, V. Closed Mon. $–$$*

Lafayette

DINING

★ **Prejean's.** Housed in a cypress cottage, this local favorite has a cozy oyster bar, red-checked cloths, and live music nightly. Huge platters of traditional and new Cajun seafood are the specialties. *3480 U.S. 167N, next to Evangeline Downs,* ☎ *318/896–3247. AE, DC, MC, V. $$*

LODGING

Holiday Inn Central–Holidome. Built around an atrium that's banked with greenery, this modern motel has rooms done in contemporary decor and 17 acres within which you can find almost everything you'd ever need for a long life. *Box 91807, 70509, ☎ 318/233–6815 or 800/942–4868, FAX 318/225–1954. 250 rooms. Facilities: restaurant, cocktail lounge, heated indoor pool with whirlpool, sauna, 2 lighted tennis courts, 24-hr jogging track, game rooms, playgrounds, picnic area, airport shuttle. AE, D, DC, MC, V. $$$*

★ **Best Western Hotel Acadiana.** Near Bayou Vermilion, this is a plush hotel whose rooms have thick carpeting, marble-top dressers, and wet bars. Even-numbered rooms face the pool. The hotel also has rooms for people with disabilities. *1801 W. Pinhook Rd., 70508, ☎ 318/233–8120 or 800/826–8386; in LA, 800/874–4664; FAX 318/234–9667. 304 rooms. Facilities: restaurant, cocktail lounge, free parking, outdoor pool. AE, D, DC, MC, V. $–$$*

Lake Charles

DINING

★ **Café Margaux.** You might feel more comfortable in a jacket and tie at this restaurant, where candlelight, tuxedoed waiters, and a 5,000-bottle mahogany wine cellar provide the setting for specialties that include rack of lamb *en croûte* and fillet of flounder with lump crabmeat and brown meunière sauce. *765 Bayou Pines, ☎ 318/433–2902. Reservations advised. AE, MC, V. Closed Sun. $$$*

LODGING

Holiday Inn, Lake Charles. Perched between the lake and the interstate, this hotel has traditional furnishings in rooms done in soothing earth tones. Hotel guests can stroll through a "casino walk" to board the **Players Riverboat Casino** (see *Gambling*, below), which docks next door. There are rooms for nonsmokers and for people with disabilities. *505 N. Lakeshore Dr., 70601, ☎ 318/433–7121 or 800/367–1814; in LA, 800/433–8809; FAX 318/436–8459. 270 rooms. Facilities: restaurant, coffee shop, gift shop, laundry, outdoor pool, free parking, video poker. AE, D, DC, MC, V. $$*

Chateau Charles Hotel & Conference Center. Set on 25 acres, the hotel includes two-bedroom suites with wet bars, microwaves, and minirefrigerators, as well as rooms for nonsmokers and for guests with disabilities. *Box 1269, 70602, ☎ 318/882–6130 or 800/935–6130, FAX 318/882–6601. 212 rooms, 4 suites. Facilities: restaurant, lounge, laundry. AE, D, DC, MC, V. $–$$*

Napoleonville

LODGING

★ **Madewood.** Expect gracious southern hospitality in this antiques-filled Greek Revival plantation mansion, which is both elegant and cozy. There are rooms in the main mansion and suites in a restored outbuilding; rates include breakfast and a candlelight dinner. *4250 Rte. 308, 70390, ☎ 504/369–7151 or 800/375–7151. 5 rooms, 3 suites. AE, D, MC, V. $$$*

Opelousas

DINING

Palace Café. This down-home coffee shop on the town square, operated by the same family since 1927, serves steaks, fried chicken, sandwiches, burgers, and seafood. Locals flock here for the homemade baklava. *167 W. Landry St., ☎ 318/942–2142. MC, V. $*

St. Martinville

DINING AND LODGING

★ **La Place d'Evangeline.** Rooms are spacious at this bed-and-breakfast on the banks of the Bayou Teche. The restaurant serves hearty portions of seafood and Cajun dishes; the homemade bread is superb. *220 Evangeline Blvd., 70582, ☎ 318/394–4010. 5 rooms. AE, MC, V. $$*

The Arts and Nightlife

The Arts

CONCERTS

Major concert attractions are booked into Lafayette's **Cajundome** (444 Cajundome Blvd., ☎ 318/265–2100) and **Heymann Performing Arts & Convention Center** (1373 S. College Rd., ☎ 318/268–5540), and into the **Lake Charles Civic Center** (900 Lakeshore Dr., Lake Charles, ☎ 318/491–1256).

THEATER

The **Lake Charles Little Theater** (813 Enterprise Blvd., Lake Charles, ☎ 318/433–7988) puts on plays and musicals. The **Théâtre 'Cadien** (Lafayette, ☎ 318/893–5655 or 318/262–5810) performs plays in French at various venues. **Lafayette Community Theater** (529 Jefferson St., ☎ 318/235–1532) offers contemporary plays with a Cajun flair.

Nightlife

CAJUN MUSIC

Mulate's in Breaux Bridge and **Prejean's** in Lafayette (*see* Dining and Lodging, *above*) and **Randol's** (2320 Kaliste Saloom Rd., Lafayette, ☎ 318/981–7080) regularly feature Cajun music and dancing. **Belizaire's** (2307 N. Parkerson Ave., Crowley, ☎ 318/788–2501) is a great place for Cajun food and dancing. **Slim's Y-Ki-Ki** (Rte. 167, Washington Rd., Opelousas, ☎ 318/942–9980), a black Cajun club, is one of the best Cajun dance venues in the state. **Fred's Lounge** (420 6th St., Mamou, ☎ 318/468–5411) is a bar with live Saturday-morning radio broadcasts (8 AM to 1 PM) and plenty of dancing. **"Rendez-Vous des Cajuns"** (Liberty Theatre, Park Ave. at 2nd St., Eunice, ☎ 318/457–6575) is a live Saturday-night radio show, mostly in French, that's been described as a combination of the "Grand Ole Opry," the "Louisiana Hayride," and the "Prairie Home Companion."

GAMBLING

Merv Griffin's 1,700-passenger **Players Riverboat Casino** (☎ 800/275–6378), whose action includes blackjack, roulette, craps, and 800 slot machines, embarks on six three-hour cruises daily.

ELSEWHERE IN THE STATE

Natchitoches and North Central Louisiana

Getting There

I–49 cuts diagonally from southeast to northwest, connecting Lafayette with Shreveport. Rte. 1 runs diagonally from the northwest corner all the way to Grand Isle on the Gulf of Mexico.

What to See and Do

Nestled in the piney hills of north-central Louisiana, **Natchitoches** (pronounced "nak-a-tish") is the oldest permanent European settlement of the Louisiana Purchase, four years older than New Orleans. The town has a quaint 33-block historic district with brick-paved streets and buildings garbed in lacy ironwork. In the center of the downtown area is pretty Cane River Lake, edged with weeping willows and rolling green lawns. If it all looks familiar to you, it's because Natchitoches appeared in the film version of *Steel Magnolias.* You can take trolley tours of town and cruises on the water. Popular attractions include the **Christmas Festival of Lights,** which draws about 150,000 people annually, and the **October Pilgrimage,** when several historic houses are open for tours.

Rte. 494 follows the lake southward from town, bordered by arching trees and dotted with handsome plantation houses. Famed primitive artist Clementine Hunter lived and worked at **Melrose Plantation** (Rte. 493, Melrose, ☎ 318/379–0055; admission charged), where nine quaint buildings can be toured. Twenty miles south of Natchitoches, the **Kate Chopin House** (Rte. 495, Cloutierville, ☎ 318/379–2233; admission charged) was home in the 19th century to Kate Chopin, author of *The Awakening,* and now houses the Bayou Folk Museum.

To the west of Natchitoches, 15 mi south of Many, lies **Hodges Gardens** (U.S. 171, ☎ 318/586–3523; admission charged), 4,700 acres of rolling pine forests with streams, waterfalls, and formal, multilevel botanical gardens, where flowers and shrubs bloom year-round. Just to the west is the huge **Toledo Bend Lake,** a camping, boating, and bass-fishing delight that lies along the Texas border.

The **Natchitoches Parish Tourist Commission** (781 Front St., Box 411, 71458, ☎ 318/352–8072) has information on the entire area, including walking and driving tour maps.

Shreveport and North Louisiana

Getting There

Shreveport Regional Airport is served by American, Continental, Delta, Northwest, TWA, and USAir. I–20 and U.S. 80 run east–west through the northern part of the state; Rte. 1 cuts diagonally from the northwest corner to the Gulf of Mexico; I–49 connects Shreveport with South Louisiana. Other north–south routes are U.S. 171, 71, 165, and 167.

What to See and Do

While South Louisiana dances to Cajun tunes and dines on Creole and Cajun fare, most of North Louisiana has more in common with Mississippi, Georgia, and other southern states; Shreveport's ties are largely to neighboring Texas. North of Alexandria, the flat marshlands and gray earth give way to stands of pine trees and bluffs of rich red clay. It is not for naught that Louisiana is known as Sportsman's Paradise. Both the north and south of the state are laced with rivers and lakes, with ample places for camping, fishing, and hunting.

Shreveport and Bossier City, joined by the Red River, comprise the largest metropolitan area in North Louisiana. A cultural center, **Shreveport** has a symphony orchestra, resident opera and ballet companies, and excellent community-theater productions. The prestigious **R. W. Norton Art Gallery** (4747 Creswell Ave., ☎ 318/865–4201) has superb European and American art, including the Southwest's largest permanent collection of works by Frederic Remington and Charles M. Russell. The **Louisiana State Museum** (Fairgrounds, ☎ 318/632–2020) has extensive displays and dioramas depicting the state's history, including a large collection of Native American artifacts from Poverty Point and other important excavations in Louisiana. The **American Rose Center** (Jefferson-Paige Rd., ☎ 318/938–5402; admission charged), headquarters of the American Rose Society, is a 118-acre pinewoods park with more than 20,000 rosebushes in more than 60 individual gardens. The place is lit up like a Christmas tree during the "Christmas in Roseland" light show, which runs from the day after Thanksgiving through New Year's Eve. Three new riverboat casinos now float on the water here: **Harrah's Casino** (Shreveport, ☎ 800/427–7247), **Isle of Capri Casino** (Bossier City, ☎ 318/678–7777 or 800/386–4753), and the **Horseshoe Riverboat Casino** (Bossier City, ☎ 800/895–0711). **Louisiana Downs** (I–20 in Bossier City, ☎ 318/551–7223; admission charged), one of the South's largest racetracks, has Thoroughbred racing from April through October.

South of Shreveport, the **Mansfield Battle Park** (Rte. 2, 4 mi south of Mansfield, ☎ 318/872–1474; admission charged) is the site of the last major Confederate victory of the War Between the States. More than 30,000 men were involved in the bitter battle. The site contains monuments and an interpretive center with audiovisual displays.

The **Shreveport-Bossier Convention & Tourist Bureau** (629 Spring St., Shreveport 71166, ☎ 318/222–9391 or 800/551–8682. Visitors centers: Southpark Mall, Jewella Rd., Shreveport 71166; 100 John Wesley Blvd., Bossier City 71111; and Pierre Bossier Mall, Airline Dr., Bossier City 71111) has free maps and information on the region. For instant information, FAX 318/864–2700.

MISSISSIPPI

By Janet Clark

Updated by Sylvia Higginbotham

Capital	Jackson
Population	2.6 million
Motto	By Virtue and Arms
State Bird	Mockingbird
State Flower	Magnolia

Visitor Information

Mississippi Division of Tourism Development (Box 22825, Jackson 39205, ☎ 601/359–3297 or 800/927–6378).

Scenic Drives

The **Natchez Trace Parkway** cuts a 313-mi swath across Mississippi from northeast of Tupelo to Natchez, passing through Jackson at the center of the state. **U.S. 90** runs along the Mississippi Sound from Alabama to Louisiana, offering views of Gulf Coast beaches, ancient live oaks, and historic homes. Along the Mississippi River, **U.S. 61**—birthplace of the blues and also known as "Blues Alley"—runs through flat Delta cotton land to the hills of Vicksburg, then through Natchez to Louisiana.

National and State Parks

NationalParks

Gulf Islands National Seashore (3500 Park Rd., Ocean Springs 39564, ☎ 601/875–9057) includes Ship, Horn, and Petit Bois islands and offers nature trails and expeditions into the marsh. Vicksburg's **National Military Park** (*see* Elsewhere in the State, *below*).

State Parks

Grand Gulf Military Monument (*see* The Natchez Trace, *below*). **J. P. Coleman State Park** (13 mi north of Iuka off U.S. 25; Rte. 5, Box 504, Iuka 38852, ☎ 601/423–6515) includes scenic Pickwick Lake, which has cabins, camping, hiking, and swimming. **Tishomingo State Park** (15 mi south of Iuka and 3 mi north of Dennis off U.S. 25; Rte. 1, Box 880, Tishomingo 38873, ☎ 601/438–6914), which vies with J.P. Coleman for the title of most spectacular Mississippi park, lies in the Appalachian foothills, making its terrain unique in Mississippi. Bring your own provisions to enjoy hiking and water sports.

THE NATCHEZ TRACE

The Natchez Trace Parkway is a long, thin park running from Nashville to Natchez, crossing early paths worn by Choctaw and Chickasaw Indians, flatboatmen, outlaws, itinerant preachers, post riders, soldiers, and settlers. Meticulously manicured by the National Park Service, it is unmarred by billboards, and commercial vehicles are forbidden to use it.

Tourist Information

Natchez–Adams County: Convention & Visitors Bureau (Box 1485, Natchez 39121, ☎ 601/446–6345 or 800/647–6724). **Natchez Trace Parkway:** Visitor Center (Rte. 1, NT–143, Tupelo 38801, ☎ 601/680–4025). **Jackson:** Metro Jackson Convention and Visitors Bureau (Box 1450, 39215, ☎ 601/960–1891 or 800/354–7695). Visitor Information Center (Jim Buck Ross Mississippi Agriculture and Forestry Museum, 1150 Lakeland Dr., ☏ 601/354–6113).

Getting There

By Plane

Jackson's **International Airport** (☏ 601/939–5631), east of the city off I–20, 10 minutes from downtown, is served by Delta, American, and Northwest Airlines.

By Car

The Natchez Trace is interrupted at Jackson, connected by I–55 and I–20, which run through the city. Natchez, the beginning of the Natchez Trace Parkway (but the end of this tour), is also served by U.S. 61.

By Train

Amtrak (☏ 800/872–7245) stops in Jackson on its way south from Memphis to New Orleans.

Exploring the Natchez Trace

The Mississippi segment of the Natchez Trace begins near Tupelo, in the northeast corner of the state in a hilly area of dense forests and sparkling streams. Enjoy some of this natural beauty at **J.P. Coleman State Park** or **Tishomingo State Park** (*see* National and State Parks, *above*).

Tupelo

At the Trace's milepost 266 is the **Natchez Trace Parkway Visitor Center** (*see* Tourist Information, *above*), offering exhibits and the *Official Map and Guide,* with detailed, mile-by-mile information from Nashville to Natchez.

Tupelo (named after the gum tree), the largest city in northern Mississippi, sits in scenic hill country. Site of the 1864 Civil War battle of the same name, it is now famous as the site of **Elvis Presley's birthplace,** a tiny, two-room shotgun house where the singer was born on January 8, 1935. The surrounding **Elvis Presley Park** includes a museum, a gift shop, and the **Elvis Presley Memorial Chapel.** *306 Elvis Presley Dr., ☏ 601/841–1245. Admission charged.*

The three-hour trip from Tupelo to Jackson can easily take an entire day if you stop to read the brown wooden markers describing historic sites, explore nature trails, and admire the neat fields, trees, and wildflower meadows along the way. At **Ridgeland,** the **Mississippi Crafts Center** (Trace milepost 102.4, ☏ 601/856–7546) displays and sells high-quality crafts in a dogtrot log cabin created by members of the Craftsman's Guild of Mississippi. Rest rooms and picnic tables are available.

Jackson

Jackson, the state capital, has an interesting downtown, with many small museums and most of the city's notable architecture. The **Jim Buck Ross Mississippi Agriculture and Forestry Museum** includes 10 old Mississippi farm buildings, as well as a working farm and a 1920s crossroads town. The general store sells snacks and souvenirs; just outside the gates, a shop sells Mississippi crafts and a down-home restaurant serves blue-plate lunches (veggies, crisp fried catfish). *1150 Lakeland Dr., ☏ 601/354–6113. Admission charged.*

The **Mississippi Museum of Art** has changing exhibits and a permanent collection of more than 40,000 works, including 19th- and 20th-century American, southern, and Mississippi art. Its high-tech, hands-on

Natchez Trace

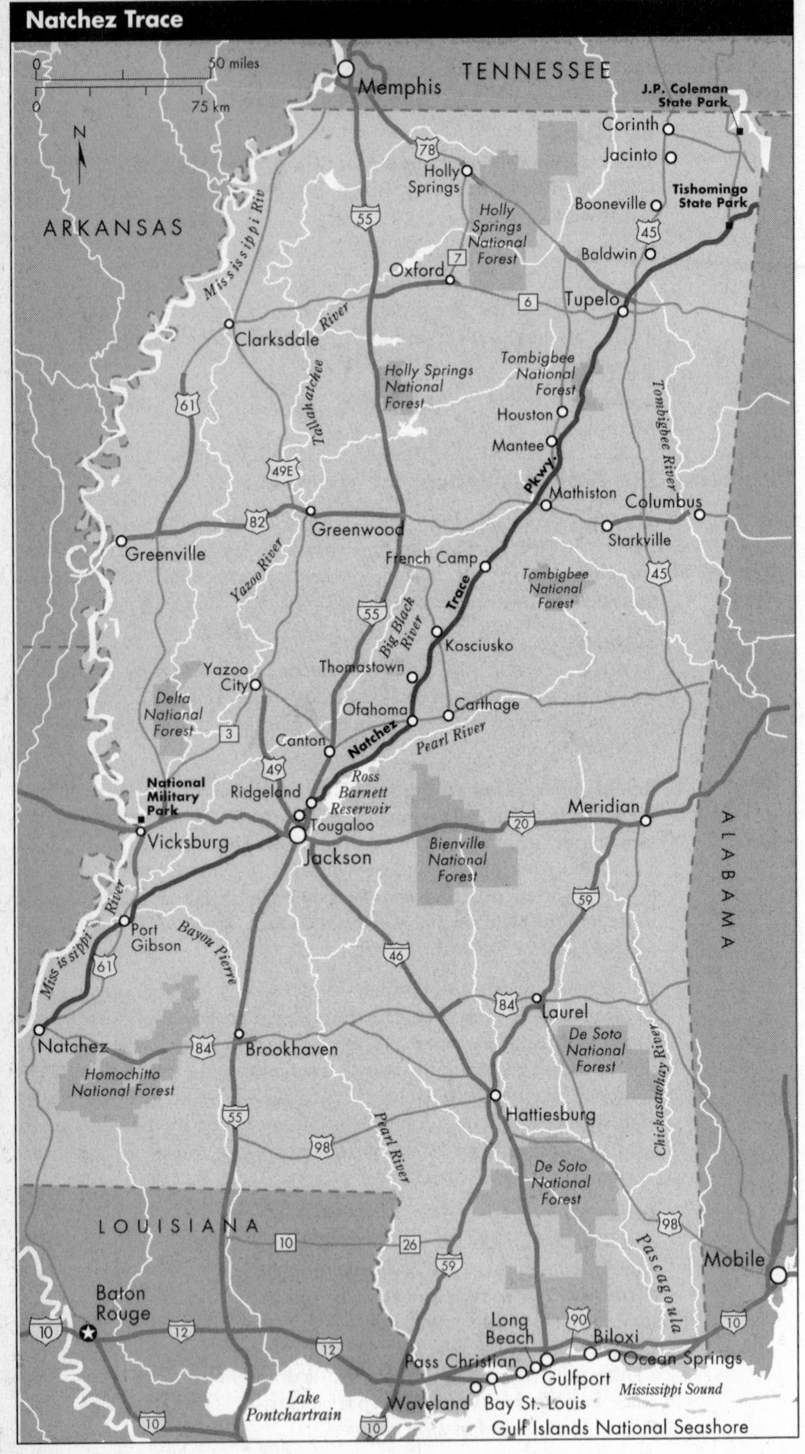

Impressions Gallery (free) combines art and education. *201 E. Pascagoula St.,* ☏ *601/960–1515. Admission charged. Closed Sun.–Mon.*

The **Governor's Mansion** has been the official home of the state's first family since its completion in 1841. It was also General W. T. Sherman's headquarters during his occupation of Jackson in 1863. It is beautifully furnished with antiques. *300 E. Capitol St.,* ☏ *601/359–3175. Tours Tues.–Fri. 9:30–11.*

The **New Capitol** (400 High St., ☏ 601/359–3114) (1903) sits in Beaux Arts splendor, its dome surmounted by a gold-plated copper eagle with a 15-ft wingspan. Elaborate architectural details inside the building include two stained-glass skylights and a painted ceiling.

The **Manship House** (1857) is a restored Gothic Revival home built by the mayor who surrendered the city to General Sherman. *420 E. Fortification St. (enter parking area from Congress St.),* ☏ *601/961–4724. Closed Sun.–Mon.*

To the south, **Port Gibson** is the earliest town to grow up along the Trace that is still in existence. Along **Church Street** many houses and churches have recently been restored; here, too, is the much-photographed **First Presbyterian Church** (1859), its spire topped by a 10-ft hand pointing heavenward. Information on the town's historic sites is available from the **Port Gibson Chamber of Commerce** (south end of Church St., ☏ 601/437–4351).

Just north of Port Gibson is **Grand Gulf Military Monument** (Rte. 2, off U.S. 61, ☏ 601/437–5911; admission charged), built on the site of the town of Grand Gulf, once the most thriving river port between New Orleans and St. Louis. Grand Gulf was partially destroyed in the 1850s, when capricious currents caused the Mississippi to change its course and flood a large section of the town. Already in decline, Grand Gulf was completely destroyed by Federal gunners during the Civil War. Children especially love the steep trail, the observation tower, the old waterwheel, and the bloodstained Civil War uniforms on display in the monument.

Natchez

Because **Natchez** had little military significance, it survived the Civil War almost untouched. Today it is famous for the opulent plantation homes and stylish town houses built between 1819 and 1860, when cotton plantations and the bustling river port poured riches into the city. A number of these houses are open year-round, but others are open only during Natchez Pilgrimage weeks, when crowds flock to see them. The pilgrimages—started in 1932 by the women of Natchez as a way to raise money for preservation—are held twice a year: three weeks in October and four weeks in March and April. Tickets are available at **Pilgrimage Tour Headquarters** (Canal St. at State St., Box 347, 39121, ☏ 601/446–6631 or 800/647–6742), where all tours originate. **Carriage tours** of downtown Natchez begin at Natchez Pilgrimage Tour Headquarters or the Eola Hotel (110 N. Pearl St.).

Rosalie (100 Orleans St., ☏ 601/445–4555), built in 1823, established the ideal form of the southern mansion, with its white columns, hipped roof, and red bricks. Furnishings purchased for the house in 1858 include a famous Belter parlor set. A trip down south is not complete without a visit to the grand and gracious **Stanton Hall** (400 High St., ☏ 601/442–6282), one of the most photographed houses in the country. Built around 1857 for cotton broker Frederick Stanton, the palatial former residence is now run as a house-museum by the Pilgrimage

Garden Club. **Longwood** (140 Lower Woodville Rd., ☎ 601/442–5193) is the largest octagonal house in the United States. Construction began in 1860, but the outbreak of the Civil War prevented its completion; unfinished and mysterious, it is guaranteed to interest both adults and children. All of these houses charge admission.

What to See and Do with Children

Jackson's **Zoological Park** (2918 W. Capitol St., ☎ 601/352–2580) features animals in natural settings, including many endangered species. Also of interest to children is the **Longwood** mansion in Natchez and the **Grand Gulf Military Monument** outside Port Gibson (*see* Exploring the Natchez Trace, *above*).

Shopping

Everyday Gourmet (2905 Old Canton Rd., Jackson, ☎ 601/362–0723; 1625 E. Country Line Rd., Jackson, ☎ 601/977–9258) stocks state products, including pecan pie, muscadine jelly, jams and chutneys, cookbooks, fine ceramic tableware, and bread and biscuit mixes.

Dining and Lodging

For price ranges, see Charts 1 (B) and 2 (B) in On the Road with Fodor's.

Jackson

DINING

Nick's. Large and elegant, this restaurant serves nouvelle versions of regional dishes. Lunch specialties are grilled catfish and pork medallions; for dinner, try eggplant stuffed with deviled crab or blackfish. *1501 Lakeland Dr.,* ☎ *601/981–8017. Jacket and tie required. AE, MC, V. $$$*

The Palette. In a light-filled gallery in the Mississippi Arts Center is one of the state's finest lunch spots. It offers such creations as Mississippi catfish sautéed in pecan butter or fresh vegetable lasagna. *201 E. Pascagoula St.,* ☎ *601/960–2003. MC, V. Closed Mon. No dinner. $$*

Ralph & Kacoo's. Here you'll dine on authentic hot and spicy Cajun food while listening to recorded music from southern Louisiana. The crawfish étoufée is superb. *100 Dyess Rd., just off I–55 and County Line Rd.,* ☎ *601/957–0702. AE, MC, V. $$*

The Mayflower. A perfect 1930s period piece with black-and-white tile floors, straight-back booths, and Formica-topped counters, this café specializes in Greek salads, fresh fish sautéed in lemon butter, and people-watching until all hours. *123 W. Capitol St.,* ☎ *601/355–4122. MC, V. $–$$*

LODGING

Edison Walthall Hotel. The cornerstone and huge brass mailbox are almost all that remain of the original 1920s Walthall Hotel, but the marble floors and paneled library/writing room almost fool you into thinking this is a restoration. The rooms have standard hotel decor, with some wicker furniture. *225 E. Capitol St., 39201,* ☎ *601/948–6161 or 800/932–6161,* FAX *601/948–0088. 208 rooms. Facilities: bar, pool, whirlpool. AE, DC, MC, V. $$$*

Millsaps-Buie House. This 1888 Queen Anne Victorian, restored as a bed-and-breakfast in 1987, is listed on the National Register of Historic Places. The guest rooms are individually decorated with antiques, and the staff is attentive. *628 N. State St., 39202,* ☎ *601/352–0221,* FAX *601/352–0221. 11 rooms. AE, DC, MC, V. $$$*

Renaissance Playa Hotel. This high-rise convention hotel in the north end of town is sleekly contemporary, but the rooms are decorated in traditional style. *1001 County Line Rd., 39211, ☎ 601/957–2800 or 800/228–9898, FAX 601/957–3191. 300 rooms. Facilities: restaurant, bar, airport van. AE, DC, MC, V. $$$*

Natchez

DINING

Natchez Landing. The view of the Mississippi River from the porch tables is enthralling, especially when the ***Delta Queen*** and the ***Mississippi Queen*** steamboats dock. Specialties of the house include barbecue (pork ribs, chicken, and beef) and catfish, fried or grilled. *35 Silver St., Under-the-Hill, ☎ 601/442–6639. AE, MC, V. $$*

Pearl Street Pasta. The fresh pasta dishes at this intimate restaurant, including pasta primavera and breast of chicken with tasso, onions, and mushrooms over angel hair pasta, suggest a taste of Italy in the Mississippi heartland. *105 S. Pearl St., ☎ 601/442–9284. AE, MC, V. $$*

Cock of the Walk. The famous original of a regional franchise, this restaurant in an old train depot overlooking the Mississippi River specializes in fried catfish fillets, fried dill pickles, hush puppies, mustard greens, and coleslaw. *200 N. Broadway, on the Bluff, ☎ 601/446–8920. AE, MC, V. $–$$*

LODGING

Dunleith. At stately, colonnaded Dunleith, a wing for overnight guests offers guest rooms with antiques, fireplaces, and wonderful views of the landscaped grounds. Guests receive a complimentary tour of the house. *84 Homochitto St., 39120, ☎ 601/446–8500 or 800/433–2445. 12 rooms. AE, MC, V. $$$*

Monmouth. This plantation mansion (ca. 1818) was owned by Mississippi governor John A. Quitman from 1826 until his death in 1858. Guest rooms—in the main house, in servants' quarters, and in garden cottages—are furnished with tester beds and antiques. *John A. Quitman Pkwy., 39120, ☎ 601/442–5852 or 800/828–4531, FAX 601/446–7762. 25 rooms. AE, MC, V. $$$*

Natchez Eola. This beautifully restored 1920s hotel has a formal lobby and small guest rooms with antique-reproduction furniture. The Eola is listed as a Historic Hotel of America by the National Trust for Historic Preservation. *110 N. Pearl St., 39120, ☎ 601/445–6000 or 800/888–9140, FAX 601/446–5310. 122 rooms. Facilities: restaurant, lounge. AE, DC, MC, V. $$$*

Ramada Hilltop Motel. This recently remodeled, comfortable motel sits on a bluff overlooking the Mississippi River to the north and Louisiana to the west. *130 John R. Junkin Dr., 39120, ☎ 601/446–6311 or 800/272–6232, FAX 601/446–6321. Facilities: restaurant, lounge, pool. AE, DC, MC, V. $$*

Tupelo

DINING

Harvey's. It's a local favorite serving consistently good chow. Specialties are prime rib and pasta. *424 S. Gloster St., ☎ 601/842–6763. AE, MC, V. Closed Sun. $$*

Jefferson Place. This rambling, late Victorian house is lively inside, with red-checked tablecloths and bric-a-brac. Popular with the college crowd, it features short orders and steaks. *823 Jefferson St., ☎ 601/844–8696. AE, MC, V. Closed Sun. $$*

Papa Vanelli's Pizzaria. Family pictures and scenes of Greece decorate the walls of this comfortably nondescript restaurant. Specialties (all homemade) include pizza with 10 toppings, lasagna, moussaka, and Greek salad. *1302 N. Gloster St., ☎ 601/844–4410. AE, D, MC, V. $*

LODGING

Ramada Inn. This modern hotel caters to business travelers and conventions as well as families. Breakfast and lunch buffets are served. *854 N. Gloster St., 38801, ☎ and FAX 601/844–4111. 230 rooms, 10 suites. Facilities: dining room, lounge with dancing, pool, laundry. AE, DC, MC, V. $$*

Trace Inn. This old, rustic inn on 15 acres near the Natchez Trace offers neat rooms and friendly service. *3400 W. Main St., 38801, ☎ 601/842–5555, FAX 601/844–3105. 134 rooms. Facilities: restaurant, pool, playground, courtesy car. AE, MC, V. $*

Nightlife

Jackson

For live entertainment on weekends, try **Hal and Mal's** (200 S. Commerce St., ☎ 601/948–0888); the **Dock** (Main Harbor Marina at Ross Barnett Reservoir, ☎ 601/856–7765); and **Rodeos** (6107 Ridgewood Rd., ☎ 601/957–9300), where patrons willingly line up outside to line-dance inside.

Natchez

After dark, head for Under-the-Hill, a busy strip of restaurants, gift shops, and bars on the river. Gambling is offered at the permanently docked riverboat casino the ***Lady Luck*** (☎ 601/445–0605), and good times are had at the **Saloon** (☎ 601/446–8023).

OXFORD AND HOLLY SPRINGS

Holly Springs and Oxford, in north Mississippi, are sophisticated versions of the Mississippi small town. Courthouse towns incorporated in 1837, they offer visitors historic architecture, arts and crafts, literary associations, a warm welcome, and those unhurried pleasures of southern life that remain constant from generation to generation: entertaining conversation, good food, and nostalgic walks at twilight. Oxford and Lafayette County were immortalized as "Jefferson" and "Yoknapatawpha County" in the novels of Oxford native William Faulkner.

Tourist Information

Holly Springs: Chamber of Commerce (154 S. Memphis St., 38365, ☎ 601/252–2943). **Oxford:** Chamber of Commerce (115 Courthouse Sq., 38655, ☎ 601/234–4651).

Getting There

By Car

Oxford is accessible from I–55; it is 23 mi east of Batesville on Rte. 6. Holly Springs, near the Tennessee state line, is reached via U.S. 78 and Rtes. 4, 7, and 311.

By Train

Amtrak (☎ 800/872–7245) stops in Batesville.

By Bus

Greyhound Lines (☎ 800/231–2222) has a station in Holly Springs (490 Craft St.).

Exploring Oxford and Holly Springs

Oxford

Courthouse Square is a National Historic Landmark. At its center is the white sandstone **Lafayette** (pronounced "Luh-*fay*-it") **County Courthouse,** rebuilt in 1873 after Union troops burned it; the courtroom on the second floor is original. There's an information center at the nearby City Hall.

University Avenue, from South Lamar Boulevard to the university, is one of the state's most beautiful sights when the trees flame orange and gold in the fall, or when the dogwoods blossom in spring. The **University of Mississippi,** the state's beloved "Ole Miss," opened in 1848. Its tree-shaded campus centers on the **Grove,** surrounded by historic buildings. Facing it is the antebellum **Barnard Observatory** (☎ 601/232–5993), newly and beautifully restored, which houses the **Center for the Study of Southern Culture,** with exhibits on southern music, folklore, and literature and the world's largest blues archive (40,000 records). The **Mississippi Room** (☎ 601/232–7408; closed weekends) in the John Davis Williams Library contains a permanent exhibit on Faulkner, including the Nobel Prize for literature he won in 1949, as well as first editions of works by other Mississippi authors.

Rowan Oak (ca. 1848) was William Faulkner's home from 1930 until his death in 1962. The two-story, white-frame house with square columns is now a National Historic Landmark owned by the university. The writer's typewriter, desk, and other personal items still evoke his presence. *Old Taylor Rd., ☎ 601/234–3284. Closed Mon.*

Faulkner's funeral was held at Rowan Oak, and he was buried in the family plot in **St. Peter's Cemetery** (Jefferson and N. 16th Sts.). Another Faulkner pilgrimage site is **College Hill Presbyterian Church** (8 mi northwest of Oxford on College Hill Rd.), where he and Estelle Oldham Franklin were married on June 20, 1929.

Holly Springs

Holly Springs, 29 mi north of Oxford on Rte. 7, contains more than 200 structures listed on the National Register of Historic Places. These include the 1858 **Montrose** (307 E. Salem Ave., ☎ 601/252–2943; admission charged), open by appointment only, and the privately owned Salem Avenue mansions **Oakleigh, Cedarhurst,** and **Airliewood.**

Dining and Lodging

For price ranges, see Charts 1 (B) and 2 (B) in On the Road with Fodor's.

Holly Springs

DINING

Phillips Grocery. Constructed in 1882 as a saloon for railroad workers, it's decorated today with antiques and crafts and serves big, old-fashioned hamburgers. *541–A Van Dorn Ave., ☎ 601/252–4671. No credit cards. Closed Sun. $*

Oxford

DINING

Downtown Grill. The Grill could be a club in Oxford, England, but the light and airy balcony overlooking the square is pure Oxford, Mississippi. Specialties include seafood gumbo and Cajun-style, spicy catfish Lafitte. *1115 Jackson Ave., ☎ 601/234–2659. AE, MC, V. $$*

Smitty's. Home-style cooking here includes red-eye gravy and grits, biscuits with blackberry preserves, fried catfish, chicken and dumplings, corn bread, and black-eyed peas. The atmosphere is down-home. *208 S. Lamar Blvd., ☎ 601/234–9111. No credit cards. $*

LODGING

Oliver-Britt House. In a restored house built about 1900, this conveniently located B&B run in a casual fashion has pleasant rooms. *512 Van Buren Ave., 38655, ☎ 601/234–8043. 5 rooms. Facility: dining room. AE, MC, V. $$*

Holiday Inn. These functional rooms have no surprises. The restaurant, however, prepares a surprisingly good breakfast. *400 N. Lamar Blvd., 38655, ☎ 601/234–3031, FAX 601/234–2834. 100 rooms. Facilities: restaurant, pool, lounge. AE, DC, MC, V. $*

The Arts

The annual **Faulkner and Yoknapatawpha Conference** is a weeklong summer event that includes lectures by Faulkner scholars and field trips in "Yoknapatawpha County." For information, contact the Center for the Study of Southern Culture (Univ. of Mississippi, Oxford 38677, ☎ 601/232–5993).

Nightlife

In Oxford, the **Gin** (E. Harrison St. and S. 14th St., ☎ 601/234–0024) offers live dance music and the **Hoka** (304 S. 14th St., ☎ 601/234–3057) is a warehouse turned movie theater and restaurant.

ELSEWHERE IN THE STATE

The Delta

Getting There

U.S. 61 runs from Memphis through the Delta to Vicksburg, Natchez, and Baton Rouge, Louisiana.

What to See and Do

Between Memphis and Vicksburg is the **Delta,** a vast agricultural plain created by the Mississippi River. Drive through it, with side trips down Rte. 1 or Rte. 8 for views of the Mississippi, timing it right for lunch in Clarksdale or Boyle and dinner at **Doe's** (502 Nelson St., ☎ 601/334–3315) in Greenville. Greenville has produced an extraordinary number of writers, including William Alexander Percy, Ellen Douglas, Hodding Carter, and Shelby Foote. The **Mississippi Welcome Center** (4210 Washington St., Vicksburg 39180, ☎ 601/638–4269) and the **Greenville/Washington County Convention and Visitors Bureau** (410 Washington Ave., Greenville 38701, ☎ 601/334–2711 or 800/467–3582) provide information on the region; the latter has details about Jim Henson's Delta boyhood and the birthplace of Kermit the Frog.

Ocean Springs

Getting There

U.S. 90 runs through the heart of Ocean Springs.

What to See and Do

On the Mississippi Gulf Coast, this oak-shaded town originated in 1699 as a French fort. It is now known as the former home of artist Walter Anderson (1903–65). He revealed his ecstatic communion with nature in thousands of drawings and watercolors, most of them kept secret until his death. The **Walter Anderson Museum of Art** (510 Washington Ave., ☎ 601/872–3164) displays his work, including his cottage studio with intricately painted walls.

Ocean Springs is also the headquarters of the **Gulf Islands National Seashore** (3500 Park Rd., ☎ 601/875–9057). On the mainland there are nature trails and ranger programs. Out in the Gulf, pristine Ship, Horn, and Petit Bois islands, for which the park is named, have beaches as white and soft as sugar—some of the country's best. Excursion boats to Ship, rimmed by about 7 mi of this remarkable sand, leave from Biloxi in summer and from Gulfport May through October, and charter operators regularly take wilderness lovers to Horn and Petit Bois, both designated wilderness areas, where camping is permitted. The **Ocean Springs Chamber of Commerce** (Box 187, 39566, ☎ 601/875–4424) has information on this area.

Vicksburg

Getting There

I–20 runs east–west and U.S. 61 north–south through Vicksburg.

What to See and Do

During the Civil War, the Confederacy and the Union vied for control of this strategic location on the Mississippi Delta across the river from Louisiana. After a 47-day siege, the city surrendered to Ulysses S. Grant on July 4, 1863, giving the Union control of the river and sounding the death knell for the Confederacy. Vicksburg's **National Military Park** is second only to Gettysburg in interest and beauty. Battle positions are marked, and monuments line the 16-mi drive through the park. *Visitor Center, Clay St. (U.S. 80), I–20 Exit 4B, ☎ 601/636–0583. Admission charged.*

Tours of grand antebellum homes and 24-hour riverfront gambling are other draws. The **Vicksburg Convention and Visitors Bureau** (Box 110, Vicksburg 39181, ☎ 601/636–9421 or 800/221–3536) has abundant information.

TENNESSEE

By Judy Ringel
Updated by Patricia Cheatham

Capital	Nashville
Population	5,099,000
Motto	Agriculture and Commerce
State Bird	Mockingbird
State Flower	Iris

Visitor Information

Tennessee Department of Tourist Development (Box 23170, Nashville 37202, ☎ 615/741–2158).

Scenic Drives

U.S. 421 from Bristol to Trade passes through the Cherokee National Forest and crosses the Appalachian Trail. **Rte. 73** south from Townsend leads through a high valley ringed by the Great Smoky Mountains to the pioneer village of Cades Cove. **Rte. 25** from Gallatin to Springfield travels through an area of Thoroughbred farms and antebellum houses. Between Monteagle and Chattanooga, **I–24** winds through the Cumberland Mountains.

National and State Parks

National Parks

Great Smoky Mountains National Park (Gatlinburg 37738, ☎ 615/436–1200) encompasses towering peaks and lush valleys, with excellent camping and fishing sites and more than 900 mi of horse and hiking trails.

State Parks

The State Parks Division of the **Tennessee Department of Environment and Conservation** (401 Church St., L&C Tower, 7th Floor, Nashville 37243, ☎ 615/532–0103 or 800/421–6683) provides information on Tennessee's 50-plus state parks. The 16,000-acre **Fall Creek Falls State Resort Park** (Rte. 3, Pikeville 37367, ☎ 615/881–5241 or 615/881–3297) has the highest waterfall east of the Rockies. Thick stands of cypress trees make **Reelfoot Lake State Resort Park** (Rte. 1, Box 296, Tiptonville 38079, ☎ 901/253–7756) in northwest Tennessee a favorite wintering ground for the American bald eagle. **Roan Mountain State Resort Park** (Rte. 1, Box 236, Roan Mountain 37687, ☎ 615/772–3303) in northeast Tennessee boasts a 600-acre natural rhododendron garden that blooms in late June.

MEMPHIS

On the bluffs overlooking the Mississippi River, Memphis is Tennessee's largest city and the commercial and cultural center of the western part of the state. It is a blend of southern tradition and modern efficiency, where aging cotton warehouses stand in the shadow of sleek new office buildings and old-fashioned paddle wheelers steam upriver past the city's newest landmark, the gleaming, stainless-steel Pyramid Arena (*see* Exploring Memphis, *below*). Memphis is perhaps best known for its music and for the two extraordinary men who introduced that music to the world: W. C. Handy, the "Father of the Blues," and Elvis Presley, the "King of Rock and Roll."

Tourist Information

Memphis: Convention & Visitors Bureau (47 Union Ave., 38103, ☎ 901/543–5300). Visitors Information Center (340 Beale St., 38103, ☎ 901/576–8171).

Arriving and Departing

By Plane

Memphis International Airport (☎ 901/922–8000), 9 mi south of downtown, is served by most major airlines and is a hub for **Northwest Airlines.** Driving time to downtown is about 15 minutes on I–240. Cab fare runs about $17. **Yellow Cab** (☎ 901/577–7700) operates a limousine service between the airport and downtown for a flat rate of $75.

By Car

Memphis is reached via the north–south I–55 or the east–west I–40. I–240 loops around the city.

By Train

Amtrak (545 S. Main St., ☎ 800/872–7245).

By Bus

Greyhound Lines (203 Union Ave., ☎ 800/231–2222).

By Boat

Memphis is one stop on the paddle-wheeler cruises of the **Delta Queen Steamboat Co.** (Robin Street Wharf, New Orleans, LA 70130, ☎ 800/543–1949). The *Delta Queen* (a National Historic Landmark) and the *Mississippi Queen* (an authentic reproduction) travel between St. Louis and New Orleans.

Getting Around Memphis

Memphis's streets are well marked, and there's plenty of parking, so the city is easily explored by car. The **Memphis Area Transit Authority** (☎ 901/274–6282) operates buses ($1) throughout downtown and the suburbs (there's an additional fare for zones outside the city limits); a trolley (50¢) runs between the north and south ends of downtown.

Exploring Memphis

Downtown

Memphis begins at the Mississippi River, which is celebrated in a 52-acre river park (☎ 901/576–6595; admission charged) on **Mud Island.** A footbridge and monorail at 125 Front Street get you to the island, where a five-block-long **River Walk** replicates the Mississippi's every twist, turn, and sandbar from Cairo, Illinois, to New Orleans. Also in the park are the **Mississippi River Museum,** the famed World War II B–17 bomber ***Memphis Belle,*** an amphitheater, shops, and a swimming pool.

Back in the city, opposite the north end of Mud Island, stands the 32-story, 22,000-seat, stainless-steel **Pyramid Arena** (1 Auction Ave., ☎ 901/526–5177; admission charged for tours), opened in 1991. For a look at Memphis's oldest dwelling, walk 20 minutes southeast to the **Magevney House** (198 Adams Ave., ☎ 901/526–4464; closed Mon.), built in the 1830s by a pioneer schoolteacher.

Heading south on 2nd Street, you'll come to the beautifully restored **Peabody Hotel** (*see* Lodging, *below*) at the corner of Union Avenue. Farther south is **Beale Street,** where W.C. Handy played the blues in the early

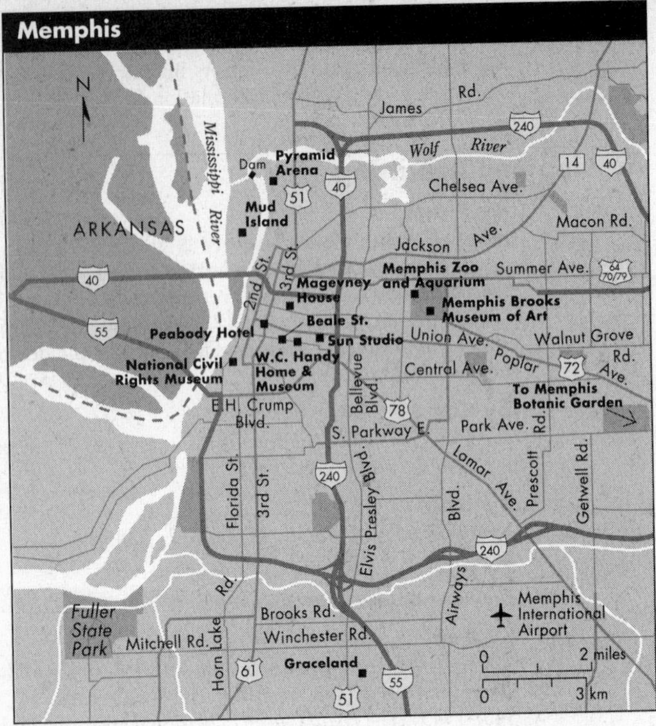

decades of the 20th century, and where clubs and restaurants are thriving once again (*see* The Arts and Nightlife, *below*). The **W.C. Handy Memphis Home and Museum** (352 Beale St., ☎ 901/522–8300; admission charged; open May–Labor Day) displays photos and other memorabilia.

South of Beale, the motel where Dr. Martin Luther King Jr. was assassinated in 1968 has been transformed into the **National Civil Rights Museum,** which documents the movement through interpretive exhibits and audiovisual displays. *406 Mulberry St.,* ☎ *901/521–9699. Admission charged (free Mon. 3–5 PM). Closed Tues.*

Other Attractions

In Overton Park, the popular 70-acre **Memphis Zoo and Aquarium** (2000 Galloway Ave., ☎ 901/725–3400) has a new 9-acre Cat Country. Also in the park, the **Memphis Brooks Museum of Art** (2080 Poplar Ave., ☎ 901/722–3500; admission charged; closed Mon.), which won a national architectural award for its 1990 renovation and addition, houses a collection of fine and decorative arts from antiquity to the present.

Graceland, the estate once owned by Elvis Presley, is 12 mi southeast of downtown. A guided tour of the Colonial-style mansion, automobile museum, and burial site reveals the spoils of stardom—from his two private jets to his gold-covered piano and his glittering stage costumes. *3717 Elvis Presley Blvd.,* ☎ *901/332–3322 or 800/238–2000 (reservations advised, especially in summer). Admission charged. Closed Tues. Nov.–Feb.*

Sun Studio, the birthplace of rock and roll, is where Elvis Presley, Jerry Lee Lewis, B.B. King, and Roy Orbison launched their careers. Tours are given daily. *706 Union Ave. (7 blocks east of downtown),* ☎ *901/521–0664. Admission charged.*

Parks and Gardens

Overton Park, a few miles east of downtown on Poplar Avenue, offers picnic areas, sports fields, hiking and biking trails, a nine-hole golf course, and a cluster of major cultural attractions. In East Memphis, the 96-acre **Memphis Botanic Garden** (750 Cherry Rd., ☎ 901/685–1566) is planted with scores of different species, from camellias to cacti.

What to See and Do with Children

At the **Children's Museum of Memphis** (2525 Central Ave., ☎ 901/458–2678), youngsters can touch, climb, and explore their way through a child-size city. A few blocks east is the **Memphis Pink Palace Museum and Planetarium** (3050 Central Ave., ☎ 901/320–6320), which features a mix of natural- and cultural-history exhibits, plus planetarium laser shows. **Chucalissa Archaeological Museum** (1987 Indian Village Dr., ☎ 901/785–3160) is a reconstruction of a Native American village that existed on the banks of the Mississippi from AD 1000 to 1500. Skilled Choctaw craftsfolk fashion jewelry, weapons, and pottery outside the C.H. Nash Museum, which houses historic versions of the same articles.

Shopping

Oak Court Mall (4465 Poplar Ave., ☎ 901/682–8928), in the busy Poplar/Perkins area of East Memphis, has nearly 70 specialty shops and two department stores. Other popular shopping centers include **Hickory Ridge Mall** (6076 Winchester at Hickory Hill, ☎ 901/367–8045) and the **Mall** (4457 Americanway at Perkins St., ☎ 901/362–9315). Off-price shopping is available at **Belz Factory Outlet Mall** (3536 Canada Rd., I–40 Exit 20, Lakeland, ☎ 901/386–3180).

Spectator Sports

Baseball

The minor-league **Memphis Chicks** (☎ 901/272–1687) play at Tim McCarver Stadium (800 Home Run La.).

Tennis

The **International Indoor Tennis Tournament** (☎ 901/765–4400) is played in February at the Racquet Club in East Memphis (511 Sanderlin Ave.).

Dining

While Memphis restaurants offer a pleasing array of cuisines, the local passion remains barbecue; the city has 70-odd barbecue restaurants. For price ranges, see Chart 1 (B) in On the Road with Fodor's.

$$$ ★ **Chez Philippe.** Chef José Gutierrez serves imaginative and sophisticated dishes in the city's most ornate surroundings. Nightly creations may include lamb with goat cheese and garlic or halibut with fried leeks and sun-dried cherry sauce. *The Peabody, 149 Union Ave., ☎ 901/529–4188. Reservations advised. AE, DC, MC, V. Closed Sun. No lunch.*

Justine's. Set in a gracefully restored Victorian mansion, Justine's offers hearty New Orleans–style Continental cuisine with an emphasis on seafood. *919 Coward Pl., ☎ 901/527–3815. Reservations required. AE, DC, MC, V. Closed Sun.–Mon. No lunch.*

$$$ **La Tourelle.** This turn-of-the-century bungalow in Overton Square has the romantic ambience of a French country inn. Five-course prix fixe meals supplement the à la carte menu. You might feel more comfort-

able in a jacket and tie. *2146 Monroe Ave., ☎ 901/726–5771. Reservations advised. MC, V.*

$$ **Cafe Max.** The atmosphere is lively at this two-story bistro in East Memphis, where menu selections emphasize pasta, seafood, and grilled meats. *6161 Poplar Ave., ☎ 901/767–3633. AE, D, MC, V. No lunch.*

$$ **Landry's Seafood House.** This converted riverfront warehouse seats 300 and packs 'em in for such seafood dishes as fried shrimp and stuffed flounder. *263 Wagner Pl., ☎ 901/526–1966. AE, DC, MC, V.*

$$ ★ **Marena's.** At this charming midtown restaurant, the menu changes monthly to highlight foods from different Mediterranean countries, including Spain, Greece, Israel, and Turkey. *11545 Overton Park, ☎ 901/278–9774. Reservations required. AE, DC, MC, V. BYOB. Closed Sun. No lunch.*

$$ ★ **Paulette's.** For two decades, this Overton Square classic has served delicious crepes and salads and excellent grilled chicken, salmon, and swordfish dishes in the Old World atmosphere of a European inn. Save room for the hot chocolate crepes. *2110 Madison Ave., ☎ 901/726–5128. AE, D, DC, MC, V.*

$ **Cafe Olé.** This popular midtown hangout offers "healthy" Mexican cuisine (no animal fats are used), including spinach enchiladas and chili rellenos. *959 S. Cooper St., ☎ 901/274–1504. AE, D, DC, MC, V.*

$ **Charlie Vergos' Rendezvous.** Tourists and locals alike flock to this downtown basement restaurant to savor Vergos's "dry" barbecued pork ribs and other barbecue specialties. *52 S. 2nd St., ☎ 901/523–2746. AE, DC, MC, V. Closed Sun.–Mon. No lunch Tues.–Thurs.*

$ ★ **Corky's.** There's always a line at this no-frills East Memphis barbecue restaurant. Once you taste the ribs (or sandwiches, or beef or pork platters), you'll understand why. *5259 Poplar Ave., ☎ 901/685–9744. AE, D, DC, MC, V.*

Lodging

Memphis hotels are especially busy during the monthlong Memphis in May International Festival and in mid-August, during Elvis Tribute Week; book well ahead at these times. For B&Bs, contact the **Bed & Breakfast Reservation Service** (Box 41621, Memphis 38174, ☎ 901/726–5920 or 800/336–2087, FAX 901/725–0194). For price ranges, see Chart 2 (B) in On the Road with Fodor's.

$$$ **Adam's Mark Memphis.** Set in the flourishing eastern suburbs near I–240, this 27-story glass tower offers sweeping vistas of the sprawling metropolis and its outskirts. *939 Ridge Lake Blvd., 38120, ☎ 901/684–6664 or 800/444–2326, FAX 901/762–7411. 380 rooms. Facilities: restaurant, coffee shop, lounge with live entertainment, health club, pool. AE, D, DC, MC, V.*

$$$ **French Quarter Suites.** This pleasant Overton Square hotel is reminiscent of a New Orleans–style inn. All suites have oversize whirlpool tubs, and some have balconies. *2144 Madison Ave., 38104, ☎ 901/728–4000 or 800/843–0353, FAX 901/278–1262. 105 suites. Facilities: restaurant, bar, health club, pool. AE, D, DC, MC, V.*

$$$ ★ **Peabody Hotel.** Even if you're not staying here, it's worth a stop to see this 12-story downtown landmark, built in 1925 and impeccably restored in 1981. The lobby preserves its original stained-glass skylights and the travertine marble fountain that is home to the hotel's resident ducks. The rooms are decorated in a variety of period styles. *149 Union Ave., 38103, ☎ 901/529–4000 or 800/732–2639, FAX 901/529–3600. 454 rooms. Facilities: 3 restaurants, lounge, bar, health club, indoor pool. AE, DC, MC, V.*

$$ **Country Suites by Carlson.** This three-story hotel in East Memphis provides many of the comforts of home, including kitchenettes. The decor is vaguely Mesoamerican, with teal carpeting and Aztec-pattern draperies. *4300 Americanway, 38118, ☎ 901/366–9333 or 800/456–4000, FAX 901/366–7835. 121 suites. Facilities: health club, pool, whirlpool. AE, D, DC, MC, V.*

$$ ★ **Holiday Inn East.** Close to I–240 and the bustling Poplar/Ridgeway office complex, this sleek 10-story hotel is popular with business travelers. *5795 Poplar Ave., 38119, ☎ 901/682–7881 or 800/465–4329, FAX 901/682–7881 ext. 7760. 246 rooms. Facilities: restaurant, lounge, health club, pool. AE, D, DC, MC, V.*

$$ **Radisson Hotel.** Across the street from the Peabody, this downtown hotel has its own lobby fountain, complete with a waterfall. Glass-walled elevators whisk guests to rooms around a 10-story atrium. *185 Union Ave., 38103, ☎ 901/528–1800 or 800/333–3333, FAX 901/526–3226. 283 rooms. Facilities: restaurant, lounge, pool, whirlpool, sauna. AE, D, DC, MC, V.*

$ **Howard Johnson Lodge East.** All units at this spacious inn have private patios or balconies; many have refrigerators and microwave ovens, while four have kitchens and whirlpool baths. The Continental breakfast is included in the price. *1541 Sycamore View, 38134, ☎ 901/388–1300 or 800/446–4656, FAX 901/388–1300 ext. 247. 84 rooms and 12 suites. Facilities: pool, coin laundry. AE, D, DC, MC, V.*

$ **La Quinta Inn–Medical Center.** Convenient to midtown, this two-story inn offers spacious, well-maintained rooms. *42 S. Camilla St., 38104, ☎ 901/526–1050 or 800/531–5900, FAX 901/525–3219. 130 rooms. Facility: outdoor pool. AE, D, DC, MC, V.*

$ **Quality Inn Hotel.** This four-story motor lodge near Graceland has spacious, well-appointed rooms with tasteful touches of country decor. *3222 Airways Blvd., 38116, ☎ 901/332–3800 or 800/221–2222, FAX 901/345–2448. 118 rooms. Facilities: pool, exercise room, coin laundry.*

The Arts and Nightlife

Call the Memphis events hot line (☎ 901/681–1111) for information about performances in the city.

The Arts

The **Orpheum Theatre** (203 S. Main St., ☎ 901/525–3000) hosts touring Broadway shows, as well as performances by **Memphis Opera** (☎ 901/678–2706) and **Memphis Concert Ballet** (☎ 901/763–0139). The **Memphis Symphony Orchestra** (3100 Walnut Grove Rd., No. 402, ☎ 901/324–3627; Sept.–May) performs at the **Vincent DeFrank Music Hall** downtown.

Nightlife

To hear the blues as they were meant to be played, head for the clubs on Beale Street. Among the most popular are **B.B. King's Blues Club** (147 Beale St., ☎ 901/524–5464), where B.B. himself occasionally performs, and **Blues Hall/Rum Boogie Cafe** (182 Beale St., ☎ 901/528–0150).

NASHVILLE

Hailed as "Music City, U.S.A." (country music, that is) and birthplace of the "Nashville Sound," Tennessee's fast-growing capital city is also a leading center of higher education, appropriately known as the Athens of the South. The city has spawned such dissimilar institutions as the "Grand Ole Opry" and Vanderbilt University, and has prospered from them both, becoming one of the mid-South's most vibrant communities in the process.

Tourist Information

Nashville: Nashville Convention & Visitors Bureau (161 4th Ave. N, 37219, ☎ 615/259–4700). Visitor information center (I–65 and James Robertson Pkwy., Exit 85, ☎ 615/259–4747).

Arriving and Departing

By Plane

Nashville International Airport (☎ 615/275–1675), about 8 mi east of downtown, is served by major airlines and is a hub for **American Airlines.** To reach downtown by car, take I–40W. Cab fare runs about $16–$18. **Downtown Airport Express** (☎ 615/275–1180) has service to downtown hotels for $8–$10.

By Car

I–65 leads into Nashville from the north and south; I–24, from the northwest and southeast; I–40, from the east and west.

By Bus

Greyhound Lines (200 8th Ave. S, ☎ 800/231–2222).

Getting Around Nashville

The central city is bisected by the Cumberland River; numbered avenues are west of and parallel to it, and numbered streets east of and parallel to it.

By Bus

Metropolitan Transit Authority (MTA) buses (☎ 615/242–4433; fare: $1.15, exact change) serve the county.

By Trolley

Nashville Trolley Company (☎ 615/862–5969; fare: 75¢) trolleys cover downtown and Music Row.

Exploring Nashville

Downtown

Downtown attractions can be covered rather easily on foot. Overlooking the river is **Fort Nashborough** (170 1st Ave. N), a replica of the crude log fort built in 1779 by Nashville's first settlers. A left onto Church Street takes you into the historic 2nd Avenue area—known as the **District**—where 19th-century buildings have been handsomely restored to house offices, restaurants, clubs, boutiques, and residences.

At the corner of 5th Avenue is the **Downtown Presbyterian Church** (5th Ave. and Church St., ☎ 615/254–7584), an Egyptian Revival tabernacle (ca. 1851) designed by noted Philadelphia architect William Strickland. Two blocks south is the **Ryman Auditorium and Museum** (116 5th Ave. N, ☎ 615/254–1445; for tickets, 615/889–6611; admission charged), the home of the "Grand Ole Opry" from 1943 to 1974—a shrine for die-hard fans. The Ryman was recently renovated and once again hosts performances.

Go north on 5th Avenue for the James K. Polk Office Building, home of the **Tennessee State Museum** (505 Deaderick St., ☎ 615/741–2692; closed Mon.), where more than 6,000 artifacts trace the history of life in Tennessee. To the west along Charlotte Avenue is the Greek Revival **State**

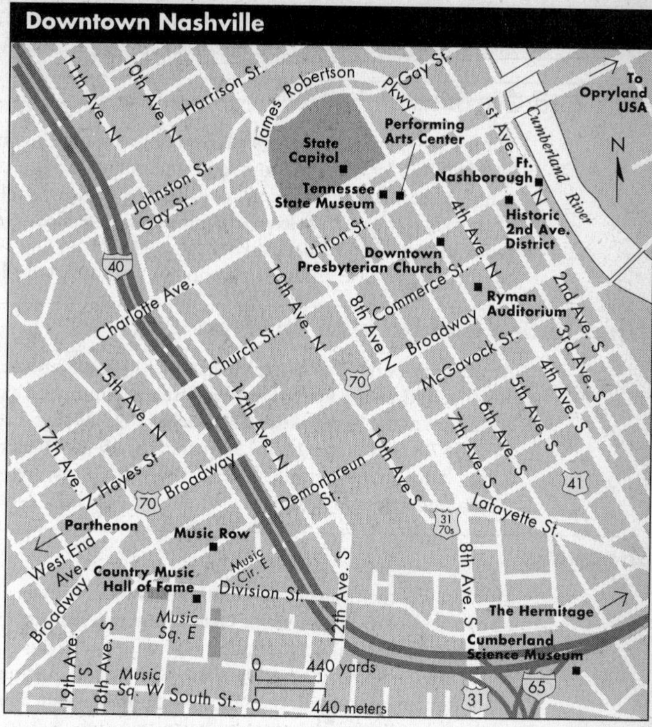

Capitol (☎ 615/741–2692), also designed by Strickland, who is interred there along with the 11th U.S. president, James K. Polk, and his wife.

Other Attractions

Music Row (Demonbreun St. exit off I–40) is the heart of Nashville's recording industry and the center of numerous country-music attractions. A ticket to the **Country Music Hall of Fame and Museum** (4 Music Sq. E, ☎ 615/255–5333) includes admission to the legendary **RCA Studio B,** a few blocks away, where Elvis, Dolly Parton, and other greats once recorded.

Opryland USA, an attraction-filled musical theme park, offers 22 rides and more than a dozen live music shows. *2802 Opryland Dr. (via Briley Pkwy.),* ☎ *615/889–6611. Admission charged. Closed weekdays Oct.–early May.*

Since 1974, Opryland has also been the home of the **"Grand Ole Opry."** Each weekend top stars perform at the nation's oldest continuous radio show, which is broadcast from the world's largest broadcast studio (it seats 4,424). *2804 Opryland Dr., 37214,* ☎ *615/889–3060 (advance ticket purchase advised). Admission charged.*

Twelve miles east of downtown (Exit 221 off I–40) is the **Hermitage,** built by the seventh U.S. president, Andrew Jackson, for his wife, Rachel. Their life and times are reflected with great care in the mansion, visitor center, and grounds. Both Jackson and his wife are entombed here. *4580 Rachel's La., Hermitage,* ☎ *615/889–2941. Admission charged.*

Two miles west of downtown in Centennial Park—built for the 1897 Tennessee Centennial Exposition—stands the **Parthenon,** an exact copy of the Athenian original and now used as an art gallery. *Athena Parthenos* is a 42-ft copy of a statue in the original Parthenon and the tallest indoor statue in the Western Hemisphere. *West End and 25th Aves., ☎ 615/862–8431. Admission charged. Closed Mon.*

Park and Gardens

The 14,200-acre **J. Percy Priest Lake** (11 mi east of downtown off I–40, ☎ 615/889–1975) is surrounded by parks where you can swim, fish, camp, hunt, hike, bike, picnic, paddle, or ride horseback. Thirty acres of gardens at the **Cheekwood–Tennessee Botanical Gardens & Museum of Art** (1200 Forrest Park Dr., ☎ 615/353–2140; admission charged) showcase annuals, perennials, and area wildflowers.

What to See and Do with Children

At the Cumberland Science Museum (800 Ridley Blvd., ☎ 615/862–5160), children are invited to touch, smell, climb, and explore. The toy collection at the **Nashville Toy Museum** (2613 McGavock Pike, ☎ 615/883–8870) spans more than 150 years. The 50-acre **Nashville Zoo** (1710 Ridge Rd. Circle, Joelton, ☎ 615/370–3333) features an African savanna and a reptile house.

Shopping

Downtown, the trilevel **Church Street Centre** (7th Ave. and Church St., ☎ 615/254–4260) features the **Castner–Knott** department store. The huge **Bellevue Center** mall in southwest Nashville (Bellevue exit from I–40W, ☎ 615/646–8690) has more than 120 stores. Antiques lovers may want to browse through the shops along **8th Avenue South.** For the latest look in country-and-western wear, two-step over to the **District.**

Dining

If you expect Nashville dining to be all corn bread, turnip greens, and grits, you're in for a surprise. Here you will find some of Tennessee's most sophisticated restaurants alongside the popular "meat-plus-threes" (diners serving meat and three kinds of vegetables). For price ranges, see Chart 1 (B) in On the Road with Fodor's.

$$$ ★ **Mario's.** Country-music stars, visiting celebrities, and local society come here to see and be seen—and to savor the memorable pastas created by Chef Sandro Bozzatto. *2005 Broadway, ☎ 615/327–3232. Reservations required. Jacket required. AE, D, DC, MC, V. Closed Sun. No lunch.*

$$$ **The Merchants.** This expensively built three-level restaurant has an outdoor patio. Specialties include fresh seafood, grilled meats, and Key lime pie. *401 Broadway, ☎ 615/254–1892. Reservations advised. AE, DC, MC, V. No lunch weekends.*

$$$ **Wild Boar.** This restaurant serves excellent Continental cuisine; its outstanding wine cellar earned it the prestigious *Wine Spectator* Grand Award in 1993. *2014 Broadway, ☎ 615/329–1313. AE, D, DC, MC, V. No lunch weekends.*

$$ ★ **F. Scott's.** This popular café and wine bar has one of the largest wine selections in town. Specialties include grilled chicken on black beans with roasted-pepper sauce, mango salsa, and smoked-tomato relish. *2210 Crestmoor, ☎ 615/269–5861. AE, D, DC, MC, V.*

$$ **Mere Bulles.** This intimate downtown restaurant offers river-view dining, a Continental menu, and an extensive wine list. *152 2nd Ave. N, ☎ 615/256–1946. Reservations advised. AE, D, MC, V.*

$$ **106 Club.** A black baby-grand piano, a shiny black enamel bar, and patrons sporting jacket and tie set the tone in this intimate art deco

dining room in suburban Belle Meade. The cuisine is a mix of California nouvelle and international favorites. *106 Harding Pl., ☎ 615/356–1300. Reservations advised. AE, D, DC, MC, V. No lunch.*

$ **Elliston Place Soda Shop.** The burgers are tasty, the sodas are frothy, and the service is friendly at this old-fashioned soda shop, where the 1950s atmosphere has been lovingly preserved. The chocolate shake is Nashville's best. *2111 Elliston Pl., ☎ 615/327–1090. No credit cards. Closed Sun.*

$ **Hermitage House Smorgasbord.** No need to be shy about helping yourself to the bountiful spread of salads, meats, vegetables, and desserts offered here. Don't miss the apple fritters. *4144 Lebanon Rd., Hermitage, ☎ 615/883–9525. MC, V.*

$ ★ **Loveless Cafe.** The appeal here is true down-home southern cooking: featherlight homemade biscuits and preserves, country ham and red-eye gravy, and fried chicken. *8400 Hwy. 100, ☎ 615/646–9700. Reservations advised. No credit cards. Closed Mon.*

$ **Old Spaghetti Factory.** This District spot offers a wide range of pasta dishes in a lively atmosphere that's great for families. *160 2nd Ave. N, ☎ 615/254–9010. D, MC, V.*

Lodging

For information on bed-and-breakfasts in the area, contact **Bed & Breakfast About Tennessee** (Box 110227, Nashville 37222, ☎ 615/331–5244 or 800/458–2421) or **Bed & Breakfast Adventures** (Box 150586, Nashville 37215, ☎ 615/383–6611). For price ranges, see Chart 2 (B) in On the Road with Fodor's.

$$$ **Loews Vanderbilt Plaza.** This beautiful hotel near Vanderbilt University has a well-deserved reputation for attentive service. *2100 West End Ave., 37203, ☎ 615/320–1700 or 800/235–6397, FAX 615/320–5019. 338 rooms, 13 suites. Facilities: 2 restaurants, 2 lounges. AE, D, MC, V.*

$$$ ★ **Opryland Hotel.** This massive, plantation-style hotel adjacent to Opryland boasts a 2-acre glass-walled conservatory filled with 10,000 tropical plants, and a skylighted cascades area with indoor streams and a half-acre lake. *2800 Opryland Dr., 37214, ☎ 615/889–1000, FAX 615/871–7741. 1,891 rooms, 150 suites. Facilities: 5 restaurants, coffee shop, 6 lounges, shops, fitness center, golf course, 3 pools, tennis. AE, D, MC, V.*

$$$ **Stouffer Renaissance Nashville Hotel.** This ultracontemporary high-rise adjoins the Nashville Convention Center and the Church Street Centre Mall. The spacious rooms have period reproduction furnishings. *611 Commerce St., 37203, ☎ 615/255–8400 or 800/468–3571, FAX 615/255–8163. 649 rooms, 24 suites. Facilities: restaurant, coffee shop, lounge, deli, health club/spa, pool. AE, D, DC, MC, V.*

$$ ★ **Courtyard by Marriott–Airport.** This handsome low-rise motor inn offers some amenities you'd expect in higher-priced hotels: spacious rooms, king-size beds, and oversize work desks. *2508 Elm Hill Pike, 37214, ☎ 615/883–9500 or 800/321–2211, FAX 615/883–0172. 133 rooms, 12 suites. Facilities: restaurant, lounge, exercise room, pool, sauna, whirlpool. AE, D, DC, MC, V.*

$$ **Hampton Inn Vanderbilt.** The rooms at this contemporary inn near Vanderbilt University are colorful and spacious. There's a hospitality suite for social or business use. *1919 West End Ave., 37203, ☎ 615/329–1144 or 800/426–7866, FAX 615/320–7112. 171 rooms. Facilities: Continental breakfast, pool. AE, D, DC, MC, V.*

$$ Holiday Inn–Briley Parkway. This hotel offers the Holidome Indoor Recreation Center, with a pool, sauna, whirlpool, game room, and more. The guest rooms are spacious and well lighted. *2200 Elm Hill Pike at Briley Pkwy., 37210, ☎ 615/883–9770 or 800/465–4329, FAX 615/391–4521. 381 rooms, 4 suites. Facilities: restaurant, lounge, pool, fitness center. AE, DC, MC, V.*

$$ Ramada Inn Across from Opryland. This contemporary, low-rise motor inn is closer to the theme park than any other hotel except the Opryland. *2401 Music Valley Dr., 37214, ☎ 615/889–0800 or 800/272–6232, FAX 615/883–1230. 290 rooms, 7 suites. Facilities: restaurant, lounge, indoor pool, whirlpool. AE, D, DC, MC, V.*

$ Comfort Inn Hermitage. Near the Hermitage, this inn offers comfortable accommodations, some with water beds or whirlpool baths. *5768 Old Hickory Blvd., 37076, ☎ 615/889–5060, FAX 615/871–4137. 106 rooms. Facilities: Continental breakfast, pool. AE, D, DC, MC, V.*

$ La Quinta Inn–Metro Center. Guest rooms are spacious and well lighted, with a large working area and an oversize bed. *2001 Metrocenter Blvd., 37228, ☎ 615/259–2130 or 800/531–5900, FAX 615/242–2650. 121 rooms. Facilities: pool. AE, DC, MC, V.*

$ ★ Wilson Inn. Three miles from Opryland, this five-story hotel is new, clean, and convenient. Many rooms have kitchens. *600 Ermac Dr., 37214 (Elm Hill Pike exit from Briley Pkwy.), ☎ 615/889–4466 or 800/333–9457, FAX 615/889–0484. 110 rooms. Facilities: Continental breakfast, pool. AE, D, MC, V.*

The Arts and Nightlife

The Arts

The **Tennessee Performing Arts Center** (505 Deaderick St., ☎ 615/737–4849) holds performances by the **Nashville Ballet** (☎ 615/244–7233), **Nashville Opera** (☎ 615/292–5710), **Nashville Symphony Orchestra** (☎ 615/329–3033), and **Tennessee Repertory Theatre** (☎ 615/244–4878). The center's **Andrew Jackson Hall** also hosts touring Broadway shows. Call **TicketMaster** (☎ 615/737–4849) for tickets and information.

Nightlife

For country music try the famous **Bluebird Cafe** (4104 Hillsboro Rd., Green Hills, ☎ 615/383–1461), where singers try out their latest material; or the **Stock Yard Bull Pen Lounge** (901 2nd Ave. N, ☎ 615/255–6464), a restaurant-lounge with live entertainment and dancing. Jazz clubs include **The Merchants** and **Mere Bulles** (for both, *see* Dining, *above*), both downtown. **Exit/In** (2208 Elliston Pl., ☎ 615/321–4400) and **Blue Sky Court** (412 4th Ave. S, ☎ 615/256–4562), convenient to downtown and Vanderbilt University, focus on rock and blues.

EAST TENNESSEE

From the misty heights of the Great Smoky Mountains to the rippling waters of the Holston, French Broad, Nolichucky, and Tennessee rivers, East Tennessee offers a cornucopia of scenic grandeur and recreational opportunities. While mountain-folk ways may persist in certain smaller communities, cities like Knoxville and Chattanooga are up-to-date and quite diverse.

Tourist Information

Chattanooga: Area Convention and Visitors Bureau (1001 Market St., 37402, ☎ 615/756–8687 or 800/322–3344). **Knoxville:** Area

Convention and Visitors Bureau (500 Henley St., 37902, ☎ 615/523-7263 or 800/727-8045).

Getting There

By Plane

Knoxville Airport (☎ 615/970-2773), served by American Eagle, ComAir, Delta, Northwest, Trans World Express, United, and USAir, is about 12 mi from town. The newly renovated **Chattanooga Airport** (☎ 615/855-2200), served by American Eagle, ASA, ComAir, Delta, Northwest Airlink, and USAir, is about 8 mi from town.

By Car

I-75 runs north-south from Kentucky through Knoxville, then to Chattanooga. I-81 heads southwest from the Virginia border at Bristol, ending at I-40 northeast of Knoxville. I-40 enters from North Carolina and continues west to Knoxville, Nashville, and Memphis.

By Bus

Greyhound Lines (☎ 800/231-2222) has stops in Chattanooga and in Knoxville.

Exploring East Tennessee

Founded in 1786, **Knoxville** was the first state capital when Tennessee was admitted to the Union in 1796. Today it is home to the main campus of the **University of Tennessee,** as well as the headquarters of the **Tennessee Valley Authority (TVA),** with its vast complex of hydroelectric dams and recreational lakes.

Historic sites in Knoxville include the 1792 **Governor William Blount Mansion** (200 W. Hill Ave., ☎ 615/525-2375; admission charged; closed Mon.), where the governor and his associates planned the admission of Tennessee as the 16th state in the Union; and the **Armstrong-Lockett House** (2728 Kingston Pike, ☎ 615/637-3163; admission charged; closed Mon. and Jan.-Feb.), an 1834 farm mansion, now a showcase of American and English furniture and English silver. The **East Tennessee Historical Center** (800 Market St., ☎ 615/544-5744; closed Mon.), housed in the 1874 U.S. Customs House, displays books, documents, and artifacts relating to the history of the state.

The $10.5 million **Knoxville Museum of Art** (410 10th St., in World's Fair Park, ☎ 615/525-6101; closed Mon.), opened in 1992, has four exhibition galleries with contemporary prints, drawings, and paintings. The **Knoxville Zoological Gardens** (Rutledge Pike S, off I-40 Exit 392, ☎ 615/637-5331; admission charged) is famous for its reptile complex and for breeding large cat species and African elephants.

Southeast of Knoxville via U.S. 441/321 is **Gatlinburg,** Tennessee's premier mountain-resort town and the northern gateway to the **Great Smoky Mountains National Park** (*see* National and State Parks, *above*). Set in the narrow valley of the Little Pigeon River (actually a turbulent mountain stream), Gatlinburg offers an abundance of family attractions, including the **Gatlinburg Sky Lift** (☎ 615/436-4307) to the top of Crockett Mountain and the **Ober Gatlinburg Tramway** (☎ 615/436-5423; closed Mar. 6-Mar. 18) to a mountaintop amusement park, ski center, and shopping mall/crafts market.

In nearby **Pigeon Forge,** about 6 mi north on U.S. 441, you'll find **Dollywood** (700 Dollywood La., ☎ 615/428-9488 or 800/365-5996; admission charged; closed Jan.-late Apr.), Dolly Parton's popular theme park. South from Gatlinburg, scenic U.S. 441 climbs to **Newfound Gap,** a haunting viewpoint on the Tennessee–North Carolina border. From here, a 7-mi spur road leads to **Clingmans Dome**—at 6,643 ft, the highest point in Tennessee.

Southwest of Knoxville off I–75 is **Chattanooga,** a city of Civil War battlefields, museums of all kinds (art, antiques, history, even knives), and a famous choo-choo (*see* Dining and Lodging, *below*). Begin your meanderings here with a stop at the new **Chattanooga Visitors Center** (2 Broad St., ☎ 615/266–7111). *Marks on the Land,* a 22-minute, 27-projector slide spectacular tracing the history of the city, is shown every half hour (admission: $1 adults, children under 6 free). Dominating Chattanooga's skyline is 2,215-ft-high **Lookout Mountain,** 6 mi away, which offers panoramic views of seven states and the world's steepest **Incline Railway** (827 E. Brow Rd., ☎ 615/821–4224; admission charged). On Lookout Mountain Scenic Highway, tours depart every 15 minutes to the famed 145-ft **Ruby Falls** (1550 Scenic Hwy., ☎ 615/821–2544; admission charged), 1,120 ft underground and only reached by elevator.

The $45 million **Tennessee Aquarium** (1 Broad St., ☎ 615/265–0695; admission charged), opened in 1992, is the world's largest freshwater aquarium, with 350 species of fish, mammals, birds, reptiles, and amphibians. Surrounding the aquarium is the new $10 million **Ross's Landing Park and Plaza,** commemorating Chattanooga's Civil War history as well as its role as a major railroad town; the open-air complex was designed by a team of world-class architects, landscape architects, and artists. Chattanooga's newest attraction is the $16.5 million **Creative Discovery Children's Museum** (4th and Chestnut Sts., adjacent to the Tennessee Aquarium, ☎ 615/757–0510; admission charged), opened in 1995, with exhibits in four main areas: invention, art, music, and science.

About 100 mi northeast of Chattanooga (take U.S. 27 to I–40E or I–75 to I–40W) is **Oak Ridge,** where atomic energy was secretly developed during World War II. The **American Museum of Science and Energy** (300 S. Tulane Ave., ☎ 615/576–3200) focuses on the uses of nuclear, solar, and geothermal energy, mainly for peaceful purposes.

What to See and Do with Children

The **Gatlinburg/Pigeon Forge area** is home to many amusement parks and offbeat museums, such as the **Guinness World Records Museum** (☎ 615/436–9100). In Knoxville, youngsters like the hands-on displays and audiovisual exhibits at the **East Tennessee Discovery Center and Akima Planetarium** (516 N. Beaman St., ☎ 615/637–1121). Children also enjoy the **Tennessee Aquarium** in Chattanooga (*see* Exploring East Tennessee, *above*) and the new **Creative Discovery Children's Museum** (*see* Exploring East Tennessee, *above*).

Shopping

The **Great Smoky Arts and Craft Community** (Glades and Buckhorn Rds. off U.S. 321N, 3 mi east of Gatlinburg, ☎ 615/436–3301), a collection of 70 shops and crafts studios along 8 mi of rambling country road, features wood carvings, corn-husk dolls, dulcimers, handmade quilts, and other Appalachian folk crafts. Chattanooga's **Warehouse Row** (12th and

Market Sts., ☎ 615/267–1111) contains factory outlets featuring such top designers as Adrienne Vittadini, Ralph Lauren, and Perry Ellis.

Sports and the Outdoors

Fishing

East Tennessee's lakes offer seasonal angling for striped bass, walleye, white bass, and muskie. Gatlinburg's streams and rivers are stocked with trout from April to November. There are boat-launch ramps (but no rentals) at **Norris Dam State Resort Park** north of Knoxville (☎ 615/426–7461) and at **Booker T. Washington State Park** near Chattanooga (☎ 615/894–4955).

Golf

East Tennessee courses open to the public include **Brainerd Golf Course** in Chattanooga (☎ 615/855–2692), **Whittle Springs Municipal Golf Course** in Knoxville (☎ 615/525–1022), and **Bent Creek Mountain Inn and Country Club** in Gatlinburg (☎ 615/436–2875).

Hiking

A scenic portion of the **Appalachian Trail** runs along high ridges in the Great Smoky Mountains National Park (Gatlinburg, ☎ 615/436–1200). The trail can be easily reached at Newfound Gap from U.S. 441.

Horseback Riding

McCarter's Riding Stables (U.S. 441 south of Gatlinburg, ☎ 615/436–5354; mid-Mar.–Oct.).

Rafting and Canoeing

East Tennessee has five white-water rivers: Ocoee, Hiwassee, French Broad, Tellico, and Nolichucky. The rafting season runs from April to early November; for canoe rentals and guided raft trips, contact **Outdoor Adventure Rafting** (Ocoee, ☎ 800/627–7636), **Wildwater, Ltd.** (Ducktown, ☎ 800/451–9972), or **Rafting in the Smokies** (Gatlinburg, ☎ 615/436–5008).

Ski Areas

Ober Gatlinburg Ski Resort (☎ 615/436–5423) has three lifts and 10 downhill slopes.

Dining and Lodging

Expect hearty food in the mountains: barbecued ribs, thick pork chops, country ham with red-eye gravy. For reservations at hotels, motels, chalets, and condominiums in Gatlinburg, contact **Smoky Mountain Accommodations Reservation Service** (526 E. Parkway, Suite 1, Gatlinburg 37738, ☎ 615/436–9700 or 800/231–2230). For B&B reservations, contact **Tennessee Bed & Breakfast Innkeepers' Association** (Box 120428, Nashville 37212, ☎ 615/321–5482 or 800/820–8144). For price ranges, see Charts 1 (B) and 2 (B) in On the Road with Fodor's.

Chattanooga

DINING

Perry's Seafood. One of Tennessee's best restaurants, Perry's specializes in grilled and sautéed fish. *850 Market St., ☎ 615/267–0007. AE, D, DC, MC, V. $$$*

The Loft. Locals and visitors alike flock to this cozy, candlelit restaurant for its clublike ambience, extensive wine list, and hearty lunch and dinner specialties. The varied entrées include broiled or blackened amberjack, king crab legs, seafood fettuccine, steaks, and prime rib—all served with soup, salad, home-baked bread, fresh vegetables, and either a baked potato or wild rice pilaf. *328 Cherokee Blvd., ☎ 615/266–3601. AE, D, DC, MC, V. $$–$$$*

★ **212 Market.** Creative American cuisine is served at this hip spot directly across from the Tennessee Aquarium. The fish entrées are especially good, the homemade breads scrumptious, and the wine list impressive. *212 Market St., ☎ 615/265–1212. AE, MC, V. $$–$$$*

Big River Grille Brewing & Works. This restored trolley warehouse is now handsomely appointed, with high ceilings, exposed brick walls, and hardwood floors. You can watch the inner workings of the microbrewery through a soaring glass wall by the bar. The sandwiches and salads are large; to wash them down, try the sampler of four brews. *222 Broad St., ☎ 615/267–2739. AE, D, DC, MC, V. $$*

LODGING

Chattanooga ChooChoo Holiday Inn. The hotel adjoins the showcase 1905 Southern Railway Terminal, now a 30-acre complex with restaurants, lounges, shops, exhibits, gardens, and an operating trolley. Guest rooms stress luxurious appointments, especially the restored Victorian-era parlor cars. *1400 Market St., 37402, ☎ 615/266–5000 or 800/872–2529, FAX 615/265–4635. 360 units, including 48 parlor cars. Facilities: 5 restaurants, lounge, indoor and outdoor pools, whirlpools, tennis courts, shops. AE, DC, MC, V. $$*

Chattanooga Marriott. This newly renovated hotel is Chattanooga's largest and is convenient to town attractions. *2 Carter Plaza, 37402, ☎ 615/756–0002 or 800/841–1674, FAX 615/266–2254. 343 rooms. Facilities: 2 restaurants, lounge, exercise room, game room, indoor and outdoor pools, valet parking. AE, DC, MC, V. $$*

★ **Radisson Read House.** The Georgian-style Read House, on the National Register of Historic Places, dates from the 1920s and has been impeccably restored to its original grandeur under a wide-ranging, $2.5 million renovation completed in June 1995. Guest rooms in the main hotel continue the Georgian motif; rooms in the annex are more contemporary. *827 Broad St., 37402, ☎ 615/266–4121 or 800/333–3333, FAX 615/267–6447. 107 rooms, 131 suites. Facilities: 2 restaurants, lounge, pool, sauna, whirlpool. AE, D, DC, MC, V. $$*

Gatlinburg

DINING

Burning Bush Restaurant. Reproduction furnishings evoke a Colonial atmosphere, but the menu leans toward Continental. Specialties include broiled Tennessee quail. *1151 Parkway, ☎ 615/436–4669. Reservations advised. AE, D, MC, V. $$*

Smoky Mountain Trout House. Trout is prepared eight ways, or you can have prime rib, country ham, or fried chicken. This restaurant is a truly rustic mountain cottage. *410 N. Parkway, ☎ 615/436–5416. AE, DC, MC, V. Closed Dec.–Mar. $$*

LODGING

★ **Buckhorn Inn.** This country inn about 6 mi outside of town has welcomed guests to its rustic rooms and cottages since 1938. The views of the Smoky Mountains are spectacular. Hearty breakfasts and dinners are included in the rates. *2140 Tudor Mountain Rd., 37738, ☎ 615/436–4668. 6 rooms, 4 1-bedroom cottages, 2 2-bedroom guest houses. MC, V. $$$*

★ **Holiday Inn Resort Complex.** Near the Convention Center and the Ober Gatlinburg aerial tramway, this hotel offers the Holidome Indoor Recreation Center, with a pool, an atrium, and other attractions. *520 Airport Rd., 37738, ☎ 615/436–9201 or 800/435–9201, FAX 615/436–*

7974. 402 rooms, including 6 suites. Facilities: 2 restaurants, lounge, 2 indoor pools, outdoor pool, whirlpool, 2 saunas, exercise room, golf, tennis. AE, D, DC, MC, V. $$

Knoxville

DINING

★ **Regas Restaurant.** This cozy Knoxville classic, with fireplaces and original art, has been around for 70 years. The specialty, prime rib, is sliced to order and served with a creamy horseradish sauce. *318 Gay St., ☎ 615/637–9805. Reservations advised. AE, D, DC, MC, V. No lunch Sat., no dinner Sun. $$–$$$*

Copper Cellar/Cumberland Grill. A favorite of the college crowd and young professionals, the original downstairs Copper Cellar has an intimate atmosphere. Upstairs, the Cumberland Grill features salads and sandwiches. Both offer outstanding desserts. *1807 Cumberland Ave., ☎ 615/673–3411. Reservations advised. AE, DC, MC, V. $$*

LODGING

★ **Hyatt Regency Knoxville.** This is a handsome, contemporary adaptation of an Aztec pyramid, atop a hill overlooking the city and nearby mountains. The nine-story atrium lobby blends modern furnishings with artwork in Mesoamerican motifs. *500 Hill Ave. SE, Box 88, 37901, ☎ 615/637–1234 or 800/233–1234, FAX 615/522–5911. 360 rooms, 27 suites. Facilities: 2 restaurants, lounge, exercise room, pool, playground. AE, D, DC, MC, V. $$$*

Luxbury Hotel. Midway between downtown Knoxville and Oak Ridge, this affordable new hotel provides oversize rooms with spacious work areas. *420 Peters Rd. N, 37922, ☎ 615/539–0058 or 800/252–7748, FAX 615/539–4887. 75 rooms, 23 suites. Facilities: Continental breakfast, pool. AE, D, DC, MC, V. $*

The Arts and Nightlife

In Chattanooga, the **Tivoli Theater** (399 McCaulley Ave., ☎ 615/757–5050) and the **Market Street Performance Hall** (221 Market St., ☎ 615/267–2498) present concerts. The **Chattanooga Little Theatre** (400 River St., ☎ 615/267–8534) stages productions year-round. In Gatlinburg, **Sweet Fanny Adams Theatre and Music Hall** (461 Parkway, ☎ 615/436–4038) stages original musical comedies and Gay '90s revues, and hotel lounges offer DJs and live entertainment.

In Knoxville, the **Bijou Theater** (803 S. Gay St., ☎ 615/522–0832) offers seasonal ballet, concerts, and plays. The "Old City" has a variety of restaurants, clubs, and shops. Try **Manhattan's** (101 S. Central St., ☎ 615/525–4463) for blues. For authentic Tex-Mex music and food there's **Amigo's** (116 S. Central St., ☎ 615/546–9505). And both **Patrick Sullivan's** (100 N. Central St., ☎ 615/694–9696) and **Hooray's** (106 S. Central St., ☎ 615/546–6729) offer saloon-style food and live rock and roll on weekends.

7 The Midwest and Great Lakes

By Holly Hughes

THE MIDWEST *is* America, that prototypical vision of neat farmland, affluent suburbs, and compact, skyscrapered downtowns strung together along purposefully straight silver highways. Sauk Centre, Minnesota, was the setting for Sinclair Lewis's *Main Street;* Muncie, Indiana, was the subject of the sociological study *Middletown, USA*. It is no accident that stand-up comedians use midwestern town names—Peoria, Sheboygan, Kokomo, Kalamazoo—to mean "the heart of the country." Nevertheless, transplanted Midwesterners spend the rest of their lives longing for broad, clear horizons; thick, shady stands of beech and maple trees; hazy summer afternoons when kids sell lemonade from sidewalk stands. People seem genuinely friendlier and more down-to-earth here.

Six states—Ohio, Indiana, Michigan, Illinois, Wisconsin, and Minnesota—occupy what was originally the Northwest Territory, a vast tract of forest and meadow awarded to the United States in the 1783 Treaty of Paris. Unlike the stark Great Plains to the west, this is gently rolling landscape, punctuated by rivers, woods, and trees. It is defined by great geographical features: to the east, the Appalachian Mountains; to the north, the Great Lakes; to the south, the Ohio River; to the west, the majestic Mississippi River.

Smarting from years of being labeled as "the sticks," midwestern cities are always trying to prove themselves, cheerfully rehabilitating their downtowns, rooting for their major-league ball teams, building gleaming convention centers and festival malls. Ohio has no fewer than five important cities (Cleveland, Cincinnati, Columbus, Dayton, and Toledo). Minnesota's major population center comprises two cities, Minneapolis and St. Paul, which means that there are twice as many parks and museums there as you'd expect. Indiana's capital, Indianapolis, is a beautifully laid-out city that's also the amateur-sports capital of the country. Michigan has Detroit, home of America's auto industry, which still offers attractions despite economic problems. Milwaukee, Wisconsin, poised on the western shore of Lake Michigan, is a rich melting pot of immigrant cultures, as is vibrant and powerful Chicago, Illinois, the region's one great metropolis.

But it's never more than an hour's drive from these cities to northern lake resorts, historic villages along sleepy back roads, utopian colonies, and pleasant university towns. Big swatches of forest and lakeshore are protected as parkland, and gorgeous scenic drives edge the Great Lakes and the dramatic bluffs of the Mississippi and Ohio river valleys.

Tour Groups

From the beauty of the Upper Peninsula and the historic sites of Mackinac Island to the bustle of such cities as Grand Rapids and Chicago, tours of the Great Lakes region offer something for everyone.

Gadabout Tours (700 E. Tahquitz Canyon Way, Palm Springs, CA 92262, ☎ 619/325–5556 or 800/952–5068) takes a three-week swing in May through St. Louis, Chicago, Indianapolis, and Holland, Michigan. **Globus** (5301 S. Federal Circle, Littleton, CO 80123, ☎ 303/797–2800 or 800/221–0090) offers 10 days in Michigan and the Great Lakes region, including Chicago; Agawa Canyon, Ontario; and Mackinac Island and Dearborn, Michigan. **Maupintour** (Box 807, Lawrence, KS 66044, ☎ 913/843–1211 or 800/255–4266) has an 8-day Great Lakes tour that goes from Chicago to the coasts and takes in scenic features

The Midwest and Great Lakes

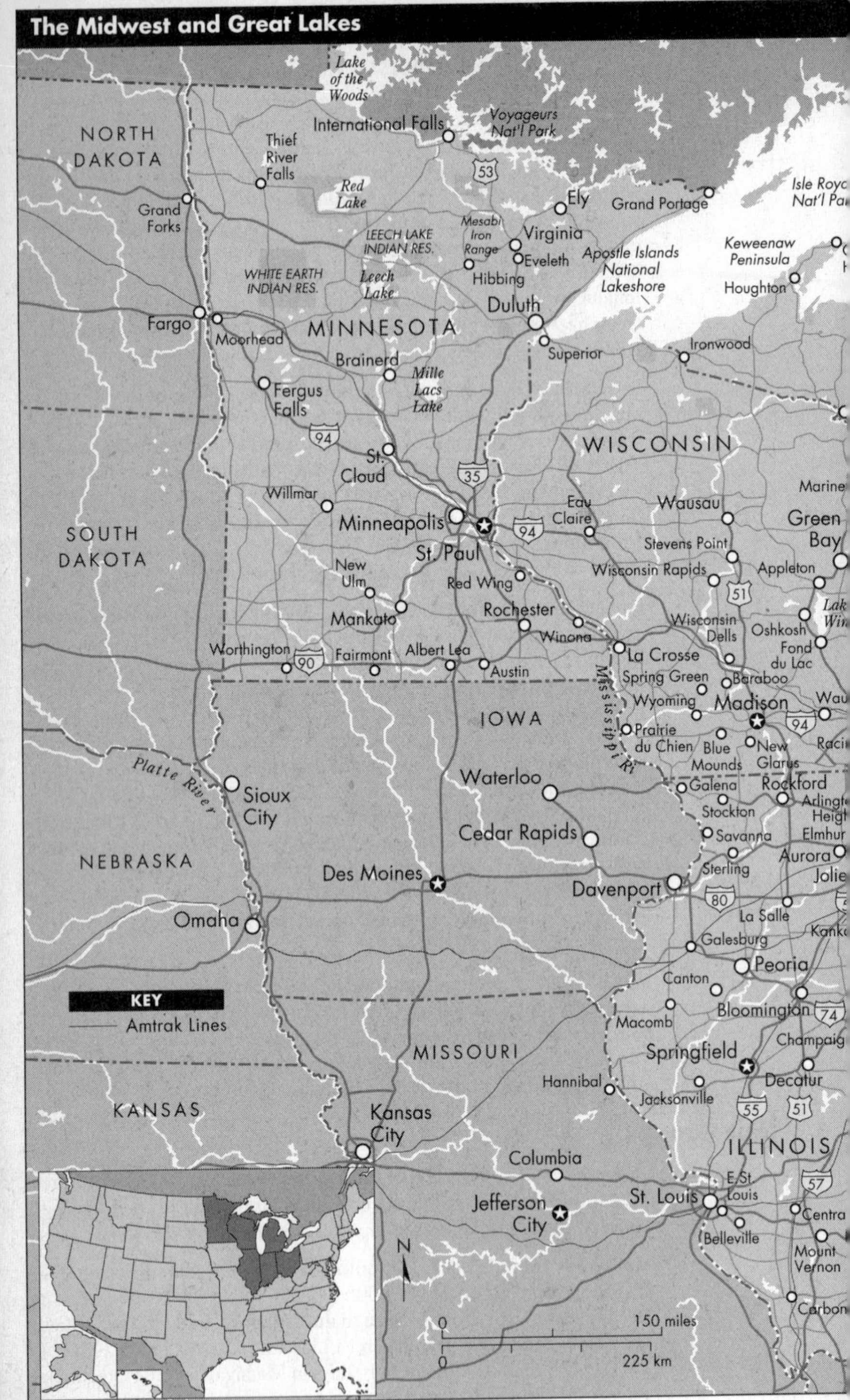

CANADA
Lake Superior
Copper Harbor
Marquette
Sault Ste. Marie
Sudbury
MICHIGAN
Iron Mountain
Escanaba
Beaver Island
Mackinac Island
Mackinaw City
Manitoulin Island
Georgian Bay
Petoskey
Northport
Alpena
Sturgeon Bay
Lake Huron
Traverse City
MICHIGAN
Toronto
Lake Ontario
Manitowoc
Cadillac
Lake Winnebago
Sheboygan
Bay City
Saginaw
Lake Michigan
Buffalo
Grand Rapids
Flint
NEW YORK
Port Huron
Milwaukee
Lansing
Racine
Battle Creek
Jackson
Lake Erie
Kenosha
Waukegan
Detroit
Ashtabula
Kalamazoo
Ann Arbor
Evanston
Chicago
Port Clinton
Cleveland
PENNSYLVANIA
South Bend
Angola
Toledo
La Porte
Gary
Auburn
Sandusky
Akron
Youngstown
Ft. Wayne
Huntington
Lima
Mansfield
Canton
Logansport
Marion
OHIO
INDIANA
Wapakoneta
Muncie
Lafayette
Danville
Anderson
Zanesville
Wheeling
Zionsville
Columbus
Crawfordsville
Dayton
Marietta
Indianapolis
Chillicothe
Terre Haute
Columbus
Cincinnati
Bloomington
Madison
WEST VIRGINIA
Wabash Riv.
Vincennes
New Albany
Corydon
Gentryville
Louisville
KENTUCKY
Ohio R.
Evansville
VIRGINIA

of Wisconsin, Mackinac Island, and coastal Michigan, winding up in Grand Rapids. **Talmage Tours** (1223 Walnut St., Philadelphia, PA 19107, ☎ 215/923–7100) offers an 8-day trip and cruise through the Great Lakes to Mackinac Island. **Tauck Tours** (Box 5027, Westport, CT 06881, ☎ 203/226–6911 or 800/468–2825) visits the coastline of Lake Michigan in 8 days, covering Holland, the Upper Peninsula, Mackinac Island, and Dearborn.

When to Go

Summer is the most popular time of year to visit the Midwest and the Great Lakes. Generally, the farther north you go, the fewer people you'll find. Prices in most places peak in July and August. Daily temperatures average in the 80s in Illinois, Indiana, and Ohio, though July and August heat waves can push them high into the 90s. In Michigan, Wisconsin, and Minnesota, temperatures run 10° cooler. These three states have the best **fall** foliage, though you can see good color in all six. Depending on the weather, the leaves usually begin to turn in mid-September and reach their most colorful by mid-October. In **winter** Michigan has the only significant downhill skiing in the region, but cross-country is extremely popular in Wisconsin and Minnesota. The Midwest usually gets at least one subzero cold snap every year. For the rest of winter, expect temperatures in the 20s and 30s, and about 10° colder in northern Michigan, Wisconsin, and Minnesota. Sudden snowstorms can make winter driving unpredictable and treacherous. **Spring** is damp and clammy, with erratic weather and temperatures ranging from the 30s to the 60s.

Festivals and Seasonal Events

Late Jan.–early Feb.: The 12-day **St. Paul (MN) Winter Carnival** celebrates winter with a sleigh and cutter parade, an ice palace, car races on the ice, and ice sculptures by artists from around the world. ☎ *612/297–6953.*

May: The month-long **Indianapolis 500 Festival** culminates in the most famous car race in the United States. ☎ *317/636–4556 or 317/241–2500.*

May 10–20: The **Holland (MI) Tulip Festival** features flowers and Dutch traditions. ☎ *616/396–4221.*

Late June–early July: Milwaukee holds **Summerfest,** a lakefront festival featuring rock, jazz, and popular music. ☎ *414/273–2680 or 800/837–3378.*

July 14–23: The **Minneapolis Aquatennial** celebrates the lakes of Minnesota with sailing regattas, waterskiing competitions, and other water-related events. ☎ *612/331–8371.*

July 15–16: The two-day **Chicago-to-Mackinac Boat Race** is one of the most challenging sailboat races in the country. ☎ *312/861–7777.*

July 29: The **Pro Football Hall of Fame Game** and induction ceremonies in **Canton, Ohio,** kick off the football season. ☎ *216/456–8207.*

Late July: The **Cincinnati Riverfront Stadium Festival** is the largest festival in the country devoted to rhythm and blues. ☎ *513/871–3900.*

Late July–early Aug.: The **Experimental Aircraft Association Fly-In** in **Oshkosh, Wisconsin,** gathers close to a million people and 30,000 aircraft from around the world. ☎ *414/426–4800.*

Early Aug.: The **Wisconsin State Fair** attracts crowds to Milwaukee for livestock and crop shows, midway attractions, and stage shows. ☎ *414/266–7000.*

Aug. 11–20: The **Illinois State Fair** in Springfield has livestock shows, car and horse races, food, and entertainment. ☎ *217/782–6661.*

Labor Day weekend: The **Detroit Montreux Jazz Festival** attracts more than 700,000 jazz fans. ☎ *313/259–5400.*

Last Sun. in Oct.: The **Chicago Marathon** draws runners from all over the world. ☎ *312/951–0660.*

Getting Around the Midwest and Great Lakes

By Plane

The region is served by most major airlines, including American, Delta, Northwest, United, and USAir. The largest airports are **Cleveland Hopkins International Airport** (☎ 216/265–6000) in Ohio; **Detroit Metropolitan Wayne County Airport** (☎ 313/942–3550) in Michigan; **General Mitchell Field** (☎ 414/747–5300), in Milwaukee, Wisconsin; **Indianapolis International Airport** (☎ 317/248–9594) in Indiana; **Minneapolis/St. Paul International Airport** (☎ 612/726–5555) in Minnesota; and **O'Hare International Airport** (☎ 312/686–2200) in Chicago, Illinois .

By Car

I–80 and I–90 converge near Cleveland and run along the northern borders of Ohio and Indiana until they split at Chicago. I–80 then cuts across Illinois into Iowa, while I–90 curves up through Wisconsin and goes across southern Minnesota. Other major arteries are I–70, crossing the southern parts of Ohio, Indiana, and Illinois; I–94, which goes from Detroit across Michigan, hugs Lake Michigan through Indiana and Illinois, then crosses Wisconsin and Minnesota; and I–75, which stretches from Sault Ste. Marie, Michigan, to Cincinnati, Ohio. State routes and county roads provide a closer look at rural areas and are in good repair throughout the region.

By Train

Amtrak (☎ 800/872–7245) is the primary passenger railroad serving the entire region. All routes go through Chicago. Among cities with commuter train service between the central city and the suburbs are Chicago (☎ 312/836–7000), Cleveland (☎ 216/621–9500), and Indianapolis (☎ 317/267–3000).

By Bus

The major intercity carrier is **Greyhound Lines** (☎ 800/231–2222). **Indian Trails** (☎ 800/248–3849) operates between Chicago and many cities in Michigan. In southern Wisconsin, **Van Galder Bus Lines** (☎ 608/257–5593 or 800/747–0094) runs from Madison and Milwaukee to Chicago's O'Hare Airport and downtown Amtrak station.

By Boat

From mid-May to October, passenger and automobile **ferry** service operates between Ludington, Michigan, and Manitowoc, Wisconsin (☎ 616/845–5555).

ILLINOIS

By Elizabeth Gardner

Updated by Julie Ann Getzlaff

Capital	Springfield
Population	11,430,602
Motto	State Sovereignty—National Union
State Bird	Cardinal
State Flower	Native violet

Visitor Information

Illinois Bureau of Tourism (100 W. Randolph St., Suite 3–400, Chicago 60601, ☎ 800/223–0121).

Scenic Drives

The Illinois part of the **Lake Michigan Circle Tour** follows the shoreline along Lake Shore Drive through Chicago and passes through the elegant suburbs of the North Shore: Evanston, Winnetka, Glencoe, Highland Park, and Lake Forest. The **Great River Road** follows the Mississippi River, stretching the length of Illinois (more than 500 mi) from East Dubuque to Cairo (pronounced "KAY-ro").

National and State Parks

National Parks

Shawnee National Forest (901 S. Commercial St., Harrisburg 62946, ☎ 618/253–7114) blankets the southern tip of Illinois with 250,000 acres of wilderness; this is where the glaciers stopped after flattening most of the rest of the state during the last Ice Age.

State Parks

Illinois has more than 100 state parks, conservation areas, fish and wildlife areas, and recreation areas. For a state park magazine giving park locations, information, and maps, write or call the **Illinois Department of Conservation** (524 S. 2nd St., Springfield 62701-1787, ☎ 217/782–7454). **Illinois Beach State Park** (Lake Front, Zion 60099, ☎ 708/662–4811), on Lake Michigan near the Wisconsin border, offers sandy beaches along 6½ mi of shoreline. **Rend Lake/Wayne Fitzgerrell State Park** (R.R. 1, Box 73, Whittington 62897, ☎ 618/439–3832) has the state's second-largest inland lake, where you can fish, sail, and swim. **Starved Rock State Park** (Box 116, Utica 61373, ☎ 815/667–4726), on the Illinois River between LaSalle and Peru, has 18 canyons formed during the melting of the glaciers.

CHICAGO

Because Chicago is not as large or as famous as New York, many Chicagoans suffer from "Second City" complex, afraid that out-of-towners won't appreciate their city's charms. But these are hard to miss, from the elegance of Michigan Avenue's shops to the stunning sweep of the lakefront skyline. The Loop, Chicago's central business district, is a living museum of skyscraper architecture, while many outlying neighborhoods retain the grace and homey quality of pre–World War II America. Chicago's arts community is world-class, and strong ethnic communities embrace immigrants from Croatia to Cambodia, all of whom leave their cultural stamp on the city.

Tourist Information

Chicago: Office of Tourism's Visitor Information Center (Chicago Cultural Center, 78 E. Washington St., 60602, ☏ 312/744–2400 or 800/487–2446; walk-in center at Pumping Station, 163 E. Pearson St.). The Mayor's Office of Special Events/General Information and Activities (121 N. La Salle St., Room 703, 60602, ☏ 312/744–3315, 312/744–3370 for taped announcement).

Arriving and Departing

By Plane

Every national airline, most international airlines, and a number of regional carriers fly into **O'Hare International Airport,** some 20 mi from downtown in the far northwestern corner of the city. One of the world's busiest airports, it is a hub for United and American Airlines. The **Chicago Transit Authority** (☏ 312/836–7000; base fare, $1.50) train station is in the underground concourse in Terminal 3; trains take you into the Loop. **Continental Airport Transport** (☏ 312/454–7799; fare, $14.75) provides express coach service to major downtown and Near North hotels. Metered taxicab service is available at O'Hare; expect to pay $25 to $30 (plus tip) to Near North and downtown locations.

Continental, TWA, and Southwest Airlines are just a few of the carriers that now use **Midway Airport,** on the city's southwest side. The **Chicago Transit Authority**'s (*see above*) Orange Line runs from Midway to the Loop, where you can transfer to other lines. **Continental Airport Transport** operates to the Loop and Near North (*see above;* $10.75).

By Car

From the east, the Indiana Toll Road (I–80/90) leads to the Chicago Skyway (also a toll road), which runs into the Dan Ryan Expressway (I–90/94); take the Dan Ryan westbound just past the turnoff for I–290 to any of the downtown eastbound exits. From the south, you can take I–57 to the Dan Ryan. From the west, follow I–80 to I–55, which is the major artery from the southwest and leads into Lake Shore Drive. From the north, I–94 or I–90 eastbound merge to form the John F. Kennedy Expressway (I–90/94) about 10 mi north of downtown.

By Train

Amtrak serves Chicago's **Union Station** (225 S. Canal St. at Jackson St., ☏ 800/872–7245).

By Bus

Greyhound Lines (630 W. Harrison St., ☏ 800/231–2222).

Getting Around Chicago

The best way to see Chicago is on foot, supplemented by public transportation or taxi. Streets are laid out in a grid, the center of which is the intersection of Madison Street, which runs east–west, and State Street, which runs north–south.

By Car

Leave your car behind if you're seeing the Loop, the Near North Side, or Lincoln Park. You'll need a car to go to the suburbs or outlying city neighborhoods. Downtown abounds with parking lots charging from $7 to $15 a day.

By Public Transportation

Chicago's extensive public transportation network includes buses and rapid-transit trains, both subway and elevated. The **Chicago Transit Authority** and the **RTA** (for both, ☎ 312/836–7000; base fare, $1.50) will provide information on how to get about on city rapid-transit and bus lines, suburban bus lines, and commuter trains.

By Taxi

Taxis are metered, with fares beginning at $1.50; each additional mi or minute of waiting time costs $1.20. Taxi drivers expect a 15% tip. Major companies are **American United Cab** (☎ 312/248–7600), **Checker Cab** (☎ 312/829–4222), and **Yellow Cab** (☎ 312/829–4222).

Orientation Tours

Bus Tours

Chicago Motor Coach Co. (☎ 312/922–8919) offers narrated tours of Chicago landmarks in double-decker buses. Tours depart from the Sears Tower (Franklin and Jackson Sts.), the bridge at Michigan and Wacker Sts., and the Water Tower (Michigan and Pearson Sts.).

Walking Tours

The **Chicago Architecture Foundation** (Archicenter, 224 S. Michigan Ave., ☎ 312/922–3432) offers downtown walking tours; bus tours; a river cruise; neighborhood tours; and tours of two Prairie Avenue Historic District homes, the Glessner House and the Henry B. Clarke House.

Water Tours

Wendella Sightseeing Boats (lower Michigan Ave. at the Wrigley Bldg., ☎ 312/337–1446) and **Mercury Skyline Cruises** (lower Wacker Dr., ☎ 312/332–1353) offer guided tours of the Chicago River and Lake Michigan. **Interlude Enterprises** (Wabash Ave. and Wacker Dr., ☎ 312/641–1210) offers lunch cruises with an architectural narration. Cruises don't run in the winter.

Exploring Chicago

Outside downtown and the Loop, Chicago is a city of neighborhoods whose rich ethnic diversity gives the city its special air.

The Loop

Walking through Chicago's central business district (defined by the "loop" of the elevated train) is like taking a course in the history of American commercial architecture. From the Monadnock Building, the tallest structure built entirely of masonry, to the Sears Tower, the tallest building of any material, Chicago's skyscrapers have unique personalities. Keep an eye out for the sculptures by Picasso, Calder, Miró, Chagall, and other artists that adorn the plazas of many buildings.

The **Chicago Cultural Center** (78 E. Washington at Michigan Ave., ☎ 312/346–3278) used to be the city's main library; it's been used primarily for exhibits, lectures, and performances since the 1970s. Two splendid Tiffany-glass domes are among its treasures. **Marshall Field's & Co.** (111 N. State St., at Randolph St.) is the city's largest department store. Undergoing a massive, multiyear renovation, it has 500 departments and a Tiffany dome of its own. Field's anchors the **State Street Mall,** a patently unsuccessful 1980s attempt to rejuvenate the Loop shopping district. The loss of millions of dollars' worth of merchandise to the April 1992 floodwaters that submerged the sub-basements of major Loop department stores did nothing to improve the situation.

The terra-cotta **Reliance Building** (State and Washington Sts.), designed by Daniel Burnham in 1890, has the distinctive Chicago window, which juts out from the surface of the building with two side windows to catch the Lake Michigan breezes. The **Richard J. Daley Center** (Dearborn and Washington Sts.), named for the late Mayor Daley, is headquarters for the Cook County court system; in the plaza is a 50-ft Cor-Ten steel sculpture by Picasso.

Across Clark Street from the Daley Center is the handsome neoclassical **Chicago City Hall/Cook County Building,** designed by Holabird and Roche in 1911. Inside are spacious halls, high ceilings, and plenty of marble. If you're lucky, you may catch the city council in session—usually a good show, with plenty of hot air. A block north is a very different civic structure: Helmut Jahn's 1985 **State of Illinois Center** (Clark and Randolph Sts.), also known as Spaceship Chicago.

A few blocks to the northwest, **333 West Wacker Drive** was designed by Kohn, Pedersen, Fox in 1983 and constructed in an unpromisingly irregular shape, dictated by the triangular parcel on which it sits. A softly curving building with forest-green marble columns, a spacious plaza, and a shimmering green-glass skin, it is particularly lovely seen at sunset from the bridge over the Chicago River at Orleans Street, when the river and surrounding buildings are mirrored in the glass.

To the south, the graceful 1973 **First National Bank** (Dearborn and Madison Sts.) was one of the first skyscrapers to slope upward from its base like the letter *A*. The adjoining plaza is a popular summer hangout at lunch. A Chagall mosaic, *The Four Seasons,* is at the northeast corner.

Farther south are two handsome examples of very early skyscrapers. The 1895 **Marquette Building** (140 S. Dearborn St.), by Holabird and Roche, features an exterior terra-cotta bas relief and interior reliefs and mosaics depicting scenes from early Chicago history. The darkly handsome **Monadnock Building** (53 W. Jackson Blvd. at Dearborn St.), with walls 6 ft thick at the base, has been beautifully restored; the north half was built by Burnham and Root in 1891, the south half by Holabird and Roche in 1893.

Across the street is the gothic-style **Fisher Building** (343 S. Dearborn St.), designed by D. H. Burnham & Co. in 1896 and exquisitely ornamented in terra-cotta with carved cherubs and fish. The **Chicago Board of Trade** (141 W. Jackson Blvd. at La Salle St.), one of the few important Art Deco buildings in Chicago, was designed in 1930 by Holabird and Roche. At the top is a gilded statue of Ceres, the Greek goddess of grain—an apt overseer of the frenetic commodities trading that goes on within.

Farther west is the **Sears Tower** (233 S. Wacker Dr. at Jackson Blvd.), the world's tallest building. A Skidmore, Owings & Merrill design of 1974, the tower has 110 stories and is almost 1,500 ft tall. The view from the skydeck is unbeatable, but there are long lines on weekends. The Wacker Drive lobby has a jolly mobile by Alexander Calder. Two blocks north of the Board of Trade is the **Rookery** (209 S. La Salle St.), an imposing red-stone building designed in 1888 by Burnham and Root; the magnificent lobby was remodeled in 1905 by Frank Lloyd Wright.

One of Louis Sullivan's outstanding works is **Carson Pirie Scott & Co.** (Madison and State Sts.), the city's "second" department store, with spectacular ornamental ironwork around the main entrance. A block south on State Street at 17 East Monroe Street is the venerable **Palmer House** hotel (*see* Lodging, *below*), with its frescoed rococo lobby one flight up from the street-level arcade.

Chicago

800W
400W
001W
001E
Walton
Locust
Chestnut
Institute Pl.
Crosby
Kingsbury
Hudson
Rush
Water Tower
North
Branch
Chicago
River
Chicago Ave.
Superior
Huron
Erie
Ontario
Ohio
Grand Ave.
Larrabee
Orleans
Franklin
Wells
La Salle
Clark
Dearborn
State
Wabash Ave.
Museum
Illinois
Hubbard
Kinzie
400N
Wacker Dr.
Water
Milwaukee
Fulton
Union
O'HARE INTERNATIONAL AIRPORT
333 West Wacker Drive
Lake
State of Illinois Center
Randolph
Richard J. Daley Center
Marshall Field & Co.
Chicago City Hall/ Cook County Building
Washington
Reliance Building
THE LOOP
State Street Mall
001N
001S
Madison
First National Bank
Carson Pirie Scott & Co.
John F. Kennedy Expwy.
Desplaines
Jefferson
Clinton
Canal
Monroe
Peoria
Green
Halsted
90
94
Adams
The Rookery
Marquette Building
Palmer House
Orchestra Hall
Quincy
Jackson Blvd.
Sears Tower
Monadnock Building
Chicago Board of Trade
Fisher Building
400S
Van Buren
Harold Washington Library Center
290
Eisenhower Expwy.
Congress Pkwy.
La Salle St. Station
Harrison
Financial
Federal
Plymouth Ct.
South Br.
Chicago River
Dan Ryan Expwy.
800S
Polk
8th
9th
11th
Taylor
500W

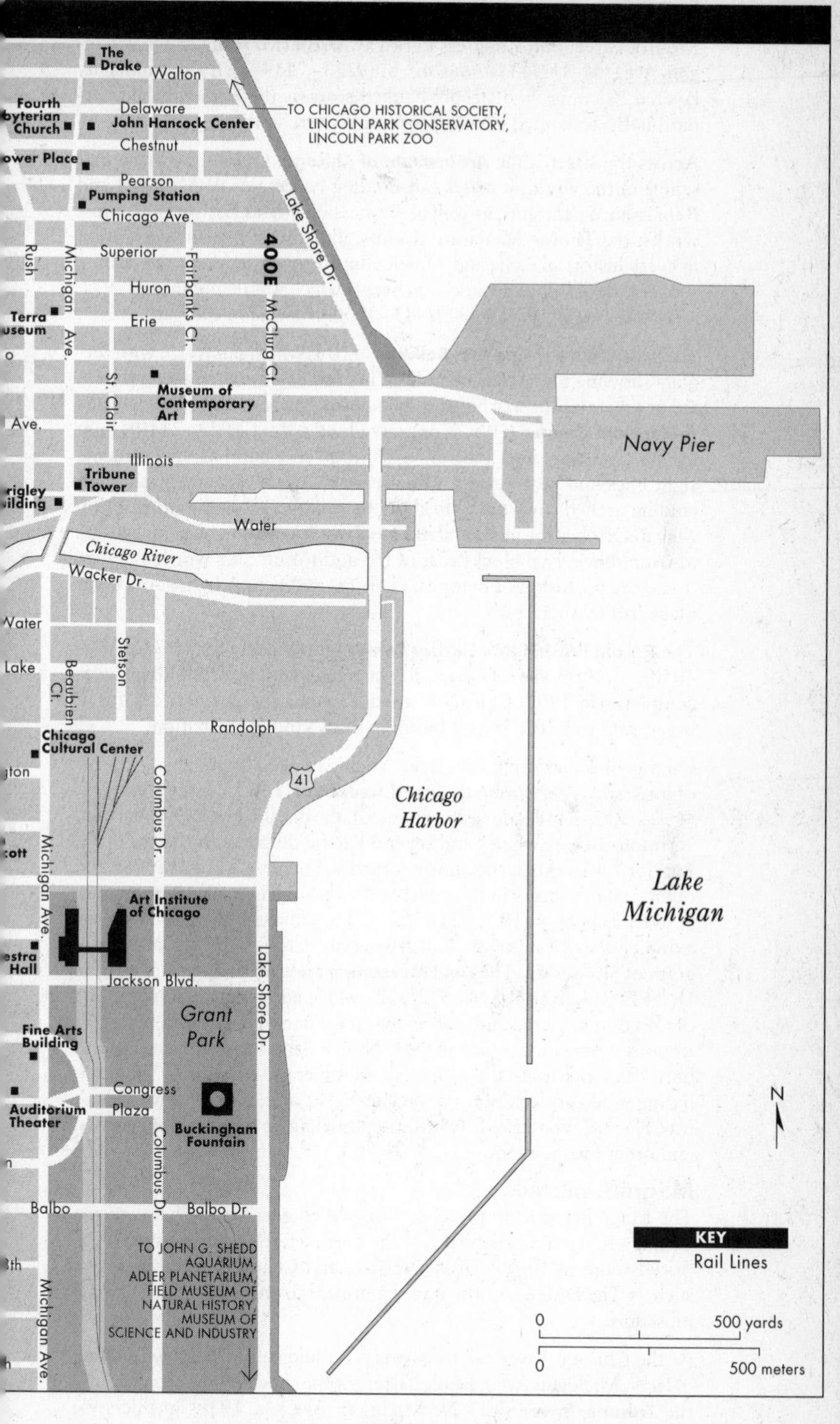
The Drake
Walton
Fourth Presbyterian Church
Delaware
John Hancock Center
TO CHICAGO HISTORICAL SOCIETY, LINCOLN PARK CONSERVATORY, LINCOLN PARK ZOO
Chestnut
Water Tower Place
Pearson
Pumping Station
Chicago Ave.
Lake Shore Dr.
Superior
400E
Rush
Michigan Ave.
Fairbanks Ct.
Huron
Terra Museum
Erie
McClurg Ct.
St. Clair
Museum of Contemporary Art
Navy Pier
Illinois
Tribune Tower
Wrigley Building
Water
Chicago River
Wacker Dr.
Water
Stetson
Lake
Beaubien Ct.
Randolph
Chicago Cultural Center
Columbus Dr.
41
Chicago Harbor
Michigan Ave.
Lake Michigan
Art Institute of Chicago
Orchestra Hall
Jackson Blvd.
Lake Shore Dr.
Grant Park
Fine Arts Building
Congress Plaza
Auditorium Theater
Buckingham Fountain
Columbus Dr.
N
Balbo
Balbo Dr.
KEY
Rail Lines
TO JOHN G. SHEDD AQUARIUM, ADLER PLANETARIUM, FIELD MUSEUM OF NATURAL HISTORY, MUSEUM OF SCIENCE AND INDUSTRY
0
500 yards
0
500 meters
Michigan Ave.

To the east lies one of Chicago's "art zones": Michigan Avenue between Monroe Street and Congress Parkway. **Orchestra Hall** (220 S. Michigan Ave., ☎ 312/435–6666 or 800/223–7114), with dramatically layered balconies and steeply banked seats, is the home of the internationally acclaimed Chicago Symphony Orchestra.

Across the street is the **Art Institute of Chicago.** One of the finest museums in the world, it offers outstanding collections of Medieval and Renaissance paintings, as well as Impressionist and Post-Impressionist works; the Thorne Miniature Rooms, illustrating interior decoration in every historical style; and a meticulous reconstruction of the trading room of the old Chicago Stock Exchange, which was demolished in 1972. *111 S. Michigan Ave., ☎ 312/443–3600. Admission charged.*

To the south is the **Fine Arts Building** (410 S. Michigan Ave.), with theaters showing foreign and art films. The handsome detailing on the exterior previews the marble and woodwork in the lobby. Nearby is the **Auditorium Theater** (50 E. Congress Pkwy., ☎ 312/922–2110), built in 1889 by Adler and Sullivan. The 4,000-seat hall has unobstructed sight lines and near-perfect acoustics; the interior ornamentation, including arched rows of lights along the ceiling, is breathtaking. From May to October, the mammoth **Buckingham Fountain** bubbles and gushes in **Grant Park,** two blocks east of the auditorium. It's worth a detour to see the profusion of nymphs, cherubs, and fish. A light show takes place from 9 to 11 PM.

The **Harold Washington Library Center** (400 S. State St., ☎ 312/747–4050), a postmodern homage to classical-style public buildings, was completed in 1991. Chicago waited 17 years for this new central library, said to be the largest building of its kind in the nation.

On a peninsula jutting into Lake Michigan at 12th Street is a cluster of museums. At the **John G. Shedd Aquarium** (1200 S. Lake Shore Dr., ☎ 312/939–2438; admission charged), the dazzling new Oceanarium, with four beluga whales and several Pacific dolphins, is the big draw. But don't miss the sharks, tarpon, turtles, and myriad smaller fish and other aquatic forms in the coral-reef exhibit. The **Adler Planetarium** (1300 S. Lake Shore Dr., ☎ 312/322–0300; admission charged for shows, exhibits free) is a museum with astronomy exhibits and a popular program of Sky Shows. The **Field Museum of Natural History** (Lake Shore Dr. at E. Roosevelt Rd., ☎ 312/922–9410; admission charged) is one of the country's great natural-history museums. The breadth of its collections is enormous; they include Native American artifacts, endless butterflies and insects, and rocks and minerals. Don't miss the fascinating (and eerie) exhibit on ancient Egypt and, if you've got kids in tow, Place of Wonder, where little ones can handle skeletons, meteorites, and other intriguing objects.

Magnificent Mile

The Magnificent Mile stretches along Michigan Avenue between the Chicago River and Oak Street, to the north. Here you'll find such high-priced shops as Gucci, Tiffany & Co., and Chanel; venerable hotels, such as The Drake and the Inter-Continental; and two fascinating art museums.

At the Chicago River are two ornate buildings: the **Wrigley Building** (410 N. Michigan Ave.), headquarters of the chewing-gum empire, and the **Tribune Tower** (435 N. Michigan Ave.), a 1930s gothic-style skyscraper. The base of the Trib Tower incorporates pieces of other buildings and monuments from around the world, including Westminster Abbey, the Parthenon, and the Pyramids.

For a waterfront detour, go down the steps to Michigan Avenue's lower level at Grand Avenue and walk east about five blocks to the very end. Here is **Navy Pier** (600 E. Grand Ave., ☏ 312/791–7437 for special events information), a former shipping pier that now has shops; restaurants and bars; a stage for music, dance, and drama performances; and a number of vessels that offer cruises on Lake Michigan. It's a pleasant place for taking in a great view of the skyline. One block south and two blocks west is **North Pier** (435 E. Illinois St.), a huge old warehouse converted into a waterfront mall with boutiques, gift shops, restaurants, the Chicago Children's Museum, and an arcade with virtual-reality games.

Follow Michigan Avenue north to Ontario Street and turn right for the **Museum of Contemporary Art** (237 E. Ontario St., ☏ 312/280–5161; admission charged; closed Mon.), a fine small museum specializing in 20th-century works. Farther north on Michigan is the **Terra Museum of American Art** (666 N. Michigan Ave., ☏ 312/664–3939; admission charged; closed Mon.), a small museum opened in the late 1980s with industrialist Daniel Terra's superb private collection. There are works here by almost every major American painter, including Whistler, Sargent, the Wyeths, and Mary Cassatt.

The **Water Tower,** one of the few buildings that survived the Chicago Fire of 1871, sits like a giant sand castle at Chicago Avenue and Pearson Street. Across the street at the **Pumping Station** is a tourist information center, where you can pick up maps and brochures and see a multimedia show about the city.

The gray-marble high rise called **Water Tower Place** (835 N. Michigan Ave.) has two department stores, Marshall Field's and Lord & Taylor; chain stores and boutiques; a cinema; and restaurants. In the next block is the sleek, 100-story **John Hancock Center** (875 N. Michigan Ave.), the local favorite for amazing views of the city. Across from it is the **Fourth Presbyterian Church** (126 E. Chestnut St.), a small gothic-style jewel with a courtyard where you can find respite from the surrounding bustle. During the week, the sanctuary offers occasional organ recitals and concerts.

At the head of the Magnificent Mile is the **Drake** (140 E. Walton Pl.; *see* Lodging, *below*), one of the city's oldest and grandest hotels; take a look at the marble-and-oak lobby, complete with cherub-laden fountain, even if you're not staying here. In nice weather you may want to cross Oak Street, in front of the main entrance, and take the underground passage that leads to Oak Street Beach and the lakefront promenade. Watch for speeding bicyclists, skateboarders, and in-line skaters.

Lincoln Park

"Lincoln Park" refers to an area that stretches from North Avenue (1600 N.) to Diversey Parkway (2800 N.), and from the lakefront on the east to about Racine Avenue (1200 W.) on the west. The adjoining lakefront park is also called Lincoln Park (causing visitors occasional confusion), though it stretches several miles farther north than the neighborhood.

The **Chicago Historical Society** (1601 N. Clark St., ☏ 312/642–4600; admission charged) is a stately brick building with a sparkling modern glass addition on the Clark Street side. Permanent exhibits include costume collections; the much-loved diorama room, which portrays scenes from Chicago's history; and a statue of Abraham Lincoln with a nose that gleams from having been rubbed by countless children.

Wandering north through **Lincoln Park** itself for half a mile will bring you to **Lincoln Park Zoo** (2200 N. Cannon Dr., ☎ 312/742–7695), whose 35 acres are home to all the requisite zoo denizens, including koala bears and several species of primates. The zoo opened in 1868, before the Chicago Fire; most of the buildings have been renovated. Just south of the zoo is **South Pond,** where you can rent paddleboats May–October. North of the zoo is the **Lincoln Park Conservatory** (2400 N. Stockton Dr., ☎ 312/742–7736), which has a palm house, a fernery, a cactus house, special exhibits, and large outdoor gardens.

At Fullerton Avenue, go west and enter the heart of the **Lincoln Park neighborhood,** where you'll pass elegant town houses and small apartment buildings from the late 1800s and early 1900s. The area declined after World War II as residents moved to the suburbs, but it was rediscovered in the 1970s, and it's not uncommon now to see million-dollar prices on some of the restored houses. The **Biograph Theater** (2433 N. Lincoln Ave., ☎ 312/348–4123), where the gangster John Dillinger met his end at the hands of the FBI, is on the National Register of Historic Places and still shows first-run movies.

Other Attractions

River North—a former warehouse neighborhood west of Michigan Avenue, bounded roughly by Clark Street, Chicago Avenue, Sedgwick Avenue, and the Chicago River—bloomed during the mid-1980s gentrification craze and now offers a number of art galleries. The Pumping Station Information Center (Michigan Ave. at Pearson St.) carries the *Chicago Gallery News,* which lists addresses, hours, and current exhibits.

The **Museum of Science and Industry,** on the lake in Hyde Park about 7 mi south of the Loop, is a treasure trove of gadgetry, applied science, and hands-on exhibits. There's a genuine German U-boat, a coal mine, Colleen Moore's Fairy Castle (a dollhouse to end all dollhouses), actual spacecraft from early NASA missions, and a giant-screen Omnimax Theater. *E. 57th St. and S. Lake Shore Dr.,* ☎ *312/684–1414. Admission charged.*

Parks and Gardens

Most of Chicago's more than 20 mi of shoreline is parkland or beach reserved for public use. A 19-mi path stretches along the lakefront, snaking through **Lincoln Park** (*see* Exploring Chicago, *above*), **Grant Park** (just east of the Loop, with acres of rose gardens), and **Jackson Park** (just south of the Museum of Science and Industry, with a wooded island and a Japanese garden) and winding past half a dozen harbors, two golf courses, Navy Pier, Buckingham Fountain, the lakefront museums, McCormick Place, and all the city's popular beaches. Bikes are the best way to cover maximum territory; they can be rented at the concession as you enter Lincoln Park at Fullerton Avenue or from **Village Cycle Center** (1337 N. Wells St., ☎ 312/751–2488). Bicycle thieves sometimes lurk in the comparatively deserted stretch south of McCormick Place; it's safe enough on weekends, but don't risk it alone during the week or at night.

There are also hundreds of parks in neighborhoods throughout the city. The **Garfield Park Conservatory** (300 N. Central Park Blvd., ☎ 312/746–5100) maintains 5 acres of plants and flowers under glass and holds four shows a year. The **Chicago Botanic Garden** (1000 Lake Cook Rd., Glencoe, ☎ 708/835–8208; $4 per car), north of the city, covers 300 acres and has 15 separate gardens and 10 greenhouses. The **Morton Arboretum** (Rte. 53, off I–88, ☎ 708/719–2465; $6 per car), in the western suburb of Lisle, has 1,500 acres of woody plants, woodlands, and outdoor gardens.

Chicago for Free—or Almost

The weekly *Reader* and other newspapers list free events. In summer, Grant Park's **Petrillo Bandshell** offers free public concerts almost every weekend and the Grant Park Symphony performs at least one night a week. Wednesdays at 12:15, the **Chicago Cultural Center** (78 E. Washington St., ☎ 312/346–3278) presents the Dame Myra Hess Memorial Concert Series, a program of recitals by rising professional classical musicians. Most **museums** have one free day a week.

What to See and Do with Children

At **Lincoln Park Zoo** (*see* Exploring Chicago, *above*), youngsters especially enjoy the Children's Zoo and the Farm-in-the-Zoo (farm animals plus a learning center with films and demonstrations). At **Brookfield Zoo** (1st Ave. and 31st St., Brookfield, ☎ 708/485–0263), one of the nation's best, the animals inhabit naturalistic settings that give visitors the feeling of being in the wild. **Kohl Children's Museum** (165 Green Bay Rd., Wilmette, ☎ 708/251–6950; admission charged) and the **Chicago Children's Museum** (465 E. Illinois St., ☎ 312/527–1000; admission charged), in the North Pier complex, have plenty of hands-on, "touch-and-feel" exhibits.

Shopping

Chicago shopping ranges from elegant department stores, small boutiques, and specialty shops to malls and bargain outlets.

Shopping Districts

The **Loop** and the **Magnificent Mile** (for both, *see* Exploring Chicago, *above*) concentrate major department and upscale specialty stores. **Oak Street** between Michigan Avenue and State Street has such top-of-the-line stores as Barney's New York (25 E. Oak St., ☎ 312/587–1700) and Giorgio Armani (113 E. Oak St., ☎ 312/751–2244). Three "vertical" malls combine department stores and specialty shops: **Water Tower Place** (835 N. Michigan Ave., *see* Exploring Chicago, *above*); the **Avenue Atrium** (900 N. Michigan Ave.); and **Chicago Place** (700 N. Michigan Ave.). The **Lincoln Park neighborhood** has several worthwhile shopping strips. Clark Street between Armitage (2000 N.) and Diversey (2800 N.) avenues is home to a number of clothing boutiques and specialty stores. From Diversey north to School Street (3300 N.) are several large antiques stores, more boutiques, and some bookstores.

Department Stores

Marshall Field's & Co. (111 N. State St., at Randolph St., ☎ 312/781–1000), the city's biggest department store, isn't—despite a $110 million renovation—as grand as it used to be, but you can still spend an entire day shopping here and not see the whole place. **Carson Pirie Scott & Co.** (1 S. State St., ☎ 312/641–7000), Chicago's "second" department store, would be a standout anywhere else. To keep up with the latest fashion trends, visit **Bloomingdale's** (Avenue Atrium, 900 N. Michigan Ave., ☎ 312/440–4460). For couture clothing, don't miss **Niemen Marcus** (737 N. Michigan Ave., ☎ 312/642–5900), which also has a great women's shoe department. **Saks Fifth Avenue** (Chicago Place, 700 N. Michigan Ave., ☎ 312/944–6500) is another must for those in search of high style.

Specialty Stores

MUSIC

Jazz Record Mart (11 W. Grand Ave., ☎ 312/222–1467) stocks a major collection of records, compact discs, and tapes, including many rare historic recordings and obscure imports. **Wax Trax Records** (1653 N. Damen Ave., ☎ 312/862–2121), the place for everything in popular music, including oldies and imports, is a "must" stop if you have teenagers with you.

Spectator Sports

Baseball

Chicago Cubs (Wrigley Field, 1060 W. Addison St., ☎ 312/404–2827; Apr.–Oct.).

Chicago White Sox (Comiskey Park, 333 W. 35th St., ☎ 312/924–1000 or 312/559–1212; Apr.–Oct.).

Basketball

Chicago Bulls (United Center, 1901 W. Madison St., ☎ 312/455–4500; Nov.–Apr.).

Football

Chicago Bears (Soldier Field, 425 E. McFetridge Dr., ☎ 312/663–5100; Aug.–Dec.).

Hockey

Chicago Blackhawks (United Center, ☎ 312/455–4500; Oct.–Apr.).

Horse Racing

Hawthorne Race Course (3501 S. Laramie Ave., Cicero, ☎ 708/780–3700; Oct.–Dec.) features flat racing. **Sportsman's Park** (3301 S. Laramie Ave., ☎ 312/242–1121) has both flat racing (Feb.–May) and harness racing (May–Oct.). **Maywood Park** (North and 5th Aves., Maywood, ☎ 312/626–4816) has harness racing (Oct.–Dec.).

Dining

Chicago has everything: from traditional aged steaks, ribs, and the ubiquitous Vienna hot dog to the loftier offerings of many excellent French and Italian restaurants to the exotic fare of Middle Eastern, Thai, and Vietnamese establishments. Most eating places listed below are in the Near North, River North, and Loop areas, within walking distance of the major hotel districts. A few are out in the city's residential neighborhoods and ethnic enclaves.

For clusters of ethnic restaurants too numerous to mention here, try Greektown (Halsted and Madison Sts.), Chinatown (Wentworth Ave. and 23rd St.), Little Italy (Taylor St. between Racine Ave. and Ashland Ave.), Argyle Street between Broadway and Sheridan Road (for Chinese and Vietnamese), Devon Avenue between 2200 W. and 3000 W. (Indian), and Clark Street from Belmont Avenue to Addison Street (Thai, Japanese, Chinese, Korean, Jamaican, Ethiopian, Mexican).

Restaurant listings appear in the monthly *Chicago* magazine and in the Friday editions of the *Chicago Tribune* and the *Sun-Times* (Weekend section). For price ranges, see Chart 1 (A) in On the Road with Fodor's.

$$$$ ★ Charlie Trotter's. This tastefully renovated Lincoln Park town house accommodates only 20 closely spaced tables. Owner and chef Charlie Trotter prepares stellar New American cuisine, incorporating flavors from around the globe into classic French dishes. The *prix fixe* degustation menus include up to seven courses and three desserts. *816*

W. Armitage Ave., ☎ *312/248–6228. Reservations required well in advance. Jacket preferred. AE, DC, MC, V. Closed Sun.–Mon. No lunch.*

$$$$ ★ **Everest.** On the 40th floor of a postmodern skyscraper in the heart of the financial district, this restaurant serves dishes squarely in the classic French tradition but with appeal to contemporary tastes. *440 S. La Salle St.,* ☎ *312/663–8920. Reservations required. Jacket required. AE, D, DC, MC, V. Closed Sun.–Mon. No lunch.*

$$$$ ★ **Le Français.** Only serious eaters should make the pilgrimage to this classic haute French outpost in the northwest suburbs. Dinner takes the entire evening, and the tab can easily top $100 per person. The menu changes nightly to reflect the best ingredients available—and the whim of the chef. Try the degustation menu, a bargain available weeknights. *269 S. Milwaukee Ave., Wheeling,* ☎ *708/541–7470. Reservations required. Jacket required. AE, D, DC, MC, V. Closed Sun. No lunch Mon., Sat.*

$$$$ **Spiaggia.** In elegant pink-and-teal quarters overlooking the lake, Spiaggia offers the most opulent Italian dining in town, with elaborate stuffed pastas, veal chops in a vodka-cream sauce, and other richly inventive dishes. Save room for dessert. The same for less can be had next door at the more casual Cafe Spiaggia. *980 N. Michigan Ave.,* ☎ *312/280–2750. Jacket required; no denim. AE, D, DC, MC, V. No lunch Sun.*

$$$$ **Trio.** Chicago's most acclaimed newcomer specializes in elaborate contemporary cuisine with Asian, French, and Italian influences. The decor is tastefully restrained, but the presentation is often whimsical: Dishes may be served on such unique objects as painters' palettes and mirrors. *1625 Hinman, Evanston,* ☎ *708/733–8746. Reservations required. Jacket required. AE, D, DC, MC, V. Closed Mon. No lunch.*

$$$ **Ambria.** In a spacious turn-of-the-century mansion, Ambria serves contemporary French food and light cuisine. Menus change seasonally; the emphasis is on using natural juices and vegetable reductions to accompany the entrées. *2300 N. Lincoln Park W,* ☎ *312/472–5959. Reservations required. AE, D, DC, MC, V. Closed Sun., holidays. No lunch.*

$$$ ★ **Arun's.** Long considered the city's best Thai restaurant, Arun's is known for its congenial staff, its elegant dining room showcasing native art, and last but not least, superbly presented dishes made with the freshest ingredients. *4156 N. Kedzie Ave.,* ☎ *312/539–1909. AE, D, DC, MC, V. Closed Mon. No lunch.*

$$$ **Le Titi de Paris.** It's worth the trip to the suburb of Arlington Heights on Chicago's northwest side for chef Pierre Pollin's classic French dishes in a refined, floral setting. *1015 W. Dundee Rd., Arlington Heights,* ☎ *708/506–0222. Reservations required. Jacket required. AE, D, DC, MC, V. Closed Sun.–Mon. No lunch Sat.*

$$$ **Morton's of Chicago.** Chicago's best steak house offers beautiful, hefty steaks cooked to perfection. Excellent service, classy ambience, and a very good wine list add to the appeal. Vegetarians and budget watchers should look elsewhere. *1050 N. State St.,* ☎ *312/266–4820. AE, D, DC, MC, V. No lunch.*

$$$ ★ **Printer's Row.** Named after its recently chic loft neighborhood in the South Loop, this warm and attractive restaurant offers inventive and satisfying American cuisine. Daily specials include at least one dish low in fat and sodium. *550 S. Dearborn St.,* ☎ *312/461–0780. Reservations required on weekends. AE, D, DC, MC, V. Closed Sun. No lunch Sat.*

$$$ ★ **Yoshi's Cafe.** Unassuming on the outside but elegant on the inside, Chef Yoshi Katsumura's restaurant features white-linen tablecloths and Asian-influenced contemporary French cuisine. Dishes are gorgeously

presented; try the saffron ravioli stuffed with lobster meat and covered with lobster sauce. *3257 N. Halsted St., ☏ 312/248–6160. Jacket required. AE, DC, MC, V. Closed Mon. No lunch.*

$$–$$$ ★ **Frontera Grill/Topolobampo.** In Frontera Grill's cozy, colorful storefront, genuine regional Mexican cooking goes way beyond burritos and chips: from charbroiled catfish (with pickled red onions and jicama salad) to garlicky skewered tenderloin (with poblano peppers, red onion, and bacon). Topolobampo, next door, shares the owners and the kitchen; it offers a more stately atmosphere and affords the chef an opportunity to experiment with more expensive ingredients. *445 N. Clark St., ☏ 312/661–1434. Reservations required at Topolobampo; advised at the grill. AE, D, DC, MC, V. Closed Sun.–Mon. No lunch Sat. at Topolobampo.*

$$–$$$ **Klay Oven.** The understated but pleasing decor and outstanding cuisine make this Chicago's best—and most expensive—Indian restaurant. Clay tandoor ovens bake mouth-watering tandoori chicken, mahimahi, and tiger prawns, and a variety of chutneys add zip to every bite. The eight-course degustation menus are excellent, as is the wine list. *414 N. Orleans St., ☏ 312/527–3999. AE, DC, MC, V. Closed Mon. No lunch weekends.*

$$ **The Berghoff.** This Loop institution has oak paneling, a bustling ambience, two huge dining rooms, and a splendid bar with Berghoff beer on tap. Expect a wait of 15 minutes or so at midday. American favorites augment the menu of German classics (Wiener schnitzel, sauerbraten). *17 W. Adams St., ☏ 312/427–3170. AE, DC, MC, V. Closed Sun., holidays.*

$$ **Cafe Ba-Ba-Reeba!** Chicago's best-known purveyor of *tapas* (varied edibles, served in small portions, that originated as accompaniments to drinks in Spanish bars), this large, open restaurant and its prominent bar are usually crowded with upscale young folk. The wide selection of cold and warm tapas ranges from stuffed cannelloni to veal with mushrooms. *2024 N. Halsted St., ☏ 312/935–5000. Large party reservations only. AE, D, DC, MC, V. Closed holidays. No lunch Mon.*

$$ ★ **Rosebud.** Specializing in good, old-fashioned southern Italian cuisine, Rosebud serves a superior red sauce, and the roasted peppers, homemade sausage, and exquisitely prepared pastas are not to be missed. The wait for a table can stretch to an hour or more, despite confirmed reservations. *1500 W. Taylor St., ☏ 312/942–1117. Reservations required. AE, D, DC, MC, V. No lunch weekends.*

$$ **Tuttaposto.** This upscale taverna specializes in Mediterranean cuisine prepared with such healthful ingredients as legumes and whole grains; the menu changes weekly. Wood-burning ovens cook seafood and meat entrées to perfection, and a small selection of regional wines complements meals nicely. For dessert, the homemade ice cream consistently receives rave reviews. *646 N. Franklin St., ☏ 312/943–6262. AE, D, DC, MC, V. No lunch weekends.*

$ **Ann Sather.** These three large, light, airy restaurants—two on the North Side, one in Hyde Park near the University of Chicago—emphasize home-style food and service. Specialties include omelets, Swedish pancakes, homemade cinnamon rolls, potato sausage, chicken croquettes, and sandwiches. *5207 N. Clark St., ☏ 312/271–6677; 929 W. Belmont Ave., ☏ 312/348–2378; 1329 E. 57th St., ☏ 312/947–9323. AE, MC, V.*

$ ★ **Pizzeria Uno/Pizzeria Due.** This is where Chicago deep-dish pizza got its start. Uno has been remodeled to resemble its franchised cousins in other cities, but its pizzas retain their light crust and distinctive tang. There's usually a shorter wait for a table at Pizzeria Due (same ownership and menu, different decor and longer hours), a block away. *Uno: 29 E. Ohio*

St., ☎ *312/321–1000. Due: 619 N. Wabash Ave.,* ☎ *312/943–2400. Reservations accepted weekday afternoons. AE, D, MC, V.*

$ **Reza's.** At this loft-like space with polished wood floors, exposed brick walls, and a relaxed ambience, everything on the menu is delicious (standouts are the tangy chicken kabobs and the lentil soup). Portions are large, but save room for one of the ultra-sweet desserts and a cup of Turkish coffee or tea. The Ontario Street restaurant in the River North area may be more convenient, but it doesn't match the Clark Street branch in decor or cuisine. *5255 N. Clark St.,* ☎ *312/561–1898; 432 W. Ontario St.,* ☎ *312/664–4500. No credit cards.*

$ **Three Happiness.** The specialty of this cavernous, kitchen-table-style Chinatown joint is its weekend dim sum brunch, served from 10 AM to 2 PM; the crowd begins to form at 9:30 on weekends. Go with a group to mix and match the little dishes of steamed and fried dumplings, rice cakes, custard squares, and other exotica. *2130 S. Wentworth Ave.,* ☎ *312/791–1228. No reservations weekends. AE, D, MC, V.*

Lodging

Chicago is the country's biggest convention town, and accommodations can be tight when major events are scheduled. Most hotels offer weekend specials when no big shows are on. Virtually every hotel chain, large or small, has at least one property in Chicago, and some have several. Hotels are concentrated in the Loop and the Near North Side. **Bed and Breakfast Chicago** (Box 14088, 60614, ☎ 312/951–0085) handles more than 50 B&Bs throughout the greater Chicago area. For price ranges, see Chart 2 (A) in On the Road with Fodor's.

$$$$ ★ **The Drake.** The grandest of Chicago's traditional hotels was built in 1920 in the style of an Italian Renaissance palace. It offers splendid lake views from two sides, and the spacious rooms are furnished with dark wood and floral upholstery for a 19th-century flavor. *140 E. Walton Pl., 60611,* ☎ *312/787–2200 or 800/553–7253,* FAX *312/951–5803. 535 rooms, 65 suites. Facilities: 3 restaurants, 2 lounges, concierge. AE, D, DC, MC, V.*

$$$$ **The Fairmont.** This 45-story neoclassical structure of Spanish pink granite is part of the Illinois Center complex and offers fine views of the lake and Grant Park. The sizable rooms are furnished in contemporary or period styles. *200 N. Columbus Dr., 60601,* ☎ *312/565–8000,* FAX *312/856–1032. 692 rooms, 72 suites. Facilities: 2 restaurants, 2 lounges, business services, valet, concierge. AE, D, DC, MC, V.*

$$$$ ★ **Four Seasons.** Occupying 17 floors in a major building, this luxurious hostelry offers spectacular lake and city views. Suggesting the decor of an English manor house, the smallish rooms have Italian marble, handcrafted woodwork, custom-woven rugs, and tasteful prints. *120 E. Delaware Pl., 60611,* ☎ *312/280–8800,* FAX *312/280–1748. 344 rooms, 121 suites, 16 apartments. Facilities: restaurant, café, lounge, health club, pool, concierge. AE, D, DC, MC, V.*

$$$$ **Sutton Place Hotel.** This ultra-modern hotel has a sleek, art-deco lobby and similarly stylish guest rooms, some of which have original photographs by Robert Mapplethorpe. Such features as VCRs, CD players, and CDs give the rooms a high-tech ambience. *21 E. Bellevue Pl., 60611,* ☎ *312/266–2100,* FAX *312/266–2103. 247 rooms, 41 suites. Facilities: restaurant, health club, concierge. AE, D, DC, MC, V.*

$$$ **Chicago Hilton and Towers.** This huge grand hotel at the south end of the Loop was lavishly restored in the mid-1980s. The ballroom is worthy of Marie Antoinette; guest rooms offer amenities and comfort. *720 S. Michigan Ave., 60605,* ☎ *312/922–4400,* FAX *312/922–5240. 1,543*

rooms. Facilities: 5 restaurants, lounge, tavern, café, pool, health club, concierge. AE, D, DC, MC, V.

$$$ ★ **Hotel Inter-Continental Chicago.** Having bought the adjacent Forum Hotel and completed a $10 million renovation of both properties in 1995, the Inter-Continental now has a dramatic lobby with a limestone-and-granite floor and a blue velvet banquette; the former Forum portion has a contemporary look. The features that earned the Inter-Continental national landmark status—such as the Italianate junior Olympic–size swimming pool—remain untouched. *505 N. Michigan Ave., Chicago 60611, ☎ 312/944–4100, FAX 312/944–4100. 844 rooms, 40 suites. Facilities: 2 restaurants, health club, pool, business services, valet, concierge. AE, D, DC, MC, V.*

$$$ **Palmer House.** Built more than a century ago by the Chicago merchant Potter Palmer, this hotel has public areas that reflect the opulence of the era, though its modern guest rooms are more ordinary. *17 E. Monroe St., 60603, ☎ 312/726–7500, FAX 312/263–2556. 1,669 rooms, 88 suites. Facilities: 6 restaurants, lounge, pool, fitness center, concierge. AE, D, DC, MC, V.*

$$$ ★ **The Raphael.** On a quiet, pretty street just off the Magnificent Mile, this hotel has Old World charm. The lobby has two-story cathedral windows, the modern guest rooms are tastefully decorated, and the staff is attentive. *201 E. Delaware Pl., 60611, ☎ 312/943–5000 or 800/821–5343, FAX 312/943–9483. 172 rooms. Facilities: restaurant, lounge. AE, D, DC, MC, V.*

$$ **City Suites Hotel.** Ten minutes north of the Loop, in the Lakeview neighborhood, this small European-style hotel is near many of Chicago's most popular restaurants, bars, theaters, and boutiques. The intimate, tastefully decorated lobby has a fireplace and a pretty floral-print carpet, and guest rooms are equally cozy, featuring chic black-and-white tile baths. This place is an excellent value. *933 W. Belmont Ave., Chicago 60657, ☎ 312/404–3400, FAX 312/404–3405. 15 rooms, 30 suites. Facilities: free movie channel, parking. AE, DC, MC, V.*

$$ ★ **Claridge Hotel.** Nestled among Victorian houses on a tree-lined Near North street, this 1930s building was fully renovated in 1987. It's intimate rather than bustling, and the decor is simple but tasteful. *1244 N. Dearborn Pkwy., 60610, ☎ 312/787–4980 or 800/245–1258, FAX 312/266–0978. 173 rooms, 3 suites. Facilities: restaurant, bar, concierge. AE, D, DC, MC, V.*

$$ **Lenox House.** Conveniently located near North Michigan Avenue, this hotel has one-room "suites," each with both a Murphy bed and a sofa bed, and a wet-bar kitchen, all done in generic '80s style. *616 N. Rush St., 60611, ☎ 312/337–1000 or 800/445–3669, FAX 312/337–7217. 330 suites. Facilities: restaurant, bar, concierge. AE, D, DC, MC, V.*

$ **Chicago International Hostel.** Dormitory-style accommodations near Loyola University in Rogers Park cost under $20 a night, including linens. Holders of International Youth Hostel cards get a discount. *6318 N. Winthrop Ave., 60660, ☎ 312/262–1011. 100 beds. Facilities: kitchen, laundry. No credit cards.*

Motels

Best Western River North (125 W. Ohio St., 60610, ☎ 312/467–0800 or 800/727–0800, FAX 312/467–1665), 149 rooms, 24 suites, restaurant, pool, health club; **$$. Comfort Inn of Lincoln Park** (601 W. Diversey Ave., 60614, ☎ 312/348–2810, FAX 312/348–1912), 74 rooms; $$. **Hojo Inn** (720 N. La Salle St., 60610, ☎ 312/664–8100, FAX 312/664–2365), 71 rooms, 4 suites, restaurant; $. **Ohio House** (600 N. La Salle St., 60610, ☎ 312/943–6000), 49 rooms, 1 suite, coffee shop; $.

The Arts and Nightlife

For listings of arts and entertainment events, check the monthly *Chicago* magazine (on newsstands) or the Friday editions of the *Chicago Tribune* or the *Chicago Sun-Times*. Two free weeklies, *The Reader* (available on Thursdays) and *New City* (available on Wednesdays), which can be found at restaurants and bars, are the best sources for what's happening in clubs and small theaters and for showings of noncommercial films.

The Arts

Chicago is a splendid city for the arts, with more than 50 theater groups, a world-class orchestra and opera company, dozens of smaller musical ensembles, and several movie theaters that go way beyond commercial Hollywood offerings.

THEATER

Half-price theater tickets are available for many productions on the day of the performance at the **Hot Tix** booth (108 N. State St., ☎ 312/977–1755; cash only). Among the many commercial theaters are the **Auditorium Theatre** (50 E. Congress Pkwy., ☎ 312/922–2110), the **Royal George Theater Center** (1641 N. Halsted St., ☎ 312/988–9000), and the **Shubert Theater** (22 W. Monroe St., ☎ 312/977–1700). Several small local ensembles have made the big jump into national prominence: **Steppenwolf** (1650 N. Halsted St., ☎ 312/335–1650), **Remains Theater** (1800 N. Clybourn Ave., ☎ 312/335–9800), and **Body Politic/Victory Gardens** (2257–61 N. Lincoln Ave., ☎ 312/871–3000). The city's oldest repertory theater, the **Goodman** (200 S. Columbus Dr., ☎ 312/443–3800), offers polished presentations of both contemporary works and classics.

MUSIC

The **Chicago Symphony** performs at Orchestra Hall (220 S. Michigan Ave., ☎ 312/435–6666 or 800/223–7114; Sept.–May) under the direction of Daniel Barenboim. In summer, James Levine takes over the baton and the symphony moves outdoors to take part in the **Ravinia Festival** (Highland Park, ☎ 312/728–4642).

OPERA

Lyric Opera of Chicago (20 N. Wacker Dr., ☎ 312/332–2244; Sept.–Jan.) performs grand opera with international stars at the Civic Opera House; tickets are difficult to come by. **Chicago Opera Theatre** (2936 N. Southport Ave., ☎ 312/292–7521) specializes in English-language productions of smaller works.

DANCE

Ballet Chicago (222 S. Riverside Plaza, ☎ 312/993–7575) is the city's only resident classical ballet troupe. **Hubbard Street Dance Company** (☎ 312/663–0853), popular for its contemporary, jazzy vitality, usually performs in the Civic Opera House.

FILM

In addition to the usual commercial theaters, Chicago has several venues for the avant-garde, vintage, or merely offbeat: **Facets Multimedia** (1517 W. Fullerton Ave., ☎ 312/281–4114), **Film Center of the Art Institute** (Columbus Dr. at Jackson Blvd., ☎ 312/443–3737), **Fine Arts Theatre** (418 S. Michigan Ave., ☎ 312/939–3700), **Music Box Theatre** (3733 N. Southport Ave., ☎ 312/871–6604), and **Chicago Filmmakers** (1543 W. Division St., ☎ 312/384–5533).

Nightlife

Chicago comes alive at night with something for everyone, from loud and loose to sophisticated and sedate. Shows usually begin at 9 PM; cover charges generally range from $3 to $7, depending on the day of the week. Many spots have a drink minimum instead of, or in addition to, a cover charge. Most bars are open until 2 AM, and some even serve until 4 AM.

BLUES CLUBS

In the years following World War II, Chicago-style blues grew into its own musical form. After fading in the '60s, Chicago blues is coming back, although more strongly on the trendy North Side than on the South Side, where it all began. The more famous clubs are **Blue Chicago** (937 N. State St., ☎ 312/642–6261), **B.L.U.E.S.** (2519 N. Halsted St., ☎ 312/528–1012), **Buddy Guy's Legends** (754 S. Wabash Ave., ☎ 312/427–0333), and **Kingston Mines** (2548 N. Halsted St., ☎ 312/477–4646). The **New Checkerboard Lounge** (423 E. 43rd St., ☎ 312/624–3240) is in a rough neighborhood but has a long pedigree.

COMEDY CLUBS

The granddaddy of them all is **Second City** (1616 N. Wells St., ☎ 312/337–3992), which usually has two different revues playing at once. The **Improv** (504 N. Wells St., ☎ 312/782–6387) aims for spontaneity. The best stand-up comedy in town is found at **Zanies** (1548 N. Wells St., ☎ 312/337–4027).

FOLK CLUBS

No Exit (6970 N. Glenwood Ave., ☎ 312/743–3355), a coffeehouse right out of the 1960s, offers folk, jazz, and poetry readings. **Old Town School of Folk Music** (909 W. Armitage Ave., ☎ 312/525–7793) mixes local talent and outstanding nationally known performers.

JAZZ CLUBS

Jazz Showcase (Blackstone Hotel, 636 S. Michigan Ave., ☎ 312/427–4846) books nationally known groups. The **Gold Star Sardine Bar** (680 N. Lake Shore Dr., ☎ 312/664–4215), a tiny spot in a splendid renovated building, books top names that attract a trendy clientele. **Pops for Champagne** (2934 N. Sheffield Ave., ☎ 312/472–1000) combines small-group jazz and a popular champagne bar. The **Green Mill** (4802 N. Broadway, ☎ 312/878–5552), a Chicago institution off the beaten track, books solid local acts.

ROCK CLUBS

Avalon Niteclub (959 W. Belmont Ave., ☎ 312/472–3020) has been around for a long time, but the acts are current. **Cabaret Metro** (3730 N. Clark St., ☎ 312/549–0203) presents nationally known and local artists and has a new dance floor downstairs. The **Cubby Bear** (1059 W. Addison St., ☎ 312/327–1662), across from Wrigley Field, offers a variety of rock, fusion, and reggae acts. In the hip Wicker Park neighborhood, the **Double Door** (1572 N. Milwaukee Ave., ☎ 312/489–3160) books top and up-and-coming local artists. **Lounge Ax** (2438 N. Lincoln Ave., ☎ 312/525–6620) offers a mix of local rock, folk, country, and reggae acts nightly. The **Wild Hare** (3530 N. Clark St., ☎ 312/327–4273) is the city's premier reggae club.

FOR SINGLES

Chicago's legendary "Rush Street" singles scene is actually on Division Street between Clark and State; here you'll find such bars as **Mother's** (26 W. Division St., ☎ 312/642–7251) and **Butch McGuire's**

(20 W. Division St., ☏ 312/337–9080) jammed with young professionals. There's another cluster of bar life in the neighborhood around Halsted and Armitage streets in Lincoln Park. **North Pier** (435 E. Illinois St.) has several popular singles spots, including the **Baja Beach Club** (☏ 312/222–1993) and **Dick's Last Resort** (☏ 312/836–7870). The quickly gentrifying Wicker Park/Bucktown area now has many bars and nightclubs, especially near the intersection of Milwaukee, Damen, and North avenues. Two of the most popular spots are **Red Dog** (1958 N. Damen Ave., ☏ 312/278–1009) and **Mad Bar** (1640 N. Damen Ave., ☏ 312/227–2277), a see-and-be-seen bar that showcases live music periodically.

GAY BARS

The area around Halsted Street between approximately Wellington Street and Addison Street has the city's highest concentration of gay bars.

Excursion to Oak Park

Getting There

Take I–290W to Harlem Avenue and exit to the left. Turn right at the top of the ramp, head north on Harlem Avenue to Chicago Avenue, turn right, and proceed to Forest Avenue.

What to See and Do

Founded in the 1850s, just west of the Chicago border, Oak Park is one of Chicago's oldest suburbs and a living museum of Prairie School residential architecture. Visit the **Frank Lloyd Wright Home and Studio** (951 Chicago Ave., corner of Forest Ave., ☏ 708/848–1500; admission charged; closed major holidays), built in 1889 and, after a long period of neglect, lovingly restored by a group of citizens working with the National Trust for Historic Preservation. A few blocks away is **Ernest Hemingway's boyhood home** (600 N. Kenilworth Ave.), a gray stucco house not open to the public. The poured-concrete **Unity Temple** (875 Lake St., ☏ 708/848–6225) was built for a Unitarian congregation in 1905. The **Oak Park Visitors Center** (158 N. Forest Ave., ☏ 708/848–1500) can provide further information on the area.

Excursion to Baha'i House of Worship

Getting There

Take Lake Shore Drive north to its end at Hollywood, then turn right onto Sheridan Road and follow it about 10 mi.

What to See and Do

Baha'i House of Worship (100 Linden Ave., Wilmette, ☏ 708/853–2300) is a sublimely lovely nine-sided building that incorporates a wealth of architectural styles and symbols from the world's religions—and symbolizes unity. The symmetry and harmony of the building are paralleled in the formal gardens that surround it.

Excursion to Joliet's Riverboat Casinos

Getting There

Joliet is about 45 mi southeast of downtown Chicago off I–55S.

What to See and Do

Two casino riverboats are docked on the Des Plaines River in Joliet. The triple-deck **Harrah's Casino** (Joliet St., ☏ 800/427–7247) floats in the heart of downtown. For a break from the gambling, try **Androttis,** an Italian restaurant at the Harrah's Pavilion on shore. The **Empress River Casino** (off Rte. 6 on Empress Dr., ☏ 708/345–6789) is a somewhat smaller boat with the full assortment of games of chance. The casino is in the southwest corner of Joliet, 50 mi from downtown Chicago. There are no betting limits, but gamblers must be 21 to board either boat. Daily cruises are available, weather permitting.

GALENA AND NORTHWESTERN ILLINOIS

The tiny town of Galena (pop. 3,900) features beautifully preserved pre–Civil War architecture, with houses in Federal, Italianate, and Gothic Revival styles; a large concentration of antiques shops; and (rare in the Midwest) hilly terrain. There's good biking, cross-country skiing, fishing, hunting, and camping in the region.

Galena's fortunes were based on the large lead deposits in the surrounding hills. Lead mining took off here in the 1820s, and Galena had a near-monopoly on shipping it down the Mississippi until the railroad came through in 1854. A depression later that decade and then the Civil War disrupted the lead trade and sent the city into an economic decline from which it never recovered. As a result, Galena today looks much as it did in the 1850s. Galena's other claim to fame is as the home of Ulysses S. Grant, commander of the Union Army in the Civil War and later the 18th president of the United States.

The region surrounding Galena is dotted with tiny towns that have been similarly bypassed by the 20th century. Among their offbeat charms are an antique-tractor museum (in Stockton) and the world's largest mallard hatchery (in Hanover). Stockton is also a time capsule of turn-of-the-century architecture, and much of Mount Carroll is registered as a National Historic District.

Tourist Information

Galena/Jo Daviess County: Convention and Visitors Bureau (101 Bouthillier St., Galena 61036, ☎ 815/777–0203 or 800/747–9377).

Getting There

By Car

From Chicago, take I–90 86 mi to Rockford, then Rte. 20W 81 mi to Galena. From Iowa, pick up Rte. 20E at Dubuque and continue 16 mi east across the Mississippi.

Exploring Galena and Northwestern Illinois

In **Galena,** the **Ulysses S. Grant Home,** built in 1860 in the Italianate bracketed style, was presented to Grant in 1865 by Galena residents in honor of his service to the Union. The family lived there until Grant's victory in the 1868 presidential election. In 1905 Grant's children gave the house to the state; now a state historic site, the house has been meticulously restored to its 1868 appearance. *500 Bouthillier St., ☎ 815/777–0248. Closed holidays.*

The **Belvedere Mansion and Gardens** centers on an 1857 Italianate mansion built for a steamboat magnate. It has been lavishly furnished by the current owners in a fashion that some locals consider gaudy; accoutrements include the famous green drapes from the movie *Gone with the Wind* and furnishings from Liberace's estate. *1008 Park Ave., ☎ 815/777–0747. Admission charged. Closed Nov.–May.*

Galena's oldest house is the 1826 **Dowling House** (220 Diagonal St., ☎ 815/777–1250; admission charged). The **Toy Soldier Collection** (310 S. Main St., ☎ 815/777–0383) has a collection of antique toy soldiers. The **Old General Store Museum** (233 S. Main St., ☎ 815/777–9129; closed weekdays Nov.–Dec., Jan.–May) re-creates a 19th-century emporium. The shops on Main Street are also fun to browse. A **trolley tour** (314 N. Main St., ☎ 815/777–1248) of the town strengthens the time-machine impression and rests hill-worn legs.

A huge swath of rolling countryside east of town, the **Galena Territory** started as a vacation-home development in the early 1980s but has taken on a life of its own as a recreation area. Hunting, fishing, and golf are popular. Watch out for deer on the back roads; they're everywhere.

Southeast of Galena, off Rte. 20 on Rte. 84, is **Hanover,** where mallards outnumber people 200 to 1. The **Whistling Wings** hatchery (113 Washington St., ☎ 815/591–3512) has 200,000 of them and offers tours by appointment. Rte. 84 along the Mississippi passes through **Savanna,** which has a number of large, well-preserved 19th-century houses. East on Rte. 52, **Mount Carroll's** rolling hills and gracious 19th-century frame and masonry buildings recall a small New England town, complete with town square. The **Campbell Center for Historic Preservation** (203 E. Seminary St., ☎ 815/244–1173) has workshops on architectural and fine-arts preservation.

To the north on Rte. 78 is **Stockton,** at 1,000 ft Illinois's highest town, where the business district preserves many of the lacy, cupola-topped structures beloved of the late Victorians. At **Arlo's Tractor Collection/Museum** (7871 S. Ridge Rd., ☎ 815/947–2593; tours by appointment only; closed Nov.–Apr.) there are 30 restored antique tractors, all in working order.

Shopping

Galena's Main Street is lined with more than 20 antiques stores and art galleries, plus a variety of boutiques, crafts shops, and bakeries. There's more good antiquing and many artists' studios in **Stockton, Warren,** and **Elizabeth.**

Sports and the Outdoors

Biking

Hilly back roads around Galena offer challenging bicycling. The **Old Stagecoach Trail** runs parallel to Rte. 20, winding through Apple River and Warren. **Chestnut Mountain Resort** (*see* Dining and Lodging, *below*) rents mountain bikes, or try Dubuque, Iowa. The county tourism office (*see* Tourist Information, *above*) has maps.

Fishing

Licenses can be purchased at marinas, bait shops, hardware stores, and other outlets, or contact the **Illinois Bureau of Tourism** (*see* Visitor Information, *above*) or the **Illinois Department of Conservation** (2612 Locust St., Sterling 61081, ☎ 815/625–2968).

Golf

Apple Canyon Lake Golf Course (14A400 Canyon Club Dr., Apple Canyon Lake, ☎ 815/492–2182), nine holes. **Eagle Ridge Inn and Resort** in Galena Territory (*see* Dining and Lodging, *below*), one 9-hole and two 18-hole courses. **Lacoma Golf Course** (8080 Timmerman Dr., East Dubuque, ☎ 815/747–3874), three 9-holes and one 18-hole course.

Hiking and Backpacking

Mississippi Palisades State Park (4577 Rte. 84N, Savanna, ☎ 815/273–2731), about 30 mi south of Galena, offers hiking with river views. More cliffs and canyons can be found at **Apple River Canyon State Park** (8763 E. Canyon Rd., north of Rte. 20 near Stockton, ☎ 815/745–3302).

Horseback Riding

Shenandoah Riding Center (Galena Territory, Rte. 20E, Galena, ☎ 815/777–2373) has lessons and trails, hay and sleigh rides.

Ski Areas

Cross-Country

Eagle Ridge Inn and Resort (*see* Dining and Lodging, *below*) maintains more than 35 mi of groomed trails. **Lacoma Golf Course** (*see* Golf, *above*) opens its 260-acre course to skiers, but you have to break your own trails. **Mississippi Palisades State Park** and **Apple River Canyon State Park** (*see* Hiking and Backpacking, *above*) have marked trails.

Downhill

It's not the Alps, or even the Catskills, but if you want downhill skiing in Illinois, try **Chestnut Mountain Resort** (*see* Dining and Lodging, *below*), with 16 runs that overlook the Mississippi.

Dining and Lodging

Galena-area restaurant fare runs to hearty steaks, burgers, and ribs. Several bakeries along Galena's Main Street offer tempting cookies and pastries. A stay in one of the area's 40-odd bed-and-breakfasts is almost de rigueur; some are right in town, others are in the Galena Territory or other rustic outlying areas. The county tourist office (*see* Tourist Information, *above*) has a complete list of B&Bs and other types of lodging; it also keeps track of vacancies. For price ranges, see Charts 1 (B) and 2 (A) in On the Road with Fodor's.

East Dubuque

DINING AND LODGING

Timmerman's Lodge and Supper Club. Perched on a bluff above the Mississippi River, this modern complex is popular with riverboat gamblers (*see* Nightlife, *below*). Most of the rooms are 1980s Holiday Inn style, but a few have antique furnishings and decor. The elegant Supper Club has spectacular views, rib-eye steaks, and candlelight. *7777 Timmerman Dr., 61025, ☎ 815/747–3181 (lodge), 815/747–3316 (Supper Club). 74 rooms, 2 suites. Facilities: restaurant, pool, sauna. AE, D, MC, V. $$*

Galena

DINING

Kingston Inn. In an 1850s building you can sample a variety of cuisines, from French (Alsatian duckling with honey-walnut sauce) to American (roast pork whiskey Jack with horseradish). They also brew their own beer. The singing waiters and waitresses are accompanied by a versatile piano player who can handle any request. *300 N. Main St., ☎ 815/777–0451. D, DC, MC, V. $$–$$$*

Cafe d'Italia. Featured in the movie *Field of Dreams*, this cozy Italian restaurant done in wood and tile serves reliable versions of minestrone, lasagna, veal parmigiana, and other standards. *301 N. Main St., ☎ 815/777–0033. AE, DC, MC, V. $$*

Baker's Oven. At this quaint bakery furnished with vintage kitchen implements and other antiques, have homemade soup, a generous sandwich, or prime rib, but save room for the delectable apple dumplings or other baked goods. *200 N. Main St., ☎ 815/777–9105. MC, V. $–$$*

DINING AND LODGING

Chestnut Mountain Resort. Perched on a bank of the Mississippi, the main building has a Swiss-chalet look; the rooms are Spartan, as befits hunters and skiers. The dining room, overlooking the river, offers adequate steak-and-burger fare and a spectacular view. *8700 W. Chestnut Rd., 61036, ☎ 815/777–1320 or 800/397–1320. 126 rooms. Facilities: restaurant, bar, tennis courts, indoor pool, alpine skiing, alpine slide, mountain bike rentals. AE, D, DC, MC, V. $$–$$$*

DeSoto House Hotel. The largest hotel in Galena has been in continuous operation for 138 years; Lincoln really did sleep here. The spacious rooms are furnished in a style reminiscent of the 1860s. An elegant curving staircase rises from the lobby to the second floor. The stately Generals' Dining Room serves straightforward steaks, chops, and seafood; the Courtyard restaurant is open for breakfast and lunch. *230 S. Main St., 61036, ☎ 815/777–0090 or 800/343–6562. 53 rooms, 2 suites. Facilities: 2 restaurants, tavern. AE, D, DC, MC, V. $$–$$$*

Farmer's Home Hotel. This restored 19th-century inn is near downtown. The rooms are furnished with original simple Victorian pieces. Breakfasts featuring organically grown ham and home-smoked salmon are a specialty. *334 Spring St., 61036, ☎ 815/777–3456 or 800/373–3456, FAX 815/777–3470. 7 rooms, 2 suites, 2-room cottage. Facilities: dining room, tavern, outdoor hot tub, bicycles. AE, D, DC, MC, V. $$–$$$*

Galena Territory

DINING AND LODGING

Eagle Ridge Inn and Resort. This rustic yet swanky complex is perfect for golfers (*see* Golf, *above*) and pretty good for everyone else. Guest rooms are spacious and plush, with sleeping and sitting areas done in dark woods and floral fabrics; all have views of lake or woodland. The formal restaurant offers excellent American cuisine. *Rte. 20E, Galena 61036, ☎ 815/777–2444. 66 rooms; 225 condominiums, town houses, and homes. Facilities: restaurant, ice-cream parlor, indoor pool, health club, children's recreation program, riding stables, alpine and cross-country skiing. AE, D, DC, MC, V. $$$$*

Motels

Best Western Quiet House Suites (Rte. 20E, Galena 61036, ☎ 815/777–2577), 42 suites, pool, fitness center, some wheelchair-accessible rooms; **$$$**. **Palace Motel** (Rte. 20W, Galena 61036, ☎ 815/777–2043), 64 rooms, Continental breakfast, outdoor pool; $$. **Grant Hills Motel** (Rte. 20E, Galena 61036, ☎ 815/777–2116), 35 rooms, Continental breakfast, outdoor pool, playground, courtesy car into town; $–$$.

Nightlife

Riverboat gambling on replicas of 19th-century boats provides a unique nightlife along the Mississippi River stretching from Galena in northern Illinois down to East St. Louis in the southern part of the state. In Galena, you board the ***Silver Eagle*** (Frentress Lake Marina, ☎ 800/745–8371), a modern casino boat that resembles a luxurious yacht rather than a paddle wheeler. There are eight cruises daily; the boat docks 10 minutes west of downtown Galena on Hwy. 20. For other gambling attractions both on the Mississippi and other inland rivers, *see* Joliet *above,* or East St. Louis and Rock Island, *below.*

ELSEWHERE IN THE STATE

Springfield

Getting There

I–55 runs north–south through the city. I–72 comes from Champaign and Decatur to the east. The Amtrak route from Chicago to St. Louis stops in Springfield.

What to See and Do

Illinois's capital has perhaps the highest concentration anywhere of sites dedicated to Abraham Lincoln. The **Lincoln Home National Historic Site** (426 S. 7th St., ☎ 217/492–4150), the **Lincoln Tomb State Historic Site** at Oak Ridge Cemetery (1500 N. Monument Ave., ☎ 217/782–2717), and the **Lincoln-Herndon Law Offices** (6th and Adams Sts., ☎ 217/785–7960) provide glimpses into his life and career before he became president. The **Old State Capitol** (Downtown Mall, ☎ 217/785–7960) has been restored to the way it looked during Lincoln's legislative years. (The "new" **state capitol building,** at 2nd Street and Capitol Avenue, dates from the 1860s.) About 20 mi northwest of Springfield is the **Lincoln's New Salem State Historic Site** (Rte. 97 near Petersburg, ☎ 217/632–4000), where Lincoln lived and studied law during his twenties.

Aside from Lincolniana, Springfield also boasts the **Dana Thomas House,** built by Frank Lloyd Wright in 1903 for a local socialite and now a state historic site. Elaborately restored in the late 1980s, it's among the most perfectly preserved examples of early Wright architecture, art glass, and furniture. *301 E. Lawrence Ave., ☎ 217/782–6776. Closed Sun.–Wed., Fri.*

The **Springfield Convention and Visitors Bureau** (109 N. 7th St., 62701, ☎ 217/789–2360 or 800/545–7300) has further information on area attractions.

Riverboat Gambling

In recent years, casino-style riverboat gambling has become one of the most popular attractions outside of Chicago. There are no betting limits in Illinois and no one under 21 is allowed in gaming areas.

East St. Louis

GETTING THERE

From downtown St. Louis, take I–40 over the Poplar Street Bridge, then I–55 to the 4th Street exit. Follow 4th Street to River Park Dr.; turn left, then left again at Front Street.

WHAT TO SEE AND DO

The ***Casino Queen*** (200 South Front St., ☎ 800/777–0777) is a side-wheeler and a romantic replica of those lavish riverboats that paddled up and down the Mississippi more than 100 years ago. Two decks are devoted to gambling; a third has a dining room. There are breakfast, lunch, and dinner cruises daily.

Rock Island

GETTING THERE

From I–80, at the Quad Cities, take I–280 to Rock Island exit on Rte. 92.

WHAT TO SEE AND DO

Jumer's Casino Rock Island (18th St. at Mississippi Riverfront, ☎ 800/477–7747) is in "The District," Rock Island's downtown arts and entertainment center. The boat's eight daily cruises feature three decks of Las Vegas–style casino action. The **Effie Afton Restaurant** (Rock Island Riverfront, ☎ 309/793–4811), docked next to the casino, is in a converted tugboat and serves lunch and dinner.

INDIANA

By Peggy Ammerman Bowman

Capital	Indianapolis
Population	5,544,154
Motto	The Crossroads of America
State Bird	Cardinal
State Flower	Peony

Visitor Information

Indiana Department of Commerce's Division of Tourism (1 N. Capitol Ave., Indianapolis 46204, ☎ 317/232–8860 or 800/289–6646).

Scenic Drives

The drive along the **Ohio River Scenic Route,** on Rtes. 56 and 156 between Madison and Aurora, takes about an hour. The 50-mi **Lincoln Heritage Trail/George Rogers Clark Trail,** on Rtes. 62 and 162 from New Albany to Gentryville, runs through the Hoosier National Forest. The 90-mi **Hoosier Heritage Trail Scenic Route,** on Rte. 66 from Newburgh through Tell City to Sulphur, begins at the Ohio River and ends up in the Hoosier National Forest. The 130-mi **U.S. Circle Tour Route** goes along U.S. 20 from the Ohio state line through the Amish country to the Indiana dune lands and Lake Michigan. The Indiana segment of the **National Road Route** spans the entire state on U.S. 40—from the Ohio border to the Illinois border—a distance of about 110 mi.

National and State Parks

National Parks

George Rogers Clark National Historical Park (401 S. 2nd St., Vincennes 47591, ☎ 812/882–1776; admission charged) pays tribute to Clark's campaign to wrest Fort Sackville from the British and to open the Western frontier. At **Indiana Dunes National Lakeshore** (1100 N. Mineral Springs Rd., Porter 46304, ☎ 219/926–7561) arctic bearberry grows next to prickly-pear cactus, and dogwoods next to jack pines along the shores of Lake Michigan. Trace the footsteps of Lincoln as a young boy at the **Lincoln Boyhood National Memorial** (Box 1816, Lincoln City 47552, ☎ 812/937–4541; admission charged). At the 188,000-acre **Hoosier National Forest** (811 Constitution Ave., Bedford 47421, ☎ 812/275–5987), Knobstone Trail wends a 60-mi path along lofty ridgetops through dense stands of oak, maple, and walnut.

State Parks

Indiana's 20 state parks are operated by the Department of Natural Resources (402 W. Washington St., Indianapolis 46204, ☎ 317/232–4124 or, in IN only, 800/622–4931) and are open daily year-round. Indiana's newest state park, **Falls of the Ohio** (914 E. Main St., New Albany 47150, ☎ 812/945–6284), showcases 220 acres of the world's largest exposed Devonian fossil beds. **Lincoln State Park** (Rte. 162, Lincoln City 47552, ☎ 812/937–4710) is adjacent to the Lincoln Boyhood National Memorial. At **Spring Mill** (Rte. 60, Box 376, Mitchell 47446, ☎ 812/849–4129), tour a restored 1800s pioneer village and gristmill, then explore two caves on foot or by boat. At **Turkey Run** (Rte. 1, Box 164, Marshall 47859, ☎ 317/597–2635), Sugar Creek is a favorite with canoeists. **Pokagon State Park** (450 Lane 100, Lake

James, Angola 46703, ☎ 219/833–2012) is a watery playground with woodlands and lakes.

INDIANAPOLIS

After undergoing a dramatic transformation in just the last 10 years, Indianapolis proudly wears the title "Cinderella City." Having long enjoyed worldwide attention each May for the Indianapolis 500, it now hosts a yearlong calendar of national and international sporting events. But it is "the greatest spectacle in racing" that sets the tone for the entire year. For 45 days leading up to the race, the entire city rolls out the red carpet with a nonstop festival. Professional and amateur sports harmonize here—it's both the testing ground for Olympic hopefuls and home turf for the Indianapolis Colts and Indiana Pacers. Equal in luster to its roster of sporting events is a dazzling cast of cultural attractions, including theater, opera, symphony, dance performances, world-class museums, and America's first downtown zoo. Among the city's natural attractions are the 4,200-acre Eagle Creek Park on the northwest side (among the nation's largest city-owned parks) and the recently completed downtown Canal Walk, a 10½-block vestige of the historic 400-mi canal system linking the Great Lakes and the Ohio River.

The 284-ft-tall monument at the center of Indianapolis that was long its most identifiable landmark is now dwarfed by jumbo sports complexes and office towers. The brick-topped street that rings the spire seems tiny compared with the wide new expressways. While new buildings make it comfortable to attend pro sports events and set a handsome scene for fine art in the city's museums, restorations of antique structures—from the nation's first Union Station and the 100-year-old State House to gracious old homes in leafy residential districts—add texture and charm.

Tourist Information

Indianapolis: City Center (210 S. Capitol Ave., 46225, ☎ 317/237–5200 or 800/323–4639). Convention & Visitors Association (1 RCA Dome, Suite 100, 46225, ☎ 317/639–4282).

Arriving and Departing

By Plane

Indianapolis International Airport is a USAir hub. The 7-mi trip from the airport to downtown takes 10 to 15 minutes; allow 25 minutes for the trip to the north side, 35 minutes to the northeast side. By taxi or limo, the cost is $17 to downtown, $35 to the north side and the northeast side. **Hoosier Cab Company** (☎ 317/243–8800) offers a special rate (with advance reservations) of $25 for service from the airport to most destinations in Marion County.

By Car

Indianapolis is a driving city. Five interstate highways, I–65, I–69, I–70, I–74, or I–465, criss-cross the city. Car rentals are available at major hotels and at the airport.

By Train

Indianapolis Union Station (350 S. Illinois St., ☎ 317/263–0550 or 800/872–7245) has Amtrak service.

By Bus

Greyhound Bus Terminal (127 N. Illinois St., ☎ 317/267–3074 or 800/231–2222).

Getting Around

It is easy to get around Indianapolis; the streets are numbered logically, and the center is comfortable for walking. **Metro buses** (☎ 317/632–1900 or 317/635–3344) run from 4:45 AM to 11:45 PM on heavily traveled routes, with shorter schedules in the suburbs. Fares (75¢, $1 during rush hour) are payable upon boarding. **Metro Taxi** (☎ 317/634–1112) and **Yellow Cab** (☎ 317/487–7777) are radio-dispatched; call ahead to be sure of getting a cab, unless you're at the airport or downtown. The fare is $2.70 for the first mile and $1.65 for each additional mile.

Exploring Indianapolis

Indianapolis's attractions extend into a wider metropolitan area than the square mile within which it was originally planned. Many of the museums, arts and entertainment venues, and shopping areas are scattered about town, generally within a 30-minute drive.

Downtown

Monument Circle is Indianapolis's centerpiece. Avenues radiate from it as in Washington, D.C. (designed by Pierre L'Enfant, of whom Indianapolis architect Alexander Ralston was a protégé). At the center of the square is the **Indiana Soldiers' and Sailors' Monument,** a 280-ft spire crowned by the 30-ft bronze *Victory,* better known as Miss Indiana. An observation deck offers a panoramic view (admission charged). Along the perimeter of the circle, the **Circle Theatre,** a vintage 1916 movie palace, is now the home of the Indianapolis Symphony Orchestra (☎ 317/262–1110; admission charged; tours by appointment), and **Christ Church Cathedral** (125 Monument Circle, ☎ 317/636–4577; tours by appointment), built in 1857, has a spire, steep gables, bell tower, and arched Tiffany-glass windows.

Assemble a meal of ethnic food at the vintage-1886 **City Market,** and savor it on the festive outdoor terrace. *222 E. Market St., ☎ 317/634–9266. Closed Sun.*

The **Indiana State Museum** showcases the state's history and culture. **Freetown Village** depicts the lifestyles of local African-Americans after the Emancipation. *202 N. Alabama St., ☎ 317/232–1637.*

The circa 1929 Gothic Tudor–style Masonic **Scottish Rite Cathedral,** contains a 54-bell carillon and a 7,500-pipe organ. *650 N. Meridian St., ☎ 317/635–2301. Closed weekends.*

Housed in a contemporary adobe-style building, the **Eiteljorg Museum of American Indian and Western Art** displays works by Frederic Remington and Georgia O'Keeffe, among others. *500 W. Washington St., ☎ 317/636–9378. Admission charged. Closed Mon. Sept.–May.*

The 19-story **Hoosier Dome,** its fiberglass roof supported by air pressure, is the home of the Indianapolis Colts and the **National Track & Field Hall of Fame.** *100 S. Capitol Ave., ☎ 317/262–3452. Admission charged. Tours daily.*

The Romanesque-style **Union Station** (39 Jackson Pl., ☎ 317/267–0700), an 1888 landmark restored and filled with shops and restaurants, features magnificent stained glass in a vaulted ceiling.

Indianapolis

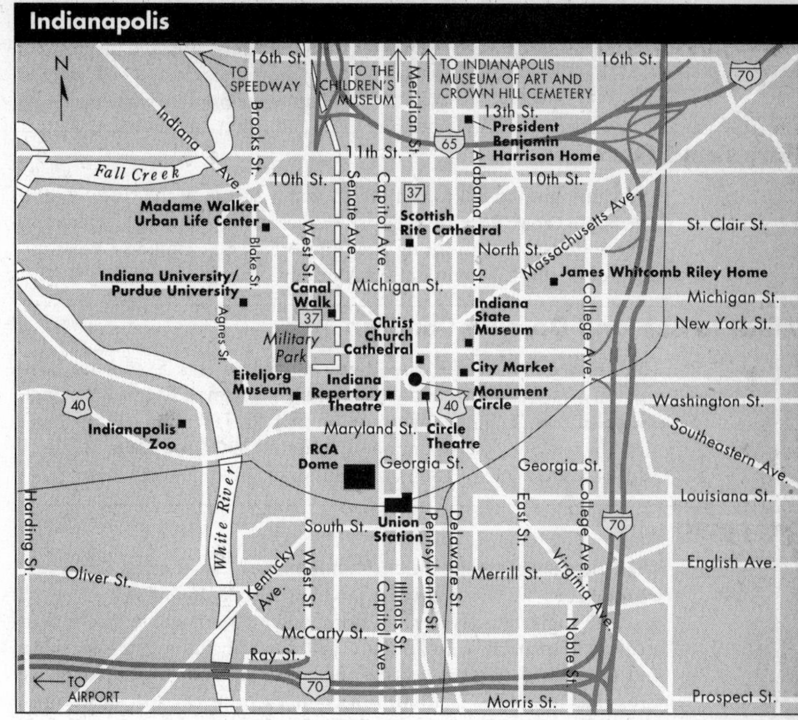

In the historic Lockerbie Square neighborhood, the **James Whitcomb Riley Home,** a memorial to the Hoosier poet, is acclaimed as one of Indiana's finest examples of Victoriana. *528 Lockerbie St., ☎ 317/631–5885. Admission charged. Closed Mon.*

Midtown/Crosstown

The **Madame Walker Urban Life Center,** in a theater where Louis Armstrong and Dinah Washington once performed, is embellished with unusual African and Egyptian motifs. *617 Indiana Ave., ☎ 317/236–2099. Admission charged. Tours by appointment.*

A Playscape, the world's largest water clock, and the Space Quest Planetarium make the **Children's Museum** one of the best in the country. Don't miss the turn-of-the-century carousel. *3000 N. Meridian St., ☎ 317/924–5431 or 317/924–5437. Admission charged. Closed Mon.*

The **Indianapolis Museum of Art** houses works by J.M.W. Turner, the old masters, and the Neo-Impressionists, as well as major Oriental and African collections. *1200 W. 38th St., ☎ 317/923–1331. Admission charged for special exhibitions. Closed Mon.*

At the **Crown Hill Cemetery,** the nation's fourth largest, notorious criminal John Dillinger cozies up to Benjamin Harrison, the 23rd president of the United States, and a host of American authors. *Indiana State Fairgrounds, 1202 E. 38th St., ☎ 317/924–1503.*

South Side

The new **Christel DeHaan Fine Arts Center** on the campus of the University of Indianapolis contains exhibition space and a 500-seat concert hall acclaimed for its acoustical qualities. *1400 E. Hanna, ☎ 317/788–3368. Admission charged for some programs.*

West Side

The **Indianapolis Motor Speedway Hall of Fame Museum** displays 30 Indy-winning cars, as well as classic and antique autos. *4790 W. 16th St., ☎ 317/248–6747. Admission charged. Closed Christmas.*

Parks and Gardens

You can jog, bike, hike, golf, or do water sports at the rustic 4,200-acre **Eagle Creek Park.** A network of recently reconstructed trails traverse woodsy terrain along the White River at **Holliday Park,** 20 minutes north of downtown off Meridian Street.

What to See and Do with Children

The **Children's** and the **Speedway museums** (*see* Exploring Indianapolis, *above*) are essential destinations for small fry; so is the **Indianapolis Zoo** (1200 W. Washington St., ☎ 317/630–2001). Don't miss the antique soda fountain at **Hook's 1890 Drug Store** (1202 E. 38th St., ☎ 317/924–1503), at the Indiana State Fairgrounds.

Shopping

The crown jewel among the city's shopping malls is the new **Circle Centre Mall** (115 W. Washington St.), which opened downtown in the fall of 1994: Eight facades in the historic downtown have been rebuilt or restored to surround a labyrinth of 120 stores, including the **Nordstrom** and **Parisian** department stores. The **Fashion Mall** (9000 Keystone Crossing, ☎ 317/574–4000) is a complex of pricey specialty stores, plus the upscale **Jacobson's** (☎ 317/574–0088) and Parisian (☎ 317/581–8200) department stores. In **Broad Ripple Village** (62nd St. and College Ave.), you'll find one-of-a-kind secondhand bookshops, boutiques, art galleries, and a variety of ethnic restaurants.

Spectator Sports

Baseball

Indianapolis Indians (Baseball Stadium, corner Washington and Maryland Sts., ☎ 317/269–3545; Apr.–Aug.).

Basketball

Indiana Pacers (Market Square Arena, 300 E. Market St., ☎ 317/263–2100; Nov.–Apr.).

Football

Indianapolis Colts (Hoosier Dome, 100 S. Capitol Ave., ☎ 317/262–3452 or 317/262–3389; Aug.–Dec.).

Ice Hockey

Indianapolis Ice (Market Square Arena, 300 E. Market St., ☎ 317/266–1234; Oct.–Apr.).

Dining

For price ranges, see Chart 1 (A) in On the Road with Fodor's.

$$$$ **Chanteclair.** A strolling violinist and beluga caviar set the tone at this elegant restaurant on the rooftop of the Airport Holiday Inn. *2501 High School Rd., ☎ 317/243–1040. Jacket and tie required. AE, D, DC, MC, V.*

$$$$ **Marker.** You'll forget you're in a hotel close to the airport when you hear the soft strains of a harp and taste appetizers such as coconut-crusted jumbo shrimp. *2544 Executive Dr., ☎ 317/248–2481. Jacket and tie required. AE, D, DC, MC, V.*

$$$ **Benvenuti.** This downtown restaurant specializes in contemporary northern Italian cuisine. Homemade lobster ravioli, grilled veal chops, and cream of roasted bell pepper soup are house specialties. *36 S. Pennsylvania St., ☎ 317/633–4915. AE, D, DC, MC, V.*

$$$ **Eller House.** Surrounded by sprawling urban development, this charming Victorian is an island of historical charm. The traditional Hoosier fare includes succulent roast turkey with dressing and chicken pot pie. *7050 E. 116th St., Fishers, ☎ 317/849–2299. AE, D, MC, V.*

$$$ **Pesto.** The sweet scent of garlic and basil wafts through the lively setting of this Italian trattoria, where waiters make the rounds bearing goat cheese pie, spinach and ricotta ravioli, and veal scallopini. *303 N. Alabama St., ☎ 317/269–0715; 2658 Lake Circle Dr., ☎ 317/875–0715. AE, D, MC, V.*

$$ **Peter's Restaurant & Bar.** Highlights of Peter's creatively prepared American cuisine include sweet-potato polenta in maple syrup and grilled pork loin covered in a cranberry-apple glaze. *8505 Keystone Crossing, ☎ 317/465–1165. AE, D, MC, V.*

$$ **Snax/Something Different.** Tapas at Snax are just enough to whet your appetite for dinner, which is served next door at Something Different. Try vegetarian rice-bean cassoulet laced with garlic, shallots, and wild mushrooms, or pheasant, squab, and partridge strudel. *2411 E. 65th St., ☎ 317/257–7115.*

$ **Arni's.** Life-size images of Marilyn Monroe, Humphrey Bogart, and other stars create a festive atmosphere. Arni's is known for its super-thin-crust pizzas, huge strombolis, and sandwiches. *3443 W. 86th St., ☎ 317/875–7034. AE, D, MC, V.*

$ **Charlie & Barney's Bar and Grille.** This chain of family-style eateries is known for its chili, which comes in five variations, including sirloin steak chili and chili pie. *1130 W. 86th St., ☎ 317/844–2399; 723 Broad Ripple Ave., ☎ 317/253–5263; 225 E. Ohio St., ☎ 317/637–5851; Merchants Plaza, 101 W. Washington St., ☎ 317/636–3101. AE, D, DC, MC, V.*

$ **MCL Cafeterias.** These no-frills cafeterias offer basics like roast beef and coconut cream pie. *10 locations, including 6010 E. 10th St., ☎ 317/356–1587; 8135 Pendleton Pike, ☎ 317/898–5455; 3630 S. East St., ☎ 317/783–2416; 5910 Crawfordsville Rd., ☎ 317/241–9497. No reservations. No credit cards.*

$ **Shapiro's Delicatessen & Cafeteria.** The strawberry cheesecake at this nationally known deli has been an Indianapolis institution since 1904. *808 S. Meridian St., ☎ 317/631–4041; 2370 W. 86th St., ☎ 317/872–7255. No credit cards.*

Lodging

For price ranges, see Chart 2 (A) in On the Road with Fodor's.

$$$$ ★ **Canterbury Hotel.** At this 60-year-old hostelry, cozy, renovated guest rooms feature armoires, queen-size four-poster beds, and luxurious baths. *123 S. Illinois St., 46225, ☎ 317/634–3000 or 800/538–8186, FAX 317/299–9257, ext. 7397. 99 rooms, 15 suites. Facilities: restaurant (jacket and tie required), bar. AE, D, DC, MC, V.*

$$$$ **University Place Conference Center and Hotel.** This hotel on the city campus of Purdue and Indiana universities coddles its intellectual clientele with handsomely appointed rooms featuring desks, easy chairs, and 18th-century reproduction furnishings. *850 W. Michigan St., 46202,*

☎ 317/269–9000 or 800/627–2700, FAX 317/231–5168. 262 rooms, 16 suites. Facilities: 2 restaurants, bar. AE, D, DC, MC, V.

$$$$ **Westin Hotel, Indianapolis.** The executive level of this high-rise is especially posh, with sleeper sofas, valet stands, hair dryers, and terrycloth robes. *50 S. Capitol Ave., 46204, ☎ 317/262–8100 or 800/228–3000, FAX 317/231–3928. 573 rooms, 38 suites. Facilities: restaurant, bar, indoor pool. AE, D, DC, MC, V.*

$$$ **Adam's Mark.** Tufted-leather sofas, wood paneling, and leaded glass make the common areas of this low building feel like an English tavern. *2544 Executive Dr., 46241, ☎ 317/248–2481 or 800/444–2326, FAX 317/248–1670. 407 rooms. Facilities: 2 restaurants, bar, 2 lounges, indoor pool, health club. AE, D, DC, MC, V.*

$$$ **Embassy Suites Downtown.** The art-deco suites of this contemporary property have separate living rooms with convertible sofas and kitchenettes. *110 W. Washington St., 46204, ☎ 317/236–1800 or 800/362–2779, FAX 317/236–1816. 360 suites. Facilities: restaurant, lounge, indoor pool. AE, D, DC, MC, V.*

$$$ **Omni Severin Hotel.** This railroad hotel has crystal chandeliers, a marble staircase, and cast-iron balustrades. Guest rooms have stark-black furnishings and white accessories. *40 W. Jackson Pl., 46225, ☎ 317/634–6664 or 800/843–6664, FAX 317/687–3619. 385 rooms, 36 suites, 11 penthouses. Facilities: restaurant, bar, indoor pool. AE, D, DC, MC, V.*

$$ **Courtyard by Marriott Downtown.** This inn across from the state-offices complex has wood veneers, marble tile, and elevators with polished-brass doors. Guest rooms have renovated baths. *501 W. Washington St., 46204, ☎ 317/635–4443 or 800/321–2211, FAX 317/687–0029. 233 rooms, 3 suites. Facilities: restaurant, outdoor pool, exercise room, playground. AE, D, DC, MC, V.*

$$ **Holiday Inn Union Station.** Baggage carts piled high with antique steamer trunks outside this inn remind you that it occupies Union Station's old train shed. Some suites are in former sleeper cars furnished with antiques and railroad memorabilia. *123 Louisiana St., 46225, ☎ 317/631–2221 or 800/465–4329, FAX 317/236–7474. 243 rooms, 33 suites. Facilities: restaurant, lounge, indoor pool. AE, D, DC, MC, V.*

$ **Fairfield Inn.** This modern-yet-modest hostelry is conveniently located just 1 mi north of I-465, near many shops and restaurants. *8325 Bash Rd., 46250, ☎ 317/577–0455, FAX 317/577–0455, ext. 702. 132 rooms. Facilities: outdoor pool, breakfast room. AE, D, DC, MC, V.*

$ **Holiday Inn Southeast.** This six-story high-rise on the beltway is popular for business and social functions. *5120 Victory Dr., 46203, ☎ 317/783–7751, FAX 317/787–1545. 140 rooms. Facilities: restaurant, lounge. AE, D, DC, MC, V.*

The Arts and Nightlife

The Arts

NUVO Newsweekly, Indianapolis Monthly magazine, Friday's edition of the *Indianapolis News,* and the Sunday edition of the *Indianapolis Star* list arts and events. Tickets for plays and concerts may be obtained through **Court Side Tickets** (6100 N. Keystone Ave., ☎ 317/254–9500), **Karma** (3540 W. 86th St., ☎ 317/876–9603), **TicketMaster** (2 W. Washington St., ☎ 317/239–1000 or 317/239–5151), **Tickets Up Front** (1099 N. Meridian St., ☎ 317/633–6400), or **Tickets on Wheels** (5987 E. 71st St., Suite 210, ☎ 317/579–6924 or 800/450–0849).

MUSIC

Indianapolis Symphony Orchestra (42 Monument Circle, ☏ 317/639–4300) performs at the Circle Theatre September to May and at Conner Prairie in summer (*see* Excursions from Indianapolis, *below*).

OPERA

Indianapolis Opera (250 E. 38th St., ☏ 317/283–3531) stages four productions from the grand-opera repertoire and one new work each season.

THEATER

Indiana's only resident professional theater, the **Indiana Repertory Theatre** (140 W. Washington St., ☏ 317/635–5252) presents major works October through May in a restored 1917 movie palace downtown.

Nightlife

Pub crawling is best in out-of-the-way neighborhoods such as Broad Ripple Village. Christmas lights and checkered flags are year-round decor at the **Chatterbox Tavern** (435 Massachusetts Ave., ☏ 317/636–0584), which attracts a varied clientele for late-night jazz. Boisterous **Rick's Café Americain** at Union Station (39 Jackson Pl., ☏ 317/634–6666) appeals to the under-30 set. The **Slippery Noodle Inn** (372 S. Meridian St., ☏ 317/631–6968), built in 1850 and once a stop on the Underground Railway, offers blues and basic food. Claiming to be Indy's first comedy club, **Crackers** (8702 Keystone Crossing, ☏ 317/846–2500) has headlined big names such as Jay Leno, Emo Phillips, and Sinbad. **Union Station** is jammed with a half dozen clubs that promise a full evening of entertainment.

Excursions from Indianapolis

Bloomington

South of Indianapolis on Rte. 37 is Indiana University, with one of the nation's 10 largest campuses. Nearby are five championship golf courses and Lake Monroe, as well as an array of ethnic restaurants. *Bloomington/Monroe County Convention and Visitors Bureau, 2855 N. Walnut St., Bloomington 47404, ☏ 812/334–8900 or 800/800–0037.*

Brown County

An hour south of Indianapolis on Rte. 135 is a woodsy area famous for its hilly terrain, fall foliage, Indiana artists' colony, and state park. Nashville, the county seat, is jammed with an amazing assortment of shops. It's especially popular with leaf-peepers in the fall; be prepared for county-wide traffic jams. *Nashville/Brown County Convention and Visitors Bureau, Box 840, Nashville 47448, ☏ 812/988–7303 or 800/753–3255.*

Columbus

On I–65 45 minutes south of Indianapolis, this affluent city of 32,000 boasts the headquarters of two *Fortune* 500 companies and more than 50 buildings designed by world-renowned architects. Guided tours (by reservation) begin at the Columbus Area Visitors Center (506 5th St., 47201, ☏ 812/372–1954).

Noblesville

Roughly 45 minutes north of downtown, just west of Rte. 37, you'll find a town center with a stately brick courthouse, a handful of shops, the Indiana Transportation Museum, and Conner Prairie, an 1830s-style frontier village. *13400 Allisonville Rd., Noblesville, ☏ 317/776–6000 or 800/966–1836. Admission charged. Closed Mon.*

Parke County

West of Indianapolis off Rte. 36 lies the covered-bridge capital of the world: 30 bridges are scattered throughout the county. Every October, various towns hold a weeklong festival, with craft fairs, quilt and antique shows, and barbecue-beef and bean-soup dinners. In late February and early March, a half-dozen sugar shacks celebrate the Parke County Maple Fair. For more information, contact the Parke County Convention and Visitors Bureau (Box 165, Rockville, ☎ 317/569–5226).

Zionsville

Slightly more than a half hour's drive from Monument Circle is an enchanting little community (pop. 5,000) of brick streets, leafy maples, and stick-style Victorian houses. It has the only recognized hunt club in the state and a quaint Main Street district.

SOUTHERN INDIANA

Dense stands of oak, hickory, and maple crown the rolling terrain that dominates southern Indiana. Tucked among the hills and valleys are riverfront towns reminiscent of the 19th century, caves that beg to be explored, and vast stretches of clear blue water.

Tourist Information

Southern Indiana: Convention and Visitors Bureau (540 Marriott Dr., Jeffersonville 47131, ☎ 812/282–6654 or 800/552–3842). **Lincoln Hills Area:** Lincoln Hills/Patoka Lake Association (Courthouse Annex, Cannelton 47520, ☎ 812/547–7028). **Madison Area:** Visitors Council (301 E. Main St., Madison 47250, ☎ 812/265–2956). **Vincennes Area:** Chamber of Commerce (Box 553, Vincennes 47591, ☎ 812/882–6440). **Evansville and New Harmony:** Evansville Convention and Visitors Bureau (623 Walnut St., Evansville 47708, ☎ 800/433–3025).

Getting There

By Car

The major road through this region is I–64. From Indianapolis, take I–70 and U.S. 41 to Vincennes, I–65 and Rte. 7 to Madison, and I–65 to New Albany. From Louisville, Kentucky, take I–65; from Cincinnati, take I–74.

By Bus

Service between Indianapolis and Vincennes is available on **Greyhound Lines** (☎ 800/231–2222) and **I-V Coaches** (☎ 317/634–3198). **White Star** (☎ 812/265–2662) travels between Madison and Indianapolis.

Exploring Southern Indiana

Indiana's oldest community, 300-year-old **Vincennes** brims over with historic sites, such as the Indiana Territory Capitol, the state's first bank and first newspaper office, a memorial to Revolutionary War general George Rogers Clark, and **Grouseland** (3 W. Scott St., ☎ 812/882–2096), home of Territory Governor William Henry Harrison. The **Old French House** (509 N. First St., ☎ 812/885–4173), dating from 1806, is one of the few surviving log-and-mud-style houses in North America. South on U.S. 41 to I–64 and southwest on Rte. 68 is **New Harmony** (Historic New Harmony Inc., Box 579, New Harmony 47631, ☎ 812/682–4482), site of two early 19th-century communes. The **Architectural Tour of Old Town** (27 N. 3rd St., ☎ 800/886–6443) traces the architectural history of Indiana's oldest city.

In the historic Riverside district of **Evansville,** columned mansions such as the **John Augustus Reitz Home** (224 S.E. 1st St., ☎ 812/423–3749) overlook the Ohio River. The **Evansville Museum of Arts and Science** (411 S.E. Riverside Dr., ☎ 812/425–2406) has American and European art from 1700 to the present, a planetarium, and a reconstructed turn-of-the-century village.

Southern Indiana is a haven for spelunkers, with **Wyandotte Caves** (Rte. 1, Leavenworth, ☎ 812/738–2782), **Squire Boone Caverns & Village** in Corydon (☎ 812/732–4831), and **Marengo Cave** (Rte. 64, Marengo, ☎ 812/365–2705).

While in **Corydon,** Indiana's first capital, you can browse through 10,000 sq ft of antiques in two downtown malls. The Federal-style **capitol building** (Chestnut and Capitol Sts., ☎ 812/738–4890) is where the state's first constitution was drafted. The **Scenic 1883 Railroad** (Walnut and Water Sts., ☎ 812/738–8000) makes a 15-mi trip through the countryside.

New Albany is the site of the French Second Empire–style **Culbertson Mansion** (914 E. Main St., ☎ 812/944–9600), with hand-painted ceilings, marble fireplaces, and delicate woodwork. The nearby **Falls of the Ohio State Park** (*see* National and State Parks, *above*) is accessible from Rte. 62.

Dubbed the "Williamsburg of the Midwest," **Madison** is an antebellum-era town whose entire main street is listed on the National Register of Historic Places. See the gleaming white Greek Revival **Lanier Mansion** (511 W. 1st St., ☎ 812/265–3526), whose portico overlooks the Ohio River. Several annual **house and garden tours** are offered; contact the Madison Area Convention and Visitors Bureau (301 E. Main St., ☎ 800/559–2956).

What to See and Do with Children

Holiday World in Santa Claus (intersection of Rte. 62 and Rte. 245, ☎ 812/937–4401 or 800/467–2682) has gift shops, museums, musical shows, water rides, and Santa himself. Bengal tigers, elephants, macaws, monkeys, and other exotic creatures inhabit the **Mesker Park Zoo** (Bement Ave., Evansville, ☎ 812/428–0715).

Sports and the Outdoors

Biking

Four routes on the **Hoosier Bikeway System** (Dept. of Natural Resources, 402 W. Washington St., Room W271, Indianapolis 46204 ☎ 317/232–4200) run through this area.

Fishing

At **Patoka Lake** (R.R. 1, Birdseye, ☎ 812/685–2464) and **Markland Dam** on the Ohio River off Rte. 156, each season brings record catches of bass, carp, and catfish.

Dining and Lodging

Southern Indiana is well supplied with roadside motels and hotels, but for the ultimate lodging experience, try one of the many local bed-and-breakfasts in the area (**Indiana Bed and Breakfast Association,** Box 1127, Goshen 46526). For price ranges, see Charts 1 (B) and 2 (B) in On the Road with Fodor's.

Clarksville/Jeffersonville/New Albany

DINING AND LODGING

Sheraton Lakeview Hotel. Ivory-colored furnishings in the rooms are dressed up with cheery floral fabrics. The Sunday brunch is a local institution. *505 Marriott Dr., Clarksville 47130, ☎ 812/283–4411 or 800/824–7740, FAX 812/288–8976. 325 rooms. Facilities: restaurant, lounge, indoor and outdoor pools. AE, DC, MC, V. $*

Corydon

LODGING

Kintner House Inn. This refurbished inn dates back to the mid-1800s and was once the headquarters of Confederate General John Hunt Morgan. *Capitol and Chestnut Sts., 47112, ☎ 812/738–2020. 14 rooms. MC, V. $$*

Madison

LODGING

Main Street Bed and Breakfast. A superbly restored 1840s Greek Revival home sits under a leafy canopy off Main Street. Bleached pine English country antiques and a morning wake-up tray add to the homey mood here. *739 Main St., 47250, ☎ 800/362–62467. 3 rooms. MC, V. $$$*

New Harmony

DINING AND LODGING

New Harmony Inn. Set on spacious grounds overlooking a small lake, this inn has a fine restaurant that draws diners from the tri-state area. *506 North St., Box 581, 47631, ☎ 812/682–4491 or 800/782–8605, FAX 812/682–4491, ext. 329. 99 rooms. Facilities: indoor pool, 2 restaurants, health spa, 2 tennis courts, fireplaces in 18 guest rooms. AE, D, MC, V. $$*

Vevay

DINING AND LODGING

Ogle Haus Inn. Whirlpool baths, dhurrie rugs, and Queen Anne–style furniture lend a note of sophistication to this modified Swiss chalet east of Madison. Its Bavarian and American cuisine draws a clientele from a 100-mi radius. *R.R. 3, Box 177, 47043, ☎ 812/427–2020 or 800/826–6299; in IN, 800/545–9360; FAX 812/427–3397. 54 rooms. Facilities: 2 restaurants, outdoor pool. AE, DC, MC, V. $$*

Vincennes

DINING AND LODGING

Executive Inn Vincennes. Amenities include a five-story, skylighted atrium and guest rooms with tufted headboards. *1 Executive Blvd., 47591, ☎ 812/886–5000 or 800/857–8154, FAX 812/886–1123. 318 rooms. Facilities: dining room, lounge, indoor pool. AE, DC, MC, V. $$*

NORTHERN INDIANA

From the shores of Lake Michigan to the tranquil setting of the Crystal Valley's Amish area, you can walk the beach and climb the dunes, then follow dusty back roads to Amish establishments.

Tourist Information

Fort Wayne: Convention and Visitors Bureau (1021 S. Calhoun St., 46802, ☎ 219/424–3700 or 800/767–7752). **Porter County:** Convention and Visitors Bureau (528 Indian Oak Mall, Chesterton 46304, ☎ 219/926–2255 or 800/283–8687). **South Bend/Mishawaka:** Convention and Visitors Bureau (401 E. Colfax Ave., South Bend 46634, ☎ 219/234–0079 or 800/392–0051).

Getting There

By Car

Major east–west roads are I–80/90 and U.S. 12 and 20. Traversing the region north–south are I–65, I–69, and U.S. 31 and 41.

By Train

South Shore Line (2702 W. Washington St., South Bend, ☎ 219/233–3111). **Amtrak** (☎ 800/872–7245).

By Bus

United Limo in Osceola (☎ 219/674–6993) provides daily service to and from Chicago. Service to and from other major midwestern cities is available on **Greyhound Lines** (4671 Terminal Dr., South Bend, ☎ 800/231–2222).

Exploring Northern Indiana

The many outdoor areas along Indiana's north coast include a National Lakeshore (*see* National and State Parks, *above)* and more. **Gibson Woods Nature Preserve** (Gibson Woods County Park, 6201 Parish Ave., Hammond, ☎ 219/844–3188) is a fine specimen of dune and swale topology.

Hordes come to **South Bend** each year to see the **University of Notre Dame**'s Fighting Irish and the century-old murals at the landmark **Golden Dome** (☎ 219/239–7367). The university's **Snite Museum of Art** (☎ 219/239–5516) contains works by Rembrandt, Chagall, and Picasso. Downtown South Bend's **East Race Waterway** attracts tubers and rafters.

The 75-mi ride east on U.S. 20 from South Bend to Angola goes through Indiana's **Amish Country**. **Amish Acres** (Rte. 19, 1600 W. Market St., Nappanee, ☎ 219/773–4188 or 800/800–4942) is a working farm with a restaurant and an inn. The **Borkhholder Dutch Village** (County Rd. 101, Nappanee, ☎ 219/773–2828) has more than 350 booths of fine arts, crafts, antiques, and collectibles.

What to See and Do with Children

Costumed interpreters recount daily life on a pioneer farm at **Buckley Homestead County Park** (3606 Belshaw Rd., Lowell, ☎ 219/696–0769). More than 222 species of jungle life, large and small, reside at the lakeside **Washington Park Zoological Gardens** (Lakefront, Michigan City, ☎ 219/873–1510).

Dining and Lodging

For inn bookings, contact the **Indiana Bed and Breakfast Association** (Box 1127, Goshen 46526). For price ranges, see Charts 1 (B) and 2 (B) in On the Road with Fodor's.

Amish Land

DINING AND LODGING

Checkerberry Inn. Set on 100 acres, this elegant hostelry boasts the state's only professional croquet course, a walking lane, and woodlands. *62644 County Rd. 37, Goshen 46526,* ☎ *219/642–4445,* FAX *219/642–4445. 11 rooms, 3 suites. Facilities: pool, croquet, tennis, restaurant. MC, V. $$$*

Essenhaus Country Inn. A three-story softly lit atrium with a potbelly stove is the centerpiece of this newly built inn. *240 U.S. 20, Middlebury 46540, ☎ 219/825–9471, FAX 219/825–9471. 31 rooms. Facilities: lounge area, game table. MC, V. $$*

Indiana Dune Lands

LODGING

Hutchinson Mansion Inn. This 1876 mansion spanning one city block is filled with stained glass windows and marble fireplaces. *220 W. 10th St., Michigan City 46360, ☎ 219/879–1700. 5 rooms, 4 suites. Facilities: library, game room. $$$*

Indian Oak Inn. Rooms in this contemporary cedar-and-fieldstone inn overlook the lake or the woods. *558 Boundary Rd., Chesterton 46304, ☎ 219/926–2200 or 800/552–4232, FAX 219/926–2200. 90 rooms, 5 suites. Facilities: heated indoor pool, whirlpool, health spa. AE, D, DC, MC, V. $$*

Carlton Lodge. A fieldstone fireplace and golden-oak woodwork create the ambience of a mountain lodge. *7850 Rhode Island Ave., Merrillville 46410, ☎ 219/756–1600 or 800/445–6343, FAX 219/756–1600, ext. 307. 112 rooms. Facilities: lounge, indoor/outdoor pool, whirlpool. AE, D, DC, MC, V. $*

South Bend

DINING AND LODGING

Marriott Hotel South Bend. The centerpiece of this sleek glass-and-limestone property is a 32,000-sq-ft atrium. *123 N. St. Joseph St., 46601, ☎ 219/234–2000 or 800/328–7349, FAX 219/234–2252. 300 rooms. Facilities: 2 restaurants, lounge, indoor pool, sauna/whirlpool. AE, D, DC, MC, V. $$$*

Works Hotel. A Singer sewing machine factory that predates the Civil War has been converted into a trendy hotel. *475 N. Niles Ave., 46617, ☎ 219/234–1954 or 800/333–5646, FAX 219/232–4807. 56 rooms. Facilities: dining room, lounge, exercise room. AE, DC, MC, V. $$*

MICHIGAN

By Don Davenport

Updated by Richard Bak

Capital	Lansing
Population	9,240,000
Motto	If You Seek a Pleasant Peninsula, Look About You
State Bird	Robin
State Flower	Apple blossom

Visitor Information

Michigan Department of Commerce Travel Bureau (Box 30226, Lansing 48909, ☎ 800/543–2937). **Information centers:** I–94 at New Buffalo and Port Huron; I–69 at Coldwater; U.S. 23 at Dundee; U.S. 2 at Ironwood and Iron Mountain; U.S. 41 at Marquette and Menominee; I–75 at St. Ignace, Sault Ste. Marie, and Monroe; U.S. 27 in a rest area 1 mi north of Clare; and Rte. 108 in Mackinaw City.

Scenic Drives

Rte. BR–15 between Pentwater and Montague follows the Lake Michigan shoreline for about 25 mi. **Rte. M–23** between Tawas City and Mackinaw City follows the Lake Huron shoreline for more than 160 mi. In the Upper Peninsula, **Rte. M–28** follows the Lake Superior shoreline between Marquette and Munising.

National and State Parks

National Parks

Isle Royale National Park (Houghton 49940, ☎ 906/482–3310), 48 mi off the Michigan coast in Lake Superior, is a wilderness park and can be reached by ferry from Houghton or Copper Harbor or by seaplane from Houghton.

Pictured Rocks National Lakeshore (Box 40, Munising 49862, ☎ 906/387–2607) in the Upper Peninsula extends 40 mi along Lake Superior between Munising and Grand Marais.

Sleeping Bear Dunes National Lakeshore (9922 Front St., Box 277, Empire 49630, ☎ 616/326–5134) encompasses 33 mi of lower Michigan's Lake Michigan shore and includes the Manitou Islands. The 71,000-acre preserve has the highest sand dunes outside the Sahara.

State Parks

Michigan has 94 state parks, including 23 in the Upper Peninsula, where a number feature spectacular waterfalls. Camping is allowed in 78 parks. A motor-vehicle permit, available at each park entrance, is required for admission. The *Michigan Travel Guide,* available from the Michigan Department of Commerce Travel Bureau (*see* Visitor Information, *above*), details the state's parks and their facilities.

Brimley State Park (Rte. 2, Box 202, Brimley 49715, ☎ 906/248–3422), overlooking Lake Superior's Whitefish Bay, is 1 of 14 parks where you may rent a tent already set up and equipped with two cots and two sleeping pads. **Porcupine Mountains State Park** (Rte. M–107, Ontanogon, ☎ 906/885–5275) and **J. W. Wells State Park** (Rte. M–35, Cedar River 49813, ☎ 906/863–9747) are 2 of 13 parks that have cabins to rent.

DETROIT

Founded seven decades before the American Revolution, Detroit is a busy industrial city that produces some 26% of the nation's autos, trucks, and tractors. The riverfront harbor is one of the busiest ports on the Great Lakes. Downtown, a constant flow of traffic moves in and out of the Detroit–Windsor Tunnel, which connects Detroit with Windsor, Ontario, directly across the Detroit River.

Nearly half of Michigan's total population lives within the metropolitan area. More than 150 ethnic groups are represented, including almost 900,000 African-Americans and more than 400,000 people of Polish descent. Detroit's Bulgarian, Belgian, and Arab populations are the largest in North America. These numbers add up to a wealth of cultural diversity that's reflected in language, music, food, art, and entertainment.

Tourist Information

Detroit Visitor Information Center (2 E. Jefferson Ave., 48226, in Hart Plaza just west of the Renaissance Center, ☏ 313/567–1170).

Arriving and Departing

By Plane

Detroit Metropolitan Wayne County Airport (☏ 313/942–3550) in Romulus, about 26 mi west of downtown Detroit, is served by most major airlines, with nearly 1,000 arrivals and departures daily.

Commuter Transportation Company (☏ 313/941–3252) operates buses from the metropolitan airport to major downtown hotels from 6:45 AM to midnight; the fare is $13 one-way, $24 round-trip. Taxis to and from the airport take about 45 minutes; the fare is about $32.

By Car

I–75 enters Detroit from the north and south, U.S. 10 from the north. Approaching from the west and northeast is I–94; from the west, I–96 and I–696. From the east, Canadian Rte. 401 becomes Rte. 3 when entering Detroit from Windsor via the Ambassador Bridge and Rte. 3B when entering via the Detroit–Windsor Tunnel.

By Train

Amtrak (16121 Michigan Ave., Dearborn, ☏ 800/872–7245).

By Bus

Greyhound Lines (1000 W. Lafayette St., ☏ 800/231–2222).

Getting Around Detroit

By Car

Detroit is the Motor City; everyone drives. Most downtown streets are one-way; a detailed map is a necessity. The main streets into downtown are Woodward Avenue (north–south) and Jefferson Avenue (east–west). Rush hours should be avoided.

By Public Transportation

The **Department of Transportation** (☏ 313/933–1300) operates bus service throughout Detroit; the fare is $1. **Suburban Mobility Authority Regional Transportation** (☏ 313/962–5515) provides suburban bus service. The **People Mover** (☏ 313/224–2160) is an elevated, automated monorail that makes a 14-minute, 2.9-mi circuit of 13 downtown stations. Trains run about every three minutes; the fare is 50¢ (tokens are sold at each station).

By Taxi

The taxi fare is $1.10 at the flag drop, plus $1.10 per mile. Taxis can be ordered by phone or hired at stands at most major hotels. The two largest companies are **Checker Cab** (☎ 313/963–7000) and **City Cab** (☎ 313/833–7060).

Exploring Detroit

Starting from the Renaissance Center, on the banks of the river downtown, you can move outward to east Detroit, then on to the near northwest side, the cultural heart of Detroit.

Downtown

Detroit's most prominent landmark, the big, brassy **Renaissance Center,** known as the Ren Cen, dominates the city's skyline with six office towers and the spectacular 73-story Westin Hotel, one of the tallest hotels in the world. This gleaming complex is a city within a city, with more than 90 retail stores, services, and restaurants. There's a People Mover stop right at the center.

Next to the Ren Cen is the **Old Mariner's Church** (☎ 313/259–2206), made famous in folksinger Gordon Lightfoot's song "The Wreck of the *Edmund Fitzgerald.*" Adjacent to the church is the 75-acre **Civic Center,** a riverfront mecca for entertainment, festivals, and sporting activities. At the heart of the Civic Center is **Philip A. Hart Plaza,** designed by Isamu Noguchi. In warm weather, lunchtime crowds come to enjoy the open spaces, the sculpture, and the computer-controlled **Dodge Fountain.**

Two blocks north is **Cadillac Square,** site of many presidential speeches and the 1872 **Civil War Soldiers' and Sailors' Monument,** designed by Randolph Rogers, who created the bronze doors of the Capitol in Washington, D.C. Just west is the **Penobscot Building,** the state's tallest office tower. The blinking red light atop its 47 stories has been part of the Detroit skyline since 1928. Two blocks north, **Capitol Park** is the site of Michigan's first capitol. A statue of Steven T. Mason, the first governor, stands over his grave in the park.

A five-minute walk north is **Grand Circus Park,** envisioned as a full circus (circle) when Detroit was rebuilt after a disastrous fire in 1805; only half was completed. A fountain in the west park honors Thomas A. Edison.

Just to the southeast, along Monroe Street, is **Greektown,** one of Detroit's most popular entertainment districts, with markets, bars, coffeehouses, shops, boutiques, and restaurants serving authentic Greek fare with an American flair. At the center of Greektown is **Trappers Alley** (508 Monroe St.), once one of the Midwest's leading fur centers and today a shopping enclave, created by restoring, remodeling, and enclosing five century-old buildings under one roof. The complex contains some 40 shops and restaurants.

Close by, the **Second Baptist Church** (Monroe and Beaubien Sts.), organized in 1836, is Detroit's oldest black congregation. It was here that blacks gathered to celebrate the Emancipation Proclamation. **Old St. Mary's Catholic Church** (Monroe and St. Antoine Sts.), built in 1885, began as a parish of German and Irish immigrants in 1833.

Two blocks south of Greektown is **Bricktown,** a collection of dining spots and bars in a refurbished corner of downtown. Characterized by a multitude of brick facades, Bricktown is a good place for a leisurely lunch, a shopping spree, or cocktails.

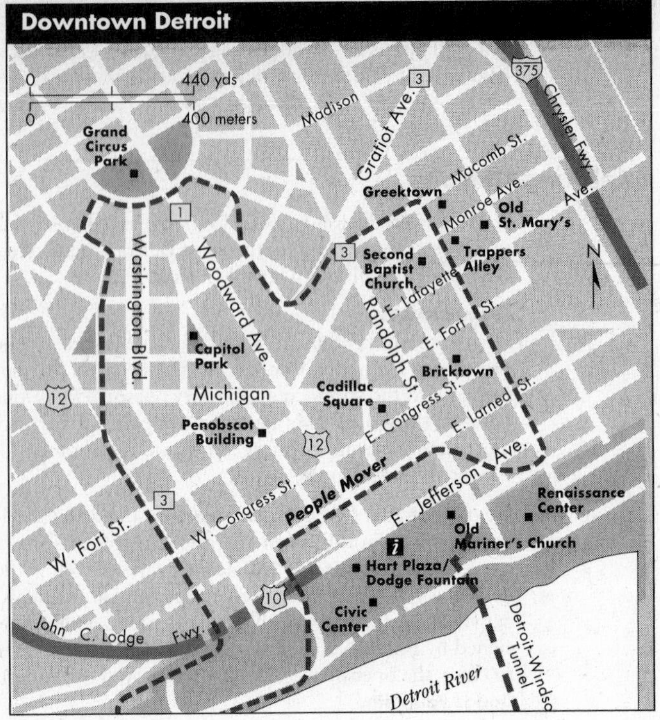

East Detroit

In the 1880s the section east of the Renaissance Center, between the river and Jefferson Avenue, blossomed with lumberyards, shipyards, and railroads. Known as **Rivertown,** the area is seeing new life today—with parks, shops, restaurants, and nightspots set in rejuvenated warehouses and carriage houses. **Stroh River Place,** opened in 1988, has attracted businesses, restaurants, and shops to a 21-acre site that stood empty for years.

Rivertown is the home of **Pewabic Pottery** (10125 E. Jefferson Ave., ☎ 313/822–0954), founded in 1907, which produced the brilliantly glazed ceramic Pewabic tiles found in buildings throughout the nation. The pottery houses a ceramic museum, a contemporary gallery, a workshop, and a learning center.

Farmers and city slickers alike have gathered in the historic, open-air **Eastern Market** (2934 Russell St., ☎ 313/833–1560) since 1892 to barter and bargain over fresh produce, meats, fish, and plants. Public shopping hours are Saturday 10–6; sales are in bulk only.

Near Northwest Detroit

The **University Cultural Center** is a world of art, history, and science clustered throughout some 40 city blocks 2½ mi from downtown via Woodward Avenue.

The **Children's Museum** (67 E. Kirby St., ☎ 313/494–1210) has exhibits on everything from dolls and toys to birds and life in other cultures. A planetarium shows the night sky in Detroit and faraway lands. The **Detroit Historical Museum** (5401 Woodward Ave., ☎ 313/833–1805) features "Collectors in Toyland," part of an ongoing exhibit of

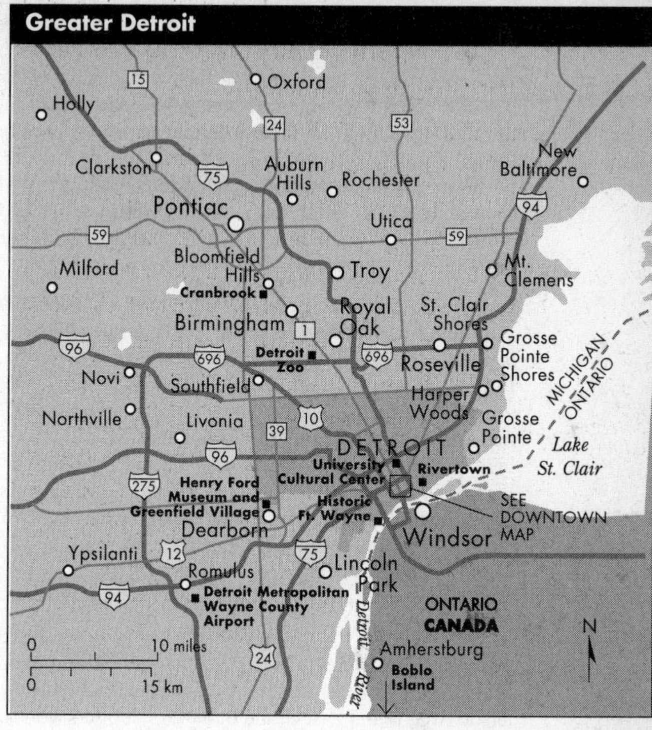

the Lawrence Scripps Wilkinson toy collection. The "Streets of Old Detroit" is a walk through the city's history from 1701.

The **Detroit Institute of Arts,** with more than 100 galleries, features 5,000 years of world-famous art treasures, including works by van Gogh, Rembrandt, and Renoir. Diego Rivera's piece *Detroit Industry,* four immense frescoes, is a must-see. *5200 Woodward Ave., ☎ 313/833–7900. Donation suggested. Closed Mon.–Tues.*

Home to 1.3 million books, the Cultural Center branch of the **Detroit Public Library** is the system's largest. Its Burton Historical Collection is the state's most comprehensive on Detroit, Michigan, and Great Lakes lore. *5201 Woodward Ave., ☎ 313/833–1000 or 313/833–1722 for recorded information. Closed Sun.–Mon.*

The **International Institute of Metropolitan Detroit** (111 E. Kirby St., ☎ 313/871–8600) is a museum, a working social agency for the foreign-born, and a lunchtime café. Its "gallery of nations" displays the arts and crafts of 43 countries. The **Museum of African-American History** (301 Frederick Douglass St., ☎ 313/833–9800) tells the story of the black experience in America through exhibits and audiovisual presentations.

Other Attractions

More than 1,200 animals from 300 species live in natural environments without bars at the **Detroit Zoological Park** (8450 W. 10 Mile Rd., Royal Oak, ☎ 810/398–0903). Highlights include the world's largest "penguinarium" and a walk-through aviary with tropical birds and plants.

Dearborn's **Henry Ford Museum and Greenfield Village,** America's largest indoor-outdoor museum, details the country's evolution from a rural to an industrial society with exhibits covering communications, transportation, domestic life, agriculture, and industry. Greenfield Village preserves 80 famous historic structures, which include the bicycle shop where the Wright brothers built their first airplane, Thomas Edison's laboratory, an Illinois courthouse where Abraham Lincoln practiced law, and the Dearborn farm where Ford himself was born. An ongoing exhibit, "The Automobile in American Life," is a lavish collection of chrome and neon that traces the country's love affair with cars. *20900 Oakwood Blvd., ☎ 313/271–1620. Admission to each site: $11.50 adults, $5.75 children; combination ticket for both sites, $20 adults, $10 children. Village buildings closed Jan.–mid-Mar.*

Cranbrook, in Bloomfield Hills, is a cultural and educational center with a graduate art academy and college preparatory schools. Historic **Cranbrook House** (380 Lone Pine Rd., ☎ 810/645–3149), a mansion built for newspaper publisher George Booth, has leaded-glass windows, art objects, and formal gardens with fountains and sculpture. **Cranbrook Academy of Art Museum** (500 Lone Pine Rd., ☎ 810/645–3312) has major exhibitions of contemporary art and a permanent collection that includes works by Eliel and Eero Saarinen and Charles Eames. **Cranbrook Institute of Science** (550 Lone Pine Rd., ☎ 810/645–3210) has intriguing hands-on physics experiments, geology displays, and dinosaur excavation exhibits.

Parks and Gardens

Belle Isle (☎ 313/267–7115), a 1,000-acre island park in the Detroit River 3 mi southeast of the city center, is reached by way of East Jefferson Avenue and East Grand Boulevard. It offers woods, walking trails, outdoor sports facilities, a nine-hole golf course, and a ½-mile-long beach.

Among Belle Isle's other attractions is the **Whitcomb Conservatory** (☎ 313/267–7134), with one of the largest orchid collections in the country. **Belle Isle Aquarium** (☎ 313/267–7159), the nation's oldest freshwater aquarium, exhibits more than 200 species of fish, reptiles, and amphibians. The **Belle Isle Nature Center** (☎ 313/267–7157) has changing exhibits and presentations on area nature. **Belle Isle Zoo** (☎ 313/267–7160; closed Nov.–Apr.) has an elevated walkway offering views of animals roaming in natural settings.

Also on Belle Isle, the **Dossin Great Lakes Museum** has displays about Great Lakes shipping, the prohibition era in Detroit, and an ongoing exhibition, "The Storm of 1913," recalling the Great Lakes' worst-ever storm. Visitors can listen to ship-to-shore radio messages and view the river and city through a periscope. *100 Strand Dr., ☎ 313/267–6440. Donation requested. Closed Mon.–Tues., holidays.*

What to See and Do with Children

Many of Detroit's attractions will interest children, including the **People Mover** (*see* Getting Around Detroit, *above*); the **Children's Museum, Detroit Historical Museum,** and **Detroit Institute of Arts** (*see* Exploring Detroit, Near Northwest Detroit, *above*); **Cranbrook Institute of Science, Detroit Zoological Park,** and **Henry Ford Museum and Greenfield Village** (*see* Exploring Detroit, Other Attractions, *above*); and **Belle Isle Aquarium, Nature Center,** and **Zoo** (*see* Parks and Gardens, *above*).

Shopping

Detroit's shops and stores are generally open Monday through Saturday from 10 to 6; many in the malls stay open until 9 PM. Some stores are open Sunday from noon to 5.

Shopping Districts

The once fashionable downtown shopping district along Woodward Avenue is now largely a collection of eclectic boutiques. In the Renaissance Center is the **World of Shops,** with some 80 retail outlets. The shops of the **Millender Center,** which can be reached by all-weather walkways from the Ren Cen or the City-County Building, include a bakery, a bank, beauty and barber shops, bookstores, and jewelers. **Trappers Alley Festival Marketplace,** in Greektown, has some 40 shops, food booths, and restaurants.

The **Eastern Market** (*see* Exploring Detroit, East Detroit, *above*) is open to the public Saturday 10–6, and stores around it are open daily. The **New Center One Mall** (in the University Cultural Center) has weatherproof skywalks connecting its more than 50 stores, galleries, and restaurants to the Fisher Building, the General Motors Building, and the Hotel St. Regis. The **Somerset Collection,** in suburban Troy, has well-known upscale chains, such as **Neiman Marcus.**

Department Stores

Crowley's (major store at New Center One, ☎ 313/874–5100) is well known for fashions for men, women, and children. **J. L. Hudson's** (major store at Fairlane Town Mall in Dearborn, ☎ 313/436–7600) is a leader in fashion and home furnishings.

Spectator Sports

Baseball

Detroit Tigers (Tiger Stadium, 2121 Trumbull Ave. at Michigan Ave., ☎ 313/962–4000; Apr.–Oct.).

Basketball

Detroit Pistons (The Palace of Auburn Hills, 2 Championship Dr., ☎ 810/377–0100; Nov.–Apr.).

Football

Detroit Lions (Pontiac Silverdome, Pontiac, 30 mi northwest of Detroit, ☎ 810/335–4151; Aug.–Dec.).

Hockey

Detroit Red Wings (Joe Louis Arena, downtown on the riverfront, ☎ 313/567–6000; Oct.–Apr.).

Dining

By Jeremy Iggers

The tremendous diversity of the Detroit restaurant scene may surprise first-time visitors. Each wave of immigrants to the city has made its culinary mark: You'll find soul-food restaurants in the inner city, a vibrant Mexican community on the west side, and Greek restaurants in Greektown. Detroiters often dine across the river in Windsor, Ontario, which offers its own rich mix of ethnic restaurants (a favorable rate of exchange makes the Canadian restaurants excellent values). For price ranges, see Chart 1 (A) in On the Road with Fodor's.

$$$$ ★ **Van Dyke Place.** The evening ritual at this restored turn-of-the-century mansion starts with dinner in main-floor dining rooms, followed by dessert and coffee in the upstairs drawing rooms. The menu offers such dishes as roast boneless quail in a potato nest. *649 Van Dyke Ave., ☎ 313/821–2620. Jacket and tie advised. AE, MC, V. No lunch Tues.–Sat.*

$$$$ ★ **The Whitney.** This former mansion of lumber baron David Whitney has been transformed into one of Detroit's most opulent restaurants. Chef Paul Grosz oversees a large menu of creative American dishes, snappy pastas, and ultrafresh seafood. *4421 Woodward Ave., ☎ 313/*

832–5700. Jacket and tie advised. AE, D, MC, V. No lunch Mon.–Sat.; Sun. brunch.

$$$ **The Caucus Club.** This venerable Detroit institution is a period piece from the era when elegant restaurants had boardroom decor, with lots of oil paintings and wood. The menu is of similar vintage: corned-beef hash, steaks, chops, Dover sole, and famous baby-back ribs. *150 W. Congress St., ☏ 313/965–4970. AE, D, DC, MC, V. Closed Sat.–Sun.*

$$$ **The Rattlesnake Club.** Superchef Jimmy Schmidt's menu offers innovative treatments of pickerel, salmon, and veal, as well as the club's signature rack of lamb. The decor is contemporary in marble and rosewood, with terrific views of the Detroit River and Windsor skyline. *300 River Pl., ☏ 313/567–4400. AE, D, DC, MC, V. Closed Sun.*

$$$ **The Summit.** This revolving restaurant on the 71st floor of the Westin Hotel has a superb view of Detroit. The menu includes charbroiled steaks and swordfish la Louisiana. *Renaissance Center, ☏ 313/568–8600. Jacket and tie advised. AE, D, DC, MC, V.*

$$ ★ **Blue Nile.** Silverware is optional when you dine Ethiopian style; richly seasoned meats and vegetables are served on communal trays covered with *injera,* a pancakelike flat bread, chunks of which are torn off to be used as scoops for the other foods. The simple but stylish casual decor features Ethiopian handicrafts. *Trappers Alley, 508 Monroe St., ☏ 313/964–6699. AE, D, DC, MC, V.*

$$ **Durango Grill.** Local culinary legend Keith Famie, always looking for fresh challenges, has created a Western café alive with buffalo heads, chaps, and a toy choo-choo running near the ceiling. Would-be cowpokes are saddled with a top-flight menu that includes whiskey ribs, rainbow trout, and buffalo burgers. *222 Sherman Dr., Royal Oak, ☏ 810/544–2887. AE, MC, V. No lunch Sun.*

$$ **Fishbone's Rhythm Kitchen Cafe.** What could be more cosmopolitan than an authentic New Orleans–style restaurant in the heart of Greektown? Like New Orleans itself, Fishbone's is loud, brash, funky, and fun. Seasonal offerings on the spicy Creole menu include gator, gumbo, crawfish, and Gulf oysters on the half shell. The best year-round bet is the whiskey ribs. *400 Monroe St., ☏ 313/965–4600. AE, D, DC, MC, V. No dinner (brunch only) Sun.*

$$ ★ **Lelli's Inn.** When Detroiters think Italian, Lelli's comes to mind. Although the decor (festoons of Christmas lights) hasn't changed in years and the waiters can be brash, the minestrone and steak Lelli are hard to beat. *7618 Woodward Ave., ☏ 313/871–1590. Jacket and tie advised. AE, DC, MC, V. No dinner Mon.*

$ **Elwood Bar & Grill.** One of the city's best preserved examples of Art Deco is right across the street from the Fox Theater, making this a popular spot for concert goers. The vast, well-tended bar, swing-era music, and lively crowd make up for the rather basic American menu. However, you won't go wrong ordering one of the soups or peppery potato chips—all homemade. *2100 Woodward Ave., ☏ 313/961–7485. AE, MC, V. No dinner Mon.*

$ **Pegasus Taverna.** Popular with the throngs who visit Greektown, the Pegasus menu includes such staples as moussaka, pastitsio, roast leg of lamb, stuffed grape leaves, and baklava. The Greektown experience isn't complete without an order of *saganaki* (flaming kasseri cheese ignited tableside) and a little retsina or ouzo to drink. *558 Monroe St., ☏ 313/964–6800. AE, D, DC, MC, V.*

$ **Traffic Jam & Snug.** No detail of hospitality is neglected at this charmingly funky hangout near the Wayne State campus. The wide-ranging menu includes an exotic selection of breads, cheeses, ice creams, sausages, and even hamburgers. *511 W. Canfield St., ☏ 313/831–9470.*

No reservations. D, DC, MC, V. No dinner Sun., Mon.; no lunch weekends.

$ **Under the Eagle.** Typical of Detroit's modestly priced little Polish cafés, the cooking at the Eagle is first-rate, with generous portions of stick-to-the-ribs roast duckling and kielbasa. For the adventuresome, there's *czarnina* (duck-blood soup). *9000 Joseph Campau St., ☎ 313/875–5905. No credit cards. Closed Wed.*

$ ★ **Wah Court.** Across the river in Windsor, Ontario, just steps from the Ambassador Bridge, is this popular no-frills Cantonese restaurant. The menu is full of such offerings as pork and duck in hot pot. Dim sum, the traditional Chinese tea snacks, are served daily, with the biggest selection on Sunday. *2037 Wyandotte Ave. W, Windsor, ☎ 519/254–1388. No reservations. MC, V.*

Lodging

Accommodations in and around the Motor City range from the pricey high-rise room-with-a-view to the more moderate and closer to the ground. Downtown, near the Renaissance Center and Civic Center, you'll find Detroit's luxury megahotels. Accommodations in suburban Troy, with its high concentration of corporate businesses, and Dearborn, where the Ford Motor Company has its headquarters, are quickly and easily reached by freeways and expressways. Most of the hotels, motels, and inns offer reduced-price weekend packages. For price ranges, see Chart 2 (A) in On the Road with Fodor's.

$$$$ ★ **Crowne Plaza Hotel Pontchartrain.** The Pontch, as it is familiarly known, is tastefully decorated with neutral shades accented by green-and-rose fabrics. The light, airy rooms all have wonderful views of the city and the river; do not, however, accept a room at the back of the hotel—which is across the street from the fire station—unless you are a heavy sleeper. *2 Washington Blvd., 48226, ☎ 313/965–0200 or 800/537–6624, FAX 313/965–9464. 416 rooms. Facilities: restaurant, lounge, concierge, heated outdoor pool, health club, complimentary limo service in city. AE, DC, MC, V.*

$$$$ ★ **Hyatt Regency Dearborn.** Opposite Ford's world headquarters, this large hotel is only five minutes from the Henry Ford Museum and Greenfield Village. *Fairlane Town Center, Dearborn 48126, ☎ 313/593–1234, FAX 313/593–3366. 771 rooms. Facilities: 3 restaurants, coffee shop, 2 lounges, indoor pool, sauna, valet parking. AE, D, DC, MC, V.*

$$$$ ★ **Omni International.** One of Detroit's newest hotels, the Omni is connected by skywalk to the Renaissance Center. The rooms are bright, large, and decorated in soothing blues and whites, with luxurious furniture. *333 E. Jefferson Ave., 48226, ☎ 313/222–7700, FAX 313/222–6509. 254 rooms. Facilities: restaurant, lounge, indoor pool, sauna, health club, 2 tennis courts, racquetball court, concierge, valet parking, People Mover station. AE, D, DC, MC, V.*

$$$$ ★ **Ritz-Carlton, Dearborn.** Since opening in 1989, the Ritz has acquired a reputation for impeccable taste and service. Its mahogany-paneled walls, overstuffed settees, Chinese jardinieres, and antique art suggest a clubby, "olde English" elegance. Reinforcing that image is a traditional afternoon high tea and hors d'oeuvres served in the lobby lounge. *300 Town Center Dr., Dearborn 48126, ☎ 313/441–2000 or 800/241–3333, FAX 313/441–2051. 308 rooms. Facilities: restaurant, grill, bar, indoor pool, sauna, fitness center. AE, D, DC, MC, V.*

$$$$ ★ **The Westin Hotel.** At 73 stories, this hotel is best summed up as megabig with megabuck prices. The rooms are neither large nor special, but each commands a waterfront view of the city and neighboring Windsor, Ontario. The lobby is sumptuously decorated in granite,

marble, brass, and earth tones. *Renaissance Center, Jefferson Ave. at Randolph St., 48243, ☎ 313/568–8000 or 800/228–3000, FAX 313/568–8146. 1,400 rooms. Facilities: restaurant, lounge, indoor pool, health club, outdoor jogging track, valet parking. AE, D, DC, MC, V.*

$$$ Dearborn Inn and Marriott Hotel. Across from the Henry Ford Museum and Greenfield Village, this property features five replicas of historic Colonial homes, honoring such famous Americans as Patrick Henry, Edgar Allan Poe, and Walt Whitman. *20301 Oakwood Blvd., Dearborn 48124, ☎ 313/271–2700 or 800/228–9290, FAX 313/271–7464. 222 rooms. Facilities: 2 restaurants, lounge, fitness center, outdoor pool, 2 tennis courts. AE, D, DC, MC, V.*

$$–$$$ Guest Quarters. This suite hotel is a feast for the eyes, with an eight-story atrium full of trees, flowers, ivy, a small fountain, and a mini-waterfall. All the decor, from carpeting to upholstery to café tablecloths, combines to create an outdoorsy ambience. A complimentary full American breakfast is served. *850 Tower Dr., Troy 48098, ☎ 810/879–7500 or 800/424–2900, FAX 810/879–9139. 251 suites. Facilities: café, lounge, indoor pool, sauna, health club. AE, D, DC, MC, V.*

$$–$$$ Mayflower Bed and Breakfast Hotel. The rooms have a homey atmosphere with lots of prints and pastels; some have whirlpool baths. Guests receive a complimentary full breakfast, and shopping, golf, and cross-country skiing are nearby. *827 W. Ann Arbor Trail, Plymouth 48170, ☎ 313/453–1620, FAX 313/453–0193. 73 rooms. Facilities: 2 restaurants, lounge. AE, D, DC, MC, V.*

$$–$$$ Somerset Inn. This inn 25 mi north of Detroit in the heart of Troy's corporate district is a favorite with the business set. Guest rooms are rather small and standard, but the entry level is lovely, with marble floors, greenery, and several small sitting rooms tucked around the perimeter. *2601 W. Big Beaver Rd., Troy 48084, ☎ 810/643–7800 or 800/228–8769, FAX 810/643–2296. 250 rooms. Facilities: restaurant, bar, 2 pools, health club. AE, D, DC, MC, V.*

$$ The Drury Inn. Decorated mostly in earth tones, the spacious rooms have brick and stucco walls and neat and clean modern furnishings, including fabric-covered tub chairs. The hotel offers a complimentary breakfast buffet. *575 W. Big Beaver Rd., Troy 48084, ☎ 810/528–3330 or 800/325–8300, FAX 810/528–3330, ext. 479. 150 rooms. Facilities: outdoor pool. AE, D, DC, MC, V.*

$$ Shorecrest Motor Inn. This pleasant, no-frills, two-story hotel is conveniently located two blocks east of the Renaissance Center and within walking distance of downtown attractions. *1316 E. Jefferson Ave., 48207, ☎ 313/568–3000 or 800/992–9616, FAX 313/568–3002, ext. 260. 54 rooms. Facilities: restaurant. AE, D, DC, MC, V.*

The Arts and Nightlife

The Arts

Detroit Monthly has a comprehensive calendar of events, as does *Metro Times,* a free weekly tabloid available in downtown stores. Also check the arts sections of the *Detroit News* and *Free Press.*

Attic Theater (7339 3rd Ave., ☎ 313/875–8284) presents Off-Broadway plays and works by new playwrights. **Detroit Repertory Theater** (13103 Woodrow Wilson Ave., ☎ 313/868–1347) is one of the city's oldest resident professional theater companies. Touring Broadway shows and nationally known entertainers appear at the **Fisher Theater** (3011 W. Grand Blvd., ☎ 313/872–1000) and the opulent **Fox Theater** (2211 Woodward Ave., ☎ 313/567–6000). **Orchestra Hall** (3177 Woodward Ave., ☎ 313/833–3700) is home to the **Chamber Music Society of Detroit** and the **Detroit Symphony.**

Nightlife

Much of Detroit's nightlife is centered in the downtown area. In Greektown, tourists crowd the **Bouzouki Lounge** (432 E. Lafayette St., ☎ 313/964–5744) to see and hear traditional Greek music, folksingers, and belly dancers. **Baker's Keyboard Lounge** (20510 Livernois Ave., ☎ 313/864–1200), a dimly lit, smoke-filled jazz club, is a Detroit institution.

In Rivertown, the **Soup Kitchen Saloon** (1585 Franklin St., ☎ 313/259–2643) is the home of the Detroit blues. The **Rhinoceros Restaurant** (265 Riopelle St., ☎ 313/259–2208) and **Woodbridge Tavern** (289 St. Aubin, ☎ 313/259–0578) are former speakeasies where downtown professionals loosen their ties and stomp their feet. Poetry readings, art exhibitions, and no-nonsense live acts give **Alvin's** (5756 Cass St., ☎ 313/832–2355) a bohemian appeal, especially among students at nearby Wayne State University.

ELSEWHERE IN THE STATE

Mackinac Island

Getting There

By car, take I–75N from Detroit to Mackinaw City. Island ferries depart from Mackinaw City and St. Ignace, at the north end of the Mackinac Bridge.

What to See and Do

No autos are allowed on **Mackinac Island** (island, town, and straits all pronounced *Mack*-i-naw), but the quaint Victorian village begs to be explored on foot. A small park at the east end of the village, along the boardwalk, offers terrific views of the Mackinac Bridge and ships passing through the straits. Farther afield, 8 mi of paved roads circle the island; bicycles rent by the hour or day at concessions near the ferry docks on Huron Street. **Mackinac Island Carriage Tours** (Main St., ☎ 906/847–3573) offers horse-drawn tours covering historic points of interest, including Ft. Mackinac, Arch Rock, Skull Cave, Surrey Hill, and the Grand Hotel.

Old Ft. Mackinac (☎ 906/847–3328), perched on a bluff above the harbor, was a British stronghold during the American Revolution and the War of 1812. Fourteen original buildings are preserved as a museum; costumed guides offer tours and reenactments. **Marquette Park,** directly below the fort along Main Street, commemorates the work of French missionary Jacques Marquette with a bark chapel patterned after those built on the island in the 1600s. The venerable **Grand Hotel** (☎ 906/847–3331), now more than a century old, charges visitors $5 just to look, but the Victorian opulence of the public rooms and the view from the world's longest porch is worth it. **Mackinac Island Chamber of Commerce** (Box 451, Mackinac Island 49757, ☎ 906/847–3783) provides information on island attractions.

Keweenaw Peninsula

Getting There

The Keweenaw, in the northwestern Upper Peninsula, is reached by U.S. 41.

What to See and Do

Curving into Lake Superior like a crooked finger, the Keweenaw (*Key*-wa-naw) was the site of extensive copper mining from the 1840s to the 1960s. The deposits were exceptionally pure, and in its heyday the

Keweenaw produced much of the world's copper. In **Hancock,** the **Arcadian Copper Mine** (☏ 906/482–7502) has a ¼-mi guided tour of workings no longer in operation. **Houghton** is home to Michigan Technical University, whose **E.A. Seaman Mineralogical Museum** (☏ 906/487–2572) has extensive displays of minerals native to the Upper Peninsula. The inland headquarters of **Isle Royale National Park** (*see* National and State Parks, *above*) are also in Houghton.

North on U.S. 41, the Victorian stone architecture in **Calumet** gives just a hint of the wealth in the copper towns during the boom days. Restoration is underway at the **Calumet Theater** (☏ 906/337–2610), which was built in 1900 and was the stage for such stars as Lillian Russell, Sarah Bernhardt, and Douglas Fairbanks, Sr. At **Coppertown, U.S.A.** (☏ 906/337–4354), a visitor center tells the story of the mines, towns, and people of the Keweenaw. Farther north, in the old mining town of **Delaware, Delaware Copper Mine Tours** (☏ 906/289–4688) provides guided walking tours through the first level of a 145-year-old mine.

At the tip of the peninsula, **Copper Harbor,** Michigan's northernmost community, is a popular spot with campers. **Fort Wilkins State Park** (☏ 906/289–4215) contains the restored buildings of an Army post established in 1844 and abandoned in 1870. The complex also has copper-mine shafts, hiking trails, and campgrounds. **Brockway Mountain Drive** climbs 900 feet above Copper Harbor to provide magnificent views of the peninsula and Lake Superior. **Keweenaw Tourism Council** (326 Shelden Ave., Houghton 49931, ☏ 906/482–2388 or 800/338–7982) provides information on peninsula attractions.

Lake Michigan Shore

Getting There

U.S. 31 edges Lake Michigan from St. Joseph to Mackinaw City.

What to See and Do

The Lake Michigan shoreline, which extends from the southwest corner of the state up to the Mackinac Bridge, is one of Michigan's greatest natural resources. Its placid waters, cool breezes, and sugary beaches (including some of the largest sand dunes in the world) have attracted generations of tourists, including such regulars as Al Capone, Ernest Hemingway, and L. Frank Baum (who wrote many of his *Wizard of Oz* books over the course of several summer vacations).

Resort towns, some of which triple in population between Memorial Day and Labor Day, dot the shoreline. **St. Joseph** is a picturesque community whose turn-of-the-century downtown and two 1,000-foot-long piers make it ideal for walkers. The artists' colony of **Saugatuck** has many fine restaurants and shops, an active gay and lesbian community, and B&Bs enough to make it a shoo-in for the title of bed-and-breakfast capital of the state. **Saugatuck Dune Rides** (☏ 616/857–2253) offers freewheeling dune-buggy rides along Lake Michigan. In neighboring **Douglas,** the **S.S. *Keewatin*** (☏ 616/857–2151), one of the Great Lakes' last classic passenger steamboats, is permanently docked as a maritime museum.

Nearby is **Holland,** home of the famous **Tulip Time Festival** (☏ 616/396–4221), held for 10 days each May. The **De Klomp Wooden Shoe and Delftware Factory** (12755 Quincy St., ☏ 616/399–1900) is the only place outside the Netherlands where earthenware is hand-painted and fired using Delft-blue glaze.

Farther north is the eastern shore's largest city, **Muskegon.** More than a Rust Belt relic, this industrial town offers the **Muskegon Winter Sports Complex** (☏ 616/744–9629), with the Midwest's only luge run. The **Frauenthal Center for the Performing Arts** (417 W. Western St., ☏ 616/722–4538) is a gaudy art deco theater that is home to traveling Broadway-quality plays, silent-film showings, the West Shore Symphony Orchestra, and the Miss Michigan Pageant. Eight miles north of town is **Michigan's Adventure Amusement Park** (Russell Rd. exit off U.S. 31, ☏ 616/766–3377), with more than 20 thrill rides, 10 water slides, a wave pool, shows, games, food, and the only two roller coasters in Michigan.

A two-hour drive north of Muskegon is **Traverse City,** the state's premier sports-vacation spot. Much to the chagrin of longtime residents, the area south of Grand Traverse Bay was "discovered" by sportsmen—and developers—about 25 years ago. Unfortunately, the roads have not kept pace with the boom in sailors, golfers, and skiers. The two-lane highways can resemble parking lots, particularly during the popular **National Cherry Festival** (☏ 616/947–1120), which draws an estimated 400,000 people each summer. For a pleasant diversion, follow Rte. 37 around the **Old Mission Peninsula,** filled with the cherry orchards and vineyards that, next to tourism, are the area's main industry. Spring, when crowds are small and the orchards are in bloom, is a good time to visit.

Some of the finest views of Lake Michigan are found farther north. Follow Rte. 119 between **Harbor Springs,** a resort village overlooking Little Traverse Bay, and **Cross Village,** where the **Chief Andrew J. Blackbird Museum** (☏ 616/526–7731) houses a collection of Ottawa and Ojibwa Native American artifacts. The **West Michigan Tourist Association** (136 E. Fulton St., Grand Rapids 49503, ☏ 616/456–8557) provides information on lakeside attractions.

MINNESOTA

By Don Davenport

Updated by Lynette Lamb

Capital	St. Paul
Population	4,375,099
Motto	Star of the North
State Bird	Common loon
State Flower	Pink lady's slipper

Visitor Information

Minnesota Office of Tourism (100 Metro Sq., 121 7th Pl. E, St. Paul 55101, ☎ 612/296–5029 or 800/657–3700; in Canada, 800/766–8687). There are 11 visitor centers around the state.

Scenic Drives

U.S. 61, along the Mississippi River between Red Wing and Winona, is often compared with the Rhine Valley in beauty; between Duluth and the Canadian border, it hugs the edge of Lake Superior for 160 mi, providing spectacular views of the lake and its rocky shoreline. **Rte. 59,** between Fergus Falls and Detroit Lakes, traverses some of central Minnesota's prime lake country.

National and State Parks

National Parks

Voyageurs National Park (*see* Elsewhere in the State, The Iron Range and Boundary Waters, *below*), in far northern Minnesota near International Falls, has 30 major lakes and is part of the watery highway that makes up the state's northern border with Canada.

State Parks

Minnesota has 65 state parks, 51 of which offer camping facilities that vary from modern to primitive sites. For information, contact the **Department of Natural Resources** (DNR Information Center, 500 Lafayette Rd., Box 40, St. Paul 55155, ☎ 612/296–6157).

Fort Snelling State Park, just south of downtown St. Paul (Rte. 5 and Post Rd., St. Paul, ☎ 612/725–2390), preserves the historic fort built at the junction of the Mississippi and Minnesota rivers in 1819. **Itasca State Park** (HCO 5, Box 4, Lake Itasca 56460, ☎ 218/266–2114) is Minnesota's oldest state park, established in 1891 to protect the headwaters of the Mississippi River, which rises from Lake Itasca. **Soudan Underground Mine State Park** (1379 Stuntz Bay Rd., Soudan 55782, ☎ 218/753–2245) offers hiking trails and tours of the Soudan Mine, Minnesota's oldest and largest iron mine, which operated until 1962. **Gooseberry Falls State Park** (1300 U.S. 61E, Two Harbors 55616, ☎ 218/834–3855) and **Temperance River State Park** (U.S. 61E, Box 33, Schroeder 55613, ☎ 218/663–7476), with roaring waterfalls and scenic vistas, are typical of parks found along Lake Superior's shore.

MINNEAPOLIS AND ST. PAUL

Drawing comparisons between Minneapolis and St. Paul is much like comparing two favorite aunts—a difficult task. St. Paul has a slightly reserved air about it; Minneapolis is brasher, noisier, and busier. Both cities have tall, gleaming glass skylines; St. Paul's is designed to blend with the city's art deco and Victorian architecture, while Minneapolis's is more eclectic. St. Paul has preserved much of its architectural heritage, while most of downtown Minneapolis is new. Both cities straddle the Mississippi River, and riverboat traffic calls at the Twin Cities from as far away as New Orleans.

There are 2.3 million people in the Greater Minneapolis/St.Paul metro region, but Minneapolis wins the population race by 96,000. The strong Scandinavian strain in the cities' ancestry has not prevented them from constructing miles-long skyway (aerial walkway) systems. Residents can drive downtown, park, walk to work, go to lunch, shop, see a show, and return to their cars without once setting foot outdoors—a blessing in the blustery Minnesota winters.

Tourist Information

Minneapolis: Convention and Visitors Association (4000 Multifoods Tower, 33 S. 6th St., 55402, ☎ 612/348–4313 or 800/445–7412). **St. Paul:** Convention and Visitors Bureau (55 E. 5th St., Suite 102, 55101, ☎ 612/297–6985 or 800/627–6101); visitor information booth, Town Square (445 Minnesota St., ☎ 612/223–5409).

Arriving and Departing

By Plane

Minneapolis/St. Paul International Airport (☎ 612/726–5555) lies between the cities on I–494, 8 mi south of downtown St. Paul and 10 mi south of downtown Minneapolis. It is served by most major domestic airlines and several foreign carriers. From the airport to either city, **Metropolitan Transit Commission** (☎ 612/349–7000) buses cost $1 ($1.25 during rush hour); taxis take about 30 minutes and charge $17–$20 to downtown Minneapolis and $12–$14 to St. Paul.

By Car

The major north–south route through the area is I–35, which divides into I–35W bisecting Minneapolis and I–35E through St. Paul. I–94 goes east–west through both cities. A beltway circles the Twin Cities, with I–494 looping through the southern suburbs and I–694 cutting through the north.

By Train

St. Paul's **Amtrak** station (730 Transfer Rd., ☎ 800/872–7245) serves both cities.

By Bus

Greyhound Lines has stations in St. Paul (25 W. 7th St., ☎ 612/222–0509 or 800/231–2222) and in Minneapolis (29 N. 9th St., ☎ 612/371–3323 or 800/231–2222).

Getting Around Minneapolis and St. Paul

Both cities are laid out on a grid, with streets running north–south and east–west. However, many downtown streets parallel the Mississippi River and run on a diagonal, and not all streets cross the river. Both downtowns have extensive skywalk systems. Many St. Paul attractions can be reached on foot, but most of those in Minneapolis require wheels. Express fare on **Metropolitan Transit Commission** (☎ 612/349–7000) buses between Minneapolis and St. Paul during rush hour is $1.75. Within each city's central business district the fare is 50¢. Outside the downtown area the fare is $1, $1.25 during peak hours (6–9 AM and 3:30–6:30 PM). Children under six ride free.

Cabs must be ordered by phone or hired at cabstands. The fare is about $3.50 for the first 1¼ mi and approximately $1.30 for each additional mile. The largest taxi firms in St. Paul are **Yellow** (☎ 612/222–4433) and **City Wide** (☎ 612/292–1616); in Minneapolis, **Blue and White** (☎ 612/333–3331) and **Yellow** (☎ 612/824–4444). **Town Taxi** (☎ 612/331–8294) serves both cities and all suburbs.

Exploring Minneapolis and St. Paul

Minneapolis

Downtown Minneapolis is easily walkable in any season. The climate-controlled skyway system connects hundreds of shops and restaurants. In general, skyways remain open during the business hours of the buildings they connect.

At the eastern edge of downtown are the Mississippi River's **Falls of St. Anthony,** discovered by Father Louis Hennepin three centuries ago. Harnessed by dams and diminished in grandeur, the historic falls are today bypassed by the **Upper St. Anthony Lock** (foot of Portland Ave.), which allows river traffic to reach industrial sections of Minneapolis. An observation deck provides views of lock operations.

Near the lock, the **Stone Arch Bridge,** a railroad bridge built over the Mississippi River in the late 19th century by railroad baron James J. Hill, was recently restored and reopened to foot and bicycle traffic. Guided walking tours of the St. Anthony Falls Historic District are offered weekends April 15–September 30 (☎ 612/627–5433).

Just north of the Mississippi, the **University of Minnesota,** with an enrollment of close to 50,000, has one of the largest campuses in the country. **Dinkytown,** on the east bank, is an area of campus bars, night spots, university shops, and record and book stores. **Seven Corners,** on the west bank, features the **West Bank Theater District,** with popular after-hours hangouts, theaters, and more night spots.

The university's **James Ford Bell Museum of Natural History** (University Ave. SE at 17th Ave., ☎ 612/624–7083; closed Mon.) has dioramas of Minnesota wildlife, a wildlife-art gallery, and a "Touch and See" room where youngsters can handle the skins, bones, and skulls of a variety of animals. The newest and most talked about building on campus is the **Weisman Art Museum** (333 E. River Rd., ☎ 612/625–9494), a wild metallic structure designed by famed avant-garde architect Frank Gehry. It features student and faculty work and a permanent collection of American art from 1900 to 1950.

Several blocks west is downtown Minneapolis, much of it built in the past 25 years. Two of the more recent additions are the 57-story **Norwest Center** (77 S. 7th St.), designed by Cesar Pelli, and its smaller companion, **Gaviidae Common** (651 Nicollet Mall), the latest downtown shopping mecca. The mirrored, 51-story **IDS Building** (80 S. 8th St.) contains **Crystal Court,** a focal point of the skyway system, with shops, restaurants, and offices. The 42-story **Piper Jaffray Tower** (222 S. 9th St.), sheathed in aqua-colored glass and the 17-story **Lutheran Brotherhood Building** (625 4th Ave. SE), dressed in copper-colored glass, are sparkling members of the skyline. At the **Foshay Tower** (821 Marquette Ave., ☎ 612/341–2522)—Minneapolis's first skyscraper, constructed in 1929—a 31st-floor observation deck provides spectacular views of the city April–October.

In the public library on **Nicollet Mall**—a mile-long pedestrian mall, running from 2nd Street to Grant Avenue, with an extensive system of skywalks connecting many shops—the **Minneapolis Planetarium** (☎ 612/372–6644) offers sky shows that tour the night sky and investigate the latest discoveries in space science.

Another downtown landmark, the inflated **Hubert H. Humphrey Metrodome** (900 S. 5th St., ☎ 612/332–0386) is home to the Minnesota Twins baseball team and the Minnesota Vikings and University of Minnesota football teams. Behind-the-scenes tours of locker rooms, the playing field, and the press box are available.

A mile south of downtown, and west of I–35W, the **Minneapolis Institute of Arts** displays more than 80,000 works of art from every age and culture, including works by the French Impressionists, rare Chinese jade, and a photography collection ranging from 1863 to the present. *2400 3rd Ave. S, ☎ 612/870–3131. Closed Mon.*

Five blocks east, the **American Swedish Institute** (2600 Park Ave., ☎ 612/871–4907) is set in a 33-room Romanesque château filled with decorative woodwork. The museum houses collections of art, pioneer items, Swedish glass, ceramics, and furniture relating to the area's Swedish heritage.

Just west of Loring Park and the I–94 loop, the **Walker Art Center** houses an outstanding collection of 20th-century American and European sculpture, prints, and photography, as well as traveling exhibits. The Walker's **Minneapolis Sculpture Garden** is the largest outdoor urban sculpture garden in the nation. *725 Vineland Pl., adjoining the Guthrie Theater, ☎ 612/375–7600. Admission charged, Thurs. free. Closed Mon., holidays.*

St. Paul

You can easily explore downtown St. Paul on foot, walking either on the streets or through the all-weather, climate-controlled skyway system. Keep in mind that the Mississippi makes a huge loop and runs east–west through St. Paul.

The **Minnesota Museum of American Art,** on the second floor of the historic Landmark Center, has a permanent collection strong in Asian and 19th- and 20th-century American art, along with changing exhibits of contemporary sculpture, paintings, and photography. *75 W. 5th St., ☎ 612/292–4355. Donation requested. Closed Mon., holidays.*

Nearby, in a 20-story building of a design known as American Perpendicular, is the City Hall and **Ramsey County Courthouse** (15 W. Kellogg Blvd., ☎ 612/266–8500). Here, Memorial Hall (4th St. entrance) features Swedish sculptor Carl Milles's towering ***Vision of Peace*** statue, the largest carved-onyx figure in the world, standing 36 feet high and weighing 60 tons.

Two blocks west is **Rice Park,** St. Paul's oldest urban park, dating from 1849. A favorite with downtowners, who eat lunch here in warm weather, it is an excellent place to stop and enjoy the flavor of the city. Facing the park on the north is the **Landmark Center** (75 W. 5th St., ☎ 612/292–3225), the restored Old Federal Courts Building, constructed in 1902. This towering Romanesque Revival structure features a six-story indoor courtyard, stained-glass skylights, and a marble-tile foyer. Housed within are the offices of many of St. Paul's cultural organizations; a branch of the **Minnesota Museum of American Art;** and the **Schubert Club Musical Instrument Museum** (☎ 612/292–3268), with an outstanding collection of keyboard instruments dating from the 1700s.

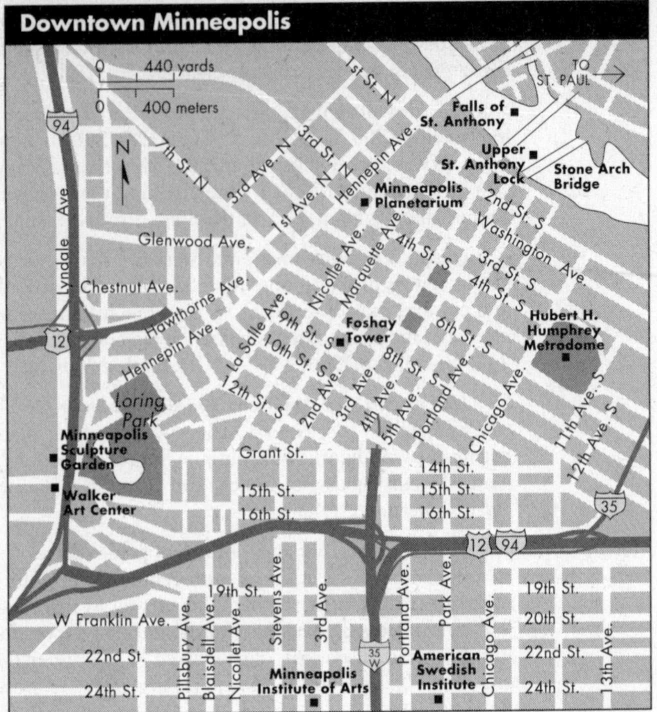

On the east side of the park is the luxurious **Saint Paul Hotel** (*see* Lodging, *below*), which hosts notables from presidents to Hollywood stars. On the south side is the block-long Italian Renaissance Revival **St. Paul Public Library.** Rice Park's most recent addition is the **Ordway Music Theater** (*see* The Arts and Nightlife, *below*), a state-of-the-art auditorium with faceted-glass walls set in a facade of brick and copper.

West of the park is the **Alexander Ramsey House,** home of the first governor of the Minnesota Territory. Built in 1872, the restored French Second Empire mansion has 15 rooms containing marble fireplaces, period furnishings, and rich collections of china and silver. *265 S. Exchange St., ☎ 612/296–8760. Admission charged. Closed Jan.–Mar.*

North of Rice Park is the **Science Museum of Minnesota,** a favorite with both local and visiting youngsters. There are exhibits on archaeology, technology, and biology; the Physical Sciences and Technology Gallery offers many exciting hands-on exhibits. In the McKnight Omnitheater, 70-mm films are projected overhead on a massive tilted screen. *30 E. 10th St., ☎ 612/221–9488. Admission charged. Closed Mon. Labor Day–*
Dec. 20.

To the northwest, the **Minnesota State Capitol** (University Ave. between Aurora and Cedar Sts., ☎ 612/296–2881), designed by the St. Paul architect Cass Gilbert, contains more than 25 varieties of marble, sandstone, and granite. Its 223-foot-high dome is the world's largest unsupported marble dome.

The Cathedral of St. Paul (239 Selby Ave., ☎ 612/228–1766), a classic Renaissance-style domed church echoing St. Peter's in Rome, lies ½ mi southwest of the capitol. Inside are beautiful stained-glass win-

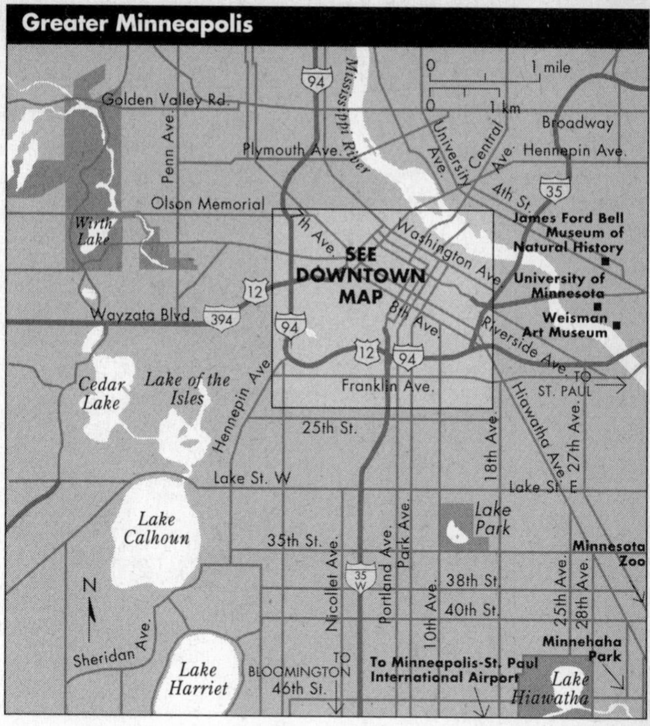

dows, statues, paintings, and other works of art as well as a small historical museum on the lower level.

Summit Avenue, which runs 4½ mi from the cathedral to the Mississippi River, has the nation's longest stretch of intact residential Victorian architecture. F. Scott Fitzgerald lived at 599 Summit in 1918, when he wrote *This Side of Paradise*. The **James J. Hill House** (240 Summit Ave., ☎ 612/297–2555), once home of the transportation pioneer and builder of the Great Northern Railroad, is a Richardsonian Romanesque mansion with carved woodwork, tiled fireplaces, and a skylighted art gallery hosting changing exhibits. The **Governor's Mansion** (1006 Summit Ave., ☎ 612/297–2161) is open for tours Thursday, May through October. **Mt. Zion Temple** (1300 Summit Ave., ☎ 612/698–3881) is the home of the oldest Jewish congregation in Minnesota (1856).

Other Attractions

In Minneapolis's Apple Valley suburb, the **Minnesota Zoo** houses some 1,700 animals in natural settings viewed by following six year-round trail systems. Other features are a monorail, a Zoo Lab, a seasonal children's zoo, bird and animal shows, and daily films and slide shows. *13000 Zoo Blvd., Apple Valley, ☎ 612/431–9200. Admission charged.*

At the confluence of the Mississippi and Minnesota rivers is **Historic Fort Snelling.** The northernmost outpost in the old Northwest Territories, it remained an active military post until after World War II. Seventeen buildings have been restored, and costumed guides portray 1820s fort life with demonstrations of blacksmithing, carpentry, and military ceremonies. A History Center has exhibits and short films on the fort. *Rtes. 5 and 55 near the International Airport south of St. Paul, ☎ 612/725–2413. Admission charged. Fort closed Nov.–Apr.; History Center closed weekends Nov.–Apr.*

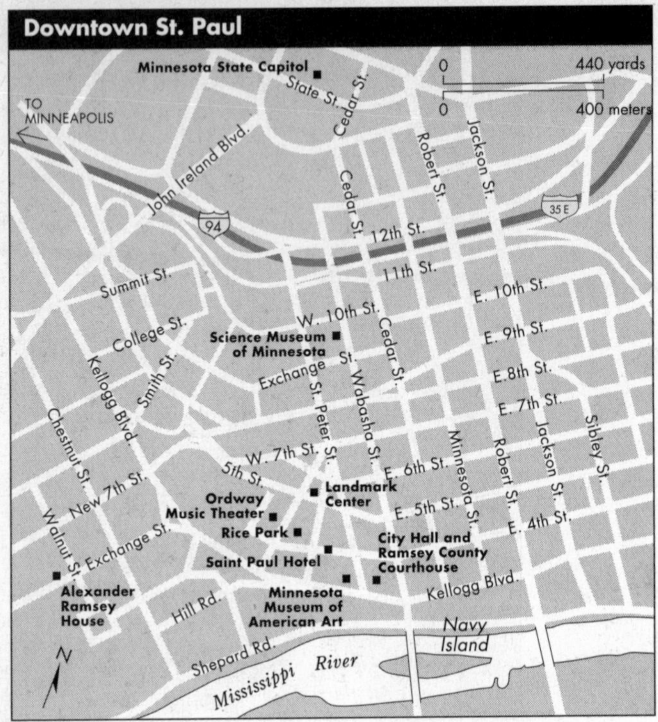

Parks and Gardens

Minneapolis

Minnehaha Park, on the Mississippi near the airport, contains Minnehaha Falls, which were made famous by Longfellow's *Song of Hiawatha.* Above the waterfall is a statue of Hiawatha and Minnehaha. Minnehaha Parkway, which follows Minnehaha Creek, offers 15 mi of jogging, biking, and roller-skating trails running west to Lake Harriet, one of the Minneapolis chain of lakes.

Wirth Park (I–394 and Theodore Wirth Pkwy.), just west of downtown, has not only bicycling and walking paths through wooded areas but also the **Eloise Butler Wildflower Garden**—a little Eden of local forest and prairie flora. Wirth also has a moderately challenging 18-hole public golf course—a popular cross-country skiing spot in winter.

St. Paul

Como Park (N. Lexington Ave. at Como Ave.) has picnic areas, walking trails, playgrounds, and tennis and swimming facilities. **Como Park Zoo** (☎ 612/488–5571) is home to large cats, land and water birds, primates, and aquatic animals. The adjacent **Como Park Conservatory** (☎ 612/489–1740), in a domed greenhouse, has sunken gardens, a fern room, biblical plantings, and seasonal flower shows.

What to See and Do with Children

At the **Children's Museum** (1217 Bandana Blvd., St. Paul, ☎ 612/644–3818; closed Mon.), youngsters can try their hand at such grown-up activities as driving a bus and playing banker or dentist in two floors of simulated settings. The **Children's Theater Company** (2400 3rd Ave. S, Minneapolis, ☎ 612/874–0400) features a season of adventurous

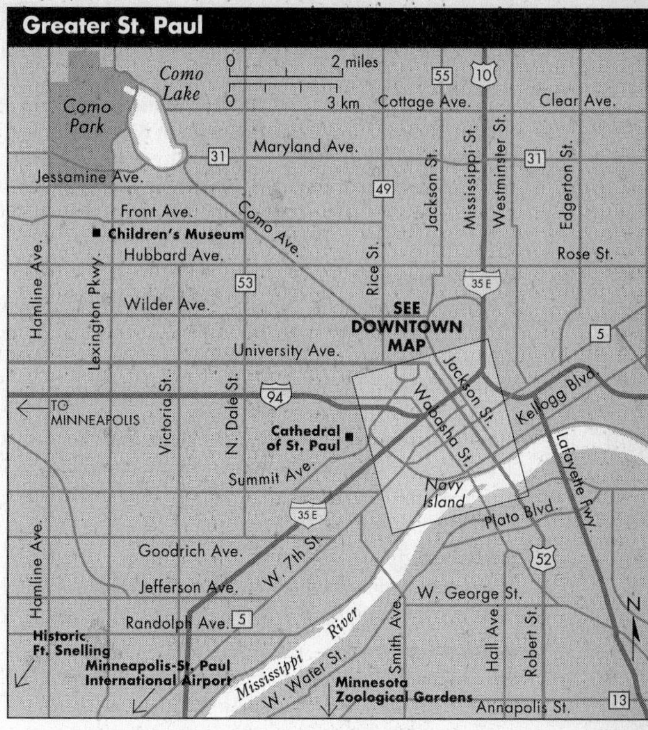

plays that appeal as much to adults as to their offspring. Among the many other Twin Cities attractions children will enjoy are **Upper St. Anthony Lock,** the **Minneapolis Planetarium,** and **Foshay Tower** (*see* Exploring Minneapolis, *above*); the **Science Museum of Minnesota** and **Minnesota State Capitol** (*see* Exploring St. Paul, *above*); the **Minnesota Zoo** and **Historic Fort Snelling** (*see* Other Attractions, *above*); and St. Paul's **Como Park Zoo** (*see* Parks and Gardens, *above*).

Shopping

The Twin Cities offer everything from tiny specialty shops to enclosed shopping malls with large department stores. The skyway systems in each city connect hundreds of stores and shops.

Minneapolis

Among the many shops along **Nicollet Mall** (*see* Exploring Minneapolis, *above*) are **Dayton's** (700 Nicollet Mall), the city's largest department store, and **Gaviidae Common** (651 Nicollet Mall), the newest downtown shopping addition, with three levels of upscale shops, including branches of **Saks Fifth Avenue** and **Neiman Marcus. The Conservatory** (800 Nicollet Mall) has a number of fine boutiques and restaurants, accented handsomely with wood and marble. **City Center** (7th St. and Hennepin Ave.) features 60 shops and 19 restaurants. **Riverplace** and **St. Anthony Main,** on the east bank of the Mississippi, have offices, restaurants, and movie theaters housed in historic structures. A few miles south is **Uptown,** a smaller shopping and entertainment mecca centered on **Calhoun Square** (Lake and Hennepin Aves.), which has more than 40 shops and several restaurants.

St. Paul

The World Trade Center (30 E. 7th St.), downtown, has more than 100 specialty shops and restaurants, including **Dayton's,** the leader in fashions for men, women, and children. **Bandana Square** (1021 Bandana Blvd. E), in the former Great Northern Railroad repair yard in northwest St. Paul, has a variety of specialty stores. **Victoria Crossing** (850 Grand Ave.) is a collection of small shops and specialty stores that provide an anchor for the dozens of other shops that span Grand Avenue from Dale Street to Prior Avenue.

Bloomington

South of Minneapolis, Bloomington is Minnesota's third-largest city (perhaps one day part of the Triplet Cities?) and home to the area's newest attraction: the **Mall of America** (Cedar Ave. and Killebrew Dr., ☎ 612/883–8800). Nicknamed "the Megamall," the world's largest enclosed mall features more than 400 stores and shops, including **Macy's, Bloomingdale's, Sears,** and **Nordstrom.** Beneath its central dome is Camp Snoopy, a large amusement park.

Spectator Sports

Baseball

Minnesota Twins (Hubert H. Humphrey Metrodome, 501 Chicago Ave. S, Minneapolis, ☎ 612/375–1116; Apr.–Oct.).

Basketball

Minnesota Timberwolves (Target Center, 600 1st Ave. N, Minneapolis, ☎ 612/337–3865; Nov.–Apr.).

Football

Minnesota Vikings (Hubert H. Humphrey Metrodome, 500 11th Ave. S, Minneapolis, ☎ 612/333–8828; Aug.–Dec.).

Beaches

With 22 lakes, Minneapolis has scores of beaches. **Thomas Beach,** at the south end of Lake Calhoun, is one of the most popular. Further information is available from the Minneapolis Parks and Recreation Board (☎ 612/661–4875).

Dining

By Karin Winegar

Despite the diverse gastronomic traditions introduced to the Twin Cities by the new immigrant population, the majority of Minnesotans of Scandinavian and German descent still demand things "toned down a bit" and are somewhat wary of any seasonings more exotic than salt and pepper. No matter what the cuisine, Minnesotans rarely dress up when they eat out. At all but the most stellar restaurants the unofficial dress code is urban-casual-but-tidy attire. For price ranges, see Chart 1 (B) in On the Road with Fodor's.

Minneapolis

$$$ **Café Un Deux Trois.** This elegant, marble-filled bistro with a 1920s feel takes up much of the main floor of the Foshay Tower, Minneapolis's first skyscraper. Food is simply and well prepared; specials include steak poivre, roasted Long Island duckling, and sautéed calf's liver. *114 S. 9th St., ☎ 612/673–0686. AE, DC, MC, V.*

$$$ **D'Amico Cucina.** From the *faux-marbre* plates and peach-and-gray linens to the black marble floors and black leather chairs, this is haute urban nouvelle with a modern Italian accent. Artistic presentations from the kitchen include fresh pastas and free-range chicken with mushroom and truffle puree. *Butler Sq., 100 N. 6th St., ☎ 612/338–2401. Jacket and tie advised. AE, DC, MC, V.*

$$$ **Goodfellow's.** The emphasis at this plush restaurant is on regional American cuisine, with such offerings as South Dakota venison, wild-rice fritters, sautéed walleye with warm new-potato salad, and cranberry-walnut compote. *Conservatory, 800 Nicollet Mall, ☎ 612/332–4800. Jacket advised. AE, D, MC, V. Closed Sun.*

$$$ **Kincaid's Steak, Chop and Fish House.** Kincaid's imposing decor of marble, brass, glass, and wood combines with eclectic cuisine to create a very up-to-date steak house. The kitchen does competent interpretations of Continental and all-American entrées, from T-bone steak to mesquite-grilled salmon to grilled rosemary lamb and baked chicken Dijon. *8400 Normandale Lake Blvd., Bloomington, ☎ 612/921–2255. Jacket and tie advised. AE, D, DC, MC, V.*

$$$ **Whitney Grille.** In the lavish Whitney Hotel, the Grille has a flower-filled garden plaza and a hushed main dining room decorated in rich woods and muted floral fabrics. Specialties include pheasant stuffed with root vegetables and mushrooms and southwestern grilled swordfish. *150 Portland Ave., ☎ 612/339–9300. Jacket advised. AE, D, DC, MC, V.*

$$ **Chez Bananas.** Inflatable palm trees, vinyl bats, and windup toys on tables set the tone for Caribbean food served—by yuppies with a sense of humor—in a warehouse storefront. Offerings include savory garlic-laced black beans and rice with chicken or fish. *129 N. 4th St., ☎ 612/340–0032. AE, D, DC, MC, V.*

$$ **Loring Cafe.** The Loring offers a terrific view of handsome Loring Park, bohemian-chic decor, and a menu that includes manicotti with lamb and Chinese chicken salad with sesame-ginger dressing. *1624 Harmon Pl., ☎ 612/332–1617. MC, V.*

$ **Black Forest Inn.** This hangout of students and artists is famous for its huge selection of bottled and tap beers, its hearty German cuisine, and its lovely courtyard. Owner Erich Christ is the real thing, and so are his plates of no-nonsense Wiener schnitzel with potato pancakes and applesauce. *1 E. 26th St., ☎ 612/872–0812. AE, D, DC, MC, V.*

$ **Bryant-Lake Bowl.** This 1930s-era eight-lane bowling alley now contains one of the Twin Cities' hippest restaurants. Impressive wine and beer lists complement such specials as smoked trout and fresh ravioli with four cheeses—and after your meal you can still bowl a few frames. The place is also known for its inexpensive breakfasts. *810 W. Lake St., ☎ 612/825–3737. MC, V.*

St. Paul

$$ **Dakota Bar and Grill.** The Twin Cities' best jazz club also serves an inventive menu of midwestern fare, including smoked pheasant fritters and salmon-walleye croquettes. Like the music, the atmosphere is contemporary and cool in color and mood. Sunday brunch is served. *Bandana Sq., 1021 E. Bandana Blvd., ☎ 612/642–1442. AE, D, DC, MC, V. No lunch.*

$$ **Khyber Pass Cafe.** In a corner storefront in a sleepy neighborhood, this small restaurant with decor that includes antique dresses, beadwork, rugs, and photos has barely a dozen tables. The small menu of sometimes-spicy Afghani cuisine includes such dishes as chicken broiled on a skewer and served with coriander chutney. *1399 St. Clair Ave., ☎ 612/698–5403. No credit cards. Closed Sun.–Mon.*

$$ **Saint Paul Grill.** The Saint Paul Hotel's stylish bistro sports contemporary decor and affords a lovely view of Rice Park. The menu is American: dry-aged steaks, a variety of fish dishes, pastas, chicken potpie, and homemade roast-beef hash. *350 Market St., ☎ 612/292–9292. AE, D, DC, MC, V.*

$ **Cafe Latté.** This furiously successful and almost always jammed cafeteria offers an eclectic selection of soups, salads, breads, and stews. The chicken chili and Caesar salad are specialties, as are all the varieties of chocolate cake. *850 Grand Ave., ☎ 612/224–5687. AE, MC, V.*

$ **Mickey's Diner.** This quintessential, streamlined, 1930s diner with lots of chrome and vinyl, a lunch counter, and a few tiny booths is listed on the National Register of Historic Places. The stick-to-the-ribs fare and great breakfasts make it a local institution. *36 W. 7th St. at St. Peter St., ☎ 612/222–5633. D, MC, V.*

Lodging

By Karin Winegar

There is no shortage of lodging in the Twin Cities. Accommodations are available in the downtowns, along I–494 in the suburbs and industrial parks of Bloomington and Richfield (known as "the strip"), and near the Minneapolis/St. Paul International Airport. A number of hotels are attached to shopping centers as well, the better to ignore Minnesota's fierce winters and summer heat. For price ranges, see Chart 2 (A) in On the Road with Fodor's.

Minneapolis

$$$ **Hyatt Regency Hotel.** A wide, sweeping lobby with a fountain and potted trees is the focal point of this hotel, within easy walking distance of downtown. Bedrooms are decorated in contemporary jade, peach, and gray fabrics and carpeting. *1300 Nicollet Mall, 55403, ☎ 612/370–1234, FAX 612/370–1463. 533 rooms, 21 suites. Facilities: restaurant, coffee shop, lounge, health club, sauna, tennis and racquetball courts, sports bar. AE, D, DC, MC, V.*

$$$ **Marriott City Center Hotel.** At this sleek, 31-story hotel within the City Center shopping mall, rooms have a contemporary look in peach and jade. *30 S. 7th St., 55402, ☎ 612/349–4000, FAX 612/332–7165. 583 rooms, 42 bilevel suites. Facilities: 2 restaurants, lounge, valet parking, health club, sauna. AE, D, DC, MC, V.*

$$–$$$ ★ **Whitney Hotel.** An 1880s flour mill converted into a small, elegant, genteel hotel, the Whitney provides suite accommodations; about half overlook the Mississippi. The lobby features rich woods, brass fixtures, and marble appointments. *150 Portland Ave., 55401, ☎ 612/339–9300 or 800/248–1879, FAX 612/339–1333. 95 suites. Facilities: restaurant, lounge, valet parking. AE, D, DC, MC, V.*

$$ **Holiday Inn Metrodome.** A 10-minute bus ride from downtown, this showy hotel is in the heart of the theater and entertainment district and is close to both the Metrodome and the University of Minnesota. *1500 Washington Ave. S, 55454, ☎ 612/333–4646 or 800/448–3663, FAX 612/333–7910. 265 rooms, 22 suites. Facilities: restaurant, lounge, indoor pool. AE, D, DC, MC, V.*

$$ **Nicollet Island Inn.** This charming 1893 limestone inn is on Nicollet Island, in the middle of the Mississippi River, with downtown Minneapolis on one shore and the Riverplace and St. Anthony Main restaurant and office complexes on the other. The comfortable rooms are decorated with Early American reproduction furniture; some have river views. *95 Merriam St., 55401, ☎ 612/331–1800, FAX 612/331–6528. 24 rooms. Facilities: restaurant, lounge, bar. AE, D, DC, MC, V.*

$$ **Park Inn International.** The desk staff is cheery enough, but the decor in the public areas is a bit somber. Rooms in the 12-story hotel have contemporary furniture and provide sweeping views of downtown. *1313 Nicollet Mall, 55403, ☎ 612/332–0371 or 800/437–7275, FAX 612/359–2160. 320 rooms, 5 suites. Facilities: restaurant, lounge, indoor pool, sauna, whirlpool, exercise room. AE, D, DC, MC, V.*

St. Paul

$$$ **Crown Sterling Suites–St. Paul.** Built in 1983, this hotel is decorated in neo–New Orleans Garden District style, with terra-cotta, brickwork, tropical plants, and a courtyard fountain. It is close to I–35E and within walking distance of major downtown businesses. *175 E. 10th St., 55101, ☎ 612/224–5400 or 800/433–4600, FAX 612/224–0957. 210 suites. Facilities: restaurant, pool, sauna, free airport pickup. AE, D, DC, MC, V.*

$$$ **Radisson Hotel Saint Paul.** This 22-story riverside tower has Oriental touches in the lobby and rooms (most with a river view) decorated in traditional American style. *11 E. Kellogg Blvd., 55101, ☎ 612/292–1900, FAX 612/224–8999. 475 rooms, 19 suites. Facilities: restaurant, indoor pool, fitness center. AE, D, DC, MC, V.*

$$$ **Saint Paul Hotel.** Built in 1910, this stately stone hotel overlooks Rice Park, the center of genteel St. Paul. Renovated in 1990, the rooms have an eclectic traditional decor. *350 Market St., 55102, ☎ 612/292–9292 or 800/292–9292, FAX 612/228–9506. 255 rooms, 10 suites. Facilities: 2 restaurants, bar. AE, D, DC, MC, V.*

$$ **Holiday Inn Express.** In what was once a paint shop for the Pacific Northern Railroad, this hotel is connected by skyway to the Bandana Square shopping center. Rooms are decorated with contemporary furnishings. *1010 W. Bandana Blvd., 55108, ☎ 612/647–1637. 103 rooms, 6 suites. Facilities: indoor pool, wading pool, whirlpool, sauna. AE, D, DC, MC, V.*

$$ **Sheraton Midway St. Paul.** This contemporary four-story hotel is in the busy district centered on Snelling and University avenues. Hallways decorated in shades of pink lead into bright, comfortable rooms (some no-smoking) with contemporary oak woodwork. *400 Hamline Ave. N, 55104, ☎ 612/642–1234 or 800/535–2339, FAX 612/642–1126. 197 rooms, 14 suites. Facilities: restaurant, lounge, indoor pool, sauna, exercise room. AE, D, DC, MC, V.*

$ **Best Western Kelly Inn.** A popular spot for state legislators whose home districts are far away, this hotel within walking distance of the state capitol has essentially remained the same clean, efficient inn for 30 years. *161 St. Anthony St., 55103, ☎ 612/227–8711, FAX 612/227–1698. 125 rooms. Facilities: restaurant, lounge, pool, sauna, children's pool. AE, DC, MC, V.*

The Arts and Nightlife

The Arts

The calendar section of the monthly *Mpls. St. Paul* magazine has extensive listings of events, as does the free monthly *Twin Cities Directory.* Events calendars are also published in the arts sections of the *St. Paul Pioneer Press and Dispatch* and the Minneapolis-based *Star Tribune,* and in the free newsweeklies *City Pages* and the *Twin Cities Reader.* **Ticketmaster** (☎ 612/989–5151) sells tickets for sporting events, concerts, theater, attractions, and special events.

MINNEAPOLIS

The West Bank theater district has the highest concentration of theaters in Minneapolis, including the **University of Minnesota Theater** (330 21st Ave. S, ☎ 612/625–4001). The award-winning **Guthrie Theater** (725 Vineland Pl., ☎ 612/377–2224 or 800/328–0542) has a repertory company known for its balance of classics and avant-garde productions. The acclaimed **Minnesota Orchestra** performs in Orchestra Hall (1111 Nicollet Mall, ☎ 612/371–5656).

ST. PAUL

The **Great American History Theater** (30 E. 10th St., ☎ 612/292–4323) presents plays about Minnesota and midwestern history. The **Penumbra Theater Company** (270 Kent St., ☎ 612/224–3180) is Minnesota's only black professional theater company. The **Ordway Music Theater** (345 Washington St., ☎ 612/224–4222) is home to the **St. Paul Chamber Orchestra** and the **Minnesota Opera.**

Nightlife

With closings at 1 AM, there's no "in the wee small hours" in the Twin Cities, but there's no lack of good places to visit. Most night spots are trendy and upscale and attract a youngish crowd. The Twin Cities also have night spots that serve a sizable gay and lesbian community.

MINNEAPOLIS

The intimate **Fine Line Music Café** (318 1st Ave. N, ☎ 612/338–8100) showcases locally and nationally known jazz and rock musicians. In a former bus station, **First Avenue** (29. N. 7th St., ☎ 612/332–1775) attracts top rock groups and is a great place for dancing; the club was featured in Prince's movie *Purple Rain.* The best gay bar in downtown Minneapolis is the **Gay Nineties** (408 S. Hennepin Ave., ☎ 612/333–7755).

ST. PAUL

Gallivan's (354 Wabasha St., ☎ 612/227–6688) is a downtown classic with a cozy fireplace and live entertainment. The **Heartthrob Cafe** (World Trade Center, 30 E. 7th St., ☎ 612/224–2783) has a vintage '50s atmosphere and 1990s high-tech lights and music. The **Dakota Bar and Grill** (Bandana Sq., 1021 E. Bandana Blvd., ☎ 612/642–1442) is one of the best jazz bars in the Midwest and features some of the Twin Cities' finest performers. Central St. Paul's popular gay bar is **Rumours** (490 N. Robert St., ☎ 612/224–0703).

ELSEWHERE IN THE STATE

Southeastern Minnesota

Getting There

From the Twin Cities, follow U.S. 61 southeast along the Mississippi River.

What to See and Do

This picturesque corner of the state has high, wooded bluffs that provide vast panoramas of the Mississippi River. The river towns and villages are noted for their charming 19th-century architecture. **Red Wing** is famous for boots and pottery, both of which bear its name. Levee Park, Bay Point Park, and Covill Park offer views of the Mississippi, which widens into Lake Pepin here. The historic **St. James Hotel** (406 Main St., ☎ 612/388–2846) has been restored to its 1875 Victorian elegance and has boutiques, shops, and an art gallery; the public spaces recall the heyday of the riverboats. Contact the **Red Wing Chamber of Commerce** (420 Levee St., Box 133, 55066, ☎ 612/388–4719) for further information.

Ten miles south on U.S. 61, **Frontenac State Park** (☎ 612/345–3401) has a fur-trading post, scenic overlooks, and Native American burial grounds.

Winona is an early lumbering town settled by New Englanders and Germans. Here **Garvin Heights Scenic Lookout** (Huff St., past U.S. 14 and U.S. 61) offers picnic facilities, hiking trails, and scenic views from atop a 575-foot bluff. The **Julius C. Wilkie Steamboat Center** (foot of Main St. in Levee Park, ☎ 507/454–1254), a replica of a steamboat, contains a museum with exhibits on steamboating and river life. Exhibits of the local Polish heritage found at the **Polish Cultural Institute** (102 N. Liberty St., ☎ 507/454–3431) include family heirlooms and many religious artifacts. For more information contact the **Winona Chamber and Convention Bureau** (67 Main St., Box 870, 55987, ☎ 507/452–2272 or 800/657–4972).

Away from the river, west of Winona on U.S. 14, is **Rochester,** home to the famous **Mayo Clinic** (☎ 507/284–2450), which offers tours of its facilities. **Mayowood,** the former residence of Dr. Charles H. Mayo, one of the brothers who founded the clinic, has 55 rooms furnished with French, Spanish, English, and American antiques; tickets for tours are purchased at the **Olmsted County History Center** (1195 County Rd. 22 SW, ☎ 507/282–9447). The **Rochester Art Center** (320 E. Center St., ☎ 507/282–8629) features exhibitions of major works by regional and national artists. The **Rochester Convention and Visitors Bureau** (150 S. Broadway, Suite A, 55904, ☎ 507/288–4331 or 800/634–8277) provides information on city attractions.

Duluth

Getting There

From the Twin Cities, head north on I–35.

What to See and Do

Set at the edge of the north-woods wilderness and the western end of Lake Superior is **Duluth,** a city of gracious old homes and one of the largest ports on the Great Lakes. **Skyline Parkway,** a 16-mi scenic boulevard above the city, offers views of Lake Superior and the harbor. Narrated boat tours of Duluth-Superior Harbor, which has 50 mi of dock line, are offered by **Vista Fleet Excursions** (5th Ave. W and the waterfront, ☎ 218/722–6218). The **Aerial Lift Bridge** (Canal Dr.), an unusual elevator bridge 386 feet long, spans the canal entrance to the harbor. Nearby, the **Depot** (506 W. Michigan St., ☎ 218/727–8025), an 1892 landmark train station, houses the **Lake Superior Museum of Transportation,** with an extensive collection of locomotives and rolling stock. **Lake Superior Zoological Gardens** (72nd Ave. W and Grand Ave., ☎ 218/723–3747) has a children's zoo and animals from all over the world. The **Duluth Convention and Visitors Bureau** (100 Lake Place Dr., 55802, ☎ 218/722–4011 or 800/438–5884) provides information on the city.

The Iron Range and Boundary Waters

Getting There

From Duluth, take U.S. 53N.

What to See and Do

The discovery of iron ore in the north woods brought an influx of immigrants, who wove a rich and varied cultural heritage. Known as "The Range" because it encompasses the huge Mesabi and Vermilion iron ranges, the region is ringed by deep forests and many lakes.

Eveleth, which produces taconite, a form of processed iron ore, is home to the **United States Hockey Hall of Fame** (801 Hat Trick Ave., ☎ 218/744–5167), where pictures, films, and artifacts tell the story of hockey in America. In **Virginia,** 2 mi north, rimmed with open-pit mines and reserves of iron ore, the **Mine View in the Sky observation platform,** at the south edge of town, overlooks part of the vast **Rochleau Mine** works. The **Virginia Historical Society Heritage Museum** (800 Olcott Park, 9th Ave. N, ☎ 218/741–1136) has exhibits on iron mining and other local history.

West of Virginia on U.S. 169 is **Hibbing,** the largest town in the Mesabi Range and the place where the Greyhound bus system began. The **Greyhound Origin Center** (Hibbing Memorial Center Bldg., 5th Ave. and 23rd St.) has displays and artifacts on the history of the company. Programs on astronomy and space exploration are offered at the **Paulucci Space Theater** (U.S. 169 and 23rd St., ☎ 218/262–6720). Tours of the **Hull-Rust Mahoning Mine,** the world's largest open-pit iron-ore mine, may be arranged during the summer at the **Hibbing Area Chamber of Commerce** (211 E. Howard St., Box 727, 55746, ☎ 218/262–3895).

Ely, east of Virginia on U.S. 169, lies in the heart of the Superior National Forest. It is the gateway to the western portion of the **Boundary Waters Canoe Area,** a federally protected area of more than 1,000 pristine lakes surrounded by dense forests. Area outfitters rent canoes and camping equipment and provide assistance in planning canoe trips. The **Vermilion Interpretive Center** (1900 E. Camp St., ☎ 218/365–3226; closed in winter) has exhibits on the Vermilion iron range, the fur trade, and Native Americans.

International Falls, at the northern terminus of U.S. 53, on the Canadian border, is known as the "icebox of the nation" because of its severe winters. The town lies at the western edge of **Voyageurs National Park** (*see* National and State Parks, *above*), where the **Rainy Lake Visitor Center** (11 mi east of International Falls on Rte. 11, ☎ 218/286–5258) offers a slide show, exhibits, maps, and information, as well as guided boat tours of the lake and other points in the park. In town is the **Koochiching County Historical Museum** (214 6th Ave., ☎ 218/283–4316), with exhibits on early settlement, gold mining, and Native Americans. The **International Falls Chamber of Commerce** (Box 169, 200 4th St., 56649, ☎ 218/283–9400 or 800/325–5766) offers brochures and information.

OHIO

Updated By
Jeff Hagan

Capital	Columbus
Population	10,847,115
Motto	With God, All Things Are Possible
State Bird	Cardinal
State Flower	Scarlet carnation

Visitor Information

Ohio Division of Travel and Tourism (Box 1001, Columbus 43266, ☎ 800/282–5393). **Ohio Historical Society** (1982 Velma Ave., Columbus 43211, ☎ 614/297–2300).

Scenic Drives

The **Lake Erie Circle Tour** consists of nearly 200 mi of state routes and U.S. highways along the Lake Erie shoreline from Toledo to Conneaut (*see* Northwest Ohio and the Lake Erie Islands, *below*). **Rte. 7,** which runs parallel to the Ohio River along the state's southeastern border, cuts through the French-settled village of Gallipolis; the site of Ohio's only significant Civil War battle, near Pomeroy; and Marietta, the historic first city of the Northwest Territory.

National and State Parks

National Parks

National monuments include the **Hopewell Culture National Historic Park** (*see* Columbus, *below*) and **Perry's Victory and International Peace Memorial** in Put-in-Bay (*see* Northwest Ohio and the Lake Erie Islands, *below*). The **William Howard Taft birthplace** (2038 Auburn Ave., Cincinnati, ☎ 513/684–3262) is a national historic site.

The **Cuyahoga Valley National Recreation Area** (15610 Vaughn Rd., Brecksville 44141, ☎ 216/526–5256) occupies 22 mi of forested valley between Cleveland and Akron, along the Cuyahoga River.

State Parks

Of the 72 state parks, 8 feature Ohio State Park Resorts (☎ 800/282–7275), which offer 16 locations for cabin rentals, swimming, boating, golf, and tennis, as well as lodging, dining, and meeting facilities. For more information, contact the **Ohio Department of Natural Resources** (Division of Parks and Recreation, Fountain Sq., Bldg. C–1, Columbus 43224, ☎ 614/265–7000).

COLUMBUS

Ohio's largest city and the state capital, Columbus is known for its entrepreneurial spirit and economic vitality. The state's largest university, Ohio State, is here, as are the headquarters of a number of Fortune 500 companies, many of whose executives claim they would not leave the city—even if they were promoted.

Tourist Information

Columbus: Visitors Center (10 W. Broad St., 43215, ☎ 614/221–6623).

Arriving and Departing

By Plane

Port Columbus International Airport, 10 mi east of downtown Columbus, is served by major airlines and by **Christman** (☎ 412/225–4000), **ComAir** (☎ 800/354–9822), **Midwest Express,** and **Skyway** (☎ 614/238–7750). A cab from the airport to downtown costs about $16; the airport shuttle costs $6.50. The least expensive ($1), but most time-consuming, way to reach downtown is on a **Central Ohio Transit Authority** bus (*see* Getting Around Columbus, *below*).

By Car

Columbus is in the center of the state, at the intersection of I–70 and I–71.

By Bus

Greyhound Lines (E. Town St. at the corner of 3rd St., ☎ 800/231–2222) serves Columbus.

Getting Around Columbus

Downtown is fairly compact and easily walkable. Some government buildings are connected to each other and to nearby buildings through underground walkways. The **Central Ohio Transit Authority** (☎ 614/228–1776), or COTA, operates buses within Columbus.

Exploring Columbus

The domeless Greek-Revival **state capitol** (corner of High and Broad Sts., ☎ 614/752–9777) building marks the heart of downtown. The building and its annex are undergoing an ambitious restoration project (scheduled to be completed by summer 1996) that includes a few wonderful modern touches, like a sunny, airy atrium connecting the two buildings. Light courts and skylights, some with stained-glass, will be reintroduced, and the number of offices will be reduced in order to approximate the building's original spaciousness. Across High Street is the **Vern Riffe Center for Government and the Arts** (77 S. High St., ☎ 614/466–2613), which contains a lively gallery of works by Ohio artists on its ground floor. "Interactive" doesn't begin to describe the fun displays at **COSI** (*see* What to See and Do with Children, *below*), also downtown.

North of downtown on High Street lies the **Short North** (☎ 614/421–1030), a strip of trendy shops, clubs, vintage clothing stores, restaurants, and art galleries that holds a Gallery Hop the first Saturday of every month. Further north on High Street, at the Ohio State University campus, is the must-see **Wexner Center for the Arts** (N. High St. at 15th Ave., ☎ 614/292–0330 or 614/292–3535), a gallery of contemporary art housed in a dramatic building designed by Peter Eisenmann.

Just south of downtown is **German Village** (☎ 614/221–8888), a neighborhood of tightly packed brick homes built by immigrants in the 19th century. Nearby is the **Brewery District** (☎ 614/621–2222), where warehouses are being turned into restaurants and shops.

South of Columbus, in Chillicothe, is the **Hopewell National Historical Park** (North of Rte. 23 on Rte. 104, ☎ 614/774–1125; admission charged Mar.–Nov.). Here, burial and ceremonial earth mounds rise from the ground in mysterious formations, the handiwork of Native Americans, mostly the Hopewell people.

What to See and Do with Children

COSI (pronounced "co-sigh"), the **Center of Science and Industry** (280 E. Broad St., Columbus, ☎ 614/228–2674), has colorful hands-on exhibits and traveling shows that kids and adults love (*see* Exploring Columbus, *above*). Four generations of gorillas live at the **Columbus Zoo** (9990 Riverside Dr., ☎ 614/645–3550), about 18 mi northwest of downtown off I–270.

Shopping

Columbus is world headquarters for Leslie Wexner's empire of clothing stores, which include **The Limited, Express, Structure, Henri Bendel, Victoria's Secret,** and **Abercrombie & Fitch,** all of which are represented downtown in **Columbus City Center** (111 S. 3rd St., ☎ 614/221–4900). You can't miss **Lazarus** (S. High and W. Town Sts., ☎ 614/463–2121), the granddaddy of Columbus department stores; its old-fashioned water tower sticks up out of the skyline like a Tootsie Roll Pop. **Ohio Factory Shops** (8000 Factory Shops Blvd., Jeffersonville 43128, ☎ 614/948–9090 or 800/746–7644), 45 minutes south of Columbus, features 75 outlets. The **Wexner Center for the Arts** (*see* Exploring, *above*) has a neat gift shop with intriguing items, some hand crafted.

Dining

Restaurants in Columbus range from yuppie chic to down home. Fine restaurants can be found in the Short North, tucked away in German Village, and in suburban neighborhoods. For price ranges, see Chart 1 (B) in On the Road with Fodor's.

$$$ **Carolyn's.** The menu changes daily at this popular restaurant in a renovated German Village house. The chef, Carolyn, experiments with regional American cuisine. *489 City Park Ave., ☎ 614/221–8100. AE, D, MC, V. Closed Sun.–Mon.*

$$ **Rigsby's Cuisine Volatile.** The new American menu devised by Kent Rigsby, who studied in San Francisco, is inventive, and the bread sticks are about a yard long. *698 N. High St., ☎ 614/461–7888. AE, D, DC, MC, V.*

$$ **Spagio.** The name is a combination of two words: "spa," for the healthy fare available here, and "gio," for geography, because its far-reaching menu evokes the flavors of the world. Those in the know are buzzing about this copper, glass, and oak-clad spot in up-and-coming Grandview. *1295 Grandview Ave., ☎ 614/486–1114. No reservations. AE, MC, V. Closed Sun.*

$ **Katzinger's Deli.** An enormous menu and a serve-yourself pickle barrel make this New York–style deli in German Village a favorite. *475 S. 3rd St., ☎ 614/228–3354. MC, V.*

$ **Schmidt's Sausage Haus.** Homemade sausage hangs from the ceiling in this old-fashioned place, redolent of the butcher shop. *240 E. Kossuth St., ☎ 614/444–6808. AE, D, DC, MC, V.*

Lodging

Downtown Columbus and nearby German Village offer a wide range of accommodations, from elegant to merely efficient. For price ranges, see Chart 2 (B) in On the Road with Fodor's.

$$$ ★ **Great Southern Hotel.** Renovated in 1995, this venerable 1897 hotel has retained much of its Victorian charm, from the rich marble-and-wood lobby to the tastefully appointed rooms. *310 S. High St., 43215, ☎ 614/228–3800 or 800/328–2073; in OH, 800/228–3789; FAX 614/228–7666. 196 rooms, 37 suites. Facilities: restaurant, lounge, parking. AE, D, DC, MC, V.*

$$$ **Hyatt Regency.** Adjacent to the convention center, this ultramodern high-rise hotel caters mainly to businesspeople. (The Hyatt on Capitol Square is more for the political crowd.) *350 N. High St., 43215, ☎ 614/463–1234, FAX 614/463–9161. 631 rooms, 21 suites. Facilities: 2 restaurants, lounge, pool, parking. AE, D, DC, MC, V.*

$$ **Courtyard by Marriott.** Refurbished in 1994, this contemporary hotel is comfortable and convenient to everything. *35 W. Spring St., 43215, ☎ 614/228–3200, FAX 614/228–3200. 149 rooms. Facilities: restaurant, lounge, access to pool and gym at YMCA next door for nominal fee, parking. AE, D, DC, MC, V.*

$ **Village Inn.** Friendly service and low rates are the draws to this no-frills German Village hotel, close to downtown. *920 S. High St., 43206, ☎ 614/443–6506, FAX 614/443–5663. 44 rooms. AE, D, DC, MC, V.*

The Arts and Nightlife

Three free weekly newspapers—the *Columbus Guardian*, the *Other Paper*, and *Columbus Alive!*—have complete listings of goings-on in the city.

The Arts

The **Columbus Symphony Orchestra** (☎ 614/224–3291) and the **BalletMet** (☎ 614/229–4860) perform at the **Ohio Theater** (55 E. State St., ☎ 614/469–1045; for tickets, 614/469–0939). **Opera/Columbus** and touring Broadway shows are at the **Palace Theatre** (34 W. Broad St., ☎ 614/469–1331; for tickets, 614/469–9850).

Nightlife

Columbus's hot spots are near the Ohio State University Campus (expect crowds on nights the OSU Buckeyes football team plays) and in the Short North. Live music is available on weekends at the **Short North Tavern** (674 N. High St., ☎ 614/221–2432) and **Union Station Cafe** (630 N. High St., ☎ 614/228–3740). **Stache's** (2404 N. High St., ☎ 614/263–5318), north of campus, showcases breakthrough rock artists, some blues acts of yesterday, and timeless eclectic music.

CINCINNATI

Cincinnati is a highly cultured, well-regulated city with a proud history, an active riverfront, and a bustling downtown. The one thing residents complain about is the weather: Because the city is in a basin along the Ohio River, summers are hot and humid.

Tourist Information

Cincinnati: Visitors Bureau (300 W. 6th St., at Plum St., 45202, ☎ 513/621–2142 or 800/246–2987).

Arriving and Departing

By Plane

Cincinnati/Northern Kentucky International Airport is 12 mi south of downtown, off I–275, in Kentucky. It is served by major airlines and by **ComAir** (☎ 800/354–9822). **Jetport Express** (☎ 606/767–3702) makes regular trips from the airport to downtown hotels ($10 one-way, $15 round-trip). Taxis downtown cost about $20.

By Car

I–71, I–75, and I–74 all converge on downtown Cincinnati.

By Train

Amtrak serves **Union Terminal** (1301 Western Ave., ☎ 800/872–7245).

By Bus

Greyhound Lines (Court St. and 1005 Gilbert Ave., ☎ 800/231–2222).

Getting Around

Downtown Cincinnati is eminently walkable. Skywalks connect hotels, convention centers, stores, and garages above street level. **Queen City Metro** (☎ 513/621–4455) runs buses out of Government Square (5th St. between Walnut and Main Sts.); there is also a downtown loop bus (No. 79) and a free shuttle that cruises 4th and 5th streets.

Exploring Cincinnati

Fountain Square (5th and Vine Sts.) is the center of downtown Cincinnati. The city is laid out along the river, with numbered streets running east–west (2nd Street is Pete Rose Way); north–south streets have names. Vine Street divides the city into east and west.

If you have only an hour in Cincinnati, spend it at **Carew Tower** (5th and Race Sts.) looking at the gorgeous Rookwood pottery in the Arcade and at the Art Deco interior of the **Omni Netherland Plaza Hotel.** Its marble, rosewood, mirrors, and murals are so richly detailed that the hotel provides an architectural walking tour.

You can cross the Ohio River into Kentucky on the **Roebling Suspension Bridge,** built by John A. Roebling, who later built the Brooklyn Bridge. **Covington Landing,** a floating entertainment complex in the form of a side-wheeler and a wharf, is west of the bridge. Beyond the wharf is **BB Riverboats** (☎ 606/261–8500), running river tours year-round. **Covington** itself, east of the bridge, is a neighborhood of fine antebellum mansions, with wonderful views from Riverside Drive.

Back on the Ohio side, the narrow streets and funky houses of **Mt. Adams,** the first hill east of downtown, are reminiscent of San Francisco. The yard of the **Immaculata Church** (Pavillion and Guido Sts.) provides a sterling view of the city.

Eden Park, on the other side of Mt. Adams, is the site of the **Cincinnati Art Museum** (☎ 513/721–5204), which has an outstanding collection of Near Eastern and ancient art, and the **Krohn Conservatory** (☎ 513/421–4086), a greenhouse and garden center with more than 5,000 species of plants. Other bastions of culture are the **Contemporary Arts Center** (115 E. 5th St., ☎ 513/345–8400 or 513/721–0390) and the **Taft Museum** (316 Pike St., ☎ 513/241–0343), famous for its Chinese porcelains.

You could spend a full day in the magnificently restored **Museum Center at Union Terminal,** which looks like a huge art-deco cabinet radio. This historical former train station houses the Museum of Natural History (*see* What to See and Do with Children, *below*), the Cincinnati Historical Society, and the **Robert D. Lindner Family OmniMax Theater** (TicketMaster, ☎ 513/749–4949). *1301 Western Ave. (off I–75 at Ezzard Charles Dr.), ☎ 513/287–7000 or 800/733–2077. Admission charged.*

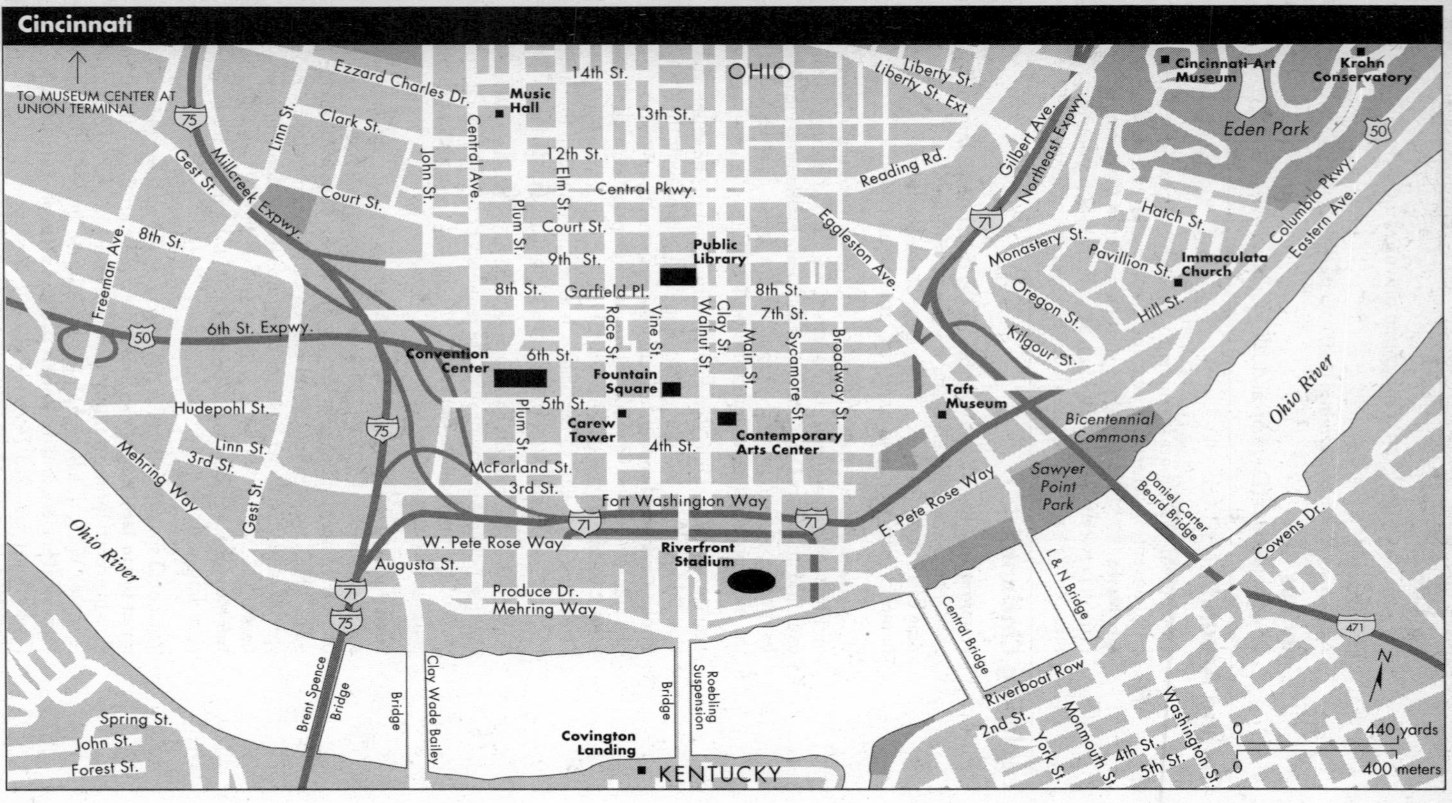
Cincinnati
TO MUSEUM CENTER AT UNION TERMINAL
OHIO
KENTUCKY
Ohio River
Ohio River
Music Hall
Cincinnati Art Museum
Krohn Conservatory
Eden Park
Immaculata Church
Public Library
Convention Center
Fountain Square
Carew Tower
Contemporary Arts Center
Taft Museum
Bicentennial Commons
Sawyer Point Park
Riverfront Stadium
Covington Landing
Daniel Carter Beard Bridge
L & N Bridge
Central Bridge
Roebling Suspension Bridge
Clay Wade Bailey Bridge
Brent Spence Bridge
Ezzard Charles Dr.
14th St.
13th St.
12th St.
Central Pkwy.
Court St.
9th St.
8th St.
Garfield Pl.
Liberty St.
Liberty St. Ext.
Reading Rd.
Gilbert Ave.
Northeast Expwy.
Columbia Pkwy.
Eastern Ave.
Hatch St.
Monastery St.
Pavillion St.
Oregon St.
Hill St.
Kilgour St.
Eggleston Ave.
8th St.
7th St.
Linn St.
Clark St.
John St.
Central Ave.
Plum St.
Elm St.
Court St.
Gest St.
Millcreek Expwy.
Freeman Ave.
8th St.
6th St. Expwy.
6th St.
Race St.
Vine St.
Walnut St.
Clay St.
Main St.
Sycamore St.
Broadway St.
5th St.
Plum St.
4th St.
Hudepohl St.
Linn St.
3rd St.
Mehring Way
Gest St.
McFarland St.
3rd St.
Fort Washington Way
E. Pete Rose Way
W. Pete Rose Way
Augusta St.
Produce Dr.
Mehring Way
Cowens Dr.
Riverboat Row
2nd St.
York St.
Monmouth St.
4th St.
5th St.
Washington St.
Spring St.
John St.
Forest St.
0 440 yards
0 400 meters
N
75
50
71
471

Parks and Gardens

Bicentennial Commons, an outdoor recreation center at Sawyer Point, on the Ohio River, uses monuments to tell the story of Cincinnati's origins as a river town. Look for the famous flying pigs, a reminder of the city's prominence as a meat-packing center.

What to See and Do with Children

The **Museum of Natural History** in the Museum Center at Union Terminal (*see* Exploring Cincinnati, *above*) has a Children's Discovery Center, a cave with real bats (behind glass), and an Ice Age diorama that lets you go behind the glass. The **Cincinnati Zoo and Botanical Center** (3400 Vine St., ☎ 513/281–4700 or 800/447–7694), famous for its white Bengal tigers, is the second-oldest zoo in the country. Follow the paw-print signs off I–75 Exit 6 or I–71 Exit 7.

Paramount's **Kings Island Theme Park,** 24 mi north of Cincinnati in Kings Mills (I–71 Exit 25A), has seven theme areas, including a water park, the longest wooden roller coaster in the world, and a wild-animal habitat. *☎ 513/398–5600 or 800/288–0808. Admission: $26.95 adults, $15.95 children 3–6 and visitors over 59. Closed Labor Day–mid-Apr. and weekdays mid-Apr.–Memorial Day.*

Shopping

Shops in the **Tower Place** (4th and Race Sts.) atrium shopping mall include the city's best-loved quality women's clothing stores, **Gidding-Jenny** and **Henry Harris.** Skywalks connect Tower Place with **McAlpin's** and **Saks Fifth Avenue** (via Carew Tower).

Spectator Sports

Baseball

Cincinnati Reds (100 Riverfront Stadium, ☎ 513/421–4510; Apr.–Oct.).

Football

Cincinnati Bengals (200 Riverfront Stadium, ☎ 513/621–3550; Aug.–Dec.).

Dining

Famous for its chili, Cincinnati has more good restaurants than the most ravenous traveler could sample in any one visit, including high-rise revolving restaurants, riverboat restaurants, and rathskellers. For price ranges, see Chart 1 (B) in On the Road with Fodor's.

$$$ ★ **The Celestial.** Request a table with a view at this classic spot on top of Mt. Adams, serving French and American cuisine. *1071 Celestial St., ☎ 513/241–4455. Jacket and tie required at dinner. AE, DC, MC, V. Closed Sun.*

$$$ **The Maisonette.** Since 1964 this has been ranked among the foremost restaurants in the United States. The food is fresh and French, the atmosphere plush and formal. *114 E. 6th St., ☎ 513/721–2260. Reservations required. Jacket required, tie advised; no jeans. AE, D, DC, MC, V. Closed Sun.*

$$ ★ **Golden Lamb.** The oldest inn in Ohio has enough Shaker furniture to qualify it as a museum. It's 33 mi north of Cincinnati, off I–71 or I–75. *27 S. Broadway, Lebanon, ☎ 513/621–8373. Reservations advised. AE, D, DC, MC, V.*

$$ **Lenhardt's.** This informal restaurant features schnitzel, Viennese and Hungarian goulash, sauerbraten, and potato pancakes. *151 W. McMillan St., ☎ 513/281–3600. AE, D, MC, V. Closed Sun., Mon., July 4, 1st 2 wks in Aug., 2 wks at Christmas.*

$$ **Montgomery Inn at the Boathouse.** The barbecued ribs are famous, and you can't get any closer to the river without swimming in it. *925 Eastern Ave., ☎ 513/721–7427. AE, D, DC, MC, V. Closed major holidays. No lunch weekends.*

$ **Rookwood Ice Cream Parlor.** Once the Tea Room at Union Terminal, this delightful green spot is decorated with vintage Rookwood pottery and serves local ice cream. *Museum Center at Union Terminal, ☎ 513/721–4985. No credit cards. Closed holidays.*

$ **Rookwood Pottery.** Families consume giant hamburgers and other American fare in wood-and-brick dining rooms that contain what were once the kilns of the famous Mt. Adams pottery. *1077 Celestial St., ☎ 513/721–5456. AE, DC, MC, V. Closed major holidays.*

Lodging

Downtown Cincinnati has several choice hotels. Many offer weekend packages including Reds or Bengals games. Staying in the suburbs is less expensive and forces you to learn your way around at least one neighborhood. For price ranges, see Chart 2 (B) in On the Road with Fodor's.

$$$ ★ **Cincinnatian Hotel.** Stars are drawn to this sedate French Second Empire–style hotel with an unusual contemporary interior. The chef at the Palace has taken the town by storm with his delectable new American cuisine. *601 Vine St., 45202, ☎ 513/381–3000 or 800/942–9000; in OH, 800/332–2020; FAX 513/651–0256. 147 rooms, 6 suites. Facilities: 2 restaurants (☎ 513/381–6006; reservations strongly advised), lounge, health club, concierge, parking. AE, D, DC, MC, V.*

$$$ ★ **Omni Netherland Plaza.** Downtown's grand Art Deco hotel is in the Carew Tower (*see* Exploring Cincinnati, *above*). Reservations are recommended for dinner at Orchids, which serves American cuisine in the exquisite Palm Court. *35 W. 5th St., 45202, ☎ 513/421–9100, FAX 513/421–4291. 621 rooms, 12 suites. Facilities: 2 restaurants, lounge, health club, pool, concierge, parking. AE, D, DC, MC, V.*

$$ **Amos Shinkle Town House B&B.** The master bedroom in this antebellum mansion, once home to the man who hired John A. Roebling to build a suspension bridge across the Ohio River, has a whirlpool bath and a chandelier in the bathroom. *215 Garrard St., Covington, KY 41011, ☎ 606/431–2118. 7 rooms with bath. Facility: parking. AE, D, DC, MC, V.*

$$ **Best Western Mariemont Inn.** Staying at this inn 10 mi east of downtown is like staying at Henry VIII's hunting lodge. Everything is in the Tudor style—even the cash machine! *6880 Wooster Pike (U.S. 50), Mariemont 45227, ☎ 513/271–2100, FAX 513/271–1057. 60 rooms. Facilities: restaurant, pub, parking. AE, D, DC, MC, V.*

$ **Caesar Creek American Youth Hostel.** Rent a sleeping bag and crash in the men's or women's dormitory, on the grounds of a state park 45 mi northeast of Cincinnati. *8823 Center Rd., Wilmington 45177, ☎ 513/521–2222. 16 beds. No credit cards.*

The Arts and Nightlife

The Arts

The **Music Hall** (1241 Elm St., ☎ 513/721–8222) is home to the **Cincinnati Symphony Orchestra** and the **Cincinnati Pops Orchestra** (☎ 513/

381–3300; performances Sept.–May at Music Hall, June–July at Riverbend), the **Cincinnati Opera** (☎ 513/241–2742; June–July), and the **Cincinnati Ballet** (☎ 513/621–5219; Oct.–May).

Nightlife

At Covington Landing, **Howl at the Moon Saloon** (foot of Madison, Covington KY, 41011, ☎ 606/491–7733) features dueling piano players and sing-alongs. In Mt. Adams, **Longworth's** (1108 St. Gregory St., ☎ 513/579–0900) has a DJ and a garden, and the **Incline** (1071 Celestial St., ☎ 513/241–4455), a sophisticated bar at the Celestial restaurant, has vocalists.

NORTHWEST OHIO AND THE LAKE ERIE ISLANDS

Between Toledo and Cleveland lies a stretch of the Lake Erie shore and a group of islands that constitute the Riviera and Madeira of Ohio. Families rent cottages at Catawba Point or Put-in-Bay (the port village of South Bass Island) and swim, fish, and boat, topping the week off with a trip to Cedar Point Amusement Park in Sandusky.

Tourist Information

Erie County: Visitors and Convention Bureau (231 W. Washington Row, Sandusky 44870, ☎ 419/625–2984 or 800/255–3743; covers Cedar Point, Kelleys Island, and Sandusky). **Ottawa County:** Visitors Bureau (109 Madison St., Port Clinton 43452, ☎ 419/734–4386 or 800/441–1271; covers Catawba, Lakeside, Marblehead, Port Clinton, and Put-in-Bay). **Greater Toledo:** Convention and Visitors Bureau (SeaGate Convention Center, 401 Jefferson Ave., 2nd Floor, 43604, ☎ 419/321–6404 or 800/243–4667). **Kelleys Island:** Chamber of Commerce (Box 783F, 43438, ☎ 419/746–2360). **Put-in-Bay:** Chamber of Commerce (Box 250–BN, 43456, ☎ 419/285–2832).

Getting There

By Plane

Toledo Express Airport, west on Rte. 2, is served by six airlines. For **Cleveland Hopkins Airport,** *see* Cleveland, *below.* **Griffing Island Airlines** (☎ 419/734–3149), out of **Port Clinton Airport** (3255 E. State Rd.), and **Griffing Flying Service** (☎ 419/626–5161), out of **Griffing–Sandusky Airport** (3115 Cleveland Rd., east of Sandusky), fly to the Lake Erie islands.

By Car

The Ohio Turnpike (I–80/90) runs 5 to 10 mi below the Lake Erie shoreline. For Toledo take Exit 4 (I–75) or Exit 5 (U.S. 280); for Port Clinton, Exit 6 (Rte. 53); for Sandusky, Exit 7 (U.S. 250). Toledo is on I–75. Rte. 2 hugs the lake between Toledo and Sandusky; Rte. 269 loops out to Marblehead.

By Train

Amtrak (☎ 800/872–7245) stops in Toledo and Sandusky.

By Bus

Greyhound Lines has national service from Toledo (811 Jefferson Ave., ☎ 800/231–2222). **Toledo Area Regional Transit Authority** (TARTA, ☎ 419/243–7433) covers Toledo and its suburbs.

By Boat

Ferries serve the Lake Erie islands from May through October. **Put-in-Bay Boat Line** (☎ 800/245–1538), from Port Clinton to Put-in-Bay, takes passengers and bicycles only and offers late-night service. **Miller Boat Line** (☎ 419/285–2421), starting in March, from Catawba to Lime Kiln Dock (on the opposite side of South Bass Island from Put-in-Bay) and to Middle Bass Island, takes passengers and cars (reservations required), as does **Neumann Boat Line** (☎ 419/798–5800), from Marblehead to Kelleys Island.

Exploring Northwest Ohio and the Lake Erie Islands

Though not a tourist town, **Toledo** has its attractions. Baseball fans won't want to miss the **Ohio Baseball Hall of Fame** (2901 Key St., off U.S. 24, Maumee, ☎ 419/893–9481), next to Ned Skeldon Stadium, where the Mud Hens play, in the Lucas County Recreation Center. The **Toledo Museum of Art** (2445 Monroe St. at Scottwood Ave., off I–75, ☎ 419/255–8000) offers a fine small collection of European and American paintings, ancient Greek and Egyptian statues, and an important collection of glass.

Vacationland begins at **Port Clinton,** which lies at the northern base of the Marblehead Peninsula, some 30 mi east of Toledo on Rte. 2. A center for fishing excursions (*see* Sports and the Outdoors, *below*), the town is also the base for a ferry to South Bass Island's **Put-in-Bay** (*see* Getting There, *above*), a port village consisting of a marina, a grassy lakefront park dotted with small cannons, and a strip of shops, bars, and restaurants featuring a vintage wooden merry-go-round. Today a wild-party town, Put-in-Bay was the site of Commodore Oliver Hazard Perry's naval victory over the British in the War of 1812. From the top of **Perry's Victory and International Peace Memorial,** a single massive Doric column east of downtown, you can see all the way to Canada. A popular day excursion is to take a ferry over to **Middle Bass Island** and sample the wares of the **Lonz Winery** (☎ 419/285–5411; May–Sept.), which looks like a European monastery.

Back on the mainland, at the eastern tip of the peninsula is **Marblehead,** site of the oldest continuously working lighthouse on Lake Erie. From here it's a short ferry ride to **Kelleys Island,** which has two remarkable geologic features: on the north shore, glacial grooves (waves in the rock) left by the Ice Age; on the south shore, prehistoric Native American pictographs.

Sandusky, a small port city with lush gardens enlivening the town square, makes a good touring base. It's near the highways and ferries and offers thousands of motel rooms as well as a few romantic Victorian hideaways.

What to See and Do with Children

Cedar Point Amusement Park is in the *Guinness Book of World Records* as having the most roller coasters in the world (11, and counting), among them the fastest and the highest wooden one. It also has Snake River Falls, the tallest, deepest, and fastest water ride in the world; a water park; and a mile-long sandy beach. *Off U.S. 250N, Sandusky,* ☎ *419/627–2350. Admission: $26.95 adults, $4.95 children under 48", children under 5 free. Closed Oct.–May, weekdays in Sept.*

Sports and the Outdoors

Beaches and Water Sports

The best Lake Erie beach is at **East Harbor State Park,** off Rte. 163, on the Marblehead Peninsula. **Cedar Point** also offers good swimming (*see* What to See and Do with Children, *above*).

Fishing

The Western Lake Erie Basin is known as the "Walleye Capital of the World." Toledo even has a **Walleye Hot Line** (☏ 419/893–9740; Mar.–May). Smallmouth bass and Lake Erie perch are also plentiful. Nonresident fishing licenses are sold at bait shops, or contact the **Division of Wildlife** (☏ 419/625–8062). There's ice fishing if the lake freezes.

The breakwater in Port Clinton and the pier at Catawba Point are both good fishing spots. Per-head fishing boats leave from Fisherman's Wharf in Port Clinton (☏ 419/734–6388) and from Battery Park Marina in Sandusky (☏ 419/625–5000), among other places.

Dining and Lodging

The chambers of commerce in Put-in-Bay and on Kelleys Island (*see* Tourist Information, *above*) give advice on lodging, which should be arranged well in advance. For price ranges, see Charts 1 (B) and 2 (B) in On the Road with Fodor's.

Catawba Point

DINING

★ **Mon Ami.** This well-established winery and restaurant has a chalet-style dining room with 4-ft-thick stone walls and a patio surrounded by wooden casks. Pasta and fresh fish are the specialties. *3845 E. Wine Cellar Rd., off N.E. Catawba Rd. (Rte. 53), ☏ 419/797–4445 or 800/777–4266. AE, MC, V. $$*

Grand Rapids

LODGING

Mill House. This country-Victorian house on the Maumee River 40 minutes from downtown Toledo was built in 1900 as a working gristmill. Today it features three Victorian-style rooms, where guests enjoy a sumptuous three-course breakfast and some great views of the gardens out back. *24070 Front St., 43522, ☏ 419/832–6455. No credit cards. $$*

Marblehead

LODGING

Old Stone House. The owners of this Federal-style mansion right on the lake keep curtains to a minimum so that nothing obscures the view. *133 Clemons St., 43440, ☏ 419/798–5922. 13 rooms share baths, 1 suite. Facility: parking. D, MC, V. $$*

Port Clinton

DINING

Garden at the Lighthouse. Up a garden path is a Victorian house, originally built for the lighthouse keeper. Fresh fish, veal, and chicken dishes are served by candlelight. *226 E. Perry St., ☏ 419/732–2151. AE, D, DC, MC, V. Closed Sun. and holidays Sept.–May. $$*

DINING AND LODGING

Island House Hotel. This 100-year-old redbrick hotel with tall windows has a dining room serving fresh fish. *102 Madison St., 43452, ☏ 419/734–2166 or 800/233–7307. 39 rooms. Facilities: restaurant, 2 lounges, parking. AE, D, DC, MC, V. $$*

LODGING

Beach Cliff Lodge. Families who fish bunk down in this unpretentious place, close to the ferry and the state park, which has freezers and fish-cleaning services. *4189 N.W. Catawba Rd., 43452, ☎ 419/797–4553. 8 rooms, 19 cottages. Facility: parking. No credit cards. $$*

Put-in-Bay

DINING

Crescent Tavern. If you can eat only one meal in Put-in-Bay, this restaurant inside a gracious Victorian house is the place. *Delaware Ave., ☎ 419/285–4211. No reservations. MC, V. $$*

Frosty's. With a bar and a pool table on one side, pizza and Formica tables on the other, this noisy place caters to rowdies and families alike. *Delaware Ave., ☎ 419/285–4741. No credit cards. $*

LODGING

Park Hotel. This white frame hotel, dating from the 1870s, has etched glass and a gracious Victorian lobby, but it's smack in the middle of the island revelry. Bring earplugs. *Box 60, 43456, ☎ 419/285–3581. 26 rooms with shared baths. MC, V. $$ (weekend rates higher).*

Sandusky

LODGING

Hotel Breakers. Built in 1905 to resemble a French château, with a five-story rotunda, stained glass, and vintage wicker furniture, this is *the* place to stay on the beach at Cedar Point, especially if you can get a turret room. *Box 5006, 44871, ☎ 419/627–2106. 400 rooms. Facilities: 4 restaurants, lounge, pool, beach, shuffleboard. D, MC, V. Closed Oct.–Apr. $$$*

Radisson Harbour Inn. This big hotel is successfully disguised as a rambling, weathered beach house. Rooms have matching spreads and draperies in patterned earth tones. *2001 Cleveland Rd. at Cedar Point Causeway, 44870, ☎ 419/627–2500. 237 rooms. Facilities: restaurant, pool, exercise room, fishing, parking. AE, D, DC, MC, V. $$*

Wagner's 1844 Inn. A block from downtown, this house is furnished with canopy beds and globe lamps in rooms and a common pool table, TV, and travel library. Continental breakfast is included in the room rate. *230 E. Washington St., 44870, ☎ 419/626–1726. 3 rooms. D, MC, V. $$*

Toledo

DINING

Tony Packo's Cafe. Before Max Klinger ever mentioned it on *M*A*S*H*, this place was famous for its Tiffany lamps and Hungarian hot dogs. Don't miss the autographed hot-dog buns. *1902 Front St., ☎ 419/691–6054. AE, D, MC, V. $*

LODGING

Holiday Inn Crowne Plaza. This is the only downtown hotel right on the Maumee River. Walkways connect it with office buildings and the convention center. Built in 1984, it was remodeled in 1995. *2 SeaGate/Summit St., 43604, ☎ 419/241–1411, FAX 419/241–8161. 243 rooms, 6 suites. Facilities: restaurant, lounge, concierge, fitness center, parking. AE, D, DC, MC, V. $$*

Motels

The majority of area motels are in and around Sandusky, on the roads to Cedar Point. Prices reflect high-season rates (June–Aug.). **Best Western Resort Inn** (1530 Cleveland Rd., Sandusky 44870, ☎ 419/625–9234), 105 rooms, restaurant, pool; *$$$*. **Comfort Inn** (11020 U.S. 250, Milan 44846, ☎ 419/499–4681 or 800/228–5150), 53 rooms, pool, exercise room; $$. **Howard Johnson's** (1932 Cleveland Rd., Sandusky 44870, ☎ 419/625–1333), 68 rooms, pool; $$.

Campground

Middle Bass Island Camping and Fishing (Apr.–Oct.: Box 69, Middle Bass Island 43446, ☎ 419/285–6121; Nov.–Mar.: 9025 Rte. 14, Streetsboro 44241, ☎ 216/626–5233) has tent and RV sites, hot showers, a beach, bike rentals, boat rentals, and charter-fishing packages.

CLEVELAND

A lot has changed in Cleveland in the 20 years since the fire on the river. The lake and the river have been cleaned up, new buildings have altered the skyline—including the stunning I.M. Pei–designed lakefront building completed in 1995—and the Flats—the industrial area along the Cuyahoga River—is booming with restaurants and nightclubs. The city is buzzing after the opening of two new sports venues: Jacobs Field, a baseball stadium for the Cleveland Indians, and the adjacent Gund Arena, which hosts basketball, hockey, indoor football, concerts, and other events. The Inner Harbor is growing steadily with the Rock and Roll Hall of Fame and Museum, finally under construction and due to open in September 1995.

Tourist Information

Cleveland: Visitor Information Center (lobby of Terminal Tower, downtown on Public Sq., ☎ 216/621–4110 or 800/321–1001).

Arriving and Departing

By Plane

Cleveland Hopkins International Airport, 10 mi southwest of downtown, is served by major airlines and several commuter lines. From here the **Rapid Transit Authority** rail system (☎ 216/621–9500) takes 20 minutes to Public Square and costs $1.50. A taxi takes twice as long and costs about $20.

Private planes land at **Burke Lakefront Airport,** on North Marginal Road, just east of downtown.

By Car

I–90 runs east–west through downtown Cleveland. I–71 and I–77 come up from the south. Driving from the east on the Ohio Turnpike (I–80), take Exit 10 to I–71N.

By Train

Amtrak (200 Memorial Shoreway NE, ☎ 800/872–7245).

By Bus

Greyhound Lines (E. 15th St. and Chester Ave., ☎ 800/231–2222).

Getting Around

The RTA rapid-transit system (☎ 216/621–9500), though not extensive, efficiently bridges east and west, with the Terminal Tower as the hub. RTA buses travel from Public Square on five downtown loop routes.

Exploring Cleveland

Begin your tour at **Terminal Tower,** Cleveland's central landmark, and **Tower City Center,** an office and shopping complex that includes the shops of the Avenue (*see* Shopping, *below*). Pick up a copy of "Walks," a brochure outlining some popular Cleveland walking tours, at the visitor center just inside the entrance to Tower City Center. Cross Public Square and walk east on Superior Avenue to the **Old Arcade** (between Superior and Euclid Aves.). Built in 1890, this is still downtown's most beautiful building. Like a nave without a cathedral, it rises five stories, with brass railings, ironwork, a bridge, and a skylight. It was here in the early '80s that the renaissance of downtown Cleveland began, with a few fast-food outlets and a shop called **Cleveland Reflections** (401 Euclid Ave., ☎ 216/566–1566), which sells souvenirs.

Walk back to Public Square and head south on Ontario Street. Here you'll find the **Gund Arena** (1 Center Court, ☎ 216/420–2000), a venue for sports events and concerts, which has a graceful design featuring sweeping lines. Next to the arena is **Jacobs Field** (2401 Ontario St., ☎ 216/420–4200), a trapezoid-shaped baseball park that looks brand-new and old-fashioned at the same time.

To see the lake, take East 9th Street to **North Coast Harbor,** formerly the East 9th Street Pier. Here you'll find the **Rock and Roll Hall of Fame and Museum** (Key Plaza, ☎ 216/781–7625; admission charged), a 150,000-sq-ft building that dramatically rises from the harbor into a glass pyramid with curving, swooping walls. Inside are a dizzying array of exhibits, including the costume John Lennon wore on the cover of the Beatles' *Sgt. Pepper's* album, a stage set from a Rolling Stones' concert, and films covering different aspects of rock music. The harbor is also the future home of the **Great Lakes Science Center** (601 Erieside Ave., ☎ 216/736–7900; admission charged), due to open in 1996, which will have a 320-seat OmniMax theater. The ***Goodtime III*** (☎ 216/861–5110; June–Sept.) gives sightseeing tours on the Cuyahoga River. At sunset, both the lake and the skyline glow.

University Circle, reached by rapid transit or a 15-minute drive from downtown, has more than 50 cultural institutions, of which the **Cleveland Museum of Art** is the centerpiece. A white marble temple set among spring-flowering trees and reflected in a lagoon, it is world-renowned for its medieval European collection, Egyptian art, and European and American paintings. *☎ 216/421–7340. Admission charged for special exhibitions. Closed Mon.*

The **Western Reserve Historical Society** has an extensive Napoleonic collection and, in the Crawford Auto-Aviation Museum, just about every old car you might want to see. *10825 East Boulevard, ☎ 216/721–5722. Admission charged. Closed Mon.*

Severance Hall (*see* The Arts and Nightlife, *below*) has the city's most beautiful Art Deco interior.

Parks and Gardens

At **Edgewater Park,** just west of downtown, there is a spot where you can swim with a startlingly close-up view of downtown. The park also includes a fishing pier, a bait shop, a fitness course, playgrounds, and picnic facilities. The stiff wind off the lake attracts a coterie of kite flyers, windsurfers, and the occasional hang glider. Drive through the **Cleveland Cultural Gardens** (Martin Luther King, Jr., Dr. in University Circle, north of Chester Ave. and south of I–90, ☎ 216/664–2517) to see gardens representing more than 20 nationalities. The **Rockefeller Park Greenhouse** (750 E. 88th St., ☎ 216/664–3103), the oldest urban civic horticultural center in the country, houses seasonal flower and plant exhibits indoors; outdoors you'll find a Japanese garden, a formal English garden, and a talking garden for people with vision impairments.

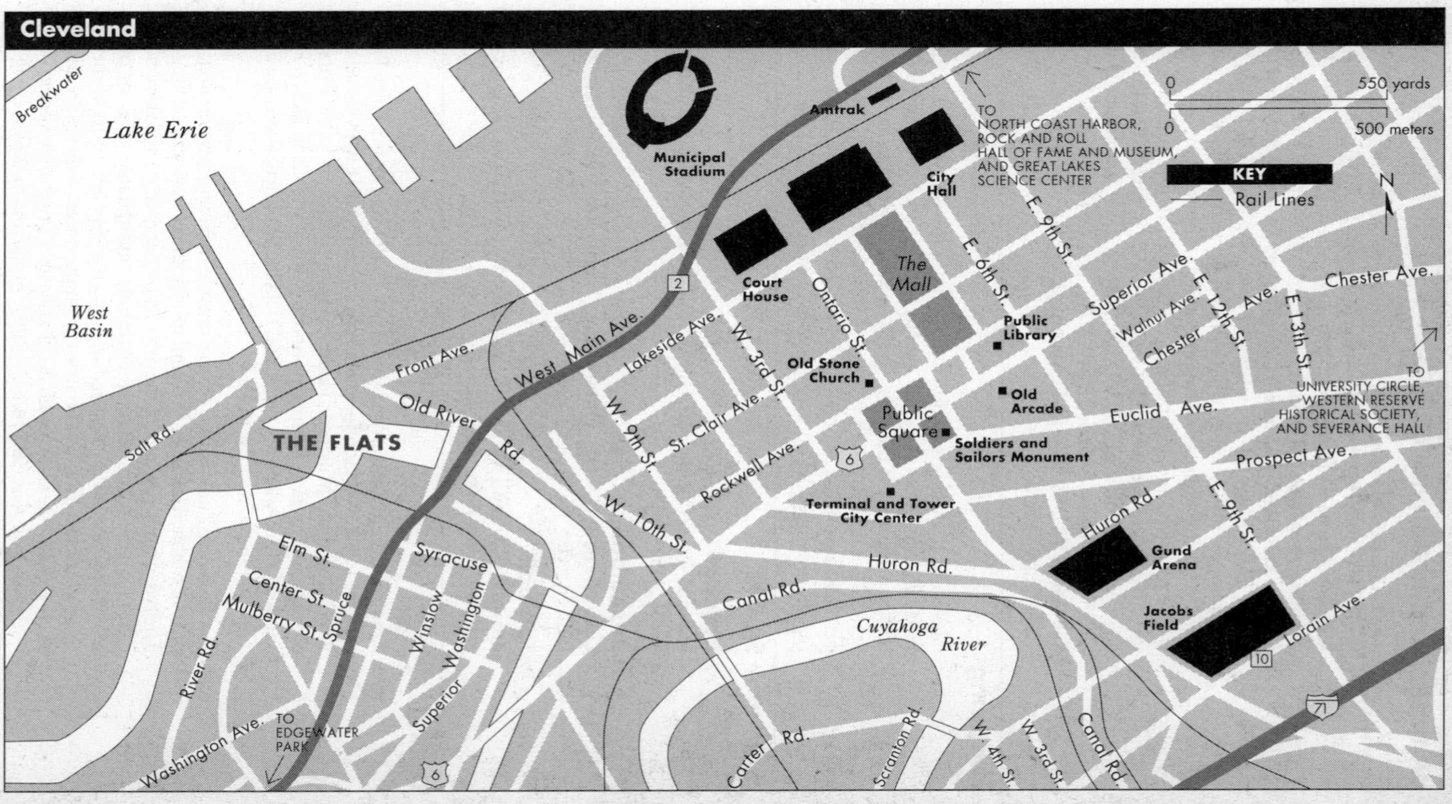
Cleveland
Breakwater
Lake Erie
West Basin
Municipal Stadium
Amtrak
City Hall
Court House
TO NORTH COAST HARBOR, ROCK AND ROLL HALL OF FAME AND MUSEUM, AND GREAT LAKES SCIENCE CENTER
0 550 yards
0 500 meters
KEY
Rail Lines
N
The Mall
E. 9th St.
E. 6th St.
Superior Ave.
Walnut Ave.
E. 12th St.
Chester Ave.
Chester Ave.
E. 13th St.
TO UNIVERSITY CIRCLE, WESTERN RESERVE HISTORICAL SOCIETY, AND SEVERANCE HALL
Public Library
Old Arcade
Euclid Ave.
Prospect Ave.
Old Stone Church
Public Square
Soldiers and Sailors Monument
Terminal and Tower City Center
Ontario St.
W. 3rd St.
Lakeside Ave.
St. Clair Ave.
W. 9th St.
Rockwell Ave.
W. 10th St.
6
2
West Main Ave.
Front Ave.
Old River Rd.
THE FLATS
Salt Rd.
Huron Rd.
Huron Rd.
Gund Arena
E. 9th St.
Jacobs Field
Lorain Ave.
10
71
Canal Rd.
Cuyahoga River
Elm St.
Center St.
Mulberry St.
Spruce
Syracuse
Winslow
Washington
Superior
River Rd.
Washington Ave.
TO EDGEWATER PARK
6
Carter Rd.
Scranton Rd.
W. 4th St.
W. 3rd St.
Canal Rd.

What to See and Do with Children

The **Children's Museum** (10730 Euclid Ave., ☎ 216/791–5437), the **Health Museum** (8911 Euclid Ave., ☎ 216/231–5010), the **Rock and Roll Hall of Fame and Museum** (North Coast Harbor, ☎ 216/781–7625), the **Museum of Natural History** (1 Wade Oval Dr., ☎ 216/231–4600), and the **Cleveland Metroparks Zoo** (Brookside Park Dr. off W. 25th St., ☎ 216/661–6500) are tried-and-true kid pleasers. Narrated tours on ***Lolly the Trolley*** (☎ 216/771–4484) leave from Burke Lakefront Airport. **Cedar Point Amusement Park** is an hour away, in Sandusky (*see* Northwest Ohio and the Lake Erie Islands, *above*). Another amusement park, **Geauga Lake** (☎ 216/562–7131; in OH, 800/843–9283; May–Sept.), is off Rte. 43 in Aurora, about 20 mi southeast of Cleveland (Ohio Turnpike Exit 13 or I–271). Just down the road from it is **Sea World** (☎ 216/995–2121, recording 216/562–8101 or 800/637–4268; June–Aug.).

Shopping

Cleveland has two glitzy downtown malls, the **Galleria** (1301 E. 9th St., ☎ 216/861–4343) and the **Avenue** (Tower City Center, ☎ 216/241–8550), with views of the river. The **West Side Market** (corner of W. 25th St. and Lorain Rd.), the world's largest indoor/outdoor farmers' market, sells freshly baked breads, fruit picked that morning, and perhaps the sharpest cheddar cheese you've ever eaten.

Spectator Sports

Baseball

Indians (Jacobs Field, 2401 Ontario St. at Carnegie Ave., ☎ 216/861–1200; Apr.–Oct.).

Basketball

Cavaliers (Gund Arena, Ontario St. at Huron Rd., ☎ 216/420–2000; Nov.–Apr.).

Football

Browns (Cleveland Municipal Stadium, ☎ 216/891–5000 or, for tickets, 216/696–3800; Aug.–Dec.).

Dining

Ethnic food is a specialty in Cleveland. A Polish dog is a spicy Polish sausage in a hot-dog bun—make sure you smother it with Cleveland's famous Stadium Mustard. There are restaurant rows in the Flats, the Warehouse District, the area around the Gund Arena and Jacobs Field, and on Coventry Road in Cleveland Heights. For price ranges, see Chart 1 (B) in On the Road with Fodor's.

$$$ **The Palazzo.** Unassuming on the outside, but with a swooning, fall-in-love ambience inside, this Italian restaurant is worth seeking out. The two granddaughters of the original owner prepare and serve northern Italian cuisine, and whether turning out updated versions of her recipes or new dishes inspired by annual trips back to Italy, they do their grandma proud. The menu changes often, but you're always likely to find a pasta dish with deliciously spicy primavera Alfredo sauce. *10031 Detroit Ave., ☎ 216/651–3900. Jacket and tie advised. AE, MC, V. Closed Sun.–Mon.*

$$$ **Sammy's.** Fresh fish, a raw bar, venison, and linguine are some of the specialties of this converted warehouse with a view of bridges over the

Cuyahoga. *1400 W. 10th St., ☎ 216/523–5560. Reservations required. AE, D, DC, MC, V. Closed Sun., holidays.*

$$ **Bohemia.** An eclectic menu and a stylish crowd make this a nice stop in the Tremont neighborhood, a part-artsy, part–eastern European enclave (hence, the name). The cozy bistro has tin ceilings and stained glass windows; the menu features such dishes as the merry prankster quesadilla (fresh baked bread stuffed with shiitake mushrooms, homemade salsa, and Monterey Jack cheese) and the Queen Jagellon (scallops and herb chicken breast over roasted-red-pepper fettucine). *900 Literary Rd., ☎ 216/566–8800. AE, MC, V. Closed Sun.*

$$ **Luchita's.** This simple Mexican restaurant is jammed on the weekends, and for good reason: great, authentic Mexican fare in generous portions, with friendly service. What more do you need? Oh, yeah, the margaritas are good, too. *3456 W. 117th St., ☎ 216/252–1169. MC, V. Closed Mon.*

$$ **Sweetwater's Café Sausalito.** Southwestern delicacies are the specialty in this laid-back Marin County–style bar and restaurant—a favorite for lunch at the Galleria. *1301 E. 9th St., ☎ 216/696–2233. AE, D, DC, MC, V. Closed Thanksgiving and Christmas.*

$ **Nate's Deli and Restaurant.** This breakfast and lunch spot on the near West Side serves traditional deli fare as well as Middle Eastern specialties. The rich and creamy hummus may be the best in town. *1923 W. 25th St., ☎ 216/696–7529. No credit cards. Closes at 6 PM Mon.–Sat. Closed Sun.*

$ **Tommy's.** This Coventry Road institution serves salads, sandwiches, and enormous milk shakes made with Cleveland's own Pierre's ice cream and served in the chilled tin in which it was made. *1824 Coventry Rd., Cleveland Heights, ☎ 216/321–7757. MC, V.*

$ **Wilbert's Bar and Grill.** A blues-and-rock club as well as a restaurant, Wilbert's has an enormous menu of Southwestern and American fare that includes some surprisingly wholesome dishes, like the vegetarian health burger (served with not-so-healthy-but-delicious homemade potato chips). Homemade tortilla chips are served with most food orders. *1360 W. 9th St., ☎ 216/771–2583. AE, D, DC, MC, V. Closed Sun.*

Lodging

Cleveland has taken great strides in correcting the shortage of hotels downtown. The Ritz-Carlton opened in 1990, the Cleveland Marriott in 1991, and at press time (spring 1995) the Wyndam Hotel was scheduled to open in Playhouse Square in July 1995. Downtown hotels offer weekend packages, whereas suburban ones have lower weekday rates. For price ranges, see Chart 2 (A) in On the Road with Fodor's.

$$$$ **Cleveland Marriott Society Center.** Attached to Society Tower, the tallest building between New York and Chicago, this hotel faces the historic Mall and abuts Public Square. Plush accommodations are complemented by fantastic views of Lake Erie and the lights and bridges of the Flats. *127 Public Sq., 44114, ☎ 216/696–9200, FAX 216/696–0966. 401 rooms, 15 suites. Facilities: restaurant, 2 lounges, fitness center, concierge, parking. AE, D, DC, MC, V.*

$$$$ **Radisson Suite Hotel.** This downtown former apartment complex debuted in 1990 as Cleveland's first all-suite hotel. Decor is modern but warmly elegant, with decidedly private club–style furnishings. *1706 E. 12th St., 44114, ☎ 216/523–8000, FAX 216/861–1266. 252 suites. Facilities: restaurant, health club. AE, D, DC, MC, V.*

$$$$ ★ **Ritz-Carlton.** The city's only four-star hotel is filled with antiques and 18th-century original artwork. The Riverview Room restaurant offers

excellent views of the Flats. *1515 W. 3rd St., 44113, ☎ 216/623–1300, FAX 216/623–0515. 208 rooms, 21 suites. Facilities: restaurant, 2 lounges, fitness center, pool, concierge, parking. AE, D, DC, MC, V.*

$$$$ **Stouffer Renaissance Cleveland Plaza Hotel.** The city's original grand hotel has a grand lobby, which features an ornate Carrara marble fountain. The rooms, done in burgundy and pale green, have period furniture and good views. *24 Public Sq., 44113, ☎ 216/696–5600, FAX 216/696–3102. 490 rooms, 50 suites. Facilities: 2 restaurants, 2 bars, health club, pool, concierge, complimentary limousine (downtown). AE, D, DC, MC, V.*

$$$ **Baricelli Inn.** Every room is different in this turn-of-the-century brownstone mansion, now a B&B, convenient to University Circle. Contemporary European and American dinners are served in the dining room. *2203 Cornell Rd., 44106, ☎ 216/791–6500, FAX 216/791–9131. 7 rooms. Facilities: Continental breakfast, restaurant (closed Sun.), parking. AE, DC, MC, V. Closed holidays.*

$$$ **Mario's International Spa and Hotel.** This rustic barn-board lodge, furnished with antiques and Victorian draperies, started out as a hair salon and grew. The restaurant has spa dining, Roman pizza, and six-course northern Italian dinners. *35 E. Garfield Rd. (Rtes. 82 and 306), Aurora 44202, ☎ 216/562–9171, FAX 216/562–2386. 14 rooms, 1 suite. Facilities: restaurant (closed Sun.), spa (closed Sun., holidays), limousine, parking. AE, D, MC, V.*

$$$ **Omni International Hotel.** Although it's on the grounds of the renowned Cleveland Clinic, there's nothing clinical about this luxurious international hotel. The Classics restaurant (no lunch Sat.; closed Sun.) serves French and Continental cuisine. *2065 E. 96th St. (at Carnegie Ave.), 44106, ☎ 216/791–1900 or 800/321–7100, FAX 216/791–7065. 292 rooms, 14 suites. Facilities: 3 restaurants, bar, access to pool and fitness center at clinic, concierge, parking. AE, D, DC, MC, V. Special rates for clinic patients.*

$$$ **Sheraton Cleveland City Center Hotel.** This hotel is geared to business travelers, with upgraded communications systems and additional phones and work space in all rooms. *777 St. Clair Ave., 44114, ☎ 216/771–7600; in OH, 800/321–1090; FAX 216/771–5129. 470 rooms, 45 suites. Facilities: restaurant, health club, conference rooms, business lounge. AE, D, DC, MC, V.*

$$ **Holiday Inn–Lakeside.** Across from Burke Lakefront Airport and convenient to the train station, this hotel, with lake views and a country-club feel, is congenial to sports fans and people who like high winds off the lake. *1111 Lakeside, 44114, ☎ 216/241–5100, FAX 216/241–7437. 370 rooms. Facilities: restaurant, bar, pool, exercise equipment, parking. AE, D, DC, MC, V.*

$$ **Ramada Inn–Southeast.** This seven-story suburban hotel, with a restful lobby done in blue and gray, is convenient to Sea World and Geauga Lake. *24801 Rockside Rd. (at I–271), Bedford Heights 44146, ☎ 216/439–2500, FAX 216/439–2500 ext. 777. 130 rooms. Facilities: restaurant, nightclub, pub, pool, parking. AE, D, DC, MC, V.*

$ **Brooklyn YMCA.** Bare-bones single rooms for men are available on a first-come, first-served basis. *3881 Pearl Rd., 44109, ☎ 216/749–2355. 69 rooms. Facilities: pool, gym, cafeteria, laundry, parking. No credit cards.*

Motels

Motels are concentrated around the Berea–Middleburg Heights exit off I–71 (near the airport), the Rockside Road/Brecksville exit off I–77, and the Chagrin Boulevard/Beachwood exit off I–271. Closer to Aurora, rates are higher in summer. **Aurora Woodlands Best Western Inn** (800 N. Aurora Rd., Aurora 44202, ☎ 216/562–9151, 146 rooms,

2 restaurants, pool, exercise room, shuttle to attractions; *$$$*. **Radisson Inn Beachwood** (26300 Chagrin Blvd., Beachwood 44122, ☎ 216/831–5150 or 800/221–2222), 188 rooms, 6 suites, restaurant, lounge, pool, fitness center; *$$*. **Budget Host Inn La Siesta Motel** (8300 Pearl Rd., Strongsville 44136, ☎ 216/234–4488), 38 rooms; *$*. **Quality Inn Airport** (16161 Brook Park Rd., Cleveland 44142, ☎ 216/267–5100 or 800/221–2222, FAX 216/267–2428), 153 rooms, restaurant, bar, 2 pools; *$*.

The Arts and Nightlife

The Arts

Playhouse Square Center (1501 Euclid Ave., at E. 17th St., ☎ 216/241–6000; Sept.–May) is home to the Cleveland Ballet, Cleveland Opera, DanceCleveland, and the Great Lakes Theater Festival. The **Cleveland Play House** (8500 Euclid Ave., ☎ 216/795–7000; Oct.–June) and **Karamu House** (2355 E. 89th St., ☎ 216/795–7070; Oct.–June) are near University Circle. **Severance Hall** (11001 Euclid Ave., ☎ 216/231–1111; Sept.–May) is home to the Cleveland Orchestra. Tickets to many events are sold through **TicketMaster** (☎ 216/241–5555).

Nightlife

Nightlife is concentrated in the Flats, where the crowd is young and into everything from darts to karaoke. **Shooter's on the Water** (1148 Main Ave., ☎ 216/861–6900) anchors the north end of the boardwalk along the west bank of the Cuyahoga River; while the **Powerhouse,** a beautifully restored former power station serving Cleveland's trolley cars, entertains at the south end with its **Improv Comedy Club** (☎ 216/696–4677) and other shops and restaurants. Trendy **Smart Bar** (1575 Merwin Ave., ☎ 216/522–1575) offers dramatic views of the river. For a look at the Flats the way it used to be, try the **Harbor Inn** (1219 Main Ave., ☎ 216/241–3232).

ELSEWHERE IN THE STATE

Neil Armstrong Air and Space Museum

Getting There

The museum is off I–75, halfway between Cincinnati and Toledo (about an hour from either city), in Wapakoneta, Neil Armstrong's hometown.

What to See and Do

Ohio is a leading producer of astronauts. The **Neil Armstrong Air and Space Museum** helps you feel what it's like to go into space. *I–75 Exit 111, ☎ 419/738–8811. Admission charged. Closed Dec.–Feb.*

Dayton

Getting There

Dayton is 54 mi north of Cincinnati on I–75, just below the interchange with I–70. **Dayton International Airport** is served by several major carriers and commuter lines.

What to See and Do

Aviation is central to the history of Dayton. The **Dayton/Montgomery County Convention and Visitors Bureau** (1 Chamber Plaza, 5th and Main Sts., 45402, ☎ 513/226–8248 or 800/221–8235; in OH, 800/221–8234) publishes a helpful visitor's guide and operates an information center at the U.S. Air Force Museum (*see below*). A self-guided tour of Dayton's Aviation Trail starts out at the **Wright Brothers Bicycle Shop**

(22 S. Williams St., ☎ 513/443–0793), where Wilbur and Orville Wright, native Daytonians, first hatched the idea for the airplane, and ends up at the **Wright Memorial,** near the field where the brothers practiced flying.

The **United States Air Force Museum** (Wright-Patterson Air Force Base, Springfield Pike [I–75 to Rte. 4, Harshman Rd. exit], ☎ 513/255–3284) is an internationally popular attraction and could easily take a full day. Exhibits tell the story of flight from Icarus to Desert Storm, with 200 planes (including the only remaining B–70) in hangars and on airfields. The Space Age is also thoroughly chronicled. The IMAX theater shows flight-related films several times daily (☎ 513/253–4629; admission charged). Also here are museum shops, a café, and picnic tables.

Canton

Getting There

Canton is 60 mi south of Cleveland, off I–77.

What to See and Do

The **Canton/Stark County Convention & Visitors Bureau** (229 Wells Ave. NW, Canton 44703, ☎ 216/452–0243 or 800/533–4302) maintains an information center on the approach road to the Hall of Fame. The **Pro Football Hall of Fame,** its dome shaped like a football in kickoff position, is a mecca to football fans. Two enshrinement halls are the serious purpose, but displays include a chronology of the game; mementos of the great players; and video replays showing great moments in football. A museum store, a snack bar, and vending machines are on the premises. *2121 George Halas Dr. NW (Fulton Rd. exit off I–77 and U.S. 62), ☎ 216/456–8207 or 216/456–7762 (recording). Admission charged.*

The **National Afro-American Museum and Cultural Center** is one of the largest African–American museums in the United States. Exhibits include black culture and history from the '40s through the '60s. Future plans include a children's mini-museum, library, art gallery, and more. *1350 Brush Row Rd., Wilberforce 45384 (Rte. 72 to Rte. 42, Brush Rd. exit), ☎ 513/376–4944. Admission charged. Closed Mon.*

WISCONSIN

By Don Davenport

Capital	Madison
Population	4,906,700
Motto	Forward
State Bird	Robin
State Flower	Wood violet

Visitor Information

Wisconsin Division of Tourism (Box 7606, Madison 53707, ☎ 608/266–2161 or 800/432–8747). **Information centers:** I–90N at Rest Area 22 near Beloit; I–94E at Rest Area 25 near Hudson; I–94N at Rest Area 26 near Kenosha; I–90E at Rest Area 31 near La Crosse; Rte. 12N at Rest Area 24 near Genoa City; Prairie du Chien, at the Rte. 18 bridge; 123 West Washington Avenue, Madison; and 305 East 2nd Street, Superior.

Scenic Drives

As part of the **Great River Road,** Rte. 35 follows the Mississippi River between Prairie du Chien and Prescott, offering many scenic vistas. Rte. 107, between Merrill and Tomahawk, travels along one of the most scenic sections of the 400-mi-long **Wisconsin River Valley.** In northeastern Wisconsin, Rtes. 57 and 42 circle the **Door County Peninsula,** providing 250 mi of spectacular Lake Michigan scenery.

National and State Parks

National Parks

Apostle Islands National Lakeshore (*see* Elsewhere in the State, *below*)

State Parks

Wisconsin's state park system includes 52 parks, nine forests, and numerous trails. Camping is allowed in 36 state parks and all state forests. The **Wisconsin Department of Natural Resources** (Bureau of Parks and Recreation, Box 7921, Madison 53707, ☎ 608/266–2181) offers information on the parks and their facilities.

Devils Lake State Park (S5975 Park Rd., Baraboo 53913, ☎ 608/356–8301) is one of the state's most popular parks, with hiking, camping, and 500-foot-high bluffs overlooking Devils Lake. **Pattison State Park** (Rte. 2, Superior 54880, ☎ 715/399–8073) offers camping, hiking, picnic facilities, and spectacular waterfalls, including the 165-foot Big Manitou Falls, Wisconsin's highest waterfall and the fourth highest east of the Rocky Mountains. **Peninsula State Park** (Rte. 42, Box 218, Fish Creek 54212, ☎ 414/868–3258) covers nearly 4,000 acres on the shores of Green Bay; offering golf, hiking, bicycling, and lakeshore camping, it is one of the state's most heavily used parks. **Wyalusing State Park** (13342 County Rte. C, Bagley 53801, ☎ 608/996–2261) stands at the confluence of the Wisconsin and Mississippi rivers, providing sweeping vistas of the river valleys.

MILWAUKEE

On the shores of Lake Michigan, Wisconsin's largest city is an international seaport and the state's primary commercial and manufacturing center. A small-town atmosphere prevails in Milwaukee, which is not so much a city as a large collection of neighborhoods. Modern steel-

and-glass high rises occupy much of the downtown area, but the early heritage persists in the restored and well-kept 19th-century buildings that share the city skyline. First settled by Potawatomi and later by French fur traders in the late 18th century, the city boomed in the 1840s with the arrival of German brewers, whose influence is still present.

Milwaukee has also become known as a city of festivals. The **Summerfest** kicks off each summer's activities on the lakefront. Another annual highlight is the **Great Circus Parade,** a July spectacle that features scores of antique circus wagons from the famed Circus World Museum in Baraboo. August brings the **state fair.**

Tourist Information

Greater Milwaukee: Convention & Visitors Bureau (510 W. Kilbourn Ave., 53203, ☎ 414/273–7222 or 800/231–0903).

Arriving and Departing

By Plane

General Mitchell International Airport (5300 S. Howell Ave., ☎ 414/747–5300), 6 mi from downtown via I–94E, is served by several domestic and international carriers. **Milwaukee County Transit System** (☎ 414/344–6711; fare $1.10, exact change) operates buses to and from the airport. Taxis between the airport and downtown take about 20 minutes; the fare range is $13 to $15.

By Car

From the north, I–43 provides controlled access into downtown Milwaukee. I–94 provides direct access to downtown from Chicago and other points south, and from the west. I–894 bypasses the metropolitan area to the south and west and provides the best connection to I–94 west and south of the city.

By Train

Amtrak (433 W. St. Paul Ave., ☎ 800/872–7245).

By Bus

Greyhound Lines (606 N. 7th St., ☎ 800/231–2222).

Getting Around Milwaukee

Lake Michigan is the city's eastern boundary; Wisconsin Avenue is the main east–west thoroughfare. The Milwaukee River divides the downtown area into east and west sections. The East–West Expressway (I–94/I–794) is the dividing line between north and south. Streets are numbered in ascending order from the Milwaukee River west well into the suburbs. Many downtown attractions are near the Milwaukee River and can be reached on foot. **Milwaukee County Transit System** (*see* By Plane, *above*) provides bus service. **Taxis** can be ordered by phone or at taxi stands; the fare is $2.50 for the first mile and $1.25 for each additional mile. The largest firm is **Yellow Cab** (☎ 414/271–1800).

Exploring Milwaukee

Downtown

Milwaukee's central business district is a mile long and only a few blocks wide. It is divided by the Milwaukee River. On the east side, the **Iron Block Building** (N. Water St. and E. Wisconsin Ave.) is one of the few remaining ironclad buildings in the United States. Its metal facade was brought in by ship from an eastern foundry and installed during the Civil War. In the 1860s, Milwaukee exported more wheat than any other

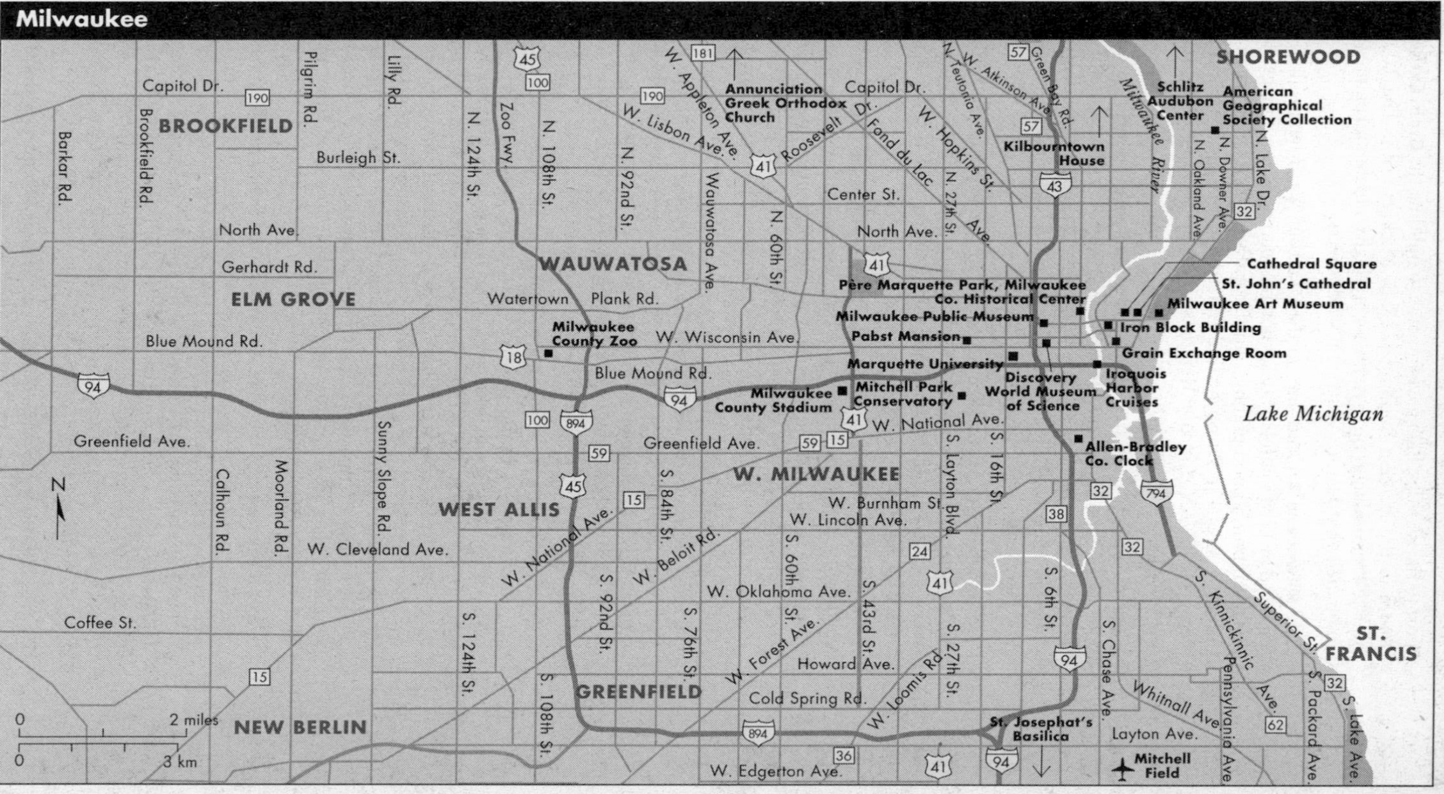
Milwaukee
SHOREWOOD
ST. FRANCIS
Lake Michigan
Milwaukee River
Schlitz Audubon Center
American Geographical Society Collection
Cathedral Square
St. John's Cathedral
Milwaukee Art Museum
Iron Block Building
Grain Exchange Room
Iroquois Harbor Cruises
Allen-Bradley Co. Clock
Kilbourntown House
Père Marquette Park, Milwaukee Co. Historical Center
Milwaukee Public Museum
Discovery World Museum of Science
Pabst Mansion
Marquette University
Mitchell Park Conservatory
Milwaukee County Stadium
Annunciation Greek Orthodox Church
Milwaukee County Zoo
St. Josephat's Basilica
Mitchell Field
W. MILWAUKEE
WAUWATOSA
WEST ALLIS
GREENFIELD
ELM GROVE
BROOKFIELD
NEW BERLIN
N. Lake Dr.
N. Downer Ave.
N. Oakland Ave.
Green Bay Rd.
W. Atkinson Ave.
N. Teutonia Ave.
W. Hopkins St.
N. 27th St.
Capitol Dr.
Fond du Lac Ave.
Roosevelt Dr.
Center St.
North Ave.
N. 60th St.
W. Appleton Ave.
W. Lisbon Ave.
Wauwatosa Ave.
N. 92nd St.
N. 108th St.
Zoo Fwy.
N. 124th St.
Lilly Rd.
Burleigh St.
Pilgrim Rd.
Gerhardt Rd.
Brookfield Rd.
Barkar Rd.
Watertown Plank Rd.
W. Wisconsin Ave.
Blue Mound Rd.
Greenfield Ave.
W. National Ave.
W. Burnham St.
W. Lincoln Ave.
W. Cleveland Ave.
W. Oklahoma Ave.
W. Beloit Rd.
W. Forest Ave.
Howard Ave.
Cold Spring Rd.
W. Edgerton Ave.
W. Loomis Rd.
Sunny Slope Rd.
Moorland Rd.
Calhoun Rd.
Coffee St.
S. 6th St.
S. 16th St.
S. Layton Blvd.
S. 27th St.
S. 43rd St.
S. 60th St.
S. 76th St.
S. 84th St.
S. 92nd St.
S. 108th St.
S. 124th St.
S. Chase Ave.
S. Kinnickinnic Ave.
Superior St.
S. Lake Ave.
S. Packard Ave.
Pennsylvania Ave.
Whitnall Ave.
Layton Ave.
32
43
57
94
794
38
41
24
59
15
36
894
181
190
45
100
18
62
N
0 2 miles
0 3 km

port in the world, which gave impetus to building the **Grain Exchange Room** in the Mackie Building (225 E. Michigan St.). The 10,000-square-foot trading room has three-story-high columns and painted ceiling panels that feature Wisconsin wildflowers.

The **Milwaukee Art Museum,** in the lakefront War Memorial Center designed by Eero Saarinen, houses notable collections of paintings, drawings, sculpture, photography, and decorative arts. Its permanent collection is strong in European and American art of the 19th and 20th centuries. *750 N. Lincoln Memorial Dr., ☎ 414/224–3200. Admission charged. Closed Mon.*

Returning to the river, stop a moment at **Cathedral Square.** This quiet park (E. Kilbourn Ave. and Jefferson St.) was built on the site of Milwaukee's first courthouse. Across the street, **St. John's Cathedral,** dedicated in 1853, was the first church built in Wisconsin specifically as a Roman Catholic cathedral.

The banks of the Milwaukee River are busy in summer, especially at noon, when downtown workers lunch in the nearby parks and public areas, such as **Père Marquette Park,** on the river at Old World 3rd Street and West Kilbourn Avenue.

Adjacent to the park, the **Milwaukee County Historical Center** (910 N. Old World 3rd St., ☎ 414/273–8288), a museum housed in a graceful former bank building, features early fire-fighting equipment, military artifacts, toys, and women's fashions. It also contains a research library with naturalization records and genealogical resources.

The river is also the departure point for cruises of Milwaukee's harbor and lakefront. **Iroquois Harbor Cruises** (Clybourn St. bridge on the west bank, ☎ 414/332–4194) offers harbor cruises aboard a 149-passenger vessel. **Celebration of Milwaukee** (502 N. Harbor Dr., ☎ 414/278–1113) and **Edelweiss Cruise Dining** (1110 N. Old World 3rd St., ☎ 414/272–3625) offer lunch and dinner cruises.

As you cross the river to the west side, notice that the east-side streets are not directly opposite the west-side streets and that the bridges across the river are built at an angle. This layout dates from the 1840s, when the area east of the river was called Juneautown and the region to the west was known as Kilbourntown. The rival communities had a fierce argument over which would pay for the bridges that connected them; so intense was the antagonism that citizens venturing into rival territory carried white flags. The Great Bridge War was finally settled by the state legislature in 1845, but the streets on either side of the river were never aligned.

A few blocks west of the river, the **Milwaukee Public Museum** has the fourth-largest collection of natural-history exhibits in the country, as well as outstanding fine arts and Native American, African, and pre-Columbian collections. Walk-through exhibits include the "Streets of Old Milwaukee," depicting the city in the 1890s; a two-story rain forest; and the "Third Planet" (complete with full-size dinosaurs), where visitors walk into the interior of the Earth to learn about its history. *800 W. Wells St., ☎ 414/278–2702. Admission charged.*

Nearby, **Discovery World—Museum of Science, Economics and Technology,** in the Milwaukee Public Central Library, has a wide range of hands-on exhibits on magnets, motors, electricity, health, and computers that introduce youngsters to science, technology, and economics. It also features the "Great Electric Show" and the "Light Wave–Laser Beam

Show" on weekends. *818 W. Wisconsin Ave., ☎ 414/765–9966. Admission charged.*

Farther west, just off Wisconsin Avenue at 16th Street on the central mall of the **Marquette University** campus, is **St. Joan of Arc Chapel** (☎ 414/288–6873), a small, stone 15th-century chapel moved from its original site near Lyon, France, and reconstructed here in 1964. One of the stones was reputedly kissed by Joan before she went to her death and is said to be discernibly colder than the others. The **Patrick and Beatrice Haggerty Museum of Art** (13th and Clybourn Sts., ☎ 414/288–7290) houses the university's collection of more than 6,000 works of art, including Renaissance, Baroque, and modern paintings, sculpture, prints, photography, and decorative arts; it also offers changing exhibitions.

Other Attractions

Away from downtown, the **Pabst Mansion,** built in 1893 for the beer baron Captain Frederick Pabst, is one of Milwaukee's treasured landmarks. The castlelike, 37-room Flemish Renaissance–style mansion has a tan pressed-brick exterior and is decorated with carved stone and terracotta ornamentation outside and carved cabinets and woodwork, ornamental ironwork, marble, tile, stained glass, and carved panels inside, all imported from a 17th-century Bavarian castle. *2000 W. Wisconsin Ave., ☎ 414/931–0808. Admission charged.*

Milwaukee's unique **Mitchell Park Conservatory** consists of three modern 85-ft-high glass domes housing tropical, arid, and seasonal plant and flower exhibits; its displays of lilies and poinsettias are spectacular at Easter and Christmas. There are picnic facilities on the grounds. *524 S. Layton Blvd., ☎ 414/649–9800. Admission charged.*

The **Milwaukee County Zoo** houses more than 3,000 wild animals and birds, including many endangered species, displayed in natural environments. It also offers educational programs, a seasonal children's zoo, narrated tram tours, miniature-train rides, picnic areas, and cross-country skiing trails. *10001 W. Bluemound Rd., ☎ 414/771–3040. Admission charged.*

North of downtown Milwaukee, the **American Geographical Society Collection,** housed in the Golda Meir Library on the University of Wisconsin–Milwaukee campus (2311 E. Hartford Ave., ☎ 414/229–6282), has an exceptional assemblage of maps, old globes, atlases, and charts, plus 180,000 books and 400,000 journals. The **University of Wisconsin–Milwaukee Art Museum** (3253 N. Downer Ave., ☎ 414/229–5070) displays a permanent collection of Greek and Russian icons and 20th-century European paintings and prints. The **UWM Fine Arts Gallery** (2400 E. Kenwood Blvd.) displays the works of students and faculty members; other changing exhibits are held at the **UWM Art History Gallery** (3203 N. Downer Ave.).

The **Charles Allis Art Museum** (1801 N. Prospect Ave., ☎ 414/278–8295) occupies an elegant Tudor-style house built in 1911 for the first president of the Allis-Chalmers Manufacturing Co. The home has stained-glass windows by Louis Comfort Tiffany and a stunning worldwide collection of paintings and objets d'art, including works by major 19th- and 20th-century French and American painters.

The Greek Revival cream-color slate **Kilbourntown House** (4400 W. Estabrook Dr., ☎ 414/273–8288), built in 1844, is listed on the National Register of Historic Places and contains an outstanding collection of mid-19th-century furniture and decorative arts.

The **Schlitz Audubon Center,** 10 mi north of downtown, is a 186-acre wildlife area of forests, ponds, marshland, and nature trails along Lake Michigan. Popular with cross-country skiers and birders, it has an environmental research and education center. *1111 E. Brown Deer Rd., ☎ 414/352–2880. Admission charged. Closed Mon., holidays.*

The **Annunciation Greek Orthodox Church** (9400 W. Congress St., ☎ 414/461–9400) was Frank Lloyd Wright's last major work; the famed Wisconsin architect called it his "little jewel." Since it opened in 1961, the blue-domed, Byzantine-style church has drawn visitors from all over the world.

Just south of downtown, the **Allen-Bradley Co. Clock** (1201 S. 2nd St.) is a Milwaukee landmark and, according to the *Guinness Book of World Records,* "the largest four-faced clock in the world." Great Lakes ships often use the clock as a navigational reference point.

Built by immigrant parishioners and local craftsmen at the turn of the century, **St. Josephat's Basilica** (2333 S. 6th St., ☎ 414/645–5623) has a dome modeled after St. Peter's in Rome. The church is adorned with a remarkable collection of relics, portraits of Polish saints and leaders, stained glass, and wood carvings.

In the Vicinity

About 15 mi north of Milwaukee off I–43 is **Cedarburg,** where the entire downtown district, most of it built of Niagara limestone by 19th-century pioneers, is on the National Register of Historic Places. **Cedar Creek Settlement** (N70 W6340 Bridge Rd., ☎ 414/375–9390 or 800/827–8020) is a collection of crafts and antiques shops in the historic Wittenberg Woolen Mill, which was built in 1864 and operated until 1969. With several levels, wooden floors, and lots of nooks and crannies, it's fun to explore. Wisconsin's last remaining **covered bridge** (off Hwy. 143) crosses Cedar Creek 3 mi north of town. The 120-foot bridge was built in 1876 and retired in 1962. Its white pine was cut and squared at a mill near Baraboo and hauled 75 mi to the bridge site. A small park beside the bridge invites picnicking.

Thirty-five miles west of Milwaukee near Eagle is the State Historical Society's living-history museum, **Old World Wisconsin,** which celebrates the state's ethnic heritage in architecture, with more than 50 historic buildings on 576 acres in the **Southern Kettle Moraine State Forest.** The restored farm and village buildings gathered from across the state depict 19th- and 20th-century rural Wisconsin. All were originally built and inhabited by European immigrants; they are grouped in German, Norwegian, Danish, and Finnish farmsteads. Costumed interpreters relate the story of immigration to Wisconsin, along with each ethnic group's role in it, and perform chores necessary to rural life a century ago, such as making soap. *S103 W37890 Hwy. 67, ☎ 414/594–2116. Admission charged. Closed Nov.–Apr.*

An hour north of Milwaukee off I–43 is **Kohler,** a planned, landscaped village surrounding the factories of the plumbing-fixtures manufacturer Kohler Co. The **Kohler Design Center** (101 Upper Rd., ☎ 414/457–3699) houses the company's ceramic-art collection, archives, artifacts from its early factory and village, and a showroom of decorator bathrooms. A guided 2½-hour tour of the factory may be arranged by reservation (☎ 414/457–4441; must be 14 or older). Guided tours of **Waelderhaus** (W. Riverside Dr., ☎ 414/452–4079), a reproduction of founder John M. Kohler's ancestral home in Austria, are offered daily. The **Woodlake Kohler Complex,** in nearby Sheboygan, comprises more than 25 shops, galleries, and restaurants—including **Artspace** (☎ 414/

452–8602), a gallery of the John Michael Kohler Arts Center. The **American Club** (Highland Dr., 53044, ☎ 414/457–8000 or 800/344–2838), built as a company-owned hotel for workers, is now a posh resort hotel on the National Register of Historic Places. The compound has two 18-hole golf courses designed by Pete Dye, a large indoor sports complex, a 500-acre wilderness preserve, and several restaurants.

Parks and Gardens

Whitnall Park (5879 S. 92nd St., in suburban Hales Corners) is one of the largest municipal parks in the nation. Its 660 acres encompass an 18-hole golf course, a variety of recreational facilities, picnic areas, and nature and cross-country skiing trails. Within the park is the internationally famous **Alfred L. Boerner Botanical Garden** (☎ 414/425–1130), with trees, shrubs, and flowers in formal and informal gardens. The park's **Wehr Nature Center** (☎ 414/425–8550) includes wildlife exhibits, woodlands and wetlands, a lake, nature trails, and wild gardens.

What to See and Do with Children

At the **Milwaukee Public Museum** (*see* Exploring Milwaukee, Downtown, *above*), the **Wizard Wing** has hands-on natural and human-history exhibits for children and families. The Milwaukee Public Central Library's **Discovery World** (*see* Exploring Milwaukee, Downtown, *above*) and the **Milwaukee County Zoo** (*see* Exploring Milwaukee, Other Attractions, *above*) both have strong appeal for the younger set. **Wm. K. Walthers, Inc.** (5601 W. Florist Ave., ☎ 414/527–0770), maker of model railroad equipment since 1932, has the world's largest single warehouse selection of trains, with a large HO-gauge layout.

Shopping

Stores range from tiny ethnic and specialty shops to enclosed shopping malls with large department stores. Using the downtown skywalk system, it's possible to browse in hundreds of stores over several blocks without once setting foot outside. Downtown Milwaukee's major shopping street is **Wisconsin Avenue** west of the Milwaukee River. The major downtown retail center, the **Grand Avenue Mall** (275 W. Wisconsin Ave.) spans four city blocks and contains more than 160 specialty shops and 17 eateries. **Historic Third Ward,** a turn-of-the-century wholesale and manufacturing district on the National Register of Historic Places, is bordered on three sides by the harbor, the river, and downtown and offers many unusual shops and restaurants. Two Milwaukee landmarks, Usinger's Sausage and Mader's Restaurant, are here. **Jefferson Street,** stretching four blocks from Wisconsin to Kilbourn, offers upscale stores and shops, including George Watts and Son, Inc., with more than a thousand patterns of china, silver, and crystal. The **Lincoln Avenue District,** minutes from downtown off I–94, has specialty shops and ethnic restaurants in a quaint, historic Polish and German neighborhood. On Milwaukee's south side, historic **Mitchell Street** is a multicultural blend of retail shops and diverse ethnic restaurants.

In the metropolitan area, **Capitol Court** (5500 W. Capitol Dr.) has more than 100 stores and shops. At **Mayfair** (2500 N. Mayfair Rd., near the Milwaukee County Zoo), more than 160 shops surround a multistory atrium complete with swaying bamboo. The 145 stores at **Northridge Shopping Center** (7700 W. Brown Deer Rd.) are anchored by a new Younkers department store and a Boston Store. The newly renovated **Southgate Mall** (3333 S. 27th St.) has 50 stores, all on one level. Wisconsin's largest shopping center, **Southridge Mall** (5300 S. 76th St., Green-dale) has more than 145 specialty stores and is anchored by five major department stores—Younkers, Boston Store, JC Penney, Sears, and Kohls.

Spectator Sports

Baseball

Milwaukee Brewers (Milwaukee County Stadium, 201 S. 46th St., ☎ 414/933–9000; Apr.–Oct.).

Basketball

Milwaukee Bucks (Bradley Center, 1001 N. 4th St., ☎ 414/227–0500; Nov.–Apr.).

Hockey

Milwaukee Admirals (Bradley Center, 1001 N. 4th St., ☎ 414/227–0500; Oct.–Apr.).

Beaches

Lake Michigan is the place to swim, but be prepared: The mid-summer water temperature is only in the 50s and 60s, and the wind adds to the chill. Among the most popular of the narrow sandy beaches are **Bradford Beach** (2400 N. Lincoln Memorial Dr.), **Doctors Beach** (1870 E. Fox Ln., Fox Point), **Grant Beach** (100 Hawthorne Ave., South Milwaukee), and **McKinley Beach** (1750 N. Lincoln Memorial Dr.). The Parks Department (☎ 414/961–6165) has information.

Dining

By Anne Schamberg

Milwaukee's culinary style was shaped to a great extent by the Germans who first settled here. Many restaurants—whether or not they are German—offer Wiener schnitzel or the meringue-based desserts called *schaumtortes*. Rye bread, sometimes crusted with coarse salt, is as common on Milwaukee tables as robins on a spring lawn. Many other ethnic groups have also donated their specialties to Milwaukee's tradition of *gemütlichkeit* (fellowship and good cheer).

Milwaukeeans like to relax and socialize when they eat out. Fashion isn't as important here as in faster-paced cities. Jackets and ties are customary at the most expensive restaurants, but only a few actually require them. For price ranges, see Chart 1 (A) in On the Road with Fodor's.

$$$$ ★ **English Room.** Milwaukee's premier hotel restaurant, in the Pfister Hotel, has a dark, Victorian elegance accented with original 19th-century paintings. The German/American menu emphasizes meat dishes, although seafood is also served; rack of lamb and chanterelle bisque are two of Chef Bob Gibbons's specialties. Service is formal, with plenty of tableside cooking. *424 E. Wisconsin Ave., ☎ 414/273–8222. AE, D, DC, MC, V. No lunch weekends.*

$$$$ ★ **Grenadier's.** Chef-owner Knut Apitz serves some of the most elegant food in Milwaukee. Imaginative dishes combine classical European style with Oriental or Indian flavors; offerings include tenderloin of veal with raspberry sauce and angel-hair pasta. The three small rooms have an air of matter-of-fact refinement; the handsome, darkly furnished piano bar also has tables. *747 N. Broadway St., ☎ 414/276–0747. Jacket required. AE, DC, MC, V. Closed Sun. No lunch Sat.*

$$$ **Boder's on the River.** Tie-back curtains, fireplaces, and lots of knickknacks give the dining rooms in this suburban restaurant a cheerful country look. The menu offers Wisconsin favorites prepared in a straightforward manner, including roast duckling and baked whitefish.

11919 N. River Rd. W43, Mequon, ☎ 414/242–0335. AE, D, DC, MC, V. Closed Mon.

$$$ Giovanni's. At this Old World–style Sicilian place one finds flocked wallpaper, crystal chandeliers, and large portions of rich Italian food. Veal steak Giovanni is excellent, but the pasta is disappointing. *1683 N. Van Buren St., ☎ 414/291–5600.AE, D, DC, MC, V. No lunch weekends.*

$$$ Harold's. Velvet-backed booths, low lighting, etched glass, and rich greenery set a romantic, if slightly generic, mood at this restaurant in the Grand Milwaukee Hotel. Oysters Rockefeller and rack of lamb Provençal are representative of the ambitious choices on the menu. There is also a selection of "traditional favorites," including steaks and fresh fillet of whitefish. *4747 S. Howell Ave., ☎ 414/481–8000. AE, DC, MC, V. No lunch weekends.*

$$$ ★ Karl Ratzsch's Old World Restaurant. In the authentic German atmosphere of this family-owned restaurant, such specialties as schnitzel, roast duckling, and sauerbraten are served by dirndl-skirted waitresses while a string trio schmaltzes it up. The main dining room is decorated with murals, chandeliers made from antlers, and antique beer steins. *320 E. Mason St., ☎ 414/276–2720. AE, D, DC, MC, V.*

$$$ Mike and Anna's. At this small, trendy restaurant in a working-class neighborhood on the south side, the changing menu features excellent nouvelle-inspired selections, such as Norwegian salmon with green mustard oil. Be sure to ask for directions when making reservations. *2000 S. 8th St., ☎ 414/643–0072. AE, MC, V. No lunch.*

$$$ ★ Steven Wade's Cafe. Noted for creative, freshly prepared food, chef and co-owner Steven Wade Klindt operates this establishment in a former suburban paint-and-wallpaper store. The changing menu might include Norwegian salmon fillet poached with vanilla sauce or coconut curried lamb. *17001 W. Greenfield Ave., New Berlin, ☎ 414/784–0774. Reservations required. AE, D, DC, MC, V. Closed Sun. No lunch Sat.*

$$ Chip and Py's. In the northern suburbs, this stylish restaurant has light gray dual-level dining rooms, a huge fireplace, and contemporary art. The eclectic menu features chicken, beef, seafood, blackened redfish, and vegetarian entrées. There's live jazz on weekends. *1340 W. Town Square Rd., Mequon, ☎ 414/241–9589. AE, D, DC, MC, V. No lunch Sun. or Tues., no dinner Mon.*

$$ Izumi's. Traditional Japanese dishes, including sushi (and tempura or noodles for those who prefer their food cooked), are the fare at this friendly, well-run restaurant. *2178 N. Prospect Ave., ☎ 414/271–5278. AE, MC, V. No lunch weekends.*

$$ Jake's. There are two locations for this longtime Milwaukee favorite that earned its reputation with perfectly prepared steaks and heaps of french-fried onion rings. The best menu choices include escargot, roast duckling, and Bailey's chocolate-chip cheesecake. *6030 W. North Ave., Wauwatosa, ☎ 414/771–0550; 21445 W. Capitol Dr., Brookfield, ☎ 414/781–7995. AE, MC, V.*

$$ Three Brothers Bar & Restaurant. Set in an 1887 tavern is one of Milwaukee's revered ethnic restaurants, serving chicken paprikash, roast lamb, Serbian salad, and homemade desserts at old metal kitchen tables. It's about 10 minutes from downtown on the near south side. *2414 S. St. Clair St., ☎ 414/481–7530. No credit cards. Closed Mon. No lunch.*

$ Crocus Restaurant and Cocktail Lounge. Tucked away on the south side is this friendly neighborhood restaurant decorated with ethnic paintings and artifacts. Good choices among the homemade Polish dishes are braised-beef roll-ups, stuffed potato dumplings, and pierogi. *1801 S. Muskego Ave., ☎ 414/643–6383. No credit cards. Closed Sun. No lunch Sat., no dinner Tues.*

$ **Elsa's on the Park.** Across from Cathedral Square Park, this chic but casual place attracts talkative young professionals for big, juicy hamburgers and pork-chop sandwiches. The decor is a crisply stylish gray, white, and black. *833 N. Jefferson St., ☎ 414/765-0615. No credit cards. No lunch weekends.*

$ **La Fuente Restaurant.** The pink stucco walls of this friendly Mexican restaurant are covered with an array of old Mexican pictures and pottery. Try the shrimp soup, steak ranchero, or *chuletas rancheras* (pork chops simmered in salsa). *625 S. 5th Ave., ☎ 414/271-8595. AE, D, DC, MC, V.*

$ **Omega V.** Plaster statuary, mosaic floors, and brocade upholstery set the Mediterranean tone at this Greek-American family-style restaurant. Menu offerings range from eggs over-easy to Athenian chicken and rice pudding. *3473 S. 27th St., ☎ 414/645-6595. No credit cards.*

$ **Watts Tea Shop.** This genteel spot for breakfast or lunch is above George Watts & Sons, Milwaukee's premier store for china, crystal, and silver. Offerings include simple breakfasts, sandwiches, a juice bar, and the special custard-filled sunshine cake. *761 N. Jefferson St., ☎ 414/276-6352. No shorts. AE, D, MC, V. Closed Sun. No breakfast Sat.*

Lodging

By Anne Schamberg

Milwaukee offers a number of options for accommodations, ranging from cozy small motels to executive suites overlooking Lake Michigan and the city. Most downtown hotels are within walking distance of the theater district, the Convention Center and Arena, and plenty of shopping and restaurants. In summer, accommodations should be booked well ahead, especially for weekends. For price ranges, see Chart 2 (A) in On the Road with Fodor's.

$$$$ ★ **Pfister Hotel.** Many of the rooms in Milwaukee's grand old hotel, built in 1893, have been combined to make suites with enlarged bathrooms. Rooms in the Tower, built in 1975, are bright and contemporary with a Victorian accent, in keeping with the original hotel. A collection of 19th-century art hangs in the elegant Victorian lobby. *424 E. Wisconsin Ave., 53202, ☎ 414/273-8222 or 800/558-8222; in WI, 800/472-4403; FAX 414/273-8222. 240 rooms, 70 suites. Facilities: 3 restaurants, nightclub, lounge, indoor pool, health club. AE, D, DC, MC, V.*

$$$ ★ **Embassy Suites–Milwaukee West.** The sweeping atrium lobby with fountains, potted plants, and glass elevators is the focal point of this hotel in the western suburbs. The two-bedroom suites are decorated in pastels and earth tones with contemporary furnishings. *1200 S. Moorland Rd., Brookfield 53005, ☎ 414/782-2900 or 800/444-6404, FAX 414/796-9159. 203 suites. Facilities: restaurant, lounge, indoor pool, whirlpool, sauna, exercise room. AE, D, DC, MC, V.*

$$$ **Hyatt Regency.** This centrally located high-rise hotel has an 18-story open atrium and a revolving restaurant on top. The rooms are airy and bright, with plush contemporary furnishings. *333 W. Kilbourn Ave., 53203, ☎ 414/276-1234, FAX 414/276-6338. 484 rooms. Facilities: 3 restaurants, 3 lounges. AE, D, DC, MC, V.*

$$$ ★ **Wyndham Milwaukee Center.** Part of the city's growing theater district, this hotel is next to the Milwaukee Center theater, by the river. The opulent lobby is tiled with Italian marble; guest rooms are contemporary, large, and pleasant, with mahogany furnishings. *139 E. Kilbourn Ave., 53202, ☎ 414/276-8686 or 800/822-4200, FAX 414/276-8007. 221 rooms. Facilities: restaurant, lounge, exercise room, sauna, whirlpool, 2 steam baths, health club. AE, D, DC, MC, V.*

$$ Grand Milwaukee Hotel. Across from the airport, the Grand is the largest hotel in the state. Renovated in 1992, the bright rooms are decorated in earth tones. The marble-walled lobby is illuminated with chandeliers; a swimming pool cools the central courtyard. *4747 S. Howell Ave., 53207, ☎ 414/481–8000 or 800/558–3862, FAX 414/481–8065. 510 rooms. Facilities: 2 restaurants, lounge, nightclub, 2 pools, health club, 7 indoor tennis courts, 6 racquetball courts, movie theater. AE, DC, MC, V.*

$$ Ramada Inn Downtown. Rough knotty-pine paneling gives the lobby of this motor hotel a casual feeling. The maroon-toned rooms are furnished in standard Ramada style. *633 W. Michigan St., 53202, ☎ 414/272–8410, FAX 414/272–4651. 154 rooms. Facilities: restaurant, lounge, outdoor pool, airport transportation. AE, D, DC, MC, V.*

$$ Sheraton Mayfair. This bustling high-rise motor hotel on the west side is convenient to the county medical complex and the Milwaukee County Zoo. Guest rooms are bright and airy, with traditional furnishings; those near the top have fine views. *2303 N. Mayfair Rd., Wauwatosa 53226, ☎ 414/257–3400, FAX 414/257–0900. 150 rooms. Facilities: restaurant, lounge, indoor pool, sauna. AE, D, DC, MC, V.*

$ Astor Hotel. Close to Lake Michigan, the Astor has the not-unpleasant air of a hotel past its heyday, which is documented with photographs of illustrious guests in the large lobby. Many of the rooms have been remodeled and furnished with antiques and period reproductions but retain old bathroom fixtures. *924 E. Juneau Ave., 53202, ☎ 414/271–4220 or 800/558–0200; in WI, 800/242–0355; FAX 414/271–6370. 96 rooms. Facilities: restaurant, lounge, garage. AE, D, DC, MC, V.*

Motels

Best Western Midway Hotel–Airport (5105 S. Howell Ave., 53207, ☎ 414/769–2100, FAX 414/769–0064), 109 rooms, restaurant, lounge, indoor pool, sauna, whirlpool, recreation area; *$$*. **Holiday Inn–South** (6331 S. 13th St., 53221, ☎ 414/764–1500, FAX 414/764–6531), 159 rooms, restaurant, lounge, indoor recreation area, heated pool, whirlpool, playground; *$$*. **Holiday Inn Express** (11111 W. North Ave., Wauwatosa 53226, ☎ 414/778–0333, FAX 414/778–0331), 122 rooms; *$*.

The Arts and Nightlife

Milwaukee Magazine (on newsstands) lists arts and entertainment events. Also check the arts section of the Sunday *Milwaukee Journal.*

The Arts

Milwaukee's theater district is in a two-block downtown area bounded by the Milwaukee River, East Wells Street, North Water Street, and East State Street. Most tickets are sold at box offices.

The **Riverside Theater** (116 W. Wisconsin Ave., ☎ 414/224–3000) and **Pabst Theater** (144 E. Wells St., ☎ 414/286–3663) host touring theater companies, Broadway shows, and other entertainment. The **Milwaukee Center** (108 E. Wells St., ☎ 414/224–9490) is home to the **Milwaukee Repertory Theater.** The **Milwaukee Symphony Orchestra, Milwaukee Ballet Company, Florentine Opera Company,** and **First Stage Milwaukee** are based at the **Performing Arts Center** (929 N. Water St., ☎ 414/273–7206). The intimate **Broadway Theatre Center** (158 N. Broadway Ave., ☎ 414/291–7800) is home to the nationally acclaimed **Skylight Opera Theatre,** the **Milwaukee Chamber Theatre,** and **Theatre X. Milwaukee Dance Theatre** (☎ 414/273–1999) and **Bauer Contemporary Ballet** (☎ 414/276–3180) perform at various venues around town.

Nightlife

The city offers a variety of nightlife, with friendly saloons (about 1,600 at last count) and a varied music scene. The **Safe House** (779 N. Front St., ☎ 414/271–2007), with a James Bond spy-hideout decor, is a favorite with young people and out-of-towners. **La Playa** (Pfister Hotel, 424 E. Wisconsin Ave., ☎ 414/273–8222) combines a South American atmosphere with the glamour of a supper club. **Major Goolsby's** (340 W. Kilbourn Ave., ☎ 414/271–3414) is regarded as one of the country's top 10 sports bars by the jocks and occasional major-league-sports stars who hang out here. Jazz fans go to the **Bombay Bicycle Club** (Marc Plaza Hotel, 509 W. Wisconsin Ave., ☎ 414/271–7250) or the **Estate** (2423 N. Murray Ave., ☎ 414/964–9923), a cozy club offering progressive jazz four nights a week.

ELSEWHERE IN THE STATE

Madison and Southern Wisconsin

Getting There

Take I–90W from Milwaukee to Madison.

What to See and Do

Madison, named after President James Madison, is the state capital and home to the University of Wisconsin. The center of the city lies on an eight-block-wide isthmus between Lakes Mendota and Monona. The Roman Renaissance–style **Wisconsin State Capitol** (☎ 608/266–0382; tours daily), built between 1906 and 1917, dominates the downtown skyline. A **farmers' market** is held on Capitol Square each Saturday from May through October. The **State Historical Society Museum** (30 N. Carroll St., Capitol Sq., ☎ 608/264–6555) has permanent and changing exhibits on Wisconsin history from prehistoric Native American cultures to contemporary social issues.

Capitol Square is connected to the university's campus by State Street, a mile-long, tree-lined shopping district of import shops, ethnic restaurants, and artisans' studios. The **Madison Art Center,** in the lobby of the Civic Center (211 State St., ☎ 608/257–0158), has a large permanent collection and frequent temporary exhibitions.

At the foot of State Street, the **University of Wisconsin,** which opened in 1849 with 20 students, now has an enrollment of 46,000. The university's **Elvehjem Museum of Art** (800 University Ave., ☎ 608/263–2246) is one of the state's best, with a permanent collection of paintings, sculpture, and decorative arts dating from 2300 BC to the present. Away from downtown, the **University Arboretum** (1207 Seminole Hwy., ☎ 608/263–7888) has more than 1,200 acres of natural plant and animal communities, such as prairie and forest landscapes, and horticultural collections of Upper Midwest specimens.

Close by, the **Henry Vilas Zoo** (702 S. Randall Ave., ☎ 608/266–4732) exhibits nearly 200 species of animals and has a children's zoo where youngsters can pet and feed animals. On Madison's south side, **Olbrich Park Botanical Gardens** (3330 Atwood Ave., ☎ 608/246–4550; admission charged) features 14 acres of outdoor rose, herb, and rock gardens and a glass-pyramid conservatory with tropical plants and flowers. The **Greater Madison Convention and Visitors Bureau** (615 E. Washington Ave., 53703, ☎ 608/255–2537 or 800/373–6376) offers information on Madison attractions.

West of Madison is **Blue Mounds,** at the eastern edge of Wisconsin's lead-mining region. **Blue Mound State Park** (1 mi northwest of village, ☎ 608/437–5711) offers glorious vistas from towers on the summit of one of the hills. **Cave of the Mounds** (Cave of the Mounds Rd., ☎ 608/437–3038; admission charged; closed weekdays mid-Nov.–mid-Mar.) is small, but it is filled with diverse and colorful mineral formations.

Nestled in a picturesque valley nearby is **Little Norway** (3576 Hwy. JG North, ☎ 608/437–8211), a restored 1856 Norwegian homestead with its original log buildings and an outstanding collection of Norwegian antiques and pioneer arts and crafts.

Another charming spot in this region is the village of **New Glarus,** founded by Swiss settlers from the canton of Glarus in 1845. It retains its Swiss character in language, food, architecture, and festivities. The **Swiss Historical Village** (612 7th Ave., ☎ 608/527–2317) contains reconstructed and original buildings from early New Glarus and displays that trace Swiss immigration to America.

Frank Lloyd Wright chose the farming community of **Spring Green** on the Wisconsin River for his home, "Taliesin," and his architectural school. Wright's influence is evident in a number of buildings in the village; notice the use of geometric shapes, low flat-roofed profiles, cantilevered projections, and steeplelike spires. Tours of **Taliesin** (3 mi south of Spring Green on Hwy. 23, ☎ 608/588–7900) buildings, designed and built by Wright, include his home and office for nearly 50 years, the 1903 Hillside Home School, galleries, a drafting studio, and a theater.

The extraordinary, multilevel, stone **House on the Rock** (5754 Hwy. 23, ☎ 608/935–3639) stands atop a 60-foot chimney of rock overlooking the Wyoming Valley. It was begun by artist Alex Jordan in the early 1940s and was opened to the public in 1961. The complex now includes re-creations of historic village streets, complete with shops, and extensive collections of dolls, cannons, musical machines, and paperweights.

The renowned **American Players Theater** (County Rte. C and Golf Course Rd., ☎ 608/588–7401) presents Shakespeare and other classics in a beautiful, wooded outdoor amphitheater near the Wisconsin River.

On the western edge of the state, **Prairie du Chien** dates from 1673, when explorers Marquette and Joliet reached the confluence of the Wisconsin and Mississippi rivers 6 mi to the south. It became a flourishing fur market in the late 17th century, and today it is a bustling river community where the steamers *Delta Queen* and *Mississippi Queen* call in summer. The **Villa Louis Mansion** (521 Villa Louis Rd., ☎ 608/326–2721) was built in 1870 by the family of the fur trader Hercules Dousman, who was Wisconsin's first millionaire. It contains one of the finest collections of Victorian decorative arts in the country. The Astor Fur Warehouse on the grounds has exhibits on the fur trade of the upper Mississippi. Nearby is **Wyalusing State Park** (*see* National and State Parks, *above*).

Wisconsin Dells and Baraboo

Getting There

Take I–90W from Milwaukee to Madison, then I–90/94 northwest to the Dells. Baraboo is off U.S. 12 to the south of I–90/94.

What to See and Do

One of the state's foremost natural attractions is the **Wisconsin Dells,** nearly 15 mi of soaring, eroded rock formations created over thousands of years as the Wisconsin River cut into the soft limestone. The two small communities encompassed by the Dells—Wisconsin Dells and Lake Delton, with a combined population of less than 4,000—draw nearly 2 million visitors annually to frolic in the water parks, play miniature golf, and enjoy the rides, shows, and other man-made attractions that today nearly overshadow the scenic wonders.

You can view the river and its spectacular rock formations on the cruise boats of **Dells Boat Tours** (☎ 608/254–8555) or aboard World War II amphibious vehicles that travel both land and water at **Dells Ducks** (☎ 608/254–6080) or **Original Wisconsin Ducks** (☎ 608/254–8751). **Noah's Ark** (☎ 608/254–6351), **Family Land** (☎ 608/254–7766), and **Riverview Park and Waterworld** (☎ 608/254–2608) offer a thrilling variety of water slides, wave pools, inner-tube and raft rides, and a host of other diversions. The notorious Confederate spy Belle Boyd, who died here while on a speaking tour in 1910, is buried in **Spring Grove Cemetery.**

When you need a break from the nonstop action, **Mirror Lake State Park** (just south of the Dells off U.S. 12, ☎ 608/254–2333) and **Rocky Arbor State Park** (2 mi north off U.S. 12, ☎ 608/254–8001) offer camping, hiking, scenery, and solitude. For more information, contact the **Wisconsin Dells Visitor and Convention Bureau** (701 Superior St., Wisconsin Dells 53965, ☎ 608/254–4636 or 800/223–3557).

South of Wisconsin Dells is **Baraboo,** where a fur-trading post run by a Frenchman named Baribault stood in the early 19th century. It is best known as the place where the five Ringling brothers began their circus careers in 1882 and where the Ringling Brothers Circus quartered in winter from 1884 to 1912. In the quarters now is **Circus World Museum** (426 Water St., ☎ 608/356–8341; admission charged; closed mid-Sept.–Apr.), a State Historical Society site that preserves the history of the more than 100 circuses that began in Wisconsin. Along with an outstanding collection of antique circus wagons, the museum presents big-top performances featuring circus stars of today. **Baraboo Chamber of Commerce** (124 2nd St., 53913, ☎ 608/356–8333 or 800/227–2266) supplies information on the town.

Door County

Getting There

Take I–43N from Milwaukee, Rte. 310E to Two Rivers, then Rte. 42N.

What to See and Do

Jutting out from the Wisconsin mainland like the thumb on a mitten, the 70-mi-long **Door County Peninsula** is bordered by the waters of Lake Michigan and Green Bay. It was named for the Porte des Morts (Door of Death), a treacherous strait separating the peninsula from nearby offshore islands. Scores of ships have come to grief in Door County waters, and even today large Great Lakes freighters often slip through the Door to seek shelter in the lee of the islands during Lake Michigan's autumn storms. Soil conditions and climate make the peninsula ideal for cherry production, and its orchards produce as much as 20 million pounds of fruit each year. The peninsula is carpeted in blossoms when the trees bloom in late May.

A visit to the peninsula can include stops at a half dozen charming lakeshore towns, each with its own flavor. First-time visitors often make a circle tour via Rtes. 57 and 42. The Lake Michigan side of the peninsula is somewhat less settled and the landscape rougher. The peninsula's rugged beauty attracts large numbers of artists, whose works are shown in studios, galleries, and interesting shops in all the villages.

Sturgeon Bay, the peninsula's chief community and a busy shipbuilding port, sits on a partially man-made ship canal connecting the waters of Lake Michigan and Green Bay. Here, the **Door County Maritime Museum** (2nd Ave. and Sunset Park, ☏ 414/743–5958) has displays on local shipbuilding and commercial fishing, and the **Door County Historical Museum** (18 N. 4th Ave., ☏ 414/743–5809) exhibits Native American relics and items from pioneer days.

Beside Rte. 57 along the peninsula's Lake Michigan side, you can see the rocky shoreline and sea caves at **Cave Point County Park** (no ☏), near Valmy. Just north of **Jacksonport,** you'll cross the 45th parallel, halfway between the equator and the North Pole.

Northport, at the tip of the peninsula, is the port of departure for the daily car ferries to **Washington Island,** 6 mi offshore; passenger ferries leave from nearby **Gills Rock.** The island's 600 inhabitants celebrate their heritage with an annual Scandinavian festival in August. Narrated tram tours aboard the Washington Island **Cherry Train** (☏ 414/847–2135) or the **Viking Tour Train** (☏ 414/854–2972) leave from the ferry dock. The island has nearly 100 mi of roads and is popular with bicyclists. You may take your own bicycle on the ferry or rent one from the ferry line at Gills Rock. To really get away from it all, take the ferry from Washington Island to remote **Rock Island State Park** (☏ 414/847–2235), a wilderness area permitting only hiking and backpack camping.

Back on the mainland, on the Green Bay side of the peninsula, the villages evoke New England in atmosphere and charm and provide exceptional views of Green Bay, where sunsets can be breathtaking. **Fish Creek** is home to the **Peninsula Players Theater** (☏ 414/868–3287), called America's oldest professional resident summer theater. Here, too, is beautiful **Peninsula State Park** (☏ 414/868–3258), which offers hiking and bicycling.

No visit to Door County would be complete without sampling the region's famed fish boil, which originated more than 100 years ago. It is a simple but delicious meal that has reached legendary status in the region. A huge caldron of water is brought to a boil over a wood fire. A basket of red potatoes is then cooked in the caldron, followed by a basket of fresh local whitefish steaks. At the moment the fish is cooked to perfection, kerosene is dumped on the fire, and the flames shoot high in the air, causing the caldron to boil over, expelling most of the fish oils and fat. The steaming whitefish is then served with melted butter, potatoes, coleslaw, and another favorite, Door County cherry pie. The **Door County Chamber of Commerce** (Box 406, Sturgeon Bay 54235-0406, ☏ 414/743–4456 or 800/527–3529) provides information on county attractions.

Bayfield and the Apostle Islands

Getting There

Take I–94W from Milwaukee to Portage, U.S. 51N to Hurley, U.S. 2W to Ashland, and then Rte. 13N to Bayfield.

What to See and Do

The commercial fishing village of Bayfield, population 700, is the gateway to the **Apostle Islands National Lakeshore,** which comprises 21 of Lake Superior's 22 Apostle Islands and a segment of mainland near Bayfield. Named by French missionaries, who mistakenly thought the islands numbered 12, the Apostles encompass 42,000 acres spread over 600 sq mi of Lake Superior. Primitive camping and hiking are allowed on most of the islands. The **Little Sand Bay Visitor Center** (13 mi north of Bayfield on Rte. 13, ☎ 715/779–3459) has exhibits and daily guided tours of a former commercial fishing operation in summer. Sailing among the islands is a favorite pastime, as is charter boat fishing for salmon. **Paragon Charters** (☎ 715/779–5634), **Catchun-Sun Charter Co.** (☎ 715/779–3111), and **Superior Charters, Inc.** (☎ 715/779–5124 or 800/772–5124), all out of Bayfield, offer captained sailboat charters among the islands. For experienced sailors, **Superior Charters, Inc.** and **Sailboats, Inc.** (☎ 800/772–5124) offer bareboat sailboat charters. **Apostle Islands Cruise Service** (City Dock, Bayfield, ☎ 715/779–3925 or 800/323–7619) gives daily sightseeing tours of the islands, weather permitting. Camper shuttle service to many of the islands is also available. **Stockton Island,** the largest island in the national lakeshore, has a visitor center (open daily, Memorial Day–Labor Day) with a park naturalist on duty; there are natural and cultural history exhibits. Guided tours of the **Raspberry Island Lighthouse** buildings and gardens are offered, as are guided tours of historic **Manitou Island Fish Camp,** on Manitou Island. Lakeshore headquarters (Washington Ave. and 4th St., Box 4, Bayfield 54814, ☎ 715/779–3397) offers publications, exhibits, and a movie about the islands.

In **Bayfield** itself is **Booth Cooperage** (1 Washington Ave., ☎ 715/779–3400)—Wisconsin's only working barrel factory and museum—where you can watch local coopers ply their trade. At **Lake Superior Big Top Chautauqua** (3 mi south of Bayfield on Rte. 13, ☎ 715/373–5851), concerts, plays, lectures, and original historical musicals are performed under canvas in the spirit of old-time tent shows. **Bayfield Chamber of Commerce** (Box 138, 54814, ☎ 715/779–3335 or 800/447–4094) provides information on other area attractions.

Bayfield is also the embarkation point to **Madeline Island,** where the village of **La Pointe** was established as a French trading post in the early 17th century, followed in 1793 by a permanent settlement. The island is reached via the car- and passenger-carrying **Madeline Island Ferry** (Washington Ave., ☎ 715/747–2051). The **Madeline Island Historical Museum** (☎ 715/747–2415), on the site of a former fur trading post, houses exhibits on island history. Narrated island tours are given by **Madeline Island Bus Tours** (Ferry Dock, La Pointe, ☎ 715/747–2051; mid-June–Labor Day). If you've a yen for the outdoors, consider renting a bicycle from **Madeline Island Bike Rentals** (☎ 715/747–2801) and touring the island on your own. **Big Bay State Park** (☎ 715/747–6425) has camping, a long sandy beach, picnic areas, and hiking and nature trails.

8 The Great Plains

By Suzanne De Galan

THE NAME GREAT PLAINS evokes an image of flat farmland stretching to the horizon, unbroken save for the occasional cluster of buildings marking a town or farmstead. Those who go there, however, know that the limitless terrain destroys as many preconceived images as it confirms. This seemingly uniform landscape actually encompasses the towering buttes that loom over the horizons of western South Dakota and the fertile river valleys that crisscross the eastern boundaries of Missouri and Kansas. Its cultural legacy owes as much to such artists as Louis Sullivan and Grant Wood as it does to the cowboy and Indian artifacts that stud the region. And although European settlement came late here, St. Louis existed more than a decade before the Declaration of Independence was signed; Coronado had explored Kansas two centuries before that.

The area that now comprises the states of Iowa, Missouri, Oklahoma, Kansas, Nebraska, and North and South Dakota saw its greatest European settlement in the 19th century. Railroad companies lured thousands of immigrants with large, inexpensive parcels of land; towns sprang up along rail lines and pioneer trails; and Native Americans were inexorably forced into smaller and smaller territories. The sod-breaking plow and hardy winter wheat helped transform the long- and short-grass prairies of the high plains into America's breadbasket. In the remaining grasslands, cattle fed where bison once reigned.

Life on the Great Plains in the 19th century was harsh and sometimes violent, but it's a life that today's residents love to re-create. Countless historical theme parks and Old West towns dot the region, along with abundant archaeological and Civil War battle sites, U.S. Army forts, pioneer trail markers, and museums of Native American and pioneer lore. Great Plains folk think nothing of journeying 100 mi to see a building covered with thousands of bushels of corn, or an arrangement of wrecked cars made to resemble the monoliths of Stonehenge. This tendency achieves its ultimate expression in Mt. Rushmore, where the 60-ft faces of four U.S. presidents have been carved into a wall of South Dakota granite.

But alongside these landmarks and oddities lies another Great Plains. To know it, you must drive its hundreds of miles of roads bisecting fields of grain, or leave the highway for one of its small towns, just to walk the Main Street and see the serene, mellow old houses. Here, somewhere between myth and reality, the true spirit of this region is revealed.

Tour Groups

Gadabout Tours (700 E. Tahquitz Canyon Way, Palm Springs, CA 92262, ☎ 619/325–5556) offers 10-day tours of the Missouri and Arkansas Ozarks that include stops in Kansas City, Branson, and Eureka Springs; 10- and 15-day cruises of the Mississippi River that wind past Iowa and Missouri towns en route to New Orleans; and 8-day tours of South Dakota's Badlands and Black Hills areas. **Maupintour** (Box 807, Lawrence, KS 66044, ☎ 913/843–1211 or 800/255–4266) features a 14-day Oregon Trail tour beginning in Kansas City and ending in Portland, Oregon, with a 1-day journey by covered wagon and tours that include Badlands National Park and Mount Rushmore National Memorial in South Dakota, and Yellowstone National Park in Wyoming.

When to Go

The traditional tourist season for most of the Great Plains is **summer,** despite the soaring temperatures and high humidity that are common throughout the region. In fact, many tourist attractions, particularly in North and South Dakota, are open only during June, July, and August. Northern states, such as the Dakotas and Nebraska, are generally cooler than southern states, with temperature averages in the 80s rather than the 90s, but you should be prepared for anything in this variable region. **Winter** weather is equally extreme, especially in Nebraska and the Dakotas, where subzero temperatures and snowy conditions are not uncommon. South Dakota offers excellent cross-country skiing and snowmobiling, but again, make sure hotels and restaurants are open. **Spring** and **fall** can be excellent times to visit, with temperatures moderate (anywhere from 40°F to 70°F) and crowds at a minimum. Fall in the Ozarks or in such places as the eastern border of Iowa has the added attraction of colorful foliage, usually in mid- to late October.

Festivals and Seasonal Events

May: At the **Oklahoma Cattlemen's Association Range Round-up** in **Guthrie,** cowhands compete in saddle bronc riding, wild-cow roping, and other contests. ☎ *405/282–3004.*

Mid-June: The **Oklahoma Mozart International Festival** features concerts, barbecues, and powwows celebrating the composer and local culture in **Bartlesville.** ☎ *918/336–9900.*

Mid-June: Nebraskaland Days is a Western hootenanny in **North Platte** that's highlighted by the Buffalo Bill Rodeo. ☎ *308/532–7939.*

Mid-June: The Red Earth Native American Cultural Festival in **Oklahoma City** attracts hundreds of Native American dancers from the United States and Canada for competitions and performances. ☎ *405/427–5228.*

July: Kansas City Blues & Jazz Festival features performances by nationally known blues and jazz artists on three stages. ☎ *800/530–5266.*

July–Aug.: Dodge City (KS) Roundup Rodeo is a five-day rodeo during the city's Dodge City Days festival. ☎ *316/225–2244.*

July 4: National Tom Sawyer Days in Mark Twain's hometown of **Hannibal, Missouri,** is a weekend's worth of activities, including a fence-painting contest. ☎ *314/221–2477.*

Early July: Black Hills and Northern Plains Indian Powwow and Exposition is the best known of many powwows held annually across **South Dakota.** ☎ *605/394–4115.*

Aug.: Iowa State Fair in **Des Moines** is a short course in farm machinery, animals, crops, and crafts; less bucolically minded visitors can enjoy carnival rides and musical entertainment. ☎ *515/262–3111.*

Early Aug.: Days of '76 in **Deadwood, South Dakota,** celebrates the town's wild and woolly gold-rush days with a parade, a rodeo, and other activities. ☎ *605/578–1876.*

Mid-Aug.: Sturgis (SD) Motorcycle Classic draws more than 175,000 bike buffs from around the country each year. ☎ *605/347–2556.*

Mid-Aug.: Pioneer Days at Bonanzaville USA transform the pioneer village of **West Fargo, North Dakota,** into a living museum for two days, with costumed shopkeepers, tradespeople, and townspeople. ☎ *701/282–2822.*

CANADA
Lake Superior
Lake Michigan
MONTANA
NORTH DAKOTA
MINNESOTA
WISCONSIN
SOUTH DAKOTA
WYOMING
IOWA
NEBRASKA
Williston
Minot
Devils Lake
Grand Forks
THEODORE ROOSEVELT NAT'L PARK
Lake Sakakawea
Carrington
Washburn
Medora
Dickinson
Mandan
Bismarck
Jamestown
Fargo
Bowman
Ellendale
STANDING ROCK INDIAN RES.
SISSETON INDIAN RES.
Buffalo
Mobridge
Aberdeen
CHEYENNE RIVER INDIAN RES.
Faith
Millbank
Watertown
Belle Fourche
Spearfish
Rapid City
Lake Oahe
Pierre
Huron
Brookings
Mount Rushmore
Wall
BLACK HILLS NAT'L FOR.
BADLANDS NAT'L PARK
Mitchell
Sioux Falls
Hot Springs
PINE RIDGE INDIAN RESERVATION
ROSEBUD INDIAN RES.
Winner
Missouri River
Chadron
Gordon
Valentine
Yankton
Vermillion
O'Neill
Sioux City
Alliance
Scottsbluff
North Platte
Bridgeport
Norfolk
Fremont
St. Paul
Minneapolis
Mississippi River
Sheldon
Spencer
Mason City
Marquette
Dubuque
Waterloo
Cedar Rapids
Marshall-town
Des Moines
Iowa City
Clinton
Davenport
Chicago

KEY
Amtrak Lines
0
150 miles
0
225 km
N
COLORADO
KANSAS
MISSOURI
ILLINOIS
OKLAHOMA
ARKANSAS
TENNESSEE
NEW MEXICO
TEXAS
THE OZARKS
OSAGE INDIAN RES.
Lake McConaughy
Ogallala
North Platte
Platte Riv
Kearney
Grand Island
Hastings
McCook
Denver
Fremont
Omaha
Council Bluffs
Lincoln
Nebraska City
Auburn
Rock Port
Beatrice
Missouri Riv
St. Joseph
Osceola
Ottumwa
Davenport
Burlington
Keokuk
Kirksville
Macon
Hannibal
Waconda Lake
Mankato
Goodland
Oakley
Russell
Scott City
Garden City
Great Bend
Hutchinson
Dodge City
Wichita
Medicine Lodge
Liberal
Guymon
Manhattan
Topeka
Lawrence
Kansas City
Independence
Sedalia
Columbia
Jefferson City
St. Charles
Alton
St. Louis
Emporia
Florence
El Dorado
Clinton
Lake of the Ozarks
Waynesville
Cape Girardeau
Coffeyville
Joplin
Springfield
Van Buren
West Plains
Poplar Bluff
Ponca City
Bartlesville
Table Rock Lake
Enid
Woodward
Tulsa
Muskogee
Clinton
Elk City
Oklahoma City
Shawnee
Amarillo
Altus
Lawton
Duncan
McAllister
Atoka
Ardmore
Hugo
Marietta

Early Sept.: United Tribes International Powwow brings Native Americans from around the country to **Bismarck, North Dakota,** to exhibit art, hold dance competitions, and celebrate cultural ties. ☎ *701/255–3285.*

Oct.: Octoberfest in **Hermann, Missouri,** draws thousands of people each weekend to celebrate this Missouri River town's German and wine-making heritage. ☎ *314/486–2744.*

Early Oct.: Norsk Hostfest in **Minot, North Dakota,** brings in crowds from throughout the region to sample Scandinavian foods, dancing, and costumes. ☎ *701/852–2368.*

Nov.: The **American Royal Livestock, Horse Show and Rodeo** is an annual celebration of **Kansas City**'s Wild West days. ☎ *816/221–5242 or 800/767–7700.*

Getting Around the Great Plains

By Plane

Major domestic carriers serve the region, including American, Continental, Delta, Northwest, United, and USAir. The largest airports are, in Missouri, **Lambert–St. Louis International Airport** (☎ 314/426–8000) and **Kansas City International Airport** (☎ 816/243–5237); in Iowa, **Des Moines International Airport** (☎ 515/256–5050); in Oklahoma, **Will Rogers World Airport** (☎ 405/681–5311) and **Tulsa International Airport** (☎ 918/838–5000); and in South Dakota, **Sioux Falls Regional Airport** (☎ 605/336–0762).

By Car

Three interstates meet at Oklahoma City: I–40, running east–west through Oklahoma; I–44, which proceeds northeast from Oklahoma City to Tulsa, Oklahoma, and through Missouri to St. Louis; and I–35, one of two major north–south arteries in the Great Plains. From Oklahoma City, I–35 proceeds north through Wichita, Kansas, Kansas City, and Des Moines. Another north–south route is I–29, which begins in Kansas City and runs along the eastern borders of Nebraska, South Dakota, and North Dakota, passing through Omaha, Sioux Falls, Fargo, and Grand Forks. Major east–west arteries are I–94 in North Dakota, which passes through Medora, the Bismarck/Mandan area, and Fargo; I–90 in South Dakota, running from Rapid City to Sioux Falls; I–80 through Nebraska and Iowa, which links North Platte, Lincoln, and Omaha with Des Moines and Iowa City; and I–70, which bisects Missouri and Kansas and links St. Louis with Kansas City and points west. Roads are generally in good condition throughout the region.

By Train

Amtrak (☎ 800/872–7245) provides some service through the Great Plains but not necessarily to the major cities, and South Dakota and Oklahoma are not served at all.

By Bus

The major intercity carrier is **Greyhound Lines** (☎ 800/231–2222). In addition, **Jefferson Lines** (☎ 612/332–8745) serves some cities in Kansas, Missouri, Iowa, and Oklahoma. **Jackrabbit Lines** (☎ 605/348–3300) serves Wall and Rapid City in western South Dakota. Many of the Greyhound stops in this region are small towns that have no ticket booth; call to check whether you must purchase your ticket in advance.

IOWA

By Marcia Andrews

Updated by Diana Lambdin Meyer

Capital	Des Moines
Population	2,216,000
Motto	Our Liberties We Prize and Our Rights We Will Maintain
State Bird	Eastern goldfinch
State Flower	Wild rose

Visitor Information

The Division of Tourism (Iowa Dept. of Economic Development, 200 E. Grand Ave., Des Moines 50309, ☎ 515/242–4705 or 800/345–4692) has 18 welcome centers along I–35 and I–80 and in towns throughout the state. For regional tourist information, call or write **Eastern Iowa Tourism Association** (116 E. 4th St., Box 485, Vinton 52349, ☎ 319/472–5135 or 800/891–3482), **Central Iowa Tourism Region** (113 1st Ave. W, Newton 50208, ☎ 515/792–7451 or 800/285–5842), and **Western Iowa Tourism Region** (502 Coolbaugh St., Red Oak 51566, ☎ 712/623–4232).

Scenic Drives

Perhaps Iowa's most beautiful scenic drive is the series of roads that takes you south along the high bluffs and verdant banks of the Mississippi River on the state's eastern border (*see* Dubuque and the Great River Road, *below*). In southeast Iowa, **Rte. 5** from Des Moines to Lake Rathbun, near Centerville, makes a nice detour for those heading south on I–35; to return to the interstate, take **Rte. 2W** from Centerville for about 50 mi.

National and State Parks

National Parks

Effigy Mounds National Monument (*see* Exploring Dubuque and the Great River Road, *below*) offers scenic hiking trails along prehistoric burial mounds. Iowa has four federal reservoir areas around large man-made lakes: **Coralville Lake** (2850 Prairie du Chien Rd. NE, Iowa City 52240, ☎ 319/338–3543), **Lake Rathbun** (Rte. 3, Centerville 52544, ☎ 515/647–2464), **Lake Red Rock** (R.R. 3, Box 149A, Knoxville 50138-9522, ☎ 515/828–7522), and **Saylorville Lake** (5600 N.W. 78th Ave., Johnston 50131, ☎ 515/276–0433 or 515/276–4656).

State Parks

Iowa's 76 state parks include 5,700 campsites, many of them with shower facilities and electrical hookups. Some well-developed parks with modern campsites, cabins, lodge rentals, and boat rentals are **Clear Lake** (☎ 515/357–4212), near Mason City; **George Wyth Memorial** (☎ 319/232–5505), near Waterloo; **Lacey-Keosauqua** (☎ 319/293–3502), near Keosauqua; and **Lake of Three Fires** (☎ 712/523–2700), near Bedford. Virgin prairie areas, part of the state park system but lacking facilities, include **Cayler Prairie,** near the Great Lakes area in northwest Iowa; **Hayden Prairie,** near the Minnesota border in the northeastern corner of the state; **Kaslow Prairie,** about 90 mi northwest of Des Moines; and **Sheeder Prairie,** about 50 mi west of Des Moines. Contact the **Department of Natural Resources** (☎ 515/281–5145) for more information.

DES MOINES

Viewed from an airplane or a car topping a hill, the capital of Iowa is a cluster of office towers that seem to pop out of a green corduroy landscape. Downtown straddles the *V* of two rivers; the '80s-built skyline faces granite government buildings and a classic gold-domed capitol across four bridges. Major businesses in this relatively hassle-free city of nearly 400,000 residents include insurance, finance, government, publishing, and agribusiness. Although hardly a glittering metropolis—the city plays annual host to a horde of farmers and agriculture buffs at the Iowa State Fair—neither is Des Moines a village. The U.S. presidential race starts here with the Iowa Caucuses, and every cultural wave breaks on Des Moines's shores—eventually.

Tourist Information

Information centers are in the **airport** lobby (☎ 515/287–4396) and in the **skywalk** above the corner of 6th and Locust streets downtown (☎ 515/286–4960).

Arriving and Departing

By Plane

Des Moines International Airport (☎ 515/256–5050), about 3 mi south of downtown, has scheduled service by major domestic airlines. The drive into town takes about 10 minutes in normal traffic. Cab fare, including tip, is less than $10. Hotel shuttles serve the route, and major car-rental companies are located in the airport.

By Car

I–80, the major east–west thoroughfare through the state, and I–35, Iowa's main north–south route, intersect northwest of Des Moines and link with I–235, which runs across the north part of town.

By Bus

Greyhound Lines (☎ 800/231–2222) and **Jefferson** (☎ 515/283–0074) share a terminal at Keosauqua Way and 12th Street.

Getting Around Des Moines

Streets in both the city and suburban Urbandale and West Des Moines are laid out in a grid, which makes getting around fairly easy, but a car is essential, as attractions are scattered about the city and suburbs. Downtown is compact enough to explore in comfortable shoes.

Exploring Des Moines

Downtown

Start from the **capitol complex** (E. 9th St. and Grand Ave., ☎ 515/281–5591) on the east bank of the Des Moines River. There you can see the elaborate murals in the rotunda of the capitol building and climb into the dome, covered in 22-karat gold leaf. Nearby, the **Botanical Center** (909 E. River Dr., ☎ 515/242–2934; admission charged) has flower exhibits and a three-story, dome-topped jungle. The **State Historical Building of Iowa** (600 E. Locust St., ☎ 515/281–5111), one block west of the capitol, shakes off any dusty-old-stuff image with its postmodern design, abstract sculpture of neon and glass, and striking fountain display. The building houses the state archives, library, and museum.

Follow Locust Street west and cross over to the west side of the Des Moines River, where some of the city's most interesting historic buildings can be found. Self-guided walking tours of the **Court Avenue District,** which contains a number of restored 19th-century warehouses and other commercial buildings, and the **Sherman Hill Historic District,** with impressive Victorian houses, are detailed in brochures from **Downtown Des Moines, Inc.** (Suite 100B, 601 Locust St., ☎ 515/245–3880). Many of the restored buildings along Court Avenue now house shops and restaurants; the area has become a popular entertainment district.

Outside the City

Living History Farms, a 600-acre open-air museum a few miles northwest of Des Moines, is well worth a half-day's exploration. The farms are a trip back in time through the sights, sounds, and smells of an 18th-century Iowa camp, two working farms of 1850 and 1900, and an 1875 town. *2600 N.W. 111th St., Urbandale, ☎ 515/278–2400. Admission charged. Closed Nov.–Apr.; call for special events in winter.*

Shopping

Valley Junction (☎ 515/223–3286), six square blocks 5 mi west of downtown, has a mix of antiques stores and contemporary shops selling country furnishings, collectibles, and Iowa souvenirs.

Dining

Des Moines's staple fare is Italian, followed closely by Chinese food, although lately there has been a trend toward more exotic cuisines, such as Thai, Indian, and Middle Eastern. Downtown, sample Court Avenue's lineup of pubs and Italian, Tex-Mex, and Cajun places. For price ranges, see Chart 1 (B) in On the Road with Fodor's.

$$$ ★ **Anna's.** In the Savery Hotel downtown, Anna's features large chandeliers, an elevated bar, and a wall of wine bottles. The menu includes prime rib and lightened versions of Continental dishes. *401 Locust St., ☎ 515/244–2151. AE, MC, V. No lunch.*

$$$ **8th Street Seafood Bar and Grill.** Lighted by skylights and flanked by a busy bar, the raised dining area seats a stylish crowd. Seafood is the draw, cooked simply and well. *1261 8th St., West Des Moines, ☎ 515/223–8808. AE, DC, MC, V. No lunch.*

$$$ **Metz Continental Cuisine.** This elegant restaurant in the Homestead Building downtown offers an upper-level bar and an intimate lower-level dining area. Exquisite entrées, such as *gibier à la Metz* (stuffed baked quail and grilled duck breast), and a sinful dessert cart highlight the menu. *303 Locust St., ☎ 515/246–1656. AE, DC, MC, V. Closed Sun.*

$$ **Cafe Su.** Dim sum appetizers are the specialty at this chic restaurant in the popular Valley Junction shopping area in West Des Moines. Contemporary decor complements the traditional Chinese cuisine. *225 5th St., ☎ 515/274–5102. AE, D, DC, MC, V. Closed Sun.*

$$ **The Greenbrier.** In the northern suburb of Johnston, this restaurant offers a large menu mixing elegant and basic fare with such choices as Iowa pork chops, rack of lamb, and fish. Frosted glass and dark wood accent the three dining rooms and bar. *5810 Merle Hay Rd., Johnston, ☎ 515/253–0124. No reservations. AE, D, MC, V. Closed Sun.*

$$ **Jesse's Embers.** Just west of downtown, Jesse's is prized for grilled prime steaks. Whether it's ribs, chicken, or seafood, top ingredients make the kitchen's reputation. The room is small, plain, and crowded with neighborhood people waiting in the bar, but service is swift. *3301 Ingersoll Ave., ☎ 515/255–6011. AE, MC, V.*

$ **Des Moines Art Center Restaurant.** For an elegant interlude with light fare, this solarium with sculpture and a pool is unique. Lunches feature soups, salads, sandwiches, and desserts. *4700 Grand Ave., ☎*

515/277–4405. MC, V. Closed Sun.–Mon. No dinner, except Thurs. by reservation.

$ ★ **Drake Diner.** The sharp, New Age look of chrome and neon adds fun to a traditional soup, salad, and sandwich menu. Students from nearby Drake University mix with older patrons. *1111 25th St., ☎ 515/277–1111. AE, D, DC, MC, V.*

$ **El Patio.** Just west of downtown, this converted bungalow filled with southwestern artifacts seats diners in colorful rooms, a porch, and a covered patio. More Tex than Mex, the food is still a cut above the fare found at chain-type Mexican restaurants. *611 37th St., ☎ 515/274–2303. AE, MC, V. No lunch.*

$ ★ **New Delhi Palace.** Classic aromatic dishes range from zingy lamb vindaloo to mild tandoori chicken; a good vegetarian choice is *palak aloo,* a savory blend of spinach and potatoes. The restaurant's peach-colored walls are hung with Indian paintings, and seating is at booths and tables with armchairs. *Parkwood Plaza, 86th and Douglas Sts., Urbandale, ☎ 515/278–2929. AE, MC, V.*

Lodging

You'll find little in the way of historic or lavish hotels here; most establishments cater to business travelers and offer modern amenities and convenient locations. Downtown renovations or newer suburban hotels dominate, with low-cost motels clustered near interstate exits and a suburban bed-and-breakfast or two (**Iowa Bed and Breakfast Innkeepers' Association,** 9001 Hickman Rd., Suite 2B, Des Moines 50322, ☎ 800/888–4667) for variety. For price ranges, see Chart 2 (B) in On the Road with Fodor's.

$$$ **Des Moines Marriott.** The downtown location on the skywalk is a plus. Rooms are plush contemporary, with unobstructed views of the city from the higher floors. The restaurant here, Quenelle's, serves rich Continental fare. *700 Grand Ave., 50309, ☎ 515/245–5500, FAX 515/245–5567. 415 rooms. Facilities: 2 restaurants, lounge, health club, pool. AE, D, MC, V.*

$$$ ★ **Embassy Suites Hotel on the River.** Across the bridge from Court Avenue attractions, this hotel has seven balconies ringing an atrium with a waterfall. Beyond this, the hotel lacks flash, but it makes up for it with free breakfasts and lots of attentive service. *101 E. Locust St., 50309, ☎ 515/244–1700, FAX 515/244–2537. 234 suites. Facilities: restaurant, 2 lounges, health club, pool, convention center. AE, MC, V.*

$$$ **Holiday Inn University Park.** On the west edge of town, the hotel's 10-story, plant-filled atrium and convention facilities draw business groups and local events. Rooms are big, with plush contemporary furnishings. *1800 50th St., West Des Moines 50265, ☎ 515/223–1800, FAX 515/223–0894. 228 rooms, 60 suites. Facilities: 2 restaurants, 2 lounges, health club, pool. AE, D, MC, V.*

$$ ★ **The Drake Inn.** Next to Drake University, this attractive, low-rise hotel has airy rooms. *1140 24th St., 50311, ☎ 515/255–4000 or 800/252–7838, FAX 515/255–1192. 52 rooms. Facilities: 2 meeting rooms. AE, D, MC, V.*

$$ **Holiday Inn Downtown.** Just north of downtown, the hotel has fresh but ordinary rooms and a few suites with whirlpool baths. *1050 6th Ave., 50314, ☎ 515/283–0151, FAX 515/283–0151. 245 rooms. Facilities: restaurant, lounge, pool. AE, D, MC, V.*

$$ **Valley West Inn.** Next to West Des Moines's big mall, the three-story inn has simply furnished rooms decorated in rosy fabrics and blond woods. *3535 Westown Pkwy., West Des Moines 50265, ☎ 515/225–*

2524 or 800/833–6755, FAX 515/225–9058. 136 rooms. Facilities: restaurant, lounge, meeting rooms, pool, whirlpool. AE, D, MC, V.

$ **Airport Comfort Inn.** Two blocks from the airport, the hotel is convenient if not quiet. The three-story building has plain rooms, big beds, and morning coffee in the lobby. *5231 Fleur Dr., 50321, ☎ 515/287–3434 or 800/221–2222. 50 rooms. Facilities: pool. AE, MC, V.*

$ ★ **Heartland Inn.** On the northeast edge of Des Moines, next to an amusement complex, this three-story building is part of a new Iowa chain. Decor is rustic. *5000 N.E. 56th St., Altoona 50009, ☎ 515/967–2400 or 800/334–3277. 87 rooms. Facilities: pool, spa, miniature golf in season. AE, D, MC, V.*

EAST-CENTRAL IOWA

This region east of Des Moines is a mix of historic towns, trim farmsteads, and forested river valleys. Cedar Rapids is the largest town in the area; Iowa City, about 25 mi south, is the home of the University of Iowa. The area is perhaps best known to tourists for the Amana colonies, a cluster of seven villages west of Iowa City that were founded in the 19th century as a utopian religious community.

Tourist Information

Amana colonies: Welcome Center (U.S. 151 and Rte. 220, Box 303, Amana 52203, ☎ 319/622–6262 or 800/245–5465), with information and a lodging reservation service. **Cedar Rapids Area:** Convention and Visitors Bureau (119 1st Ave. SE, 52401, ☎ 319/622–3828 or 800/735–5557). **Iowa City/Coralville:** Visitors Bureau (325 E. Washington St., Iowa City 52240, ☎ 319/337–6592).

Getting There

By Plane

The **Cedar Rapids/Iowa City Municipal Airport** (☎ 319/362–8336), 7 mi south of Cedar Rapids and just off I–380, is served by American Eagle, Delta, USAir, TWA, Northwest/Northwest Airlink, and United.

By Car

I–80, the state's major east–west thoroughfare, runs from Des Moines east to Iowa City. From Iowa City, I–380N passes Lake Macbride on the way to Cedar Rapids. From Cedar Rapids, U.S. 151 meanders southwest for about 25 mi through a rural farmscape to Middle Amana, the start of the cluster of Amana colonies.

Exploring East-Central Iowa

Start your tour at the southwestern point of the region's roughly triangular shape, at the **Amana colonies,** encompassing the seven villages of Amana (where the **welcome center** is located; *see* Tourist Information, *above*), West Amana, South Amana, High Amana, East Amana, Middle Amana, and Homestead. Although the descendants of the German/Swiss immigrants who founded the community voted to end its communal way of life in 1932, much of this life is preserved here. A 25-mi circuit of the area takes in restored buildings, such as barn and kitchen museums and a schoolhouse. Crafts hunters favor the shopping opportunities here, where members of the Amana community still manufacture prized woolen goods, furniture, wine, cheese, and more.

North of the Amanas on U.S. 151 is **Cedar Rapids.** In the 19th and early 20th centuries, waves of Czechoslovakian immigrants settled in

Eastern Iowa

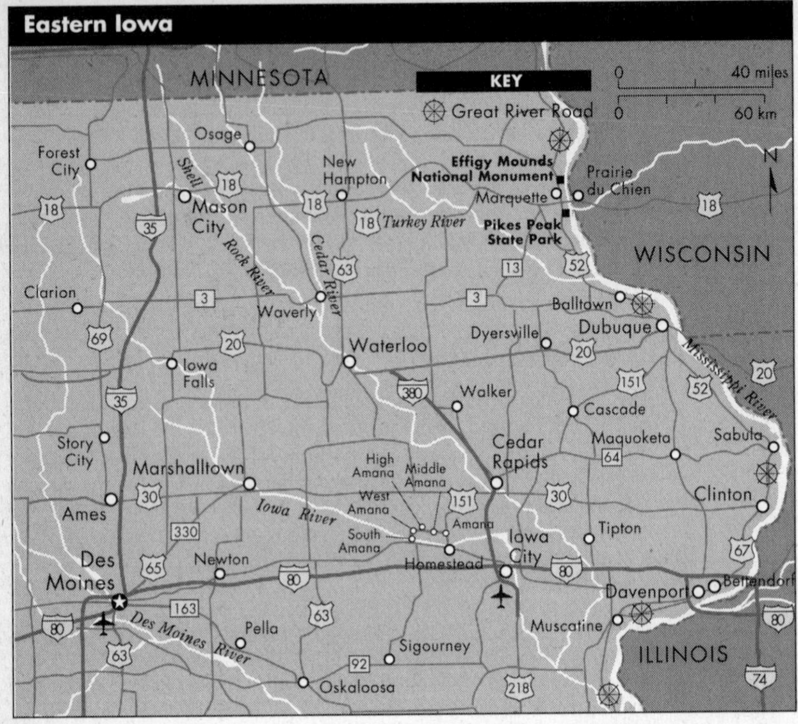

this manufacturing town; a sampling of their heritage is on view at the **Czech Village, Museum and Immigrant Home** (10–119 16th Ave. SW, ☎ 319/362–8500; admission charged; closed Sun.). The city also boasts the world's largest permanent collection of paintings by renowned native son Grant Wood at its **Museum of Art** (410 3rd Ave. SE, ☎ 319/366–7503).

South of here on I–380 is **Iowa City,** where the **University of Iowa's** hilly campus on the Iowa River is dominated by its **old capitol** (for tours, ☎ 319/335–0548), which served as the seat of state government until the capital was moved to Des Moines in the mid-19th century. Today the Greek Revival building is part of the university.

West Branch, just west of Iowa City on I–80, is home to the **Herbert Hoover Presidential Library and Birthplace** (Parkside Dr. and Main St., ☎ 319/643–2541 or 319/643–5301; admission charged). Here you can see the simple cottage where the future president was born to Quaker parents in 1874; the house contains period furnishings, many of them original.

Shopping

The commercial hub of Amana shopping is the eight-block center of Amana, just east of the welcome center. The **Woolen Mill Salesroom** (800 48th Ave., ☎ 319/622–3432) sells all manner of woolens, from clothing for men, women, and kids, to blankets; you can take a self-guided tour of the mill. On weekdays at the **Furniture and Clock Shop** (724 48th Ave., ☎ 319/622–3291), you can watch craftspeople making the products sold here. The **Old Fashioned High Amana Store** (☎ 319/622–3797), 2 mi west of the welcome center, is fragrant, creaky, and full of old-timey gifts. A block away, the **Amana Arts Guild Cen-**

ter (☎ 319/622–3678) sells high-quality quilts and crafts. **Little Amana,** at I–80 and U.S. 151, is more of a quick-stop outlet for woolens, gifts, and souvenirs than a typical Amana village. The **Tanger Factory Outlet Center** (Exit 220 off I–80, Williamsburg, ☎ 800/727–6885) has 55 stores selling mainly women's designer clothing at discounted prices.

Dining and Lodging

Amana kitchens are well known for both quality and quantity. Try the locally made rhubarb wine served at many establishments here. Hotels in Cedar Rapids tend to cater to business travelers, but the Amanas, like many Iowa towns, are home to a burgeoning number of B&Bs (**Iowa Bed and Breakfast Innkeepers' Association,** 9001 Hickman Rd., Suite 2B, Des Moines 50322, ☎ 800/888–4667). Iowa City has a fair number of decent chain hotels and motels. For price ranges, see Charts 1 (B) and 2 (B) in On the Road with Fodor's.

Amana Colonies

DINING

Ox Yoke Inn. Traditional German-American food is served in an old-country-inspired setting, including walls lined with beer steins. *Main St., Amana, ☎ 319/622–3441. AE, D, MC, V. $$*

Bill Zuber's Restaurant. The comfortable surroundings haven't changed much since the 1950s. Neither has the menu, which is a primer on German cuisine: lots of baked or fried meat, plus salad, vegetables, and dessert, all for a reasonable price. *Main St., Homestead, ☎ 319/622–3911. AE, D, MC, V. $*

★ **Brick Haus Restaurant.** In the middle of prime Amana shopping, the restaurant features long tables covered in checkered cloths and lots of *wiener schnitzel mit spätzle* (breaded, deep-fried veal with homemade soft noodles). *Box 285, Amana, ☎ 319/622–3278. AE, D, MC, V. $*

LODGING

Amana Holiday Inn. For the most part this is standard Holiday Inn material, enlivened by such rustic touches as a pool and sauna in a barn-like setting. *Exit 225 off I–80, Box 187, Little Amana 52203, ☎ 319/668–1175 or 800/633–9244, FAX 319/668–2853. 156 rooms. Facilities: restaurant, lounge. AE, D, MC, V. $$*

★ **Rawson's Bed & Breakfast.** Once a kitchen workers' dormitory when Homestead still practiced communal living, this unique establishment has two large, distinctive rooms, with exposed beams and brick walls, and one suite. All three feature excellent period furnishings and fabrics and lavish baths. *Box 118, Homestead 52235, ☎ 319/622–6035. 2 rooms, 1 suite. D, MC, V. $$*

Die Heimat Country Inn. This two-story B&B has small rooms decorated with locally made, traditional furnishings and deluxe rooms with canopy beds. *Box 160, Homestead 52236, ☎ 319/622–3937. 19 rooms. Facilities: meeting rooms, picnic tables, barbecue grills. D, MC, V. $*

Cedar Rapids

LODGING

Collins Plaza. In this seven-balcony hotel north of downtown, rooms are large, with traditional furnishings and pastel colors. *1200 Collins Rd. NE, 52402, ☎ 319/393–6600 or 800/541–1067, FAX 319/393–2308. 221 rooms. Facilities: 2 restaurants, lounge, pool, spa, airport shuttle. AE, D, MC, V. $$$*

Iowa City

DINING

Givanni's. Neon lights enhance the exposed-brick walls at this popular Italian/American/vegetarian restaurant in the downtown pedestrian mall. *109 E. College St., ☎ 319/338–5967. AE, D, DC, MC, V. $$*

Motel

Heartland Inn (3315 Southgate Ct. SW, Cedar Rapids 52304, ☎ 319/362–9012 or 800/334–3277), 87 rooms, pool, spa; *$*.

DUBUQUE AND THE GREAT RIVER ROAD

The mighty Mississippi River forms the eastern border of Iowa, and the top third of this border, from the Minnesota line to Dubuque, combines the oldest settlements, highest bluffs, and closest river access of the entire stretch. This tour follows the Great River Road, a network of federal, state, and county roads, as it winds its way from the northeast corner of the state along this magnificent stretch of riverbank.

Tourist Information

Tourist Information Center (Port of Dubuque Welcome Center, 3rd St. and Ice Harbor, Dubuque 52001, ☎ 319/556–4372 or 800/798–8844).

Getting There

By Car

Link up with the Great River Road from the north on U.S. 18 at Prairie du Chien, Wisconsin, or pick up the scenic route anywhere along Iowa's eastern border. For its entire length, the Great River Road is marked with a 12-spoke pilot's wheel symbol.

By Bus

Greyhound Lines (☎ 800/231–2222) links Dubuque to most major cities from the bus station (2255 Kerper Blvd.).

Exploring Dubuque and the Great River Road

Spectacular views of the Mississippi start at the **Municipal Park** in Lansing and continue at the **Effigy Mounds National Monument** (☎ 319/873–3491), north of McGregor. Here hiking trails run alongside eerie prehistoric Native American burial mounds in animal shapes. One-, four-, and six-hour walks lead to cliff-top views of the upper Mississippi River valley.

From **Pikes Peak State Park** (☎ 319/873–2341), 3 mi south of McGregor, the view includes the Wisconsin River as it links up with the Mississippi. The stretch of road approaching Balltown, 7 mi north of Dubuque, reveals green hills rolling down to the river.

Dubuque is full of river merchants' homes, some of them lavish Victorian houses turned B&Bs, snuggled against the limestone cliffs that back this small harbor town. Here you can get out of your car and explore **Cable Car Square** (☎ 319/583–5000) at 4th and Bluff streets, site of two dozen shops and restaurants. Ride **Fenelon Place Elevator** to the top of a 200-foot bluff for a sweeping view of the city.

What to See and Do with Children

Dyersville, 25 mi west of Dubuque on U.S. 20, found fame as a setting for the movie *Field of Dreams.* The field, about 3 mi north of town, has been preserved as a tourist attraction. Dyersville itself has several interesting museums, including the **National Farm Toy Museum** (1110 16th Ave. SE, ☎ 319/875–2727; admission charged).

Dining and Lodging

Ethnic and family-style restaurants line Dubuque's 4th Street at Cable Car Square. As with the rest of the state, B&Bs are abundant here (**Iowa Bed and Breakfast Innkeepers' Association,** 9001 Hickman Rd., Suite 2B, Des Moines 50322, ☎ 800/888–4667). For price ranges, see Charts 1 (B) and 2 (B) in On the Road with Fodor's.

Balltown

DINING

★ **Breitbach's Country Dining.** This funky, rambling piece of folk architecture has a good home-style kitchen. *563 Balltown Rd., ☎ 319/552–2220. No credit cards. $*

Dubuque

DINING

The Ryan House. A restored Victorian house provides a lavish period setting for updated, lightened Continental cuisine. *1375 Locust St., ☎ 319/556–5000. AE, D, MC, V. $$–$$$*

Yen Ching. This café offers predictable Chinese food, with a few spicy Hunan dishes for variety. *926 Main St., ☎ 319/556–2574. AE, MC, V. Closed Sun. $$*

LODGING

★ **The Hancock House.** This meticulously restored Victorian perched halfway up a bluff has four-poster beds, lace-covered windows, and ornate fireplaces. *1105 Grove Terr., 52001, ☎ 319/557–8989, FAX 319/583–0813. 9 rooms. Facilities: Continental breakfast. D, MC, V. $$$*

The Redstone Inn. Coming across this establishment is like finding a British manor on the prairie. Bedrooms are grand, and baths are lavish. *504 Bluff St., 52001, ☎ 319/582–1894. 15 rooms. Facilities: lounge, breakfast. AE, D, MC, V. $$*

Stout House. This sturdy red-stone mansion has vivid Victorian furnishings. *1105 Locust St., 52001, ☎ 319/552–1894. 6 rooms (some share baths). AE, D, MC, V. $$*

ELSEWHERE IN THE STATE

Iowa's Great Lakes

Getting There

Take I–80W from Des Moines to U.S. 71N to Spirit Lake.

What to See and Do

The Iowa Great Lakes lie in the northwest corner of the state. The region has six lakes (including West Okoboji—one of only three blue-water lakes in the world) and a dozen vacation resorts. Climb aboard the ***Queen II*** excursion boat (Arnolds Park, ☎ 712/332–5159) for a tour of West Okoboji. **Iowa Great Lakes Chamber of Commerce** (Box 9, Arnolds Park 51331, ☎ 712/332–2107) has more information on the area.

Riverboat Gambling on the Mississippi River

Getting There

From Des Moines, take I–80E to Davenport and follow signs to the riverfront.

What to See and Do

Davenport, the largest of the four "Quad Cities," was the first city in the nation to introduce casino riverboat gambling. In downtown Davenport, with plenty of hotels, restaurants, and antiques shops within walking distance, the **President Riverboat Casino** (130 West River Dr., ☎ 800/262–8711), listed as a National Historic Landmark, is as big as a football field, with five decks decorated in Victorian splendor.

The Covered Bridges Region

Getting There

Take I–35S from Des Moines to U.S. 92W, which leads into Madison County.

What to See and Do

Made famous by Robert James Waller's novel *The Bridges of Madison County,* Madison County, 50 mi southwest of Des Moines, has six covered bridges that date back to the 1880s. A covered bridge festival (☎ 515/462–1185) is held here each October. In Winterset, the Birthplace of John Wayne is furnished with family memorabilia and authentic turn-of-the-century pieces; in the gift shop, a VCR plays Wayne's films. *224 S. Second St.,* ☎ *515/462–1044. Admission charged.*

KANSAS

By Janet Majure

Updated by Michael and Linda Kephart Flynn

Capital	Topeka
Population	2,531,000
Motto	To the Stars Through Difficulties
State Bird	Western meadowlark
State Flower	Helianthus

Visitor Information

Kansas Department of Commerce, Travel & Tourism Division (700 S.W. Harrison St., Suite 1300, Topeka 66603, ☎ 913/296–2009 or 800/252–6727). **Visitor information centers:** on I–70W in Kansas City, on I–70E in Goodland, on I–35N at South Haven, and in Topeka (Capitol, 10th and Harrison Sts.).

Scenic Drives

Rte. 177S from I–70 to historic Council Grove provides lovely views—especially in late afternoon or early morning—of the undulating Flint Hills.

National and State Parks

National Parks

Federal sites include **Ft. Larned National Historic Site** (*see* The Santa Fe Trail Region, *below*); **Ft. Scott National Historic Site** (Old Fort Blvd., Fort Scott 66701, ☎ 316/223–0310), which centers on a fort built in 1842 to keep the peace in Native American territory; and the **Cimarron National Grassland** (Box J, 242 E. Hwy. 56, Elkhart 67950, ☎ 316/697–4621), less than a mile from central Elkhart, which offers a self-guided automobile tour of key Sante Fe Trail sites.

State Parks

Kansas has 24 state parks, most associated with recreational lakes, run by the **Department of Wildlife and Parks** (512 S.E. 25th Ave., Pratt 67124, ☎ 316/672–5911). Two of the best are **Scott County State Park** (R.R. 1, Box 50, Scott City 67871, ☎ 316/872–2061), containing archaeological evidence of the northernmost Native American pueblo and the first white settlement in Kansas, and **Milford State Park** (8811 State Park Rd., Milford 66514, ☎ 913/238–3014), with a 37,000-acre reservoir, a nature center, and an arboretum.

EAST-CENTRAL KANSAS

Heading west from Kansas City across this land, you'll follow in the footsteps of pioneers who traveled the Oregon, Santa Fe, Smoky Hill, and Chisholm trails. Native American history, Civil War sites, and a taste of the Old West loom large along this 150-mi stretch.

Tourist Information

Abilene: Convention & Visitors Bureau (201 N.W. 2nd St., 67410, ☎ 913/263–2231 or 800/569–5915). **Kansas City, Kansas:** Convention & Visitors Bureau (727 Minnesota Ave., 66117, ☎ 913/321–5800); Overland Park Convention & Visitors Bureau (10975 Benson Dr., Suite 360, 66210, ☎ 913/491–0123 or 800/262–7275). **Lawrence:** Convention & Visitors Bureau (734 Vermont St., 66044, ☎ 913/865–4411).

Topeka: Convention & Visitors Bureau (1275 S.W. Topeka Blvd., 66612, ☎ 913/234–1030 or 800/235–1030).

Getting There

By Plane

The biggest airport serving the area is **Kansas City International Airport** in Missouri (*see* Missouri). USAir Express serves Topeka's **Forbes Field** (☎ 913/862–6515).

By Car

I–70W enters the area from Kansas City, Missouri; I–70E, from Colorado. Most attractions are just off the interstate. Note: Kansas weather is extremely variable. Listen to the radio for forecasts, as ice storms, heavy snowfalls, flash floods, and high winds can make driving treacherous.

By Train

Amtrak (☎ 800/872–7245) serves Lawrence, Topeka, and Kansas City.

By Bus

Greyhound Lines (800/231–2222) connects Kansas City, Kansas, Lawrence, Topeka, and Abilene en route to Denver. **Jefferson Lines** (☎ 800/735–7433) serves Kansas City, Overland Park, and Lawrence.

Exploring East-Central Kansas

Along I–70 you'll encounter an array of historic sites and recreational opportunities. **Kansas City,** which straddles the border between Kansas and Missouri, was a major provisioning point for frontier travelers in the 19th century. For information on the Missouri side of Kansas City, *see* Missouri.

On the Kansas side, the **Mahaffie Farmstead & Stagecoach Stop** served the Santa Fe Trail, one of the routes established in the 19th century for trade and, later, westward expansion. Guided tours are given of the stone house, one of three buildings here that are listed on the National Register of Historic Places. *1100 Kansas City Rd., Olathe, ☎ 913/782–6972. Admission charged. Closed Mon.–Tues. June–Aug., weekends Sept.–May, Jan., major holidays.*

In the Kansas City suburb of Fairway, the **Shawnee Methodist Mission** (3403 W. 53rd St., ☎ 913/262–0867), a state historic site, was begun in 1839 as a school to teach English and trade skills to Native Americans. In Overland Park, another suburb, college sports history is recounted through photographs, videos, and sound tracks at the **National Collegiate Athletic Association Visitors Center** (6201 College Blvd., ☎ 913/339–0000).

West about 40 mi on I–70 is **Lawrence.** The town was rebuilt after being raided and burned for its antislavery views during the Civil War by William Quantrill and a band of Confederate sympathizers; many structures dating from this time remain. Stroll Massachusetts Street through the lovely downtown area, whose turn-of-the-century buildings and retail shops retain a small-town flavor.

A few blocks away is the scenic main campus of the 29,000-student **University of Kansas.** Lining Jayhawk Boulevard are an assortment of university buildings, including the Romanesque-style structure of native limestone that houses one of the school's four museums: the **University of Kansas Natural History Museum** (Dyche Hall, ☎ 913/864–4540), which displays fossils, mounted animals, and rotating exhibits. Also in Lawrence is **Haskell Indian Nations University** (23rd and

Barker Sts., ☎ 913/749–8448), which has provided higher education for Native Americans since 1884.

Continue west on I–70 for about 30 mi to **Topeka** and see the outstanding Classical Revival state **capitol** (10th and Harrison Sts., ☎ 913/296–3966), begun in 1866 and completed nearly 40 years later. Lobby murals include a striking depiction of abolitionist John Brown by regionalist artist John Steuart Curry. The ornate senate chambers, featuring bronze columns and variegated-marble accents, are magnificent. West of downtown, the **Kansas Museum of History** (6425 S.W. 6th St., ☎ 913/272–8681), perversely situated in a modernist box of a building, explains Kansas's history from the Native American era to the present. Just outside Topeka, the **Combat Air Museum** (Hangars 602–604, Forbes Field, ☎ 913/862–3303; admission charged) offers two hangars full of military aircraft dating from World War I. **Historic Ward–Meade Park** (124 N. Fillmore St., ☎ 913/295–3888) is as lovely as it is historic, with a restored mansion, a cabin, a train depot, a one-room schoolhouse, and botanical gardens.

The countryside to the west is a sea of treeless hills. Extending from Nebraska to Oklahoma, the **Flint Hills** include the last large vestiges of bluestem or tallgrass prairie that once covered much of the Great Plains.

The small town of **Abilene,** about 85 mi west of Topeka, is famous for cattle drives and for Dwight D. Eisenhower. The **Eisenhower Center** complex includes the late president's **boyhood home**—the 19th-century clapboard looks out of place among the surrounding limestone buildings—as well as the **Eisenhower Museum,** the **Eisenhower Presidential Library,** and the **Place of Meditation,** a chapel where the president; his wife, Mamie; and their son Doud Dwight, are interred. The museum displays memorabilia of Eisenhower's life, from his youth in Abilene to his success as a general during World War II through his popular presidency. *S. Buckeye St. at 4th St., ☎ 913/263–4751. Admission charged for museum. Closed major holidays.*

Other Abilene attractions include the **Dickinson County Historical Museum** (412 S. Campbell St., ☎ 913/263–2681), offering exhibits on the life of the Plains Indians, and the **Greyhound Hall of Fame** (407 S. Buckeye St., ☎ 913/263–3000), documenting the history of this illustrious canine breed.

What to See and Do with Children

Children will enjoy the dinosaur bones and live snakes at Lawrence's **University of Kansas Natural History Museum** and Discovery Place at Topeka's **Kansas Museum of History,** with hands-on exhibits about 19th-century clothes, tools, and household items (for both, *see* Exploring East-Central Kansas, *above*). **Gage Park** in Topeka (635 Gage Blvd., ☎ 913/295–3838) has a carousel and is home to the **Topeka Zoo** (☎ 913/272–5821). In Olathe, **Golfland/Sunsplash** (20005 W. 153rd St., ☎ 913/764–3204) is a family-oriented golf and water theme park.

Shopping

Lawrence Riverfront Factory Outlets (1 Riverfront Plaza, Lawrence, ☎ 913/842–5511), at the north end of downtown, has nearly 50 stores. The **Tanger Center** (1035 N. 3rd St., Lawrence, ☎ 913/842–6290), about a mile north of downtown, offers more than 50 factory outlet stores from major-name manufacturers of clothing, shoes, and other goods.

Sports and the Outdoors

Fishing

Most of this region follows the Kansas River, where a series of large-scale flood-control reservoirs affords good fishing for walleye, bass, and crappie. Good sites include **Clinton State Park** (798 N. 1415 Rd., Lawrence 66049); **Perry State Park** (R.R. 1, Box 464A, Ozawkie 66070), near Topeka; **Tuttle Creek State Park** (5020–B Tuttle Creek Blvd., Manhattan 66502); and **Milford State Park** (*see* National and State Parks, *above*). Licenses are required and can be purchased at county clerks' offices, state park offices, and some retail outlets. The **Kansas Department of Fish and Game** (☎ 316/672–5911) has further information.

Hiking and Backpacking

Kansas's reservoirs (*see* Fishing, *above*) are bordered by state parks with marked nature trails. The **Konza Prairie** (5 mi off I–70 at Exit 307, McDowell Creek Rd., ☎ 913/532–6620), an 8,600-acre section of Flint Hills tallgrass prairie set aside for research and preservation, has a self-guided nature trail.

Spectator Sports

Basketball

Not only did the University of Kansas hire basketball's inventor as its first coach, but the **Jayhawks** are consistently among the top-10 college basketball teams in the country. Games are memorable—if you can get a cherished ticket (☎ 913/864–3141; Nov.–Mar.).

Horse and Dog Racing

The **Woodlands** (99th St. and Leavenworth Rd., Kansas City, ☎ 913/299–9797) offers greyhound racing year-round, horse racing in late summer.

Dining and Lodging

Typical Kansas roadhouse fare is chicken-fried steak and fried chicken. In cities, good barbecue and Mexican food can be found. Accommodations range from business-class hotels in the Kansas City suburb of Overland Park to the basic roadside motels that predominate in the western part of the region to B&Bs (**Kansas Bed & Breakfast Association,** Rte. 1, Box 93, WaKeeney 67672). For price ranges, see Charts 1 (B) and 2 (B) in On the Road with Fodor's.

Abilene

DINING

Kirby House. The traditional midwestern fare served here is nothing special, but the quietly elegant setting, in a restored Victorian mansion, makes up for it. *205 N.E. 3rd St., ☎ 913/263–7336. D, MC, V. $–$$*

Kansas City

DINING

★ **Tatsu's French Restaurant.** At this expanded and renovated refuge of low-key elegance in a colorless suburban shopping strip, traditional French cuisine with an Oriental accent flourishes. *4603 W. 90th St., Prairie Village, ☎ 913/383–9801. Jacket and tie advised. AE, MC, V. Closed Sun. No lunch Sat. $$–$$$*

★ **Hayward's Pit Bar-B-Que.** Locals flock to this hillside restaurant for piles of succulent smoked beef, ribs, chicken, pork, and sausage. The combination plate lets you try three of them. *11051 Antioch Rd., Overland Park, ☎ 913/451–8080. Reservations accepted except after 6 PM Fri. and Sat. AE, MC, V. $–$$*

LODGING

Doubletree Hotel. Adjacent to two major highways, a business park, and a scenic public jogging trail, this 18-story hotel is convenient to shopping, restaurants, and a bowling alley. The public spaces have an Asian motif, complete with botanical prints, cloisonné vases, and folding screens; guest rooms are decorated in shades of taupe and teal. *10100 College Blvd., Overland Park 66210, ☎ 913/451–6100, FAX 913/451–3873. 357 rooms, 18 suites. Facilities: restaurant, lounge, health club, indoor pool, hot tub, racquetball. AE, D, DC, MC, V. $$$*

★ **Overland Park Marriott Hotel.** This upscale hotel in a suburban business area has a lobby with marble floor and traditionally furnished rooms. The concierge level has slightly larger rooms and a lobby/lounge serving food and drinks. *10800 Metcalf Ave., Overland Park 66210, ☎ 913/451–8000, FAX 913/451–5914. 390 rooms, 7 suites. Facilities: 2 restaurants, lounge, health club, pool. AE, D, DC, MC, V. $$$*

Lawrence

DINING

★ **Free State Brewing Co.** Kansas's first brew pub to open since 1886 serves such dishes as fish and chips and a Burgundy beef sandwich (shredded beef brisket on a baguette, smothered with gravy) to complement the selection of beers made here. Brewery tours are offered on Saturday. *636 Massachusetts St., ☎ 913/843–4555. Reservations for parties of 10 or more. AE, D, MC, V. $–$$*

LODGING

★ **Eldridge Hotel.** This historic downtown hotel offers attractive suites that include a parlor and wet bar; rooms on the top (fifth) floor afford good views. The downtown location means some traffic noise but great convenience. *701 Massachusetts St., 66044, ☎ 913/749–5011 or 800/527–0909, FAX 913/749–4512. 48 suites. Facilities: restaurant, bar, hot tub. AE, D, DC, MC, V. $$*

Topeka

DINING AND LODGING

Heritage House. This turn-of-the-century clapboard home, once the site of the Menninger Clinic, has B&B rooms ranging from the dramatic to the cozy. Third-floor rooms have less light and more noise. The intimate restaurant serves a frequently changing Continental menu for lunch and dinner. *3535 S.W. 6th St., 66606, ☎ 913/233–3800, FAX 913/233–9793. 11 rooms with bath. Facilities: restaurant (reservations preferred; jacket and tie advised). AE, D, DC, MC, V. $$–$$$*

LODGING

Club House Inn. In western Topeka near the Kansas Museum of History, this modern, white, stucco B&B inn features spacious rooms, many overlooking a landscaped courtyard, and suites with kitchenettes. *924 S.W. Henderson St., 66615, ☎ 913/273–8888 or 800/258–2466, FAX 913/273–5809. 121 rooms, 17 suites. Facilities: outdoor pool, hot tub. AE, D, DC, MC, V. $$*

Motels

Representatives of such chains as Motel 6, Super 8, and Econo Lodge are along I–70 (*see* Appendix, Toll-Free Numbers). **Best Western Inn** (2210 N. Buckeye St., Abilene 67410, ☎ 913/263–2050, FAX 913/263–7230), 62 rooms, 1 suite, restaurant, lounge, indoor pool, hot tub; $.

Campgrounds

Four Seasons RV Acres (6 mi east of Abilene off I–70, 2502 Mink Rd., 67410, ☎ 913/598–2221 or 800/658–4667). **KOA Campgrounds of Lawrence** (1473 Hwy. 40, Lawrence 66044, ☎ 913/842–3877). **KOA**

Campground (Rte. 1, Grantville 66429, ☎ 913/246–3419). Camping is also available in state parks at reservoirs (*see* Sports and the Outdoors, *above*).

Nightlife

The New Theatre (9229 Foster St., Overland Park, ☎ 913/649–7469), an Equity "theater-restaurant," stages first-run and recent musicals and comedies in a dramatic auditorium.

THE SANTA FE TRAIL REGION

Although the Santa Fe Trail spans the entire state, the towns in western Kansas are most closely associated with its lore and history. This is the Kansas we know from film and myth: remote, flat, treeless, littered with tumbleweeds, windy, but imbued with a romance linked with such names as Wyatt Earp and Dodge City. Towns sprang up here first along the trail, then near the railroad lines that followed. Today, agriculture is the mainstay. Tourism is growing, but don't expect resorts.

Tourist Information

Dodge City: Convention & Visitors Bureau (4th and Spruce Sts., 67801, ☎ 316/225–8186). **Hutchinson:** Convention & Visitors Bureau (117 N. Walnut St., 67501, ☎ 316/662–3391). **Larned:** Chamber of Commerce (502 Broadway, 67550, ☎ 316/285–6916 or 800/747–6919).

Getting There

By Plane

Dodge City Regional Airport (☎ 316/227–8679), about 2 mi east of downtown, is served by USAir Express.

By Car

From Kansas City or Topeka, take I–70W to I–135S, then Rte. 61 to Hutchinson. Eastbound travelers enter Dodge City via U.S. 50 or U.S. 56.

By Train

Amtrak (☎ 800/872–7245) serves Hutchinson and Dodge City.

By Bus

Greyhound Lines (☎ 800/231–2222) connects with **TNM&O Coaches** (☎ 316/276–3731) to provide service to Dodge City from Wichita. The **Hutchinson Shuttle Service** (☎ 316/662–5205) connects with Great Bend, Newton, Wichita, and other cities in central Kansas.

Exploring the Santa Fe Trail Region

Hutchinson is home to the state fairgrounds, with some of the world's largest grain elevators, but what really makes this small town worth a visit is the recently expanded **Kansas Cosmosphere & Space Center.** Housing more than $100 million worth of space exhibits, the center's museum has the largest collection outside the Smithsonian Institution. Various displays—including interactive exhibits—explain the history of space exploration and solutions to the many challenges of human flight. The center also has a planetarium and an Omnimax theater. *1100 N. Plum St., ☎ 316/662–2305 or 800/397–0330. Admission charged. Closed Dec. 25.*

Head west on 4th Street (which becomes County Road 636) for about 30 mi and keep a sharp lookout for signs to the **Quivira National Wildlife Refuge** (R.R. 3, Box 48A, Stafford 67578, ☎ 316/486–2393). More than 250 bird species have been spotted here, including golden and bald eagles, pelicans, and cranes.

Drive north through the refuge, then turn west on County Road 484, which becomes Rte. 19, to **Larned,** where the **Santa Fe Trail Center** (2 mi west of town on Rte. 156, ☎ 316/285–2054) details the history of the trail and displays artifacts from early-20th-century prairie life. About 4 mi farther west on Rte. 156 is **Fort Larned National Historic Site** (R.R. 3, ☎ 316/285–6911; admission charged), a meticulously restoration of a prairie fort that was completed in 1868 to protect travelers on the Santa Fe Trail and, later, railroad workers. Buffalo Soldiers (post–Civil War regiments of black soldiers) were stationed here. The site includes a museum, restored barracks, and other buildings; a video paints a distinctly unromantic picture of the fort's history and mission.

Turn south on the first road west of Ft. Larned, which intersects with U.S. 56. Follow this southwest to **Dodge City,** which capitalizes on its 19th-century reputation as the "wickedest little city in America." Founded 5 mi west of Ft. Dodge in anticipation of the arrival of the Santa Fe railroad, the town thrived on the drinking and gambling of buffalo hunters and cowboys. It was here that lawmen Bat Masterson and Wyatt Earp earned their fame.

Dodge City's **Boot Hill Museum** includes exhibits on Native American history, the Santa Fe Trail, and the town's early life; Front Street, a reconstruction of houses, saloons, and other businesses that existed before the original town burned in 1885; and a Boot Hill cemetery re-creation (the remains of those buried here were moved years ago). In summer, gunfights, medicine shows, and stagecoach rides are staged daily. *Front St., ☎ 316/227–8188. Admission charged.*

Follow U.S. 50W for 9 mi to the **Santa Fe Trail tracks,** a 140-acre preserve where, more than 120 years later, ruts from wagons on the trail are still visible in the sandy prairie earth.

Sports and the Outdoors

Hiking

At **Dillon Nature Center** in Hutchinson (3002 E. 30th St., ☎ 316/663–7411), a National Recreation Trail system takes in woods, prairie, and wetlands.

Spectator Sports

Rodeo

The Professional Rodeo Cowboys Association's biggest Kansas rodeo is the **Dodge City Roundup Rodeo** (☎ 316/225–2244), held for five days each summer during the Dodge City Days festival.

Dining and Lodging

Motels hold sway in this part of the state, and you'll find few fancy restaurants, though many offer fresh and flavorful food. If you're traveling in summer, make reservations early for lodging; for restaurants, reservations on weekends are advised. Note: "Red beer" on menus means beer mixed with tomato juice. (It's good—really!) Kansas's liquor laws vary from county to county; in "dry" counties, alcohol is served only

The Santa Fe Trail Region

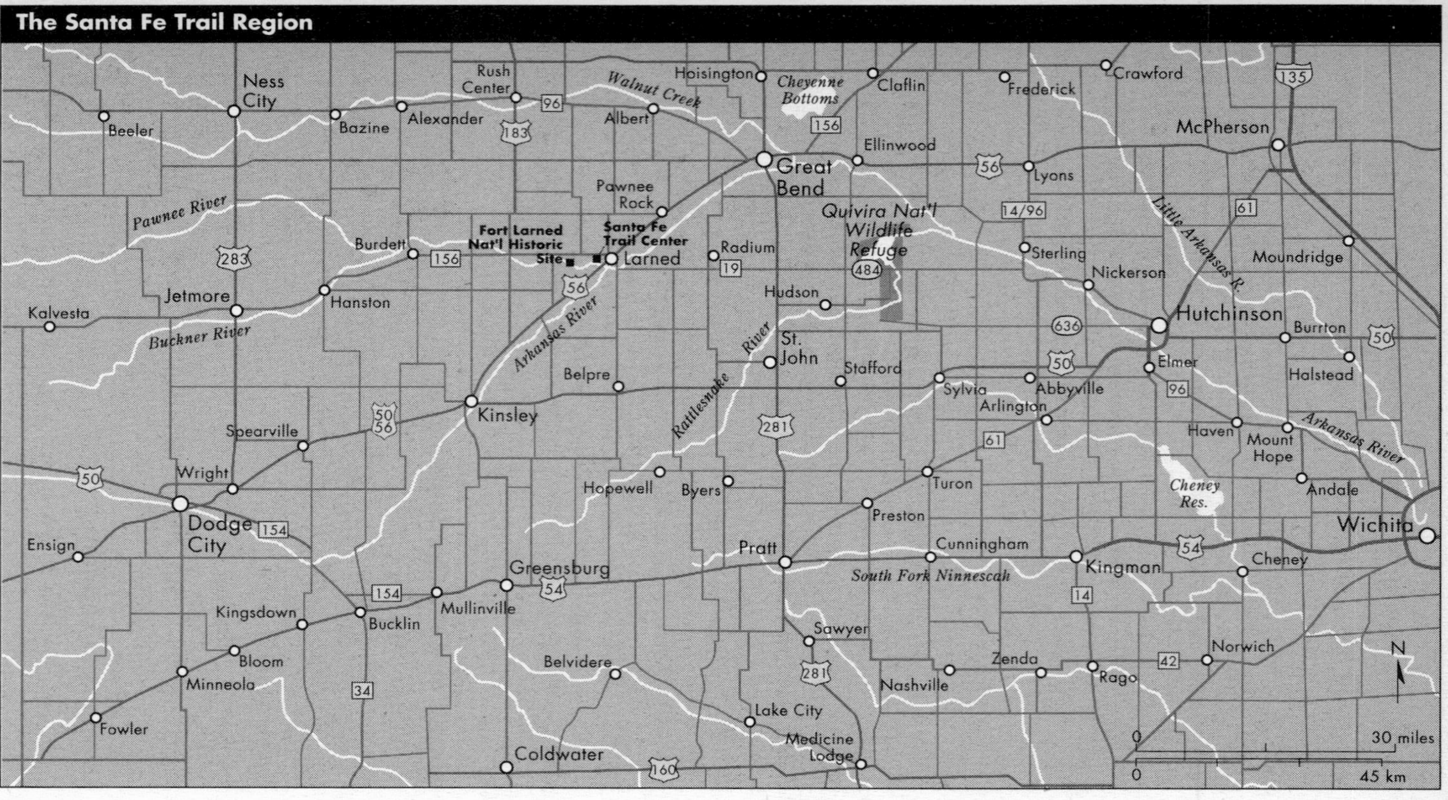

in private clubs, to which many hotels offer courtesy memberships (ask when you call to reserve). For price ranges, see Charts 1 (B) and 2 (B) in On the Road with Fodor's.

Dodge City

DINING

El Charro. Mexican dishes such as "enchilada delights," topped with cheese, lettuce, tomato, and sour cream, bring in crowds. The pleasant, low-key dining room has baskets of silk flowers hanging from beamed ceilings, and ornate, dark-wood chairs. *1209 W. Wyatt Earp Blvd., ☎ 316/225–0371. MC, V. Closed Sun. $–$$*

★ **Saigon Market.** Fresh ingredients for Vietnamese dishes are cooked to order and colorfully presented in the restaurant half of this market, which is housed in a funky strip mall. The "French" coffee (a strong blend served with condensed milk over ice) could be dessert. *1202 E. Wyatt Earp Blvd., ☎ 316/225–9099. No reservations. No credit cards. Closed Mon. $–$$*

LODGING

Silver Spur Lodge & Convention Center. You'll find clean, pleasant, undistinguished rooms at this sprawling complex just five minutes from Front Street. *1510 W. Wyatt Earp Blvd., 67801, ☎ 316/227–2125, FAX 316/227–2030. 121 rooms, 3 suites. Facilities: 2 restaurants, lounge, outdoor pool. AE, D, DC, MC, V. $$*

Hutchinson

DINING

★ **Anchor Inn.** Two large, brick-walled rooms in older downtown buildings are the setting for Mexican dishes using the restaurant's distinctive homemade flour tortillas. Portions are bounteous. *126–128 S. Main St., ☎ 316/669–0311. No reservations weekend nights. MC, V. Closed Sun. May–Sept. $*

Roy's Hickory Pit BBQ. This tiny restaurant seating 36 serves barbecued pork spare ribs, beef brisket, sausage, ham, and turkey. There's nothing else on the menu except beans, salad, and bread—but who needs more? *1018 W. 5th St., ☎ 316/663–7421. No reservations. No credit cards. Closed Sun.–Mon. $*

LODGING

★ **Ramada Inn Hutchinson.** Rooms in the "minidome" section of this busy convention hotel look onto a quiet landscaped courtyard. Main-dome rooms open onto a recreation area that has a putting green and a swimming pool. *1400 N. Lorraine St., 67501, ☎ 316/669–9311 or 800/362–5018, FAX 316/669–9830. 220 rooms, 7 suites. Facilities: restaurant, lounge, indoor pool, 2 tennis courts, exercise room. AE, D, DC, MC, V. $$*

Larned

DINING

Harvest Inn. Chicken, steaks, and seafood are on the menu at this family restaurant; food is also served in the accompanying bar, the Grain Club. *718 Ft. Larned Ave., ☎ 316/285–3870. No reservations. D, MC, V. $–$$*

Motels

EconoLodge and Super 8 are in Dodge City (*see* Appendix, Toll-Free Numbers). **Best Western Townsman Inn** (123 E. 14th St., Larned 67550, ☎ 316/285–3114, FAX 316/285–7139), 44 rooms, pool; $. **Quality Inn City Center** (15 W. 4th St., Hutchinson 67501, ☎ 316/663–1211, FAX 316/663–6636), 98 rooms, restaurant, lounge, outdoor pool;

$. **Scotsman Inn** (322 E. 4th St., Hutchinson 67501, ☎ 316/669–8281, FAX 316/669–8282), 48 rooms; $.

Campgrounds

Gunsmoke Campground (R.R. 2, W. Hwy. 50, Dodge City 67801, ☎ 316/227–8247). **Melody Acres RV Park** (1009 E. Blanchard St., Hutchinson 67501, ☎ 316/665–5048). **Watersports Campground** (500 E. Cherry St., Dodge City 67801, ☎ 316/225–9003 or 316/225–8044).

Nightlife

In Dodge City, the **Boot Hill Museum Repertory Co.** (*see* the Boot Hill Museum in Exploring the Santa Fe Trail Region, *above*) puts on a 19th-century Long Branch Variety Show. Also in Dodge City, the **Longhorn Saloon** (706 N. 2nd St., ☎ 316/225–3546) has a restaurant as well as a 1,350-sq-ft wooden dance floor for Western stomping.

ELSEWHERE IN THE STATE

Wichita

Getting There

Wichita lies about 190 mi southwest of Kansas City on the Kansas Turnpike (I–35). Most visitors arrive by car or fly into **Wichita Mid-Continent Airport** (☎ 316/946–4700), served by most major domestic carriers.

What to See and Do

Originally a frontier town, Wichita is known today as the "Air Capital of the World"—Beech, Cessna, and Learjet are based here, and Boeing has a major installation. The city is also home to such corporate giants as Coleman, which manufactures camping equipment, and Pizza Hut.

Tourist attractions include the **Indian Center Museum** (650 N. Seneca St., ☎ 316/262–5221), featuring artifacts from numerous tribes, including the Crow and the Sioux; the **Old Cowtown Museum** (1871 Sim Park Dr., ☎ 316/264–0671), a re-creation of a 19th-century town; **Botanica, the Wichita Gardens** (701 N. Amiden, ☎ 316/264–0448); and the **Wichita Greyhound Park** (10 mi from downtown Wichita on I–135, ☎ 316/755–4000 or 800/872–2894). The **Convention and Visitors Bureau** (100 S. Main St., Suite 100, 67202, ☎ 316/265–2800 or 800/288–9424) has more information.

MISSOURI

By Lori Dodge Rose

Updated by Michael and Linda Kephart Flynn

Capital	Jefferson City
Population	5,117,073
Motto	Let the Welfare of the People Be the Supreme Law
State Bird	Eastern bluebird
State Flower	Hawthorn

Visitor Information

The **Missouri Division of Tourism** (Truman State Office Bldg., Box 1055, Jefferson City 65102, ☎ 314/751–4133; in MO, 800/877–1234) operates six tourist information centers to serve travelers as they enter Missouri on major interstates.

Scenic Drives

Rte. 21 from St. Louis to Doniphan in extreme southern Missouri passes through national forests and rugged hill country. Scenic routes in the Ozark Mountains of southwestern Missouri include **Rte. 76, Rte. 248,** and **U.S. 65** south of Springfield.

National and State Parks

National Parks

The **Ozark National Scenic Riverways** (National Park Service, Box 490, Van Buren 63965, ☎ 314/323–4236) includes the Current and Jacks Fork rivers, two south-central Missouri rivers that were the first to be federally protected. Both offer good canoeing. The **Mark Twain National Forest** (401 Fairgrounds, Rolla 65401, ☎ 314/364–4621) in southern Missouri offers a wealth of outdoor opportunities.

State Parks

Lake of the Ozarks State Park (*see* Exploring the Ozarks, *below*) is the largest state park in Missouri. The popular **Missouri River State Trail,** known to locals as the Katy Trail, is a walking and cycling path, much of it along the Missouri River between Sedalia and St. Charles. Other significant parks include **Elephant Rocks** (Belleview 63623, ☎ 314/697–5395), **Johnson's Shut-ins** (Middle Brook 63656, ☎ 314/546–2450), **Mastodon State Park** (Imperial 63052, ☎ 314/464–2976), and **Onondaga Cave State Park** (Leasburg 65535, ☎ 314/245–6576). For more information, contact the **Missouri Department of Natural Resources** (Division of State Parks, 101 Adams St., Jefferson City 65101, ☎ 314/751–2479 or 800/334–6946).

ST. LOUIS

Founded as a French fur-trading settlement on the west bank of the Mississippi River in 1764, St. Louis today is best known for its soaring silver arch so impressive to travelers entering the city from the east. In its early days, the city thrived as a river port, then as a rail hub, and today it's the world headquarters for such diverse corporations as Anheuser-Busch and McDonnell Douglas. The building of the Gateway Arch more than 25 years ago did more than commemorate the city's role in westward expansion—it helped spark the rebirth of a downtown that had been abandoned in the rush for the suburbs.

Tourist Information

St. Louis: Convention and Visitors Commission (10 S. Broadway, Suite 1000, 63102, ☎ 314/421–1023 or 800/888–3861) is open weekdays from 8:30 to 5. **Visitor centers** are at the airport and downtown (308 Washington Ave., ☎ 314/241–1764). The **Missouri Tourist Information Center** (☎ 314/869–7100) is just west of the Missouri–Illinois border on I–270 at the Riverview exit.

Arriving and Departing

By Plane

Lambert–St. Louis International Airport (☎ 314/426–8000), 10 mi northwest of downtown on I–70, has scheduled flights by most major domestic and foreign carriers. It's about 20 minutes by car from the airport to downtown St. Louis; taxis cost about $20. Transportation is also provided to downtown stops by the **Bi-State** bus (☎ 314/231–2345) and to downtown hotels by **Airport Express** shuttle vans (☎ 314/429–4950).

By Car

From I–70, I–55, and I–44, follow the exits for downtown St. Louis. From U.S. 40 (I–64) from the west, exit at Broadway.

By Train

Amtrak (550 S. 16th St., ☎ 314/331–3300 or 800/872–7245).

By Bus

Greyhound Lines (1450 N. 13th St., ☎ 800/231–2222).

Getting Around St. Louis

Downtown sights can be explored on foot, but for the city's more far-flung attractions, you'll need a car. **MetroLink** (☎ 314/231–2345), the city's light rail system, stops near major attractions downtown. Rides are free between Laclede's Landing and Union Station weekdays from 10 AM to 3 PM.

Exploring St. Louis

Downtown

Any visit to the Gateway City should include a trip to the top of the **Gateway Arch,** rising 630 feet above the Mississippi River. This magnificent centerpiece of the 91-acre **Jefferson National Expansion Memorial Park** was built in 1966 to commemorate the city where thousands of 19th-century pioneers stopped for provisions before traveling west. A tram takes visitors up the inside of each leg of the arch to an observation room, where you get a terrific view of the city and the mighty Mississippi. Below it is the underground visitor center and the **Museum of Westward Expansion.** *On the riverfront at Market St., ☎ 314/425–4465. Admission charged.*

Just down the steps from the arch is the Mississippi riverfront and its cobblestone levee, where permanently moored riverboats house a handful of mostly fast-food restaurants. The ***Huck Finn, Tom Sawyer,*** and ***Becky Thatcher*** (☎ 314/621–4040), replicas of 19th-century steamboats, offer one-hour sightseeing trips. North of the arch is **Laclede's Landing,** nine square blocks of cobblestone streets and restored 19th-century warehouses now filled with shops, galleries, restaurants, and nightspots.

Downtown St. Louis

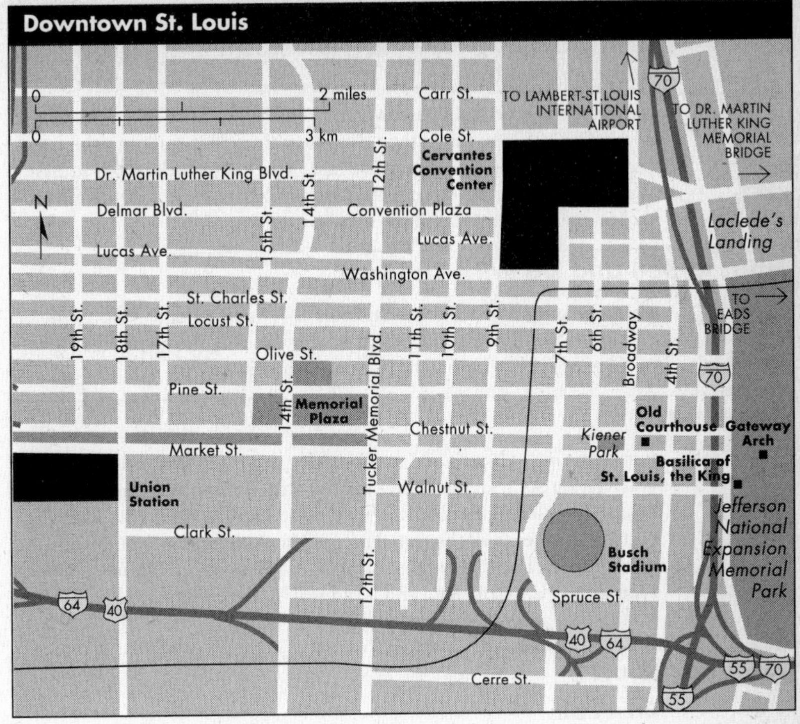

Back on the west edge of the arch grounds is St. Louis's oldest church, **Basilica of St. Louis, the King** (209 Walnut St.), a simple Greek Revival structure built 150 years ago that is a favorite setting for weddings. One block west on Market Street, the **Old Courthouse** (11 N. 4th St., ☎ 314/425–4465) houses displays and photographs of early St. Louis.

South of the courthouse is **Busch Stadium,** home of the St. Louis Cardinals (*see* Spectator Sports, *below*). On the northeast side of the stadium is the **St. Louis Cardinals Hall of Fame,** displaying sports memorabilia and audio and video highlights of the city's baseball history. ☎ *314/421–3263. Admission charged. Closed weekends Jan.–Mar.*

Other Attractions

St. Louis is home to the world's largest brewer, **Anheuser-Busch,** makers of Budweiser beer. Tours at the company's world headquarters in south St. Louis include the stables where some of the famous Clydesdale horses are kept. *12th and Lynch Sts., tel 314/577–2626. Closed Sun.*

On the west edge of town is **Forest Park** (north of U.S. 40 between Kingshighway and Skinker Blvds.). On its grounds are the **St. Louis Zoo** (☎ 314/781–0900), which includes a high-tech education center, and the **St. Louis Art Museum** (☎ 314/721–0072), whose pre-Columbian and German Expressionist collections are outstanding. **St. Louis Science Center** (5050 Oakland Ave., ☎ 314/289–4444) contains exhibits on ecology, space, and humanity.

A mind-boggling collection of mosaics covers the walls, ceilings, and three domes of the **Cathedral of St. Louis** (Lindell Blvd. and Newstead Ave., ☎ 314/533–2824), also known as the New Cathedral.

The **Missouri Botanical Garden,** known locally as Shaw's Garden for founder Henry Shaw, is a 15-minute drive southwest of downtown.

Highlights include an impressive Japanese garden and a tropical rain forest housed in a geodesic dome. *4344 Shaw Ave., ☎ 314/577–5100. Admission charged.*

St. Louisans love **Ted Drewes** frozen custard (6726 Chippewa St., ☎ 314/481–2652) so much they'll stand in lines that spill into the street, but don't worry—the lines move fast. You'll label yourself a tourist if you have to ask what a concrete is (it's frozen custard so thick it won't budge even when you flip the cup upside down).

What to See and Do with Children

Six Flags over Mid-America–St. Louis (I–44 and Allenton Rd., Eureka, ☎ 314/938–4800), about 30 mi southwest of St. Louis, thrills visitors of all ages with amusement rides and shows.

Shopping

For browsing in boutiques and specialty shops, try **Union Station** (18th and Market Sts.), an impressive former train station, and **Laclede's Landing** (*see* Exploring St. Louis, *above*). The **Central West End,** along Euclid Avenue east of Forest Park, is an area of hip boutiques and restaurants. The city's most sophisticated shoppers head for **Plaza Frontenac** (Clayton Rd. and Lindbergh Blvd., ☎ 314/432–0604), home to nearly 50 upscale stores.

Spectator Sports

Baseball

The **St. Louis Cardinals** (Busch Stadium, 250 Stadium Plaza, ☎ 314/421–3060; Apr.–Oct.).

Dining

St. Louis's Hill neighborhood has an Italian restaurant on nearly every corner; other ethnic restaurants are found throughout the city. Even the abundant steak houses carry an Italian dish or two. The Central West End and Laclede's Landing have a number of restaurants, as does Clayton, the St. Louis County seat, about 7 mi west of downtown. For price ranges, see Chart 1 (B) in On the Road with Fodor's.

$$$ **Cardwell's.** Diners can eat in the airy café, with marble-top tables and French doors, or in the more formal, elegant dining room. The frequently changing menu at this Clayton restaurant may include salmon with a sesame-seed crust; poultry mixed grill, with marinated quail, squab, and duck; or maybe even wild boar. *8100 Maryland St., ☎ 314/726–5055. AE, MC, V. Closed Sun.*

$$$ **Sidney Street Cafe.** Tables for two in the atrium and a candlelit dining room lend romance to this former storefront in the Benton Park neighborhood. The eclectic cuisine includes raspberry or tequila-lime chicken. *2000 Sidney St., ☎ 314/771–5777. AE, D, DC, MC, V. Closed Sun.–Mon.*

$$$ ★ **Tony's.** After more than 40 years at the north edge of downtown, this highly acclaimed restaurant has moved to the more central Equitable Building to make room for construction of the city's new domed stadium. Run by the Bommarito family for three generations, Tony's still offers superb Italian dishes and prime steaks and remains a favorite place for celebrating special occasions. *410 Market St., ☎ 314/231–7007. Jacket and tie required. AE, D, DC, MC, V. Closed Sun. No lunch.*

$$ **Blue Water Grill.** Grilled seafood with a Southwestern flair is the specialty at this small, festive restaurant near the Hill. On Monday night, diners can mix and match "Flying Saucers," an assortment of miniature entrées. *2607 Hampton Ave., ☎ 314/645–0707. MC, V. Closed Sun.*

$$ ★ **Cunetto's House of Pasta.** There's usually a wait at this popular restaurant on the Hill, but relaxing in the cocktail lounge is part of the experience. Once seated, you'll find plenty of veal and meat dishes from which to choose, as well as more than 30 different pastas. *5453 Magnolia Ave., ☎ 314/781–1135. No reservations at dinner. AE, DC, MC, V. Closed Sun.*

$ ★ **Blueberry Hill.** This St. Louis original, in the hip University City neighborhood, was into pop memorabilia long before the Hard Rock Cafe. Order a burger and a Rock & Roll beer, plunk a quarter into the famous 2,000-tune jukebox, and let the good times roll. *6504 Delmar Blvd., ☎ 314/727–0880. No reservations. AE, D, DC, MC, V.*

$ **Rigazzi's.** Generous, inexpensive servings of pasta keep locals coming back to this no-frills pasta house on the Hill. *4945 Daggett St., ☎ 314/772–4900. AE, MC, V. Closed Sun.*

Lodging

Most of St. Louis's big hotels are downtown or in Clayton, about 7 mi west. To check out the growing number of B&Bs in town, call or write **Bed and Breakfasts of St. Louis, River Country of Missouri and Illinois** (1900 Wyoming St., St. Louis 63118, ☎ 314/771–1993). For price ranges, see Chart 2 (A) in On the Road with Fodor's.

$$$ **Hotel Majestic.** This small European-style hotel downtown is often the choice of visiting celebrities. The more than 80-year-old building was renovated in 1987 and filled with reproduction antiques. *1019 Pine St., 63101, ☎ 314/436–2355 or 800/451–2355, FAX 314/436–0223. 91 rooms, 3 suites. Facilities: restaurant, lounge, valet parking. AE, D, DC, MC, V.*

$$$ **Hyatt Regency St. Louis at Union Station.** Most of the rooms are in a contemporary garden setting beneath the arched trusses of Union Station's original train shed. The Regency Club offers deluxe rooms and suites on the concierge club level. *1 St. Louis Union Station, 63103, ☎ 314/231–1234, FAX 314/436–6827. 538 rooms, 22 suites. Facilities: 2 restaurants, 2 lounges, health club, outdoor pool, valet parking. AE, D, DC, MC, V.*

$$$ **Ritz-Carlton, St. Louis.** In Clayton, this recent addition to the luxury-hotel scene is filled with chandeliers and museum-quality oil paintings. Some rooms on the top floors have views of the downtown St. Louis skyline. *100 Carondelet Plaza, Clayton 63105, ☎ 314/863–6300, FAX 314/863–3525. 301 rooms, 32 suites. Facilities: 2 restaurants, 2 lounges, health club, indoor pool. AE, D, DC, MC, V.*

$$ ★ **Drury Inn–Union Station.** Leaded-glass windows and marble columns give historic charm to this former YMCA. There's no bellman here, but you do have complimentary breakfasts and an excellent location next door to Union Station. *201 S. 20th St., 63103, ☎ 314/231–3900, FAX 314/231–3900. 176 rooms, 11 suites. Facilities: restaurant, indoor pool. AE, D, DC, MC, V.*

$ **Budgetel Inn West Port.** Rooms are of a standard size at this reliable chain hotel near West Port Plaza, the site of some of the city's finest shops. The hotel offers complimentary Continental breakfast. *12330 Dorsett Rd., 63043, ☎ 314/878–1212, FAX 314/878–3409. 145 rooms, 15 suites. AE, D, DC, MC, V.*

Motels

Fairfield Inn by Marriott (9079 Dunn Rd., 63042, ☎ 314/731–7700, FAX 314/731–7700, ext. 709), 135 rooms, pool; *$*. **Red Roof Inn** (5823 Wilson St., ☎ 314/645–0101, FAX 314/645–0101, ext. 444), 110 rooms; *$*.

The Arts and Nightlife

The Arts

The **Fabulous Fox Theatre** (527 N. Grand Blvd., ☎ 314/534–1678) hosts major shows and concerts. The **Riverport Amphitheatre** (14141 Riverport Dr., ☎ 314/298–9944) stages big-name concerts. The **St. Louis Symphony Orchestra** presents programs at **Powell Symphony Hall** (718 N. Grand Blvd., ☎ 314/534–1700). For tickets to major events, call **Dialtix** (☎ 314/291–7600).

Nightlife

Much of St. Louis's nightlife can be found in the redeveloped areas of **Laclede's Landing,** on the riverfront, and in **Soulard,** on the south edge of downtown. For gambling, head to the **President Riverboat Casino** (800 N. 1st St., ☎ 314/622–3000 or 800/772–3647) or upriver to the **Alton Belle Riverboat Casino** (219 Piasa St., Alton, IL, ☎ 618/474–7500 or 800/336–7568). To find out who's playing where, consult the *St. Louis Post-Dispatch*'s Thursday calendar section or the free weekly paper *The Riverfront Times.*

KANSAS CITY

With more fountains (more than 200) than any city except Rome and more boulevard miles (155) than Paris, Kansas City is attractive and cosmopolitan. This spread-out metropolitan area, which straddles the Missouri–Kansas line, has a rich history as a frontier trade center and river port, where wagon trains were outfitted before heading west on the Santa Fe and Oregon trails. Through the years it has been home to the nation's second-largest stockyards, saxophone player Charlie "Bird" Parker and his Kansas City–style bee-bop, and some of the best barbecue in the world.

Tourist Information

Greater Kansas City: The Convention and Visitors Bureau (1100 Main St., Suite 2550, ☎ 816/221–5242 or 800/767–7700) is in City Center Square in downtown Kansas City. Its **Visitor Information Phone** (☎ 816/691–3800) offers a weekly recording of activities. The **Missouri Information Center** (I–70 and Blue Ridge Cutoff, ☎ 816/889–3330) overlooks the Truman Sports Complex.

Arriving and Departing

By Plane

Kansas City International Airport (☎ 816/243–5237), 30 minutes northwest of downtown on I–29, is served by major domestic airlines. Taxi service is zoned; the maximum fare from the airport to downtown Kansas City is $26. **KCI Shuttle** buses (☎ 816/243–5950; fare $11) will take you to major downtown hotels.

By Car

From I–70 or I–35, exit at Broadway for downtown. If you're coming from the airport, I–29 from the north merges with I–35 north of the city.

By Train

Amtrak (2200 Main St., ☎ 816/421–3622 or 800/872–7245).

By Bus

Greyhound Lines (11th St. and Troost Ave., ☎ 800/231–2222).

Getting Around Kansas City

Attractions are located throughout the metropolitan region, making cars important for visitors. However, **Kansas City Trolley's** replica trolleys (☎ 816/221–3399) travel between downtown, Crown Center, Westport, and the Country Club Plaza; the drivers are usually entertaining and well versed in local history.

Exploring Kansas City

Plaza, Midtown, Downtown

Kansas City's **Country Club Plaza** (47th and Main Sts., ☎ 816/753–0100) is known for its more than 180 fine shops and restaurants, its Spanish-style architecture, and its annual display of holiday lights from Thanksgiving to January, when hundreds of thousands of gaily colored bulbs outline the plaza's buildings. Here you'll also find many of the city's fountains and statues. Several blocks east of the plaza is the **Nelson-Atkins Museum of Art** (4525 Oak St., ☎ 816/561–4000), known principally for its outstanding Oriental art collection and its Henry Moore Sculpture Garden on the south grounds.

Before there was a Kansas City, there was a **Westport** (north of the Plaza at Broadway and Westport Rd., ☎ 816/756–2789), built along the Santa Fe Trail as an outfitting center for the wagon trains heading west. Today this area is filled with renovated and new buildings housing trendy shops, restaurants, and nightspots.

On the crest of a hill at the north edge of **Penn Valley Park,** north of Westport, is the **Liberty Memorial** (100 W. 26th St., ☎ 816/221–1918), dedicated to those who served in World War I. From the 217-foot tower's observation deck you get a panoramic view of the city.

Just across Main Street to the east is **Crown Center** (Grand Ave. and Pershing Rd., ☎ 816/274–8444), an 85-acre shopping, entertainment, office, and hotel complex. In summer, free Friday night concerts are held on the terrace; a covered outdoor ice-skating rink is open in winter. Kansas City–based Hallmark Cards, the largest maker of greeting cards in the world, built Crown Center and has its headquarters here. You can stop by the **Hallmark Visitor's Center** (☎ 816/274–3613; closed Sun.), which features a display on the history of the greeting-card industry and a bow-making machine (you get to keep the bow).

Downtown, the **Treasures of the Steamboat *Arabia*** museum houses goods—from French perfume to buttons to coffee pots—salvaged from the *Arabia's* muddy grave 132 years after it sank in the Missouri River in 1856. *4th and Grand Sts., ☎ 816/471–4030. Admission charged.*

Other Attractions

Just east of Kansas City is **Independence,** once the home of President Harry S. Truman. His life and career are the focus at the **Harry S. Truman Library and Museum** (U.S. 24 and Delaware St., ☎ 816/833–1225) and the **Truman Home** (219 N. Delaware St., ☎ 816/254–9929; ticket center, 223 Main St.; closed Mon.), the summer White House for Harry and Bess Truman during his administration.

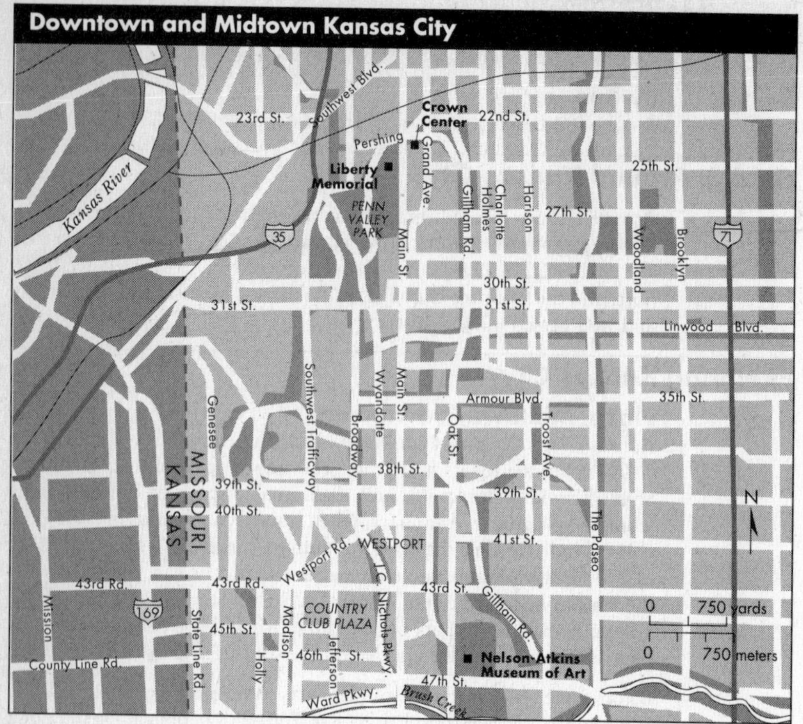

Fleming Park (22807 Woods Chapel Rd., ☏ 816/795–8200) in Blue Springs, south of Independence, features the 970-acre **Lake Jacomo,** as well as **Missouri Town 1855** (☏ 816/881–4431), a reproduction 1800s town created from more than 30 transplanted period houses, barns, stores, and outbuildings. Staff and volunteers dress in period clothing at this living-history museum.

Shopping

Kansas City's finest shopping is on **Country Club Plaza,** and a number of specialty shops and boutiques are concentrated in **Westport** and at **Crown Center** (for all, *see* Exploring Kansas City, *above*).

Spectator Sports

Baseball

Kansas City Royals (Kauffman Stadium, Truman Sports Complex, I–70 and Blue Ridge Cutoff, ☏ 816/921–8000; Apr.–Oct.).

Football

Kansas City Chiefs (Arrowhead Stadium, Truman Sports Complex, ☏ 816/924–9400; Aug.–Dec.).

Dining

Kansas City is best known for its steaks and barbecue, although locals argue over which places serve the best. Both Country Club Plaza and Westport have a variety of good eating places, from elegant restaurants to sidewalk cafés to neighborhood joints dispensing barroom grub. For price ranges, see Chart 1 (B) in On the Road with Fodor's.

$$$ **Cafe Allegro.** Among the favorite entrées at this trendy restaurant are salmon with Chinese mustard glaze and tuna tartare. The brick interior is hung with paintings by local artists, and candles and fresh flowers grace the tables. *1815 W. 39th St., ☎ 816/561–3663. AE, DC, MC, V. No lunch weekends.*

$$$ ★ **Plaza III–The Steakhouse.** This handsome, nationally known restaurant on Country Club Plaza serves excellent steaks, prime rib, and seafood; its steak soup is legendary. *4749 Pennsylvania Ave., ☎ 816/753–0000. AE, D, DC, MC, V. No lunch Sun.*

$$$ **Savoy Grill.** Locals often choose this historic, turn-of-the-century beauty when celebrating a special occasion. Maine lobster or a T-bone steak from the restaurant's own herd are good choices here. *219 W. 9th St., ☎ 816/842–3890. AE, D, DC, MC, V. No lunch Sun.*

$$ **Golden Ox.** It's a little out of the way, but this steak house, featuring prime rib in a comfortable Western atmosphere, is still extremely popular. *1600 Genesee St., ☎ 816/842–2866. AE, D, DC, MC, V. No lunch Sun.*

$$ ★ **West Side Cafe.** This has become one of Kansas City's hottest spots—in more ways than one. The spicy tandoori chicken highlights a menu of Indian, Greek, and North African food. Seating is limited, so arrive early or be ready for a wait. *723 Southwest Blvd., ☎ 816/472–0010. AE, D, MC, V. No dinner Sun.–Tues.*

$ ★ **Arthur Bryant's.** Although there are reportedly more than 70 barbecue joints in Kansas City, Bryant's—low on decor but high on taste—tops the list for many Kansas Citians, who don't mind standing in line to order from the counter. *1727 Brooklyn Ave., ☎ 816/231–1123. AE, MC, V.*

$ **Ponak's.** This large, popular restaurant is in the flourishing Hispanic neighborhood along Southwest Boulevard. Among the menu items are soft tacos, tamales, enchiladas, and *menudo,* a Mexican soup made with tripe and hominy. *2856 Southwest Blvd., ☎ 816/753–0775. No reservations weekend nights. AE, MC, V.*

Lodging

Kansas City offers a core of major hotels within walking distance of Country Club Plaza and Westport or in the Crown Center complex. For a listing of B&Bs, contact **Bed and Breakfast Kansas City** (Box 14781, Lenexa, KS 66285, ☎ 913/888–3636). For price ranges, see Chart 2 (B) in On the Road with Fodor's.

$$$ ★ **The Raphael.** Built in 1927 as apartments, the Raphael today enjoys its status as the only intimate, European-style hotel in the city. Despite its small size, many of the rooms are large and have excellent views of the Plaza. *325 Ward Pkwy., 64112, ☎ 816/756–3800 or 800/821–5343, FAX 816/756–3800. 123 rooms, 72 suites. Facilities: restaurant, lounge, valet parking. AE, D, DC, MC, V.*

$$$ ★ **Ritz-Carlton.** This luxury hotel filled with crystal chandeliers, imported marble, and fine art was completely renovated in 1990. Some of the luxuriously appointed rooms have balconies and views of the Plaza. *401 Ward Pkwy., 64112, ☎ 816/756–1500, FAX 816/756–1635. 373 rooms, 28 suites. Facilities: 2 restaurants, 2 bars, health club, outdoor pool, valet parking. AE, D, DC, MC, V.*

$$$ **Westin Crown Center.** Part of the Crown Center complex, the Westin features a bustling lobby complete with a five-story waterfall and natural limestone cliff. All rooms have views; the best face Crown Center Square to the east. *1 Pershing Rd., 64108, ☎ 816/474–4400, FAX 816/391–4438. 725 rooms, 49 suites. Facilities: 3 restaurants, health club, outdoor pool, putting green, tennis courts. AE, D, DC, MC, V.*

$$ **Drury Inn–Stadium.** Across from the sports complex, this chain hotel offers clean, comfortable rooms; for a few dollars more, you can have a "minisuite" with a king-size bed, a recliner, and a microwave. *3830 Blue Ridge Cutoff, 64133, ☎ 816/923–3000, FAX 816/923–3000. 133 rooms, 1 suite. Facilities: outdoor pool. AE, D, DC, MC, V.*

$$ **Quarterage Hotel.** Larger rooms at this intimate, brick hotel in Westport have either a queen-size bed or two doubles; smaller, less expensive rooms have one double and a balcony. *560 Westport Rd., 64111, ☎ 816/931–0001 or 800/942–4233, FAX 816/931–8891. 123 rooms. Facilities: health club, sauna. AE, D, DC, MC, V.*

$ **EconoLodge of KCI.** This inexpensive option for airport lodging offers free transportation to area restaurants. *11300 N.W. Prairie View, 64153, ☎ 816/464–5082. 58 rooms, 1 suite. AE, D, DC, MC, V.*

The Arts and Nightlife

The Arts

The **Folly Theater** (12th and Central Sts., ☎ 816/842–5500) and the larger **Midland Center for the Performing Arts** (1228 Main St., ☎ 816/471–8600) have shows and concerts. The **Lyric Opera** of Kansas City and the **Kansas City Symphony** perform at the **Lyric Theatre** (11th and Central Sts., ☎ 816/471–7344). For information on upcoming events, check the Friday and Sunday editions of the *Kansas City Star.* Call **TicketMaster** (☎ 816/931–3330) for tickets to main events.

Nightlife

Much of Kansas City's nightlife can be found in the Westport and Plaza areas. The **Grand Emporium** (3832 Main St., ☎ 816/531–1504) is *the* place in town for blues. The city is justly proud of its jazz heritage, and live performances are featured at several establishments; call the **Jazz Hotline** (☎ 816/763–1052).

THE OZARKS

From wooded mountaintops and clear, spring-fed streams, to the water playgrounds of Lake of the Ozarks and Table Rock Lake, the Ozark hill region of southern Missouri offers limitless recreation and striking beauty. Branson, second only to Nashville as the nation's country-music capital, attracts 5 million visitors a year to its star-studded theaters.

Tourist Information

Greater Lake of the Ozarks: Convention and Visitors Bureau (Box 98, Lake Ozark 65049, ☎ 314/365–3371 or 800/325–0213). **Table Rock Lake/Kimberling City Area:** Chamber of Commerce (Box 495, Kimberling City 65686, ☎ 417/739–2564). **Branson:** Branson Lakes Area Chamber of Commerce (Box 220, 65616, ☎ 417/334–4136). **Springfield:** Convention and Visitors Bureau and Tourist Information Center (3315 E. Battlefield Rd., 65804-4048, ☎ 417/881–5300 or 800/678–8766).

Getting There

By Car

Many of the towns and attractions in this wide-ranging region can be reached from I–44, which cuts diagonally across the state from St. Louis to Springfield (about 210 mi). Branson lies about 40 mi south of Springfield on U.S. 65. The Lake of the Ozarks is centrally located between St. Louis and Kansas City.

Exploring the Ozarks

Central Missouri's **Lake of the Ozarks,** formed by the damming of the Osage River in 1931, is the state's largest lake, with 1,300 mi of shoreline sprawling over 58,000 acres. In summer, crowds of vacationing families descend on the numerous resorts, motels, and tourist attractions; better times to visit may be spring, when the dogwoods are blooming, and fall, when the wooded hills come alive with color.

Lake of the Ozarks State Park (U.S. 54, ☎ 314/348–2694), just south of Osage Beach, encompasses 90 mi of shoreline and offers hiking trails, other recreational activities, and tours of **Ozark Caverns,** one of Missouri's 5,000 or so caves. ☎ *314/346–2500. Admission charged. Closed Dec.–Feb.*

You're deep in the country's "Bible Belt" when you reach **Springfield** (off I–44), home to two Bible colleges and a theological seminary and near several sights and cultural events with religious themes. For many people, though, the first stop in Springfield has little to do with religion. The enormous **Bass Pro Shops Outdoor World** (1935 S. Campbell Ave., ☎ 417/887–1915), dubbed the "Sportsman's Disney World," has cascading waterfalls, a wildlife trophy collection, a boat showroom, sporting goods shops—and about 6 million visitors a year.

The visitor center at **Wilson's Creek National Battlefield** (Rte. ZZ and Farm Rd. 182, ☎ 417/732–2662), southwest of Springfield, documents the first major Civil War battle to be fought west of the Mississippi. In Mansfield, roughly 40 mi east of Springfield on U.S. 60, is the **Laura Ingalls Wilder Home** (Rte. A, ☎ 417/924–3626), a National Historic Landmark, where the much-loved children's author wrote her "Little House" books. Museum displays include Laura's handwritten manuscripts (written with pencil on school tablets) and Pa's fiddle. About 70 mi west of Springfield is the **George Washington Carver National Monument** (off Rte. V, ☎ 417/325–4151), honoring the birthplace of Carver, the famous black botanist and agronomist.

About 40 mi south of Springfield on U.S. 65 is **Lake Taneycomo,** the first of Missouri's man-made lakes. Along its riverlike length, small resorts are concentrated in towns such as Forsyth and Rockaway Beach. Its larger, more developed neighbor, **Table Rock State Park** (Branson, ☎ 417/334–4704), has boating, picnicking, and plenty of motels, resorts, and commercial campgrounds. Kimberling City is the main resort town here.

With more than 60,000 seats in such star-studded venues as the Roy Clark Celebrity Theatre and the Cristy Lane Theatre (*see* The Arts and Nightlife, *below*), **Branson** is becoming a mecca for country-music fans to rival Nashville. Most of the town's recent growth has taken place along Rte. 76, already crowded with miniature-golf courses, bumper-car concessions, souvenir and hillbilly-crafts shops, motels, and resorts.

A few miles west of Branson is the **Shepherd of the Hills Homestead and Outdoor Theatre,** a working pioneer homestead with a gristmill, a sawmill, and smith and wheelwright shops. The *Shepherd of the Hills* inspirational drama is performed outdoors here. *Rte. 76,* ☎ *417/334–4191. Admission charged. Closed Jan.–Apr.*

What to See and Do with Children

The Ozarks region is well suited to family vacations, with boating, swimming, and many roadside attractions, such as miniature golf and water parks. **Silver Dollar City** (Rte. 76, ☎ 417/338–8100), just west of Branson, features Ozark artisans demonstrating traditional crafts, along with rides and music shows. Nearby, **White Water** (Rte. 76, Branson, ☎ 417/334–7488) is the place for water-soaked rides and activities.

Shopping

Osage Village (U.S. 54, Osage Beach, ☎ 314/348–2065) is a major factory-outlet mall with about 115 stores.

Sports and the Outdoors

Canoeing

The Ozarks have some of the finest "floating" streams in the country, such as the **Current** and **Jacks Fork rivers,** two waterways protected as the **Ozark National Scenic Riverways** (*see* National and State Parks, *above*). For a list of outfitters, contact the Missouri Division of Tourism (*see* Visitor Information, *above*).

Fishing

Bull Shoals Lake, Lake Taneycomo, and **Table Rock Lake** all offer excellent fishing, including bass, catfish, and trout. Other good spots include **Lake of the Ozarks** and **Truman Lake.** Contact the **Missouri Department of Conservation** (Box 180, Jefferson City 65102, ☎ 314/751–4115) for information on permits, costs, and seasons.

Hiking and Backpacking

The partially completed **Ozark Trail** passes through national and state forest and parkland, as well as private property. For information and maps, contact the **Missouri Department of Natural Resources** (Division of State Parks, 101 Adams St., Jefferson City 65101, ☎ 314/751–2479 or 800/334–6946) or individual state parks (*see* National and State Parks, *above*).

Dining and Lodging

To find out about B&Bs in the area, contact the **Ozark Mountain Country Bed and Breakfast** reservation service (Box 295, Branson 65616, ☎ 417/334–4720 or 800/695–1546). For price ranges, see Charts 1 (B) and 2 (B) in On the Road with Fodor's.

Branson Area

DINING

★ **Candlestick Inn.** Fresh local trout is a specialty at this restaurant overlooking Lake Taneycomo. The two elegant dining rooms have floor-to-ceiling glass. *Rte. 76E, Branson, ☎ 417/334–3633. AE, D, DC, MC, V. Closed 1st 2 wks of Jan. No lunch. $$*

Outback Steak and Oyster Bar. This rustic, Australian-inspired oysters-and-steak place has a veranda overlooking its own swamp, where a fake crocodile rests on a log. Servers wear khaki and greet you with "G'day!" *1914 Rte. 76W, Branson, ☎ 417/334–6306. AE, D, MC, V. $$*

LODGING

Holiday Inn Branson. Although this modern hotel is not on Lake Taneycomo, some rooms have views of it. Service is friendly, and the location is convenient to area attractions. *1420 Rte. 76W, Box 340, Branson 65616, ☎ 417/334–5101, FAX 417/334–0789. 220 rooms, 6 suites. Facilities: restaurant, lounge, outdoor pool. AE, D, DC, MC, V. $$*

Kimberling Inn Resort and Conference Center. This small resort motel on Table Rock Lake is within walking distance of the Kimberling City Shopping Village, where there are crafts shops, restaurants, and bowling. *Box 159B, Kimberling City 65686, ☎ 417/739–4311 or 800/833–5551. 120 rooms. Facilities: 3 restaurants, lounge, 3 outdoor and indoor pools, miniature golf, tennis court, boat rentals. AE, D, DC, MC, V. $$*

Lake of the Ozarks

DINING

Blue Heron. This seasonal restaurant serving steak and seafood is popular with lake visitors, who enjoy cocktails poolside before moving to the dining room overlooking the lake. *Bus. Rte. 54 and Rte. HH, Osage Beach, ☎ 314/365–4646. No reservations. AE, D, MC, V. Closed Sun.–Mon. and Dec.–Feb. No lunch. $$*

Shooters 21. This large, popular lakeside bar and restaurant has both casual and fine dining. Bar fare includes such favorites as spicy chicken wings, potato skins, and burgers. *Lake Rd. 54–56, Osage Beach, mile marker 21, ☎ 314/348–2100. AE, D, MC, V. $–$$*

LODGING

★ **Lodge of the Four Seasons.** Featuring a highly rated, 18-hole, Robert Trent Jones golf course, two other courses, and fine dining in the Toledo Room, this deluxe resort offers drastically reduced winter rates. *Box 215, Lake Ozark 65049, ☎ 314/365–3000 or 800/843–5253, FAX 314/865–8525. 311 rooms, 23 suites. Facilities: 3 restaurants, 2 lounges, 11 indoor and outdoor pools, 17 indoor and outdoor tennis courts, lake swimming, 45 holes of golf. AE, D, DC, MC, V. $$$*

★ **Marriott's Tan-Tar-A Resort and Golf Club.** One of the top choices in the region for vacations and business meetings, the resort features numerous recreational opportunities and fine dining at its Windrose restaurant. *Rte. KK, Osage Beach 65065, ☎ 314/348–3131 or 800/826–8272, FAX 314/348–3206. 750 rooms, 250 suites. Facilities: 5 restaurants, 3 lounges, health club, 5 indoor and outdoor pools, 6 indoor and outdoor tennis courts, 27 holes of golf. AE, D, DC, MC, V. $$$*

Holiday Inn Resort and Conference Center. The hotel does not have lake access, but some slightly more expensive rooms do have a view. *Bus. Rte. 54, Box 1930, Lake Ozark 65049, ☎ 314/365–2334 or 800/532–3575, FAX 314/365–6887. 213 rooms, 4 suites. Facilities: restaurant, lounge, 3 indoor and outdoor pools, miniature golf, exercise room. AE, D, DC, MC, V. $$*

Springfield

DINING

Hemingway's Blue Water Cafe. In the Bass Pro Shops Outdoor World (*see* Exploring the Ozarks, *above*), this restaurant offers seafood, steaks, pasta, and poultry in a tropical atmosphere. *1935 S. Campbell Ave., ☎ 417/887–3388. AE, D, MC, V. $$$*

LODGING

Radisson Inn and Conference Center. The rooms at this hotel in the south part of town are clean and comfortable; the lobby is more ornate, with a deep green and burgundy color scheme and marble-topped desks. *3333 S. Glenstone Ave., 65804, ☎ 417/883–6550, FAX 417/883–5720. 199 rooms, 1 suite. Facilities: restaurant, lounge, indoor and outdoor pool. AE, D, DC, MC, V. $$*

University Plaza Holiday Inn. Boasting the largest conference center in Missouri, this hotel has guest rooms arranged around a nine-story atrium. *333 John Q. Hammons Pkwy., 65806, ☎ 417/864–7333, FAX 417/831–5893, ext. 7177. 271 rooms, 24 suites. Facilities: 2 restaurants, 2 lounges, indoor and outdoor pool, 2 tennis courts, exercise room. AE, D, DC, MC, V. $$*

Motels

EconoLodge (2808 N. Kansas Expressway, Springfield 65803, ☎ 417/869–5600), 83 rooms; *$*. **Red Roof Inn** (2655 N. Glenstone Ave., Springfield 65803, ☎ 417/831–2100), 112 rooms; *$*.

Campgrounds

In the Lake of the Ozarks area: **Deer Valley Park and Campground** (Sunrise Beach, ☎ 314/374–5277; closed mid-Oct.–mid-Apr.); **Lake of the Ozarks State Park** (*see* Exploring the Ozarks, *above*); **Majestic Oaks Park** (Lake Ozark, ☎ 314/365–1890; closed Nov.–Mar.). In the Branson area: **Blue Mountain Campground** (Branson, ☎ 800/779–2114); **Port of Kimberling Marina and Campground** (Kimberling City, ☎ 417/739–5377); **Silver Dollar City Campground** (Branson, ☎ 417/338–8189 or 800/477–5164; closed Nov.–Mar.).

The Arts and Nightlife

Among the music shows in the Lake of the Ozarks region is the **Kin-Fokes Country Music Show** (Camdenton, ☎ 314/346–6797). Music theaters in Branson include **Andy Williams Moon River Theater** (☎ 417/334–4500), **Baldknobbers Hillbilly Jamboree Show** (☎ 417/334–4528), **Cristy Lane Theater** (☎ 417/335–5111), **Grand Palace** (☎ 417/336–4636), **Jim Stafford Theater** (☎ 417/335–8080), **Mel Tillis Theater** (☎ 417/335–6635), **Mickey Gilley's Family Theater** (☎ 417/334–3210), **Presleys' Mountain Music Jubilee** (☎ 417/334–4874), **Roy Clark Celebrity Theater** (☎ 417/334–0076), and the **Shoji Tabuchi Show** (☎ 417/334–7469). Contact the Branson Lakes Area Chamber of Commerce (*see* Tourist Information, *above*) for a complete listing.

ELSEWHERE IN THE STATE

Hannibal

Getting There

Hannibal is about two hours north of St. Louis on U.S. 61.

What to See and Do

Hannibal is Mark Twain country. His boyhood home is preserved at the **Mark Twain Home and Museum** (208 Hill St., ☎ 314/221–9010). The **Mark Twain Cave** (Rte. 79, ☎ 314/221–1656) is where Tom Sawyer and Becky Thatcher got lost in Twain's classic *Adventures of Tom Sawyer.* Contact the **Hannibal Visitors and Convention Bureau** (320 Broadway, Box 624, 63401, ☎ 314/221–2477).

Ste. Genevieve

Getting There

Ste. Genevieve is about 60 mi south of St. Louis on I–55.

What to See and Do

Numerous historic homes in this small river town, the oldest permanent settlement in Missouri, include examples of 18th-century French Creole architecture, characterized by vertical log construction. The **Great River Road Interpretive Center** (66 S. Main St., 63670, ☎ 314/883–7097) houses the tourist information office.

St. Joseph

Getting There

St. Joseph is about an hour north of Kansas City on I–29.

What to See and Do

During the short experiment called the Pony Express, riders set out on the 2,000-mi trip to Sacramento, California, from what is now St. Joseph's **Pony Express National Memorial** (914 Penn St., ☏ 816/279–5059). Nearby is the **Jesse James Home** (12th and Penn Sts., ☏ 816/232–8206), where the notorious outlaw was shot and killed by a member of his own gang for the reward money. The bullet hole in the wall is still visible. The **St. Joseph Convention and Visitors Bureau** (Box 445, 109 S. Fourth St., 64502, ☏ 816/233–6688 or 800/785–0360) has more information.

NEBRASKA

Updated by Michael and Linda Kephart Flynn

Capital	Lincoln
Population	1,578,000
Motto	Equality Before the Law
State Bird	Western meadowlark
State Flower	Goldenrod

Visitor Information

The **Nebraska Department of Economic Development, Division of Travel and Tourism** (Box 94666, Lincoln 68509, ☎ 800/228–4307) staffs 24 rest and information areas along I–80.

Scenic Drives

Rte. 2, from Grand Island west to Crawford, is a long, lonesome road through the Sandhills that traverses 332 mi of delicate wildflowers, tranquil rivers, and placid cattle. The 130-mi drive north on **U.S. 83** from North Platte to Valentine offers a fine view of the Sandhills' native shortgrass prairie. **U.S. 26** from Ogallala to Scottsbluff is a 128-mi historic segment of the Oregon Trail, passing such natural landmarks as Ash Hollow; Courthouse, Jail, and Chimney rocks; and Scotts Bluff National Monument.

National and State Parks

National Parks

Homestead National Monument, near Beatrice (Rte. 3, Box 47, 68310, ☎ 402/223–3514), commemorates the post-1862 homestead movement and the pioneers who braved the rigors of the prairie frontier. **Nebraska National Forest,** at Halsey (Box 38, 69142, ☎ 308/533–2257), is the largest man-planted forest in the country.

State Parks

The **Nebraska Game and Parks Commission** (Box 30370, Lincoln 68503, ☎ 402/471–0641) manages and provides information on the seven state parks. Among them are **Fort Robinson State Park** (*see* Exploring Northwest Nebraska, *below*); **Eugene T. Mahoney State Park** and **Platte River State Park** (*see* Exploring Southeast Nebraska, *below*); and **Indian Cave State Park,** in the state's southeast corner (2 mi north and 5 mi east of Shubert, Box 30, 68437, ☎ 402/883–2575).

SOUTHEAST NEBRASKA

This is a land of mixed blessings; one of city sophistication and country charm. Visitors can tour museums and historic buildings, shop in restored warehouses, ride riverboats, and board a vintage steam locomotive.

Tourist Information

Lincoln: Convention and Visitors Bureau (1221 N St., 68508, ☎ 402/434–5335 or 800/423–8212). **Nebraska City:** Convention and Visitors Bureau (806 1st Ave., 68410, ☎ 402/873–6654). **Omaha:** Greater Omaha Convention and Visitors Bureau (6800 Mercy Rd., Suite 202, 68106, ☎ 402/444–4660 or 800/332–1819).

Getting There

By Plane

Eppley Airfield, about 3 mi from downtown Omaha, is served by most domestic carriers, as well as **GP Express** (☎ 800/525–0280) and **United Express** (☎ 800/554–5111). Cab fare from the airport to downtown is about $8. **Lincoln Municipal Airport,** about 3 mi from downtown Lincoln, is served by several major airlines as well as GP Express. Cabs to downtown cost about $10. **Eppley Express** (☎ 308/234–6066 or 800/888–9793) runs an airport minibus from Lincoln Municipal Airport to Eppley Airfield ($16 fare).

By Car

I–80W from Des Moines links with Omaha (I–480 serves downtown Omaha) and Lincoln. U.S. 75S from Omaha leads to Nebraska City. From Lincoln, Rte. 2 goes to Nebraska City. To get to Beatrice, take U.S. 77S from Lincoln.

By Train

Amtrak's (☎ 800/872–7245) *Desert Wind, Pioneer,* and *California Zephyr* stop in Lincoln and Omaha.

By Bus

Omaha and Lincoln are served by **Greyhound Lines** (☎ 800/231–2222). Local bus service is provided in Lincoln by **StarTran** (☎ 402/476–1234) and in Omaha by **Metro Area Transit** (☎ 402/341–0800).

Exploring Southeast Nebraska

Nebraska's multistory state capitol building dominates the Lincoln skyline; the river city of Omaha is the region's center of commerce and industry. Minutes away from both downtowns are expansive prairies, state parks, and attractions that chronicle the opening of the West to settlement.

Start your tour in **Omaha,** where the **Henry Doorly Zoo** (3701 S. 10th St., ☎ 402/733–8401; admission charged) has the world's largest indoor rain forest, the Lied Jungle, and a saltwater aquarium. From here, it's about 2 mi north to the **Western Heritage Museum** (801 S. 10th St., ☎ 402/444–5072; admission charged), which documents Omaha history from 1880 to 1954; exhibits include a replica of the 1911 *Vin Fiz,* the first biplane to cross North America. Then head west on U.S. 6 to Father Flanagan's **Boys Town** (138th St. and W. Dodge Rd., ☎ 402/498–1140), the only official village in the nation created just for children. Founded in 1917 and made famous by the 1938 movie with Spencer Tracy and Mickey Rooney, the town includes schools, churches, and farmland.

Travel south on 144th Street and east on Rte. 370, about 40 minutes in all, to **Bellevue,** home of the **Strategic Air Command Museum** (2510 SAC Pl., ☎ 402/292–2001). Here you can stroll beneath the wings of aircraft that changed the course of history, see missiles huge and small, view rare film footage, and browse through an extensive collection of military artifacts.

In Fremont, about 50 mi northwest of Bellevue, board the historic **Fremont and Elkhorn Valley Railroad** (1835 N. Somers Ave., ☎ 402/727–0615 or 800/942–7245). The steam-powered train travels through 15 mi of lush Elkhorn Valley and offers dinner and mystery trips.

About 60 mi south of Fremont are the **Eugene T. Mahoney State Park** (near Ashland, ☎ 402/944–2523) and the **Platte River State Park**

(Rte. 50, then 2 mi west on Spur 13E near Louisville, ☎ 402/234–2217). Both provide campsites and cabins, riding, swimming, hiking, buffalo-stew cookouts, and spectacular vistas of the Platte River valley.

Take I–80W to **Lincoln,** home of the **University of Nebraska** and the state government. Scan the city's skyline from atop the **Nebraska Capitol** (1445 K St., ☎ 402/471–3191), a 400-foot spire that towers over the surrounding plains. A five-minute drive north will take you to the **State Museum of Natural History** (at the university, 14th and U Sts., ☎ 402/472–2642), nicknamed "Elephant Hall" for its huge collection of extinct animals that once roamed the Great Plains. A 20-minute drive west takes you to **Nine-Mile Prairie** (1 mi west of N.W. 48th St. and Fletcher Ave.), where you can park your car and get out to hike the natural prairies.

From Lincoln, you can take Rte. 2 southeast to U.S. 75, then U.S. 136 southeast to Brownville. At the Brownville State Recreation Area, the ***Spirit of Brownville*** riverboat (☎ 402/825–6441 or 712/625–2791) offers sightseeing, dining, and dancing cruises on the mighty Missouri River. Just south of Brownville Bridge is the **Capt. Meriwether Lewis and Missouri River History Museum** (☎ 402/825–3341), featuring a restored side-wheeler dredge once used on the river.

U.S. 75N brings you to **Nebraska City,** a tidy town rimmed with historic sites and apple orchards, including the **Arbor Day Farm** (100 Arbor Ave., ☎ 402/873–8710), where you can buy apples, cider, and desserts year-round.

Hop the **Nebraska City Trolley** (☎ 402/873–3000) at stops throughout town. It links historic sites to 11 downtown factory outlets clustered around 8th and 1st Corso streets and to the **VF Factory Outlet Mall** (1001 Rte. 2, ☎ 402/873–7727), with merchandise from dishes to sweaters. The trolley also stops at **John Brown's Cave** (1908 4th Corso St., ☎ 402/727–5630), a museum, a historic village, and a cave once used to hide runaway slaves.

Nearby is the **Arbor Lodge State Historical Park and Arboretum.** On the grounds are the 52-room mansion and greenhouse of J. Sterling Morton, the 19th-century politician and lover of trees who inaugurated the first Arbor Day, now observed nationwide as a day for planting trees. *2nd and Centennial Aves., ☎ 402/873–7222. Admission charged.*

Shopping

Nebraska Furniture Mart (700 S. 72nd St., Omaha, ☎ 402/397–6100 or 800/359–1200) is reputed to be the largest furniture store west of the Mississippi. Omaha's **Old Market** (between 10th and 13th Sts., ☎ 402/346–4445) is a collection of boutiques, galleries, and restaurants in the oldest part of town. Lincoln's charming restored warehouse shopping district, **Historic Haymarket** (between 7th and 9th Sts., from O to S Sts., ☎ 402/435–7496), features quaint antiques stores, novelty gift shops, and some fine restaurants. Find bargains at Nebraska City's outlets (*see* Exploring Southeast Nebraska, *above*).

Sports and the Outdoors

Fishing

The 13 Salt Valley lakes surrounding Lincoln, especially **Branched Oak** (N.W. 140th St. and W. Raymond Rd.) and **Pawnee** (N.W. 98th and W. Adams Sts.), offer a variety of fish, including largemouth bass, northern pike, walleye, and channel catfish. For more information contact the **Game and Parks Commission** (☎ 402/471–0641).

Spectator Sports

Football

The **University of Nebraska Cornhuskers** are a football powerhouse. Although tickets for games (Sept.–Nov.) are nearly impossible to get, check the Husker Ticket Outlet (117 S. Stadium St., ☎ 402/472–3111).

Dining and Lodging

Dining choices in this varied region range from international cuisine to pizza to quiche. Lodging runs from full-service hotels to comfortable bed-and-breakfasts (**Bed and Breakfast of Nebraska,** Rte. 2, Box 17, Elgin 68636, ☎ 402/843–2287). For price ranges, see Charts 1 (B) and 2 (B) in On the Road with Fodor's.

Brownville

LODGING

Thompson House Bed and Breakfast. This Victorian three-story house has a game room and parlor. Rooms are decorated with antiques, including kerosene lamps. *Box 162, 68321, ☎ 402/825–6551. 5 rooms. MC, V. $$$*

Lincoln

DINING

★ **Billy's.** The elegance of a bygone era is complemented by a fascinating collection of political memorabilia and antiques in this upscale restaurant that offers everything from steak Diane to charbroiled chicken. *1301 H St., ☎ 402/474–0084. AE, MC, V. $$*

Misty's Restaurant. Adorned with Cornhusker football paraphernalia, this is considered by locals to be the prime-rib palace of the Plains. *6235 Havelock Ave., ☎ 402/466–8424. AE, D, MC, V. $$*

Rock 'n' Roll Runza. Waitresses on roller skates serve Runzas—a hamburger-cabbage sandwich—at this '50s-style restaurant. *210 N. 14th St., ☎ 402/474–2030. AE, MC, V. $*

★ **Valentino's Restaurant.** Besides pizza with original, home-style, or deep-dish crust, the restaurant also serves Italian specials and dessert pizzas with such toppings as cherry and cream cheese. *3457 Holdrege St., ☎ 402/467–3611. MC, V. $*

LODGING

The Cornhusker. The lobby of this elegant hotel has a grand curving staircase, oak accents, and an Italian marble floor. East- and south-wing rooms have good views of downtown Lincoln. *333 S. 13th St., 68508, ☎ 402/474–7474, FAX 402/474–1847. 277 rooms, 12 suites. Facilities: restaurant, pool, exercise room, sauna. AE, D, DC, MC, V. $$$*

★ **Rogers House Bed and Breakfast.** Built in 1914, this ivy-covered brick mansion was converted into a B&B in 1984 by the current owners. The antiques-filled rooms with oak floors include a living room with fireplace and a sunroom where guests can have breakfast. *2145 B St., 68502, ☎ 402/476–6961. 12 rooms. AE, MC, V. $$*

Nebraska City

DINING

★ **Teresa's Family Restaurant.** Booths line the walls of this casual, family-style place where old-fashioned food, such as homemade lemon pie and meat loaf, is offered at yesterday's prices. *812 Central Ave., ☎ 402/873–9100. MC, V. $*

★ **Ulbrick's.** This converted gas station and café is nothing fancy, but the made-from-scratch, family-style dinners of fried chicken, creamed corn and cabbage, and homemade egg noodles are exceptional. *1513 S. 11th St., ☎ 402/873–5458. Reservations advised Sun. No credit cards. $*

LODGING

Whispering Pines. Nestled among pines on 6½ quiet acres, this 112-year-old, two-story brick house has been completely refurbished as a B&B and filled with antiques. *Rte. 2, 68410, ☎ 402/873–5850. 4 rooms. MC, V. $*

Omaha

DINING

Bohemian Cafe. Gaily painted Czech plates hang on the walls of this family-style restaurant, where you can try such ethnic favorites as goulash. *1406 S. 13th St., ☎ 402/342–9838. D, MC, V. $$*

Johnny's Café. Since 1922 this has been *the* place to eat near the famous Omaha Stockyards. Mouthwatering steaks are the specialty, but seafood and midwestern dishes are offered as well. *4702 S. 27th St., ☎ 402/731–4774. AE, MC, V. $$*

★ **Mr. C's.** Christmas lights surround you at this Italian steak house. Here the lasagna and manicotti are as good as the sirloin. *5319 N. 30th St., ☎ 402/451–1998. AE, DC, MC, V. $$*

Austins. Throw your peanut shells on the floor at this casual eatery where the atmosphere is Western and the food pure country. Chicken-fried steak, prime rib, and barbecued ribs are the specialties. *12020 Anne St., ☎ 402/896–5373. AE, MC, V. No reservations. $*

Garden Café. Home-style cooking with everything made from scratch is what this café in the historic Old Market is known for. Noteworthy are the potato casseroles, soups, salads, and desserts. *12th and Harvey Sts., ☎ 402/422–1574. AE, DC, MC, V. $*

Neon Goose. The mood is lively at this recently remodeled restaurant with piano bar. Good menu choices here are the unusual quiches and the melt-in-your-mouth omelets. *1012 S. 10th St., ☎ 402/341–2063. AE, D, DC, MC, V. $*

LODGING

Marriott Hotel. Built in the 1980s, this six-story hotel in suburban Omaha offers comfort but little flash. There's a gift shop here, and you can take advantage of nearby shopping at the upscale Regency Fashion Court area. *10220 Regency Circle, 68114, ☎ 402/399–9000, FAX 402/399–0223. 297 rooms, 4 suites. Facilities: 2 restaurants, pool, exercise equipment, gift shop. AE, D, DC, MC, V. $$$*

★ **Red Lion Hotel.** This 19-story hotel has a luxurious, chandeliered lobby and spacious rooms with mauve and mint-green color schemes. It's in the heart of downtown, close to the Old Market and Creighton University. *1616 Dodge St., 68102, ☎ 402/346–7600, FAX 402/346–5722. 413 rooms, 18 suites. Facilities: restaurant, pool, sauna. AE, D, DC, MC, V. $$$*

Motels

Oak Creek Inn (2808 S. 72nd St., Omaha 68124, ☎ 402/397–7137), 102 rooms, pool, whirlpool, sauna, spa/exercise room; *$$*. **Harvester Motel** (1511 Center Park Rd., Lincoln 68512, ☎ 402/423–3131), 80 rooms, pool, cocktail lounge; *$*.

Campgrounds

Indian Cave State Park (*see* National and State Parks, *above*) and **Eugene T. Mahoney State Park** (*see* Exploring Southeast Nebraska, *above*) offer excellent tent and RV camping.

NORTHWEST NEBRASKA

Here the Great Plains end and the Old West begins—a rugged, beautiful land with dramatic buttes and bluffs, Ponderosa pines, craggy ridges, and canyons.

Tourist Information

Alliance: Box Butte Visitors Committee (Alliance Chamber of Commerce, Box 571, 69301, ☎ 308/762–1520). **Chadron:** Chamber of Commerce (Box 646, 69337, ☎ 308/432–4401). **Scottsbluff:** United Chamber of Commerce (1517 Broadway St., 69361, ☎ 308/632–2133 or 800/788–9475). **Valentine:** Visitors Center (Box 201, 69201, ☎ 402/376–2969 or 800/658–4024).

Getting There

By Car

From Omaha and Lincoln, take I–80W about 275 mi to U.S. 26, which closely follows the Oregon and Mormon trails to Scottsbluff. To bypass Kearney and North Platte, take I–80 to Grand Island, then scenic Rte. 2 to the north, which runs parallel to I–80 through Nebraska's Sandhills.

Exploring Northwest Nebraska

Head west on U.S. 26 to Bridgeport, then 4 mi south on Rte. 88. From the road you can see **Courthouse and Jail rocks,** sandstone outcroppings that pioneers used as landmarks on the trail west. Four miles south of Bayard, at the junction of U.S. 26 and Rte. 92, the **Chimney Rock National Historic Site** (☎ 308/586–2581) is an even more impressive outcropping that pioneers described as "towering to the heavens." Oregon Trail wagon ruts are still visible at the **Scotts Bluff National Monument** (3 mi west of Gering on Rte. 92, ☎ 308/436–4340), an enormous bluff that rises out of the rocky plains. Once described as the "Lighthouse of the Plains," it now features a museum at its base.

About 60 mi north of Mitchell on Rte. 29, the **Agate Fossil Beds National Monument** features fossil deposits dating back 20 million years. A museum (☎ 308/668–2211) preserves and displays fossils and Native American artifacts, including personal items that belonged to Chief Red Cloud.

Continue north on Rte. 29, then east on U.S. 20 to **Fort Robinson State Park** (☎ 308/665–2900), where activities include trail rides, historic tours, cookouts, swimming, trout fishing, hiking, and stagecoach rides.

Sports and the Outdoors

Hiking and Backpacking

Fort Robinson State Park (*see* Exploring Northwest Nebraska, *above*) and **Chadron State Park** (8 mi south of Chadron on U.S. 385, ☎ 308/432–6167) offer an abundance of trails.

Dining and Lodging

Travelers to the region chow down at casual, out-of-the-way restaurants, wagon-train cookouts, and ranches. Inexpensive cattle ranches and B&Bs (**Bed and Breakfast of Nebraska,** Rte. 2, Box 17, Elgin, NE 68636, ☎ 402/843–2287) provide charming alternatives to chain mo-

Western Nebraska

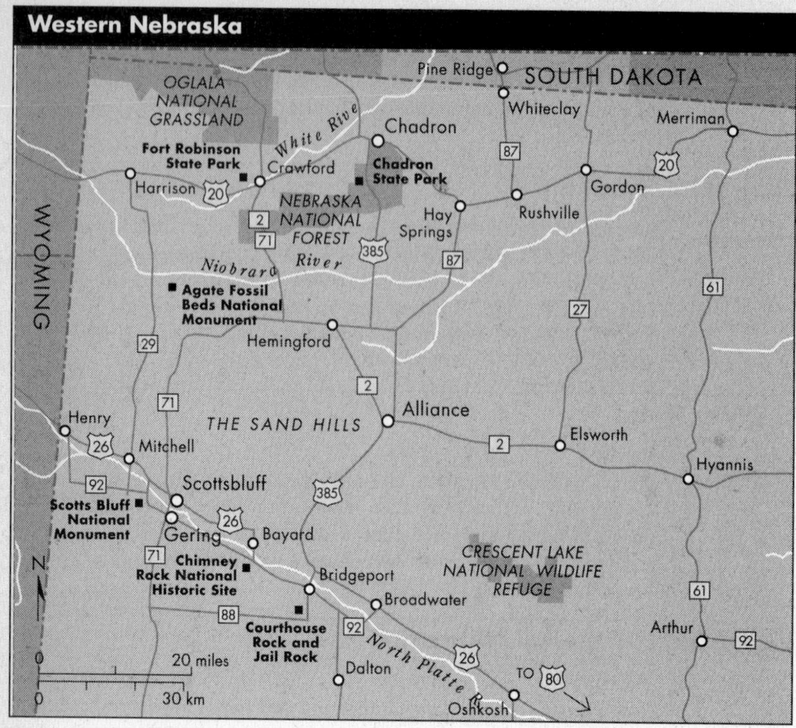

tels. For price ranges, see Charts 1 (B) and 2 (B) in On the Road with Fodor's.

Bayard

DINING AND LODGING

★ **Oregon Trail Wagon Train.** Enjoy sleeping under the stars and eating cookouts of stew, spoon bread, and vinegar pudding on covered-wagon tours through some of Nebraska's remaining short-grass prairies. One- to six-day treks are available. *Rte. 2, Box 502, 69334, ☎ 308/586–1850. Reservations required. MC, V. $$$*

Crawford

LODGING

Fort Robinson State Park Lodge. Dating back to the 1800s, this historic fort in Fort Robinson State Park includes a two-story lodge with large verandas and tall columns. Built in 1909 as an enlisted men's barracks, the lodge now has modern rooms with private baths but no telephones or TVs. *3 mi west of Crawford, Box 392, Crawford, 69339, ☎ 308/665–2900. 23 rooms with bath. MC, V. $*

Oshkosh

DINING

S & S Cafe. This café serves hearty fish dishes, thick steaks, and juicy burgers. The atmosphere is completely unpretentious—there's even a bullet hole in the wall near the clock. *Hwy. 26, ☎ 308/772–3811. MC, V. $*

Scottsbluff

DINING

Grampy's Pancake House. This large, family-style restaurant is divided into three dining rooms with booths and tables, where tasty breakfasts such as strawberry pancakes are featured. Lunch and dinner are also served here. *1802 E. 20th Pl., ☎ 308/632–6906. MC, V. $*

Motels

Scottsbluff Inn (1901 21st Ave., Scottsbluff 69361, ☎ 308/635–3111), 138 rooms, pool, sauna, weight room, restaurant/lounge; *$$*. **Landmark Inn** (246 Main St., Bayard 69334, ☎ 308/586–1375), 10 rooms; *$*. **Town Line Motel** (Box 423, Crawford 69339, ☎ 308/665–1450), 24 rooms (7 with kitchenettes); *$*.

Ranches

Verde Valley Guest Ranch. Bed-and-breakfast or all-inclusive packages are offered at this working cattle ranch 60 mi north of Lake McConaughy. Rooms are available in the 1915 Mission-style home or in modern cabins. Those who opt for the meal-and-activities plan can take part in riding, hunting, sailing, and swimming. *Box 228, Hyannis 69350, ☎ 308/458–2220. 7 rooms, 3 cabins. Facilities: dining room, pool, recreational activities. MC, V. $$–$$$*

Meadow View Ranch Bed and Breakfast Bunkhouse. Guests stay in the converted bunkhouse of this 5,000-acre working ranch 18 mi from the South Dakota border. Accommodations include a kitchenette, a living room, and two bedrooms. Complimentary breakfast is served in the ranch kitchen, and picnic lunches are packed on request. Activities include fishing, hiking in the nearby Sandhills, wagon rides, and cattle drives. *HC 91, Box 29, Gordon 69343, ☎ 308/282–0679. Bunkhouse sleeps 7. No credit cards. Closed Nov.–Apr. $$*

Campgrounds

Chadron State Park (*see* Hiking and Backpacking, *above*) and **Fort Robinson State Park** (*see* Exploring Northwest Nebraska, *above*) offer tent and RV camping.

ELSEWHERE IN THE STATE

Lake McConaughy and Ogallala

Getting There

From Lincoln and Omaha, take I–80W to Ogallala.

What to See and Do

Lake McConaughy State Recreation Area and the **Kingsley Dam** (9 mi north of Ogallala on Rte. 61, ☎ 308/284–3542) annually attract thousands of visitors who come to camp, fish, go boating, and enjoy the natural white-sand beaches here. In Ogallala, **Front Street** (☎ 308/284–6000) depicts an 1880s Main Street and features nightly western shows Memorial Day through Labor Day. Nearby are **Mansion on the Hill** (☎ 308/284–4066), a museum with exhibits on 19th-century cattle drives, and **Boot Hill Cemetery,** three blocks west of the mansion.

Red Cloud

Getting There

From Lincoln and Omaha, take I–80W to Grand Island, then U.S. 34S to U.S. 281, then U.S. 281S.

What to See and Do

Red Cloud was the home of Pulitzer Prize–winning author Willa Cather. The **Willa Cather Historical Center** (338 N. Webster St., ☎ 402/746–3285) is dedicated to the author, who loved the Plains—610 acres of which are preserved as the **Cather Memorial Prairie** (5 mi south of Red Cloud).

The Great Platte River Road

Getting There

From Omaha and Lincoln, take I–80W.

What to See and Do

Westward-bound pioneers on the Mormon and Oregon trails once hugged the shores of the Platte River, a verdant natural pathway. Today I–80 follows the same route, cutting through the state's heartland and affording glimpses of this pioneer past. **Sculpture gardens** dot the landscape along the highway for 500 mi across the Nebraska plains. At nine rest areas large stone and metal artwork constitutes what some critics have called a "museum without walls."

In **Grand Island,** the **Stuhr Museum of the Prairie Pioneer** (junction of U.S. 34 and U.S. 281, ☎ 308/385–5316) houses Native American artifacts and features a 60-building "Railroad Town," complete with a steam-powered train. From early March to mid-April, visitors flock to an area near Grand Island and Kearney to witness the migration of thousands of Sandhill cranes as they pause here before resuming their flight north. The **Platte River Whooping Crane Habitat Maintenance Trust** (☎ 308/384–4633) and the **Lillian Rowe Audubon Sanctuary** (☎ 308/468–5282) offer tours.

Fort Kearny State Historical Park (4 mi south of I–80 on Rte. 44 and 4 mi east of L–50A, ☎ 308/234–9513) has a re-created stockade and interpretive exhibits detailing the role of the outpost on the frontier.

Harold Warp's Pioneer Village (junction of U.S. 6, U.S. 34, and Rte. 10 in Minden, ☎ 308/832–1181) has an extensive collection of pioneer memorabilia; horse-drawn, covered-wagon rides; and crafts demonstrations. **Gothenburg's** downtown Ehmen Park contains an original **Pony Express Station** (☎ 308/537–2680). The Wild West comes alive in **North Platte,** where Buffalo Bill Cody and his famous Wild West show began. You can tour his ranch house in the **Buffalo Bill Ranch State Historical Park** (☎ 308/535–8035), 6 mi northwest of North Platte. **Hastings Museum** (1330 N. Burlington Ave., ☎ 402/461–2399; admission charged) has exhibits on natural history and the history of the frontier; related films are shown in its IMAX theater.

Sandhills/Valentine Region

Getting There

From Lincoln and Omaha, take I–80W to Grand Island. Go north on U.S. 281 to Rte. 22 and then follow it west 9 mi to Rte. 11N. At Burwell, follow Rte. 91W to U.S. 183N to U.S. 20W to Valentine.

What to See and Do

Fort Hartsuff State Historical Park (3 mi north of Elyria, off Rte. 11, ☎ 308/346–4715) is a restored 1870s infantry post with guides in period uniforms and costumes.

For a glimpse of the Great Plains as they once were, you can take a drive through hundreds of miles of mixed-grass prairie, where outdoor attractions beckon. The **Niobrara River** draws canoeists from throughout the state. Outfitters include **Dryland Aquatics** (Box 33C, Sparks 69220, ☎ 402/376–3119), **A&C Canoe Rentals** (518 N. Ray St., Valentine 69201, ☎ 402/376–2839), **Brewers Canoers** (433 E. U.S. 20, Valentine 69201, ☎ 402/376–2046), **Graham Canoe Outfitters** (HC 13, Box 16A, Valentine 69201, ☎ 402/376–3708), and **Little Outlaw Canoe & Tube Rentals** (Box 15, Valentine 69201, ☎ 402/376–1822). Native wildlife is abundant at the **Valentine National Wildlife Refuge** (HC 14, Box 67, Valentine 69201, ☎ 402/376–1889), south of Valentine on U.S. 83. Its 70,000 acres of prairie and wetlands shelter ducks, geese, hawks, eagles, deer, coyotes, beavers, and other species. There are trails for driving or hiking through this open country; information kiosks are located at entrances to the refuge.

Nearby, the **Fort Niobrara National Wildlife Refuge** (HC 14, Box 67, Valentine 69201, ☎ 402/376–1889), 5 mi east of Valentine on Rte. 12, has a more forested terrain and larger species, such as bison, elk, and Longhorn cattle.

NORTH DAKOTA

By Kevin Bonham

Updated by Sue Berg

Capital	Bismarck
Population	638,800
Motto	Liberty and Union, Now and Forever, One and Inseparable
State Bird	Western meadowlark
State Flower	Wild prairie rose

Visitor Information

North Dakota Tourism Department (Liberty Memorial Bldg., 604 E. Blvd., Bismarck 58505, ☎ 701/328–2525 or 800/435–5663). **Welcome centers:** along I–94E, 1 mi west of Beach; off I–94 the Oriska rest area, 12 mi east of Valley City; off I–29N at the Lake Agassiz Rest Area, 8 mi south of Hankinson interchange; along I–29S, 1 mi north of the Pembina interchange; one block west of the junction of U.S. 2 and U.S. 85 in Williston; at the junction of U.S. 12 and U.S. 85 in Bowman; at the 45th Street interchange off I–94W in Fargo; and on U.S. 2, 10 mi east of Grand Forks at Fisher's Landing.

Scenic Drives

The **Pembina Gorge** in northeast North Dakota is a beautiful forested valley created by glaciers and the winding Pembina River; from I–29 at the Joliette exit near the northern boundary of the state, drive west on Rte. 5, then north on Rte. 32 to Walhalla. Theodore Roosevelt National Park's **South Unit loop road** begins near park headquarters in Medora and winds 36 mi through an eerie world of lonesome pinnacles and spires, steep gorges and ravaged buttes. The 26-mi **North Unit loop road** begins at the park entrance along U.S. 85, 15 mi south of Watford City; the high ground above the Little Missouri River has dramatic overlooks, and a lower area near the visitor center features a series of slump rocks, huge sections of bluff that gradually slid intact to the valley floor.

National and State Parks

National Park

Theodore Roosevelt National Park (*see* Exploring the Badlands, *below*).

State Parks

North Dakota's state parks are open year-round. Among the most scenic are **Cross Ranch State Park,** 50 mi north of Bismarck, off Rte. 200A (HCR2 Box 152, Sanger 58567, ☎ 701/794–3731); two parks on U.S. 2 and Hwy. 19 that are part of **Devils Lake State Parks** (Box 165, Devils Lake 58301, ☎ 701/766–4015); **Fort Abraham Lincoln State Park** (*see* Exploring the Missouri River Corridor, *below*); and **Icelandic State Park,** on Rte. 5, 5 mi west of Cavalier (HCR3 Box 64A, Cavalier 58220, ☎ 701/265–4561). All parks listed offer camping facilities.

MISSOURI RIVER CORRIDOR

The Missouri River is both a geographic and a symbolic barrier between the two North Dakotas—the east and the west. The state capital of Bismarck, on the east bank of the river, is a busy political hub, while a short drive northwest leads to sprawling Lake Sakakawea, where urban life seems a world away.

Tourist Information

Bismarck-Mandan: Convention and Visitors Bureau (Box 2274, 523 N. 4th St., Bismarck 58501, ☎ 701/222–4308). **Minot:** Convention and Visitors Bureau (1015 S. Broadway, 58701, ☎ 701/857–8206).

Getting There

By Plane

Bismarck Municipal Airport (☎ 701/222–6502) and **Minot International Airport** (☎ 701/857–4724) are served by Northwest, Frontier, and United Express. Both airports are about 5 mi from downtown; cab fare is about $5.

By Car

I–94, the state's major east–west thoroughfare, runs through the Bismarck-Mandan area. U.S. 83 runs north from Bismarck to Minot, the state's fourth-largest city. U.S. 2 runs east–west along the top half of the state, including Minot.

By Train

Amtrak (☎ 800/872–7245) stops in Minot and Williston.

By Bus

Greyhound Lines (☎ 800/231–2222) and **Triangle Transportation** (☎ 701/223–6576) serve Bismarck and Minot.

Exploring the Missouri River Corridor

As with the rest of North Dakota, most of the attractions described here are open in the summer only (often Memorial Day–Labor Day); be sure to call ahead before you visit. The 19-story **state capitol** building (600 E. Boulevard Ave., 58505, ☎ 701/328–2480) in north **Bismarck** is visible for miles across the Dakota prairie; tours of the limestone-and-marble Art Deco structure, built in the 1930s, are offered weekdays year-round and also on weekends Memorial Day to Labor Day. Just down the hill is the **North Dakota Heritage Center** (612 E. Blvd., ☎ 701/328–2666), which serves as the state museum and archives. Exhibits include Native American and pioneer artifacts and natural-history displays. The **Former Governor's Mansion** (4th St. and Ave. B, ☎ 701/224–2666) is an elegant Victorian structure containing political memorabilia and period furnishings. The ***Lewis and Clark Riverboat*** (☎ 701/255–4233) offers summer cruises on the Missouri River, plying the same route taken by the traders, trappers, and settlers of the last century.

The boat is slated to dock at **Fort Abraham Lincoln State Park** (Rte. 2, Mandan, ☎ 701/663–9571). You can also reach the park from Bismarck by crossing the river on I–94 to Mandan, then either traveling 4 mi south on Rte. 1806 or taking the 9-mi **Fort Lincoln Trolley** (☎ 701/663–9018) from south Mandan. Among the reconstructed buildings at the fort are the barracks (where you can stay overnight for $15) and the **Custer House** (admission charged), a replica of the 1870s house where Gen. George Armstrong Custer lived with his wife, Libby, before his fateful expedition to Little Big Horn. Nearby is the reconstructed **On-A-Slant Indian Village** (admission charged), once home to the Mandan tribe.

From Bismarck, take U.S. 83 to Washburn, then Rte. 200A west to the **Knife River Indian Villages National Historic Site** (¼ mi north of Stanton, ☎ 701/745–3309). The area preserves depressions formed by the Hidatsa and Mandan Indians' earth lodges, circular mud and timber structures. Pottery shards and other artifacts are displayed at the museum and interpretive center. There's also a full-size replica of an earth lodge.

Twenty miles north is the 600-sq-mi **Lake Sakakawea,** affording countless recreational opportunities including swimming and boating. State parks and small resort communities are sprinkled along its shores. Free tours of the **Garrison Dam Power Plant** are conducted by the U.S. Army Corps of Engineers (☎ 701/654–7441). For more information on the lake, contact the Tourism Department (*see* Visitor Information, *above*).

Sports and the Outdoors

Biking

The 246-mi **Lewis and Clark Bike Tour** follows the Missouri River along Rtes. 1804, 200, and 22, from the South Dakota border to the Montana border. Contact the Tourism Department (*see* Visitor Information, *above*) for details. **Dakota Cyclery** (211 S. 3rd St., Bismarck, ☎ 701/222–1218) rents bicycles and can provide information about area biking.

Fishing

Walleye and northern pike are the big catches on Lake Sakakawea. The **North Dakota Game and Fish Department** (100 N. Bismarck Expressway, Bismarck 58501, ☎ 701/328–6300) provides a list of area fishing guides. The ***North Dakota Hunting and Fishing Guide*** outlines seasons and regulations and is available through the Tourism Department (*see* Visitor Information, *above*).

Hiking

The 17-mi **Roughrider Trail** along Missouri River bottomland is a treasure. For details, contact the Parks and Recreation Department (1835 E. Bismarck Expressway, Bismarck 58504, ☎ 701/328–5357).

Dining and Lodging

For a listing of area B&Bs, contact the Tourism Department (*see* Visitor Information, *above*). For price ranges, see Charts 1 (B) and 2 (B) in On the Road with Fodor's.

Bismarck

DINING

★ **Peacock Alley Bar and Grill.** In what was once the historic Patterson Hotel, this restaurant enjoys local fame as the former scene of countless political deals; period photographs recall those heady days. The menu features seafood specials such as Cajun firecracker shrimp and such regional dishes as pheasant in white-wine sauce. *422 E. Main St., ☎ 701/255–7917. AE, MC, V. $$*

Fiesta Villa. This family-run Mexican restaurant is suitably housed in a Spanish mission-style building, with arched doorways and high ceilings. Beef or chicken fajitas are a good choice here, and they go well with the excellent margaritas. *4th and Main Sts., ☎ 701/222–8075. AE, D, MC, V. $*

LODGING

Radisson Inn. Rooms here are spacious and comfortable, with overstuffed chairs and soothing pastel color schemes. The hotel is across from Bismarck's largest shopping mall, Kirkwood Plaza. *800 S. 3rd St., 58504, ☎ 701/258–7700, FAX 701/224–8212. 306 rooms, 8 suites. Facilities: restaurant, lounge, indoor pool, sauna, health club. AE, D, DC, MC, V. $$*

Mandan

DINING

Captain's Table Restaurant. As the name suggests, the decor follows a maritime theme. Menu selections hail from around the world; the specialty is a peppery South American–style steak whose recipe is a closely guarded secret. *Best Western Seven Seas Inn, I–94, Exit 152, ☎ 701/663–3773. AE, D, DC, MC, V. $$*

★ **Mandan Drug.** For a fun lunch (the place is open 9–6), follow a sandwich or homemade soup with an old-fashioned cherry soda or a Brown Cow—that's a root beer float with chocolate ice cream. The homemade candy is hard to resist. *316 Main St., ☎ 701/663–5900. MC, V. Closed Sun. $*

LODGING

Best Western Seven Seas Inn and Convention Center. Nautical decor fills the public areas, from scrimshaw displays to 200-year-old anchors to carpeting made to resemble ship's planking. Rooms continue the theme with maritime art. *I–94, Exit 152, 2611 Old Red Trail, 58554, ☎ 701/663–7401 or 800/597–7327, FAX 701/663–0025. 103 rooms, 4 suites. Facilities: restaurant, lounge, casino, pool. AE, D, DC, MC, V. $$*

Minot

LODGING

★ **Best Western International Inn.** Larger-than-average rooms have contemporary furnishings at this modern, three-story hotel on a hill above downtown Minot. *1505 N. Broadway, 58703, ☎ 701/852–3161 or 800/735–4493, FAX 701/838–5538. 265 rooms, 6 suites. Facilities: restaurant, lounge, casino, pool. AE, D, DC, MC, V. $$*

Motel

Expressway Inn (200 E. Bismarck Expressway, Bismarck 58504, ☎ and FAX 701/222–2900 or ☎ 800/456–6388), 163 rooms, outdoor pool, indoor hot tub, game room; *$$*

Campgrounds

Fort Abraham Lincoln State Park (*see* Exploring the Missouri River Corridor, *above*). **Lake Sakakawea State Park** (*see* National and State Parks, *above*).

Nightlife

Gambling

Prairie Knights Casino (CH 1, Box 26A, Mandan 58554, ☎ 701/255–7777), on Standing Rock Reservation, 44 mi south of Mandan on Rte. 1806, is the fanciest of the five reservation casinos in North Dakota, with murals by Native American artists and first-class food. The games (slots, blackjack, poker), bar, and two restaurants are open 24 hours a day. At press time, **The Lodge at Prairie Knights,** a 70-room hotel, was under construction and slated for a June 1995 opening (for more information, call 800/425–8277).

THE BADLANDS

Theodore Roosevelt, who ranched in western North Dakota in the late 1800s, once said, "I would never have been president if it had not been for my experiences in North Dakota." He was talking about the Badlands, where a national park named after him is now the heart of this wide-open country, largely unchanged since the president's time.

Tourist Information

Medora: Convention and Visitors Bureau (c/o Rough Riders, 1 Main St., Box 198, 58645, ☎ 701/623–4422 in season, 701/623–4444 or 701/223–4800 off-season). **Williston:** Convention and Visitors Bureau (10 Main St., Box G, 58801, ☎ 701/774–9041).

Getting There

By Plane

Bismarck Municipal Airport (*see* Missouri River Corridor, *above*) is the nearest large airport. The commuter airline United Express serves **Williston Airport** (☎ 701/774–8594) and **Dickinson Airport** (☎ 701/225–5856).

By Car

I–94 crosses the Badlands, with an exit at Medora at the entrance to the South Unit of Theodore Roosevelt National Park. U.S. 85 links the park's North and South units.

By Bus

Greyhound Lines (☎ 800/231–2222) stops in Dickinson and Medora.

Exploring the Badlands

Theodore Roosevelt National Park (Box 7, Medora 58645, ☎ 701/623–4466) is divided into two units, which are separated by 50 mi of Badlands and the **Little Missouri Grasslands.** Scenic loops through both (*see* Scenic Drives, *above*) are marked with low speed limits to protect the bison, wild horses, mule deer, pronghorn antelope, and bighorn sheep that roam here. You can get a panoramic view of the Badlands from the park's **Painted Canyon Overlook and Visitors Center** (☎ 701/623–4466) on I–94, 7 mi east of Medora, a good place to start a tour. The center provides picnic tables from which to enjoy the sweeping vista.

If you're up for an hour-long horseback ride in the **South Unit** of the park, contact **Peaceful Valley Ranch** (☎ 701/623–4496), 7 mi north of the park entrance. They'll take you on some of the park's 80 mi of marked horse trails. The visitor center will provide you with maps if you prefer to hike.

The **North Unit,** off U.S. 85 south of Watford City, offers the same scenic driving and hiking opportunities but in a less crowded setting. This is a good place to spot the wildlife you may have missed in the South Unit.

Outside the park, historic **Medora** is a walkable small town with a number of tiny shops, museums, and other attractions. The **Château de Mores,** an elegant 26-room mansion on a bluff overlooking the town, was built in the mid-1880s by the Marquis de Mores, a French nobleman who ran a short-lived cattle and meat-packing industry from here. You can see a collection of antique dolls in the **Medora Doll House;** Native American artifacts, wildlife exhibits, and wax figures depicting frontier days in the **Museum of the Badlands;** or the three-screen, multimedia show ***The Rough Rider Time Machine*** in the Town Hall Theater. The **Schafer Heritage Center,** opened in 1995, is an art gallery with an exhibit about Harold Schafer, who since the early 1960s has been investing his Mr. Bubble fortune in rebuilding Medora. For information on these and other Medora attractions, contact the Medora Convention and Visitors Bureau (*see* Tourist Information, *above*).

Fort Buford State Historic Site (☎ 701/572–9034; admission charged; closed mid-Sept.–mid-May), 22 mi southwest of Williston via Rte. 1804, is built around the 1866 fort that once imprisoned famous Na-

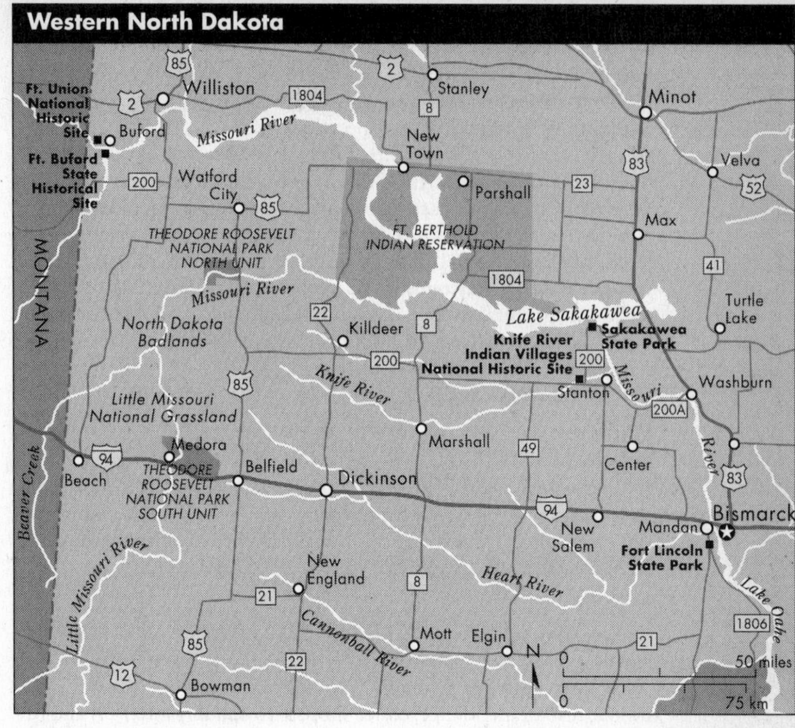

tive American leaders, including Sioux leader Sitting Bull and Nez Percé Chief Joseph. Two miles north of here on Rte. 58 is the **Fort Union Trading Post** (☏ 701/572–9083). This national historic site presents a reconstruction of the fur trading post of John Jacob Astor's American Fur Company. Ft. Union dominated the fur trade along the upper Missouri River from 1829 to 1866 and hosted such notable visitors as Prince Maximilian of Germany and John James Audubon.

Shopping

Specialty shops lining Medora's Main Street include **Dakota Arts and Crafts** (☏ 701/623–4805), offering a variety of crafts items, gifts, and souvenirs, and **Chateau Nuts** (☏ 701/623–4825), which stocks every nut imaginable in quantities large enough to make a squirrel's heart race.

Sports and the Outdoors

Biking

The loop roads in the North and South Units of Theodore Roosevelt National Park are challenging and scenic.

Hiking and Backpacking

Both units of Theodore Roosevelt National Park offer spectacular hiking and backpacking opportunities. The Little Missouri National Grasslands, which stretches between the two park units, is also a popular spot (for information, contact the Tourism Department, *see* Visitor Information, *above*).

Dining and Lodging

For price ranges, see Charts 1 (B) and 2 (B) in On the Road with Fodor's.

Medora

DINING

★ **Rough Rider Hotel Dining Room.** Housed in a two-story wood-frame building, this rustic restaurant features barbecued buffalo ribs, along with prime rib and other beef specialties. *Main St., ☎ 701/623–4444. AE, MC, V. Closed Sun.–Thurs. Oct.–Apr. $$*

Chuckwagon Cafeteria. This large, wood-paneled cafeteria with Western decor often hosts patio cookouts. Main courses include prime rib and ham, and a large array of side dishes, soups, and salads are offered. *Main St., ☎ 701/623–4444. MC, V. Closed Sept.–mid-May. $*

Trapper's Kettle Restaurant. Be prepared for reminders of the fur trade—traps, furs, stuffed and mounted animals, and a canoe, which holds the buffet. Go for chili topped with melted cheese. There's also a branch in Williston. *I–29 and U.S. 2, ☎ 701/575–8585; in Williston, U.S. 2 and U.S. 85, ☎ 701/774–0241. AE, D, DC, MC, V. $*

Williston

DINING

★ **El Rancho Restaurant.** The Old West atmosphere here was replaced by the earthy colors and art of the Southwest, but beef—especially prime rib—remains the specialty. Seafood and chicken are also on the menu. *1623 2nd Ave. W, ☎ 701/572–6321. AE, D, DC, MC, V. $$*

Motels

Badlands Motel (Box 198, Medora 58645, ☎ 701/623–4422), 116 rooms, pool; closed Oct.–Apr.; $. **El Rancho Motor Hotel** (1623 2nd Ave. W, Williston 58801, ☎ and FAX 701/572–6321 or 800/433–8529), 92 rooms, restaurant, lounge, coffee shop; $. **Hospitality Inn** (I–94 and Rte. 22, Dickinson 58601, ☎ 701/227–1853 or 800/422–0949, FAX 701/225–0090), 146 rooms, 3 suites, restaurant, lounge, casino, pool, Jacuzzi, sauna, game room; $. **Medora Motel** (E. River Rd., Medora 58645, ☎ 701/623–4422), 190 rooms, pool; $.

Campgrounds

Cottonwood Campground (5 mi inside Theodore Roosevelt National Park, ☎ 701/623–4466). **Medora Campground** (Medora, ☎ 701/623–4435). **Red Trail Campground** (Box 367, Medora, ☎ 701/623–4317 or 800/621–4317).

Nightlife

The ***Medora Musical*** (☎ 701/623–4444), in the outdoor **Burning Hills Amphitheater,** is a stage-show tribute to Western Americana featuring everything from singing to history to fireworks.

ELSEWHERE IN THE STATE

The Lakes Region

Getting There

U.S. 2 is the principal east–west route through the region, connecting with I–29 at Grand Forks. U.S. 281 runs north–south through the region, with secondary roads leading to lakes and area attractions. Devils Lake is served by **United Express. Amtrak** stops in Devils Lake and Rugby.

What to See and Do

Devils Lake, the heart of the lakes region, is surrounded by hundreds of smaller lakes and prairie potholes. A major breeding ground for North America's migratory waterfowl, the area offers fine birding. Devils Lake itself has excellent jumbo perch and walleye fishing and uncrowded beaches. For more information on fishing in the area, contact the **Game and Fish Department** (100 N. Bismarck Expressway, Bismarck 58501, ☎ 701/328–6300). On the Devils Lake Sioux Indian Reservation is the **Fort Totten Historic Site** (Rte. 57, ☎ 701/766–4441; admission charged; closed mid-Sept.–mid-May), the best-preserved military fort west of the Mississippi River. Built in 1867, it later served as one of the nation's largest government-run schools for Native Americans.

At Rugby, west of Devils Lake on U.S. 2, is the **geographical center of North America.** Marked by a stone monument, the landmark includes a spacious **Geographical Center Historical Museum** (☎ 701/776–6414; admission charged; closed mid-Sept.–mid-May) containing thousands of objects, such as 19th-century farming equipment and antique cars. The **International Peace Garden** (☎ 701/263–4390; admission charged), 13 mi north of Dunseith on U.S. 281, is a 2,300-acre garden straddling the border between Canada and the United States and planted as a symbol of peace between the two nations. In addition to the 100,000 flowers planted annually, the garden includes an 18-foot floral clock, a Peace Tower, and a Peace Chapel. For more information, contact **Devils Lake Tourism & Promotion** (Box 879, Devils Lake 58301, ☎ 701/662–4903).

Dining

For price ranges, see Chart 1 (B) in On the Road with Fodor's.

Birchwood. Cajun specialties and delicious prime rib are staples at this lakeside restaurant bordering Canada. *North of Rte. 43, Lake Metigoshe, ☎ 701/263–4283. MC, V. $$*

Mr. & Mrs. J's. The "Pig-out Omelette" is the specialty; a huge salad bar complements Mexican and traditional foods. *U.S. 2E, Devils Lake, ☎ 701/662–8815. MC, V. $*

Campground

Grahams Island State Park (Rte. 1, Box 165, Devils Lake 58301, ☎ 701/766–4015) is 15 mi southwest of Devils Lake off Rte. 19.

The Red River Valley

Getting There

I–94 links Fargo with Minneapolis–St. Paul to the east and with Billings, Montana, to the west. I–29 connects Fargo with Grand Forks, 75 mi north, and with Sioux Falls, South Dakota, to the south. **Hector International Airport** (☎ 701/241–1501), in Fargo, and **Grand Forks International Airport** (☎ 701/746–2580) are served by Northwest, Frontier, and United Express. **Amtrak** (☎ 800/872–7245) also serves both cities. **Greyhound Lines** (☎ 800/231–2222) provides service to Fargo and Grand Forks.

What to See and Do

The **Red River of the North** forms the eastern boundary of North Dakota with Minnesota. The fertile valley formed by the river was the destination of Scandinavian and other northern European immigrants in the late 19th century and still contains more than one-third of the state's population. The region is an enormous shopping hub, drawing bargain hunters from Minnesota, Canada, and the rest of North Dakota.

In the southeast corner of the state, off I–29, is **Wahpeton,** where you can ride on the restored 1926 **Prairie Rose Carousel** (10 mi east of I–29; rides cost $1) and visit the nearby **Ehnstrom Nature Center and Chahinkapa Park Zoo** (☎ 701/642–8709; admission charged), with such native species as eagles, bison, and elk. Ten miles west is Mooreton's

Bagg Bonanza Farm (☎ 701/224–8989; admission charged; closed Mon.), a national historic site that recreates the "bonanza" farm life of the late 1800s and early 1900s. Nine of the 21 buildings have been restored. Head north 50 mi on I–29 to **Fargo,** the state's largest city. **Bonanzaville USA** (Exit 65, I–29, West Fargo, ☎ 701/282–2822; admission charged) is a pioneer village and museum with 40 original and re-created buildings that show life in 1880s Dakota Territory. **Roger Maris Baseball Museum** (West Acres Shopping Center, I–29 and 13th Ave. S) honors baseball's all-time best single-season home-run hitter.

Seventy-five miles north of Fargo on I–29 is **Grand Forks,** the state's cultural and technological center. It's home to the **North Dakota Museum of Art** (Centennial Dr., ☎ 701/777–4195) and the **Center for Aerospace Sciences** (4125 University Ave., ☎ 701/777–2791), both at the **University of North Dakota.** Seventy miles north of Grand Forks via I–29, the **Pembina State Museum** (☎ 701/328–3567), opened in summer 1995, has exhibits on North Dakota history and an observation tower. Farther north, in **Icelandic State Park** (*see* National and State Parks, *above*), the **Pioneer Heritage Interpretive Center** (☎ 701/265–4561) uses artifacts and exhibits to showcase the ethnic diversity of the region. For further information on the area, contact the **Fargo/Moorhead Convention and Visitors Bureau** (2001 44th St. SW, Fargo 58103, ☎ 800/235–7654), **Grand Forks Convention and Visitors Bureau** (202 N. 3rd St., Suite 200, 58203, ☎ 800/866–4566), or **Wahpeton Visitors Center** (120 N. 4th St., 58075, ☎ 701/642–8559 or 800/892–6673).

Dining

For price ranges, see Chart 1 (B) in On the Road with Fodor's.

Old Broadway. Featuring Gay '90s decor under 18-ft ceilings, with a plethora of antiques, the restaurant is in the circa-1903 Stern's clothing store. Ribs, smoked on the premises, are popular. *22 N. Broadway, Fargo, ☎ 701/237–6161. AE, D, DC, MC, V. $$*

Sanders 1907. Tiny, elegant, and intimate, Sanders has lots of mirrors, exceptional local artwork, and exuberant rosemaling on its booths. Fabulous pâté; wonderful salads and breads; such entrées as prime rib cooked with garlic, basil, rosemary, and olive oil; and desserts like walnut torte and "Chocolate Decadence" make this a delightful gastronomic experience. *312 Kittson Ave., Grand Forks, ☎ 701/746–8970. AE, DC, MC, V. $$*

OKLAHOMA

By Matt Schofield

Updated by Barbara Palmer

Capital	Oklahoma City
Population	3,299,150
Motto	Labor Conquers All Things
State Bird	Scissor-tailed flycatcher
State Flower	Mistletoe

Visitor Information

Oklahoma Tourism and Recreation Department (Box 60789, Oklahoma City 73146, ☏ 405/521–2409 or 800/652–6552). **State Historical Society** (2100 N. Lincoln St., Oklahoma City 73105, ☏ 405/521–2491).

Scenic Drives

Rte. 49 through the granite peaks of the Wichita Mountains Wildlife Refuge (*see* Exploring Southwestern Oklahoma, *below*) and **Rte. 10,** which follows the Spring, Neosho, and Illinois rivers from Wyandotte through Grove to Gore (*see* Exploring Northeastern Oklahoma, *below*) are both scenic. **Rte. 1** through the northern section of the Ouachita National Forest (*see* National and State Parks, *below*), from Talihina east about 50 mi to the state border, makes a beautiful drive in autumn, when the forest foliage is most colorful.

National and State Parks

National Parks

The **Ouachita National Forest** (HC64, Box 3467, Heavener 74937, ☏ 918/653–2991) in southeastern Oklahoma is a scenic region of small mountain ranges.

State Parks

Oklahoma has 50 state parks, and all but 2 offer camping. Some of the best parks are **Alabaster Caverns State Park** (Rte. 1, Box 32, Freedom 73842, ☏ 405/621–3381), **Beavers Bend State Park** (Box 10, Broken Bow 74728, ☏ 405/494–6300), **Great Salt Plains State Park** (*see* Elsewhere in the State, *below*), **Quartz Mountain State Park** (*see* Exploring Southwestern Oklahoma, *below*), and **Red Rock Canyon State Park** (Box 502, Hinton 73047, ☏ 405/542–6344).

OKLAHOMA CITY

Where else but in Oklahoma will you find oil wells pumping on the grounds of the state capitol? The state's dual themes of oil and the American West can be explored in Oklahoma City's museums and historic centers. Twenty miles north on I–35 is Victorian Guthrie, the state capital from territorial days until after statehood, 1889–1910. Much of the town is now included in a 1,400-acre historic district, the largest on the National Register.

Tourist Information

Oklahoma City: Convention and Visitor's Bureau (123 Park Ave., 73102, ☏ 405/278–8900 or 800/225–5652). **Guthrie:** Chamber of Commerce (212 W. Oklahoma St., Box 995, 73044, ☏ 405/282–1947 or 800/299–1889). The *Daily Oklahoman*'s Friday weekend section and the *Gazette* (a free weekly distributed in restaurants and hotels) list events.

Arriving and Departing

By Plane

The **Will Rogers World Airport** (☎ 405/681–5311), in the southwest section of the city, is served by major domestic airlines. It's about a 20-minute drive from downtown on I–44N; cab fare is about $14. There's no bus service from the airport, but several hotels in town offer transportation.

By Car

Interstates 35, 40, and 44 form a loop around the downtown area. I–235 cuts through the middle of town. Downtown exits include Walker Ave. and Lincoln Blvd.

By Bus

Greyhound Lines (427 W. Sheridan St., ☎ 800/231–2222).

Getting Around Oklahoma City

A car is a necessity here; although the downtown can be explored on foot, the rest of the city is spread out. Traffic is rarely a problem.

Exploring Oklahoma City

Oklahoma City sprawls over four counties, but the major points of interest are all within 10 mi of one another and generally northeast of the downtown area.

At the limestone and granite **Oklahoma State Capitol** (N.E. 23rd St. and Lincoln Blvd., ☎ 405/521–3356) those oil wells you see on the grounds aren't just for show: Although the earliest well dried up in 1986, the remainder actually do pump oil.

A few blocks away are the farmhouse, barn, and gardens of the **Harn Homestead and 1889er Museum;** the farm is on land claimed during the Run of 1889, which opened central Oklahoma to settlement. The Harn family donated land for the capitol (and later regretted not retaining the mineral rights). *313 N.E. 16th St., tel 405/478–2412. Admission charged. Closed Sun.–Mon.*

The **National Cowboy Hall of Fame and Western Heritage Center,** north of the capitol off I–44, has vast collections of paintings, sculpture, and artifacts, including John Wayne's kachina collection. A sod house, saloon, and mine are part of a re-created frontier town. At press time, four additional galleries were scheduled to open in 1995. *1700 N.E. 63rd St., ☎ 405/478–2250. Admission charged.*

The **Kirkpatrick Center** (2100 N.E. 52nd St., ☎ 405/427–5461), about 2½ mi south via Martin Luther King Avenue, houses science and art museums, a Native American museum, the International Photography Hall of Fame, and four other institutions.

Next door, at the **Oklahoma City Zoological Park,** machine-made mists and a waterfall help create a natural habitat for Western lowland gorillas, orangutans, and chimpanzees. *2101 N.E. 50th St., ☎ 405/424–3344. Admission charged.*

Directly north of the zoo is **Remington Park,** where thoroughbred and quarter-horse pari-mutuel races are scheduled in fall, spring, and summer. Call ahead for race dates and reservations. *1 Remington Pl., 73111, ☎ 405/424–9000 or 800/456–9000. Admission charged.*

A walk through the **Crystal Bridge Tropical Conservatory,** a glass botanical tube at the I. M. Pei–designed **Myriad Gardens,** takes visitors through habitats that range from desert to rain forest, complete with a 35-foot waterfall. *301 W. Reno Ave., ☎ 405/297–3995. Admission charged. Closed Christmas.*

Shopping

The **Choctaw Indian Trading Post** (1520 N. Portland St., ☎ 405/947–2490) is a good source for Native American artifacts, art, and crafts. **Route 66** (50 Penn Place, 5000 N. Pennsylvania Ave., ☎ 405/848–6166) gallery and gift shop sells jewelry and sculpture by regional artists, plus T-shirts, caps, and calendars commemorating the old highway's neon glory days.

Dining

Remember, you're in beef country: Plain food and large portions of meat are standard here. The Bricktown neighborhood, a renovated section of downtown, is a favorite dining spot for locals. For price ranges, see Chart 1 (B) in On the Road with Fodor's.

$$$ ★ **Coach House.** The dark-wood-paneled walls of this small, cozy restaurant are covered with images of the hunt, a theme reflected in the menu, which features pheasant, quail, and venison. Other specialties include scallops with roasted corn cakes and individual chocolate cakes. *6437 Avondale Dr., ☎ 405/842–5000. AE, MC, V.*

$$ ★ **Sand Plum.** In historic downtown Guthrie, about 20 minutes north of Oklahoma City, this elegant Victorian-style restaurant serves an enormous Sunday brunch buffet, with everything from Caesar salad to eggs Benedict to cheesecake. *202 W. Harrison St., Guthrie, ☎ 405/282–7771. AE, MC, V.*

$ **Bricktown Brewery.** Even the shrimp are steamed in beer in this airy brew pub, where blowups of historical photographs are displayed against exposed brick. Land Run Lager and Copperhead Ale complement a menu heavy on comfort foods: chicken pot pie, fish-and-chips, and bratwurst. *1 Oklahoma Ave., ☎ 405/232–2739. AE, DC, MC, V.*

$ ★ **Cattlemen's Steak House.** Beef is the star attraction at this classic steak house, where diners are surrounded by Western murals and paraphernalia such as cattle branding irons. Spur-wearing cowboys have been spotted in the restaurant, which is in the heart of Stockyard City, home to saddlers, Western-wear stores, and the Oklahoma National Stockyards, the nation's largest. *1309 S. Agnew Ave., ☎ 405/236–0416. AE, D, DC, MC, V.*

$ **County Line.** Pretty Boy Floyd was a regular when this was a Prohibition-era roadhouse. Now the Deco-style barbecue restaurant serves smoked baby-back ribs and chicken, accompanied by loaves of freshly baked bread and eucalyptus-scented hot towels. *1226 N.E. 63rd St., ☎ 405/478–4955. AE, D, DC, MC, V.*

Lodging

Hotels here offer few surprises. The more expensive ones have restaurants, clubs, and lounges, but rooms generally differ little from those in moderately priced establishments. If you don't plan to spend a lot of time at the hotel, you may be better off stopping at one of the chain motels along the highways. For price ranges, see Chart 2 (B) in On the Road with Fodor's.

$$$ Century Center Hotel. At this 15-story glass-and-stone building in the heart of downtown, some floors are decorated in Southwestern pastels and bleached wood, while others enfold you in mauve and deep green. All rooms have traditional-style furniture and state-of-the-art electronics. *1 N. Broadway, 73102, ☎ 405/235–2780, FAX 405/272–0369. 399 rooms, 13 suites. Facilities: restaurant, lounge, pool. AE, D, DC, MC, V.*

$$$ Clarion Hotel and Conference Center. The furnishings from Jimmy and Tammy Faye Bakker's bankrupt Christian theme park and hotel have found a home here: Expect turndown service, lighted make-up mirrors, and lots of maroons, mauves, and pinks. The hotel is conveniently located near museums, the capitol, and expressways. *4345 N. Lincoln Blvd., 73105, ☎ 405/528–2741 or 800/252–7466, FAX 405/525–8185. 68 rooms. Facilities: restaurant, lounge. AE, D, DC, MC, V.*

$$ Harrison House Bed and Breakfast Inn. Rooms are furnished in turn-of-the-century antiques and named for former Guthrie residents, such as Tom Mix (he tended bar down the street) and Carry Nation. Specify one of the 21 rooms in the original inn or the adjacent Freeman Block; other rooms are not nearly as charming. *124 W. Harrison St., Guthrie 73044, ☎ 405/282–1000 or 800/375–1001, FAX 405/282–4304. 30 rooms with bath. AE, D, DC, MC, V.*

$$ Hilton Inn. A marble-floored lobby and a neutral color scheme in the rooms—not to mention the 18 new cabana rooms facing the pool and hot tub—give the place a tropical feel. Be sure to ask about corporate rates when you call, as the hotel frequently makes them available to noncorporate guests. *2945 N.W. Expressway, 73112, ☎ 800/848–4811, FAX 405/843–4829. 212 rooms, 4 suites. Facilities: restaurant, lounge, outdoor pool, hot tub. AE, D, DC, MC, V.*

$ Comfort Inn. This motel shares its restaurant and lounge with the adjacent Clarion hotel, but rooms here can be as much as a third cheaper. *1345 Lincoln Blvd., 73105, ☎ 405/528–2741, FAX 405/525–8185. 240 rooms, 13 suites. Facilities: restaurant, lounge, outdoor pool. AE, D, DC, MC, V.*

Motels

Motel 6 has several locations here: Airport (820 S. Meridian, 73108, ☎ 405/946–6662, FAX 405/946–4058), 128 rooms, outdoor pool; North (11900 N.E. Expressway, 73131, ☎ 405/478–8666, FAX 405/478–7442), 101 rooms, outdoor pool; South (1417 N. Moore Ave., 73160, ☎ 405/799–6616, FAX 405/799–5053), 121 rooms, outdoor pool; Midwest City (6166 Tinker Diagonal, Midwest City 73110, ☎ 405/737–6676, FAX 405/737–2216), 93 rooms, outdoor pool. All are inexpensive ($).

Ranch

$$$ ★ Island Guest Ranch. At this 2,800-acre working ranch 90 mi north of Oklahoma City, guests help herd cattle, ride horses, fish, hike, and attend staged powwows and team roping and penning in the ranch's own rodeo arena. Rooms, each with private bath, are in two rustic bunkhouses; hearty meals are served in the main log lodge. Rates include all meals and activities; reservations should be made at least several weeks in advance. The owners will meet you at the airport upon request. *Ames 73718, ☎ 405/753–4574, FAX 405/753–4574. 10 rooms. MC, V. Closed Oct.–Mar.*

NORTHEASTERN OKLAHOMA

The Ozarks lap over from Arkansas into northeastern Oklahoma, making the Grand Lake O' the Cherokees a popular vacation spot. Cowboys still roam the range, both on horseback and in pickup trucks, and rodeos and Western museums are abundant. The infamous Cherokee Trail of Tears—along which thousands of Cherokee traveled in the 1830s when they were forcibly resettled from their Georgia homes—ended here. And with a dozen more Native American tribes headquartered here, powwows and tribal museums are plentiful. Today tribal governments are vital once again and Native American art, language, and customs are actively preserved.

Tourist Information

Tahlequah: Chamber of Commerce (123 E. Delaware St., 74464, ☎ 918/456–3742). **Tulsa:** Visitor Information Center and Chamber of Commerce (616 S. Boston St., 74119, ☎ 918/585–1201).

Getting There

By Plane

Tulsa International Airport (☎ 918/838–5000), about 10 mi northeast of downtown Tulsa, is served by major domestic airlines. Average cab fare to the downtown area is about $12. Major hotels have shuttle bus service.

By Car

In Tulsa, I–44 and I–244 form a downtown loop. The Keystone, Cherokee, and Broken Arrow expressways also lead downtown. From Tulsa, U.S. 75 leads north to the Bartlesville area. I–44 is the main route northeast from Tulsa and connects with many smaller, more scenic highways. A 400-mi segment of old Rte. 66 travels through Oklahoma; the 100-mi leg that connects with I–35 north of Oklahoma City and I–44 just west of Tulsa is the easiest to follow. Watch for old gas stations, shady city parks, and tiny grocery stores in towns such as Chandler and Sapulpa. Rte. 66 parallels I–44 northeast of Tulsa, where classic landmarks include **Arrowood Trading Post** (2700 N. Old Highway 66, Catoosa, ☎ 918/266–3663) and the **Buffalo Ranch** (1 mi north of Afton on Rte. 66, ☎ 918/257–4544).

By Bus

Greyhound Lines (317 S. Detroit St., ☎ 800/231–2222) serves Tulsa.

Exploring Northeastern Oklahoma

The friendly city of **Tulsa** has a number of cultural attractions. About 3 mi from the downtown area is the **Gilcrease Museum** (1400 Gilcrease Museum Rd., ☎ 918/596–2700). Its collection, dedicated to Western art and Americana, includes paintings by such artists as Frederic Remington and James McNeill Whistler, as well as a wide-ranging selection of Native American art and artifacts. A few miles southeast of downtown is the **Philbrook Museum of Art** (2727 S. Rockford Rd., ☎ 918/749–7941). Housed in the Italianate villa of former oil baron Waite Phillips, the collection runs the gamut from Italian Renaissance to Native American art. The oil money that built Tulsa in the 1920s left a legacy of Art Deco architecture second in size only to that of Miami, Florida. Stop by the Chamber of Commerce (*see* Tourist Information, *above*) for a walking-tour map including more than a dozen downtown buildings.

Northwest of Tulsa and 8 mi north of Pawhuska on the Tallgrass Prairie Drive is the **Tallgrass Prairie Reserve** (☎ 918/287–4803), a 52,000-acre swath of unbroken tallgrass prairie that is home to a bison herd, a cowboy bunkhouse, and hiking trails. From Pawhuska, take Rte. 60 west to Rte. 123, through the **Prairie Wild Horse Refuge**

Northeastern Oklahoma

(☎ 918/336-1564), home to 1,200 horses that travelers can spot on either side of the highway.

Also on Rte. 123 is **Woolaroc,** perhaps the top attraction in the state. It includes a drive-through wildlife preserve where bison and 40 other species roam (visitors must remain in their vehicles). The preserve surrounds a museum packed with Western lore: gun and rifle exhibits; Native American artifacts; Western art, including works by Remington and Russell; and such memorabilia as Theodore Roosevelt's saddle. The historic Woolaroc lodge, formerly used by oilman Frank Phillips, is filled with every animal trophy imaginable. *Box 1647, Bartlesville 74005, ☎ 918/336-0307. Admission charged. Closed Mon. Labor Day–Memorial Day.*

Follow Rte. 123 north to **Bartlesville,** site of the **Frank Phillips Home** (1107 S. Cherokee St., ☎ 918/336-2491), a 26-room Greek Revival mansion built in 1909. A couple of blocks northwest is the **Price Tower,** designed by Frank Lloyd Wright, which houses the **Bartlesville Museum** (6th and Dewey Sts., ☎ 918/336-8708). Wright envisioned the 19-story building, completed in 1956, as a "tower in a country town." Its magnificent cantilevered exterior, adorned with copper plates and gold-tinted glass, is a landmark on the small city's skyline. The interior contains many of Wright's original furnishings.

Southeast of Bartlesville by way of Nowata lies the **Dog Iron Ranch and Will Rogers Birthplace** (near Oologah, ☎ 918/275-4201). The great humorist's childhood home, built in 1875, is a two-story log-and-clapboard structure containing period furnishings; you'll also find Longhorn cattle and barnyard animals on the grounds. Nearby, on Rte. 88 in Claremore, is the **Will Rogers Memorial** (☎ 800/324-9455), where

Rogers and his family are buried. The site contains a museum and a theater that shows Rogers's movies and newsreels.

You can take I–44 and U.S. 59 to **Grove** and the **Grand Lake O' the Cherokees.** Numerous recreational options here include a dinner cruise or sightseeing tour aboard the ***Cherokee Queen*** riverboat (☎ 918/786–4272).

Travel south about 50 mi on Rte. 10—a scenic drive through a region of dense forest, hills, and lakes—to **Tahlequah,** home to the Cherokee Nation. The **Cherokee Heritage Center,** 3 mi south of town off U.S. 62, offers daily summer performances of the drama *Trail of Tears;* the **Cherokee National Museum/Adams Corner** here includes a re-creation of the 16th-century Cherokee village Tsa-La-Gi. *Willis Rd.,* ☎ *918/456–6007. Admission charged. Closed weekends Sept.–May; Sun., June–Aug.*

Head southwest on U.S. 62 to Okmulgee. Okmulgee's sandstone **Creek Council House** (106 W. 6th St., ☎ 918/756–2324), on a shady square, has been meticulously restored. The two-story structure was the center of Creek political life from 1878 until the turn of the century, when tribal governments were liquidated. It's now a museum, a library, and a center for the preservation of the Creek language.

The Cherokee were hardly the region's first settlers, as the **Spiro Mounds Archaeological State Park** attests. The park contains remains of 12 earthen mounds used as dwellings by the Spiro, an ancient people who lived here from about AD 900 to 1400. A 1½-mi trail runs alongside the mounds, and a visitor center contains artifacts. *6 mi northwest of Spiro,* ☎ *918/962–2062. Closed Mon. May–Oct.; Mon.–Tues. Nov.–Apr.*

Shopping

Lyon's Indian Store (401 E. 11th St., Tulsa, ☎ 918/582–6372) sells contemporary Native American beadwork and prints, and artifacts collected during the years the Lyon family ran a trading post for Pawnee Bill are on display. **Mister Indian's** (1000 S. Main St. in nearby Sapulpa, ☎ 918/224–6511) sells both Native American and Western gear; you'll also find notices of area powwows on its bulletin board. Cherry Street, a popular six-block stretch between Utica and Peoria avenues along 15th Street, is home to antiques stores, bars, bakeries, sandwich shops, and a brewery installed in what was once a school. At the **First Edition Book Shop** (1502 E. 15th St., ☎ 918/582–1967), the Native American and Americana collections make for a good browse.

Sports and the Outdoors

Fishing

Tulsa World's sports section has up-to-date fishing information, or check with the **Department of Wildlife and Conservation** (☎ 405/521–2221). Fishing licenses can be purchased in most tackle shops.

Hiking and Backpacking

Every park in the area has hiking trails. For general information, call the **Tourism and Recreation Department** (*see* Visitor Information, *above*).

Dining and Lodging

Tulsa probably has the best dining in the state, and you'll look hard to find any restaurants that qualify as expensive. Outside the city there are always the fast-food chains; a better option may be to pack a picnic lunch. Tulsa also offers a fair number of comfortable though unexciting hotels. For price ranges, see Charts 1 (B) and 2 (B) in On the Road with Fodor's.

Bartlesville

LODGING

★ **Hotel Phillips.** From the street, this seven-story yellow-brick hotel looks like a 1950s-era hospital, but you'll find lots of wood and rich upholstery inside. Managed by the Marriott hotel chain, the hotel caters to business travelers—on weekdays, the *Wall Street Journal* is delivered to your door. *821 S. Johnstone Ave., 74003, ☎ 918/337–6600 or 800/331–0706, FAX 918/336–0350. 165 rooms. Facilities: restaurant, bar, fitness room. AE, D, DC, MC, V. $$*

Tulsa

DINING

Bravo Ristorante. In the formal dining room of the Adam's Mark hotel, traditional Italian cuisine is served by a waitstaff composed of both professional and student vocalists who deliver arias with your meal. The wine list is extensive. *Adam's Mark Hotel, 100 E. 2nd St., ☎ 918/582–9000. AE, D, MC, V. $$*

Jamil's. A good choice for families, this residence-turned-restaurant features smoked chicken and ribs served with complimentary tabouli and cabbage rolls in an old-fashioned, homey atmosphere. *2833 E. 51st St., ☎ 918/742–9097. AE, D, DC, MC, V. No lunch. $$*

Metro Diner. This neon- and chrome-filled reproduction of a '50s-era diner serves burgers, french fries and gravy, blue-plate specials, and cream pies. *3001 E. 11th St., Rte. 66, ☎ 918/592–2616. AE, D, MC, V. $*

★ **Nelson's Buffeteria.** This lively, old-fashioned lunchroom shows off 1940s decor and the best chicken-fried steak in town. Food is served cafeteria-style. *514 S. Boston St., ☎ 918/584–9969. No credit cards. Closed weekends. No dinner. $*

LODGING

Adam's Mark Hotel. Next door to the Performing Arts Center, this plush hotel is connected to a shopping mall with an indoor ice skating rink. Each room has a stocked minibar and tiny balcony. The staff is considered the best in Tulsa. *100 E. 2nd St., 74103, ☎ 918/582–9000 or 800/444–2326, FAX 918/569–2232. 456 rooms, 8 suites. Facilities: restaurant, 2 lounges, fitness room, indoor pool, outdoor pool. AE, D, DC, MC, V. $$$*

Doubletree Inn Downtown. Visitors are welcomed with chocolate chip cookies in this modern high rise that features contemporary decor in hues of green, rose, and mauve. A skywalk connects the hotel to the Tulsa Convention Center. *616 W. 7th St., 74127, ☎ 918/587–8000, FAX 918/560–2261. 386 rooms, 32 suites. Facilities: 2 restaurants, bar, spa. AE, D, DC, MC, V. $$$*

★ **Southern Hills Marriott.** Rooms are generally spacious and comfortable; those on higher floors have good views of either downtown or the river. *1902 E. 71st St., 74136, ☎ 918/493–7000, FAX 918/481–7147. 370 rooms, 13 suites. Facilities: 2 restaurants, 2 lounges, health club. AE, D, DC, MC, V. $$$*

La Quinta Inn. This no-frills chain hotel is squeaky clean and conveniently located near the airport. *35 N. Sheridan Rd., 74115, ☎ 918/836–3931, FAX 918/836–5428. 99 rooms, 2 suites. Facilities: pool. AE, D, DC, MC, V. $$*

Motels

Best Western Trade Winds East Motor Hotel (3337 E. Skelly Dr., Tulsa 74135, ☎ 918/743–7931, FAX 918/743–4308), 156 rooms, lounge; $. **Motel 6** (1011 S. Garnett Rd., 74128, ☎ 918/234–6200, FAX 918/234–9421; 154 rooms, outdoor pool, $; and 5828 W. Skelly Dr., 74107, ☎ 918/445–0223, FAX 918/445–2750; 153 rooms, outdoor pool, $).

Campgrounds

Tenkiller State Park (HCR 68, Box 1095, Vian 74962, ☎ 918/489–5643) and **Greenleaf State Park** (Rte. 1, Box 119, Braggs 74423, ☎ 918/487–5196), both near Gore, have cabins and campgrounds, as does **Osage Hills State Park** (Red Eagle Rte., Box 84, Pawhuska 74056, ☎ 918/336–4141), near Bartlesville. **Sequoyah State Park** (Rte. 1, Box 198–3, Hulbert 74441, ☎ 918/772–2046) offers camping with a swimming beach, marina, and heated pool, 54 cabins, and a 101-room lodge (☎ 918/772–2545).

The Arts

Tulsa has an active cultural scene. The **Tulsa Ballet Theatre** (4512 S. Peoria Ave., ☎ 918/749–6006; Sept.–Apr.) is a nationally acclaimed company. The **Tulsa Philharmonic** (2901 S. Harvard Ave., ☎ 918/747–7445; Sept.–May) and the **Tulsa Opera** (1610 S. Boulder, ☎ 918/582–4035; Nov.–Apr.) hold most of their performances at the Performing Arts Center downtown.

SOUTHWESTERN OKLAHOMA

The frontier doesn't seem far away in this rugged, sparsely populated region; oceans of grass are broken by blue granite mountains, and almost every small town has a saddle shop. During the 19th century this was the domain of the buffalo and the Kiowa and Comanche tribes; travelers may still spot Native American tepees and brush arbors in rural areas during the summer.

Tourist Information

Anadarko: Chamber of Commerce (Box 366, 73005, ☎ 405/247–6651). **Lawton:** Chamber of Commerce (Box 1376, 73502, ☎ 405/355–3541).

Getting There

By Plane

The **Will Rogers World Airport** gives the best access to the region (*see* Oklahoma City, *above*).

By Car

As with the rest of the state, you'll need a car to tour this region. Most of the area falls between I–44 and I–40 southwest of Oklahoma City; U.S. and state highways on our tour connect with these interstates.

By Bus

Greyhound Lines (15 N.E. 20th St., ☎ 800/231–2222) serves Lawton.

Exploring Southwestern Oklahoma

Lawton makes a good base for exploring the region. The **Museum of the Great Plains** (601 Ferris Ave., ☎ 405/581–3460; admission charged) features a tiny re-created town, a Spanish-sword display, and an outdoor fort.

A short drive north on I–44 brings you to the main entrance to the **Fort Sill Military Reservation,** built in 1869 in an effort to subdue the Native Americans of the southern plains. Seven original buildings contain exhibits on the fort's history. Geronimo's Guardhouse is named for the famous Chiricahua Apache warrior who died at the fort in 1909, a prisoner of war. The Fort Sill Apache tribe dances the Apache Fire Dance here in September. ☏ *405/351–5123. Closed major holidays.*

A few miles farther north, I–44 crosses U.S. 49, which runs along the northern border of Fort Sill and westward to the **Wichita Mountains Wildlife Refuge,** one of the most beautiful areas in the state. Here the wildlife is thick and the scenery—pines, cliffs, and still, clear lakes—often breathtaking. The refuge is home to bison, Longhorn cattle, and other species. The best rock climbing and mountain biking in the state is to be found here; hiking trails are abundant and camping is permitted, but backcountry camping and biking are by permit only. *Rte. 1, Indiahoma,* ☏ *405/429–3222. Guided tours by reservation.*

From the western end of the refuge, U.S. 54 and 62 lead southwest to Altus. From here travel north on U.S. 283/Rte. 44 to **Quartz Mountain State Park** (Lone Wolf, ☏ 405/563–2238), site of a state-run resort (*see* Dining and Lodging, *below*). The scenery alone is worth the trip—bare rock outcroppings reflected in pristine Altus Lake, and in spring, wildflowers in abundance—but you can also explore caves, visit the park's nature center, or take advantage of the guided tours and special programs offered throughout the year.

Some 100 mi east lies the largely Native American community of **Anadarko,** site of the **Southern Plains Indian Museum and Crafts Center** (715 E. Central St., ☏ 405/247–6221). Just east of the museum is the **National Hall of Fame for Famous American Indians** (U.S. 62E, ☏ 405/247–5555), an outdoor collection of busts depicting well-known Native Americans. Southeast of town, **Indian City USA** (Rte. 8, ☏ 405/247–5661) is a re-creation of life in seven Native American villages. At the **Susan Peters Gallery** (112 W. Main St., ☏ 405/247–7151 or 800/256–3724), you'll find original works and prints by such Oklahoma Native American artists as T. C. Cannon and the Kiowa Five.

Sports and the Outdoors

Fishing

The best bets are Altus Lake or any of the lakes at the Wichita Mountains Wildlife Refuge (*see* Exploring Southwestern Oklahoma, *above*). The sports section in the *Daily Oklahoman* has fishing reports for the lakes in the area, or contact the **Department of Wildlife and Conservation** (☏ 405/521–3855).

Hiking and Backpacking

Check specific parks (*see* National and State Parks, *above*) or contact the state tourism department (*see* Visitor Information, *above*).

Dining and Lodging

This is not an area where either shines. Try to pack lunches when you can for picnics in parks; at night you'll probably have to content yourself with chain restaurants. Unless you plan on camping, your hotel will probably be little more than a convenient base for exploring a fascinating region. For price ranges, see Charts 1 (B) and 2 (B) in On the Road with Fodor's.

Altus

DINING

Val's It's About Time. This pub-style restaurant is so packed with memorabilia—license plates, hubcaps, and an old tuba—you might miss the vintage Altus high school band uniform hanging on the wall. Steaks,

ribs, chicken-fried steak, and seafood are featured on the menu. *800 N. Main St., ☎ 405/482–4580. AE, D, MC, V. $–$$*

LODGING

Best Western. Popular with business travelers, this hotel offers a number of rooms with hair dryers, refrigerators, and two phones. *2804 N. Main St., 73521, ☎ 405/482–9300 or 800/338–8163, FAX 405/482–2245. 101 rooms, 3 suites. Facilities: indoor pool. AE, D, DC, MC, V. $*

Lawton

DINING

Chi's Fong Village. Tablecloths and better-than-average service at fast-food prices have made this place a favorite with locals. Orange chicken, barbecued spare ribs, and Happy Family—shrimp, beef, chicken, and pork stir-fry—are standards on the buffet. *6204 N. Cache Rd., ☎ 405/536–2435. AE, D, MC, V. $*

★ **Woody's BBQ.** Enjoy pork ribs or beef brisket in one of two rustic dining rooms featuring ceiling fans and wood trim. Side dishes include okra, fried mushrooms, and "wood chips" (fried potatoes with melted cheese and bacon). *1107 W. Lee Blvd., ☎ 405/355–4950. MC, V. $*

LODGING

Holiday Inn. Executive rooms at this downtown hotel feature king-size beds, refrigerators, and wet bars. *3134 Cache Rd., 73505, ☎ 405/353–1682, FAX 405/353–2872. 171 rooms. Facilities: restaurant, outdoor pool. AE, D, DC, MC, V. $$*

Howard Johnson Lodge and Convention Center. The public areas of this low-rise stucco hotel just off I–44 have eclectic decor ranging from Victorian-style frosted glass to a rustic "chandelier" of antlers. Standard rooms have a teal-and-burnt-orange color scheme; decor in suites ranges from pastel accents in the bridal suite to high-tech glass and chrome in the whirlpool suites. *1125 E. Gore St., 73501, ☎ 405/353–0200, FAX 405/353–6801. 142 rooms, 11 suites. Facilities: restaurant, indoor pool, tennis courts. AE, D, DC, MC, V. $$*

Lone Wolf

LODGING

★ **Quartz Mountain Resort.** One of Oklahoma's five state-run resorts in state parks, this establishment offers guests the choice of rooms in the main stone-and-wood lodge, cabins, or a 64-bed dormitory. A park naturalist leads wildflower walks in spring and bald eagle watches in winter; there's also a golf course that's a regional favorite. *Rte. 1, 73655, ☎ 405/563–2424, FAX 405/563–9125. 45 lodge rooms, 16 cabins, 64 dorm beds. Facilities: restaurant, pool, nature center, golf course, other sports facilities. AE, D, DC, MC, V. $$*

Meers

DINING

Meers Store. All that's left of a boomtown that grew up during a brief gold rush in 1901 is this eatery and a federal seismographic station by the cash register. The restaurant's claim to fame is not gold but the Meersburger—a 7-inch-wide, pure Longhorn beef burger. You'll also find steaks, barbecue, and homemade ice cream on the menu. *Rte. 115, 4 mi east of the Wichita Mountains Wildlife Refuge, ☎ 405/429–8051. No credit cards. $*

Motels

Hospitality Inn (202 E. Lee St., Lawton 73501, ☎ 405/355–9765, FAX 405/355–2360), 106 rooms, coffee shop next door, laundry, outdoor pool; $. **Ramada Inn** (601 N. 2nd St., Lawton 73507, ☎ 405/355–7155, FAX 405/353–6162), 98 rooms, restaurant, lounge, outdoor pool; $.

Campgrounds

In addition to its lodge, Quartz Mountain State Park (*see* Exploring Southwestern Oklahoma, *above*) also has camping facilities. For camping information on other state parks in the area, contact the state tourism department (*see* Visitor Information, *above*).

ELSEWHERE IN THE STATE

Great Salt Plains State Park/ Salt Plains National Wildlife Refuge

Getting There

Take I–35N from Oklahoma City to U.S. 60 (which becomes U.S. 64), then head west. The drive takes about two hours. Expect gravel and dirt roads as you approach the salt flats.

What to See and Do

This park attracts visitors from around the world, probably because they get to keep the selenite crystals (sand and clay formations trapped inside crystalized gypsum) they dig up in the park's salt flats. The salt flats are part of a wildlife refuge with hiking and drive-through trails where whooping cranes, bald eagles, and terns can be spotted; an adjacent state park offers camping and water sports on Great Salt Plains Lake. *Rte. 1, Box 28, Jet 73749,* ☎ *405/626–4731. Digging Apr.–mid-Oct.*

SOUTH DAKOTA

By Doug Cunningham

Updated by Konnie LeMay

Capital	Pierre
Population	699,999
Motto	Great Faces, Great Places
State Bird	Chinese ring-necked pheasant
State Flower	Pasqueflower

Visitor Information

South Dakota Department of Tourism (711 E. Wells Ave., Pierre 57501, ☏ 800/732–5682). Call the **Department of Transportation** for maps of summer road construction (☏ 605/773–3571) and winter road-condition reports (☏ 605/773–3536).

Scenic Drives

The beautiful **Needles Highway** (Rte. 87) and **Iron Mountain Road** (U.S. 16A) run through Custer State Park (*see* National and State Parks, *below*). U.S. 85 follows scenic **Spearfish Canyon.**

National and State Parks

National Parks

For **Badlands National Park** and **Black Hills National Forest,** *see* The West, *below.* **Jewel Cave National Monument,** 50 mi southwest of Rapid City on U.S. 16 (R.R. 1, Box 60aa, Custer 57730, ☏ 605/673–2288), gets its name from the calcite formations in the world's fourth-longest—and the United States' second-longest—cave. **Wind Cave National Park,** 50 mi south of Rapid City on U.S. 385 (R.R. 1, Box 190, Hot Springs 57747, ☏ 605/745–4600), is 28,000 acres of prairie and forest above the world's ninth-longest cave.

State Park

Custer State Park (HC 83, Box 70, Custer 57730, ☏ 605/255–4464 or 605/255–4515 for campground reservations) has 73,000 spectacular acres of grasslands and pine-covered hills that are home to bison, deer, bighorn sheep, prairie dogs, and pronghorn.

THE WEST

Unlike the agricultural eastern half of the state, this is a land of prairies, pine forests, and desolate, rocky landscapes. It's also where most of the state's tourists come, to visit such places as Deadwood, the 19th-century mining town turned gambling mecca, and Mt. Rushmore, where the stern grandeur of these giant carvings remains after more than 50 years.

Getting There

By Plane

Rapid City Regional Airport (☏ 605/393–9924), 10 mi southeast of downtown via Rte. 44, is served by Northwest Airlines, Skywest (a Delta connection), and United Express.

By Car

Unless you are traveling with a package tour, a car is essential here. Make rental reservations early; Rapid City has a large number of business travelers, and rental agencies are often booked. I–90 bisects the state slightly south of its center; it leads to Wall and Rapid City. From Rapid City, U.S. 14 leads to towns and attractions in the northern part of the Black Hills, while U.S. 16 winds through its southern half. Rte. 44 is an alternate route between the Black Hills and the Badlands. The Black Hills have seven tunnels with limited clearance; they are marked on state maps and in the state's tourism booklet.

By Bus

Gray Line of the Black Hills (Box 1106, Rapid City 57709, ☎ 605/342–4461 or 800/456–4461) offers bus tours of the region, including trips to Mt. Rushmore, Black Hills National Forest, and Deadwood. **Jack Rabbit Lines** (☎ 800/444–6287) serves Wall; Rapid City; and Pierre, the capital.

The Black Hills

Tourist Information

Black Hills, Badlands and Lakes Association (900 Jackson Blvd., Rapid City 57702, ☎ 605/341–1462, FAX 605/341–4614). **Rapid City:** Chamber of Commerce and Convention & Visitors Bureau (Civic Center, Box 747, 444 N. Mt. Rushmore Rd., 57709, ☎ 605/343–1744 or 800/487–3223, FAX 605/348–9217).

Exploring the Black Hills

As with the rest of the state, many of the region's attractions are open only in the summer; be sure to call ahead before you visit. To the locals, **Rapid City** is West River, meaning west of the Missouri. (The tamer souls, perhaps more firmly rooted to the plains, live East River.) South Dakota's second-largest city, this cross between Western town and progressive community is a good base from which to explore the Black Hills. Cowboy boots are common here, and business leaders often travel by pickup truck or four-wheel-drive vehicle. Yet the city supports a convention center and a modern, acoustically advanced performance hall and boasts more than its share of bookstores downtown and a modern shopping mall on the outskirts.

The **Sioux Indian Museum** (515 West Blvd., ☎ 605/348–0557) exhibits art and crafts from the Sioux and other Native American tribes. The museum's Tipi Shop sells Native American–made earrings, drums, shields, and art. In Box Elder, just outside Rapid City, is the **South Dakota Air & Space Museum** (I–90 Exit 66, ☎ 605/385–5188). Outside the Ellsworth Air Force Base (base tours offered in summer), it features a ⅗-size Stealth bomber model, Gen. Dwight D. Eisenhower's Mitchell B–25 bomber, and numerous other planes, as well as a once-operational missile silo.

The vast **Black Hills National Forest** (R.R. 2, Box 200, Custer 57730, ☎ 605/673–2251) covers 1.3 million acres on the state's western edge. Its most famous attraction is **Mt. Rushmore National Memorial** (Keystone, 21 mi southwest of Rapid City on U.S. 16, ☎ 605/574–2523), the granite cliff where the faces of Presidents Washington, Jefferson, Lincoln, and Theodore Roosevelt are carved. Sculptor Gutzon Borglum labored at this monumental task for more than 14 years; it was finally finished by his son, Lincoln, in 1941. The memorial is spectacular in the morning light and at night, when a special lighting ceremony (nightly June–mid-Sept.) dramatically illuminates the carving.

Also in Keystone, the **Rushmore-Borglum Story** museum (342 Winter St., ☎ 605/666–4448; admission charged) contains newsreel footage of the original blasting of the rock face, as well as exhibits and drawings about the project and its artist. Fifteen miles southwest of here on

The Black Hills

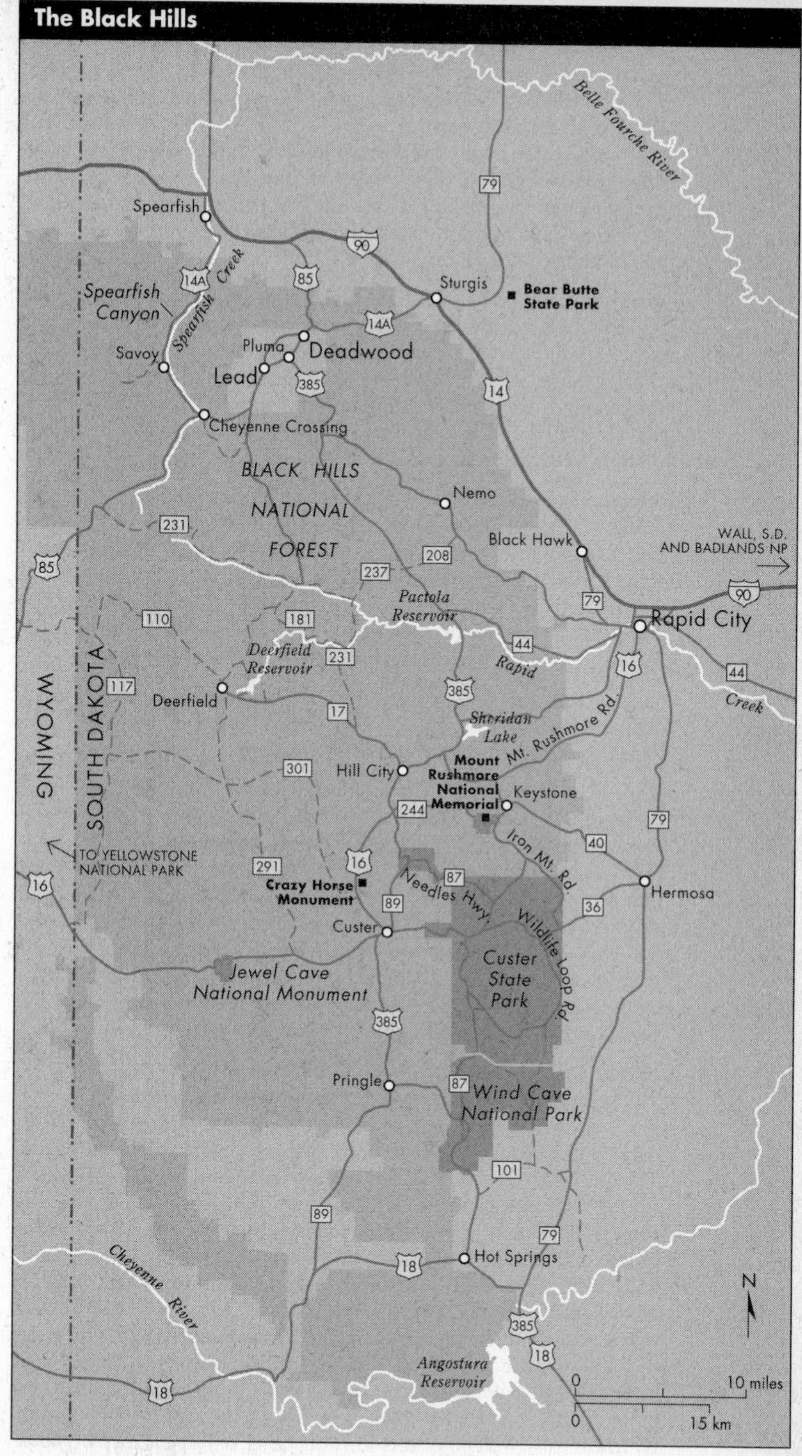

U.S. 385, another monumental likeness is emerging; when finished, the **Crazy Horse Memorial** (☎ 605/673–4681; admission charged) will depict the Lakota warrior who defeated General Custer at Little Bighorn. The site includes a visitor center and the **Indian Museum of North America.** Expect frequent blasting at this work-in-progress, which will be the world's largest sculpture when completed. Southeast of here is **Wind Cave National Park** (*see* National and State Parks, *above*). In Lakota tradition, it was from this cave that the first Lakota people were tricked by *Iktomi* (spider person) into stepping from their home underground and coming to live on the surface.

Lead (pronounced "Leed"), 50 mi north of Rapid City via I–90 and Alt. Rte. 14A, is a mining community born in the Black Hills gold-rush frenzy of the late 19th century. **Homestake Mining Co. Surface Tours** (101 W. Main St., ☎ 605/584–3110) offers tours of the aboveground operations of the country's oldest operating gold mine. Free ore samples are available. The town itself contains a number of historic houses, many once home to immigrant miners.

Sturgis, 29 mi northwest of Rapid City via I–90, is a sleepy town of about 5,600 whose population swells to between 50,000 and 130,000 the second week in August. Since 1938, the **Black Hills Motor Classic** (Sturgis Rally & Races, Box 189, Sturgis 57785, ☎ 605/347–6570, FAX 605/347–3245) has drawn motorcyclists and enthusiasts from around the world; many businesses turn their buildings over to sellers of leather goods, rally T-shirts, and other biker-related paraphernalia for the week.

In Spearfish, about 45 mi northwest of Rapid City via I–90, the ***Black Hills Passion Play*** (☎ 605/642–2646; admission charged) has since 1939 been recounting the last seven days in the life of Christ.

The films *Dances With Wolves* (which won the 1990 Academy Award for best picture) and *Thunderheart* have generated new interest, and new businesses, in the Black Hills. **Prairie Adventures** (Moon Meadows Rd. and Hwy. 16,Rapid City 57702, ☎ 605/342–4578) displays photos and shows a video taken during the making of *Dances With Wolves*. **Affordable Adventures** (Box 546, Rapid City 57709, ☎ 605/342–7691, FAX 605/341–4614) has a combination package for touring movie-location sites, including some in Spearfish Canyon and Badlands National Park; the guides specialize in year-round tours of the nearby Oglala Lakota Sioux reservation of Pine Ridge.

What to See and Do with Children

The fossilized remains of ancient mammoths at the **Mammoth Site** (one block north of the U.S. 18 bypass, Hot Springs, ☎ 605/745–6017; admission charged) should prove fascinating to children and adults alike. The site, discovered in 1974, is believed to contain up to 100 mammoths (50 have been unearthed so far) in the sinkhole where they came to drink some 26,000 years ago. A visitor center is built over the area; excavation is in progress. **Flintstones, Bedrock City** (intersection of U.S. 16 and 385, Custer, ☎ 605/673–4079) is a full-scale tribute to the enduring cartoon characters, complete with a curio shop, a train ride, a drive-in restaurant serving brontoburgers, and camping. **Bear Country U.S.A.** (8 mi south of Rapid City on U.S. 16, ☎ 605/343–2290; admission charged) is a drive-through wildlife park featuring black bears, wolves, and most other North American wildlife, and a walk-through Wildlife Center with bear cubs, wolf pups, and other offspring. In Rapid City, **Storybook Island** (near intersection of Jackson Blvd. and Sheridan Lake Rd.) lets children romp through scenes from fairy tales and nursery rhymes, and

Dinosaur Park (Skyline Dr.), listed on the National Register of Historic Places, features large plaster dinosaurs and a great view of the city.

Shopping

Rapid City stores carry Western souvenirs, crafts, and clothing. **eggs-pressions!** (1635 Deadwood Ave., ☎ 800/551–9138) offers an "eggstraordinary" collection of crafted eggwork, from jewelry to the bejeweled, the whimsical to the ornate. Nearly every gift shop here carries the locally famous Black Hills gold, a combination of metals that produce distinctive green and red tints; you can watch jewelry being made at the **Heirloom Black Hills Gold & Silver Co.** (603 Main St., ☎ 605/341–3671). **Prairie Edge Trading Co. & Galleries** (606 Main St., ☎ 605/342–3086) displays fine art and crafts of the Plains Indians, as well as works by various other Great Plains artists, in a three-story, restored 1886 building. A turn-of-the-century-style trading company in the same building has books, regional crafts, and a world-class collection of Italian glass beads. **Sioux Trading Post** (415 6th St., ☎ 605/348–4822 or 800/456–3394) has a broad range of authentic Plains Indian art, crafts, music, and books and offers a catalogue for mail orders. **Everybody's Book Store** (515 6th St., ☎ 605/341–3224) has a fine selection of used books, as well as new books on Native Americans and by regional authors. **Prince & Pauper Bookshop** (612 St. Joseph St., ☎ 605/342–7964 or 800/354–0988) has a large selection of books by regional and Native American authors.

Rushmore Mall (just off I–90 outside Rapid City, ☎ 605/348–3378) contains such specialty shops as **Leather Unlimited** (for coats and jackets) as well as department and Western stores. Among the latter is **RCC-Western Stores** (☎ 605/341–6633), which has one of the largest selections of boots in the area and can outfit you from head to toe in the latest Western fashions.

For Native American art, jewelry, baskets, and other goods, check out the gift shop of the **Museum of North America,** 15 mi southwest of Keystone on U.S. 385 (*see* Exploring the Black Hills, *above*).

Dining

For price ranges, see Chart 1 (B) in On the Road with Fodor's.

$$ Firehouse Brewing Co. This former firehouse serves up hearty fare, such as buffalo sausage, marinated buffalo steak, and rancher's (beef) pie. A wide variety of beers, from light to stout, are brewed on the premises. *610 Main St., Rapid City, ☎ 605/348–1915. AE, D, DC, MC, V.*

$$ Fireside Inn Restaurant & Lounge. Seating in one of the two dining rooms here is around a huge slate fireplace. The large menu includes prime rib, seafood, and Italian dishes. *6.5 mi west of Rapid City on Rte. 44, ☎ 605/342–3900. Reservations for 6 or more only. MC, V.*

$$ Landmark Restaurant and Lounge. This hotel restaurant is popular for its lunch buffet and for specialties that include prime rib, beef Wellington, freshwater fish, and buffalo brochettes. *Alex Johnson Hotel, 523 6th St., Rapid City, ☎ 605/342–1210. AE, D, DC, MC, V.*

$ Circle B Ranch. Chuck-wagon suppers include barbecued beef, biscuits, and all the trimmings. The ranch also offers Western shows and wagon and trail rides. *16 mi west of Rapid City on U.S. 385, 1 mi north of junction with Rte. 44, ☎ 605/348–7358. Reservations required. D, MC, V. Closed Sept.–May. No lunch.*

$ Flying T Chuckwagon. At this converted barn, ranch-style meals of barbecued beef, potatoes, and baked beans are served on tin plates. Afterward, diners settle back to watch a Western show featuring music and cowboy comedy. *6 mi south of Rapid City on U.S. 16, ☎ 605/342–1905. No credit cards. Closed mid-Sept.–late May. No lunch.*

$ World Famous Roadkill Cafe. Started by two bike-rally enthusiasts, the café promises on its Day-Glo menu to bring food "From your grill to ours!" including "The Chicken That Didn't Quite Cross the Road," "Smidgen of Pigeon," and the daily special "Guess That Mess!" The café actually offers standard fare from breakfast to tuna melt and buffalo and beef burgers, and a car-filling collection of Road Kill cookbooks and novelty items. *1333 Main St., Sturgis, ☎ 605/347–4502. No reservations. MC, V.*

Lodging

For price ranges, see Chart 2 (B) in On the Road with Fodor's.

During the summer, reservations are helpful and often required to ensure lodging; calling two or three days ahead is usually adequate. In addition to the hotels described here, several chains, including Howard Johnson's, Best Western, and Holiday Inn, have properties in and around Rapid City (*see* Appendix, Toll-Free Numbers).

$$–$$$ Alex Johnson Hotel. Western elegance pervades this nine-story-tall historic landmark located downtown. The lobby features leather wing chairs, a soaring, beamed ceiling, and a torch chandelier made out of Lakota war lances. The rooms are furnished with replicas of the original furniture that was here when the hotel opened in 1928. The hotel was officially dedicated to the Lakota Indians, so Native American patterns and artwork are dominant. *523 6th St., Rapid City 57701, ☎ 605/342–1210 or 800/888–2539. 85 rooms, 35 suites. Facilities: restaurant, pub, lounge, gift shop. AE, D, DC, MC, V.*

$$ Holiday Inn Rushmore Plaza. Opened in 1990, this eight-story hotel has a lobby with an atrium, glass elevators, and a 60-ft waterfall. Rooms have modern decor and mauve and gray tones. *505 N. 5th St., Rapid City 57701, ☎ 605/348–4000, FAX 605/348–9777. 157 rooms, 48 suites. Facilities: restaurant, lounge, pool, exercise room. AE, D, DC, MC, V.*

Campgrounds

For information on state campgrounds, contact the **Department of Game, Fish and Parks** (523 E. Capitol Ave., Pierre 57501, ☎ 605/773–3485). Among private facilities is **Rushmore Resort and Campground** (Box 124, Keystone 57751, ☎ 605/666–4605).

Deadwood

Tourist Information

Deadwood-Lead: Chamber of Commerce (460 Main St., Deadwood 57732, ☎ 605/578–1876 or 800/999–1876, FAX 605/578–1033).

Exploring Deadwood

Traveling through western South Dakota without stopping in Deadwood, 41 mi northwest of Rapid City, would have to qualify as sinful. Following the legalization of gambling in 1989, town planners rushed to revitalize and refurbish this once-infamous gold-mining boomtown for the projected onslaught of visitors. Streets have been repaved with cobblestones, and Main Street utility lines have been buried in order to keep all traces of the 20th century from impinging on visitors. Gaming halls and casinos now make up almost every storefront downtown; the refurbished old hotels have their own gambling rooms.

If a place with gambling can be wholesome, this is it (the maximum bet is $5), but it wasn't always so. This is the Old West town where Wild Bill Hickok was shot during a poker game and where Poker Alice

Tubbs was famous for smoking big cigars. **Mt. Moriah Cemetery,** above Deadwood, is the final resting place for Hickok, Calamity Jane, and other notorious Deadwood residents. From there, one has a panoramic view of Deadwood. The **Adams Memorial Museum** (54 Sherman St., ☎ 605/578–1714) has three floors of displays, including the first locomotive used in the Black Hills, photographs of the town's early days, and a gun collection.

Dining

For price ranges, see Chart 1 (B) in On the Road with Fodor's.

$$ **Jake's.** The fine-dining restaurant takes up the fourth floor of the Midnight Star, a renovated former clothing store owned by actor Kevin Costner and his brother. (The rest of the building contains a bar and grill and a gaming hall.) Popular dishes include steak and pork medallions. *677 Main St., ☎ 605/578–1555. AE, D, DC, MC, V.*

$$ ★ **1903 Historic Franklin Dining Room.** Turn-of-the-century elegance is the theme at this restaurant in the Historic Franklin Hotel. Beef is a specialty, but there's also a large variety of pastas and seafood. *700 Main St., ☎ 605/578–1465. AE, D, MC, V.*

Lodging

For price ranges, see Chart 2 (B) in On the Road with Fodor's.

$$–$$$ ★ **Bullock Hotel.** This 1895 hotel has been meticulously restored to its ornate Victorian origins. The first floor, containing the gaming hall, has high ceilings and brass and crystal chandeliers. Guest rooms are furnished with Victorian reproductions and have large windows. *633 Main St., 57732, ☎ 605/578–1745 or 800/336–1876. 26 rooms, 2 suites. Facilities: restaurant, lounge, gambling. AE, D, MC, V.*

$$–$$$ ★ **Historic Franklin Hotel and Gambling Hall.** The front rooms have views of Main Street in this turn-of-the-century hotel in the heart of the gambling district. Wide wooden stairways to upper floors contribute to the historic feel. *700 Main St., 57732, ☎ 605/578–2241 or 800/688–1876. 62 rooms. Facilities: restaurant, 2 bars, gambling, ski packages. AE, D, DC, MC, V.*

$$ **Goldiggers Hotel and Gaming Establishment.** In the gaming hall downstairs, the look is more Vegas than Wild West, but the rooms upstairs have a period look, with dark wood and burgundy tones. *629 Main St., 57732, ☎ 605/578–3213 or 800/456–2023, FAX 605/578–3762. 9 rooms, 2 suites. Facilities: restaurant, lounge, gambling. AE, D, MC, V.*

Campgrounds

For information on state campgrounds, contact the **Department of Game, Fish and Parks** (523 E. Capitol Ave., Pierre 57501, ☎ 605/773–3485). Among private campgrounds around Deadwood are **Custer Crossing Campground and Store** (HCR 73, Box 1527, Deadwood 57732, ☎ 605/584–1009), 15 mi south of town; **Deadwood KOA** (Box 451, Deadwood 57732, ☎ 605/578–3830), 1 mi west of town; and **Wild Bill's Campground** (HCR 73, Box 1101, Deadwood 57732, ☎ 605/578–2800) on U.S. 385.

The Badlands

Tourist Information

Black Hills, Badlands and Lakes Association (*see* The Black Hills, *above*). **Wall:** USDA Forest Service Buffalo Gap National Grasslands Visitor Center (Box 425, Wall 57790, ☎ 605/279–2125).

Exploring the Badlands

Badlands National Park, 80 mi east of Rapid City off I–90, can seem like another planet. Millions of years of erosion have left these 244,000 acres with desolate gorges, buttes, and ridges colored in rust, pink, and gold. Scenic overlooks are marked. The Ben Reifel Visitor Center, 2 mi north of Interior via Rte. 377, or, from I–90, off Exits 131 or 110, offers information and maps. *Box 6, Interior 57750, ☎ 605/433–5361. Admission charged Apr.–Nov.*

South of the park, on the Pine Ridge Indian Reservation, is the **Wounded Knee Massacre monument,** where more than 300 Sioux, mostly women and children, were killed when soldiers opened fire after a brief skirmish in 1890.

If you're traveling on I–90 you'll see the ubiquitous signs every few miles ticking off the mileage to **Wall Drug** (☎ 605/279–2175), the pharmacy turned tourist mecca that enticed Depression-era travelers with offers of free ice water. The store has nearly every tourist trinket imaginable, plus a restaurant that seats more than 500, a bookstore, a chapel, a selection of knives and boots, and Western art. **Wall** itself, a sleepy community on the edge of the Badlands, has several motels and restaurants.

Dining

For price ranges, see Chart 1 (B) in On the Road with Fodor's.

$–$$ **Cactus Family Restaurant and Lounge.** This downtown Wall restaurant specializes in delicious hot cakes and pies. A giant roast-beef buffet is sometimes offered in summer. *519 Main St., Wall, ☎ 605/279–2561. D, MC, V.*

$ **Cedar Pass Lodge Restaurant.** This restaurant at a rustic hotel specializes in Indian tacos (a slice of pan-fried bread covered with traditional taco fixings). It also serves up hearty meat-and-potatoes fare. *Badlands National Park, Interior, ☎ 605/433–5460. AE, D, DC, MC, V. Closed mid-Nov.–Mar.*

$ ★ **Elkton House Restaurant.** This comfortable restaurant with sun room and wood paneling has fast service and a terrific hot roast beef sandwich, served on white bread with gravy and mashed potatoes. *South Blvd., Wall, ☎ 605/279–2152. D, MC, V.*

Lodging

For price ranges, see Chart 2 (B) in On the Road with Fodor's.

$ ★ **Cedar Pass Lodge.** In Badlands National Park, the lodge's wood-frame cabins with knotty-pine interiors have a 1950s look. Each one- or two-bedroom cabin has a private bath. *Box 5, Interior 57750, ☎ 605/433–5460. 24 cabins. Facilities: restaurant, gift shop. AE, D, DC, MC, V. Closed Oct.–Apr.*

Motel

$ **Badlands Budget Host Motel** (HC 54, Box 115, Interior 57750, ☎ 605/433–5335 or 800/388–4643), 15 rooms, pool, playground, convenience store; closed mid-Sept.–May.

Campgrounds

Among private campgrounds in the area is **Circle 10 Campground** (Rte. 1, Box 51½, Philip 57567, ☎ 605/433–5451. For information on state campgrounds, contact the **Department of Game, Fish and Parks** (523 E. Capitol Ave., Pierre 57501, tel. 605/773–3485).

Sports and the Outdoors

Fishing

Some of the best fishing in the state lies to the east of this area, in the large lakes along the Missouri River, but mountain streams throughout the Black Hills offer good trout fishing. Custer State Park has trout fishing in several lakes. For more information, contact the state Department of Tourism's **fishing division** (☎ 800/445–3474).

Hiking

The **Centennial Trail,** 111 mi long, runs through the Black Hills National Forest, from the Plains Indians' sacred site at Bear Butte in the north to Wind Cave National Park, passing from grasslands into the high-country hills. For more information, contact the state Department of Tourism (*see* Visitor Information, *above*).

Snowmobiling

With about 300 mi of marked and groomed trails, the Black Hills is one of the premier spots in the country for snowmobiling. A map of the trail network is available from the Department of Tourism (*see* Visitor Information, *above*). For trail conditions, updated three times weekly, call 800/445–3474.

Ski Areas

The Black Hills' winter-sports magazine, *Romancing the Snow,* has information on cross-country and downhill skiing and is available from the Black Hills, Badlands and Lakes Association (*see* Tourist Information, *above*). For ski reports, call 800/445–3474.

Cross-Country

The Black Hills offer skiing on 600 mi of abandoned logging roads, railroad beds, and fire trails, as well as several trail networks including the **Big Hill,** 16 mi of trails on the rim of Spearfish Canyon. Information is available from **Ski Cross Country** (701 3rd St., Spearfish 57783, ☎ 605/642–3851), a ski equipment and rental shop.

Downhill

Deer Mountain Ski Area (Box 622, Deadwood 57732, ☎ 605/584–3230) has 25 trails, a 700-ft vertical drop, and one triple chair and two Poma lifts. Lessons, rentals, and cross-country trails are available. **Terry Peak Ski Area** (Box 774, Lead 57754, ☎ 605/584–2165) offers a 1,052-ft vertical drop, five chairlifts, and state-of-the-art snowmaking. A rental shop, lessons, and a lodge are available.

ELSEWHERE IN THE STATE

Sioux Falls

Getting There

Sioux Falls is in the southeastern corner of the state, at the intersection of I–90 and I–29. **Sioux Falls Regional Airport** (☎ 605/336–0762) is served by most major domestic carriers and by Mesaba (through Northwest Airlines).

What to See and Do

Sioux Falls, the state's largest city, is an ideal starting point for most attractions in the eastern part of the state. The city is a commercial hub; restaurants, hotels, and shops are numerous. The **Great Plains Zoo and Delbridge Museum of Natural History** (805 S. Kiwanis Ave., ☎ 605/339–7059; admission charged) contains, besides its live-animal displays, one of the world's largest collections of mounted animals. The **Old Courthouse Museum** (200 W. 6th St., ☎ 605/335–4210) is a massive Romanesque-style structure made of a native red stone called Sioux quartzite. It houses exhibits on the history of the area, including Native American artifacts. The **Pettigrew Home and Museum** (131 N. Duluth Ave., ☎ 605/339–7097) was built in 1889 and was later the home of South Dakota's first full-term senator, Richard F. Pettigrew. The Queen Anne–style home contains period furnishings and Native American and natural-history exhibits.

Mitchell

Getting There

Mitchell is 70 mi west of Sioux Falls on I–90.

What to See and Do

The city of Mitchell trumpets the "world's only" **Corn Palace** (604 N. Main St., ☎ 605/996–7311 or 800/257–2676). This fanciful structure, built in 1892, is topped by gaily painted Moorish domes, with a facade covered with multicolored corn, grain, and grasses in various designs and murals. Inside is an exhibition hall built to showcase the state's agricultural production. The exterior designs are changed annually. Across the street is the **Enchanted World Doll Museum** (615 N. Main St., ☎ 605/996–9896; admission charged), with 4,000 antique and modern dolls displayed in 400 scenes. For further information contact the **Mitchell Department of Tourism** (Box 776, 57301, ☎ 605/996–7311 or 800/257–2676, FAX 605/996–8273).

DeSmet

Getting There

From Sioux Falls, follow I–29N for 49 mi, then U.S. 14W for about 37 mi.

What to See and Do

Fans of the *Little House* children's book series may want to visit the town where author Laura Ingalls Wilder lived for 15 years. The Ingalls family moved to DeSmet in 1879 and lived first in a shanty, then in a farmhouse, and then in town in a house that Pa Ingalls built in 1887. The first and last homes are open to the public and contain period furnishings and memorabilia. The community is also home to the annual **Laura Ingalls Wilder Pageant** (Laura Ingalls Wilder Memorial Society, Box 344, DeSmet 57231, ☎ 605/854–3383 or 605/854–3181), held late June–early July.

Pierre

Getting There

Pierre (pronounced "Peer") is on U.S. 83, about 225 mi west of Sioux Falls.

What to See and Do

The **state capitol** (500 E. Capitol Ave., ☎ 605/773–3765), a magnificent Greek Revival building completed in 1910, has a rich interior decorated with mosaic floors, stained-glass skylights, allegorical murals, and an impressive columned staircase. The state historical society has a museum and archives at the **Cultural Heritage Center** (900 Governors Dr., ☎ 605/773–3458; admission charged). Exhibits focus on the history of the state with emphasis on the city of Pierre, which evolved from a French trading post in the early 1800s. The first of three phases for a "South Dakota Experience" permanent exhibit was completed in 1992. It offers a taste of the state from 1743, the year European trappers first arrived, through the beginning of the 20th century. The second phase, completed in the fall of 1994, focuses on the life of the Plains Indians prior to 1743. The third phase, not scheduled for completion until the year 2000, will cover 20th-century events. (For tourist office, *see* Visitor Information, *above.*)

9 The Southwest

By Edie Jarolim

A REGION THAT SEEMS TO DEMAND superlatives, the Southwest is the ruggedly beautiful, wide-open land out of which America's myths continue to emerge. Cowboys and Indians, Old World conquistadors and new religions, the rise and fall of fortunes in gold, copper, and oil—all feed into the vision of an untamed territory with limitless horizons.

Of course, Phoenix, Dallas, and Salt Lake City are sophisticated metropolises, and Santa Fe is coming to rival Los Angeles in wealth and number of art galleries per square foot. Las Vegas is sui generis, an unbridled, peculiarly American phenomenon. Foodies all over the country sing the praises of the delicately spiced Southwestern cuisine, an outgrowth of Asian immigration into the area, now duplicated in cosmopolitan restaurants nationwide. Nor is there a region that has better Mexican food, whether you like it Tex-Mex, Sonoran, or New Mexican style. Southwestern furnishings—an eclectic blend that might include Mission chests, Navajo blankets, Mexican tinwork mirrors, *ristras* (strings of red chili peppers), and even bleached cow skulls à la Georgia O'Keeffe—have become so popular in upscale homes that they're a bit of a cliché.

But other, more ancient cultures vie here with contemporary ones. The country's largest Indian reservation, that of the Navajo nation, occupies millions of acres traversing state boundaries, and dozens of other tribes—among them Hopi, Zuni, and Apache—live in the region as well. It is their vanishing civilization and, above all, the area's natural phenomena—spectacular canyons, a vast salt lake, eerily towering rock formations, and clear, lambent light—that continue to capture the imagination of visitors and residents alike. The Southwestern landscape is a glorious lesson in geologic upheaval, to be learned at such sites as Arches National Park in Utah, Carlsbad Caverns in New Mexico, and the Grand Canyon in Arizona.

Clearly anything is possible in such an unrestrained place. The heyday of the Western movie may be over, but when 1990s screen heroines Thelma and Louise light out for freedom, they find it in the Southwest, still the most natural setting for outlandish deeds and grand gestures.

Tour Groups

The tours of this region reveal natural splendors from the Grand Canyon to Zion National Park and such famous cities as San Antonio, Sante Fe, and Las Vegas.

Brennan Tours (1402 3rd Ave., Suite 717, Seattle, WA 98101, ☎ 206/622–9155 or 800/237–7249) offers an 8-day tour of the canyonland parks of Utah, Arizona, and Nevada, including the Grand Canyon, Monument Valley, and Bryce and Zion national parks. **Domenico Tours** (751 Broadway, Bayonne, NJ 07002, ☎ 201/823–8687 or 800/554–8687) offers a 9-day excursion through Texas, including a visit to the Alamo. **Gadabout Tours** (700 E. Tahquitz Canyon Way, Palm Springs, CA 92262, ☎ 619/325–5556 or 800/952–5068) follows the "Blue Bonnet Trail" for a two-week tour of Texas. A number of 5- to 7-day tours head to destinations in Arizona, Nevada, and Utah (Grand Canyon, Tucson, Lake Powell and Zion National Park, and Reno). Many more in-depth tours of the region are also available. **Globus** (5301 S. Federal Circle, Littleton, CO 80123, ☎ 303/797–2800 or 800/221–0090) has an 8-day "Best of Texas" tour with a side trip to New Orleans and a

13-day "Parks and Canyons Spectacular" tour, which swings through six western states. Nine- and 12-day "Sunny Southwest" tours cover Arizona in depth, leaving from San Diego. For similar tours at bargain prices, check out Globus's budget-minded affiliate, **Cosmos Tourama** (same address). **Maupintour** (Box 807, Lawrence, KS 66044, ☎ 913/843–1211 or 800/255–4266) offers four tours of Arizona or Arizona–Utah combinations, from 8 days to two weeks. A 12-day tour hits the highlights of "Southwest Indian Lands." Other 8-day tours cover "Grand New Mexico" and southwest Texas and Big Bend National Park. **Tauck Tours** (Box 5027, Westport, CT 06881, ☎ 203/226–6911 or 800/468–2825) has a number of 8-day tours. These include Texas in depth; New Mexico in depth, visiting Carlsbad Caverns, Santa Fe, and Albuquerque; "Arizona Resorts"; and "Canyonlands of Arizona and Utah."

When to Go

In the semiarid climate of most of the Southwest, **spring** is the season of choice, with cool, fresh, clear weather. In March and April, when temperatures average in the 70s, short-lived wildflowers produce carpets of extravagant color in many parts of the region, including some deserts as well as temperate areas like east Texas. **Summer** is dry and often very hot, sometimes unpleasantly so, across the Southwest; but water sports abound, and dramatic mountain chains offer another cool respite. Summer thunderstorms are typical in most areas. After spring, **fall**—September to November, in general—is the preferred time to visit, with temperatures falling back into the 70s and 80s, and gorgeous foliage to be seen in many areas. Skiers flock to slopes across the Southwest in **winter.** In general, temperatures vary greatly even within the same state and season because of the great variety of microclimates in the Southwest's mountains, deserts, plains, and forests.

Festivals and Seasonal Events

Late Jan.: The **Cowboy Poetry Gathering** in **Elko, Nevada,** has become famous both for the authentic characters it draws from around the Southwest and for the gentle quality of the verse these rough-hewn men and women produce. ☎ *702/738–7508.*

Early Feb.: The **Tubac (AZ) Festival** is the state's oldest arts-and-crafts show, a nine-day extravaganza that includes exhibitions, strolling performers, and food galore. ☎ *602/398–2704.*

Mid.-Feb.: Washington's Birthday Celebration in **Laredo, Texas,** and **Nuevo Laredo,** its sister city across the border, is a binational celebration of parades and fiestas honoring the first successful New World revolutionary. ☎ *210/722–0589.*

Feb.–Mar.: Twenty thousand animals are shown at **Houston**'s **Livestock Show & Rodeo,** a truly Texas-size event held under the curved roof of the Astrodome. Rodeos and country music abound. ☎ *713/791–9000.*

Early Mar.: High-quality artwork is the norm at the **Heard Museum Guild Indian Fair and Market,** a juried invitational for Native American artists held in **Phoenix, Arizona.** ☎ *602/252–8840.*

Late Apr.: Native Americans celebrate **American Indian Week** in **Albuquerque, New Mexico,** with dance, arts and crafts, and a trade show at the Indian Pueblo Cultural Center. ☎ *505/843–7270.*

Late Apr.: Fiesta San Antonio (TX), more than a century old, commemorates the Battle of San Jacinto with a festival of music, food, sports, art shows, and the River Parade. ☎ *210/227–5191.*

The Southwest

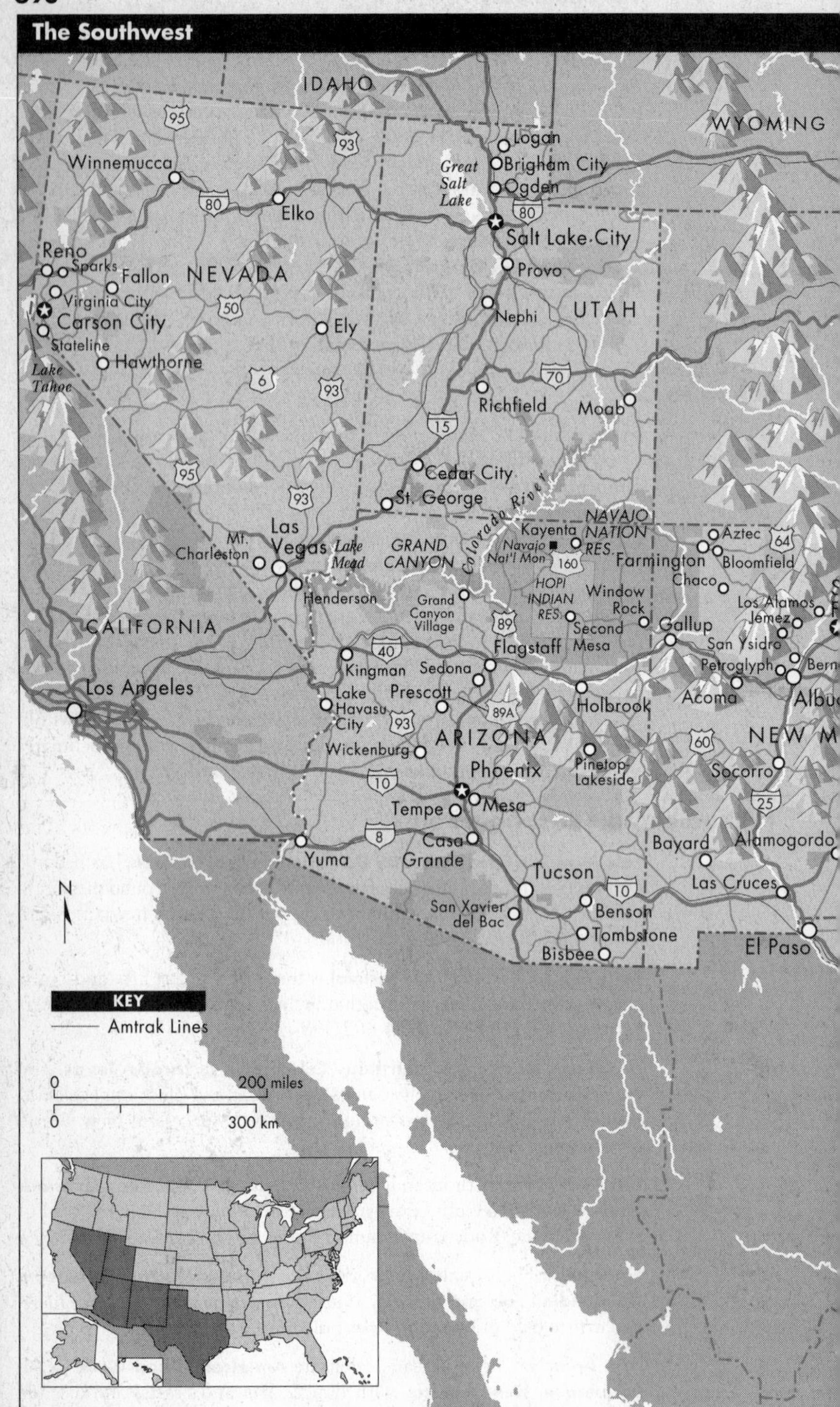

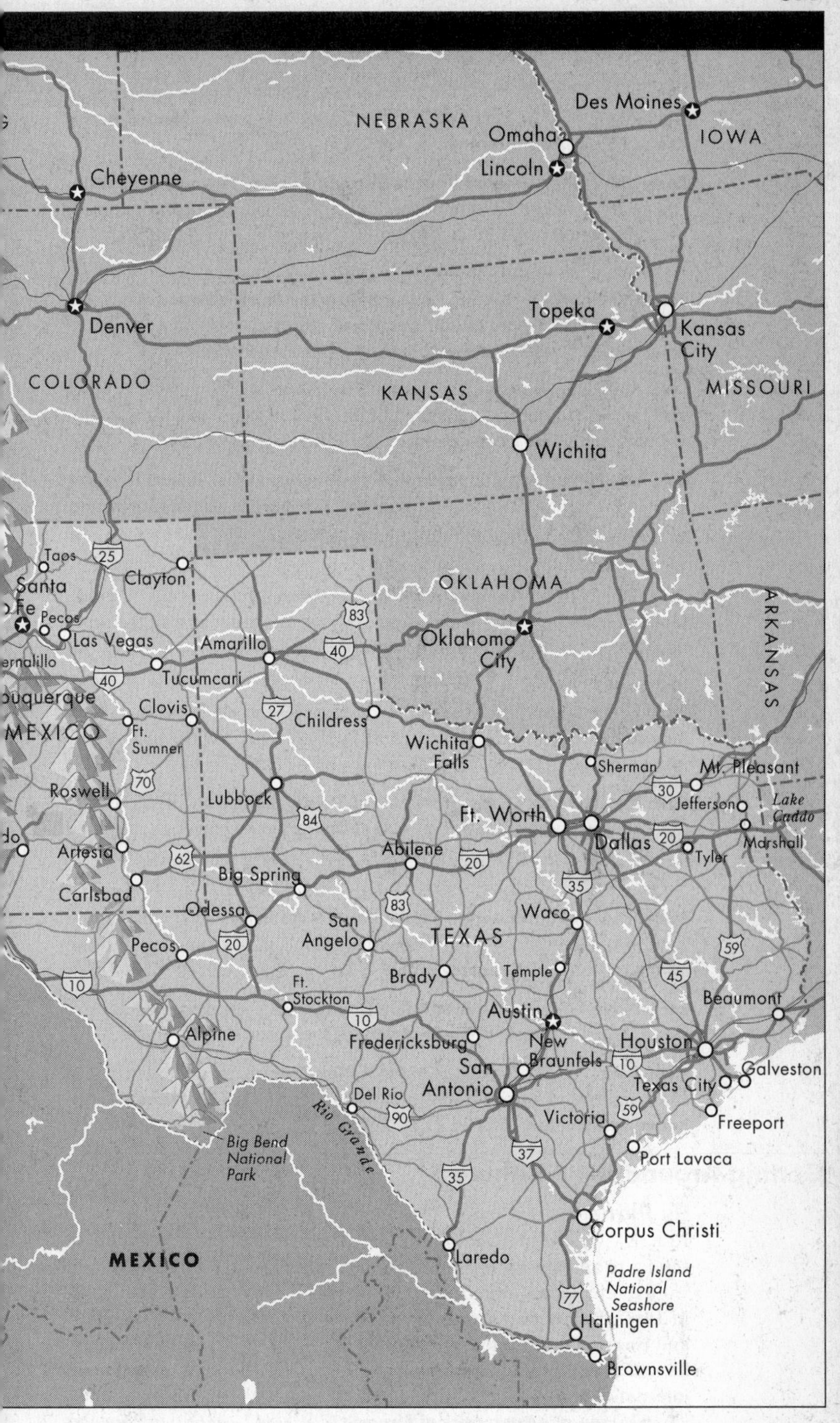
NEBRASKA
Des Moines
Omaha
IOWA
Lincoln
Cheyenne
Topeka
Kansas City
Denver
COLORADO
KANSAS
MISSOURI
Wichita
Taos
Santa Fe
Clayton
OKLAHOMA
Pecos
Las Vegas
Amarillo
Oklahoma City
ARKANSAS
Tucumcari
Clovis
Childress
Ft. Sumner
Wichita Falls
Sherman
Mt. Pleasant
Roswell
Lubbock
Jefferson
Lake Caddo
Ft. Worth
Dallas
Marshall
Tyler
Artesia
Abilene
Big Spring
Carlsbad
Odessa
Waco
San Angelo
TEXAS
Pecos
Temple
Brady
Ft. Stockton
Beaumont
Austin
Alpine
Fredericksburg
New Braunfels
Houston
San Antonio
Galveston
Texas City
Del Rio
Rio Grande
Victoria
Freeport
Big Bend National Park
Port Lavaca
Corpus Christi
MEXICO
Laredo
Padre Island National Seashore
Harlingen
Brownsville

May 5: Cinco de Mayo, a fiesta celebrating Mexican history and heritage, is held in many cities and towns across the Southwest.

Late June: New Mexico's craftspeople are world-famous, and some of the best of them display and sell their work at the **New Mexico Arts & Crafts Fair** in **Albuquerque.** ☎ *505/884–9043.*

Early July: The **National Basque Festival** in **Elko, Nevada,** celebrates the heritage of the Basque people (recruited from northern Spain for their remarkable shepherding abilities) in the American West. ☎ *702/738–7547.*

July 8–10 and 13–17: The popular **Mormon Miracle Pageant** is a musical drama of American and Mormon history, set against the backdrop of the Temple in **Manti, Utah.** ☎ *801/835–3000.*

Late July: The **Fiesta de Santiago y Santa Ana,** a colorful street party and fair, which began as a trade fair nearly 300 years ago, is the major annual event in **Taos, New Mexico.** ☎ *505/758–3873 or 800/732–8267.*

Late July–Early Aug.: The **Festival of the American West,** hosted for more than 20 years by Utah State University in **Logan,** is famous for its fair and a multimedia pageant entitled "The West: America's Odyssey." ☎ *801/750–1143.*

Aug. 23–27: The **Nevada State Fair,** in **Reno,** offers a week of rides, farm-animal competitions, livestock shows, fast food, and all the other accoutrements of a real state fair. ☎ *702/688–5767.*

Mid-Sept.: On the first weekend after Labor Day, Zozobra, or "Old Man Gloom," is burned to open the annual **Fiestas de Santa Fe** in **New Mexico.** During the celebration, Santa Fe Plaza is filled with music, dancing, and food vendors. ☎ *505/984–6760 or 800/777–2489.*

Late Sept.–Late Oct.: The **State Fair of Texas,** the nation's largest state fair, holds its three-week annual run at **Dallas**'s State Fair Park, declared a National Historic Landmark in 1986 for its Art Deco architecture. ☎ *214/421–8716.*

Mid-Oct.: The **Albuquerque International Balloon Fiesta,** in which more than 600 colorful hot-air balloons rise in spectacular unison with the dawn, is probably **New Mexico**'s best-known event. ☎ *505/821–1000.*

Early Nov.: The outdoor **Fine Folk Festival,** with 250 performers, draws some 150,000 people to **Mesa, Arizona,** every year. ☎ *602/890–2613.*

Early Dec.: The ghost town of **Madrid, New Mexico,** is reawakened with street lights and an arts-and-crafts festival during the **Christmas Openhouse Celebration.** ☎ *505/473–0743.*

Getting Around the Southwest

By Plane

America West, American, Delta, and Southwest all provide extensive service to and among the Southwestern states; Continental, TWA, and United offer more limited service. The region's major airports include, in Texas, **Dallas–Fort Worth International Airport** (☎ 214/574–8888) and **Houston Intercontinental Airport** (☎ 713/230–3100); in Nevada, **Reno Cannon International Airport** (☎ 702/328–6868) and **McCarran International Airport** (☎ 702/261–5743) in Las Vegas; in New Mexico, **Albuquerque International Airport** (☎ 505/842–4366); in Phoenix, Arizona, **Sky Harbor International Airport** (☎ 602/273–3300); and in Utah, **Salt Lake International Airport** (☎ 801/575–2400).

By Car

The Southwest is traversed by the country's two major east–west highways: I–80, the northern route, which passes through Salt Lake City, Utah, and Reno, Nevada; and I–40, which enters Texas at the Oklahoma border, heading to Los Angeles by way of Amarillo, Texas, Albuquerque, New Mexico, and Flagstaff, Arizona. Other east–west arteries include I–10, which links New Orleans and Los Angeles via Houston, San Antonio and El Paso, Texas, and Tucson and Phoenix, Arizona; and I–20, which connects Dallas and El Paso. The major north–south routes of the region are I–15, which heads south from Salt Lake City to Las Vegas; I–25, from Denver to El Paso by way of Albuquerque; and I–35, from Oklahoma to the Mexican border by way of Dallas and Fort Worth.

By Train

Amtrak (☎ 800/872–7245) serves all the states of the region, with one major line between New Orleans and Los Angeles, and another passing through southeastern Colorado to Albuquerque and Flagstaff.

By Bus

Greyhound Lines (☎ 800/231–2222) provides service to towns and cities throughout the region.

ARIZONA

By Edie Jarolim

Updated by Edie Jarolim and Susana C. Sedgwick

Capital	Phoenix
Population	3,670,000
Motto	God Enriches
State Bird	Cactus wren
State Flower	Saguaro cactus

Visitor Information

Arizona Office of Tourism (1100 W. Washington St., Phoenix 85007, ☎ 800/842–8257).

Scenic Drives

The drive from the South Rim to the North Rim of the Grand Canyon follows U.S. 89 through the **Arizona Strip,** a starkly beautiful, largely uninhabited part of the state. Almost all of the Grand Canyon drives are breathtaking, especially the West Rim Drive on the South Rim and the dirt-road drive to Point Sublime on the North Rim. Fall foliage is spectacular on U.S. 89A from Flagstaff to Sedona via **Oak Creek Canyon.** From Tucson, I–10 east of Benson passes through the startling rock formations of **Texas Canyon.**

National and State Parks

National Parks

Among the state's national parks are **Canyon de Chelly** (*see* Northeast Arizona, *below*), **Grand Canyon National Park** (*see* Grand Canyon National Park, *below*), **Petrified Forest National Park** (*see* Northeast Arizona, *below*), and **Saguaro National Monument** (*see* Tucson and Southern Arizona, *below*). For Native American ruins in scenic settings, visit **Walnut Canyon National Monument** and **Wupatki National Monument** (*see* Elsewhere in the State, *below, for both*) in the Flagstaff area, **Tuzigoot National Monument** south of Sedona, and **Navajo National Monument** (*see* Northeast Arizona, *below*). Little-visited spots of unusual beauty include **Sunset Crater Volcano National Monument** (*see* Elsewhere in the State, *below*), west of Flagstaff, and **Chiricahua National Monument,** in the southeast part of the state.

State Parks

Arizona's state parks run a wide spectrum, from the relatively tiny 54-acre **Slide Rock** (Box 10358, Sedona 86339), near Sedona, to 13,000-acre **Lake Havasu** (1350 W. McCulloch Blvd., Lake Havasu City 86403). Boating and water-sports enthusiasts congregate at **Alamo Lake State Park** (Box 38, Wenden 85257), north of Wenden, while **Catalina** and **Picacho Peak state parks** (Box 36986, Tucson 85704), near Tucson, are the best bets for desert activities. **Painted Rocks Park** (2015 W. Deer Valley Rd., Phoenix 85027), west of Gila Bend, is distinctive for its Native American rock carvings. All have hiking trails and, except for Slide Rock, campgrounds. For a taste of the state's lively frontier history, visit **Riordon Historical State Park** in Flagstaff, **Jerome State Historic Park** in north-central Arizona, **Tombstone Courthouse State Historic Park, Tubac Presidio Historic Park** (*see* Tucson and Southern Arizona, *below*) and Yuma Territorial Prison State Historic Park, in the south. For additional information, contact the **Arizona State Parks Department** (1300 W. Washington St., Phoenix 85007, ☎ 800/842–8257).

GRAND CANYON NATIONAL PARK

Not even the finest photographs pack a fraction of the impact of a personal experience of the Grand Canyon. This awesome, vastly silent ancient erosion of the surface of our planet is 277 mi long, 17 mi across at its widest spot, and more than 1 mi deep at its lowest point. Its twisted and contorted layers of rock reveal a fascinating geological profile of the Earth. All around you, otherworldly stone monuments change colors with the hours.

Tourist Information

Grand Canyon National Park (Box 129, Grand Canyon 86023, ☎ 520/638–7888). **South Rim visitor center** (Grand Canyon Village, east of El Tovar Hotel, ☎ 520/638–7888); **North Rim visitor center** (Grand Canyon Lodge, ☎ 520/638–2611). South Rim accommodations: **Grand Canyon National Park Lodges** (Box 699, Grand Canyon 86023, ☎ 520/638–2401); North Rim accommodations: **Grand Canyon Lodge** (Box 400, Cedar City, UT 84720, ☎ 801/586–7686, FAX 801/586–3157). North and South Rim camping: **MISTIX** (Box 85705, San Diego, CA 92186–5705, ☎ 800/365–2267). A free newspaper, the *Guide,* containing a detailed area map, is available at both rims. Before you go, write to Grand Canyon National Park (*see above*) for a complimentary *Trip Planner.*

Getting There

By Plane

McCarran International Airport in Las Vegas (☎ 702/261–5743) is the primary hub for flights to **Grand Canyon National Park Airport** (☎ 520/638–2446). Carriers include **Air Nevada** (☎ 800/634–6377); **Las Vegas Fliers,** who provide ground transportation as well (☎ 800/343–2632); and **Scenic Airlines** (☎ 800/535–4448). You can make connections from **Sky Harbor International Airport** in Phoenix (☎ 520/273–3300) with **Scenic Airlines** (☎ 800/634–6801). The **Tusayan Grand Canyon Shuttle** (☎ 520/638–0871) operates between Grand Canyon airport and the nearby towns of Tusayan and Grand Canyon Village. **Fred Harvey Transportation Company** (☎ 520/638–2822 or 520/638–2631) provides taxi service.

By Car

In general, the best access to the Grand Canyon is from Flagstaff (*see* Elsewhere in the State, *below*), either northwest on U.S. 180 (81 mi) to Grand Canyon Village on the South Rim or, for a scenic route, north on U.S. 89 to Rte. 64W. To visit the North Rim, some 210 mi from Flagstaff, follow U.S. 89N to Bitter Springs, then take U.S. 89A to the junction of Rte. 67. From the west on I–40, the most direct route to the South Rim is via Rte. 64 to U.S. 180. Summer traffic approaching the South Rim is very congested around Grand Canyon Village. The more remote North Rim is closed to automobiles after the first heavy snow of the season, usually reopening around mid-May.

By Train

The town closest to the Grand Canyon served by **Amtrak** is Flagstaff (☎ 520/774–8679 or 800/872–7245). From Williams, you can take the historic **Grand Canyon Railway** (☎ 800/843–8724) to the South Rim.

By Bus

Greyhound Lines stops at Flagstaff and Williams. From both towns, **Nava-Hopi Tours** (☎ 800/892–8687 or, in Flagstaff, 520/774–5003; fax 520/774–7715) offers bus service to the canyon's South Rim.

Exploring Grand Canyon National Park

Access to both the South Rim and North Rim areas of the Grand Canyon is carefully managed by the National Park Service. Unfortunately, large crowds converge on the South Rim every summer, and there is talk of limiting auto access to the area. Still, the most trafficked spots are popular for good reason. Don't forget that a walk, however brief, into the canyon itself opens up a totally new and extraordinary perspective.

South Rim

Mather Point, at the outskirts of Grand Canyon Village, affords the first glimpse of the canyon from one of the most impressive and accessible vista points on the rim.

Scenic overlooks on the 25-mi-long **East Rim Drive** include **Yaki Point,** where the popular Kaibab Trail starts the canyon descent to the inner gorge; **Grandview Point,** which supports large stands of ponderosa and piñon pine, oak, and juniper; and **Moran Point,** a favorite spot for photographers. Three miles east of Moran Point, at the **Tusayan Ruins and Museum** (☎ 520/638–2305), partially intact rock dwellings offer evidence of early habitation in the gorge. From **Lipan Point,** the widest spot in the canyon, you get an astonishing visual profile of the area's geologic history. The highest point along the tour is **Desert View** and the **Watchtower,** site of a lookout tower with a panoramic view of the Grand Canyon (☎ 520/638–2736; admission charged) and a trading post with Native American art (*see* Shopping, *below*).

Back in Grand Canyon Village, the paved **Village Rim Trail** (about 1 mi round-trip) starts at **Hopi House,** one of the canyon's first curio stores (*see* Shopping, *below*). Stops along the way include the historic **El Tovar Hotel,** the jewel in the crown of the country's national park system (*see* Dining and Lodging, *below*); **Lookout Studio,** a combination lookout point, museum, and gift shop; **Bright Angel Trailhead,** the starting point for the best known trail to the bottom of the canyon; and **Bright Angel Lodge,** with a fireplace made of regional rocks arranged in layers that match those of the canyon.

On the **West Rim Drive, Trailview Overlook** affords an unobstructed view of the distant San Francisco Peaks, Arizona's highest mountains. At **Maricopa Point,** you'll see the towering headframe of an early Grand Canyon mining operation. The **Abyss** reveals a sheer canyon drop of 3,000 ft. **Pima Point** provides a bird's-eye view of the Tonto Plateau and the Tonto Trail, which winds for more than 70 mi through the canyon. **Hermits Rest,** the westernmost viewpoint, and the Boucher Trail, which descends from it (*see* Sports and the Outdoors, *below*), were named for Louis Boucher, a 19th-century prospector who had a roughly built home down in the canyon. The West Rim Drive is closed to auto traffic in summer; from late May through September, free shuttle buses leave daily from Grand Canyon Village for Hermits Rest.

North Rim

The relative solitude of the North Rim, set in deep forest near the 9,000-ft crest of Kaibab Plateau in the isolated Arizona Strip, is well worth the extra miles on the road. From central Arizona, the only route into this area is more than 200 mi of lonely road to the northwest of

Grand Canyon National Park

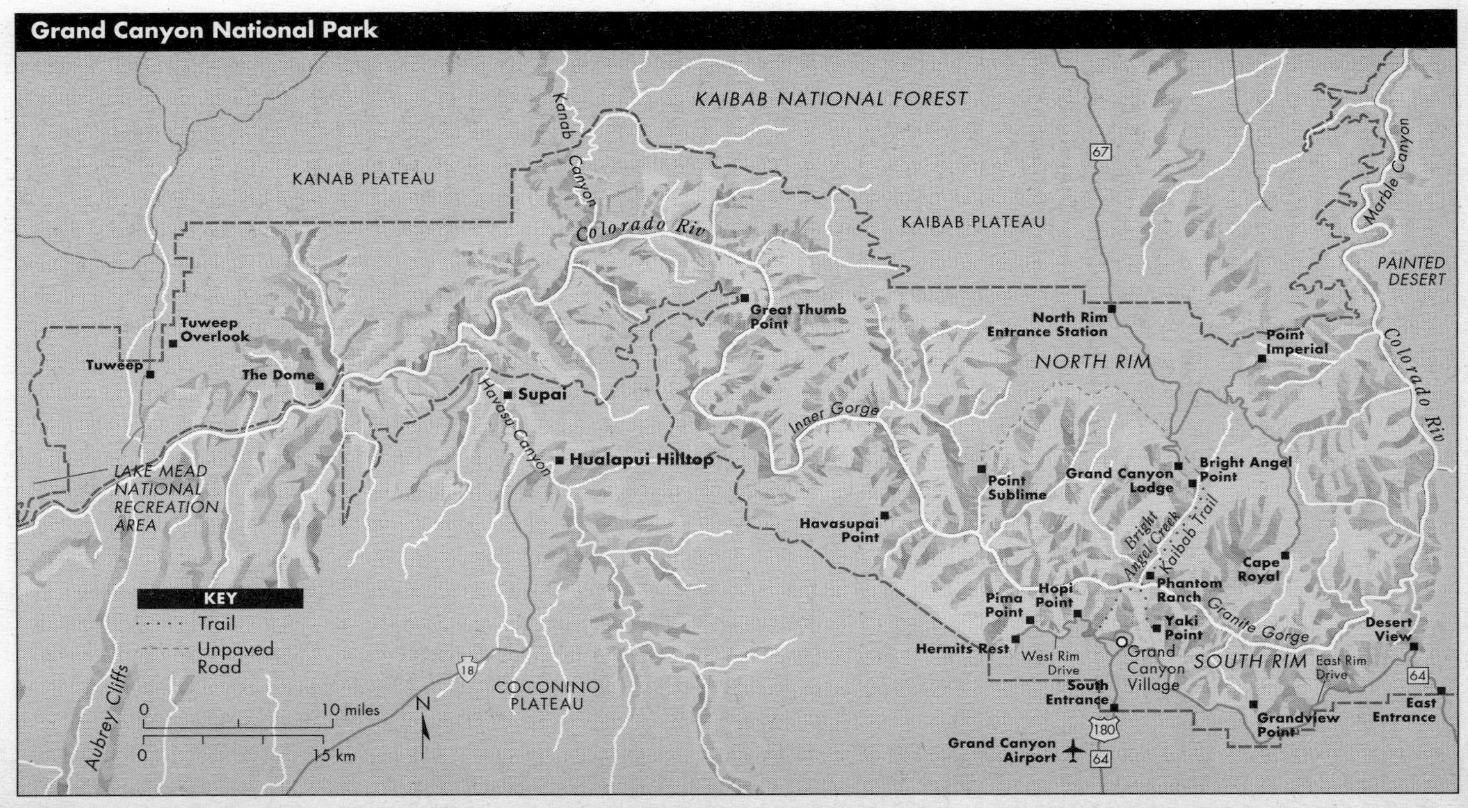

Flagstaff. In winter, heavy snows close highway access to, and facilities in, the North Rim.

The trail to **Bright Angel Point,** one of the most awe-inspiring overlooks on either rim, starts on the grounds of the **Grand Canyon Lodge** (*see* Dining and Lodging, *below*), a massive stone structure built in 1928 by the Union Pacific Railroad. Two of the North Rim's most popular outlooks are **Point Imperial,** at 8,803 ft the canyon's highest viewpoint, and **Cape Royal,** the southernmost viewpoint on the North Rim.

What to See and Do with Children

Free daily programs conducted by the National Park Service may appeal especially to children. Gentle horses can be rented at the **Moqui Lodge** (Tusayan, ☎ 520/638–2424). Short mule rides suitable for young children leave from Grand Canyon Lodge to the easier trails along the North Rim; make reservations with **Canyon Trail Rides** (☎ 520/638–2292 or 801/679–8665 off-season).

Shopping

Native American items sold at most of the lodges and at major gift shops are authentic. Among the most interesting places to browse or buy are the **Desert View Trading Post** (East Rim Dr., ☎ 520/638–2360), offering a mix of Southwest souvenirs and Native American crafts; the **El Tovar Hotel Gift Shop** (near the rim in Grand Canyon Village, ☎ 520/638–2631), where silver jewelry is featured; **Hopi House** (east of El Tovar Hotel, ☎ 520/638–2631), with a wide variety of Native American artifacts, some of museum quality; and **Cameron Trading Post** (54 mi north of Flagstaff on U.S. 89, ☎ 520/679–2231 or 800/338–7385), with Navajo, Hopi, Zuni, and New Mexico Pueblo jewelry, rugs, baskets, and pottery.

Sports and the Outdoors

Hiking

One of the most popular and scenic hiking paths from the South Rim to the bottom of the canyon (8 mi), the well-maintained **Bright Angel Trail** has a steep (4,460-ft) ascent and should be attempted only by persons in good physical condition. The 9-mi **Hermit (Boucher) Trail,** which starts at Hermits Rest and offers some inspiring views of Hermit Gorge and the Redwall and Supai formations, isn't maintained and is suitable only for experienced long-distance hikers. The steep **South Kaibab Trail** begins near Yaki Point on East Rim Drive near Grand Canyon Village and connects at the bottom of the canyon with the **North Kaibab Trail,** the only maintained trail into the canyon from the North Rim. Plan on five days if you want to hike the gorge from rim to rim. **Note:** For hikes into the gorge, carry 1-1½ gallons of water per day and drink frequently, about every 10 minutes, especially in summer. To avoid fatigue, take along high-energy snacks, such as trail mix, bananas, and fig bars.

Park rangers or visitor-center personnel have detailed area maps of the many canyon trails. Overnight hikes require a permit; write **Backcountry Reservations Office** (Box 129, Grand Canyon 86023). It's wise to make a reservation in advance. If you arrive without one, go to the Backcountry Reservations Office either near the entrance to Mather Campground on the South Rim or at the North Rim's ranger station.

Mule Trips

Mule trips down the precipitous trails to the inner gorge are nearly as well known as the canyon itself. Inquire at the **Reservations Depart-**

ment (Box 699, Grand Canyon 86023, ☎ 520/638–2401) about prices and restrictions for riders, and book months in advance.

Rafting

Reservations for white-water rafting trips, which last from one to several days, must often be made more than six months ahead of time. Outfitters include **Canyoneers, Inc.** (☎ 520/526–0924; outside AZ, 800/525–0924), **Diamond River Adventures** (☎ 520/645–8866 or 800/343–3121), **Expeditions Inc.** (☎ 520/779–3769), and **Wilderness River Adventures** (☎ 520/645–3296 or 800/992–8022). **Fred Harvey Transportation Company** (☎ 520/638–2822) specializes in smooth-water rafting day trips. For a complete list of river-raft companies, contact the **River Permits Office** (Grand Canyon National Park, Box 129, Grand Canyon 86023, ☎ 520/638–7888).

Dining and Lodging

Restaurants throughout Grand Canyon country and northwestern Arizona cater to tourists who are moving at a good clip from one place to another; they generally offer standard American fare at reasonable prices.

It's difficult to find rooms in the South Rim area in summer. The North Rim is less crowded but has limited lodging facilities. Make reservations as soon as your itinerary is firmed up, even as much as six months in advance. If you can't find accommodations in the immediate South Rim area, try the nearby communities of Williams or Flagstaff. Camping inside the park is permitted only in designated areas. For information on park camping and reservations, contact **MISTIX** (*see* Tourist Information, *above*). The Arizona Office of Tourism (*see* Visitor Information, *above*) offers a campground directory. For price ranges, see Charts 1 (B) and 2 (B) in On the Road with Fodor's.

South Rim

DINING AND LODGING

El Tovar Hotel. Reminiscent of a grand European hunting lodge, El Tovar has maintained a tradition of excellent service and luxury since 1905. The hotel's fine restaurant, set in a room of hand-hewn logs and beamed ceilings, serves Continental dishes such as veal française. *Box 699, Grand Canyon 86023, ☎ 520/638–2401 (reservations) or 520/638–2631, FAX 520/638–9247. 65 rooms, 10 suites. Facilities: restaurant, cocktail lounge, gift shop. AE, D, DC, MC, V. $$$*

Bright Angel Lodge. Built in 1935, this log-and-stone structure a few yards from the canyon rim offers rooms in the main lodge or in quaint cabins (some with fireplaces) scattered among the pines. The restaurant, overlooking the Abyss, is informal but memorable. *Box 699, Grand Canyon 86023, ☎ 520/638–2401 (reservations) or 520/638–2631, FAX 520/638–9247. 30 rooms (19 shared baths), 47 cabins. Facilities: restaurant, cocktail lounge, soda fountain, gift shop. AE, D, DC, MC, V. $$–$$$*

LODGING

Maswik Lodge, Yavapai Lodge, Moqui Lodge, Kachina Lodge, and **Thunderbird Lodge.** The five other Fred Harvey Company lodges on the South Rim are all comfortable and well appointed. Moqui is on U.S. 180, just outside the park, while the others are in Grand Canyon Village. *Box 699, Grand Canyon 86023, ☎ 520/638–2401 (reservations) or 520/638–2631, FAX 520/638–9247. 1,000 rooms. Facilities: restaurants. AE, D, DC, MC, V. $$–$$$*

CAMPING

In Grand Canyon Village, **Mather Campground** (contact MISTIX; *see* Tourist Information, *above*) has RV and tent sites, and **Trailer Village** (Box 699, Grand Canyon 86023, ☎ 520/638–2401) has RV sites. Commercial and Forest Service campgrounds outside the park include **Flintstone Bedrock City** (Grand Canyon Hwy., HCR 34, Box A, Williams 86046, ☎ 520/635–2600), with tent and RV sites; **Grand Canyon Camper Village** (Box 490, Grand Canyon 86023, ☎ 520/638–2887) in Tusayan, with RV and tent sites; and **Ten X Campground** (Kaibab National Forest, Tusayan Ranger District, Box 3088, Grand Canyon 86023, ☎ 520/638–2443), with family sites.

Bottom of the Canyon

DINING AND LODGING

Phantom Ranch. Dormitory accommodations for hikers and cabins for hikers and mule riders nestle in a grove of cottonwood trees at the bottom of the canyon. The restaurant has a limited menu, with meals served family style. Arrangements—and payment—for both food and lodging should be made 9–11 months in advance. *Box 699, Grand Canyon 86023, ☎ 520/638–2401 (reservations) or 520/638–2631. 4 dorms with shared bath, 11 cabins with outside shower. Facilities: dining room. AE, D, DC, MC, V. $*

CAMPING

Indian Gardens, about halfway down the canyon, and **Bright Angel,** near the bottom, are free campgrounds; contact the Backcountry Reservations Office (*see* Sports and the Outdoors, *above*).

North Rim

DINING AND LODGING

★ **Grand Canyon Lodge.** The premier lodging facility on the North Rim, this historic property offers comfortable, though not luxurious, accommodations in an extraordinary setting. Surprisingly sophisticated Continental fare is served in the huge dining room. *TW Recreational Services, Box 400, Cedar City, UT 84720, ☎ 801/586–7686 (reservations) or 520/638–2611, FAX 801/586–3157. 44 rooms, 157 cabins (4 cabins are wheelchair accessible). Facilities: dining room, cafeteria, lounge, shop, visitor center. D, DC, MC, V. $$*

CAMPING

North Rim Campground (contact MISTIX; *see* Tourist Information, *above*) inside the park has RV and tent sites. Forest Service facilities outside the park include **Demotte Campground** (Kaibab National Forest, North Kaibab Ranger District, Box 248, Fredonia 86022, ☎ 520/643–7395), also with tent and RV sites.

NORTHEAST ARIZONA

Most of northeast Arizona, a vast and lonely land of shifting red dunes and soaring buttes, belongs to the Navajo and Hopi peoples. Throughout the area, excellent Native American arts and crafts may be found in shops, galleries, and trading posts. Visitors are also welcome to observe certain ancient cultural traditions, such as Hopi ceremonial dances; however, the privacy, customs, and laws of the tribes should be respected. Within the stunning landscapes of Navajo National Monument and Canyon de Chelly, both on the Navajo reservation, the mysterious ruins of ancient Anasazi tribes can be haunting. These Native American ancestors first wandered here thousands of years ago. Just below the southeastern boundary of the Navajo reservation, straddling I–40, Petrified Forest National Park is an intriguing geologic open book of the Earth's distant past. Above the far northwestern corner of the Navajo reservation on U.S. 80 lies Glen Canyon Dam. Behind it more than 120 mi of Lake Powell's emerald waters are held in precipitous canyons of erosion-carved stone.

Tourist Information

Glen Canyon Recreation Area (Box 1507, Page 86040, ☎ 520/645–8200). **Hopi Tribe Office of Public Relations** (Box 123, Kykotsmovi 86039, ☎ 520/734–2441). **Navajo Tourism Department** (Box 663, Window Rock 86515, ☎ 520/871–6659, 520/871–7371, or 520/871–6436). **Page/Lake Powell:** Chamber of Commerce (106 S. Lake Powell Blvd., Box 727, Page 86040, ☎ 520/645–2741).

Getting There

By Plane

No major airlines fly directly to this area. You'll need to make flight connections in Phoenix (*see* Metropolitan Phoenix, *below*) to travel on to either Flagstaff's airport (*see* Grand Canyon National Park, *above*) or to **Page Municipal Airport** (☎ 520/645–2494) near Lake Powell.

By Car

From the east or west, I–40 passes through Flagstaff, a good entry point to the region. From the north or northwest, U.S. 89 brings you to Page. From the northeast, U.S. 64 leads west from Farmington, New Mexico.

A tour of Navaho and Hopi country involves driving long distances among widely scattered communities, so a detailed road map is essential. Especially recommended is the map of the northeast put out by the Navajo Tourism Department (*see* Tourist Information, *above*). In this sparsely populated area, service stations are rare, so be sure to take care of necessary maintenance before your trip. Never drive into dips or low-lying road areas during a heavy rainstorm; flash floods are very sudden and extremely dangerous.

By Train

Amtrak stops in Flagstaff (☎ 520/774–8679 or 800/872–7245), a good jumping-off point for a car trip into the area.

By Bus

Greyhound Lines (☎ 800/231–2222) goes to Phoenix and Flagstaff. Travel by the **Navajo Transit System** (☎ 520/729–4002), which has fixed routes throughout the reservation, is slow.

Exploring Northeast Arizona

Some 115 mi east of Flagstaff off I–40, **Petrified Forest National Park** is strewn with fossilized tree trunks whose wood cells were replaced over the centuries by brightly hued mineral deposits. The park's 94,000 acres include portions of the **Painted Desert,** a colorful but essentially barren and waterless series of windswept plains, hills, and mesas. Also look for fascinating Native American petroglyphs. *Box 2217, Petrified Forest, AZ 86028, ☎ 520/524–6228. Admission charged.*

Northeast of Petrified Forest, **Window Rock** is the capital of the Navajo Nation and the business and social center for families from the surrounding rural areas. Visit the **Navajo Nation Museum** (Rte. 264, next to Navajo Nation Inn, ☎ 520/871–6673; closed weekends in winter), which is devoted to Navajo art, culture, and history. The adjoining **Navajo Arts and Crafts Enterprise** (*see* Shopping, *below*) displays local work.

Northwest of Window Rock, **Canyon de Chelly** (pronounced "duh-SHAY"), nearly 84,000 acres, is one of the Southwest's most extraordinary national monuments. Thousand-year-old pictographs made by the Anasazi people decorate some of its sheer cliff walls, and gigantic stone formations rise hundreds of feet above small streams, hogans, tilled fields, peach orchards, and grazing lands. Paved rim drives offer marvelous views. There are also horseback tours of the canyon. *Box 588, Chinle 86503, ☎ 520/674–5500 or 520/674–5501.*

At the approximate center of the Navajo reservation lies the 4,000-sq-mi **Hopi reservation,** a series of stone-and-adobe villages built on high mesas. On **First Mesa** is the town of **Walpi,** built on solid rock and surrounded by steep cliffs. Its 30 residents defy modernity and live without electricity and running water.

In **Second Mesa's** oldest and largest village, **Shungopavi,** the famous Hopi snake dances—no longer open to the public—are held in August of even-numbered years. Also on Second Mesa is the **Hopi Cultural Center,** with a pueblo-style museum, shops, and a good restaurant and motel (*see* Dining and Lodging, *below*). *Museum ☎ 520/734–6650. Admission charged to museum.*

Kykotsmovi, at the eastern base of **Third Mesa,** is known for its greenery and peach orchards. It is the site of Hopi Tribal Headquarters. Atop Third Mesa, **Oraibi,** established around AD 1150, is widely believed to be the oldest continuously inhabited community in the United States.

Monument Valley, on the Utah border north of Kayenta, will look familiar if you've seen Westerns. This sprawling expanse of soaring red buttes, eroded mesas, deep canyons, and naturally sculpted rock formations was also populated by the Anasazi and has been home to generations of Navajo. Within this vast area lies the 30,000-acre **Monument Valley Navajo Tribal Park** and its scenic 17-mi self-guided tour. *Visitor center, 3½ mi off U.S. 163, 24 mi north of Kayenta, ☎ 801/727–3287. Admission charged.*

At **Navajo National Monument,** southwest of Monument Valley off U.S. 160, two unoccupied 13th-century cliff pueblos, **Keet Seel** and **Betatakin,** stand under the overhang of soaring orange and ocher cliffs. The largest Native American ruins in Arizona, these pueblos, too, were built by the Anasazi, whose reasons for abandoning them prior to AD 1300 are still disputed by scholars. *HC71 Box 3, Tonalea 86044, ☎ 520/672–2366.*

For information on the construction of **Glen Canyon Dam** and **Lake Powell,** 136 mi north of Flagstaff on U.S. 89, stop at the **Carl Hayden Visitor Center** (Glen Canyon Dam, ☎ 520/645–8405 or 520/645–8404). The best way to see eerie, man-made Lake Powell as it twists through rugged canyon country is by boat (*see* Sports and the Outdoors, *below*). Take a half-day excursion to **Rainbow Bridge National Monument,** a 290-ft red sandstone arch that straddles one of the lake's coves.

Shopping

You may find exactly what you want, at a good price, from a roadside vendor, but the following have dependable selections of Native American wares. **Cameron Trading Post** (54 mi north of Flagstaff on U.S. 89, ☎ 520/679–2231 or 800/338–7385) is one of the Southwest's few remaining authentic trading posts. **Navajo Arts and Crafts Enterprise** in Window Rock (off Rte. 264, next to Navajo Nation Inn, ☎ 520/871–4108 or 800/662–6189, FAX 520/871–5466) stocks fine authentic

Navajo products. **Hubbell Trading Post** (Rte. 264, 1 mi west of Ganado, ☎ 520/755–3254) is famous for its "Ganado red" Navajo rugs and has a good collection of crafts.

Sports and the Outdoors

Boating

Rental boats and water-sports equipment, as well as excursion boats, are available at **Wahweap Marina** (U.S. 89, 5 mi north of Page, ☎ 520/645–1085 or 800/528–6154).

Hiking

There's excellent hiking in **Canyon de Chelly.** Guides are required for all but the White House Ruin Trail; contact the visitor center. In addition to casual hikes along the rim areas, **Navajo National Monument** offers guided hikes (☎ 520/672–2367) to Betatakin (early May–mid-Oct.); a permit is needed for the unsupervised longer hike to Keet Seel (Memorial Day–Labor Day).

Horseback Riding

Edward Black (☎ 800/551–4039 or 801/739–4285) gives long and short trail rides from his stable in the Monument Valley area. Also, year-round rides are offered at **Bigman's** (☎ 520/677–3219).

Dining and Lodging

Northeast Arizona is vast, and few communities offer places to eat; Page, Window Rock, Fort Defiance, Ganado, Chinle, Holbrook, Hopi Second Mesa, Keams Canyon, Tuba City, Kayenta, Goulding's Trading Post/Monument Valley, and Cameron all have restaurants and fast-food service. No alcoholic beverages are sold on the Navajo and Hopi reservations, and possession or consumption of alcohol is against the law in these areas.

Similarly, half the battle in this big land is knowing in which of the scattered communities lodging can be found. Towns noted above also offer accommodations. In summer, it is especially wise to make reservations. For price ranges, see Charts 1 (B) and 2 (B) in On the Road with Fodor's.

Cameron

DINING AND LODGING

Cameron Trading Post and Motel. A good place to stop if you're driving from the Hopi mesas to the Grand Canyon, this motel offers attractive Southwestern-style rooms. Hearty fare—including traditional fry bread, Navajo tacos, and Navajo stew—is served in the wood-beamed dining room. *54 mi north of Flagstaff on U.S. 89, Box 339, 86020, ☎ 520/679–2231 or 800/338–7385, FAX 520/679–2350. 62 units. Facilities: café, restaurant, market, curio shop, art gallery, RV park. AE, DC, MC, V. $$*

Chinle/Canyon de Chelly

DINING AND LODGING

Holiday Inn Canyon de Chelly. Opened in late 1992 on the site of a former trading post, this Navajo-staffed complex has pastel-toned contemporary-style rooms. Restaurant service can be erratic, but the food more than compensates. *BIA Rte. 7, Box 1889, Chinle, AZ 86503, ☎ 520/674–5000 or 800/234–6835, FAX 520/674–8264. 108 rooms. Facilities: restaurant, pool, gift shop. AE, D, DC, MC, V. $$$*

Thunderbird Lodge. At the mouth of Canyon de Chelly, this pleasant establishment with manicured lawns and cottonwood trees has stone-

and-adobe units with inviting Navajo decor. In a cafeteria, an inexpensive American menu is prepared by an all-Navajo staff. *½ mi south of canyon visitor center, Box 548, 86503, ☎ 520/674–5841 or 800/679–2473. 72 rooms. Facilities: cafeteria, gift shop. AE, D, DC, MC, V. $$*

CAMPING

Cottonwood Campground (Canyon de Chelly National Monument, near visitor center, Box 588, Chinle 86503, ☎ 520/674–5500) has individual and group sites.

Hopi Reservation–Second Mesa

DINING AND LODGING

★ **Hopi Cultural Center Motel.** This pleasant pueblo-style lodging high atop Second Mesa offers immaculate rooms with white walls and charming Native American decor. A comfortable, inexpensive restaurant serves traditional Native American dishes, including Hopi bluecorn pancakes and *nok qui vi* (lamb stew). *Rte. 264, Box 67, 86043, ☎ 520/734–2401. 33 units. Facilities: restaurant, gift shop, museum. DC, MC, V. $$*

Kayenta

LODGING

Holiday Inn. Typical of the chain except for the Southwestern decor, this accommodation near Monument Valley has comfortable rooms. It also has one of the few swimming pools in the western end of Indian country. *South of junction U.S. 160 and 163, Box 307, 86033, ☎ 520/697–3221 or 800/465–4329, FAX 520/697–3349. 160 rooms. Facilities: restaurant, pool, gift shop. AE, D, DC, MC, V. $$$*

Wetherill Inn Motel. This clean and cheerful two-story motel without frills was named for frontier explorer John Wetherill. There is a café nearby. *U.S. 163, Box 175, 86033, ☎ 520/697–3231. 54 rooms. AE, D, DC, MC, V. $$*

Keams Canyon

DINING

Keams Canyon Restaurant. At this typical rural roadside spot, you'll find American dishes and a few Native American items, including Navajo tacos. *Keams Canyon Shopping Center (off Rte. 264), ☎ 520/738–2296. MC, V. No dinner weekends. $*

CAMPING

Keams Canyon Campground (near Keams Canyon trading post on Rte. 264, ☎ 520/738–2297) offers free camping at two sites.

Lake Powell/Page

DINING AND LODGING

★ **Wahweap Lodge.** On a promontory above Lake Powell, the lodge serves as the center for area recreational activities. Many guest rooms, nicely furnished in oak and Southwestern colors, have lake views. The semicircular Rainbow Room gives a panoramic view of the lake; specialties on the extensive Southwestern-standard American menu include coho salmon with Dijon mustard cream sauce. *U.S. 89, 5 mi north of Page, Box 1597, Page 86040, ☎ 520/645–2433 or 800/528–6154. 350 rooms. Facilities: restaurant, cocktail lounge, gift shop, rental boats, cruises, fishing and water-skiing equipment, river-rafting excursions, houseboats. AE, D, DC, MC, V. $$$*

Weston's Empire House. This classic 1950s-style motel is on Page's main street, 7 miles north of Lake Powell. The smoky bar is the real Western thing. *Box 1747 (107 S. Lake Powell Blvd.), 86040, ☎ 520/645–2406 or 800/551–9005, FAX 520/645–2647. 69 rooms. Facilities: restaurant, bar/lounge, pool, cable TV. MC, V. $$*

Monument Valley, Utah

DINING AND LODGING

Goulding's Lodge. Featuring cozy rooms with Southwestern-design bedspreads, Native American art, and spectacular views of Monument Valley, this comfortable motel often serves as the headquarters for film location crews. The motel's Stagecoach Restaurant serves good standard fare and some Native American dishes. *2 mi west of U.S. 163, just north of UT border, Box 360001, Monument Valley, UT 84536, ☏ 801/727–3231 or 800/874–0902. 62 rooms. Facilities: restaurant; indoor heated pool and trading post history museum (both closed Nov. 15–Mar. 15). AE, D, DC, MC, V. $$$*

CAMPING

Mitten View Campground (Monument Valley Navajo Tribal Park, near visitor center, ☏ 801/727–3287) has some sites available year-round. **Good Sam Campground** (off U.S. 163, near Goulding's Trading Post, ☏ 801/727–3232, ext. 425) operates mid-March–October.

Navajo National Monument

CAMPING

Navajo National Monument (*see* Exploring Northeast Arizona, *above*) has two campgrounds with free RV and tent sites that are open May to October.

Window Rock

DINING AND LODGING

Navajo Nation Inn. Native American government officials frequent this motel in the Navajo Nation's tribal capital. Spanish Colonial furniture and Navajo art decorate the rooms. An inexpensive restaurant serves American and Navajo fare, including fry bread, tacos, and mutton stew. *North side of Rte. 264, Box 2340, 86515, ☏ 520/871–4108 or 800/662–6189. 56 units. Facilities: restaurant, pool. AE, DC, MC, V. $$*

SEDONA AND FLAGSTAFF

Located in north-central Arizona, these two locations are important stops for Southwest travelers—Sedona for its stunning natural beauty and Flagstaff as a base for exploring the Grand Canyon and Navajo-Hopi country.

Sedona

Sedona is perhaps the most attractive stopover en route north from Phoenix to the Grand Canyon. Startling formations of deep-red rocks, like Capitol Butte or Bell Rock, gently caress what is almost always a clear blue sky—made to seem even bluer by the dark green of forests. Filmmakers in the 1940s and '50s saw this as a quintessential wild-west landscape and shot more than 80 films in the area. Now a sort of art colony, Sedona is also a center of interest to New Age enthusiasts, who believe the area contains important vortices (energy centers).

Arriving and Departing

Sedona is 125 mi north of downtown Phoenix and 27 mi south of Flagstaff, at the southern end of Oak Creek Canyon on U.S. 89A.

Exploring Sedona

Scenic hiking spots include **Long Canyon, Devil's Kitchen,** and the Native American ruins in **Boynton Canyon,** and there are almost limitless other opportunities for hikes and walks. Stop at the **Sedona Ranger District** office (250 Brewster Rd., ☏ 520/282–4119, open weekdays 7:30–4:30) for more information. In addition, **Red Rock State Park** (☏

520/282–6907) is 5 mi southwest of Sedona, and **Slide Rock State Park** (☎ 520/282–3034) is 8 mi to the north in beautiful Oak Creek Canyon. **Jerome,** about 37 mi southwest on U.S. 89A, is a former mining boomtown perched on Cleopatra Hill. Come here for outstanding views and for funky boutiques. For information on the area, contact **Sedona–Oak Creek Canyon Chamber of Commerce** (North U.S. 89A and Forest Rd., Box 478, Sedona 86339, ☎ 520/282–7722 or 800/288–7336).

Back in town, touristy shopping is the main activity: **Tlaquepaque Mall** (Rte. 179, ☎ 520/282–4838) offers the largest concentration of upscale shops. The **Chapel of the Holy Cross** (Chapel Rd., ☎ 520/282–4069) is worth a visit for its striking architecture and stunning vistas.

Dining

$$$ **L'Auberge de Sedona.** One of the most romantic restaurants in Arizona, L'Auberge is done in country-French style; ask for a table overlooking Oak Creek. The six-course prix-fixe menu ($55) might include wild game consommé with duck ravioli or filet mignon with foie gras, wild mushrooms, and truffle sauce. *L'Auberge La., ☎ 520/282–1667. Reservations required. Jacket required. AE, D, DC, MC, V.*

$$ ★ **Heartline Café.** This pretty, plant-filled café serves tasty Southwestern-style food, such as grilled salmon marinated in tequila and lime. A sampler for two allows you and your companion to try all of the luscious desserts on the menu. *1610 W. U.S. 89A, ☎ 520/282–0785. AE, D, MC, V. No lunch Sun.*

Lodging

$$$ ★ **Enchantment Resort.** Set in spectacular Boynton Canyon, Enchantment has excellent sports facilities. All rooms are in pueblo-style casitas and have dazzling views of the surrounding forest and canyons. Many offer fireplaces and kitchenettes, and two have private pools. *525 Boynton Canyon Rd., 86336, ☎ 520/282–2900 or 800/826–4180, FAX 520/282–9249. 162 rooms. Facilities: 5 pools, tennis courts, hiking, 6-hole pitch-and-putt course, fitness center, spa, and restaurant. AE, D, MC, V.*

$$ **Sky Ranch Lodge.** An excellent value in an expensive town, the lodge has simply furnished rooms with Southwestern touches, such as Mexican tiles surrounding the dressers. Some have fireplaces and others balconies offering terrific views of Sedona's red-rock canyons. *Airport Rd., Box 2579, 86339, ☎ 520/282–6400, FAX 520/282–7682. 92 rooms (20 with kitchenettes), 2 cottages. Facilities: pool, whirlpool. MC, V.*

Flagstaff

The largest city in north-central Arizona, Flagstaff is set against a lovely backdrop of pine forests and the snowcapped San Francisco Peaks. As gateway to the Grand Canyon, the city is burgeoning with motels and restaurants.

Arriving and Departing

Flagstaff is 138 mi north of Phoenix, and 80 mi south of the Grand Canyon, at the junction of I–40 and I–17.

Exploring Flagstaff

The **downtown historic district,** near the Santa Fe railroad station, offers a glimpse of the city in its prime, as does the huge **Riordan Mansion** (1300 Riordan Ranch St., ☎ 520/779–4395), built by two lumber-baron brothers. The **Lowell Observatory** (1400 W. Mars Hill, ☎ 520/774–2096) offers educational programs on the night sky and allows visitors to peer through its 24-inch telescope on some evenings (schedules vary seasonally).

Five miles north of town on U.S. 180 is the exit for **Arizona Snowbowl** (☎ 520/779–1951), a ski lodge with fine skiing in winter; come in summer for excellent views and good hiking trails. In a lovely pine forest about 10 mi southeast of Flagstaff on I–40 is **Walnut Canyon National Monument** (Walnut Canyon Rd., ☎ 520/526–3367), site of 14th-century Anasazi cliff dwellings. The 2,000-sq-mi San Francisco Volcanic Field, about 20 mi north of Flagstaff on U.S. 89, is home to **Sunset Crater Volcano National Monument** (☎ 520/556–7042) and the adjacent **Wupatki National Monument** (☎ 520/556–7040), both well worth visiting for their beauty as well as for their windows into the area's geologic and Native American history.

The **Flagstaff Visitors Center** (1 E. Rte. 66, ☎ 520/774–9541 or 800/842–7293) has information on the area.

Dining

$$$ ★ Cottage Place. This elegant restaurant in a homey little 1920s cottage has an American-Continental menu with innovative touches. Try a charbroiled tiger shrimp appetizer and rack of lamb tenderloin *au poivre. 126 W. Cottage Ave., ☎ 520/774–8431. AE, MC, V. Closed Mon. No lunch.*

$ Café Espress. A wholesome, natural food, all-day restaurant, Café Espress serves a largely vegetarian menu (red meat is excluded). Hearty stir-fried vegetables, pasta dishes, daily soups, tasty fish or chicken specials, delicious homemade deserts, and a friendly atmosphere (work of local artists hangs on the walls) all come at prices that will make you feel good, too. *16 N. San Francisco St., ☎ 520/774–0541. MC, V.*

Lodging

$$$ Inn at Four Ten. This quiet but convenient downtown B&B offers several spacious two-room suites in a beautifully restored 1907 building. A full breakfast is served. *410 N. Leroux St., 86001, ☎ 520/774–0088 or 800/774–2008. 8 suites with bath. Facility: kitchenette. AE, MC, V.*

$$$ Little America of Flagstaff. Rooms in this popular hotel on wooded grounds are surprisingly ornate, with brass chandeliers and French Provincial–style furnishings. It's one of the few places in town that offer room service. *2515 E. Butler Ave., Box 3900, 86004, ☎ 520/779–2741 or 800/352–4386, FAX 520/779–7983. 248 rooms. Facilities: restaurant, 24-hr coffee shop, gift shop, cocktail lounge, pool, courtesy van, service station. AE, D, DC, MC, V.*

The Arts and Nightlife

The Arts

Between the **Flagstaff Symphony Orchestra** (☎ 520/774–5107), **Theatrikos Community Theater** (11 W. Beaver St., ☎ 520/774–1662), and Northern Arizona University's **School of Performing Arts** (☎ 520/523–3731), you're bound to find something cultural. In July, the **Flagstaff Festival of the Arts** (Box 1607, Flagstaff 86002, ☎ 520/774–7750 or 800/266–7740) fills the air with music.

Other annual events are the **All Indian Powwow** (☎ 520/526–6593) and **Festival of Native American Arts** (☎ 520/779–6921), both held in the summer. The **Coconino Center for the Arts** (2300 N. Fort Valley Rd., ☎ 520/779–6921) hosts a **Festival of Native American Arts** each summer from late June through mid-August. The center also sponsors the **Trappings of the American West** from mid-May to early June, which focuses on cowboy art—from painting and sculpture to cowboy poetry.

Nightlife

For live music, the **Museum Club** (3404 E. Rte. 66, ☎ 520/526–9434) is a honky-tonk where there's usually a country-swing band; **Main Street Bar and Grill** (14 S. San Francisco St., ☎ 520/774–1519) has bluegrass, jazz, or rock; **Charly's** (23 N. Leroux St., ☎ 520/779–1919) attracts a loyal local following to its late-night jazz and blues bands; and **Monsoon's** (22 E. Rte. 66, ☎ 520/774–7929) books good alternative and reggae bands.

METROPOLITAN PHOENIX

America's newest, fastest-growing major urban center, metropolitan Phoenix lies at the northern tip of the Sonoran Desert in the Valley of the Sun, named for its 330-plus days of sunshine each year. Now-chic Scottsdale began in 1901 as "30-odd tents and a half-dozen adobe houses" put up by seekers of healthful desert air. Glendale and Peoria on the west side and Tempe, Mesa, Gilbert, and Chandler on the east constitute the nation's third-largest Silicon Valley. Excellent hiking, golf, shopping, and dining and some of the best luxury resorts in the country make Phoenix desirable as a vacation spot as well as a business destination.

Tourist Information

Phoenix: Chamber of Commerce (Bank One Plaza, 201 N. Central Ave., Suite 2700, Phoenix 85073, ☎ 602/254–5521). **Phoenix and Valley of the Sun:** Convention and Visitors Bureau (Arizona Center, 400 E. Van Buren St., Suite 600, Phoenix 85004; Hyatt Regency Phoenix, 2nd and Adams Sts.; ☎ 602/254–6500 for both).

Arriving and Departing

By Plane

Sky Harbor International Airport (☎ 602/273–3300), 3 mi east of downtown Phoenix, is home base for **America West** and a hub for **Southwest.** It is also served by other major airlines. Tempe is 10 minutes from the airport; Glendale and Mesa are 25 minutes away, and Scottsdale and Sun City 30–45 minutes. **Phoenix Transit** buses (☎ 602/253–5000) connect with downtown Phoenix or Tempe for $1. A **taxi** trip to downtown Phoenix costs from $6.50 to $12. **Supershuttle** vans (☎ 602/244–9000) charge at least 25% less than taxi fares for longer trips.

By Car

From the west, you'll probably come to Phoenix on I–10. I–40 enters Arizona in the northwest; U.S. 93 continues to Phoenix. From the east, I–10 brings you from El Paso into Tucson, then north to Phoenix. The northeastern route, I–40 from Albuquerque, leads to Flagstaff, where I–17 goes south to Phoenix.

By Train

Amtrak (4th Ave. and Harrison St., ☎ 602/253–0121 or 800/872–7245).

By Bus

Greyhound Lines (525 E. Washington St., ☎ 602/271–7426 or 800/231–2222).

Getting Around Metropolitan Phoenix

If you plan to see anything beyond Phoenix, Scottsdale, or Tempe's pedestrian-friendly downtowns, you will need a car.

Exploring Metropolitan Phoenix

A stroll through the east end of downtown Phoenix will take you to **Heritage Square,** a city-owned block of renovated turn-of-the-century houses in a parklike setting. **Museo Chicano** (25 E. Adams, ☎ 602/257–5536; admission charged) is a center for Latin American art. Also downtown, the **Heard Museum** (22 E. Monte Vista Rd., ☎ 602/252–8840; admission charged), set in a classic Arizona adobe house, is the nation's leading museum of Native American art and culture.

Nearby **Scottsdale**'s downtown is rich in historic sites, nationally known art galleries, and lots of clever boutiques. Historic Old Scottsdale, with its rustic storefronts and wooden sidewalks, has a look of the Old West.

In the Vicinity

An hour's drive south of Phoenix, **Casa Grande Ruins National Monument** provides insight into the culture of the Hohokam Indians, who began farming in this area more than 1,500 years ago. *1 mi north of Coolidge on Rte. 87, ☎ 602/723–3172. Admission charged.*

What to See and Do with Children

Children can get involved with the hands-on exhibits at the **Arizona Museum for Youth** (35 N. Robson St., Mesa, ☎ 602/644–2467; admission charged). Attractions in Phoenix's Papago Park include the **Hall of Flame** (6101 E. Van Buren St., ☎ 602/275–3473; admission charged), where retired fire fighters lead tours, and the **Phoenix Zoo** (455 N. Galvin Pkwy., ☎ 602/273–7771; admission charged). **Mystery Castle** (800 E. Mineral Rd., Phoenix, ☎ 602/268–1581; admission charged) is chock-full of amusing oddities.

Shopping

The valley is a shopper's delight, with everything from glitzy malls in Phoenix and Mesa to charming boutiques and galleries in downtown Scottsdale (5th Ave.). Among the best malls are the **Arizona Center** (455 N. 3rd St., Phoenix, ☎ 602/271–4000), shops and restaurants in a downtown park; **Fiesta Mall** (1445 W. Southern Ave., Mesa, ☎ 602/833–4540), shopping and restaurants for the east valley; **Metrocenter** (I–17 and Peoria Ave., Phoenix, ☎ 602/997–2641), the state's largest; **Scottsdale Fashion Square** (Scottsdale and Camelback Rds., Scottsdale, ☎ 602/990–7800), a step upscale; and **Biltmore Fashion Park** (24th St. and Camelback Rd., Phoenix, ☎ 602/955–8400), even more exclusive.

Sports and the Outdoors

Hiking

Phoenix has some of the most well-trod hiking trails in the world. **Squaw Peak Park** (2701 Squaw Peak Dr., just north of Lincoln, ☎ 602/262–7901) is a favorite two-hour hike and has up to 10 mi of interconnected trails. **Camelback Mountain,** in Echo Canyon Park (McDonald and Tatum Streets), is a more challenging climb, taking anywhere from one to three hours. **South Mountain Park** (1019 S. Central Ave., ☎ 602/495–0222) is the jewel of the city's Mountain Park Preserves and the largest city park in America. Its mountains and arroyos contain more than 40 mi of multi-use trails. Rangers can help you plan hikes to see some of the 200 Native American petroglyph sites in the park.

Golf

The Valley of the Sun is a mecca for world-reknown, year-round golf. More than 100 courses, from par 3 to PGA championship links, are available. For a detailed listing, contact the **Arizona Golf Association** (11801 N. Tatum Blvd., Phoenix 85028, ☎ 602/944–3035).

Spectator Sports

Baseball

Seven major-league-baseball teams train in the Phoenix area (Feb.–Apr.). Contact the **Mesa Convention and Visitor's Bureau** (120 N. Center St., Mesa 85201, ☎ 602/969–1307) for information.

Golf

The PGA's **Phoenix Open** (☎ 602/585–4334) is held each January at the Tournament Players Club in Scottsdale.

Rodeos

The **Parada del Sol** takes place each January–February (Box 292, Scottsdale 85252, ☎ 602/990–3179). In early May, the **Rodeo of Rodeos** (4133 N. 7th St., Phoenix, ☎ 602/263–8671) is one of the Southwest's oldest and best.

Dining

Steak houses, from cowboy to fancy, abound in the area, as do excellent Mexican restaurants. Lighter, spicier, and generally more upscale fare may be found in Phoenix at the numerous restaurants serving Southwestern-international. For price ranges, see Chart 1 (B) in On the Road with Fodor's.

$$$ **Christopher's.** Here a bistro worthy of the Champs-Elysées shares an open kitchen with an elegant, monogrammed-linen-and-silver modern restaurant. Classic fish, veal, and chicken are flawlessly cooked, sauced, and presented—with delightful Southwestern touches. *2398 E. Camelback Rd., ☎ 602/957–3214. Reservations required. Jacket and tie required. AE, DC, MC, V.*

$$$ **Compass Room.** The Southwestern fare matches the spectacular views at Hyatt Regency Phoenix's rotating-crown room. Honey-mesquite salmon and prime rib are favorites. *122 N. 2nd St., ☎ 602/252–1234. Reservations advised. Jacket and tie required. AE, D, DC, MC, V.*

$$$ **La Hacienda.** Set in the chichi Scottsdale Princess Resort, this lovely tile-roof hacienda shows what happens when Sonoran food goes haute cuisine. It doesn't get much better, amigo. *7575 E. Princess Dr., 1 mi north of Bell Rd., Scottsdale, ☎ 602/585–4848. Reservations advised. AE, DC, MC, V.*

$$$ **Marquesa.** In two soft-hued, intimate rooms at the Scottsdale Princess, Catalan food is given an exciting Southwestern interpretation. The stunning presentations of such dishes as paella with lobster, chicken,pork, shellfish, and chistora match the flavors. *7575 E. Princess Dr., Scottsdale, ☎ 602/585–4848. Reservations required. Jacket and tie advised. AE, DC, MC, V.*

$$$ ★ **Vincents on Camelback.** One of the handful of Southwestern cuisine's originators, Vincent Guerithault is among the West's master chefs. His specialties include duck tamales and grilled lobster with smoky chipotle-chili pasta. *3930 E. Camelback Rd., ☎ 602/224–0225. AE, DC, MC, V.*

$$ Greekfest. Greek cooking meets haute cuisine in a tasteful Athens-style taverna. The feather-light spinach-pie appetizers, the sweet and succulent lamb, and fresh stuffed grape leaves make a memorable meal. *1940 E. Camelback Rd., ☎ 602/265–2990. Reservations advised. AE, D, DC, MC, V.*

$$ Mint Thai. At this tiny, graceful place southeast of Mesa you'll find the valley's most varied Thai menu. The *rama* beef in peanut sauce, prepared with delicacy and power, is amazing. *1111 N. Gilbert Rd., Gilbert, ☎ 602/497–5366. Reservations advised on weekends. AE, MC, V.*

$$ Rustler's Rooste. Decorated in a playful miner-cowpoke style, this droll Western restaurant has great views of Phoenix and excellent steaks, juicy barbecued ribs and chicken, and homemade ice cream. *7777 S. Pointe Pkwy., ☎ 602/431–6474. AE, D, DC, MC, V.*

$ Adrian's. At this local favorite, set in a modest creek-rock building with wrought-iron grilles and a tiny outdoor patio, you'll find coastal Mexican dishes as well as excellent Sonoran fare. *2334 E. McDowell Rd., ☎ 602/273–7957. No reservations. No credit cards.*

$ ★ Los Dos Molinos. Don't come for atmosphere but for pure, hot New Mexico–style cooking: homemade fresh green and red chile, shrimp veracruz, and other spicy delights. *260 S. Alma School Rd., Mesa, ☎ 602/835–5356; 8646 S. Central Ave., Phoenix, ☎ 602/243–9113. No reservations. No credit cards.*

Lodging

Famous for its world-class resorts, metropolitan Phoenix has a considerable array of lodging options, from luxury and executive hotels to no-frills roadside motels. For price ranges, see Chart 2 (B) in On the Road with Fodor's.

$$$ ★ The Buttes. This is the Phoenix area's best hotel buy, joining dramatic architecture, classic Southwestern design, and stunning valley views. The rooms are moderate in size and comfortable. *2000 Westcourt Way, Tempe 85282, ☎ 602/225–9000 or 800/843–1986, FAX 602/438–8622. 353 rooms. Facilities: 2 restaurants, pool, health club, saunas, shops. AE, D, DC, MC, V.*

$$$ Hilton Suites. A new, more luxurious version of the frequent-traveler suites concept, this property, close to downtown, is likely to become a classic. The design is modern, colorful, and bold. *10 E. Thomas Rd., Phoenix 85012, ☎ 602/222–1111, FAX 602/265–4841. 226 suites. Facilities: restaurant, bar, pool, exercise room, sauna, gift shop. AE, D, DC, MC, V.*

$$$ ★ Ritz-Carlton. This sand-colored, neo-Federal mid-rise facing Biltmore Fashion Park mall hides a well-appointed luxury hotel that pampers the traveler. A compact, elegant health club and the daily high tea are highlights. *2401 E. Camelback Rd., Phoenix 85016, ☎ 602/468–0700, FAX 602/468–9883. 281 rooms, 14 suites. Facilities: 2 restaurants, 2 bars, pool, 2 saunas, tennis courts, concierge, gift shop, valet parking. AE, D, DC, MC, V.*

$$ ★ Best Western Executive Park. One of downtown's hidden jewels, this small facility is simply but elegantly decorated. Prints by Southwestern masters line the walls. *1100 N. Central Ave., Phoenix 85004, ☎ 602/252–2100 or 800/528–1234, FAX 602/340–1989. 107 rooms. Facilities: restaurant, bar, pool, health club, sauna. AE, D, DC, MC, V.*

$$ Camelback Courtyard by Marriott. This four-story hostelry delivers compact elegance in its public areas and no-frills comfort in its rooms and suites. *2101 E. Camelback Rd., Phoenix 85016, ☎ 602/955–5200 or 800/321–2211, FAX 602/955–1101. 155 rooms, 11 suites. Facilities: restaurant, bar, exercise room, pool, spa. AE, D, DC, MC, V.*

$$ **Doubletree Suites.** Two miles north of the airport, this is the best of a dozen nearby choices. Suites are modest in size, with teal, peach, and green furnishings. *320 N. 44th St., Phoenix 85008, ☎ 602/225–0500 or 800/800–3098, FAX 602/225–0957. 242 suites. Facilities: restaurant, bar-lounge, pool, health club, sauna, shops, free airport shuttle. AE, D, DC, MC, V.*

$ **Ambassador Inn.** Close to the airport and shopping and recreational facilities, this cheerful hotel is set around an enclosed courtyard with a fountain. *4727 E. Thomas Rd., Phoenix 85018, ☎ 602/840–7500 or 800/624–6759, FAX 602/840–5078. 170 rooms. Facilities: restaurant, bar, pool, exercise room, spa, free airport shuttle 7 AM–10 PM. AE, D, DC, MC, V.*

$ **Motel 6 Scottsdale.** Though amenities aren't a priority here, the best bargain in Scottsdale lodging is steps away from Scottsdale Fashion Square and Camelview Plaza, and close to the specialty shops of 5th Avenue. *6848 E. Camelback Rd., Scottsdale 85251, ☎ 602/946–2280, FAX 602/949–7583. 122 rooms. Facilities: pool, spa. AE, D, DC, MC, V.*

Resorts

For price ranges, see Chart 2 (A) in Chapter 1.

$$$$ ★ **Hyatt Regency Scottsdale at Gainey Ranch.** Modern and dramatic, this is Scottsdale's finest resort. Gondolas on a manmade lagoon and hot-air balloons are among the unusual diversions. *7500 E. Doubletree Ranch Rd., Scottsdale 85258, ☎ 602/991–3388 or 800/233–1234, FAX 602/483–5550. 493 rooms. Facilities: 3 restaurants, lounge, 10 pools, 8 tennis courts, 3 golf courses, health club, concierge floor. AE, D, DC, MC, V.*

$$$$ **Pointe Hilton on South Mountain.** The Southwest's largest resort, it's also the most convenient—close to the airport, downtown Phoenix, and the eastern valley. Accommodations are lavishly designed and decorated. *7777 S. Pointe Pkwy., Phoenix 85044, ☎ 602/438–9000 or 800/876–4683, FAX 602/431–6535. 638 suites. Facilities: 4 restaurants, 3 pools, health center, saunas, stable, tennis, golf, hiking trails, shops. AE, D, DC, MC, V.*

The Arts and Nightlife

Cultural and entertainment events are listed in the free weekly *New Times* newspaper, distributed Wednesday; the Friday and Sunday Life sections of the *Arizona Republic;* and the Marquee section of Saturday's *Phoenix Gazette.*

The Arts

Downtown Phoenix's **Symphony Hall** (225 E. Adams St., ☎ 602/262–7272) and **Herberger Theater Center** (222 E. Monroe St., ☎ 602/252–8497) are home to many performing-arts groups. The developing "cultural district" 2 mi north, around Deck Park, offers several more.

Nightlife

Nightclubs, restaurants, resorts, and upscale bars abound in the **Arizona Center** in downtown Phoenix and in Scottsdale and downtown Tempe.

TUCSON AND SOUTHERN ARIZONA

Arizona's second-largest city, Tucson feels like a small town, albeit one enriched by its deep Hispanic and Old West roots. With a large university and myriad resorts, the city affords visitors many cultural and recreational options. It's also the gateway to southern Arizona, a relatively undiscovered treasure of mountains, deserts, canyons, and dusty little cowboy towns. Of particular interest are Bisbee and Tombstone, which give visitors a taste of what Arizona was like in its mining and cowboy heydays.

Tourist Information

Metropolitan Tucson: Convention and Visitors Bureau (130 S. Scott Ave., Tucson 85701, ☎ 520/624–1817 or 800/638–8350). **Bisbee:** Chamber of Commerce (7 Naco Rd., Box BA, 85603, ☎ 520/432–5421). **Tombstone:** Chamber of Commerce (Schiefflin Hall, Fremont and 4th Sts., Box 995, 85638, ☎ 520/457–3911.

Getting There

By Plane

Tucson International Airport (☎ 520/573–8000), 8½ mi south of downtown, is served by 13 carriers, many of which serve Mexico as well as domestic destinations.

By Car

From Phoenix, 111 mi to the northwest, or from the east, take I–10 to Tucson. From the south, take I–19. East of Tucson, U.S. 80 cuts south from I–10 to Tombstone and Bisbee.

By Train

Amtrak (400 E. Toole Ave., ☎ 520/623–4442 or 800/872–7245) serves Tucson and vicinity.

By Bus

Greyhound Lines (2 S. 4th Ave. at E. Broadway, ☎ 800/231–2222) serves the Tucson area. **Arizona Shuttle Service** (☎ 520/795–6771) runs express buses from Phoenix's Sky Harbor Airport to Tucson.

Exploring Tucson and Southern Arizona

Because of its higher elevation, **Tucson**'s climate is more temperate than that of its rival, Phoenix. As a result, it offers outdoor activities year-round, including historical tours. The city covers more than 500 sq mi in a valley ringed by mountains, so a car is necessary. The downtown area, just east of I–10 off of the Broadway-Congress exit, is easy to navigate on foot.

The **Presidio district** in downtown Tucson encompasses more than 130 years of the city's architectural history, including the original walled **El Presidio del Tucson**—a Spanish fortress built in 1776 when Arizona was still part of New Spain.

The city divides the **Saguaro National Park** (☎ 520/883–6366) into two sections; the one west of town is the most heavily visited. Both are forested by the huge saguaro cactus, a native of the Sonoran Desert that is known for its towering height (often 50 ft) and arms that reach out in strange configurations.

Near Saguaro National Park West, the **Arizona-Sonora Desert Museum** is one of the state's most popular tourist attractions. In this desert microcosm, birds and animals busy themselves in a natural habitat ingeniously planned to allow the visitor to look on without disturbing them. *2021 N. Kinney Rd., ☎ 520/883–2702. Admission charged.*

Among the museums on the University of Arizona campus that give insight into the area's past, present, and future are the **Center for Creative Photography** (☎ 520/621–7968), the **Arizona Historical Society's Museum** (☎ 520/628–5774), the **Arizona State Museum** (☎ 520/621–

6302), and the **Grace H. Flandrau Science Center and Planetarium** (☎ 520/621–4515; admission charged).

Just southwest of Tucson, the 1692 **Mission San Xavier del Bac** (I–19 Exit 92, San Xavier Rd., ☎ 520/294–2624) is the oldest Catholic church in the United States still serving the community for which it was built: the Tohonó O'odham Indian tribe. Inside this beautiful Spanish/Moorish-style structure contains a wealth of painted statues, carvings, and frescoes.

Tombstone is 67 mi southeast of Tucson on U.S. 80. Born on the site of a wildly successful silver mine, the town was headquarters of many of the West's rowdies in the late 1800s. The famous shoot-out at the OK Corral and other gunfights are replayed on Sunday on the town's main drag, **Allen Street.** As you enter Tombstone from the northwest, you'll pass **Boot Hill Graveyard,** where the victims of the OK Corral shoot-out are buried. The **Tombstone Courthouse State Historic Park** (Toughnut and 3rd Sts., ☎ 520/457–3311; admission charged) offers an excellent introduction to the town's past.

Once a mining boomtown, **Bisbee,** set on a mountainside 24 mi south of Tombstone, is now an artists' colony. Arizona's largest pit mine yielded some 94 million tons of copper ore before mining activity halted in the early 1970s; at the **Lavender Pit Mine** you can still see the huge crater left by the process. The **Mining and Historical Museum** (5 Copper Queen Plaza, ☎ 520/432–7071; admission charged) is filled with old photos and artifacts from the town's heyday. Behind the museum is the venerable **Copper Queen Hotel** (*see* Dining and Lodging, *below*), home away from home to such guests as "Black Jack" Pershing, John Wayne, and Teddy Roosevelt. The **Copper Queen mine tour** (478 N. Dart Rd., ☎ 520/432–2071; admission charged), led by retired miners, is an entertaining way to learn about the town's history.

What to See and Do with Children

Children will enjoy the **Arizona–Sonora Desert Museum** (*see* Exploring Tucson and Southern Arizona, *above*). Unfortunately, a fire at the nearby **Old Tucson Studios** (201 S. Kinney Rd., in Tucson Mountain Park, ☎ 520/883–0100), where more than 250 Westerns have been shot over the past 50 years, has destroyed much of the place. Plans to rebuild had not been announced at press time.

Shopping

In Tucson, **Desert House Crafts** (2837 N. Campbell Ave., ☎ 520/323–2132) and the **Kaibab Shops** next door (☎ 520/795–6905) carry a broad selection of fine Southwestern crafts and clothing.

Hard-core bargain hunters usually head for **Nogales,** the Mexican border town 63 mi south of Tucson on I–19. For work by regional artists, try the **Tubac** artists' community, 45 mi south of Tucson, just off I–19 at Exit 34.

Sports and the Outdoors

Golf

Tucson has five **municipal golf courses** (Tucson Parks and Recreation Dept., ☎ 520/791–4336), as well as many excellent **resort courses,** such as those at Loews Ventana Canyon (☎ 520/299–2020), Tucson National Golf and Conference Resort (☎ 520/297–2271), Westin La Paloma (☎ 520/742–6000), and Sheraton Tucson El Conquistador (for

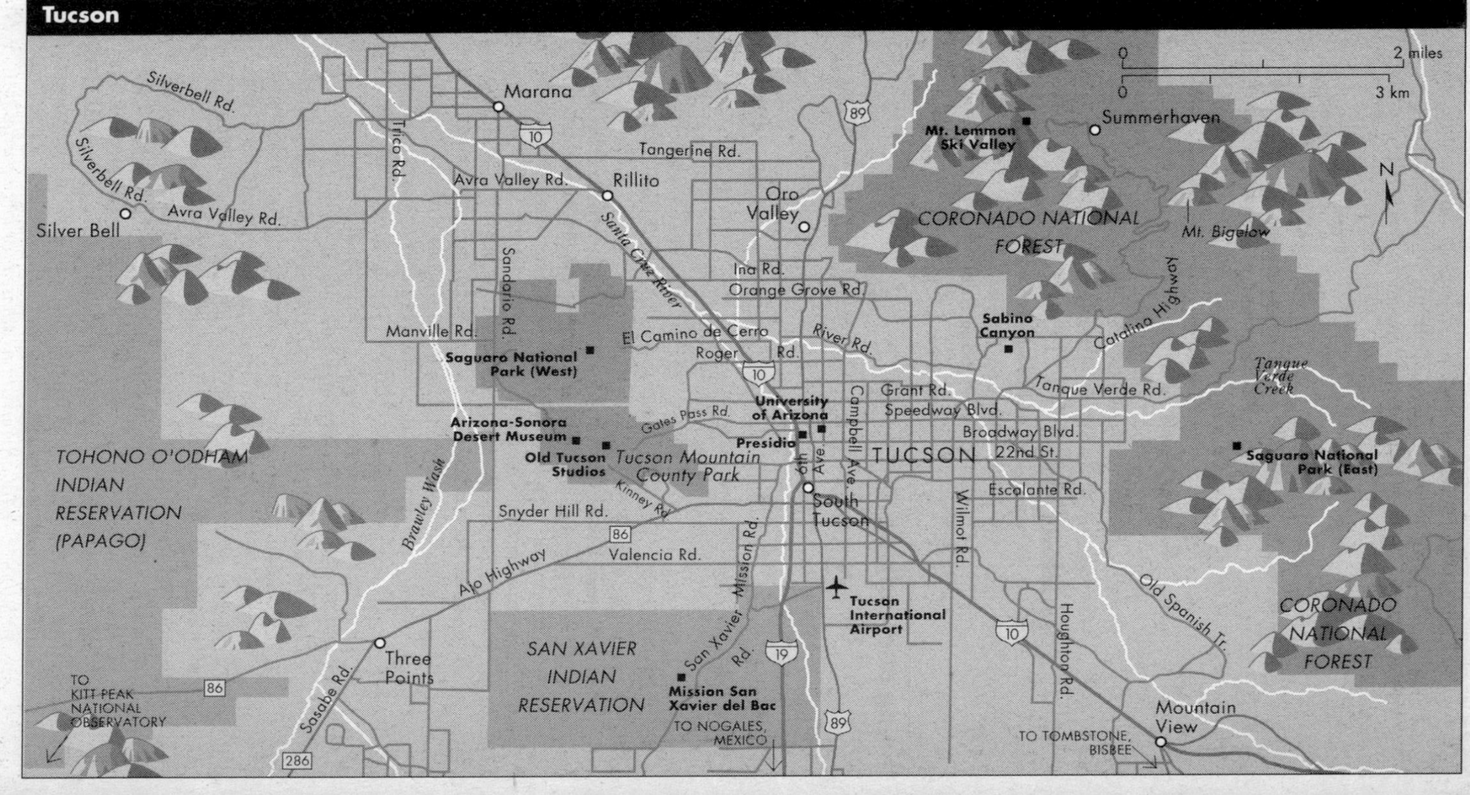

0
2 miles
0
3 km
N
Silverbell Rd.
Marana
89
10
Tangerine Rd.
Trico Rd.
Silverbell Rd.
Avra Valley Rd.
Rillito
Silver Bell
Avra Valley Rd.
Oro Valley
Mt. Lemmon Ski Valley
Summerhaven
CORONADO NATIONAL FOREST
Mt. Bigelow
Sandario Rd.
Santa Cruz River
Ina Rd.
Orange Grove Rd.
Catalina Highway
Sabino Canyon
Manville Rd.
El Camino de Cerro
River Rd.
Roger Rd.
Saguaro National Park (West)
Tanque Verde Creek
Tanque Verde Rd.
Grant Rd.
Speedway Blvd.
University of Arizona
Gates Pass Rd.
Campbell Ave.
Broadway Blvd.
Arizona-Sonora Desert Museum
Presidio
6th Ave.
TUCSON
22nd St.
Saguaro National Park (East)
TOHONO O'ODHAM INDIAN RESERVATION (PAPAGO)
Old Tucson Studios
Tucson Mountain County Park
Kinney Rd.
South Tucson
Escalante Rd.
Brawley Wash
Snyder Hill Rd.
86
Valencia Rd.
Mission Rd.
Wilmot Rd.
Ajo Highway
Tucson International Airport
Old Spanish Tr.
Houghton Rd.
CORONADO NATIONAL FOREST
Three Points
SAN XAVIER INDIAN RESERVATION
San Xavier Rd.
19
Mission San Xavier del Bac
TO KITT PEAK NATIONAL OBSERVATORY
86
Sasabe Rd.
286
TO NOGALES, MEXICO
89
TO TOMBSTONE, BISBEE
Mountain View

the last, *see* Dining and Lodging, *below*). For information about other courses in the area, send $2.50 for the *Tucson and Southern Arizona Golf Guide* (Tucson Guide Quarterly Inc., Box 42915, Tucson 85733, ☎ 520/322–0895).

Hiking

Great hiking opportunities around Tucson can be found at **Tucson Mountain Park, Mt. Lemmon, Sabino Canyon,** and **Kitt Peak.** A little-visited treasure, **Chiracahua National Monument** (about two hours east of Tucson off of Route 10, south of Bowie) affords spectacular rugged rock vistas. Directly south of Tucson, the Huachuca Mountains, home of **Ramsey Canyon,** are a bird-watcher's paradise. The Santa Ritas, just south of Tucson, host another bird lovers' haven, **Madera Canyon.** The local chapter of **Sierra Club** (☎ 520/620–6401) welcomes out-of-town visitors on their weekend hikes.

Horseback Riding

Tucson stables include **Desert-High Country Stables** (6501 W. Ina Rd., ☎ 520/744–3789), **Pantano Stables** (4450 S. Houghton Rd., ☎ 520/751–4235), and **Pusch Ridge Stables** (13700 N. Oracle Rd., ☎ 520/825–1664).

Dining and Lodging

For price ranges, see Charts 1 (B) and 2 (B) in On the Road with Fodor's.

Tucson

DINING

★ **Janos.** This historic Presidio district restaurant offers delightfully innovative Southwestern cuisine, such as adobe of grilled salmon and lobster chipotle buerre blanc. Come here for a special, big-splurge evening. *150 N. Main Ave.,* ☎ *520/884–9426. Reservations advised. AE, DC, MC, V. Closed Sun. Nov.–mid-May; Sun.–Mon. mid-May–Nov. $$$*

Ventana Room. A triumph of understated elegance, this dining room serves splendid desert views with its updated Continental cuisine. Specials might include medallions of venison with dried cherry sauce. *Loews Ventana Resort, 7000 N. Resort Dr.,* ☎ *520/299–2020. Reservations advised. Jacket required. AE, D, DC, MC, V. No lunch. $$$*

Bocatta. Decked out in florals and Victoriana, this romantic restaurant augments its northern Italian menu—penne with chicken, artichokes, and pine nuts, say—with southern French touches. The owner's "fast-food" restaurant, Pronto (2955 E. Speedway Blvd., ☎ 520/326–9709) is great for a quick, inexpensive bite. *5605 E. River Rd.,* ☎ *520/577–9309. AE, DC, MC, V. Lunch Fri. only. $$–$$$*

Café Terra Cotta. Everything about this restaurant says Southwest, from the decor to the food. Contemporary specialties include prawns stuffed with herbed goat cheese, and pork tenderloin with black beans. *4310 N. Campbell Ave.,* ☎ *520/577–8100. AE, D, DC, MC, V. $$–$$$*

★ **Kingfisher.** This chic new restaurant has already developed a loyal following for its excellent American regional cuisine, its selection of small batch bourbon, and its late (for Tucson) dining hours. *2564 E. Grant Rd.,* ☎ *520/323–7739. AE, D, MC, V. No lunch Sun. $$–$$$*

★ **Café Poca Cosa.** This colorful and lively restaurant tucked into a corner of the Park Inn/Santa Rita's lobby is cheerful and thoroughly Mexican. Ingredients are fresh, and service is excellent. *88 E. Broadway,* ☎ *520/622–6400. Reservations advised for large parties. MC, V. No dinner Sun. $$*

Pinnacle Peak Steakhouse. Tourists love this cowboy steak house—it's fun, it's Tucson, and the food ain't half bad either. *6541 E. Tanque Verde Rd., ☎ 520/296–0911. No reservations. AE, D, DC, MC, V. $–$$*

LODGING

★ **Arizona Inn.** Although this landmark 1930s-era inn is close to the university and downtown, it is secluded on 14 acres of lushly landscaped grounds. All rooms have patios and lovely period furnishings. *2200 E. Elm St., 85719, ☎ 520/325–1541 or 800/933–1093, FAX 520/881–5830. 83 rooms. Facilities: 2 restaurants, lounge, pool, 2 tennis courts, croquet, library, gift shop. AE, MC, V. $$$*

Embassy Suites Tucson–Broadway. This centrally located hotel offers two-room suites (with kitchenette) opening onto a plant-filled atrium. Extras include a free cooked-to-order breakfast and complimentary happy hour. *5335 E. Broadway, 85711, ☎ 520/745–2700 or 800/353–2779, FAX 520/790–9232. 142 suites. Facilities: outdoor heated pool, salon. AE, D, DC, MC, V. $$$*

Peppertrees. Just off of the University of Arizona campus, this pleasant bed-and-breakfast has lodgings in a beautiful Victorian house and a bungalow-style house next door. Some units have full kitchens and washer/dryers—ideal for families. *724 E. University Blvd., 85719, ☎ 520/622–7167 or 800/348–5763, FAX 520/622–5959. 3 rooms, 2 guesthouses, 1 studio. MC, V. $$–$$$*

★ **Windmill Inn.** Located in a chic shopping plaza, this new all-suites property offers well-designed, modern rooms, each with a microwave, two TVs, and three phones. Complimentary coffee, muffins, and a newspaper are delivered to your door. *4250 N. Campbell Ave., 85718, ☎ 520/577–0777 or 800/547–4747, FAX 520/577–0045. Facilities: pool, laundry room, free local calls. $$*

★ **Casa Tierra.** For a real desert experience, come to this B&B on 5 acres near Saguaro National Park. Rooms in the beamed-ceiling adobe house are arranged around a garden courtyard. *11155 W. Calle Pima, 85743, ☎ and FAX 520/578–3058. 3 rooms. Facility: hot tub. No credit cards. Closed June–Aug. $–$$*

Hotel Congress. This downtown hotel, built in 1919 in Art Deco style, attracts a hip young crowd who enjoy the convenient location, popular (and loud on weekends) Club Congress, and low room rates. *311 E. Congress St., 85701, ☎ 520/622–8848 or 800/722–8848, FAX 520/792–6366. 40 rooms. Facilities: restaurant, bar, hair salon, nightclub. AE, MC, V. $*

Ranches

Tanque Verde Ranch. One of the country's oldest guest ranches covers more than 600 acres in the beautiful Rincon Mountains. The rooms are furnished in tasteful Southwestern style; most have patios and fireplaces. Rates include meals. *14301 E. Speedway Blvd., 85748, ☎ 520/296–6275 or 800/234–3833, FAX 520/721–9426. 65 rooms. Facilities: restaurant, indoor and outdoor pools, tennis courts, spa, exercise room, horseback riding. AE, D, MC, V. $$$*

White Stallion Ranch. Many scenes from the television show *High Chaparral* were shot on this family-run ranch, set on 3,000 desert mountain acres. Rates include excellent, hearty meals. Rooms are plain but comfortable. *9251 W. Twin Peaks Rd., 85743, ☎ 520/297–0252 or 800/782–5546, FAX 520/744–2786. 29 rooms. Facilities: pool, tennis, volleyball, horseback riding, petting zoo. No credit cards. Closed May–Sept. $$$*

Resorts

★ **Sheraton Tucson El Conquistador.** This friendly golf and tennis resort is nestled in the foothills of the Santa Catalinas. Both private casitas and the main hotel building offer appealing rooms in light woods and pastels. Biosphere 2, famous for its new age experiments in survival, is just up the road. *10000 N. Oracle Rd., Tucson, 85737, ☎ 520/742–7000 or 800/325–7832, FAX 520/544–1228. 432 rooms. Facilities: 5 restaurants, golf, tennis, racquetball, horseback riding, 3 pools, 2 fitness centers, sauna, whirlpool. AE, D, DC, MC, V. $$$*

Westward Look Resort. Set on 80 acres in the Santa Catalina foothills, Westward Look has a warm, welcoming atmosphere. It's less expensive than other Tucson area resorts, and it's closer to city sights and activities. *245 E. Ina Rd., Tucson, 85704, ☎ 520/297–1151 or 800/722–2500, FAX 520/297–9023. 244 rooms. Facilities: 2 restaurants, lounge, 3 pools, spas, tennis courts. AE, D, DC, MC, V. $$$*

Spa

For price range, *see* Chart 2 (A) in Chapter 1.

Canyon Ranch. At this well-known health spa surrounded by spectacular desert scenery, guests are pampered while shaping up in the rigorous program. The food is unobtrusively healthful, and rooms are luxuriously furnished in muted Southwestern tones. *8600 E. Rockcliff Rd., Tucson, 85715, ☎ 520/749–9000 or 800/742–9000, FAX 520/749–1646. 112 rooms, 41 suites. Facilities: restaurant; 4 pools; tennis, squash, basketball, and racquetball courts; extensive workout equipment; spa complex; health center. AE, D, MC, V. $$$$*

Campgrounds

The public campground closest to Tucson is at **Catalina State Park** (11570 N. Oracle Rd., ☎ 520/628–5798). Recreational vehicles can park in any number of facilities around town; the **Metropolitan Tucson Convention and Visitors Bureau** (*see* Tourist Information, *above*) can provide information about specific locations.

Bisbee

DINING

★ **Café Roka.** One of the best bargains in southern Arizona, this chic northern Italian restaurant in a historic building offers delicious pasta dinners (including soup and salad) at very reasonable prices. *35 Main St., ☎ 520/432–5153. MC, V. $$*

Stenzel's. Set in a rustic wood cabin, Stenzel's serves up good ribs and grilled chicken and outstanding fettuccine Alfredo. There's a decent wine list. *207 Tombstone Canyon, ☎ 520/432–7611. MC,V. $$*

LODGING

★ **Copper Queen Hotel.** This turn-of-the-century hotel in the heart of downtown has thin walls but a lot of Victorian charm; ask for a renovated room. The boom-days memorabilia throughout is fascinating. *11 Howell Ave., Drawer CQ, 85603, ☎ 520/432–2216 or 800/247–5829, FAX 520/432–4298. 43 rooms. Facilities: dining room, saloon, pool, gift shop. AE, D, DC, MC, V. $$–$$$*

Clawson House. Terrific views of town from the sun porch, a light-filled kitchen, and generous but healthy breakfasts are among the reasons to seek out this B&B on Old Bisbee's Castle Rock. *116 Clawson Ave., Box 454, 85603, ☎ 520/432–5237 or 800/467–5237. 3 rooms, 2 share bath. D, DC, MC, V. $$*

Tombstone

DINING

Longhorn Restaurant. Set up to look like an old saloon, the Longhorn is decorated with posters and artifacts from Tombstone's wilder days. Burgers, sandwiches, steaks, and some Mexican dishes are served. *Allen and 5th Sts., ☎ 520/457–3405. MC, V. $–$$*

LODGING

Best Western Look-Out Lodge. This motel off U.S. 80 on the way into town has a lot of character. Rooms have Western-print bedspreads, Victorian-style lamps, and views of the Dragoon Mountains and desert valley. *U.S. 80W, Box 787, 85638, ☎ 520/457–2223 or 800/528–1234, FAX 520/457–3870. 40 rooms. AE, D, DC, MC, V. $$*

Tombstone Boarding House. Two meticulously restored 1880s adobes sit side-by-side in a quiet residential neighborhood; guests of this friendly B&B sleep in one house and go next door to have a hearty country breakfast in the other. *108 N. Fourth St., Box 906, 85638, ☎ 520/457–3716. 8 rooms, 2 share bath. Facilities: piano and TV in living room. No credit cards. $$*

The Arts and Nightlife

The Arts

The **Tucson Symphony Orchestra** (☎ 520/882–8585) and the **Arizona Opera Company** (☎ 520/293–4336) perform in the Tucson Convention Center's Music Hall (260 S. Church St., ☎ 520/791–4836). The **Arizona Theatre Company** (☎ 520/622–2823) is at Tucson's Temple of Music and Art (330 S. Scott Ave., ☎ 520/884–4875) September through May.

Nightlife

In Tucson, **Cactus Moon** (5470 E. Broadway, ☎ 520/748–0049), **Maverick** (4702 E. 22nd St., ☎ 520/748–0456), and **Wild Wild West** (4385 W. Ina Rd., ☎ 520/744–7744) are lively country-western nightclubs.

NEVADA

Updated by Deke Castleman

Capital	Carson City
Population	1,470,000
Motto	Battle Born
State Bird	Mountain bluebird
State Flower	Sagebrush

Visitor Information

Nevada Commission on Tourism (Capitol Complex, Carson City 89710, ☎ 702/687–4322 or 800/237–0774).

Scenic Drives

The **Loneliest Road in America** is Rte. 50, which cuts across the central part of the state from Carson City to Ely. **Rte. 93** north from Las Vegas runs more than 500 mi through long desert valleys, and passes 13,061-ft **Wheeler Peak,** the second-highest point in the state. For a good look at the Southwest desert, particularly in the spring, take **U.S. 93/95** southeast from Las Vegas, turning east onto Rte. 147 in Henderson, which takes you through Lake Mead National Recreation Area to Valley of Fire State Park (*see* Las Vegas, *below*).

National and State Parks

National Parks

Great Basin National Park (off U.S. 93 at the Nevada–Utah border, Baker 89311, ☎ 702/234–7331) is 77,092 acres of dramatic mountains, lush meadows, alpine lakes, limestone caves, and a stand of bristlecone pines (the oldest living trees in the world), with many areas for camping, hiking, and picnicking.

State Parks

For information on Nevada's 23 state parks, contact the state tourism office (*see* Visitor Information, *above*). **Washoe Lake State Recreation Area** (4855 E. Lake Blvd., off U.S. 395, Carson City 89704, ☎ 702/687–4319), with views of the majestic Sierra Nevada, is popular for fishing and horseback riding.

LAS VEGAS

Las Vegas is known around the world as a fantasy land for adults. Its name, meaning "the meadows," was created by a Spanish scouting party who found a spring here in the 1820s. Mormons settled the valley briefly in 1855, but until the turn of the century it was little more than a handful of ranches and homesteads. In 1905 the San Pedro, Los Angeles, and Salt Lake Railroad founded the town of Las Vegas as a watering stop for its steam trains. The construction of Hoover Dam in the 1930s brought a new wave of settlers seeking jobs.

The Las Vegas that we know today began shortly after World War II when mobster Benjamin "Bugsy" Siegel decided to build a gambling resort in the desert. (Gambling had been legalized in the state in 1931.) Bugsy built his Flamingo with money borrowed from fellow mobsters who, when the Flamingo flopped, rubbed him out. The resort eventually recovered and casino-hotels on the Las Vegas Strip caught on. Now the city is home to nine of the 10 largest hotels in the world.

Tourist Information

Contact the **Las Vegas Chamber of Commerce** (711 E. Desert Inn Rd., 89109, ☎ 702/735–1616)or the **Convention & Visitors Authority** (3150 Paradise Rd., 89109, ☎ 702/892–0711).

Arriving and Departing

By Plane

McCarran International Airport (☎ 702/261–5743), about two mi from the south end of the Strip, is served by major airlines. Taxi fare from the airport to Strip hotels is about $9–$12; to the downtown hotels, about $15–$18. But the best and least expensive way to reach your hotel ($4–$6 per person) is by **Bell Trans Limousine** (☎ 702/739–7990), which you will find near the taxis.

By Car

Major highways leading into Las Vegas are I–15 from Los Angeles and Salt Lake City, U.S. 95 from Reno, and U.S. 93 from Arizona.

By Train

Amtrak serves downtown's Union Station (1 N. Main St., ☎ 702/386–6896 or 800/872–7245).

By Bus

Greyhound Lines (200 S. Main St., ☎ 800/231–2222).

Getting Around Las Vegas

Taxis, which can easily be found in front of every hotel, are the best way to get around the city. The **Strip bus** (Citizen's Area Transit or CAT, ☎ 702/228–7433; fare $1.50) links the Strip and the downtown, with stops near major hotels. If you want to drive out of town or explore the desert, you can rent a car, but be sure to gas up before you go; you won't find many stations out there.

Exploring Las Vegas

Las Vegas is a relatively small city and is easy to explore on foot, but beware: During the extremely hot months of June, July, and August, walking outside for an extended length of time is not recommended.

The downtown casino center may be only four blocks long, but it is the most brightly lit four blocks in the world, and is best seen at night, when it comes alive. If you recognize this stretch, it is because you have seen it in so many movies. The focal point of **downtown** is **Jackie Gaughan's Plaza Hotel and Casino** (1 N. Main St.), built on the site of the old Union Pacific train station—the only train station in the world that is actually inside a casino.

Among the downtown hotel-casinos, the **Golden Nugget** (129 E. Fremont St., ☎ 702/785–7111) has a particularly attractive lobby where you can see an enormous, 61-pound gold nugget. **Binion's Horseshoe** (128 E. Fremont St., ☎ 702/382–1600) is an old-fashioned gambling joint that has a display of $1 million in cash. The **Four Queens Hotel** (202 E. Fremont St., ☎ 702/385–4011) is the home of the biggest slot machine in the world: 18 ft long and 7 ft high, with room for six players.

The **Strip**—a 3½-mi stretch of Las Vegas Boulevard South—begins at the **Sahara Hotel** (at No. 2535, ☎ 702/737–2111), which was built in 1952 and has a clock on top of its tallest tower. The **Guinness World of Records Museum** (at No. 2780, ☎ 702/792–3766; admission charged) honors such record holders as the tallest man in the world and has videos of records actually being set. Next door, **Circus Circus** (at No. 2880, ☎ 702/734–0410)—the first Las Vegas hotel to cater to families with children—has a midway with carnival games, free circus acts, and a theme park called **Grand Slam Canyon** (☎ 702/794–3939), which boasts the world's largest indoor roller coaster. The **Candlelight Wedding Chapel** (at No. 2855, ☎ 702/735–4179) is the busiest chapel in town.

Towers sprout from all sides at the **Riviera Hotel** (2901 Las Vegas Blvd. S, ☎ 702/734–5110). The reclusive billionaire Howard Hughes lived in the penthouse of the **Sheraton Desert Inn** (at No. 3145, ☎ 702/733–4444), and owned the **Frontier Hotel** (at No. 3120, ☎ 702/794–8200), as well. The **Sands** (at No. 3355, ☎ 702/733–5000) was the home of the "Rat Pack"—Frank Sinatra, Dean Martin, and friends—in the '60s. At the $670-million palace known as the **Mirage** (at No. 3400, ☎ 702/791–7111), a volcano erupts in a front yard landscaped with a towering waterfall, lagoons, and tropical plants; inside is a glassed-in tigers' den. Adjacent to the Mirage, the **Treasure Island** resort (at No. 3300, ☎ 702/894–7111) re-creates Robert Louis Stevenson's novel—pirates and sailors engage in ship-to-ship cannon battles in Buccaneer Bay out front.

The **Imperial Palace Hotel and Casino** (at No. 3535, ☎ 702/731–3311) is the home of the **Imperial Palace Auto Collection** (admission charged), more than 300 antique and classic cars, many of them formerly owned by the famous or the infamous, such as Adolf Hitler and Al Capone. The **Flamingo Hilton** (at No. 3555, ☎ 702/733–3111),with one of the most beautiful neon signs in the city, was the first luxury resort on the Strip, established by Bugsy Siegel in 1946.

The high stakes at the opulent **Caesars Palace** (at No. 3570, ☎ 702/731–7110) attract serious gamblers. **Bally's** (at No. 3645, ☎ 702/739–4111) is colossal. Across the strip from Bally's, the Mirage company is building **Beau Rivage,** an $800-million megaresort with a 30-acre man-made lake. The emerald green **MGM Grand** (at No. 3799, ☎ 702/891–1111) houses the largest casino in the world—so large that it's divided into four separate casinos, delineated by different carpeting. The sprawling grounds of the **Tropicana** (at No. 3801, ☎ 702/739–2222) are especially attractively landscaped. The blue-and-pink castlelike **Excalibur** (at No. 3850, ☎ 702/597–7777), built on a medieval/Renaissance theme, is the world's second-largest hotel. **New York–New York,** a 1,700-room hotel-casino, is being built on the lot across from Excalibur; when completed in 1997, it will feature a replica of the New York City skyline and a roller coaster. **Luxor** (at No. 3900, ☎ 702/262–4000) is a 30-story Egyptian-style pyramid complete with the "River Nile," which has barge tours around the casino. Two miles off the Strip is the **Liberace Museum** (1775 E. Tropicana Ave., ☎ 702/798–5595; admission charged) in three buildings: one for the entertainer's pianos and cars, one for the costumes, and the third for general memorabilia.

In the Vicinity

The awe-inspiring **Hoover Dam** (Rte. 93 east of Boulder City, ☎ 702/293–8321; admission charged), about 25 mi east of Las Vegas, was constructed in the 1930s to tame the destructive waters of the Colorado River and produce electricity. Tours into the 727-ft-high, 660-ft-thick dam are offered every day but Christmas.

Las Vegas

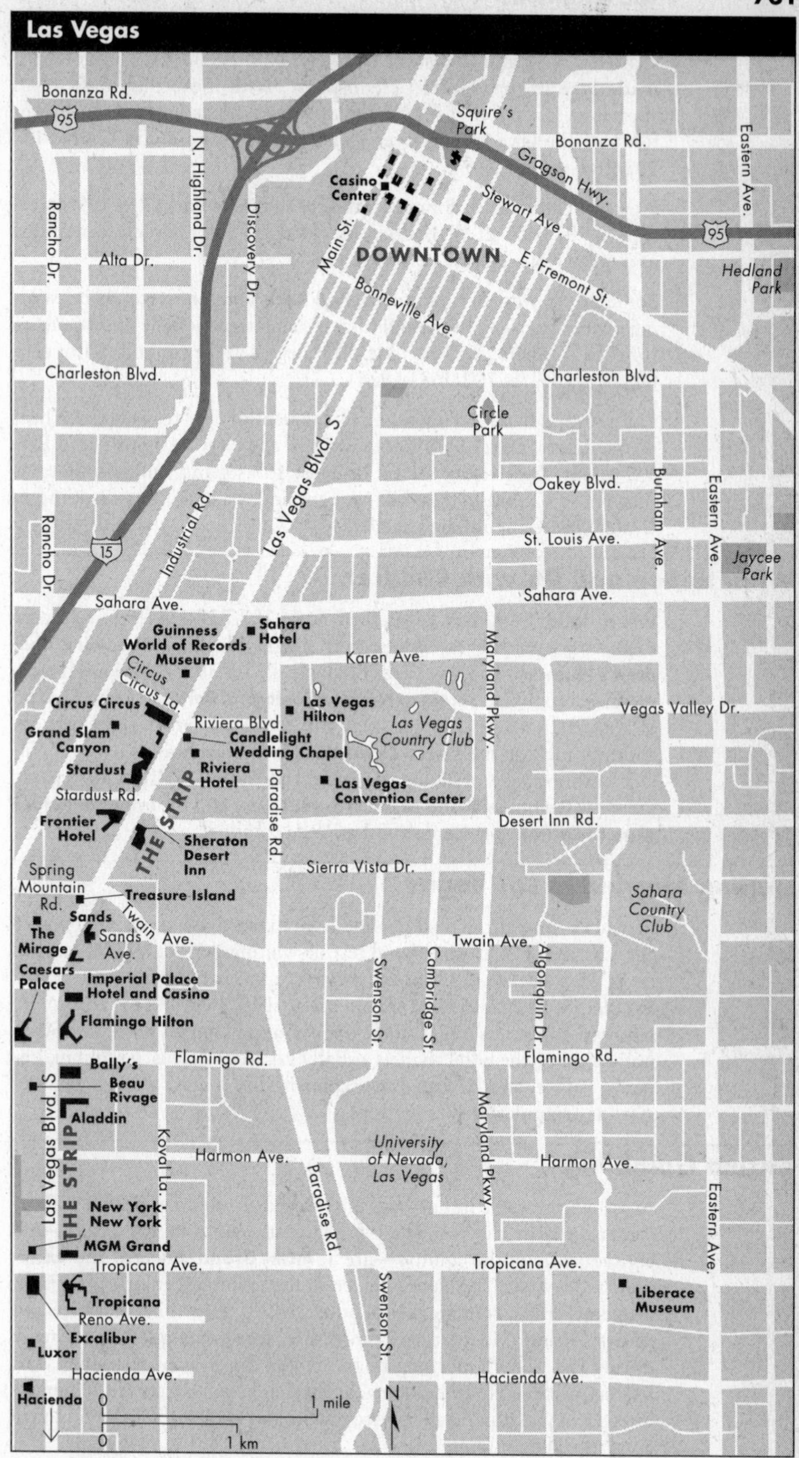

Bonanza Rd.
95
Squire's Park
Bonanza Rd.
Gragson Hwy.
Eastern Ave.
N. Highland Dr.
Casino Center
Stewart Ave.
Discovery Dr.
Rancho Dr.
Main St.
95
Alta Dr.
DOWNTOWN
E. Fremont St.
Hedland Park
Bonneville Ave.
Charleston Blvd.
Charleston Blvd.
Circle Park
Las Vegas Blvd. S
Oakey Blvd.
Burnham Ave.
Eastern Ave.
Industrial Rd.
Rancho Dr.
15
St. Louis Ave.
Jaycee Park
Sahara Ave.
Sahara Ave.
Guinness World of Records Museum
Sahara Hotel
Karen Ave.
Circus Circus La.
Maryland Pkwy.
Circus Circus
Las Vegas Hilton
Vegas Valley Dr.
Las Vegas Country Club
Riviera Blvd.
Grand Slam Canyon
Candlelight Wedding Chapel
Stardust
Riviera Hotel
Paradise Rd.
Las Vegas Convention Center
Stardust Rd.
THE STRIP
Frontier Hotel
Sheraton Desert Inn
Desert Inn Rd.
Spring Mountain Rd.
Sierra Vista Dr.
Treasure Island
Sahara Country Club
Sands
The Mirage
Twain Ave.
Sands Ave.
Twain Ave.
Swenson St.
Cambridge St.
Algonquin Dr.
Caesars Palace
Imperial Palace Hotel and Casino
Flamingo Hilton
Flamingo Rd.
Flamingo Rd.
Bally's
Beau Rivage
Aladdin
Las Vegas Blvd. S
Koval La.
Maryland Pkwy.
Harmon Ave.
University of Nevada, Las Vegas
Harmon Ave.
THE STRIP
New York-New York
MGM Grand
Paradise Rd.
Eastern Ave.
Tropicana Ave.
Tropicana Ave.
Swenson St.
Tropicana
Liberace Museum
Reno Ave.
Excalibur
Luxor
Hacienda Ave.
Hacienda Ave.
Hacienda
0
1 mile
0
1 km
N

The construction of the dam created **Lake Mead** (Alan Bible Visitor Center, U.S. 93 and Lakeshore Dr., ☎ 702/293–8906), the largest man-made lake in the Western Hemisphere, with more than 500 mi of shoreline. It is popular for boating, fishing, and swimming. For water tours of the lake and Hoover Dam, contact **Lake Mead Cruises** (☎ 702/293–6180).

North of Lake Mead, dramatic **Valley of Fire State Park** (Rte. 169, Overton, ☎ 702/397–2088) contains distinctively colored rock formations and mysterious Pueblo petroglyphs.

Some 20 mi west of downtown, **Red Rock Canyon** descends in twisting ravines from sandstone cliffs that are an internationally known mecca for rock climbers. A 13-mi loop drive begins at the canyon visitor center (Rte. 159, ☎ 702/363–1921).

For a respite from the noise and excitement of Las Vegas and the heat of the desert, travel 35 mi northwest of the city on U.S. 95 and Rte. 157 to **Mt. Charleston,** a land of dense forests and rangy mountains that reach 12,000 ft. The hiking, camping, picnicking, and skiing in winter (Lee Canyon) are excellent.

What to See and Do with Children

Wet n' Wild (2600 Las Vegas Blvd. S, ☎ 702/737–3819) is a 26-acre theme park with every water ride imaginable. **Lied Discovery Children's Museum** (833 Las Vegas Blvd. N, ☎ 702/382–3445) has hands-on science exhibits. **Southern Nevada Zoological Park** (1775 N. Rancho Dr., ☎ 702/648–5955) is a small but nice zoo. Other good bets for children include the **Circus Circus** midway; **Excalibur**'s Medieval Village, a shopping and dining complex, and Fantasy Faire, a kid's game area; the **Guinness World of Records Museum;** and the **Imperial Palace Auto Collection** (*see* Exploring Las Vegas, *above*).

Getting Married in Las Vegas

Nevada is one of the easiest—and least expensive—states in which to get married. There is no blood test or waiting period; all you have to do is get a license ($35) at the Marriage License Bureau (200 S. 3rd St., 89155, ☎ 702/455–3146; after hours, 702/455–4415) and you're ready to go. In Las Vegas, there are about 25 chapels along the Strip, not including the hotel chapels at Bally's, Circus Circus, Excalibur, Imperial Palace, and Riviera (*see* Exploring Las Vegas, *above*). Services start at around $40.

Casino Gambling

Most major hotels in Las Vegas (as well as in Reno and Lake Tahoe) center on large casinos. The three largest casinos in Las Vegas—and consequently in the country—are at **MGM Grand, Riviera,** and **Excalibur** (*see below*). The games played in the casinos are slots, blackjack, baccarat, craps, roulette, keno, poker, wheel of fortune, and race and sports betting. Most larger casinos offer free gaming lessons, usually during the "slow" morning hours. If you don't want to bother with lessons, just head for the slot machines; thanks to progressive computer-linked slot jackpots, such as Megabucks and Quartermania, wins have gone into the millions.

Like the hotels, casinos have different themes attracting different folks. Some of the better ones are listed below.

Binion's Horseshoe Hotel and Casino (128 E. Fremont St., ☎ 702/382–1600), home of the World Series of Poker, has a Wild West theme and attracts serious gambling aficionados.

Caesars Palace (3570 Las Vegas Blvd. S, ☎ 702/731–7110), a sprawling ersatz temple for serious gamblers with money to burn, lays on the ancient-Rome theme, complete with toga-clad cocktail waitresses and Cleopatra's Barge lounge.

Circus Circus (2880 Las Vegas Blvd. S, ☎ 702/734–0410) casino is under a pink-and-white big top. Kids of all ages can watch circus performers and play games on the mezzanine.

Excalibur (3850 Las Vegas Blvd. S, ☎ 702/597–7777) recalls the days of King Arthur, with strolling entertainers and a jousting tournament in the showroom. The casino is cavernous and cacophonous; the 2,630 slot machines add to the hubbub.

Flamingo Hilton (3555 Las Vegas Blvd. S, ☎ 702/733–3111) bears little resemblance to the "classy joint" created by Bugsy Siegel in the 1940s. The splendiforous pink-flamingo theme is rampant in the huge casino, which is always mobbed. A 15-acre water park with four pools was recently added.

Golden Nugget Hotel and Casino (129 E. Fremont St., ☎ 702/385–7111) is Victorian in theme, replete with white marble, gold leaf, gold-plated elevators, and palm trees. The world's largest gold nugget, weighing 61 pounds, is displayed near the lobby.

Jackie Gaughan's Plaza Hotel and Casino (1 N. Main St., ☎ 702/386–2110) is the only casino in the world with its own train station; Amtrak stops here twice daily.

Las Vegas Hilton (3000 W. Paradise Rd., ☎ 702/732–5111) has the largest sports book in the world, with 46 video screens.

Luxor (3900 Las Vegas Blvd. S, ☎ 702/262–4000) re-creates ancient Egypt with its 29-million-cubic-ft pyramid. The casino is roomy, regal, and round.

MGM Grand Hotel and Theme Park (3805 Las Vegas Blvd. S, ☎ 702/891–1111), which opened in December 1993, is the world's largest casino, with 3,500 slot machines, more than 100 gaming tables, and a *Wizard of Oz* theme.

The Mirage (3400 Las Vegas Blvd. S, ☎ 702/791–7111) transports you to the South Seas, with thatch-roofed gaming areas and tropical plants and flowers flanking an indoor stream and pond. High rollers—those comfortable with $1,000 minimum bets—gamble in a separate, glassed-in area.

Sheraton Desert Inn (3145 Las Vegas Blvd. S, ☎ 702/733–4444) is small, relaxed, and elegant, appealing to the most exclusive clientele in town.

Tropicana (3801 Las Vegas Blvd. S, ☎ 702/739–2222) is lush and tropical, with a stunning pool area complete with swim-up blackjack in summer.

Shopping

Las Vegas's best shopping is on the Strip at the **Fashion Show Mall** (3200 Las Vegas Blvd. S, ☎ 702/369–8382), a collection of 150 shops and department stores, including Saks Fifth Avenue and Neiman Marcus. **Forum Shops at Caesars** (3500 Las Vegas Blvd. S, ☎ 702/893–4800), a complex of 70 specialty stores adjacent to Caesars Palace, dazzles shoppers with a replicated Roman street, complete with columns, piazzas, fountains, and a cloud-filled dome ceiling. You'll find Gucci, Ann Taylor, the Museum Company, and the Warner Bros. Studio Store alongside several popular restaurants. **Boulevard Mall** (3528 S. Maryland Pkwy., ☎ 702/735–8268), about 3 mi from the Strip, serves Las

Vegans who live on the east side of town. **Meadows Mall** (4300 Meadows La., ☎ 702/878–4849) is on the northwest side of town and has a big merry-go-round for kids. **Gamblers General Store** (800 S. Main St., ☎ 702/382–9903) carries all manner of gambling paraphernalia.

Spectator Sports

Boxing

Some of the major hotels, such as **Caesars Palace** and the **Mirage,** present championship bouts.

Golf

The annual PGA **Las Vegas Invitational** takes place in October at the Sheraton Desert Inn (☎ 702/382–6616).

Rodeo

The **National Finals Rodeo** is held in December at the University of Nevada's Thomas and Mack Center (☎ 702/731–2115).

Dining

Foods from some 40 countries are represented in Las Vegas restaurants. Dining options range from elegant gourmet meals at the best hotels to buffets, for which the city is known. Most hotels have buffets at breakfast ($3–$4), lunch ($4–$6), and dinner ($6–$8). The cheapest buffet is at **Circus Circus,** the two best are at the **Rio** and **Palace Station.** The best Sunday champagne brunch is the Sterling Brunch at **Bally's.** For price ranges, see Chart 1 (A) in On the Road with Fodor's.

$$$$ **Chin's.** An upscale Chinese restaurant with a bright, contemporary decor, Chin's offers such specialties as strawberry chicken and pepper orange roughy. *Fashion Show Mall, 3200 Las Vegas Blvd. S,* ☎ *702/733–8899. AE, D, DC, MC, V.*

$$$$ ★ **Palace Court.** This flagship restaurant of Caesars Palace is under a beautiful dome in a round room with greenery and floor-to-ceiling picture windows. The fare is classic French; chateaubriand is a specialty. *3570 Las Vegas Blvd. S,* ☎ *702/731–7731. Jacket required. AE, D, DC, MC, V.*

$$$ ★ **Le Montrachet.** This quiet place away from the chatter of the slot machines, with elaborate table settings and pastoral scenes on the walls, is the pride of the Las Vegas Hilton. The menu changes with the season, but the rack of lamb is always good. *3000 W. Paradise Rd.,* ☎ *702/732–5111. Jacket required. AE, D, DC, MC, V.*

$$$ **Pamplemousse.** The loving creation of Georges LaForges, a former Las Vegas maître d', this restaurant looks like a little French country inn. There is no menu; the waiter recites the daily specials and their method of preparation. *400 E. Sahara Ave.,* ☎ *702/733–2066. Jacket required. AE, D, DC, MC, V.*

$$ **Alpine Village.** You can't miss this place: It looks like a Swiss chalet, inside and out. The fare is German-Swiss; the sauerbraten is something special. Below the main restaurant is a lively rathskeller with oompah music. *3003 Paradise Rd.,* ☎ *702/734–6888. AE, D, DC, MC, V.*

$$ **Battista's Hole in the Wall.** Battista Locatelli, a former opera singer, prides himself on the quality of his mostly northern Italian food, as well as on the cleanliness of his kitchen. Decorated with wine bottles, garlic, and celebrity photos, the restaurant offers lots of specials, with all the free wine you can drink. *4041 Audrie St.,* ☎ *702/732–1424. AE, D, DC, MC, V. No lunch.*

$$ ★ **Bertolini's.** This sidewalk café inside the Forum Shops at Caesars can be noisy, but the northern Italian fare is first-rate. Order individual piz-

zas, soups, salads, and luscious gelato and sorbet. *3570 Las Vegas Blvd. S, ☎ 702/735–4663. AE, MC, V.*

$$ **Ricardo's.** This large restaurant has terrific south-of-the-border food (especially the burritos), great margaritas, and a strolling mariachi band. *2380 E. Tropicana Ave., ☎ 702/798–4515. AE, D, DC, MC, V.*

$$ **The Steak House.** In the center of a dark, quiet room reminiscent of 1890s San Francisco, with wood paneling and antique brass, steaks aged to perfection are cooked over an open-hearth charcoal grill. *Circus Circus, 2880 Las Vegas Blvd. S, ☎ 702/794–3767. AE, D, DC, MC, V. No lunch.*

$$ ★ **The Tillerman.** Seafood flown in fresh from the West Coast daily is served in a garden setting under a skylight. The yellowfin tuna is especially reliable. *2245 E. Flamingo Rd., ☎ 702/731–4036. No reservations. AE, D, DC, MC, V.*

$ **Roberta's.** This is Las Vegas's most venerable "bargain gourmet" room, at the historic El Cortez downtown. You won't believe the prices, especially for a 16-ounce prime rib or a pound of king crab legs. *El Cortez, 600 Fremont St., ☎ 702/386–0692. AE, MC, V. No lunch.*

Lodging

Las Vegas lodging ranges from virtual palaces to simple motels. The hotels tend to be a better bet for value; for instance, Circus Circus—one of the largest resort hotels in the world—has among the lowest prices in town. The largest and most lavish hotels are on the Strip; downtown hotels are generally less expensive. For price ranges, see Chart 2 (A) in On the Road with Fodor's.

$$$$ ★ **Caesars Palace.** This hotel caters to an upscale clientele with world-class service, superstar entertainers like Diana Ross and David Copperfield, and lavish restaurants. Its casino is full of fancy people making sizable wagers. Guest rooms are opulent, even by Las Vegas standards, and many have Roman tubs. *3570 Las Vegas Blvd. S, 89109, ☎ 702/731–7110 or 800/634–6661, FAX 702/731–6636. 1,301 rooms, 217 suites. Facilities: 9 restaurants, lounge, casino, showroom, health spa, 2 pools, 4 tennis courts, IMAX movie theater, shopping mall. AE, D, DC, MC, V.*

$$$$ **Sheraton Desert Inn.** Surrounded by its private golf course and offering town houses as well as televised gambling lessons, the hotel is one of the town's more restrained. The elegant rooms have a southwestern ambience. *3145 Las Vegas Blvd. S, 89109, ☎ 702/733–4444 or 800/634–6906, FAX 702/733–4774. 726 rooms, 95 suites. Facilities: 5 restaurants, lounge, casino, showroom, health club and spa, 10 tennis courts, golf course. AE, D, DC, MC, V.*

$$$ **Golden Nugget Hotel.** Its attractive white-and-green exterior is shaded with palm trees; the lobby is beautiful as well, with gold, white marble, and etched glass. Guest rooms reflect the same elegance. *129 E. Fremont St., 89101, ☎ 702/385–7111 or 800/634–3454, FAX 702/386–8362. 1,801 rooms, 106 suites. Facilities: 5 restaurants, lounge, casino, showroom, health club, pool. AE, D, DC, MC, V.*

$$$ ★ **The Mirage.** At one of the most extravagant and impressive hotels in the world, the colors and lush foliage outside and in bring to mind a tropical resort. Outside the block-long hotel is a series of waterfalls, surrounding a volcano that erupts every 15 minutes after dark. *3400 Las Vegas Blvd. S, 89109, ☎ 702/791–7111 or 800/627–6667, FAX 702/791–7446. 2,825 rooms, 224 suites. Facilities: 9 restaurants, lounge, casino, showroom, exercise facility, pool, 4 tennis courts. AE, D, DC, MC, V.*

$$ **Bally's.** This is the only hotel in the city with two full-size showrooms: one for headliners and one for "Jubilee!," the long-running production show. Many of the attractive guest rooms are suites, and some have round beds under mirrored ceilings. A $25-million elevated monorail was recently completed to link the MGM Grand Hotel and Bally's. *3645 Las Vegas Blvd. S, 89109, ☎ 702/739–4111 or 800/634–3434, FAX 702/739–4405. 2,567 rooms and 265 suites. Facilities: 7 restaurants, lounge, casino, 2 showrooms, health spa, pool, 10 tennis courts. AE, D, DC, MC, V.*

$$ **Excalibur.** This pink-and-blue turreted castle is the second-largest resort hotel in the world and has a King Arthur theme. This and its inexpensive food make it appeal mostly to families. *3850 Las Vegas Blvd. S, ☎ 702/597–7777 or 800/937–7777, FAX 702/597–7009. 4,032 rooms. Facilities: 7 restaurants, lounge, casino, showroom, pool, shops. AE, D, DC, MC, V.*

$$ **Flamingo Hilton.** The first luxury hotel in Las Vegas, once surrounded only by desert, the Flamingo now offers dramatic views of the busiest intersection of the Strip from contemporary rooms done in bright colors and soft textures. *3555 Las Vegas Blvd. S, 89109, ☎ 702/733–3111 or 800/732–2111, FAX 702/733–3528. 3,334 rooms, 196 suites. Facilities: 8 restaurants, lounge, casino, showroom, health spa, 4 pools, 4 tennis courts. AE, D, DC, MC, V.*

$$ **Harrah's Las Vegas.** A Las Vegas–neon Mississippi River gambling boat marks the entrance to what was formerly the largest Holiday Inn in the world. The rooms are modest by Strip standards, decorated in muted tones and dark-wood furniture. *3475 Las Vegas Blvd. S, 89109, ☎ 702/369–5000 or 800/634–6765, FAX 702/369–5008. 1,725 rooms. Facilities: 5 restaurants, lounge, casino, showroom, exercise room, pool. AE, D, DC, MC, V.*

$$ **Las Vegas Hilton.** Lasers emanating from the Hilton pierce the night sky, and with 29 floors and three wings, the hotel is one of the most recognizable in town. The rooms are large, and decorated in soft colors; those on the higher floors have great views. A Star Trek theme park is planned to open in late 1996. *3000 Paradise Rd., 89109, ☎ 702/732–5111 or 800/732–7117, FAX 702/794–3611. 3,174 rooms and suites. Facilities: 11 restaurants, lounge, casino, showroom, spa, pool, putting green, 6 tennis courts, youth hotel. AE, D, DC, MC, V.*

$$ **Luxor.** This bronze-color pyramid recalls ancient Egypt with interior waterways and a replica of King Tut's tomb. "Inclinators" rise to the top floor at a 39° angle. *3900 Las Vegas Blvd. S, 89119, ☎ 702/262–4000 or 800/288–1000, FAX 702/262–4454. 2,521 rooms, 14 suites. Facilities: 7 restaurants, lounge, casino, showroom, entertainment complex, shops. AE, D, DC, MC, V.*

$$ **MGM Grand Hotel and Theme Park.** This movieland-theme megaresort is the largest in the world. Four emerald green hotel towers reflect a *Wizard of Oz* theme; a 33-acre theme park re-creates Hollywood backlots with rides and performances. *3799 Las Vegas Blvd. S, 89119, ☎ 702/891–1111 or 800/929–1111, FAX 702/891–1030. 4,272 rooms, 733 suites. Facilities: 9 restaurants, lounge, casino, showroom, indoor arena, outdoor amusement park, comedy club, health club, pool, tennis courts, child-care center, game room. AE, D, DC, MC, V.*

$$ **Rio Suite Hotel.** These red-and-blue 21-story towers contain all suites. Ask for a unit on one of the top floors and on the east side, facing the Strip. A recent $74-million expansion created casino space, a parking garage, and a new tower. *3700 W. Flamingo Rd. (at Valley View), 89109, ☎ 702/252–7777 or 800/888–1808, FAX 702/253–6090. 860 suites. Facilities: 8 restaurants, lounge, showroom, casino, health club, pool. AE, D, DC, MC, V.*

$$ Riviera Hotel. One of the city's most famous and venerable hotels, the Riviera has one of the largest casinos in the world. The location is convenient to the upper Strip and Convention Center. *2901 Las Vegas Blvd. S, 89109, ☎ 702/734–5110 or 800/634–6753, FAX 702/794–9663. 2,220 rooms. Facilities: 5 restaurants, food court, casino, 4 showrooms, health club, pool, 2 tennis courts. AE, D, DC, MC, V.*

$$ Sands Hotel. This 1950s landmark, the first circular building in town, rises 16 stories, with a cluster of low rises around a V-shaped pool. Upper-floor tower rooms offer some of the only outdoor balconies on the Strip. John F. Kennedy, Richard Nixon, and Ronald Reagan were guests in the Presidential Suite. *3355 Las Vegas Blvd. S, 89109, ☎ 702/733–5000 or 800/634–6901, FAX 702/733–5632. 715 rooms. Facilities: 4 restaurants, lounge, casino, showroom, health club, 2 pools, putting green, 6 tennis courts, convention center. AE, D, DC, MC, V.*

$$ Treasure Island Resort. This hotel, which opened in November 1993, is based on Robert Louis Stevenson's novel, set in the South Seas. There's a re-created 18th-century pirate village and a monorail to the Mirage. *3300 Las Vegas Blvd. S, 89109, ☎ 702/894–7111 or 800/944–7444, FAX 702/894–7446. 2,912 rooms. Facilities: 5 restaurants, lounge, casino, showroom, health club, pool, shopping arcade. AE, D, DC, MC, V.*

$$ Tropicana. Two high-rise towers loom above the most beautiful grounds in Las Vegas, complete with waterfalls and swans. Room decor is tropical, with bamboo and pastels. *3801 Las Vegas Blvd. S, 89109, ☎ 702/739–2222 or 800/634–4000, FAX 702/739–2469. 1,818 rooms, 94 suites. Facilities: 6 restaurants, lounge, casino, showroom, health club, 3 pools, 4 tennis courts, racquetball. AE, D, DC, MC, V.*

$ Circus Circus. Catering primarily to families with children, the hotel has painted circus tents in the hallways and a generally chaotic atmosphere. The brightly decorated rooms (red carpets and chairs; red, pink, and blue striped wallpaper) are small but clean. *2880 Las Vegas Blvd. S, 89109, ☎ 702/734–0410 or 800/634–3450, FAX 702/734–2268. 2,793 rooms. Facilities: 5 restaurants, casino, 3 pools, wedding chapel, large RV park. AE, D, DC, MC, V.*

$ Jackie Gaughan's Plaza Hotel and Casino. This casino-hotel was built on the original site of the Union Pacific train station and now houses an Amtrak station. Rooms are decorated in light mauve tones; those facing east have a great view of downtown. *1 Main St., 89101, ☎ 702/386–2110 or 800/634–6575, FAX 702/382–8281. 1,037 rooms. Facilities: 3 restaurants, lounge, casino, showroom, pool. AE, D, DC, MC, V.*

$ Sahara Las Vegas Hotel. Like many of its neighbors, the Sahara began as a small motor hotel and built itself up by adding towers. Unlike its neighbors, it hasn't expanded its small casino, preferring instead to serve as a business hotel for the convention center down the street. The older rooms are small; tower rooms are larger and those that face south overlook the Strip. *2535 Las Vegas Blvd. S, 89109, ☎ 702/737–2111 or 800/634–6666, FAX 702/791–2027. 2,100 rooms. Facilities: 5 restaurants, lounge, casino, showroom, health club, 2 pools. AE, D, DC, MC, V.*

$ Sam's Town Hotel and Casino. This friendly hotel outside town on U.S. 95 presents an Old West theme that feels authentic because the place is so close to the desert. Some rooms offer views of the desert and mountains; the inside-facing rooms overlook a brand new 18-story courtyard complete with trees, creeks, and a waterfall. *5111 Boulder Hwy., 89122, ☎ 702/456–7777 or 800/634–6371, FAX 702/454–8014. 650 rooms. Facilities: 5 restaurants, lounge, casino, pool, bowling alley, RV park. AE, D, DC, MC, V.*

$ Stardust. From its first incarnation as a motor hotel to its recent 32-story tower, the Stardust is one of the best-known hotels on the Strip. The newer tower rooms are the best. *3000 Las Vegas Blvd. S, 89109,*

☎ 702/732–6111 or 800/634–6757, FAX 702/732–6296. 2,500 rooms. Facilities: 6 restaurants, lounge, casino, showroom, health club, pool, 2 tennis courts. AE, D, DC, MC, V.

Motels

Days Inn–Town Hall (4155 Koval La., 89109, ☎ 702/731–2111 or 800/634–6541, FAX 702/731–1113), 360 rooms, coffee shop, pool; $. **Motel 6** (195 E. Tropicana Ave., 89109, ☎ 702/798–0728, FAX 702/798–5657), 877 rooms, 2 pools; $. **Westward Ho** (2900 Las Vegas Blvd. S, 89109, ☎ 702/731–2900 or 800/634–6651, FAX 702/731–6154), 1,000 rooms, restaurant, 7 pools; $

The Arts and Nightlife

The Arts

Most arts events in Las Vegas are associated with the **University of Nevada, Las Vegas** (☎ 702/895–3011). For additional information, call the **Allied Arts Council** (☎ 702/731–5419).

Nightlife

Perhaps no city in America—or even in the world—has more to do at night than Las Vegas.

SHOWROOMS

Hotel showrooms seat from several hundred to 2,000. Most are luxurious and intimate, with few, if any, bad seats. The old-style seating system involves arriving early and tipping the maitre d' or captain. The new trend is reserved seating, which eliminates the waiting and the hassle. When a show is expected to sell out, hotel guests are given ticket preference.

The four main kinds of entertainment offered in showrooms are **headliner shows,** such as Frank Sinatra, Julio Iglesias, and Diana Ross; **big production shows,** such as "Jubilee!" at Bally's or the Tropicana's "Folies Bergères," which include major song and dance numbers and smaller specialty acts, while topless showgirls strut their stuff; **small production shows,** such as "Melinda, First Lady of Magic" at the Lady Luck; and the **lounge shows,** offered all over town, where pop bands play dance music and the only price of admission is the cost of a drink or two.

The major hotels' entertainment offerings are as follows (*see* Exploring Las Vegas *or* Lodging, *above,* for addresses and phone numbers): **Bally's,** headliners and large production show; **Caesars Palace,** headliners; **Excalibur,** large production show; **Flamingo Hilton,** large production show; **Harrah's Las Vegas,** small production show; **Imperial Palace,** small production show; **Las Vegas Hilton,** Andrew Lloyd Weber's *Starlight Express*; **MGM Grand,** headliners and large and small production shows; **Mirage,** Siegfried & Roy; **Rio,** large production show; **Riviera,** large and small production shows; **Sahara,** small production show; **Stardust,** large production show; **Sheraton Desert Inn,** headliners; **Treasure Island,** Cirque du Soleil; **Tropicana,** large production show.

COMEDY CLUBS

MGM Grand has **Catch a Rising Star,** the Riviera has **An Evening at the Improv,** and the Tropicana has the **Comedy Stop.**

JAZZ

The **Four Queens Hotel**'s Monday night jazz program, hosted by Alan Grant, is broadcast on National Public Radio.

RENO

Reno, once the gambling and divorce capital of the country, is smaller, less crowded, friendlier, and prettier than Las Vegas. Established in 1859 as a trading station at a bridge over the Truckee River, Reno grew with the nearby silver mines, the railroad, and gambling, and is getting a boost from the new National Bowling Stadium—the only one of its kind in the country—as well as the new 1,700-room Silver Legacy downtown. Its first major casinos opened in 1935.

Tourist Information

Reno-Sparks Convention and Visitors Authority (4590 S. Virginia St., Reno 89502, ☎ 702/827–7366 or 800/367–7366).

Arriving and Departing

By Plane

Reno–Tahoe International Airport (☎ 702/328–6400), served by national and regional airlines, is on the east side of the city and minutes from downtown.

By Car

The major highways leading to Reno are I–80 (east–west) and U.S. 395 (north–south).

By Train

Amtrak (135 E. Commercial Row, ☎ 702/329–8638 or 800/872–7245).

By Bus

Greyhound Lines (155 Stevenson St., ☎ 702/322–2970 or 800/231–2222).

Getting Around Reno

Reno is such a small city that the best way to get around it is on foot or by taxi. Taxis (like rental cars) are easily hired at the airport and in front of the major hotels; the main taxi firms are **Reno-Sparks Cab Co.** (☎ 702/333–3333), **Whittlesea Checker** (☎ 702/322–2222), and **Yellow** (☎ 702/355–5555). **Reno Citifare** (☎ 702/348–7433) provides local bus service. Many large hotels have courtesy buses on call.

Exploring Reno

One advantage Reno has over Las Vegas is weather: Its summer temperatures are much more agreeable and thus much more pleasant for strolling. The city's focal point is the famous Reno Arch, a sign over the upper end of Virginia Street proclaiming it "The Biggest Little City in the World."

As in Las Vegas, gambling is a favorite pastime. While not as garish as their Vegas counterparts, Reno's casinos still offer plenty of glitter and glitz. With the exception of the Reno Hilton, Peppermill, Clarion, and John Ascuaga's Nugget, they are crowded into five square blocks downtown. **Reno Tahoe Gaming Academy** (300 E. 1st St., ☎ 702/329–5665) conducts a behind-the-scenes tour of the Club Cal–Neva. Some of the better casinos are listed below.

Circus Circus (500 N. Sierra St., ☎ 702/329–0711 or 800/648–5010), marked by a neon clown sucking a lollipop, is the best stop for families with children. Complete with clowns, games, fun-house mirrors, and circus acts, the midway overlooking the casino floor is open from 10 AM to midnight.

Club Cal-Neva (38 E. 2nd St., ☎ 702/323–1046) is the best place in town to gamble, with low limits and optimal rules.

Fitzgeralds (255 N. Virginia St., ☎ 702/785–3300) celebrates the luck of the Irish with a large green casino and a leprechaun mascot. On the second floor in the Lucky Forest you can kiss the only Blarney stones ever to leave Ireland; on the third floor admire a collection of more than 50 antique slot machines.

Flamingo Hilton (255 N. Sierra St., ☎ 702/322–1111 or 800/648–4882) reproduces its Vegas counterpart, complete with a gigantic neon pink-feathered flamingo.

Harold's (250 Virginia St., ☎ 702/329–0881), opened in 1935, was the first major casino in Nevada. A famous advertising campaign was responsible for the HAROLD'S CLUB OR BUST signs seen for years around the world. It boasts "Long-Hands Meters" on both crap tables, which keep track of the number of rolls made by each shooter.

Harrah's (219 N. Center St., ☎ 702/786–3232 or 800/648–3773), which debuted in 1937 as the Tango Club, was Reno's second large casino. A pair of sprawling buildings covers almost two city blocks and contains a sports casino with a new sports book and a children's arcade. There are low minimums and friendly patrons and workers.

Nevada Club (224 N. Virginia St., ☎ 702/329–1721) takes you back to the 1940s. Its slots are old-fashioned one-arm bandits; line up three cherries and you might win a classic hot rod. There's a World War II–era diner on the second floor, along with penny slots.

Four casinos lie outside the downtown area: **Reno Hilton** (2500 E. 2nd St., ☎ 702/789–2000 or 800/648–5080), with 100,000 square ft, is the largest casino in Reno; **Peppermill** (2707 S. Virginia St., ☎ 702/826–2121 or 800/648–6992) is the gaudiest, glitziest, and noisiest; **Clarion** (3800 S. Virginia St., ☎ 702/825–4700 or 800/723–6500) has the best buffet in Reno; and **John Ascuaga's Nugget** (1100 Nugget Ave., Sparks, ☎ 702/356–3300 or 800/648–1177) is the classiest.

Besides the hotel-casinos, Reno has a number of cultural attractions. On the University of Nevada campus, the sleekly designed **Fleischmann Planetarium** (1600 N.Virginia St., ☎ 702/784–4811) offers films and star shows. The **Nevada Historical Society** (1650 N. Virginia St., ☎ 702/688–1190) features mining exhibits and Native American artifacts. The **Nevada Museum of Art** (160 W. Liberty St., ☎ 702/329–3333), the state's largest, has changing exhibits. More than 220 antique and classic automobiles, including an Elvis Presley Cadillac, are on display at the **William F. Harrah Foundation National Automobile Museum** (Mill and Lake Sts., ☎ 702/333–9300).

Downtown River Walk (S. Virginia St. and the river, ☎ 702/334–2077) is a festive scene year-round and often hosts special events featuring street performers, musicians, dancers, food, art displays, and games. **Victorian Square** (Victorian Ave. between Rock and Pyramid, Sparks), fringed by restored turn-of-the-century houses and Victorian-dressed casinos and storefronts, is a parklike setting with a bandstand-gazebo.

In the Vicinity

Only 25 mi from Reno (U.S. 395S to Rte. 341), **Virginia City** was once the largest city in Nevada, with more than 20,000 residents and 110 saloons. The Comstock Lode, one of the largest gold and silver deposits ever discovered, was responsible for Virginia City's boom (1860–1880). Today it's one of the liveliest and most authentic historic mining towns in the West. Little has changed in more than 100 years. You can still belly up to the grand mahogany bar and hear honky-tonk piano music at the **Bucket of Blood** (☎ 702/847–0322) saloon on C Street. The lavish interiors of **Mackay Mansion** (D St., ☎ 702/847–0173) and the **Castle** (B St., no ☎) offer a glimpse into the past with such adornments as Oriental rugs, Italian marble, and Brussels lace, as well as table settings made from the silver mined beneath these houses. **Virginia & Truckee Railroad** (Washington and F Sts., ☎ 702/847–0380) takes visitors on historic steam-powered locomotives through the Comstock mining region. Virginia City's most famous resident was Mark Twain, who lived here from 1861 to 1864 while working as a reporter for the *Territorial Enterprise;* the **Mark Twain Museum** (109 S. C St., ☎ 702/847–0454) has mementos of his life. For more information, contact the **Virginia City Chamber of Commerce** (S. C St.; Box 464, 89440, ☎ 702/847–0311).

South of Virginia City is **Carson City,** the state capital. The **Nevada State Museum** (600 N. Carson St., ☎ 702/687–4810; admission charged), once a U.S. mint, has exhibits on early mining days, antique gaming devices, and willow baskets woven by Washoe artists. The **Nevada State Railroad Museum** (2180 S. Carson St., ☎ 702/687–6953) has an extensive historic collection of passenger and freight cars and two restored Virginia & Truckee trains. The **Carson City Chamber of Commerce** (1900 S. Carson St., ☎ 702/882–1565) has information on the town's attractions.

Genoa, the oldest settlement in Nevada, is a quaint Victorian town about 20 mi south of Carson City just west of U.S. 395. **Mormon Station State Historic Park** (Foothill Rd. and Genoa La., ☎ 702/687–4379) contains an early log cabin and Mormon artifacts. **Walley's Hot Springs Resort** (2001 Foothill Rd., ☎ 702/782–8155) has hot mineral pools dating from 1862.

What to See and Do with Children

Of particular interest to children in Reno are the **Fleischmann Planetarium** and the **William F. Harrah Foundation National Automobile Museum** (*see* Exploring Reno, *above*). **Wilbur D. May Great Basin Adventure** (1502 Washington St., ☎ 702/785–4153), in Rancho San Rafael Park, traces the evolution of the Great Basin through mining and other exhibits, including a dinosaur pit; also available here are a petting zoo, pony rides, and a touch-and-feel discovery room. In nearby Sparks, **Wild Island** (250 Wild Island Ct., ☎ 702/331–9453) is a family theme park that includes a water park, a 36-hole minigolf course, and a state-of-the-art video arcade.

Shopping

The **Park Lane Mall** (310 E. Plumb La., ☎ 702/825–7878) is the older and cozier indoor shopping center in town; check out the Made in Nevada store. The **Meadowood Mall** (Virginia St. at McCarran Blvd., ☎ 702/827–8450) is a newer, more spacious and upscale mall. **Harold's Club Antique Slots** (250 N. Virginia St., ☎ 702/329–0881) sells slot and video poker machines for about $600.

Dining

Reno dining options range from plush gourmet restaurants and extensive hotel buffets to interesting little eateries scattered around the city. As in Las Vegas, the least expensive places are the hotel-casino breakfast, lunch, and dinner buffets. The best are at the **Clarion, John Ascuaga's Nugget** (*see* Exploring Reno, *above*) and the **Eldorado** (*see* Lodging, *below*). For price ranges, see Chart 1 (B) in On the Road with Fodor's.

$$$ **Harrah's Steak House.** The hotel-casino's dark and romantic restaurant serves excellent steaks. *219 N. Center St., ☎ 702/786–3232. AE, D, DC, MC, V.*

$$$ **Le Moulin.** Located in the Peppermill casino, the intimate Le Moulin has subdued lighting and touches of neon and art deco. The fare, as you would expect, is French. There's a prime-rib-and-lobster early-bird special from 5 to 7. *2707 S. Virginia St., ☎ 702/826–2121. AE, D, DC, MC, V. No lunch.*

$$$ **19th Hole.** This restaurant on the Lakeridge Golf Course has a great view of the city and nearby mountains. The menu offers American and Continental food. *1200 Razorback Rd., ☎ 702/825–1250. D, MC, V.*

$$ **Café de Thai.** The soups, salads, wok dishes, and satay are all divine, concocted by a Thai chef trained at the Culinary Institute. *3314 S. McCarran, ☎ 702/829–8424. MC, V.*

$$ **La Strada.** This excellent northern Italian restaurant is upstairs from the Eldorado casino. The pastas and sauces are homemade, and the gourmet pizzas are wood-fired. *345 N. Virginia St., ☎ 702/786–5700. AE, D, DC, MC, V. No lunch.*

$$ **Presidential Car.** On the third floor of Harold's, this restaurant has an excellent view of Reno Arch. The menu includes prime rib, steak, and seafood, and death-by-chocolate cake. *250 N. Virginia St., ☎ 702/329–0881. AE, MC, V.*

$ **Bertha Miranda's Mexican Restaurant.** Begun as a little hole-in-the-wall, it has grown into a highly successful establishment. The food is made fresh by Bertha's family. Be sure to try the salsa. *336 Mill St., ☎ 702/786–9697. MC, V.*

$ **La Trattoria.** The food of southern Italy is served at this family-owned and -operated restaurant. Ravioli in red-wine sauce is a specialty. *719 S. Virginia St., ☎ 702/323–1131. DC, MC, V.*

$ **Louis' Basque Corner.** Basque shepherds once populated northern Nevada, and this is a great place to sample authentic Basque food, which is served family-style at large tables covered with red cloths in a wood-paneled dining room. Dishes include oxtail, shrimp, and tongue. *301 E. 4th St., ☎ 702/323–7203. AE, DC, MC, V.*

$ **Nugget Diner.** This is a classic Americana diner; seating is on stools at front and back counters. The Awful Awful burger is renowned, as is the prime rib. *Nugget Casino, 233 N. Virginia St., ☎ 702/323–0716. MC, V.*

Lodging

Most of Reno's hotels are downtown. For price ranges, see Chart 2 (B) in On the Road with Fodor's.

$$$ **Flamingo Hilton.** This sister hotel of the Las Vegas Flamingo sports a new porte cochere and million-dollar sign. The guest rooms facing west have a nice view of the mountains. *255 N. Sierra St., 89501, ☎ 702/322–1111 or 800/648–4822. 604 rooms. Facilities: 4 restaurants, lounge, showroom, casino. AE, D, DC, MC, V.*

$$$ **Harrah's.** This is one of the most luxurious hotels in downtown Reno. Large, conservatively decorated guest rooms overlook downtown and the whole mountain-ringed valley. *219 N. Center St., 89501, ☎ 702/788–3773 or 800/648–3773. 565 rooms. Facilities: 4 restaurants, casino, showroom, health club, pool, shopping arcade. AE, MC, V.*

$$$ **Reno Hilton.** This 27-story hotel near the airport, formerly Bally's, has just undergone a massive two-year, $72-million renovation that changed its theme from Hollywood to the western United States. The casino and public areas now feature rivers, trees, and lush vegetation of the Northwest, and mountainscapes and rock formations of the Southwest. *2500 E. 2nd St., 89595, ☎ 702/789–2000 or 800/648–5080. 2,001 rooms. Facilities: 6 restaurants, lounge, casino, showroom, health club, pool, tennis courts, shopping arcade, wedding chapel. AE, D, DC, MC, V.*

$$ **Eldorado.** Known for its fine food and attention to detail, the Eldorado is completing an all-suites tower. Rooms overlook the mountains. *345 N. Virginia St., 89501, ☎ 702/786–5700 or 800/648–5966. 800 rooms. Facilities: 8 restaurants, lounge, casino, pool. AE, D, DC, MC, V.*

$$ **John Ascuaga's Nugget.** This casino-hotel in neighboring Sparks offers some of the largest and most luxurious rooms around, as well as a resident elephant named Bertha. *1100 Nugget Ave., Sparks 89431, ☎ 702/356–3300 or 800/648–1177. 983 rooms. Facilities: 7 restaurants, lounge, casino, showroom, indoor pool, free shuttle to downtown Reno. AE, D, DC, MC, V.*

$ **Circus Circus.** This smaller version of the giant Las Vegas hotel has the same atmosphere. The rooms, though small and garish, are good value—when you can get one. *500 N. Sierra St., 89503, ☎ 702/329–0711 or 800/648–5010. 1,625 rooms. Facilities: 3 restaurants, lounge, casino. AE, DC, MC, V.*

$ **Comstock.** The lobby and casino reflect an Old West theme. Rooms are small, with Victorian-style decor and city or mountain views. *200 W. 2nd St., 89501, ☎ 702/329–1880 or 800/648–4866. 310 rooms. Facilities: 3 restaurants, lounge, casino, health club, pool. MC, V.*

$ **Peppermill.** The home of Reno's most colorful casino is 3 mi from downtown, but its rooms are plush and sedate. *2707 S. Virginia St., 89502, ☎ 702/826–2121 or 800/648–6992. 631 rooms. Facilities: 3 restaurants, lounge, casino, health club, pool. AE, D, DC, MC, V.*

The Arts and Nightlife

The Arts

Most of the arts in Reno—such as the **Nevada Festival Ballet** (☎ 702/329–2552), the **Nevada Opera Association** (☎ 702/786–4046), the **Reno Philharmonic** (☎ 702/825–5905), and the **Performing Arts Series** (☎ 702/826–0880)—center on the **University of Nevada, Reno** (☎ 702/784–1110).

Nightlife

As in Las Vegas, Reno area nightlife breaks down into four categories: headliners, big production shows, small production shows, and lounge acts. Offerings at the major Reno hotels (*see* Lodging, *above*, for addresses and phone numbers): **Circus Circus,** continual circus acts; **Flamingo Hilton,** large production show; **Harrah's Reno,** headliners and small production shows; **John Ascuaga's Nugget,** headliners (mostly country-western); **Reno Hilton,** headliners and large production show.

LAKE TAHOE

Southwest of Reno, Lake Tahoe's vast expanse of crystal-blue water surrounded by rugged peaks is a playground for natives and visitors alike. Half in Nevada and half in California, it is the largest alpine lake in North America, 22 mi long and 12 mi wide. The region offers outstanding skiing in winter; boating, fishing, and mountain sports in summer; and casino entertainment year-round.

Tourist Information

In Lake Tahoe, contact the **Tahoe-Douglas Chamber of Commerce** (Hwy. 50, at the Round Hill Shopping Center, Box 7139, Stateline 89449, ☎ 702/588–4591) or the **Incline Village/Crystal Bay Visitors and Convention Bureau** (969 Tahoe Blvd., Incline Village 89451-9508, ☎ 702/832–1606 or 800/468–2463).

Getting There

By Plane

The closest major airport to Lake Tahoe is **Reno–Tahoe International Airport** (*see* Reno, *above*). However, two regional airlines offer limited service from several California cities to the **Lake Tahoe Airport** (☎ 916/542–6180) near Stateline.

By Car

From Reno, U.S. 395S through Carson City to U.S. 50 leads to South Lake Tahoe; U.S. 395S to Rte. 431 leads to North Lake Tahoe.

Exploring Lake Tahoe

A scenic drive circling Lake Tahoe (Rtes. 28 and 89) offers stunning lake, forest, and mountain vistas. You also can explore the lake aboard the ***MS Dixie II*** (Zephyr Cove, ☎ 702/588–3508). **Crystal Bay,** the northernmost community on the Nevada shore, has a small-town, outdoorsy feel, along with several casinos.

To the south, affluent **Incline Village** has lakeshore residences, weekend condos, inviting shopping areas, and, south of town, the **Ponderosa Ranch,** a Hollywood-style Western town based on the TV series *Bonanza. Rte. 28,* ☎ *702/831–0691. Admission charged. Closed Nov.–Apr.*

At the south end of the lake—just before the neon signs of **Stateline,** where four towering and two low-rise casinos cluster in one block just east of the Nevada–California border (*see* Dining and Lodging, *below*)—a road takes you southeast to the **Heavenly Ski Area** (☎ 702/586–7000), where the tram lifts you to fantastic skiing in winter and unbeatable views over the water year-round.

What to See and Do with Children

Aside from water sports on the lake, **Ponderosa Ranch** (*see* Exploring Lake Tahoe, *above*) is the chief attraction for children.

Sports and the Outdoors

Fishing

The lake is renowned for mighty mackinaws and rainbow trout. Nonresident fishing permits are available at most sporting-goods stores. For more information, call the **Department of Wildlife** (☎ 702/688–1500).

Golf

Edgewood at Tahoe (Stateline, ☎ 702/588–3566; 18 holes). **Glenbrook Golf Course** (Glenbrook, ☎ 702/749–5201; 9 holes). **Incline Village Championship Golf Course** (955 Fairway Blvd., ☎ 702/832–1144; 18 holes). **Incline Village Executive Course** (690 Wilson Way, ☎ 702/832–1150; 18 holes).

Hiking

More than 100 mi of hiking trails traverse the area, many through high mountain passes and along streams and meadows with sweeping views. Contact the **U.S. Forest Service** (☎ 916/573–2600) for information.

Ski Areas

Lake Tahoe offers more than 15 world-class alpine (downhill) resorts and nearly a dozen Nordic (cross-country) skiing centers—all within an hour of one another. Elevations range from 6,000 to 10,000 ft, with vertical drops up to nearly 4,000 ft. More than 150 lifts operate during the season, which usually lasts from November through May.

Cross-Country

Diamond Peak (1210 Ski Way, Incline Village 89450, ☎ 702/832–1177) has 22 mi of groomed high-elevation track with skating lanes.

Downhill

Diamond Peak (*see* Cross-Country, *above*) has seven lifts, 29 runs, and a 1,840-ft vertical drop. **Heavenly Ski Area** (Box 2180, Stateline 89449, ☎ 916/541–1330 or 800/243–2836), straddling the Nevada–California border, has 25 lifts, 71 trails (including the longest run in Tahoe), and a 3,600-ft drop. **Mt. Rose** (22222 Mt. Rose Hwy., Reno 89511, ☎ 702/849–0704) has the highest base elevation in the area, with unequaled powder skiing, five lifts, 41 runs, and a 1,440-ft drop.

Dining and Lodging

For price ranges, see Charts 1 (B) and 2 (B) in On the Road with Fodor's.

Incline Village/Reno

DINING

Galena Forest Inn. Set at the foot of the mountains, the Galena appropriately serves Swiss-Austrian alpine fare. Try the forest terrine of venison and rabbit. *17025 Mt. Rose Hwy., ☎ 702/849–2100. D, MC, V. No lunch. $$$*

Lone Eagle Grille. This restaurant in the Hyatt Regency Hotel has one of the best views of the lake. Specialties include duck, fish, and steak; there's a salad and dessert buffet. *Country Club Dr. at Lakeshore, Incline Village, ☎ 702/831–1111. AE, D, DC, MC, V. $$*

Stateline

DINING

Empress Court. Plush velvet booths and etched-glass partitions provide the setting for traditional Chinese cuisine. Try the grilled-squab salad. *Caesars Tahoe, Rte. 50, ☎ 702/588–3515. AE, DC, MC, V. No lunch. $$$*

Sage Room Steak House. A historic landmark in Lake Tahoe, this romantic restaurant is a descendant of the Wagon Wheel Saloon and Gambling Hall, the beginning of Harvey's Resort. Sautéed prawns Mediterranean are excellent. *Harvey's Resort Hotel/Casino, Rte. 50, ☎ 702/588–2411. AE, D, DC, MC, V. $$*

The Summit. This 16th-floor restaurant affords a wonderful view. The creative menu includes artfully presented salads, seafood entrées, and decadent desserts. *Harrah's Casino/Hotel Lake Tahoe, Rte. 50,* ☎ *702/588–6611. AE, D, DC, MC, V. $$*

El Vaquero. Wrought iron, a fountain, and tiles give this restaurant an authentic Old Mexico feel. The traditional Mexican fare includes enchiladas and chimichangas. At the Taco Cart, you can make your own. *Harvey's Resort Hotel/Casino, Rte. 50,* ☎ *702/588–2411. AE, D, DC, MC, V. $*

The Forest. On the 18th floor of Harrah's, this restaurant offering buffet-style dining has the best view of any buffet in Nevada. The interior simulates a forest. *Rte. 50,* ☎ *702/588–6611. No reservations. AE, DC, MC, V. $*

LODGING

Caesars Tahoe. Once you negotiate the lobby stairs and casino areas, you find hallways with faux Corinthian columns and plush rooms in fantasy-land color schemes, such as hot pink and mint green. The indoor pool has a waterfall and a swim tunnel. *Box 5800, 89449,* ☎ *702/588–3515 or 800/648–3353. 440 rooms, 50 suites. Facilities: 5 restaurants, lounge, casino, showroom, health club, pool, tennis courts. AE, D, DC, MC, V. $$$*

★ **Harrah's Casino/Hotel Lake Tahoe.** The rooms are large and comfortable, and all have two full bathrooms, complete with telephones and TVs. Most rooms also have excellent views of the lake and the mountains. *Rte. 50, Box 8, 89449,* ☎ *702/588–6606 or 800/648–3773. 533 rooms, 79 suites. Facilities: 7 restaurants, casino, showroom, health club, indoor pool. AE, DC, MC, V. $$$*

Hyatt Regency Lake Tahoe. Rooms are large and attractive, with warm color schemes and lake views. Amenities include a private beach, water sports, Camp Hyatt for kids, and a forest-theme casino. *Country Club Dr. at Lakeshore, Incline Village 89450,* ☎ *702/832–1234 or 800/233–1234. 460 rooms. Facilities: 3 restaurants, lounge, casino, health club, pool, beach. AE, DC, MC, V. $$$*

Harvey's Resort Hotel/Casino. This family-owned hotel is Lake Tahoe's largest resort. The rooms are comfortably furnished in American traditional style, with soft colors. Most have a view of the lake and the mountains. *Rte. 50, Box 128, 89449,* ☎ *702/588–2411 or 800/648–3361. 740 rooms. Facilities: 8 restaurants, lounge, casino, health spa, tennis courts. AE, D, DC, MC, V. $$*

Nightlife

Lake Tahoe nightlife centers on the top-name entertainment and production shows at the casino-hotels. **Caesars Tahoe** and **Harrah's** (*see* Lodging, *above*) both present headliners.

NEW MEXICO

By Ron Butler
Updated by Carmella Padilla

Capital	Santa Fe
Population	1.5 million
Motto	It Grows as It Goes
State Bird	Roadrunner
State Flower	Yucca

Visitor Information

New Mexico Department of Tourism (Lamy Bldg., 491 Old Santa Fe Trail, Santa Fe 87503, ☎ 505/827–7400 or 800/545–2070, FAX 505/827–7402). **USDA Forest Service, Southwestern Region** (Public Affairs Office, 517 Gold Ave. SW, Albuquerque 87102, ☎ 505/842–3292). **Indian Pueblo Cultural Center** (2401 12th St. NW, Albuquerque 87102, ☎ 505/843–7270).

Scenic Drives

An alternative to the more direct route from Santa Fe to Taos, the old **High Road** takes you through rolling hillsides studded with orchards and tiny picturesque villages set against a rugged mountain backdrop. No visit to northern New Mexico is complete without the 100-mi trip through the **Enchanted Circle,** a breathtaking panorama of deep canyons, passes, alpine valleys, and towering mountains of the verdant Carson National Forest. **Rte. 66,** America's most nostalgic highway, includes a colorful stretch that now constitutes Albuquerque's Central Avenue. The old route between Albuquerque and Santa Fe, the **Turquoise Trail** (Rte. 14), snakes up through a portion of Cibola National Forest and a number of ghost towns.

National and State Parks

National Park

Carlsbad Caverns National Park (*see* Elsewhere in the State, *below*) is a spectacular system of caves and rock formations.

State Parks

New Mexico's 40 state parks range from the high mountain lakes and pine forests of the north to the Chihuahuan Desert lowlands in the south. Pristine and unspoiled, they offer every conceivable outdoor recreational facility. For maps and brochures, contact the **State Parks and Recreation Division** (Energy, Minerals, and Natural Resources Dept., 408 Galisteo St., Box 1147, Santa Fe 87504-1147, ☎ 505/827–7465 or 800/451–2541, FAX 505/827–4001).

Native American Reservations

Two general classifications of Native Americans live in New Mexico: the Puebloans, who established an agricultural civilization here many centuries ago, and the descendants of the nomadic tribes who came into the area much later—the Navajos, Mescalero Apaches, and Jicarilla Apaches. The settlements of various **Pueblo** tribes are described in the Santa Fe and Albuquerque sections below.

The **Jicarilla Apaches** live on a 750,000-acre reservation in north-central New Mexico. The tribe has a well-defined tourist program promoting big-game hunting, fishing, and camping on a 15,000-acre game preserve; for details, contact the **Jicarilla Apache Tribe** (Box 507, Dulce 87528, ☎ 505/759–3242).

A reservation of a half-million acres of timbered mountains and green valleys in southeastern New Mexico is home to the **Mescalero Apaches.** The tribe owns and operates one of the most elegant luxury resorts in the state, Inn of the Mountain Gods, as well as Ski Apache, 16 mi from Ruidoso. Contact the **Mescalero Apache Tribe** (Box 176, Mescalero 88340, ☎ 505/671–4494) for additional information.

The **Navajo Reservation,** home to the largest Native American group in the United States, covers 16 million acres in New Mexico, Arizona, and Utah. There are a few towns on the reservation, but for the most part it is a vast area of stark pinnacles, colorful rock formations, high desert, and mountains. The tribe encourages tourism; write or call the **Navajo Nation Tourism Office** (Box 663, Window Rock, AZ 86515, ☎ 602/871–6659 or 602/871–7371, FAX 602/871–7381).

SANTA FE

With its crisp, clear air and bright, sunny weather, New Mexico's capital couldn't be more welcoming. Perched on a 7,000-ft-high plateau at the base of the Sangre de Cristo Mountains, Santa Fe is surrounded by the remnants of a 2,000-year-old Pueblo Indian civilization and filled with evidence of the Spanish, who founded the city as early as 1607. The rows of chic art galleries (Santa Fe claims to be the country's third most important art center, after New York and Los Angeles), smart restaurants, and shops selling Southwestern furnishings and apparel combine to make it uniquely appealing. Its population, an estimated 60,000, swells to nearly double that during the peak summer season and again in the winter when skiers arrive, lured by the challenging slopes of the Santa Fe Ski Area and those of nearby Taos Ski Valley.

Tourist Information

Santa Fe: Chamber of Commerce (510 N. Guadalupe St., Suite L, De Vargas Center N, 87504, ☎ 505/983–7317). Convention and Visitors Bureau (201 W. Marcy St., Box 909, 87504, ☎ 505/984–6760 or 800/777–2489, FAX 505/984–6679).

Arriving and Departing

By Plane

Albuquerque International Airport (☎ 505/842–4366), 65 mi southwest of Santa Fe, serves both cities. Major airlines link it with the rest of the country. **Mesa Airlines** (☎ 505/473–4118 or 800/637–2247) operates air-shuttle service between Albuquerque and **Santa Fe Municipal Airport** (☎ 505/473–7243).

By Car

Santa Fe is accessible from points north and south on I–25 or U.S. 84/285.

By Train

Amtrak's (☎ 800/872–7245) nearest station is in Lamy, 17 mi from Santa Fe (☎ 505/988–4511), to which it is linked by an Amtrak shuttle-bus service (☎ 505/982–8829 in Santa Fe).

By Bus

Texas New Mexico & Oklahoma Coaches (858 St. Michaels Dr., ☎ 505/471–0008).

Getting Around Santa Fe

The downtown area is easily maneuvered on foot. The city's new public bus system is limited in scale so you'll need a car to visit attractions in the outer reaches. Otherwise, public transportation in town is monopolized by **Capital City Cab Company** (☎ 505/438–0000).

Exploring Santa Fe

The heart of Santa Fe is its historic **Plaza.** Established as early as 1607 as the city's social and political hub, it was later the terminus of the Santa Fe Trail, where freight wagons unloaded after completing their arduous journeys. Today the Plaza is lined with shops, art galleries, and restaurants. Bordering the north side is the oldest public building in the United States: the Pueblo-style **Palace of the Governors,** which houses a **history museum** (☎ 505/827–6483; admission charged to visitors over 17; closed Mon. Jan.–Feb.). Under the building's portal, **Native American vendors** from area pueblos display and sell their wares. Across the street, the Pueblo Revival **Museum of Fine Arts** (107 W. Palace Ave., ☎ 505/827–4455; admission charged to visitors over 18; closed Mon. Jan.–Feb.) emphasizes the work of regional artists, including Georgia O'Keeffe, as well as the early painters of the Santa Fe and Taos art colonies. Across the street from the southeast corner of the Plaza is Santa Fe's landmark hotel, **La Fonda** (*see* Lodging, *below*).

A block east, the magnificent French Romanesque–style **St. Francis Cathedral** (231 Cathedral Pl., ☎ 505/982–5619) houses the crypt of its builder, Jean Baptiste Lamy, Santa Fe's first archbishop, and the 17th-century statue *La Conquistadora* (Our Lady of the Conquest), carried to Santa Fe by the Spanish explorer Don Diego de Vargas.

Across the street, in an expanded state-of-the-art facility in the renovated former post office, is the **Institute of American Indian Arts Museum** (108 Cathedral Pl., ☎ 505/988–6281; admission charged), which houses the more than 8,000-object National Collection of Contemporary Indian Art. Its paintings, photography, and traditional crafts showcase the work of students and teachers, past and present, of the prestigious **Institute of American Indian Arts,** which was founded as a one-room studio classroom in the early 1930s. Allan Houser, Fritz Scholder, Kevin Red Star, and Earl Biss are only a few of the top-flight Native American artists associated with the school.

A number of the city's sights trace the path of the **Old Santa Fe Trail.** The **Loretto Chapel** (211 Old Santa Fe Trail, ☎ 505/984–7971; admission charged) is known for the "Miraculous Staircase"—an engineering marvel many of the faithful consider to have been built by St. Joseph—that leads to the choir loft. The adobe **San Miguel Mission** (401 Old Santa Fe Trail, ☎ 505/983–3974), built in about 1625 by the Tlaxcala Indians and the oldest church still in use in the United States, houses the San Jose Bell, said to have been cast in Spain in 1356, and a number of priceless statues and paintings. **Barrio De Analco** (now called East De Vargas St.), lined with historic houses, is believed to be one of the oldest continuously inhabited streets in the United States.

The fascinating **Museum of International Folk Art** (706 Camino Lejo, ☎ 505/827–6350; admission charged; closed Mon. in winter) is the premier museum of its kind in the world, with textiles, dolls, jewelry, ornaments, and other folk-art objects from many countries. Behind the museum is the privately owned **Wheelwright Museum of the American Indian** (704 Camino Lejo, ☎ 505/982–4636), housed in a building shaped like a traditional Navajo hogan and displaying works of all Native American cultures. The **Museum of Indian Arts and Culture** (708 Camino Lejo, ☎ 505/827–6344; admission charged; closed Mon. in winter) focuses on the history and contemporary culture of New Mexico's Pueblo, Navajo, and Apache tribes.

In the Vicinity

Situated on a rolling mesa at the base of the rugged Sangre de Cristo, about 60 mi northeast of Santa Fe, **Taos** is an enchanted town of romantic courtyards, stately elms and cottonwood trees, narrow streets, and adobe walls. It's also a world-famous art and literary center, and a popular ski resort in winter. The **Taos Pueblo**—2 mi north of the commercial center of Taos, at the base of the 12,282-ft-high Taos Mountain—is the home of the Taos Tiwa–speaking Indians, whose apartment house–style pueblo dwelling is one of the oldest continuously inhabited communities in the United States. A farming and ranching community of adobe houses, **Ranchos de Taos,** 4 mi south of town, has one of the most beautiful churches in the Southwest, which was painted numerous times by Georgia O'Keeffe. With its massive, buttressed adobe walls and graceful towers, the **San Francisco de Asis Church** is a revered sanctuary to local parishioners, as well as a prime example of early Mission architecture.

Just under 200 mi northwest of Santa Fe, in **Chaco Culture National Historical Park,** are the remains of 13 fully developed pueblos and about 400 smaller settlements. The most spectacular is Pueblo Bonito, the largest prehistoric Southwest Indian dwelling ever excavated. Its magnificent kivas, a 1,200-mi network of paved roads, and a solstice marker testify that the area was the highest point in the Anasazi culture, which peaked in about AD 1150. *Star Rte. 4, Box 6500, Bloomfield 87413, ☎ 505/988–6716 or 505/988–6727. Admission charged.*

Forty-five minutes northwest of Santa Fe, **Los Alamos,** birthplace of the atomic bomb, spreads over fingerlike mesas at an altitude of 7,300 ft. While research continues at the Los Alamos National Laboratory (in such fields as lasers, nuclear energy, superconductivity, and medicine), the area also abounds with interesting archaeological sites, including **Bandelier National Monument** (HCR1, Box 1, Suite 15, Los Alamos 87544, ☎ 505/672–3861; admission charged), featuring the remains of one of the largest Anasazi Indian civilizations.

About 25 mi southeast of Santa Fe, **Pecos National Historic Park** is the site of a once flourishing Indian pueblo. An early trading center, Pecos was the largest and easternmost pueblo reached by the Spanish conquistadors in 1541. Franciscan priests built a mission church here in the 1620s, but the pueblo was abandoned in 1838, presumably due to disease. *Box 418, Pecos 87552, ☎ 505/757–6032. Admission charged.*

Pueblos near Santa Fe

The Native American pueblos near Santa Fe vary in their craft specialties and the recreational facilities they offer to tourists. Most have ceremonial dances on feast days that are open to the public, but policies on taking photographs, tape recording, or sketching differ from pueblo to pueblo. Permission to visit is sometimes required, and in some cases admission is charged. Call ahead for regulations.

Jemez Pueblo (Box 100, Jemez 87024, ☎ 505/834–7359), the state's sole Towa–speaking pueblo, is noted for its polychrome pottery and fine yucca-frond baskets. The beautiful **San Jose de los Jemez Mission,**

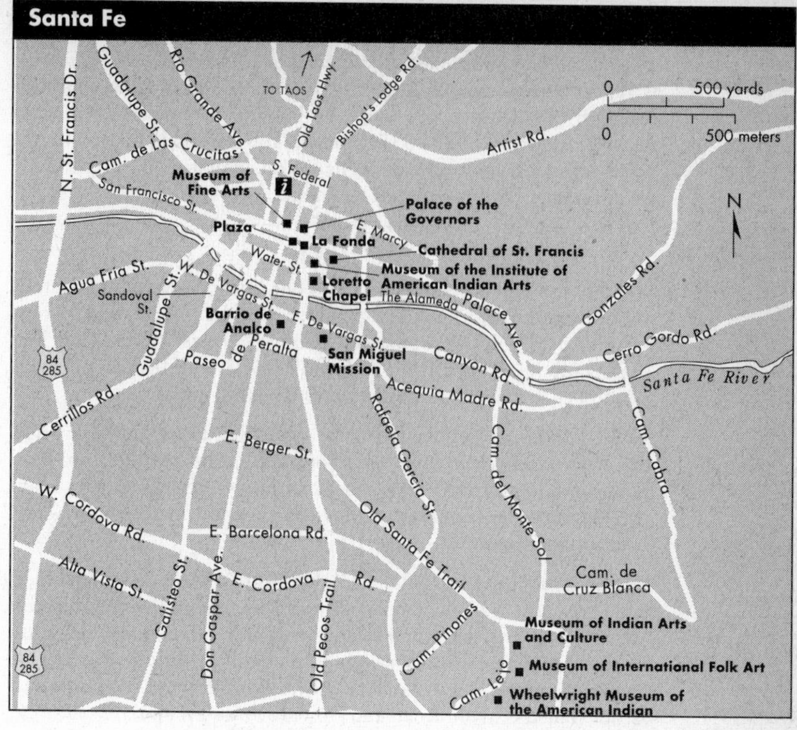

a great stone structure built in 1622, is at the Jemez State Monument (Box 143, Jemez Springs 87025, ☎ 505/829–3530) 13 mi north.

Pojoaque Pueblo (Rte. 11, Box 71, Santa Fe 87501, ☎ 505/455–2278) features a cultural center and museum for all Tewa-speaking Indian tribes (different from the Tiwa- and Towa-speaking tribes mentioned above). The pueblo also operates an official state tourist center, which offers an extensive selection of northern New Mexican Indian arts and crafts.

San Ildefonso Pueblo (Rte. 5, Box 315-A, Santa Fe 87501, ☎ 505/455–2273) was the home of the most famous of all pueblo potters, Maria Martinez, whose exquisite polished black-on-black pottery is revered among collectors. The pueblo still boasts a number of highly acclaimed potters, as well as other artists and craftspeople, many of whom open their homes to prospective buyers. San Ildefonso is one of the more active pueblos in maintaining its ceremonial dances and customs.

The picturesque **San Juan Pueblo** (Box 1099, San Juan 87566, ☎ 505/852–4400) is headquarters of the Eight Northern Indian Pueblos Council. In its beautiful arts center, the Oke Oweenge Crafts Cooperative, the pueblo's distinctive redware and micaceous clay pottery can be purchased. Two handsome kivas, a New England–style church, and a restaurant complete this largest of New Mexico's Tewa-speaking landmarks.

Santa Clara Pueblo (Box 580, Espanola 87532, ☎ 505/753–7326) is the home of the beautiful 740-room **Puye Cliff Dwellings,** a national landmark. It is also famous for its shiny red-and-black engraved pottery and for its many well-known painters and sculptors. Pueblo tours are offered on weekdays.

What to See and Do with Children

The **Museum of International Folk Art** (*see* Exploring Santa Fe, *above*) is a great place to take children any day, but its **Saturdays Are for Kids** program is especially fun. **Santa Fe Children's Museum** (1050 Old Pecos Trail, ☎ 505/989–8359), one of the few attractions Santa Fe offers for small children, features hands-on exhibits in the arts and sciences that are both fun and educational.

Shopping

Santa Fe has 150 art galleries and no one knows how many painters; the Convention and Visitors Bureau (*see* Tourist Information, *above*) has a full listing. The *Wingspread Collector's Guide* (Wingspread, Box 13566, Albuquerque 87192, ☎ 505/292–7537 or 800/873–4278) is a good bet if you are seriously interested in buying art here.

People also come to the city to buy something called Santa Fe Style, characterized by clean lines and strong colors and including an eclectic blend of items from various local cultures—everything from Spanish Mission–style furniture to Mexican tinwork mirrors and Native American blankets.

Canyon Road, once an Indian trail that led to distant Pecos Pueblo, is Santa Fe's most famous shopping district. **Downtown,** an approximately five-block district with the Plaza at its center, offers a mix of shops, galleries, and restaurants ranging from the eclectic to the cliché. **Guadalupe Street,** a few blocks southwest of the Plaza, has in the past decade joined Canyon Road and Downtown as a major area to stroll, browse, and shop.

Santa Fe's Wild West era is alive and well in the many stores that feature Western wear and memorabilia. **Jane Smith Ltd.** (122 W. San Francisco St., ☎ 505/988–4775) showcases pricey but exquisite handmade men's and women's Western wear. **Santa Fe Western Mercantile** (6820 Cerrillos Rd., ☎ 505/471–3655) offers a seemingly inexhaustible supply of hats, boots, jeans, buckles, and belts. **Trader Jack's Flea Market** (7 mi north of Santa Fe on U.S. 84/285) has a wide variety of vintage and contemporary Western bargains from roughly Easter to Thanksgiving, weather permitting.

Montecristi Custom Hat Works (118 Gallisteo St., ☎ 505/983–9598) is where the smart set goes for custom-made straw Panama hats. Felt toppers with bejeweled and unusual (rattlesnake skin) hatbands are also featured.

Sports and the Outdoors

Horseback Riding

Bishop's Lodge (Bishop's Lodge Rd., ☎ 505/983–6377). **Santa Fe Detours** (100 E. San Francisco St., ☎ 505/983–6565 or 800/338–6877).

Hot-Air Ballooning

Rocky Mountain Tours (1323 Paseo de Peralta, ☎ 505/984–1684 or 800/231–7238).

River Rafting

New Wave Rafting Company (107 Washington Ave., ☎ 505/984–1444 or 800/984–1444). **Los Rios River Runners** (Box 2734, Taos 87571, ☎ 505/776–8854 or 800/544–1181, FAX 505/776–1842). **Santa Fe Rafting Company and Outfitters** (☎ 505/988–4914 or 800/467–7238).

Ski Areas

Ski New Mexico (1210 Luisa St., Suite 8, Santa Fe 87501, ☎ 505/982–5300) and **Santa Fe Central Reservations** (320 Artist Rd., ☎ 505/983–8200 or 800/982–7669) provide information on skiing in the area.

Cross-Country

Carson National Forest (Box 558, Taos 87571, ☎ 505/758–6200) has 440 mi of trails. **Enchanted Forest Cross-Country Ski Area** (Box 521, Red River 87558, ☎ 505/754–2374) near Taos has 18 mi of trails. The **New Mexico Ski Touring Club** (☎ 505/821–0309 or 505/988–6940) maintains an extensive trail system and organizes ski tours on weekends.

Downhill

Northern New Mexico offers five **downhill** ski resorts within a 90-mi radius, with Taos hailing as one of the premier ski areas in the world. **Angel Fire Resort** (Drawer B, Angel Fire 87710, ☎ 505/377–6401 or 800/633–7463), 2,180-ft drop, 59 trails, 6 lifts. **Red River Ski Area** (Box 900, Red River 87558, ☎ 505/754–2382), 1,600-ft drop, 44 trails, 7 lifts. **Santa Fe Ski Area** (1210 Luisa St., Suite 10, Santa Fe 87505, ☎ 505/982–4429 or 505/983–9155), 1,650-ft vertical drop, 38 trails, 7 lifts. **Sipapu Lodge and Ski Area** (Box 29, Vadito 87579, ☎ 505/587–2240), 865-ft drop, 19 trails, 3 lifts. **Taos Ski Valley** (Box 90, Taos Ski Valley 87525, ☎ 505/776–2291), 2,612-ft drop, 72 trails, 11 lifts.

Spectator Sports

Horse Racing

Santa Fe Downs (off I–25, 20 mi south of Santa Fe, ☎ 505/471–3311; mid-June–Labor Day).

Dining

A delicious mixture of Pueblo Indian, Spanish, Mexican, and American-frontier cooking, Santa Fe cuisine is like none other. The city has nearly 200 restaurants to suit all tastes and budgets, from a riot of fast-food outlets on the outskirts, particularly along Cerrillos Road, to elegant (and often pricey) spots Downtown. For price ranges, see Chart 1 (B) in On the Road with Fodor's.

Santa Fe

$$–$$$$ ★ **Coyote Cafe.** Formerly a Greyhound bus depot, this is now one of the trendiest spots in town, thanks to the cheerful ambience and an imaginative menu, which changes daily. Northern New Mexican offerings include a 26-ounce rib-eye steak called the Cowboy, served with barbecued black beans and red chile-dusted onion rings. *132 W. Water St., ☎ 505/983–1615. Reservations required. AE, D, DC, MC, V.*

$$$ ★ **The Compound.** This restaurant shimmers with Old World elegance. The American-Continental menu includes chicken in champagne, roast loin of lamb, Russian caviar, and New Zealand raspberries. *653 Canyon Rd., ☎ 505/982–4353. Reservations required. Jacket and tie required. AE. Closed Sun.–Mon. No lunch.*

$$$ ★ **Pink Adobe.** One of the best-known restaurants in town, the Pink Adobe serves Continental, New Orleans Creole, and local New Mexican favorites in several cozy dining rooms in a three-century-old adobe. *406 Old Santa Fe Trail, ☎ 505/983–7712. Reservations required. AE, D, DC, MC, V.*

$$–$$$ **Cafe Escalera.** The menu at this popular spot changes daily and features such fresh Mediterranean-influenced fare as a fried oyster sandwich. Order the matchstick potatoes, to be dipped in homemade ketchup. The sumptuous desserts are always homemade. *130 Lincoln Ave., ☎ 505/989–8188. Reservations required. AE, MC, V.*

$$–$$$ ★ **Ristorante La Traviata.** Possibly the best restaurant in Santa Fe, this intimate eatery offers memorable regional Italian dishes in a simple but tasteful setting. Excellent appetizers like tuna carpaccio and Caesar salad gear diners up for even better entrées, including veal sautéed in a white wine cream sauce topped with fresh shaved Oregon truffles. The *tiramisù* dessert is heavenly. *95 W. Marcy St., ☎ 505/984–1091. Reservations required. AE, MC, V.*

$–$$$ ★ **Cafe Pasqual's.** Only a block southwest of the Plaza, this cheerful, informal place serves regional specialties and possibly the best breakfast in town. Forget the pancakes and order the corned beef hash or the *chorizo burrito* (Mexican sausages, scrambled eggs, home fries, and scallions wrapped in a flour tortilla and doused with red or green chile). Expect a line outside. *210 Don Gaspar Ave., ☎ 505/983–9340. Reservations required for dinner. AE, MC, V.*

$$ ★ **El Nido.** A favorite of Santa Fe Opera fans and performers, this institution has been serving in its cozy, firelit rooms for more than 50 years. The menu features seafood—including excellent broiled salmon and swordfish steak—as well as choice aged beef, prime rib, and New Mexican specialties. *U.S. 285, 10 mi north of Santa Fe to Tesuque exit, then ¼ mi more to restaurant, ☎ 505/988–4340. Reservations required. D, MC, V. Closed Mon.*

$$ **La Tertulia.** Almost as well known for its splendid Spanish Colonial art collection as for its fine New Mexican cuisine and extraordinary house sangria, this lovely restaurant is set in a converted 19th-century convent. *416 Agua Fria St., ☎ 505/988–2769. Reservations required. AE, D, MC, V. Closed Mon.*

$$ **Ore House on the Plaza.** This restaurant is perfectly located, with a dining balcony overlooking the Plaza. Seafood and steaks are artfully prepared; margaritas come in 80 flavors. *50 Lincoln Ave., ☎ 505/983–8687. Reservations required. AE, MC, V.*

$–$$ **Plaza Café.** This busy-beehive restaurant has been a fixture on the Plaza since 1918. From all appearances, the decor hasn't changed much since then—a red leather banquette, black Formica tables, tile floors, and vintage Santa Fe photos, all topped by a coffered tin ceiling. Standard American fare is featured, along with an interesting mix of Southwestern and Greek specialties; try the *huevos rancheros* (eggs over corn tortillas smothered with chile and cheese) or the Greek meat loaf. Choose from a good selection of beers and wines. *54 Lincoln Ave., ☎ 505/982–1664. No reservations. D, MC, V.*

$ **Guadalupe Cafe.** A favorite of locals, this informal café features New Mexican items, including any of a half-dozen enchiladas served with tasty red or green chile and sizable *sopaipillas* (fluffy fried bread). The raspberry pancakes are one of many breakfast favorites that keep diners crammed into the waiting area every morning. *313 Guadalupe St., ☎ 505/982–9762. D, MC, V.*

$ **The Shed.** Great homemade desserts and tasty New Mexican cuisine make this a favorite for lunch and Thursday, Friday, and Saturday dinners. Housed in a rambling adobe hacienda dating from 1692, the restaurant is decorated throughout with festive folk art. Try the red-chile enchiladas or *posole* (hominy stew), and definitely don't miss the mocha cake dessert. *113½ E. Palace Ave., ☎ 505/982–9030. No reservations. No credit cards. Closed Sun.*

Taos

$$$–$$$$ ★ **Brett House.** The former home and literary salon of Lady Dorothy Brett, friend and traveling companion of Frieda and D. H. Lawrence, offers

superb views of the Sangre de Cristo Mountains and excellent Southwestern and international cuisine. *Rtes. 7 and 150, ☏ 505/776–8545. Reservations required. MC, V.*

$$$ **Apple Tree.** Situated in a historic adobe Territorial house, this cozy and casual restaurant is a popular luncheon, early dinner, and Sunday brunch spot. A series of intimate dining rooms connected by open archways have pastel walls and wooden tables flanked with straw-seated chairs. Among the excellent entrées are mango chicken, enchiladas, shrimp quesadillas, and lamb steak (made from organically raised local lambs). Two homemade soups are prepared daily. *123 Bent St., ☏ 505/758–1900. Reservations required. D, MC, V.*

$$ ★ **Lamberts.** Established in 1989 in a remodeled Victorian house, this upscale restaurant has quickly become a local favorite. The menu changes according to what's available fresh from the market, and the results are always excellent. Entrées range from grilled lamb chops to grilled salmon with basil butter, and the wine list features an array of fine California vintages. *309 Paseo del Pueblo Sur, ☏ 505/758–1009. AE, DC, MC, V.*

$ **Bent Street Deli.** Featuring one of the best Reuben sandwiches this side of New York City, this small deli offers great soups, sandwiches, and desserts in a convenient location not far from Taos Plaza. Try the Taos sandwich: sliced turkey, fresh green chile, bacon, and guacamole, all rolled in a flour tortilla. *120 Bent St., ☏ 505/758–5785. MC, V.*

Lodging

Hotel rates, which fluctuate considerably from place to place, are generally lower from November through April (excluding the Thanksgiving and Christmas holidays), after which they soar. B&Bs in Santa Fe and Taos often offer less expensive—and usually charming—accommodations (**Bed and Breakfast of New Mexico,** Box 2805, Santa Fe 87504, ☏ 505/982–3332). For price ranges, see Chart 2 (A) in On the Road with Fodor's.

Santa Fe

$$$$ **Eldorado Hotel.** One of the city's most luxurious hotels, the Eldorado, in the heart of downtown, has rooms furnished in Southwestern style. Many have balconies, and all offer mountain views. The Old House restaurant is above average. *309 W. San Francisco St., 87501, ☏ 505/988–4455 or 800/955–4455, FAX 505/988–4455 ext. 143. 219 rooms. Facilities: 2 restaurants, bar, pool, nightly entertainment, shopping arcade. AE, D, DC, MC, V.*

$$$$ ★ **Inn of the Anasazi.** One of Santa Fe's newest hotel showpieces offers rooms with beamed ceilings, kiva fireplaces, and handcrafted furnishings. Amenities include concierge service and an amazing restaurant featuring innovative takes on local and regional cuisine. *113 Washington Ave., 87501, ☏ 505/988–3030 or 800/688–8100, FAX 505/988–3277. 51 rooms, 8 suites. Facilities: restaurant, wine cellar. AE, D, DC, MC, V.*

$$$–$$$$ ★ **La Fonda.** The oldest hotel in Santa Fe, this may be the only hotel in the world that can boast having had both Kit Carson and John F. Kennedy as guests. Each room is unique, featuring hand-carved and painted Spanish Colonial–style furniture and motifs painted by local artists. *100 E. San Francisco St., 87501, ☏ 505/982–2952 or 800/523–5002, FAX 505/988–2952. 160 rooms, 35 suites. Facilities: restaurant, lounge, bar, pool, spa. AE, D, DC, MC, V.*

$$$–$$$$ **La Posada de Santa Fe.** This Victorian-era inn near the Plaza sits on 6 acres of beautifully landscaped gardens and expansive green lawns. Most rooms—20 of which are separate bungalows—have fireplaces, beamed

ceilings, and Native American rugs; five rooms in the main building are drenched in Victorian decor. *330 E. Palace Ave., 87501, ☎ 505/986–0000 or 800/727–5276, FAX 505/982–6850. 119 rooms. Facilities: restaurant, bar, pool, health-club privileges. AE, DC, MC, V.*

$$–$$$$ **Territorial Inn.** This elegantly remodeled, 100-year-old Victorian home is just one block north of the Plaza. Some rooms have their own fireplaces, and a hot tub is enclosed in a gazebo in the back garden. *215 Washington Ave., 87501, ☎ 505/989–7737, FAX 505/986–9212. 10 rooms. MC, V.*

$$$ **Inn of the Governors.** This unpretentious inn is two blocks from the Plaza and one of the nicest hotels in town. Standard rooms have a Mexican theme, with bright colors, hand-painted folk art, Southwestern fabrics, and handmade furnishings. *234 Don Gaspar Ave. (at Alameda St.), 87501, ☎ 505/982–4333 or 800/234–4534, FAX 505/989–9149. 100 rooms. Facilities: restaurant, piano bar, pool, parking. AE, DC, MC, V.*

$$–$$$ **Hotel Santa Fe.** Owned by the Picuris Pueblo Indians, this 1991 hotel—the largest off-reservation Indian-owned hotel in the country—offers rooms decorated in traditional Southwestern style. Its gift shop offers works of Picuris and other Pueblo Indian artists at prices lower than those of most nearby retail stores, and guests get an additional 25% discount. *1501 Paseo de Peralta, 87504, ☎ 505/982–1200 or 800/825–9876, FAX 505/984–2211. 40 rooms, 91 suites. Facilities: bar, deli. AE, D, DC, MC, V.*

Taos

$$–$$$$ **Sagebrush Inn.** Graceful portals, romantic patios, and charming adobe architecture make this one of the prettiest hotels in town. Many of the rooms have kiva fireplaces; some have balconies looking onto the mountains. Georgia O'Keeffe once lived and painted here. *S. Santa Fe Rd., Rte. 68, Box 557, 87571, ☎ 505/758–2254 or 800/428–3626, FAX 505/758–5077. 80 rooms. Facilities: 2 restaurants, lounge, nightly entertainment, pool, spas, tennis courts. AE, D, DC, MC, V.*

$$$ ★ **Hotel La Fonda de Taos.** Built in 1937, La Fonda catered to European and American celebrities in its heyday. Today it is well past its prime, but the locale—on the south side of Taos's Plaza—is ideal and the experience of staying there enchanting. The lobby is a showcase of framed newspaper and magazine stories, posters, photos, paintings, and Native American artifacts. In the office of owner Saki Karavas is one of Taos's most celebrated "treasures," a collection of erotic paintings by Taos resident D. H. Lawrence that were banned in England in 1929; a fee of $3 gets you in for a peek. *108 S. Plaza, 87571, ☎ 505/758–2211 or 800/833–2211, FAX 505/758–8508. 23 rooms. AE, MC, V.*

$$$ **Taos Inn.** Only steps from the Plaza, this sprawling hotel is a prized local landmark—parts of the structure date from the 1600s—exemplifying rustic Southwestern charm. Guest rooms are individually furnished, featuring Southwestern motifs; Indian-style, wood-burning fireplaces; and furniture built by local artists. *125 Paseo del Pueblo Norte, 87571, ☎ 505/758–2233 or 800/826–7466, FAX 505/758–5776. 39 rooms. Facilities: restaurant, bar, lounge, library, wine shop. AE, DC, MC, V.*

$$–$$$ ★ **Mabel Dodge Luhan House.** This Pueblo Indian–style structure, set on spectacular grounds, was the home of heiress and Taos socialite Mabel Dodge Luhan. The 12 guest rooms in the main house boast Italian influences and are furnished with turn-of-the-century pieces; rooms in the newer guest house have regional hand-carved furnishings. *242 Morada La., 87571, ☎ 505/758–9456 or 800/846–2235, FAX 505/751–0431. 19 rooms (6 share baths). MC, V.*

$ **Koshari Inn.** Nestled under centuries-old silver aspens in the foothills of Taos Canyon is this beautifully converted former motel. Rooms are spacious, with handmade furnishings; each has a private entrance. *1.8 mi east of the Plaza on Kit Carson Rd., Box 6612, 87571, ☎ 505/758–7199. 12 units. Facility: pool. MC, V.*

Resorts

$$$$ ★ **Rancho Encantado.** This elegantly casual 168-acre resort offers a full range of activities in the piñon-covered hills above the sprawling Rio Grande Valley. Guest rooms have fine Spanish and Western antiques; some have fireplaces and/or private patios. The restaurant also serves Western-style fare. *Rte. 592, near Tesuque, 8 mi north of Santa Fe (Rte. 4, Box 57C), 87504, ☎ 505/982–3537 or 800/722–9339, FAX 505/983–8269. 12 rooms, 10 suites, 30 2-bedroom condos. Facilities: restaurant, 2 pools, spa, tennis, horseback riding, hiking, jogging. AE, D, DC, MC, V.*

$$$–$$$$ ★ **Austing Haus.** This enormous timber-frame building offers stunning views of the Taos Ski Valley from its glass-paneled front. Guest rooms are spare and functional, and the dining room is excellent. *Taos Ski Valley Rd. (Rte. 150), Box 8, Taos 87525, ☎ 505/776–2649 or 800/748–2932. 36 rooms, 8 suites, 4 chalets. Facilities: restaurant, 3 hot tubs, satellite TV. D, MC, V.*

$$$–$$$$ **Bishop's Lodge.** Three miles north of downtown Santa Fe, in the rolling foothills of the Sangre de Cristo Mountains, this incredible 1,000-acre resort was the retreat of Jean Baptiste Lamy, the first archbishop of Santa Fe. Guests stay in 11 one- and three-story lodges. The dining room is one of the area's best. *Bishop's Lodge Rd., Santa Fe 87504, ☎ 505/983–6377 or 800/732–2240, FAX 505/989–8739. 88 rooms. Facilities: restaurant, bar, pool, whirlpool, horseback riding, hiking, skeet shooting, tennis, golf, supervised children's programs. AE, D, MC, V.*

$$–$$$$ **Quail Ridge Inn Resort.** Five miles north of Taos Plaza, the Quail Ridge Inn condominium resort offers a touch of modern elegance against a magnificent natural backdrop. What it lacks in rustic charm it makes up for in a host of recreational amenities, from organized trail rides to ski packages to hot-tub soaks. *Taos Ski Valley Rd. (Rte. 150), Box 707, Taos 87571, ☎ 505/776–2211 or 800/624–4448, FAX 505/776–2949. 115 rooms, 60 suites. Facilities: restaurant, lounge, fitness center, pool, hot tub, tennis courts, squash, volleyball. D, DC, MC, V.*

Campgrounds

La Bajada Welcome Center (La Bajada Hill, 13 mi southwest of Santa Fe on I–25, ☎ 505/471–5242) provides information on private campgrounds. The **Santa Fe National Forest** (1220 S. St. Francis Dr., Box 1689, 87504, ☎ 505/988–6940), right in the city's backyard, has public sites open from May through October. Inside the city, **Los Campos Recreation Vehicle Park** (3574 Cerrillos Rd., 87501, ☎ 505/473–1949) is the only full-service RV park within the city limits. Operated by the Tesuque Pueblo Indians, **Tesuque Pueblo RV Campground** (U.S. 285/Rte. 5, Box 360-H, Santa Fe, ☎ 505/455–2661) has hookups and tent sites.

The Arts and Nightlife

Check the entertainment listings in Santa Fe's daily newspaper, the *New Mexican,* or the weekly *Santa Fe Reporter,* published on Wednesdays, for special performances and events.

The Arts

Artistically and visually the city's crown jewel, the famed **Santa Fe Opera** (U.S. 285, ☎ 505/982–3855) is housed in a modern open-air amphitheater carved into a hillside 7 mi north of the city and features some of the world's best operatic voices. The **Santa Fe Symphony** (☎ 505/983–3530; Sept.–May) performs at Sweeney Center (201 W. Marcy St.). The **Santa Fe Pro Musica** (☎ 505/988–4640) plays at the Lensic Theater (211 W. San Francisco St.; Sept.–May). The **Santa Fe Chamber Music Festival** (☎ 505/983–2075; July–Aug.) brings an extraordinary array of internationally known musicians to the St. Francis Auditorium of the Museum of Fine Arts (in the Plaza).

Nightlife

The lounges, hotels, and night spots of Santa Fe offer a wide variety of entertainment options. **Badlands** (213 W. Alameda St., ☎ 505/820–2985) offers a mix of live and Deejay rock, disco, and alternative dance music. **El Farol** (808 Canyon Rd., ☎ 505/983–9912) features live blues, jazz, and folk entertainment in a rustic centuries-old abode. **Rodeo Nites** (2911 Cerrillos Rd., ☎ 505/473–4138) attracts a country-western crowd.

ALBUQUERQUE

A large city—its population is nearing the half-million mark—Albuquerque spreads out in all directions, with no apparent ground rules. The city seems as free-spirited as the hot-air balloons that take part in its annual October International Balloon Fiesta. Like the rest of New Mexico, Albuquerque blends its cultures—Native American, Spanish, and Anglo—well.

Albuquerque began as an important trade and transportation station on the Old Chihuahua Trail, an extension of the Santa Fe Trail that wound down into Mexico. The original four-block downtown, known as Old Town, is the city's tourist hub, with galleries and trendy Mexican and New Mexican restaurants.

Tourist Information

Albuquerque: Convention and Visitors Bureau (Springer Sq. Bldg., 121 Tijeras Ave. NE, Box 26866, 87125, ☎ 505/243–3696 or 800/284–2282).

Arriving and Departing

By Plane

Albuquerque International Airport (☎ 505/842–4366) is 5 mi south of downtown; the trip takes 10–15 minutes. Taxis charge about $7 (plus 50¢ for each additional rider). **Sun Tran** buses (☎ 505/843–9200), which cost 75¢, pick up at the sunburst signs about every 15 minutes.

By Car

I–25 enters Albuquerque from points north and south; I–44, from points east and west.

By Train

Amtrak (☎ 800/872–7245) serves **Albuquerque Station** (214 1st St. SW, ☎ 505/842–9650).

By Bus

Greyhound Lines: Transportation Center (300 2nd St. SW, ☎ 800/231–2222).

Exploring Albuquerque

Albuquerque sprawls in all directions, so you'll need transportation to get wherever you're going. Historic and colorful Rte. 66 is Albuquerque's Central Avenue, unifying, as nothing else, the diverse areas of the city—Old Town cradled at the bend of the Rio Grande, the University of New Mexico to the east, and Nob Hill, a lively strip of restaurants, boutiques, galleries, and shops, farther east. The river and the railroad tracks, running almost neck and neck and traversed by Central Avenue, divide the city into quadrants: SW, NW, SE, NE.

The city began in 1706, in Old Town, and tree-shaded **Old Town Plaza** remains the heart of Albuquerque's heritage. The **San Felipe de Neri Church** (2005 North Plaza NW, ☎ 505/243–4628), enlarged and expanded several times over the years, faces the plaza, its massive adobe walls and other original sections intact. Most of the old adobe houses surrounding the plaza have been converted into shops, galleries, and restaurants.

The striking 1986 glass-and-sand-colored **New Mexico Museum of Natural History** offers an active volcano, a frigid Ice Age cave, dinosaurs, and an Evolator (short for Evolution Elevator), a six-minute high-tech ride through 35 million years of New Mexico's geologic history. *1801 Mountain Rd. NW, ☎ 505/841–8837. Admission charged.*

A short drive north of Old Town, the **Indian Pueblo Cultural Center** holds the largest collection of Native American arts and crafts in the Southwest, a valuable resource for the study of the region's first inhabitants. The spectacular two-story center is owned and operated by the 19 Pueblo tribes of New Mexico, each of which has an alcove devoted to its arts and crafts. Free performances of ceremonial dances are given on most weekends and on special holidays. *2401 12th St. NW, ☎ 505/843–7270. Admission charged.*

For an overview of Albuquerque—and half of New Mexico, for that matter—head for **Sandia Crest,** the 10,678-ft summit of the Sandia Mountains. **Sandia Peak Aerial Tramway,** the world's longest aerial tramway, makes an awesome 2.7-mi climb from a point outside the city limits to the top of Sandia Peak. At sunset the desert skies are a kaleidoscope of colors. *10 Tramway Loop NE, ☎ 505/296–9585 or 505/298–8518. Admission: $12.50 adults, $9.50 senior citizens and children 5–12. Closed weekdays 2nd and 4th wks of Apr.*

In the Vicinity

So named because early 19th-century settlers believed they had stumbled upon the Halls of Montezuma, **Aztec Ruins National Monument,** a 3½- to 4-hour drive northwest of Albuquerque, contains 500 rooms laid out in an E-shaped plan around a plaza. Archaeologists restored the 12th-century Great Kiva to mint condition in 1934. *U.S. 550, Box 640, Aztec 87410, ☎ 505/334–6174. Admission charged.*

Coronado State Monument and Park, a prehistoric Indian pueblo once known as Kuaua, sits on a bluff overlooking the Rio Grande near Bernalillo, 20 mi north of Albuquerque, and is believed to have been the headquarters of Coronado's army of 1,200, who came seeking the legendary Seven Cities of Gold in 1540. *Off I–25 on Rte. 44, Box 95, Bernalillo 87004, ☎ 505/867–5589 or 505/867–5351. Admission charged.*

About 160 mi southeast of Albuquerque—near the cemetery, just off Rte. 212, where Billy the Kid is buried, and the adjacent museum devoted to him—**Fort Sumner State Monument** displays artifacts and photographs relating to the fort and the Bosque Redondo Reservation. At the latter, 9,000 Navajos and Mescalero Apaches were interned from 1863 to 1868, brought to the site by Kit Carson after the infamous "Long Walk" from their original homeland in Canyon de Chelly, Arizona. *Off I–40 and U.S. 84, Box 356, Ft. Sumner 88119,* ☎ *505/355–2573. Admission charged. Closed Tues.–Wed.*

At the site of five extinct volcanoes, 8 mi west of Albuquerque, **Petroglyph National Monument** contains more than 17,000 ancient rock drawings, inscribed on the 17-mi-long West Mesa escarpment as early as AD 1300. *6900 Unser Blvd. NW, Albuquerque 87120,* ☎ *505/897–8814. Parking charge.*

Pueblos near Albuquerque

A series of terraced adobe pueblos, dominated by the massive mission church of San Estevan del Rey, **Acoma** (Box 309, Acoma 87034, ☎ 505/252–1139), also known as Sky City, sits atop a 367-ft mesa that rises abruptly from the valley floor 64 mi west of Albuquerque. Its one-time population of several thousand has dwindled to a mere 50 who live in the village without electricity or running water. This pueblo may be visited on guided tours only, and visitors can buy the tribe's prized thin-shelled pottery from pueblo artists.

The **Santo Domingo Pueblo** (Box 99, Santo Domingo 87052, ☎ 505/465–2214), off I–25 at the Santo Domingo exit between Albuquerque and Santa Fe, operates a Tribal Cultural Center, where its outstanding *heishi* (shell) jewelry is sold. The August 4 Corn Dance is one of the most colorful and dramatic of all the Pueblo ceremonial dances.

The sun symbol appearing on the New Mexican flag was adopted from the **Zia Pueblo** (135 Capital Square Dr., San Ysidro 87053-6013, ☎ 505/867–3304), at its present site (40 mi northwest of Albuquerque) since the early 1300s. Skillful Zia potters produce fine polychrome wares, and the watercolors of the tribe's painters are highly prized.

What to See and Do with Children

At the **Old Coal Mine Museum** (Madrid Star Rte., Madrid 87010, ☎ 505/473–0743), about 30 mi north of Albuquerque, children love exploring the mine tunnel, climbing aboard a 1906 steam train, and nosing through antique buildings. Sprawled over 60 acres, Albuquerque's **Rio Grande Zoological Park** (903 10th St. SW, ☎ 505/843–7413) is home to more than 1,300 animals from around the world, including a rare snow leopard. The **Tinkertown Museum** (Rte. 536, Sandia Park, ☎ 505/281–5233) houses a delightful world of miniature carved-wood characters, including an animated Western village and a tiny circus.

Shopping

As in most large, sprawling western cities, Albuquerque's main shopping areas are malls and shopping centers. Hours are generally weekdays 10–9, Saturday 10–6, and Sunday noon–6.

Among the major shopping centers are **Coronado Center** (Louisiana and Menaul Blvds., ☎ 505/881–2700), New Mexico's largest mall; **Fashion Square** (1100 San Mateo Blvd., ☎ 505/265–6931); **First Plaza Galeria** (20 First Plaza NW, ☎ 505/242–3446); and **Winrock Center** (Louisiana Blvd. exit off I–40, ☎ 505/883–6132). The **Antique Specialty Mall** (4516 Central Ave. SE, ☎ 505/268–8080) specializes in memorabilia from the early 1880s to the 1950s. **Nob Hill,** a seven-block strip stretching along Central Avenue from Girard to Washington streets, is the city's newest and trendiest shopping district. Neon-lighted boutiques, restaurants, galleries, and performing arts spaces encourage plenty of strolling and people-watching.

Sports and the Outdoors

Contact the **Albuquerque Parks and Recreation Department** (400 Marquette NW, Box 1293, Albuquerque 87103, ☎ 505/768–3490) for information on its network of parks and recreational programs, including golf courses, paved tracks for biking and jogging, swimming pools, tennis courts, ball fields, playgrounds, and even a shooting range.

Hot-Air Ballooning

Reliable firms include **Braden's Balloons** (3212 Stanford NE, ☎ 505/281–2714) and **World Balloon Corporation** (4800 Eubank NE, ☎ 505/293–6800).

The **Albuquerque International Balloon Fiesta** (8309 Washington Pl. NE, 87113, ☎ 505/821–1000) attracts more than 650 hot-air balloons each October in the world's largest gathering of balloonists. An estimated 1.5 million people attend the nine-day aerial extravaganza to watch as the balloons float over Albuquerque's backyards.

Dining

Many of Albuquerque's favorite dining spots specialize in northern New Mexico–style cooking, but French, Continental, Mediterranean, Italian, and standard American fare are also readily available. You can dress as casually as you like. Restaurants in the major business hotels tend to be a bit more formal. For price ranges, see Chart 1 (B) in On the Road with Fodor's.

$$$ **Nicole's.** This local favorite, in the Albuquerque Marriott, highlights creatively prepared dishes such as red chile fettuccine and sumptuous desserts including a chocolate macadamia nut pie. The setting is elegant and the service excellent. *2101 Louisiana NE, ☎ 505/881–6800. Reservations required. AE, D, DC, MC, V.*

$$–$$$ **Stephens.** This popular dining spot features an open, contemporary Southwestern look and an award-winning wine list. The classical menu includes delectable rack of lamb and piñon tequila chicken; a special spa menu is available for those who want to count calories. *1311 Tijeras Ave. NW, ☎ 505/842–1773. Reservations required. AE, DC, MC, V. No lunch weekends.*

$$ ★ **Artichoke Cafe.** In a turn-of-the-century brick building just east of downtown, the café offers New American, Italian, and some French dishes and specializes in broiled salmon, veal, and lamb. Its large modern dining room, decorated with the work of local artists, spills onto a small courtyard. *424 Central Ave. SE, ☎ 505/243–0200. Reservations required. AE, D, DC, MC, V. Closed Sun. No lunch Sat.*

$$ **Maria Teresa.** A restored 1840s adobe in Old Town furnished in handsome English antiques is the setting for this appealing restaurant. The menu offers aged beef, seafood, chicken, and New Mexican specialties, such as *carne adovada* (cubed pork marinated in red chile). *618 Rio Grande Blvd. NW, ☎ 505/242–3900. AE, DC, MC, V.*

$$ **Monte Vista Fire Station.** Now a national historic landmark, this spacious, airy restaurant was once a working firehouse. The New American menu includes a wide variety of seafood, beef, and pasta dishes; highlights are wild-mushroom ravioli and crab cakes. *3201 Central Ave. NE, ☎ 505/255–2424. AE, D, DC, MC, V. No lunch weekends.*

$$ ★ **Scalo Northern Italian Grill.** The trendy Nob Hill set gathers at this informal eatery to have first-rate dishes such as spinach fettuccini with grilled chicken breast, sun-dried tomatoes, and piñon nuts, or thin-crust pizza. An open kitchen is at the hub of this multilevel restaurant, which also features a full-service bar with fine Italian wines. *3500 Central Ave. SE, in the Nob Hill Business Center, ☎ 505/255–8781. Reservations required. AE, D, MC, V. No lunch Sun.*

$ **66 Diner.** This former transmission shop on old Rte. 66 is now a glitzy art deco establishment with black-and-white tile floors and turquoise-and-pink vinyl seats. Burgers, blue-plate specials—pot roast, chicken-fried steak, beef stew—and the separate soda fountain all add to the tone of 1950s nostalgia. *1405 Central Ave. NE, ☎ 505/247–1421. AE, D, MC, V.*

Lodging

Albuquerque's hotels offer a comfortable mix of modern conveniences and Old West flavor, with accommodations ranging from budget motels to bed-and-breakfasts to soaring hotel towers. All are uniformly friendly and folksy, and incorporate much of the Southwest heritage in their decor and design. For price ranges, see Chart 2 (B) in On the Road with Fodor's.

$$$ **Albuquerque Marriott.** This luxury property uptown near some of the city's best shopping areas is geared to vacationers as well as executive travelers. Furnishings are contemporary, with Southwest touches. *2101 Louisiana Blvd. NE, 87110, ☎ 505/881–6800 or 800/334–2086, FAX 505/888–2982. 411 rooms. Facilities: 2 restaurants, lounge, health club, 2 pools, free airport transfers. AE, D, DC, MC, V.*

$$$ **Hyatt Regency Albuquerque.** Adjacent to the Convention Center in the heart of downtown are the two soaring, desert-colored towers of this totally modern and luxurious hotel. The spacious guest rooms are finished in contemporary southwestern style with a mauve, burgundy, and tan color scheme. *330 Tijeras Ave. NW, 87102, ☎ 505/842–1234, FAX 505/766–6710. 395 rooms. Facilities: restaurant, 2 lounges, health club, outdoor pool. AE, D, DC, MC, V.*

$$–$$$ ★ **Casas de Sueños.** Long a gathering spot for artists and now a bed-and-breakfast on a 2-acre compound adjacent to Old Town, "Houses of Dreams" offers casitas attractively decorated with beehive fireplaces, pigskin furniture, regional paintings, and Native American rugs. *310 Rio Grande Blvd. SW, 87104, ☎ 505/247–4560 or 800/242–8987, FAX 505/842–8493. 17 casitas. AE, D, DC, MC, V.*

$$–$$$ **La Posada de Albuquerque.** Opened by Conrad Hilton in 1939 (he honeymooned here with Zsa Zsa), this historic hotel in the heart of downtown oozes charm and character. Native American war-dance murals ornament the wall behind the reception desk. The guest rooms vary in size from small to spacious and are decorated with Southwest and Native American themes; many have fireplaces. *125 2nd St. NW, 87102, ☎ 505/242–9090 or 800/777–5732, FAX 505/242–8664. 114 rooms. Facilities: 2 restaurants, bar, gift shop, free airport and Old Town transfers. AE, D, DC, MC, V.*

$$–$$$ **William E. Mauger Estate.** In this elegant downtown 1897 Queen Anne residence, four guest rooms are Victorian style, the other two art deco. Full breakfasts are served in guests' rooms or in the parlor. *701 Roma Ave. NW, 87102, ☎ 505/242–8755. 8 rooms. AE, DC, MC, V.*

$$ **Radisson Inn.** This two-story motor hotel at the airport has a southwestern-Spanish flavor, with arched balconies, desert colors, a courtyard pool, and indoor and outdoor dining. The guest rooms are comfortable, if not luxurious. *1901 University Blvd. SE, 87106, ☎*

505/247–0512, FAX 505/843–7148. 157 rooms. Facilities: restaurant, lounge, outdoor pool, spa, free airport transfers. AE, D, DC, MC, V.

$ **University Lodge.** Located in the middle of Nob Hill, six blocks east of the University of New Mexico, this small hotel has standard furnishings and is clean and comfortable. *3711 Central Ave. NE, ☎ 505/266–7663. 52 rooms. Facilities: outdoor pool. AE, D, DC, MC, V.*

Campgrounds

Fifteen minutes south of Albuquerque on I–25, the **Isleta Lakes and Recreation Area** (Box 383, Isleta 87022, ☎ 505/877–0370) has complete campground facilities with tent sites and RV hookups. Within the city limits, **Albuquerque KOA Central** (12400 Skyline Rd. NE, 87123, ☎ 505/296–2729) and **Albuquerque North KOA** (555 S. Hill Rd., Bernalillo 87004, ☎ 505/867–5227) have tent sites and RV hookups.

The Arts and Nightlife

To find out what's on in town, check the *Albuquerque Journal* on Friday and Sunday or the *Albuquerque Tribune* on Thursday.

The Arts

The **New Mexico Symphony Orchestra** (3301 Menaul NE, Suite 4, ☎ 505/881–8999) is the state's largest performing arts organization.

Nightlife

El Rey Theatre (624 Central Ave. SW, ☎ 505/243–7546) presents live blues, rock, alternative, jazz, metal, and country sounds in a renovated 1941 theater. **Dingo Bar** (303 Gold Ave. SE, ☎ 505/243–0663) is a small downtown nightclub drawing big crowds with its live mix of jazz, blues, punk, pop, and world-beat dance offerings.

ELSEWHERE IN THE STATE

Carlsbad Caverns National Park

Getting There

In the southeastern part of the state, the park is 320 mi from Albuquerque via I–25, U.S. 380, and U.S. 285, and 167 mi west of El Paso, Texas, via U.S. 180. **Mesa Airlines** (☎ 800/637–2247; in Carlsbad, 505/885–0245) offers air-shuttle service between Albuquerque airport and **Cavern City Air Terminal** in Carlsbad.

What to See and Do

Carlsbad Caverns National Park (3225 National Parks Hwy., Carlsbad 88220, ☎ 505/785–2232 or 505/785–2233) contains one of the world's largest and most spectacular cave systems: 77 caves, with huge subterranean chambers, fantastic rock formations, and delicate mineral sculptures. Only two caves are open to the public. At **Carlsbad Cavern,** the descent to the 750-ft level is made by foot or elevator; either way, you can see the Big Room, large enough to hold 14 Houston Astrodomes. **New Cave** (☎ 505/785–2232; reservations required a day in advance), 25 mi from the main cavern, is much less accessible: The last few miles of the roadway are gravel, and the mouth of the cave is a ½-mi climb up a 500-ft rise.

The park is the area's main lure, but the town of **Carlsbad** (Chamber of Commerce, 302 S. Canal St., 88220, ☎ 505/887–6516) and such nearby attractions as **Living Desert State Park** (1504 Miehls Dr., Carlsbad 88220, ☎ 505/887–5516) are also well worth visiting.

Dining

For price ranges, *see* Charts 1 (B) and 2 (B) in On the Road with Fodor's.

$–$$ **Lucy's.** A family-owned oasis of great Mexican food, Lucy's is adorned in Southwestern decor. Here you can enjoy such items as chapa chicken chacos (chicken tacos with guacamole) and Tucson-style chimichangas (chicken, beef, or brisket with chili, cheese, and seasonings). *701 S. Canal St., ☎ 505/887–7714. MC, V.*

Lodging

$$ **Best Western Motel Stevens.** An old favorite with both locals and tour groups, this is a reliable, well-operated place. Guest rooms feature bright desert colors, mirrored vanities, and modern furnishings; some have kitchenettes and/or private patios. Be sure to visit the Silver Spur bar and lounge on Saturday night. *1829 S. Canal St., 88220, ☎ 505/887–2851 or 800/528–1234, FAX 505/887–6338. 202 rooms. Facilities: restaurant, lounge, pool. AE, D, DC, MC, V.*

TEXAS

By Mark Potok

Capital	Austin
Population	16,841,000
Motto	Friendship
State Bird	Mockingbird
State Flower	Bluebonnet

Visitor Information

Texas Department of Tourism (Box 5064, Austin 78763, ☎ 800/888–8839).

Scenic Drives

In far southwest Texas, **Rte. 170** from Lajitas through Presidio and into the Chinati Mountains is one of the most spectacular drives in the state, plunging over mountains and through canyons along the Rio Grande (thus its name, "El Camino del Rio," or River Road). **U.S. 83** from Leakey to Uvalde is a roller coaster of a ride through the lush western edges of the central Texas Hill Country. In the northern panhandle, **I-27** from Lubbock to Amarillo carries travelers through the buffalo grass and sheer cliffs of the Llano Estacado ("Staked Plain," so named because the lack of trees forced pioneers to tie their horses to stakes). From Center, a small town near the Louisiana border, south into the Sabine National Forest, **Rte. 87** takes you over several dramatic lakes and through one of the huge pine forests for which east Texas is famous.

National and State Parks

National Parks

Big Bend National Park (U.S. 385 from Marathon; Superintendent, Big Bend National Park 79834, ☎ 915/477–2291) is the state's premier natural attraction. This overwhelming landscape, laid bare by millions of years of erosion, includes spectacular canyons, a junglelike floodplain, the sprawling Chihuahuan Desert, and the cool woodlands of the Chisos Mountains. Spread out over 801,163 acres, Big Bend teems with animal life, from relatively rare black bears and mountain lions to coyotes, javelinas, gray foxes, beavers, deer, and jackrabbits. More than 430 bird species have been identified here, including such favorites as the roadrunner and such rarities as the Colima warbler. The park is crosshatched with hundreds of miles of trails, dirt roads, and paved roads and offers wild backcountry camping (with permits). For the more timid, there are ranger-led walks, campgrounds, a trailer park, and other amenities. River outfitters offer rafting trips through remote canyons of the Rio Grande (☎ 915/424–3219 or 800/545–4240 to reserve spots for longer trips).

Davy Crockett National Forest (Ratcliff Lake; 1240 E. Loop 304, Crockett, 75835, ☎ 409/544–2046)—a 161,500-acre park in the "piney woods" of east Texas about 20 mi east of the historic town of Crockett on Rte. 7—offers camping, canoeing on the Neches River, a dramatic 19-mi hiking trail, and picnicking facilities and concessions around Ratcliff Lake.

Aransas National Wildlife Refuge (Rte. 2040, Tivoli, ☎ 512/286–3559), on a peninsula jutting 12 mi into the Gulf of Mexico near Rockport, is the principal wintering ground of the endangered whooping crane. The best time to spot it and some 300 other species of birds is between November and March.

State Parks

You can call a central reservations number (☎ 512/389–8900) to book any campsite in the Texas state park system. **Caddo Lake State Park** (Rte. 43, ☎ 903/679–3351), on the southern shore of the lake near Karnack, offers camping, cabins, fishing, swimming, and boating.

Named after the local term for "high plains," **Caprock Canyons State Park** (Rte. 1065, Quitaque, ☎ 806/455–1492) in the panhandle is marked by canyons, striking geologic formations, and an abundance of wildlife, including African aoudad sheep, mule deer, and golden eagles.

Enchanted Rock State Park (Rte. 965, Llano, ☎ 915/247–3903), near Fredericksburg in the Hill Country, is so named because of the noises emitted by the underground heating and cooling of its massive, 500-foot-high dome of solid granite. The rock is the reputed site of ancient human sacrifices.

Fishing is king at **Inks Lake State Park** (Rte. 29 and Park Rd. 4, Barnet, ☎ 512/793–2223), northwest of Austin at the edge of the Hill Country. Surrounding the lake's crystal-clear waters are extensive amenities, including facilities for camping, trailers, boats, and golf.

Set on the High Plains east of the panhandle town of Canyon, **Palo Duro Canyon State Park** (Rte. 217 and Park Rd. 5, ☎ 806/488–2227) is a place of rock spires and precipitous cliffs, long a favorite spot for Texan tourists. When movie director Steven Spielberg was looking for the world's most dramatic sunset for 1989's *Indiana Jones and the Last Crusade,* he found it in Palo Duro Canyon near this park. The site of the last great battle with the Comanches, the park today offers an outdoor amphitheater backed by a 600-foot cliff, where the historical drama *Texas,* written by a local playwright, is presented late June through August (Mon.–Sat.; reservations recommended, ☎ 806/655–2181).

HOUSTON AND GALVESTON

The oil crash of the early 1980s hit once-flamboyant Houston as few other places in Texas, and the resulting strange contrast between the downtown's glass-and-steel magnificence and its boarded-up buildings may be the city's most noticeable feature; however, the city's economic pace has clearly quickened in recent years. Another cause of remarkable juxtapositions is a total lack of zoning—unique among major American cities—that has yielded such results as the shacks of the poverty-stricken Fourth Ward pushing hard up against the glittering skyscrapers built during the boom years. There have been several recent attempts to pass laws that would regulate development.

The nation's fourth-largest city is still an international business hub and the energy capital of the United States, a fact evidenced by the Texas-size conventions that occasionally fill its major hotels to bursting point. Its port still thrives, and its highways, while plentiful, can be nightmarish with roaring traffic. Large and varied foreign communities and a plenitude of fine ethnic restaurants and world-class cultural institutions lend Houston a distinct cosmopolitan flavor that Dallasites will claim but cannot capture. This is truly a city for city lovers.

Galveston, 50 mi to the southeast, is Houston's touristy stepchild. An island in the Gulf of Mexico, connected by causeway and bridge to the mainland, it is an odd mix of Victorian architecture and Coney Island–like beach developments. Although virtually all of its architecture dates from after 1900, when an unheralded hurricane and consequent tidal waves swept over this 32-mi-long sandbar, Galveston has managed to recapture a historic feel long lost to its northern neighbor. Once a faded has-been, the city is now enjoying a tourist-fueled renaissance evident in energetic renovation efforts. It is artsy, even precious, and well stocked with hotels and restaurants catering to visitors.

Tourist Information

Galveston Island: Convention & Visitors Bureau (2106 Seawall Blvd., in the Moody Center, ☎ 409/763–4311 or 800/351–4237; in TX, 800/351–4236), Strand Visitors Center (2016 Strand, ☎ 409/765–7834). **Greater Houston:** Convention & Visitors Bureau (801 Congress Ave., 77002, ☎ 713/227–3100 or 800/365–7575). Information booths are near the baggage areas at Hobby and Intercontinental airports.

Arriving and Departing

By Plane

Houston's two major airports are, between them, served by about 22 airlines. (Be sure to check which airport you will be using, as many airlines serve both.) **Southwest Airlines** (☎ 713/237–1221 or 800/435–9792) offers particularly extensive, frequent, and inexpensive service among nine Texas cities. More convenient to downtown is **W. P. Hobby Airport** (☎ 713/643–4597), 9 mi to the southeast. During rush hour, the trip into the city will take about 45 minutes; taxi fare runs about $20. **Houston Intercontinental Airport** (HIA; ☎ 713/230–3100), 15 mi north of downtown and closer to the Galleria area, is the city's international airport. The trip downtown during peak hours takes up to an hour; cab fare will run you up to $30. **Shuttles** (☎ 713/523–8888) to several Houston locations serve both Hobby ($10) and HIA ($15); **city express bus service** (☎ 713/635–4000) to HIA costs $1.20. **Galveston Limousine Service** (☎ 713/223–2256 in Houston; 409/765–5288 or 409/744–0563 in Galveston; 800/640–4820 in TX) offers hourly service to island locations from both Houston airports for $15–$18.

By Car

Houston is ringed by the I–610 beltway. A tighter loop, comprising several expressways, circles the downtown and provides remarkable views of the city, especially at dawn and dusk. Radiating out from these rings like spokes of a wheel are I–10, heading east to Louisiana and west to San Antonio; U.S. 59, northeast to Longview or southwest to Victoria; and I–45, southeast to Galveston (about an hour away) or north to Dallas. Traffic on all these highways can be extremely heavy during rush hours.

By Train

In Houston, **Amtrak** (☎ 713/224–1577 or 800/872–7245) trains run out of the old **Southern Pacific Station** (902 Washington Ave.).

Galveston's **Center for Transportation and Commerce** (2500 Strand, ☎ 409/765–5700) serves as the terminal for the **Texas Limited** (☎ 713/522–8895 or 800/374–7475), a rail line that connects to Houston's **Eureka Station** (567 T.C. Jester St.). Available for group charters only, the train has seven restored cars from the 1920s to the 1940s.

By Bus

Greyhound Lines (2121 Main St., Houston, ☎ 800/231–2222). **Texas Bus Lines** (49th St. and Broadway, Galveston, ☎ 409/765–7731).

Getting Around Houston and Galveston

Both Houston and Galveston almost demand cars. Attractions are spread out, and public transportation is sketchy. Houston has a city bus system (Metro, ☎ 713/635–4000), but it is difficult for visitors to learn its intricacies. Similarly, Galveston offers island bus service, but of far more interest is the **Treasure Island Tour Train** (2106 Seawall Blvd., ☎ 409/765–9564), which departs regularly from just outside the Convention & Visitors Bureau (*see* Tourist Information, *above*) for tours of local sights.

Exploring Houston and Galveston

Houston

Houston can be neatly divided into three major areas: (1) downtown, a homage to modernism that spurred one architecture critic to declare the city "America's future" and that includes the theater district; (2) an area a couple of miles south of downtown that includes some of the Southwest's leading museums, as well as Rice University and the internationally renowned Texas Medical Center; and (3) the ritzy shopping area west of downtown that is centered on the Galleria.

DOWNTOWN

You may want to start by taking in the entire urban panorama from the observation deck of I. M. Pei's **Texas Commerce Tower** (600 Travis St.; closed weekends), at 75 stories the city's tallest building and the world's highest composite tube tower. Nearby **Texas Street** is 100 feet wide, precisely the width needed to accommodate 14 Texas longhorns horn tip to horn tip in the days when cattle were driven to market along this route. Downtown's major attractions are clustered at this northwest corner, and you can get another perspective on the architecture that distinguishes the city by relaxing in **Tranquillity Park,** between Walker and Rusk streets east of Smith Street. This cool, human-scaled oasis of fountains and diagonal walkways among the skyscrapers was built to commemorate the first words of man on the moon: "Houston, Tranquillity Base here. The Eagle has landed." The plaque claiming that America has "the only system of government" capable of such a feat conveniently ignores *Sputnik* and the entire history of space exploration, but it is a true reflection of the city's bursting Texas chauvinism.

The park forms the threshold to the theater district, whose major buildings are a few steps away. The **Jesse H. Jones Hall for the Performing Arts** (615 Louisiana St.), home to the Houston Symphony Orchestra and the Society for the Performing Arts, is a huge hall that appears almost encased by a second, colonnaded building; its teak auditorium is more attractive than the exterior. The **Alley Theatre** (615 Texas Ave.), a fortresslike but innovative low-lying structure, is the venue of the city's only resident professional theater company. The **Gus S. Wortham Theater Center** (550 Prairie Ave.), where the Houston Grand Opera and the Houston Ballet perform in two side-by-side theaters, was completed in 1987. Just behind the Wortham, **Sesquicentennial Park** was built two years later as the first phase of a beautification of the shore of Buffalo Bayou, the minor body of water bounding downtown's north end. **City Hall** (901 Bagby St.), just northwest of Tranquillity Park, is an unremarkable building whose chief interest lies in its allegorical interior murals.

On the west side of downtown, running south from Tranquillity Park, is the **Smith–Louisiana corridor,** two daunting canyons formed by towers of glass and steel, most of which were erected before oil prices plunged

Houston

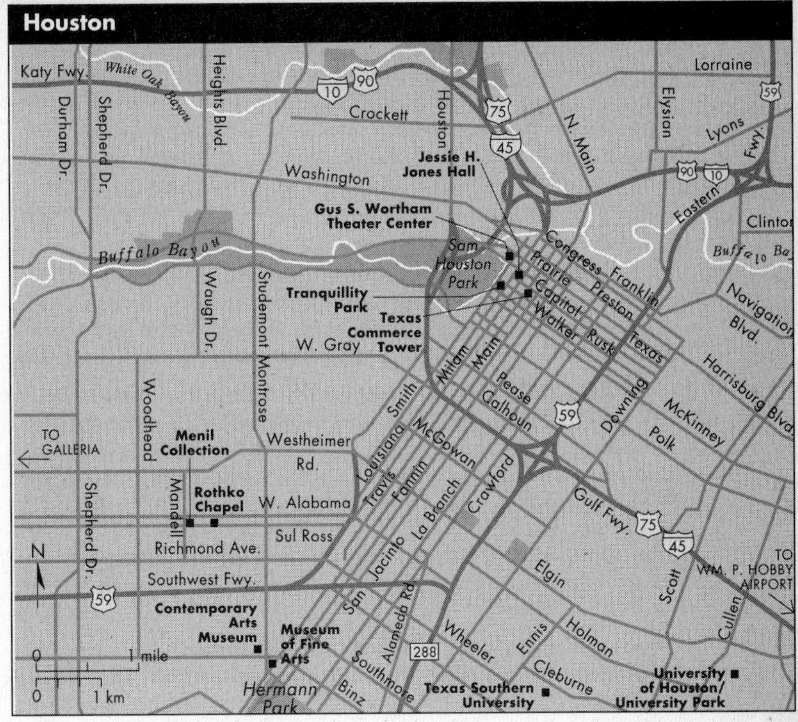

in 1983. A walk down these streets may be the truest measure of the city's modernism, intensified by the **outdoor sculptures** of Joan Miró, Claes Oldenburg, Louise Nevelson, and Jean Dubuffet. (Dubuffet's *Monument au Fantôme,* on Louisiana Street between Lamar and Dallas streets, is a particular delight to children.) The downtown area may leave you with an eerie sense of emptiness, but there is a good reason for that beyond the universal depopulation of America's urban centers: More than 70 of the major business and government buildings downtown are connected by a 6.7-mi labyrinth of **underground tunnels,** used by those in the know as a welcome escape from the humidity for which Houston is justly infamous.

A last stop downtown, particularly if you have children, might be the lobby of the **Hyatt Regency Houston** (1200 Louisiana St.). Garish and decorated with potted plants and brass aplenty, the lobby's atrium soars 30 stories, circled by balconies and topped by a revolving restaurant cocktail lounge. A ride up in the glass-enclosed cabs of the powerful elevators is dramatic, a sure winner with kids, and a trifle frightening.

THE MUSEUM DISTRICT

Four miles south of downtown on Main Street lies leafy **Rice University,** Texas's finest institution of higher learning; the **Texas Medical Center,** a sprawling complex best known for the famous M. D. Anderson Cancer Center; and the three world-class museums that are the city's cultural crown jewels.

The **Museum of Fine Arts'** collection is remarkable for its completeness, if exhausting in size. Housed in a complicated series of wings and galleries—many of which were designed by Ludwig Mies van der Rohe—the museum now also owns the **Bayou Bend Collection** of American decorative arts, housed across town in the River Oaks mansion neighborhood (1 Westcott St., ☎ 713/639–7758; tours by reservation only). Highlights of the museum's vast offerings include the Straus collection of Renaissance and 18th-century works and the notable Samuel Kress collection of Italian and Spanish Renaissance paintings. Impressionism is also well represented in such paintings as *The Rocks,* an 1888 van Gogh that prefigures some of the artist's later, more extravagant brush strokes. *1001 Bissonnet (north of Rice U.), between Montrose and Main Sts., ☎ 713/639–7300. Admission charged (free Thurs.). Closed Mon.*

The **Contemporary Arts Museum,** in an aluminum-sheathed trapezoid across the street, is the home of avant-garde art in Houston. It is noteworthy for the traveling exhibits that pass regularly through its spaces. *5216 Montrose St., ☎ 713/526–0773. Admission charged. Closed Mon.*

The **Menil Collection,** 10 minutes away by car on a small side street, is the city's biggest cultural surprise. Opened in 1987 in a spacious building designed by the Italian architect Renzo Piano, the museum's airy galleries contain treasures as diverse as tribal African sculpture and Andy Warhol's paintings of Campbell's soup cans. Also here are works by Léger, Picasso, Braque, and other major modern artists. Check out the wonderful Matisse cutouts, executed when the artist's eyes were failing and he could no longer paint. *1515 Sul Ross St., ☎ 713/525–9400. Closed Mon.–Tues.*

Just down the street is the moody **Rothko Chapel** (3900 Yupon St. at Sul Ross St., ☎ 713/524–9839), an octagonal sanctuary hung with 14 paintings by Mark Rothko. At first they appear as simple black panels; only when you come close can you see the subtle coloring. Outside the chapel, created as a site for religious meditation by all faiths, is Barnett Newman's sculpture *Broken Obelisk,* symbolizing the life and assassination of Martin Luther King, Jr.

THE GALLERIA AREA

On the west side of Houston, near the intersection of Westheimer Road and I–610, is the **Galleria,** one of the world's swankiest shopping malls. Here 4 major department stores and 300 shops groan with an abundance of fashionable apparel and other pricey goods; hundreds more stores and sumptuous restaurants line the surrounding streets. Foreign shoppers are known to travel to Houston for no other reason than to spend money at the Galleria. Several deluxe hotels are also found in the area, and River Oaks, a street of multimillion-dollar mansions, is conveniently nearby.

Galveston

History is the main draw in Galveston, a city that was once the largest in Texas. Its wealthy classes built the houses that are now being restored to their former glory in a frenzy of tourist-driven rehabilitation. These homes, and some beautifully restored iron-front commercial buildings, are concentrated on the northern, bay side of the island—especially along a street known as the Strand—and on Broadway, a boulevard that runs east–west through Galveston's midsection. Also hugging the north rim of the island, from 9th to 51st streets, is the harbor, port to about 100 small fishing boats and shrimp trawlers and to the *Elissa,* the tall ship that is Galveston's pride and joy. The south, ocean side of the island is lined with beaches (*see* Beaches, *below*), hotels, parks, and restaurants.

THE STRAND AND BROADWAY

The heart of historic Galveston—and the nucleus of its newfound prosperity—is the **Strand,** especially the five blocks that run from 25th to

20th Street (now on the National Register of Historic Places). When Galveston was still a powerful port city—before the Houston Ship Channel was dug, diverting most boat traffic inland—this stretch of former stores, offices, and warehouses was known as the Wall Street of the South.

At its foot is the **Center for Transportation and Commerce** (which also houses the **Railroad Museum,** 2500 Strand, ☎ 409/765–5700; admission charged), an art-deco building that was once the Santa Fe Railroad terminal. As you stroll up the street, you'll pass dozens of trendy shops—some of them quite beautiful—and the few four-and five-story iron-front buildings that have not yet been restored, where workers are busily scurrying about to bring in still more shops, restaurants, and bars. A block away is the **Tremont House,** a onetime dry-goods warehouse converted into a hotel that conjures up visions of coaches, top hats, and Victorian elegance. Today the hotel is the best on the island. Still, it's not hard to see how new all this redevelopment is: Just at the edges of this gilded renaissance, tawdry topless bars and windowless "clubs" beckon with signs like "Lipstick Lounge" and "Exotic Dancers."

A 20-minute walk or 5-minute drive to the south is Broadway, home of the "Broadway Beauties"—not employees of the above-mentioned lounges but, rather, three of the finest examples of historic restoration in Texas. The Victorian **Bishop's Palace** (1402 Broadway, ☎ 409/762–2475; admission charged; closed Tues.), listed on the National Register of Historic Places, was built in 1886 for Col. Walter Gresham. The man had a fondness for fireplaces, to which the 11 rare stone and wood mantels in the limestone-and-granite castle amply attest. The building's most outstanding feature, however, is the wooden main staircase, a work of art that took 61 craftsmen seven years to carve.

Ashton Villa (2328 Broadway, ☎ 409/762–3933; admission charged) is a formal Italianate villa built in 1859 of brick—appropriately so, as owner James Moreau Brown started out as a poor mason. A freethinking man, Brown had to install curtains to shield daintier guests from the naked Cupids painted on one wall. His daughter, Miss Bettie, was quite a liberated woman for her era, smoking cigars in public and raising money for the poor. Three blocks away is the 1894 **Moody Mansion** (2618 Broadway, ☎ 409/762–7668; admission charged), another brick mansion, with interiors of exotic woods and gilded trim. Taped voices replicate "typical" period conversations based on historical documents.

North of Broadway, the **East End Historical District** is a trove of wooden Victorian houses built for people somewhat less wealthy. Sealy and Ball streets are particularly lovely. For a sense of how the other half lived in this slaveholding society, stop by the twin "shotgun houses" at 1722–24 Winnie Street, typical of the way poor of all colors long lived in much of Texas.

THE ELISSA

In 1961, a marine archaeologist and naval historian named Peter Throckmorton spotted a rotting iron hulk in the shipyards outside Athens, Greece. While it looked much like hundreds of other Greek cargo ships, Throckmorton realized the 150-foot boat was what remained of a beautiful square-rigger constructed almost a century earlier, in 1877. Through successive owners, its bark rig had been cut down to a single cargo mast, its proud sailing bow sliced off to change its telltale profile during a spell as a smuggler. Today, after almost 20 years of work, the Scottish-built *Elissa*—the oldest ship on the Lloyd's Register—has been restored to its former glory by the Galveston Historical Foundation and hundreds of volunteers. The ship, which in the last century carried cargoes to Galveston Harbor, may be toured above and below decks and is the centerpiece of the **Texas Seaport Museum.** *Pier 21, ☎ 409/763–1877. Admission charged.*

Parks and Gardens

Houston

A short drive south of downtown on Main Street is **Hermann Park,** 545 acres of luxuriant trees, lawns, duck-graced reflecting pools, picnic areas, and an 18-hole golf course. Sitting on the northern perimeter of the Texas Medical Center, the park is also home to the Houston Zoo and the Museum of Natural Science (*see* What to See and Do with Children, *below*), the Garden Center, and the Miller Outdoor Theater. This park is the city's playground.

Memorial Park, several miles west of downtown, is 1,500 acres of mostly virgin woodland, a wonderful spot for walkers, joggers, and bikers.

The small downtown **Sam Houston Park,** bounded by Bagby, McKinney, and Dallas streets, preserves a few of the city's 19th-century buildings. Tickets for daily guided tours are available at the Heritage Society (☎ 713/655–1912), on the Bagby side.

Galveston

Stewart Beach Park (Seawall Blvd. at Broadway, ☎ 409/765–5023) offers a complete bathhouse, an amusement park, bumper boats, a miniature golf course, and even bungee jumping.

Toward the western, unpopulated end of the island, **Galveston Island State Park** (13 Mile Rd., ☎ 409/737–1222) is a 2,000-acre natural habitat ideal for birding and walking.

What to See and Do with Children

Houston

In Hermann Park, the Zoological Gardens, commonly known as the **Houston Zoo** (1513 N. MacGregor St., ☎ 713/525–3300), includes a petting zoo, an aquarium, and other attractions. In the same park, a miniature train and paddleboat rides are favorites with children. The excellent **Museum of Natural Science** (1 Hermann Circle Dr., ☎ 713/639–4600), also on park grounds, includes the **Baker Planetarium** and **Wortham IMAX Theatre,** with a six-story-high projection screen.

Astroworld and Waterworld (8400 Kirby Dr., at I–610, ☎ 713/799–1234), forming one of the country's major amusement complexes, are perennial favorites. Among the 100 rides are the "Texas Cyclone," a terrifying roller coaster, and the "Thunder River" water ride. Other attractions for children include the **Houston Fire Museum** (2403 Milam St., ☎ 713/524–2526), the **Houston Police Museum** (17000 Aldine Westfield Rd., ☎ 713/230–2300), and the wacky **Orange Show** (2402 Munger St., ☎ 713/926–6368; closed Jan.–Feb.), an irreverent and bizarre labyrinth built over 26 years by a Houston eccentric as a tribute to the orange—a Houston must-see.

Adults as well as children may enjoy **Space Center Houston,** 25 mi south of Houston (I–45 to the Alvin exit, then 3 mi east on NASA Rd. 1, ☎ 713/244–2100). Tram tours take you through NASA's adjacent **Johnson Space Center,** where several rockets are displayed. When it's not in use, you can visit Mission Control as well.

Galveston

The island's main draws for children, inevitably, are its 32 mi of beaches and the beachside rides at **Stewart Beach Park** (*see* Parks and Gardens, *above*). Other choices are the **Lone Star Flight Museum** (at Scholes Field Municipal Airport, ☎ 409/740–7722) and the collection of classic automobiles at **David Taylor Classics** (1918 Mechanic St., ☎ 409/765–6590).

Shopping

Houston

The city's premier shopping area is the **Galleria** (Post Oak Blvd. and Westheimer Rd.), famed for high-quality stores like Neiman Marcus, Marshall Field's, and Tiffany & Co. On **Post Oak Boulevard** north to San Felipe is another stretch of luxury stores. East of the Galleria, **Westheimer Road** offers an array of galleries and artsy shops. Probably the most expensive merchandise found in a Houston mall is at the **River Oaks Shopping Center** (Shepherd Dr. and Gray St.). Good boots and other Western gear are available at **Stelzig's Western Wear** (3123 Post Oak Blvd.). Downtown, the **Parks Shops in Houston Center** (1200 McKinney St.), with 70 stores, is a recently built mall that provides a convenient entrance to the city's tunnel system (another is at the downtown Hyatt Regency), which is lined with retail shops. Tunnel maps are free at most banks.

Galveston

The historic stretch of the Strand is the best place to shop in Galveston. The **Old Strand Emporium** (2112 Strand, ☎ 409/763–9445) is a charming deli and gourmet grocery. Antiques, collectibles, and peanut products are found at the **Old Peanut Butter Warehouse** (100 20th St., ☎ 409/762–8358).

Spectator Sports

Houston

BASEBALL

Houston Astros (Astrodome, 8400 Kirby Dr., ☎ 713/799–9500; Apr.–Oct.).

BASKETBALL

Houston Rockets (The Summit, 10 Greenway Plaza, ☎ 713/627–0600; Nov.–Apr.).

FOOTBALL

Houston Oilers (Astrodome, Loop 610, Kirby and Fannin Sts, ☎ 713/797–9111; Aug.–Dec.).

HOCKEY

Houston Aeros (The Summit, 10 Greenway Plaza, ☎ 713/627–2376; Oct.–Apr.).

SOCCER

Houston Hotshots (The Summit, 10 Greenway Plaza, ☎ 713/468–5100; June–Sept.).

Beaches

Galveston

Galveston's ocean beaches are all open to the public. The eastern end of the island, especially around Stewart Beach Park, is rife with amenities of all kinds, including rentals of surfboards, sailboats, chairs, and umbrellas. To the west are less crowded beaches, with a quieter, more natural atmosphere.

Dining

For price ranges, see Chart 1 (B) in On the Road with Fodor's.

Houston

$$$ **Anthony's.** In a new location on trendy Westheimer Boulevard and with an expanded Continental menu, Anthony's was named one of America's top new restaurants by *Esquire* magazine in 1994—and rightly so. Chef Bruce McMillian changes the menu frequently, but the veal Gragnon, prepared with shallots, artichokes, and marsala, is usually available and always superb. *4007 Westheimer Blvd., ☎ 713/961–0552. Jacket and tie advised. AE, DC, MC, V.*

$$$ **Cafe Annie.** Don't be put off by the shopping-strip entrance—the food served up at large, isolated tables is the finest American cuisine in town. The mussel soup and the venison are favorites, but the rabbit enchiladas may be the café's most unusual offering. *1728 Post Oak Blvd., ☎ 713/840–1111. Reservations required. Jacket and tie advised. AE, D, DC, MC, V. Closed Sun.*

$$ **Athens Bar & Grill.** It's not easy to find, in an industrial area near the ship channel, but you can tell it's authentic when Greek sailors stride in late at night and begin breaking plates. There's live music nightly, belly dancing on weekends. *8037 Clinton Dr., ☎ 713/675–1644. Reservations required. AE, DC, MC, V. Closed Sun.*

$$ **Spanish Flower.** A bit of a trek north of downtown, this is *the* Mexican restaurant for those in the know in Houston. It's open 24 hours a day (except on Tuesday night)—a cheerful place of ceramic tiles, potted plants, and outdoor dining. *4701 N. Main St., ☎ 713/869–1706. AE, D, DC, MC, V.*

$ **This Is It.** And so it is, if you're looking for genuine soul food. In the Fifth Ward just west of downtown, this eatery offers a buffet of oxtails, pork hocks, chitterlings, black-eyed peas, and the like. This can be a tough neighborhood, so you may want to stick to lunch. *239 W. Gray St., ☎ 713/523–5319. No credit cards.*

Galveston

$$$–$$$$ **Wentletrap.** Light woods and brick abound in this fine Continental restaurant in the Strand historic district. The veal medallions are a local favorite, the ever-changing seafood dishes trustworthy. *2301 Strand, ☎ 409/765–5545. AE, DC, MC, V. Closed Sun. eve.*

$$ **Gaido's.** Founded in 1911 by the Gaidos, this restaurant is still in the same politically important Italian family and still serves some of the best seafood in town. Try their famous grilled red snapper, lump crabmeat, or oysters as you gaze out picture windows at the gulf. *39th and Seawall Blvd., ☎ 409/762–9625. AE, MC, V.*

$–$$ **Benno's on the Beach.** There's a Coney Island feel to this little red, white, and blue joint, cited by some as the best place in Galveston for deep-fried seafood. *1200 Seawall Blvd., ☎ 409/762–4621. AE, MC, V.*

$ **Shrimp N' Stuff.** You can tell by the mix—including cops, businesspeople, and high-school students—that this place, with a brick-walled courtyard, is a great deal for fresh seafood. *3901 Ave. O, ☎ 409/765–5708. AE, DC, MC, V.*

Lodging

For price ranges, see Chart 2 (A) in On the Road with Fodor's.

Houston

$$$$ **Ritz-Carlton.** With hallways perfumed by exotic flowers and rooms affording dramatic views, the Ritz is convenient to the Galleria, the museum district, and the superposh River Oaks neighborhood. *1919 Briar Oaks La., 77027, ☎ 713/840–7600 or 800/241–3333, FAX 713/840–8036. 207 rooms, 25 suites. Facilities: 2 restaurants, bar, tearoom, rooftop pool, health club, valet parking. AE, D, DC, MC, V.*

$$$ **Hyatt Regency Houston.** Every room opens onto a balcony overlooking the dramatic atrium, and the revolving rooftop restaurant/cocktail lounge, Spindletop, offers panoramic views of the city. Convenient to all downtown locations, this hotel is a business traveler's choice. *1200 Louisiana St., 77002, ☎ 713/654–1234, FAX 713/951–0934, telex 775–791. 907 rooms, 52 suites. Facilities: 4 restaurants, 2 bars, pool, nearby health club, valet parking. AE, D, DC, MC, V.*

$$ **Allen Park Inn.** This pleasant motor inn, with rooms circling an outdoor swimming pool, is convenient to downtown, fairly priced, and well maintained. *2121 Allen Pkwy., 77019, ☎ 713/521–9321 or 800/231–6310, FAX 713/521–9321, ext. 350. 249 rooms, 22 apartments. Facilities: restaurant, 2 bars, health club. AE, D, DC, MC, V.*

$–$$ **Sara's Bed & Breakfast & Inn.** A pretty example of the Queen Anne–style architecture that populates the Houston Heights neighborhood, about 4 mi northwest of downtown, this turn-of-the-century B&B has a cupola, several porches, and a family atmosphere. *941 Heights Blvd., 77008, ☎ 713/868–1130 or 800/593–1130. 10 rooms (5 share bath), 1 suite. AE, DC, MC, V.*

Galveston

$$$$ **San Luis Hotel and Condominiums.** Balconied rooms overlooking the gulf are the norm at this spiffy if isolated high-rise resort complex, where hotel rooms are in one wing and more expensive condominiums in another. *5222 Seawall Blvd., 77551, ☎ 409/744–1500 or 800/445–0090; in TX, 800/392–5937; FAX 409/744–8452. 244 hotel rooms, 106 condominiums. Facilities: 2 restaurants, 2 bars, entertainment, pool, health club, tennis courts. AE, D, DC, MC, V.*

$$$ **Tremont House.** Walking into this hotel, right off the Strand in the heart of old Galveston, is a progressive pleasure, from the Victorian elegance of its facade to the hand-carved 1888 mahogany bar of the narrow, four-story atrium that forms the lobby. But it's not until you reach your room, decorated in elegant black-and-white vertical patterns and Italian tile, with soaring ceilings and 11-foot windows, that you truly appreciate the grandeur. *2300 Mechanic's Row, 77550, ☎ 409/763–0300 or 800/874–2300, FAX 409/763–1539. 116 rooms. Facilities: restaurant, bar, access to health club. AE, DC, MC, V.*

$–$$ **Commodore.** Hard on the beach, this is a functional hotel with a large pool and gulf views from many room balconies. *3618 Seawall Blvd., 77552, ☎ 409/763–2375 or 800/231–9921, FAX 409/763–2379. 91 rooms. AE, D, DC, MC, V.*

The Arts and Nightlife

The Arts

HOUSTON

Houston's performing-arts scene is a busy one, as reflected in the venues described above (*see* Exploring Houston, Downtown). Ticket information on the city's **symphony orchestra, opera, ballet,** and **So-**

ciety for the Performing Arts, which books dance, orchestras, and solo artists, may be obtained by calling 713/227–5134. Dramas are regularly presented at the **Alley Theatre** (615 Texas Ave., ☎ 713/228–9341 or 800/733–7469). Complete listings of events are carried in the *Houston Chronicle, Houston Post,* and *Key Magazine.*

GALVESTON

The recently restored **Grand 1894 Opera House** (2020 Post Office St., ☎ 409/765–1894 or 800/821–1894), where performances of various kinds are held from time to time, is worth visiting for the architecture alone. Sarah Bernhardt and Anna Pavlova once played this storied stage, which is just 70 feet from the farthest seat. The **Strand Street Theater** (2317 Ship's Mechanic Row, ☎ 409/763–4591) is another venue for occasional dramas.

Nightlife

HOUSTON

Possibly the most interesting bar in Houston is a brick-fronted hole-in-the-wall, **La Carafe** (813 Congress Ave., ☎ 713/229–9399), in the oldest commercial building in Houston. A top venue for an eclectic mix of pop performers—from the Neville Brothers to fiddler Vassar Clements—is **Fitzgerald's** (2706 White Oaks Dr., ☎ 713/862–7580).

SAN ANTONIO AND THE HILL COUNTRY

The Alamo—symbol either of Texan heroism or of Anglo arrogance—is by no means the only reason to visit San Antonio. A mélange of easily mingling ethnic groups, it is in many ways Texas's most beautiful and atmospheric city. To the northwest is the Hill Country, an anomaly in generally flat Texas, rich with pretty landscapes, early American history, and echoes of the linen-to-silk story of Lyndon Baines Johnson, the nation's 36th president.

Tourist Information

Hill Country: Tourism Association (1001 Junction Hwy., Kerrville 78028, ☎ 210/895–5505). **Bandera:** Convention & Visitors Bureau (1206 Cypress St.; Box 171, 78003, ☎ 210/796–3045 or 800/364–3833). **Fredericksburg:** Convention & Visitors Bureau (106 N. Adams St., 78624, ☎ 210/997–6523). **Kerrville:** Convention & Visitors Bureau (1700 Sidney Baker St., 78028, ☎ 210/792–3535 or 800/221–7958). **San Antonio:** Alamo Visitor Center (216 E. Crockett St.; Box 845, 78293, ☎ 210/225–8587); Convention & Visitors Bureau (121 Alamo Plaza South, 78205, ☎ 210/270–8700 or 800/447–3372; also has booths at the airport).

Getting There

By Plane

More than a dozen airlines serve the **San Antonio International Airport** (☎ 210/821–3411), about a 15-minute drive north of downtown. Inexpensive shuttle services (☎ 210/366–3183) operate 24 hours a day. **Southwest Airlines** (☎ 210/617–1221 or 800/435–9792) provides regional service.

By Car

Good highways serve San Antonio from most directions, including I–35 from Dallas and I–10 from Houston. I–410 rings the city, and several highways take you downtown.

San Antonio

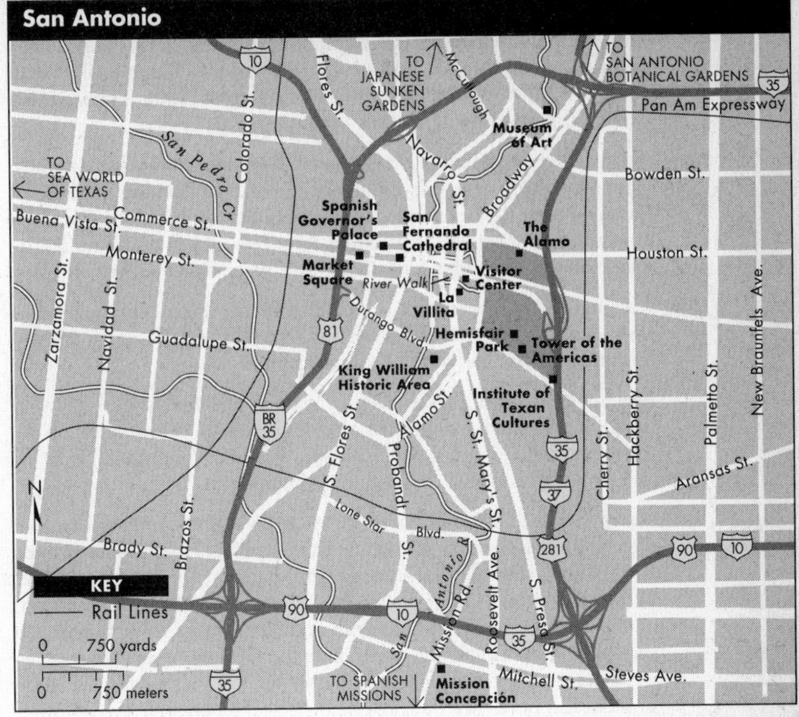

By Train

Amtrak serves San Antonio's station (1174 E. Commerce St., ☎ 210/223–3226 or 800/872–7245), with daily trains north to Fort Worth, Dallas, east Texas, and Chicago; east to New Orleans and beyond; and west to Los Angeles.

By Bus

Buses run out of San Antonio's **Greyhound station** (500 N. St. Mary's St., ☎ 800/231–2222) to all major cities as well as to most local towns.

Exploring San Antonio and the Hill Country

Much of San Antonio can be explored on foot, although some of its attractions will require transportation. For the Hill Country, a car is a must; you can cover several towns in a day, catching some of the landscapes in between as you drive.

San Antonio

At the heart of San Antonio, the **Alamo** (Alamo Plaza, ☎ 210/225–1391) stands as a repository of Texas history, a monument to the 189 volunteers who died there in 1836 during a 13-day siege by the Mexican dictator General Santa Anna. They fought not for Texan independence, but for adherence to the liberal 1824 constitution of Mexico, of which Texas was then a part. When the Alamo was finally breached on March 6, at dreadful cost to the Mexican Army, the slaughter that followed would be remembered in history as the major turning point of the Texas Revolution. Santa Anna claimed victory, but, as a liberal aide wrote privately, "One more such 'glorious victory' and we are finished." Three weeks later, at Goliad, Santa Anna ordered the massacre of 343 Texan prisoners. But he was captured and the revolution completed on April 21, when Sam Houston led his sharpshooting volunteers—crying "Remember the Alamo! Remember Goliad!"—to victory against two-to-one odds at San Jacinto. Today the Alamo is filled with guns and other paraphernalia belonging to William Travis, Davy Crockett, James Bowie, and the other martyrs.

Another sight on Alamo Plaza is the 1859 **Menger Hotel.** In its moody, mahogany bar—a precise replica of the pub in London's House of Lords—Teddy Roosevelt supposedly recruited his Rough Riders, cowboys off the Chisholm Trail drank to excess and fought, and cattlemen closed deals with a handshake over three fingers of rye whiskey.

Recently, there's been talk of redoing Alamo Plaza—getting rid of some of the tackier souvenir shops and restoring several historic walls—but this plan has met with much opposition.

Beginning and ending at the Alamo, the **Texas Star Trail** is a 2.6-mi walking tour designated by blue disks in the sidewalks. Information on the trail, which takes you past 80 historic sites and landmarks, is available at the Alamo Visitor Center at Alamo Plaza.

Nearby, reached by dozens of stairways, is **River Walk,** or Paseo del Rio, the city's leading tourist attraction. Built a full story below street level, River Walk is several miles of scenic stone pathways built on both banks of the San Antonio River downtown. In some places it is peaceful and quiet, in others a mad conglomeration of restaurants, bars, hotels, and strolling mariachi bands, all of which can be seen from river taxis or charter boats—as Queen Elizabeth II did on her 1991 visit. Near La Mansion del Rio hotel (*see* Lodging, *below*), at the Navarro Street Bridge, the huge red-brick retail and entertainment complex known as South Bank opened in 1995, anchored by a new branch of the Hard Rock Cafe. Each January, when parts of the river are drained to clear the bottom of debris, locals revel in the River Bottom Festival and Mud Parade. A pleasure at all times, River Walk should be experienced at night.

Southeast of the walk is **HemisFair Park,** onetime site of a World's Fair and currently home to the 750-foot **Tower of the Americas** (☎ 210/299–8615), where an observation deck and a rotating restaurant offer bird's-eye views of the city. Just beyond is the **Institute of Texan Cultures** (HemisFair Plaza, ☎ 210/558–2300), a university-run, interactive museum focusing on the 27 ethnic groups who made Texas what it is today. Among the many exhibits you'll find an elaborately engraved 16th-century conquistador's helmet of the type favored by Vasquez de Coronado; the "Castroville Hearse"; and a full-size, walk-through replica of a sharecropper's house.

A little farther south is the **King William Historic Area,** settled by leading German merchants in the late 19th century. The elegant Victorian mansions, set in a quiet, leafy neighborhood, are a pleasure to behold; Madison and Guenther streets are particularly pretty for a stroll or drive. A few houses, like the 1876 **Steves Homestead** (509 King William St., ☎ 210/225–5924), offer daily tours. While you're in the vicinity, you might want to stop in at **Guenther House** (205 E. Guenther St., ☎ 210/227–1061). Home of the adjacent Pioneer Flour Mills' founding family, it was built in 1860 and today offers tours, a small museum of mill memorabilia, a gift shop, and a cheerful restaurant serving fine German pastries and full breakfasts and lunches.

Continuing south from downtown, you can pick up the **Mission Trail,** connecting four of the Spanish stone missions built along the San Antonio River (the first of which, established in 1718, later came to be known as the Alamo). Meant to Christianize the Native Americans, these religious outposts were surrounded by presidios. All are beautiful, in their way. **Mission Concepción** (807 Mission Rd.) is known for its frescoes; **San José** (6539 San José Dr.), "Queen of Missions," has had its outer wall, Native American dwellings, granary, and workshops restored; **Espada** (10040 Espada Rd.), the southernmost, is a favorite of serious students and includes an Arab-inspired aqueduct that was part of the missions' famous *acequia* water-management system. Pick up trail maps at the downtown information centers, as the missions are hard to find (☎ 210/229–5701).

Heading back downtown, you'll pass close by the **Lone Star Brewery** (600 Lone Star Blvd., ☎ 210/270–9467)—"Home of the National Beer of Texas"—which makes for an interesting tour. The grounds also contain the old Buckhorn Bar, once San Antonio's leading saloon; a cottage used by the writer O. Henry; and the **Buckhorn Hall of Horns, Fins and Feathers** (☎ 210/270–9467), said to contain the world's largest collection of animal horns. Back in town, just west of the river, the **San Fernando Cathedral** (Commerce and Flores Sts.) is where Santa Anna raised his no-quarter flag for the Alamo defenders to tremble at. The seat of a bishopric, it was visited by Pope John Paul II in 1987. Nearby is the beautiful **Spanish Governor's Palace,** seat of Spanish power in Texas. *105 Plaza de Armas, ☎ 210/224–0601. Admission charged.*

San Antonio's arts scene is marked by a strong Southwestern flavor. The **San Antonio Museum of Art** (200 W. Jones Ave., ☎ 210/829–7262) houses pre-Columbian, Native American, Spanish colonial, and other art. The **Southwest Craft Center** (300 Augusta St., ☎ 210/224–1848) is filled with crafts but may be most remarkable for its building, once an Ursuline school for girls.

The Hill Country

It's a long, pleasing drive through the Hill Country from San Antonio. Starting a slow, clockwise loop to the northwest, it's less than an hour's trip to the Kerrville area on I–10. However, you may want to catch the far prettier Rte. 16, a hilly road that leads to **Bandera** (population: 877). One of the nation's oldest Polish communities (dating from 1855) and site of an 1854 Mormon colony, Bandera is today replete with working and guest ranches. On I–10, **Boerne** (population: 4,274) is another early immigrant settlement, founded by Germans and named after a German writer. One of its fine early buildings is the **Kuhlmann-King House,** which can be toured by appointment with the local historical society (402 E. Blanco St., ☎ 210/249–2030 or 210/249–8000). Nearby **Cascade Caverns** (Exit 543 off I–10, ☎ 210/755–8080) is a dramatic, active wet cave with a 90-foot underground waterfall and visitor facilities including RV camping and a pool.

Kerrville, a town of little obvious interest, is said to have the best climate in the nation. This has led to a proliferation of hotels, children's summer camps, guest ranches, and religious centers. **Kerrville State Park,** 500 acres along the cypress-edged Guadalupe River, is a good place to spot the white-tail deer that abound in the area. From Kerrville, it's 24 mi to **Fredericksburg,** probably the Hill Country's prettiest town and the heart of its predominantly German-American population. Its main street (duly co-signed as Hauptstrasse) is a sort of German version of a classic Western movie scene —but lined with chic stores, antiques shops, and small German eateries rather than rowdy saloons. One of Fredericksburg's famous sons was Chester W. Nimitz, commander in chief of the U.S. Pacific fleet in World War II. The restored Nimitz Steamboat Hotel now forms part of the **Admiral Nimitz Museum** (340

E. Main St., ☎ 210/997–4379), which displays restored hotel rooms, exhibits on the war in the Pacific, and a "Garden of Peace" donated by the Japanese people.

Heading east, you may want to duck onto Rte. 1376 and into **Luckenbach** (population: 25)—a speck on the map made famous by the Waylon Jennings and Willie Nelson duet "Let's Go to Luckenbach, Texas"; by the late humorist Hondo Crouch, who once owned the general store; and by the chili contests that draw people from nearby states. Founded in 1850, the hamlet remains largely unchanged, with one unpainted general store and tavern, a rural dance hall, and a blacksmith's shop. The rustic little complex is open daily except Wednesday, but you may want to stop by on Sunday afternoon, when informal groups of fiddlers, guitarists, and banjo pickers gather under the live oaks.

Anyone who has read a biography of Lyndon Johnson will want to visit **Johnson City** to see the place where the gawky, huge-eared child who would one day lead America through some of its most troubled moments grew up. While his was not a Horatio Alger story, Johnson certainly came from an unremarkable town—a dusty, poor place that was no doubt one reason for the burning ambition that marked his rise. His small white-frame boyhood home is about the nicest place in town, and it is not spectacular. A short walk takes you to Johnson Settlement, the ranch complex once owned by LBJ's family, and an 1856 dogtrot cabin similar to those the early Johnsons lived in. Free bus tours of these sites and of Johnson's birthplace, one-room school, and grave depart several times a day from the **LBJ State Historical Park** (☎ 210/644–2252 or 210/644–2478), just east of Stonewall on U.S. 290. Exhibits also highlight the history of the Hill Country.

Nearby **Blanco,** the onetime county seat that also figures in the Johnson clan's long history, is ornamented by a fine bit of classic Texas: the Second Empire–style **Old Blanco County Courthouse.** About 6 mi northwest of Blanco (turn west by the Laundromat on Park Rd. 23, left on Rte. 102, then right on Rte. 103) is the **myrrh-weeping icon of New Sarov** at Christ of the Hills Eastern Orthodox Monastery (☎ 210/833–5363). The icon, a rendition of the Mother of God, is said to have begun five months of weeping on May 7, 1985, and still weeps on occasion. The monks and nuns who inhabit the place claim thousands of miracles, including cures of deadly diseases, through the anointing with tears that is offered to all visitors.

The drive back to San Antonio on U.S. 281 is a pretty one, but if you have time, go by way of **San Marcos** on Rte. 32. This road, which skips along parts of a ridge called the **Devil's Backbone,** is a classic Hill Country drive, replete with deer sightings and appealing landscapes.

What to See and Do with Children

San Antonio

In the heart of San Antonio are several attractions that will keep children occupied for hours. The **Cowboy Museum and Gallery** (209 Alamo Plaza, ☎ 210/229–1257), a surprisingly zippy little museum with goodies like a Sioux necklace made of human-finger bones, faces the Alamo. Nearby, in the Rivercenter mall, the **Alamo IMAX Theatre** (849 E. Commerce St., ☎ 210/225–4629 or 800/354–4629) shows the 45-minute *Alamo . . . the Price of Freedom* on a giant screen five times a day. The **San Antonio Zoo** (3903 N. St. Mary's St., ☎ 210/734–7183) has the nation's third-largest animal collection—including koala bears—most kept in outdoor habitats. The **Buckhorn Hall of Horns, Fins**

The Hill Country

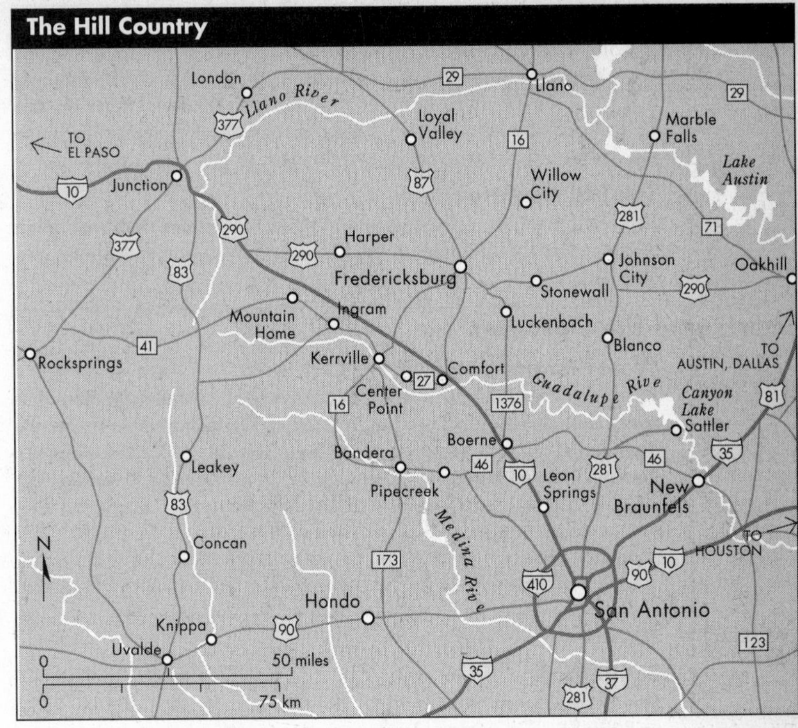

and Feathers and the **Institute of Texan Cultures** (*see* Exploring San Antonio, *above*) are other child-pleasing possibilities.

West of downtown, the $140 million **Sea World of Texas** (Ellison Dr. and Westover Hills Blvd., ☎ 210/523–3000 or 800/527–4757; in TX, 800/722–2762) has five stadiums and the usual complement of killer whales, walruses, otters, and dolphins. Nearby, **Fiesta, Texas** (I–10 West and Loop 1604, ☎ 210/697–5050), a $100 million park split up into four thematic areas—Hispanic, German, Western, and 1950s Rock 'n' Roll— features rides, music, and restaurants.

The Hill Country

Cascade Caverns (*see* Exploring the Hill Country, *above*) are near Boerne. The remarkable **Natural Bridge Caverns** (follow signs from Rte. 1863 between San Antonio and New Braunfels, ☎ 210/651–6101) are a mile-long series of awesome, multicolored subterranean rooms and corridors. On Rte. 306, 2 mi southwest of Sattler, you'll find **Dinosaur Flats,** with 100-million-year-old "thunder lizard" tracks.

Shopping

San Antonio

With its rich ethnic heritage, the city is a wonderful place to buy Mexican imports, most inexpensive and many of high quality. **El Mercado** is the Mexican market building that is part of **Market Square** (514 W. Commerce St., ☎ 210/299–8600). The building contains about 30 shops, including stores that offer blankets, Mexican dresses, men's *guayabera* shirts, and strings of brightly painted papier-mâché vegetables. Another area of Market Square worth visiting is the lively **Farmer's Market,** which underwent a $2.1 million renovation in 1994. **La Villita** (418 Villita St., ☎ 210/299–8610), a restored village a few blocks south of downtown, is now a conglomeration of crafts shops and small restaurants, some in adobe buildings dating from the 1820s. It's noteworthy for its Latin American importers and the demonstrations of its resident glass-blower. **Rivercenter** (849 E. Commerce St., ☎ 210/225–0000) is a fairly standard, if very ritzy, shopping mall right on the river. **Paris Hatters** (119 Broadway, ☎ 210/223–3453), run for three generations by the Cortez family, is a truly atmospheric place to buy Western hats.

The Hill Country

While the area generally is no shopping mecca, **Fredericksburg**'s main street is lined with antiques shops, imaginative stores, and Western saloons.

Sports and the Outdoors

Water Sports

Rafting, tubing, and canoeing are popular on the Guadalupe River between Canyon Lake north of San Antonio and New Braunfels. Try **Jerry's Rentals** (River Rd. north of New Braunfels, ☎ 210/625–2036) or **Rockin' R River Rides** (☎ 210/629–9999) or **Gruene River Co.** (☎ 210/625–2800), both on the river in New Braunfels. Canyon Lake, one of the most scenic lakes in Texas with its surrounding steep evergreen hills, has two yacht clubs, two marinas, a water-skiing club, and excellent fishing—an 86-pound flathead catfish is just one local record.

Spectator Sports

Basketball

San Antonio Spurs (Alamodome, 100 Montana St., ☎ 210/554–7787 or 800/688–7787; Nov.–Apr.).

Horse Racing

Retama Park (I–35, San Antonio, ☎ 210/651–7000; Wed.–Sun. Apr.–July and Sept.–Nov.)

Dining and Lodging

The Bandera and Kerrville visitors bureaus (*see* Tourist Information, *above*) have information on guest ranches. The Hill Country is chock-full of bed-and-breakfasts, particularly in tourist towns like Fredericksburg. Ask for listings at local convention and visitors bureaus, or try the reservations services **Be My Guest** (402 W. Main St., Fredericksburg 78624, ☎ 210/997–7227 or 210/997–8555) and **Gastehaus Schmidt** (231 W. Main St., Fredericksburg 78624, ☎ 210/997–5612). For price ranges, see Charts 1 (B) and 2 (A) in On the Road with Fodor's.

San Antonio

DINING

Polo's. Inside the elegant Fairmount hotel, Polo's is equally elegant and chic. A blend of Southwestern nouvelle and Oriental cuisine—fare that has made the cover of *Texas Monthly*—the menu includes delights like black pasta stuffed with lobster and crab. *401 S. Alamo St., ☎ 210/224–8800. Jacket and tie advised. AE, DC, MC, V. $$$*

The Bayous. Overlooking a pleasant curve of River Walk, the restaurant has a chef who specializes in fine Creole cookery—crawfish pasta, blackened fish, oyster specialties, and the like. *517 N. Presa St., ☎ 210/223–6403. AE, DC, MC, V. $$–$$$*

Rio Rio Cantina. The Tex-Mex fare served here is unusually imaginative. The restaurant sits on one of the busier—sometimes annoyingly so—stretches of River Walk. *421 E. Commerce St., ☎ 210/226–8462. AE, D, DC, MC, V. $$*

County Line Barbecue. Texas is famous for its barbecued ribs, smoked brisket, and related fare. In San Antonio there's only one contender. *On Rte. 1604, ½ mi west of U.S. 281, ☎ 210/496–0011. AE, MC, V. $–$$*

Mi Tierra. At Market Square directly across from the entrance to El Mercado, this huge, cheerful, and famous restaurant boasts good Tex-Mex food, wandering mariachis, and a Mexican bakery, all 24 hours a day! *218 Produce Row, ☎ 210/225–1262. AE, DC, MC, V. $*

LODGING

Fairmount. This historic luxury hotel made the *Guinness Book of World Records* when its 3.2-million-pound brick bulk was moved six blocks—and across a bridge—to its present location. It's marked by a superrefined but grandmotherly atmosphere of canopy beds, overstuffed chairs, and marble baths. *401 S. Alamo St., 78205, ☎ 210/224–8800 or 800/642–3363; in TX, 800/642–3339; FAX 210/224–2767. 19 rooms, 17 suites. Facilities: restaurant, bar. AE, DC, MC, V. $$$$*

La Mansion del Rio. A Spanish motif marks this large hotel on a quiet portion of the River Walk. Inside and out it's replete with Mediterranean tiles, archways, and soft wood tones. Rooms are very modern. *112 College St., 78205, ☎ 210/225–2581 or 800/531–7208; in TX, 800/292–7300; FAX 210/226–1365. 322 rooms, 15 suites. Facilities: 2 restaurants, bar, pool. AE, D, DC, MC, V. $$$–$$$$*

★ **Menger Hotel.** Since its 1859 opening, the Menger has lodged Robert E. Lee, Ulysses S. Grant, Teddy Roosevelt, Oscar Wilde, Sarah Bernhardt, even Roy Rogers and Dale Evans—all of whom must have appreciated the charming, three-story Victorian lobby, its sunny dining room, and the flowered courtyard. Rooms in the oldest part of the hotel have four-poster beds and antique-patterned wallpapers; new rooms are spacious and tastefully modern. *204 Alamo Plaza, 78205, ☎ 210/223–4361 or 800/345–9285, FAX 210/228–0022. 320 rooms, 23 suites. Facilities: restaurant, outdoor pool, health club, shops, bar. AE, D, DC, MC, V. $$$*

Ramada Emily Morgan. On the other side of Alamo Plaza, this neo-Gothic hotel is named for the so-called Yellow Rose of Texas, the beautiful mulatto slave who supposedly occupied Santa Anna's attentions at San Jacinto while sending secret messages encouraging the Texans to attack (this tale is discounted by most serious historians). *705 E. Houston St., 78205, ☎ 210/225–8486 or 800/824–6674, FAX 210/225–7227. 177 rooms. Facilities: 2 restaurants, bar, outdoor pool/whirlpool, exercise room, sauna. AE, D, DC, MC, V. $$–$$$*

Bullis House. The rooms in this historic mansion are spacious and well restored—and a good deal in a town where lodging is surprisingly expensive. The premises also include a modern youth hostel in a separate building next door. *621 Pierce St., 78208, ☎ 210/223–9426. 7 rooms, 6 share bath; hostel, 40 beds. Facilities: pool. AE, D, MC, V. $*

The Hill Country

DINING

Friedhelm's. This Bavarian restaurant is known as the best in town, no small feat in a place of such intense Germanic influence. Try the Bavarian schnitzel, a breaded cutlet topped with Emmentaler cheese and jalapeño sauce. *905 W. Main St., Fredericksburg, ☎ 210/997–6300. AE, D, MC, V. Closed Mon. $–$$*

LODGING

Holiday Inn Y.O. Ranch. This sprawling, ranch-theme hotel is named after a well-known 50,000-acre dude ranch to which regular excursions are arranged. The large rooms carry out the Western theme with such decor as cattle horns. *2033 Sidney Baker St., Kerrville 78028, ☎*

210/257–4440; in TX, 800/531–2800; FAX *210/896–8189. 188 rooms, 12 suites. Facilities: restaurant, bar, ballroom, pool, hot tub, tennis. AE, D, DC, MC, V. $$–$$$*

The Arts and Nightlife

The Arts

At San Antonio's **Mexican Cultural Institute** (600 HemisFair Plaza, ☎ 210/227–0123), Mexican culture is depicted in film, dance, art, and other exhibits. A 1929 movie/vaudeville theater has been restored to its baroque splendor as the **Majestic Performing Arts Center** (224 E. Houston St., ☎ 210/226–5700), a venue for touring Broadway shows and home to the San Antonio Symphony Orchestra. **Kerrville** annually hosts one of the country's largest folk festivals.

Nightlife

Around the 3000 block of San Antonio's **North St. Mary's Street,** you'll find a colorful assortment of bars and restaurants in converted commercial buildings, many featuring live entertainment. **River Walk** favorites include **Durty Nellie's Pub** (Hilton Palacio del Rio, 200 S. Alamo St., ☎ 210/222–1400), where sing-alongs are popular, but a more interesting choice may be the **Landing** (Hyatt Regency Hotel, 123 Losoya St., ☎ 210/223–7266), where the world-class Jim Cullum's Jazz Band has attracted the attention of foreign and U.S. critics for its superb Dixieland jazz. Another great choice is the **Menger Hotel bar** (*see* Exploring San Antonio, *above*).

DALLAS AND FORT WORTH

These twin cities, separated by 30 mi of suburbs, may be the oddest couple of all in a state of odd couples. Dallas—one of those unfortunate places whose chief global fame emanates from a TV show—is glitzy and ritzy, a swelling, modernistic business metropolis whose inhabitants go to bed early and to church on Sunday. Fort Worth, sneered at as "Cowtown" by its neighbors, lives in the shadow of its wild history as a rip-roaring cowboy town, a place of gunfights and cattle drives—even though its cultural establishment is superior to Dallas's and it has seen a downtown rebirth in recent years. It's said that Fort Worth parents tell their children to be polite to everyone—that fellow in the faded jeans and cowboy hat could well be the president of the bank. In Dallas, no such care is necessary; people ostentatiously act the part their class has assigned them.

Tourist Information

Dallas: Convention & Visitors Bureau (1201 Elm St., Suite 2000, 75270, ☎ 214/746–6677, 214/746–6679 for a recorded schedule of events, or 800/232–5527); information booths at the municipal airport, Love Field, Union Station, and the West End Market Place. **Fort Worth:** Convention & Visitors Bureau (415 Throckmorton St., 76102, ☎ 817/336–8791 or 800/433–5747); information booths at the Sid Richardson Collection of Western Art, at the Fort Worth Museum of Science and History, and in the Stockyards.

Arriving and Departing

By Plane

One of the rare successful collaborations between the rival cities is the **Dallas–Fort Worth International Airport** (☎ 214/574–6720), 17 mi from the business districts of each town. The world's second-busiest airport, it is surprisingly easy to use, though encumbered by slow transportation between terminals. It may cost $30 or more to get to downtown Dallas by taxi, usually about $25 to downtown Fort Worth. Cheaper van service is offered by the 24-hour **Supershuttle** (☎ 817/329–2000); the **Airporter Bus Service** (☎ 817/334–0092) serves a downtown Fort Worth terminal and some hotels. Ritzier service comes from **Lone Star Limousine** (☎ 214/238–8884).

Love Field (Cedar Springs at Mockingbird La., Dallas, ☎ 214/670–6073), a $10–$15 taxi ride from downtown Dallas, is the hub of **Southwest Airlines** (☎ 214/263–1717 or 800/435–9792), offering extensive service within Texas, to many cities in the four contiguous states, and, with stops, to destinations as far away as Chicago and California.

By Car

The Metroplex, as the Greater Dallas–Fort Worth area is known, is well served by interstates. The main approaches include I–35 from Oklahoma to the north and Waco to the south; I–30 from Arkansas; I–20 from Louisiana or New Mexico; and I–45 from Houston. The twin cities are linked by I–20, the southern route, and I–30, generally the more useful road. Dallas is circled by the I–635 ring road, known as the LBJ Freeway, while Fort Worth is looped by I–820.

By Train

Amtrak (☎ 800/872–7245) serves both cities with daily trains to east Texas and Chicago, and others heading south to San Antonio. Dallas's terminal is **Union Station** (400 Houston St., ☎ 214/653–1101); in Fort Worth, it's the old **Santa Fe Depot** (1501 Jones St., ☎ 817/332–2931), built in 1900.

By Bus

Greyhound Lines (☎ 800/231–2222) has stations in Dallas (205 S. Lamar St.) and Fort Worth (901 Commerce St.).

Getting Around Dallas and Fort Worth

As much as anywhere in Texas, a car is necessary to see Dallas and Fort Worth, and getting around by car is relatively easy. Both cities have bus systems, but service is sketchy and sometimes just plain bad.

Exploring Dallas and Fort Worth

Dallas

Many thousands visit Dallas mainly because of the city's unhappy legacy as the site of the assassination of President John F. Kennedy, which occurred downtown. Also downtown is one of the most remarkable, and recent, flowerings of skyscraping architecture anywhere—that same skyline familiar to the world from the "Dallas" television show—and this is accompanied by the offerings of a revitalized West End, where restaurants and shops fill a former warehouse district. Nearby are several major cultural institutions, and only a little farther away, Deep Ellum is the hip-hopping center of the city's countercultural scene. A short car trip from downtown are historic areas that give a sense of the old Dallas. And to the north, where the city's conservative, wealthy establishment has long been entrenched, there's shopping galore.

DOWNTOWN

On November 22, 1963, shots that would shock the world rang out on Dealey Plaza, at the west end of downtown, as the presidential motorcade rounded the corner from Houston Street onto the Elm Street approach to the Triple Underpass. Eventually, the Warren Commission would conclude—to the continuing disbelief of a majority of Americans—that President Kennedy was killed by Lee Harvey Oswald, acting alone and firing from the sixth floor of the **Texas School Book Depository.** Today, a first-rate exhibit in the building—called **The Sixth Floor**—documents the hate-filled times, the enduring vision of Camelot, riveting details of the assassination, and a remarkably evenhanded account of the conspiracy theories that continue to emerge. The spot from which Oswald is said to have shot is maintained exactly as it was. At the end of the exhibit is a moving log of brief messages written by visitors. *411 Elm St., ☎ 214/653–6666. Admission charged.*

Just outside, on the Elm Street side of the building and to the right, is the **grassy knoll** from which many believed a second gunman fired. Visitors inevitably congregate directly across the street, on **Dealey Plaza,** to look up at the so-called sniper's perch. A short walk away, at Main and Market streets, is the stark **cenotaph** designed like an empty house by architect Philip Johnson as a tribute to Kennedy, who was a personal friend.

Around the corner, the **West End Historic District** is an area of brick warehouses built between 1900 and 1930 and brought back to life in 1976. Now filled with restaurants, shops, and pedestrian activity, it is one of the city's biggest draws for visitors both day and night. It is anchored by the **West End Market Place** (603 Munger Ave., ☎ 214/748–4801), once a candy and cracker factory and now a lively, five-story shopping and eating center built around an atrium.

A few blocks south, facing the cenotaph, is the **Old Red Courthouse** (Main and Houston Sts.). This Romanesque building of red sandstone went up in 1892 and is one of the city's oldest surviving structures and a familiar landmark. On adjacent Dallas County Historical Plaza, the **John Neely Bryan Cabin** is the reconstructed 1841 log cabin and trading post that was the city's first building.

The most remarkable thing about the center of downtown, where most of the famous Dallas skyline sprouts, is the fact that it is so new—almost all its major skyscrapers were completed in the 1980s. I. M. Pei, the New York architect who for so long has favored Texas, has had a very strong influence here. His **First Interstate Bank Tower** (1445 Ross Ave.), with its huge, green-glass triangular shapes, was built in 1986 and is arguably the city's finest skyscraper. See it at dusk, when the sun's reflections can be incredible. **Dallas City Hall** (1500 Marilla St.), with a facade that angles out sharply over a large plaza edged by three spiky flagpoles, is another striking Pei concoction. To one side, in Pioneer Plaza, stands Robert Summer's interpretation of life on the old Shawnee Trail—70 longhorn steer and three cowboys—said to be the largest bronze sculpture in the world. The installation was completed in 1995.

One building Dallasites have developed an abiding love for is **First Republic Bank Plaza** (901 Main St.), whose 70 stepped stories are outlined in green argon lights and visible for miles. Another dramatic feature of the skyline is **Reunion Tower** (300 Reunion Blvd.), where the Hyatt Regency's lit-up restaurant and bar is known for spectacular views of the city. Set among nearby tall buildings, **Thanks-Giving Square** (Pacific Ave. and Ervay St.) is a small, triangular plaza designed by Philip Johnson on the theme of gratitude. With its spiraling chapel and quiet gardens, it is a peaceful spot, perfect for lunch or resting tired feet.

The **Arts District** is on the north edge of downtown and is anchored by the **Dallas Museum of Art** (1717 N. Harwood St., ☎ 214/922–1200). The museum itself is gorgeous—a series of low, white limestone galleries built off a central barrel vault—and an impressive new wing, the Museum of the Americas, focuses on American art before the arrival of Europeans. In the main museum, make a point of seeing Claes Oldenburg's *Stake Hitch,* a huge stake and rope, along with the remarkable pre-Columbian collection. The **Morton H. Meyerson Symphony Center** (2301 Flora St., ☎ 214/670–3600) is a place of sweeping, dramatic curves, ever-changing vanishing points, and surprising views. This 1989 building, another Pei offering, is far more interesting inside than out. Just in front, ***De Musica*** is a solid iron sculpture, reminiscent of musical notes, by the great Spanish Basque sculptor Eduardo Chillida.

OTHER ATTRACTIONS

Deep Ellum, a 20-minute walk east from downtown, was born as the city's first black neighborhood. Today it is the throbbing center of Dallas's avant-garde, a place of trend-setting art galleries, bars, clubs, and restaurants. The area centers on Commerce, Main, and Elm streets; its name is a phonetic rendering of "Deep Elm," pronounced with a Southern drawl.

Just southeast of this area, **Fair Park** (1300 Robert B. Cullum Blvd., ☎ 214/890–2911) is a 277-acre collection of artfully arranged rare Art Moderne buildings. Most of the grounds date from the 1936 Texas Centennial Exhibition, although the park has hosted the Texas State Fair since 1886. Murals and sculptures line the park's central esplanade, and in the **Hall of State** (3939 Grand Ave., ☎ 214/421–4500) more murals tell the story of Texas in heroic terms. The park also contains six major exhibit spaces: the **African-American Museum** (☎ 214/565–9026); the **Age of Steam Railroad Museum** (☎ 214/428–0101), with the world's largest steam locomotives; the **Dallas Aquarium** (☎ 214/670–8443); the **Dallas Civic Garden Center** (☎ 214/428–7476), a large conservatory with a French-style formal park; the **Museum of Natural History** (3535 E. Grand Ave., ☎ 214/421–3466), a place of dinosaurs and mammoths; and **The Science Place** (☎ 214/428–5555).

In **East Dallas,** Swiss Avenue has the city's best representations of two distinct periods. On lower Swiss Avenue (2900 block), nearer downtown, the **Wilson Block Historic District** is an unaltered block of turn-of-the-century frame houses, restored as offices for nonprofit groups. The **Swiss Avenue Historic District** (particularly the 5000–5500 blocks) has a large number of setback Prairie-style and other mansions.

Just north of downtown, bustling bars and restaurants line trendy **McKinney Avenue.** A restored **trolley** (☎ 214/855–5267) runs up McKinney from outside the Dallas Museum of Art (at St. Paul and Ross Sts.). Farther north, you'll find a Dallas oddity in the **Biblical Arts Center** (7500 Park La., ☎ 214/691–4661; closed Sun. morn. and Mon.), where there's a replica of Christ's tomb at Calvary and where sound and light bring a 124-by-20-ft biblical mural to life. In this north end of town are famous shopping malls like **NorthPark Center** and the **Galleria** (*see* Shopping, *below*).

Fort Worth

Downtown Fort Worth is where you'll find the city's financial core, most of its historic buildings, and Sundance Square, the restored turn-of-the-century commercial neighborhood that is one of its greatest attractions. A few miles north, past a decrepit industrial area, the Stockyards and adjacent Western-theme stores, restaurants, and ho-

Downtown Dallas

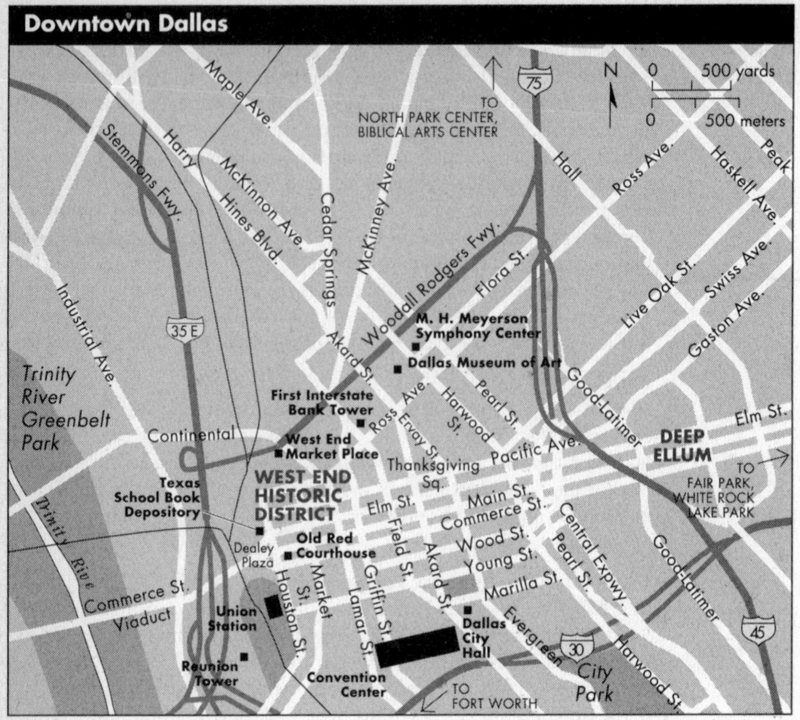

tels cluster around Main Street and Exchange Avenue. Just west of downtown, out Lancaster Avenue, the cultural district is home to four well-known museums, a fading coliseum complex, and several parks.

DOWNTOWN

Fort Worth's much underrated downtown gracefully manages something that few American cities do: an attractive marriage of modern glass-and-steel towers and the human-scale Victorian buildings of a century ago. The billionaire Bass brothers of Fort Worth are to be thanked for what may be the most eye-pleasing juxtaposition of scale: Rather than tear down several blocks of brick buildings to accommodate the twin towers of their giant City Center development, they created **Sundance Square** (bounded by Houston, Commerce, 2nd, and 3rd Sts.) by restoring the area as a center of tall-windowed restaurants, shops, nightclubs, and offices. It was here, on Main between 2nd and 3rd streets, that "King of the Gamblers" Luke Short, owner of the White Elephant Saloon, shot the colorful gunslinger Jim Courtright dead. The square's name recalls the Sundance Kid (Harry Longbaugh), who with Butch Cassidy (Robert Leroy Parker) hid out around 1898 in the nearby neighborhood, south and east of the present square, known as **Hell's Half-Acre.** This was a violent quarter of dank saloons, drunken cowboys, and dirty brothels. When a local prostitute was nailed to an outhouse, outraged citizens passed laws against guns and gambling—only to rescind them as soon as the local economy screeched to a halt. The **Sid Richardson Collection of Western Art** (309 Main St., ☎ 817/332–6554) conjures up parts of this dark world in the idealized oils of Frederic Remington and Charles Russell.

Also in Sundance Square, **Fire Station No. 1** (203 Commerce St., ☎ 817/732–1631) houses an exhibit on 150 years of city history. The 1907 building, which fronts on the street where cattle headed for the Chisholm Trail used to pass, once held the city's mascot panthers. Local firemen with a sense of humor acquired the pair after a Dallas newspaper claimed Fort Worth was so quiet that a panther could sleep downtown. Bored, they finally escaped.

The wedge-shaped **Flatiron Building** (1000 Houston St.), also downtown, is topped by gargoyles and panthers. Built in 1907 as medical offices, it was patterned on similar Renaissance Revival structures in New York and Philadelphia. Nearby, the former **Hotel Texas,** now the Radisson Plaza (815 N. Main St., ☎ 817/870–2100), is a downtown landmark, the place where President Kennedy slept the night before he was assassinated.

The **Tarrant County Courthouse** (100 E. Weatherford St.), on the north edge of downtown, is an 1895 Beaux Arts building of native red granite. Main Street heads north from the courthouse onto the **Paddock Viaduct,** which takes traffic over the bluff where early pioneers kept watch for Comanches, then leads directly to the Stockyards, several miles north. On the way there's a grim reminder of one of the darker aspects of Texas history: the former **Ku Klux Klan Building** (1012 N. Main St.), now the Ellis Pecan Company.

THE STOCKYARDS

The **Fort Worth Stockyards Historic District** recalls the prosperity brought to the city in 1902, when two major Chicago meatpackers, Armour and Swift, set up plants here to ship meat across the country in refrigerator cars—a new innovation. In the **Livestock Exchange Building** (131 E. Exchange Ave.), where cattle agents kept their offices, you'll find the **Stockyards Museum** (☎ 817/625–5082). Across the street, the **Stockyard Station** (130 E. Exchange Ave., ☎ 817/625–9715) is a fast-growing marketplace of shops and restaurants, all housed in former sheep pens. Nearby, **Cowtown Coliseum** (121 E. Exchange Ave., ☎ 817/625–1025) is the site of Saturday night rodeos. Also here are what's left of a complex of cattle pens; horse and mule barns; and, of course, **Billy Bob's Texas** (2520 Rodeo Plaza, ☎ 817/624–7117), billed as "the world's largest honky-tonk." Exchange Avenue is lined with restaurants, clubs, Western-wear stores, and famous spots like the **White Elephant Saloon** and the **Stockyards Hotel.** The **Tarantula Excursion Train** (2318 8th Ave., ☎ 817/625–7245; round-trip fare: $10 adults, $5.50 children) offers tours from its south-of-downtown base to the Stockyards. Information on the area is available at the **Stockyards Visitors Center** (130 E. Exchange Ave., ☎ 817/624–4741).

THE CULTURAL DISTRICT

Architect Louis Kahn's last and finest building was the **Kimbell Art Museum,** six long concrete vaults with skylights running the length of each. Mirrored light filters dreamily through these into large, airy galleries. "This light," Kahn explained, "will give a glow of silver to the room without touching the objects directly, yet give the comforting feeling of knowing the time of day." The envy of the curating world for its large acquisitions budget, the Kimbell has wonderful collections of early-20th-century European art and old masters. Two of the many extraordinary paintings are Munch's *Girls on a Jetty* and Goya's *The Matador Pedro Romero,* depicting the great bullfighter who killed 5,600 of the animals. *3333 Camp Bowie Blvd., ☎ 817/332–8451. Closed Mon.*

The city's three other major museums are all short walks from the Kimbell. The **Amon Carter Museum** (3501 Camp Bowie Blvd., ☎ 817/738–1933; closed Mon.), designed by Philip Johnson, is a collection of

American art centered on Remingtons and Russells. The **Modern Art Museum of Fort Worth** (1309 Montgomery St., ☎ 817/738–9215; closed Mon.) focuses on such painters as Picasso, Rauschenberg, and Warhol. Biology, geology, computer science, and astronomy are the order of the day at the **Fort Worth Museum of Science and History** (1501 Montgomery St., ☎ 817/732–1631; admission charged).

In the same area, the **Will Rogers Center** (3301 W. Lancaster Ave., ☎ 817/871–8150) is a partially restored coliseum-and-stock-pen complex named after the humorist and Fort Worth booster, who described the city as "where the West begins" (and Dallas as "where the East peters out"). The center is used for horse shows (at press time, a major new equestrian arena was scheduled to open in 1995) and other farm shows, the most famous of which is the annual Southwestern Exposition and Livestock Show, a livestock event held in late January or early February.

Parks and Gardens

Dallas

Fair Park (*see* Exploring Dallas, *above*), with its many museums and formal gardens, is one of the city's most visited parks; in October it hosts the three-week State Fair of Texas. At **White Rock Lake Park** (8300 Garland Rd., ☎ 214/670–8283), a beautiful and popular 9.3-mi jogging and bicycling path circles the sailboat-dotted lake. Bikes and skates can be rented along the Garland Road side of the lake, where you'll also find the **Dallas Arboretum** (8525 Garland Rd., ☎ 214/327–8263), 66 acres of gardens and lawns. Just south of downtown, **Old City Park** (1717 Gano St., ☎ 214/421–5141) is an outdoor museum of historic log cabins, antebellum mansions, and a Victorian bandstand, all set against the Dallas skyline.

Fort Worth

Downtown, **Water Gardens Park** (15th and Commerce Sts.) is a series of man-made waterfalls, walkways, and green areas that provide a cool respite from the surrounding pavement. At night, the Philip Johnson creation is illuminated and particularly striking. Just south of the cultural district, the **Fort Worth Botanic Garden** (3220 Botanic Garden Dr. at University Dr., ☎ 817/871–7686) lies on one edge of Trinity Park; its biggest draw is the tranquil **Japanese Garden.**

What to See and Do with Children

Midway between Dallas and Fort Worth, two major theme parks on I–30 beckon children of all ages: **Six Flags over Texas** (exit at Rte. 360S, ☎ 817/530–6000), with parachute drops, the world's largest wooden roller coaster, and other rides; and **Wet 'N Wild** (exit at Rte. 360N, ☎ 817/265–3356; closed Oct.–Apr.), with water rides like the 300-foot "Kamikaze." **Ripley's Believe It or Not/Palace of Wax** (601 E. Safari Pkwy., ☎ 214/263–2391) is a little closer to Dallas. Northeast of Dallas, the **Mesquite Rodeo** (1818 Rodeo Dr., Mesquite, ☎ 214/285–8777) is the biggest around.

Dallas

The many museums of **Fair Park** (*see* Exploring Dallas, *above*) are the premier attractions for kids. Older children are as fascinated as their parents by **The Sixth Floor** (*see* Exploring Dallas, *above*), with its interactive exhibits on the Kennedy assassination. The highlight of the **Dallas Zoo** (621 E. Clarendon St., ☎ 214/946–5154) is the "Wilds of Africa" exhibit, featuring a monorail and lowland gorillas in a natural habitat. Consider a pilgrimage to the **graves of Bonnie Parker**

(Crown Hill Cemetery, 9700 Webbs Chapel Rd.) **and Clyde Barrow** (Western Heights Cemetery; follow signs on Fort Worth Ave. near Winnetka St.).

Fort Worth

The **Stockyards** is surely the favorite kids' spot, followed by the **Fort Worth Museum of Science and History** and its Omni theater giant-screen presentations (for both, *see* Exploring Fort Worth, *above*).

Shopping

Dallas

Ever since 1873, when Dallas ensured its future by finagling the intersection of two intercontinental rail lines (by sneaking in an amendment to the railroads' enabling law), the city has been the great Southwestern mecca of American commerce. The **Galleria** (LBJ Fwy. and Dallas North Tollway, ☎ 214/702–7100), with 190 retailers, is one of Dallas's best-known upscale malls. **NorthPark Center** (Central Expressway and Northwest Hwy., ☎ 214/363–7441), developed as the nation's first indoor mall by art collector Ray Nasher, offers a variety of upscale shops and department stores—and rotating exhibits of world-class art on its walls. In downtown Dallas, the original **Neiman Marcus** (1618 Main St., ☎ 214/746–6911) is a huge draw.

The **West End Market Place** (603 Munger Ave., ☎ 214/748–4801) has a tourist bent. If you're in the mood for the fresh fruit and vegetables for which the Rio Grande Valley is famous, stop by the **Dallas Farmer's Market** (1010 S. Pearl St., ☎ 214/748–2082), on the southeast edge of downtown. There are some fine clothing stores on trendy **McKinney Avenue,** and nearby, the elegant **Crescent** (500 Crescent Ct.) offers *very* ritzy shops. Around the corner, on a street of fine restaurants and shops, the best place for Mexican masks, clothing, jewelry, rugs, and more is **Mariposa** (2817 Routh St., ☎ 214/871–9103).

Fort Worth

Both Fort Worth's attitude and its economy have always pointed west, and that's reflected in the shopping you'll find here. Most visitors head right to the **Stockyards,** where there are several good Western-wear outlets. Check out **Fincher's** (115 E. Exchange Ave., ☎ 817/624–7302), a Western store since 1902 and before that a bank; you can still walk into the old vaults. A great place for boots is the nearby **M. L. Leddy's Boot and Saddlery** (2455 N. Main St., ☎ 817/624–3149).

Downtown, **Sundance Square** is a perennial draw, with several small stores; better shopping, however, is generally found in the attached **Tandy Center** (200 Throckmorton St., ☎ 817/390–3720), a large and modern indoor mall. For fine small items, try the **major museums' gift shops. Barber's Book Store** (215 W. 8th St., ☎ 817/335–5469), specializing in Texana and rare and fine books, is the oldest bookshop in Texas.

Spectator Sports

Dallas

BASEBALL

Texas Rangers (The Ballpark at Arlington, 1000 Ballpark Way, Arlington, off I–30, ☎ 817/273–5100; Apr.–Oct.).

BASKETBALL

Dallas Mavericks (Reunion Arena, 777 Sports St., ☎ 214/748–1808; Nov.–Apr.).

FOOTBALL

Dallas Cowboys (Texas Stadium, 2401 E. Airport Fwy., Irving, ☏ 214/579–5000; Aug.–Dec.).

HOCKEY

Dallas Stars (Reunion Arena, 777 Sports St., ☏ 214/467–8277; Oct.–Apr.).

Dining

For price ranges, see Chart 1 (A) in On the Road with Fodor's.

Dallas

$$$$ **French Room.** Wonderfully detailed nouvelle touches—such as veal that comes looking like a delicately wrought hummingbird—match the world-class service and exquisite baroque style of the dining room of this famous restaurant, in the Adolphus hotel. *1321 Commerce St., ☏ 214/742–8200. Reservations required. Jacket and tie required. AE, D, DC, MC, V. Closed Sun. No lunch.*

$$$ **Jennivine.** An intimate yet bustling feel reminiscent of an English pub makes this upscale Continental restaurant a local favorite. Try the excellent rack of lamb. *3605 McKinney Ave., ☏ 214/528–6010. Reservations required. AE, DC, MC, V. Closed Sun.*

$$ ★ **Calle Doce.** Head and shoulders above the Tex-Mex that most Americans think of as Mexican food is *cocina veracruzana,* superb cuisine from the Gulf of Mexico city of Veracruz. Come to this restaurant, frequented by power brokers and others who seek the very best, for such seafood delights as *huachinango* (red snapper smothered in sweet red peppers and onions) and *ceviche* (shellfish marinated in lime). *415 W. 12th St., ☏ 214/941–4304. AE, DC, MC, V.*

$ **Hoffbrau.** They have steak, but it's the best hamburgers in town that make the Western-theme Hoffbrau famous. *3205 Knox St., ☏ 214/559–2680. AE, DC, MC, V.*

$ **Mia's.** Film and stage celebrities mix with the unwashed masses in this crowded, upbeat Tex-Mex restaurant. You'll have to stand while you wait for seating, but it's worth it. *4322 Lemmon Ave., ☏ 214/526–1020. MC, V. Closed Sun.*

Fort Worth

$$$ **Saint-Emilion.** Practically hidden away in a brick chalet set back from the street, one of Fort Worth's very best restaurants offers great food and wine for the money. The country-French cuisine, such as roast duck, is matched by a list of 120 French and California wines. *3617 W. 7th St., ☏ 817/737–2781. AE, D, DC, MC, V. No lunch Sun.*

$$ **Joe T. Garcia's.** The city's best-known Tex-Mex restaurant, where margaritas are used to soak up huge portions, is adjacent to its own bakery/breakfast/lunch room. Joe T.'s is conveniently located on the way from downtown to the Stockyards. *2201 N. Commerce St., ☏ 817/626–4356. No credit cards.*

$–$$ **Benito's.** In the hospital district just south of downtown, this popular Tex-Mex spot open until 3 AM is known for its tamales and rare seasonal Mexican beers, such as Noche Buena. *1450 W. Magnolia Ave., ☏ 817/332–8633. AE, MC, V.*

$ **Bailey's Barbeque.** Although almost no one gets to sit down in this tiny hole-in-the-wall, it's been crowded since 1931 with judges, lawyers, and other courthouse folk. *826 Taylor St., ☏ 817/335–7469. No credit cards. No dinner. Closed weekends.*

Lodging

For price ranges, see Chart 2 (A) in On the Road with Fodor's.

Dallas

$$$$ **Adolphus.** Beer baron Adolphus Busch created this Beaux Arts building, Dallas's finest old hotel, in 1912, sparing nothing in the way of rich ornamentation inside and out. Widely admired by students of architecture, it was lavishly restored in 1981 at a cost of $60 million. *1321 Commerce St., 75202, ☎ 214/742–8200 or 800/221–9083, FAX 214/651–3588. 431 rooms, 27 suites. Facilities: 2 restaurants, 3 bars, access to health club. AE, D, DC, MC, V.*

$$$ **Hyatt Regency.** A typical Hyatt with its soaring atrium and its glass-and-brass look, this downtown hotel is best known for the panoramic views from the restaurant atop its 50-story tower. *300 Reunion Blvd., 75207, ☎ 214/651–1234 or 800/233–1234, FAX 214/782–8126. 943 rooms, 49 suites. Facilities: 3 restaurants, 3 bars, health club, jogging track, 2 tennis courts, sauna, whirlpool, pool. AE, D, DC, MC, V.*

$$–$$$ **Stoneleigh.** Just north of downtown, this fading brick hotel has long been favored by celebrities—including Oliver Stone while filming his movie on the Kennedy assassination. It is convenient to many restaurants and home to the Dallas Press Club. *2927 Maple Ave., 75201, ☎ 214/871–7111 or 800/255–9299, FAX 214/871–9379. 103 rooms, 27 suites. Facilities: restaurant, bar, pool. AE, D, DC, MC, V.*

$–$$ **La Quinta–North Central.** Although this is standard motor-inn fare, the location, on Central Expressway a short drive north of downtown, is excellent. *4440 N. Central Expressway, 75206, ☎ 214/821–4220 or 800/531–5900, FAX 214/821–7685. 101 rooms. Facilities: pool. AE, D, DC, MC, V.*

Fort Worth

$$$ **Worthington.** Built in 1981 of white concrete, this 12-story, ultramodern hotel stretches along two city blocks, forming a dramatic glassed-in bridge (where lunch, brunch, and tea are served) over Houston Street. There's a spare austerity to its rooms and a square-lined look to the large lobby. *200 N. Main St., 76102, ☎ 817/870–1000 or 800/433–5677; in TX, 800/772–5977; FAX 817/332–5679. 509 rooms, 69 suites. Facilities: 3 restaurants, bar, 2 tennis courts, pool, gym, whirlpool, sundeck. AE, D, DC, MC, V.*

$$–$$$ **Radisson Plaza.** The former Hotel Texas was once a great cattlemen's hotel, attested to by the steers celebrated in its terra-cotta frieze. Modernized but still rich with history, the hotel lodged President Kennedy in Suite 850 the night before his death; other suites have housed such famous guests as Rudolph Valentino and Jack Dempsey. *815 N. Main St., 76102, ☎ 817/870–2100 or 800/333–3333, FAX 817/882–1300. 516 rooms, 26 suites. Facilities: restaurant, bar, pool, health club, shops, sauna. AE, D, DC, MC, V.*

$$–$$$ **Stockyards.** A storybook place that's seen more than its share of cowboys, rustlers, gangsters, and oil barons, the hotel has been used in many a movie, including some shots in the Bonnie and Clyde Room, where the duo stayed in 1933. In the Booger Red Saloon, the barstools are saddles. *109 E. Exchange Ave., 76106, ☎ 817/625–6427 or 800/423–8471, FAX 817/624–2571. 46 rooms, 6 suites. Facilities: restaurant, bar. AE, D, DC, MC, V.*

$$ **Miss Molly's.** Once a prim little inn, then a raucous bordello, this place above the Star Cafe just outside the Stockyards has been reincarnated as an attractive bed-and-breakfast. *109½ W. Exchange Ave., 76106, ☎ 817/626–1522 or 800/996–6559. 7 rooms with shared bath, 1 suite. AE, DC, MC, V.*

The Arts and Nightlife

The Arts

DALLAS

The top performing-arts attraction in Dallas is whatever's at the **Morton H. Meyerson Symphony Center** (*see* Exploring Dallas, *above*), home to the **Dallas Symphony Orchestra** (☎ 214/871–4099). The **Dallas Theater Center** is a resident company that performs at the **Kalita Humphreys Theater** (3636 Turtle Creek Blvd., ☎ 214/526–8210), the only theater ever designed by Frank Lloyd Wright. The **Majestic Theatre** (1925 Elm St., ☎ 214/880–0137), a beautifully restored 1920s vaudeville/movie palace, hosts various groups, including the **Dallas Opera** (☎ 214/443–1043). In Fair Park, the **Starplex** (1818 1st Ave., ☎ 214/421–1111) hosts most big-name bands that come to town. The **Dallas Black Dance Theater** (2627 Flora St., ☎ 214/871–2376) has become locally famous.

FORT WORTH

The **Casa Mañana Theater** (3101 W. Lancaster Ave., ☎ 817/332–9319), a theater-in-the-round under one of Buckminster Fuller's first geodesic domes, plays host to the city's summer-musicals series. Other local theaters include the **Fort Worth Theater** (3505 W. Lancaster Ave., ☎ 817/738–6509) and **Stage West** (3055 S. University Dr., ☎ 817/784–9378).

Nightlife

DALLAS

Much of Dallas bar life swirls around lower and upper **Greenville Avenue,** north of downtown. On lower Greenville, **Flip's** (1520 Greenville Ave., ☎ 214/824–9944) has a pleasant outdoor terrace, while **Poor David's Pub** (1924 Greenville Ave., ☎ 214/821–9891) may be the top club venue for popular music in a town known for a good music scene. On upper Greenville, stop at the **San Francisco Rose** (3024 Greenville Ave., ☎ 214/826–2020) for a quiet drink and a bite to eat inside or outdoors. For country music and dancing, try **Cowboy's** (7331 Gaston Ave., ☎ 214/321–0115). Journalists hang out at what could easily pass for a real Chicago newspaper bar, **Louie's** (1839 N. Henderson St., ☎ 214/826–0505).

A younger, more avant-garde scene is found in Deep Ellum, where **Club Dada** (2720 Elm St., ☎ 214/744–3232) is one of several trend-setting music venues. **Adair's** (2624 Commerce St., ☎ 214/939–9900) is more of a neighborhood bar, complete with pool tables, while **Crescent City Cafe** (2615 Commerce St., ☎ 214/745–1900) offers Creole cuisine.

FORT WORTH

The area around the Stockyards, in particular, is crammed with saloons of distinctly Western flavor. The best may be the **White Elephant Saloon** (100 E. Exchange Ave., ☎ 817/624–8241), whose owner brought keno to Fort Worth. But the most famous is **Billy Bob's Texas** (2520 Rodeo Plaza, ☎ 817/624–7117), built in an old cattle-pen building and offering big country-music names regularly. Downtown offers one extraordinary spot: the **Caravan of Dreams** (312 Houston St., ☎ 817/877–3000), a performing-arts center with a rooftop cactus garden that has to be seen to be believed. The club is a world-class music venue, specializing in jazz and blues greats, but also pulling in top eclectic performers like Lyle Lovett. It's worth a visit just to see the famous jazz, dance, and theater murals.

ELSEWHERE IN THE STATE

East Texas

Getting There

Between Dallas and Shreveport, Louisiana, lies east Texas, whose main east–west artery is I–20. Marshall, the heart of the region, is about a three-hour drive from Dallas or a half hour from the Louisiana line. Daily **Amtrak** trains serve Marshall.

What to See and Do

Heading into east Texas from the Dallas–Fort Worth area, you'll pass two great boundaries: a natural line, marking the start of a piney, hilly region totally unlike the Great Plains, and a man-made one, the beginning of what was the slaveholding part of the United States. In every way, east Texas—a region once dependent on cotton—feels more Southern than Western, a fact of which the local architecture will continually remind you. After Texas seceded from the union in 1861, **Marshall** became the seat of civil authority west of the Mississippi and the wartime capital of Missouri; five Confederate generals are buried in its cemetery. The town is full of historic homes, some of which—like the **Starr Family Home** (407 W. Travis St., ☏ 903/935–3044)—can be toured; others are small hostelries. One of its charms is the beautiful **Stagecoach Road** (take Poplar St., which heads east from U.S. 59, and follow markers); in places, the stages cut some 20 feet into the ground on this undisturbed section of the old main road to Shreveport. Off U.S. 59, signs lead to **Marshall Pottery** (☏ 903/938–9201), a huge working pottery.

Jefferson, a 20-minute drive north, is one of Texas's most historic towns, a charming place on Big Cypress Bayou that once served hundreds of steamboats coming up from New Orleans. When his offer to run track through the town was rebuffed, railroad baron Jay Gould is said to have angrily scrawled in the register of the Excelsior House hotel the prophetic words "The End of Jefferson." Today the superb **Excelsior House** (211 W. Austin St., ☏ 903/665–2513), built in the 1850s, is a tribute to the restorer's art (reservations are required months in advance). Across the street is **Gould's Private Railroad Car** (admission charged).

Caddo Lake, hung with Spanish moss and edged with bald cypresses, is a fishing mecca straddling the Texas-Louisiana border. At various times it has been home to the beleaguered Caddo Indians, to bootleggers hiding out in its dense shore growth, to the great spiritual singer Leadbelly (reared at Swanson's Landing), to a thriving steamboat traffic from New Orleans, and to all manner of legend. **Caddo Lake State Park** (*see* National and State Parks, *above*) is on the south shore.

Dining

For price ranges, see Chart 1 (B) in On the Road with Fodor's.

$$ **Black Swan.** The specialty here is Southern cooking with a touch of Creole, served either inside the beautiful historic home or outdoors, on a second-floor balcony overlooking the main street. *210 W. Austin St., Jefferson, ☏ 903/665–8922. MC, V. Closed Tues.–Wed.*

Lodging

For price ranges, see Chart 2 (B) in On the Road with Fodor's.

$$–$$$ **Pride House.** Ornate woodwork and original stained glass distinguish this old Victorian mansion, one of Jefferson's finest B&Bs. *409 E. Broadway, Jefferson 75657, ☏ 903/665–2675. 10 rooms. MC, V.*

$$ **Caddo Cottage.** This is the place for a family looking for a quiet time along one of the most beautiful parts of Caddo Lake. *Taylor Island, Uncertain 75661, ☏ 903/789–3988. 1 apartment, sleeps 4. No credit cards.*

El Paso

Getting There

At Texas's far southwest corner, El Paso is 11 hours' drive from San Antonio; about 12 from Dallas–Fort Worth; 6 from Santa Fe, New Mexico; and 5 from Phoenix, Arizona. **El Paso International Airport** (Southwest is the major local carrier, ☏ 800/435–9792) and **Amtrak** (Union Station, 700 San Francisco St., ☏ 800/872–7245) serve the city.

What to See and Do

Dramatically situated a few miles between the southern end of the Rockies and the northern terminus of Mexico's Sierra Madre range, **El Paso** (established by the Spanish in 1598) was a major stopping point on the way west during the California gold rush. Outside the city, in El Paso's lower valley, are several important historic sites. **Mission Ysleta** (Old Pueblo Rd., Zaragosa exit off I–10 east of El Paso, ☏ 915/859–9848), circa 1681, is the oldest Spanish mission in the Southwest. The adjacent **Tigua Indian Reservation** (119 S. Old Pueblo Rd., ☏ 915/859–3916), home of the oldest ethnic group in Texas, offers Tigua pottery, jewelry, art, and replicas of ancient Native American homes. To the south are **Soccoro Mission** (328 S. Nevares, ☏ 915/859–7718), famed for its fine vigas—the carved ceiling beams that mark local architecture—and **San Elizario Presidio** (1556 San Elizario Rd., ☏ 915/851–2333), a fort built to protect the missions.

Across the Rio Grande is the Mexican city of **Juarez,** which offers often sensational shopping; try the **El Paso–Juarez International Trolley** (Santa Fe and Main Sts., ☏ 915/544–0061). **Scenic Drive** (north on Mesa St., then right on Rim Rd.) offers panoramic views of El Paso. **Transmountain Road** (off I–10 west of downtown) takes you through "Smuggler's Gap," a dramatic cut across the Franklin Mountains. For more information, contact the **El Paso Convention & Visitors Bureau** (1 Civic Center Plaza, 79901, ☏ 915/534–0600 or 800/351–6024).

Dining

For price ranges, see Chart 1 (B) in On the Road with Fodor's.

$$ **Tigua Indian Reservation.** In a cheerful, feather-and-pottery-bedecked dining room adjacent to the reservation gift shop, this Mexican-flavored restaurant offers delightful Tigua twists. *122 Old Pueblo Rd., ☏ 915/859–3916. AE, D, MC, V. Closed Mon.–Tues.*

Lodging

For price ranges, see Chart 2 (B) in On the Road with Fodor's.

$$$ **Camino Royal Paso del Norte.** This elegant brick downtown hotel is listed on the National Register of Historic Places. The jewel of the lobby is the dark-wood circular Dome Bar, which sits under a superb 1912 Tiffany skylight. Guest rooms are functional and large. *101 S. El Paso St., 79901, ☏ 915/534–3000 or 800/722–6466, FAX 915/534–3024. 375 rooms. Facilities: 2 restaurants, bar, nightclub, pool, exercise room, sauna. AE, D, DC, MC, V.*

South Padre Island

Getting There

In the southeast corner of the state, near the Mexican border town of Matamoros, South Padre Island is reached by a bridge across the Intracoastal Waterway from Port Isabel, which, in turn, is accessible from Rtes. 48 and 100.

What to See and Do

At the southern tip of one of the largest barrier islands in the world—113-mile-long Padre Island—the resort town and white-sand beaches of South Padre Island (population: 1,677) attract college students at spring break but delight nature-seekers, beach and sun lovers, and fishermen the rest of the year. To the north, the 80½-mile **Padre Island National Seashore** (9405 South Padre Island Dr., Corpus Christi 78418, ☏ 512/949–8173; admission charged) is entirely natural, unchanged from the days when scavenging Karankawa Indians roamed among its sand dunes, sea oats, and beach morning glories. For further information, contact the **South Padre Island Convention & Visitors Bureau** (600 Padre Island Blvd.; Box 3500, 78597, ☏ 210/761–6433 or 800/343–2368).

Austin

Getting There

Between Dallas–Fort Worth and San Antonio on I–35, Austin is accessible from Houston via U.S. 290. **Robert Mueller Municipal Airport** (☏ 512/472–3321) handles local flights.

What to See and Do

Austin, created as capital of the new Republic of Texas in 1839, is perhaps the least Texan of cities: a liberal enclave in a generally conservative state and a heavily treed, hilly town in a land more commonly known for its monotonous flatness. Austin is famous throughout the Southwest for its thriving **music scene,** which plays itself out on scores of blues, country, rock, jazz, and other stages. It is also home to the nation's largest urban **bat colony,** found under the Congress Avenue bridge during the summer months. The **state capitol** (11th and Congress Sts., ☏ 512/463–0063) is a striking building of pink Texas granite; after a major restoration, tours are expected to resume in 1995. The **Lyndon B. Johnson Presidential Library and Museum** (2313 Red River Rd. on the University of Texas campus, ☏ 512/482–5136) has a replica of the president's Oval Office and exhibits on his political life and programs. Further information is available at the **Austin Convention & Visitors Bureau** (201 E. 2nd St., 78701, ☏ 512/478–0098 or 800/888–8287).

UTAH

By Stacey Clark

Capital	Salt Lake City
Population	1,916,000
Motto	Industry
State Bird	California gull
State Flower	Sego lily

Visitor Information

Utah Travel Council (Council Hall, Capitol Hill, Salt Lake City 84114, ☎ 801/538–1030 or 800/200–1160). Nine **regional visitor information centers** offer brochures and travel advice (call the Utah Travel Council for locations), and **welcome centers** are near all major entrances to the state. **Utah Centennial Commission** (324 S. State St., Suite 234, Salt Lake City 84111, ☎ 801/531–1996) can send you a calendar of centennial events for 1996.

Scenic Drives

From Logan, **U.S. 89** runs north through a limestone canyon with steep, striated walls, cresting above Bear Lake on the Utah–Idaho border. In northeastern Utah, **U.S. 191** jogs north out of Vernal past geologic formations up to a billion years old before meeting **Rte. 44,** which gives an elongated view of Flaming Gorge National Recreation Area amid scents of desert sage and juniper. A colorful guide, *Utah Scenic Byways and Backways,* is available at regional visitor information centers and welcome centers.

National and State Parks

National Parks

Utah has five national parks, including **Bryce Canyon** and **Zion** (*see* Exploring Southwestern Utah, *below*) and **Canyonlands** and **Arches** (*see* Exploring Southeastern Utah, *below*). Once called "Land of the Sleeping Rainbow" because of its colorfully striped cliffs, **Capitol Reef National Park** (Torrey 84775, ☎ 801/425–3791), reached via Rte. 24 off I–70/U.S. 50, has still-flourishing riverside orchards planted by early settlers. Petroglyphs line the canyon walls near the Fremont River.

Utah's six national monuments include the excavations at **Dinosaur National Monument** (Box 128, Jensen 84035, ☎ 801/789–2115), the limestone caverns of **Timpanogos Cave** (Rte. 3, Box 200, American Fork 84003, ☎ 801/756–0351), and the giant, stream-formed spans of **Natural Bridges National Monument** (Box 1, Lake Powell 84533, ☎ 801/259–5239). **Glen Canyon National Recreation Area** (*see* Exploring Southeastern Utah, *below*) and **Flaming Gorge National Recreation Area** (Box 278, Manila 84046, ☎ 801/784–3445) offer fishing and boating on huge reservoirs.

State Parks

The **Division of State Parks** (1636 W. North Temple St., Salt Lake City 84116, ☎ 801/538–7221) publishes a directory of Utah's 45 state parks. **Goblin Valley State Park** (Box 637, Green River 84525, ☎ 801/564–3633), off I–70 on Rte. 24 in eastern Utah, has acres of wind-eroded sandstone "goblins" around a desert campground. **This Is The Place State**

Park (2601 Sunnyside Ave., Salt Lake City 84108, ☏ 801/584-8391), on the east bench of the Salt Lake Valley, details the trek of Mormon pioneers and re-creates an 1850s township, complete with cooking, crafts, and blacksmithing demonstrations.

SALT LAKE CITY

On July 24, 1847, Mormon leader Brigham Young looked out over the Salt Lake Valley and announced to the ragged party behind him, "This is the right place." So began the religious settlement that would become Salt Lake City. The conservative influence of the Church of Jesus Christ of Latter-day Saints, as the Mormon church is officially known, continues to shape the city. Nevertheless, it has come a long way from its pioneer origins to its current position as a major winter-sports destination, a center for biomedical research, and the gateway to the natural wonders of southern Utah.

Tourist Information

Salt Lake City: Convention and Visitor's Bureau (180 S. West Temple St., ☏ 801/521-2822).

Arriving and Departing

By Plane

Salt Lake International Airport (☏ 801/575-2400) is 7 mi north of downtown. Major hotels provide shuttles, and **Utah Transit Authority** (☏ 801/287-4636) buses link the airport to regular city routes. Taxi fare to downtown averages $10-$15, including tip.

By Car

I-15 runs north-south through Salt Lake, I-80 east-west. I-215 circles the valley.

By Train

Amtrak (☏ 800/872-7245) serves the city's **Rio Grande Depot** (320 Rio Grande St., ☏ 801/531-0189).

By Bus

Greyhound Lines (160 W. South Temple St., ☏ 800/231-2222).

Getting Around Salt Lake City

Salt Lake City streets are laid out geometrically and numbered in increments of 100 in each direction, with Temple Square as their root. It is easy to get around by car; parking is inexpensive, and streets and highways are less crowded than those in comparable urban areas. **Utah Transit Authority** (☏ 801/287-4636; fare: 75¢, with a free fare zone in downtown shopping areas) buses and trolleys serve the valley.

Exploring Salt Lake City

City attractions fan out from Temple Square. To the north is the Capitol Hill district, to the south are shopping and arts locations, to the east lie the ski resorts of the Wasatch Mountains, and to the west is the Great Salt Lake.

Historic **Temple Square** (North Visitors' Center, 50 W. North Temple St., ☏ 801/240-2534) is the 10-acre core of sites central to Mormonism. Two visitor centers house exhibits and art with religious themes. The Mormon Tabernacle Choir performs on Thursday and Saturday in the squat, domed **Salt Lake Tabernacle.** While the six-spired granite **Salt Lake Temple** itself is closed to all but church members, the other buildings and monuments on the beautifully landscaped grounds are open to the public free of charge. In winter, the trees twinkle with thousands of lights for the holiday season.

East of Temple Square, across Main Street, the **Joseph Smith Memorial Building** (☎ 801/240–1266) is a Mormon community center where visitors can learn how to do genealogical research through a computer program and watch an hour-long film on early Mormon history and the emigration of Mormons to the Salt Lake Valley in the mid-19th century. The center also has two restaurants.

Directly west of Temple Square are the **Museum of Church History and Art** (☎ 801/240–3310), displaying Mormon artifacts, paintings, fabric art, and sculptures; and the **Family History Library** (☎ 801/240–2331), offering free public access to the Mormons' huge collection of genealogical records.

On the corner of South Temple and State streets is the 1854 **Beehive House** (☎ 801/240–2671), the home of Brigham Young while he served as territorial governor. The **Lion House** (☎ 801/363–5466) next door received the overflow of Young's large family; it is now a social center and restaurant.

The renaissance-revival-style **state capitol** (☎ 801/538–3000), completed in 1915, sits on a hill at the north end of State Street. In addition to marble-walled legislative and Supreme Court chambers, the building has interesting statues and plaques tucked into niches on the main floor. Depression-era murals in the rotunda depict events from Utah's past. Scattered on the grounds are a number of historical monuments, including a bronze statue of a young soldier, honoring Vietnam veterans.

The **Pioneer Memorial Museum,** west of the capitol grounds, holds thousands of artifacts, including tools and carriages from the late 1800s and a doll and toy collection. *300 N. Main St., ☎ 801/538–1050. Closed Sun.*

The **Marmalade District**—the streets bisecting the west slope of Capitol Hill—contains many original pioneer houses. Other well-preserved historic houses are on South Temple Street east of Temple Square. Among them is the **Kearns Mansion,** at No. 603 (☎ 801/538–1005), the governor's residence; tours are offered. Also on South Temple Street is the recently restored early 20th-century **Catholic Church of the Madeleine** (331 E. South Temple St., ☎ 801/328–8941). The 26th-floor observation deck of Salt Lake's tallest structure, the **LDS Church Administration Building** (50 E. North Temple St., ☎ 801/240–2452), offers the best views of the city.

In the Vicinity

About 17 mi west of downtown via I–80 is the **Great Salt Lake.** Water flows into it with no outlet other than evaporation, so minerals and salts remain trapped, causing the lake to be more saline than any other body of water on Earth except the Dead Sea. There is one beach with showers, and sailboats dot the lake with color on summer days. The south and west shores and neighboring wetlands are prime nesting grounds for many species of migratory, shore, and wading birds.

Southeast of Salt Lake City, the **Wasatch Mountains** part in two scenic canyons (Rte. 190 and Rte. 210). Resorts here offer arts festivals and concerts in summer and skiing in winter (*see* Ski Areas, *below*); **Snow-**

bird Resort, one of the country's outstanding ski areas, has a 125-passenger tram that delivers mountaintop views year-round.

Utah's premier ski destination and only bona-fide resort town, **Park City** (*see* Ski Areas, *below*), 29 mi east of Salt Lake City on I–80, is home to the U.S. Ski Team and Ski Association. In addition to its three ski areas, it offers a historic **Main Street,** with a museum, art galleries, shops, and restaurants in restored buildings; several elegant bed-and-breakfasts; three golf courses; and a factory-outlet mall. It also offers Deer Valley Resort, where both the slopes and the clientele are equally manicured.

Two-and-a-half hours' drive east on U.S. 40 from Salt Lake City, in the northeast part of the state, is **Dinosaur National Monument** (*see* National Parks, *above*), which showcases the remains of Jurassic giants, colorful canyons and deserts, and petroglyphs. The Green and Yampa rivers offer white-water rafting opportunities; some stretches of the Green River are great for placid float trips and wildlife viewing.

Parks and Gardens

Red Butte Gardens (☎ 801/581–5322), east of the University of Utah campus, has 150 acres of trees, shrubs, herbs, wildflowers, and stream-fed pools tucked into a private canyon in the Wasatch foothills. A concert series is held each summer.

What to See and Do with Children

The **Children's Museum of Utah** (840 N. 300 West, ☎ 801/328–3383) lets kids explore a 727 jet plane, a semitruck, strange light effects, and an archaeological dig. **Raging Waters** (1200 W. 1700 South, ☎ 801/973–4020), Utah's largest water park, has 11 pools and 19 rip-roaring slides. **Hansen Planetarium** (15 S. State St., ☎ 801/538–2098) is a dignified buff-faced building with free exhibits and a domed theater for daily star shows. **Hogle Zoo** (2600 Sunnyside Ave., ☎ 801/582–1631) has 1,200 animals. Bring walking shoes and a hat; exhibits are spread out, and shade is at a premium. **Wheeler Historic Farm** (6351 S. 900 East, ☎ 801/264–2212) has a well-stocked trout pond and daily "chore tours." There is an admission charge at all of these attractions.

Shopping

Crossroads Plaza (50 S. Main St., ☎ 801/531–1799) has four floors of stores, theaters, and restaurants. The neighboring **ZCMI Center** (36 S. State St., ☎ 801/321–8743) features 80 stores and restaurants. **Trolley Square** (600 S. 700 East, ☎ 801/521–9877) once housed electric trolleys; today it has the city's most varied shopping, as well as restaurants and movie theaters.

Spectator Sports

Basketball

Utah Jazz (Delta Center, 300 W. South Temple St., ☎ 801/355–3865; Nov.–Apr.).

Ski Areas

Utah's dry powder offers exceptional downhill and cross-country skiing. Lift lines are short and tickets are reasonable at all ski areas; those listed below are about 25 mi southeast of Salt Lake City. **Solitude Nordic Center** (Rte. 190, ☎ 801/536–5774 or 800/748–4754) and **White Pine Touring** (Park City, ☎ 801/649–8701) offer cross-country skiing

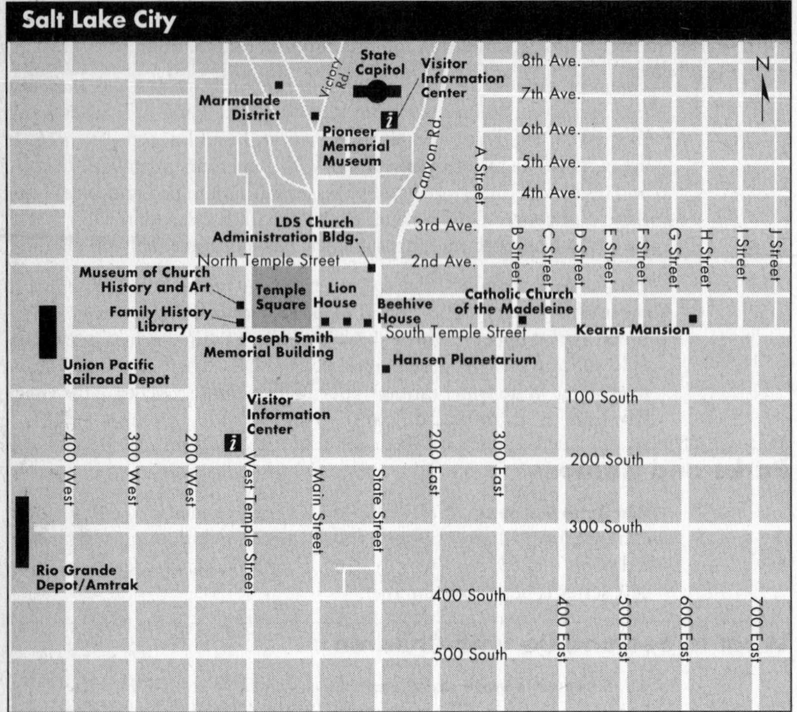

tours, rentals, lessons, and advice. For more information, call **Ski Utah** (☎ 801/534–1779; snow report, ☎ 801/521–8102).

Alta (Rte. 210, ☎ 801/742–3333), 39 runs, 8 lifts, 2,100-ft vertical drop. **Brighton** (Rte. 190, ☎ 801/943–8309 or 800/873–5512), 64 runs, 7 lifts, 1,745-ft drop. **Deer Valley** (Rte. 224, ☎ 801/649–1000), 66 runs, 13 lifts, 2,200-ft drop. **Park City Ski Area** (Rte. 224 off I–80, ☎ 801/649–8111 or 800/222–7275), 89 runs, 13 lifts, gondola, 3,100-ft drop. **Snowbird** (Rte. 210, ☎ 801/742–2222 or 800/453–3000), 47 runs, 8 lifts including high-speed tram, 3,100-ft drop. **Solitude** (Rte. 190, ☎ 801/534–1400), 63 runs and bowls, 7 lifts, 2,030-ft drop, 12 mi of groomed cross-country track. **Sundance** (U.S. 189 off I–15, ☎ 801/225–4107 or 800/892–1600), 41 runs, 4 lifts, 2,150-ft drop. **Wolf Mountain** (Rte. 92, ☎ 801/649–5400), 58 runs, 7 lifts, 2,200-ft drop.

Dining

Dining in Salt Lake offers variety and lots of food for your money. Liquor laws have some peculiarities, but mixed drinks, wine, and beer are available at most restaurants; when in doubt, call ahead. For price ranges, see Chart 1 (B) in On the Road with Fodor's.

$$$$ ★ **Glitretind.** A source of Deer Valley's unsurpassed reputation in ski-resort dining, this fabulous restaurant is worth breaking open the piggy bank for. How does saffron sauce and Caspian caviar with your New England lobster sound? Or grilled chicken breast stuffed with goat cheese? This is the stuff that magazines rave about when Deer Valley is the topic of discussion. *Stein Eriksen Lodge, Deer Valley,* ☎ *801/645–6455. AE, DC, MC, V.*

Salt Lake City Vicinity

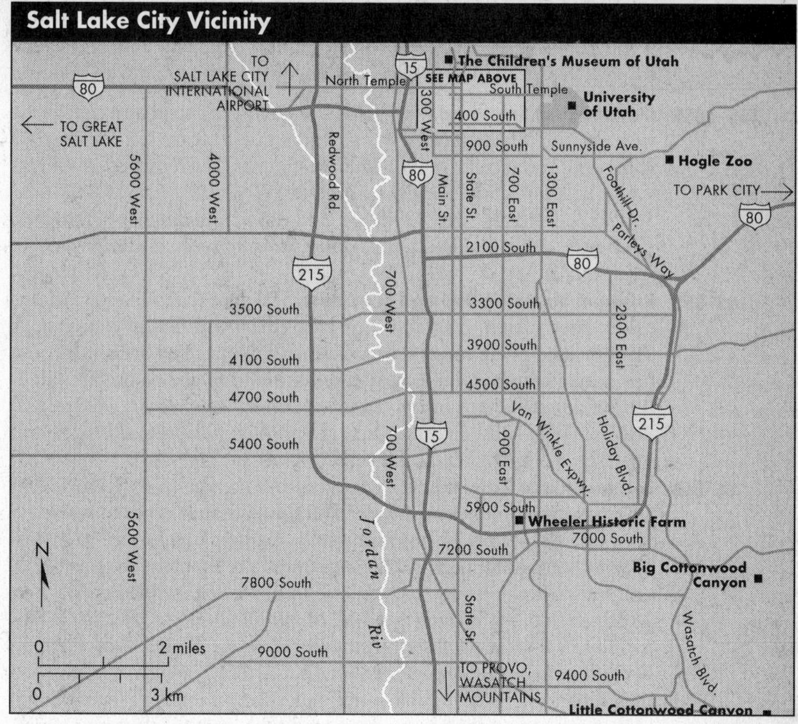

$$$ ★ **Santa Fe Restaurant.** In a stream-side lodge with mountain views, Southwestern concoctions are highlighted by fresh herbs and unusual sauces. *2100 Emigration Canyon Rd., ☎ 801/582–5888. MC, V.*

$$ ★ **Baci Trattoria.** The combination of northern and southern Italian food served in surroundings of marble and stained glass makes Baci a feast for the eyes and the taste buds. *134 W. Pierpont Ave., ☎ 801/328–1500. AE, MC, V. Closed Sun.*

$$ **Lamb's Restaurant.** Having opened its doors in 1919, Lamb's claims to be Utah's oldest operating restaurant. The decor is reminiscent of a turn-of-the-century diner, and the menu has beef, chicken, and seafood dishes, plus a selection of sandwiches. *169 S. Main St., ☎ 801/364–7166. AE, D, DC, MC, V. Closed Sun.*

$$ **Market Street Grill.** The stylish black-and-white decor is catchy, but the food steals the show. The large menu includes creatively prepared seafood, steaks, and chicken. *48 Market St., ☎ 801/322–4668. AE, MC, V.*

$ ★ **Squatter's Pub Brewery.** It seems delightfully sinister to enjoy home-brewed beer in a state like Utah, but that's exactly what you'll find here. Combining a lively atmosphere with great food and drink, Squatter's comes highly recommended by locals and visitors alike. In addition to the popular Squatterburger, the Sicilian-style pizza, and the generous plate of fish-and-chips, you'll also find killer bread pudding as well as six different ales. *147 W. Broadway, ☎ 801/363–2739. AE, D, DC, MC, V.*

Lodging

Salt Lake lodgings stretch from the airport east to the downtown area and south on State and Main streets. Contact the **Utah Hotel and**

Motel Association (9 Exchange Pl., Suite 812, Salt Lake City 84111, ☎ 801/359–0104) for further suggestions. Prices vary widely with the seasons. For price ranges, see Chart 2 (A) in On the Road with Fodor's.

$$$–$$$$ Cliff Lodge at Snowbird Resort. This angular gray structure echoes the surrounding Wasatch Mountains. Large guest rooms with wide glass walls offer spectacular views winter or summer. The redwood-and-brass lobby is sumptuous. *Snowbird Resort 84092, ☎ 801/521–6040 or 800/453–3000, FAX 801/742–3204. 532 rooms. Facilities: 3 restaurants, 2 lounges, spa, 2 pools, valet parking, laundry service, laundry room. AE, D, DC, MC, V.*

$$–$$$ ★ Brigham Street Inn Bed and Breakfast. The decor in each room of this solid Queen Anne mansion was created by a different designer. A black-walled living room is dramatic yet inviting. The breakfast room has a long common table near the marble fireplace or private tables for two with wing chairs. *1135 E. South Temple St., 84102, ☎ 801/364–4461, FAX 801/521–3201. 9 rooms. Facilities: dining room, off-street parking. AE, D, DC, MC, V.*

$$–$$$ Shadow Ridge Resort. Just a few feet from the Park City Resort Center, you can amble to the slopes in less time than it takes to warm up your car. Accommodations range from a single hotel room to a two-bedroom condominium suite. All rooms are attractively furnished, and the staff is friendly and experienced. *50 Shadow Ridge St., Box 1820, 84060, ☎ 801/649–4300 or 800/451–3031, FAX 801/649–5951. 150 rooms. Facilities: restaurant, lounge, heated outdoor pool, hot tub, sauna, laundry room. AE, DC, MC, V.*

$$ Little America. Private, double-tiered wings flank a central 17-story building; sunny tower rooms are decorated with gentle colors and generously upholstered furniture. The lobby and mezzanine have enormous brick fireplaces. *500 S. Main St., 84102, ☎ 801/363–6781 or 800/453–9450, FAX 801/596–5911. 850 rooms. Facilities: 2 restaurants, lounge, exercise room, pool, laundry room, underground parking, airport shuttle. AE, D, DC, MC, V.*

$$ ★ Peery Hotel. This four-story gray-brick hotel opened in 1910. Most guest rooms are furnished with eclectic antique reproductions and fanciful linens. The plush lobby lends itself to loitering. *110 W. 3rd South, 84102, ☎ 801/521–4300 or 800/331–0073, FAX 801/575–5014. 77 rooms. Facilities: 2 restaurants, 2 lounges, pool, sauna, exercise room, laundry room, airport shuttle. AE, D, DC, MC, V.*

$ Airport Inn. This chunky, redbrick motel near the freeway and airport offers good value. The rooms are generically furnished but reasonably quiet, considering the location. *2333 W. North Temple St., 84116, ☎ 801/539–0438, FAX 801/539–8852. 100 rooms. Facilities: restaurant, lounge, airport shuttle. AE, D, DC, MC, V.*

$ ★ Skyline Inn. On the edge of a quiet neighborhood, and near restaurants and shopping, this tan stucco motel is well maintained and friendly. *2475 E. 1700 South, 84108, ☎ 801/582–5350. 24 rooms. Facilities: pool, hot tub. AE, D, DC, MC, V.*

The Arts and Nightlife

A calendar of events is available at the **Salt Lake Convention and Visitors Bureau** (*see* Tourist Information, *above*). The ***Salt Lake Tribune*** carries daily arts and entertainment listings.

The Arts

Salt Lake's best arts bets are **Ballet West** (50 W. 200 South, ☎ 801/355–2787), **Pioneer Theater Company** (300 S. 1340 East St., ☎ 801/581–6961), **Salt Lake Acting Company** (168 W. 500 North, ☎ 801/363–0525),

Utah Opera Company (50 W. 200 South, ☎ 801/355–2787), and **Utah Symphony** (Abravanel Hall, 123 W. South Temple St., ☎ 801/533–5626). Concerts are presented at the **Delta Center** (300 W. South Temple St., ☎ 801/325–2000).

Nightlife

Many night spots are private clubs, meaning a membership is required (temporary memberships cost about $5). Weekends are wild at the **Dead Goat Saloon** (165 S. West Temple St., ☎ 801/328–4628), a subterranean hangout with live music and a busy dance floor. **Port O' Call** (78 W. 400 South, ☎ 801/521–0589) serves mountains of nachos and features popular local bands. The art deco–style **Zephyr Club** (301 S. West Temple St., ☎ 801/355–5646) has live blues, rock, reggae, and dancing. **The Bay** (404 S. West Temple St., ☎ 801/363–2623) is a smoke- and alcohol-free club with three dance floors.

SOUTHWESTERN UTAH

Southwestern Utah is a colorful mingling of desert, red-rock formations, and pristine forests. Heading the list of natural wonders are Zion and Bryce Canyon national parks, where clear air and high elevations create spectacular hundred-mile vistas. The picturesque towns of St. George, Cedar City, and Springdale offer historic sites and year-round warm weather.

Tourist Information

Color Country Travel Bureau (906 N. 14th West, Box 1550, St. George 84771, ☎ 801/628–4171 or 800/233–8824).

Getting There

By Plane

St. George and **Cedar City airports** are served by **Skywest Airlines** (☎ 800/453–9417).

By Car

I–15 and U.S. 89 pass north–south through the region.

By Bus

Greyhound Lines (☎ 800/231–2222) stops in St. George and Cedar City.

Exploring Southwestern Utah

At **Bryce Canyon National Park,** millions of years of geologic mayhem have created gigantic bowls filled with strange pinnacles and quilted drapes of stone. An 18-mi scenic drive skirts the western rim, offering views of the amphitheaters. *Rte. 12, Bryce Canyon 84717, ☎ 801/834–5322. Admission charged. Some roads closed Nov.–Mar.*

Cedar City is the setting for the state's premier theatrical event: the **Utah Shakespearean Festival** (☎ 801/586–7878; June–Sept.), offering feasts, bawdy Elizabethan skits, and performances in an open-air replica of the Globe Theatre.

The Virgin River carved the towering cliffs of Zion Canyon and still flows along its floor. Spring-fed hanging gardens sprout lush greens along the walls. **Zion National Park** offers roads, tram tours, and horseback and hiking trails for exploring the beauties of the vividly hued canyon and its tributaries. It can be very crowded in summer. *Rte. 9, Springdale 84767, ☎ 801/772–3256. Admission charged.*

Nearby, the sleepy and picturesque towns of **Virgin, Rockville,** and **Springdale** dot the desert at the base of lofty red cliffs. To the west, in **St. George,** you can tour the historic district and **Brigham Young's Winter Home** (89 W. 200 North, ☎ 801/673–5181). In **Santa Clara,** the 130-year-old **house of missionary Jacob Hamblin** (3386 Santa Clara Dr., ☎ 801/673–2161) has cotton plants and a vineyard.

Sports and the Outdoors

Biking

Rte. 9 through Zion, the **Bryce Canyon Scenic Loop,** and **Rte. 18** through Snow Canyon offer classic southwestern scenery. **Bicycle Utah** (☎ 801/649–5806) offers a free directory of biking routes.

Golf

St. George attracts golfers year-round to seven public courses, including **Dixie Red Hills** (1000 North 700 West, ☎ 801/634–5852; 9 holes) and **South Gate** (1075 Tonaquint Dr., ☎ 801/628–0000; 18 holes). The **Washington County Travel Council** (☎ 801/634–5747 or 800/869–6635) has information.

Hiking and Backpacking

Bryce and Zion national parks (*see* Exploring Southwestern Utah, *above*) have many trails of varying difficulty. Zion's paved **Gateway to the Narrows Trail** follows the Virgin River. Bryce's moderately difficult **Navajo Loop Trail** has views of towering Thor's Hammer.

Dining and Lodging

Southwestern Utah offers several dining and lodging options. **Accommodations Referral Service** (☎ 800/259–3343) and **R & R Tours** (☎ 801/628–7710) provide area-wide recommendations. For price ranges, see Charts 1 (B) and 2 (B) in On the Road with Fodor's.

Bryce Canyon

DINING AND LODGING

Bryce Lodge. The lobby and dining room of this rustic 1920s wood-and-sandstone lodge have high ceilings with exposed beams and massive stone fireplaces. The sturdily furnished guest rooms are geared to informal travelers. *Bryce Canyon National Park, Box 400, Cedar City 84720, ☎ 801/586–7686, FAX 801/586–3157. 114 rooms. Facilities: restaurant ($$). AE, DC, MC, V. Closed Nov.–Apr. $$–$$$*

Ruby's Inn. Five two-story buildings contain the motel-like, simply decorated guest rooms; the rough-hewn public areas are in a more rustic structure. The restaurant serves basic American fare, with creative specials. *Rte. 63, Box 1, 84717, ☎ 801/834–5341 or 800/528–1234, FAX 801/834–5265. 368 rooms. Facilities: restaurant, pool, hot tub. AE, D, DC, MC, V. $$*

Cedar City

DINING

★ **Milt's Stage Stop.** Locals and an increasing number of tourists have discovered terrific food and inviting atmosphere of this dinner spot in beautiful Cedar Canyon. It's known for its 12-ounce rib-eye steak, prime rib, and fresh crab, lobster, and shrimp dishes. The splendid views of the surrounding mountains delight patrons year-round. *5 mi east of town on Rte. 14, ☎ 801/586–9344. AE, D, DC, MC, V. $$*

St. George

DINING

Pancho and Lefty's. The Mexican cuisine served here varies from authentic tamales wrapped in corn husks to avocado-laced taco salads. The decor is spirited, and the margaritas are tart. *1050 S. Bluff St., ☎ 801/628–4772. AE, MC, V. $$*

LODGING

★ **Seven Wives Inn Bed and Breakfast.** Guest rooms in two neighboring pioneer homes are named after the wives of the innkeeper's polygamous grandfather. The furnishings include quilts from the late 1800s, lace canopies, and massive wood and iron beds. *217 N. 100 West, 84770, ☎ 801/628–3737 or 800/600–3737. 13 rooms. Facilities: dining room, pool, off-street parking. AE, D, DC, MC, V. $$*

Springdale

DINING

★ **Bit and Spur Restaurant and Saloon.** This low-slung eatery serves innovative and healthy Southwestern-style Mexican food. Works by local artists fill the pine-paneled interior, while the patio features bright flowers and scents from the herb garden. *1212 Zion Park Blvd., ☎ 801/772–3498. MC, V. Closed Tues.–Wed. Nov.–Feb. $$*

Flannigans. Whether you sit inside or out, Zion Canyon is the focus at this modern wood-and-glass restaurant where grilled steaks and fresh vegetables are artfully prepared. *428 Zion Park Blvd., ☎ 801/772–3244. MC, V. $$*

LODGING

★ **Cliffrose Lodge and Gardens.** Acres of lawn, trees, and gardens surround the low, rambling stucco wings of this hotel on the banks of the Virgin River, ¼ mi from Zion. The ample rooms are decorated in desert hues. *281 Zion Park Blvd., 84767, ☎ 801/772–3234 or 800/243–8824, FAX 801/772–3900. 36 rooms. Facilities: pool. AE, D, MC, V. $$*

Campgrounds

The region has nearly 100 national park and forest, state park, and private campgrounds from which to choose; for more information contact the **Utah Travel Council** (*see* Visitor Information, *above*). **Snow Canyon State Park** (Box 140, Santa Clara 84765, ☎ 801/628–2255) and the larger **Watchman Campground** (Zion National Park, Springdale 84767, ☎ 801/772–3256) have tent sites and RV hookups.

SOUTHEASTERN UTAH

For years southeastern Utah has captured the imagination of filmmakers, serving as the site of such Western and adventure films as *Stagecoach, Indiana Jones and the Last Crusade,* and *Thelma and Louise.* Highlighting this canyon country, rugged Arches and Canyonlands national parks invite exploration by way of scenic drives, four-wheeling, hiking, rock-climbing, river-running, and cycling.

Tourist Information

Grand County: Travel Council (Main and Center Sts., Box 550, Moab 84532, ☎ 801/259–1370 or 800/635–6622).

Getting There

By Plane

Alpine Air (☎ 801/575–2839) flies daily from Salt Lake City to **Canyonlands Field,** in Moab.

By Car

I–70 runs east–west through the region; U.S. 191 slices north–south.

Exploring Southeastern Utah

Arches National Park, just northwest of Moab, has spectacular sandstone formations carved by wind and water from an ancient seabed. Trails and two scenic roads lead among towering pillars and arches. *Box 907, Moab 84532, ☎ 801/259–8161. Admission charged.*

The landscape of nearby **Canyonlands National Park** is divided into three geologically distinct districts, each with its own visitor center. Scenic loops, trails, and four-wheel-drive roads lead to views of massive canyons or uplifts crowded with stone spires and other bizarre features. *Rte. 313, Moab 84532, ☎ 801/259–7164. Admission charged.*

A sweeping view of the Canyonlands' multicolor upside-down geography is found at **Dead Horse Point State Park** (Rte. 313, ☎ 801/259–2614), named for a band of wild horses once stranded on this isolated peninsula. **Glen Canyon National Recreation Area** (☎ 602/645–2471) surrounds **Lake Powell,** a stark mingling of water and stone that resulted from the construction of Glen Canyon Dam on the Colorado River. Renting a houseboat is the optimal way to explore the canyons and coves.

The town of **Moab,** below I–70 on Rte. 128, has become a mecca for mountain bikers. Sudden popularity hasn't harmed Moab's laid-back atmosphere, but B&Bs, motels, museums, and bike shops have sprouted up everywhere. Just south of Moab, Utah's only commercial winery, **Arches Vineyard** (2182 S. U.S. 191, ☎ 801/259–5397; closed Jan.–Feb.), gives tours and has a tasting room.

Sports and the Outdoors

Biking

Southeastern Utah has hundreds of charted mountain-biking trails, including the **Moab Slickrock Trail,** 4 mi east of town, a 10-mi roller-coaster route marked only by dashes of paint on raw rock; and **Gemini Bridges,** where a steep ascent is followed by a ride over wavy slickrock and two giant stone spans. For rentals and advice, try **Rim Tours** (1233 S. U.S. 191, Moab, ☎ 801/259–5223 or 800/626–7335).

Hiking and Backpacking

The **Moab Visitor Center** (☎ 801/259–1370) offers advice on trails. Remember to bring water along on any hike in this thirsty region. The 2½-mi **Devils Garden Trail** in Arches National Park passes 10 stunning arches. **Delicate Arch** is at the end of a moderate 1½-mi march over undulating slickrock. Canyonlands National Park's **Chesler Park Trail** leads you 3 mi to a wide, grass-and-sagebrush flat ringed by huge red-and-white-banded stone needles.

Rafting

The sport of river-running began here with John Wesley Powell's explorations. Outfitters offer float trips and wild white-water treks through black-granite-walled **Westwater Canyon** and the crashing rapids of **Cataract Canyon,** on the Colorado River; or through **Desolation** and **Gray canyons** on the Green River, both of which shelter Anasazi Indian ruins. **Raft Utah** (☎ 801/566–2662) publishes a free directory.

Dining and Lodging

Southeastern Utah is not luxurious, but clean and comfortable lodging is available throughout. Cuisine leans toward fast food and hearty meals using local produce. **Moab–Canyonlands Central Reservations** (☎ 801/259–5125 or 800/748–4386) offers suggestions. The following are all in Moab. For price ranges see Charts 1 (B) and 2 (B) in On the Road with Fodor's.

Dining

$$ ★ **Center Café.** This is Moab's version of nouvelle cuisine, and a successful one at that. It features the likes of cioppino, roast game hen, and prawns and pasta baked in paper. A prix-fixe menu and a wine list are also available. *92 E. Center St., ☎ 801/259–4295. AE, MC, V. Closed Dec.–Mar. No lunch.*

$ **Poplar Place.** This two-story mock-adobe restaurant and watering hole has gourmet pizzas, pasta, and salads. *11 E. 1st North, ☎ 801/259–6018. MC, V. Closed Dec.–Mar.*

Lodging

$$$ **Pack Creek Ranch.** This guest ranch on a forested mountain loop offers rustic log cabins and activities ranging from horseback riding—followed by a massage—to cross-country skiing and weekend entertainment. *La Sal Mt. Loop Rd., Box 1270, 84532, ☎ 801/259–5505, FAX 801/259–8879. 9 cabins and 1 ranch house that sleeps up to 12. Facilities: kitchens, hot tub, sauna, pool. AE, D, MC, V.*

$$ ★ **Sunflower Hill Bed and Breakfast.** Country touches mark the decor of this stucco-and-weathered-wood dwelling built at the turn of the century and enlarged and renovated in the early 1990s. The breakfast spread might include yogurt, homemade bread, or huge fruit muffins. *185 N. 3rd East, 84532, ☎ 801/259–2974. 6 rooms and suites (2 share bath). Facilities: kitchenette in common area, outdoor hot tub. MC, V.*

$ **The Virginian.** The friendly staff is this plain two-story motel's best feature. Rooms look out on surrounding rusty cliffs. *70 E. 2nd South, 84532, ☎ 801/259–5951. 20 rooms. Facilities: kitchenettes. AE, D, DC, MC, V.*

Campgrounds

The **Moab Visitor Center** (*see* Sports and the Outdoors, *above*) has a campground directory detailing everything from overflow areas with no facilities to year-round commercial campgrounds. **Dead Horse Point State Park** (Box 609, Moab 84532; *see* Exploring Southeastern Utah, *above*) has a campground with spectacular views, a museum, a picnic area, flush toilets, and 21 campsites with hookups. **Moab KOA** (3225 S. U.S. 191, Moab 84532, ☎ 801/259–6682) and **Slickrock Campground** (U.S. 191, 1 mi north of town, Moab 84532, ☎ 801/259–7660) have tent sites, full hookups, showers, laundry, and swimming pools.

10 The Rockies

By Carolyn Price

CALL THE IDAHO INFORMATION LINE, and you'll be asked to press "5" on your touch-tone phone if you would like to report a wolf sighting. Check in with the state's tourist promotion offices, and more than likely you'll be talking to a state-employed prison inmate earning $1 an hour for his or her trouble.

Wolves and outlaws haven't left the Rocky Mountain states of Idaho, Montana, Wyoming, and Colorado, and they remain part of the unpredictable charms and crimes of nature and human action that thrived in the Old West: the click of cowboy spurs and the rustling of leather chaps, the sins of Native American betrayals and broken treaties, the energy and innocence of wide-open spaces, boomtowns, and the search for gold.

But most of all, there are the mountains—a 4,000-mi-long chain that stretches from Alaska to northern New Mexico. Begun about 70 million years ago when sandstone, shale, granite, marble, and volcanic rock surged and split and gave under the plow of glacial ice, the Rockies emerged to run intermittently along what is now the Idaho–Montana boundary down to a central section sloping through western Wyoming's Yellowstone and Grand Teton national parks and into northern Colorado.

This mountain backdrop still inspires the kind of fear and wonder it did in mountain men and Native Americans. What you'll see from atop these summits is a landscape of breathtaking beauty and variety. The westernmost state, Idaho, has terrain encompassing everything from fruit orchards to the tallest sand dunes in the United States. Montana claims 25 million acres of public land, most of it aloft in the northern Rockies. Its Glacier National Park is home to the ptarmigan, wolf, mountain goat, and moose. Wyoming, the ninth-largest and least populated state in the Union, is studded with thermal pools, bubbling hot springs, and, within a square-mile area in Yellowstone National Park, one-fourth of the Earth's geysers. In Colorado, the ski capital of the United States, high-country lakes, meadows frosted with blue columbine, and treeless alpine tundra assemble in one sweeping vista, while the mile-high city of Denver and the university town of Boulder attract visitors and settlers from all corners of the globe.

Tour Groups

Going West Tours (Livery Travel, 25 Neill Ave., Helena, MT 58601, ☎ 406/443–1410) offers five- to seven-day bus tours through Glacier, Yellowstone, and Little Bighorn national parks. **Maitland Travel Services, Inc.** (38 2nd St. E, Kalispell, MT 59901, ☎ 406/755–1032) arranges custom individual tours of Glacier National Park and other destinations in the Rockies. **Off the Beaten Path** (109 E. Main St., Bozeman, MT 59715, ☎ 406/586–1311) offers individually tailored tours ranging from hiking trips in the Canadian Rockies and Yellowstone to horse-pack and fly-fishing trips throughout the western Rockies. **Rocky Mountain Holiday Tours** (Box 842, Fort Collins, CO 80522, ☎ 303/482–5813) organizes custom tours (fly/drive) mainly to Colorado, Wyoming, South Dakota, Utah, Arizona, and New Mexico.

When to Go

Many visitors think the Rockies have only two seasons: skiing and hiking. But for those willing to risk sometimes-capricious weather, fall and

CANADA
MONTANA
IDAHO
WYOMING
NORTH DAKOTA
SOUTH DAKOTA
WATERTON-GLACIER INT'L PEACE PARK
BLACKFEET INDIAN RES.
Sand Point
Libby
Kalispell
Flathead Lake
FLATHEAD INDIAN RES.
Coeur d'Alene
Kellogg
COEUR D'ALENE INDIAN RES.
Avery
Moscow
Dworshak Res.
Lewiston
NEZ PERCE INDIAN RES.
Missoula
Lincoln
Fairfield
Cut Bank
Shelby
Conrad
Havre
Milk River
FORT BELKNAP INDIAN RES.
Malta
Scobey
Westby
FORT PECK INDIAN RES.
Wolf Point
Sidney
Fort Benton
Great Falls
Missouri River
Fort Peck Lake
Circle
Jordan
Lewistown
Glendive
Helena
Harlowton
Roundup
Ingomar
Yellowstone R.
Baker
Miles City
Deer Lodge
Anaconda
Butte
Forsyth
Billings
Elk City
Riggins
Wisdom
Bozeman
Livingston
CROW INDIAN RES.
N. CHEYENNE INDIAN RES.
Broadus
BIGHORN CANYON NAT'L REC. AREA
Snake River
New Meadows
Salmon
Dillon
Lima
Challis
YELLOWSTONE NAT'L PARK
Sheridan
Devil's Tower
Gilette
Rapid City
Weiser
Payette
Emmett
Caldwell
Nampa
Boise
Stanley
SAWTOOTH NAT'L REC AREA
Butte City
Dubois
Cody
Buffalo
Worland
GRAND TETON NAT'L PARK
WIND RIVER
Thermopolis
Newcastle
Midwest

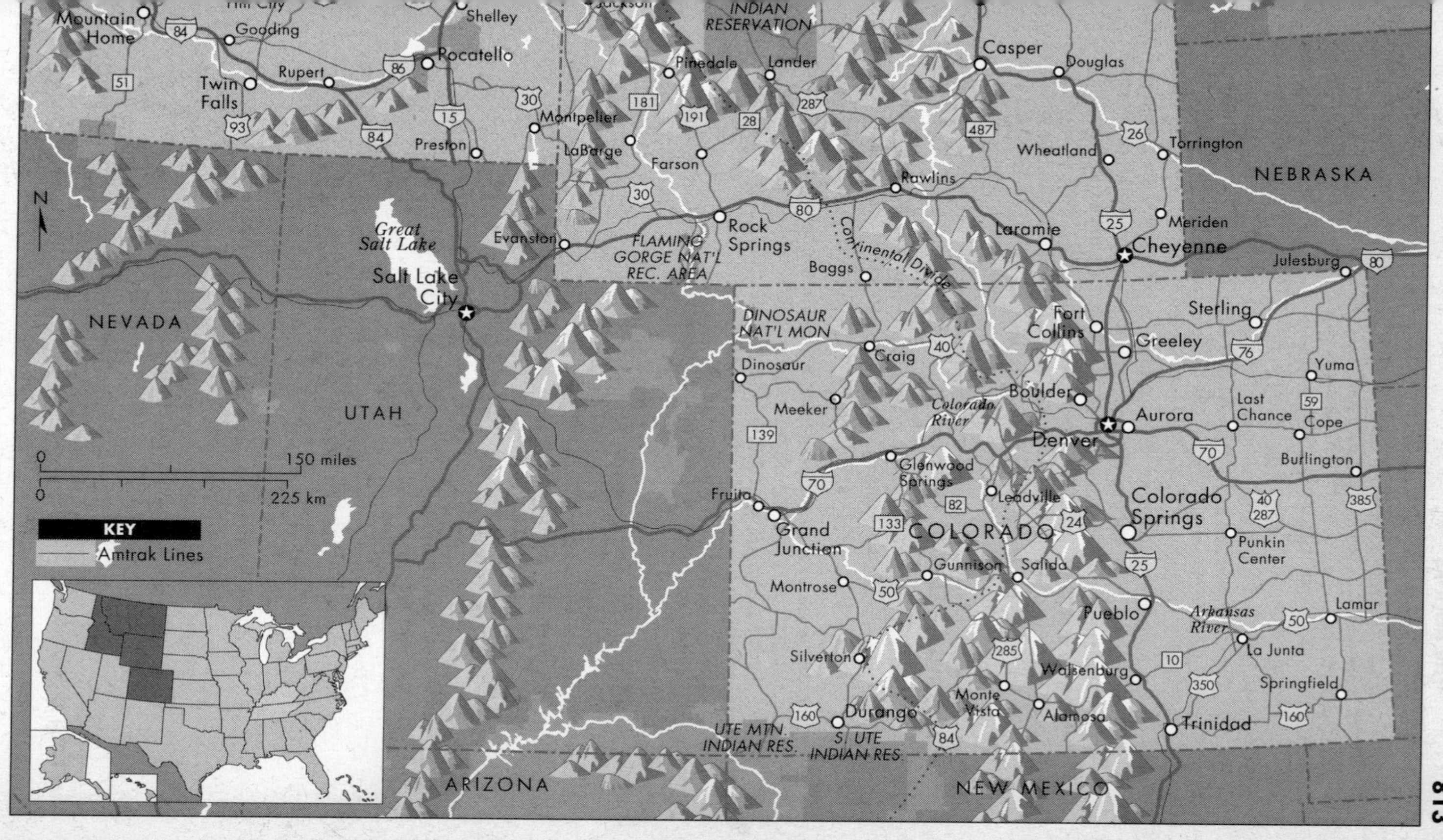
Mountain Home
Gooding
Shelley
Pocatello
Rupert
Twin Falls
Preston
Montpelier
LaBarge
Farson
Pinedale
Lander
INDIAN RESERVATION
Casper
Douglas
Wheatland
Torrington
NEBRASKA
Rawlins
Rock Springs
FLAMING GORGE NAT'L REC. AREA
Evanston
Great Salt Lake
Salt Lake City
Baggs
Continental Divide
Laramie
Meriden
Cheyenne
Julesburg
NEVADA
UTAH
DINOSAUR NAT'L MON
Dinosaur
Craig
Meeker
Colorado River
Fort Collins
Greeley
Sterling
Yuma
Boulder
Denver
Aurora
Last Chance
Cope
Burlington
Glenwood Springs
Leadville
Fruita
Grand Junction
COLORADO
Colorado Springs
Punkin Center
Gunnison
Salida
Montrose
Pueblo
Arkansas River
Lamar
La Junta
Silverton
Walsenburg
Springfield
Monte Vista
Alamosa
Durango
Trinidad
UTE MTN. INDIAN RES.
S. UTE INDIAN RES.
ARIZONA
NEW MEXICO
N
150 miles
225 km
KEY
Amtrak Lines

spring are the Rockies' best-kept secrets. **Spring** is a good time for fishing, rafting the runoff, or birding and wildlife viewing. **Fall** may be the prettiest season of all, with golden splashes of aspen on the mountainsides, more wildlife at lower elevations, and excellent fishing during spawning. You will also pay less during these shoulder seasons, and you may have a corner of Yellowstone all to yourself. Driving in the **winter** is chancy, and, although the interstates are kept open even in fearsome weather, highway passes like the Going-to-the-Sun Highway in Glacier National Park can be blocked from late October to June. High altitude (over 7,000 ft above sea level) and latitude (the nearer you get to Canada) result in longer winters. Winter visitors should prepare for the possibility of temperatures below zero—but the climate is dry, so the cold is less cruel. Wilderness snowbanks can linger through June, so backcountry hikers generally crowd in from July through Labor Day. **Summer** temperatures rarely rise into the 90s, but the thinner atmosphere at high altitudes makes it necessary for visitors to shield themselves from ultraviolet rays.

Festivals and Seasonal Events

Early Jan.: National Western Stock Show and Rodeo in **Denver** is the biggest in the world, attracting all the stars of the rodeo circuit for two weeks. ☎ *303/892–1505 or 303/295–1660 for the box office.*

3rd week in June: Telluride (CO) Bluegrass & Country Music Festival has become so popular that the organizers have had to limit the number of spectators to 10,000. *1539 Pearl St., Suite 200, Boulder, CO 80302,* ☎ *800/624–2422.*

Late June–mid-Aug.: Colorado Shakespeare Festival, in **Boulder,** presents three full-scale traditional and nontraditional Shakespeare productions and one non-Shakespearean play Tuesday–Sunday nights. The actors are recruited from around the country. ☎ *303/492–2783.*

Late June–late Aug.: Aspen Music Festival and School. Students from around the world perform with faculty, and world-class soloists and conductors are also featured. ☎ *303/925–3254.*

July–Aug.: Grand Teton Music Festival, the most important classical music concert series in the northern Rockies, attracts musicians from the nation's finest orchestras. *Box 490, Teton Village, Jackson Hole, WY 83025,* ☎ *307/733–1128.*

Last 2 weeks in July: Cheyenne (WY) Frontier Days, the rodeo "Daddy of 'em all," includes evening shows featuring the biggest names in country music, as well as parades and very popular pancake breakfasts. ☎ *800/227–6336 or 800/543–2339 in WY.*

Nov.: Join the **Eagle Watch** to see hundreds of bald eagles gather annually in Canyon Ferry State Park, **near Helena, Montana,** during freshwater salmon spawning. This is one of the few places outside Alaska where you can see the eagles in such concentration. The best time to go is in November, but the eagles gather here from October to late December. ☎ *406/442–4120.*

Getting Around

By Plane

The new **Denver International Airport** opened in March 1995. Several domestic airlines fly from Denver and Salt Lake into **Jackson Hole Airport** (☎ 307/733–4767) in Wyoming, with additional service during the ski season, including direct flights from Chicago by American Airlines. The **Boise Air Terminal** (☎ 208/382–3110) in Idaho is served by Delta, SkyWest, United, and other airlines. In Montana, the **Missoula Airport** (☎ 406/543–7001) and **Glacier Park International Airport** (☎ 406/752–1028), in Kalispell, are served by major domestic airlines. **Salt Lake City Airport** (☎ 801/575–2400) also provides an access point to Wyoming and Idaho.

By Car

Major interstates crisscross the region, winding their way through accessible mountain passes. The busiest, but least scenic, east–west thoroughfare is I–80, which crosses southern Wyoming, passing through Cheyenne and Laramie in the southeast corner. To reach Yellowstone National Park, you must either make the long drive north from Rock Springs or come south from I–90, which crosses southern Montana. In Colorado, I–70 runs east–west, passing through Denver and Grand Junction in the west and passing south of Rocky Mountain National Park. I–15 runs north from Salt Lake City into Idaho and connects with I–84, which heads west to Boise and on to Portland. I–90 passes through Sheridan in northeast Wyoming before crossing Montana and northern Idaho; it comes within 100 mi of Glacier National Park, which can be reached by going north from Missoula on U.S. 93 and east on U.S. 2. I–15 goes along the east side of the park; you can reach Glacier by driving west on U.S. 89. I–25 comes up from New Mexico and passes through Colorado Springs and Denver in Colorado; Cheyenne and Casper in Wyoming; and then joins I–90 in Montana. Throughout the Rockies, drivers should be extremely cautious about winter travel, when white-outs and ice are not uncommon. Because major airports are few and far between, the Rockies are a favorite of car travelers and campers, and the busy driving season is summer. Major attractions such as Glacier and Yellowstone National Park are well away from the interstates, requiring visitors to drive dozens or even hundreds of miles on scenic, two-lane highways to the entrances.

By Train

Amtrak (☎ 800/872–7245) connects the Rockies to both coasts and all major American cities; trains run through Boise, Salt Lake City, and Denver, with other stops in between. Routes have switched back and forth between Colorado and southern Wyoming in recent years. Amtrak trains also run through northern Montana, with stops in Essex and Whitefish, along the border of Glacier National Park. Connecting motor-coach services are provided in the summer from Pocatello, Idaho, to Yellowstone National Park.

By Bus

Greyhound Lines (☎ 800/231–2222) has extensive service throughout Colorado and connects major cities throughout the region, including Cheyenne, Boise, Pocatello, and Missoula. Various smaller bus lines connect with Greyhound to provide service to smaller communities as well as the parks.

COLORADO

By Sandra Widener

Updated by Jordan Simon

Capital	Denver
Population	3,294,394
Motto	Nothing Without Providence
State Bird	Lark bunting
State Flower	Columbine

Visitor Information

You can call the state of Colorado's **toll-free number** (☎ 800/433–2656) for a comprehensive travel guide. **Colorado Travel-Bank** (☎ 303/320–8550; modem, 303/671–7669).

Scenic Drives

Colorado has 17 designated scenic routes, which are marked by signs featuring a blue columbine. The 232-mi **San Juan Skyway** passes through historic ranching and mining towns, such as Durango, Silverton, Ouray, Telluride, and Cortez. The **Peak-to-Peak Highway** follows Rtes. 119, 72, and 7 through gold-mining towns to Rocky Mountain National Park.

National and State Parks

National Parks

Great Sand Dunes National Monument (35 mi northeast of Alamosa off Rte. 150, Mosca 81146, ☎ 719/378–2312), with shimmering mountains of sand almost 700 ft high, has a year-round campground and a nature trail. **Mesa Verde National Park** (U.S. 160, 8 mi east of Cortez, Mesa Verde Natl. Park 81330, ☎ 970/529–4465) features the remarkable, well-preserved cliff dwellings of the ancient Anasazi Indians; lodging, restaurants, and camping are crowded in summer. **Rocky Mountain National Park** (Hwy. 36, Estes Park 80517, ☎ 970/586–2371) offers a picture-book vision of craggy mountains, abundant wildlife, and deep-blue mountain lakes in more than 250,000 acres, with camping, hiking, lodging, and scenic drives. There is also lodging in nearby Estes Park.

State Parks

The state's 40 parks offer opportunities to hike, fish, sail, and take in idyllic views. The **Colorado Division of Parks** (Dept. of Natural Resources, 1313 Sherman St., Denver 80203, ☎ 303/866–3437) provides information.

DENVER

Denver is a city where winter weather reports often begin with skiing conditions, and where weekends are often occupied with trips to the mountains to hike, camp, and fish after the lifts shut down for the summer. The sharp-edged new skyscrapers, clean streets, and dozens of well-used parks evoke the image of a young, forward-looking city, but much of what made Denver what it is lies in its Western past. Areas like LoDo, for instance, a historic part of lower downtown, buzz with jazz clubs, restaurants, and art galleries housed in century-old buildings.

Tourist Information

Denver Metro Convention and Visitors Bureau (225 W. Colfax Ave., 80202, ☎ 303/892–1112).

Arriving and Departing

By Plane

The new **Denver International Airport** (☎ 303/270–1900), opened in March 1995 23 mi from downtown Denver, has flights by most major carriers. Cab fare downtown should average about $40; **RTD,** the local bus service (*see* Getting Around Denver, *below*), can also get you there. The **Airporter** (☎ 303/333–5873; reservations required) offers express-bus service from the airport to downtown hotels.

By Car

I–70 (east–west) and I–25 (north–south) intersect near downtown.

By Train

Amtrak serves **Union Station** (17th St. at Wynkoop St., ☎ 800/872–7245).

By Bus

Greyhound Lines (1055 19th St., ☎ 800/231–2222).

Getting Around Denver

A free shuttle-bus service operates frequently down the length of the 16th Street Mall. For explorations beyond downtown, a car is best, although buses and taxis are available.

By Car

Despite a number of one-way streets, driving in Denver is not difficult, and finding a spot in a parking lot is usually easy. Traffic on I–25 and I–70 can be congested during rush hours.

By Public Transportation

The region's public **bus** service, **RTD** (☎ 303/299–6000 or 303/299–6700), has routes throughout Denver and to outlying towns, such as Boulder, Longmont, and Nederland. RTD's **light rail system** began operating in October 1994, serving Denver's downtown and southwest regions. Buy bus and rail tokens ($1) at grocery stores or with exact change on the bus; rail tokens are also available from machines in the train stations.

By Taxi

Cabs are available at the airport and usually at major hotels. Companies offering 24-hour service include **Yellow Cab** (☎ 303/777–7777; $1.40 minimum, $1.20 per mi) and **Metro Taxi** (☎ 303/333–3333; $1.40 minimum, $1.40 per mi).

Orientation Tours

Gray Line (☎ 303/289–2841) offers a 2½-hour city tour, a mountain parks tour, and a mountain casino tour.

Exploring Denver

Denver presents its official face to the world at the **Civic Center.** The three-block park, with lawns, gardens, and a Greek amphitheater, forms a backdrop for the **state capitol** (1475 Sherman St., ☎ 303/866–2604; closed Sun.) and the **City and County Building,** which are at opposite ends. The dome of the 1894 capitol is periodically recovered with hammered gold leaf as a reminder of the state's mining heritage. The

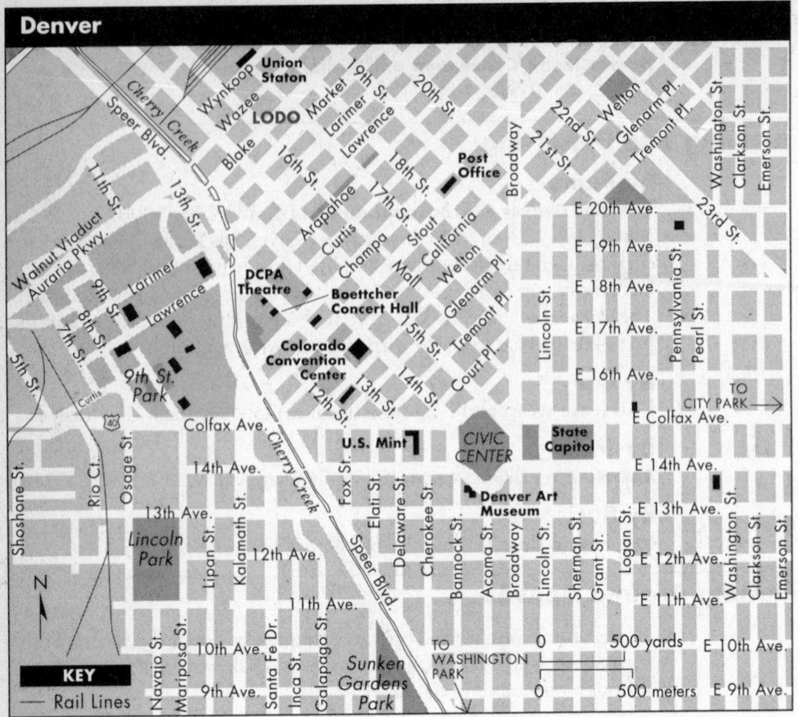

balcony at its base affords a panoramic view of the Rockies. Just off the park are the **Colorado History Museum** (1300 Broadway, ☎ 303/866–3682; admission charged), with Colorado and Western memorabilia and dioramas, plus special exhibits; and the **Denver Art Museum** (100 W. 14th Ave., ☎ 303/640–2793; closed Mon., major holidays), with an excellent collection of Native American art, as well as that by Old Masters and Impressionists, and textiles, pottery, and period rooms.

Close by is the **Denver Mint** (officially known as the United States Mint), the source of all coins marked with a *D*. There are tours of this facility, where more than 5 billion coins are stamped yearly—and where the third-largest hoard of gold in the United States is on display. *W. Colfax Ave. and Cherokee St.,* ☎ *303/844–3582. Closed weekends.*

Free shuttle buses are the only vehicles allowed on the **16th Street Mall,** which features shade trees, outdoor cafés, historic buildings, and shopping. Hop off the bus at Tremont Place and walk over a block to the **Museum of Western Art** (1727 Tremont Pl., ☎ 303/296–1880; admission charged), a frontier-era bordello that now celebrates artistic heroes of the Western myth: Frederic Remington, Albert Bierstadt, and Charles Russell. On the way back, peek inside the **Brown Palace** (321 17th St.; *see* Lodging, *below*), Denver's hotel empress, built in 1892 and still proud of her antique charms.

Farther down the mall is the 330-ft-tall **D&F Tower** (16th St. at Arapahoe St.), built to emulate the campanile of St. Mark's Cathedral in Venice, and **Tabor Center** (16th St. at Lawrence St.), a cheery shopping mall. South on Curtis Street is the **Denver Center for the Performing Arts** (14th and Curtis Sts.), a huge space-age complex of theaters and a symphony hall.

Across from Tabor Center behind Writer Square is historic **Larimer Square** (Larimer and 15th Sts.), Denver's most charming shopping area, which showcases some of the city's oldest retail buildings and finest specialty shops. Farther into LoDo, north of Larimer Square between Speer Boulevard and Larimer Street, lies an equally historic, but quirkier, area featuring art galleries, nightclubs, and restaurants that offer everything from the hautest cuisine to the most down-home coffee-shop fare.

East of downtown, the **Molly Brown House** (1340 Pennsylvania St., ☎ 303/832–4092; admission charged), a Victorian confection, celebrates the life and times of the scandalous unsinkable one, while the **Grant-Humphreys Mansion** (770 Pennsylvania St., ☎ 303/894–2506; admission charged) is a testament to the proper Denver society that looked down on Molly at the turn of the century.

Northeast of downtown in **City Park,** the popular **Denver Zoo** features a nursery for baby animals and a polar bear exhibit where visitors can watch the bears swim underwater. *E. 23rd St. between York St. and Colorado Blvd., ☎ 303/331–4110. Admission charged.*

Also in City Park is the **Denver Museum of Natural History,** a rich combination of traditional collections and intriguing hands-on exhibits, plus a planetarium and an IMAX movie theater with a four-story screen. *2001 Colorado Blvd., ☎ 303/322–7009. Admission charged.*

Parks and Gardens

Denver has one of the largest city park systems (☎ 303/698–4900) in the country, with more than 20,000 acres in the city and nearby mountains. **City Park** features lakes, tennis, golf, museums, and the zoo (*see* Exploring Denver, *above*). Flower gardens and lakes abound in **Washington Park** (east of Downing St. between Virginia Ave. and Louisiana Ave.); this is where young Denver goes to run, rollerblade, bike, play volleyball and tennis, and hang out.

On the east side of the city are the **Denver Botanic Gardens** (1005 York St., ☎ 303/331–4010; admission charged), a flowering retreat. The conservatory houses a rain forest; outside are a Japanese garden, a rock garden, and gorgeous horticulture displays at their height in summer. **Platte River Greenway** is a 20-mi biking, jogging, and rollerblading path that follows Cherry Creek and the Platte River, much of it through downtown Denver.

What to See and Do with Children

At the **Denver Children's Museum** (2121 Children's Museum Dr., ☎ 303/433–7444), interactive exhibits include a working TV station and an outdoor, all-year beginners' ski hill.

Shopping

Denver is one of the top places to buy recreational equipment and clothing. You can also pick up a pair of cowboy boots and other Western apparel at Western stores.

Shopping Districts

The **Cherry Creek** shopping district, 2 mi from downtown, is Denver's best. On one side of 1st Avenue at Milwaukee Street is the **Cherry Creek Shopping Mall,** a classy granite-and-glass behemoth containing some of the nation's finest retailers. On the other side is **Cherry Creek North,** with art galleries and specialty shops. Historic **Larimer Square** (14th and Larimer Sts.) is the center of Denver specialty shopping, with antiques, housewares, and clothing boutiques. On the 16th Street Mall are **Tabor Center** and other large downtown retailers.

Specialty Stores

South Broadway between 1st Avenue and Evans Street has blocks of antiques stores; prices are sometimes lower than elsewhere.

ANTIQUE BOOKS

Tattered Cover (1st Ave. at Milwaukee St., ☎ 303/322–7727) has overstuffed armchairs, four stories of books (more than 175,000 titles), afternoon lectures and musicales, and a knowledgeable staff.

SPORTING GOODS

Gart Brothers Sports Castle (1000 Broadway, ☎ 303/861–1122) is a huge, multistory shrine to Colorado's love of the outdoors.

WESTERN WEAR

Denver Buffalo Company Trading Post (1109 Lincoln St., ☎ 303/832–0884) has top-of-the-line Western clothing and high-quality souvenirs, not to mention a restaurant specializing in buffalo—low in fat and cholesterol. **Miller Stockman** (16th St. Mall at California St., ☎ 303/825–5339) is an old-line Denver retailer selling the genuine article.

Spectator Sports

Baseball

Colorado Rockies (Coors Stadium, downtown at 22nd and Wazee Sts., ☎ 303/762–5437; Apr.–Oct.).

Basketball

Denver Nuggets (McNichols Sports Arena, just west of downtown across I–25, ☎ 303/893–3865; Nov.–Apr.).

Football

Denver Broncos (Mile High Stadium, ☎ 303/433–7466; Aug.–Dec.).

Dining

Beef, buffalo, and burritos have an honored spot in Denver's culinary history, but more sophisticated fare—from Vietnamese to casual French—is enthusiastically supported throughout the city. Cruise LoDo or 17th Avenue east from downtown for inventive kitchens, and check out Federal Street for cheap ethnic eats. For price ranges, see Chart 1 (A) in On the Road with Fodor's.

$$$$ ★ **Cliff Young's.** Young presides over his elegant art deco restaurant with meticulous care, showering diners with attention while the kitchen prepares New American standbys such as free-range veal with a sly Asian gloss. *700 E. 17th Ave., ☎ 303/831–8900. Jacket and tie advised. AE, D, DC, MC, V. No lunch weekends.*

$$$ **Buckhorn Exchange.** The neighborhood has deteriorated, but this Denver landmark continues to pull in crowds eager to eat elk, buffalo, and beef on checkered tablecloths and gawk at the enormous collection of memorabilia and animal heads. *1000 Osage St., ☎ 303/534–9505. AE, D, DC, MC, V. No lunch weekends.*

$$$ ★ **Strings.** This light, airy spot with its wide-open kitchen is one place in Denver to see and be seen. The food is casual-contemporary; one specialty is spaghetti with caviar and asparagus in champagne-cream sauce. *1700 Humboldt St., ☎ 303/831–7310. AE, D, DC, MC, V. No lunch Sun.*

$$$ ★ **Zenith American Grill.** Chef Kevin Taylor's creative variations on the Southwestern theme include such standouts as velvety yet fiery smoked

corn soup with avocado salsa and Texas venison with caramelized apples. The attractive space has a cool, high-tech look. *1750 Lawrence St., ☎ 303/820–2800. Reservations required. AE, MC, V. No lunch weekends.*

$$ ★ **Barolo Grill.** This restaurant looks like a chichi farmhouse, as if Laura Ashley went gaga over an Italian count—dried flowers in brass urns, straw baskets, and hand-painted porcelain. The food is bold yet classic; healthful yet flavorful. Choose from wild boar stewed with apricots; risotto croquettes flavored with minced shrimp; or smoked salmon pizza. *3030 E. 6th Ave., ☎ 303/393–1040. AE, MC, V. Closed Sun.–Mon. No lunch.*

$$ **Imperial Chinese Seafood Restaurant.** Denver's best Chinese food is served in a graceful dining room featuring Chinese art. Try the steamed sea bass with ginger, Hunan, or black-bean sauce. *1 Broadway, ☎ 303/698–2800. Reservations only for 4 or more. AE, DC, MC, V. No lunch Sun.*

$$ **Le Central.** Here you find authentic, informal, delicious French food in a bistro atmosphere. Favorites on the hearty menu are bouillabaisse, cassoulet, and *entrecôte au poivre* (peppered rib steak). A Sunday brunch is served. *112 E. 8th Ave., ☎ 303/863–8094. No credit cards. No lunch Sat.*

$ **Bluebonnet Café and Lounge.** Its location in a fairly seedy neighborhood southeast of downtown doesn't stop the crowds from lining up early. The early Western decor, the Naugahyde, and the fantastic jukebox set an upbeat mood for killer margaritas and the best burritos and green chili in town. *457 S. Broadway, ☎ 303/778–0147. MC, V.*

$ **T-WA Inn.** This popular South Asian hole-in-the-wall serves great food, including delicate Vietnamese spring rolls and daily specials. *555 S. Federal Blvd., ☎ 303/922–4584. AE, MC, V.*

$ ★ **Wynkoop Brewing Company.** With its beer brewed on the premises, in a converted LoDo building, and its hearty pub fare, the Wynkoop has become a fast favorite of trendy Denver. Try the shepherd's pie or grilled marlin sandwich, then check out the gallery, pool hall, and cabaret for a full night's entertainment. *1634 18th St., ☎ 303/297–2700. No reservations weekends. AE, D, DC, MC, V.*

Lodging

Denver's lodging choices range from the stately Brown Palace to the YMCA, with B&Bs and other options in between. **Bed & Breakfast Rocky Mountains** (673 Grant St., 80203, ☎ 303/860–8415) handles B&Bs throughout the state. **Hostelling International–Rocky Mountain Council** (☎ 303/442–1166) provides information about hostels in 13 Colorado locations. For price ranges, see Chart 2 (A) in On the Road with Fodor's.

$$$$ ★ **Brown Palace Hotel.** This grand dame of Colorado lodgings has housed everyone from President Eisenhower to the Beatles. The downtown hotel's dramatic eight-story lobby is topped by a glorious stained-glass ceiling. Rooms are decorated in Victorian style. *321 17th St., 80202, ☎ 303/297–3111 or 800/321–2599, FAX 303/293–9204. 205 rooms, 25 suites. Facilities: 4 restaurants, 2 bars, concierge, parking. AE, D, DC, MC, V.*

$$$ **Burnsley.** Since its face-lift in the 1980s, this 16-story, Bauhaus-style tower on the southeastern edge of downtown has offered a quiet haven close to the center. The modern suites all have balconies and full kitchens. *1000 Grant St., 80203, ☎ 303/830–1000 or 800/231–3915, FAX 303/830–7676. 82 suites. Facilities: restaurant, bar, pool, parking. AE, DC, MC, V.*

$$$ ★ **Loews Giorgio.** The 12-story steel-and-black glass facade conceals the unexpected and delightful Italian baroque motif within. Rooms are spacious and elegant, with Continental touches. The only drawback of this property is its location: halfway between downtown and the Denver Tech Center. *4150 E. Mississippi Ave., ☎ 303/782–9300 or 800/345–9172, FAX 303/758–6542. 200 rooms, 19 suites. Facilities: restaurant, bar, access to nearby health club, complimentary Continental breakfast, complimentary airport shuttle. AE, D, DC, MC, V.*

$$$ ★ **Oxford.** This fine hotel was a Denver fixture in the Victorian era; now, completely refurbished in turn-of-the-century style, it is the city's most charming small hotel. Guest rooms are exquisitely furnished in French and English antiques. *1600 17th St., 80202, ☎ 303/628–5400 or 800/228–5838, FAX 303/628–5413. 81 rooms. Facilities: restaurant, 2 bars, health club (fee), valet parking. AE, D, DC, MC, V.*

$$ **Castle Marne.** This historic house with balconies, a four-story turret, and intricate stone- and woodwork is east of downtown in a shabbily genteel area near several fine restaurants. The B&B's rooms are decorated with antiques and art. *1572 Race St., 80206, ☎ 303/331–0621 or 800/926–2763, FAX 303/331–0623. 9 rooms. Facilities: game room, parking. AE, D, DC, MC, V.*

$$ ★ **Queen Anne Inn.** North of downtown in a reclaimed historic area, this B&B (composed of two adjacent Victorian houses) makes a romantic getaway, with fresh flowers, antiques, and turn-of-the-century charm. Full breakfast and an afternoon Colorado-wine tasting are free to guests. *2147 Tremont Pl., 80205, ☎ 303/296–6666. 10 rooms, 4 suites. AE, D, MC, V.*

$$ **Red Lion.** This airport hotel at the edge of town is a good bet if you plan to sidestep Denver and head immediately for the mountains. The rooms are unexceptional; service is efficient. *3203 Quebec St., 80207, ☎ 303/321–3333 or 800/547–8010, FAX 303/329–5233. 567 rooms. Facilities: 2 restaurants, 2 bars, exercise equipment, indoor pool, parking. AE, D, DC, MC, V.*

$ **Comfort Inn/Downtown.** The advantages to this hotel are its reasonable rates and its location, right across from—and connected to—the Brown Palace in the heart of downtown. Rooms higher up have smashing panoramic views. *401 17th St., 80202, ☎ 303/296–0400 or 800/221–2222, FAX 303/297–0774. 229 rooms. Facilities: restaurant, bar, valet parking. AE, D, DC, MC, V.*

$ ★ **Holiday Chalet.** This turn-of-the-century house turned hotel is in the heart of Capitol Hill, immediately east of downtown. It's full of charm, with stained-glass windows and homey touches, and each room has a kitchenette stocked for breakfast. *1820 E. Colfax St., 80218, ☎ 303/321–9975 or 800/626–4497, FAX 303/377–6556. 10 rooms. AE, D, DC, MC, V.*

$ **YMCA.** The old standby has clean, basic rooms, some with private baths, and a great location downtown. *25 E. 16th Ave., 80202, ☎ 303/861–8300. 185 rooms. Facility: restaurant. MC, V.*

The Arts and Nightlife

Friday's *Denver Post* and *Rocky Mountain News* list entertainment events, as does *Westword,* a weekly published on Wednesday. **TicketMan** (☎ 303/430–1111) sells tickets to major events. The **Ticket Bus** (16th St. Mall at Curtis St., no ☎) sells tickets from 10 to 6 weekdays, and half-price tickets the day of the performance.

The Arts

The modern **Denver Center for the Performing Arts** (13th and Curtis Sts., ☎ 303/893–3272) complex houses most of the city's large concert halls and theaters.

DANCE

Colorado Ballet (☎ 303/837–8888) specializes in classical ballet. **Colorado Contemporary Dance** (☎ 303/892–9797) brings national dance companies to Denver. Both perform at various locations around town.

MUSIC

The **Colorado Symphony Orchestra** (☎ 303/986–8742) performs at Boettcher Concert Hall (13th and Curtis Sts.). The **Denver Chamber Orchestra** (☎ 303/825–4911) usually plays at historic Trinity Methodist Church (18th St. and Broadway).

THEATER

The **Denver Center Theater Company** (☎ 303/893–4100) offers fine repertory theater. **Robert Garner Attractions** (☎ 302/893–4100) brings Broadway-caliber plays to the city.

Nightlife

Downtown and **LoDo** host most of Denver's nightlife. Downtown features more mainstream entertainment, while LoDo is home to rock clubs and small theaters. Remember that Denver's altitude makes you react sooner to alcohol.

COMEDY

Comedy Works (1226 15th St., ☎ 303/595–3637) features local and nationally known stand-up comics.

COUNTRY AND WESTERN

The **Grizzly Rose** (I–25 Exit 215, ☎ 303/295–1330) has miles of dance floor, national bands, and country-and-western dancing lessons.

JAZZ

El Chapultepec (20th St. at Market St., ☎ 303/295–9126) is a smoky, unpretentious place where visiting jazz musicians end up after hours.

ROCK

Herman's Hideaway (1578 S. Broadway, ☎ 303/778–9916) is a favorite for hot local bands and national acts; some blues and reggae, too. **Rock Island** (Wazee and 15th Sts., ☎ 303/572–7625) caters to the young, restless, and hip.

Excursions from Denver

Boulder

Home of the **University of Colorado,** Boulder is a quintessential college town but also home to a hard-core group of professional athletes who live to bike and run. The atmosphere is peaceful, new-age, and cultural, with the gorgeous backdrop of the mountains. One of the city's main attractions is the **Pearl Street Mall,** a see-and-be-seen pedestrian street with benches, grassy spots, great shopping, and outdoor cafés. Weekdays 11–2, the **Celestial Seasonings Plant** (4600 Sleepytime Dr., ☎ 303/530–5300) offers free tours; you'll see the tea ingredients in their raw forms (the Mint Room is off-limits, due to its potent scent), and see how they're blended. Rich in lectures, theater, and music year-round, Boulder celebrates classical music each summer at its **Colorado Music Festival** (Chautauqua Park, ☎ 303/449–1397).

GETTING THERE

From Denver, take I–25N to the Boulder Turnpike (Hwy. 36). Denver's RTD buses make the 27-mi commute to Boulder regularly.

Central City and Blackhawk

Abandoned mines on the side of the scenic road that leads to these historic towns testifies to their silver- and gold-mining heritage. Now, however, low-stakes **gambling** has arrived, and the jingle of slot machines is a constant. The narrow, winding streets are edged with brick storefronts from the last century. The **Central City Opera House** (☎ 303/292–6700), a small Victorian jewel in the center of town, offers opera in summer.

GETTING THERE

From I–70, take Hwy. 58 to Golden; from there, take Hwy. 6 up Clear Creek Canyon and Hwy. 119 northwest 1 mi past Blackhawk to Central City, for a total of 35 mi from Denver.

Georgetown

With its multitude of **gingerbread Victorian houses** on quiet streets, Georgetown provides a tantalizing glimpse of Colorado's heady mining past. The town, a National Historic District, has restaurants, small shops, and the **Georgetown Loop Railroad** (☎ 303/569–2403), a 3-mi narrow-gauge line that travels into the mountains and back.

GETTING THERE

Take I–70W to the Georgetown exit, 46 mi from Denver.

Golden

Coors (13th and Ford Sts., ☎ 303/277–2337) operates the world's largest brewery in Golden and offers a free half-hour tour that covers the basics of brewing beer and ends with a trip to the tasting rooms. Tours run daily except Sun.

GETTING THERE

From I–70, take Hwy. 58 to Golden.

COLORADO SPRINGS AND ENVIRONS

At the center of the state, 65 mi south of Denver, is Colorado's second-largest city, Colorado Springs. As well as its natural wonders, such as Pike's Peak, of "Pike's Peak or Bust" fame, the region has such man-made attractions as the Air Force Academy and the Broadmoor resort.

Tourist Information

Colorado Springs: Convention and Visitors Bureau (104 S. Cascade Ave., ☎ 719/635–7506 or 800/368–4748).

Getting There

By Plane

Colorado Springs Municipal Airport (5750 E. Fountain Blvd., ☎ 719/596–0188), 20 mi from the city, is served by domestic airlines.

By Car

From Denver take I–25S.

By Bus

Greyhound Lines (120 S. Weber St., ☎ 800/231–2222). **Springs Transit Management** (127 E. Kiowa St., ☎ 719/475–9733) serves local routes.

Exploring Colorado Springs and Environs

The city of **Colorado Springs** has wide, tree-lined streets and Victorian houses, but its main feature is the mix of attractions around it. The **U.S. Olympic Center** (1 Olympic Plaza, ☎ 719/578–4500) offers tours of the sprawling complex where hundreds of young athletes train. The **Broadmoor** (1 Lake Ave.; *see* Dining and Lodging, *below*) is a rambling ensemble of pink stucco Italian Renaissance–style hotel buildings, golf courses, gardens, an ice rink where Olympic skaters practice, and a picture-perfect lake skimmed by black swans. The **Carriage House Museum** on the grounds displays an old stagecoach, vintage cars, and carriages used at Presidential inaugurals.

Two routes—a cog railway (515 Ruxton Ave., Manitou Springs, ☎ 719/685–5401) and a toll road (10 mi west on Hwy. 24, left at marked exit at Cascade)—lead up to breathtaking views atop **Pike's Peak,** the summit Zebulon Pike claimed could never be scaled by humans. The **Air Force Academy** (10 mi north on I–25, Exits 156B and 150B, ☎ 719/472–2555) is notable for its forest-and-mountain setting and its strikingly futuristic Cadet Chapel, with 17 spires that rise 150 ft. The academy offers guided tours in summer. The **Garden of the Gods** (off Ridge Rd., north of U.S. 24, ☎ 719/578–6939) offers picnic spots and hikes among 1,350 acres of weird, windswept red rock formations and unusual plant life.

Cripple Creek (24 mi west to Divide, then 20 mi south on Hwy. 67), until recently a creaky old mining town once known for vast deposits of gold, has gone upscale with the legalization of low-stakes gambling. The **Cripple Creek and Victor Narrow Gauge Railroad** (north end of town, ☎ 719/689–2640; closed Nov.–Apr.) runs a 4-mi route past old mines and older mountains.

Head east on U.S. 50 to reach one of the Rockies' most powerful sights. The 1,030-ft-deep **Royal Gorge,** often called the Grand Canyon of Colorado, was carved by the Arkansas River over 3 million years ago. It's spanned by the world's highest **suspension bridge.** Other activities at the gorge include riding the astonishing aerial tram (2,200 ft long and 1,178 ft above the canyon floor) and descending aboard the **Scenic Railway** (the world's steepest incline rail) to stare at the sun and the bridge 1,000 ft above. There is also a theater that presents a 25-minute multimedia show, outdoor musical entertainment in the summer, and the usual assortment of food concessions and gift shops. *Royal Gorge Complex, ☎ 719/275–7507. Admission charged.*

What to See and Do with Children

The **Cheyenne Mountain Zoo** (4250 Cheyenne Mountain Zoo Rd., ☎ 719/475–9555), set on a mountainside, is a haven for endangered species—more than 100—and a home to hundreds of other animals, most in habitats closely resembling their natural ones. Famous films such as *True Grit* and *Cat Ballou* were shot in **Buckskin Joe Park and Railway** (off Hwy. 50, Cañon City, ☎ 719/275–5485; admission charged), which vividly evokes the Old West. Children love the horse-drawn trolley rides, horseback rides, and gold panning, while adults appreciate the live entertainment in the Crystal Palace and Saloon. At the **North Pole and Santa's Workshop** (Exit 141 of Hwy. 24 W, ☎ 719/684–9432; admission charged), energetic elves bustle about this colorful shrine to the commercialization of Christmas. Kids can feed deer, ride a Ferris wheel and carousel, try their luck in an arcade, visit

Central Colorado

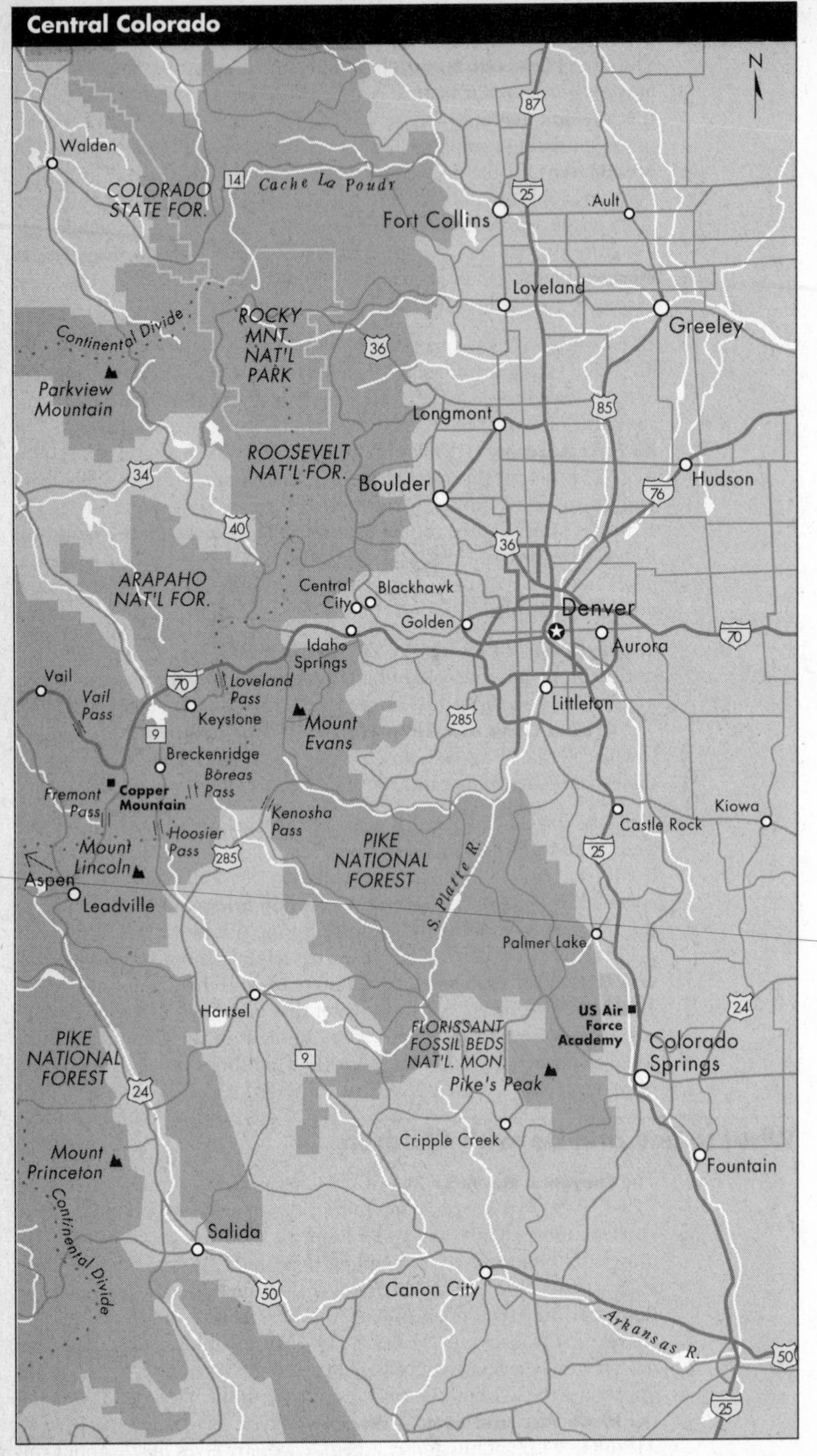

Santa at the height of summer, and stuff themselves in the Candy Kitchen, Sugar Plum Terrace, or old-fashioned ice-cream parlor.

Shopping

Castle Rock Factory Shops (20 mi south of Denver on I–25, ☎ 303/688–4494) has more than 50 clothing and home-furnishings stores.

Sports and the Outdoors

Biking

Pike National Forest (Ranger District Office, 601 S. Weber St., Colorado Springs 80903, ☎ 719/636–1602) has mountain-bike trails.

Fishing

Lovers of trout-stream fishing flock to the **South Platte** (Rte. 67, 28 mi north of Woodland Park). **Elevenmile Reservoir** (Hwy. 24W to west edge of town of Lake George) has rainbow trout, kokanee salmon, and pike.

Golf

The **Broadmoor** (1 Lake Ave., ☎ 719/634–7711) has three 18-hole courses.

Hiking and Backpacking

Check the **Convention and Visitors Bureau** (*see* Tourist Information, *above*) for information and maps. Some of the best trails are in **Pike National Forest** (*see* Biking, *above*).

Horseback Riding

Academy Riding Stables (4 El Paso Blvd., ☎ 719/633–5667) rents horses for guided tours through Garden of the Gods park (*see* Exploring Colorado Springs and Environs, *above*). Reservations are necessary.

Dining and Lodging

Steaks and other basic Western foods, along with Mexican food, are the most popular menu options hereabouts. The Colorado Springs Convention and Visitors Bureau (*see* Tourist Information, *above*) offers lodging assistance. For price ranges, see Charts 1 (B) and 2 (B) in On the Road with Fodor's.

Colorado Springs

DINING

Flying W Ranch. Chuckwagon suppers of barbecued beef, beans, biscuits, applesauce, and spice cake are served around a campfire at this working ranch. Afterward, a cowboy band gives a Western show. In winter, steak-house dinners are served inside. *3330 Chuckwagon Rd., ☎ 719/598–4000. Reservations required. No credit cards. Closed Sun.–Thurs. Oct.–May. $$*

Margarita. Plants, adobe walls, terra-cotta tile, and mosaic tables lend an air of refinement to this fine eatery, whose constantly changing menu is an intriguing hybrid of Mexican and Continental influences. *7350 Pine Creek Rd., ☎ 719/598–8667. AE, MC, V. Closed Mon. No dinner Sun. $$*

DINING AND LODGING

★ **The Broadmoor.** This resort is a Colorado legend. The lovely 1918 buildings house plush, traditional rooms; the restaurants serve everything from formal French to Sunday brunch. There are even two notable museums here—the International Skating Hall of Fame and Museum (Peggy Fleming trained here), and the original owner's prodigious collection of antique carriages. *1 Lake Ave., 80901, ☎ 719/634–7711* *or 800/634–7711, FAX 719/577–5779. 483 rooms, 67 suites. Facilities: 8 restaurants, 3 bars, health club, 12 tennis courts, 3 golf courses, 3 pools, 3 squash courts, ice skating, horseback riding, shopping arcade, beauty salon, cinema, paddleboat and mountain-bike rentals, children's programs. D, DC, MC, V. $$$*

LODGING

★ **Hearthstone Inn.** Rooms at this B&B are individually decorated with antiques and stylish country prints. Breakfast runs to such delicacies as corn pancakes with maple syrup and fruit compote. *506 N. Cascade Ave., 80903, ☎ 719/473–4413 or 800/521–1885. 25 rooms, 2 share bath. No smoking. AE, MC, V. $$*

Manitou Springs

DINING

Briarhurst Manor. An 1878 stone mansion provides the setting for chef Sigi Krauss's offerings. Dishes such as chateaubriand are prepared with Colorado ingredients and a European touch. *404 Manitou Ave., ☎ 719/685–1864. AE, D, DC, MC, V. Closed Sun., 1st 2 wks of Jan. No lunch. $$$*

Motels

Le Baron Hotel (314 W. Bijou, Colorado Springs 80905, ☎ 719/471–8680 or 800/477–8610, FAX 719/471–0894), 206 rooms, restaurant, lounge, pool, fitness room; *$$.* **Palmer House/Best Western** (I–25, near Exit 145, 3010 North Chestnut St., Colorado Springs 80907, ☎ 719/636–5201 or 800/223–9127, FAX 719/636–3108), 150 rooms, restaurant, lounge, pool; *$$.*

NORTHWESTERN COLORADO

As you climb west from Denver, the mountains rear up, pine forests line the road, and the legendary Colorado of powder skiing, alpine scenery, and the great outdoors begins. As once-primitive mining towns have attracted skiers and scenery buffs, sophisticated dining and lodging have followed.

Tourist Information

Aspen Chamber Resort Association (328 E. Hyman Ave., ☎ 970/925–5656; 425 Rio Grande Pl., ☎ 970/925–1940); **Glenwood Springs Chamber Resort Association** (1102 Grand Ave., ☎ 970/945–6589 or 800/221–0098); **Steamboat Springs Chamber Resort Association** (1201 Lincoln Ave., ☎ 970/879–0880 or 800/922–2722); **Summit County Chamber of Commerce** (Main St., Frisco, ☎ 970/668–5000); **Vail Valley Tourism and Convention Bureau** (100 E. Meadow Dr., ☎ 970/476–1000).

Getting There

By Plane

Aspen Airport (☎ 970/920–5385) is 7 mi east of town; most flights connect from Denver. **Steamboat Springs Airport** (☎ 970/879–1204) is 3 mi northwest of town. Vail Valley is served by the **Eagle County Airport** (☎ 970/524–9490), 35 mi west of Vail. All are served by regional and national airlines, but Vail has scheduled service only during ski season.

By Car

I–70 is the main route to the Summit County resorts, Vail, and Glenwood Springs. From Glenwood Springs, Hwy. 82 heads to Aspen. Hwy. 36 leads to Rocky Mountain National Park and Estes Park; Hwy. 40 heads to Steamboat Springs.

By Train

Amtrak (☏ 800/872–7245) stops in Glenwood Springs, Granby, and Winter Park.

By Bus

Greyhound Lines (☏ 800/231–2222) serves most major mountain towns.

Exploring Northwestern Colorado

Estes Park is the northern gateway to **Rocky Mountain National Park** (*see* National and State Parks, *above*), where Trail Ridge Road (closed in winter) provides a spectacular ride over one of the highest auto routes in the world. On the west side of the park is **Grand Lake,** the largest natural lake in Colorado, which has a lovely shoreline and boasts the world's highest yacht club.

The closest resort skiing from Denver is off I–70 at **Winter Park,** a family-oriented resort particularly good for intermediate skiers. It is popular with Denverites, who often travel there via the Ski Train (☏ 303/296–4754) on weekends. The mountains of **Summit County,** 70 mi from Denver off I–70, attract climbers, hikers, and skiers. The county's four ski resorts have interchangeable lift tickets. **Copper Mountain** has some terrain for most abilities, with an emphasis on intermediate skiers. The extremely well-designed ski area complements the first Club Med in North America. **Keystone Resort**'s hallmark is meticulous service in a planned village centered on a man-made lake. The resort encompasses the ski areas of **Keystone,** focused on beginning and intermediate skiers, and **A-Basin** and **North Peak,** for serious skiers. Shuttle buses serve these areas from Keystone. **Breckenridge** is an old mining town transformed into a resort with history, renovated buildings, and a sense of place, as well as fine skiing, particularly for intermediate and advanced skiers. For a change from resort atmosphere and prices, head to **Lake Dillon,** a large reservoir popular with boaters. Up U.S. 40 from I–70, **Steamboat Springs** offers the amenities of the others, plus great, uncrowded skiing for all abilities and a real Western feel.

West of Summit County is **Vail,** celebrated home of the largest ski mountain in North America, with acres of skiing for every ability. Constructed from the ground up to look like a European ski village, it is huge, varied in its attractions, and pricey. It tends to be more conservative and family-oriented than Aspen (*see below*). **Beaver Creek** was created for those seeking an even more exclusive atmosphere; this is another instant Bavarian village, with more class and more expense. Its ski area is geared toward intermediate and advanced skiers.

At the turnoff for Aspen on I–70 is **Glenwood Springs,** where the main attraction, besides the scenery, is the **Yampah Hot Springs** (Pine St., ☏ 970/945–7131; admission charged), the world's largest outdoor mineral hot springs, a clean, well-run complex.

You know all about **Aspen:** the glitz, the rich, the chic-by-jowl actresses and moguls who jam this tiny town during the ski season. It's expensive—and worth it, if your passion is people-watching in an exquisitely restored mining town that happens to offer great skiing. Many prefer the other seasons, though, for the beauty of the place or the summer **Aspen Music Festival** (☎ 970/925–3254).

Within Aspen's orbit are several ski areas, each geared to a different level of ability. Skiers can get a multiday ticket to all four mountains: **Tiehack** serving primarily beginners and low-intermediate skiers; **Aspen Highlands,** for intermediate skiers, with some of the highest vertical drops and best views; **Snowmass,** a perfect intermediate hill; and for experts, **Aspen Mountain,** which hosts international competitions.

What to See and Do with Children

Most ski resorts offer special programs and activities for children, especially **Winter Park** (which was the first with programs for children), **Copper Mountain, Keystone,** and **Vail.** In summer, **Breckenridge** and **Winter Park** open alpine slides.

Shopping

The town of **Silverthorne** features an outlet shopping complex (I–70 at Silverthorne, ☎ 970/468–9440) with about 50 stores.

Sports and the Outdoors

Biking

Mountain biking is increasingly popular in the region; trails are everywhere. Check with visitor centers.

Boating

Sailing regattas are common at **Grand Lake.** Rent fishing boats and motorboats at **Beacon Landing Marina** (Grand Co. Rd. 64, 6 mi south of Grand Lake, off Hwy. 34, ☎ 970/627–3671). **Lake Dillon Marina** (Dillon, ☎ 970/468–5100) rents sail and motorboats.

Fishing

Grand Lake, with trout lurking in its depths, and the connected reservoirs, **Shadow Mountain Lake** and **Lake Granby,** are popular. **Dillon Reservoir** is stocked with salmon and trout. The **Lower Blue River,** below Dillon Reservoir, is a Gold Medal catch-and-release area, as is the **Upper Fryingpan River** near Aspen.

Golf

Sheraton Steamboat Golf Club (2200 Village Inn Ct., ☎ 970/879–2220) was designed by Robert Trent Jones Jr. Jack Nicklaus designed the course at the **Breckenridge Golf Club** (200 Clubhouse Dr., ☎ 970/453–9104), where reservations are almost mandatory. The difficult **Eagle/Vail Golf Course** (0431 Eagle Dr., Avon, ☎ 970/949–5267) has reduced fees in fall and spring.

Hiking and Backpacking

To find out about parks and wilderness areas with great hiking and backpacking, contact **Holy Cross Ranger District Office** (24747 Hwy. 24, Minturn, near Vail, ☎ 970/827–5715), **Aspen Ranger District Office** (806 W. Hallam St., ☎ 970/925–3445), and **Dillon Ranger District Office** (Blue River Pkwy., Silverthorne, ☎ 970/468–5400).

Rafting

The **Colorado River** is popular for both white-water enthusiasts and beginners; so is the **Arkansas River,** near Buena Vista. Contact rafting firms through the **Colorado River Outfitters Association** (☎ 303/369–4632) in Denver.

Ski Areas

For **snow conditions** at Colorado resorts, call 303/831–7669.

Cross-Country

Aspen/Snowmass Nordic Trail System (☎ 970/923–3148) contains 81 km (50 mi) of trails through the Roaring Fork Valley. **Breckenridge Nordic Ski Center** (☎ 970/453–6855) maintains 31 km (19 mi) of trails in its system. **Copper Mountain/Trak Cross-Country Center** (☎ 303/986–2882) offers 26 km (16 mi) of groomed track and skate lanes. **Devil's Thumb Ranch/Ski Idlewild** (Devil's Thumb, 10 mi north of Winter Park; Ski Idlewild, Winter Park, ☎ 970/726–5632) are full-service resorts with 53 km (33 mi) of groomed trails between them. **Frisco Nordic Center** (112 N. Summit Blvd., ☎ 970/668–0866) has nearly 40 km (25 mi) of one-way loops. **Keystone Nordic Center at Ski Tip Lodge** (☎ 970/468–4275) provides 29 km (18 mi) of prepared trails and 56 km (35 mi) of backcountry skiing winding through Arapahoe National Forest. **Steamboat Ski Touring Center** (☎ 970/879–8180) has trails on the golf course. **Vail/Beaver Creek Cross-Country Ski Centers** (☎ 970/476–5601, ext. 4390) provide information on the many trails in the Vail Valley.

Downhill

Aspen Highlands (1600 Maroon Creek Rd., Aspen 81611, ☎ 970/925–1220) has 597 acres of runs, 9 lifts, and a 3,635-ft vertical drop. **Aspen Mountain** (Box 1248, Aspen 81612, ☎ 970/925–1220) has 631 acres of runs, a gondola, 7 lifts, and a 3,262-ft drop. **Beaver Creek** (Box 7, Vail 81658, ☎ 970/949–5750) has 1,125 acres of runs, 10 lifts, and a 3,340-ft drop. **Breckenridge** (Box 1058, Breckenridge 80424, ☎ 303/452–3000) has 1,915 acres of runs, 16 lifts, and a 3,398-ft drop. **Copper Mountain** (Box 3533, Copper Mountain 80443, ☎ 970/968–2882) has 1,360 acres of runs, 19 lifts, and a 2,601-ft drop. **Keystone** (Box 38, Keystone 80435, ☎ 970/468–2316) has 1,737 acres of runs, 19 lifts, and a 2,900-ft drop. **Snowmass** (Box 5566, Snowmass Village 80446, ☎ 970/923–2010) has 2,500 acres of runs, 15 lifts, and a 4,087-ft drop. **Steamboat** (2305 Mt. Werner Circle, Steamboat Springs 80487, ☎ 970/879–6111) has 2,500 acres of runs, a gondola, 20 lifts, and a 3,685-ft drop. **Tiehack** (Box 1248, Aspen 81612, ☎ 970/925–1220) has 410 acres of runs, 7 lifts, and a 2,030-ft drop. **Vail** (Box 7, Vail 81658, ☎ 970/476–5677) has 4,014 acres of runs, a gondola, 24 lifts, and a 3,250-ft drop. **Winter Park** (Box 36, Winter Park 80482, ☎ 970/726–5514) has 1,358 acres of runs, 20 lifts, and a 3,060-ft drop.

Dining and Lodging

Dining in Colorado's resorts can be an exquisite, unforgettable experience. It can also cost you plenty. The celebrity atmosphere of towns like Aspen and Vail attracts celebrity chefs, and hot restaurants come and go as quickly as they do in New York. If you don't want to spend the money to eat with the stars, consider heading to nearby towns, where the atmosphere—and the prices—are more down-home Western.

The ski resorts make getting accommodations as easy as possible. To hook travelers up with many different kinds accommodations, there are central numbers: Aspen, 800/262–7736; Beaver Creek, 800/622–3131; Breckenridge, 800/221–1091; Copper Mountain, 800/458–8386; Keystone, 800/222–0188; Steamboat Springs, 800/922–2722; Vail, 800/525–3875; Winter Park, 800/453–2525. Condos are the most common and, because they have kitchens, can help cut down on food expenses. For price ranges, see Charts 1 (A) and 2 (A) in On the Road with Fodor's.

Aspen

DINING

Restaurant at the Little Nell. In plush, upholstered surroundings accented by brass railings and wide windows, Chef George Mahaffey uses local delicacies to create such dishes as roast rack of Colorado lamb with saffron couscous and pan-braised vegetables. *675 E. Durant Ave., ☎ 970/920–6330. AE, D, DC, MC, V. $$$$*

★ **Syzygy.** Upstairs and unmarked, this restaurant is for those who like sleek modern design, track lighting, and sophisticated food that blends international flavors. *520 E. Hyman, ☎ 970/925–3700. AE, MC, V. $$$*

LODGING

★ **Hotel Jerome.** The century-old brick building has been refurbished with the charm of the original Victorian style in each room. *330 E. Main St., 81611, ☎ 970/920–1000 or 800/331–7213, FAX 970/925–2784. 44 rooms with bath, 49 suites. Facilities: 2 restaurants, 2 bars, pool, whirlpool, underground parking, shuttle bus to slopes and airport. AE, DC, MC, V. $$$–$$$$*

Snowflake Inn. This is another property with wildly divergent accommodations, all quite comfortable and decorated mostly in tartans or bright colors. *221 E. Hyman Ave., 81611, ☎ 970/925–3221 or 800/247–2069, FAX 970/925–8740. 38 units. Facilities: heated outdoor pool and Jacuzzi, sauna, laundry facilities. AE, MC, V. $$*

Beaver Creek

LODGING

Hyatt Regency Beaver Creek. The public rooms are a striking blend of soaring Western space, huge stone fireplaces, an enormous antler chandelier, and upholstered comfort. Guest rooms are decorated in forest green and maroon. Guests leave the hotel and click on their skis. Watch for much lower rates off-season. *Box 1595, Avon 81620, ☎ 970/949–1234 or 800/233–1234, FAX 970/949–4164. 295 rooms, 3 suites, 26 condos. Facilities: 3 restaurants, deli, 2 lounges, children's programs, 5 tennis courts, pool, 6 hot tubs, health club, ski valet. AE, D, DC, MC, V. $$$$*

Breckenridge

LODGING

Williams House. From the cozy front parlor, done up in pink and ultramarine, with a crackling mantel fireplace and floral spreads, to the exquisite dollhouse-like accommodations, the Williams House is a dream bed-and-breakfast. Best of all are the affable hosts: Avid skiers ("Cold cereal on powder days," they warn), the owners Fred Kinat and Diane Jaynes take guests to their secret stashes and on hikes in summer. *303 N. Main St., ☎ 970/453–2975. 4 rooms. AE. $–$$*

Glenwood Springs

LODGING

Hotel Colorado. Teddy Roosevelt and others stayed at this grande dame of Northwest Colorado to take advantage of the adjacent hot springs, and the public rooms have been returned to their former glory. The bedrooms are huge and sparsely furnished. *526 Pine St., 81601, ☎ 970/945–6511 or 800/544–3998, FAX 970/945–7030. 96 rooms, 26 suites. Facilities: 2 restaurants, bar, exercise room, beauty salon. AE, D, DC, MC, V. $–$$*

Grand Lake

LODGING

Grand Lake Lodge. Set majestically above Grand Lake and bordering Rocky Mountain National Park, the lodge is actually a collection of rustic cabins that accommodate two to 25 guests. Some have wood-burning stoves for heat, others share baths, but all share a comfortable, well-worn atmosphere. *Box 269, 80447,* ☎ *970/627–3967 in summer or 970/759–5848. 40 cabins, 10 share bath. Facilities: restaurant, bar, pool, horseback riding (fee), hiking trails, mountain-bike rental. AE, D, MC, V. Closed mid-Sept.–May. $$*

Keystone

DINING AND LODGING

★ **Ski Tip Lodge.** From the tranquil atmosphere to the public room's huge picture windows overlooking a forest, the lodge is special. So is the American regional food. Built in the 1880s, the B&B reflects the era in its period-furnished rooms. It is ½ mi from the slopes. *Box 38, 80435,* ☎ *970/468–4202 or 800/222–0188. 24 rooms, 2 share bath. Facilities: restaurant, bar. AE, D, DC, MC, V. $$–$$$*

Steamboat Springs

DINING

★ **La Montaña.** This Mexican/Southwestern establishment is probably Steamboat's most popular restaurant. Among the standouts are red chili pasta in a shrimp, garlic, and cilantro sauce; mesquite-grilled interwoven strands of elk, lamb, and chorizo sausage; and elk loin crusted with pecan nuts and bourbon cream sauce. *Après Ski Way and Village Dr.,* ☎ *970/879–5800. D, MC, V. No lunch. $–$$*

LODGING

Sky Valley Lodge. This homey property is a few miles from downtown, amid glorious scenery that contributes to the get-away-from-it-all feel of the inn. Warm English-country-style rooms are decorated in restful mountain colors and feature touches such as fruits and dried flowers. *31490 E. Hwy. 40, 80477,* ☎ *970/879–7749 or 800/538–7519,* FAX *970/879–7749. 24 rooms. Facilities: hot tub, ski shuttle. AE, MC, V. $$*

Vail

DINING

★ **Sweet Basil.** For a fine meal in a cheery, intimate atmosphere, this can't be beat. The menu is creative, with such offerings as salmon pillard with bok choy, sesame puree, and tomato-cilantro sauce. *193 E. Gore Creek Dr.,* ☎ *970/476–0125. AE, MC, V. $$–$$$*

LODGING

★ **Sonnenalp.** This centrally located Bavarian-style hotel run by a German family offers small rooms with an authentically German alpine feeling. Accommodations are in three buildings: the pretty Swiss Chalet, the rustic Austria Haus, and the more contemporary Bavaria Haus. The restaurants are superb. *20 Vail Rd., 81657,* ☎ *970/476–5656 or 800/654–8312. 186 rooms. Facilities: 4 restaurants, 3 bars, 3 pools, European health spa. DC, MC, V. $$$–$$$$*

Winter Park

DINING AND LODGING

★ **Gasthaus Eichler.** This is Winter Park's most romantic dining spot, with quaint Bavarian decor, antler chandeliers, and stained-glass windows, all glowing in the candlelight. Featured are veal and grilled items, in addition to scrumptious German classics such as sauerbraten, *kassler rippchen*, and *rindsrollater.* The Eichler also offers 15 cozy Old World rooms, with down comforters, lace curtains, armoires, cable TV, and Jacuzzi tubs. *Winter Park Dr.,* ☎ *970/726–5133 or 800/543–3899. AE, D, MC, V. No lunch. $$*

Ranches

★ **C Lazy U Ranch.** Near Rocky Mountain National Park, this rambling, Southwestern-style wooden lodge has fireplaces and Navajo rugs in its rooms and cabins. The fare ranges from old-fashioned ranch food (steak and barbecue) to lighter, health-conscious dishes, such as mountain trout stuffed with artichokes. *Box 379, Granby 80446, ☎ 970/887–3344, FAX 970/887–3917. 19 rooms, 20 cabins. Facilities: dining room, 2 tennis courts, volleyball and racquetball courts, pool, sauna, horseback riding, cross-country skiing, sleigh rides, ice skating. No credit cards. Summer and holiday 1-week minimum stay. $$$–$$$$*

Home Ranch. This rustic, updated, Western lodge in the Steamboat Springs area has some Stickley furniture in the white-walled rooms. Each log cabin has a wood-burning stove and a hot tub. *Box 822, Clark 80428, ☎ 970/879–1780 or 800/223–7094, FAX 970/879–1795. 8 cabins, 6 lodge rooms. Facilities: dining room, sauna, pool, horseback riding, guided hiking and fishing. AE, MC, V. $$$–$$$$*

Campgrounds

Campgrounds are everywhere in the state and national forests (*see* Sports and the Outdoors, *above,* for addresses and telephone numbers). Reserve camping spaces for many of the national forest campgrounds by calling 800/283–2267. **Tiger Run Resort** (3 mi north of town on Hwy. 9, Box 815, Breckenridge 80424, ☎ 970/453–9690) is a resort for RVs, with tennis, a pool, and a game room. **Winding River Resort Village** (Box 629, Grand Lake 80447, ☎ 970/627–3215) is a combination campground and low-cost dude ranch in a beautiful forest.

SOUTHWESTERN COLORADO

This area encompasses ski areas and red-rock deserts, cowboy hangouts and haunts of ancient cultures. The feeling is less glamorous and more down-home; you may see a cowboy in the distance riding off after a stray, or walk into a bar where ranchers discussing stock prices sit next to climbers enthusing over an ascent route.

Tourist Information

Southwest Colorado Tourism Center (Box 2102, Montrose 81402, ☎ 800/933–4340). **Durango:** Chamber of Commerce (111 S. Camino Del Rio, Box 2587, 81302, ☎ 970/247–0312 or 800/525–8855). **Telluride:** Chamber of Commerce (666 W. Colorado Ave., Box 653, 81435, ☎ 970/728–3041).

Getting There

By Plane

Durango–La Plata County Airport (☎ 970/247–8143) is 14 mi east of Durango, and **Montrose Regional Airport** (☎ 970/249–3203) is about 1 mi from Montrose. **Gunnison County Airport** (☎ 970/641–2304) is 23 mi south of Crested Butte. **Telluride Regional Airport** (☎ 970/728–5313) is about 2 mi from Telluride.

By Car

Hwy. 141 from Grand Junction to Hwy. 145 leads to Telluride; Hwy. 550 is the route from Durango to Silverton and Ouray.

By Bus

Greyhound Lines (☎ 800/231–2222) serves Durango and such major mountain towns as Purgatory, Silverton, Ouray, Ridgeway, and Montrose.

Exploring Southwestern Colorado

Telluride is another old mining town turned ski resort, with a difference: Its relative isolation in a box canyon makes it more laid-back than many Colorado resorts, and its beauty is legendary. The resort provides terrain for skiers of all abilities. The summer brings nationally known festivals of film (☎ 970/728–4401), bluegrass (☎ 800/624–2422), and jazz (☎ 970/728–7009). South of Telluride is a complete change of scene: **Mesa Verde** (*see* National and State Parks, *above*), where the forests give way to dramatic red rock cliff dwellings fashioned by the Anasazi, believed to be the ancestors of the Pueblos, more than seven centuries ago.

East is **Durango,** a surprisingly large town with dramatic views of the San Juan Mountains that still cherishes its frontier traditions. A trip on the **Durango and Silverton Narrow Gauge Railroad** (479 Main Ave., ☎ 970/247–2733) is worth the trouble of making reservations well in advance. The eight-hour round-trip, on tracks laid between the two towns in 1881, offers unspoiled scenery, dramatic gorge crossings, and rails dug into the mountainside. **Silverton** is a much smaller, more untouched frontier mining town.

Ouray, about 25 mi up the twisty, breathtaking Million-Dollar Highway, is a charming, sleepy Western town surrounded by the magnificent red San Juan Mountains. Don't miss the **Ouray Hot Springs Pool** (☎ 970/325–4638) or, for a more rustic dip, **Orvis Hot Springs** (☎ 970/626–5324). Farther north, up Hwy. 135, is **Crested Butte,** an old Victorian mining town tucked away in another gorgeous setting that serves as base for the excellent Crested Butte ski area 2 mi away, most suited for high-intermediate and expert skiers.

Sports and the Outdoors

Biking

The mountainous trails are challenging for experienced riders. Rent bikes in Durango and Crested Butte.

Fishing

The **Dolores River,** in the San Juan National Forest (*see* Hiking and Backpacking, *below*), and the **Animas River,** near Durango, are good for trout. The **Vallecito Reservoir,** also near Durango, has pike, trout, and salmon. At **Ridgway State Park** (☎ 970/626–5822), 10 mi north of Ouray, you can catch rainbow trout.

Golf

Some of the best 18-hole courses in the area are **Hillcrest Golf Course** (2300 Rim Dr., Durango, ☎ 970/247–1499), **Tamarron** (40292 Rte. 550N, north of Durango, ☎ 970/259–2000), **Telluride Golf Club** (Telluride Mountain Village, ☎ 970/728–3856), and **Skyland Country Club** (385 Country Club Dr., outside Crested Butte, ☎ 970/349–6127).

Hiking and Backpacking

The 469-mi **Colorado Trail,** from Durango to Denver, is a major route. The **San Juan National Forest District Office** (701 Camino del Rio, Room 101, Durango, ☎ 970/247–4874) has information on trails in the area.

Rafting

Rafting is popular on the San Miguel, Dolores, Gunnison, and Animas rivers. Arrange trips through the **Colorado River Outfitters Association** (☎ 303/369–4632).

Ski Areas

For snow conditions at Colorado resorts, call 303/831–7669.

Cross-Country

Trails abound; check with local tourist offices for details. **Purgatory Ski Touring Center** (Purgatory Ski Area, No. 1 Skier Pl., Durango 81301, ☎ 970/247–9000) offers 16 km (25 mi) of trails; **Telluride Nordic Center** (free shuttle from alpine ski area; ☎ 970/728–7570) has 30 km (48 mi) of trails.

Downhill

Crested Butte (off Rte. 135, Box A, 81225, ☎ 970/349–2222) has 1,160 acres of runs, 13 lifts, and a 2,775-ft vertical drop. **Purgatory–Durango** (Hwy. 550, ☎ 970/247–9000) has 722 acres of runs, 9 lifts, and a 2,029-ft drop. **Telluride** (Rte. 145, Box 11155, 81435, ☎ 970/728–3856) has 1,050 acres of runs, 10 lifts, and a 3,522-ft drop.

Dining and Lodging

For price ranges, see Charts 1 (B) and 2 (B) in On the Road with Fodor's.

Crested Butte

DINING

★ **Slogar.** Set in a lovingly renovated Victorian tavern awash in lace and stained glass, this restaurant turns out some of the plumpest, juiciest fried chicken west of the Mississippi. *2nd and Whiterock Sts., ☎ 970/349–5765. MC, V. No lunch. $*

Durango

DINING

Ariano's. Pasta made fresh daily and a sure touch with meats makes this northern Italian restaurant one of Durango's most popular. Veal scaloppine sautéed with fresh sage and garlic is among the featured dishes. *150 E. 6th St., ☎ 970/247–8146. No reservations. AE, MC, V. $$*

Red Snapper. If you're in the mood for fresh, creatively prepared seafood, head for this congenial place, furnished with more than 200 gallons' worth of aquariums. Of course, steaks and prime rib are also available (this is a meat-and-potatoes town). *144 E. 9th St., ☎ 970/259–3417. AE, MC, V. No lunch. $$*

LODGING

★ **Strater Hotel.** Author Louis L'Amour made this jewel of a restored Victorian hotel his home during frequent trips to town. The meticulously decorated accommodations match the Victorian charm of the public parlors. *699 Main Ave., 81301, ☎ 970/247–4431 or 800/247–4431, FAX 970/259–2208. 93 rooms. Facilities: restaurant, 2 bars, whirlpool. AE, DC, MC, V. $$*

Ouray

DINING AND LODGING

St. Elmo Hotel. Originally a miner's hotel, this B&B is welcoming and intimate, with Victorian antiques and charm. The Bon Ton Restaurant downstairs serves northern Italian food. *426 Main St., 81427, ☎ 970/325–4951. 9 rooms. Facilities: restaurant, bar, hot tub, sauna. D, MC, V. $$*

LODGING

Box Canyon Lodge and Hot Springs. The attraction here is the private mineral springs, used first by the Ute, then by Coger Sanitarium (formerly on site). Soak away your cares in two redwood tubs full of steaming 103°–107° water, with the stunning mountain views around you.

The rooms are nondescript, but modern and comfortable, with all amenities. *45 3rd St., ☎ 970/327–5080. 40 rooms. Facilities: 2 natural hot tubs. AE, DC, MC, V. $$*

Silverton

LODGING

Wyman Hotel. Rooms in this 1902 red sandstone building have cathedral ceilings and arched windows and are furnished with period antiques, brass lamps, and, believe it or not, VCRs. *1371 Greene St., ☎ 970/387–5372. 18 rooms. AE, MC, V. Closed mid-Oct.–early May. $–$$*

Telluride

DINING

★ **La Marmotte.** This rustic restaurant, decorated like a French country cottage, is the place to go in town for a special meal. The French owners and chefs change the menu constantly, serving such dishes as duck confit or lamb with red bell pepper sauce and white beans. *150 W. San Juan Ave., ☎ 970/728–6232. AE, MC, V. No lunch. $$$*

LODGING

San Sophia Inn. If you eschew Victorian frills, this is the inn for you: There's no trace of Laura Ashley here, except for the brass beds and down comforters. Rooms, while smallish, are luxurious, done in handsome desert shades with pine armoires. *330 W. Pacific St., ☎ 970/728–3001 or 800/537–4781. 16 rooms. Facilities: hot tub, underground parking. AE, MC, V. $$$–$$$$*

Ranches

San Juan Ranch. In the gorgeous Uncompagre Valley north of Ouray, this simple Southwestern-style ranch has comfortable, unpretentious '50s decor and hearty yet health-conscious American cooking, with plenty of homegrown vegetables served family style (meals are included in the rates). *Hwy. 23, Box 2882, Ridgway 81432, ☎ 970/626–5360 or 800/331–3015, FAX 970/626–5457. 9 units. Facilities: dining room, children's program, horseback riding, whirlpool, sauna, free airport shuttle. 3-day minimum stay in winter, 1 week in summer. AE, MC, V. $$*

Skyline Ranch. Burlap walls, pine furniture, and down comforters deck the rooms in the slab-wood buildings of this rustic Western ranch. The horseback riding and fly-fishing are great. In winter, guests cross-country ski or head for downhill skiing at Telluride. The cuisine is French-American, with a menu that changes daily. *Off Hwy. 145, 8 mi south of Telluride; Box 67, Telluride 81435, ☎ 970/728–3757, FAX 970/728–6728. 10 lodge rooms, 6 cabins. Facilities: restaurant (Dec.–Mar.: breakfast included, lunch and dinner open to public; Apr.–Nov.: meals included, closed to public), whirlpool, sauna, free shuttle to airport and ski area. AE (winter only), MC, V. $–$$*

Campgrounds

Ranger District Offices (*see* Hiking and Backpacking, *above*) have information on campgrounds in the state and national forests. **KOA** has a campground near Durango (east on Hwy. 160, ☎ 970/247–0783; closed mid-Oct.–May).

IDAHO

Updated by Susan English

Capital Boise
Population 1,036,500
Motto It Is Perpetual
State Bird Mountain bluebird
State Flower Syringa

Visitor Information

Idaho Travel Council (Dept. of Commerce, 700 W. State St., Box 83720, Boise 83720, ☎ 208/334–2470 or 800/635–7820).

Scenic Drives

Idaho has 10 official scenic drives, detailed in a map available from the Idaho Travel Council (*see* Visitor Information, *above*). The **Lake Coeur d'Alene Scenic Route** follows Rtes. 3 and 97 for 70 mi along the eastern shore of one of the most beautiful lakes in the world. The **Sawtooth Scenic Byway** between Ketchum and Challis passes through spectacular mountain scenery with plenty of wildlife.

National and State Parks

National Parks

Eight national forests are entirely within Idaho's borders, and seven more intrude from surrounding states, giving the state more than 21 million acres of protected land. **Challis National Forest** (HC63, Box 1671, Challis 83226, ☎ 208/879–2285) has some 2½ million acres and the state's highest peak. **Sawtooth National Forest** (2647 Kimberly Rd. E., Twin Falls 83301, ☎ 208/737–3200) includes the **Sawtooth National Recreation Area** (Star Rte., Ketchum 83340, ☎ 208/726–7672) and within that the **Sawtooth Wilderness Area** (*see* Ketchum/Sun Valley and Sawtooth, *below*). **Silent City of the Rocks National Reserve** (Box 169, Almo 83312, ☎ 208/824–5519) is an eerie landscape of rock formations outside Almo in south-central Idaho.

State Parks

The **Idaho Department of Parks & Recreation** (Box 83720, Boise 83720-0065, ☎ 208/334–4199) maintains 24 state parks, ranging from undeveloped, natural areas to full-scale recreational facilities. **Harriman State Park** (Rte. 20 near Yellowstone, HC 66, Box 500, Island Park 83429, ☎ 208/558–7368) has a world-famous fly-fishing stream (Henry's Fork of the Snake River) and is part of a 16,000-acre wildlife refuge. **Ponderosa State Park** (Box A, 83638, ☎ 208/634–2164) is a beautiful forested park outside McCall, popular in summer and winter.

SOUTHERN IDAHO

The southern third of Idaho is a richly diverse region of mountains, desert, and farms. Roughly bisected by the Snake River, southern Idaho is predominantly agricultural in flavor, although it offers waterfalls higher than Niagara, weird volcanic formations where the lunar astronauts trained, and some of Ernest Hemingway's favorite fishing holes.

Idaho

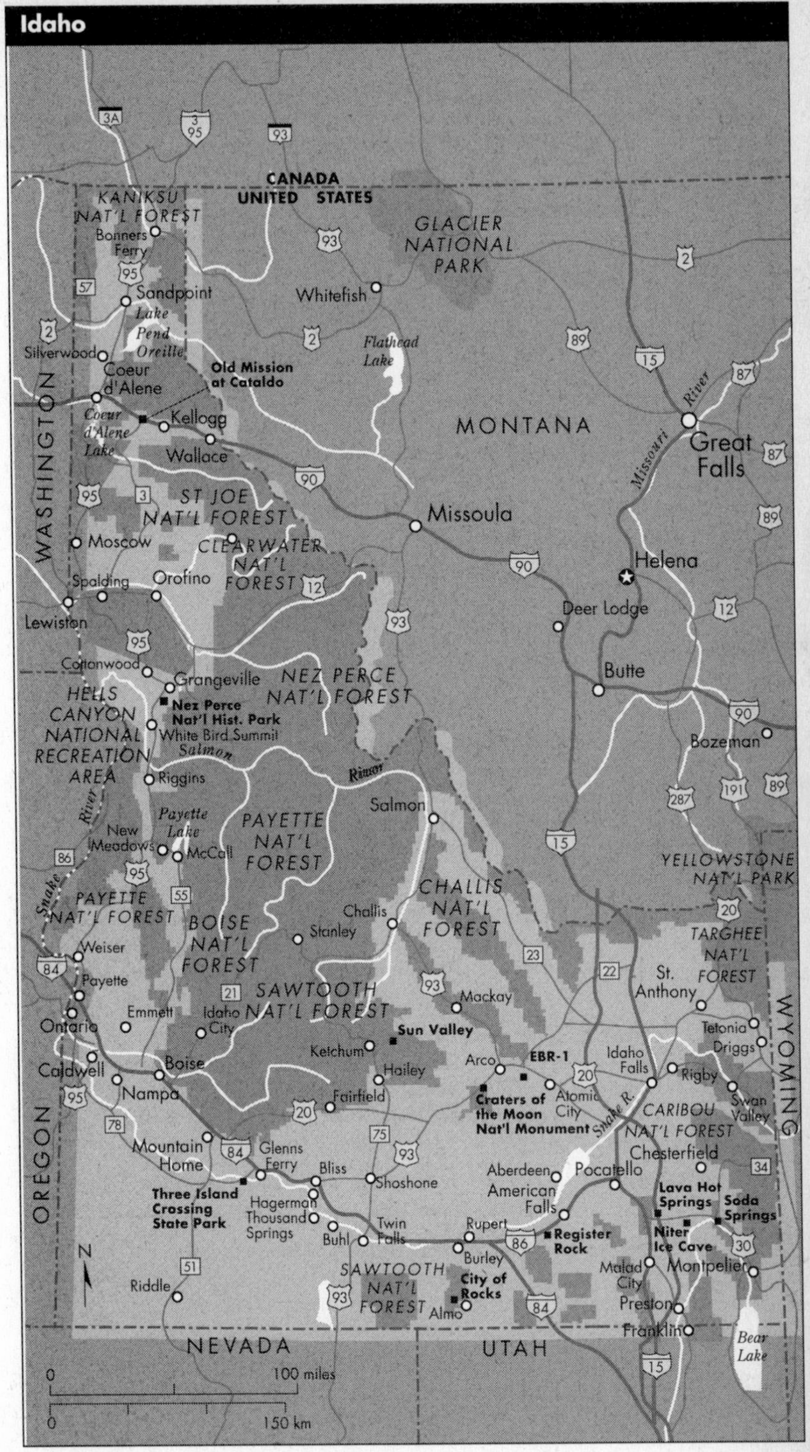
CANADA
UNITED STATES
KANIKSU NAT'L FOREST
Bonners Ferry
Sandpoint
Lake Pend Oreille
Silverwood
Coeur d'Alene
Old Mission at Cataldo
Coeur d'Alene Lake
Kellogg
Wallace
GLACIER NATIONAL PARK
Whitefish
Flathead Lake
MONTANA
Great Falls
Missouri River
Missoula
Helena
Deer Lodge
Butte
Bozeman
WASHINGTON
ST JOE NAT'L FOREST
CLEARWATER NAT'L FOREST
Moscow
Spalding
Orofino
Lewiston
Cottonwood
Grangeville
NEZ PERCE NAT'L FOREST
Nez Perce Nat'l Hist. Park
HELLS CANYON NATIONAL RECREATION AREA
White Bird Summit
Salmon River
Riggins
Salmon
PAYETTE NAT'L FOREST
Payette Lake
New Meadows
McCall
Snake River
CHALLIS NAT'L FOREST
YELLOWSTONE NAT'L PARK
TARGHEE NAT'L FOREST
BOISE NAT'L FOREST
Challis
Stanley
Weiser
Payette
SAWTOOTH NAT'L FOREST
Mackay
St. Anthony
Tetonia
Driggs
WYOMING
Emmett
Idaho City
Ontario
Sun Valley
Ketchum
Hailey
Arco
EBR-1
Idaho Falls
Rigby
Swan Valley
Caldwell
Boise
Nampa
Fairfield
Craters of the Moon Nat'l Monument
Atomic City
Snake R.
CARIBOU NAT'L FOREST
Chesterfield
Mountain Home
Glenns Ferry
Bliss
Shoshone
Aberdeen
Pocatello
American Falls
OREGON
Three Island Crossing State Park
Hagerman
Thousand Springs
Buhl
Twin Falls
Rupert
Burley
Register Rock
Lava Hot Springs
Soda Springs
Niter Ice Cave
Malad City
Montpelier
Riddle
City of Rocks
Almo
Preston
Franklin
Bear Lake
NEVADA
UTAH
N
0
100 miles
150 km

Getting There

By Plane

Boise Municipal Airport (☎ 208/383–3110), 3 mi from downtown, is served by national and regional airlines. The **Boise Urban Stages** (☎ 208/336–1010) shuttle bus to town costs 75¢; taxis cost $7–$10.

By Car

Boise is best reached by I–84 or I–15 from the south and by I–90 from the north.

By Train

Amtrak (1701 Eastover Terr., in the Morrison-Knudsen building, Boise, ☎ 800/872–7245).

By Bus

Greyhound Lines (1212 W. Bannock St., Boise, ☎ 800/231–2222) serves Boise, Twin Falls, Pocatello, and Idaho Falls.

Boise

Tourist Information

Boise: Convention and Visitors Bureau (168 N. 9th St., Suite 200, 83702, ☎ 208/344–7777 or 800/635–5240).

Exploring Boise

Founded in 1863 in the foothills of the Rockies on the Boise River as an Oregon Trail military post, Idaho's capital is now a tree-shaded, modern government, cultural, and business center. The **Boise Tour Train** (☎ 208/342–4796), a rubber-wheeled "train" pulled by a replica of an 1890 puffer-belly locomotive, offers one-hour tours (May–Oct.) starting from Julia Davis Park. At the other end of the tour is the **Idaho Historical Museum** (610 N. Julia Davis Dr., ☎ 208/334–2120), with an exhibit of an Old West saloon, and the **Boise Art Museum** (670 S. Julia Davis Dr., ☎ 208/345–8330), which has displays of traditional and contemporary works.

Down Warm Springs Boulevard is the **Old Idaho Penitentiary,** built in 1870 and in use until 1973. It now houses the **Idaho Transportation Museum,** the **Electricity Museum,** and the **Printing Museum.** *2445 Old Pen Rd., ☎ 208/334–2844. Admission charged.*

What to See and Do with Children

The **Discovery Center of Idaho** (131 W. Myrtle St., ☎ 208/343–9895; admission charged) is a hands-on science learning center for children. **Birds of Prey World Center** (5666 W. Flying Hawk La., ☎ 208/362–3716; admission charged) is the world's largest collection of living raptors.

Dining

For price ranges, see Chart 1 (B) in On the Road with Fodor's.

$$$ ★ **Peter Schott's.** This intimate restaurant on the first floor of the Idanha Hotel is generally regarded as the best restaurant in central Idaho. A local celebrity with his own two-minute cooking show, Schott calls his food New American cuisine, but he also throws in a little northern Italian. Fresh fish dominates the menu, and the wine list is complete (155 selections) but not extravagant. *928 Main St., ☎ 208/336–9100. AE, D, DC, MC, V. Closed Sun. No lunch.*

$$ ★ **Milford's Fish House.** In historic Old Boise, this seafood and steak house has 1940s decor. The Northwest salmon is terrific. *405 S. 8th St., ☎ 208/342–8382. AE, MC, V.*

$$ **Sandpiper.** Candlelight, high ceilings, oak tables, and live music on weekends make this a popular gathering place for politicians and businesspeople. Steaks and prime rib are the specialties. *1100 W. Jefferson St., ☎ 208/344–8911. AE, D, DC, MC, V.*

$ **Tablerock Brewpub & Grill.** Boise's first microbrewery has a Southwestern decor, with white pine, cacti, and prints by Native American artists. The diverse menu has something for everyone. *705 Fulton St., ☎ 208/342–0944. AE, D, DC, MC, V.*

Lodging

For price ranges, see Chart 2 (B) in On the Road with Fodor's.

$$$ **Idanha Hotel.** Close to business and shopping areas, this French château–style bed-and-breakfast with its distinctive turrets opened in 1901. Step back in time in the antiques-filled, turn-of-the-century rooms. *928 Main St., 83702, ☎ 208/342–3611. 45 rooms. Facilities: Continental breakfast, restaurant. AE, D, DC, MC, V.*

$$$ ★ **Owyhee Plaza Hotel.** The distinctive carved-stone ornamentation of this 1910 downtown hotel has put it on the National Register of Historic Places. Rooms are bright and spacious yet old-fashioned; some have balconies with mountain views. *1109 Main St., 83702, ☎ 208/343–4611 or 800/233–4611. 100 rooms. Facilities: 2 restaurants, health club, pool. AE, MC, V.*

$$ ★ **Idaho Heritage Inn.** Tom and Phyllis Lupher operate this B&B in a former governor's mansion about a mile east of downtown. Each room is very different, but all have names with political themes. Antiques, wallpaper, and old-style bed frames retain an early 1900s feel. A full breakfast is included. *109 W. Idaho St., 83702, ☎ 208/342–8066. 6 rooms. Facilities: dining room, sun room. AE, D, MC, V.*

$$ **Red Lion Inn Downtowner.** This modern seven-story hotel on the edge of downtown has good views, simply furnished large rooms, and live entertainment at night. *1800 Fairview St., 83702, ☎ 208/344–7691. 182 rooms. Facilities: coffee shop, pool. AE, D, DC, MC, V.*

Motels

Best Western Airport Motor Inn (2660 Airport Way, 83705, ☎ 208/384–5000), 50 rooms, airport limo; *$$*. **Boisean Motel** (1300 S. Capitol Blvd., 83706, ☎ 208/343–3645 or 800/365–3645), 136 rooms, restaurant, pool; *$$*. **Boise Super 8 Lodge** (2773 Elder St., 83705, ☎ 208/344–8871), 110 units; *$*.

Campgrounds

There are private campgrounds throughout the state; the **Idaho Travel Council** (*see* Visitor Information, *above*) offers a free directory. Camping is also available in nearly all of the state and national parks; contact the state parks department (*see* National and State Parks, *above*).

The Arts

Idaho Shakespeare Festival holds performances in the open-air theater in Boise's Park Center (412 S. 9th St., ☎ 208/336–9221; June–Sept.). The **Boise Philharmonic** performs September through May at the Morrison Center for Performing Arts (☎ 208/344–7849). The **National Old Time Fiddler's Contest** (☎ 208/549–0450), held in mid-June in Weiser, is the largest such competition in North America.

Shoshone to Craters of the Moon

Tourist Information

South Central Idaho: Travel Committee (858 Blue Lake Blvd., Twin Falls 83301, ☎ 800/255–8946).

Exploring Shoshone to Craters of the Moon

Five miles northeast of Twin Falls, in a rugged valley between towering walls of rock, the Snake River plunges 212 ft over the magnificent **Shoshone Falls.** The best viewing times are from October to April, when the river waters upstream are not being diverted for irrigation. The nearby massive Snake River Canyon is an awe-inspiring, vertiginous gash in the earth.

U.S. 26/93 heads northeast from Shoshone 60 mi to the **Craters of the Moon National Monument** (Box 29, Arco 83213, ☎ 208/527–3257 or 208/527–3207), where eerie spatter cones and heaps of volcanic cinders dot charred-looking, windswept lava fields. The similarity between this area and the pockmarked surface of the moon is so striking that NASA has brought astronauts here for training.

Ketchum/Sun Valley and Sawtooth

Tourist Information

Salmon River: Chamber of Commerce (Box 289, Riggins 83549, ☎ 208/628–3778). **Stanley-Sawtooth:** Chamber of Commerce (Box 8, Stanley 83278, ☎ 208/774–3411). **Sun Valley–Ketchum:** Chamber of Commerce (Box 2420, Sun Valley 83353, ☎ 208/726–3423 or 800/634–3347).

Exploring Ketchum/Sun Valley and Sawtooth

Sun Valley, America's first destination ski resort (1935) and site of the world's first chair lifts (*see* Ski Areas, *below*), is now a world-class winter and summer sport center. Nearby, in a valley surrounded by the peaks of Idaho's central Rockies, lies the town of **Ketchum.** Just outside town, beside Trail Creek, the **Ernest Hemingway Memorial** commemorates the writer's last years, which were spent in Ketchum, where he fished in Silver Creek. He is buried in the town cemetery.

One of the more scenic routes in the Rockies is the 68-mi stretch of the **Sawtooth Scenic Byway** from Ketchum, over Galena Summit, and down into the **Sawtooth Wilderness Area** to Stanley. Pick up a free cassette tape for the ride at the **Sawtooth National Recreation Area Headquarters** (☎ 208/726–7672), 8 mi north of Ketchum on Hwy. 75. Drop it off at the ranger station in Stanley, or vice versa if you're headed south.

Stop at **Galena Summit** and view the Sawtooths, as well as the landscape of the headwaters of the Salmon River. Known as the River of No Return, for the many pioneers lost trying to make it up the rugged river from Lewiston, the Salmon today is a prime lure for rafters (*see* Sports and the Outdoors, *below*).

At the Stanley ranger station, pick up another cassette for a similar trip down Hwy. 21 along the South Fork of the Payette River. Drop the tape off in Lowman and continue on into Boise.

Dining

For price ranges, see Chart 1 (B) in On the Road with Fodor's.

$$$ Evergreen. The French-American menu features lamb Madeira, roast duck, and Idaho trout. Dining is in four small, friendly rooms with soft lighting, antiques, and a French-vineyards theme. *171 1st Ave., Ketchum, ☎ 208/726–3888. AE, MC, V. Closed May, Nov. No lunch.*

$$$ Peter's. This local favorite is a casual, bright bistro offering northern Italian and Austrian dishes. Veal, pork, fresh fish, and other seafood get some exotic treatments. *6th St. and 2nd Ave., Ketchum, ☎ 208/726–9515. AE, MC, V. No lunch weekends.*

$$ **The Christiana.** This is as old-line as Sun Valley gets. Hemingway had cocktails here during his final months. The menu reflects that heritage with beef fillet in béarnaise sauce, salmon in hollandaise, and other traditional favorites. *Sun Valley Rd. and Walnut St., Ketchum,* ☎ *208/726–3388. AE, MC, V.*

$ **Gretchen's.** This rustic, cozy restaurant offers breakfast, lunch, and dinner. The salmon and trout are fresh and especially well prepared, and the hamburgers are enormous. The young staff is very enthusiastic. *Sun Valley Village,* ☎ *208/622–2097. AE, MC, V.*

Lodging

For price ranges, see Chart 2 (A) in On the Road with Fodor's.

$$$$ **Nob Hill Inn.** This small luxury hotel with European decor, marble, and tile is right in the center of town and has a fine dining room, Restaurant Felix. *960 N. Main St., Box 800, Ketchum 83340,* ☎ *208/726–8010 or 800/526–8010. 24 rooms, 4 suites. Facilities: restaurant, breakfast, indoor/outdoor pool, sauna. AE, MC, V.*

$$$ **Best Western Christiania Lodge.** This two-story U-shaped gray wood motel near the center of town has rooms with contemporary decor; some have fireplaces. *651 Sun Valley Rd., Box 2196, Ketchum 83340,* ☎ *208/726–3351 or 800/535–3241. 38 rooms. Facilities: Continental breakfast, outdoor heated pool, hot tub. AE, D, DC, MC, V.*

$$$ **Sun Valley Lodge and Inn.** At this Bavarian-style resort hotel at the foot of Bald Mountain's perfect slopes, the Lodge has an elegant European tone while the Inn is more sporty. Accommodations range from luxury suites to family units. The formal Lodge dining room features French cuisine. *Sun Valley Rd., Sun Valley 83353,* ☎ *208/622–4111 or 800/786–8259. 560 units. Facilities: 13 restaurants, 3 bars, lounge, 3 pools, sauna, stables, 18 tennis courts, summer children's program. AE, D, DC, MC, V.*

$$ **Bald Mountain Lodge.** On the National Register of Historic Places and right in the center of town, this 1929, one-story, log hotel has tastefully decorated rooms, many in knotty pine. *151 S. Main St., Box 426, Ketchum 83340,* ☎ *208/726–9963. 10 rooms, 20 apartments. AE, D, DC, MC, V.*

Ranches

For price ranges, see Chart 2 (A) in On the Road with Fodor's.

$$$ **Diamond D Ranch.** At the end of 28 mi of hair-raising dirt road near Stanley comes the payoff: snowcapped mountains all around, homey meals, cozy rooms with a Laura Ashley touch, and a big fireplace surrounded by overstuffed chairs. *Box 1555, Boise 83701,* ☎ *208/336–9772. 4 rooms, 2 apartments, 4 cabins. Facilities: pool, hot tub, sauna. No credit cards. Closed Dec.–Apr.; hunters only Oct.–Nov.*

$$ **Salmon River Lodge.** This wilderness guest ranch offers family-style meals, hunting, fishing, horseback riding, and water trips. Cozy rooms with a rustic cedar finish can sleep four or more. On the river 70 mi from Salmon, the lodge is accessible only by the proprietors' boat. *Box 927, Salmon 83467,* ☎ *208/756–3033 or 800/635–4717. 8 rooms. Facilities: buffet, lounge with fireplace. AE, MC, V. Closed Dec.–Feb.*

Sports and the Outdoors

Fishing

Idaho is one of the best states in the union for fishing, with 39 species of game fish. The season generally runs from the Saturday before Memorial Day through November. The **Idaho Department of Fish &**

Game (Box 25, 600 S. Walnut St., Boise 83707, ☎ 208/334–3700) provides information and licenses.

Hiking and Backpacking

For information on hiking through the wilderness, contact **Stanley-Sawtooth Chamber of Commerce** (*see* Tourist Information, *above*) or **Idaho Outfitters and Guides Association** (Box 95, Boise 83701, ☎ 208/342–1919).

Rafting

The king of Idaho's rafting routes is the **Middle Fork of the Salmon River,** which starts about 20 mi above Stanley, then runs northeast for about 135 mi to join the main stream. Reserve well ahead for May and June. For information about trips and guides, contact the Stanley-Sawtooth chamber (*see* Tourist Information, *above*).

Ski Areas

Cross-Country

The Idaho winter backcountry is ideal for Nordic skiing, with an extensive network of groomed trails. Contact **Idaho Outfitters and Guides Association** (*see* Sports and the Outdoors, *above*) or individual ski areas for more information.

Downhill

Bogus Basin (2405 Bogus Basin Rd., Boise 83702, ☎ 208/332–5100), 58 runs, 6 lifts, 1,800-ft drop. **Brundage** (Box 1062, McCall 83638, ☎ 208/634–4151), 38 runs, 4 lifts, 1,800-ft drop. **Pebble Creek** (Box 370, Inkom 83245, ☎ 208/775–4452), 24 runs, 3 lifts, 2,000-ft drop. **Sun Valley** (Sun Valley 83353, ☎ 800/635–8261 or 800/786–8259), 80 runs, 17 lifts, 3,400-ft drop.

NORTHERN IDAHO

Northern Idaho has the greatest concentration of lakes anywhere in the country. Its clean, watery setting is home to a major population of ospreys, as well as to numerous bald eagles. Coeur d'Alene, the region's principal town, makes a good base for exploration.

Getting There

By Plane

The nearest airport is **Spokane International** (☎ 509/455–6455), 20 mi from Coeur d'Alene, in eastern Washington.

By Car

The major highways serving northern Idaho are I–90 east–west and U.S. 95 north–south.

By Train

Amtrak (☎ 800/872–7245) serves Sandpoint, about 40 mi north of Coeur d'Alene.

By Bus

Greyhound (1527 Northwest Blvd., Coeur d'Alene, ☎ 800/231–2222).

Hells Canyon and Lewis and Clark Country

Tourist Information

Lewiston: Chamber of Commerce (2207 E. Main St., 83501, ☎ 208/743–3531 or 800/473–3543). **Moscow:** Chamber of Commerce (411 S. Main St., 83843, ☎ 208/882–1800).

Exploring Hell's Canyon

Travel north from Boise up I–80 to Payette, and turn right on U.S. 95. Roughly 140 mi north is **Riggins,** headquarters for many white-water rafting and kayaking outfitters. (Note the time-zone change: Pacific time to the north, Mountain time to the south.)

About 15 mi west of Riggins is **Hell's Canyon**—at 5,500 ft, the deepest gorge in North America, even deeper than the Grand Canyon. The best way to see the canyon is by one- to six-day float or jet-boat trips on the Snake River (for outfitters, contact the state tourist office or Lewiston Chamber of Commerce; reserve well ahead). Check in at **Hell's Gate State Park** (Snake River Ave., 4 mi south of Lewiston, ☎ 208/743–2363) if you want to follow one of the rough roads through the rugged **Hell's Canyon National Recreation Area.**

Rte. 12, which cuts east across Idaho from Lewiston to Lolo Pass on the Montana border, follows the route on which Sacajawea, the famous female Indian guide, led Lewis and Clark through the rugged wilderness. The **Nez Percé National Historic Park Headquarters** (☎ 208/843–2261) has extensive information about the explorers; the surrounding trails are groomed for cross-country skiers in the winter.

Dining

For price ranges, see Chart 1 (B) in On the Road with Fodor's.

$$ ★ **Jonathan's.** In this huge, elegant two-level restaurant, inverted umbrellas float above candlelit tables. The American eclectic fare includes steaks, ribs, seafood from Seattle, Mexican dishes, pastas, poultry, and salads. *301 D St., Lewiston, ☎ 208/746–3438. AE, DC, MC, V.*

$$ **Zany's.** This offbeat restaurant has a carousel horse, a bathtub, and other miscellany hanging from the ceiling; jukeboxes; and an old-fashioned soda counter. It serves steaks, barbecued chicken, salads, pastas, and even some Mexican fare. *2006 19th Ave., Lewiston, ☎ 208/746–8131. AE, D, MC, V.*

Lodging

For price ranges, see Chart 2 (B) in On the Road with Fodor's.

$$ ★ **Carriage House Bed and Breakfast.** On a tree-shaded street of historic houses, this B&B offers a 1900 French Provincial–style main house with a dining room and a gift shop, and a separate guest house with country antiques in bedrooms above a shared sitting room. *611 5th St., Lewiston 83501, ☎ 208/746–4506. 2 suites. MC, V.*

$ **Sacajawea Motor Inn.** Built in 1950, this oft-remodeled motel edged with flower beds captures the flavor of the region. Rooms are decorated in earth tones, with sled chairs and well-lighted desks. *1824 Main St., Lewiston 83501, ☎ 208/746–1393 or 800/333–1393. 90 rooms, 4 suites. Facilities: restaurant, lounge, exercise room, pool, hot tub, laundry. AE, D, DC, MC, V.*

Coeur d'Alene

Tourist Information

Coeur d'Alene: Convention & Visitors Bureau (Box 1088, 83816, ☎ 208/664–0587). **North Idaho:** Travel Committee (Box 928, Sandpoint 83864, ☎ 208/263–2161).

Exploring Coeur d'Alene

Coeur d'Alene, the largest city in Idaho's panhandle, has become a major recreation center because of its superb location on the beautiful lake for which it is named. Surrounded by a lush green forest, the lake is home to the largest population of ospreys in the western United States. In summer, the cruiser ***Mish-An-Nock*** (☎ 800/688–5253) takes passengers on excursions around the lake. Along the lakefront, the luxurious **Coeur d'Alene Resort** (*see* Dining and Lodging, *below*) has the world's largest floating boardwalk, which is open to the public. For a history lesson on this city born during the gold rush of 1883, stop in at the **Museum of North Idaho** (Northwest Blvd. at the city park, ☎ 208/664–3448) or the enormous **old mission at Cataldo** (☎ 208/682–3814), built in 1850 entirely by hand.

What to See and Do with Children

Silverwood Theme Park (U.S. 95, Athol, ☎ 208/772–0515) is a perfectly reconstructed turn-of-the-century mining town, with rides on a narrow-gauge steam train or in a vintage biplane.

Dining

For price ranges, see Chart 1 (B) in On the Road with Fodor's.

$$$ **Cedars Floating Restaurant.** This restaurant is actually *on* the lake, giving it wonderful views. Beer-garden steak is a specialty. *U.S. 95, ¼ mi south of I–90, ☎ 208/664–2922. AE, DC, MC, V. No lunch.*

$$ **Beachhouse.** Overlooking Silver Beach Marina with docking facilities for diners, this casual waterfront restaurant features pasta and seafood on its varied menu. *2 mi east of Coeur d'Alene on I–90 at Silver Beach, ☎ 208/664–6464. MC, V. Closed Nov.–Mar.*

$ **Jimmy D's.** This Continental sidewalk café is popular with locals as well as visitors. The specialties are fresh seafood and pasta, and the wine list features more than 100 selections. *320 Sherman Ave., ☎ 208/664–9774. AE, MC, V.*

Dining and Lodging

For price ranges, see Chart 2 (A) in On the Road with Fodor's.

$$$$ **Coeur d'Alene Resort.** On the shores of Lake Coeur d'Alene, this world-class resort offers plush guest rooms with fireplaces or lake-view lanais. The restaurant, Beverly's, has a beautiful view of the lake and the mountains, as well as cuisine of the Northwest and a superb wine cellar. *2nd and Front Sts., 83814, ☎ 208/765–4000 or 800/688–5253. 338 rooms. Facilities: 2 restaurants, 3 lounges, exercise equipment, sauna, 2 pools, 18-hole golf course, bowling alley, private beach. AE, D, DC, MC, V.*

Lodging

For price ranges, see Chart 2 (B) in On the Road with Fodor's.

$$$ **Blackwell House.** This B&B in a charming Victorian jewel of a house is close to the lake and to shopping. Its quaint, elegant rooms have wing chairs and antique beds, and the bathtubs are big and old-fashioned. *820 Sherman Ave., 83814, ☎ 208/664–0656. 8 rooms, 2 share bath. MC, V.*

$$ **Warwick Inn.** Just a block from the lake's sand beach and boardwalk, this small B&B offers large guest rooms with lace curtains and quilts. *303 Military Dr., 83814, ☎ 208/765–6565. 3 rooms, 2 share bath. AE, MC, V.*

Motels

Bennett Bay Inn (5144 E. Coeur d'Alene Lake Dr., 83814, ☎ 208/664–6168 or 800/368–8609), 21 units (some with kitchens), pool; *$$*.

Pines Resort Motel (1422 Northwest Blvd., 83814, ☎ 208/664–8244), 65 rooms, restaurant, lounge, indoor/outdoor pool; *$*.

The Northern Lakes

Tourist Information

Priest Lake: Chamber of Commerce (Box 174, Coolin 83821, ☎ 208/443–3191). **Sandpoint:** Chamber of Commerce (Box 928, 83864, ☎ 208/263–2161).

Exploring the Northern Lakes

Sandpoint is a resort town on the shores of **Pend Oreille,** the largest lake in northern Idaho and completely surrounded by mountains. At the southern end of the lake, 4,000-acre **Farragut State Park** (☎ 208/683–2425) offers forest walks, picnic areas, and camping.

Rte. 57 provides access to remote **Priest Lake,** with 70 mi of densely wooded shoreline, and the **Upper Priest Lake Scenic Area,** just a jump from the Canadian border. The **Grove of Ancient Cedars,** on the west side of Priest Lake, is a stand of virgin forest with trees up to 12 ft across and 150 ft high.

Dining and Lodging

For price ranges, see Charts 1 (B) and 2 (B) in On the Road with Fodor's.

$$$ **Hill's Resort.** You have a choice of cabins or condos, all with kitchenettes and some with fireplaces. The restaurant features steaks and oysters, and there's dancing in the summer. *HCR 5, Box 162A, Priest Lake 83856, ☎ 208/443–2551. 48 units. D, MC, V.*

$–$$ ★ **Connie's Best Western.** This may be the best-maintained motel in Idaho. Rooms are spotless and tastefully decorated for a motel, with special touches like marbleized wallpaper. At **Connie's Café,** locals gather for breakfast at the counter, but the basic fare—pancakes, cereal, sandwiches (often big enough for two), steaks—is also served in the café, cocktail lounge, or dining room with fireplace. *323 Cedar St., 83864, ☎ 208/263–9581 or 800/528–1234. 53 rooms. Facilities: restaurant, outdoor pool, whirlpool, meeting/banquet rooms. AE, D, MC, V.*

Ranch

$ **Shreffler's.** There's nothing fancy about this working ranch, nestled between the Selkirk Mountains and the Cabinet Range high in Idaho's panhandle, but the owners offer real hospitality. *200 W. Center Valley Rd., Sandpoint 83864, ☎ 208/263–5038. 4 rooms (shared baths). No credit cards.*

Sports and the Outdoors

Fishing

Lake Pend Oreille is famous for kamloops, Lake Priest for mackinaw, Lake Coeur d'Alene for cutthroat trout and chinook salmon. The St. Joe and Coeur d'Alene rivers are good for stream angling. (*See* Southern Idaho, Fishing, *above,* for general information.)

Hiking

Extensive trail systems run through the **Selway Bitterroot Wilderness,** the **Frank Church River of No Return Wilderness,** and the **Gospel Hump Wilderness.** For information and guides, contact **Idaho Outfitters and Guides Association** (Box 95, Boise 83701, ☎ 208/342–1919).

Rafting

The **Salmon** and the **Selway** rivers are suitable for rafting. For information, contact the **Salmon River Chamber of Commerce** (*see*

Ketchum/Sun Valley and Sawtooth, Tourist Information, *above*) or **Idaho Outfitters and Guides Association** (*see* Hiking, *above*).

Ski Areas

Schweitzer (Box 815, Sandpoint 83864, ☎ 208/263–9555 or 800/831–8810), 48 runs, six lifts, 2,400-ft vertical drop. **Silver Mountain** (610 Bunker Ave., Kellogg 83837, ☎ 208/783–1111), 52 runs, six lifts, 2,200-ft drop.

MONTANA

By Ellen Meloy
Updated by
Kristin Rodine

Capital Helena
Population 799,065
Motto Oro y Plata (gold and silver)
State Bird Western meadowlark
State Flower Bitterroot

Visitor Information

Travel Montana (Dept. of Commerce, 1424 9th Ave., Helena 59620, ☎ 406/444–2654 or 800/847–4868).

Scenic Drives

The **Beartooth Highway,** U.S. 212 from Red Lodge to Yellowstone National Park, is a slow but spectacular 68-mi route over a 10,947-ft mountain pass (open June–mid-Oct.). **I–15** and **U.S. 287** and **89,** for 187 mi between Helena and East Glacier, parallel the Rocky Mountain Front as it rises dramatically from the eastern plains. The 50-mi-long **Going-to-the-Sun Road** runs through Glacier National Park (*see* The Flathead and Western Montana, *below*).

National and State Parks

Millions of acres of Big Sky Country—Montana's nickname for its vast wide-open spaces—are public reserves, including national parks, monuments, and recreation areas, eight national wildlife refuges, 10 national forests, and 15 wilderness areas. Although most of Yellowstone National Park is in Wyoming, it is a logical part of a Montana itinerary.

National Parks

Glacier National Park (*see* The Flathead and Western Montana, *below*) crowns the Continental Divide on the Montana–Canada border. **Little Bighorn Battlefield National Monument** (*see* Bighorn Country, *below*) preserves the battle site in southeastern Montana.

State Parks

The **Montana Department of Fish, Wildlife and Parks** (1420 E. 6th Ave., Helena 59620, ☎ 406/444–3750) manages 41 state parks, including **Bannack State Park** west of Dillon, a ghost town of homes, saloons, and a gallows. **Missouri Headwaters State Park** near Three Forks marks the site where Lewis and Clark came upon the confluence of the three rivers that form the Missouri.

THE FLATHEAD AND WESTERN MONTANA

Stunning peaks and lush intermontane valleys offer superb recreation and some of the Rockies' most dazzling landscapes. The northwest, or Flathead region, is a destination resort area with such attractions as Flathead Lake and Glacier National Park. In western Montana south of the Flathead, forests, lakes, and meadows mix with ranch country and small valley towns.

Tourist Information

Glacier Country: Regional Tourism Commission (Box 1396, Dept. 507–10–21, Kalispell 59903, ☎ 406/756–7128 or 800/338–5072).

Getting There

By Plane

Glacier Park International Airport (☎ 406/257–5994) in Kalispell and the **Johnson Bell Missoula Airport** (☎ 406/728–4381) are served by major domestic airlines.

By Car

I–90 and U.S. 93 pass through Missoula. U.S. 93 and Rte. 35 lead off I–90 to Kalispell in the Flathead; from there, U.S. 2 leads to Glacier park. From Great Falls, take I–15 then U.S. 89 to St. Mary, at the east entrance to Glacier's Going-to-the-Sun Road (open June–Sept., depending on snowfall; off-season, leave 89 for U.S. 2 at Browning for West Glacier).

By Train

Amtrak (☎ 800/872–7245) stops in Essex, Whitefish, West Glacier, and East Glacier.

By Bus

Intermountain Bus Co. (☎ 406/755–4011) stops in Kalispell. **Greyhound Lines** (☎ 800/231–2222) serves Missoula.

Exploring the Flathead and Western Montana

The Flathead

The Flathead's towns are atypical of Montana in that they are relatively close to one another. Bigfork, Kalispell, and Whitefish make good touring bases; many attractions are within a day's drive.

Glacier National Park (National Park Service, West Glacier 59936, ☎ 406/888–5441) preserves more than a million spectacular acres of peaks, waterfalls, lakes, and wildlife best seen from a hiking trail (*see* Sports and the Outdoors, *below*) or on horseback. The 50-mi **Going-to-the-Sun Road,** the park's only through road, is a cliff-hanger and unsuitable for oversize vehicles; guided bus tours (☎ 406/226–9311) leave from either end. Most of the park, including this road, is closed to vehicles in winter.

South of Kalispell is deep, pristine **Flathead Lake,** the largest freshwater lake west of the Mississippi. An 85-mi loop drive around it takes in cherry orchards, parks, sweeping views of the Mission and Swan ranges, and the arts community of **Bigfork,** with professional repertory theater at the **Bigfork Summer Playhouse** (Electric Ave., ☎ 406/837–4886).

Western Montana

In addition to being a forestry and trade center, **Missoula,** 60 mi south of Kalispell via U.S. 93, is home of the **University of Montana** and a thriving community of writers and artists. The Clark Fork, Bitterroot, and Blackfoot rivers converge here—it's not unusual to see anglers casting just down from the movie theater. The **Missoula Museum of the Arts** (335 N. Pattee St., ☎ 406/728–0447) exhibits contemporary works.

East of town, Rte. 200 leads to the **Seeley–Swan Valley,** densely forested and studded with lakes. View loons and other waterfowl from turnouts along the 18-mi **Clearwater Chain-of-Lakes** scenic route (Rte. 83 from

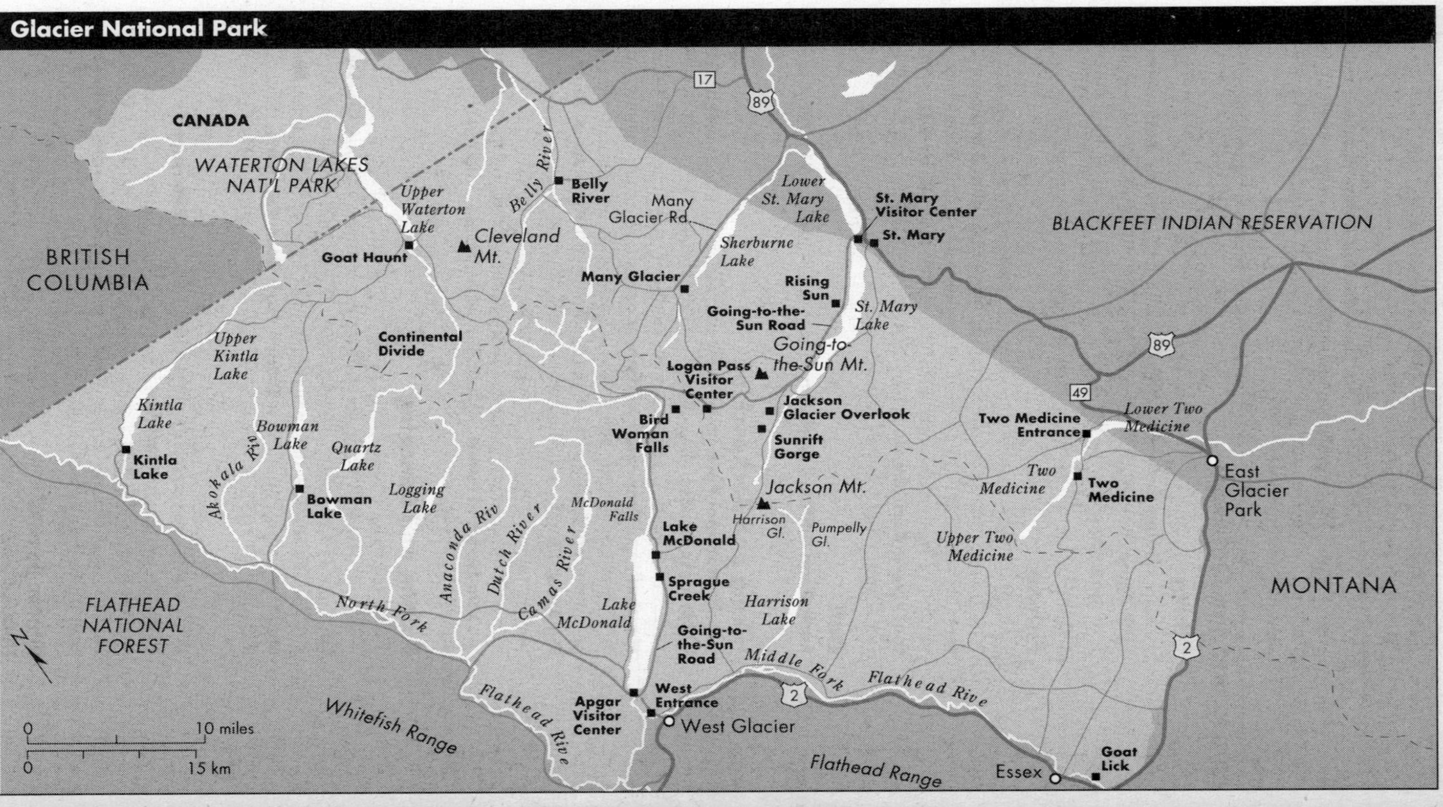
Glacier National Park
CANADA
WATERTON LAKES NAT'L PARK
BRITISH COLUMBIA
Upper Waterton Lake
Goat Haunt
Cleveland Mt.
Belly River
Belly River
Many Glacier Rd.
Many Glacier
Lower St. Mary Lake
St. Mary Visitor Center
St. Mary
BLACKFEET INDIAN RESERVATION
Sherburne Lake
Rising Sun
Going-to-the-Sun Road
St. Mary Lake
Going-to-the-Sun Mt.
Continental Divide
Upper Kintla Lake
Kintla Lake
Kintla Lake
Logan Pass Visitor Center
Bird Woman Falls
Jackson Glacier Overlook
Sunrift Gorge
Two Medicine Entrance
Lower Two Medicine
East Glacier Park
Bowman Lake
Bowman Lake
Quartz Lake
Logging Lake
Akokala Riv
Anaconda Riv
Dutch River
Camas River
McDonald Falls
Lake McDonald
Sprague Creek
Lake McDonald
Jackson Mt.
Harrison Gl.
Pumpelly Gl.
Two Medicine
Two Medicine
Upper Two Medicine
MONTANA
FLATHEAD NATIONAL FOREST
North Fork
Harrison Lake
Going-to-the-Sun Road
Middle Fork
Flathead Rive
West Entrance
Apgar Visitor Center
West Glacier
Flathead Rive
Whitefish Range
Flathead Range
Essex
Goat Lick
17
89
89
49
2
2
N
0
10 miles
0
15 km

along the 18-mi **Clearwater Chain-of-Lakes** scenic route (Rte. 83 from Salmon Lake to Rainy Lake).

South of Missoula on U.S. 93, the **Bitterroot Valley** stretches between the Sapphire Mountains and the Bitterroots, one of the northern Rockies' most rugged ranges. Jesuit missionaries founded **St. Mary's Mission** in 1841 at **Stevensville.**

Sports and the Outdoors

Biking

Glacier's **Going-to-the-Sun Road** is a challenging ride. **Backcountry Bicycle Tours** (Box 4029, Bozeman 59772, ☎ 406/586–3556) organizes five- to seven-day trips in Glacier National Park as well as the rest of the state.

Fishing

Fish for cutthroat and bull trout in the **Flathead River** or northern pike, Mackinaw, and other lake species in **Flathead Lake. Big Dipper Charters** (Kalispell, ☎ 406/257–3234 or 800/453–3234) offers boats and guides. In western Montana, fish the **Clark Fork, Bitterroot,** or **Blackfoot rivers; Rock Creek,** a blue-ribbon trout stream; or **Seeley Lake.** Local stores sell fishing licenses.

Golf

Eagle Bend Golfing Community (Box 960, Bigfork 59911, ☎ 406/837–7300), 18 holes.

Hiking and Backpacking

Glacier National Park has 730 mi of trails at all ability levels; **Glacier Wilderness Guides** (Box 535M, West Glacier 59936, ☎ 406/888–5466 or 800/521–7238) leads backcountry trips. The **Great Bear, Bob Marshall,** and **Scapegoat wilderness areas** (Flathead National Forest, 1935 3rd Ave. E, Kalispell 59901, ☎ 406/755–5401) constitute a million-acre refuge along the Continental Divide. The **Jewel Basin Hiking Area,** 13 mi east of Bigfork, off Rte. 83, is a short, minimal-ascent trail to high-country lakes and superb views, designed for children and inexperienced hikers. For information on backcountry hiking, contact the **Lolo National Forest** (Bldg. 24, Fort Missoula, Missoula 59801, ☎ 406/329–3814).

Rafting and Canoeing

The three forks of the Flathead River constitute 10% of the nation's Wild and Scenic River system. Rafting outfitters include **Glacier Raft Co.** (Box 218M, West Glacier 59936, ☎ 406/888–5454 or 800/332–9995). Canoes take the calmer waters of Glacier Park's **Lake McDonald.** For canoe rentals try **Glacier Park Boat Company** (Box 5262, Kalispell 59903, ☎ 406/888–5727 May–Sept. or 406/752–5488 Oct.–Apr.).

In the west, most stretches of the **Clark Fork** and **Bitterroot** are runnable by raft or canoe; the **Blackfoot** is more difficult. Outfitters include **Western Waters** (5455 Keil Loop, Missoula 59802, ☎ 406/543–3203). Northeast of Missoula near Seeley Lake, the **Clearwater River Canoe Trail** follows an easy 4-mi stretch.

Water Sports

Flathead Lake supports a large sailing community, countless water-skiers and windsurfers, and cruises on the ***Port Polson Princess*** (Polson, ☎ 406/883–2448).

Ski Areas

For ski reports call 406/444–2654 or 800/847–4868.

Cross-Country

Trails are found at **Glacier National Park,** in the **Flathead National Forest,** and in the **national forests** near Missoula (for information on all these sites, *see* Sports and the Outdoors, *above*). On Glacier's southern border, the **Izaak Walton Inn** (U.S. 2, Essex 59916, ☎ 406/888–5700) has 18 mi of groomed trails.

Downhill

Big Mountain (Box 1400, Whitefish 59937, ☎ 406/862–1900 or 800/858–5439) is Montana's largest resort, with 61 marked runs, 9 lifts, and a 2,300-ft vertical drop.

Dining and Lodging

The Flathead breaks the West's traditional steak-and-burger mold by offering sophisticated dining (dress: neat but casual) and fine wines. Lodging in Glacier is seasonal (June–September); reserve well in advance here, and for the summer and ski seasons in the Flathead. For price ranges, see Charts 1 (B) and 2 (B) in On the Road with Fodor's.

Bigfork

DINING

Coyote Roadhouse. Behind a simple stucco facade lies a cozy place serving Cajun, Sicilian, and Mexican specialties. *8083 Rte. 35, ☎ 406/837–4250. AE, MC, V. $$*

Glacier National Park

DINING AND LODGING

Lodges. Glacier's grand lodges date from the early 1900s, when the Great Northern Railroad brought tourists to this remote park. The rooms in all the lodges are rustic—no TVs—but quite comfortable. **Glacier Park Lodge,** connected to East Glacier's Amtrak station by a brief walk through a garden, offers 154 rooms, golf, and a pool. **Lake McDonald Lodge,** a former hunting refuge near West Glacier, has 100 rooms in cabins, motel units, and a lodge on the lake (with boat rentals and fishing). **Many Glacier Hotel,** 12 mi west of Babb overlooking Swiftcurrent Lake, is the park's largest lodge, offering 208 rooms, boat tours, and fishing. *Glacier Park, Inc.: June–Labor Day, East Glacier 59434, ☎ 406/226–5551; Labor Day–May, Greyhound Tower, Station 1210, Phoenix, AZ 85077, ☎ 602/207–6000. Facilities: restaurants, bars, trail rides. D, MC, V. Closed Labor Day–May. $$–$$$*

Missoula

DINING

Alley Cat Grill. French, Indonesian, and seafood specials are served in a pleasant bistro atmosphere. *125½ Main St., ☎ 406/728–3535. MC, V. $$*

Zimorino's Red Pies Over Montana. The menu is Italian—thick-crust pizzas, lasagna, and other dishes. *424 N. Higgins Ave., ☎ 406/549–7434. MC, V. $*

LODGING

Goldsmith's Inn. This B&B, formerly the home of a University of Montana president, was moved to its present riverside location and restored. One room has a fireplace. The large front deck overlooks the river. *809 E. Front St., 59801, ☎ 406/721–6732. 7 units. AE, MC, V. $$–$$$*

Motels

Village Red Lion Motor Inn (100 Madison St., Missoula 59801, ☎ 406/728–3100 or 800/547–8010, FAX 406/728–2530), 172 rooms, coffee shop, restaurant, lounge, whirlpool, outdoor pool, gift shop; *$$–$$$*. **Best Western Outlaw Inn** (1701 Hwy. 93S, Kalispell 59901, ☎ 406/755–6100 or 800/237–7445, FAX 406/756–8994), 220 rooms, restaurant, lounge, casino, whirlpools in some rooms, 2 indoor pools; *$$*.

Ranch

Montana's guest ranches (for Travel Montana's listing, *see* Visitor Information, *above*) range from working ranches to deluxe cowless spreads. Those listed throughout this chapter are categorized as either *$$* (less than $1,000 per week) or *$$$* ($1,000–$1,900), double occupancy.

Averill's Flathead Lake Lodge. Reserve at least a year in advance for this deluxe 2,000-acre dude ranch on the shores of Flathead Lake. The decor is rustic Western. There's a big stone fireplace in each lodge. Rates are AP, with a one-week minimum. *Box 248, Bigfork 59911, ☎ 406/837–4391, FAX 406/837–6977. 18 rooms, 20 cottages. Facilities: dining room, sailing, waterskiing, fishing, tennis, horseback riding, hiking, cookouts. MC, V. Closed Nov.–Apr. $$$*

Hot Springs

Lost Trail Hot Springs Resort. On the Montana–Idaho border, 90 mi south of Missoula, in the Bitterroot National Forest, this resort offers rustic rooms in log cabins and a hot tub and swimming pools fed straight from the hot springs. The resort is also close to recreation areas at Lost Trail Pass. *Off U.S. 93, Box 8321, Sula 59871, ☎ 406/821–3574, FAX 406/821–4012. 18 rooms in 3 lodges; 7 cabins for 2–8 people each. Facilities: restaurant, casino, lounge, pools, nearby skiing, RV spaces. AE, MC, V. $–$$*

Campgrounds

Glacier National Park's 10 campgrounds are available on a first-come, first-served basis; they fill by noon. Other public campgrounds are in national forests and state parks (*see* Sports and the Outdoors, *above*). Look for private campgrounds with RV services near towns, or check Travel Montana's directory (*see* Visitor Information, *above*).

SOUTHWESTERN MONTANA

Montana's pioneer history began here, and the full range of the early mining frontier—from rough-and-tumble camps to the mansions of the magnates—is still evident. In the stunning high country north and west of Yellowstone National Park you'll find some of the state's best ski terrain and world-class fishing.

Tourist Information

Gold West Country: Regional Tourism Commission (1155 Main St., Deer Lodge 59722, ☎ 406/846–1943 or 800/879–1159). **Yellowstone Country:** Regional Tourism Commission (Box 1107, Red Lodge 59068, ☎ 406/446–1005 or 800/736–5276).

Getting There

By Plane

Major domestic airlines fly to Helena, Bozeman, and Butte.

By Car

I–15 passes through Helena. Use I–90 for Butte and Bozeman. U.S. 191, 89, 287, and 212 link the region with Yellowstone.

By Bus

Intermountain Bus Co. stops in Helena (☎ 406/442–5860) and Butte (☎ 406/723–3287). **Greyhound Lines** serves Bozeman (☎ 406/587–3110). In summer, **Karst Stages** (☎ 800/332–0504) runs between Bozeman, Livingston, and Yellowstone.

Exploring Southwestern Montana

The humble mining origins of **Helena,** Montana's capital, are visible in its earliest commercial district, **Reeder's Alley.** However, by 1888, the "Queen City of the Rockies" boasted major gold rushes and 50 resident millionaires. The mansions on the **West Side** and commercial buildings on the main street, **Last Chance Gulch,** preserve the era's grace and opulence.

Helena's vibrant arts scene includes dramatic performances and movies in the two auditoriums within the **Myrna Loy Theater** (15 N. Ewing St., ☎ 406/443–0287). The **Archie Bray Foundation** (2915 Country Club Ave., ☎ 406/443–3502), a nationally known center for ceramic arts, offers tours. The **Montana Historical Society Museum** (225 N. Roberts St., ☎ 406/444–2694) and **Holter Museum of Art** (12 E. Lawrence Ave., ☎ 406/442–6400) showcase valuable collections of folk and Western painting and historic memorabilia.

While the millionaires lived in Helena, the miners lived in **Butte,** a tough, wily town with a rich ethnic mix. The **Berkeley Pit,** a mile-wide open-pit copper mine, sits at the edge of the **Butte National Historic District.** Near Deer Lodge, the **Grant-Kohrs Ranch National Historic Site** (316 Main St., Deer Lodge 59722, ☎ 406/846–2070) preserves the home and outbuildings of a 19th-century ranch, still worked by cowboys and draft horses.

Bozeman, 50 mi east of Butte on I–90, is a regional trade center, a place crazy for food, art, and the outdoors. It is also home to **Montana State University,** whose **Museum of the Rockies** (600 W. Kagy Blvd., ☎ 406/994–3466; admission charged) offers paleontology exhibits, a hands-on dinosaur playroom, planetarium shows, and Western art and history exhibits.

South of town, U.S. 191 follows the Gallatin River to **West Yellowstone,** the gateway to **Yellowstone National Park** (*see* Wyoming). On the U.S. 89 approach to the park, **Livingston** sits at the head of **Paradise Valley,** bisected by the **Yellowstone River.** Another route to Yellowstone, U.S. 212, leads to **Red Lodge,** a town of distinct ethnic flavors passed down from early miners. Late summer is **rodeo season** in Livingston, Red Lodge, and Big Timber.

Sports and the Outdoors

Fishing

Few trout streams rival the **Missouri, Beaverhead,** and **Big Hole rivers;** outfitters include the **Complete Fly Fisher** (Wise River, ☎ 406/832–3175). Livingston, Ennis, and West Yellowstone are base towns for the superb fly-fishing on the **Yellowstone, Madison,** and other local rivers; **Dan Bailey's Fly Shop** (209 W. Park St., Livingston, ☎ 406/222–1673 or 800/356–4052) is a Montana legend. Licenses are sold at local stores.

Golf

Big Sky Golf Course (Rte. 64, Big Sky, ☎ 406/995–4706), 18 holes.

Hiking and Backpacking

Areas include the **Gates of the Mountains** near Helena (☎ 406/449–5201), the **Anaconda-Pintler Wilderness** near Anaconda (☎ 406/496–3400), and the **Lee Metcalf Wilderness** near Bozeman and **Absarokee-Beartooth Wilderness** near Livingston (☎ 406/587–6701).

Rafting and Canoeing

The **Missouri River** north of Helena is easy for rafts and canoes. **Bear Trap Canyon,** on the Madison River near Ennis, and **Yankee Jim,** on the Yellowstone near Gardiner, require white-water experience or an outfitter, such as the **Yellowstone Raft Co.** (☎ 406/848–7777 or 800/858–7781).

Ski Areas

For ski reports, call 406/444–2654 or 800/847–4868.

Cross-Country

In winter, many national forest roads and trails become backcountry ski trails (*see* Sports and the Outdoors, *above*). **Lone Mountain Ranch** (Box 160069, Big Sky 59716, ☎ 406/995–4644) offers 47 mi of groomed and tracked trails, food, and lodging.

Downhill

Big Sky resort (*see* Dining and Lodging, *below*) has 55 runs, 10 lifts, and a 3,030-ft vertical drop.

Dining and Lodging

For price ranges, see Charts 1 (B) and 2 (B) in On the Road with Fodor's.

Big Sky

DINING AND LODGING

Big Sky Ski and Summer Resort. At this resort in Gallatin Canyon 43 mi south of Bozeman, come back to large, bright rooms in the ski lodge or condominiums after enjoying the extensive outdoor activities. *Box 160001, 59716, ☎ 406/995–4211 or 800/548–4486, FAX 406/995–5001. 204 lodge rooms, 94 condo rooms. Facilities: restaurants, health club, outdoor pool, golf, horseback riding, fishing, gondola rides, skiing. AE, D, DC, MC, V. Closed mid-Apr.–early June, late Sept.–mid-Dec. $$–$$$*

Bozeman

LODGING

Voss Inn. This 1883 Victorian house in the historic district is furnished with period antiques. The hosts offer guided tours of Yellowstone in their Jeep; prices, which include breakfast and lunch, vary depending on the number of participants (a tour for four people costs $53 per person). *319 S. Willson Ave., 59715, ☎ 406/587–0982. 6 rooms with bath. No smoking. AE, MC, V. $$*

Helena

DINING

The Windbag. Named for the hot political debates you're likely to overhear while dining on burgers, seafood, and light dishes, this saloon was a bordello until the 1970s. *19 S. Last Chance Gulch, ☎ 406/443–9669. AE, D, MC, V. $$*

LODGING

The Sanders. Wilbur Fisk Sanders, frontier politician and vigilante, once lived in this gracious 1875 mansion, now a centrally located B&B on the National Historic Register. *328 N. Ewing St., 59601, ☎ 406/442–3309, FAX 406/443–1361. 7 rooms. AE, MC, V. $$–$$$*

Motels

Bozeman Inn (1235 N. 7th Ave., Bozeman 59715, ☎ 406/587–3176 or 800/648–7515, FAX 406/585–3591), 50 rooms, restaurant, lounge, pool, sauna, hot tub; *$$*. **Jorgenson's** (1714 11th Ave., Helena 59601, ☎ 406/442–1770; in MT only, 800/272–1770; FAX 406/449–0155), 107 rooms, restaurant, lounge, indoor pool, laundry; *$*.

Ranch

For price range, *see* Ranch *under* Dining and Lodging *in* The Flathead and Western Montana, *above*.

Lazy K Bar. This venerable dude ranch, built in 1880, sits on 22,000 acres below the Crazy Mountains. It is a working ranch, and guests do a lot of riding, including actual cattle moving and other ranch work, if they choose. Rates are AP, with a one-week minimum stay. *Box 550, Big Timber 59011, ☎ and FAX 406/537–4404. Facilities: horseback riding, fishing, square dancing, children's wrangler. No credit cards. Closed Oct.–May. $$*

Hot Springs

Chico Hot Springs Lodge. Built at the turn of the century, this resort is nestled against the Absarokee Mountains 29 mi north of Yellowstone. The dining room is famous, as are the mineral hot springs. Accommodations are in condominiums or the old lodge, as well as cabins and two small motels. *Pray 59065, ☎ 406/333–4933, FAX 406/333–4694. 85 rooms. Facilities: restaurant, pools, ski trips. D, MC, V. $–$$*

Campgrounds

Public campgrounds are in national forests and state parks; private ones with RV services are near towns, or check Travel Montana's directory (*see* Visitor Information, *above*). In peak season, campgrounds near Yellowstone fill early in the day.

The Arts

The **New World Symphony** performs in Big Sky (*see* Big Sky Resort, *above*) during the **Big Sky Arts Festival** in July. Big Timber hosts August's **Montana Cowboy Poetry Gathering** (Big Timber Chamber of Commerce, ☎ 406/932–5131).

BIGHORN COUNTRY

Cowboy culture seems overpowering in southeastern Montana, but this is truly Indian land. A stunning country of rimrock, badlands, wide-open grasslands, and rugged mountains, it is still the home of the Northern Cheyenne and the Crow. Billings is a convenient base for touring.

Tourist Information

Custer Country: Regional Tourism Commission (Rte. 1, Box 1206A, Hardin 59034, ☎ 406/665–1671).

Getting There

By Plane

Major domestic airlines fly to **Logan International Airport** in Billings (☎ 406/657–8495).

By Car

The main routes between Yellowstone and Broadus, in the southeast corner of the state, are I–94, I–90, U.S. 212, and Rte. 59.

By Bus

Greyhound Lines (☎ 800/231–2222) and **Rimrock Stages** (☎ 406/549–2339 or 800/255–7655) serve Billings.

Exploring Bighorn Country

Booms in coal, oil, and gas made **Billings** Montana's largest town. Sprawled between steep-faced rimrocks and the Yellowstone River, it has big-city services and a stockman's heart. In summer the town puts on a nightly rodeo.

Southeast of Billings on I–94 lie the **Crow** and **Northern Cheyenne Indian reservations. Crow Fair** (☎ 406/638–2601), held in Crow Agency for five days in August, draws visitors from all over the West for parades, rodeos, dancing, and horse races.

On the Montana–Wyoming border is **Bighorn Canyon National Recreation Area** (Fort Smith 59035, ☎ 406/666–2412); **Ok-A-Beh Marina** (604 S. 1st St., Hardin 59034, ☎ 406/665–2216) rents boats for exploring the canyon.

Fifteen miles southeast of Hardin on I–90, **Little Bighorn Battlefield National Monument** (National Park Service, Crow Agency 59022, ☎ 406/638–2621) preserves the site where, in 1876, the Cheyenne and Sioux defended their lives and homeland in a bloody battle with General George Armstrong Custer. A museum and guided tours help to unravel the history.

Sports and the Outdoors

Fishing

Trout anglers fish the **Yellowstone River** above Columbus. Downriver, expect walleye, bass, and warmer-water fish. The **Bighorn River** below Yellowtail Dam near Pryor is trout heaven; lake species inhabit the reservoir above the dam.

Hiking and Backpacking

The northern region of the arid **Pryor Mountains,** south of Billings, is on the Crow Reservation; permits for backcountry travel are issued by the Crow Tribal Council (Crow Agency 59022, ☎ 406/638–2601). The southern Pryors are in Custer National Forest (2602 1st Ave. N, Billings 59103, ☎ 406/657–6361).

Rafting and Canoeing

Canoes, rafts, and drift boats suit the **Yellowstone River** and the **Bighorn River** below Yellowtail Dam.

Ski Area

Red Lodge Mountain (Box 750, Red Lodge 59068, ☎ 406/446–2610 or 800/444–8977), an hour southwest of Billings, has 35 runs, six lifts, and a 2,016-ft vertical drop.

Dining and Lodging

For price ranges, see Charts 1 (B) and 2 (B) in On the Road with Fodor's.

Billings

DINING AND LODGING

Radisson Northern Hotel. This historic 1905 building in downtown Billings was destroyed by fire in 1940, then rebuilt. Although remodeled, it still provides a sense of the city's past. The decor in the rooms follow an American West theme; views are glorious. The Golden Belle restaurant serves fine Continental cuisine in an atmosphere that's fancier than usual for Montana. *Broadway at 1st Ave. N, Box 1296, 59101, ☎ 406/245–5121 or 800/333–3333, FAX 406/259–9862. 160 rooms. Facilities: restaurant, lounge. AE, D, DC, MC, V. $$–$$$*

Motel

Ponderosa Inn Best Western (220 Central Ave., Billings 59401, ☎ and FAX 406/761–3410), 104 rooms, restaurant, lounge, pool, sauna; *$$.*

Campgrounds

Public campgrounds are in **Custer National Forest** or **Bighorn Canyon National Recreation Area;** private ones are near towns, or check Travel Montana's listing (*see* Visitor Information, *above*).

ELSEWHERE IN THE STATE

Central and Eastern Montana

Getting There

I–15 and U.S. 89 traverse the region north–south; U.S. 2 and I–94, east–west.

What to See and Do

Montana's heartland is open grasslands and, rising abruptly from the plains, the sheer escarpment of the Rocky Mountain Front. In Great Falls, the **C. M. Russell Museum** (400 13th St. N, ☎ 406/727–8787) has a formidable collection of works by the cowboy artist. Cowboy life thrives in **Miles City,** which in May hosts the **Miles City Bucking Horse Sale,** three days of horse trading, rodeo, and street dances. For more information on the region, contact the **Russell Country Regional Tourism Commission** (Box 1366, Great Falls 59403, ☎ 406/761–5036 or 800/527–5348) and the **Missouri River Country Regional Tourism Commission** (Box 11990, Wolf Point 59201, ☎ 406/653–3600).

WYOMING

By Geoffrey O'Gara

Updated by Candy Moulton

Capital	Cheyenne
Population	453,588
Motto	Equal Rights
State Bird	Meadowlark
State Flower	Indian paintbrush

Visitor Information

Wyoming Division of Tourism (I–25 at College Dr., Cheyenne 82002, ☎ 307/777–7777; for recording/ski reports, ☎ 800/225–5996). **Information centers** in Cheyenne, Evanston, Jackson, and Sheridan are open year-round; in Sundance, Pine Bluffs, and Chugwater, and near Laramie, they close in winter.

Scenic Drives

North of Cody and east of Yellowstone is the 60-mi **Beartooth Highway,** U.S. 212. It is a summer trip, switchbacking as it does across Beartooth Pass, at 10,947 ft the state's highest highway. Add a few miles and take the **Chief Joseph Scenic Highway** (Rte. 296, south from Beartooth Highway toward Cody) to see the gorge carved by the Clarks Fork of the Yellowstone River. There is more scenery than service on these roads, so gas up in Cody or at the northeastern end of the route, in Red Lodge, Montana.

National and State Parks

National Park

Devils Tower National Monument (east of Gillette, 27 mi north of I–90; Box 8, Devils Tower 82714, ☎ 307/467–5283), a stone stump rising 1,280 ft above the Belle Fourche River, has been especially popular since it was featured in the film *Close Encounters of the Third Kind.*

State Parks

Wyoming's state parks are listed in brochures and on the Division of Tourism's state road map. Historic sites include **South Pass City** (125 South Pass Main, South Pass City 82520, ☎ 307/332–3684), a history-rich gold camp near the Oregon Trail, and the **Wyoming Territorial Prison Park** (975 Snowy Range Rd., Laramie 82070, ☎ 800/845–2287), where Butch Cassidy once did time. **Hot Springs State Park** in Thermopolis, on U.S. 20, has the world's largest hot spring.

YELLOWSTONE, GRAND TETON, AND JACKSON

When John Colter's descriptions of Yellowstone were reported in St. Louis newspapers in 1810, most readers dismissed them as tall tales. Colter had left the Lewis and Clark expedition to trap and explore in a region virtually unknown to whites, and his reports of giant elk roaming among fuming mud pots and waterfalls and geysers in a wilderness of evergreens and towering peaks were just too farfetched to be taken seriously. Sixty years and several expeditions later, however, the nation was convinced, and in 1872 Yellowstone became the country's first national park.

The Snake River emerges from Yellowstone country into the Teton Valley, where it makes its way south and west at the foot of the Grand Tetons. In the valley of Jackson Hole, just south of Grand Teton National Park and nestled between the Tetons and the Gros Ventre Mountains, the town of Jackson has been hosting visitors for over a century. The spot was first a rendezvous for fur trappers, then the gateway to the nearby parks and dude ranches, and later the center of a booming ski industry.

Tourist Information

Grand Teton National Park (National Park Service, Moose 83012, ☎ 307/739–3300 or 307/739–3399). **Yellowstone National Park** (National Park Service, Mammoth 82190, ☎ 307/344–7381). **Jackson Hole:** Chamber of Commerce (Box E, 83001, ☎ 307/733–3316). Visitors Council (Box 982, Dept. 8, 83001, ☎ 800/782–0011).

Getting There

By Plane

Several airlines have daily service from Denver and Salt Lake City into **Jackson Hole Airport** (reservations, ☎ 307/733–7682), 9 mi north of town and about 40 mi south of Yellowstone National Park. Major car-rental agencies serve the airport. **Yellowstone Regional Airport** (☎ 307/587–5096), at Cody, on the east side of the park, is served by commuter airlines out of Denver. (*See* Montana *for information on additional service.*)

By Car

To reach Yellowstone through the Teton Valley and Jackson Hole, turn north off I–80 at Rock Springs and take U.S. 191 the 177 mi to Jackson; Yellowstone is about 60 mi farther north on U.S. 191/89. You can also approach Yellowstone from the east through Cody on U.S. 14/16/20; for north and west entrances, *see* Montana. Grand Teton National Park is about 10 mi north of Jackson on U.S. 191/89.

By Train

The **Amtrak *Pioneer*** (☎ 800/872–7245) travels across Wyoming's southern tier, with one stop eastbound and westbound each Monday, Wednesday, and Friday in Evanstown, Green River, Rock Springs, Rawlins, Laramie, and outside Cheyenne. Rock Springs and Evanstown are the stops for those heading to Yellowstone; cars can be rented at the stations.

By Bus

There is no direct bus service to Jackson. In ski season, **START** buses (☎ 307/733–4521) operate between town and Jackson Hole Ski Resort, and the **Targhee Express** (☎ 307/733–3101 or 800/827–4433) crosses Teton Pass to the Grand Targhee Ski Resort. **TW Recreational Services** (☎ 307/344–7901) has bus tours of Yellowstone in summer and snow-coach tours in winter.

Exploring Yellowstone, Grand Teton, and Jackson

Yellowstone

Yellowstone preserves and provides access to natural treasures such as **Yellowstone Lake,** with its 110-mi shoreline and lake cruises, wildlife, waterfowl, and trout fishing; **Grand Canyon of the Yellowstone,** 24 mi long, 1,200 ft deep, in shades of red and ocher surrounded by emerald-green forest; spectacular **Mammoth Hot Springs;** and 900 mi of horse trails, 1,000 mi of hiking trails, and 370 mi of public roads. Visitor

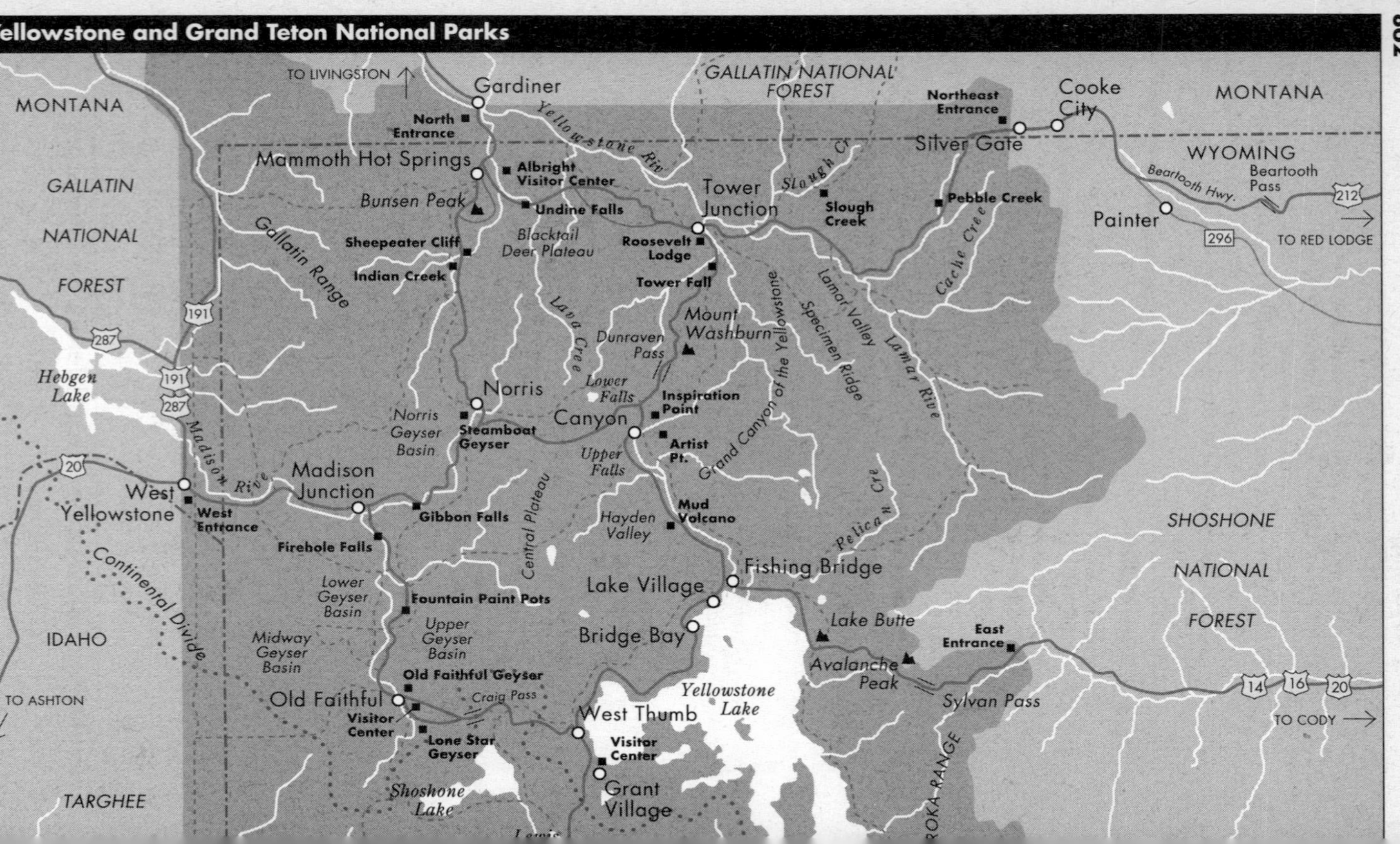
Yellowstone and Grand Teton National Parks
TO LIVINGSTON
Gardiner
GALLATIN NATIONAL FOREST
Northeast Entrance
Cooke City
MONTANA
MONTANA
North Entrance
Yellowstone Riv
Silver Gate
WYOMING
Beartooth Pass
Beartooth Hwy.
Mammoth Hot Springs
Albright Visitor Center
GALLATIN
Tower Junction
Slough Cr.
Slough Creek
Pebble Creek
Painter
Bunsen Peak
Undine Falls
NATIONAL
TO RED LODGE
Blacktail Deer Plateau
Roosevelt Lodge
Sheepeater Cliff
Gallatin Range
Cache Cree
Indian Creek
Tower Fall
FOREST
Lava Cree
Mount Washburn
Grand Canyon of the Yellowstone
Specimen Ridge
Lamar Valley
Lamar Rive
Dunraven Pass
Hebgen Lake
Lower Falls
Norris
Inspiration Point
Norris Geyser Basin
Steamboat Geyser
Canyon
Artist Pt.
Madison Rive
Madison Junction
Upper Falls
West Yellowstone
West Entrance
Gibbon Falls
Central Plateau
Hayden Valley
Mud Volcano
Pelican Cre
SHOSHONE
Firehole Falls
Continental Divide
Fishing Bridge
Lake Village
NATIONAL
Lower Geyser Basin
Fountain Paint Pots
Lake Butte
FOREST
Upper Geyser Basin
Bridge Bay
IDAHO
Midway Geyser Basin
East Entrance
Old Faithful Geyser
Avalanche Peak
Yellowstone Lake
TO ASHTON
Old Faithful
Craig Pass
Sylvan Pass
Visitor Center
West Thumb
TO CODY
Lone Star Geyser
Visitor Center
ROKA RANGE
Grant Village
TARGHEE
Shoshone Lake
212
296
191
287
191
287
20
14
16
20

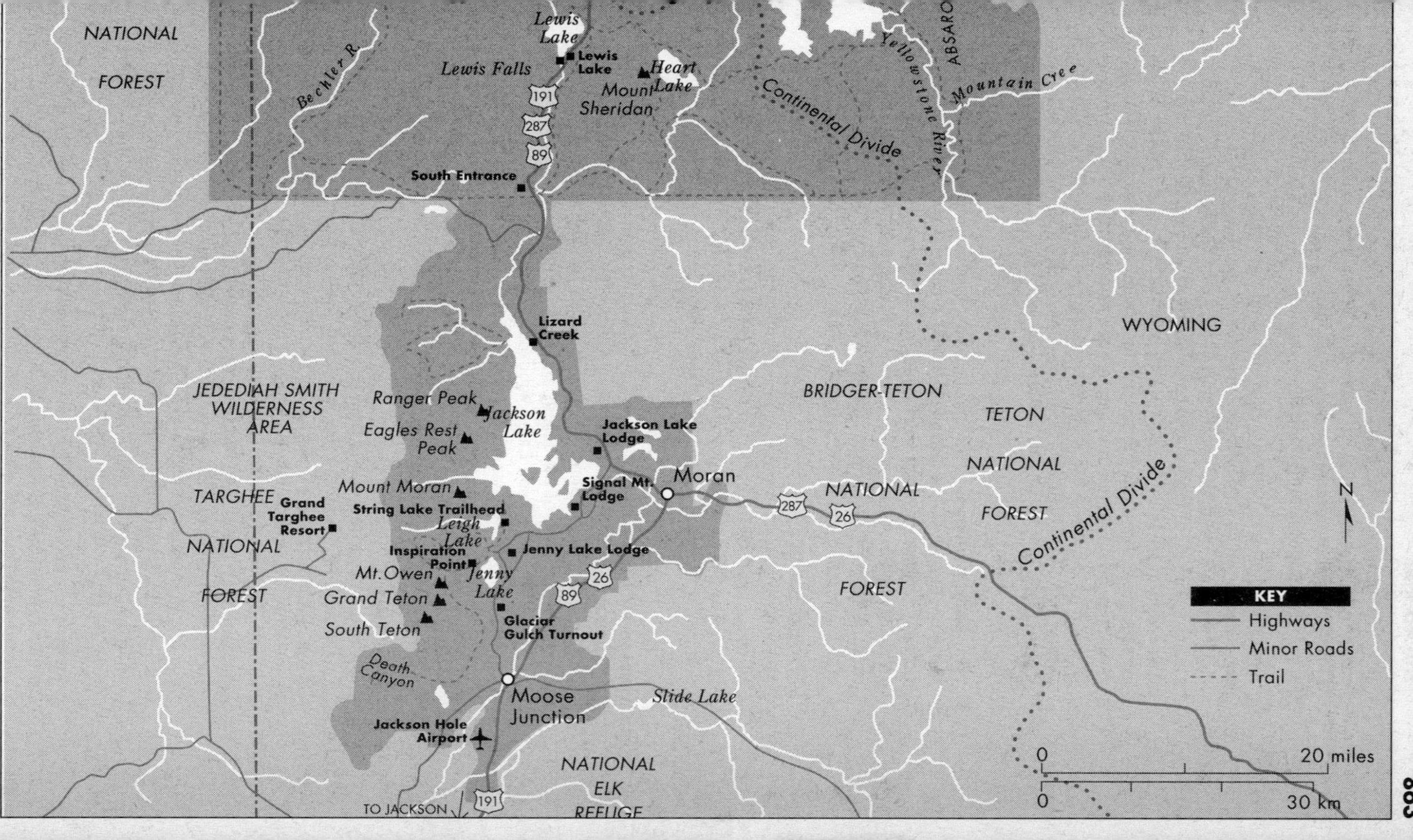
NATIONAL
FOREST
Lewis Lake
Lewis Lake
Lewis Falls
Heart Lake
Mount Sheridan
Bechler R.
191
287
89
South Entrance
Continental Divide
Yellowstone River
ABSARO
Mountain Cree
WYOMING
Lizard Creek
JEDEDIAH SMITH WILDERNESS AREA
Ranger Peak
Jackson Lake
Eagles Rest Peak
Jackson Lake Lodge
BRIDGER-TETON
TETON
NATIONAL
Moran
Signal Mt. Lodge
Mount Moran
TARGHEE
Grand Targhee Resort
String Lake Trailhead
Leigh Lake
NATIONAL
287
26
NATIONAL
FOREST
Continental Divide
N
Inspiration Point
Jenny Lake Lodge
Mt. Owen
Jenny Lake
26
89
FOREST
FOREST
Grand Teton
South Teton
Glacier Gulch Turnout
KEY
Highways
Minor Roads
Trail
Death Canyon
Moose Junction
Slide Lake
Jackson Hole Airport
NATIONAL
ELK
REFUGE
TO JACKSON
191
0
20 miles
0
30 km

centers throughout the park offer guided hikes, evening talks, and campfire programs (check the park newsletter *Discover Yellowstone*). Park service literature and warnings about dealing with the wildlife—grizzly bears and bison, especially—should be taken seriously.

Roads from all five park entrances eventually join the figure-8 **Grand Loop Road,** which makes many areas of the park accessible by vehicle. If you enter from the south, start at the Old Faithful area. The best-known geyser is, of course, **Old Faithful,** the dependable crowd pleaser that erupts every hour or so. Wooden walkways lead among the other geysers, mud pots, and colorful springs and along the nearby **Firehole River.** Stay on the walkways—geysers can be dangerous. Elk and bison frequent this area. Near the west entrance is **Norris Geyser Basin;** among its hundreds of springs and geysers is the unpredictable **Steamboat Geyser,** which came back to life in 1978 and shoots water more than 300 ft into the air.

Near **Canyon Village,** at the middle of the loops, is a short hike to **Inspiration, Grandview,** and **Lookout points,** where the vistas explain why Colter's accounts seemed so outlandish. The **North Rim Trail** leads to views of the cascading waters of the 308-ft **Upper** and 109-ft **Lower falls.** In the northeast corner of the park is the beautiful **Lamar Valley,** which attracts bison in the summer.

Grand Teton

Just south of Yellowstone, connected by the John D. Rockefeller Memorial Parkway (U.S. 89), is **Grand Teton National Park,** established in 1929 and expanded to its present size when the Rockefeller family donated land that it owned in Jackson Hole.

Technical climbers rope up and drag themselves to the 13,770-ft summit of the **Grand** (usually led by an experienced guide), but day hikers find many rewards, too, from a journey up **Cascade Canyon** to a ramble along a lakeshore. **Jenny, Leigh,** and **Jackson lakes** are strung out along the base of the Tetons and are popular with fishermen, canoeists, and, on Jackson Lake, windsurfers and sailors. Rafting along the **Snake River** allows views of moose or bison and a variety of smooth or fast-moving water. **Willow Flats** and **Oxbow Bend** are both excellent places to see waterfowl, and **Signal Mountain Road** affords a top-of-the-park view of the Tetons.

Jackson

The nearby national parks deserve some of the credit for the growth of Jackson, but the town has an identity and a Western swing all its own. With its raised wooden sidewalks, cowboys strolling about, and old-fashioned storefronts and lettering on shop windows, Jackson may resemble a Western-movie set, but it's the real thing. There are hot debates about whether and how much to control development, and most locals want to avoid what they call "Aspenization." For the time being, the town remains compact and folksy, a place where genuine cowboys rub shoulders with the store-bought variety and where the antler-arched square, the whoop-it-up nightlife, and the surrounding wilderness are pretty much intact.

Jackson is walk-around size, and easy to relax in after a stint of white-water rafting, hiking, or skiing. Whether your idea of relaxing is epicurean meals, lolling in a hot tub, or dancing at the Cowboy Bar, Jackson is a good host.

What to See and Do with Children

A favorite family spot is **Granite Hot Springs,** south of Jackson off U.S. 191, 10 mi into Bridger–Teton National Forest along a gravel road. There is a shady campground by a creek, a hot-springs pool, hikes, and scenery. From December 15 through March, the **National Elk Refuge** (675 E. Broadway, Jackson, 83001, ☎ 307/733–0277; admission charged), just north of Jackson, offers trips on horse-drawn sleighs through the herd of more than 7,000 elk in their winter preserve.

Shopping

Shopping in Jackson is centered on the town square. Western wear and outdoor clothing, some of it locally made, dominate in such stores as **Wyoming Outfitters** (165 N. Center St., ☎ 307/733–3877), **Jackson Hole Clothiers** (45 E. Deloney St., ☎ 307/733–7211), and **Hideout Leather** (40 N. Center St., ☎ 307/733–2422). Specialists in the latest outdoor equipment include **Teton Mountaineering** (170 N. Cache St., ☎ 307/733–3595) and **Skinny Skis** (65 W. Deloney St., ☎ 307/733–6094). **Trailside Americana** (105 N. Center St., ☎ 307/733–3186) features Western jewelry and art. For photographic art, try **Tom Mangelsen Images of Nature Gallery** (170 N. Cache St., ☎ 307/733–6179).

Sports and the Outdoors

In Jackson there are guides and services to cater to almost every interest. The **Jackson Hole Chamber of Commerce** (*see* Tourist Information, *above*) has information on various winter and summer activities and lists of outfitters. For sporting opportunities in the parks, which include skiing, horseback riding, hiking, and climbing, contact the visitor centers.

Boating

Hire boats on Jackson Lake through **Colter Bay Marina** (☎ 307/733–2811) or **Signal Mountain Marina** (☎ 307/543–2831).

Climbing

Mountain climbers get a leg up from **Jackson Hole Mountain Guides** (☎ 307/733–4979) or **Exum Mountain Guides** (☎ 307/733–2297).

Fishing

There are blue-ribbon trout streams all through this country, and Jackson Lake has set some records for Mackinaw trout. The necessary license for fishing in Yellowstone and Grand Teton is free at entrance gates or park offices. For fishing elsewhere, licenses can be bought at sporting-goods or general merchandise stores; or contact **Wyoming Game and Fish** (5400 Bishop Blvd., Cheyenne 82002, ☎ 307/777–4600). Fly shops in Jackson include **Jack Dennis Sporting Goods** (on the square, ☎ 307/733–3270) and **High Country Flies** (165 N. Center St., ☎ 307/733–7210).

Golf

Jackson Hole Golf Club (off U.S. 89, 8 mi north of Jackson, ☎ 307/733–3111) and **Teton Pines Golf Club** (3450 N. Clubhouse Dr., ☎ 307/733–1733) both have 18 holes.

Rafting

There are peaceful, scenic floats on the Upper Snake, including the beautiful Oxbow, which you can navigate yourself by canoe or kayak. Guided rafting trips are available from such outfits as **Barker-Ewing Scenic** (in Moose, ☎ 307/733–1000 or 800/448–4202), **Snake River**

Kayak & Canoe School (Jackson, ☎ 307/733–3127 or 800/824–5375), and **Triangle X** (Moose, ☎ 307/733–5500). For bouncier guided white-water trips in Snake River Canyon, try **Dave Hansen Whitewater** (Jackson, ☎ 307/733–6295) or **Lewis & Clark Expeditions** (Jackson, ☎ 307/733–4022 or 800/824–5375). Canoes and kayaks can be rented in Jackson from **Leisure Sports** (1075 S. U.S. 89, ☎ 307/733–3040) and **Teton Aquatics** (155 W. Gill St., ☎ 307/733–3127).

Ski Areas

Cross-Country

In winter, cross-country skiing and snowshoeing are permitted in parts of both Yellowstone and Grand Teton national parks and surrounding forests. One of the best spots is **Togwotee Pass,** within Bridger–Teton and Shoshone national forests (U.S. 26/287), where **Togwotee Mountain Lodge** (Box 91, Moran 83013, ☎ 307/543–2847) offers 13½ mi of groomed tracks. **Spring Creek Ranch Resort** (*see* Dining and Lodging, *below*) has 8 mi of trails; **Jackson Hole Nordic Center** (Box 290, Teton Village 83025, ☎ 307/733–2292) has 12.

Downhill

Grand Targhee Ski Resort (Box SKI, Alta 83422, ☎ 307/353–2300 or 800/827–4433), 64 runs, four lifts, 2,200-ft vertical drop. **Jackson Hole Ski Resort** (Box 290, Teton Village 83025, ☎ 307/733–2292 or 800/443–6931), 58 runs, nine lifts, 4,139-ft drop (the longest of any U.S. ski area), some snowmaking. **Snow King** (Box SKI, Jackson 83001, ☎ 307/733–5200 or 800/522–5464), 400 acres of slopes, three lifts, 1,571-ft drop.

Dining and Lodging

You can make reservations for a stay in Jackson or Jackson Hole Ski Resort through **Central Reservations** (☎ 800/443–6931). **Bed & Breakfast Rocky Mountains** (906 S. Pearl St., Denver 80209, ☎ 303/744–8415) handles B&Bs throughout the region. For price ranges, see Charts 1 (B) and 2 (B) in On the Road with Fodor's.

Grand Teton

Three of the park's lodges are operated by **Grand Teton Lodge Company** (Box 240, Moran 83013, ☎ 307/543–2811; AE, DC, MC, V).

DINING AND LODGING

Jackson Lake Lodge. This low-slung, massive brown stone edifice has huge windows overlooking Willow Flats. Guest rooms in the adjacent buildings are larger and more appealingly decorated than those in the main lodge. The Mural Room's menu sometimes features local game, such as venison or antelope. *Off U.S. 89 north of Jackson Lake Junction; Grand Teton Lodge Co.* (see above). *385 rooms. Facilities: 2 restaurants, pool. Closed mid-Oct.–late May. $$$*

★ **Jenny Lake Lodge.** The most exclusive of the resorts, set amid pines and a wildflower meadow, has cabins and rooms that are rustic yet luxurious, with sturdy pine beds covered with handmade quilts and electric blankets. The dining-room menu emphasizes Rocky Mountain cuisine, including roast prime rib of buffalo or breast of pheasant with pheasant sausage. *Jenny Lake Rd.; Grand Teton Lodge Co.* (see above). *30 cabins. Facilities: restaurant, lounge. Closed mid-Oct.–late May. $$$*

★ **Signal Mountain Lodge.** On the shore of Jackson Lake, the main building is of volcanic stone and pine shingle; inside is a cozy lounge with a fireplace, a piano, and Adirondack furniture. Guest rooms are in a separate cluster of cabinlike units. The Aspens restaurant offers such dishes as shrimp linguine and medallions of elk. *Park Inner Teton Rd., Box 50, Moran 83013, ☎ 307/543–2831. 79 units, some with kitchenettes. Facilities: restaurant, bar, marina. AE, DC, MC, V. Closed mid-Oct.–early May. $$–$$$*

Colter Bay Village. Near the shore of Jackson Lake, the resort is made up of log cabins and less-expensive tent cabins (canvas-covered wood frames). The Chuckwagon restaurant is family-oriented, with lasagna, trout, and barbecued spare ribs. *Off U.S. 89; Grand Teton Lodge Co.* (see above). *250 cabins (30 share bath), 72 tent cabins (communal bath). Facilities: 2 restaurants, bar, laundromat. Closed late Sept.–early June (tent cabins have slightly shorter season). $$*

Jackson

DINING

★ **Blue Lion.** In this homey, light-blue clapboard house, the fare ranges from rack of lamb to fresh seafood. *160 N. Milward St., ☎ 307/733–3912. AE, D, MC, V. $$$*

The Bunnery. This pine-paneled whole-grain restaurant and bakery serves irresistible breakfasts, from omelets with blue cheese, mushrooms, and sautéed spinach to home-baked pastry; and sandwiches, burgers, and Mexican fare later in the day. *130 N. Cache St., Hole-in-the-Wall Mall, ☎ 307/733–5474. No reservations. MC, V. $$*

★ **Nani's.** The ever-changing menu at this cozy restaurant may offer braised veal shanks with saffron risotto and other regional Italian cooking. *240 N. Glenwood St., ☎ 307/733–3888. DC, MC, V. $$*

DINING AND LODGING

★ **Spring Creek Ranch.** Outside of town on Gros Ventre Butte, this luxury resort offers beautiful views of the Tetons and a number of amenities, including cooking in some units, horseback riding, tennis, and cross-country skiing and sleigh rides in winter. Aside from 36 hotel rooms, there's a changing mix of studios, suites, and condos with lofts, called "choates." The comfortable restaurant, the **Granary,** its lodgepole interior decorated with Native American artwork, serves fine food; lead off with Dungeness crab and Havarti cheese wrapped in phyllo dough, followed by poached salmon in cucumber dill sauce with wild rice. *1800 Spirit Dance Rd., Box 3154, 83001, ☎ 307/733–8833 or 800/443–6139, FAX 307/733–1524. 117 units. Facilities: restaurant (reservations required; $$$), pool, tennis courts, horseback riding, Nordic skiing. AE, D, DC, MC, V. $$–$$$*

LODGING

Painted Porch Bed & Breakfast. Eight miles north of town is this 1901 farmhouse with rooms decorated with antiques; some have Japanese soaking tubs. *Teton Village Rd., Box 3965, 83001, ☎ 307/733–1981. 4 rooms. MC, V. $$$*

Cowboy Village Resort. Each of the pine-log cabins in this complex on a quiet side street offers bunk beds and a kitchenette, making it a popular spot for families and groups of friends who don't mind close quarters. *120 S. Flat Creek Dr., 83001, ☎ 307/733–3121, FAX 307/739–1955. 82 cabins. Facilities: 2 whirlpools. AE, D, MC, V. $$*

Teton Village

DINING

★ **Mangy Moose.** Folks pour in here off the ski slopes with big appetites and a lot to talk about. It's noisy, but the trendy, eclectic American fare is decent. *South end of Teton Village, ☎ 307/733–4913. AE, MC, V. $$*

DINING AND LODGING

★ **Alpenhof.** In the heart of the Jackson Hole Ski Resort (*see* Ski Areas, *above*), this European-style hotel is the lodge closest to the lifts. The restaurant, which serves veal, wild game, and seafood, is small, quiet, and comfortable. *Box 288, 83025,* ☎ *307/733–3242,* FAX *307/739–1516. 41 rooms. Facilities: restaurant, bistro, bar, pool, whirlpool, sauna. AE, D, MC, V. $$$*

Yellowstone

The lodgings and restaurants within Yellowstone are operated by **TW Recreational Services** (Yellowstone National Park, 82190; for lodging reservations, ☎ 307/344–7311, FAX 307/344–2456; AE, D, DC, MC, V). There are numerous services, from gas stations to snack bars, throughout the park.

DINING AND LODGING

★ **Lake Yellowstone Hotel.** At the north end of the lake is the park's oldest (late 1800s) and most elegant resort, with a columned, pale-yellow neoclassical facade. The spacious lobby's tall windows overlook the lake, and some rooms have brass beds and vintage fixtures. The cabins are comparatively rustic. The restaurant offers such items as Thai curried shrimp or fettuccine with smoked salmon and snow peas. *Lake Village. 250 rooms and cabins. Facilities: restaurant (☎ 307/242–3701; reservations required). Closed late Sept.–mid-May. $$–$$$*

★ **Old Faithful Inn.** You can loll in front of the lobby's immense stone fireplace and look up six stories at wood balconies that seem to disappear into the night sky. Guest-room decor ranges from brass beds to Victorian cherry wood to inexpensive motel-style furniture. The dining room, a huge hall centered on a fireplace of volcanic stone, serves shrimp scampi and chicken *forestière,* among other delights. *Old Faithful. 327 rooms (77 share bath). Facilities: restaurant (☎ 307/344–7901, ext. 4999; dinner reservations required), cocktail lounge, gift shop. Closed mid-Oct.–mid-Dec., mid-Mar.–early May. $$*

Mammoth Hot Springs Hotel. Sharing its grounds with the park headquarters, this spot is a little far from some of the major attractions. The lobby has Art Deco touches; the cabins are small and ranged around "auto courts." The dining room offers regional American fare, including prime rib and chicken with Brie and raspberry sauce. The Terrace Grill, across from the lodge, is an airy room with large windows that bring in the outdoors, offering fast-food and cafeteria-style service. *Mammoth. 140 cabins, 4 with hot tubs. Facilities: 2 restaurants (dining room ☎ 307/344–7901, ext. 531455), lounge, horseback riding. Closed mid-Sept.–mid-Dec., mid-Mar.–late May. $–$$*

Old Faithful Snow Lodge. The compact, drab-looking motel tucked off to one side of the Old Faithful complex is one of only two park lodgings that stay open in winter. The rooms are nondescript motel style, but the lobby's wood-burning stove is a popular gathering spot in winter. The small restaurant serves family fare. *Old Faithful. 31 rooms (30 share bath), 34 cabins. Facilities: restaurant (no lunch early Sept.–mid-Oct.), gift shop. Closed mid-Oct.–mid-Dec., mid-Mar.–mid-May. $*

★ **Roosevelt Lodge.** Near the Lamar Valley in the park's northeast corner, this simple, homey log lodge is more ranch house than resort. The dining room serves barbecued ribs, Roosevelt beans, and other Western fare. Accommodations are in nearby cabins. *Tower-Roosevelt. 8 cabins with bath, 78 with nearby common shower cabin. Facilities: restaurant (no reservations), lounge, gift shop. Closed early Sept.–early June. $*

Motels

Antler Motel (43 W. Pearl St., Jackson 83001, ☎ 307/733–2535 or 800/522–2406), 107 rooms, hot tub; $$$. **Days Inn** (1280 W. Broadway, Jackson 83001, ☎ 307/739–9010, FAX 307/733–0044), 74 rooms, Continental breakfast, whirlpool, sauna; $$$. **Virginian Motel** (750 W. Broadway, Jackson 83001, ☎ 307/733–2792, FAX 307/733–9513), 159 rooms, restaurant, pool; $$. **Motel 6** (1370 W. Broadway, Jackson 83001, ☎ 307/733–1620, FAX 307/734–9175), 155 rooms, outdoor heated pool; $.

Campgrounds

Grand Teton

The **National Park Service** (Drawer 170, Moose 83012, ☎ 307/739–3300) has five campgrounds within the park; none have RV hookups, but all have fire grates and rest rooms. The privately run **Colter Bay Trailer Village** (Grand Teton Lodge Co., Box 240, Moran 83013, ☎ 307/543–2855) has full RV hookups.

Yellowstone

Among the 11 **National Park Service** (Box 168, Yellowstone National Park 82190, ☎ 307/344–7381) campsite areas in Yellowstone, **Bridge Bay** (420 sites, marina) is the largest and **Slough Creek** (32 tent-trailer sites) is the smallest. There are also 300 backcountry campsites, for which you need a permit from the park rangers.

ELSEWHERE IN THE STATE

Cheyenne

Getting There

I–25 comes north the 100 mi from Denver. Commuter airlines fly between Denver and **Cheyenne Municipal Airport** (☎ 307/634–7071) and **Greyhound** (☎ 800/231–2222) provides bus service. **Amtrak** stops 10 mi outside the city, and a shuttle bus takes passengers into town.

What to See and Do

For a whiff of corral dust, don't miss the **Frontier Days** rodeo (☎ 800/227–6336) the last week of July—a reminder that the state's capital city was once known as "Hell on Wheels." Outside the gold-domed **state capitol** is a statue of Esther Hobart Morris, who earned Wyoming its "equality state" motto: The first woman to hold U.S. public office, she was appointed a justice of the peace in 1870. Women got the vote in 1869, and in 1924 Mrs. Nellie Taylor Ross became the state's and the nation's first elected female governor.

The **Frontier Days Old West Museum** (Frontier Park, 4501 N. Carey Ave., ☎ 307/778–7290 or 800/778–7290) displays buggies, stagecoaches, and buckboards. A favorite lodging place with travelers and state legislators is the **Hitching Post Inn** (1700 W. Lincolnway, ☎ 307/638–3301 or 800/528–1234, FAX 307/638–3301).

Cody

Getting There

Cody is 52 mi east of Yellowstone on U.S. 14/16/20.

What to See and Do

Most people use Cody as a way station en route to or from Yellowstone's east entrance, but the town has a museum that makes it a required stop for anyone interested in the history of the American West. The **Buffalo**

Bill Historical Center (720 Sheridan Ave., ☎ 307/587–4771; admission charged) has a **Plains Indian Museum,** the **Cody Firearms Museum,** the **Buffalo Bill Museum,** and the **Whitney Gallery of Western Art.** For information about the many fine guest ranches between Cody and Yellowstone, contact the **Wapati Valley Association** (1231 Yellowstone Hwy., ☎ 307/587–9595). In town, the **Irma Hotel** (1192 Sheridan Ave., 82414, ☎ 307/587–4221) has an ornate cherry-wood bar and some rooms in turn-of-the-century Western style. For further information, contact the **Cody Chamber of Commerce** (☎ 307/587–2297).

Sheridan

Getting There

Commuter airlines fly from Denver to **Sheridan County Airport** (☎ 307/674–4222). **Powder River Transportation** (☎ 800/237–7211) buses connect with national carriers. I–90 comes into Sheridan 130 mi from Billings, Montana, and I–25 comes 140 mi north from Casper.

What to See and Do

This is authentic cowboy country, with a touch of dudish sophistication. **Eaton's Ranch** (Wolf 82844, ☎ 307/655–9285), on Wolf Creek near Sheridan, began hosting guests in 1904, making it the granddaddy of all dude ranches. The **Equestrian Center** (☎ 307/674–5179), 12 mi south of town toward Big Horn, offers polo matches on summer weekends, as well as horse shows and steeplechase. Mosey into **King's Saddlery and Ropes** (184 N. Main St., ☎ 307/672–2702 or 800/443–8919), where you can look at (and try out) hundreds of lariats, as well as hand-tooled leather saddles that sell for thousands of dollars. For information, contact the **Sheridan Chamber of Commerce** (Box 707, 82801, ☎ 307/672–2485).

11 The West Coast

By Larry Peterson

ALTHOUGH OFTEN with an arched eyebrow, the rest of America keeps a careful watch on its West Coast, knowing that the latest thing there will almost surely be coming to a sporting-goods store, bookstore, menu, college campus, voter referendum, church, shopping mall, TV or computer screen, CD player, or theater near them. Soon.

This is the far edge of the frontier, the last stop of westward expansion. The region is shaped as much by its people's unwavering conviction that reality can be pretty much remade to their liking as by its geography. This fact characterizes and unifies cities as different as Seattle, Portland, San Francisco, Los Angeles, and San Diego. The essence of the area is also built on preconceived notions getting turned on in their heads: The Spanish came in search of a mythical paradise filled with gold and found fertile land; the Americans came for the land and found the gold; Lewis and Clark came looking for the Northwest Passage and found a damp, plentiful wilderness. Current notions ripe for debunking include the many clichés that the West Coast has generated about itself and the character of its citizens: The feet-on-the-ground Northwest gave us Jimi Hendrix, David Lynch, and the Simpsons. From eccentric, extravagant San Francisco came Joes DiMaggio and Montana. Southern California's hotbed of hedonism spawned Richard Nixon and Ronald Reagan.

Though more and more camouflaged by the hand of man, nature continues to offer a critical perspective on human pursuits. The ragged edges of Washington's Olympic Peninsula and the Oregon coast illustrate the power of the ocean; the mountains surrounding Seattle offer a sobering sense of scale, as does the view from Yosemite's valley floor; and tremors along the San Andreas fault tick off nanoseconds on Earth's geological clock. Every city and town along the West Coast sits amid some grand gesture of nature, and the challenge of how to preserve it is a source of both tension and creativity.

After three centuries of exploration and migration, the West Coast remains a place of myth and expectation, a land of promise. As America's proving ground for new ideas, the region continues to exert its magnetic pull on the imagination of people the world over.

Tour Groups

In the western states, where distances are long, group tours provide an attractive alternative to driving.

Domenico Tours (751 Broadway, Bayonne, NJ 07002, ☎ 201/823–8687 or 800/554–8687) has 7- to 18-day tours of California, as well as shorter excursions that include such events as the Tournament of Roses. **Gadabout Tours** (700 E. Tahquitz Canyon Way, Palm Springs, CA 92262, ☎ 619/325–5556) offers regional tours, including "Hearst Castle Rail Caper," "California Wine Country," and "Pacific Ports of Call" in the Northwest. **Gray Line of Seattle** (720 S. Forest St., Seattle, WA 98134, ☎ 206/624–5813 or 800/544–0739) has 2- to 7-day regional tours, including a "Northwest Triangle" of Seattle, Vancouver, and Victoria. **Maupintour** (Box 807, Lawrence, KS 66044, ☎ 913/843–1211 or 800/255–4266) explores the coast, with stops at San Diego, San Francisco, Portland, and Seattle.

When to Go

You can take a West Coast vacation anytime of the year. Weather in coastal areas is generally mild year-round, with the rainy season running from October through March. Expect to encounter heavy coastal fog throughout the summer. Inland areas such as Napa Valley, the Columbia Gorge, and the High Sierras can be hot in summer, with temperatures reaching up to 90° in the plains and mountains; in California's central valley and desert regions, summer temperatures can soar above 110°. The ski season in the High Sierras and Cascades runs from October through March, occasionally into April and May. Those who want to enjoy the sun-drenched delights of the desert should plan a trip between October and May; the wildflowers are at their peak in April. Whenever you visit the West Coast, expect temperatures to vary widely from night to day, sometimes by as much as 40°. Most West Coast attractions are open daily year-round, but summer is the busiest tourist season, when you can expect the most congestion and the highest prices.

Festivals and Seasonal Events

Jan. 1: Tournament of Roses in **Pasadena, California,** features a parade of over 50 floral floats, equestrian units, and marching bands, followed by the Rose Bowl football game. ☎ *818/449–4100.*

Late Jan.–early Feb.: AT&T Pebble Beach (CA) National Pro-Am pairs 180 top professional golfers with amateurs from business, sports, and entertainment. ☎ *408/649–1533.*

Feb.: Chinese New Year celebrations are held in **San Francisco and Los Angeles,** complete with dragon parades, fireworks, and sumptuous feasts. ☎ *415/982–3000 in San Francisco or 213/617–0396 in Los Angeles.*

Mid-Feb.–late Oct.: Oregon Shakespeare Festival, held in **Ashland,** presents four plays by Shakespeare—plus seven other plays by both classical and contemporary playwrights—in repertory in three theaters; tours, concerts, and lectures are also offered. ☎ *503/482–4331.*

Early Mar.: Mendocino (CA) Whale Festival combines whale-watching with art viewing, wine tasting, lighthouse tours, music, and merriment. ☎ *707/961–6300.*

Memorial Day Weekend: Sacramento Jazz Jubilee brings more than 100 jazz bands to **Sacramento, California,** for four days of jamming. ☎ *916/372–5277.*

Early June: Portland (OR) Rose Festival features a rose show, carnivals, celebrity entertainment, a hot-air balloon race, a national air show, visiting bands, and a world-class auto show. ☎ *503/227–2681.*

Mid-June–early July: Oregon Bach Festival brings stellar musicians to **Eugene** for concerts, recitals, lectures, chamber music, and opera. ☎ *503/346–5666.*

Late July: Pacific Northwest Arts & Crafts Fair brings the work of Northwest artists to **Bellevue, Washington.** ☎ *206/454–4900.*

Early Aug.: Old Spanish Days Fiesta is **Santa Barbara**'s biggest event, with parades, a carnival, a rodeo, and dancers in the Spanish marketplace. ☎ *805/962–8101.*

Early Aug.: Mt. Hood Festival of Jazz brings acclaimed jazz musicians to **Gresham, Oregon,** for a tuneful weekend. ☎ *503/666–3810.*

West Coast (Northern)

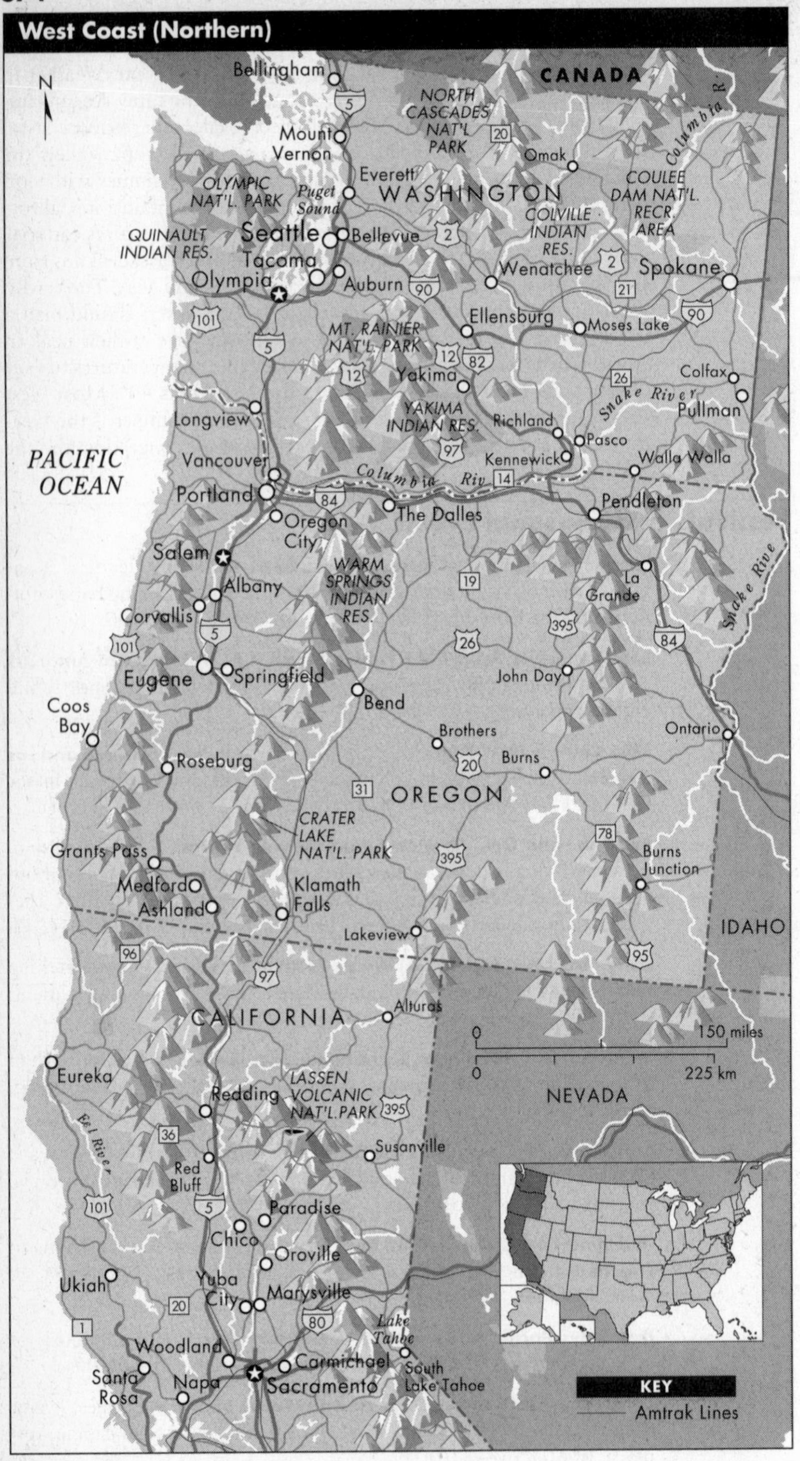

West Coast (Southern)

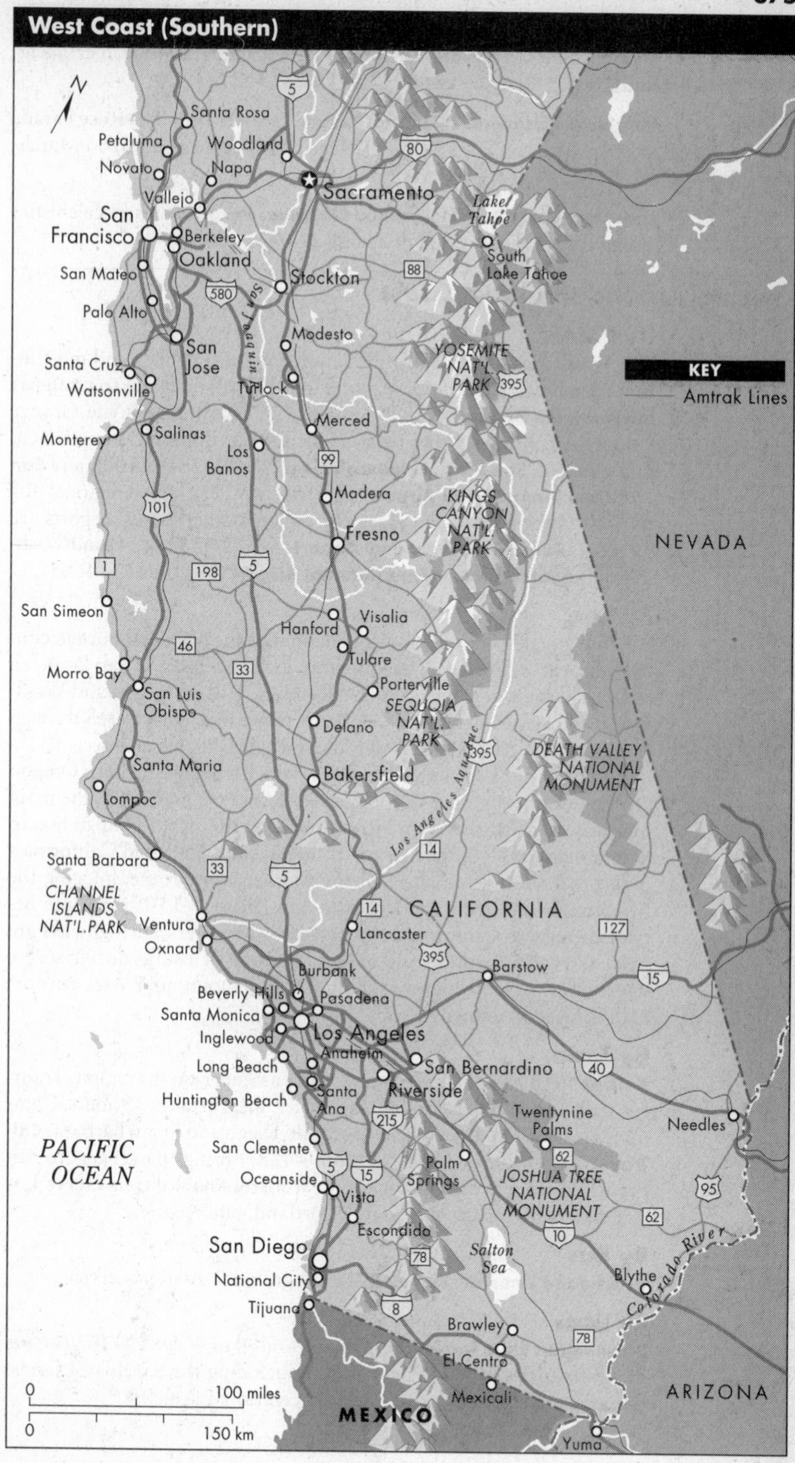

Late Aug.–Oct.: Renaissance Pleasure Faire draws revelers in Elizabethan-style costumes to **Novato, California,** for weekends of music, merriment, and theater. ☎ *415/892–0937 or 800/523–2473.*

Late Nov.: Pasadena's Doo Dah Parade satirizes the city's Rose Parade with such participants as the Briefcase Drill Team and Kazoo Marching Band. ☎ *818/449–3689.*

Late Nov.–early Dec.: Hollywood Christmas Parade features celebrities riding festively decorated floats. ☎ *213/469–2337.*

Getting Around the West Coast

By Plane

The West Coast is served by all major domestic airlines and most international carriers. Major airports in California include **Los Angeles International Airport** (☎ 310/646–5252), plus John Wayne Orange County Airport and other regional airports at Burbank, Long Beach, and Ontario; **San Diego Lindbergh Field** (☎ 619/231–2100); and **San Francisco International Airport** (☎ 415/876–2222), plus regional airports at Oakland and San Jose. The region's other major airports are Oregon's **Portland International Airport** (☎ 503/335–1234) and Washington's **Seattle-Tacoma International Airport** (☎ 206/433–4645).

By Car

I–5 runs north–south from the Canadian to the Mexican border, connecting Seattle, Portland, Sacramento, Los Angeles, and San Diego en route. The coastal route is designated Hwy. 101 in Oregon and Washington and Hwy. 1 in most of California, where much of it travels through coastal valleys. Major east–west routes include I–90, which bisects Washington from Spokane to Seattle; I–84, which traverses eastern Oregon and travels through the Columbia Gorge to Portland; I–80, the main highway crossing the High Sierras in California from Lake Tahoe to San Francisco; I–10, the historic route through Southern California's desert to Los Angeles; and I–8, the southernmost route, hugging the Mexican border from El Centro to San Diego. I–15 is the route between Southern California and Las Vegas. The interstate highways are open all year, but you should expect temporary closures during severe winter storms. State highways crossing high mountain passes are normally closed in winter.

By Train

Amtrak (☎ 800/872–7245) serves rail passengers in the region. Trains run daily between Seattle and Los Angeles; the trip takes 35 hours. Commuter trains serve Los Angeles from San Diego and Santa Barbara. **CalTrain** (☎ 415/508–6200 or 800/660–4287) brings passengers to San Francisco from peninsula locations. **Transcontinental** trains serve Los Angeles, San Francisco/Oakland, Portland, and Seattle.

By Bus

Greyhound Lines (☎ 800/231–2222) provides intercity service.

By Boat

Washington State Ferries (☎ 206/464–6400 or 800/843–3779) serve 20 destinations around Puget Sound, including the San Juan Islands. Ferries can accommodate cars and recreational vehicles.

CALIFORNIA

By Aaron Shurin and Bobbi Zane

Capital	Sacramento
Population	32,140,000
Motto	Eureka
State Bird	Valley quail
State Flower	Golden poppy

Visitor Information

California Division of Tourism (801 K St., Suite 1600, Sacramento 95814, ☎ 916/322–1397 or 800/462–2543, FAX 916/322–3402).

Scenic Drives

The land- and seascapes along the nearly 400 mi of coastline between San Francisco Bay and the Oregon border are beautiful and rugged; switchbacked **Hwy. 1** is punctuated by groves of giant redwood trees, tiny coastal towns, and secluded coves and beaches. **U.S. 395** north from San Bernardino rises in elevation gradually from the Mojave Desert to the Sierra foothills and on to the east entrance to Yosemite National Park. **Highway 49** winds 325 mi through northern California's historic Gold Country.

National and State Parks

National Parks

At **Yosemite National Park** (Box 577, Yosemite National Park, CA 95389, ☎ 209/372–0200), glacial granite peaks and domes rise more than 3,000 ft. Yosemite Valley offers hiking, backpacking, and spectacular scenery at every turn; Yosemite Falls, at 2,425 ft, is the highest waterfall in North America. Hotel rooms or cabins are reserved through Yosemite Concession Services Corporation (5410 E. Home Ave., Fresno 93727, ☎ 209/252–4848), campsites through MISTIX (☎ 800/365–2267). Just north of San Francisco is the **Point Reyes National Seashore** (☎ 415/663–1092), whose shoreline and sand dunes attract lots of birds and migrating whales.

State Parks

California's more than 200 state parks are maintained by the **Department of Parks and Recreation** (Box 942896, Sacramento 94296, ☎ 916/653–6995). **Anza Borrego Desert** (☎ 619/767–5311), northeast of San Diego, has fascinating flora and rock formations. **Big Basin Redwoods** (☎ 408/338–6132), near Santa Cruz, has 18,000 acres of the big trees. **Leo Carillo State Beach** (☎ 818/880–0350), north of Malibu, has tide pools, hiking trails, and picnic areas. **Pismo Beach** (☎ 805/489–2684), near San Luis Obispo, offers a wide stretch of beach and many recreational facilities.

SAN FRANCISCO

San Francisco is a relatively small city, with just over 750,000 residents nested on a 46.6-sq-mi tip of land between San Francisco Bay and the Pacific Ocean. Its residents cherish the city's colorful past, and many older buildings have been spared from demolition and nostalgically converted into modern offices and shops. Despite acts of God, the indifference of developers, and the mixed record of the city's Planning

Commission, much of architectural and historical interest remains. Bernard Maybeck, Julia Morgan, Willis Polk, and Arthur Brown, Jr., are among the noted architects whose designs still grace the city's downtown and neighborhoods.

First-time visitors won't want to miss Golden Gate Park, the Palace of Fine Arts, the Golden Gate Bridge, or a cable-car ride on Nob Hill. A walk down the Filbert Steps or through Macondray Lane, though, or a peaceful hour gazing east from Ina Coolbrith Park, can be equally inspiring.

Much of the city's neighborhood vitality comes from the distinct borders provided by its hills and valleys, and many areas are so named: Nob Hill, Twin Peaks, Eureka Valley. San Francisco neighborhoods are self-aware, and they retain strong cultural, political, and ethnic identities. Experiencing San Francisco means visiting the neighborhoods: the colorful Mission District, gay Castro, countercultural Haight Street, serene Pacific Heights, bustling Chinatown, and still-exotic North Beach.

Exploring involves navigating a maze of one-way streets and restricted parking zones. Public parking garages or lots tend to be expensive, as are hotel parking spaces. Cable cars, buses and trolleys can take you to or near many of the area's attractions. Many of the following exploring tours include information on public transportation.

Tourist Information

San Francisco: Convention and Visitors Bureau (201 3rd St., Suite 900, 94103, ☎ 415/974–6900).

Arriving and Departing

By Plane

San Francisco International Airport (SFO, ☎ 415/761–0800), 20 minutes south of the city off U.S. 101, is served by most major airlines. **Oakland Airport** (☎ 510/577–4000), across the bay but not much farther from the city, provides additional air access through several domestic airlines. The **SFO Airporter** (☎ 415/495–8404; $8 one-way, $14 round-trip) bus runs every 20 minutes between downtown and SFO. **SuperShuttle** (☎ 415/558–8500; $11 first person, $8 each additional person) will take you from SFO to anywhere within the city limits in 30–50 minutes, depending on traffic and your destination. **Taxis** between downtown and either airport take 20–30 minutes and cost about $30.

By Car

I–80 comes into San Francisco from the east, crossing the Bay Bridge from Oakland. U.S. 101 runs north–south through the city and across the Golden Gate Bridge.

By Train

Amtrak (☎ 800/872–7245) trains stop in Oakland (Jack London Sq., 245 2nd St.) and Emeryville (5885 Landregan St.); shuttle buses connect the Emeryville station and San Francisco's Ferry Building on the Embarcadero. CalTrain serves the southern peninsula from San Francisco's **Southern Pacific** depot (4th and Townsend Sts., ☎ 800/660–4287).

By Bus

Greyhound Lines (☎ 800/231–2222) serves San Francisco's **Transbay Terminal** (1st and Mission Sts.).

Getting Around San Francisco

By Car

Driving in the city is a challenge. Watch out for one-way streets, curb your wheels when parking on hills, and check street signs for parking restrictions—of which there are many.

By Public Transportation

Most of the light-rail and bus lines of **MUNI** (Municipal Railway System, ☎ 415/673–6864) operate continuously; standard fare is $1 for adults, and exact change is required. Three **cable-car** lines crisscross downtown; information and tickets ($2) can be obtained at the main turnaround at Powell and Market streets and at major stops. **BART** (Bay Area Rapid Transit, ☎ 415/992–2278) sends its sleek air-conditioned trains to the East Bay and south to Daly City; wall maps list destinations and fares. Trains run Monday–Saturday 6 AM–midnight, Sunday 9 AM–midnight.

By Taxi

Rates are high—$1.70 just to get in—and it's difficult to hail a passing cab. For a radio-dispatched taxi, try **Yellow Cab Co.** (☎ 415/626–2345).

Orientation Tours

Gray Line (350 8th St., ☎ 415/558–9400) offers a variety of city tours on buses and double-deckers. The **Great Pacific Tour** (518 Octavia St., ☎ 415/626–4499) takes 3½ hours; German-, French-, Spanish-, and Italian-speaking guides are available.

Walking Tours

Trevor Hailey's **Castro District Tour** (☎ 415/550–8110) focuses on the history and development of the city's gay and lesbian community. The **Chinese Cultural Heritage Foundation** (☎ 415/986–1822) offers a Heritage Walk and a Culinary Walk through Chinatown.

Exploring San Francisco

Touring San Francisco is best done one neighborhood at a time and on foot—although the hills are a challenge. Dependable walking shoes are essential. You'll need a jacket for the dramatic temperature swings, especially in summer, when fog rolls in during the afternoon. Starting from Union Square, which is more or less in the center of things, we'll go through nearby Chinatown, and Nob Hill, then south to the Civic Center area; east through the Financial District to the Embarcadero along San Francisco Bay; then north and west through North Beach, Telegraph Hill, Fisherman's Wharf, and the Golden Gate Bridge, and on to Golden Gate Park and the Pacific Ocean.

Union Square

The landmark of Union Square is the grand **Westin St. Francis Hotel** (335 Powell St., ☎ 415/397–7000), San Francisco's second-oldest, on the southeast corner of Post and Powell streets. After a day exploring the stores of this major shopping district (*see* Shopping, *below*), you can relax over a traditional tea in the Westin's dramatic art deco **Compass Rose** lounge.

Across Union Square is tiny **Maiden Lane,** which runs for two blocks between Stockton and Kearny streets. From 11 AM to 5 PM the lane is closed to vehicles and becomes a chic and costly mall. **140 Maiden Lane,** the only Frank Lloyd Wright building in San Francisco, is reminiscent of his later Guggenheim Museum in New York.

South of Market (SoMa)

The vast tract of downtown land south of Market Street along the waterfront and northeast of the Mission district is known as SoMa (patterned after New York City's SoHo). For years, the area was a stomping ground for alternative artists, recent immigrants, and the gay leather set. Although many artists cleared out when urban renewal began, they still hang out in SoMa and show their work in several galleries that remain on the cutting edge of San Francisco's art scene.

In the mid-1960s, the San Francisco Redevelopment Agency grabbed 87 acres of run-down land and planned the largest building project in the city's history: **Yerba Buena Center.** After more than two decades, it has finally taken shape, although parts of it are still under construction and still other portions aren't past the blueprint stage. The complex is on the block surrounded by 3rd, Mission, Howard, and 4th streets and comprises galleries, an outdoor performance stage, two theaters, a sculpture garden, two restaurants, and a gift shop. On the eastern edge of the block is the **Center for the Arts** (701 Mission St., ☎ 415/978–2278); the focus here is on the multicultural arts, from the community-based to the international.

The centerpiece of the SoMa arts scene is the **San Francisco Museum of Modern Art** (151 3rd St., ☎ 415/357–4000; admission charged), designed by Swiss architect Mario Botta. A number of the city's best galleries are nearby, including **Capp Street Project** (525 2nd St., ☎ 415/495–7101), the **Ansel Adams Center** (250 4th St., ☎ 415/495–7000; admission charged), and the **Cartoon Art Museum** (814 Mission St., ☎ 415/546–3922; admission charged).

Four blocks south of the SFMOMA is **South Park,** a tree-filled square with a playground, several cafés and restaurants, and inviting benches. The park is bordered by 2nd, 3rd, Bryant, and Brannan streets and is a great place for a quiet break.

Chinatown

The dragon-crowned, green-tile **Chinatown Gate** at Bush Street and Grant Avenue is the main entrance to Chinatown. The bustling, noisy, colorful stretches of Grant Avenue and Stockton Street are difficult to navigate on foot, but by car it's worse, and parking is almost impossible. Join the residents as they stroll and shop for fresh fish, vegetables, and baked goods. Almost 100 restaurants are squeezed into these 14 blocks.

Among the many interesting architectural examples here are the **Chinese Six Companies** building (843 Stockton St.), with curved roof tiles and elaborate cornices, and the **Old Chinese Telephone Exchange** (now the Bank of Canton; 743 Washington Street), a three-tiered pagoda built just after the '06 earthquake.

To learn about the area's rich immigrant history, go to the **Chinese Cultural Center,** which exhibits the work of Chinese-American artists and offers Saturday-afternoon tours of Chinatown (*see* Walking Tours, *above*). *Holiday Inn, 750 Kearny St.,* ☎ *415/986–1822.* ⏲ *Tues.–Sat. 10–4.*

Nob Hill

North of Union Square is **Nob Hill,** home to the city's elite as well as some of its finest hotels. The 1906 earthquake destroyed the neighborhood mansions that had been built by Gold Rush millionaires and the later railroad barons. Although not the grandest of the bunch, the shell of railroad magnate James Flood's Italianate-style brownstone mansion (1000 California St.) managed to survive the quake, was slightly remodeled, and now houses the exclusive **Pacific Union Club. Grace Cathedral** (1051 California St.) is the seat of the Episcopal church in San Francisco. The gothic structure took 53 years to build and has bronze doors cast from Ghiberti's *Gates of Paradise* in Florence. The **Mark Hopkins Inter-Continental Hotel** atop Nob Hill is known for the view from its **Top of the Mark** lounge (1 Nob Hill, ☎ 415/392–3434).

Civic Center

City Hall (Polk St., between Grove and McAllister Sts.), a granite-and-marble masterpiece modeled after the Capitol in Washington, faces the long **Civic Center Plaza** with a fountain, walkways, and flowerbeds. (The plaza is "home" to many transients, and caution is advised after dark.) City Hall is closed for seismic repairs until 1998. Across Van Ness Avenue, between McAllister and Hayes streets, is the **Performing Arts Center** complex, which includes the **War Memorial Opera House** and the **Louise M. Davies Symphony Hall.**

To the west of the Civic Center area, in a neighborhood known as the Western Addition, is the much-photographed row of six identical Victorian houses along Steiner Street, at the east end of Alamo Square. If you're walking, the safest route—in the daytime—is up Fulton Street to Steiner Street; avoid the area completely at night.

The Financial District

Bounded by the Union Square area, Telegraph Hill, Mission Street, and the Embarcadero, San Francisco's Financial District is distinguished from the rest of town by its cluster of steel-and-glass high rises and older, more decorative architectural monuments to commerce. The city's signature high-rise is the 853-ft **Transamerica Pyramid** (600 Montgomery St., ☎ 415/983–4100), whose 27th-floor public viewing area affords spectacular vistas. Dominating the skyline, however, is the 52-story **Bank of America** tower. High atop this granite monolith, the **Carnelian Room** (555 California St., ☎ 415/433–7500) is a good spot for a sunset dinner or cocktails.

Other notable structures in this district include the **Russ Building** (235 Montgomery St.), a gothic twin to the Chicago Tribune Tower; the **Mills Building and Tower** (220 Montgomery St.), of white marble and brick; and the **Pacific Stock Exchange** (Pine and Sansome Sts.). The ceiling and entry in the **Stock Exchange Tower** (155 Sansome St.), an Art Deco gem, are of black marble.

The Embarcadero

The tower of the 1896 **Ferry Building,** on the Embarcadero at the foot of Market Street, made it the tallest building in town for many years. Obscured from view for the past three decades by the elevated Embarcadero Freeway, the tower was returned to prominence when the 1989 earthquake forced the roadway's dismantling. Ferries still sail from here to Sausalito (*see* Excursion to Sausalito, *below*), Larkspur, and Tiburon. The Embarcadero's waterfront promenade, which extends to the **San Francisco–Oakland Bay Bridge,** is great for walking and jogging and has a fine view of Treasure Island and the East Bay.

Across from the Ferry Building, at the end of Market Street, is the huge **Embarcadero Center,** a complex of eight buildings that include more than 100 shops, 40 restaurants, five movie theaters, and two hotels. A three-tier pedestrian mall links the buildings. The **Hyatt Regency Hotel** (5 Embarcadero, ☎ 415/788–1234) is noted for its lobby and 20-story

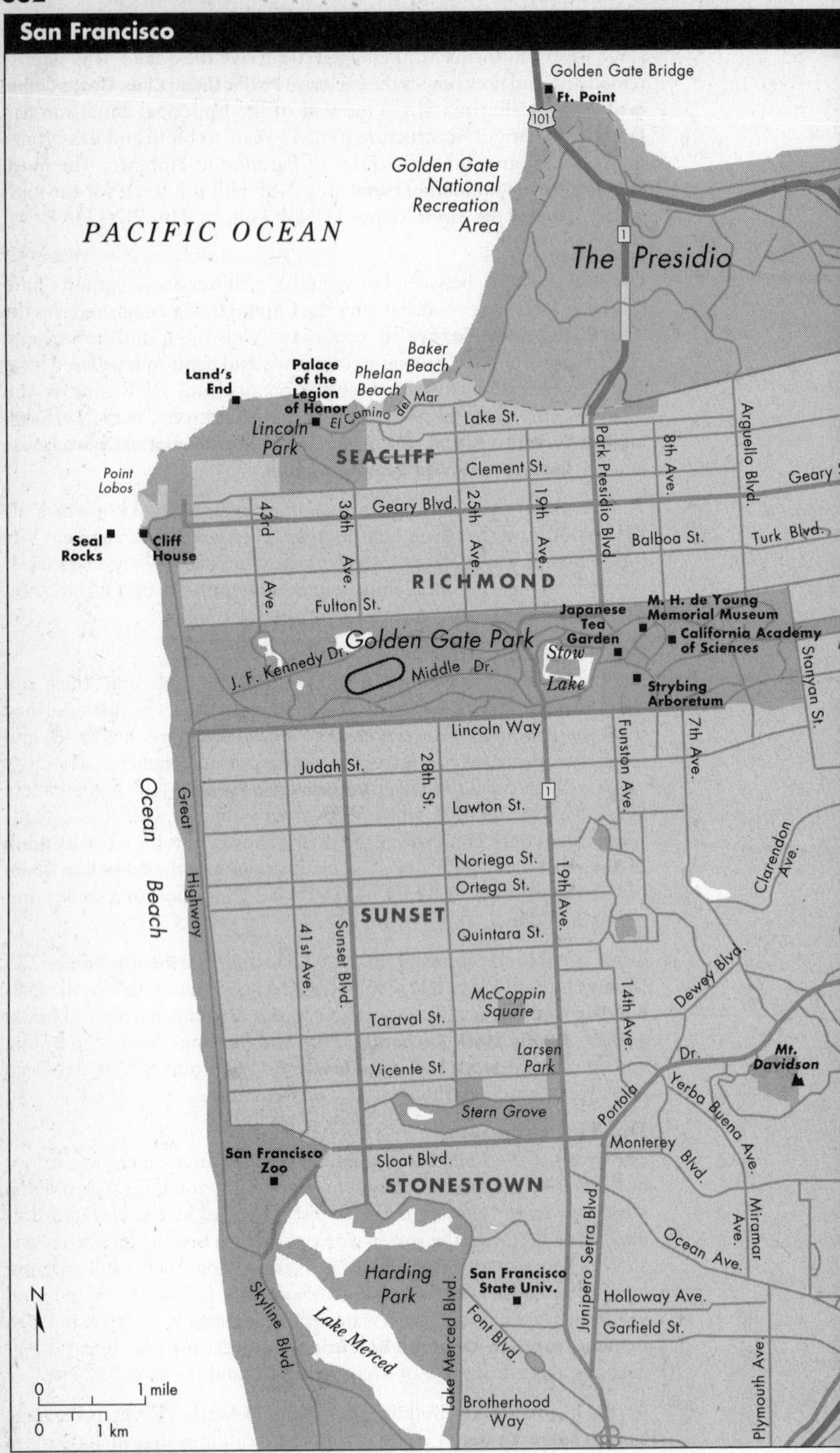
Golden Gate Bridge
Ft. Point
101
Golden Gate National Recreation Area
PACIFIC OCEAN
1
The Presidio
Baker Beach
Phelan Beach
Palace of the Legion of Honor
Land's End
El Camino del Mar
Lake St.
Lincoln Park
SEACLIFF
Clement St.
Point Lobos
Geary Blvd.
Seal Rocks
Cliff House
43rd Ave.
36th Ave.
25th Ave.
19th Ave.
Park Presidio Blvd.
8th Ave.
Arguello Blvd.
Geary S
Balboa St.
Turk Blvd.
RICHMOND
Fulton St.
Japanese Tea Garden
M. H. de Young Memorial Museum
California Academy of Sciences
Golden Gate Park
J. F. Kennedy Dr.
Middle Dr.
Stow Lake
Strybing Arboretum
Stanyan St.
Lincoln Way
Funston Ave.
7th Ave.
Judah St.
28th St.
Lawton St.
Ocean Beach
Great Highway
Noriega St.
Ortega St.
19th Ave.
Clarendon Ave.
SUNSET
Quintara St.
41st Ave.
Sunset Blvd.
McCoppin Square
14th Ave.
Dewey Blvd.
Taraval St.
Larsen Park
Vicente St.
Dr.
Mt. Davidson
Portola
Yerba Buena Ave.
Stern Grove
Monterey Blvd.
San Francisco Zoo
Sloat Blvd.
STONESTOWN
Miramar Ave.
Ocean Ave.
Harding Park
San Francisco State Univ.
Junipero Serra Blvd.
Holloway Ave.
Garfield St.
Skyline Blvd.
Lake Merced
Lake Merced Blvd.
Font Blvd.
Brotherhood Way
Plymouth Ave.
N
0
1 mile
0
1 km

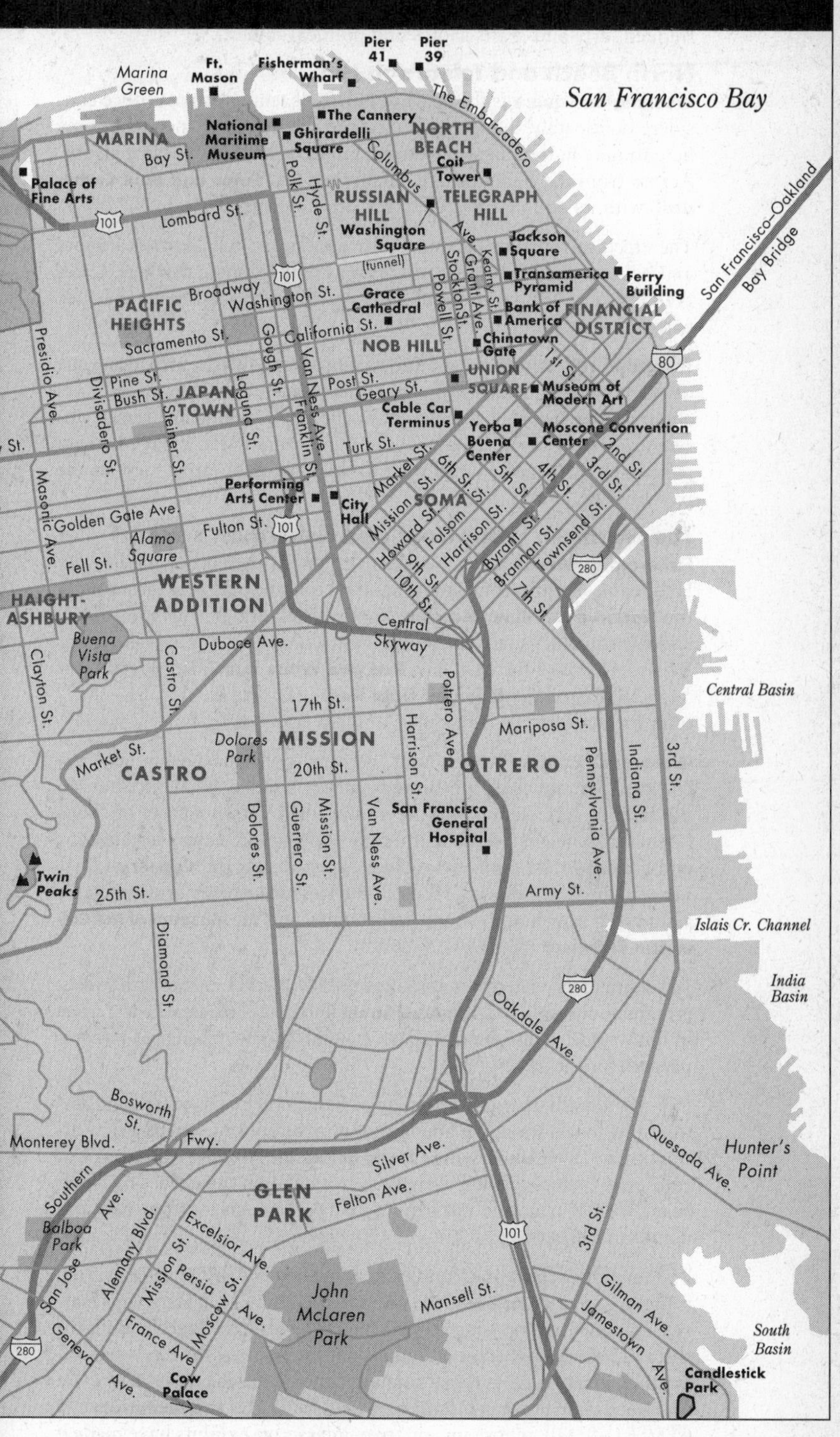

San Francisco Bay
Pier 41
Pier 39
Fisherman's Wharf
Ft. Mason
Marina Green
MARINA
The Cannery
National Maritime Museum
Ghirardelli Square
NORTH BEACH
The Embarcadero
Coit Tower
Palace of Fine Arts
Bay St.
RUSSIAN HILL
TELEGRAPH HILL
Columbus
Lombard St.
Polk St.
Hyde St.
Washington Square
Jackson Square
(tunnel)
Transamerica Pyramid
Ferry Building
San Francisco–Oakland Bay Bridge
Broadway
Washington St.
Grace Cathedral
PACIFIC HEIGHTS
Bank of America
FINANCIAL DISTRICT
California St.
NOB HILL
Chinatown Gate
Sacramento St.
Presidio Ave.
Gough St.
Van Ness Ave.
Powell St.
Stockton St.
Grant Ave.
Kearny St.
1st St.
Pine St.
Bush St.
JAPAN TOWN
Post St.
UNION SQUARE
Museum of Modern Art
Geary St.
Divisadero St.
Steiner St.
Laguna St.
Franklin St.
Cable Car Terminus
Yerba Buena Center
Moscone Convention Center
Turk St.
Market St.
6th St.
5th St.
4th St.
3rd St.
2nd St.
Performing Arts Center
City Hall
Mission St.
SOMA
Golden Gate Ave.
Fulton St.
Masonic Ave.
Howard St.
Folsom St.
Harrison St.
Bryant St.
Brannan St.
Townsend St.
Alamo Square
Fell St.
9th St.
10th St.
7th St.
WESTERN ADDITION
HAIGHT-ASHBURY
Buena Vista Park
Central Skyway
Duboce Ave.
Clayton St.
Castro St.
Potrero Ave.
Central Basin
17th St.
Mariposa St.
Dolores Park
MISSION
Harrison St.
Pennsylvania Ave.
Indiana St.
3rd St.
Market St.
CASTRO
20th St.
POTRERO
Dolores St.
Guerrero St.
Mission St.
Van Ness Ave.
San Francisco General Hospital
Twin Peaks
25th St.
Army St.
Islais Cr. Channel
Diamond St.
India Basin
Oakdale Ave.
Bosworth St.
Monterey Blvd.
Fwy.
Quesada Ave.
Hunter's Point
Silver Ave.
Southern
GLEN PARK
Felton Ave.
Balboa Park
Ave.
Alemany Blvd.
Excelsior Ave.
3rd St.
San Jose Ave.
Mission St.
Persia Ave.
Moscow St.
John McLaren Park
Mansell St.
Gilman Ave.
Jamestown Ave.
South Basin
Geneva Ave.
France Ave.
Cow Palace
Candlestick Park

hanging garden. In front of the hotel is **Justin Herman Plaza,** site of frequent arts-and-crafts shows and political rallies.

North Beach and Telegraph Hill

Washington Square is the heart of North Beach, which was once considered Little Italy, though nowadays the elderly Italian men who come here to take in the sun share the park benches with Chinese matrons. Across from the park is the Romanesque **Sts. Peter and Paul Cathedral,** with its double-turreted terra-cotta towers.

The streets surrounding the cathedral are packed with Italian delicatessens and bakeries, coffeehouses, and, increasingly, Chinese markets. Cafés are the arteries of North Beach, and the aroma of fresh roasted coffee permeates the air.

Telegraph Hill, which rises to the east of North Beach, provides some of the best views in town. From Filbert Street, the Greenwich Stairs climb to **Coit Tower,** a monument to the city's volunteer firemen. Inside are the works of 25 muralists, most notably the great Mexican painter Diego Rivera. From the top there's a panoramic view of the bay, bridges, and islands.

The Northern Waterfront and Fisherman's Wharf

Fisherman's Wharf and the waterfront are at the end of the Powell-Hyde cable-car line from Union Square. From the cable-car turnaround, the **National Maritime Museum** (foot of Polk St., ☎ 415/556–3002) and Ghirardelli Square are to the west; Fisherman's Wharf and piers 39 and 41 are to the east. The **Red and White Fleet** (Pier 41, ☎ 415/546–2628) and the **Blue and Gold Fleet** (Pier 39, ☎ 415/781–7877) offer bay cruises.

Ghirardelli Square (North Point, between Polk and Larkin Sts.) is a complex of renovated 19th-century factory buildings that once housed the famous chocolate maker; it is now filled with a variety of shops (including one that sells Ghirardelli chocolates), cafés, restaurants, and galleries. Just east of the Hyde Street Pier is the **Cannery** (2801 Leavenworth St.). Built in 1894 for the Del Monte Fruit and Vegetable Cannery, it now houses shops, restaurants, and the **Museum of the City of San Francisco** (☎ 415/928–0289).

Just south of the waterfront area, between Hyde and Leavenworth streets, is that famous stretch of **Lombard Street** known as "the crookedest street in the world." This series of sharp switchbacks was designed to compensate for the steep grade.

Pier 39, already the most popular of San Francisco's waterfront destinations for its shopping and entertainment options, opens a new attraction in 1996: **Underwater World at Pier 39.** Moving walkways will transport visitors through a space surrounded on three sides by water filled with marine life indigenous to the Bay Area—from fish and plankton to sharks.

To the west of the waterfront area, at the edge of the Marina district, is the rosy, rococo **Palace of Fine Arts** (Baker and Beach Sts.), with massive columns, an imposing rotunda, and a swan-filled lagoon. Built for the 1915 Panama–Pacific International Exposition, the city's semiofficial celebration of its rebuilding after the earthquake, the palace is a cherished San Francisco landmark. Inside is the **Exploratorium** (☎ 415/561–0360), whose imaginative, interactive exhibits have made it one of the best science museums in the world.

To reach the **Golden Gate Bridge** from here, walk along the bay or take MUNI Bus 28 to the toll plaza. Nearly 2 mi long, the bridge looks serene and airy, yet it's tough enough to withstand 100 mph winds. Even when conditions are gusty and misty (as they frequently are), a walk across the bridge offers unparalleled views of the skyline, the bay, the Marin County headlands, and the Pacific Ocean.

Golden Gate Park and the Western Shore

Golden Gate Park, in the northwest part of town, is ideal for strolling, especially on Sunday, when it is closed to car traffic. A cluster of museums in its eastern section includes the **M. H. de Young Memorial Museum** (☏ 415/863–3330), with American art; adjoining it are the galleries of the **Asian Art Museum** (☏ 415/668–8921). The **California Academy of Sciences** (☏ 415/750–7145), a natural-history museum, is excellent. The **Steinhart Aquarium** (☏ 415/750–7145) features a cylindrical 100,000-gallon tank, the Fish Roundabout, which is home to 14,000 creatures and a coral reef. The **Strybing Arboretum** (☏ 415/661–0668) features Californian, Australian, Mediterranean, and South African plants. A long walk west brings you to Ocean Beach and the Pacific. At the north end of the beach is **Cliff House** (1066 Point Lobos Ave., ☏ 415/386–3330), a restaurant where you can dine to the sound of crashing surf.

What to See and Do with Children

In **Golden Gate Park** (*see* Exploring San Francisco, *above*), the playground has a vintage carousel, and the **Steinhart Aquarium** has a "Touching Tide Pool." The **Exploratorium** in the Palace of Fine Arts (*see* Exploring San Francisco, *above*) is wonderful for children. **Pier 39** (at the eastern end of North Point St. at the Embarcadero) has a carousel, roving entertainment, food stalls, and a population of noisy sea lions that bask on the north side of the pier from time to time. Another good bet is the **San Francisco Zoo** (Sloat Blvd. at Great Hwy., ☏ 415/753–7083), at the south end of Ocean Beach.

Shopping

Shopping is a primary activity in San Francisco, where choices include everything from the most elegant boutiques and department stores to discount outlets and vintage-clothing stores.

Shopping Districts

Union Square is flanked by such department stores as **Macy's, Saks Fifth Avenue,** and **Neiman Marcus,** with **Tiffany & Co.** (252 Grant Ave.) and **Brooks Brothers** (201 Post St.) nearby.

Fisherman's Wharf is the hub of waterfront shopping and sightseeing attractions: **Pier 39, Ghirardelli Square,** and the **Cannery** (*see* Exploring San Francisco, *above*) offer shops, restaurants, a festive atmosphere, a view of the bay, and cable-car access.

Jackson Square, a preserve of beautiful Victorian town houses, also features a dozen or so of San Francisco's finest antiques dealers. The **Embarcadero Center** and **Chinatown** (*see* Exploring San Francisco, *above*) are nearby.

The area south of Market (**SoMa,** *see* Exploring, *above*), just below the Financial District, is packed with discount outlets in warehouses wedged between hip restaurants and art galleries. On Saturday, the factory outlets between 2nd, 10th, Townsend, and Howard streets open their doors to the public, offering discounts of as much as 50%. In the **660 Factory Outlets Center** (660 3rd St.) alone, there are two floors of shops.

The **Haight-Ashbury** district attracts a lot of visitors who want a look into the flower-power past. Gentrification has changed the area—the virtual world headquarters of hippiedom in the '60s—and there are now some interesting shops, particularly on the 1500 block of Haight Street.

Specialty Stores

ANTIQUES

Paris 1925 (1954 Union St., ☎ 415/567–1925) specializes in jewelry and vintage watches. **Telegraph Hill Antiques** (580 Union St., ☎ 415/982–7055) features artwork, china and porcelain, bronzes, crystal, and Victoriana. (*See also* Jackson Square in Shopping Districts, *above.*)

ART

Vorpal Gallery (393 Grove St., ☎ 415/397–9200) exhibits graphic arts, postmodern paintings, drawings, and sculpture.

BOOKS

City Lights (261 Columbus Ave., ☎ 415/362–8193), stomping ground of the 1960s Beat poets, is well stocked with poetry, contemporary literature and music, and translations of Third World literature.

CLOTHING

Gianni Versace (Post and Kearny Sts.) has boutiques for men (☎ 415/956–7957) and women (☎ 415/956–7977) at the Crocker Galleria. **Eileen West** (2915 Sacramento St., ☎ 415/982–2275) has dresses, lingerie, and linens by this San Francisco designer.

GIFTS

Gump's (135 Post St., ☎ 415/982–1616) sells dinnerware, flatware, glassware, Asian artifacts, antiques, and furniture.

Spectator Sports

Baseball

San Francisco Giants (Candlestick Park, off U.S. 101, ☎ 415/467–8000; Apr.–Oct.). **Oakland A's** (Oakland Coliseum, off I-880 at 66th Ave., ☎ 510/638–0500; Apr.–Oct.).

Basketball

Golden State Warriors (Oakland Coliseum, tickets available through BASS, ☎ 510/762–2277; Nov.–Apr.).

Football

San Francisco 49ers (Candlestick Park, ☎ 415/468–2249; Aug.–Dec.). Games sell out far in advance.

Dining

San Francisco may have more restaurants per capita than any other American city. The Bay Area gave us "California cuisine," which uses the freshest local produce, occasional Asian flavorings, and classic French cooking techniques. This style is well represented in the city—as is every conceivable ethnic cuisine. For price ranges, see Chart 1 (A) in On the Road with Fodor's. Reservations necessary, except as noted.

$$$$ **Ernie's.** This reliable old-timer now serves light versions of French classics and some Italian dishes. As for decor, Ernie's is still steeped in the aura of Gay Nineties San Francisco. *847 Montgomery St., ☎ 415/397–5969. Jacket and tie required. AE, DC, MC, V. No lunch.*

$$$$ ★ **Masa's.** The artistry of the presentation is as important as the French cuisine in this understated, elegant, flower-filled dining spot. *Vintage Court Hotel, 648 Bush St., ☎ 415/989–7154. Reservations advised far in advance. Jacket and tie required. AE, D, DC, MC, V. Closed Sun.–Mon. and first 2 wks in Jan. No lunch.*

$$$ **Garden Court.** The classic European menu, stunning stained-glass ceiling, Ionic columns, and crystal chandeliers combine to make the ultimate old San Francisco dining experience. The Sunday brunch is extravagant. *Sheraton Palace Hotel, Market and New Montgomery Sts., ☎ 415/546–5000. Jacket and tie required. AE, D, DC, MC, V.*

$$$ **Hayes Street Grill.** Up to 15 kinds of seafood are featured each night. The fish is superbly fresh, simply grilled, and served with a choice of sauces ranging from tartar to a spicy Szechuan concoction. *320 Hayes St., ☎ 415/863–5545. AE, D, DC, MC, V. Closed some holidays. No lunch weekends.*

$$$ ★ **Postrio.** In Wolfgang Puck's open kitchen and stunning three-level bar and dining area, the food is Californian with Mediterranean and Asian overtones and emphasizes pastas, grilled seafood, and freshly baked breads. *545 Post St., ☎ 415/776–7825. Jacket and tie required. AE, D, DC, MC, V.*

$$$ ★ **Stars.** This huge dining room with a clublike ambience is the culinary temple of Jeremiah Tower, an acknowledged co-creator of California cuisine. The menu ranges from grills to ragouts to sautés—some daringly creative and some classical. *150 Redwood Alley, ☎ 415/861–7827. AE, DC, MC, V. No lunch weekends.*

$$ **Fog City Diner.** The long, narrow dining room emulates a railroad dining car. The cooking is inspired by U.S. regional cuisine. *1300 Battery St., ☎ 415/982–2000. D, DC, MC, V.*

$$ ★ **Harbor Village.** Classic Cantonese cooking, dim-sum lunches, and fresh seafood from its own tanks are the hallmarks of this very fine restaurant. *4 Embarcadero Center, ☎ 415/781–8833. Reservations advised for dinner; no reservations for weekend lunch. AE, DC, MC, V.*

$$ ★ **LuLu.** Chef Reed Hearon has brought a touch of the French–Italian Riviera to a stunningly renovated warehouse. Sharing dishes family-style is the custom here. Next door is the quieter LuLu Bis, serving prix-fixe dinners. *816 Folsom St., ☎ 415/495–5775. AE, DC, MC, V. No lunch at LuLu Bis. No lunch Sun. at LuLu.*

$ **Capp's Corner.** At this family-style trattoria, diners sit elbow-to-elbow and feast on bountiful five-course Italian dinners. *1600 Powell St., ☎ 415/989–2589. Reservations advised. AE, D, DC, MC, V. No lunch weekends.*

$ **Chevy's.** At this branch of a popular Mexican minichain, the emphasis is on the freshest ingredients and sauces. Of note are the fajitas and the grilled quail and seafood. *4th and Howard Sts., ☎ 415/543–8060. Reservations required for 8 or more. AE, MC, V.*

$ **Mifune.** Bowls of thin, brown *soba* (buckwheat) and thick, white *udon* (wheat) are the traditional Japanese specialties served at this North American outpost of an Osaka-based noodle empire. *Japan Center Building, West Wing, 1737 Post St., ☎ 415/922–2728. No reservations. AE, D, MC, V.*

Lodging

San Francisco has world-class hotels, renovated older buildings with European charm, Victorian homes transformed into bed-and-breakfasts, and representatives of most chains. Less expensive motel and hotel rooms can be found in the Civic Center and Lombard areas; truly budget accommodations are available at the **YMCA Central Branch** (220

Golden Gate Ave., ☎ 415/885–0460). For free assistance with hotel reservations try **San Francisco Reservations** (☎ 800/333–8996). For price ranges, see Chart 2 (A) in On the Road with Fodor's.

$$$$ ★ **Four Seasons Clift.** This stately landmark is one of San Francisco's most acclaimed hotels for its elegant style and service. Rooms, some rich with dark woods and burgundies, others refreshingly pastel, all have large writing desks, plants, and flowers. *495 Geary St. (Union Sq.), 94102, ☎ 415/775–4700 or 800/332–3442, FAX 415/441–4621. 329 rooms. Facilities: restaurant, lounge, exercise room, meeting rooms. AE, DC, MC, V.*

$$$$ ★ **Huntington Hotel.** Attentive, discreet service is the hallmark of this Nob Hill hotel. Rooms and suites are all individually appointed in such opulent materials as soft leathers, raw silks, and velvets. *1075 California St. (Nob Hill), 94108, ☎ 415/474–5400 or 800/227–4683; in CA, 800/652–1539; FAX 415/474–6227. 140 rooms. Facilities: restaurant, lounge. AE, D, DC, MC, V.*

$$$$ ★ **Ritz-Carlton, San Francisco.** Rated one of the top three hotels in the world by *Condé Nast Traveler,* the Ritz-Carlton is renowned for its grandeur and warm, attentive service. Rooms are elegant and spacious, and every bath is appointed with double sinks, hair dryers, and vanity tables. *600 Stockton St., at California St. (Nob Hill), 94108, ☎ 415/296–7465 or 800/241–3333, FAX 415/291–0288. 336 rooms. Facilities: 2 restaurants, 3 lounges, indoor pool, health club, shops. AE, D, DC, MC, V.*

$$$$ **Sherman House.** This magnificent landmark mansion on a low hill in residential Pacific Heights is San Francisco's most luxurious small hotel. Rooms are individually decorated with Biedermeier, English Jacobean, or French–Second Empire antiques. *2160 Green St. (Pacific Heights), 94123, ☎ 415/563–3600 or 800/424–5777, FAX 415/563–1882. 14 rooms. AE, DC, MC, V.*

$$$ ★ **Hotel Majestic.** One of the city's first grand hotels, the Majestic offers romantic rooms with French and English antiques and four-poster canopy beds. Most rooms have a fireplace. *1500 Sutter St. (Civic Ctr.), 94109, ☎ 415/441–1100 or 800/869–8966, FAX 415/673–7331. 57 rooms. Facilities: restaurant, lounge. AE, DC, MC, V.*

$$$ **Inn at the Opera.** This hotel hosts guests from the music, dance, and opera worlds. Rooms, some smallish, are decorated with creamy pastels and dark wood furnishings; the ones in the back are the quietest. *333 Fulton St. (Civic Ctr.), 94102, ☎ 415/863–8400 or 800/325–2708; in CA, 800/423–9610; FAX 415/861–0821. 48 rooms. Facilities: restaurant, lounge. AE, DC, MC, V.*

$$$ ★ **Petite Auberge.** The French countryside was imported to downtown San Francisco to create this charming, teddy-bear-festooned B&B inn. Its sister hotel next door, the White Swan, has an English-country flavor. *863 Bush St. (Union Sq.), 94108, ☎ 415/928–6000, FAX 415/775–5717. 26 rooms. AE, DC, MC, V.*

$$ **The Cartwright.** This is a family-owned hotel with a friendly, personal touch and an ideal location. Rooms have brass or carved-wood beds and small refrigerators. *524 Sutter St. (Union Sq.), 94102, ☎ 415/421–2865 or 800/227–3844, FAX 415/421–2865. 114 rooms. Facility: coffee shop. AE, D, DC, MC, V.*

$$ **King George.** Behind the George's white-and-green Victorian facade, the rooms are compact but nicely furnished in classic English style, with walnut furniture and a pastel-and-earthtone color scheme. The hotel has a reputation for conscientious service. *334 Mason St. (Union Sq.), 94102, ☎ 415/781–5050 or 800/288–6005, FAX 415/391–6976. 144 rooms. AE, D, DC, MC, V.*

$ **Adelaide Inn.** The bedspreads don't match the drapes, but the rooms are clean and cheap at this friendly small hotel popular with Europeans. *5 Isadora Duncan Ct. (off Taylor St., between Geary and Post Sts.), 94102, ☎ 415/441–2474, FAX 415/441–0161. 18 rooms with shared baths. Facilities: breakfast room, refrigerators. AE, MC, V.*

$ **Marina Inn.** Charming B&B accommodations are offered here at motel prices. English country-style rooms have private bath. Complimentary Continental breakfast is served in the central sitting room. *3110 Octavia St. (at Lombard St.), 94123, ☎ 415/928–1000 or 800/274–1420, FAX 415/928–5909. 40 rooms. Facility: lounge. AE, MC, V.*

$ ★ **San Remo Hotel.** This small European-style hotel with daily and weekly rates has tiny rooms but is tidy and pleasingly decorated. Rooms share six tiled shower rooms, one bathtub chamber, and six scrupulously clean toilets. *2237 Mason St. (near Fisherman's Wharf), 94133, ☎ 415/776–8688 or 800/352–7366, FAX 415/776–2811. 62 rooms, 1 with private bath. AE, DC, MC, V.*

The Arts and Nightlife

The best guide to arts and entertainment events in San Francisco is the pink "Datebook" section of the *Sunday Examiner-Chronicle*. The *Bay Guardian* and *S.F. Weekly*, free weeklies available throughout the city, list more neighborhood, avant-garde, and budget-priced events. **BASS** (☎ 510/762–2277) offers charge-by-phone ticket service. Half-price, same-day tickets to many stage shows go on sale at 11 AM Tuesday–Saturday at the **TIX Bay Area** (☎ 415/433–7827) ticket booth on the Stockton Street side of Union Square.

THEATER

The **American Conservatory Theater** (ticket office next to the Geary Theater, 405 Geary St., ☎ 415/749–2228), a repertory company, specializes in classics. The **Curran** (445 Geary St., ☎ 415/474–3800) hosts touring companies.

MUSIC

The **San Francisco Symphony** plays from September to May in the Louise M. Davies Symphony Hall (201 Van Ness Ave. at Grove St., ☎ 415/431–5400).

OPERA

Productions of the **San Francisco Opera** (War Memorial Opera House, 301 Van Ness Ave. at Grove St., ☎ 415/864–3330), presented from September through December, are often sold out; standing-room tickets are usually available. (Note: The SFO will move to two nearby venues in 1996, while the opera house undergoes seismic retrofitting.)

DANCE

The **San Francisco Ballet** (War Memorial Opera House, ☎ 415/703–9400) performs classical and contemporary works from February through May. (Note: The SFB will perform in several other venues in 1996, while the opera house undergoes seismic retrofitting.)

FILM

The Bay Area has a large number of first-run and revival movie theaters. The **San Francisco International Film Festival** (☎ 415/931–3456) takes place late April–early May.

Nightlife

Nob Hill is noted for its piano bars and lounges with panoramic views, **North Beach** for its bistros and dwindling topless scene, **Union Street**

for its singles scene, **South of Market** (SoMa) for its alternative clubs, and the **Castro** for gay bars.

COMEDY CLUBS

Cobb's Comedy Club (2801 Leavenworth St., at Beach St., ☎ 415/928–4320) features stand-up comedians. The **Punch Line** (444-A Battery, ☎ 415/397–7573) launched comics Jay Leno and Whoopi Goldberg.

DANCE CLUBS

DNA Lounge (375 11th St. near Harrison St., ☎ 415/626–1409), a long-time SoMa haunt, serves up alternative independent rock, funk, and rap, often live, sometimes recorded.

Metronome Ballroom (1830 17th St., ☎ 415/252–9000) is a lively yet mellow smoke- and alcohol-free Friday–Sunday spot for ballroom dancing.

JAZZ CLUBS

Jazz at Pearl's (256 Columbus Ave., ☎ 415/291–8255) is a romantic and sophisticated spot for jazz.

NIGHTCLUBS

The **Great American Music Hall** (859 O'Farrell St., ☎ 415/885–0750), one of the country's great eclectic nightclubs, has top blues, folk, jazz, and rock entertainers; it also books top comics.

ROCK CLUBS

Bottom of the Hill (1233 17th St., at Texas St., ☎ 415/626–4455) showcases alternative rock and blues. **Slim's** (333 11th St., ☎ 415/621–3330) specializes in basic rock, jazz, and blues.

FOR SINGLES

The **Balboa Cafe** (3199 Fillmore St., ☎ 415/921–3944) is a yuppie hangout famous for its burgers. The **Hard Rock Cafe** (1699 Van Ness Ave., ☎ 415/885–1699) features the usual rock-and-roll motif. **Johnny Love's** (1500 Broadway, ☎ 415/931–8021) is a restaurant and singles scene that often hosts good jazz and blues.

GAY AND LESBIAN NIGHTLIFE

San Francisco's large and active gay/lesbian community supports a multitude of bars, comedy clubs, cabarets, and discos. Check the *San Francisco Bay Times* (☎ 415/626–8121) or *Odyssey* (☎ 415/621–6514) for the latest one-night-a-week clubs. On Thursdays, the **Box** (at City Nights, 715 Harrison St., ☎ 415/647–8258) has house, hip-hop, and funk sounds for a mixed gay/lesbian crowd. The cozy **Elephant Walk** (Castro and 18th Sts., no ☎) is one of few Castro area bars where the music level allows for conversation. The **End Up** (6th and Harrison Sts., ☎ 415/543–7700), with a spacious dance floor and an open-air courtyard, hosts several popular gay and lesbian one-night clubs. At the **Midnight Sun** (4067 18th St., ☎ 415/861–4186), giant video screens play nightly to a packed house.

Excursions from San Francisco

Berkeley and Oakland

Berkeley is the home of the 178-acre **University of California at Berkeley,** a center of student protests in the 1960s. Along Telegraph Avenue south of the campus is a student-oriented business district with a dog-eared counterculture ambience. Food lovers will want to head for that cradle of California cuisine, **Chez Panisse Cafe & Restaurant** (1517 Shattuck Ave., ☎ 510/548–5525; closed Sun.). In the elegantly appointed redwood-paneled dining room downstairs and the less pricey and more informal café upstairs, Alice Waters masterminds the culinary wizardry and Jean-Pierre Moullé performs as head chef, together producing such treats as roast truffled breast of guinea hen and a variety of distinctive pasta dishes.

Oakland has long been viewed as a warmer and more spacious alternative to San Francisco, and many residents commute to work across the bay from vintage houses in Oakland's hillside neighborhoods. It is also an important industrial town and the second-largest port in California. The revitalized Jack London Square, waterfront, and downtown area have attracted long-overdue attention to the city. The **Oakland Museum** (1000 Oak St., ☏ 510/834–2413; admission charged) displays Californian art, history, and natural sciences through engaging exhibits and films.

GETTING THERE

By car, follow I–80 across the Bay Bridge; exit at University Avenue for Berkeley, or pick up I–580 and exit at Grand Avenue for Oakland. By BART, Berkeley is 45 minutes to an hour from the city; exit at the downtown Berkeley stop, then take the shuttle to the campus. Oakland is a 45-minute BART ride from San Francisco; exit at the Lake Merritt station for the museum.

Sausalito

This hillside town on Richardson Bay, an inlet of San Francisco Bay in Marin County, feels at once like an artist colony and something out of the Mediterranean with its usually sunny weather, resort-town ambience, yacht harbor, and superb views of the Richardson and San Francisco bays. The main street, Bridgeway, has waterfront restaurants on one side and shops, hotels, and residential neighborhoods climbing the wooded hills on the other. At the south end is an esplanade with expansive views. The **Village Fair** (777 Bridgeway), just behind the marina, is a four-story former warehouse that has been converted into a warren of clothing, crafts, and gift boutiques. Along the northern shores of Richardson Bay are some of the 400 houseboats that make up Sausalito's famous **"floating-homes community."**

GETTING THERE

By car, cross the Golden Gate Bridge and drive north a few miles to the Sausalito exit. **Golden Gate Ferry** (☏ 415/332–6600) and the **Red and White Fleet** (☏ 415/546–2628) cruise regularly from the Embarcadero and Fisherman's Wharf on breathtaking 30-minute trips to (and from) the island.

THE WINE COUNTRY

California's Napa and Sonoma counties produce some of the world's finest wines. In the Napa Valley, every inch of soil is in the service of one of the 200 or so local wineries, and traffic on the two-lane stretch of Hwy. 29 from Napa to Calistoga slows to a crawl on weekends, when visitors jam the gift shops and restaurants. In Sonoma County, the pace is less frenetic. The wineries in both counties range from charming and rustic to palatial and high-tech, but the land that surrounds them is consistently striking.

Tourist Information

Napa Valley: Conference and Visitors Bureau (1310 Napa Town Center, 94559, ☏ 707/226–7459). **St. Helena:** Chamber of Commerce (1080 Main St., Box 124, 94574, ☏ 707/963–4456 or 800/767–8528).

Sonoma County: Convention and Visitor's Bureau (5000 Roberts Lake Rd., Rohnert Park 94928, ☎ 707/586–8100 or 800/326–7666). **Russian River Wine Road** (Box 46, Healdsburg 95448, ☎ 707/433–6782).

Getting There

By Plane

The San Francisco and Oakland airports (*see* San Francisco, *above*), served by most major carriers, are just over an hour's drive away.

By Car

Although traffic on the two-lane country roads can be heavy, the best way to get around the Wine Country is by car. There are three major paths through the area: U.S. 101 north from Santa Rosa, Hwys. 12 and 121 through Sonoma County, and Hwy. 29 north from Napa. From San Francisco, cross the Golden Gate Bridge and follow U.S. 101 to Santa Rosa and head north, or take the exit east on Hwy. 37 and north on Hwy. 121 into Sonoma. Another route runs over San Francisco's Bay Bridge and along I–80 to Vallejo, where you can pick up Hwy. 29 north to Napa.

By Train

The **Napa Valley Wine Train** (☎ 707/253–2111 or 800/522–4142; in CA only, 800/427–4124) serves lunch, dinner, and a weekend brunch on a restored Pullman car as it runs between Napa and St. Helena.

By Bus

Greyhound Lines (☎ 800/231–2222) runs buses from the Transbay Terminal at 1st and Mission streets to Sonoma and Santa Rosa. **Sonoma County Area Transit** (☎ 707/585–7516) and **Napa Valley Transit** (☎ 707/255–7631) provide local transportation.

Exploring the Wine Country

Napa

Along Hwy. 29 north of the town of **Napa** toward Calistoga are some of California's most important wineries. In Yountville is **Domaine Chandon,** owned by Moët-Hennessey and Louis Vuitton. You can take a tour or sample flutes of the luxurious sparkling wine made by the *méthode champenoise* for $3–$4 a glass. *California Dr.,* ☎ *707/944–2280. Closed Mon.–Tues., Nov.–Apr., major holidays.*

Many wineries are between Yountville and St. Helena. At **Robert Mondavi** (7801 St. Helena Hwy., Oakville, ☎ 707/259–9463), the 60-minute tour is encouraged before imbibing. The wine at **V. Sattui** (111 White La., St. Helena, ☎ 707/963–7774) is only sold on the premises; the tactic draws crowds, as does the huge gourmet delicatessen with its exotic cheeses and pâtés.

Calistoga, at the valley's north end, was founded as a spa and remains notable for its mineral water, hot mineral springs, mud baths, steam baths, and massages. **Dr. Wilkinson's Hot Springs** (1507 Lincoln Ave., ☎ 707/942–4102; reservations recommended) offers all of these services.

The **Silverado Trail** runs parallel to Hwy. 29 north of Napa. It leads to some distinguished wineries: **Clos du Val** (5330 Silverado Trail, ☎ 707/259–2200), **Stag's Leap Wine Cellars** (5766 Silverado Trail, ☎ 707/944–2020), and, just off the Trail, the **Rutherford Hill Winery** (200 Rutherford Hill Rd., ☎ 707/963–7194).

Sonoma

East of U.S. 101 and west of the Napa Valley, Hwy. 12 runs through the hills of Sonoma County. In the town of **Sonoma** is the landmark **Buena Vista Carneros Winery** (18000 Old Winery Rd., ☎ 707/938–1266), where California wine making got its start in 1857. Today the wines are produced elsewhere, but there are tours, a gourmet shop, an art gallery, a wine museum, and great picnic spots.

The wineries off U.S. 101 in Sonoma County are located along winding side roads. For a historic overview, start at the imposing **Korbel Champagne Cellars** (13250 River Rd., Guerneville, ☎ 707/887–2294), housed in a former railway station. The **Hop Kiln Winery** (6050 Westside Rd., Healdsburg, ☎ 707/433–6491) is located in a hops-drying barn that dates from the early 1900s. **Lytton Springs Winery** (650 Lytton Springs Rd., Healdsburg, ☎ 707/433–7721) produces Sonoma Zinfandel, a dark, fruity wine with a high alcohol content.

What to See and Do with Children

Old Faithful Geyser of California (1299 Tubbs La., 1 mi north of Calistoga, ☎ 707/942–6463) is a 60-ft tower of steam and vapor that erupts every 40 minutes or so. At the **Petrified Forest** (4100 Petrified Forest Rd., 5 mi west of Calistoga, ☎ 707/942–6667) you'll see the effects of volcanic eruptions from Mt. St. Helena that occurred 3.4 million years ago. Most wineries permit children on tours, though anyone under 21 may not sample wines.

Shopping

Most wineries will ship purchases, but don't expect bargains. Area supermarkets stock a wide selection of local wines at lower prices.

Sports and the Outdoors

Hot-Air Ballooning

This sport has become part of the scenery in the Wine Country. Many hotels arrange excursions, or contact **Balloons Above the Valley** (☎ 707/253–2222) or **Napa Valley Balloons** (☎ 707/944–0228 or 800/253–2224).

Dining and Lodging

For price ranges, see Charts 1 (A) and 2 (A) in On the Road with Fodor's. Reservations are strongly advised at the dining spots listed below.

Calistoga

DINING

All Seasons Cafe. This sun-filled bistro serves a seasonal menu accented with organic greens, wild mushrooms, local game, house-smoked beef, and salmon coupled with a superb listing of local wines at bargain prices. *1400 Lincoln Ave., ☎ 707/942–9111. MC, V. Closed Wed. $$–$$$*

LODGING

Mountain Home Ranch. This rustic ranch, established in 1913, is set on 300 wooded acres, with hiking trails, a creek, and a fishing lake. It has just one TV and no ☎s. *3400 Mountain Home Ranch Rd., 94515, ☎ 707/942–6616, FAX 707/942–9091. 6 rooms, 11 cabins. Facilities: 2 pools, tennis court. MC, V. Closed Dec.–Jan. $$*

Rutherford

DINING

★ **Auberge du Soleil.** The dining terrace of this hilltop inn, looking down across groves of olive trees to the Napa Valley vineyards, is the closest you can get to the atmosphere, charm, and cuisine of southern France without a passport. *180 Rutherford Hill Rd., ☎ 707/963–1211. Jacket and tie advised. AE, D, MC, V. $$$$*

St. Helena

LODGING

Meadowood Resort. Set on 256 wooded acres is this rambling country lodge, with separate five-suite bungalows and smaller lodges clustered on the hillside. The decor is New England seashore, and some rooms have fireplaces. *900 Meadowood La., 94574, ☎ 707/963–3646 or 800/458–8080, FAX 707/963–3532. 82 rooms. Facilities: 2 restaurants, bar, room service, 2 pools, hot tub, massage, sauna, steam room, 9-hole golf course, 7 tennis courts, croquet, health club. AE, D, DC, MC, V. $$$$*

Santa Rosa

DINING

★ **John Ash & Co.** The chef emphasizes presentation, innovation, and freshness and uses mainly seasonal foods grown in Sonoma County. The two-level dining room overlooks vineyards. *4430 Barnes Rd., ☎ 707/527–7687. Jacket advised. AE, MC, V. Closed Mon. $$$*

Sonoma

LODGING

Thistle Dew Inn. Half a block from Sonoma Plaza, this Victorian inn features collector-quality arts-and-crafts furnishings and antique quilts. Welcome bonuses include a hot tub and free use of the inn's bicycles. *171 W. Spain St., 95476, ☎ 707/938–2909 or 800/382–7895. 6 rooms. AE, MC, V. $$$*

Yountville

DINING

★ **Mustard's Grill.** Grilled fish, steak, local fresh produce, and an impressive selection of wines are offered in an unassuming, usually crowded dining room. *7399 St. Helena Hwy., ☎ 707/944–2424. D, DC, MC, V. $$$*

ELSEWHERE IN NORTHERN CALIFORNIA

The Gold Country

Getting There

Sacramento Metropolitan Airport (☎ 916/929–5411) is served by most major domestic airlines. **Greyhound** (☎ 800/231–2222) serves Sacramento, Auburn, Grass Valley, and Placerville from San Francisco. The most convenient way to see the area is by car, since few towns have public transportation. I–80 intersects with Hwy. 49, the main route through the region, at Auburn; U.S. 50 intersects with Hwy. 49 at Placerville.

What to See and Do

When gold was discovered at **Coloma** in 1848, people came from everywhere in the world to get some, and when the rush was over California was a very different place. Today, clustered along Hwy. 49 are restored villages and ghost towns, antiques shops, crafts stores, and vineyards.

The heart of the Gold Country lies on Hwy. 49 between Nevada City and Jamestown. In **Nevada City** is the 1865 **Nevada Theatre,** California's oldest in continuous use. In **Grass Valley** is the **Empire Mine** (10791 E. Empire St., ☎ 916/273–8522; admission charged), now a state park with exhibits on gold mining. The **Marshall Discovery State Historical Park** (☎ 916/622–3470; admission $5 per car), 8 mi north of Placerville on Hwy. 49, has a replica of **Sutter's Mill,** where it all started. In **Columbia State Historic Park** (☎ 209/532–4301) you can ride a stagecoach, pan for gold, or watch a blacksmith working at his anvil. The **Railtown 1897 State Historic Park** (☎ 209/984–3953) in **Jamestown** includes 26 acres of trains, a station, and a roundhouse.

Sacramento, the California state capital, is the largest Gold Country city. The **Visitor Information Center** (1104 Front St., ☎ 916/442–7777) in the city's Old Town will key you in to such attractions as the **Discovery Museum** (101 I St., ☎ 916/264–7057) and the **California State Railroad Museum** (125 I St., ☎ 916/448–4466), which displays 21 restored locomotives and railroad cars.

Lake Tahoe

Getting There

Reno-Tahoe International Airport, 58 mi northeast of the lake, is used by national and regional airlines (*see* Nevada). **Lake Tahoe Airport** on Hwy. 50, 3 mi south of the lakeshore, is served by **Transworld Express,** which flies from Los Angeles and San Francisco. **Amtrak** (☎ 800/872–7245) and **Greyhound Lines** (800/231–2222) also serve the area. **South Tahoe Area Ground Express** (☎ 916/573–2080) and **Tahoe Area Regional Transit** (☎ 916/581–6365) offer local buses. The 198 mi northeast of San Francisco can be driven in about four hours. The major route is I–80 through the Sierra Nevada; U.S. 50 from Sacramento is the direct route to the south shore. Caution: Tire chains are sometimes necessary in winter.

What to See and Do

Visitors to Lake Tahoe's California side, where gambling isn't legal, come here to ski, hike, fish, camp, and boat in the spectacular mountains 6,000 ft above sea level in the High Sierra. Ski resorts, such as Incline Village and Squaw Valley, open at the end of November and operate as late as May, when the U.S. Forest Service's **Lake Tahoe Visitors Center** (☎ 916/573–2674) opens on the south shore. Tourist information is also provided at the **Lake Tahoe Visitors Authority** (☎ 916/544–5050 or 800/288–2463).

The 72-mi shoreline is best seen along a route through wooded flatlands and past beaches, climbing to vistas on the rugged west side of the lake. It should take about three hours but can be slow going in summer and on holiday weekends.

Past South Lake Tahoe, where the shore route becomes Hwy. 89, is the **Pope-Baldwin Recreation Area** (☎ 916/541–5227), where three grand century-old mansions are open to the public. The **Lake Tahoe Visitors Center** (☎ 916/573–2674) on Taylor Creek is also near the site of a onetime Washoe Indian settlement, and there are trails through meadow, marsh, and forest. **Emerald Bay** is famed for its jewellike shape and color.

The ***Tahoe Queen*** (☎ 916/541–3364), a glass-bottom stern-wheeler, cruises on the lake and visits Emerald Bay year-round from Ski Run marina, off U.S. 50 in South Lake Tahoe. Beyond Emerald Bay is **D. L. Bliss State Park** (☎ 916/525–7277), with 6 mi of shorefront and 268 family campsites. At Tahoe City, Hwy. 89 turns north to **Squaw Valley,** site of the 1960 Winter Olympics.

THE CENTRAL COAST

From San Francisco south for several hundred miles, the California coastline shows off its beauty and power. Raging surf splashing rugged rocks, hidden tidal pools, and wind-warped trees mark the journey. Several towns provide entertainment, but the Pacific Ocean dominates. Coast-hugging Hwy. 1, sometimes precariously narrow, is the route of choice; it's slow and winding, but the surpassingly beautiful views make considerations of time seem unimportant.

Tourist Information

Monterey Peninsula Chamber of Commerce (Box 1770, 380 Alvarado St., Monterey 93942, ☎ 408/649–1770). **Visitor Information Center** (1 Santa Barbara St. at Cabrillo Blvd., Santa Barbara, ☎ 805/965–3021).

Getting There

By Plane

Monterey Peninsula Airport (☎ 408/648–7000) and **Santa Barbara Municipal Airport** (☎ 805/683–4011) are served by airlines including American Eagle, United, United Express, and Skywest.

By Car

Driving Hwy. 1 along the coast offers the richest rewards. U.S. 101 can be taken to Salinas, from which Hwy. 68 goes to Monterey. From San Francisco, I–280 connects with Hwy. 17 just south of San Jose and gets you to the coast near Santa Cruz.

By Train

Amtrak's *Coast Starlight* makes stops in Santa Barbara, San Luis Obispo, and Salinas on its run from Los Angeles to Seattle.

Exploring the Central Coast

As you pick up Hwy. 1 heading south out of San Francisco, you'll be driving along a clifftop past long beaches and coves on your right and artichoke and pumpkin fields on your left. About 75 mi south of the city is the seaside and college town of **Santa Cruz,** with an old-time boardwalk and an amusement park where one of the last clackety wooden roller coasters still dips and dives.

About an hour south of Santa Cruz, the Monterey Peninsula curves into the Pacific, with seaside forests of gnarled Monterey cypress. The town of **Monterey** is rich in California history. Its "Path of History" is a 2-mi self-guided tour through **Monterey State Historic Park** (☎ 408/649–7118). **Custom House,** built by the Mexican government in 1827 and believed to be the oldest government building west of the Rockies, is a logical starting place. The next stop along the path is the **Pacific House** (☎ 408/649–2907), a former hotel and saloon that is now a museum of early California life displaying gold-rush relics, historic photographs, and a costume gallery.

Inevitably, visitors are drawn toward Monterey's waterfront, if only because of the barking of sea lions. They're best seen along **Fisherman's Wharf,** an aging and touristy pier that children enjoy. From the wharf, a footpath leads to **Cannery Row,** where the old tin-roof canneries made famous by John Steinbeck's book have been converted into restaurants, art galleries, and minimalls. The **Monterey Bay Aquarium** (886 Cannery Row, ☎ 408/648–4888 or, in CA, 800/756–3737) is a window on the sea waters beyond. Among standout exhibits are a three-story Kelp Forest, a bat-ray petting pool, a 55,000-gallon sea-otter tank, and an enormous outdoor artificial tide pool. A new wing, the first floor of which is scheduled to open in March 1996, will be devoted to open-ocean and deep-sea habitats.

The celebrated **17-Mile Drive** offers a chance to explore an 8,400-acre microcosm of the coastal landscape around Monterey and neighboring Carmel. This is where you'll find the **Lone Cypress,** a weather-sculpted tree on a rocky outcrop above the waves. On **Seal Rock** and **Bird Rock,** just offshore, you can watch the creatures sunning themselves en masse. Also along the drive is the famous **Pebble Beach Golf Links.**

Carmel is a quaint village where buildings have no street numbers and live music is banned in the local watering holes. Before it became an art colony in the early 20th century and long before it became a shopping mecca, Carmel was an important religious center for Spanish California. Mission San Carlos Borromeo del Rio Carmelo, or the **Carmel Mission** (Rio Rd. and Lasuen Dr., ☎ 408/624–3600), was founded in 1770 and served as headquarters for the mission system. Its stone buildings and tower dome have been beautifully restored, and a tranquil garden is nearby. Another example of Carmel's architectural heritage is the poet Robinson Jeffers's wondrous **Tor House** (26304 Ocean View Ave., ☎ 408/624–1813). The stone cottage is handmade, as is the abutting Hawk tower, set with stones from Carmel's coastline and even one from the Great Wall of China. The town's greatest beauty is in the rugged coastline and surrounding cypress forests, best seen at **Carmel River State Park** (off Scenic Rd., south of Carmel Beach and the larger **Point Lobos State Reserve** (☎ 408/624–4909 for both), a 1,250-acre headland just south of Carmel. At the latter, the Sea Lion Point Trail is a good spot to observe sea lions, otters, harbor seals, and seasonally migrating whales.

Another sort of migration takes place in the adjacent town of **Pacific Grove,** where each year (Oct.–Mar.) orange-and-black monarch butterflies take up residence in the pine and eucalyptus groves and hang from branches like fluttering veils.

Travel 13 mi south of Carmel for the quintessential view of California's coast from the elegant concrete arch of **Bixby Creek Bridge.** Just south of it, the **Point Sur Light Station,** atop a sandstone cliff, heralds the beginning of **Big Sur.** One of the few places where you can actually reach the water is **Pfeiffer Beach** (follow the road just past the Big Sur Ranger Station for 2 mi); at the foot of the cliffs are huge, picturesque sea-washed rocks, one with a hole cut through it by the waves. On the ocean side of Hwy. 1, set high above the waves, is the restaurant **Nepenthe** (*see* Dining and Lodging, *below*). A few miles south, at the **Julia Pfeiffer Burns State Park** (☎ 408/667–2315), a trail leads up a small valley to a waterfall; the park also offers picnic and camping areas, as well as beach access.

About 30 mi south on Hwy. 1, **Hearst Castle,** officially known as the Hearst San Simeon State Historical Monument, reigns in solitary splendor. Buses take you up the hill to newspaper magnate William Randolph Hearst's grandiose mansion, which has extravagant marble halls, lush swimming pools, and an extensive art collection. Begun in 1919 and never officially completed (work stopped in 1947), this grand place was meant not only as a residence but as a showcase for Hearst's magnificent collection of European art and antiquities. *Reservations usually required: ☎ 805/927–2020 or 800/444–4445. Admission: day tours $14 adults, $8 children 6–12, under 6 free; evening sunset tours $25 adults, $13 children 6–12, under 6 free. Tours daily 8:20 AM–3 PM (later in summer); tours most Fri. and Sat. evenings Mar.–May and Sept.–Dec. Reservations may be made up to 8 wks in advance. AE, D, MC, V.*

The coastal ribbon of Hwy. 1 ends at **Morro Bay. Morro Rock,** with the sheltered harbor on one side and the Pacific surf on the other, is a preserve for peregrine falcons. At **San Luis Obispo,** just south, halfway between San Francisco and Los Angeles, are such historic sites as the 1772 **Mission San Luis Obispo de Tolosa** (☎ 805/543–6850) downtown. Drop by the garish, goofy **Madonna Inn** (100 Madonna Rd., off U.S. 101, ☎ 805/543–3000) if only for a drink and a look at the bar's gilt cherubs and pink bar stools.

Santa Barbara has long been a weekend getaway and second-home retreat for the wealthy and celebrated from Los Angeles. Nestled between the hills and the ocean, the town is blessed with a temperate climate, is bursting with flowers, and seems like the most relaxed place in the world. It also retains its Spanish character, with wide tree-shaded streets, red-tile-roofed arcades downtown, and courtyards filled with upscale boutiques and restaurants. The landmark **Mission Santa Barbara** (2201 Laguna St., ☎ 805/682–4713), which inspired much of the downtown architecture, is set in the hills above town. Downtown are the Spanish-Moorish–style **Santa Barbara Courthouse** (1100 Anacapa St., ☎ 805/962–6464), adorned with scenic murals from Hollywood's heyday; the Spanish-style **Santa Barbara Public Library** (40 E. Anapamu St.); the **Santa Barbara Museum of Art** (1130 State St., ☎ 805/963–4364), whose collections include Greek and Roman antiquities and paintings by Grandma Moses; **El Presidio State Historic Park** (123 E. Cañon Perdido St., ☎ 805/966–9719), a military stronghold built by the Spanish in 1782; and **El Paseo** (State and De la Guerra Sts.), a shopping arcade built around an old adobe home. Along the waterfront, not far from downtown, is **Stearns Wharf** (Cabrillo Blvd. at State St.), a pier holding shops, eateries, and the Museum of Natural History's **Sea Center,** which features a display of marine life. Just north of town, with 65 acres of native plants, is the **Santa Barbara Botanic Garden** (1212 Mission Canyon Rd., ☎ 805/682–4726).

What to See and Do with Children

The **Monterey Bay Aquarium** (*see* Exploring the Central Coast, *above*) will entertain most children, as will the **boardwalk and amusement park** in Santa Cruz. The **Santa Barbara Zoo** (500 Niños Dr., ☎ 805/962–6310) has a scenic railroad and a barnyard petting zoo. At Santa Barbara's East Beach is an elaborate **jungle-gym area.**

Shopping

In Monterey and Carmel you'll find many art galleries and shops selling arts and crafts by local artists. Among the artists whose work is shown at **Photography West Gallery** (Ocean Ave. and Dolores St., Carmel, ☎ 408/625–1587) is Ansel Adams, who resided nearby for many years. Santa Barbara's downtown **State Street** is a shopping mecca; the open-air **Paseo Nuevo** mall (700 and 800 blocks of State St.) houses upscale boutiques and larger stores. Many antiques shops are clustered in Victorian buildings on State and nearby **Brinkerhoff Avenue.**

Sports and the Outdoors

Biking

The Monterey Peninsula is prime biking territory, with paths following some of the choicest parts of the shoreline; rentals are available from **Bay Bikes** (640 Wave St., Monterey, ☎ 408/646–9090). In Santa Barbara, the **Cabrillo Bike Lane** passes the city zoo, a bird refuge, beaches, and the harbor; rent bikes, quadricycles, and skates from **Beach Rentals** (8 W. Cabrillo Blvd., ☎ 805/966–6733).

Fishing

Charter boats leave from Monterey, Morro Bay, and Santa Barbara. Most fishing trips—from such outfits as **Monterey Sport Fishing** (96 Fisherman's Wharf, Monterey, ☎ 408/372–2203) or **SEA Landing** (Cabrillo Blvd. at Bath, Santa Barbara, ☎ 805/963–3564)—include equipment rental, bait, fish cleaning, and a one-day license.

Golf

Pebble Beach Golf Links (17-Mile Dr., ☎ 408/625–8518; reservations essential), with its sweeping ocean views, is one of the world's most famous courses. At nearby **Spyglass Hill** (Spyglass Hill Rd., ☎ 408/624–3811), the holes are unforgiving, but the views offer consolation. In Santa Barbara are the **Santa Barbara Golf Club** (Las Positas Rd. and McCaw Ave., ☎ 805/687–7087) and **Sandpiper Golf Course** (7925 Hollister Ave., Goleta, ☎ 805/968–1541).

Whale-Watching

On their annual migration between the Bering Sea and Baja California, 45-ft gray whales can be spotted at many points not far off the coast. The migration south takes place from December through February; the journey north, from late February to mid-May.

Beaches

In general, the shoreline north of San Luis Obispo is rocky and backed by cliffs, the water rough and often cold, and sunbathing limited to only the warmest hours of the early afternoon. Still, the boardwalk at **Santa Cruz, Point Lobos State Reserve** in lower Monterey Bay, **Big Sur,** and **Morro Bay** provide unparalleled beach experiences. **Pismo Beach** marks the first of the classic southern California beaches, with long, low stretches of sand. The shoreline from **Point Concepcion** down through Santa Barbara and into Ventura County contains some of the best beaches anywhere.

Near Santa Barbara, **East Beach** has lifeguards, volleyball courts, a jogging-and-biking trail, a jungle-gym play area, and a bathhouse with a gym, showers, and changing rooms. **Arroyo Burro Beach,** just west of Santa Barbara, is a state preserve, with a small grassy area with picnic tables and sandy beaches below the cliffs. West of Santa Barbara on Hwy. 1 are **El Capitan, Refugio,** and **Gaviota** state beaches, each with campsites, picnic tables, and fire pits. East of the city is the state beach at **Carpinteria,** a sheltered, sunny, and often crowded beach.

Dining and Lodging

For price ranges, see Charts 1 (A) and 2 (A) in On the Road with Fodor's. Dining reservations advised, except as noted.

Big Sur

DINING

Nepenthe. The 800-ft-high cliff site, overlooking lush meadows and the ocean, was once owned by Orson Welles. The food is adequate—from roast chicken with sage to sandwiches and hamburgers—but it's the location that warrants a stop. *Hwy. 1, south end of town, ☎ 408/667–2345. Reservations required for large parties. AE, MC, V. $$*

DINING AND LODGING

Ventana Inn. Here you'll find California chic: restful *and* hip. The 12 cottagelike buildings are scattered in clusters on a hillside above the Pacific. Rooms are country-style, with quilts, natural wood interiors, and tile floors. Rates include Continental breakfast and afternoon wine and cheese. The attractive stone and wood Ventana Restaurant serves California cuisine with Continental influences. *Hwy. 1, 93920, ☎ 408/667–2331, FAX 408/667–2419. 59 rooms. Facilities: restaurant, 2 pools, spa, fitness room. Minimum stay 2 nights on weekends, 3 on holidays. AE, D, DC, MC, V. $$$$*

LODGING

Big Sur Lodge. This lodge within Pfeiffer Big Sur State Park is the best place in Big Sur for families. Motel-style cottages—some with fireplaces or kitchens—are set around a meadow surrounded by redwood and oak trees. *Hwy. 1, Box 190, 93920, ☎ 408/667–2171, FAX 408/667–2824. 61 rooms. Facilities: pool, sauna. MC, V. $$–$$$*

Cambria

DINING

★ **Hamlet at Moonstone Gardens.** This patio in the middle of a plant nursery is perfect for lunch. An upstairs dining room overlooks the Pacific and the gardens. The fish of the day comes poached in white wine; other entrées range from hamburgers to rack of lamb. The extensive cellar has offerings from more than 50 wineries. *Hwy. 1, east side, ☎ 805/927–3535. MC, V. Closed Dec. $–$$*

Carmel

DINING

Crème Carmel. This bright and airy small restaurant has a California-French menu that changes seasonally. Specialties include charbroiled Muscovy duck with celery root puree and green peppercorn, and beef tenderloin prepared with cabernet. *San Carlos St., near 7th Ave., ☎ 408/624–0444. AE, DC, MC, V. No lunch. $$$*

LODGING

★ **Highlands Inn.** The hotel's setting, on high cliffs above the Pacific, gives it outstanding views in a region famous for them. The plush spa suites and condominium-style units feature wood-burning fireplaces and ocean-view decks; some have full kitchens. *Hwy. 1, Box 1700, 93921, ☎ 408/624–3801 or 800/538–9525; in CA, 800/682–4811; FAX 408/626–1574. 142 rooms. Facilities: 2 restaurants, pool, entertainment. AE, D, DC, MC, V. $$$$*

Monterey

DINING

★ **Fresh Cream.** Locals love this spot for French cuisine with light, imaginative California accents. Dishes include rack of lamb Dijoinnaise and roast duck in black currant sauce. *100 Pacific St., ☎ 408/375–9798. AE, DC, MC, V. Closed Mon. No lunch. $$$*

The Fishery. A mixture of Asian and Continental influences characterizes both food and decor. Specialties include broiled swordfish with saffron butter and fresh Hawaiian tuna teriyaki. *21 Soledad Dr., ☎ 408/373–6200. MC, V. Closed Sun. and Mon. No lunch. $$*

LODGING

★ **Spindrift Inn.** This Cannery Row hotel has a private beach and rooftop garden. Rooms are spacious, with sitting areas, Oriental rugs, fireplaces, canopied beds, down comforters, and other luxuries. Room rates include Continental breakfast and afternoon tea. *652 Cannery Row, 93940, ☎ 408/646–8900 or 800/841–1879, FAX 408/646–5342. 41 rooms. AE, D, DC, MC, V. $$$–$$$$*

Monterey Motor Lodge. Its location near El Estero Park gives this motel an edge over similarly priced competitors. A large secluded courtyard with pool is another plus. *55 Aguajito Rd., 93940, ☎ 408/372–8057 or 800/558–1900, FAX 408/655–2933. 45 rooms. Facilities: restaurant, pool. AE, D, DC, MC, V. $–$$*

Morro Bay

DINING

★ **Margie's Diner.** This mom-and-pop diner-café serves generous portions of all-American favorites: ham or steak and eggs, omelets, chili, burgers, hot and cold sandwiches, fried chicken steak, and deep-dish apple pie. The milkshakes are terrific. *1698 N. Main St., ☎ 805/772–2510. No reservations. No credit cards. $*

Pacific Grove

DINING

★ **Old Bath House.** This romantic converted bathhouse overlooks the water at Lovers Point. The Continental menu here makes the most of local seafood and produce. When they're available, the salmon and Monterey Bay prawns are particularly worth ordering. *620 Ocean View Blvd., ☎ 408/375–5195. AE, D, DC, MC, V. No lunch. $$$*

San Simeon

DINING

San Simeon Restaurant. The imitation Greek columns, statues, and tapestries in the ocean-view dining room here are reminders of your proximity to Hearst Castle. The menu is standard American; prime rib is the big draw. *Hwy. 1, east side, ☎ 805/927–4604. Reservations advised in summer. AE, D, MC, V. $–$$*

Santa Barbara

DINING

★ **Citronelle.** The accent at this offspring of Los Angeles' famed Citron is on French Riviera–style dishes: light and delicate, but loaded with intriguing good tastes. The desserts here are unmatched anywhere in SoCal. Sweeping harbor views can be seen from the dining room. *901 E. Cabrillo, ☎ 805/963–0111. AE, D, DC, MC, V. $$$*

Castagnola Seafood Restaurant. This unassuming spot just two blocks from the beach serves wonderfully good, fresh broiled fish. The homemade clam chowder is excellent. *205 Santa Barbara St., ☎ 805/962–8053. No reservations. AE, D, MC, V. $–$$*

Roy. This tiny downtown storefront is a real bargain. Owner/chef Leroy Gandy serves a $10 fixed-price dinner and Sunday brunch menu that includes a small salad, fresh soup, and a tempting roster of Cal-Mediterranean main courses: shrimp ravioli, marinated leg of lamb with eggplant ratatouille, and grilled salmon with pineapple-orange-mango chutney and a mint-butter sauce. Expect a long wait on weekends. *7 W. Carrillo St., ☎ 805/966–5636. No reservations. AE, MC, V. Closed Mon. No lunch except Sun. brunch. $*

LODGING

★ **Four Seasons Biltmore.** This grande dame of Santa Barbara hostelries is more formal than other city accommodations, with lush gardens and palm trees galore. *1260 Channel Dr., 93108, ☎ 805/969–2261, FAX 805/969–5715. 170 rooms, 12 cottages (4–6 rooms in each). Facilities: 2 restaurants, 2 pools, 2 health clubs, 3 tennis courts. AE, DC, MC, V. $$$$*

Ambassador by the Sea. Near the harbor and Stearns Wharf, this place has a real California beach feel. Sun decks overlook the ocean and bike path. *202 W. Cabrillo Blvd., 93101, ☎ 805/965–4577, FAX 805/965–9937. 32 rooms, 2 with kitchenettes. Facility: pool. AE, D, DC, MC, V. $$–$$$*

★ **Motel 6.** Low price and great location near the beach are the pluses for this no-frills place. Reserve well in advance all year. *443 Corona Del Mar Dr., 93103, ☎ 805/564–1392 or 805/891–6161. 52 rooms. Facilities: heated pool. AE, D, DC, MC, V. $*

The Arts

The Carmel-Monterey area's top performing-arts venue is the **Sunset Community Cultural Center** (San Carlos, between 8th and 10th Aves., Carmel, ☎ 408/624–3996), which presents concerts, lectures, and headline performers. The **Arlington Theater** (☎ 805/963–4408) is home to the Santa Barbara Symphony.

LOS ANGELES

Los Angeles is a wholly 20th-century city, created, defined, dependent upon, and thrust into prominence only by the advances of the modern age: automobiles, airplanes, and the movies. It is a center of power and wealth, where the arts flourish and the rich and celebrated make their homes. Also a landing place for hundreds of thousands of immigrants, it is among the most ethnically diverse cities in the nation, with thriving Hispanic, Korean, Chinese, Japanese, and Middle Eastern cultures.

Tourist Information

Los Angeles: Convention and Visitors Bureau (633 W. 5th St., Suite 6000, 90071, ☎ 213/624–7300).

Arriving and Departing

By Plane

Los Angeles International Airport (LAX, ☎ 310/646–5252), about 25 mi west of downtown and 10 mi from Beverly Hills, is served by over 85 major airlines. Four smaller regional airports—located in **Burbank, Long Beach, Orange County,** and **Ontario**—also serve the greater Los Angeles area. Taxis to downtown cost about $24 (request a flat fee—metered fares are more) and take 20–60 minutes, depending on traffic. **SuperShuttle** (☎ 310/782–6600) services downtown hotels for about $12 ($13 to Disneyland hotels); fares to private residences vary. **Airport Coach** (☎ 714/938–8900 or 800/772–5299) provides service from LAX to the Pasadena ($12 one-way/$20 round-trip, $7/$12 children 3–11) and Anaheim ($14/$22, $8/$14) areas.

By Car

I–5 (called the Golden State or Santa Ana Freeway here) runs north–south. I–10 (Santa Monica Freeway) heads east cross-country. I–15 comes into the area from the northeast and continues down to San Diego.

By Train

Amtrak (☎ 800/872–7245) serves Los Angeles's **Union Station** (800 N. Alameda St.).

By Bus

Greyhound Lines (208 E. 6th St., ☎ 800/231–2222).

Getting Around Los Angeles

Los Angeles was designed to be traversed by car. Freeways, whose names can change along the route, are the most efficient way to get from one end of the city to another.

By Public Transportation

The **Southern California Metropolitan Transit Authority** (MTA; ☎ 213/626–4455; fare $1.10, 25¢ for each transfer) provides infrequent bus service and is expanding with the **Metrorail Blue Line,** which runs daily, 5 AM–10 PM, from downtown Los Angeles to Long Beach. The fare is $1.10. The **Metro Red Line** runs from Union Station to MacArthur Park; the fare is $1.10. The line will extend to Hollywood by 1998. **DASH** (Downtown Area Short Hop; ☎ 213/485–7201) is a system of minibuses that serve the downtown area. DASH runs weekdays 6:30 AM–6 PM, Saturday 10 AM–5 PM. Stops are every two blocks or so, and you pay 25¢ every time you get on, no matter how far you go.

By Taxi

Cabs must be ordered by phone, from such companies as **Independent Cab. Co.** (☎ 213/385–8294 or 310/569–8214) and **United Independent Taxi** (☎ 213/653–5050). The metered rate is $1.60 per mile.

Orientation Tours

Starline (☎ 213/463–3333) offers tours to movie stars' homes, Disneyland, Universal Studios, the *Queen Mary,* Santa Catalina Island, and other attractions.

Exploring Los Angeles

Los Angeles is best approached as clusters of destinations, each to be explored separately.

Downtown Los Angeles

Downtown's historic and ethnic neighborhoods can be explored on foot or by DASH minibuses. John Portman's 1974 **Westin Bonaventure Hotel** (404 S. Figueroa St., ☎ 213/624–1000) projects five shimmering cylinders 35 stories into the sky, crowned by a revolving rooftop bar. Pyramidal skylights mark the **Museum of Contemporary Art** (250 S. Grand Ave., ☎ 213/626–6222; admission charged), which opened in 1986 and was designed by renowned Japanese architect Arata Isozaki. The permanent collection includes works from the 1940s to the present; artists represented include Mark Rothko, Franz Kline, and Susan Rothenberg.

On weekends especially, **Chinatown**'s colorful shops, exotic markets, and restaurants attract crowds of shoppers, drawn not only from the 15,000 Chinese and Southeast Asian (mostly Vietnamese) inhabitants of Chinatown, but from the entire city. The southern edge of Chinatown merges with downtown Los Angeles's Spanish and Mexican history. The historic buildings of the 44-acre **El Pueblo de Los Angeles**

Historical Monument (visitor center, Sepulveda House, 622 N. Main St., ☎ 213/628–1274) celebrate the birthplace of Los Angeles (no one knows exactly where the original 1781 settlement was). Fiestas are held nearly every weekend on **Olvera Street,** a genuine Mexican-style marketplace with shops, stalls, restaurants, and the oldest downtown building (1818).

South of Olvera Street, **City Hall** (200 N. Spring St.) is recognizable from its roles as a backdrop on *Dragnet.* Further south, along 1st and San Pedro streets, stretches **Little Tokyo,** with Japanese shops, restaurants, and sushi bars. The **Japanese American Cultural and Community Center** (244 S. San Pedro St., ☎ 213/628–2725) presents exhibits, theater, and concerts.

Amid shops and sidewalk vendors along Broadway catering to the Hispanic community, **Grand Central Market** (317 S. Broadway, ☎ 213/624–2378) has exotic produce, herbs, and meats. The gentrified Victorian-era **Bradbury Building** (304 S. Broadway, ☎ 213/626–1893) has a filigreed, glassed-in courtyard and open balconies. This can be an exhilarating slice-of-life walk, but be sure to keep a sharp eye out for pickpockets while exploring this area.

In South-Central Los Angeles is **Exposition Park** (Figueroa St. at Exposition Blvd.), site of the 1932 Olympics and home of the **Memorial Coliseum,** the **Sports Arena,** and the **Swim Stadium** that were used in the 1984 Olympics, as well as two impressive museums: the **California Museum of Science and Industry** (☎ 213/744–7400) and the **Natural History Museum** (☎ 213/744–3466; admission charged).

Hollywood

The cradle of the movie industry, Hollywood is rife with landmarks of its glamorous past. The **Capitol Records Building** (1756 N. Vine St.) was built in 1956 to resemble a stack of records. The **Palace** (1735 N. Vine St., ☎ 213/467–4571) opened as the Hollywood Playhouse in 1927 and for years presented vaudeville shows; it was later a TV studio and now hosts rock concerts and late-night weekend dancing. The Art Deco **Pantages Theater** (6233 Hollywood Blvd.), originally a movie house, hosted the Oscars in the 1950s and now features large-scale Broadway musicals. **Frederick's of Hollywood** (6608 Hollywood Blvd., ☎ 213/466–8506) is the famous name in risqué lingerie, and also features a bra museum. **Mann's Chinese Theater** (6925 Hollywood Blvd., ☎ 213/464–8111), originally Grauman's Chinese, invented the gala premiere; its famous courtyard holds the footprints of more than 160 movie celebrities.

The **Hollywood Walk of Fame** immortalizes the names of movie and other greats on brass plaques embedded in pink stars along the city's sidewalks. Since the first stars were installed in 1960, more than 2,300 have been added. Marlon Brando is at 1765 Vine Street, Clark Gable at 1608 Vine, John Wayne at 1541 Vine, and Marilyn Monroe at 6774 Hollywood Boulevard.

Five miles north of Hollywood, in the San Fernando Valley, off U.S. 101 (the Hollywood Freeway), **Universal Studios and CityWalk** shows off the (glamorized) inner workings of the film industry in its tremendously popular five- to seven-hour tram tours of the backlot, featuring special effects and stage shows. *100 Universal City Pl., ☎ 818/508–9600. Admission: $31 adults, $24.95 senior citizens and children 3–11. Box office open daily 9–7. AE, MC, V.*

Not far away, at **Warner Bros. Studios,** you can observe the day-to-day action of movie making on a two-hour walking tour of whatever is being filmed at the time. *4000 Warner Blvd., Burbank, ☎ 818/954–1744. Admission: $27, children under 10 not admitted. Reserve 1 wk in advance. Tours on the hour, weekdays 9–4. AE, MC, V.*

Wilshire Boulevard

Along 16-mi Wilshire Boulevard are many of the city's best museums and tallest office buildings, the heart of Beverly Hills and the opulent Westside, and the seaside cliffs of Santa Monica. Hispanic, Filipino, Korean, and Middle Eastern communities occupy the side streets from the Harbor Freeway west to Fairfax Avenue. The large **Koreatown Plaza** mall is on the corner of Western and San Marino avenues.

At the southeast corner of Wilshire and Western Avenue sits the **Wiltern Theater** (3780 Wilshire Blvd.), one of the city's best examples of full-strength Art Deco architecture. The 1930s zigzag design was recently restored to its splendid turquoise hue.

Hancock Park (Wilshire Blvd. at Curson Ave.) is built atop the **La Brea Tar Pits,** from which over 100 tons of fossils have been removed. Many are on view next door at the **George C. Page Museum** (5801 Wilshire Blvd., ☎ 213/936–2230; admission charged). Also in the park is the **Los Angeles County Museum of Art** (5905 Wilshire Blvd., ☎ 213/857–6000; admission charged), containing collections of paintings and decorative arts, a sculpture garden, and Japanese art. North of Hancock Park (near CBS) is the **Farmer's Market** (6333 W. 3rd St., ☎ 213/933–9211), a partly covered marketplace with food stalls, a few boutiques, and vendors selling high-priced produce.

The Westside

L.A.'s Westside—encompassing West Hollywood, Beverly Hills, Bel Air, and UCLA—epitomizes what most people think of as the southern California good life: palatial hilltop homes, chic shops, and star-studded restaurants. **West Hollywood** is trendy, stylish, and home to both the bizarre and the beautiful. **Melrose Avenue** is a test kitchen for the avant-garde in quirky shops and a clutch of great eateries offering Thai, Mexican, yogurt, or burgers and fries. **Sunset Strip**—the stretch of Sunset Boulevard through West Hollywood—became a movie-star stomping ground in the 1930s, headquarters to the suave TV detectives of *77 Sunset Strip* in the 1950s, and today the center of a lively rock club scene. **Spago** (*see* Dining, *below*), the reigning champion of celebrity hangouts, is just off Sunset on Horn Avenue.

As it runs through **Beverly Hills,** Sunset Boulevard becomes a broad, tree-shaded avenue, with immaculately manicured lawns fronting mansions of every conceivable style. Perfectly coiffed and clad shoppers stroll among the chic shops of Rodeo, Camden, and Beverly drives. **Westwood,** home to the **University of California at Los Angeles,** straddles the hillsides between Wilshire and Sunset boulevards west of Beverly Hills. UCLA offers walking tours of the campus (☎ 310/206–8147), and on weekends the surrounding area offers lively nightlife. Royce Hall, one of the original buildings on campus, has been indefinitely closed due to earthquake damage.

Santa Monica and the Beach Cities

Wilshire Boulevard ends at Ocean Avenue in **Santa Monica,** a mix of senior citizens, yuppies, and the contingent of homeless people who hang out at **Palisades Park,** a palm-shaded stretch of green atop the cliffs above the beach. All are attracted to the **Santa Monica Pier** (☎

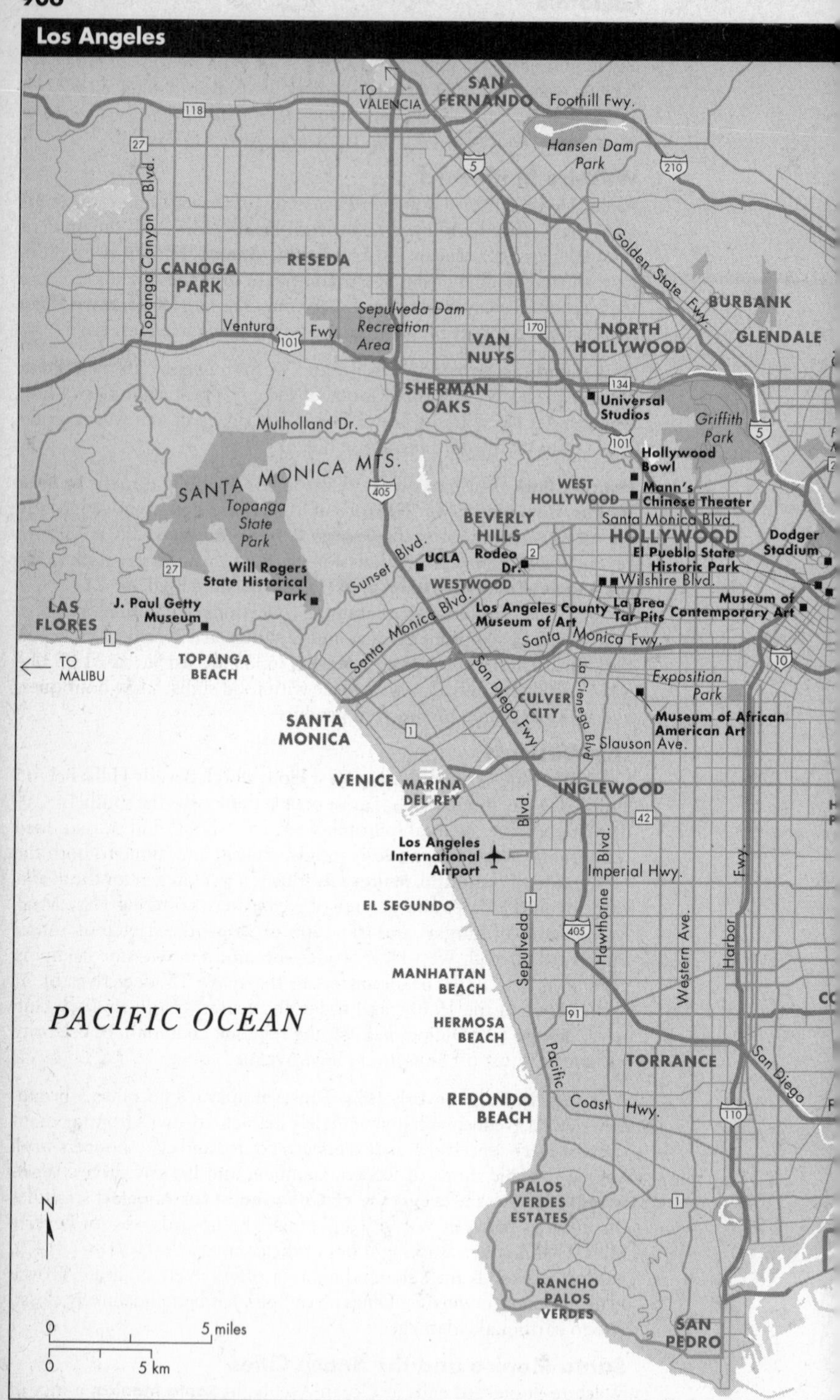

Los Angeles
TO VALENCIA
SAN FERNANDO
Foothill Fwy.
Hansen Dam Park
118
27
5
210
Topanga Canyon Blvd.
CANOGA PARK
RESEDA
Golden State Fwy.
BURBANK
GLENDALE
Sepulveda Dam Recreation Area
Ventura
101
Fwy
VAN NUYS
170
NORTH HOLLYWOOD
SHERMAN OAKS
134
Universal Studios
Griffith Park
Mulholland Dr.
SANTA MONICA MTS.
405
Hollywood Bowl
WEST HOLLYWOOD
Mann's Chinese Theater
Topanga State Park
BEVERLY HILLS
Santa Monica Blvd.
HOLLYWOOD
Dodger Stadium
El Pueblo State Historic Park
Sunset Blvd.
UCLA
Rodeo Dr.
2
Will Rogers State Historical Park
WESTWOOD
Wilshire Blvd.
LAS FLORES
J. Paul Getty Museum
Santa Monica Blvd.
Los Angeles County Museum of Art
La Brea Tar Pits
Museum of Contemporary Art
Santa Monica Fwy.
TO MALIBU
TOPANGA BEACH
San Diego Fwy.
La Cienega Blvd.
Exposition Park
10
CULVER CITY
Museum of African American Art
SANTA MONICA
Slauson Ave.
VENICE
MARINA DEL REY
INGLEWOOD
42
Los Angeles International Airport
Imperial Hwy.
Hawthorne Blvd.
Harbor Fwy.
EL SEGUNDO
Sepulveda Blvd.
MANHATTAN BEACH
Western Ave.
PACIFIC OCEAN
HERMOSA BEACH
91
TORRANCE
San Diego
Pacific Coast Hwy.
REDONDO BEACH
110
PALOS VERDES ESTATES
N
RANCHO PALOS VERDES
SAN PEDRO
0 5 miles
0 5 km

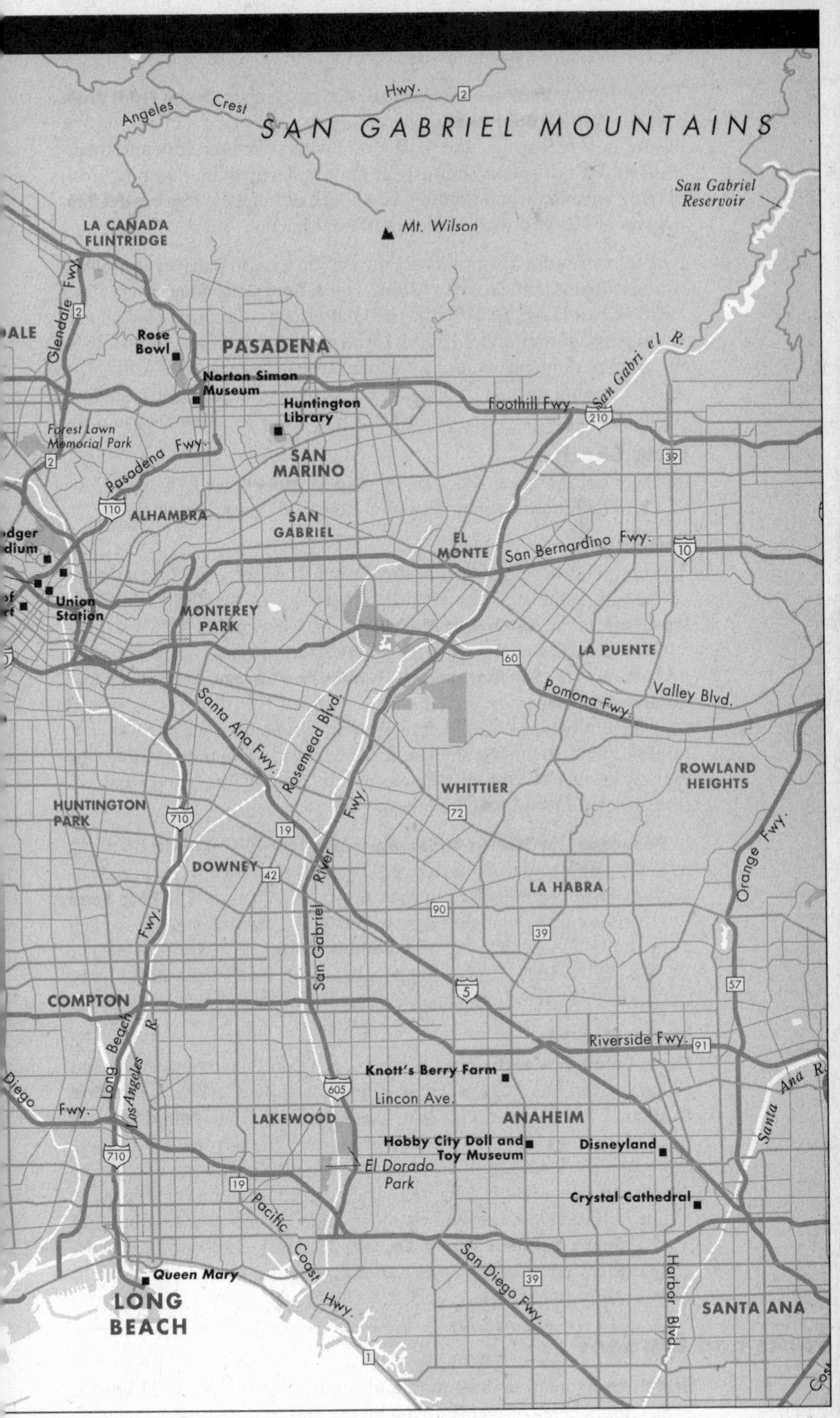

Angeles Crest Hwy.
2
SAN GABRIEL MOUNTAINS
San Gabriel Reservoir
Mt. Wilson
LA CANADA FLINTRIDGE
Glendale Fwy.
2
ALE
Rose Bowl
PASADENA
San Gabriel R.
Norton Simon Museum
Huntington Library
Foothill Fwy.
210
Forest Lawn Memorial Park
Pasadena Fwy.
2
SAN MARINO
39
110
ALHAMBRA
SAN GABRIEL
EL MONTE
San Bernardino Fwy.
10
dger dium
Union Station
MONTEREY PARK
LA PUENTE
60
Pomona Fwy.
Valley Blvd.
Santa Ana Fwy.
Rosemead Blvd.
ROWLAND HEIGHTS
WHITTIER
HUNTINGTON PARK
710
Fwy.
72
19
Orange Fwy.
DOWNEY
42
River
LA HABRA
90
39
San Gabriel
Fwy.
COMPTON
5
57
Riverside Fwy.
91
Long Beach
Los Angeles R.
Knott's Berry Farm
605
Lincon Ave.
Santa Ana R.
Diego Fwy.
LAKEWOOD
ANAHEIM
Hobby City Doll and Toy Museum
Disneyland
710
El Dorado Park
19
Crystal Cathedral
Pacific Coast Hwy.
San Diego Fwy.
39
Queen Mary
LONG BEACH
Harbor Blvd.
SANTA ANA
1

310/394–7554), with its 46-horse antique carousel, gift shops, arcade, cafés, and psychic adviser.

To the south is **Venice,** known for the active scene on **Ocean Front Walk** and the **Venice Boardwalk.** Whatever the next craze in fashion or leisure is, you'll see it here first, along with street vendors and musicians and Californians seriously at play: rollerblading, pumping iron, playing volleyball, and tanning. Just south of Venice is **Marina del Rey,** the world's largest man-made small-boat harbor.

North from Santa Monica along the Pacific Coast Highway is **Malibu,** the beachfront home to many stars. The **J. Paul Getty Museum** (17985 Pacific Coast Hwy., ☎ 310/458–2003) houses a collection of Greek and Roman antiquities and 13th- to 19th-century paintings. Admission is free, but parking reservations are required. If you take MTA Bus 434 to the museum instead of driving (a way to get into the Getty on days when parking is full up), the operator will give you an admission pass.

Long Beach

To the south, in Long Beach, is the ***Queen Mary*** (Pier J, ☎ 310/435–3511). The famous ocean liner now houses shops and restaurants.

Pasadena

The communities northeast of downtown L.A. were the first suburbs of the city, established by wealthy Angelenos in the 1880s. In **Highland Park** is the **Southwest Museum** (234 Museum Dr., ☎ 213/221–2163; admission charged), with a collection of Native American art and artifacts. In **San Marino** is the **Huntington Library, Art Gallery and Botanical Gardens** (Oxford Rd., ☎ 818/405–2100; donations), spread over 130 hilly acres. The complex's collections number more than 6 million items, including the Dead Sea Scrolls, a Gutenberg Bible, the earliest known edition of Chaucer's *Canterbury Tales,* and first editions by Ben Franklin and Shakespeare.

In **Pasadena,** the **Norton Simon Museum** (411 W. Colorado Blvd., ☎ 818/449–6840; admission charged) houses Impressionist paintings, as well as masterpieces by Rembrandt, Goya, and Picasso. The **Rose Bowl** (991 Rosemont Ave.) is the home of the New Year's Day game, as well as of the UCLA Bruins. Nearby **Gamble House** (4 Westmoreland Pl., ☎ 818/793–3334; admission charged), built by Charles and Henry Greene in 1908, is the ultimate in California Craftsman-style architecture.

In the Vicinity

Santa Catalina Island, 26 mi offshore, is a good day trip or weekend getaway from Los Angeles. From San Pedro and Long Beach, **Catalina Express** (☎ 310/519–1212) provides boat service and **Island Express** (☎ 310/491–5550) offers helicopter service. No private cars are permitted on the island (golf carts can be rented), but the main town of Avalon is easily explored on foot. The rest of the island is made up of rolling hills (on which buffalo roam), secluded beaches, and nature preserves. **Santa Catalina Island Co.** (☎ 310/510–2000 or 800/428–2566) offers escorted bus tours of the interior, coastal cruises, and glass-bottom-boat rides.

Parks and Gardens

Griffith Park (junction of Ventura and Golden State Fwys., ☎ 213/665–5188) offers acres of picnic areas, hiking and bridle trails, a carousel, and pony rides. Also in the park are the **Los Angeles Zoo** (☎ 213/666–4090), one of the major zoos in the United States and noted for its breeding in captivity of endangered species such as the California condor;

Travel Town (5200 Zoo Dr., ☎ 213/662–5874), with railcars, planes, and classic cars; and the **Planetarium and Observatory** (Los Feliz Blvd. and Vermont Ave., ☎ 213/664–1191), offering planetarium and Laserium shows and an expansive view of the city below.

What to See and Do with Children

In Valencia, **Six Flags Magic Mountain** offers shows and 260 acres of rides, including the world's largest looping roller coaster and a simulated white-water wilderness adventure. *26101 Magic Mountain Pkwy., ☎ 805/255–4111. Admission: $30 adults, $15 children 4' tall and under (under age 3 free), $18 senior citizens. Hours vary seasonally.*

In San Pedro, the **Cabrillo Marine Aquarium** (3720 Stephen White Dr., ☎ 310/548–7562) has seaquariums, a see-through tidal tank, and a touch tank.

Shopping

You can find anything you want in Los Angeles's shops: brand names in department stores in any mall; one-of-a-kind items along Melrose Avenue; designer originals on Rodeo Drive; art in galleries on La Cienega Boulevard; specialty foods at ethnic neighborhood shops and the Farmer's Market (*see* Exploring Los Angeles, *above*).

Shopping Districts

Rodeo Drive in Beverly Hills is the world-famous street with such pricey shops as **Fred Hayman** (273 N. Rodeo Dr., ☎ 310/271–3000) for designer men's and women's fashions; or **Bijan** (420 N. Rodeo Dr., ☎ 310/273–6544), where you shop by appointment for designer men's fashions. The **Cooper Building** (860 S. Los Angeles St., ☎ 213/622–1139) in downtown L.A. contains eight floors of outlet shops. For vintage styles or the weird, go to **Melrose Avenue** between La Brea and Crescent Heights. The stylish **Beverly Center** (Beverly Blvd. at La Cienega Blvd.) has more than 200 upscale stores and boutiques. **Santa Monica Promenade** and **Montana Avenue** feature boutique after boutique of quality goods.

Department Stores

Los Angeles has branches of many national chains, including **Bloomingdale's, Neiman Marcus, Saks Fifth Avenue,** and **Sears.** Most malls have such regional stores as the upscale **Nordstrom** and **Bullocks** or the more middle-of-the-road **Robinson-May** and **Broadway.**

Specialty Stores

BOOKS

Book Soup (8818 Sunset Blvd., West Hollywood, ☎ 213/659–3110) has film and photography books, international magazines, and frequent book-signings.

GIFTS AND CRAFTS

Tesoro (319 S. Robertson, Blvd., Beverly Hills, ☎ 310/273–9890) stocks trendy ceramics, Southwestern blankets, and contemporary art.

MUSIC

Aron's Records (1150 N. Highland Ave., Hollywood, ☎ 213/469–4700) carries new releases and an extensive selection of old records.

Spectator Sports

Baseball

Dodgers (Dodger Stadium, 1000 Elysian Park Ave., downtown, ☎ 213/224–1400; Apr.–Oct.).

Basketball

Lakers (Forum, 3900 West Manchester Ave., Inglewood, ☎ 310/419–3182; Nov.–Apr.). **Clippers** (L.A. Sports Arena, 3939 S. Figueroa St., downtown, ☎ 213/748–8000; Nov.–Apr.).

Football

Raiders (Memorial Coliseum, 3939 S. Figueroa St., ☎ 310/322–5901; Aug.–Dec.).

Hockey

L.A. Kings (Forum, ☎ 310/673–6003; Oct.–Apr.).

Horse Racing

Santa Anita Race Track (Arcadia, ☎ 818/574–7223; late Dec.–Apr., Oct.–mid-Nov.). **Hollywood Park** (near the Forum in Inglewood, ☎ 310/419–1500; Apr.–mid-July, mid-Nov.–Dec. 24).

Beaches

Los Angeles County beaches (and state beaches operated by the county) have lifeguards. Public parking (for a fee) is available at most. Most state beaches have picnic and rest-room facilities, and most city beaches are backed by a boardwalk with plenty of services.

Leo Carillo State Beach

This beach is fun at low tide, when tide pools emerge. There are hiking trails, sea caves, and tunnels; whales, dolphins, and sea lions can often be seen. *35000 block of Pacific Coast Hwy. (PCH), Malibu, ☎ 818/880–0350.*

Surfrider Beach/Malibu Lagoon State Beach

The steady 3- to 5-ft waves make this beach north of Malibu Pier a great long-board surfing spot. The International Surfing Contest is held here in September. The lagoon is sanctuary for many birds. *23200 PCH, Malibu, ☎ 310/880–0350.*

Manhattan State Beach

Here are 44 acres of sandy beach for swimming, diving, surfing, and fishing, backed by a grassy park with duck pond and picnic facilities. *West of Strand, Manhattan Beach, ☎ 310/372–2166.*

Paradise Cove

With its pier and equipment rentals, this sandy beach is a mecca for sportfishing boats. *28128 PCH, Malibu, ☎ 310/457–9891.*

Playa del Rey

This underrated spot stretches almost 2 mi from Marina del Rey and attracts a young crowd. *6660 Esplanade, Playa del Rey, no ☎.*

Redondo State Beach

This wide beach is usually packed in summer, and parking is limited. *Foot of Torrance Blvd., Redondo Beach, ☎ 310/372–2166.*

Santa Monica Beach

The widest stretch of beach on the Pacific coast, and one of the most popular, this spot offers bike paths, facilities for the disabled, playgrounds, and volleyball, *Santa Monica Blvd. and Ocean Ave., Santa Monica, ☎ 310/394–3266.*

Topanga Canyon State Beach

This great surfing spot is a rocky beach that stretches from the mouth of the canyon down to Coastline Drive. *18700 block of PCH, Malibu, ☎ 310/394–3266.*

Westward Beach/Point Dume State Beach

This sandy beach is ½ mi long, with tide pools and sandstone cliffs. It's a favorite surfing spot among older surfers for its slow long-breaking waves. *South end of Westward Beach Rd., Malibu, ☎ 310/457–9891.*

Will Rogers State Beach

This wide, sandy beach is several miles long and has steady, even surf. Parking is limited, but there's plenty of beach, volleyball, and bodysurfing action parallel to the pedestrian bridge. *15800 PCH, Pacific Palisades, ☎ 310/394–3266.*

Zuma Beach County Park

Malibu's largest and sandiest beach, this is a favorite surfing spot and teen hangout. *30050 PCH, Malibu, ☎ 310/457–9891.*

Dining

Los Angeles's dining scene features foods influenced by the city's myriad cultures, as well as cuisines haute, healthy, and retro. Each ethnic neighborhood has its own wonderful restaurants: Chinese in Monterey Park, Mexican in East Los Angeles, Korean in Koreatown, and Jewish in delis on Fairfax on the Westside. Parking can be difficult; most restaurants listed here offer valet parking except as noted. Note: The city's no-smoking ordinance applies to all restaurants: If you want to smoke, choose a restaurant with an outdoor area or a full-scale bar. Some of the incorporated cities around Los Angeles make their own rules, so call ahead. For price ranges, see Chart 1 (A) in On the Road with Fodor's.

$$$$ ★ **Rex Il Ristorante.** Two floors of a historic Art Deco building were remodeled to resemble the dining salon of the 1930s Italian luxury liner *Rex*. The cuisine is the lightest of *nuova cucina* in small portions at big prices. *617 S. Olive St. (Downtown), ☎ 213/627–2300. Reservations required. Jacket and tie required. AE, DC, MC, V. Closed Sun. No lunch Sat.–Wed.*

$$$ ★ **Hotel Bel-Air.** The Bel-Air's restaurant is appealing not only for the ambience of its country-garden setting but also for the first-rate California–Continental cuisine. *701 Stone Canyon Rd. (Bel Air), ☎ 310/472–1211. Jacket and tie advised at dinner. AE, DC, MC, V.*

$$$ ★ **L'Orangerie.** French specialties at this elegant restaurant include caviar-topped coddled eggs served in the shell, squab with foie gras, pot-au-feu, and apple tart served with a jug of double cream. *903 N. La Cienega Blvd. (West Hollywood), ☎ 310/652–9770. Reservations required. Jacket and tie required. AE, D, DC, MC, V. Closed Mon. No lunch Sat.–Sun.*

$$$ **Pacific Dining Car.** Set in a 1920s railroad car is one of L.A.'s oldest restaurants, known for well-aged steaks, rack of lamb, and an extensive California wine list. It's a favorite haunt of politicians, lawyers, and postgame Dodger fans. *1310 W. 6th St. (Downtown), ☎ 213/483–6000. AE, DC, MC, V.*

$$–$$$ ★ **Granita.** Wolfgang Puck's Malibu eatery has stunning interior details; even the blasé locals are impressed. The menu here favors seafood items, and there's also spicy shrimp pizza with sun-dried tomatoes and herb pesto, roasted Chinese duck with dried fruit chutney, and Caesar salad with oven-baked bruschetta. *23725 W. Malibu Rd. (Malibu), ☎ 310/*

456–0488. Reservations required far ahead, especially for weekends. D, DC, MC, V. No lunch Mon.–Tues.

$$–$$$ ★ **Spago.** At this restaurant that propelled Wolfgang Puck into the culinary spotlight, the proof is in the tasting: grilled baby Sonoma lamb, pizza with Santa Barbara shrimp, and baby salmon. It's also the place to see *People* magazine live, but noisy. *1114 Horn Ave. (West Hollywood), ☎ 310/652–4025. Reservations required. Jacket required. D, DC, MC, V. No lunch.*

$$–$$$ **West Beach Cafe.** At this first of Bruce Marder's string of innovative upscale restaurants, best bets are the filet mignon taco, braised lamb shank, ravioli with port and radicchio, and possibly L.A.'s best hamburger and fries. *60 N. Venice Blvd. (Venice), ☎ 310/823–5396. AE, D, DC, MC, V.*

$$ **Border Grill.** At this very trendy, very loud storefront place, the menu ranges from crab tacos to vinegar-and-pepper grilled turkey to pickled pork sirloin. *1445 4th St. (Santa Monica), ☎ 310/451–1655. AE, D, DC, MC, V.*

$$ ★ **Gladstone's 4 Fish.** The view alone makes this the most popular restaurant along this section of the coast. Familiar seashore fare is prepared adequately and served in large portions. Best bets: crab chowder, steamed clams, and chili. *17300 Pacific Coast Hwy. (Pacific Palisades), ☎ 310/454–3474. AE, D, DC, MC, V.*

$$ ★ **Restaurant Katsu.** This stark, simple, perfectly designed sushi bar serves the most exquisite sushi delicacies in all of southern California. *1972 N. Hillhurst Ave. (Hollywood), ☎ 213/665–1891. AE, DC, MC, V. No lunch weekends.*

$–$$ **California Pizza Kitchen.** An immaculate, pleasingly modern dining room is supplemented with counter service by the open kitchen. Pizzas feature a wide choice of toppings; the pastas are equally interesting and carefully prepared. *207 S. Beverly Dr. (West Hollywood), ☎ 310/275–1101. AE, D, DC, MC, V. No valet parking.*

$–$$ **Mon Kee Seafood Restaurant.** The place is crowded and messy, but the cooking is excellent and the ingredients are fresh. The garlic crab is addictive; the steamed catfish is a masterpiece of gentle flavors. *679 N. Spring St. (Downtown), ☎ 213/628–6717. AE, DC, MC, V. Pay parking lot.*

$ **Chan Dara.** In this Swiss chalet you'll find excellent Thai food. Try the noodle dishes, especially those with crab and shrimp. *310 N. Larchmont Blvd. (Hollywood), ☎ 213/467–1052. AE, MC, V. On-street parking.*

$ **El Cholo.** This restaurant has been packing 'em in since the 1920s for good bathtub-size margaritas, a zesty assortment of tacos, make-your-own tortillas, and (June–Sept.) green-corn tamales. *1121 S. Western Ave. (Hollywood), ☎ 213/734–2773. AE, DC, MC, V.*

$ **Nate 'n' Al's.** This gathering place for Hollywood comedians, writers, and their agents serves first-rate matzo-ball soup, lox and scrambled eggs, cheese blintzes, potato pancakes, and the best deli sandwiches west of Manhattan. *414 N. Beverly Dr. (West Hollywood), ☎ 310/274–0101. AE, MC, V. Free parking.*

Lodging

You can find almost any sort of accommodation in Los Angeles, from a motel room to a poolside bungalow. Because of L.A.'s sprawl, select a hotel that is close to where you want to be. For price ranges, see Chart 2 (A) in On the Road with Fodor's.

$$$$ ★ **Bel Age Hotel.** This all-suite, European-style hotel boasts such extravagant touches as multi-line phones with voice mail, original art, private terraces, and courtesy limousine service. South-facing suites have

terrific views of the skyline. *1020 N. San Vicente Blvd., West Hollywood 90069, ☎ 310/854–1111 or 800/424–4443, FAX 310/854–0926. 200 suites. Facilities: 3 restaurants, lounge, business center, pool. AE, DC, MC, V.*

$$$$ **Biltmore Hotel.** Built in 1923, this landmark hotel has hosted several U.S. presidents. Italian artist Giovanni Smeraldi painted the lobby ceiling; imported Italian marble adorns the Grand Avenue Bar. Furnishings are conservative contemporary; rooms on two executive floors have desks equipped for business travelers. *506 S. Grand Ave., 90071, ☎ 213/624–1011 or 800/245–8673, FAX 213/612–1545. 685 rooms. Facilities: 3 restaurants, lounge, entertainment, health club (fee). AE, DC, MC, V.*

$$$$ **Regent Beverly Wilshire.** This famous hotel faces Rodeo Drive and the Hollywood Hills, and its clientele tends to be as glamorous as its Italian Renaissance–style surroundings. Guest rooms have appropriate period furnishings and glorious marble bathrooms. Style and service are emphasized, with limos to the airport, a multilingual staff, and a great restaurant. Much of the movie *Pretty Woman* was filmed here. *9500 Wilshire Blvd., Beverly Hills 90212, ☎ 310/275–5200 or 800/421–4354; in CA, 800/427–4354; FAX 310/274–2851. 300 rooms, 48 suites. Facilities: 3 restaurants, pool, health spa, business center. AE, D, DC, MC, V.*

$$$ ★ **Doubletree Hotel LAX.** Rooms and suites at this three-winged airport hotel are decorated in muted earth tones and contemporary furnishings; many suites have private outdoor spas. The luxurious lobby is decorated in marble and brass. The Trattoria Grande restaurant features pasta and seafood specialties. *5400 W. Century Blvd., 90045, ☎ 310/216–5858 or 800/222–8733, FAX 310/645–8053. 729 rooms. Facilities: 2 restaurants, lounge, pool, sauna, fitness center, parking (fee). AE, D, DC, MC, V.*

$$$ **Radisson Hollywood Roosevelt.** The site of the first Academy Awards ceremony, this hotel across from Mann's Chinese Theatre has an Art Deco lobby and a pool decorated by David Hockney. Most rooms have pastel decor with pine furniture; for a treat, try one of the 40 Hollywood-theme suites. *7000 Hollywood Blvd., Hollywood 90028, ☎ 213/466–7000 or 800/950–7667, FAX 213/462–8056. 311 rooms. Facilities: 3 restaurants, lounge, valet parking. AE, D, DC, MC, V.*

$$ **Barnabey's Hotel.** Modeled after a 19th-century English inn, with four-poster beds, lace curtains, and antiques, Barnabey's also has an enclosed greenhouse pool. *3501 Sepulveda Blvd. (at Rosecrans Ave., Manhattan Beach), 90266, ☎ 310/545–8466 or 800/552–5285, FAX 310/545–8621. 126 rooms. Facilities: 2 restaurants, lounge, pool. AE, D, DC, MC, V.*

$$ **Figueroa Hotel.** This hotel has kept its charming Spanish style intact as it enters its second half-century. There's a poolside bar. *939 S. Figueroa St. (Downtown), 90015, ☎ 213/627–8971 or 800/421–9092; in CA, 800/331–5151; FAX 213/689–0305. 285 rooms. Facilities: 3 restaurants, coffee shop, lounge, pool, free parking. AE, DC, MC, V.*

$$ **Holiday Inn–LAX.** This hotel appeals to families as well as business types. Rooms are serviceable. Amenities include multilingual telephone operators and touring information. *9901 La Cienega Blvd., 90045, ☎ 310/649–5151 or 800/624–0025, FAX 310/670–3619. 403 rooms. Facilities: restaurant, pool, exercise room, pay parking. AE, D, DC, MC, V.*

$ **Best Western Royal Palace Hotel.** Just off I–405, this good value for families has only suites with kitchenettes. Rooms are decorated with modern touches, lots of wood, and mirrors. *2528 S. Sepulveda Blvd. (West Los Angeles), 90064, ☎ 310/477–9066 or 800/251–3888, FAX*

310/478–4133. 55 suites. Facilities: pool, exercise room, laundry. AE, D, DC, MC, V.

$ Carmel Hotel. This old (1920s) but clean hotel is a block from the beach, Santa Monica Shopping Plaza, movie theaters, and many fine restaurants. *201 Broadway, Santa Monica 90401, ☎ 310/451–2469 or 800/445–8695, FAX 310/393–4180. 102 rooms. Facilities: restaurant, pay parking. AE, DC, MC, V.*

$ Orchid Hotel. One of the smaller downtown hotels, this offers clean, no-frills accommodations at a good price. *819 S. Flower St. (Downtown), 90017, ☎ 213/624–5855, FAX 213/624–8740. 63 rooms. Facilities: nearby pay parking, coin-operated laundry. AE, DC, MC, V.*

The Arts and Nightlife

The Calendar section of the *Los Angeles Times* is the best source of information for local events. Tickets can be purchased by phone from **TeleCharge** (☎ 800/762–7666), **TicketMaster** (☎ 213/480–3232), or **Good Time Tickets** (☎ 213/464–7383).

The Arts

THEATER

Plays are presented at two of the three theaters at the **Music Center** (135 N. Grand Ave.): the **Ahmanson Theatre** (☎ 213/972–7211) and the 742-seat **Mark Taper Forum** (☎ 213/972–7353). The **Center Theatre Group at Mark Taper Forum** is a resident company but also books its shows into various theaters and mounts its own productions. The **James A. Doolittle Theatre** (1615 N. Vine St., Hollywood, ☎ 213/851–9750) presents dramas. **Westwood Playhouse** (10886 Le Conte Ave., Westwood, ☎ 310/208–6500 or 310/208–5454) offers musicals and comedies year-round.

MUSIC

The **Dorothy Chandler Pavilion** (135 N. Grand Ave., ☎ 213/972–7211) is home to the Los Angeles Philharmonic Orchestra and offers other large-scale productions. **Ambassador Auditorium** (300 W. Green St., Pasadena, ☎ 818/304–6161) presents a regular concert season. The **Hollywood Bowl** (2301 Highland Ave., Hollywood, ☎ 213/850–2000) offers an outdoor summer season of classical and popular music. The outdoor **Greek Theater** (2700 N. Vermont Ave., ☎ 213/665–1927) offers a summer jazz/popular/pops schedule.

Nightlife

COMEDY

Comedy Store (8433 Sunset Blvd., Hollywood, ☎ 213/656–6225) showcases comedians, including the top names. The **Improvisation** (8162 Melrose Ave., West Hollywood, ☎ 213/651–2583; 321 Santa Monica Blvd., Santa Monica, ☎ 310/394–8664) features comedy and some music.

DANCE CLUBS

Bar One (9229 Sunset Blvd., Beverly Hills, ☎ 310/271–8355) is a hot and hip dance club. **Coconut Teaszer** (8117 Sunset Blvd., Los Angeles, ☎ 213/654–4773) has dancing to live music and a great barbecue menu. Its pool tables are always crowded.

LIVE MUSIC

Studio musicians often sit in at the **Baked Potato** (3787 Cahuenga Blvd. W, North Hollywood, ☎ 818/980–1615), a club near Universal Studios. The **Lighthouse** (30 Pier Ave., Hermosa Beach, ☎ 310/372–6911) offers a broad spectrum from reggae to big-band. **Marla's Jazz Supper Club** (2323 W. Martin Luther King Jr. Blvd., Los Angeles, ☎

213/294–8430), owned by Marla Gibbs of *The Jeffersons* and *227,* swings with blues and jazz.

The **Roxy** (9009 Sunset Blvd., West Hollywood, ☎ 310/276–2222), classy and comfortable, is L.A.'s premier rock club, though it presents stage productions as well. The **Viper Room** (8852 Sunset Blvd., West Hollywood, ☎ 310/358–1880), part-owned by actor Johnny Depp, presents pop, rock, blues, and jazz/fusion performers.

ORANGE COUNTY

Orange County sits between Los Angeles to the north and San Diego to the south. Though primarily suburban, it is one of the top tourist destinations in California, with attractions such as Disneyland, pro sports, and miles of beaches.

Tourist Information

Anaheim Area: Convention and Visitors Bureau (Anaheim Convention Center, 800 W. Katella Ave., 92802, ☎ 714/999–8999); Visitor Information Hot Line (☎ 714/635–8900).

Getting There

By Plane

John Wayne Orange County Airport (Santa Ana, ☎ 714/252–5252) is served by a number of major carriers.

By Car

I–405 (San Diego Fwy.) and I–5 (Santa Ana Fwy.) run north–south through Orange County, then merge into I–5 south of Laguna.

By Train

Amtrak (800/872–7245) has nine daily stops in Fullerton, Anaheim, Santa Ana, San Juan Capistrano, and San Clemente.

By Bus

Greyhound Lines (☎ 800/231–2222) serves Orange County.

Exploring Orange County

Inland Orange County

Anaheim is the home of **Disneyland.** Visitors enter the Magic Kingdom by way of Walt Disney's idealized turn-of-the-century **Main Street. Tomorrowland** is the site of the special-effects, sci-fi extravaganza Star Tours; *Captain Eo,* Michael Jackson's 3-D movie; the thrilling Space Mountain ride; and the Monorail. **Fantasyland** features rides based on children's stories. **Frontierland** depicts the Wild West. The highlight of **Adventureland** is the Indiana Jones thrill ride. **New Orleans Square** is the setting for Pirates of the Caribbean, a boat ride through a scene lavish with animated characters, and the Blue Bayou restaurant. The **Haunted Mansion** nearby is full of holographic ghosts. In **Critter Country** is Splash Mountain, a flume ride that drops 52 ft at 40 mph. **Mickey's Toontown,** a new "land" opened in 1993, is a child-size interactive community that's home to Mickey and other cartoon characters. Children can talk to manholes, sample Minnie's perfume, and bounce off the walls at Goofy's house. Along with the various thrill-rides and high-tech wizardry are the strolling Disney characters, a daily parade on Main Street, and fireworks nightly in summer. *1313 Harbor Blvd.,* ☎ *714/999–4565. Admission: $33 adults, $27 senior citizens, $25 children 3–11.*

Nearby in **Buena Park** is **Knott's Berry Farm,** a 150-acre complex of food, shops, rides, and other attractions. The park's thrill rides include the Boomerang, Bigfoot Rapids, and the Parachute Sky Jump. Areas of the park are themed: **Camp Snoopy** is especially for tiny tots and features a kid-size roller coaster, petting zoo, and playhouse; at the spooky **Mystery Lodge** visitors can commune with the native peoples of the Northwest coast; **Fiesta Village** features the Montezooma's Revenge roller coaster and the wild Jaguar roller coaster. **Ghost Town,** the park's original attraction, is a replica of an 1880s mining town. Across Beach Boulevard from the main portion of Knott's is a replica of Philadelphia's Independence Hall. And don't miss Knott's Chicken Dinner restaurant (and the boysenberry pies) that started it all in 1934. *8039 Beach Blvd., ☎ 714/220–5200. Admission: $28.50 adults, $18.50 senior citizens and children 3–11.*

Just east of Knott's is the **Movieland Wax Museum,** which re-creates the famous in wax. *7711 Beach Blvd., ☎ 714/522–1155. Admission: $12.95 adults, $6.95 children.*

Garden Grove is the site of the impressive **Crystal Cathedral** (12141 Lewis St., ☎ 714/971–4013), the domain of televangelist Robert Schuller.

The Coast

Pacific Coast Highway is the main thoroughfare for all the beach towns along the coast. **Huntington Beach** is a popular surfer hangout; you can watch the action from the **Huntington Pier.** To the south is **Newport Beach,** a Beverly-Hills-by-the-sea; nearly 10,000 boats bob in the *U*-shape **Newport Harbor,** which arcs out into a peninsula sheltering eight small islands. A three-car ferry serves **Balboa Island,** with its Victorian **Balboa Pavilion,** a turn-of-the-century architectural gem. The **Newport Harbor Art Museum** (850 San Clemente Dr., ☎ 714/759–1122; admission charged) holds a collection of works by California artists.

Farther south is the town of **Corona del Mar,** with an exceptional beach. In **Laguna Beach,** art galleries in town coexist with the volleyball games and sun worship on nearby Main Beach; in July and August, the **Pageant of the Masters** (☎ 714/494–1147) features living models re-creating famous paintings. **San Clemente** is a popular surfing spot and the site of Richard Nixon's Western White House. In March, migrating swallows and spectacle-loving tourists flock to **Mission San Juan Capistrano** (Camino Capistrano and Ortega Hwy., ☎ 714/248–2048; admission charged).

Sports and the Outdoors

Biking

A **bike path** runs from Marina del Rey down to San Diego with only minor breaks. For rentals, try **Rainbow Bicycles** (Laguna, ☎ 714/494–5806) or **Team Bicycle Rentals** (Huntington Beach, ☎ 714/969–5480).

Water Sports

Water-sports equipment rentals are near most piers. **Hobie Sports** has three rental locations (2 in Dana Point, ☎ 714/496–2366; Laguna, ☎ 714/497–3304). **Balboa Boat Rentals** in Newport Harbor (☎ 714/673–7200) and **Emcarcadero Marina** at Dana Point (☎ 714/496–6177) rent sail and power boats.

Spectator Sports

Baseball

California Angels (Anaheim Stadium, 2000 Gene Autry Way, ☎ 714/634–2000; Apr.–Oct.).

Hockey

Mighty Ducks of Anaheim (The Arrowhead Pond of Anaheim, 2695 E. Katella, for tickets, ☎ 714/740–2000; Oct.–Apr.).

Beaches

The beaches in Orange County are among the finest and most varied in southern California, offering fine swimming and many services. Posted warnings about undertow should be taken seriously; it can be quite strong.

Huntington Beach State Beach is a long stretch of flat, sandy beach with changing rooms, concessions, fire pits, and lifeguards. **Lower Newport Bay** is a sheltered enclave that includes a 740-acre preserve for ducks and geese. **Newport Dunes Resort** offers picnic facilities, changing rooms, and a boat launch. **Corona del Mar State Beach** has sandy beaches backed by rocky bluffs, and tide pools and caves. **Laguna** has the county's best spot for scuba diving in the **Marine Life Refuge,** from Seal Rock to Diver's Cove. **Main Beach,** a sandy arc just steps from downtown Laguna, is a popular picnic and volleyball venue. In South Laguna, **Aliso County Park** has recreational facilities and a fishing pier. **Doheny State Park,** near Dana Point Harbor, has food stands, camping, and a fishing pier. **San Clemente State Beach** has camping facilities and food stands and is renowned for its surf.

Dining and Lodging

For price ranges, see Charts 1 (A) and 2 (A) in On the Road with Fodor's. Reservations advised except as noted.

Anaheim

DINING

JW's. This French-country dining room serves well-prepared classic fare, such as roast saddle of lamb, venison, and wild boar. *Marriott Hotel, 700 Convention Way, ☎ 714/750–8000. Jacket suggested. AE, D, DC, MC, V. $$$*

The Catch. This very reliable restaurant across the street from Anaheim Stadium features hearty portions of steak, seafood, and salads. *1929 S. State College Blvd., Anaheim, ☎ 714/634–1829. AE, DC, MC, V. No lunch weekends. $$–$$$*

LODGING

Disneyland Hotel. This 60-acre resort is connected to the theme park by monorail. The towers and tropical village make for unique accommodations; rooms are decorated in soft pastels and have balconies with views of Disneyland or the hotel marina. *1150 W. Cerritos Ave., 92802, ☎ 714/778–6600, FAX 714/956–6597. 1,136 rooms. Facilities: 6 restaurants, pool, 10 tennis courts. AE, DC, MC, V. $$$$*

Inn at the Park Hotel. This venerable hotel, a longtime favorite of conventioneers, has large rooms, all with balconies and views of Disneyland. The pool area is especially attractive and spacious. *1855 S. Harbor Blvd., 92802, ☎ 714/750–1811 or 800/421–6662, FAX 714/971–3626. 500 rooms. Facilities: restaurant, lounge, pool, exercise room, spa, video games. AE, D, DC, MC, V. $$$*

Ramada Hotel Maingate. This clean, reliable member of the chain is across the street from Disneyland and has a free shuttle. *1460 S. Harbor Blvd., 92802, ☎ 714/772–6777 or 800/447–4048, FAX 714/999–1727. 465 rooms. Facilities: restaurant, pool, Jacuzzi, game room. AE, D, DC, MC, V. $$*

Hampton Inn. Here you'll find basic lodging at a basic price a short drive from Disneyland. *300 E. Katella Way, 92802, ☎ 714/772–8713 or 800/426–7866, FAX 714/778–1235. 136 rooms. Facilities: pool, complimentary breakfast. AE, D, DC, MC, V. $*

Costa Mesa

DINING

Mandarin Gourmet. Dollar for bite, owner Michael Chang provides what the critics and locals consider the best Chinese cuisine in the area. *1500 Adams Ave., ☎ 714/540–1937. AE, DC, MC, V. $$*

Dana Point

DINING AND LODGING

★ **Ritz-Carlton Laguna Niguel.** One of California's most highly respected hotels, the Ritz offers beach access, a spectacular ocean view, the Dining Room restaurant, a lavishly decorated lobby, and spacious rooms with balconies, French doors, and some fireplaces. *1 Ritz-Carlton Dr., 92677, ☎ 714/240–2000 or 800/241–3333, FAX 714/240–0829. 393 rooms. Facilities: 3 restaurants, 3 lounges, 2 pools, health club, 4 tennis courts, golf course. AE, D, DC, MC, V. $$$$*

Laguna Beach

DINING

Las Brisas. A spectacular coastline view from the clifftop terrace, great margaritas, irresistible guacamole, and nouvelle Mexican dishes make this a local favorite. *361 Cliff Dr., ☎ 714/497–5434. AE, D, DC, MC, V. $$*

LODGING

Surf and Sand Hotel. At this hotel right on the beach, rooms sport soft sand colors, wooden shutters, and private balconies. *15555 S. Coast Hwy., 92651, ☎ 714/497–4477 or 800/524–8621, FAX 714/494–7653. 157 rooms. Facilities: 2 restaurants, 2 lounges, pool, private beach, concierge. AE, D, DC, MC, V. $$$$*

Newport Beach

DINING

★ **Antoine.** The lovely, candlelit dining room, made for romance and quiet conversation, serves the best French cuisine of any hotel in southern California. *Sutton Place Hotel, 4500 MacArthur Blvd., ☎ 714/476–2001. Jacket and tie required. AE, DC, MC, V. No lunch. $$$$*

Crab Cooker. If you don't mind waiting in line, this shanty of a place serves fresh fish grilled over mesquite at low, low prices. *2200 Newport Blvd., ☎ 714/673–0100. No reservations. No credit cards. $*

LODGING

★ **Four Seasons Hotel.** Marble and antiques fill the airy lobby. The guest rooms, decorated in Southwestern colors, have spectacular views. *690 Newport Center Dr., 92660, ☎ 714/759–0808 or 800/332–3442, FAX 714/759–0568. 285 rooms. Facilities: 2 restaurants, pool, 2 tennis courts. AE, D, DC, MC, V. $$$$*

Sutton Place Hotel. This ultramodern hotel has an eye-catching ziggurat design. Luxuriously appointed rooms have minibars and built-in hair dryers. *4500 MacArthur Blvd., 92660, ☎ 714/476–2001 or*

800/810–6888, FAX 714/476–0153. 435 rooms. Facilities: 2 restaurants, lounge, pool, 2 tennis courts, health club, Jacuzzi, concierge. AE, D, DC, MC, V. $$$$

The Arts

Orange County Performing Arts Center (600 Town Center Dr., Costa Mesa, ☎ 714/556–2787) presents symphony orchestras, opera companies, and musicals. Summer concert series are presented at **Irvine Meadows Amphitheater** (8800 Irvine Center Dr., ☎ 714/855–4515) and **Pacific Amphitheater** (Orange County Fairgrounds, Costa Mesa, ☎ 714/740–2000).

SAN DIEGO

One of California's most attractive cities, San Diego is the birthplace of Spanish California. Its combination of history, pleasing climate, outdoor recreation and sports, and cultural life makes it a popular destination.

Tourist Information

San Diego: International Information Center (11 Horton Plaza, 92101, ☎ 619/236–1212); Mission Bay Visitor Information Center (2688 E. Mission Bay Dr., off I–5, 92109, ☎ 619/276–8200).

Arriving and Departing

By Plane

San Diego International Airport at Lindbergh Field (☎ 619/231–2100) is 3 mi northwest of downtown and is served by most domestic and many international air carriers. **Cloud 9 Shuttle** (☎ 619/278–8877 or 800/974–8885) has door-to-door service to anywhere in San Diego County, often for less than a taxi. **San Diego Transit** (☎ 619/233–3004) Rte. 2 buses leave the airport every 10–15 minutes and cost $1.50. Taxi fare is $6–$8 (plus tip) to most center-city hotels.

By Car

I–5 runs north–south. I–8 comes into San Diego from the east, I–15 from the northeast.

By Train

Amtrak (800/872–7245) trains arrive at **Santa Fe Depot** (Kettner Blvd. and Broadway, ☎ 619/239–9021).

By Bus

Greyhound Lines (120 W. Broadway and Los Angeles St., ☎ 800/231–2222).

Getting Around San Diego

It's best to have a car, but avoid the freeways during rush hours. The **San Diego Trolley** (☎ 619/233–3004) travels the 20 mi from downtown to within 100 ft of the Mexican border; other trolleys on the line serve Seaport Village, the Convention Center, and inland areas. **Harbor Hopper** (☎ 800/300–7447) is a water-taxi service.

Exploring San Diego

Downtown

The **Embarcadero** is a waterfront walkway lined with restaurants and cruise-ship piers. The **Maritime Museum** (1306 N. Harbor Dr., ☎ 619/

234–9153; admission charged) has a collection of restored ships, including the windjammer ***Star of India.***

Just south of the museum is the **Seaport Village** shopping mall (☎ 619/235–4014), three connected shopping plazas designed to reflect the architectural styles of early California; from here water taxis cross the bay to **Coronado,** a city of numerous Victorian houses whose most prominent landmark is the historic turreted and gingerbreaded **Hotel del Coronado** (*see* Lodging, *below*)—the first electrically lighted hotel. Another Coronado landmark is the **North Island Naval Air Station** (☎ 619/545–8167), from which Charles Lindbergh took off on his flight around the world. You can drive to Coronado via the 2.2-mi San Diego–Coronado Bridge, which offers a stunning view of the San Diego skyline.

In downtown San Diego, the **Gaslamp Quarter** is a 16-block National Historic District containing most of the city's Victorian-era commercial buildings. The **Gaslamp Quarter Association** (William Heath Davis House, 410 Island Ave., ☎ 619/233–5227) has walking-tour brochures and maps.

Balboa Park encompasses 1,400 acres of cultural, recreational, and environmental delights, including a theater complex and public gardens. Among the park's several museums are the **Museum of Man** (☎ 619/239–2001), one of the finest anthropological museums in the country; the **Hall of Champions Sports Museum** (☎ 619/234–2544); and the **Museum of Photographic Arts** (☎ 619/239–5262). Laserium and Omnimax shows are given in the **Reuben H. Fleet Space Theater and Science Center** (☎ 619/238–1233). All the above sights charge admission. The **Botanical Building** (no ☎; closed Thurs.) houses more than 500 types of tropical and subtropical plant species and a stunning orchid collection.

Balboa Park's most famous attraction is the **San Diego Zoo,** where more than 3,200 animals of 777 species roam in habitats built around natural canyons. The zoo is also an enormous botanical garden with one of the world's largest collections of subtropical plants. *☎ 619/234–3153. Admission: $13 adults, $6 children 3–11; bus tour additional. ⏲ Fall–spring, daily 9–4; summer, daily 9–9.*

San Diego's Spanish and Mexican history and heritage are most evident in **Old Town San Diego State Historic Park** (☎ 619/220–5422), a six-block district. **Old Town Plaza** contains many historic buildings. **Bazaar del Mundo** is a shopping complex with gardens, exotic shops, and outdoor restaurants, built to represent a colonial Mexican square. **Robinson-Rose House,** once the commercial center of old San Diego, is now park headquarters.

Mission Bay Park contains beaches, playgrounds, and the Giant Dipper roller coaster at **Belmont Park.**

At **Sea World**'s ocean-oriented amusement park, the Shamu whale show, Mission: Bermuda Triangle, Penguin Encounter, shark exhibit, and tide pools are popular attractions. Rocky Point Preserve houses Alaskan sea otters salvaged from the 1989 *Exxon-Valdez* oil spill and allows visitors to interact with bottlenose dolphins. *Sea World Dr. at I–8, ☎ 619/226–3901. Admission: $28.95 adults, $20.95 children 3–11; parking $5. ⏲ 10–dusk, later in summer.*

Thirteen miles north of downtown San Diego, in the upscale village of **La Jolla,** is the **San Diego Museum of Contemporary Art** (700 Prospect St., ☎ 619/454–3541; admission charged), which is currently being renovated and is not slated to open until early 1996. Until then, contemporary art will only be shown in the museum's small downtown annex (1001 Kettner Blvd., ☎ 619/234–1001). The **Stephen Birch Aquarium-Museum** (2300 Expedition Way, ☎ 619/534–3474; admission charged) at the **Scripps Institution of Oceanography** is the largest oceanographic exhibit in the country; tanks filled with colorful saltwater fish and a simulated submarine ride are among the attractions. North of La Jolla is **Torrey Pines State Beach and Reserve** (☎ 619/755–2063; admission charged), with a museum, hiking trails, and beaches. A short drive east of Oceanside along Hwy. 76 takes you to the 1798 **Mission San Luis Rey** (☎ 619/757–3651; admission charged), California's largest and best-preserved mission; its museum has an extensive collection of old Spanish vestments.

Shopping

San Diego's shopping areas are a mélange of self-contained megamalls, historic districts, quaint villages, funky neighborhoods, and chic suburbs.

Horton Plaza (☎ 619/238–1596), occupying six square blocks downtown (Broadway and G St., from 1st to 4th Aves.), is a multilevel postmodern mall with department stores, one-of-a-kind shops, fast-food counters, classy restaurants, a farmer's market, movies, and live theater. Across from Horton Plaza, the **Paladion** (1st Ave. between G and F Sts., ☎ 619/232–1627) houses such tony boutiques as Cartier, Tiffany, and Gucci.

The **Gaslamp Quarter** features art galleries, antiques shops, and other specialty stores. **La Jolla/Golden Triangle**'s trendy boutiques line Girard Avenue and Prospect Street; and **Coast Walk,** along Prospect Street, offers shops, galleries, and restaurants. **Old Town** has **Bazaar del Mundo, La Esplanade,** and **Old Town Mercado,** with international goods, toys, souvenirs, and arts and crafts.

Spectator Sports

Baseball

San Diego Padres (Jack Murphy Stadium, 9449 Frials Rd., ☎ 619/283–4494; Apr.–Oct.).

Football

San Diego Chargers (Jack Murphy Stadium, ☎ 619/280–2111; Aug.–Dec.).

Horse Racing

Del Mar Thoroughbred Club (Del Mar Fairgrounds, ☎ 619/755–1141; July–Sept.).

Beaches

Coronado Beach

This wide stretch of uncrowded sandy beach is perfect for sunbathing or Frisbee throwing. There are rest rooms and fire rings; parking can be difficult on busy days. *From the bridge, turn left on Orange Ave., then follow signs.*

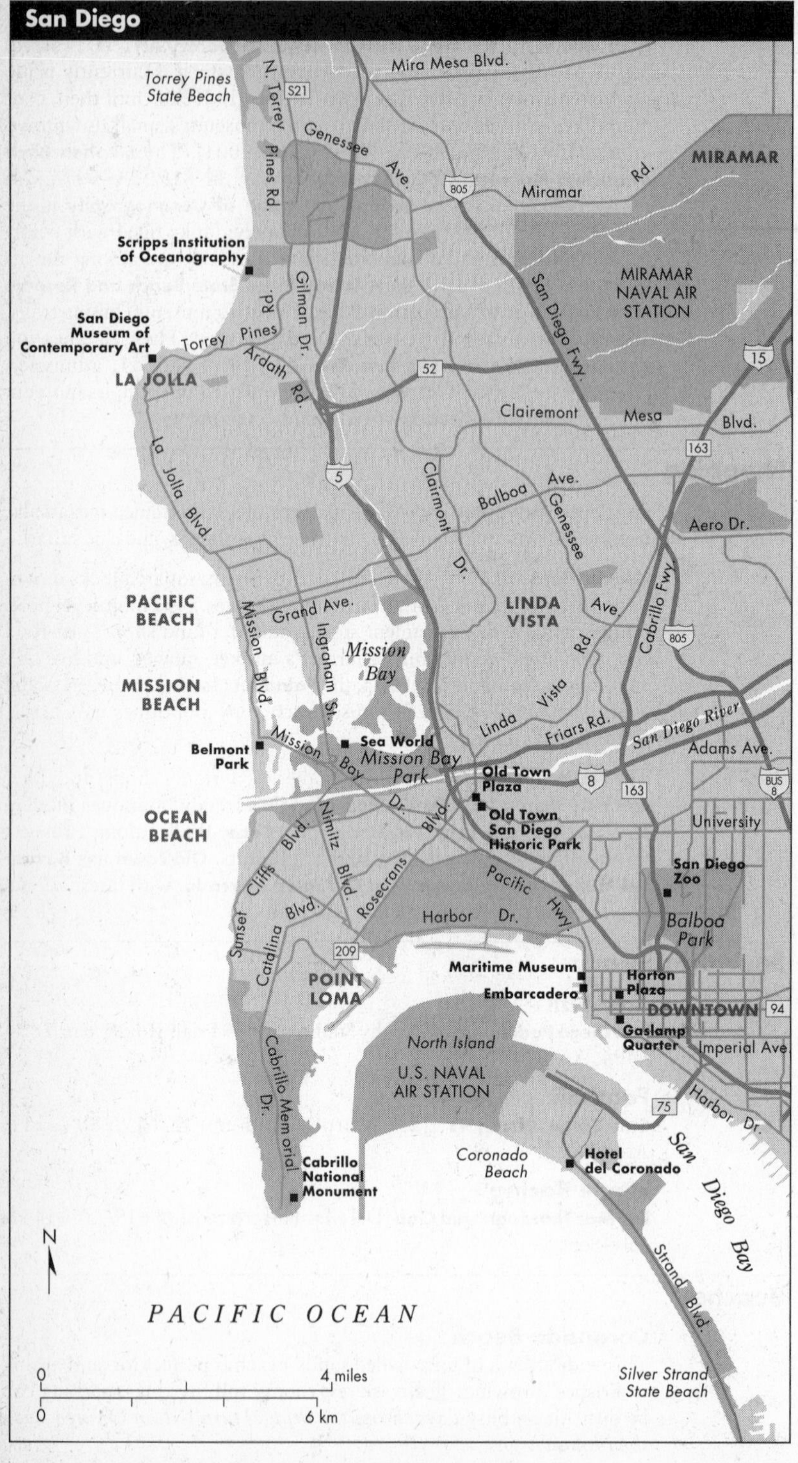
San Diego
Torrey Pines State Beach
N. Torrey Pines Rd.
S21
Mira Mesa Blvd.
Genessee Ave.
805
Miramar Rd.
MIRAMAR
Scripps Institution of Oceanography
Gilman Dr.
San Diego Fwy.
MIRAMAR NAVAL AIR STATION
San Diego Museum of Contemporary Art
Torrey Pines Rd.
Ardath Rd.
LA JOLLA
52
15
Clairemont Mesa Blvd.
163
5
Clairmont Dr.
Balboa Ave.
Genessee Ave.
La Jolla Blvd.
Aero Dr.
PACIFIC BEACH
Mission Blvd.
Grand Ave.
Ingraham St.
Mission Bay
LINDA VISTA
Cabrillo Fwy.
805
MISSION BEACH
Linda Vista Rd.
Friars Rd.
San Diego River
Adams Ave.
Belmont Park
Sea World
Mission Bay Park
Mission Bay Dr.
Old Town Plaza
8
163
BUS 8
OCEAN BEACH
Nimitz Blvd.
Old Town San Diego Historic Park
University
Sunset Cliffs Blvd.
Rosecrans Blvd.
Pacific Hwy.
San Diego Zoo
Catalina Blvd.
Harbor Dr.
Balboa Park
209
Maritime Museum
Embarcadero
Horton Plaza
POINT LOMA
DOWNTOWN
94
Gaslamp Quarter
Imperial Ave.
North Island
U.S. NAVAL AIR STATION
Cabrillo Memorial Dr.
75
Harbor Dr.
Coronado Beach
Hotel del Coronado
San Diego Bay
Cabrillo National Monument
N
Strand Blvd.
PACIFIC OCEAN
0
4 miles
0
6 km
Silver Strand State Beach

Imperial Beach

Surfers and swimmers congregate at this beach, which has lifeguards in summer, parking, rest rooms, and food vendors nearby. *Take Palm Ave. west from I–5 to the water.*

La Jolla Cove

The cove is a favorite of rough-water swimmers, but Children's Pool, a shallow lagoon at the south end, is a safer haven. *Follow Coast Blvd. north to signs; or take the La Jolla Village Dr. exit from I–5, head west to Torrey Pines Rd., turn left and drive down the hill to Girard Ave., turn right and follow signs.*

Mission Beach/Pacific Beach

The boardwalk is popular with strollers, roller skaters, and bicyclists. The south end is filled by surfers, swimmers, and volleyball players. Pacific Beach is a teen hangout; it's crowded in summer, and parking is a challenge. There are rest rooms and restaurants. *Exit I–5 at Garnet Ave. and head west to Mission Blvd.*

Silver Strand State Beach

On Coronado, this beach has relatively calm water, an RV campground ($14 per night), and other facilities. Parking is free Labor Day through February; at other times the fee is $4 per car. *Take the Palm Ave. exit off I–5 west to Hwy. 75; turn right and follow signs.*

Dining

San Diego's gastronomic reputation rests primarily on its seafood. A city that once stood solidly in the meat-and-potatoes camp now also boasts Afghani, Thai, Vietnamese, and other ethnic cuisines. For price ranges, see Chart 1 (A) in On the Road with Fodor's. Reservations advised except as noted.

$$$ ★ **Dobson's.** The perennial favorite here is mussel bisque. Fish, veal, fowl, and beef entrées are menu highlights. *956 Broadway Circle, ☎ 619/231–6771. Jacket advised. AE, DC, MC, V. Closed Sun. No lunch Sat.*

$$$ ★ **George's at the Cove.** Service is excellent at this art-filled dining room with a view of La Jolla Cove, and an imaginative, well-prepared menu featuring seafood, pasta, beef, and veal. The charbroiled apple-smoked salmon entrée and any of the shellfish pastas are recommended. *1250 Prospect St., La Jolla, ☎ 619/454–4244. AE, D, DC, MC, V.*

$$$ **Top O' the Cove.** This romantic restaurant with a view of La Jolla Cove turns out beautifully garnished, luxury fare dressed with creamy and well-seasoned sauces. The extensive wine list has received countless awards. *1216 Prospect St., La Jolla, ☎ 619/454–7779. AE, DC, MC, V.*

$$–$$$ ★ **Trattoria La Strada.** This lively Tuscan restaurant's dishes include *antipasto di mare,* with tender shrimp and shellfish, and salad La Strada, with wild mushrooms, walnuts, and shaved parmesan. The pastas, particularly the *pappardelle all'anitra* (wide noodles with a duck sauce), are excellent. *702 5th Ave., ☎ 619/239–3400. AE, D, DC, MC, V. No lunch weekends.*

$$ **Cafe Pacifica.** The menu changes according to the day's catch. Light, interesting sauces and imaginative garnishes are teamed with simply cooked fillets of salmon, sea bass, and swordfish. *2414 San Diego Ave., ☎ 619/291–6666. AE, D, DC, MC, V. No lunch Sat.–Mon.*

$$ ★ **Palenque.** This family-run restaurant in Pacific Beach serves a good selection of Mexican dishes, including chicken with mole, served in the regular chocolate-based or green chili version, and *camarones en chipotle,* large shrimp cooked in a chili and tequila cream sauce (an old family recipe of the proprietor). *1653 Garnet Ave., Pacific Beach,* ☎ *619/272–7816. AE, D, DC, MC, V.*

$–$$ ★ **Bayou Bar and Grill.** Seafood gumbo, duck esplanade, and fresh Louisiana Gulf seafood dishes are among the Cajun and Creole specialties served here. Desserts include praline cheesecake and Creole pecan pie. *329 Market St.,* ☎ *619/696–8747. AE, D, DC, MC, V. No lunch Mon.–Tues.*

$ **Hob Nob Hill.** The pot roast, fried chicken, and corned beef here have a truly homemade taste. The place has been under the same ownership since 1944, and its dark, wooden booths and patterned carpet lend a vintage feel. *2271 1st Ave.,* ☎ *619/239–8176. AE, D, MC, V.*

$ ★ **Thai Chada.** Try any of the noodle dishes, the Tom Ka Kai chicken soup (with coconut milk, lemon grass, lime juice, and scallions), or the roast duck curry. *142 University Ave.,* ☎ *619/297–9548. AE, D, DC, MC, V. No lunch Sun.*

Lodging

Most hotels have parking except as noted below. For price ranges, see Chart 2 (A) in On the Road with Fodor's.

$$$–$$$$ **Catamaran Resort Hotel.** Children under 18 stay free at this hotel with a tropical feel. Rooms are in six two-story buildings or a high rise with spectacular views. Some have kitchens. Two resident parrots are often poised on a perch in the lushly landscaped lobby, replete with a koi fish pond. *3999 Mission Blvd., 92109,* ☎ *619/488–1081 or 800/288–0770,* FAX *619/490–3328 (reservations) or 619/488–1619 (front desk). 312 rooms. Facilities: restaurant, coffee shop, nightclub, 2 bars, pool, spa, exercise room, water-sports rentals. AE, D, DC, MC, V.*

$$$–$$$$ **Hotel del Coronado.** Rooms and suites in the 1888 original Victorian building are charmingly quirky. A newer high rise has more standard accommodations. *1500 Orange Ave., Coronado 92118,* ☎ *619/435–6611 or 800/468–3533,* FAX *619/522–8262. 691 rooms. Facilities: 3 restaurants, deli, pool, Jacuzzi, steamroom, sauna, 8 tennis courts, croquet, beach, bicycles. AE, D, DC, MC, V.*

$$$–$$$$ ★ **La Valencia.** This centrally located pink-stucco hotel is a La Jolla landmark. It has a courtyard for patio dining and an elegant lobby where guests congregate to enjoy the ocean view. Rooms have a romantic European ambience. *1132 Prospect St., La Jolla 92037,* ☎ *619/454–0771,* FAX *619/456–3921. 100 rooms. Facilities: 3 restaurants, bar, pool, sauna, hot tub, exercise room, library. AE, D, DC, MC, V.*

$$$–$$$$ ★ **Westgate Hotel.** Antiques, Italian marble counters, and bath fixtures with 14-karat-gold overlays typify the opulent furnishings here. High tea, breathtaking views, and nearby Horton Plaza are other highlights. *1055 2nd Ave., 92101,* ☎ *619/238–1818 or 800/221–3802; in CA, 800/522–1564;* FAX *619/557–3737. 223 rooms. Facilities: 3 restaurants, lounge, exercise room. AE, D, DC, MC, V.*

$$–$$$ **Heritage Park Bed & Breakfast Inn.** This romantic 1889 Queen Anne mansion is decorated with 19th-century antiques. Rates include breakfast. *2470 Heritage Park Row, 92110,* ☎ *619/295–7088 or 800/995–2470. 9 rooms (2 share bath). AE, MC, V.*

$$ ★ **Best Western Hanalei Hotel.** The feel here is tropical inside and out. Golf access and free transport to local malls and Old Town are provided. *2270 Hotel Circle N, 92108,* ☎ *619/297–1101 or 800/882–*

0858, FAX 619/297-6049. 412 rooms. Facilities: 2 restaurants, bar, pool, spa, free parking. AE, D, DC, MC, V.

$$ **Torrey Pines Inn.** This contemporary-style hotel adjacent to the Torrey Pines Golf Course commands an expansive coastline view. *11480 Torrey Pines Rd., La Jolla 92037, ☎ 619/453-4420 or 800/995-4507, FAX 619/453-0691. 74 rooms. Facilities: restaurant, coffee shop, 2 bars, pool. AE, D, DC, MC, V.*

$ ★ **La Pensione.** This budget hotel in a quiet downtown neighborhood has a pretty central courtyard and rooms with harbor views and some kitchenettes. *1700 India St., 92101, ☎ 619/236-8000 or 800/232-46835, FAX 619/236-8088. 81 rooms. Facility: laundry. AE, MC, V.*

$ **Mission Bay Motel.** A half-block from the beach, this motel offers modest units within walking distance of great restaurants and nightlife. *4221 Mission Blvd., 92109, ☎ 619/483-6440. 50 rooms. Facility: pool. MC, V.*

$ **Padre Trail Inn.** This family-style motel is within walking distance of Old Town, shopping, and dining. *4200 Taylor St., 92110, ☎ 619/297-3291 or 800/255-9988, FAX 619/692-2080. 100 rooms. Facilities: restaurant, bar, pool. AE, D, DC, MC, V.*

The Arts and Nightlife

San Diego enthusiastically supports opera, symphony, and a wide range of theaters. Book tickets well in advance through **TicketMaster** (☎ 619/220-8497).

The Arts

Old Globe Theatre (Simon Edison Centre, Balboa Park, ☎ 619/239-2255) presents classics, experimental works, and a summer Shakespeare Festival. **Copley Symphony Hall** (1245 7th Ave., ☎ 619/699-4200) is home to the San Diego Symphony, whose season runs October–May. **Civic Theatre** (202 C St., ☎ 619/236-6510) is where to catch the San Diego Opera from January to April.

Nightlife

San Diego's nightlife ranges from quiet piano bars to cutting-edge rock. **Casbah** (2501 Kettner Blvd., ☎ 619/232-4355) showcases rock, reggae, and funk bands every night. **Humphrey's** (2241 Shelter Island Dr., ☎ 619/523-1010) offers the city's best jazz and folk. **Leo's Little Bit O' Country** (680 W. San Marcos Blvd., San Marcos, ☎ 619/744-4120) hosts C&W dancing. The **Comedy Store** (916 Pearl St., La Jolla, ☎ 619/454-9176) hosts local and national talent. The popular **Pacific Beach Bar and Grill** (860 Garnet Ave., Pacific Beach, ☎ 619/272-4745) has a huge patio, billiards, and satellite sports.

ELSEWHERE IN SOUTHERN CALIFORNIA

Palm Springs

Getting There

Palm Springs is about a two-hour drive east of Los Angeles and a three-hour drive northeast of San Diego. From L.A.. take the I-10E to Hwy. 111. From San Diego take I-15N to Hwy. 60, then I-10E to Hwy. 111. **Palm Springs Municipal Airport** is served by national and regional airlines.

What to See and Do

A desert playground for Hollywood celebrities since the 1930s, Palm Springs has plenty of attractions: luxurious resorts, nearly year-round golf and tennis, shopping, celebrity watching, and top-name entertainment. The area's natural attractions include the desert landscape of **Joshua Tree National Park** (I–10S to the Cottonwood Visitor Center or I–10N to Hwy. 62 to the Oasis Visitor Center, ☎ 619/367–7511). The oddly shaped trees, with their branches raised like arms, and the sculptural outcroppings of rocks are entrancing. There are over 500 campsites within the park and more in private campgrounds around it. The vast **Anza Borrego Desert State Park** (☎ 619/767–5311), in the southern portion of the region, explodes into color each spring when the wildflowers bloom. The **Palm Springs Desert Resorts Bureau** (69–930 Hwy. 111, Suite 201, Rancho Mirage 92270, ☎ 619/770–9000 or 800/417–3529) and **Palm Springs Visitor Information Center** (2781 N. Palm Canyon, 92262, ☎ 800/347–7746) can provide helpful information.

For an overview of the area, take a ride up the **Palm Springs Aerial Tramway** (1 Tramway Rd., ☎ 619/325–1391). **Palm Canyon Drive** is the main shopping strip, with Saks Fifth Avenue as the centerpiece and shops offering jewelry, resort wear, and sportswear. **El Paseo** (48980 Seminole Dr., Cabazon) is the trendiest shopping spot in the desert.

As befits the home of the **Bob Hope Desert Classic** (Jan.) and the **Dinah Shore Championship** (Mar. or Apr.), golf courses abound in the area. The most famous are connected with resorts and private country clubs, but two that are open to the public are **Palm Springs Golf Course** (1885 Golf Club Dr., ☎ 619/328–1005) and **Tommy Jacobs' Bel Aire Greens** (1001 El Cielo Rd., ☎ 619/327–0332).

Dining and Lodging

The restaurant scene in Palm Springs benefits from so much L.A. influence. Full-service hotels and resorts are the city's strong suit, though there are plenty of basic lodging options. For price ranges, see Charts 1 (A) and 2 (A) in On the Road with Fodor's.

DINING

Palomino Euro Bistro. One of the hot spots in the desert, this restaurant specializes in grilled and roasted entrées: spit-roasted garlic chicken, oak-fired thin-crust pizza, and oven-roasted prawns. *73–101 Hwy. 111, ☎ 619/773–9091. AE, D, DC, MC, V. No lunch Sat. $$*

LODGING

★ **Ritz-Carlton Rancho Mirage.** The poshest gem in the desert has all the amenities: restaurants, pools, bar, fitness center, and tennis courts. The rooms are comfortably furnished in 18th- to 19th-century style; they have marble baths and French doors opening onto a balcony or patio. *68–900 Frank Sinatra Dr., Rancho Mirage 92270, ☎ 619/321–8282, FAX 619/321–6928. 240 rooms. AE, D, DC, MC, V. $$$$*

Korakia Pensione. This historic Moorish-style home is furnished with antiques, fireplaces, and handmade furniture. Room rates include full breakfast. *257 S. Patencio Rd., ☎ 619/864–6411. 12 rooms. Facilities: pool, kitchen in some rooms. No credit cards. $$–$$$*

Death Valley

Getting There

From the west (about 300 mi from Los Angeles), exit U.S. 395 at either Hwy. 190 or 178. From the southeast (about 140 mi from Las Vegas), take Hwy. 127 north from I–15 and Hwy. 178 past Funeral Peak, Badwater, Dante's View, and Zabriskie Point to Hwy. 190 at Furnace Creek. Reliable maps are a must; AAA provides the most detailed ones.

What to See and Do

Death Valley National Park (visitor center, Furnace Creek, ☎ 619/786–2331), the lowest point in the country, is a desert wonderland, with 14 sq mi of sand dunes, 200 sq mi of crusty salt flats, 11,000-ft mountains, and hills and canyons of many hues. In the northwest section is **Scotty's Castle** (north on Hwy. 190), a $2.5 million Moorish-style mansion built by a onetime cowboy and performer in Buffalo Bill's Wild West Show. **Harmony Borax Works** (south on Hwy. 190) illustrates the mining history of the valley, from which the 20-mule teams hauled borax to the railroad at Mojave. **Dante's View,** 5,000 ft up in the Black Mountains, offers a view of both the lowest (Badwater) and highest (Mt. Whitney) points in the United States.

OREGON

By Jeff Kuechle

Capital	Salem
Population	3,082,000
Motto	The Union
State Bird	Western meadowlark
State Flower	Oregon grape

Visitor Information

Oregon State Welcome Center (12348 N. Center Ave., Portland 97217, ☎ 503/285–1631) and the **Oregon Economic Development Tourism Division** (595 Cottage St. NE, Salem 97310, ☎ 800/547–7842).

Scenic Drives

The **Crown Point Scenic Highway** twists and turns its way above I–84 through the heavily wooded, waterfall-laced fairyland east of Portland. **U.S. 101** follows the unspoiled, monolith-studded Oregon coastline all the way from Washington to California. **Hwy. 138** from Roseburg to Crater Lake is a National Scenic Byway (*see* Elsewhere in the State, Ashland/The Rogue Valley, *below*).

National and State Parks

National Parks

Crater Lake National Park (Box 7, Crater Lake 97604, ☎ 503/594–2211) began 6,800 years ago, when Mt. Mazama decapitated itself in a huge explosion. Rain and snowmelt eventually filled the caldera, creating a sapphire-blue lake so clear that sunlight penetrates to a depth of 400 ft. Visitors can drive or hike the park's 25-mi Rim Drive, explore a variety of nature trails, and (in summer) take guided boat trips around the lake itself. **Newberry National Volcanic Monument,** 25 mi southeast of Bend, contains over 50,000 acres of lakes, lava flows, and spectacular geological features administered by the Deschutes National Forest (1645 Hwy. 20E, Bend 97701, ☎ 503/388–2715). **Oregon Caves National Monument** (20000 Caves Hwy., Cave Junction 97523, ☎ 503/592–3400) offers guided tours of the "Marble Halls of Oregon." **Oregon Dunes National Recreation Area** (855 Highway Ave., Reedsport 97467, ☎ 503/271–3611), a 47-mi swath of camel-colored sand, is popular with campers, hikers, mountain bikers, dune-buggy enthusiasts, and even dogsledders.

State Parks

Oregon's 225 state parks run the gamut from sage-scented desert to mountains to sea. The **Oregon State Parks and Recreation Department** (525 Trade St. SE, Salem 97310, ☎ 800/452–5687) has information on the parks and facilities.

PORTLAND

Portland has earned a reputation as one of the best-planned and most relaxing cities in America. Straddling the banks of the wide, salmon-filled Willamette River, it blends flower-filled parks, efficient mass transit, skyscrapers, and beautifully restored historic buildings. As one of the United States' most important gateways to the Pacific Rim, Portland has gained noticeable sophistication in recent decades.

Tourist Information

Portland/Oregon Visitors Association (World Trade Center 3, 28 S.W. Salmon St., 97204, ☎ 503/222–2223; in OR, 800/345–3214; outside OR, 800/962–3700). **Portland Guides** are easily spotted in their green jackets walking the sidewalks downtown; they can assist with directions, answer questions about the city, and even give recommendations on top spots to eat, drink, and rest your feet.

Arriving and Departing

By Plane

Portland International Airport (☎ 503/335–1234) is in northeast Portland, about 10 mi from the city center, and is served by major domestic carriers. Taxi (**Portland Taxi,** ☎ 503/256–5400; **Broadway Cab,** ☎ 503/227–1234), bus (**Raz Transportation,** ☎ 503/246–3301), and hotel shuttle services connect the airport to downtown. A taxi ride downtown from the airport costs about $22, and the bus is $7.

By Car

I–84 (Banfield Fwy.) and Hwy. 26 (the Sunset) run east–west; I–5 and I–205 run north–south.

By Train

Amtrak serves Union Station (800 N.W. 6th Ave., ☎ 503/273–4865 or 800/872–7245).

By Bus

Greyhound Lines (550 N.W. 6th Ave., ☎ 800/231–2222).

Getting Around Portland

The metro area is laid out in a logical grid system, with numbered avenues running north–south and named streets running east–west. The efficient **MAX light-rail line** links east Portland suburbs with the Lloyd Center district, the Convention Center, Memorial Coliseum, and the downtown core. The **Tri-Met bus system** covers the metro area extensively. Call 503/238–7433 for schedules and routes for both Tri-Met and MAX.

Exploring Portland

Downtown

Start a tour downtown, with its lively shops, restaurants, galleries, museums, and theaters. In previous incarnations, the site of **Pioneer Courthouse Square** was the city's first school, an elegant hotel, and a parking lot. Now it's the city's main gathering place and people-watching venue. Nearby is the **Portland Center for the Performing Arts** (corner of S.W. Broadway and S.W. Main St., ☎ 503/796–9293), the elegant hub of the city's arts community. Within its richly paneled confines is the 2,776-seat **Arlene Schnitzer Concert Hall,** while the 916-seat **Intermediate Theater** and the 292-seat **Delores Winningstad Theater** are just across the street in the new Performing Arts Building.

Pass westward through the tree-lined South Park Blocks, a series of city blocks that form a vast, green boulevard of statues and fountains, on your way to the **Portland Art Museum.** The Northwest's oldest arts facility, the museum contains 35 centuries of Asian, European, and Native American art. *1219 S.W. Park Ave., ☎ 503/226–2811. Admission charged (except 4–9 PM first Thurs. of month). Closed Mon.*

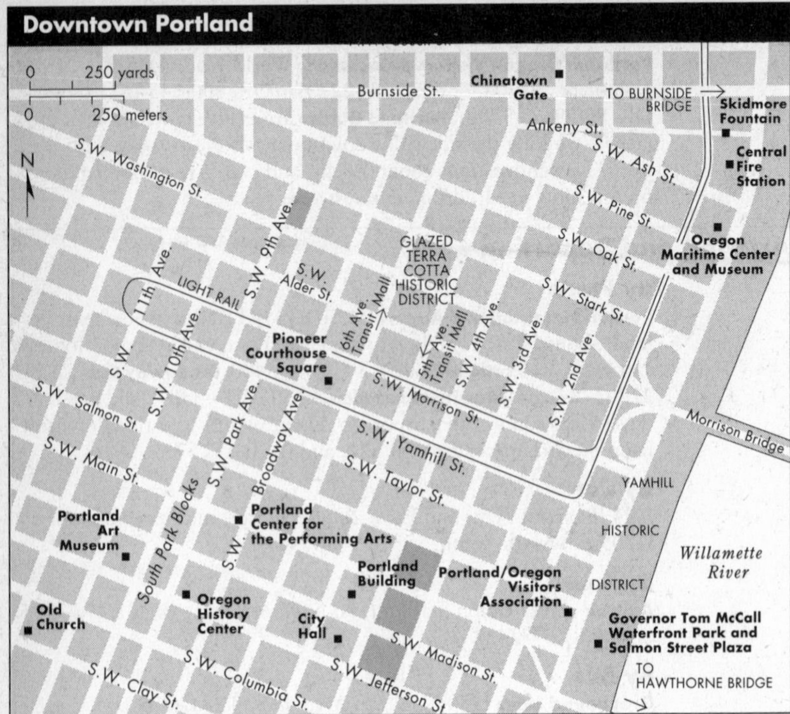

Across the South Park Blocks you'll note towering murals of Lewis and Clark and the Oregon Trail. The paintings frame the entrance to the **Oregon History Center,** where the state's history from prehistoric times to the present is documented. *1200 S.W. Park Ave., ☎ 503/222–1741. Admission charged.*

The **Old Church,** built in 1882, is a prime example of carpenter-Gothic architecture, complete with rough-cut lumber, tall spires, and original stained-glass windows. Free concerts on one of the few operating Hook and Hastings pipe organs are presented on Wednesday at noon. *1422 S.W. 11th Ave., ☎ 503/222–2031. Closed Sun.–Mon.*

Southward on Madison Street is architect Michael Graves's **Portland Building** (1120 S.W. 5th Ave.), one of the country's first postmodern designs. *Portlandia,* the second-largest hammered-copper sculpture in the world (after the Statue of Liberty), kneels on the second-story balcony. Inside is the **Metropolitan Center for Public Art** (☎ 503/823–5111). Across Madison Avenue is the classically styled **City Hall,** built in 1895, with columns on two of its faces and high ceilings, marble hallways, and pillars inside.

The **World Trade Center** (28 S.W. Salmon St.) is a trio of buildings connected by sky bridges and designed by Portland architect Robert Frasca. Cross Front Avenue to **Governor Tom McCall Waterfront Park.** The grassy 2-mi expanse, a former expressway, follows the curve of the Willamette north to Burnside Street; it's a popular venue for festivals, concerts, picnics, jogging, and biking.

Cross Front Avenue, and you're in the heart of the **Yamhill and Skidmore National Historic Districts,** which preserve many fine examples of 19th-century cast-iron architecture. The former commercial waterfront of Portland is now a district of galleries, fountains, and shops.

The main mast of the battleship **Oregon,** which served in three wars, stands at the foot of Oak Street. Across Front Avenue is the **Oregon Maritime Center and Museum** (113 S.W. Front Ave., ☎ 503/224–7724), whose exterior features prime street-level examples of cast-iron architecture. Inside are models of ships that once plied the Columbia River. Next door is the **Jeff Morris Memorial Fire Museum** (111 S.W. Front Ave.) in the central Fire Station, which houses antique pumps and other equipment.

Nearby, **Portland Saturday Market** (100 S.W. Ankeny St., ☎ 503/222–6072), also open on Sunday, features live entertainment and some 300 merchants selling an assortment of ethnic foods, art, and crafts from March through Christmas.

In the 1890s Portland's Chinese community was the second largest in the United States. Today it is compressed into several blocks in the northwest part of town, with fine restaurants, shops, and grocery stores. **Chinatown Gate** (N.W. 4th Ave. and Burnside St.) can be recognized by its 5 roofs, 64 dragons, and 2 huge lion dogs; it is the official entrance to **Chinatown.**

In the Vicinity

Pittock Mansion, 1,000 ft above the city, offers superb views of the skyline, rivers, and Cascade Mountains. The 1909 mansion, which combines French Renaissance and Victorian decor, was built by Henry Pittock, former editor of the *Oregonian.* Set in its own scenic park, the opulent manor has been restored and is filled with art and antiques of the 1880s. *3229 N.W. Pittock Dr., ☎ 503/823–3624. Admission charged.*

What to See and Do with Children

The **Children's Museum** (3037 S.W. 2nd Ave., ☎ 503/823–2227) offers hands-on play with changing interactive exhibits. The **Oregon Museum of Science and Industry** (1945 S.E. Water Ave., ☎ 503/797–4000), in a restored steam plant on the east bank of the Willamette, has touring exhibits, permanent displays, a planetarium, and an Omnimax theater.

Shopping

For local products, try the several **Made In Oregon** shops, at Portland International Airport, Lloyd Center, the Galleria, Old Town, Washington Square, or Clackamas Town Center. Merchandise ranges from books to distinctive myrtle wood, local wines, and fine Pendleton woolen products.

Pioneer Place (700 S.W. 5th Ave., ☎ 503/228–5800) is the jewel in the city's shopping crown. More than 80 specialty shops are anchored by a gleaming **Saks Fifth Avenue.** Next door is the original **Meier & Frank** (621 S.W. 5th Ave., ☎ 503/223–0512) department store, a Portland landmark since 1857. **Nordstrom** (701 S.W. Broadway, ☎ 503/224–6666), famous for personal service, features quality apparel and accessories and a large shoe department. **Nike Town** (930 S.W. 6th Ave., ☎ 503/221–6453) is part sports shrine, part sales outlet for Nike's many sportswear lines.

With more than 1 million new and used volumes, **Powell's City of Books** (1005 W. Burnside St., ☎ 503/228–4651) is one of the largest bookstores in the world. **Norm Thompson** (1805 N.W. Thurman St., ☎ 503/

221–0764) features one-of-a-kind Northwest gifts. The **Portland Pendleton Shop** (900 S.W. 4th Ave., ☎ 503/242–0037) carries men's and women's wear, including the Oregon mill's famous Pendleton shirts and blankets.

Spectator Sports

Basketball

Portland Trail Blazers (Memorial Coliseum, 1401 N. Wheeler St., east end of Broadway Bridge, ☎ 503/234–9291; Nov.–Apr.).

Dining

Bounteous local produce from land and sea receives star billing at Portland's many dining establishments, and recent Pacific Rim immigrants have added depth and spice to the restaurant scene. For price ranges, see Chart 1 (B) in On the Road with Fodor's.

$$$ ★ **Genoa.** Small, crowded, and intimate, Genoa seats 35 people for sumptuous four- and seven-course northern Italian dinners. The menu changes to take advantage of seasonal bounty. *2832 S.E. Belmont St., ☎ 503/238–1464. Reservations required. AE, D, DC, MC, V. Closed Sun. No lunch.*

$$$ **L'Auberge.** Here you can dine simply beside the lounge fireplace or splurge on a six-course meal in the candlelit formal dining room. L'Auberge continues to stay at the forefront of the Pacific Northwest cuisine scene. *2601 N.W. Vaughn St., ☎ 503/223–3302. AE, D, DC, MC, V. No lunch; Sun., bar menu only.*

$$ **Esparza's Tex-Mex Cafe.** The only thing wilder than the colorful, jackalope-festooned decor at this bustling neighborhood café is the cuisine that issues from chef-owner Joe Esparza's kitchen—dishes like smoked-buffalo enchiladas, calf-brain tacos, and the best *chiles rellenos* this side of El Paso. *2725 S.E. Ankeny St., ☎ 503/234–7909. MC, V. Closed Sun.–Mon.*

$$ ★ **Indigine.** Owner-chef Millie Howe wows regulars with her original cuisine, which draws flavors from India, Latin America, Indonesia, and Italy. The surroundings are intimate, with a pleasing Japanese simplicity. *3725 S.E. Division St., ☎ 503/238–1470. MC, V. Closed Sun.–Mon. No lunch.*

$$ **Jake's Famous Crawfish.** Portland's best-known restaurant celebrated its 100th birthday in 1992. White-coated waiters serve up fresh Northwest seafood, selected from a lengthy sheet of daily specials, in a warren of old-fashioned wood-paneled dining rooms. *401 S.W. 12th Ave., ☎ 503/226–1419. AE, D, DC, MC, V. No lunch weekends.*

$ **Bangkok Kitchen.** Don't be daunted by the bland decor—the quality of the food makes up for it. Owner-chef Srichan Miller juggles lime, cilantro, coconut milk, lemongrass, curry, and (above all) hot peppers with great virtuosity. Order your dishes mild or medium-hot unless you have an asbestos tongue. *2534 S.E. Belmont St., ☎ 503/236–7349. No credit cards. Closed Sun.–Mon. No lunch Sat.*

$ ★ **Yen Ha.** The vibrant flavors of Vietnam find full expression at Yen Ha, thronged nightly with Asians and Caucasians alike. Superb rice-paper rolls (filled with shrimp, pungent bean threads, and fresh mint and dipped in peanut sauce) and exquisite noodle dishes are among the star attractions. *8640 S.W. Canyon Rd. (west Portland), ☎ 503/292–0616; 6820 N.E. Sandy Blvd. (east Portland), ☎ 503/287–3698. MC, V. Closed Mon.*

Brew Pubs

Portland is the microbrewery mecca of North America. Its dozen-odd small breweries and affiliated pubs offer both satisfying dining and good value. Among the standouts are the **B. Moloch Heathman Bakery and Pub** (901 S.W. Salmon St., ☎ 503/227–5700) and the **Pilsner Room** (309 S.W. Montgomery St., ☎ 503/220–1865), which offer a variety of local brews and inexpensive nouvelle pub cuisine. The **Bridgeport Brew Pub** (1313 N.W. Marshall St., ☎ 503/241–7179) serves thick hand-thrown pizzas, washed down with creamy pints of Bridgeport real ale. **McMenamins Edgefield** (2126 S.W. Halsey St., Troutdale, ☎ 503/492–4686) is the showpiece of the vast microbrewing empire of the McMenamin brothers, a 12-acre estate with its own pub, restaurant, movie theater, 105-room inn, winery, and brewery.

Lodging

There is a full array of national and regional chain offerings near the airport. The city center and waterfront support a variety of elegant new and historic hotels. B&Bs cluster in the West Hills and across the river in the Lloyd Center/Convention Center area. **Northwest Bed & Breakfast** (☎ 503/243–7616) is a good source of reservations for Portland and the entire coastal region. For price ranges, see Chart 2 (B) in On the Road with Fodor's.

$$$ **The Benson.** Portland's grandest hotel, built in 1912, has received a $30 million face-lift, restoring it to its original turn-of-the-century grandeur. Elegance is everywhere, from walls paneled in Russian walnut to the muted tinkling of the lobby's grand piano to the opulent guest rooms. *309 S.W. Broadway, 97205, ☎ 503/228–2000 or 800/426–0670, FAX 503/226–4603. 287 rooms. Facilities: 3 restaurants, 2 lounges, fitness room, gift shop, valet parking, airport-shuttle service, concierge. AE, D, DC, MC, V.*

$$$ ★ **The Heathman.** Superior service, an award-winning restaurant, and a library of signed first editions by authors who have been guests here have earned the Heathman a reputation for quality. The guest rooms have original artwork by Northwest artists. *1009 S.W. Broadway, 97205, ☎ 503/241–4100 or 800/551–0011, FAX 503/790–7110. 151 rooms. Facilities: restaurant, bar, fitness room. AE, D, DC, MC, V.*

$$$ **Hotel Vintage Plaza.** From the names of the rooms to a complimentary wine hour each evening, this luxury hotel, opened in 1991, takes its theme from the area's wine country. Suites feature full living areas appointed in hunter green, deep plum, cerise, and gold. *422 S.W. Broadway, 97205, ☎ 503/228–1212 or 800/243–0555, FAX 503/228–3598. 107 rooms, some wheelchair accessible. Facilities: restaurant, complimentary breakfast, piano lounge, concierge, fitness room, business center, valet parking. AE, D, DC, MC, V.*

$$$ **Red Lion/Lloyd Center.** At Oregon's second-largest hotel, service runs like a well-oiled machine. Many of the large rooms with balconies have views of the mountains or the city center. Lloyd Center shopping and MAX light rail are across the street. *1000 N.E. Multnomah St., 97232, ☎ 503/281–6111 or 800/547–8010, FAX 503/284–8553. 476 rooms, some wheelchair accessible. Facilities: 3 restaurants, 2 lounges, whirlpool, outdoor pool, weight room, airport shuttle. AE, D, DC, MC, V.*

$$$ **Shilo Inn Suites Hotel.** Each suite has three TVs, a VCR, a microwave, four phones, a refrigerator, a wet bar, and two oversize beds. *11707 N.E. Airport Way, 97220, ☎ 503/252–7500 or 800/222–2244, FAX 503/254–0794. 200 rooms, some wheelchair accessible. Facilities: Continental breakfast, restaurant, lounge, whirlpool, indoor pool,* *spa, exercise room, steam room, business service center, free parking, airport shuttle. AE, D, DC, MC, V.*

$$ Best Western Inn at the Convention Center. Rooms were redecorated in 1989 in pleasing creams and rusts at this property across the street from the convention center. *420 N.E. Holladay St., 97232, ☎ 503/233–6331, FAX 503/233–2677. 97 rooms. Facilities: restaurant, laundry, free parking. AE, D, DC, MC, V.*

$$ Portland Guest House. This northeast Portland 1890s stick-style Victorian, with its fresh dusty heather exterior paint and original oak floors, was transformed into a cozy B&B in 1987. Rooms are done in white on white with Victorian walnut antique furniture and original Pacific Northwest art. *1720 N.E. 15th Ave., 97212, ☎ 503/282–1402. 7 rooms, 2 share bath. AE, DC, MC, V.*

$ Downtown Portland YWCA. The baths are down the hall, but the beds are new in this recently renovated Y for women 18 and older. With rates around $10–$35 a night, it's a rare lodging bargain. *1111 S.W. 10th Ave., 97205, ☎ 503/223–6281, FAX 503/223–5988. 23 rooms, plus an 8-bed hostel (all share bath). Facilities: full athletic club, laundry facilities, communal kitchenette, phones. MC, V.*

$ Mallory Hotel. This refurbished Portland stalwart is eight blocks from the city center. The rooms are on the small side but tastefully decorated in white and natural wood. *729 S.W. 15th Ave., 97205, ☎ 503/223–6311 or 800/228–8657, FAX 503/223–0522. 144 rooms. Facilities: restaurant, lounge, free parking. AE, D, DC, MC, V.*

Motels

Riverside Inn (50 S.W. Morrison St., 97204, ☎ 503/221–0711, FAX 503/274–0312), 141 rooms, restaurant, lounge, health club; *$–$$*. **Portland Silver Cloud Inn** (2426 N.W. Vaughn St., 97210, ☎ 503/242–2400, FAX 503/242–1770), 81 rooms, Continental breakfast, laundry, fitness room, whirlpool; *$*.

The Arts and Nightlife

The *Oregonian* (on newsstands) and *Willamette Week* (available free in the metro area) list arts and entertainment events. **Portland Area Theatre Alliance** (☎ 503/241–4902) has current listings.

The Arts

The **Portland Center Stage** performs from November to April at Portland's **Intermediate Theater** (1111 S.W. Broadway, ☎ 503/248–6309). The Portland Center for the Performing Arts (☎ 503/248–4496) offers rock concerts, lectures, and Broadway musicals. The **Oregon Symphony** (☎ 503/228–1353) performs more than 40 concerts each season at the **Arlene Schnitzer Concert Hall. Portland Opera** (☎ 503/241–1802) and the **Oregon Ballet Theater** (☎ 503/222–5538) perform at the **Civic Auditorium** (S.W. 3rd Ave. and Clay St. downtown).

Nightlife

With its theaters, movie houses, bars, nightclubs, and comedy clubs, Portland's downtown core is the best bet for nightlife. **Rock 'N' Rodeo** (220 S.E. Spokane St., ☎ 503/235–2417) is the current hot spot for country-and-western music and line dancing. **Embers** (110 N.W. Broadway, ☎ 503/222–3082) is a full-throttle disco, complete with dangling mirror balls and a highly eclectic (but rhythmically gifted) clientele. The **Dublin Pub** (6821 Beaverton-Hillsdale Hwy., ☎ 503/297–2889) has a great selection of beers and Irish folk music. The top jazz venues in

Portland are **Brasserie Montmartre** (626 S.W. Park Ave., ☎ 503/224–5552) and **Jazz De Opus** (33 N.W. 2nd Ave., ☎ 503/222–6077). For comedy try **Harvey's Comedy Club** (436 N.W. 6th Ave., ☎ 503/241–0338), which presents headliners with a national reputation.

THE OREGON COAST

Oregon has 400 mi of white-sand beaches, not a grain of which is privately owned. Hwy. 101 parallels the coast from Astoria south to California, past stunning monoliths of sea-tortured rock, brooding headlands, hidden beaches, haunted lighthouses, tiny ports, and, of course, the placid Pacific.

Tourist Information

Astoria: Chamber of Commerce (111 W. Marine Dr., 97103, ☎ 503/325–6311). **Bay Area:** Chamber of Commerce (50 E. Central St., Coos Bay 97420, ☎ 503/269–0215 or 800/824–8486). **Cannon Beach:** Chamber of Commerce (2nd and Spruce Sts., 97110, ☎ 503/436–2623). **Florence Area:** Chamber of Commerce (270 Hwy. 101, 97439, ☎ 503/997–3128). **Lincoln City:** Visitors Center (801 N.W. Hwy. 101, 97367, ☎ 503/994–2164 or 800/452–2151).

Getting There

By Plane

Portland International (*see* Portland, *above*) is the closest major airport.

By Car

The best way to see the coast is by car, following twisting, slow-paced, two-lane Hwy. (U.S.) 101. Hwy. 26 (the Sunset) is the main link to Portland.

By Bus

Greyhound Lines (☎ 800/231–2222) serves coastal communities such as Coos Bay, Florence, and Lincoln City. **RAZ Transportation** (☎ 503/246–3301) serves Astoria and Seaside.

Exploring the Oregon Coast

Astoria, founded in 1811 where the mighty Columbia River meets the sea, is believed to be the first official settlement established by the United States on the West Coast. Here Lewis and Clark wept with joy at their first sight of the Pacific. The Victorian houses of fur, timber, and fishing magnates still dot the flanks of Coxcomb Hill; many are now inviting bed-and-breakfasts. The **Astor Column,** a 125-ft-tall monolith atop Coxcomb Hill, patterned after Trajan's Column in Rome, rewards a climb up 164 spiral stairs with breathtaking views over Astoria, the Columbia, the Coast Range, and the sea.

The **Columbia River Maritime Museum** has exhibits ranging from the fully operational lightship *Columbia* to poignant personal belongings from some of the 2,000 ships that have been wrecked at the mouth of the river since 1811. *Foot of 17th St. at Marine Dr., ☎ 503/325–2323. Admission charged.*

Nine miles south of Astoria is the **Fort Clatsop National Memorial** (Hwy. 101, ☎ 503/861–2471), a replica of the log stockade depicted in Clark's journal, commemorating the achievement of Lewis and Clark. Farther south are **Tillamook Head** and **Ecola State Park** (☎ 503/436–

2844), a popular playground of sea-sculpted rock, sandy beach, tide pools, green headlands, and panoramic views.

Thirty miles south of Astoria is refined, artistic **Cannon Beach,** whose proximity to Portland has endowed it with a fabulous weathered-cedar shopping district, some of the coast's most beautiful beachfront homes, and a subtle, moneyed hauteur. **Haystack Rock,** a 235-ft offshore monolith a short walk across a sandy beach, is a bird sanctuary—and one of the most photographed sites on the coast.

South of Neahkahnie Mountain, **Tillamook** invites travelers to taste the cheese that has made the area world-famous, at the factory on U.S. 101. The **Three Capes Scenic Loop,** west of town, encompasses magnificent coastal scenery, a lighthouse, offshore wildlife refuges, sand dunes, camping areas, and hiking trails.

The bustling little towns of **Lincoln City** and **Newport,** united in spirit if 25 mi apart geographically, are known for excellent seafood and lodgings.

Newport's charming old bay front is a fine place for an afternoon stroll, with its fishing fleet, weathered buildings, art galleries, steaming crab kettles, and seafood markets. **Marina Square** (250 S.W. Bay Blvd., ☎ 503/265–2206; admission charged) includes undersea gardens and a wax museum. Across Yakina Bay is the **Oregon Coast Aquarium** (2820 S.E. Ferry Slip Rd., ☎ 503/867–3123; admission charged). It features 2.5 acres of pools, cliffs, and sandy shores; four indoor galleries (the largest in North America); and a theater devoted to whales.

South of Newport, the coast takes on a very different character—slower-paced, less touristy, far less crowded, but just as rich in scenery and outdoor sporting activities. The peaceful coastal village of **Florence** is the northern gateway to the **Oregon Dunes National Recreation Area** (855 Highway Ave., Reedsport 97467, ☎ 503/271–3611), a 47-mi swath of undulating lion-colored sand. The dunes, some more than 500 ft high, are a vast and exuberant playground for children, particularly the sandy slopes surrounding cool Cleawox Lake.

Umpqua River Lighthouse State Park (west of U.S. 101) adjoins an operating lighthouse and encompasses a small freshwater lake and campground. Next to it are a whale-watching station, 500-ft-high sand dunes, and the **Douglas County Coastal Visitors Center** (☎ 503/271–4631), which has local history exhibits.

Coos Bay is the Oregon coast's largest metropolitan area, and although its tourist amenities are somewhat rustic, it still makes a good home base for exploring the region. At lovely **Golden and Silver Falls State Park** (off U.S. 101, 24 mi northeast of Coos Bay, ☎ 503/888–4902), Glenn Creek pours over a high rock ledge deep in the old-growth forest. West of Coos Bay, the Cape Arago Highway presents spectacular scenery at three state parks (☎ 503/888–4902): **Sunset Bay** with a white-sand beach, picnicking, and campgrounds; **Shore Acres,** once the estate of a timber baron, with a 7.5-acre formal garden and a glass-enclosed storm-watch viewpoint; and **Cape Arago,** a prime site for viewing sea lions and whales. At nearby **South Slough National Estuarine Reserve** (Seven Devils Rd., ☎ 503/888–5558), rich tidal estuaries support life ranging from algae to bald eagles and black bears.

Bullards Beach State Park (☎ 503/347–2209), 1 mi north of Bandon, spreads over miles of shoreline and impressive sand dunes. It has a campground as well as the restored **Coquille River Lighthouse. Cape Blanco**

Western Oregon

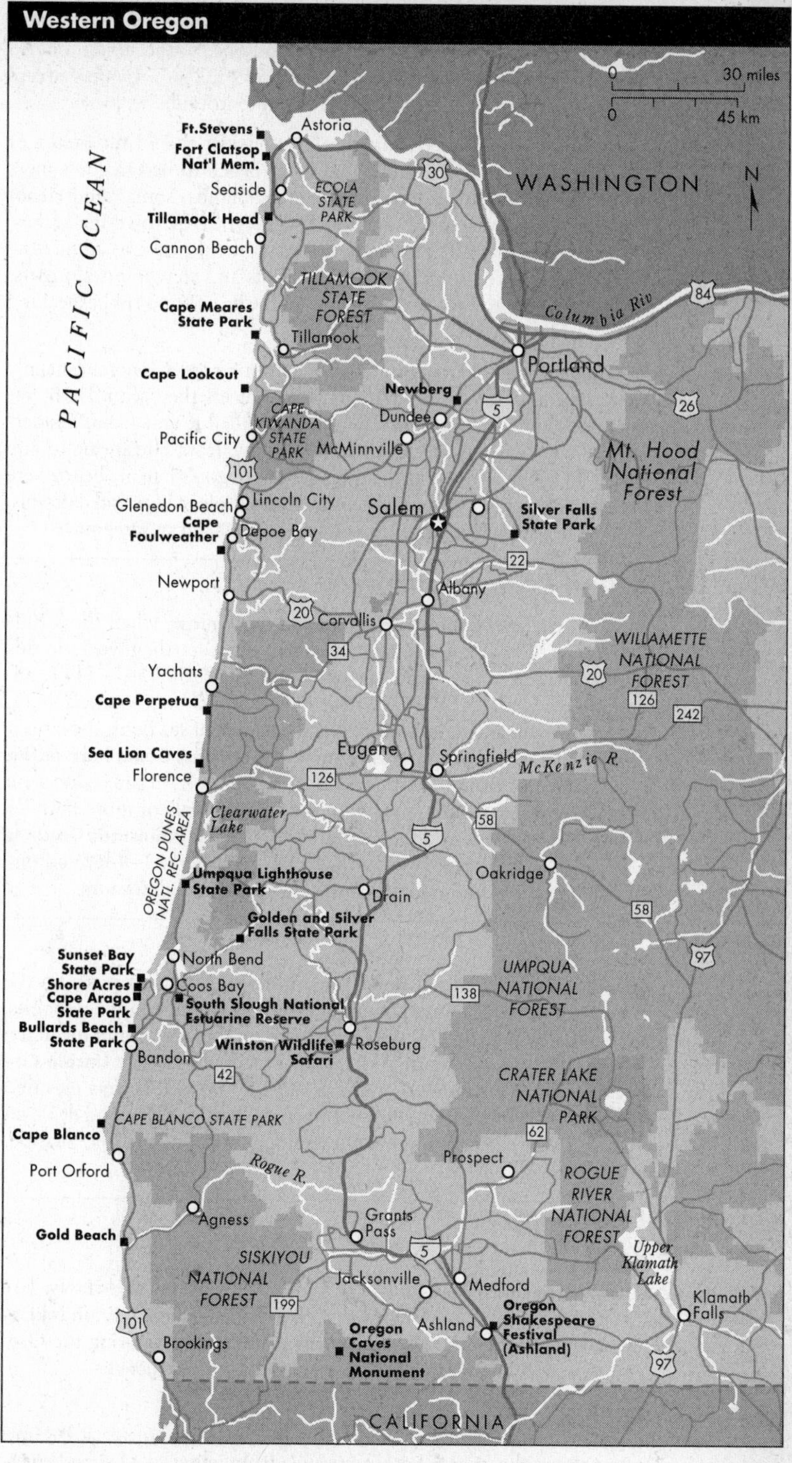
0
30 miles
0
45 km
N
PACIFIC OCEAN
WASHINGTON
CALIFORNIA
Ft.Stevens
Astoria
Fort Clatsop Nat'l Mem.
Seaside
ECOLA STATE PARK
Tillamook Head
Cannon Beach
TILLAMOOK STATE FOREST
Cape Meares State Park
Tillamook
Columbia Riv
Portland
Cape Lookout
Newberg
Dundee
CAPE KIWANDA STATE PARK
Pacific City
McMinnville
Mt. Hood National Forest
Glenedon Beach
Lincoln City
Cape Foulweather
Depoe Bay
Salem
Silver Falls State Park
Newport
Albany
Corvallis
WILLAMETTE NATIONAL FOREST
Yachats
Cape Perpetua
Sea Lion Caves
Florence
Eugene
Springfield
McKenzie R.
Clearwater Lake
OREGON DUNES NATL. REC. AREA
Umpqua Lighthouse State Park
Drain
Oakridge
Golden and Silver Falls State Park
Sunset Bay State Park
North Bend
Shore Acres
Coos Bay
Cape Arago State Park
South Slough National Estuarine Reserve
UMPQUA NATIONAL FOREST
Bullards Beach State Park
Winston Wildlife Safari
Roseburg
Bandon
CRATER LAKE NATIONAL PARK
CAPE BLANCO STATE PARK
Cape Blanco
Port Orford
Rogue R.
Prospect
ROGUE RIVER NATIONAL FOREST
Agness
Gold Beach
Grants Pass
Upper Klamath Lake
SISKIYOU NATIONAL FOREST
Jacksonville
Medford
Klamath Falls
Oregon Shakespeare Festival (Ashland)
Ashland
Oregon Caves National Monument
Brookings
30
84
26
5
22
20
34
126
242
58
97
138
42
62
199
101

Lighthouse, west of the community of Sixes, was built in 1878 and is still operating. It is the most westerly lighthouse in the contiguous 48 states. Adjacent **Cape Blanco State Park** (☎ 503/332–6774) offers sweeping views of rocks and beaches, plus a campground.

Many knowledgeable coastal travelers consider the 63-mi stretch of U.S. 101 between Port Orford and Gold Beach to be Oregon's most beautiful. The highway soars up green headlands, some hundreds of feet high, past awesome sea-sculpted scenery: caves, towering arches, natural and man-made bridges. One caution: Take time to admire the scenery, but make use of the many turnouts and viewpoints along the way—this close to California, traffic can be heavy, and rubbernecking dangerous.

Gold Beach, about 30 mi north of the California border, is notable mainly as the place where the wild Rogue River meets the ocean. Daily jet-boat excursions roar up the scenic, rapids-filled Rogue from Wedderburn, Gold Beach's sister city across the bay, from late spring to late fall. Gold Beach also marks the entrance to Oregon's banana belt, where milder temperatures encourage a blossoming trade in lilies and daffodils. You'll even see a few palm trees here—a rare sight in Oregon.

What to See and Do with Children

May brings the **Cannon Beach Sandcastle Contest,** when thousands throng the beach to view imaginative and often startling works in this most transient of art forms. **Sea Lion Caves** (☎ 503/547–3111; admission charged), off U.S. 101 near Florence, is a huge vaulted chamber where kids can get a close view of hundreds of sea lions, the largest of which weigh 2,000 pounds or more. **West Coast Game Park Safari** (7 mi south of Brandon on U.S. 101, ☎ 503/347–3106; admission charged; closed weekdays in winter) offers animals of more than 75 exotic species, some of which children can pet. At **Prehistoric Gardens** (13 mi south of Port Orford on U.S. 101, ☎ 503/332–4463; admission charged), kids come face-to-face with life-size dinosaurs.

Shopping

Hemlock Street, Cannon Beach's main drag, is the best place on the coast to browse for unusual clothing, souvenirs, picnic supplies, books, and gifts. Newport's **Bay Boulevard** is a good place to find local artwork, gifts, and foodstuffs. There are bargains galore at **Lincoln City Factory Stores** (Hwy. 101, ☎ 503/996–5000), which has elevated shopping to a sport along the central coast. Particularly good deals on vintage items can be found in the antiques malls in Astoria, Seaside, and Lincoln City.

Sports and the Outdoors

Biking

The **Oregon Coast Bike Route** (☎ 503/378–3432) parallels Hwy. 101 and the coast from Astoria south to Brookings. For mountain bikers, the **Oregon Dunes National Recreation Area** (*see* Exploring the Oregon Coast, *above*) near Florence offers a unique challenge.

Fishing

Huge salmon, delectable Dungeness crab, and dozens of species of bottom fish are the quarry here, accessible from jetties, docks, and riverbanks from Astoria to Brookings. Charter boats and guides are plentiful; contact local chambers of commerce (*see* Tourist Information, *above*) for information on seasons, rates, and schedules.

Golf

The Oregon coast has about 20 public and private courses, including (from north to south) **Salishan Golf Links** (Gleneden Beach, ☎ 503/764–3600), the coast's most challenging course, with 18 holes; Newport's 9-hole **Agate Beach Golf Club** (☎ 503/265–7331); 18-hole **Ocean Dunes Golf Links** in Florence (☎ 503/997–3232); and Gold Beach's 9-hole **Cedar Bend Golf Course** (☎ 503/247–6911).

Beaches

Virtually the entire 400-mi coastline of Oregon is clean, quiet white-sand beaches, accessible to all. Thanks to its sea-sculpted stone, **Face Rock Wayside,** just outside Bandon, is thought by many to have the most beautiful walking beach in the state. The placid semicircular lagoon at **Sunset Bay State Park** on Cape Arago is Oregon's safest swimming beach. Fossils, clams, mussels, and other eons-old marine creatures embedded in soft sandstone cliffs make **Beverly Beach State Park** (5 mi north of Newport) a favorite with young beachcombers.

Dining and Lodging

For price ranges, see Charts 1 (B) and 2 (B) in On the Road with Fodor's.

Astoria

DINING

Pier 11 Feed Store Restaurant & Lounge. This spacious restaurant, overlooking the Columbia from a renovated pier/warehouse, serves hearty and abundant fish, steaks, and prime rib. *Foot of 10th St.,* ☎ *503/325–0279. D, MC, V. $$*

LODGING

★ **Franklin Street Station Bed & Breakfast.** The ticking of clocks and the mellow marine light shining through leaded-glass windows set the tone at this B&B, built in 1900. Breakfasts are huge, hot, and satisfying. *1140 Franklin Ave., 97103,* ☎ *503/325–4314 or 800/448–1098. 6 rooms. MC, V. $–$$*

Brookings

DINING

Mama's Authentic Italian Food. Home-style Italian food is served in this small, simply furnished, and always busy restaurant. *703 Chetco Ave.,* ☎ *503/469–7611. AE, MC, V. $*

LODGING

★ **Chetco River Inn.** Acres of private forest surround this remote-but-splendid modern fishing lodge 15 mi up the Turquoise River from Brookings. Fishing guides are available upon request, as are eclectic dinners cooked by the B&B's owner, Sandra Burgger; she's also a font of information on the many hiking trails in the area. Quilts and fishing gear decorate the comfortable bedrooms. *21202 High Prairie Rd., 97415,* ☎ *503/469–8128 (radio phone) or 800/327–2688. 4 rooms (2 with shared bath). MC, V. $$*

Cannon Beach

DINING

The Bistro. Cannon Beach's most romantic restaurant is small, candlelit, and intimate. The four-course, fixed-price menu features imaginative, Continental-influenced renditions of fresh local seafood dishes. *263 N. Hemlock St.,* ☎ *503/436–2661. MC, V. Closed Wed. and Jan. No lunch weekdays. $$$*

Dooger's. This comfortable family-style eatery's fresh, well-prepared seafood, exquisite clam chowder, and low prices keep 'em coming back for more. *1371 S. Hemlock St., ☎ 503/436–2225. MC, V. $–$$*

DINING AND LODGING

★ **Stephanie Inn.** With its tastefully decorated, luxuriously appointed rooms—most have a Jacuzzi bathtub, fireplace, minifridge, wet bar, VCR, cable TV, and patio—and outstanding oceanside location overlooking Haystack Rock at Cannon Beach, the smoke-free Stephanie Inn is rapidly becoming *the* place on the Oregon coast. This rising star also features terrific five-course prix fixe dinners of innovative Pacific Northwest cuisine. Generous country breakfasts are included in the tariff, as are evening wine and hors d'oeuvres. *2740 S. Pacific Rd., 97110, ☎ 503/436–2221 or 800/633–3466, FAX 503/436–9711. 46 rooms. Facilities: dining room, espresso bar, library, massages, video library, free shuttle into town. Reservations required for dinner. AE, D, DC, MC, V. $$$–$$$$*

LODGING

Hallmark Resort. This rapidly growing oceanfront resort offers cozy rooms—many with fireplaces, kitchens, and/or whirlpools—and some of the best views in Cannon Beach. *1400 S. Hemlock St., 97110, ☎ 503/436–1566 or 800/345–5676. 127 rooms. Facilities: restaurant, lounge, indoor pool, sauna, whirlpool, weight room, kiddie pool, refrigerators, covered parking. AE, D, DC, MC, V. $$$–$$$$*

Coos Bay

DINING

Blue Heron Bistro. You'll get subtle preparations of local seafood, chicken, and homemade pasta with an international flair at this busy bistro. There are no flat spots on the far-ranging menu; the innovative soups and desserts are also excellent. *100 Commercial St., ☎ 503/267–3933. MC, V. $$*

Portside Restaurant. This unpretentious spot with picture windows overlooking the busy Charleston boat basin buys directly from the fishermen moored outside. Try the steamed Dungeness crab with drawn butter, a local specialty, or the all-you-can-eat seafood buffet on Friday night. *8001 Kingfisher Rd. (follow Cape Arago Hwy. from Coos Bay), ☎ 503/888–5544. AE, D, DC, MC, V. No lunch weekends. $$*

LODGING

This Olde House B&B. The charm and care that have gone into the renovation of this sprawling Victorian, four blocks up the hill from downtown Coos Bay, are matched only by the charm and warmth of its owners. *202 Alder Ave., 97420, ☎ 503/267–5224. 4 rooms, 3 share bath. Facilities: breakfast. No credit cards. $–$$*

Florence

DINING

Bridgewater Seafood Restaurant. The venerably salty ambience of Florence's photogenic bay-front Old Town permeates this spacious fish house. Steaks, salads, and, of course, plenty of fresh seafood are the mainstays at this creaky-floored Victorian-era restaurant. *1297 Bay St., ☎ 503/997–9405. MC, V. $$*

Gleneden Beach

DINING AND LODGING

Salishan Lodge. For most visitors, this is the Oregon coast's best-known resort. Nestled into a 750-acre hillside forest preserve, Salishan embodies a uniquely Oregonian elegance—from the soothing, silvered-cedar ambience of its guest rooms (which have fireplaces), to its collections of wine (20,000 bottles at last count) and original art. The dining room is famous for its seasonal Northwest cuisine. *Hwy. 101, 97388, ☎ 503/764–3600 or 800/452–2300. 205 rooms. Facilities: 3 restaurants, bar, private beach access, indoor pool, whirlpool and saunas, indoor and outdoor tennis courts, 18-hole golf course, weight room, nature trails, massages, beauty salon, gift shop, art gallery, playground, pets welcome. AE, D, DC, MC, V. $$–$$$*

Gold Beach

DINING AND LODGING

★ **Tu Tu Tun Lodge.** This famous, richly appointed fishing resort perches above the clear blue Rogue River, 7 mi upstream from Gold Beach. The units are furnished with rustic charm; private decks overlook the river and the surrounding old-growth forest. Huge amounts of satisfying, straightforward American fare are served. *96550 North Bank Rogue, 97444, ☎ 503/247–6664, FAX 503/247–0672. 16 rooms, 2 suites, 1 2-bedroom house, 1 3-bedroom house. Facilities: restaurant, bar, heated outdoor pool, hiking, boat dock and ramp, guided fishing, jet-boat excursions. Dining room closed Nov.–Apr. MC, V. $$–$$$$*

LODGING

Ireland's Rustic Lodges. Original one- and two-bedroom cabins filled with rough-and-tumble charm, plus newer motel rooms, are set amid spectacular landscaping. Each unit has a fireplace and a deck overlooking the sea. *1120 S. Ellensburg Ave. (just off Hwy. 101), 97444, ☎ 503/247–7718. 7 cabins, 30 motel rooms. No-smoking rooms available. No credit cards. $–$$*

Lincoln City

DINING

★ **Bay House.** This charming bungalow serves meals to linger over while you enjoy views across sunset-gilded Siletz Bay. The Northwest cuisine includes Dungeness crab cakes with roasted chile chutney, fresh halibut Parmesan, and roast duckling with fig-plum sauce. The wine list is extensive, the service impeccable. *5911 S.W. Hwy. 101, ☎ 503/996–3222. AE, D, MC, V. Closed Mon.–Tues. Nov.–Apr. No lunch. $$–$$$*

Lighthouse Brew Pub. This westernmost outpost of the Portland-based McMenamins microbrewery empire features ales brewed on the premises, good food, and cheerfully eccentric decor. Families are welcome. *4157 N. Hwy. 101 (in Lighthouse Sq. shopping center), ☎ 503/994–7238. No reservations. MC, V. $*

LODGING

Ester Lee Motel. Perched on a seaside bluff, this small whitewashed motel attracts a devoted repeat business through value and simplicity. For the price, there are some nice amenities, including wood-burning fireplaces, full kitchens, and cable TV in all rooms. *3803 S.W. Hwy. 101, 97367, ☎ 503/996–3606. 53 rooms. D, MC, V. $*

Newport

DINING

Mo's. A half-dozen Mo's restaurants are scattered from Cannon Beach to Florence; arguably, the best of the bunch is in Newport. The chowder is legendary—a creamy potion flavored with bacon and onion and studded with tender potatoes and clams. The menu of fresh local seafood is simply prepared at family prices. Kids love this place. *622 S.W. Bay Blvd., ☎ 503/265–2979. Other locations: Lincoln City (860 S.W. 51st St., ☎ 503/996–2535), Florence (1436 Bay St., ☎ 503/997–*

2185), Otter Rock (925 1st St., ☎ 503/765–2442, closed in winter). No reservations. D, MC, V. $

DINING AND LODGING

★ **Sylvia Beach Hotel.** At this restored 1912 B&B, each of the antiques-filled guest rooms (some with decks) is named for a famous writer and decorated on that theme. In the Poe Room, for instance, a pendulum swings over the bed. Upstairs is a well-stocked library with fireplace, slumbering cat, and too-comfortable chairs. Breakfast is a hearty buffet. *267 N.W. Cliff St., 97365, ☎ 503/265–5428. 20 rooms. Facilities: restaurant. No smoking. AE, MC, V. $–$$*

Yachats

LODGING

Ziggurat. It's hard to miss this terraced, pyramid-shape inn just south of Yachats, one of the most charming small communities on the coast. Two large suites take up the first floor, living and dining areas fill the second, and a third guest room fills the top floor of this unique, art-filled home. *95330 Hwy. 101, ☎ 503/547–3925. 3 rooms. Facilities: breakfast, library. No smoking. No credit cards. $$*

Campgrounds

Nineteen state parks along the coast include campgrounds. Most feature full hookups and tent sites. Many are near the shore, and some contain group facilities and hiker/biker or horse camps. The **Oregon State Parks and Recreation Department** (*see* National and State Parks, *above*) has details. **Honeyman State Park** (84505 Hwy. 101, Florence 97439, ☎ 503/997–3641) adjoins the Oregon Dunes National Recreation Area. Reserve well ahead.

ELSEWHERE IN THE STATE

Mt. Hood and Bend

Getting There

Mt. Hood lies about an hour east of Portland on U.S. 26; the only way to get there is by car. Continue east on U.S. 26, then south on U.S. 97, for the resort town of Bend, two hours beyond Mt. Hood. **Bend–Redmond Airport** (☎ 503/548–2148) is served by **Horizon Airlines** (☎ 800/547–9308) and **United Express** (☎ 800/241–6522).

What to See and Do

Mt. Hood, 11,245 ft high and surrounded by the 1.1-million-acre **Mt. Hood National Forest** (2955 Northwest Division, Gresham 97030, ☎ 503/666–0700), is an all-season playground that attracts more than 7 million visitors annually for skiing, camping, hiking, fishing, or day trips to breathe the resinous mountain air. Historic **Timberline Lodge** (off U.S. 26 a few miles east of Government Camp; Timberline 97028, ☎ 503/272–3311 or 800/547–1406) has withstood howling winter storms on the mountain's flank for over 60 years; it's a popular spot for romantic getaways. There is year-round skiing on the slopes above.

Hood River is the self-proclaimed sailboarding capital of the world. **Columbia Gorge Sailpark** (Port Marina, ☎ 503/386–2000), on the river downtown, offers a boat basin, a swimming beach, jogging trails, and picnic tables.

The skiing is also excellent in **Bend,** which occupies a tawny high-desert plateau in the very center of Oregon, framed on the west by three 10,000-ft Cascade peaks. With its plentiful dining and lodging options,

Bend makes a fine base camp for skiing at nearby Mt. Bachelor, whitewater rafting on the Deschutes River, world-class rock-climbing at Smith Rocks State Park, and other outdoor activities. Don't miss the archaeological and wildlife displays at the **High Desert Museum** (59800 S. U.S. 97, 6 mi south of Bend, ☎ 503/382–4754; admission charged). **Newberry Crater National Monument** (25 mi southeast of Bend, ☎ 503/388–2715) provides recreation for cross-country skiers, snowmobilers, fishermen, and hikers.

Willamette Valley/Wine Country

Getting There

I–5, the state's main north–south freeway, runs straight down the center of the Willamette Valley from Portland.

What to See and Do

Oregon's wine country occupies the wet, temperate trough between the Coast Range to the west and the Cascades to the east. More than 40 wineries dot the hills between Portland and Salem, and dozens more are scattered from Newport as far south as Ashland, on the California border. Although tiny in comparison with California's, Oregon's wine industry is booming. Cool-climate varietals such as Pinot Noir and Riesling have gained the esteem of international connoisseurs.

Most of the vineyards welcome visitors, and a day of touring, tasting, and picnicking is a popular local excursion. The best way to tour is by car. "Discover Oregon Wineries," an indispensable, annually updated map and guide to the wine country, is available free at wine shops and wineries or by calling the **Oregon Wine Growers' Association** (☎ 503/228–8403). **Northwest Bed & Breakfast** (☎ 503/243–7616) is a good source of reservations for the area's extensive B&B network.

Newberg, a graceful old pioneer town at a broad bend in the Willamette River southwest of Portland, is the site of the **Hoover–Minthorne House** (115 S. River St., ☎ 503/538–6629; admission charged), the boyhood home of President Herbert Hoover. Built in 1881, the beautifully preserved and well-landscaped frame house includes many of the original furnishings. To the south, the idyllic orchard land around **Dundee** produces 90% of America's hazelnut crop.

Salem, the state capital, makes a good base of operations; in addition to its hotels, B&Bs, and restaurants, there are some fine gardens and museums. A brightly gilded 23-ft-high bronze statue of the Oregon Pioneer atop the 106-ft capitol dome is the centerpiece of Salem's **Capitol Building** (900 Court St., ☎ 503/378–4423), where Oregon's legislators convene every two years. Nearby are the tradition-steeped brick buildings of **Willamette University,** the oldest college in the West, founded in 1842. Just south of downtown, **Bush's Pasture Park** (600 Mission St. SE, ☎ 503/363–4714; admission charged) includes a Victorian mansion with 10 fireplaces and an art center with two exhibition galleries. **Deepwood Estate** (1116 Mission St. SE, ☎ 503/363–1825; admission charged), on the National Register of Historic Places, encompasses 105 acres of lawns, formal English gardens, and a fanciful 1894 Queen Anne mansion with splendid interior woodwork and original stained glass. **Silver Falls State Park** (26 mi east of Salem, ☎ 503/873–8681) covers 8,700 acres and includes 10 waterfalls accessible to hikers.

At **Albany,** 24 mi south on I–5, visitors can take self-guided driving tours of three historic districts that have, among them, 350 homes and every major architectural style popular in the United States since 1850. Tour maps are available at the **Albany Chamber of Commerce** (435 W. 1st St., 97321, ☎ 503/926–1517).

Eugene, Oregon's second-largest city, is the home of the **University of Oregon** (the setting for *National Lampoon's Animal House*) and the **Willamette Science and Technology Center** (2300 Leo Harris Pkwy., ☎ 503/687–3619; admission charged), where imaginative hands-on scientific exhibits and a planetarium absorb children and adults alike.

To the south, the sleepy farming community of **Roseburg** is on the Umpqua River, famous among fishermen. West of town are a dozen of the region's wineries. The **Douglas County Museum** (Fairgrounds, I–5 Exit 123, ☎ 503/440–4507) has an exceptional fossil collection. **Wildlife Safari** (3 mi west of I–5, Winston, ☎ 503/679–6761; admission charged) is a drive-through wildlife park with a petting zoo, elephant rides, a restaurant, and an RV park. **Hwy. 138** from Roseburg to Crater Lake National Park is a National Scenic Byway. It takes you through rugged canyons and past several waterfalls, numerous camping areas, and some mountain lakes.

Ashland/The Rogue Valley

Getting There

Ashland is midway between Portland and San Francisco on I–5, about 15 mi north of the California border. **Jackson County Airport** (☎ 503/772–8068) in nearby Medford is served by **Horizon Airlines, United,** and **United Express.**

What to See and Do

Ashland is home to the Tony Award–winning **Oregon Shakespeare Festival** (15 S. Pioneer St., ☎ 503/482–4331), which annually attracts more than 400,000 visitors to this relaxing Rogue Valley town. The local arts scene, a warm climate, and a critical mass of opulent B&Bs and sumptuous restaurants make this an exceptionally pleasant place for a holiday. There is excellent downhill and Nordic skiing atop 7,523-ft-high **Mt. Ashland;** to the west, the famous Rogue River boils and churns through the rugged, remote **Kalmiopsis Wilderness** in Siskiyou National Forest (☎ 503/471–6516). The local wineries are also worth a visit.

Nearby **Jacksonville** preserves the look and feel of an Old West pioneer settlement; the entire town is a National Historic Landmark. Each summer Jacksonville hosts the **Peter Britt Festival** (☎ 503/773–6077 or 800/882–7488), a concert series featuring some of the world's best jazz and classical musicians. **Crater Lake National Park** (*see* National and State Parks, *above*) is about 80 mi northeast along Hwy. 62.

WASHINGTON

By Tom Gauntt

Updated by Loralee Wenger

Capital	Olympia
Population	4.9 million
Motto	By-and-by
State Bird	Willow goldfinch
State Flower	Rhododendron

Visitor Information

Washington Tourism Development Division (Box 42500, Olympia, 98504-2500, ☎ 360/586–2088 or 800/544–1800).

Scenic Drives

About 90 mi north of Seattle, starting from just south of Bellingham on I–5, Hwy. 11 loops 25 mi around **Chuckanut Bay.** On one side of Hwy. 11 is the steep, heavily wooded Chuckanut Mountain, and on the other are sweeping views of Puget Sound and the San Juan Islands. The area is also dotted with fine restaurants. Near the Oregon border, Hwy. 14 winds east from Vancouver into the **Columbia River National Scenic Area.** The road clings to the steep slopes of the gorge most of the time and features several tunnels and picturesque towns such as Carson, known for its hot springs, and White Salmon, renowned for windsurfing.

National and State Parks

National Parks

Mt. Rainier National Park (Superintendent's Office, Tahoma Woods, Star Rte., Ashford 98304, ☎ 360/569–2211), about 85 mi southeast of Seattle, comprises 14,411-ft Mt. Rainier—the fifth-highest mountain in the lower 48 states—and nearly 400 sq mi of surrounding wilderness. The visitor center has exhibits, films, and a 360-degree view of the summit and surrounding peaks. For a vision of the apocalypse, head for the **Mount St. Helens National Volcanic Monument** (42218 N.E. Yale Bridge Rd., Amboy, WA 9860, ☎ 306/750–3900). The visitor center is on Hwy. 504, 5 mi east of the Castle Rock exit off I–5. The monument is 45 mi east of Castle Rock. Although the crater still steams and small earthquakes are common, excellent views are available within 10 mi of the mountain. **Olympic National Park** (600 E. Park Ave., Port Angeles 98362, ☎ 360/452–0330) is one of the most outstanding pieces of natural beauty in the United States, with such diversified areas as the wilderness coastline, the lush green of the temperate Hoh Rain Forest, some 60 active glaciers, and the alpine beauty of Hurricane Ridge. **North Cascades National Park** (2105 Hwy. 20, Sedro Woolley 98284, ☎ 360/856–5700), a little-known park about 120 mi northeast of Seattle, holds some of the state's most rugged mountains, high, craggy peaks, and jewellike lakes.

For information about any of the national parks and monuments in Washington, contact the **U.S. Forest Service and National Park Service Outdoor Recreation and Information Center** (915 2nd Ave. No. 442, Seattle 98174, ☎ 206/220–7450).

State Parks

Leadbetter Point State Park (Robert Gray Dr., 2 mi south of Ilwaco, Box 488, 98624, ☎ 360/642–3078), at the northernmost tip of the

Long Beach Peninsula, is a wildlife refuge, good for bird-watching. The dunes at the very tip are closed April to August to protect the nesting snowy plover. Black brants, sandpipers, turnstones, yellowlegs, sanderlings, knots, and plovers are among the 100 species known to inhabit the point.

SEATTLE

Whether it's a double, tall, decaf nonfat latte with a dash of nutmeg or a standard cup of java, coffee has transformed Seattle's reputation from soggy and mossy to rich, dark, and steamy. Since 1971, when three enterprising young men first started Starbucks, the city's premier coffee company, Seattle has risen to claim its place as the nation's coffee capital. On nearly every block downtown and dotting Seattle neighborhoods, visitors will find espresso carts and coffee shops.

In the days when Starbucks began setting the stage for caffeine mania, Seattle was largely a city of Boeing employees who exited to the Olympic and Cascade mountains as often as possible to hike, backpack, and climb. Wearing corduroy slacks and a plaid wool shirt with a slide rule in the pocket was de rigueur.

Today Seattle has grown into a major cultural center, and its sophistication is evident in its architecture, food, fashion, and arts. The city is a magnet for people who are drawn by its blend of urban sophistication, easygoing charm, and ready access to spectacular outdoor recreation. The arts are strong and innovative, and the restaurants—from tiny International District dumpling stands to posh world-class dining rooms—serve a steady supply of visitors, longtime residents, and newcomers, all caught up in the act of simultaneously discovering and celebrating this place. Surrounding it all are still the old familiars, the mountains and the water.

Tourist Information

Seattle/King County: Drop by the Convention and Visitors Bureau (800 Convention Pl., at the I–5 end of Pike St., 98101, ☏ 206/461–5840) or the information booth at Westlake Center (400 Pine St., street level, ☏ 206/467–1600) or write to the Visitor Information Center (520 Pike St., Suite 1300, 98101, ☏ 206/461–5840).

Arriving and Departing

By Plane

Seattle-Tacoma International Airport (Sea-Tac) is 20 mi south of downtown, and is served by major American and some foreign airlines. A cab ride to downtown takes about 30 to 45 minutes, and the fare is about $25. **Gray Line Airport Express** (☏ 206/626–6088) buses run to and from major downtown hotels. Fare: $7.50 one-way, $13 round-trip.

By Car

I–5 enters Seattle from the north and south, I–90 from the east.

By Train

Amtrak (303 S. Jackson St., ☏ 800/872–7245).

By Bus

Greyhound Lines (8th Ave. and Stewart St., ☏ 800/231–2222).

Getting Around Seattle

A car is the handiest way to cover metropolitan Seattle, but bus service is convenient and efficient, too. Despite occasional steep hills, downtown is good for walking.

By Car

Driving can be a chore, what with hills, tunnels, reversible express lanes, and frustrating rush hours. Main thoroughfares into downtown are Aurora Avenue (called the Alaskan Way Viaduct through town) and I–5.

By Public Transportation

Metropolitan Transit (☎ 206/553–3000) provides a free-ride service in the downtown-waterfront area until 7 PM; fares to other destinations range from 85¢ to $1.60, depending on the zone and time of day. The elevated **Monorail,** a futuristic leftover from the 1962 Seattle World's Fair, runs the 2 mi from the Seattle Center to Westlake Center; the fare is 80¢.

By Taxi

Cab hailing is not a Seattle sport. Fare is $1.80 at the flag drop and $1.80 per mile. Major companies are **Farwest** (☎ 206/622–1717) and **Yellow Cab** (☎ 206/622–6500).

Orientation Tours

Bus Tour

Gray Line (Sheraton Hotel, 1400 6th Ave., ☎ 206/626–5208) offers guided bus tours of the city and environs, from a daily 2½-hour spin to a 6-hour "Grand City Tour," offered in spring, summer, and fall.

Boat Tour

Argosy Cruises (Pier 55, ☎ 206/623–1445) offers one-hour tours of Elliott Bay, the port of Seattle, and various other locations.

Walking Tour

The **Underground Tour** (☎ 206/682–4646 or 206/682–1511) explores the Pioneer Square area, including the now-below-ground sections that have been built over.

Exploring Seattle

Downtown

Downtown Seattle is bounded by the Kingdome to the south, the Seattle Center to the north, I–5 to the east, and the waterfront to the west. You can reach most points of interest by foot, bus, or the Monorail. Remember, though, that Seattle is a city of hills, so wear your walking shoes.

The **Seattle Art Museum** (100 University St., ☎ 206/625–8900; admission charged) opened in 1991. The five-story building, designed by postmodern theorist Robert Venturi, is a work of art in itself, its limestone exterior with vertical fluting accented by terra-cotta, cut granite, and marble. Inside are extensive collections of Asian, Native American, African, Oceanic, and pre-Columbian art, a café, and a gift shop.

Pike Place Market (1st Ave. at Pike St., ☎ 206/682–7453) is a Seattle institution, begun in 1907 when the city issued permits allowing farmers to sell produce from their wagons parked at Pike Place. Urban renewal almost closed the market, but citizens rallied and voted it a historical asset. Sold here are fresh seafood (which can be packed in dry ice for your flight home), produce, cheese, Northwest wines, bulk spices, teas, coffees, and arts and crafts.

At the base of the Pike Street Hillclimb at Pier 59 is the **Seattle Aquarium** (☎ 206/386–4320; admission charged), showcasing Northwest marine life. Sea otters and seals swim and dive in their pools, and the "State of the Sound" exhibit shows aquatic life and the ecology of Puget Sound.

A couple blocks east of Pier 51, at the foot of Yesler Way, is **Pioneer Park,** where an ornate iron-and-glass pergola stands. This was the site of Henry Yesler's pier and sawmill and of Seattle's original business district. An 1889 fire destroyed many of the wood-frame buildings in the area now known as **Pioneer Square,** but the residents rebuilt them with brick and mortar. Also in the square is the **Klondike Gold Rush National Historical Park** (117 S. Main St., ☎ 206/553–7220).

Southeast of Pioneer Square is the **International District** (known locally as the ID), where a third of the residents are Chinese, a third are Filipino, and the rest from elsewhere in Asia. The ID began as a haven for Chinese workers after they'd finished the Transcontinental Railroad. Today the district includes many Chinese, Japanese, and Korean restaurants, as well as herbalists, massage parlors, and acupuncturists. The **Nippon Kan Theater** (628 S. Washington St., ☎ 206/224–0181) was historically the focal point for Japanese-American activities, including Kabuki theater. Renovated and reopened in 1981 as a national historic site, it presents many Asian-oriented productions.

North of Downtown

From **Westlake Center** (*see* Shopping, *below*), a shopping complex completed in 1989, you can pick up the Monorail to **Seattle Center,** a 74-acre complex built for the 1962 Seattle World's Fair. It includes an amusement park, theaters, a new coliseum, exhibition halls, museums, and shops. Also here is the **Space Needle,** a Seattle landmark, which is visible from almost anywhere in the downtown area and looks like something from *The Jetsons*. The glass elevator to the observation deck offers an impressive view of the city, and there's a popular restaurant.

From downtown or the Seattle Center, Hwy. 99 (Aurora Ave. N) heads north across the Aurora Bridge to the 45th Street exit, then to the **Woodland Park Zoo** (N. 50th St. and Fremont Ave., ☎ 206/684–4800; admission charged), where many animals are free to roam within sections of the zoo's 92 acres.

A short drive east is the 33,500-student **University of Washington** (locals call it the U-Dub), founded in 1861. On the northwestern corner of the campus is the **Thomas Burke Memorial Washington State Museum** (17th Ave. NE and N.E. 45th St., ☎ 206/543–5590; donation suggested), Washington's natural-history and anthropological museum. Near the university's Husky Stadium is the **Museum of History and Industry** (2700 24th Ave. E, ☎ 206/324–1125; admission charged).

Parks and Gardens

Seattle's setting makes it a natural for parks and gardens. At **Washington Park Arboretum** (2300 Arboretum Dr. E, ☎ 206/325–4510), near the university, Rhododendron Glen and Azalea Way are in bloom from March through June. The Hiram M. Chittenden Locks, better known as the **Ballard Locks** (3015 N.W. 54th St., west of the Ballard Bridge, ☎ 206/783–7059; visitor center closed Tues.–Wed. in winter), close the 8-mi-long Lake Washington Ship Canal connecting freshwa-

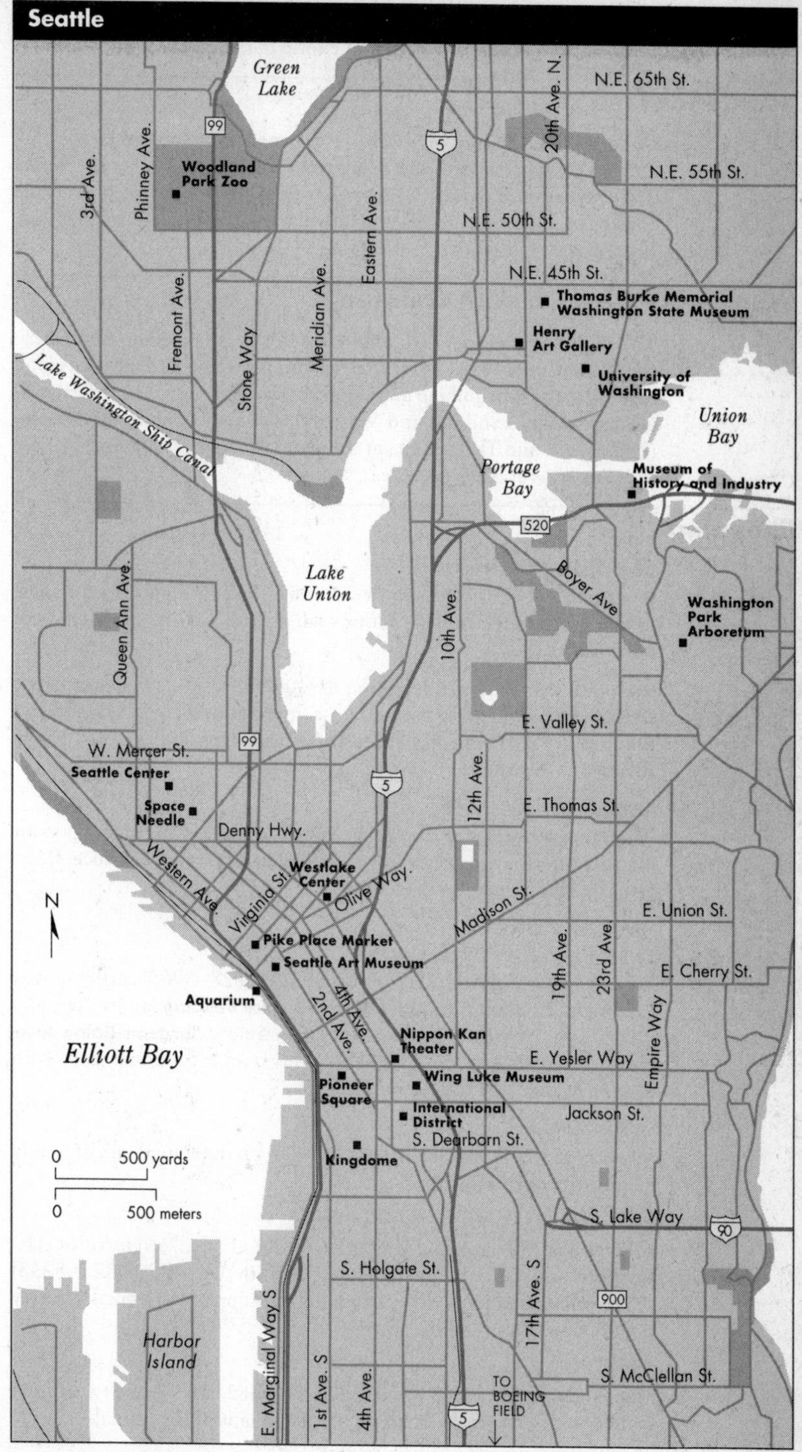
Seattle
Green Lake
N.E. 65th St.
99
5
20th Ave. N.
Woodland Park Zoo
Phinney Ave.
3rd Ave.
N.E. 55th St.
Eastern Ave.
N.E. 50th St.
N.E. 45th St.
Thomas Burke Memorial Washington State Museum
Fremont Ave.
Meridian Ave.
Henry Art Gallery
Stone Way
University of Washington
Lake Washington Ship Canal
Union Bay
Portage Bay
Museum of History and Industry
520
Lake Union
Boyer Ave.
Queen Ann Ave.
10th Ave.
Washington Park Arboretum
E. Valley St.
W. Mercer St.
Seattle Center
12th Ave.
Space Needle
E. Thomas St.
Denny Hwy.
Western Ave.
Westlake Center
Virginia St.
Olive Way
Madison St.
E. Union St.
Pike Place Market
Seattle Art Museum
E. Cherry St.
19th Ave.
23rd Ave.
Aquarium
4th Ave.
2nd Ave.
Empire Way
Nippon Kan Theater
Elliott Bay
E. Yesler Way
Pioneer Square
Wing Luke Museum
International District
Jackson St.
S. Dearborn St.
0 500 yards
Kingdome
0 500 meters
S. Lake Way
90
S. Holgate St.
900
17th Ave. S
Harbor Island
S. McClellan St.
E. Marginal Way S
1st Ave. S
4th Ave.
TO BOEING FIELD

ter Lake Washington to Puget Sound; alongside the canal is a 7-acre **ornamental garden** of native and exotic plants, shrubs, and trees.

Seattle for Free

Gallery Walk (☎ 206/587–0260) is an open house hosted by Seattle's art galleries that explores new exhibits the first Thursday of every month. The **Out to Lunch Series** (☎ 206/623–0340) is outdoor concerts held weekdays at noon in various downtown parks, plazas, and atriums mid-June–early September.

What to See and Do with Children

The **Children's Museum** (fountain level of Seattle Center, 305 Harrison St., ☎ 206/441–1768) features an infant-toddler area with a giant, soft ferryboat for climbing and sliding and offers intergenerational programs, special exhibits, and workshops. **Seattle Children's Theater** (2nd Ave. N and Thomas St., at the Seattle Center, ☎ 206/441–3322) presents several plays each year.

Shopping

Shopping Districts

City Centre (1420 5th Ave., ☎ 206/467–9670), a gleaming marble tower, houses such upscale shops such as Ann Taylor and Barneys of New York.

Westlake Center (1601 5th Ave., ☎ 206/467–1600) is a three-story steel-and-glass building with 80 upscale shops and covered walkways that connect it to branches of Seattle's major department stores, **Nordstrom** and **The Bon.**

Food Market

Pike Place Market (*see* Exploring Seattle, *above*), a partially open-air market, offers a wide selection of fresh meat, seafood, produce, flowers, and crafts from vendors' stalls.

Specialty Stores

ANTIQUES AND JEWELRY

Antique Importers (640 Alaskan Way, ☎ 206/628–8905) carries mostly English oak and pine antiques. **Fourth & Pike Building** (at 4th Ave. and Pike St.) houses many retail-wholesale jewelers. **Turgeon-Raine Jewelers** (1407 5th Ave., ☎ 206/447–9488) is an exceptional store with a sophisticated but friendly staff.

MEN'S APPAREL

Mario's (1513 6th Ave., ☎ 206/223–1461) carries a good mix of trendy and designer fashions for men.

OUTDOOR WEAR AND EQUIPMENT

Eddie Bauer (5th Ave. and Union St., ☎ 206/622–2766) features classic sports and outdoor apparel. **REI** (1525 11th Ave., ☎ 206/323–8333) sells clothing and a full array of outdoor equipment in a creaky, funky building on Capitol Hill.

TOYS

Magic Mouse Toys (603 1st Ave., ☎ 206/682–8097) has two floors stuffed with toys, from small windups to giant plush animals.

WOMEN'S APPAREL

Boutique Europa (1015 1st Ave., ☎ 206/624–5582; 1420 5th Ave., ☎ 206/587–6292) features sophisticated European clothing. On the edge of the Pike Place Market, **Local Brilliance** (1535 1st Ave., ☎ 206/343–

5864) showcases fashions by local designers. **Nubia's** (1507 6th Ave., ☎ 206/622–0297) is a small shop but has an excellent selection of unconstructed knits for women's business and casual wear, belts, beads, and other accessories.

Spectator Sports

Baseball

Seattle Mariners (Kingdome, 201 S. King St., ☎ 206/628–3555; Apr.–Oct.).

Basketball

Seattle SuperSonics (Seattle Center Coliseum, 1st Ave. N, ☎ 206/281–5850; Nov.–Apr.).

Football

Seahawks (Kingdome, ☎ 206/827–9777; Aug.–Dec.).

Dining

For price ranges, see Chart 1 (A) in On the Road with Fodor's.

$$$$ ★ **Canlis.** This sumptuous restaurant is a Seattle institution. Its famous steaks—and its equally famous oysters from Quilcene Bay and fresh fish in season—are cooked to a turn. *2576 Aurora Ave. N, ☎ 206/283–3313. Jacket required. AE, DC, MC, V. Closed Sun. No lunch.*

$$$ **Campagne.** Overlooking Pike Place Market and Elliott Bay, Campagne is intimate and urbane, with white walls, picture windows, and colorful modern prints setting the tone. The flavors of Provence pervade the menu in such dishes as chicken stuffed with goat cheese and fresh herbs, and salmon in a cognac-and-champagne butter sauce. *Inn at the Market, 86 Pine St., ☎ 206/728–2800. Jacket required. AE, MC, V.*

$$ **Place Pigalle.** Despite its French name, this is a very American restaurant and popular with locals. Large windows look out over Elliott Bay and, in good weather, are open to admit the salt breeze. The menu features seasonal meals of seafood and local ingredients. *Pike Place Market, ☎ 206/624–1756. MC, V. Closed Sun.*

$$ ★ **Wild Ginger.** The specialty is Pacific Rim cookery, including tasty southern Chinese, Vietnamese, Thai, and Korean dishes served in a warm, clubby dining room. Daily specials are based on seasonally available products. *1400 Western Ave., ☎ 206/623–4450. AE, DC, MC, V. No lunch Sun.*

$ ★ **Emmet Watson's Oyster Bar.** This small seafood place is hard to find (it's in the back of Pike Place Market's Soames–Dunn Building and fronts a small courtyard), but it's worth the effort. The oysters are fresh and offered in a number of varieties; the beer list, too, is ample, featuring 25 or more selections from local microbrews to fancy imports. *Pike Place Market, 1916 Pike Pl., ☎ 206/448–7721. No reservations. No credit cards. No dinner Sun.*

$ **Salvatore Ristorante Italiano.** You'll wait for a table at this small storefront, but regulars don't consider that much of a drawback. Go for the individual pizzas or one of the specials—which always include pasta dishes and meat and fish courses—that are chalked onto the blackboard above the kitchen window. The wine list has some locally rare Italian bottlings. *6100 Roosevelt Way NE, ☎ 206/527–9301. No reservations. MC, V. Closed Sun. No lunch.*

Lodging

Seattle boasts an abundance of lodgings, from deluxe downtown hotels to smaller, less expensive digs in the University District. For information on the ever-growing number of B&Bs, contact the **Pacific Bed & Breakfast Agency** (701 N.W. 60th St., Seattle 98107, ☎ 206/784–0539) or the **Washington State Bed-and-Breakfast Guild** (2442 N.W. Market St., Seattle 98107, ☎ 800/647–2918). For price ranges, see Chart 2 (A) in On the Road with Fodor's.

$$$–$$$$ ★ **Alexis.** At this intimate hotel in a restored 1901 building near the waterfront, guest rooms are decorated in contemporary subdued colors. Some suites feature Jacuzzi jets and wood-burning fireplaces. The hotel has a no-tipping policy. *1007 1st Ave., 98104, ☎ 206/624–4844 or 800/426–7033, FAX 206/621–9009. 39 rooms, 15 suites. Facilities: restaurant, café, bar, access to health club. AE, DC, MC, V.*

$$$–$$$$ ★ **Four Seasons Olympic Hotel.** Restored to its 1920s grandeur, the Olympic is Seattle's most elegant hotel. Its public rooms are furnished with marble, thick rugs, wood paneling, and potted plants. The less luxurious guest rooms feature a homey ambience with comfortable reading chairs and floral-print fabrics. *411 University St., 98101, ☎ 206/621–1700 or 800/223–8772, FAX 206/682–9633. 450 rooms. Facilities: 3 restaurants, health club, indoor pool. AE, DC, MC, V.*

$$–$$$ **Edgewater.** The only hotel on Elliott Bay, the Edgewater was famous for guests fishing from their waterside windows. In 1988 new ownership banned the fishing but remodeled and redecorated the rooms in a comfortably rustic style with unfinished wood furnishings and plaid fabric in red, green, and blue. *Pier 67, 2411 Alaskan Way, 98121, ☎ 206/728–7000 or 800/624–0670, FAX 206/441–4119. 234 rooms. Facilities: restaurant, bar. AE, DC, MC, V.*

$$–$$$ ★ **Inn at the Market.** This sophisticated but unpretentious hotel is adjacent to the Pike Place Market. It combines the best aspects of a small, deluxe hotel with the informality of the Pacific Northwest, offering a lively setting that's perfect for travelers who prefer personality over big-hotel amenities. Rooms are spacious, have contemporary furnishings and ceramic sculptures, and offer views of the city, Elliott Bay, the Pike Place Market, and the hotel courtyard. *86 Pine St., 98101, ☎ 206/443–3600, FAX 206/448–0631. 65 rooms. Facilities: access to health club and spa, room service, no-smoking rooms available. AE, D, DC, MC, V.*

$$ ★ **Meany Tower Hotel.** Built in 1931 and remodeled several times, this pleasant hotel a few blocks from the University of Washington campus features a contemporary ambience, with a muted peach color scheme and brass fixtures, and careful, attentive service. Nearly all the rooms have views of the Cascades or the Olympic Mountains, the University of Washington, or Lake Union. The tiled baths include old-fashioned pedestal sinks. *4507 Brooklyn Ave. NE, 98105, ☎ 206/634–2000, FAX 206/634–2000. 155 rooms. Facilities: restaurant, lounge, no-smoking rooms available. AE, DC, MC, V.*

$ **Seattle YMCA.** A member of the American Youth Hostels Association, this Y offers rooms that are clean and plainly furnished with a bed, phone, desk, and lamp. Single and double dorm units can accommodate four people each. *909 4th Ave., 98104, ☎ 206/382–5000. 198 beds. Facilities: pool, health club. MC, V.*

Motels

Doubletree Suites (16500 Southcenter Pkwy., Tukwila 98188, ☎ 206/575–8220, FAX 206/575–4743), 221 suites, restaurant, lounge, health club, indoor pool, whirlpool, sauna; *$$$*. **Doubletree Inn** (205 Strander Blvd., Tukwila 98188, ☎ 206/246–8220, FAX 206/575–4749), 200 rooms, dining room, coffee shop, lounge, outdoor pool; *$$*. **University Plaza Hotel** (400 N.E. 45th St., 98105, ☎ 206/634–0100, FAX 206/633–2743), 135 rooms, restaurant, lounge, fitness room, outdoor heated pool; *$*.

The Arts and Nightlife

The Arts

In recent years Seattle has gained a reputation as a world-class theater town; it also has a strong music and dance scene, with local, national, and international artists. The Friday *Seattle Times* and *Post-Intelligencer* detail the coming week's events. *Seattle Weekly,* which hits newsstands on Wednesday, has detailed coverage and arts reviews.

To charge tickets, call **TicketMaster** (☎ 206/628–0888). **Ticket/Ticket,** with two locations (401 Broadway E and 1st Ave. and Pike St., ☎ 206/324–2744), sells half-price, same-day tickets for cash only.

DANCE

Pacific Northwest Ballet (Opera House, Seattle Center, ☎ 206/441–2424) is a resident company and school that presents 60–70 performances annually.

MUSIC

Seattle Symphony (Opera House, Seattle Center, ☎ 206/443–4747) presents some 120 concerts September–June in and around town. A new $99-million Symphony Hall at Second Avenue and University Street is set to open in 1997. **Northwest Chamber Orchestra** (☎ 206/343–0445), the Northwest's only professional chamber orchestra, presents a full spectrum of music, from Baroque to modern, at various venues.

OPERA

Seattle Opera (Opera House, Seattle Center, ☎ 206/389–7600), considered one of the top companies in America, presents six productions during its August–May season.

THEATER

The **Seattle Repertory Theater** (Bagley Wright Theater, Seattle Center, 155 Mercer St., ☎ 206/443–2222) presents high-quality programming from classics to new works. The **New City Arts Center** (1634 11th Ave., ☎ 206/323–6800) features experimental performances by the resident company and in conjunction with national and international artists. The **Empty Space Theater** (3509 Freemont Ave. N, ☎ 206/547–7500) has a strong reputation for introducing new playwrights. The **Group Theatre** (Center House lower level, Seattle Center, ☎ 206/441–1299) presents socially provocative works by old and new artists of varied cultures and colors. **A Contemporary Theater** (ACT; 100 W. Roy St., ☎ 206/285–5110) develops works by new playwrights, including at least one world premiere every year; ACT will move into the Eagle's Auditorium (7th Ave. and Union St.) in mid-1996.

Nightlife

For a relatively small city, Seattle has a strong and diverse music scene. On any given night, you can hear high-quality sounds at a wide variety of night spots.

BARS AND NIGHTCLUBS

Bars with waterfront views are plentiful hereabouts. **Pescatore** (5300 34th Ave. NW, ☎ 206/784–1733) is in Ballard, with large windows overlooking the Ship Canal. **Adriatica** (1107 Dexter Ave. N, ☎ 206/285–5000), a Mediterranean restaurant and lounge in an Arts and Crafts–style building, sits above Lake Union's west side. **Arnie's Northshore Restaurant** (1900 N. Northlake Way, ☎ 206/547–3242) has a lounge with giant windows overlooking Gas Works Park and Lake Union. A Seattle favorite, **Ray's Boathouse** (6049 Seaview Ave. NW, ☎ 206/789–

3770) is perched on the shore of Shilshole Bay, a perfect spot for watching the sun set behind the Olympic Mountains.

BLUES/R&B CLUB

The **Ballard Firehouse** (5429 Russell St. NW, ☎ 206/784–3516) is a music mecca in Ballard, with an emphasis on the blues.

COMEDY CLUB

Comedy Underground (222 Main St., ☎ 206/628–0303), a Pioneer Square club that's literally underground, beneath Swannie's, presents stand-up comedy and open-mike nights.

DANCE CLUBS

Fenix Underground (323 2nd Ave. S, ☎ 206/467–1111) is one of several popular clubs in Pioneer Square. At street level, **Fenix** (315 2nd Ave. S, ☎ 206/467–1111) also features recorded dance music. On Capitol Hill, **Neighbours** (1509 Broadway E, ☎ 206/324–5358) attracts a good mix of gay men and everyone else.

GRUNGE CLUBS

Seattle has become a center for grunge music, producing such top bands as Nirvana, Pearl Jam, and Alice in Chains. Somewhat reminiscent of '70s acid rock, grunge populated the soundtrack of the movie *Singles,* which was filmed in Seattle. The **Off-Ramp Cafe** (109 Eastlake Ave. E, ☎ 206/628–0232) features grunge and rock. You will find a variety of music at the **OK Hotel** (212 Alaskan Way S, ☎ 206/621–7903), including grunge, acoustic, jazz, and even poetry readings.

JAZZ CLUB

Dimitriou's Jazz Alley (2037 6th Ave., ☎ 206/441–9729) is a downtown club with nationally known performers every night but Sunday. Excellent dinners are served before the first show.

ROCK CLUBS

Central Saloon (207 1st Ave. S, ☎ 206/622–0209) is a crowded Pioneer Square saloon with an ever-changing roster of local and national rock acts. **Crocodile Cafe** (2200 2nd Ave., ☎ 206/448–2114) rocks with live local groups Tuesday through Saturday.

Excursion to Whidbey and the San Juan Islands

Getting There

BY PLANE

From Seattle-Tacoma International Airport, **Harbor Airlines** (☎ 800/359–3220) flies to San Juan Island and Whidbey Island. **Kenmore Air** (☎ 206/486–1257 or 800/543–9595) flies floatplanes from Lake Union in Seattle to the San Juan Islands. **West Isle Air** (☎ 360/293–4691 or 800/874–4434) flies to San Juan Island from Anacortes and Bellingham.

BY CAR

By car from Seattle, drive north on I–5 to La Conner; go west on Rte. 536 to Rte. 20W and follow signs to Anacortes; then pick up the ferry for the San Juan Islands. Whidbey Island can be reached by ferry from Mukilteo, or you can drive from Seattle along I–5, then head west on Hwy. 20 and cross the dramatic Deception Pass via the bridge at the north end of the island.

BY FERRY

The **Washington State Ferry System** (☎ 206/464–6400 or 800/843–3779) provides car and passenger service from Mukilteo, on Hwy. 525, 30 mi north of Seattle, to Clinton on Whidbey Island and from Anacortes, about 90 mi north of Seattle, to the San Juan Islands. **San Juan Islands Shuttle Express** (Alaska Ferry Terminal, 355 Harris Ave. No. 105, Bellingham 98225, ☎ 206/671–1137) provides daily passenger service from Bellingham to Orcas Island and San Juan Island's Friday Harbor with a narrative talk on the wildlife and natural history of the area. You can also take a three-hour whale-watching trip out of Friday Harbor.

What to See and Do

Whidbey Island and the San Juan Islands are the jewels of Puget Sound. Because, except for Whidbey, they are reachable only by ferry, airplane, or private boat, the islands beckon souls longing for a quiet change of pace, whether it be kayaking in a cove, walking a deserted beach, or nestling by the fire in an old farmhouse. The islands are a popular weekend getaway spot for Seattleites. The **San Juan Tourism Cooperative** (Box 65, Lopez 98261, ☎ 360/468–3663) can provide information.

Whidbey Island is mostly rural, with undulating hills, gentle beaches, and little coves. **Langley** is a quaint town that caters to locals and tourists with a number of inviting bed-and-breakfast inns, a handful of good restaurants, shops, and galleries. It sits atop a 50-ft-high bluff overlooking the southeastern shore. A little over half the way up this 50-mi-long island is **Coupeville,** site of many restored Victorian houses and one of the largest National Historic Districts in the state. The town was founded in 1852 by Captain Thomas Coupe; his house, built in 1853, is one of the state's oldest.

Ebey's Landing National Historic Reserve (☎ 360/678–4636), headquartered in Coupeville, is a 17,000-acre area including Keystone, Coupeville, and Penn Cove. Established by Congress in 1978, the reserve is the first and largest of its kind, dotted with 91 nationally registered historic structures, farmland, parks, and trails. At **Deception Pass State Park** (☎ 360/675–2417), at the north end of the island, take in the spectacular view and stroll among the madrona trees, with their peeling reddish-brown bark.

The other major islands are **Lopez Island,** with old orchards, weathered barns, and sheep and cow pastures; **Shaw Island,** where Franciscan nuns in traditional habits run the ferry dock; **Orcas,** a large, mountainous, horseshoe-shaped island with marvelous hilltop views and several good restaurants; and **San Juan Island,** with the colorful, active waterfront town of Friday Harbor. Lopez, Orcas, and San Juan all feature a number of excellent bed-and-breakfast accommodations.

Bicycling, boating, fishing, and camping are favored activities on the islands, but the small villages also teem with antiques shops and art galleries. There are a few restaurants that should not be missed. On Orcas, **Christina's** (North Beach Rd. and Horseshoe Hwy., ☎ 360/376–4904; *$$–$$$*) is very romantic, with low light and views of the water; it emphasizes fresh local seafood, with some of the best salmon entrées in the Northwest. Along a country road on San Juan Island, the **Duck Soup Inn** (3090 Roche Harbor Rd., ☎ 360/378–4878; *$$$*) has a French bistro–style menu of fresh local fish. On Whidbey Island, **Garibyan Brothers Café Langley** (113 1st St., Langley, ☎ 360/221–3090; *$$*) offers Mediterranean fare in a casual atmosphere.

Excursion to Tacoma

Getting There

Tacoma is about 35 mi south of Seattle via I–5. Sea-Tac airport is about a 30-minute drive away. The city is served by major bus, train, and air carriers.

What to See and Do

If it weren't so close to Seattle, Tacoma would be quite a draw. As it is, Tacoma huddles in Seattle's shadow. Because of a variety of industrial aromas emanating from Tacoma, Seattleites often make fun of the city. Nevertheless, Tacoma offers many good arts performances, renovated historical theaters, wonderfully restored residential neighborhoods, fine bay views, and a world-class zoo. (**Tacoma–Pierce County Visitors and Convention Bureau,** 906 Broadway, Tacoma 98402, ☎ 206/627–2836.)

Union Station (1717 Pacific Ave., ☎ 206/931–7884) is an heirloom from the golden age of railroads, when Tacoma was the western terminus for the transcontinental Northern Pacific Railroad. Built by Reed and Stem, architects of New York City's Grand Central Station, the massive copper-domed, Beaux Arts–style depot was opened in 1911 and shows influences ranging from the Roman Pantheon to the 16th-century Italian Baroque. It now houses federal district courts. The rotunda is open to the public and features a large exhibit of Dale Chihuly art glass. The renovation of Union Station has prompted more redevelopment in the area. In 1996, the **Washington State Historical Society** (315 N. Stadium Way, ☎ 206/593–2830; admission charged) will move to a new facility near Union Station. The museum houses exhibits on the natural, Native American, pioneer, maritime, and industrial history of the state. While in the area, catch a meal at the **Swiss** (1904 S. Jefferson Ave., ☎ 206/572–2821), located in a distinctive 1913 building that was once the Swiss Hall; you'll find good pub fare and a selection of Northwest microbrews.

Downtown on Broadway is Antique Row, with numerous antiques shops, two restored theaters, and unusual, funky boutiques. For example, visit **Good Kitty, Bad Kitty** (765 Broadway, ☎ 206/383–4232) for everything feline—from coffee mugs to fabrics designed by a Tacoma artist. The **Tacoma Art Museum** (1123 Pacific Ave., ☎ 206/272–4258; admission charged) contains a rich collection of American and French paintings, as well as Chinese jades and imperial robes. In **Wright Park** (6th and Division Sts., I and J Sts., ☎ 206/591–5331), a pleasant 30-acre park just north of downtown, is the **W. W. Seymour Botanical Conservatory,** a Victorian-style greenhouse with an extensive collection of exotic flora.

Northeast of Tacoma is the 700-acre **Point Defiance Park,** one of the largest urban parks in the country. Within it is the **Point Defiance Zoo and Aquarium,** founded in 1888 and now one of the top zoos in America. Using the Pacific Rim as its theme, it has blossomed (since an extensive renovation in 1986) into an impressive example of humane and innovative trends in zoo administration. *5400 N. Pearl St., ☎ 206/305–1000. Zoo admission charged. Closed Thanksgiving, Christmas.*

Excursion to Olympia

Getting There

Olympia is on I–5, about 60 mi southwest of Seattle and 25 mi southwest of Tacoma.

What to See and Do

The pace of life in **Olympia,** Washington's state capital, is largely determined by the legislative season: When they're in session, it's hopping; when they're not, it's fairly quiet. You can tour the stately **Legislative Building** (Capitol Way between 10th and 14th Aves., ☎ 206/586–8687), a handsome Romanesque structure with a 287-ft dome that closely resembles the capitol building in "the other Washington." Behind it is the modern **State Library,** with collections of works by Northwest authors and art by Mark Tobey and Kenneth Callahan. If history and politics make you hungry, stop by **La Petite Maison** (2005 Ascension Way, ☎ 206/943–8812; *$$$*), where imaginative French food is served in a converted 1890s farmhouse.

THE OLYMPIC PENINSULA

The rugged Olympic Peninsula is the northwestern corner of the continental United States. Much of it is wilderness, with the Olympic National Park and National Forest at its heart. The peninsula has tremendous variety: the wild Pacific shore, the sheltered waters along the Hood Canal and the Strait of Juan de Fuca, the rivers of the Olympic's rain forests, and the towering Olympic Mountains.

Tourist Information

North Olympic Peninsula Visitor & Convention Bureau (Box 670, Port Angeles 98362, ☎ 360/452–8552 or 800/942–4042). **Port Angeles:** Visitor Center (121 E. Railroad Ave., 98362, ☎ 360/452–2363).

Getting There

By Plane

Horizon Air (☎ 800/547–9308) flies into Port Angeles from Seattle-Tacoma airport. Private charter airlines fly into Port Angeles, Forks, and Hoquiam.

By Car

U.S. 101 loops around the Olympic Peninsula, which can be reached from Olympia via Rtes. 8 and 101 and from Tacoma, 50 mi away, via Hwy. 16.

By Bus

Port Angeles-Seattle Bus Line (☎ 360/452–8311) serves the Olympic Peninsula.

By Ferry

The **Washington State Ferry System** (☎ 206/464–6400 or 800/843–3779) provides car and passenger service from downtown Seattle to Bremerton. The **Black Bally Ferry Line** (☎ 360/457–4491) operates between Port Angeles on the Olympic Peninsula and Victoria, British Columbia.

Exploring the Olympic Peninsula

From Olympia, go west along Hwy. 101 and Rtes. 8 and 12 to Gray's Harbor and the twin seaports of **Hoquiam** and **Aberdeen.** From Hoquiam, you can drive north on Rte. 109, which sticks to the coast and passes through resorts and ample beach areas such as **Copalis Beach, Pacific Beach,** and **Moclips** on its way to the Quinault Indian Reservation and the tribal center of **Taholah.** The town itself is rustic and offers little in the way of tourist attractions, the main draw here, as elsewhere on the peninsula, being the vast pristine scenery.

Hwy. 109 dead-ends at Taholah, and you must backtrack to return to U.S. 101. About 20 mi north of Aberdeen on Hwy. 101 is the Hoh Road, which goes east to the **Hoh Rain Forest,** part of the Olympic National Park. This complex and rich, temperate ecosystem of conifers, hardwoods, grasses, mosses, and other flora shelters such wildlife as elks, otters, beavers, salmon, and flying squirrels. The average rainfall here is 145 inches a year. The **Hoh Visitor Center,** at the campground and ranger center at road's end, has information, nature trails, and interpretive displays. *Upper Hoh Rd., 1.5 mi north of the Hoh River Bridge; visitor center is 20 mi farther,* ☎ *360/374–6925. Admission charged. Visitor center open year-round but often unstaffed Sept.–May.*

North on U.S. 101 is the small logging town of **Forks,** renowned for its lavish three-day Fourth of July celebrations, which feature logging-truck parades, lots of fireworks, and a demolition derby. From here, La Push Road leads west about 15 mi to **La Push,** a coastal village and the tribal center of the Quileute Indians. Several points along this road have short trails with access to the ocean, fabulous views of offshore islands, and dramatic, stark rock formations.

Returning to U.S. 101, which swings to the east as you go north from Forks, you go through the **Sol Duc River Valley,** famous for its salmon fishing. The **Soleduck Fish Hatchery** (☎ 360/327–3246) has interpretive displays on fish breeding. A few miles past the tiny town of Sappho are the deep azure waters of **Lake Crescent.** The area has abundant campsites, resorts, trails, canoeing, and fishing. The original lodge buildings of 1915 (*see* Dining and Lodging, *below*)—well worn but comfortable—are still in use.

Twelve miles south on Soleduck Road (which meets U.S. 101 1 mi west of the western tip of Lake Crescent) is an entrance to Olympic National Park and to **Sol Duc Hot Springs,** where you can dip into three hot sulfur pools ranging from 98° to 104°. ☎ *360/327–3583. Admission charged. Closed Oct.–mid-May.*

Back on U.S. 101 east, you will soon come to **Port Angeles,** a bustling commercial fishing port and an access route to Canada. The town hosts the visitor center for **Olympic National Park** (*see* National Parks, *above*), at 3002 Mt. Angeles Road. A bus will take you, or you can drive up the road up to **Hurricane Ridge,** 17 mi south of Port Angeles, which rises nearly a mile above sea level as it enters the park and offers spectacular views of the Olympics, the Strait of Juan de Fuca, and Vancouver Island.

A wide variety of animal life, present and past, can be found in the charming town of **Sequim** (pronounced "squim"), 17 mi east of Port Angeles on U.S. 101, at the **Museum and Arts Center** in the Sequim–Dungeness Valley (175 W. Cedar St., ☎ 360/683–8110), where you can view the remains of an Ice Age mastodon and exhibits on the early Klallam Indians and the town's pioneer history. In the fertile plain at the mouth of the Dungeness River, 4 mi northwest of Sequim, the **Dungeness National Wildlife Refuge** (☎ 360/457–8451) is home to thousands of migratory waterfowl, as well as clams, oysters, and seals.

About 10 mi east of Sequim, Rte. 20 turns northward 12 mi to **Port Townsend.** Its waterfront is lined with handsome brick buildings from the 1870s that have been carefully restored and house a variety of attractive shops and restaurants. High up on the bluff are large gingerbread-trimmed Victorian homes, many of which have been turned into elegant B&Bs.

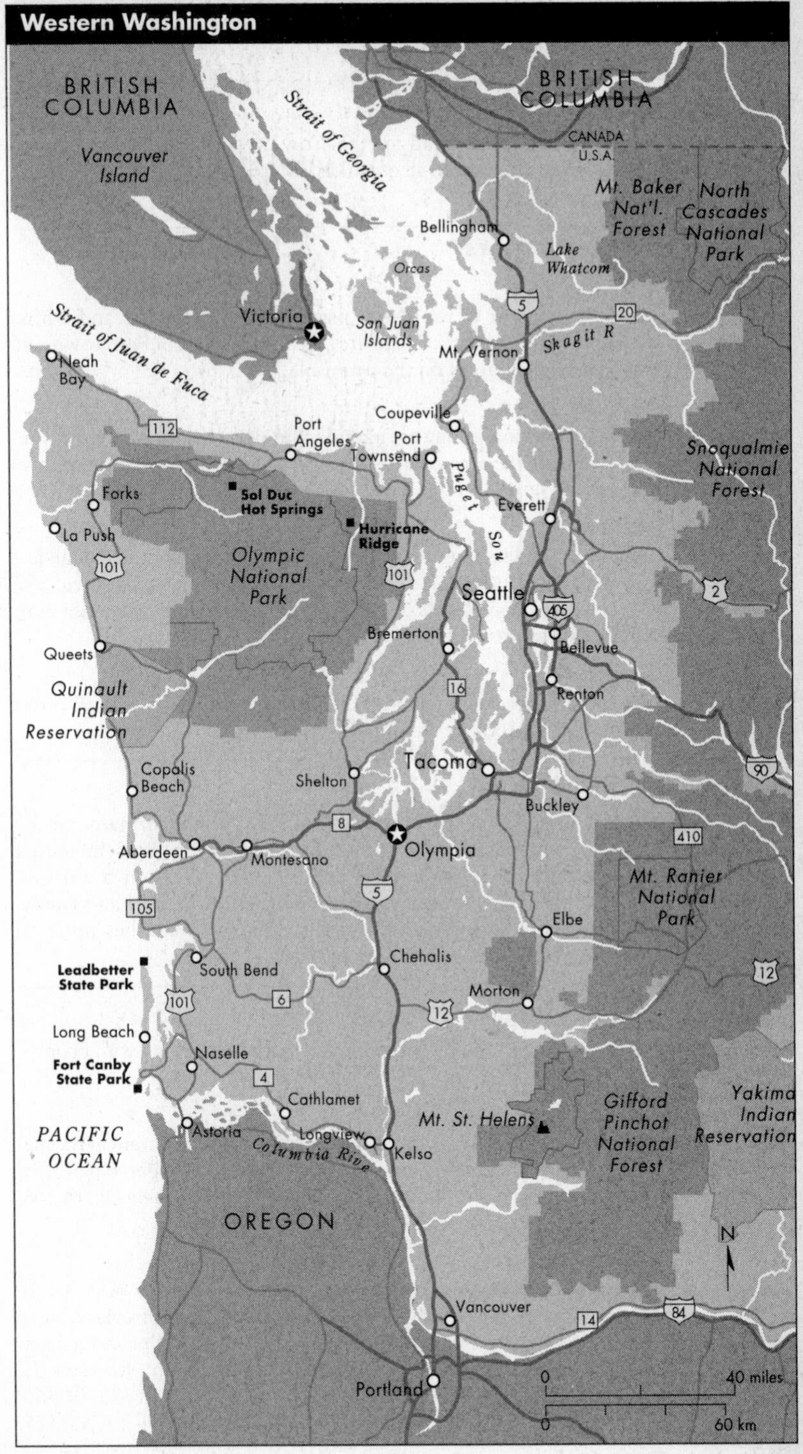
Western Washington
BRITISH COLUMBIA
Vancouver Island
Strait of Georgia
BRITISH COLUMBIA
CANADA
U.S.A.
Mt. Baker Nat'l. Forest
North Cascades National Park
Bellingham
Lake Whatcom
Orcas
Victoria
San Juan Islands
Strait of Juan de Fuca
Neah Bay
Mt. Vernon
Skagit R
Coupeville
Port Angeles
Port Townsend
Puget Sou
Snoqualmie National Forest
Forks
Sol Duc Hot Springs
Hurricane Ridge
La Push
Everett
Olympic National Park
Seattle
Bremerton
Bellevue
Queets
Renton
Quinault Indian Reservation
Tacoma
Copalis Beach
Shelton
Buckley
Aberdeen
Montesano
Olympia
Mt. Ranier National Park
Elbe
Leadbetter State Park
South Bend
Chehalis
Morton
Long Beach
Naselle
Fort Canby State Park
Cathlamet
Gifford Pinchot National Forest
Yakima Indian Reservation
Mt. St. Helens
PACIFIC OCEAN
Astoria
Longview
Kelso
Columbia Rive
OREGON
N
Vancouver
Portland
0
40 miles
0
60 km

Driving south on Hwy. 101 through the sawmill town of **Shelton** will bring you back to Olympia.

Shopping

Confirmed shoppers head for the array of waterfront boutiques and stores in **Port Townsend,** all of which feature a good selection of Northwest arts and crafts.

Sports and the Outdoors

Biking

Biking is popular in the flatter parts of Port Townsend and within Olympic National Park. There are bike-rental shops in Port Townsend and other resort areas on the peninsula.

Fishing

Trout and salmon fishing are abundant in rivers throughout the peninsula. Contact the area tourist office (*see* Tourist Information, *above*) for details.

Hiking

Both ocean and mountain areas offer numerous hiking trails for all levels. Contact the **Olympic National Forest** (1835 Blacklake Blvd. SW, Olympia 98512-5623, ☎ 360/956–2400) or **Olympic National Park Visitor Center** (☎ 360/452–0330).

Skiing

Hurricane Ridge (*see* Exploring the Olympic Peninsula, *above*) offers 25 mi of cross-country ski trails.

Beaches

Beaches abound on the Olympic Peninsula, although many are on tribal or private land and are not generally accessible. Remember that the North Pacific is not for swimming—unless you wear a wet suit. For walking and exploring, the main beaches are **Copalis** and **Pacific,** north of Hoquiam; a series of scenic, unnamed beaches north of **Kalaloch;** and **Rialto Beach,** near La Push.

Dining and Lodging

For price ranges, see Charts 1 (B) and 2 (B) in On the Road with Fodor's.

Gig Harbor

DINING

★ **Neville's Shoreline.** This pleasant, accommodating restaurant at the marina specializes in seafood—try the simply but well-prepared pan-fried oysters—and serves a Sunday brunch. *8827 N. Harborview Dr.,* ☎ *206/851–9822. AE, MC, V. $$*

LODGING

★ **Sandpiper Beach Resort.** This modern, four-story complex offers clean, attractive suites; most have a sitting room, dining area, fireplace, small kitchen, porch, bedroom, and bath. This is definitely the place for a getaway; no in-room phones, no pool, no TV, no restaurant. *Rte. 109 (1½ mi south of Pacific Beach), Box A, 98571,* ☎ *360/276–4580,* FAX *360/276–4464. 30 rooms. Facilities: gift shop, espresso bar. MC, V. $$–$$$.*

Port Angeles

DINING

C'est Si Bon. This locally famous spot run by a French couple is probably the most elegant restaurant on the decidedly informal Olympic

Peninsula. The walls are adorned with art, the tables with fine linen, and windows offer a good view of the flower-laden terrace and the Olympic Mountains. The cuisine, of course, is French. *2300 Hwy. 101E (4 mi east of town), ☎ 360/452–8888. Reservations advised. AE, DC, MC, V. Closed Mon. No lunch. $$$*

LODGING

Sol Duc Hot Springs Resort. The comfortable, casual resort has minimally outfitted cabins and dates from the turn of the century. Some cabins are more rustic with knotty pine walls, while others are more modern. There are plenty of hiking trails in the area. *12 mi south of Hwy. 101 on Soleduck Rd., Box 2169, 98362, ☎ 360/327–3583, FAX 360/327–3398. 32 units, camping and RV facilities. Facilities: restaurant (reservations required), 3 hot springs, outdoor pool. AE, D, MC, V. Closed mid-Oct.–mid-May. $$–$$$*

Lake Crescent Lodge. This old but comfortable accommodation with a big main lodge and small cabins overlooks the beautiful deep-blue Lake Crescent. Units in the lodge are minimal—bathrooms down the hall, dimly lit rooms—but the setting makes up for sparse amenities. *HC–62, Box 11, 98362, ☎ 360/928–3211, FAX 360/928–3253. Facilities: restaurant, fishing, boating. AE, DC, MC, V. Closed mid-Nov.–Apr. $–$$*

Port Townsend

DINING

★ **Fountain Café.** This small café off the main tourist drag is one of the best restaurants in town. You can count on seafood and pasta specialties with imaginative twists, such as oysters in an anchovy wine sauce. *920 Washington St., ☎ 360/385–1364. AE, MC, V. $$*

Salal Café. Featuring home-style cooking and daily specials, this cooperatively run restaurant shines among early morning breakfast joints. Try one of many variations on the potato-egg scramble for lunch. Seafood and regional American-style meals are good, portions ample, and prices reasonable. *634 Water St., ☎ 360/385–6532. No reservations. No credit cards. Closed Tues. No dinner. $*

LODGING

James House. Commanding a spot on the bluff overlooking downtown and the waterfront, this splendid, antiques-filled Victorian B&B provides visitors with a great sense of how the well-heeled lived in the late 1800s. *1238 Washington St., 98368, ☎ 360/385–1238. 12 rooms. MC, V. $$$*

Palace Hotel. This friendly hotel in the historic section of downtown is tastefully decorated to reflect its 1889 construction date and its one-time history as a bordello. *1004 Water St., 98368, ☎ 360/385–0773 or 800/962–0741, FAX 360/946–5287. 15 units, 5 with kitchenette. Facilities: restaurant. AE, D, MC, V. $$*

Quinault

LODGING

Lake Quinault Lodge. This deluxe lodge is set on a perfect glacial lake in the midst of the Olympic National Forest. Built in 1926 of cedar shingles, the lodge has delightfully decorated public rooms with antique reproductions and a fireplace. *S. Shore Rd., Box 7, 98575, ☎ 360/288–2571, FAX 360/288–2901. 89 rooms. Facilities: restaurant, bar, whirlpool, indoor pool, sauna, games room. AE, MC, V. $$$*

Campgrounds

Camping areas abound on the Olympic Peninsula. Some of the best within the Olympic National Park are **Hoh River, Mora,** and **Fairholm**

(☎ 360/452–0330). Elsewhere on the peninsula: **Bogachiel State Park** (☎ 360/374–6356) near Forks (closed after dusk in winter); **Fort Flagler State Park** (☎ 360/385–1259) near Port Townsend (closed for overnight camping Nov.–Feb.); **Ocean City State Park** (148 State Rte. 115, Hoquiam 98550, ☎ 360/289–3553); and **Pacific Beach State Park** (☎ 360/276–4297). Also see **Sol Duc Hot Springs Resort** (*see* Dining and Lodging, *above*).

LONG BEACH PENINSULA

If the waters of the Pacific and the Columbia River met in a less turbulent manner, a huge seaport might sit at the river's mouth. Instead, the entrance to the Columbia is sparsely populated, dotted with fishing villages and cranberry bogs. Although only a 3½-hour drive southwest of Seattle and two hours northwest of Portland, the Long Beach Peninsula is worlds away from either city. Just north of the river's mouth, the peninsula separates the Pacific Ocean and Willapa Bay and is known for excellent bird-watching, beachcombing, hiking, history, and a handful of gourmet restaurants.

Tourist Information

Long Beach: Visitors Bureau (intersection of Hwys. 101 and 103, Seaview 98631, ☎ 360/642–2400 or 800/451–2542).

Getting There

By Car

Long Beach is accessible from the east via Hwy. 4, which connects with I–5 near Longview, and from the north and south via U.S. 101.

Exploring Long Beach Peninsula

U.S. 101 crosses the broad Columbia River between Astoria, Oregon, and Megler, Washington, in a high, graceful span. Just beyond, on Hwy. 103, is **Ilwaco,** a small fishing community of about 600. The **Ilwaco Heritage Museum** (115 S.E. Lake St., ☎ 360/642–3446; admission charged) uses dioramas to present the history of southwestern Washington, beginning with the Native Americans.

A couple of miles south is the **Cape Disappointment Lighthouse,** first used in 1856 and one of the oldest lighthouses on the West Coast. The cape was named by English fur trader Captain John Meares in 1788 in honor of his unsuccessful attempt to find the Northwest Passage.

Fort Canby State Park (3 mi west of Ilwaco, off U.S. 101 (☎ 360/642–3078) was an active military installation until 1957, when it was turned over to the Washington State Parks and Recreation Commission. Now it is best known for great views of the Columbia River Bar during winter storms. The **Lewis & Clark Interpretive Center** documents the 8,000-mi round-trip journey of the famous pair and their Corps of Volunteers for Northwest Discovery from Wood River, Illinois, to the mouth of the Columbia. ☎ *360/642–3029 or 360/642–3078.*

The town of **Long Beach** caters to tourists with beach activities and an old-fashioned amusement park with go-carts and bumper cars. About halfway up the peninsula is **Ocean Park,** the area's commercial center. A few miles north is **Oysterville,** established as an oystering town in 1854. When the native shellfish were fished to extinction, a Japanese oyster was introduced, but the town never made a comeback. Tides have washed away homes, businesses, and a Methodist church, but the village still exists. Maps inside the vestibule of the restored **Oysterville Church** direct you through town, which is now on the National Register of Historic Places. At the northern tip of the peninsula is **Leadbetter State Park** (*see* National and State Parks, *above*).

Shopping

The **Bookvendor** (101 Pacific Ave., Long Beach, ☎ 360/642–2702) stocks an extensive supply of children's books, classics, and travel books, as well as art supplies. **North Head Gallery** (600 S. Pacific Ave., Long Beach, ☎ 360/642–8884) has the largest selection of Elton Bennett originals, plus Bennett reproductions and works from other Northwest artists.

Sports and the Outdoors

Biking

Good areas for bicycling on the peninsula's 20 mi include Fort Canby and North Head roads, Sandridge Road to Ocean Park and Oysterville, U.S. 101 from Naselle to Seaview, and Rte. 103 along Willapa Bay. There are rentals available in virtually every town.

Fishing

Salmon, rock cod, lingcod, flounder, perch, sea bass, and sturgeon are popular and plentiful for fishing. A guide is available from the **Port of Ilwaco** (Box 307, 98624, ☎ 360/642–3145). Clamming season varies depending on the supply; for details call the **Washington Department of Fisheries** (☎ 360/902–2250) or the **Fisheries' shellfish lab** (☎ 360/665–4166). There are tackle shops all over Long Beach Peninsula, and most sell the necessary fishing licenses.

Golf

There are two nine-hole golf courses: the **Peninsula Golf Course** (☎ 360/642–2828), at the north end of Long Beach, and the **Surfside Golf Course** (☎ 360/665–4148), 2 mi north of Ocean Park.

Hiking

Hiking trails are available at **Fort Canby** and **Leadbetter** state parks (*see, respectively,* Exploring Long Beach Peninsula, *above, and* National and State Parks, *above*).

Dining and Lodging

For price ranges, see Charts 1 (B) and 2 (B) in On the Road with Fodor's.

Ilwaco

LODGING

Inn at Ilwaco. This B&B is set in a renovated New England–style church, built in 1928. The guest rooms—most of them upstairs in the old Sunday-school rooms—are cozily furnished with some antiques, armoires, and eyelet or printed chintz curtains and coverlets. *120 Williams St. NE, 98624, ☎ 360/642–8686. 9 rooms, 2 share bath. MC, V. $$$*

Long Beach

DINING

My Mom's Pie Kitchen. Though this place in a mobile home keeps limited hours, it's worth dropping by for such specialty pies as banana whipped cream, chocolate almond, sour-cream raisin, and fresh raspberry. Also on the menu are clam chowder and quiche. *Hwy. 103 and 12th St. S, ☎ 360/642–2342. MC, V. Closed Sun.–Tues. No dinner. $*

Seaview

DINING

★ **Shoalwater Restaurant.** The dining room at the Shelburne Inn (*see* Lodging, *below*) has been acclaimed by *Gourmet* and *Bon Appétit*. Seafood brought from the fishing boats to the restaurant's back door is as fresh as it can be; mushrooms and salad greens are gathered from the peninsula's woods and gardens. *Pacific Hwy. and N. 45th St., ☏ 360/642–4142. AE, MC, V. $$$*

42nd Street Cafe. This middle-of-the-road restaurant is nestled comfortably between deep-fried seafood and expensive gourmet fare, emphasizing home-cooked food on a menu that changes daily. *Hwy. 103 and 42nd St., ☏ 360/642–2323. V. $$*

LODGING

Shelburne Inn. This bright and cheerful, antiques-filled inn built in 1896 is on the National Register of Historic Places. It is also right on the highway, which can make it noisy, so the best picks are rooms on the west side. *4415 Pacific Way, Box 250, Seaview 98644, ☏ 360/642–2442, FAX 360/642–8904. 16 rooms. Facilities: restaurant (*see Dining, above*), pub. AE, MC, V. $$$*

Sou'wester. A stay here is a bohemian experience. Choose from rooms and apartments in a historic lodge, cabins, or classic mobile-home units on the surrounding property just behind the beach. The lodge was built in 1892 as the summer retreat for Henry Winslow Corbett, a Portland banker, timber baron, shipping and railroad magnate, and U.S. senator. *Beach Access Rd., Box 102, 98644, ☏ 360/642–2542. 3 rooms with shared bath and kitchen, 4 cabins, 8 trailers. D, MC, V. $*

Campgrounds

Camping is available at **Fort Canby State Park** (Box 488, Ilwaco 98624; *see* Exploring Long Beach Peninsula, *above*) and **Chinook County Park** (Box 261, Chinook 98614, ☏ 360/777–8442).

ELSEWHERE IN THE STATE

Yakima Valley

Tourist Information

Yakima Valley Visitor and Convention Bureau (10 N. 8th St., Yakima, 98901-2515, ☏ 509/575–1300).

Getting There

The valley is along I–82 between Yakima and the tri-city area of Richland, Kennewick, and Pasco. From Seattle, drive east on I–90 to Ellensburg and south on Hwy. 97 (about 180 mi). Yakima has a small airport with limited service from Seattle, Spokane, and Portland on United Airlines. There is no passenger train service, but the area is served by Greyhound buses, which stop in Yakima, Toppenish, Sunnyside, Wapato, and Prosser.

What to See and Do

The attraction here, aside from the views of 12,688-ft Mt. Adams and 14,410-ft Mt. Rainier to the west, is an abundance of wineries. Dozens of small operations dot this fertile area, which has an excellent reputation for producing fine wines. Some of the best-known vineyards are **Hogue Cellars, Château Ste. Michelle,** and **Quail Run Winery.** The **Yakima Valley Wine Grower Association** (Box 39, Grandview 98930) publishes maps of the region and a brochure that lists local wineries with tasting-room tours.

Spokane

Getting There

Spokane Airport is served by Horizon, Northwest, and United airlines. Amtrak and Greyhound both serve Spokane. By car, Spokane can be reached by I–90 (east–west) and Hwy. 195 (north–south).

What to See and Do

Billed as the "Capital of the Inland Empire," Spokane (pronounced Spo-*can*) seems like a bit of the Midwest dropped into the Far West. The 380,000 residents of the area don't necessarily embrace Seattle as the state's cultural capital or Olympia as the seat of government. Wedged against the Idaho border (which locals cross regularly in search of outdoor recreation), Spokane is separated from Seattle by a good 300 mi and the formidable Cascade Range.

In town, the main attraction is **Riverfront Park,** 100 acres covering several islands in the Spokane River and including a spectacular falls. While Spokane has extensive historic areas, it may be best remembered for hosting the 1974 World's Fair. Ultramodernist buildings from that exposition still remain, and today house an IMAX theater, a skating rink, and exhibition space. In sharp architectural contrast is the town's 1902 **Great Northern Railroad Station,** with its tall stone clock tower.

Just 30 mi east of town on I–90 is Idaho's **Lake Coeur d'Alene** (*see* Idaho), which features fishing, camping, hiking, water sports, and a wide variety of resort accommodations.

12 The Pacific

By Paula Consolo and Jillian Stone

THE TWO YOUNGEST STATES IN THE UNION, Alaska and Hawaii, have more in common than their images might suggest. Both are thousands of miles from the U.S. mainland, both have dramatic landscapes, and both have significant populations of indigenous people. The two states also share a reliance on water—rivers, lakes, and the Pacific Ocean, which supply a means of transportation, a source of food, and a host of recreational possibilities. Humpback whales also forge a link, summering in Alaska's Inside Passage and Prince William Sound, then swimming the 4,000 mi to Hawaii to mate, calve, and nurse their young in the warm waters off Maui, the Big Island, and Oahu. Although Alaskan and Hawaiian stores are stocked with the same aspirin and the same cereal found in any mainland state, there is something of the exotic in both places—albeit in very different forms.

Alaska, with its vast, austere wilderness and extreme weather, is a demanding land, but it rewards exploration with temperate summers, a frontier atmosphere, and flora and fauna rarely accessible elsewhere on the planet. From the nation's highest mountain, Mt. McKinley, to the islands, glaciers, and fjords of the southeast, the state provides superb hiking, boating, and fishing—and scenery as majestic and unspoiled as any in North America.

Hawaii's gentle climate and tremendous diversity make it a welcoming and endlessly fascinating place. Each of the eight major volcanic islands has its own character; some offer lush tropical scenery and stunning white beaches, others provide dramatic cliffs or beaches with black sand. If you enjoy rampant commercialism in a spotlessly clean, well-groomed environment, Oahu's Waikiki is the place for you. From pineapple plantations to active volcanoes in spectacular mountain ranges; from cheerful towns to remote, exquisite natural refuges, Hawaii's islands lure visitors with myriad delights.

Packages and Tours

A tour of Alaska could mean a cruise through waters where seals cling to icebergs, a soaring flight over a mammoth glacier, and/or a visit to Mt. McKinley (packages combining land and sea travel are known as cruise-tours). Tours of Hawaii are equally diverse, ranging from rugged hikes through lush forests and along volcanic slopes to luxurious idling on white-sand beaches.

In Alaska

Tours through Alaska differ mainly in the type of travel employed. Independent travelers to Alaska can create their own itineraries by contacting **Knightly Tours** (Box 16366, Seattle, WA 98116, ☎ 206/938–8567 or 800/426–2123). Those wishing to join a group can contact the following tour operators.

AIR TOURS

Contact **Alaska Airlines Vacations** (Box 68900, SEARV, Seattle, WA 98168, ☎ 800/468–2248).

CRUISE TOURS

Contact **Holland America Westours** (300 Elliott Ave. W., Seattle, WA 98119, ☎ 206/281–3535 or 800/426–0327); **Princess Cruises & Tours** (2815 2nd Ave., Suite 400, Seattle, WA 98121, ☎ 206/728–4202 or

800/426–0442); or **Alaska Sightseeing/Cruise West** (Suite 700, 4th & Battery Bldg., Seattle, WA 98121, ☎ 206/441–8687 or 800/426–7702).

MOTORCOACH TOURS

Contact **Collette Tours** (162 Middle St., Pawtucket, RI 02860, ☎ 401/728–3805 or 800/832–4656); **Domenico Tours** (751 Broadway, Bayonne, NJ 07002, ☎ 201/823–8687 or 800/554–8687); **Cosmos/Globus** (5301 S. Federal Circle, Littleton, CO 80123, ☎ 303/797–2800 or 800/221–0900); **Maupintour** (Box 807, Lawrence, KS 66044, ☎ 913/843–1211 or 800/255–4266); **Mayflower Tours** (1225 Warren Ave., Box 490, Downers Grove, IL 60515, ☎ 708/960–3430 or 800/323–7604). **Tauck Tours** (Box 5027, Westport, CT 06881, ☎ 203/226–6911 or 800/468–2825).

In Hawaii

Vacations to Hawaii come either as guided tours or pre-arranged air and land packages for independent travelers. (*See* Motorcoach Tours, *above* for contact information for the following operators.)

GUIDED TOURS

Contact **Collette Tours; Cosmos/Globus; Maupintour**; and **Tauck Tours.**

INDEPENDENT PACKAGES

Contact **Collette, Cosmos/Globus,** or **GoGo Tours** (69 Spring St., Ramsey, NJ 07446, ☎ 800/821–3731).

When to Go

Alaska

Most visitors come to Alaska in **summer,** when mild temperatures and the midnight sun prevail. Predictably, hotels and campgrounds are crowded, and prices are often higher than in the off-season: Advance planning is essential. The farther north you go in summer, the longer the days; Fairbanks in June is never really dark, although the sun does set for a couple of hours. In the Interior, temperatures can easily reach the 80s and 90s in June and July. The rest of the state is cooler, and rain is common in coastal areas. Mosquitoes are fierce in summer, especially in wilderness areas; never travel without repellent. **Fall** in Alaska is an abbreviated three weeks, when trees and bushes blaze with color and daytime temperatures are still pleasant. It comes as early as late August in the Interior and in September further south. **Winters** are extremely cold in the Interior (daytime temperatures of 0° or lower), but many Alaskans prefer that season, because it opens up most of the state for travel by snowmobile and dogsled. In the southeast's temperate maritime climate, though, temperatures rarely dip below freezing. **Spring** is often a month-long soggy period of thawing and freezing, starting at the beginning of April.

Hawaii

Hawaii's long days of sunshine and fairly mild year-round temperatures allow for 12 months of pleasurable island travel. In resort areas near sea level, the average afternoon temperature during the coldest months of December and January is 80°F; during the hottest months of August through October, temperatures can reach the low 90s. The northern shores of each island usually receive more rain than those in the south. Mid-December through mid-April and July through August are peak travel times, which means accommodation rates can be 10%–15% higher.

Festivals and Seasonal Events

Alaska

Mid-Feb.: Anchorage Fur Rendezvous includes the three-day world-championship dogsled sprint through city streets, plus hundreds of other winter activities. ☎ *907/277–8615.*

Early Mar.: Iditarod Trail Sled Dog Race officially covers 1,049 mi (the number was chosen because Alaska was the 49th state) from Anchorage to Nome. The route can take up to two weeks to complete. Most people witness the start in Anchorage or the finish in Nome. ☎ *907/376–5155.*

Late Aug.: Alaska State Fair in Palmer, north of Anchorage, is a traditional celebration complete with cooking, handicrafts, livestock, and brewing competitions. ☎ *907/745–4827.*

Hawaii

Mar. or Apr.: Merrie Monarch Festival in Hilo on the Big Island is a full week of ancient and modern hula competitions beginning Easter Sunday. Tickets must be purchased months in advance. ☎ *808/935–9168.*

June: King Kamehameha Day honors Hawaii's first king (who united the islands) with parades and ceremonies statewide.

Sept.–Oct.: Aloha Festivals are a statewide celebration dating from 1946. ☎ *808/944–8857.*

Getting Around

Alaska

The **Alaska Pass** (☎ 800/248–7598 or 800/89–82–85 from the U.K.) offers discounted one-price travel on train, bus, and boat travel throughout Alaska, British Columbia, and the Yukon.

BY PLANE

Alaska's major gateway airports are **Anchorage International Airport** (☎ 907/266–2437), **Fairbanks International Airport** (907/474–2500), and **Juneau International Airport** (☎ 907/789–7821). Carriers serving the state include Alaska Airlines, MarkAir, Northwest, Delta, and United.

BY CAR

Alaska has few roads for its size, and most are concentrated between Anchorage, Fairbanks, and the Canadian Yukon. In southeast Alaska, travel between communities is almost exclusively by boat or airplane. In south-central Alaska and the Interior, most highways have only two lanes, and a few are dirt roads. The following are paved highways that are open year-round: The Alaska Highway enters the state from Canada near Tok and continues west to Fairbanks. The Glenn Highway begins at Tok and travels south to Anchorage. The Richardson Highway runs north–south between Valdez and Delta Junction, where it meets the Alaska Highway. The Seward Highway heads south from Anchorage through the Kenai Mountains to Seward, with the branch Sterling Highway heading southwest to Soldotna, Kenai, and Homer. The George Parks Highway runs north from Anchorage, past Denali National Park to Fairbanks.

BY TRAIN

The **Alaska Railroad** (☎ 907/265–2494 in Anchorage, 907/456–4155 in Fairbanks, or 800/544–0552) runs mainline service from Seward through Anchorage to Fairbanks. A secondary line links Portage, southeast of Anchorage, with Whittier on Prince William Sound. Travel

The Pacific Region

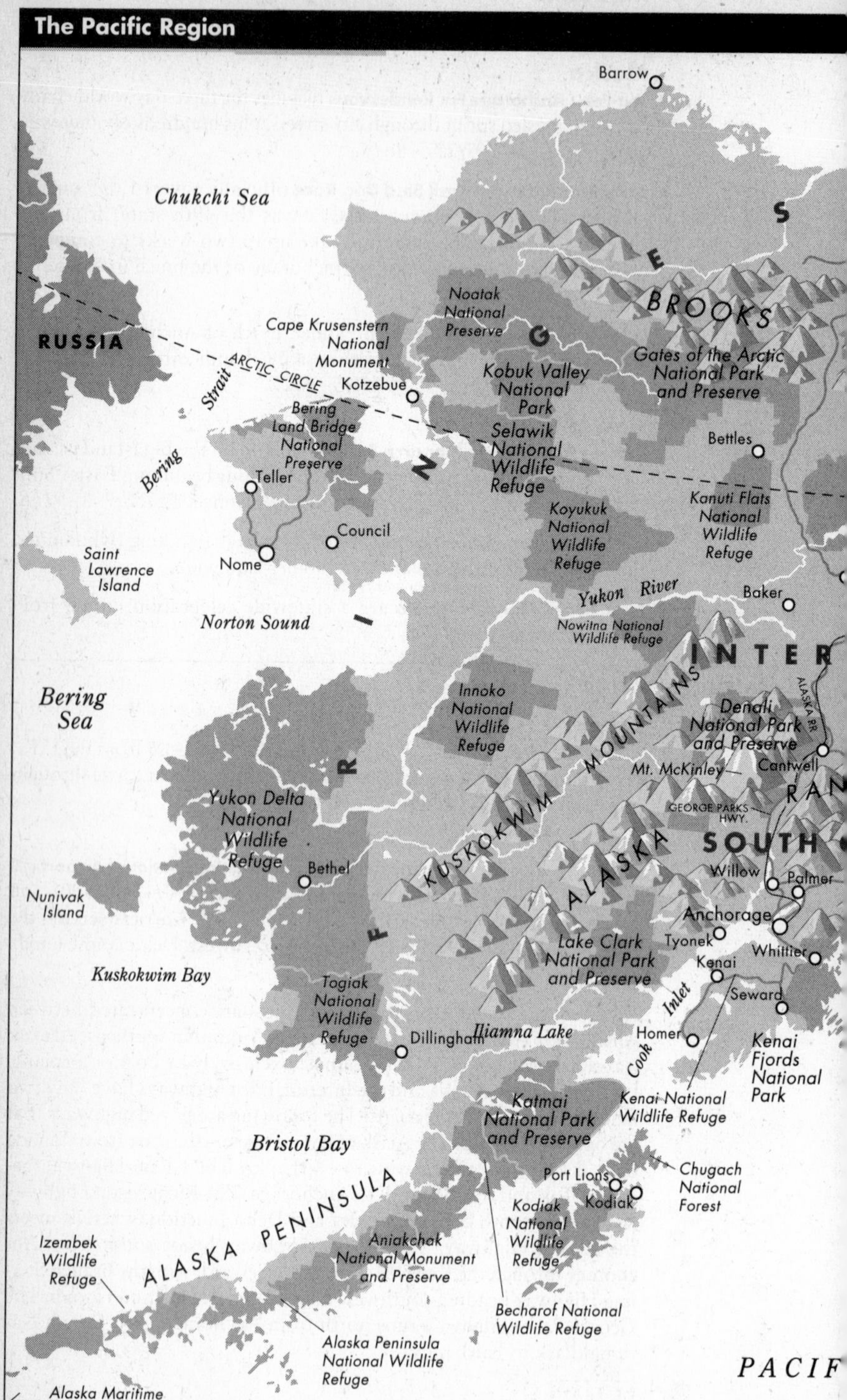
Barrow
Chukchi Sea
BROOKS RANGE
RUSSIA
ARCTIC CIRCLE
Bering Strait
Noatak National Preserve
Cape Krusenstern National Monument
Kotzebue
Kobuk Valley National Park
Gates of the Arctic National Park and Preserve
Bering Land Bridge National Preserve
Selawik National Wildlife Refuge
Bettles
Teller
Council
Nome
Koyukuk National Wildlife Refuge
Kanuti Flats National Wildlife Refuge
Saint Lawrence Island
Yukon River
Baker
Norton Sound
Nowitna National Wildlife Refuge
INTER
Bering Sea
Innoko National Wildlife Refuge
Denali National Park and Preserve
ALASKA RR
Cantwell
Mt. McKinley
KUSKOKWIM MOUNTAINS
GEORGE PARKS HWY.
Yukon Delta National Wildlife Refuge
SOUTH
Bethel
ALASKA RANGE
Willow
Palmer
Nunivak Island
Anchorage
Tyonek
Lake Clark National Park and Preserve
Whittier
Kenai
Seward
Kuskokwim Bay
Togiak National Wildlife Refuge
Cook Inlet
Dillingham
Iliamna Lake
Homer
Kenai Fjords National Park
Kenai National Wildlife Refuge
Katmai National Park and Preserve
Bristol Bay
Port Lions
Kodiak
Chugach National Forest
ALASKA PENINSULA
Kodiak National Wildlife Refuge
Izembek Wildlife Refuge
Aniakchak National Monument and Preserve
Becharof National Wildlife Refuge
Alaska Peninsula National Wildlife Refuge
PACIF
Alaska Maritime National Wildlife Refuge

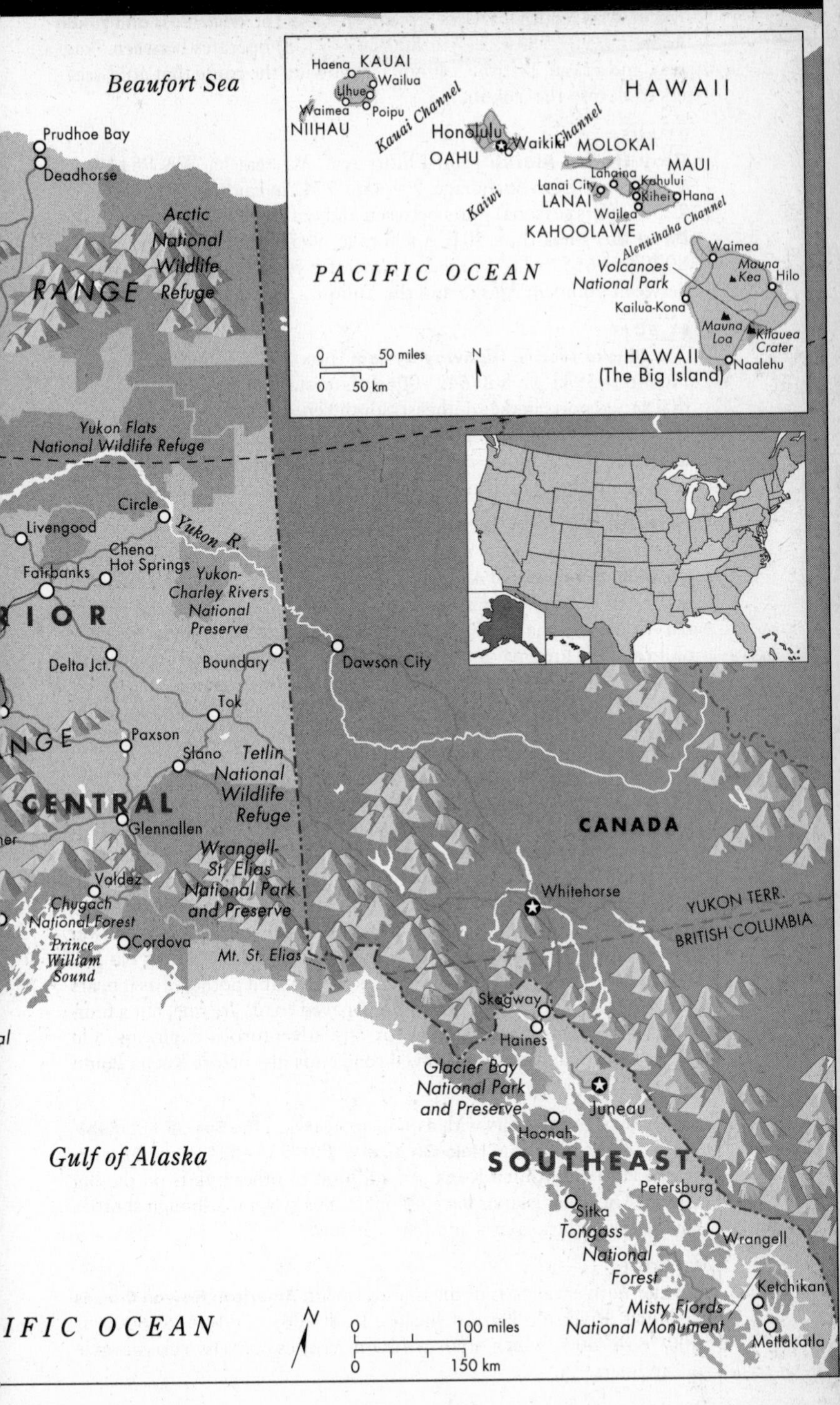

Beaufort Sea
Prudhoe Bay
Deadhorse
Arctic National Wildlife Refuge
RANGE
Yukon Flats National Wildlife Refuge
Circle
Yukon R.
Livengood
Chena Hot Springs
Fairbanks
Yukon-Charley Rivers National Preserve
RIOR
Delta Jct.
Boundary
Dawson City
Tok
NGE
Paxson
Slano
Tetlin National Wildlife Refuge
CENTRAL
Glennallen
Wrangell-St. Elias National Park and Preserve
Valdez
Chugach National Forest
Prince William Sound
Cordova
Mt. St. Elias
CANADA
Whitehorse
YUKON TERR.
BRITISH COLUMBIA
Skagway
Haines
Glacier Bay National Park and Preserve
Juneau
Hoonah
SOUTHEAST
Petersburg
Sitka
Wrangell
Tongass National Forest
Ketchikan
Misty Fjords National Monument
Metlakatla
Gulf of Alaska
IFIC OCEAN
N
0 100 miles
0 150 km
HAWAII
KAUAI
Haena
Wailua
Lihue
Waimea
Poipu
NIIHAU
Kauai Channel
Honolulu
Waikiki
OAHU
Channel
MOLOKAI
MAUI
Lahaina
Kahului
Lanai City
Kihei
Hana
LANAI
Wailea
Kaiwi
KAHOOLAWE
Alenuihaha Channel
PACIFIC OCEAN
Waimea
Volcanoes National Park
Mauna Kea
Hilo
Kailua-Kona
Mauna Loa
Kilauea Crater
HAWAII (The Big Island)
Naalehu
0 50 miles
0 50 km
N

to Seward is in the summer only; the rest of the route operates year-round, with reduced services September–May. The **White Pass and Yukon Route** (☎ 907/983–2217 or 800/343–7373) operates between Skagway and Fraser, British Columbia, following the route that gold-seekers took into the Yukon.

BY BUS

Gray Line of Alaska (300 Elliott Ave. W, Seattle, WA 98119, ☎ 907/277–5581 in Anchorage, 907/456–7742 in Fairbanks, or 800/544–2206) offers seasonal tours between and within Alaskan cities. **Alaska Direct Bus Lines** (Box 501, Anchorage, 99510, ☎ 907/277–6652 or 800/780–6652 May 1 to Oct. 1) operates year-round intercity service between points in Alaska and the Yukon.

BY BOAT

The **Alaska Marine Highway System** (Box 25535, Juneau 99802, ☎ 907/465–3941 or 800/642–0066) is a state-operated ferry system that serves ports in the southeast, south-central, and southwest regions of the state. You cannot get from southeast to south-central Alaska by ferry; the boats do not cross the Gulf of Alaska. For information on cruise-ship travel in the state, *see* Cruise Tours, *above.*

Hawaii

BY PLANE

Honolulu International Airport (☎ 808/836–6411), on Oahu, is served by American, Continental, Delta, Northwest, TWA, United, and Hawaiian Airlines. Aloha and Hawaiian airlines fly interisland between Honolulu and the four major Neighbor Island airports: **Keahole** (Big Island, ☎ 808/329–2484), also served by United; **Hilo International** (Big Island, ☎ 808/934–5801); **Kahului** (Maui, ☎ 808/872–3893), also served by American, Delta, and United; and **Lihue** (Kauai, ☎ 808/246–1400).

BY CAR

No Hawaiian island can be circumnavigated completely by car. The Big Island's roads are well maintained, although lava has closed the road from Kalapana to just east of Kamoamoa in Hawaii Volcanoes National Park. On Maui, highways are in good shape, although a four-wheel-drive vehicle is necessary for the road east of Hana. Kauai's main route runs south from Lihue and west to Polihale Beach; a narrower northern route runs to Haena, the beginning of the roadless Na Pali Coast. Molokai's main route becomes narrow and potholed as it nears Halawa Valley in the east. Lanai's few paved roads are fine, but a four-wheel-drive vehicle is essential for any adventurous exploring. On Oahu's Waianae Coast, the paved road ends just before Kaena Point.

BY BUS

Honolulu is the only city with a municipal service, **The Bus** (☎ 808/848–5555). The county-run **Hele-On Bus** (☎ 808/935–8241) operates between Hilo and Kailua-Kona , in addition to other points on the Big Island. The other islands have no public bus system, although shuttles run between the airports and major hotels.

BY BOAT

An alternative way to tour the islands is with **American Hawaii Cruises** (2 North Riverside Plaza, Chicago, IL 60606, ☎ 312/466–6000 or 800/765–7000), which offers weeklong cruises on its two classic-style ocean liners.

ALASKA

By Barbara Hodgin and Mary Engel

Updated by M. T. Schwartzman

Capital	Juneau
Population	570,000
Motto	North to the Future
State Bird	Willow ptarmigan
State Flower	Forget-me-not

Visitor Information

Alaska Division of Tourism (Box 110801, Juneau 99811, ☎ 907/465–2010, FAX 907/465–2287). The **Alaska Public Lands Information Center** (605 W. 4th Ave., Suite 105, Anchorage 99501, ☎ 907/271–2737) is a clearinghouse of information on state and federal lands, including hiking trails, cabins, and campgrounds inside and outside the parks. The **Department of Fish and Game** (Box 25526, Juneau 99802; for seasons and regulations, ☎ 907/465–4180; for licenses, ☎ 907/465–2376) can answer questions about sportfishing. The **Alaska Native Tourism Council** (1577 C St., Suite 304, Anchorage 99501, ☎ 907/274–5400, FAX 907/263–9971) represents the state's native-run attractions.

Cruising

About one-third of Alaska's visitors arrive by cruise ship. Most cruises leave from Vancouver, British Columbia, on a week-long itinerary up the Inside Passage of Alaska's southeast panhandle, visiting Ketchikan, Sitka, Juneau, and either Haines or Skagway. Many include a day in Glacier Bay National Park, but check to confirm which cruises schedule such a visit. The major cruise tour operators serving Alaska are **Princess Cruises and Tours** (2815 2nd Ave., Suite 400, Seattle, WA 98121, ☎ 206/728–4202 or 800/426–0442) and **Holland America Line/Westours** (300 Elliott Ave. W, Seattle, WA 98119, ☎ 206/281–3535 or 800/426–0327). For a small-ship cruise-tour, contact **Alaska Sightseeing/Cruise West** (4th & Battery Bldg., Suite 400, Seattle, WA 98121, ☎ 206/441–8687 or 800/426–7702). State ferries provide year-round budget service for passengers and vehicles (*see* Getting There *in* Southeast, *below*) on similar routes.

National and State Parks

Alaska has more land in national parks, wilderness areas, and national wildlife refuges than all the other states combined.

National Parks

Denali National Park and Preserve (*see* The Interior, *below*) is home to North America's tallest peak, Mt. McKinley. **Glacier Bay National Park and Preserve** (Box 140, Gustavus 99826, ☎ 907/697–2230), in the southeast, is a marine preserve where 16 spectacular glaciers meet tidewater and seals float on icebergs. **Katmai National Park and Preserve** (*see* Elsewhere in the State, *below*), a volcanic moonscape on the Alaska Peninsula, is home to huge coastal brown bears that share the Brooks River with trout fishermen. On the Kenai Peninsula south of Anchorage is **Kenai Fjords National Park** (*see* South Central, *below*). The nation's largest national forest, the **Tongass** (101 Egan Dr., Juneau 99801, ☎ 907/586–8751) stretches the length of the panhandle, and the country's largest national park, **Wrangell–St. Elias** (Box 29, Glennallen 99588, ☏ 907/822–5234), east of Anchorage, is six times the size of Yellowstone.

State Parks

Chugach State Park (HC 52, Box 8999, Indian 99540, ☏ 907/345–5014) near Anchorage has scores of hiking trails, good fishing on lakes and streams, and state-owned recreational cabins for rent. **Denali State Park** (HC 32, Box 6706, Wasilla 99654, ☏ 907/745–3975) has some of the best views of Mt. McKinley.

SOUTHEAST

Southeast Alaska is a maritime region of thousands of islands blanketed by old-growth spruce forest. The waters abound in Pacific salmon (five species) and sea mammals. The shore is home to deer, bears, and coastal communities that cling to the mountainsides. The wet climate inspires locals to call galoshes "Juneau tennis shoes," although summer does bring some breathtakingly beautiful sunny days. Tlingit, Haida, and Tsimshian villages, as well as museums and cultural centers in the region's larger communities, offer insights into Native American cultures.

Tourist Information

Tourism Council (Box 20710, Juneau 99802, ☏ 907/586–4777; for a travel planner, 800/423–0568; FAX 907/463–4961).

Getting There

Southeast Alaska is mainly accessible by air or water. The mainland road system (south from Fairbanks through the Canadian Yukon) connects only with tiny northern communities after hundreds of miles of wilderness road. Cruise ships (*see* Cruising, *above*) or state ferries are the most common means of transportation for visitors.

By Plane

Regular jet service is available from Pacific Coast and southwestern U.S. cities to Ketchikan, Wrangell, Petersburg, Sitka, and Juneau (Juneau International Airport, ☏ 907/789–7821). The area is served by Alaska Airlines (☏ 800/426–0333), MarkAir (☏ 800/627–5247), and in summer by Delta Airlines (☏ 800/221–1212). Floatplane and wheel-plane service to the villages is available from the region's larger communities.

By Car

Ferries to southeast Alaska leave from Bellingham, Washington, or from Prince Rupert, British Columbia. From the north, the Alaska and Haines or Klondike highways lead to Skagway and Haines, and ferries continue south through the region.

By Ferry

The **Alaska Marine Highway System** (Box 25535, Juneau 99802, ☏ 907/465–3941 or 800/642–0066, FAX 907/277–4829) is an extensive network of large and small vessels that links most southeast communities. All ferries take cars (reservations necessary in summer) and have cafeterias or restaurants; most also have staterooms, but many Alaskans camp out on deck in tents or on the lounges' floors. The system makes connections with **BC Ferries** in Prince Rupert, British Columbia.

Southeast and South Central Alaska

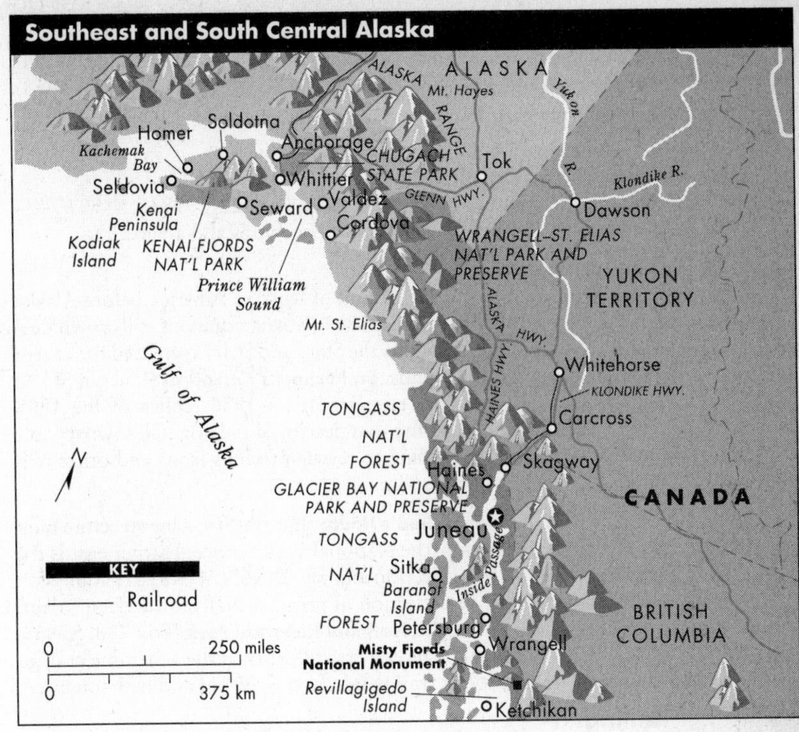

Ketchikan

Tourist Information

Ketchikan: Visitors Bureau (131 Front St., 99901, ☎ 907/225–6166 or 800/770–3300; for brochures, ☎ 800/770–2200; FAX 907/247–6166).

Exploring Ketchikan

Ketchikan is a fishing and logging town at the south end of the panhandle. Its centerpiece is **Creek Street,** the historic red-light district, now home to quaint shops built on stilts over Ketchikan Creek. Ten miles north of town, the **Totem Bight State Historical Park** (N. Tongass Hwy., ☎ 907/247–8574) displays beautiful totem poles—many dating from the 1930s but replicating much older totem poles—as does the village of **Saxman** (☎ 907/225–5163), 2 ½ mi south of Ketchikan. Original totem poles, some dating back nearly 200 years, can be seen at the **Totem Heritage Center** (601 Deermont St., ☎ 907/225–5900; admission charged). The city, in fact, contains the largest collection of totem poles in the world.

Shopping

Silver Lining Seafoods (1705 Tongass Ave., ☎ 907/225–6664), north of the city dock, has excellent locally smoked seafoods and fish-motif postcards, sweatshirts, and T-shirts by local artist Ray Troll.

Dining

For price ranges, see Chart 1 (B) in On the Road with Fodor's.

$$$ ★ **Salmon Falls Resort.** Fresh local seafood is served in a lovely log building overlooking the Inside Passage. Located 17 mi north of town, it's a good choice after a visit to Totem Bight park. *Mile 17, N. Tongass Hwy., ☎ 907/225–2752. AE, MC, V.*

B&Bs

Alaska Bed and Breakfast Association (369 S. Franklin St., Suite 200, Juneau 99801, ☎ 907/586–2959, FAX 907/463–4453 or 800/493–4453).

Sitka

Tourist Information

Sitka: Visitors Bureau (Centennial Bldg., Box 1226, 99835, ☎ 907/747–5940, FAX 907/747–3739) provides brochures and advice.

Exploring Sitka

This historic town was the capital of Russian America before Alaska was sold to the United States in 1867. Russian cannons still crown **Castle Hill,** and the flagpole where the Stars and Stripes replaced the czarist Russian standard still stands. **St. Michael's Cathedral** (Lincoln St., ☎ 907/747–8120; donation requested) is a 1976 replica of the 1848 church. During the 1966 fire that destroyed the original, townspeople entered the burning building to rescue precious icons and other religious objects, now on display.

Nearby is the **Russian Bishop's House** (Lincoln St.), a log structure built in 1842 and restored by the National Park Service. Farther east is the **Sheldon Jackson Museum** (Lincoln St., ☎ 907/747–8981; admission charged), with its fine collection of priceless Native American, Aleut, and Eskimo items. In **Sitka National Historical Park** (Box 738, 99835, ☎ 907/747–6281), Tlingit carvers still work at the venerable craft of carving totems; a forest trail winds among 15 old and new totems.

Dining

For price ranges, see Chart 1 (B) in On the Road with Fodor's.

$$$ **Channel Club.** Consistently fine steaks and seafood are served in nautical surroundings, including glass fishnet floats and whalebone carvings. *2906 Halibut Point Rd., ☎ 907/747–9916. AE, DC, MC, V.*

Lodging

For price ranges, see Chart 2 (B) in On the Road with Fodor's.

$$$ **Westmark Shee Atika.** The lobby and rooms in this Westmark chain outpost recreate the feeling of a rustic lodge. Many rooms overlook Crescent Harbor and islands beyond; others have mountain and forest views. *330 Seward St., 99835, ☎ 907/747–6241 or 800/544–0970, FAX 907/747–5486. 100 rooms. Facilities: restaurant, bar. AE, D, DC, MC, V.*

B&Bs

See Ketchikan, *above.*

Juneau

The state capital clings to the mountainside along a narrow saltwater channel. It was born as a gold-rush town in 1880 and remained an active gold-mining center until World War II. Today the number-one employer here is the state government, with transportation and tourism important runners-up.

Tourist Information

Juneau: Log Cabin Information Center (134 3rd St., 99801, ☎ 907/586–2201, FAX 907/586–6304).

Exploring Juneau

Although Juneau's hills are steep, most visitors can explore the charming town on foot. Houses downtown date from the gold rush. Along

South Franklin Street, the **Red Dog Saloon** preserves the rough-and-tumble spirit of '98, while the Victorian **Alaskan Hotel** is more genteel. The tiny, onion-domed **St. Nicholas Russian Orthodox Church** (5th and Gold Sts.; donation requested), constructed in 1894, is the oldest original Russian church in Alaska. The **Alaska State Museum** (395 Whittier St., ☎ 907/465–2901; admission charged), near the waterfront, highlights the state's rich cultural heritage, with Eskimo and Native American artifacts, gold-rush memorabilia, and natural-history displays.

Shopping

Along South Franklin Street, the **Alaska Steam Laundry Building** has shops and a good coffeehouse downstairs. Across the street, the **Senate Building Mall** houses a charming Christmas store and other import shops. **Taku Smokeries** has two retail outlets here selling locally smoked seafood and a new restaurant downtown.

Dining

For price ranges see Chart 1 (B) in On the Road with Fodor's.

$$$ ★ **Silverbow Inn.** In the oldest operating bakery in the state (circa 1890), Alaskan seafood and steaks are served. The fare is complemented by wine from an award-winning wine list. *120 2nd St., ☎ 907/586–4146. AE, D, DC, MC, V.*

$$$ **The Summit.** The funky frame exterior belies this restaurant's prestigious reputation. In the small, candlelit interior, diners have their choice of nearly two dozen excellent local fish and shellfish dishes. *455 S. Franklin St., ☎ 907/586–2050. AE, D, DC, MC, V. No lunch.*

$$ **The Fiddlehead.** Healthy, eclectic food ranging from black beans with rice to pasta with smoked salmon is served in a comfortable setting of light wood, stained glass, and a view of Mt. Juneau. The homemade bread is delicious. *429 Willoughby Ave., ☎ 907/586–3150. AE, D, DC, MC, V.*

Lodging

For price ranges see Chart 2 (B) in On the Road with Fodor's.

$$$ **Baranof Hotel.** This grande dame of Juneau hotels has been refurbished over the years to reflect the decor of its 1930s origins, but rooms are furnished in a simple, contemporary style. *127 N. Franklin St., 99801, ☎ 907/586–2660 or 800/544–0970, FAX 907/586–8315. 193 rooms, 16 suites. Facilities: restaurant, bar, coffee shop. AE, D, DC, MC, V.*

There are also three restored historic hotels in downtown Juneau: The 1890s **Silverbow Inn** (120 2nd St., 99801, ☎ 907/586–4146 or 800/586–4146, FAX 907/586–4242), 6 rooms, restaurant; *$$$*. The 1913 **Alaskan Hotel** (167 S. Franklin St., 99801, ☎ 907/586–1000 or 800/327–9347, FAX 907/463–3775), 40 rooms, lounge; *$$*. The 1898 **Inn at the Waterfront** (455 S. Franklin St., 99801, ☎ 907/586–2050, FAX 907/586–2999), 28 rooms, restaurant, lounge; *$$*.

B&Bs

See Ketchikan, *above*.

Sports and the Outdoors

Fishing

Southeast Alaskans are blessed with great salmon fishing off city docks and on beaches where creeks meet salt water. Another option is to take an air taxi to a remote spot for a day's fishing or an extended stay (*see* Wilderness Camps and Lodges, *below*). Fishing licenses are available in most grocery and sporting-goods stores.

Kayaking and Rafting

You can bring your own kayak aboard state ferries or hire a local outfitter—such as **Alaska Discovery Wilderness Adventures** (5449 Shaune Dr., Suite 4, Juneau 99801, ☎ 907/780–6226 or 800/586–1911)—for a guided Inside Passage or Glacier Bay excursion. For rafting on the Mendenhall River, contact **Alaska Travel Adventures** (9085 Glacier Hwy., Suite 204, Juneau 99801, ☎ 907/789–0052; in AK only, 800/478–0052). Guided sea-kayaking tours of nearby Misty Fjords National Monument in Tongass National Forest are available from **Southeast Exposure** (Box 9143, Ketchikan 99901, ☎ 907/225–8829).

Ski Areas

The **Eaglecrest** ski area, across the channel from Juneau on Douglas Island, has 31 trails, three lifts, a ski school, and equipment rental. *155 S. Seward St., Juneau 99801, ☎ 907/586–5284 or 907/586–5330 for recorded ski conditions. ⏲ Dec.–Apr.*

Cross-country skiing is popular in all southeast communities. Check with local visitor centers for the location of trails groomed for diagonal and skate skiing.

Campgrounds

State and national forest campgrounds are available near all southeast communities (*see* Alaska Public Lands Information Center *in* Visitor Information, *above*). The *Milepost,* available in most Alaska and Washington bookstores, lists campgrounds throughout the state.

Wilderness Camps and Lodges

Accommodations range from spartan bunkhouses to luxury lodges where guests dress for candle-lit dinners. One agency that books area lodges is **Alaska Sportfishing Packages** (Box 9170, Seattle, WA 98109, ☎ 206/216–2920 or 800/426–0603, FAX 206/216–2908).

SOUTH CENTRAL

South-central Alaska is home to most of the state's population and many of its most popular attractions. A visit starts in Anchorage, then continues south to the fishing and artists' communities of the Kenai Peninsula.

Getting There

By Plane

Anchorage International Airport (☎ 907/266–2437), about 6 mi from downtown, is served by Alaska Airlines, Continental, MarkAir, Northwest, Delta Airlines, and United. Commuter-plane service is available to Denali National Park, Homer, and Kenai. A cab from Anchorage airport to downtown costs about $15 plus tip. Some hotels have shuttles.

By Car

To get to Anchorage from Tok, on the Alaska Highway near the Canadian border, head southwest on the Glenn Highway. From Fairbanks travel south on the George Parks Highway. From Anchorage, the Seward and Sterling highways lead south to the Kenai Peninsula.

By Ferry

The south-central section of the **Alaska Marine Highway** ferry system (*see* Southeast, *above*) links communities on Prince William Sound, the

Gulf of Alaska, and Cook Inlet. Connections to and from Anchorage can be made in Whittier and Seward. There is no ferry service between the south-central and southeast parts of the state.

By Train

The **Alaska Railroad** (☎ 800/544–0552; in Anchorage, 907/265–2494; in Fairbanks, 907/456–4155; FAX 907/265–2323) offers mainline service between Seward, Anchorage, Denali National Park, and Fairbanks, and secondary service between Portage and Whittier.

By Bus

Gray Line of Alaska (in season: ☎ 907/277–5581 [Anchorage] or 907/456–7742 [Fairbanks]; off-season: 800/544–2206) serves Anchorage, Denali, and Fairbanks.

Anchorage

Tourist Information

Anchorage: Convention and Visitors Bureau (1600 A St., Suite 200, Anchorage 99501, ☎ 907/276–4118; events hot line, 907/276–3200; FAX 907/278–5559). Log Cabin Information Center (W. 4th Ave. and F St., ☎ 907/274–3531).

Exploring Anchorage

Anchorage is a young, spirited city in a spectacular setting between mountains and sea. With nearly half the state's population residing here, it's home to everything from oil industry high rises to backwoods cabins with resident dogsled teams.

The **Anchorage Museum of History and Art** (W. 7th Ave. and A St., ☎ 907/343–6173; admission charged) has a permanent display of artwork depicting Alaska as seen by explorers, resident painters, and latter-day visitors and an outstanding exhibit on Native Alaskan life. Just north of downtown, at **Ship Creek,** you can see salmon jump in summer as they head upstream to spawn; there's a platform for easy viewing.

At **Earthquake Park,** at the west end of Northern Lights Boulevard, you can survey the damage wrought by the 1964 quake, when houses tumbled into the ocean. Trees have claimed the earth mounds and ponds created by the quake's force. The nearby floatplane base at **Lake Hood** is the world's largest and busiest. For a scenic walk, stroll along the **Coastal Trail,** which runs along Knik Arm. Plan a sunset visit, when the sun moves slowly across the horizon and bathes the trail in golden light. The trailhead is at the western end of West 2nd Avenue.

What to See and Do with Children

The **Imaginarium** (725 W. 5th Ave., ☎ 907/276–3179; admission charged) is an interactive science museum with a shop that sells educational toys.

Shopping

If Alaska has a shopping mecca, Anchorage is it. The gift shops along 4th Avenue sell T-shirts and trinkets. The **Alaska Native Arts and Crafts Association** (333 W. 4th Ave., ☎ 907/274–2932) offers genuine—if pricey—local baskets, carvings, and beadwork.

Spectator Sports

Most Alaskans are doers rather than watchers of sports. One exception is the vastly popular dogsled racing. On winter weekends, the **Anchorage Sled Dog Racing Association** (☎ 907/562–2235) hosts races.

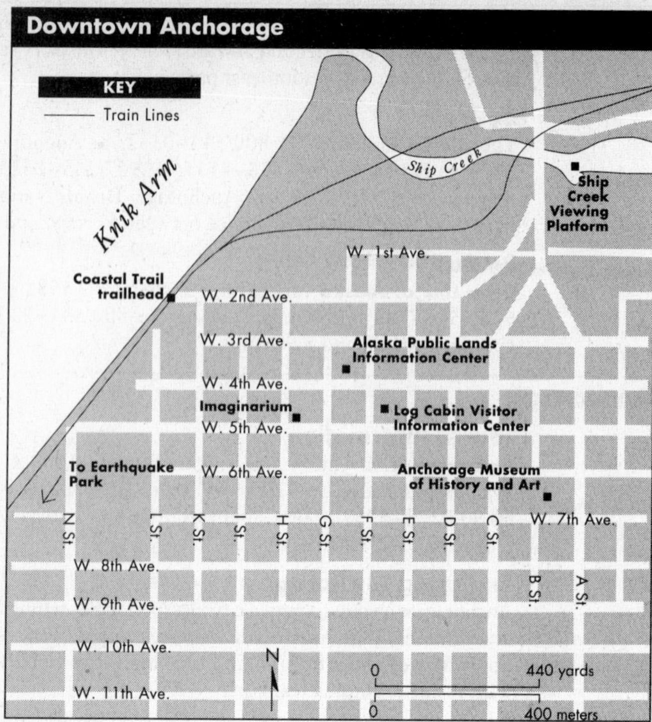

The **Fur Rendezvous,** world-championship dogsled races, are held in downtown Anchorage in mid-February. March brings the famous, 1,049-mi Iditarod.

Dining

For price ranges, see Chart 1 (B) in On the Road with Fodor's.

$$$ **Aladdin's.** In a strip-mall setting on the south side of the city, the former director of catering for the Anchorage Hilton serves eclectic dishes from throughout the Mediterranean, complemented by an equally interesting wine list. *4420 Old Seward Hwy., ☎ 907/561–2373. AE, D, DC, MC, V. Closed Sun.*

$$$ ★ **Marx Brothers Cafe.** Innovative American cuisine, such as wild game and caramelized rack of lamb, is served in the second-oldest house in Anchorage, originally constructed for the engineers who built the Alaska Railroad. There are more than 500 selections on the wine list. *627 W. 3rd Ave., ☎ 907/278–2133. Reservations required. AE, DC, MC, V. No lunch. Closed Sun.*

$$$ ★ **Seven Glaciers Restaurant.** Perched high on a mountain at 2,300 ft, dining here is both a culinary experience and a scenic adventure, as you first must board a high-speed tram to get to the restaurant. The decor combines the high-tech and the rustic; meat, fish, and fowl dishes are served "architecturally," meaning that your steak may arrive standing on its side. *Alyeska Resort, Girdwood, ☎ 907/754–2237. Reservations required. AE, D, MC, V. Closed Tues.–Wed. No lunch.*

$$–$$$ **Double Musky.** It's worth the 40-mi trip south of town and the wait once you arrive. The little building set among spruce trees is casually decorated with Mardi Gras memorabilia, the better to prepare you

for the fine Cajun dishes and huge, tender steaks to come. *Crow Creek Rd., Girdwood, ☎ 907/783–2822. No reservations. AE, D, DC, MC, V.*

$$–$$$ **Simon and Seafort's Saloon and Grill.** Large windows overlook Cook Inlet at this brass-and-wood restaurant. Fresh local seafood in interesting sauces and great rack-roasted prime rib are the specialties of the house, but there are also pastas, salads, and chicken dishes. *420 L St., ☎ 907/274–3502. AE, DC, MC, V. No lunch Sun.*

$ **Downtown Deli.** This classic delicatessen offers sandwiches, salads, and local fish in a casual, woodsy atmosphere. *525 W. 4th Ave., ☎ 907/276–7116. AE, D, DC, MC, V.*

Lodging

For price ranges, see Chart 2 (B) in On the Road with Fodor's.

$$$ **Anchorage Hotel.** Many original details have been restored in this charming, centrally located small hotel, built in 1916. Rooms are decorated in pastel colors. *330 E St., 99501, ☎ 907/272–4553 or 800/544–0988, FAX 907/277–4483. 26 rooms, 10 suites. Facility: pub. AE, D, DC, MC, V.*

$$$ ★ **Hotel Captain Cook.** This three-tower hotel takes up a full city block. The South Pacific decor includes teak paneling in public spaces and teak furniture in the rooms. *W. 4th Ave. and K St., 99501, ☎ 907/276–6000 or 800/843–1950, FAX 907/278–5366. 562 rooms, 77 suites. Facilities: 4 restaurants, indoor pool, health club. AE, D, DC, MC, V.*

$$$ **Voyager Hotel.** This small four-story hotel features full kitchens in all rooms and bathrooms that were recently remodeled with pedestal sinks and wainscoting. Some rooms have views of the Cook inlet. *501 K St., 99501, ☎ 907/277–9501 or 800/247–9070, FAX 907/274–0333. 38 rooms. Facilities: restaurant, lounge. AE, D, DC, MC, V.*

$ **Anchorage International Hostel.** In a cinder-block building downtown, guests share dorm-style rooms and a kitchen on each floor. *700 H St., 99501, ☎ 907/276–3635, FAX 907/276–7772. Capacity: 95. MC, V.*

B&Bs

Alaska Private Lodgings: Stay With a Friend (Box 200047, Anchorage 99520, ☎ 907/258–1717, FAX 907/258–6613).

The Arts and Nightlife

The **Alaska Center for the Performing Arts** (621 W. 6th Ave., ☎ 907/263–2900) is home to a local opera company, symphony orchestra, and theater companies. The **Fly-by-Night Club** (3300 Spenard Rd., ☎ 907/279–7726) stages popular revues with lots of good boogie-woogie music and tacky jokes. The *Anchorage Daily News* publishes a weekend activity guide every Friday.

The Kenai Peninsula

Tourist Information

Kenai Penisula: Tourism Marketing Council (11127 Frontage Rd., Suite 201, 99611, ☎ 907/283–3850 or 800/535–3624, FAX 907/283–2838). **Soldotna:** Visitor Information Center (Box 236, Soldotna 99669, ☎ 907/262–1337, FAX 907/262–3566). **Homer:** Visitor Center (Box 541, 99603, ☎ 907/235–7740, FAX 907/235–8766). **Seward:** Visitor Information Center (Mile 2, Seward Hwy., Box 749, 99664, ☎ 907/224–8051, FAX 907/224–5353).

Exploring the Kenai Peninsula

Thrusting into the Gulf of Alaska south of Anchorage, the **Kenai Peninsula** is a glacier-hewn landscape offering magnificent wildlife viewing and fishing from its spectacular coastline. In summer, the

Alaska Railroad runs a passenger train daily to **Seward,** a small fishing and timber town on Resurrection Bay, but most people drive the three hours from Anchorage. Tour boats leave Seward's busy downtown harbor for excursions that include visits to sea lions and bird rookeries and close-up visits to tidewater glaciers.

Seward is the jumping-off point for **Kenai Fjords National Park** (Box 1727, Seward 99664, ☎ 907/224–3175), a dramatic coastal parkland of sheer cliffs, waterfalls, and deep-green spruce. **Mariah Charters** (☎ 907/224–8623 in season, 907/243–1238 off-season) has tours of the park.

At the southern terminus of the Seward Highway, 225 mi from Anchorage, lies **Homer,** in a breathtaking setting at the end of a sand spit that juts into Kachemak Bay. The town's buildings are picturesque, and you can comb the beach, fish off the docks, or charter a boat for halibut fishing (*see* Sports and Outdoor Activities, *below*). Wildlife abounds in the bay, and most fishing charters include a chance to view whales, seals, porpoises, and birds close up. If you walk along the docks at the end of the day, you can see fishermen unloading their catch. Across from the end of the Homer spit is **Halibut Cove,** perhaps the prettiest spot in Alaska and reachable only by the Kachemak Bay ferry. **Seldovia,** on the other side of Kachemak Bay from Homer, has onion-domed Russian churches and excellent fishing.

Dining

For price ranges, see Chart 1 (B) in On the Road with Fodor's.

$$ **Harbor Dinner Club.** Run by the same family since 1962, this eatery serves local halibut and salmon in a simply appointed dining room with a view of Resurrection Bay and the mountains. *220 5th Ave., Seward, ☎ 907/224–3012. AE, D, DC, MC, V.*

$$ ★ **The Saltry.** This restaurant with a deck over the water has the best seafood, including fine sushi, in south-central Alaska. To get there, take the half-hour ride on the Kachemak Bay Ferry from Homer Harbor. *Halibut Cove (boat and dining reservations through Central Charter Booking Agency, ☎ 907/235–7847; in AK only, 800/478–7847). AE, V.*

Lodging

For price ranges, see Chart 2 (B) in On the Road with Fodor's. For information on wilderness camps and lodges, *see* Southeast, *above.*

$$$ **Land's End.** The three wings of this hotel—starboard, port, and midship—are appointed in a mix of nautical and contemporary decor. All rooms facing the bay have small balconies for watching the sunset. *Box 273, 4786 Homer Spit Rd., Homer 99603, ☎ 907/235–2500; in AK only, 800/478–0400; FAX 907/235–0420. 61 rooms, 12 suites. Facilities: restaurant, lounge, gift shop. AE, D, DC, MC, V.*

$$ **Van Gilder Hotel.** This aging but dignified three-story stucco building is listed on the National Register of Historic Places. Rooms are a bit shabby but serviceable; some have brass beds, pedestal sinks, and claw-foot tubs. The staff is friendly. *308 Adams St., Seward 99664, ☎ 907/224–3079 or 800/204–6835, FAX 907/224–3689. 26 rooms. Facilities: tour desk. AE, D, DC, MC, V.*

Sports and the Outdoors

Biking

Most south-central highways are suitable for biking on the shoulder. Anchorage has more than 125 mi of bike trails. The **Matanuska Valley** is an increasingly popular place for farm-road rides. Bikes are available for rent at many hotels and at **Downtown Bicycle Rental** (6th Ave. and B St., Anchorage, ☎ 907/279–5293) and **Adventures and Delights** (K St., between 4th and 5th Aves., ☎ 907/276–8282).

Fishing

All south-central coastal communities have fishing charters, outfitters, and guides. Although Anchorage does not have good saltwater fishing—glacial runoff makes the water too murky—the freshwater lakes are stocked. In Homer, **Central Charter Booking Agency** (4241 Homer Spit, 99603, ☎ 907/235–7847; in AK only, 800/478–7847) books salmon and halibut charters. **Alaska Wildland Adventures** (Box 389, Girdwood 99587, ☎ 800/334–8730; in AK only, 800/478–4100) offers a variety of float and fish packages on the Kenai River, world-famous for its huge salmon runs. Licenses are sold in most grocery and other retail stores.

Hiking and Backpacking

Many hiking trails in south-central Alaska have public cabins for rent along the way (*see* Alaska Public Lands Information Center *in* Visitor Information, *above*).

Kayaking and Rafting

Floating is available on hundreds of rivers within a small area. **Nova River Runners** (Box 1129, Chickaloon 99674, ☎ 907/745–5753; in AK only, 800/746–5753) offers guided day trips on the Chickaloon and Matanuska. **Ketchum Air Service** (Box 190588, Anchorage 99519, ☎ 907/243–5525 or 800/433–9114) provides drop-off and pick-up service and full outfitting for wilderness float trips.

Ski Areas

The **Alyeska Resort** (Box 249, Girdwood 99587, ☎ 907/754–1111 or 800/880–3880; for recorded ski conditions, 907/754–7669), about 40 mi south of Anchorage, is the largest in the state, with 470 acres of skiable terrain, a 3,125-ft vertical drop, 61 trails, seven lifts, and a new 60-passenger tram. It also has a 300-room hotel, a ski school, and a mountain-top restaurant (*see* Dining, *above*). **Hilltop Ski Area** (7015 Abbot Rd., Anchorage 99516, ☎ 907/346–1446; for recorded ski conditions, 907/346–2167), 10 mi from downtown Anchorage, has two lifts, nine trails, a vertical drop of 300 ft, ski instruction, cross-country trails, and a national-grade half-pipe for snowboarders.

Campgrounds

In Anchorage, the city-operated **Centennial Camper Park** (Box 196650, 99519, ☎ 907/333–9711; closed mid-Oct.–Apr.) has 88 spaces and showers. For Kenai Peninsula campgrounds, contact the Alaska Public Lands Information Center (*see* Visitor Information, *above*).

THE INTERIOR

The Alaska and George Parks highways offer access to this diverse area, a vast wilderness of birch and spruce forest, tundra valleys, and abundant wildlife. Its crown jewel is Denali National Park, 250 mi north of Anchorage. En route here from Anchorage, visitors travel through green Matanuska Valley farm country. North of Fairbanks, two hot springs retreats welcome visitors year-round.

Getting There

By Plane

Year-round, Alaska Airlines, MarkAir, Delta, and United fly a daily nonstop jet service between Anchorage and Fairbanks (Fairbanks International Airport, ☎ 907/474–2500). In summer, Alaska Airlines flies nonstop between Seattle and Fairbanks. Also in summer, Northwest flies to Fairbanks from Minneapolis. A number of bush carriers originate in Fairbanks and will take you to otherwise inaccessible destinations in the region.

By Car

Much of the Interior is inaccessible by road. One exception is the George Parks Highway, which runs from Anchorage to Fairbanks. Hardy RVers and campers drive the Alaska Highway through British Columbia and the Yukon to Fairbanks; it takes at least a week.

By Train

The **Alaska Railroad** (☎ 800/544–0552; in Anchorage, 907/265–2494; in Fairbanks, 907/465–4155; FAX 907/265–2323) offers service between Anchorage and Fairbanks via Denali.

Denali National Park

Tourist Information

Denali National Park and Preserve (Superintendent, Box 9, Denali National Park 99755; in winter, ☎ 907/683–2294; in summer, 907/683–1266; recorded information, 907/683–9640; FAX 907/683–9612 year-round; admission charged).

Exploring Denali National Park

Denali is 6 million acres of wilderness, including the majestic **Mt. McKinley**—at 20,320 ft the highest peak in North America. Along with panoramic vistas of unspoiled taiga and tundra, the park is the natural habitat of bears, wolves, moose, Dall sheep, and caribou. To enhance viewing opportunities, the only road through the park is closed to private vehicles, except those with campground permits for sites inside the park. Visitors ride shuttle buses (☎ 800/622–7275; $12–$30 depending on turnaround point) on the 11-hour round-trip excursion to **Wonder Lake,** famous for its views of wading moose and Mt. McKinley. If you tire of the ride, you can get out and walk, then catch another bus (they leave from the park entrance every half hour starting at 5 AM) in either direction to continue your journey. The park also offers naturalist walks and dogsled demonstrations; check with the **Visitor Access Center** near the park entrance for the day's schedule. Denali is open year-round, but services and accommodations are limited from September to May. For information on camping, *see* Campgrounds, *below.*

Dining

There's not a great variety of food available at the park. All hotels have their own restaurants. For price ranges, see Chart 1 (B) in On the Road with Fodor's.

$ **Lynx Creek Pizza & Pub.** This funky frame building is popular with young park workers for after-work beer and pizza; try the reindeer-sausage topping. *Parks Hwy., 1½ mi north of park entrance,* ☎ *907/683–2548. No reservations. AE, D, MC, V. Closed Sept.–May.*

Lodging

For price ranges, see Chart 2 (B) in On the Road with Fodor's.

$$$ **Denali National Park Hotel.** The main attractions of this hotel—the only one inside the park—are its location near the railroad station and its theater, and that it hosts free naturalist films and ranger talks daily. Rooms are simple, some in old Pullman cars. *Box 87, Denali National Park 99755,* ☎ *907/276–7234 or 907/683–2215,* FAX *907/258–3668. 100 rooms. Facilities: cafeteria, snack shop, lounge, auditorium. AE, D, MC, V. Closed Sept.–May.*

$$$ **Denali Princess Lodge.** This large log complex above the Nenana River is the most luxurious hotel at the park. Suites have whirlpools, and the lounge features a fireplace. *Parks Hwy., 1 mi north of park entrance,* ☎ *907/683–2282,* FAX *907/683–2545. Reservations: 2815 2nd Ave., Suite 400, Seattle, WA 98121,* ☎ *800/426–0500,* FAX *206/443–1979. 280 rooms. Facilities: 2 restaurants, tour desk, bike rentals, outdoor hot tubs, meeting rooms, lounge with fireplace, bar. AE, MC, V. Closed mid-Sept.–mid-May.*

$ **Denali Hostel.** A wood-frame bunkhouse offers shared accommodations and bus service to and from the park. It's located 10 mi north, near Healy. *Box 801, Denali National Park 99755,* ☎ *907/683–1295. No credit cards. Closed mid-Sept.–mid-May.*

WILDERNESS LODGES

$$$ **Camp Denali.** This rustic compound in the heart of the park has cabins lit by gaslight. Its authentic charm and delicious home cooking make it a popular place to stay in Denali. A knowledgeable staff will acquaint you with the surrounding wilderness. *Box 67, Denali National Park 99755; in summer,* ☎ *907/683–2290,* FAX *907/683–1568; in winter,* ☎ *603/675–2248,* FAX *603/675–9125. 17 cabins. Closed early Sept.–early June.*

$$$ **Denali Wilderness Lodge.** Built as a hunting camp to supply gold rush-era miners, this complex of more than two dozen log buildings is reachable only by bush plane from an air strip at Denali National Park. Activities include horseback riding, hiking, bird watching, and wildlife photography. *Box 50, 99755,* ☎ *907/683–1287 or 800/541–9779. 6 rooms in lodge, 16 cabins. Closed Sept.–late May.*

Campgrounds

There are seven campgrounds in Denali. Three are open to private vehicles for tent and RV camping; three are reached by shuttle bus and are restricted to tent camping; and one is for backpackers only. For more information, contact the Park Superintendent (*see* Tourist Information, *above*). Several private campgrounds can be found outside the park along the highway, such as **Grizzly Bear Cabins and Campground** (Box 7, Denali National Park 99755, ☎ 907/683–2696). For general campsite information and availability, contact the Alaska Public Lands Information Center (*see* Visitor Information, *above*).

Fairbanks

Tourist Information

Fairbanks: Convention and Visitors Bureau Information Cabin (550 1st Ave., 99701, ☎ 907/456–5774 or 800/327–5774, events hot line 907/456–4636, FAX 907/452–2867).

Exploring Fairbanks

Built on the banks of the Chena River, Fairbanks was founded by gold miners early in the century and later became a transportation hub for all of the Interior. Today it's the state's second-largest city, although its atmosphere is more that of a frontier town. Its residents—who cope with incredible winter temperatures (lows reach –50°F), darkness or twilight almost around the clock in winter, and ice fog—consider themselves the hardiest of Alaskans.

One of Fairbanks's main attractions is the **University of Alaska.** On its grounds are the **Large Animal Research Station** (☎ 907/474–7207; admission charged), home to live musk-ox and caribou, and the **University of Alaska Museum** (☎ 907/474–7505; admission charged), whose collection includes a 36,000-year-old mummified steppe bison. The **Geophysical Institute** (☎ 907/474–7558) shows a video on the aurora borealis on Thursday at 2 PM in summer (June 1–Sept. 1). The west ridge of the campus affords an excellent view of the **Alaska Range** to the south.

Another big draw in Fairbanks is the **Alaskaland Park** (Airport Way and Peger Rd., ☎ 907/459–1087; closed Labor Day–Memorial Day; admission charged), on the Chena River near downtown. Among its numerous attractions are museums, a theater, an art gallery, a native village, and a reconstructed gold-rush town.

Spectator Sports

The **North American Open Sled Dog Championship** is held in downtown Fairbanks in March. Check with the visitors bureau (*see* Tourist Information, *above*) for details. **Ice hockey** is a passion here: The amateur **Gold Kings** (☎ 907/456–7825) and the University of Alaska **Nanooks** (☎ 907/474–7205) draw big crowds at their arenas October through March.

Dining

For price ranges, see Chart 1 (B) in On the Road with Fodor's.

$$ ★ **Pump House Restaurant.** A restored mining pump station is the setting for good seafood, steaks, and an oyster bar. *Mile 1.3, Chena Pump Rd., ☎ 907/479–8452. AE, MC, V.*

Lodging

For hotel price ranges, see Chart 2 (B) in On the Road with Fodor's.

$$$ ★ **Sophie Station.** At this all-suite hotel near Fairbanks International Airport, every room has a kitchen. *1717 University Ave., 99709, ☎ 907/479–3650 or 800/528–4916, FAX 907/479–7951. 147 rooms. AE, D, DC, MC, V.*

$$$ **Westmark Fairbanks.** Close to downtown, this full-service member of Alaska's biggest chain is built around a courtyard on a quiet street. Rooms are contemporary and comfortable. *813 Noble St., ☎ 907/456–7722 or 800/544–0970, FAX 907/451–7478. 240 rooms. Facilities: restaurant, lounge, tour desk, gift shop. AE, D, DC, MC, V.*

B&Bs

Alaska Fairbanks B&B (902 Kellum St., 99701, ☎ 907/452–4967, FAX 907/451–6955).

Hot Springs Retreats

The discovery of natural hot springs in the frozen wilderness just north of Fairbanks sent early miners scrambling to build communities around this heaven-sent phenomenon. Today the area is a popular excursion for Fairbanks residents, who come to soak in the pools filled with hot spring water and to enjoy excellent fishing, hiking, and cross-country skiing. The springs are also a favorite spot to view the famed northern lights.

$$–$$$ **Chena Hot Springs Resort.** This resort, just 60 mi from Fairbanks on Chena Hot Springs Road, is the closest and most popular destination among locals. There's a campground with RV hookups, as well as hotel rooms furnished with antique wardrobes and rustic cabins (electricity,

no water). Nonguests can pay to use the heated pool and eat in the restaurant. *Box 73440, Fairbanks 99707, ☎ 907/452–7867; in AK only, 800/478–4681; FAX 907/456–3122. 47 rooms in hotel, 7 cabins. Facilities: restaurant, lounge, spring-heated pool, 3 Jacuzzis, hot tub. AE, D, DC, MC, V.*

$$ **Circle Hot Springs Resort.** A 2½-hour drive from Fairbanks on the Steese Highway, this spa retains the original hotel dating from 1930. There are also one- or two-bedroom cabins with Jacuzzis and kitchenettes. The entire complex is naturally heated by the hot springs. *Box 254, Central 99730, ☎ 907/520–5113. 24 rooms (most with shared bath), 12 cabins. Facilities: restaurant, lounge, spring-heated pool, indoor Jacuzzi. MC, V.*

Sports and the Outdoors

Canoeing

The Chena River is popular for canoeing, both in Fairbanks and out in the wilderness. Entry points are marked along Chena Hot Springs Road. Avoid the Tanana River, with its swift and tricky current and hidden sandbars.

Fishing

Char, grayling, and pike are abundant in the lakes and rivers of the Interior. The Chena River between Fairbanks and Chena Hot Springs is especially popular for grayling fishing.

Hiking and Backpacking

Skilled wilderness travelers can hike anywhere in Denali National Park, with the exception of areas occasionally closed because of bear-related dangers. There are well-marked beginner trails near the park entrance.

Rafting

Several companies offer white-water trips on the thrilling **Nenana River,** which parallels the George Parks Highway near the Denali entrance. Try **Denali Raft Adventures** (Drawer 190, Denali National Park 99755, ☎ 907/683–2234) or **McKinley Raft Tours** (Box 138, Denali National Park 99755, ☎ 907/683–2392).

Wilderness Camps and Lodges

See Southeast, *above.*

ELSEWHERE IN THE STATE

The Arctic

Tourist Information

For information on native-run attractions in **Barrow** and **Kotzebue,** contact the Alaska Native Tourism Council (*see* Visitor Information, *above*). For information on **Nome,** contact the Convention and Visitors Bureau (Box 240, Nome 99762, ☎ 907/443–5535, FAX 907/443–5832).

Getting There

You must fly to destinations in the Arctic, as no public highways lead there (the Dalton Highway to Prudhoe Bay is closed to private traffic past Chandalar). **Alaska Airlines Vacations** (SEARV, Box 68900, Seattle, WA 98168, ☎ 800/468–2248) runs air-tours of the Arctic from Anchorage and Fairbanks. **Princess Tours** (2815 2nd Ave., Suite 400, Seattle, WA 98121, ☎ 800/835–8907) offers packages.

What to See and Do

The gold-rush town of **Nome** sits just below the Arctic Circle. Colorful saloons and low-slung, ramshackle buildings help perpetuate its vintage gold-camp aura, present since ore was discovered here in 1898. **Kotzebue,** on the other hand, is a proud Eskimo community north of Nome that preserves its heritage in the **Living Museum of the Arctic** (☎ 907/442–3301; admission charged in summer) and a cultural camp where elders pass on traditions to the next generation. In town, salmon dries on wooden racks and Eskimo boats rest in yards. At the top of the state, tours of the **Prudhoe Bay** area explore the oil-industry life there, as well as the wildlife and tundra surrounding it. In Barrow, the northernmost community in the United States, the sun rises on May 10th and doesn't set for nearly three months.

Kodiak and Katmai National Park and Preserve

Tourist Information

Alaska's Southwest (3300 Arctic Blvd., Suite 203, Anchorage 99503, ☎ 907/562–7380, FAX 907/562–0438).

Getting There

Alaska Airlines (☎ 800/426–0333) flies a daily nonstop jet service to Kodiak from Anchorage. For packages to Kodiak, contact **Alaska Airlines Vacations** (SEARV, Box 68900, Seattle, WA 98168, ☎ 800/468–2248). At the base of the Alaska Peninsula, 290 mi southwest of Anchorage, Katmai is accessible only by plane to King Salmon and then floatplane for the 20-minute hop to the park.

What to See and Do

Kodiak, the largest island in the United States, is home to the Kodiak brown bear, the largest land mammal in North America. It also was the original capital of Russian Alaska, before the seat of colonial government was moved to Sitka. Visitors can go halibut fishing, sea kayaking, or flightseeing for bears. Katmai is a relatively primitive park compared with the likes of Denali, but therein lies its charm. The peaceful valley became a land of steaming fumaroles after the 1912 eruption of Mt. Novarupta and the collapse of nearby Mt. Katmai's peak. The residents who fled the area, now dubbed the **Valley of Ten Thousand Smokes,** have been replaced by sports lovers and tourists. Fishermen flock here for trophy rainbow trout and salmon. Hiking, boat tours, and wildlife viewing are other Katmai attractions. **Katmailand Inc.** (4700 Aircraft Dr., Suite 2, Anchorage 99502, ☎ 907/243–5448 or 800/544–0551) offers tours; or contact **Katmai National Park and Preserve** (Box 7, King Salmon 99613, ☎ 907/246–3305).

The Aleutian and Pribilof Islands

Tourist Information

For tourism information on the Aleutian chain and the Pribilof Islands, contact Alaska's Southwest (*see* Katmai, *above*).

Getting There

About the only practical way to see these areas is through a package tour. Schedules are flexible, as weather often delays flights to and from the islands. Contact **Reeve Aleutian Airways** (4700 W. International Airport Rd., Anchorage 99502, ☎ 907/243–4700 or 800/544–2248) for flight and package-tour information. The **Alaska Marine Highway** (*see* Southeast, *above*) serves the Aleutian Islands in summer.

What to See and Do

The **Aleutian Islands** stretch 1,000 mi from the Alaska Peninsula toward Japan. This semivolcanic, treeless archipelago of 20 large and several hundred smaller islands makes Alaska the westernmost point (as well as the *easternmost* point!) on the continent. The Aleut natives who live in the tiny settlements here work in canneries or as fishermen and guides. Out here, where the wind blows constantly and fog is common, can be found some of the most spectacular bird-watching opportunities in the country, with abundant terns, guillemots, murres, and puffins, as well as species unique to the islands. The Japanese invaded the Aleutian Islands during World War II, and at Dutch Harbor on Unalaska Island visitors can still see concrete bunkers, gun batteries, and a partially sunken ship.

Each spring the largest northern fur-seal herd in the world comes to the tiny green **Pribilof Islands,** in the Bering Sea about 200 mi northwest of Cold Bay. Most tours fly to **St. Paul,** one of the largest islands and home to the descendants of Aleut-Russians, whose churches, names, and facial features reveal their heritage.

HAWAII

By Marty Wentzel

Capital	Honolulu
Population	1,209,000
Motto	The Life of the Land Is Perpetuated in Righteousness
State Bird	Nene (Hawaiian goose)
State Flower	Hibiscus

Visitor Information

Hawaii Visitors Bureau (2270 Kalakaua Ave., Suite 801, Honolulu 96815, ☏ 808/923–1811; in NY, 212/947–0717).

Scenic Drives

On the eastern tip of Oahu, the 10-mi stretch of **Kalanianaole Highway** from Hanauma Bay to Waimanalo is a cliff-side road resembling those of the California coast. On the Big Island, **Hwy. 19** north out of Hilo runs along the rugged Hamakua Coast to Waipio Valley, past sugarcane fields and spectacular ocean views. From Paia to Hana, Maui's **Hana Highway** (Hwy. 36) is a winding, 55-mi coastal route that spans numerous rivers and passes tropical waterfalls. From the town of Waimea, Kauai's **Waimea Canyon Drive** meanders upward past panoramas of Waimea Canyon, culminating at the 4,120-ft Kalalau Lookout.

National and State Parks

National Parks

Some of Hawaii's best national park service attractions are **Hawaii Volcanoes National Park, Puuhonua o Honaunau National Historic Park,** and **Puukohola National Historic Site** (*see* The Big Island of Hawaii, *below*); **Haleakala National Park** (*see* Maui, *below*); **Kalaupapa** (*see* Elsewhere in the State, *below*); and **USS *Arizona* Memorial** (1 Arizona Memorial Pl., Honolulu 96818–3145, ☏ 808/422–0561). A 20-minute drive west from downtown Honolulu, the memorial shields the hulk of the USS *Arizona,* which sank with 1,102 men aboard when the Japanese attacked Pearl Harbor on December 7, 1941.

State Parks

Popular state parks include **Hapuna Beach State Recreation Area** (*see* The Big Island, *below*), **Kokee State Park** (*see* Kauai, *below*), and **Wailua River State Park** (Wailua Marina, Kapaa, Kauai 96746, ☏ 808/822–5065), where you can see the sites of ancient villages and an enormous, fern-laced lava tube. For brochures and other information, write to the **District Office of the Hawaii Department of Land and Natural Resources,** Division of State Parks (Box 621, Honolulu 96809, ☏ 808/587–0300).

HONOLULU AND WAIKIKI

Honolulu, on the island of Oahu, is worlds apart from any other city in the country. Here the salad of cultures is artfully tossed in a blend that is harmonious yet allows each culture to retain its distinct flavor and texture. Its downtown sector combines a royal history with the modern-day action of a major metropolitan center. Just 3½ mi from downtown is Waikiki, a tourist mecca par excellence. Set on the sunny, dry side of Oahu, Waikiki touts the natural splendors of the islands while offering the glittering atmosphere that makes it a resort of international renown.

Tourist Information

Hawaii Visitors Bureau (*see* Visitor Information, *above*).

Arriving and Departing

By Plane

Honolulu International Airport (☏ 808/836–6411) is only 20 minutes from Waikiki. U.S. carriers serving Honolulu include American, Continental, Delta, Hawaiian, Northwest, TWA, and United. A cab from the airport to downtown costs about $20 plus tip. **TransHawaiian Services** (☏ 808/533–8765) runs a shuttle service to Waikiki ($7 adults, $4 children under 12). Some hotels also provide shuttle service; ask when you make reservations.

Getting Around Honolulu and Waikiki

By Car

There's no need to rent a car if you don't want to leave Waikiki. Driving in rush hour (6:30–8:30 AM and 3:30–5:30 PM) is frustrating because of traffic, parking limitations, and numerous one-way streets. If you do plan to rent, reservations are suggested year-round.

By Public Transportation

You can ride **The Bus** (☏ 808/848–5555) all around Oahu for a mere 85¢.

By Taxi

You can usually get a cab outside your hotel. The two biggest taxicab companies are **Charley's** (☏ 808/531–1333) and **SIDA of Hawaii, Inc.** (☏ 808/836–0011).

Orientation Tours

The **Pearl Harbor and Punchbowl Tour** offered by Polynesian Adventure Tours (☏ 808/833–3000) includes a Navy launch out to the ***Arizona* Memorial.** In downtown Honolulu, the **Chinatown Walking Tour** (☏ 808/533–3181) provides a fascinating peek at Oahu's oldest neighborhood.

Exploring Honolulu and Waikiki

Directions are often given in terms of *mauka* (toward the mountains) and *makai* (toward the ocean), or they may refer to Diamond Head (east, toward the famous volcanic landmark) and *ewa* (west).

Downtown Honolulu

The **Hawaii Maritime Center,** across Ala Moana Boulevard from Alakea Street, features exhibits honoring Hawaii's relationship with the sea. *Pier 7, ☏ 808/536–6373. Admission charged.*

Nearby, at King and Richards streets, is **Iolani Palace** (☏ 808/522–0832), built in 1882 and the only royal palace in America. The Victorian structure has been beautifully restored and is open for guided tours Wednesday–Saturday. Tickets must be reserved in advance.

Across King Street is **Aliiolani Hale,** the old judiciary building that served as the parliament hall during the monarchy era. In front is the gilded statue of Kamehameha I, the Hawaiian chief who unified the islands.

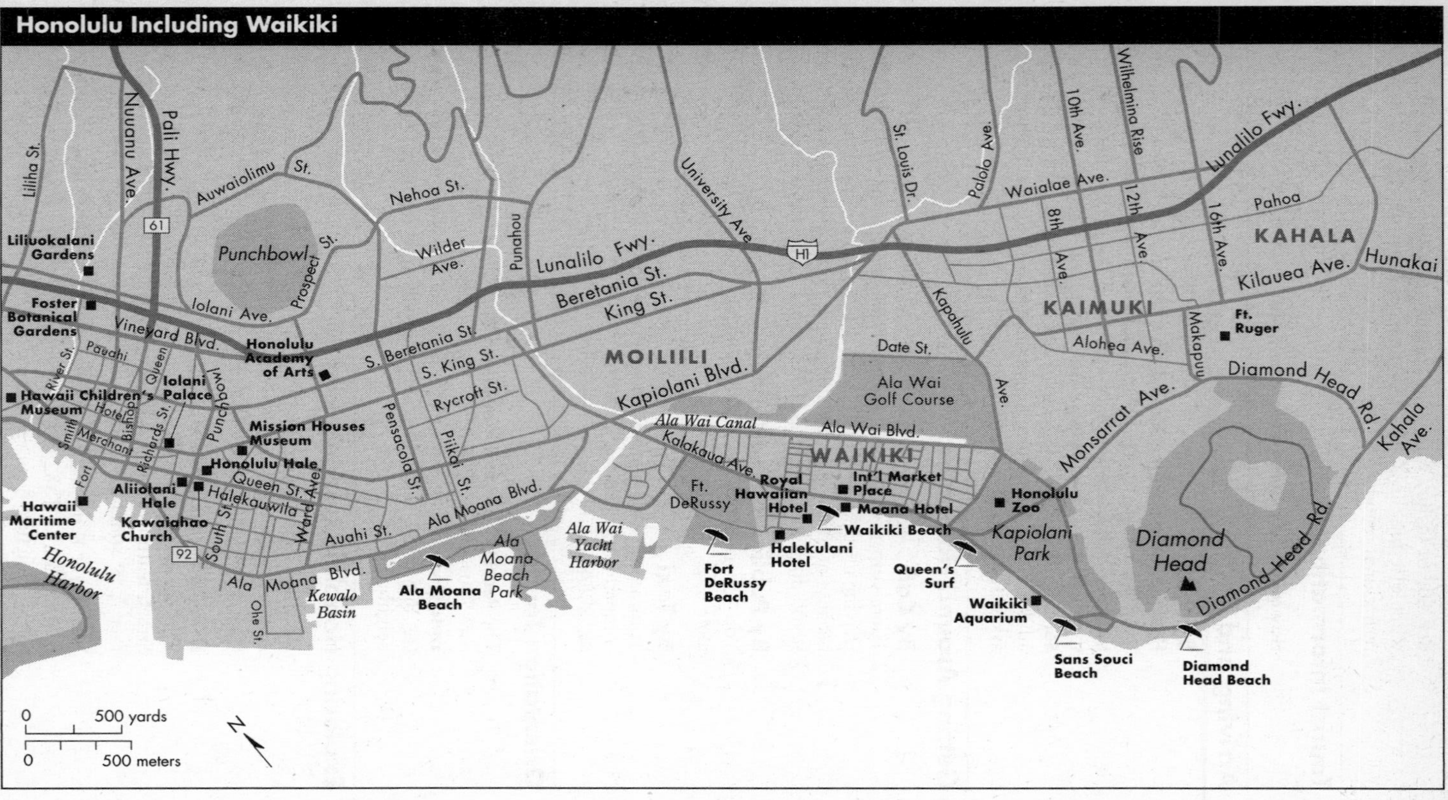
Honolulu Including Waikiki
Liliha St.
Nuuanu Ave.
Pali Hwy.
61
Auwaiolimu St.
Liliuokalani Gardens
Punchbowl
Prospect St.
Nehoa St.
Wilder Ave.
Punahou
Foster Botanical Gardens
Iolani Ave.
Vineyard Blvd.
Honolulu Academy of Arts
Pauahi
River St.
Queen
Iolani Palace
Hawaii Children's Museum
Hotel
Bishop
Smith
Merchant
Richards St.
Punchbowl
Mission Houses Museum
Honolulu Hale
Fort
Aliiolani Hale
Queen St.
Halekauwila
Ward Ave.
Hawaii Maritime Center
Kawaiahao Church
South St.
92
Honolulu Harbor
Ala Moana Blvd.
Ohe St.
Kewalo Basin
Auahi St.
Ala Moana Blvd.
Ala Moana Beach
Ala Moana Beach Park
S. Beretania St.
S. King St.
Rycroft St.
Pensacola St.
Piikoi St.
Lunalilo Fwy.
Beretania St.
King St.
MOILIILI
Kapiolani Blvd.
University Ave.
H1
Ala Wai Canal
Kalakaua Ave.
Ft. DeRussy
Ala Wai Yacht Harbor
Fort DeRussy Beach
Royal Hawaiian Hotel
Halekulani Hotel
WAIKIKI
Int'l Market Place
Moana Hotel
Waikiki Beach
Ala Wai Blvd.
Ala Wai Golf Course
Date St.
St. Louis Dr.
Palolo Ave.
Kapahulu Ave.
Queen's Surf
Waikiki Aquarium
Honolulu Zoo
Kapiolani Park
Sans Souci Beach
Monsarrat Ave.
Diamond Head
Diamond Head Rd.
Diamond Head Beach
Waialae Ave.
10th Ave.
8th Ave.
Wilhelmina Rise
12th Ave.
KAIMUKI
Alohea Ave.
Makapuu
16th Ave.
Ft. Ruger
Lunalilo Fwy.
Pahoa
KAHALA
Kilauea Ave.
Hunakai
Diamond Head Rd.
Kahala Ave.
0 500 yards
0 500 meters
N

Honolulu Hale (530 S. King St. at Punchbowl St.), the city hall, is a Mediterranean Renaissance–style building constructed in 1929. Across the street is **Kawaiahao Church** (957 Punchbowl St., ☎ 808/522–1333), built in 1842 of massive blocks of solid coral. The church witnessed the coronations, weddings, and funerals of generations of Hawaiian royalty. Next door is the **Mission Houses Museum** (553 S. King St., ☎ 808/531–0481), home of the first U.S. missionaries in Hawaii after their arrival in 1820. The mission's three main structures—the **Hale La'au** wood-frame house, the **Printing Office,** and the **Chamberlain House**—are among the oldest buildings on the islands.

Waikiki

The impressive **Halekulani Hotel** (2199 Kalia Rd., ☎ 808/923–2311) is built on the site of a 1917 hotel—a portion of the old structure remains—that was the setting for the first of the Charlie Chan detective novels, *The House Without a Key.* The hotel's modern version features a massive floral arrangement in the lobby and a pool with an orchid mosaic at the bottom. Follow the paved ocean walk to the pink **Royal Hawaiian Hotel** (2259 Kalakaua Ave., ☎ 808/923–7311), built in 1921 when Waikiki was still a sleepy paradise. Cross the street and walk toward Diamond Head to the **International Market Place** (2330 Kalakaua Ave., ☎ 808/923–9871), with its spreading banyan tree and dozens of souvenir stands. On the makai side of the street is the oldest hotel in Waikiki, the **Sheraton Moana Surfrider** (2365 Kalakaua Ave., ☎ 808/922–3111), which underwent a major renovation in 1989. The beaux arts style building includes a room with hotel memorabilia dating from the turn of the century.

At the Diamond Head end of Waikiki, the **Honolulu Zoo** (151 Kapahulu Ave., ☎ 808/971–7171; admission charged) is home to thousands of furry and finned creatures. It's not the biggest zoo in the country, but its 40 lush acres certainly make it one of the prettiest. **Kapiolani Park,** a vast green playing field, is where you'll find the **Waikiki Shell** (2805 Monsarrat Ave., ☎ 808/521–2911), Honolulu's outdoor concert arena. Next door, the **Kodak Hula Show** (☎ 808/833–1661) has been wowing crowds for more than 50 years. The **Waikiki Aquarium** (2777 Kalakaua Ave., ☎ 808/923–9741; admission charged), the third-oldest aquarium in America, harbors more than 300 species of marine life.

The hike to the summit of **Diamond Head** (Monsarrat Ave. near 18th Ave., ☎ 808/971–2525) offers a marvelous view of Oahu's southern coastline. The entrance is about 1 mi above Kapiolani Park. Drive through the tunnel to the inside of the crater, park, and start walking. It's a half-hour jaunt to the top.

What to See and Do with Children

In addition to the creatures on display at the zoo and aquarium (*see* Exploring Honolulu and Waikiki, *above*), porpoises are on view in the lagoon at the **Kahala Hilton** (5000 Kahala Ave., ☎ 808/734–2211).

Shopping

Just outside Waikiki is the **Ala Moana Shopping Center** (1450 Ala Moana Blvd., ☎ 808/946–2811 for special event information), a 50-acre open-air mall with major department stores, including Liberty House. **Ward Centre** (1200 Ala Moana Blvd.) has 30 upscale boutiques and eateries, including R. Field Wine Co. and Compadres, for Mexican food. **Ward Warehouse** (1050 Ala Moana Blvd.) is a two-story mall with 65 shops and restaurants. In Waikiki there's the **International Market**

Place (*see* Exploring Honolulu and Waikiki, *above*). Also in Waikiki, the **Royal Hawaiian Shopping Center** (2201 Kalakaua Ave., ☎ 808/922–0588 for special event information) is three stories high and three blocks long, with 120 stores.

Beaches

Honolulu

Ala Moana Beach Park, across from Ala Moana Shopping Center, is the most popular beach for families because the protective reef keeps waters calm. Facilities include bathhouses, indoor and outdoor showers, lifeguards, concession stands, and tennis courts. **Hanauma Bay,** a 30-minute drive east of Waikiki, is a marine preserve with outstanding snorkeling, a snack bar, bathhouses, and gear rental.

Waikiki

Fort DeRussy Beach, the widest part of Waikiki Beach, has volleyball courts, picnic tables, showers, and food stands. **Queen's Surf,** across from the Honolulu Zoo, is named for Queen Liliuokalani's beach house, which once stood here. Sand here is soft, and the beach slopes gently to the water; it attracts a mixture of families and gays. **Sans Souci,** across from Kapiolani Park, is a favorite of singles in skimpy bathing suits. Its shallow waters are safe for children.

Dining

The strength of Hawaii's tourist industry has attracted some of the finest chefs in the world to Oahu's hotels, where you'll find the best dining on the island. A variety of restaurants serve fine ethnic food, especially Chinese, Japanese, and Thai. No matter what or how you eat, you'll probably pay higher prices in Waikiki than in the rest of Hawaii. For price ranges, see Chart 1 (A) in On the Road with Fodor's.

$$$$ ★ **Bali by the Sea.** An oceanside setting provides glorious views of Waikiki Beach, outdone only by such upscale international entrées as roast duck with papaya puree and poached mahimahi and opakapaka, a pair of island fish served with two sauces. *Hilton Hawaiian Village, 2005 Kalia Rd., ☎ 808/941–2254. Reservations required. Dress: collared shirt. AE, D, DC, MC, V. No dinner Sun.*

$$$$ ★ **La Mer.** In the exotic atmosphere of a Mandalay mansion is served a unique blend of French and Hawaiian cuisine. A standout among entrées is *onaga* (a local fish) baked in a thyme and rosemary rock salt crust with a sauce of fresh herbs. *Halekulani Hotel, 2199 Kalia Rd., ☎ 808/923–2311. Reservations required. Jacket required. AE, D, DC, MC, V. No lunch.*

$$$$ **Maile.** The glamorous and glittering signature restaurant of the "hotel of the stars" has moved upstairs and now has an ocean view. Steaks and meats are the pride of the Maile, including roast duckling Waialae with fruit sauce. *Kahala Mandarin Oriental Hotel, 5000 Kahala Ave., ☎ 808/734–2211. Reservations required. Jacket advised. AE, D, DC, MC, V. No lunch.*

$$$$ ★ **Michel's at the Colony Surf.** With mirrors, piano music, chandeliers, and panoramas of the sea, this is easily the most romantic restaurant in town. The Continental fare includes pepper steak flamed with Jack Daniels whiskey. *Colony Surf Hotel, 2895 Kalakaua Ave., ☎ 808/923–6552. Reservations required. Jacket required at dinner. AE, D, DC, MC, V.*

$$$ **Hy's Steak House.** Things always seem to go well at Hy's, from the steak tartare to the cherries jubilee. The atmosphere is snug, and you can watch the chef work behind glass. *Waikiki Park Heights Hotel,*

2440 Kuhio Ave., ☎ 808/922–5555. Reservations required. AE, D, DC, MC, V. No lunch.

$$$ ★ **Restaurant Suntory.** Here is Japanese dining at its most elegant. Choose from the sushi bar, rooms devoted to *teppanyaki* (food prepared on an iron grill) or *shabu-shabu* (thinly sliced beef boiled in broth), or a private room. *Royal Hawaiian Shopping Center, 2233 Kalakaua Ave., ☎ 808/922–5511. AE, DC, MC, V.*

$$$ **The Secret.** Formerly the Third Floor, this elegant restaurant has a European feel, with extravagant food displays, dim lights, and huge wicker chairs. Try abalone sautéed with lemon and served with capers on basmati rice. *Hawaiian Regent Hotel, 2552 Kalakaua Ave., ☎ 808/922–6611. Reservations required. AE, DC, MC, V. No lunch.*

$$ **Golden Dragon.** Szechuan, Cantonese, and unconventional nouvelle Chinese cuisine is served in this dining room by the sea. Among the best items is the beggar's chicken (whole chicken baked in a clay pot), which must be ordered 24 hours in advance. *Hilton Hawaiian Village, 2005 Kalia Rd., ☎ 808/946–5336. Reservations required. AE, D, DC, MC, V. No lunch.*

$$ ★ **Keo's Thai Cuisine.** Hollywood celebrities have discovered this orchid-filled nook, where the Evil Jungle Prince (chicken, shrimp, or vegetables in a sauce of fresh basil, coconut milk, and red chili) is tops. *625 Kapahulu Ave., ☎ 808/737–8240. Reservations required. AE, DC, MC, V. No lunch.*

$$ **Tripton's American Cafe.** The spare Napa Valley ambience (a real change of pace from the relentless glitter of nearby Waikiki) and inventive American cuisine—including seasonal specialties and knockout desserts—make this a favorite of local residents as well as visitors. *Diamond Head Center, 449 Kapahulu Ave., ☎ 808/737–3819. AE, DC, MC, V.*

$ ★ **California Pizza Kitchen.** A tiled and mirrored glass atrium showcases designer pizzas with such toppings as Thai chicken, Peking duck, and Caribbean shrimp. There's another branch (☎ 808/955–5161) on Ala Moana Boulevard in Waikiki. *Kahala Mall, 4211 Waialae Ave., ☎ 808/737–9446. No reservations. AE, MC, V.*

$ **Compadres Mexican Bar and Grill.** The outdoor terrace is fun for margaritas and chips. Inside, lively photographs and colorful paintings create a festive setting for fajitas, chili rellenos, and nachos. *Ward Centre, 1200 Ala Moana Blvd., ☎ 808/591–8307. No reservations. AE, MC, V.*

$ **Hau Tree Lanai.** Next to Sans Souci Beach and shaded by a huge hau tree, this outdoor café provides relaxing ocean views to accompany the American entrées. At breakfast try the Belgian waffle or salmon omelet. *New Otani Kaimana Beach Hotel, 2863 Kalakaua Ave., ☎ 808/921–7066. Reservations required at dinner. AE, DC, MC, V.*

$ **Maple Garden.** The fine reputation of this restaurant is founded on the spicy Mandarin cuisine, not on the no-frills decor. A consistent favorite is the eggplant in hot garlic sauce. *909 Isenberg St., ☎ 808/941–6641. AE, DC, MC, V.*

Lodging

Oahu's best accommodations are in or near Waikiki, with a few places of note in Honolulu. Except for the peak months of January, February, and August, you'll have no trouble getting a room if you call first. For B&Bs in the area contact **Hawaii's Best Bed and Breakfasts** (Box 563, Kamuela 96743, ☎ 808/885–4550). (Note: All mailing addresses are in Honolulu.) For price ranges, see Chart 2 (A) in On the Road with Fodor's.

$$$$ ★ **Halekulani Hotel.** This sleek, modern hotel has fresh marble-and-wood rooms, some with breathtaking ocean views. It also offers two of the finest restaurants in Honolulu, and a pool with a giant orchid mosaic. *2199 Kalia Rd., 96815, ☎ 808/923–2311 or 800/367–2343, FAX 808/926–8004. 456 rooms. Facilities: 3 restaurants, 3 lounges, fitness room, pool. AE, D, DC, MC, V.*

$$$$ ★ **Hilton Hawaiian Village.** Waikiki's largest resort includes four towers, a botanical garden, and a pond with penguins. Rooms are done in raspberry or aqua, with rattan and bamboo furnishings. *2005 Kalia Rd., 96815, ☎ 808/949–4321 or 800/445–8667, FAX 808/947–7898. 2,542 rooms. Facilities: 6 restaurants, 5 lounges, 3 pools. AE, D, DC, MC, V.*

$$$$ **Ihilani Resort and Spa.** This sleek, 15-story hotel is the first of a new resort development west of Honolulu that provides a neighbor island atmosphere only 25 minutes from the airport. Rooms have marble bathrooms and private lanais. *92-1001 Olani St., Kapolei 96707, ☎ 808/679–0079 or 800/626-4446. 387 rooms. Facilities: 4 restaurants, 2 pools, golf course, tennis, spa. AE, DC, MC, V.*

$$$$ **Kahala Mandarin Oriental Hotel.** Formerly the Kahala Hilton, this hotel, in an elegant neighborhood minutes away from Waikiki, is the choice of stars, kings, and presidents. The lobby features chandeliers, tropical flower displays, and a musician playing a grand piano. The large rooms have his-and-her dressing rooms and parquet floors. Three distinguished restaurants are here. *5000 Kahala Ave., 96816, ☎ 808/734–2211. 309 rooms, 60 cottages. Facilities: 3 restaurants, 2 lounges, health club, pool. AE, D, DC, MC, V.*

$$$ ★ **Colony Surf.** This is a small oceanside hotel with impeccable personal service; each unit is equipped with a full kitchen. Location is a plus, on the quiet east end of Waikiki near Diamond Head. *2895 Kalakaua Ave., 96815, ☎ 808/923–5751 or 800/252–7873, FAX 808/922–8433. 50 units. Facilities: 2 restaurants, 2 lounges. AE, D, DC, MC, V.*

$$$ **Outrigger Waikiki Hotel.** At this beachfront property, each room has a Polynesian motif and a lanai, and some have kitchenettes. *2335 Kalakaua Ave., 96815, ☎ 808/923–0711 or 800/688–7444. 530 rooms. Facilities: 6 restaurants, 6 lounges, pool. AE, D, DC, MC, V.*

$$$ **Waikiki Joy.** In the heart of Waikiki, this gem has some rooms with refrigerators, others with kitchens, wet bars, or king-size beds. Every room has a whirlpool, a deluxe stereo system, and a bedside control panel. *320 Lewers St., 96815, ☎ 808/923–2300 or 800/922–7866, FAX 808/924–4010. 93 rooms. Facilities: restaurant, lounge, pool, sauna. AE, D, DC, MC, V.*

$$$ ★ **Waikiki Parc.** Despite the main entrance down a narrow side street, this hotel's location just one block from Waikiki's beach is a real plus. Rooms have rattan furniture and blue-and-white decor. *2233 Helumoa Rd., 96815, ☎ 808/921–7272 or 800/422–0450, FAX 808/923–1336. 298 rooms. Facilities: 2 restaurants, pool. AE, D, DC, MC, V.*

$$ ★ **Manoa Valley Inn.** Tucked away in a lush valley 2 mi from Waikiki, this inn was built in 1919 and renovated when it was converted into a B&B in 1982. Rooms have antique four-poster beds, marble-top dressers, and patterned wallpaper. *2001 Vancouver Dr., 96822, ☎ 808/947–6019 or 800/634–5115. 8 rooms, 1 cottage. AE, MC, V.*

$$ **New Otani Kaimana Beach.** Polished to a shine, it sits right on the beach across from Kapiolani Park. Rooms are small but nicely appointed, with soothing pastels and off-white furnishings. *2863 Kalakaua Ave., 96815, ☎ 808/923–1555 or 800/356–8264, FAX 808/922–9404. 125 rooms. Facilities: 2 restaurants, lounge. AE, D, DC, MC, V.*

$$ **Outrigger Reef Hotel.** A beachfront location and moderate rates are this hotel's selling points. Rooms are done in mauves and pinks; many have lanais. *2169 Kalia Rd., 96815, ☎ 808/923–3111 or 800/688–*

7444, FAX *808/924–4957. 885 rooms. Facilities: 2 restaurants, 4 lounges, nightclub, shops, pool. AE, D, DC, MC, V.*

$ **Continental Surf.** This budget Waikiki high rise is two blocks from the ocean and convenient to shopping and dining. Rooms, with standard modern decor and Polynesian hues, have limited views; some have kitchenettes. *2426 Kuhio Ave., 96815,* ☎ *808/922–2755,* FAX *808/922–2765. 140 rooms. AE, DC, MC, V.*

$ **Edmunds Hotel Apartments.** This low-priced spot on the Ala Wai Canal has views of the mountains. The rooms are small and nondescript but include kitchenettes. *2411 Ala Wai Blvd., 96815,* ☎ *808/923–8381. 12 rooms. No credit cards.*

$ ★ **Royal Grove Hotel.** A flamingo-pink Waikiki landmark, this hotel has a family atmosphere. Rooms have no real theme or views but do come with kitchens. *15 Uluniu Ave., 96815,* ☎ *808/923–7691. 87 rooms. Facilities: pool. AE, DC, MC, V.*

The Arts and Nightlife

The Arts

MUSIC

The **Honolulu Symphony** (1441 Kapiolani Blvd., Honolulu, ☎ 808/942–2200) performs pops, classics, and summer "starlight" programs.

THEATER

The **Diamond Head Theater** (520 Makapuu Ave., Honolulu, ☎ 808/734–0274) presents experimental, contemporary, and classic works, including musicals and dramas.

Nightlife

COCKTAIL AND DINNER SHOWS

At the **Maile Lounge** (Kahala Mandarin Oriental Hotel, 5000 Kahala Ave., ☎ 808/734–2211), folks swing on the small dance floor to Kit Samson's Sound Advice band.

DINNER CRUISES

Patterned after an ancient Polynesian vessel, **Alii Kai Catamaran's** (Pier 8, street level, Honolulu, ☎ 808/524–6694)*Alii Kai* takes 1,000 passengers on a deluxe dinner cruise, complete with two open bars and a Polynesian show. **Windjammer Cruises** (2222 Kalakaua Ave., Honolulu, ☎ 808/922–1200) ferries you along Oahu's south shores on the 1,500-passenger *Rella Mae,* done up like a clipper ship.

LUAUS

The **Royal Luau** (2259 Kalakaua Ave., Waikiki, ☎ 808/923–7311) takes place at the venerable Royal Hawaiian and is a notch above many others on the island.

NIGHTCLUBS

Rumours (Ala Moana Hotel, 410 Atkinson St., Honolulu, ☎ 808/955–4811) provides video and disco dancing with high-tech lights.

ROCK CLUBS

A two-story, smoky dive called **Anna Bannana's** (2440 S. Beretania St., Waikiki, ☎ 808/946–5190) has fresh, loud, and sometimes avant-garde live music.

Excursions from Honolulu and Waikiki

The **North Shore of Oahu** is the flip side of Honolulu. Instead of high rises there are old homes and stores, some converted into businesses catering to tourists, surfers, and beach bums. The area's wide, uncrowded beaches, rural countryside, and slower pace are reminiscent of Hawaii's other islands.

Getting There

On the Diamond Head end of Waikiki, go toward the mountains on Kapahulu Avenue and follow the signs to the Lunalilo Freeway (H–1). Follow H–1 northwest to H–2 through Wahiawa, where the road becomes two-way. Follow the signs to Haleiwa, which marks the official beginning of the north shore.

Haleiwa is a sleepy plantation town that has come of age, with contemporary boutiques and galleries. Northeast of Haleiwa the road continues past such famous beaches as **Waimea Bay,** where winter waves can crest at 30 ft. Across the street is **Waimea Valley** (☎ 808/638–8511), a lush area for wildlife, walks, and cliff-diving shows.

East of here is the **Polynesian Cultural Center,** 40 acres containing lagoons and seven re-created South Pacific villages, where a spectacular evening luau and revue is offered. *55–370 Kamehameha Hwy., Laie, ☎ 808/293–3333 or 808/923–1861. Admission to villages, demonstrations, and American dinner: $47 adults, $30 children. Closed Sun.*

THE BIG ISLAND OF HAWAII

Nearly twice as large as all the other Hawaiian Islands combined, this youngest island of the chain is still growing: Since 1983, the lava spewed intermittently by Kilauea, the world's most active volcano, has added more than 70 acres to the island. A land of superlatives, the Big Island is also the most diverse island. You can hike into a crater, catch a marlin weighing hundreds of pounds, or simply sunbathe on 266 mi of coastline.

Tourist Information

Hawaii Visitors Bureau (250 Keawe St., Hilo 96720, ☎ 808/961–5797; 75–5719 Alii Dr., Kailua-Kona 96740, ☎ 808/329–7787).

Getting There

Visitors to the west side of the island fly into Kona's **Ke-ahole Airport** (☎ 808/329–2484). Those staying on the east side fly into **Hilo International Airport** (☎ 808/934–5801). Both airports are served by Aloha Airlines and Hawaiian Airlines; United flies into Kona.

Exploring the Big Island

The Big Island is so large and varied that it's best to split it up when exploring. Spend a night in the county seat of Hilo, visit the cow town of Waimea, head to Volcanoes National Park for some hiking, then wind up on the west coast, home of the best beaches, weather, and nightlife.

Hilo and the Hamakua Coast

Hilo is nicknamed the City of Rainbows because of its frequent showers, but rain or shine, this east-coast town is truly beautiful. In the last few years its old-time buildings have been the focus of a refurbishment that has revitalized the downtown area.

The morning catch is auctioned at the **Suisan Fish Market** (85 Lihiwai, ☎ 808/935–8051). Stop by at about 7:30 AM to see sellers hawking aku, ahi, and other fish.

Farther west is the **Lyman House,** built in 1839 by missionaries from Boston. The unique collection at the adjacent **Lyman Museum** ranges from carved wooden cuspidors to historical dress. *276 Haili St., ☏ 808/935–5021. Admission charged. Closed Sun.*

About 10 mi north of Hilo and 5 mi inland is **Akaka Falls State Park,** where two waterfalls provide dramatic photo opportunities. Hwy. 19 continues through sleepy little towns to **Honokaa,** where the first macadamia trees were planted in Hawaii in 1881. Eight miles west of Honokaa is **Waipio,** where you can make arrangements for a four-wheel-drive tour of **Waipio Valley** (☏ 808/775–7121), where there are 2,000-ft cliffs and 1,200-ft waterfalls. Back on Hwy. 19, the top attraction in **Waimea** (also known by its older name, Kamuela) is the **Parker Ranch Visitor Center and Museum** (☏ 808/885–7655), which delves into the history of the island's ranching with life-size replicas and a 22-minute video.

Hawaii Volcanoes National Park

Thirty miles southwest of Hilo is **Hawaii Volcanoes National Park,** a 344-sq-mi park established in 1916 that features an abundance of attractions inspired by Kilauea. Just beyond the park entrance is **Kilauea Visitor Center,** where displays and a movie focus on past eruptions. Next door is the **Volcano Art Center** (☏ 808/967–7511), built in 1877 as a lodge and featuring the work of local artists. Across the street is the **Volcano House** (☏ 808/967–7321), a charming old lodge dating from 1941, with a huge stone fireplace. Windows in the restaurant and bar provide picture-perfect views of Kilauea Caldera and its steaming fire pit, Halemaumau Crater. Drive around the caldera to see the **Thomas A. Jaggar Museum** (☏ 808/967–7643), with seismographs and filmstrips of current and previous eruptions. *Box 52, Volcano 96718, ☏ 808/967–7311. Admission charged.*

Kailua-Kona

Much of the action in this touristy seaside village on the island's west coast centers on **Kailua Pier,** where the fishing fleet arrives each evening. During the big-game tournaments each summer, daily catches are weighed in here. Nearby, the two-story **Hulihee Palace** (75–5718 Alii Dr., ☏ 808/329–1877) served as King Kalakaua's summer residence in the 1880s. Across the street is **Mokuaikaua Church** (☏ 808/329–0655), built in 1836, though the original church was founded in 1820 by Hawaii's first missionaries. Toward the end of the mile-long strip is **Waterfront Row** (75–5770 Alii Dr., ☏ 808/329–8502), a trendy assemblage of shops and restaurants.

Kohala Coast

If you're staying in Kona, you can tour the Kohala Coast by driving north from Kailua-Kona on Hwy. 19 past luxury resorts and sweeping stretches of old lava flows. Stop at the **Puukohola National Historic Site** visitor center (Box 44340, Kawaihae 96743, ☏ 808/882–7218), which tells the story of the three stone temples (one of them is submerged just offshore) built here by King Kamehameha's men in 1791.

What to See and Do with Children

The 65-ft ***Atlantis*** submarine offers a 50-minute underwater ride from Kailua-Kona's pier. Sign up at King Kamehameha's Kona Beach Hotel (75–5660 Palani Rd., ☏ 808/329–6626; $79 adults, $39 children under 13). **Puuhonua o Honaunau** (Hwy. 160, Honaunau, ☏ 808/328–2326; admission charged), about 14 mi south of Kailua-Kona, is a 180-acre national historical park offering demonstrations of Hawaiian crafts, games, and canoe making; the park includes tidal pools and a picnic area.

Shopping

In Hilo, **Prince Kuhio Shopping Plaza** (111 E. Puainako) offers specialty boutiques and larger stores. The upscale hotels of the **Kohala Coast** provide quality goods at high prices. In Waimea, **Parker Square** (Kawaihae Rd.) houses many shops and specialty boutiques, including the popular **Gallery of Great Things** (☎ 808/885–7706), which sells fine art and handicrafts.

Sports and the Outdoors

Camping and Hiking

Popular areas are the 13,796-ft **Mauna Kea,** in the northeast, and Hawaii Volcanoes National Park. For more information, contact the **Department of Parks and Recreation** (25 Aupuni St., Hilo 96740, ☎ 808/961–8311).

Fishing

More than 50 charter boats are available for hire, most of them out of Honokohau Harbor, just north of Kailua. For bookings call the **Kona Activities Center** (☎ 808/329–3171 or 800/367–5288).

Golf

On the Kohala Coast, the **Mauna Kea Beach Resort** (1 Mauna Kea Beach Dr., ☎ 808/882–7222) has an 18-hole course, and the **Francis I'i Brown Golf Course** (Mauna Lani Resort, ☎ 808/885–6655) is known for its two 18-hole courses.

Sailing/Snorkeling

Captain Zodiac Raft Expedition (Kailua, ☎ 808/329–3199) offers a four-hour snorkel cruise off the Kona coast.

Scuba Diving

The Kona coast has calm waters for diving. Outfitters include **Big Island Divers** (75–5467 Kaiwi St., Kailua-Kona 96740, ☎ 800/488–6068). Many Kohala Coast resorts, such as Waikoloa Resort, hold scuba-diving classes for guests.

Skiing

Skiing on 13,796-ft Mauna Kea is for experienced adventure skiers only; the best months are February and March. Currently the ski area has no lodge or lifts. **Ski Guides Hawaii** (Box 1954, Kamuela 96743, in ski season, ☎ 808/885–4188) furnishes transportation, guides, and equipment.

Beaches

Onekahakaha Beach Park, a protected white-sand beach 3 mi south of Hilo, is a favorite of local families. Close to Kailua-Kona, the most popular beach is **Kahaluu Beach Park,** where the swimming, snorkeling, and fine facilities attract weekend crowds. Currents can pull swimmers away from the beach when the surf is high. On the Kohala Coast, **Anaehoomalu Beach** (Royal Waikoloan Resort) is an expanse perfect for water sports. Equipment rentals and instructors are on call at the north end. The long white **Kauna'oa Beach** (Mauna Kea Beach Resort) is one of the most beautiful on the island. Beware, though, of the high surf that pounds the shore during winter months. Amenities here are hotel-owned. Between the Mauna Kea Beach and Mauna Lani resorts, **Hapuna State Recreation Area** is a ½-mi crescent of sand flanked by rocky points. The surf can be hazardous in winter, but calmer summer water makes it ideal for swimming, snorkeling, and scuba diving.

Dining and Lodging

With so many good restaurants on the scene, choosing a place to eat in the western part of the Big Island is difficult. The Kohala Coast is somewhat pricey, while Hilo dining has remained fairly inexpensive and family-oriented. The same theme is true of accommodations. The Kohala Coast costs more, while in Hilo there is only one expensive listing. You can find good deals on charming accommodations by contacting **Hawaii's Best Bed and Breakfasts** (Box 563, Kamuela 96743, ☎ 808/885–4550 or 800/262–9912). For price ranges, see Charts 1 (B) and 2 (B) in On the Road with Fodor's.

Hawaii Volcanoes National Park

DINING

★ **Ka Ohelo Room.** What makes this restaurant so special is its mountain-lodge setting at the edge of Kilauea Crater. Try the fresh catch of the day or the prime rib. *Volcano House,* ☎ *808/967–7321. AE, D, DC, MC, V. $*

Hilo

DINING

Sandalwood Room. This is Hilo's most elegant restaurant, with one side open to a stretch of lawn overlooking the coastline. The menu features local items such as fresh fish and Japanese-style grilled chicken. *Hawaii Naniloa Hotel, 93 Banyan Dr.,* ☎ *808/969–3333. AE, D, DC, MC. $$$*

★ **Pescatore's.** Lace curtains and a miniature waterfall provide a quaint backdrop to traditional Italian dishes such as eggplant parmigiana and seafood *fra diavolo* (shrimp, clams, and fresh fish in spicy marinara sauce). *235 Keawe St.,* ☎ *808/969–9090. DC, MC, V. $$*

Roussel's. This Cajun-Creole eatery has arched doorways, high ceilings, and 16 tables with cane-back chairs. Recommended are shrimp Creole, with a piquant tomato sauce, and trout Alexander, which combines a boneless fish fillet with lobster, shrimp, mushrooms, and sherry. *60 Keawe St.,* ☎ *808/935–5111. AE, DC, MC, V. No lunch weekends. $$*

LODGING

Hawaii Naniloa Hotel. Renovations in 1990 did wonders for this hotel, whose rooms are decorated in beige and rose. The 10- and 12-story towers are connected by a lobby to shops. *93 Banyan Dr., 96720,* ☎ *808/969–3333 or 800/367–5360,* FAX *808/969–6622. 325 rooms. Facilities: 3 restaurants, bar, health club, pool. AE, D, DC, MC, V. $$$*

Arnott's Lodge. This plain, tidy dwelling in a wilderness setting has dorm rooms for up to four people—semiprivate, double, and private rooms, and suites. It's best for active visitors who don't mind sharing a kitchen and a TV room. *98 Apapane Rd., 96720,* ☎ *808/969–7097 or 800/368–8752,* FAX *808/961–9638. 9 rooms. DC, MC, V. $*

Kailua-Kona

DINING

Jameson's by the Sea. Sit outside next to the ocean or just inside the picture windows for glorious sunset views over Magic Sands Beach. The co-owner and chef serves three or four island fish specials daily, plus a tasty baked shrimp stuffed with crab and garnished with hollandaise sauce. *77–6452 Alii Dr.,* ☎ *808/329–3195. AE, D, DC, MC, V. No lunch weekends. $$–$$$*

LODGING

★ **King Kamehameha's Kona Beach Hotel.** Though its rooms are not particularly special, this is the only centrally located Kailua-Kona hotel—right next to the pier—with a white-sand beach. There's a shopping mall in the lobby. *75–5660 Palani Rd., 96740,* ☎ *808/329–2911 or 800/367–2111,* FAX *808/329–4602. 460 rooms. Facilities: 2 restaurants, 2 lounges, pool, sauna, tennis courts, shops. AE, D, DC, MC, V. $$$*

Kona Islander Inn. Turn-of-the-century plantation-style architecture in a setting of palms and torchlit paths makes this older apartment hotel across the street from Waterfront Row a good value. *75–5776 Kuakini Hwy., 96740,* ☎ *808/329–3181 or 800/922–7866,* FAX *808/326–9339. 142 rooms. Facilities: pool. AE, DC, MC, V. $$*

Kohala Coast and Waimea

DINING

★ **Canoe House.** This open-air beachfront restaurant surrounded by fish ponds serves Pacific Rim cuisine, such as wok-fried sesame shrimp on crisp noodles with *lilikoi* (passion fruit) glaze and steamed mahimahi with ginger-scallion salsa and baby Chinese cabbage. *Mauna Lani Bay Hotel, 1 Mauna Lani Dr.,* ☎ *808/885–6622. Jacket advised. AE, D, DC, MC, V. $$$*

★ **Merriman's.** Peter Merriman earns rave reviews for his imaginative Hawaiian cuisine using fresh local ingredients, including vegetarian selections. Try opakapaka (an island fish) ravioli in orange-dill sauce, and tangy lilikoi mousse. *Opelo Plaza II, corner of Rte. 19 and Opelo Rd., Kamuela,* ☎ *808/885–6822. AE, MC, V. $$*

LODGING

★ **Kona Village Resort.** Accommodations at this resort in Kaupulehu-Kona are in thatched-roof huts by the sea or around fish ponds. The extra-large rooms have no telephones, TVs, or radios but do come with ceiling fans and bright tropical prints. *Box 1299, Kailua-Kona, 96745,* ☎ *808/325–5555 or 800/367–5290,* FAX *808/325–5124. 125 units. Facilities: 2 restaurants, 2 bars, 2 pools, 2 hot tubs, beach, shops. AE, D, DC, MC, V. Closed 1 wk in Dec. $$$*

Ritz-Carlton, Mauna Lani. On 32 acres of secluded beachfront property, this branch of the famous chain has an island flavoring. Rooms are furnished warmly, with marble-top side tables and massive wooden highboys with elaborate carvings. Along with the top-drawer amenities are a host of recreational facilities, on both land and sea. The tennis setup here may just be the best on the island. *1 N. Kaniku Dr., Kohala Coast 96743,* ☎ *808/885–2000 or 800/845–9905,* FAX *808/885–5778. 596 rooms. Facilities: pool, 11 tennis courts, 2 golf courses, health club, sauna. AE, D, DC, MC, V. $$$*

Waimea Country Lodge. In the cool upcountry, the lodge has rustic rooms that look out on green pastures. All units have heaters and some have kitchenettes. The lodge has no restaurant, but a number of good Waimea establishments are nearby. *Box 2559, Kamuela 96743,* ☎ *808/885–4100,* FAX *808/885–6711. 21 rooms. AE, MC, V. $$*

Nightlife

The hottest place on the island is the **Second Floor,** a disco at the Hilton Waikoloa Village (425 Waikoloa Beach Dr., Kamuela 96743, ☎ 808/885–1234). In Hilo, **d'Angora's** (101 Apuni St., ☎ 808/934–7888) offers dancing to disco music. Luaus and Polynesian revues are especially popular on the island's west side. **Kona Village Resort** (☎ 808/325–5555) offers the most authentic island entertainment.

MAUI

Maui is known internationally for its perfect beaches, heady nightlife, and sophisticated resorts. The island offers a range of experiences, from the sun, fun, and nightlife of the West Maui "Gold Coast" to the laid-back lifestyle of Hana to the east. Maui also has outstanding restaurants and lavish landscapes, all of which are presided over by a 10,023-ft dormant volcano named Haleakala, where you can see a sunrise like none other on earth.

Tourist Information

Maui Visitors Bureau (1727 Wili Pa Loop, Wailuku 96793, ☎ 808/244–3530).

Getting There

Maui's major airport, **Kahului Airport** (☎ 808/872–3800 or 808/872–3830), at the center of the island, is served by United, American, Delta, Hawaiian Airlines, and IslandAir. If you're staying in West Maui, you might be better off flying into **Kapalua–West Maui Airport** (☎ 808/669–0228), served by Aloha IslandAir. At press time, upstart Mahalo Airlines was planning to begin Honolulu–Kapalua service in 1995, filling the gap left by Hawaiian Airlines, which abandoned its West Maui routes in 1994. The landing strip at **Hana Airport** (☎ 808/248–8208) is served by Aloha IslandAir.

Exploring Maui

West Maui

The road that follows the island's northwest coast passes through the beach towns of **Napili, Kahana,** and **Honokowai,** all packed with condos and a few restaurants. South of these is **Lahaina,** former capital of the islands and a 19th-century whaling town. On the ocean side of **Front Street,** where many old buildings have been renovated, is a **banyan tree** planted in 1873 and the largest of its kind in Hawaii. Docked nearby at Lahaina Harbor is the brig ***Carthaginian II*** (☎ 808/661–3262), built in Germany in the 1920s and now open as a museum. Also worth a visit is the **Baldwin Home** (696 Front St., ☎ 808/661–3262; admission charged), where missionary doctor Dwight Baldwin dwelled beginning in 1836. The **Seamen's Hospital** (1024 Front St., ☎ 808/661–3262) was built in the 1830s as a royal party house for King Kamehameha III and later turned into a hospital.

Central Maui

Kahului is an industrial and commercial town that most tourists pass through on their way to and from the airport. Get on its main street, Kaahumanu Avenue (Hwy. 32), and take a right on Puunene Avenue (Hwy. 350). On the right is the **Alexander & Baldwin Sugar Museum,** which details the rise of sugarcane on the islands. *3957 Hansen Rd., Puunene, ☎ 808/871–8058. Admission charged. Closed Sun.*

Back on Kaahumanu Avenue, follow signs toward **Wailuku** and take a right on Kahului Beach Road. Continue on the beach road until you reach Kanaloa Avenue, make a left, and soon you'll find **Maui Zoological and Botanical Gardens** (☎ 808/243–7337), with a small children's zoo and native Hawaiian gardens. Follow Kaahumanu Avenue to **Wailuku's Historical District,** much of which is on the National Register of Historic Places. A right on Market Street off Main Street takes you to the **Iao Theater** (68 N. Market St., ☎ 808/242–6969), dating

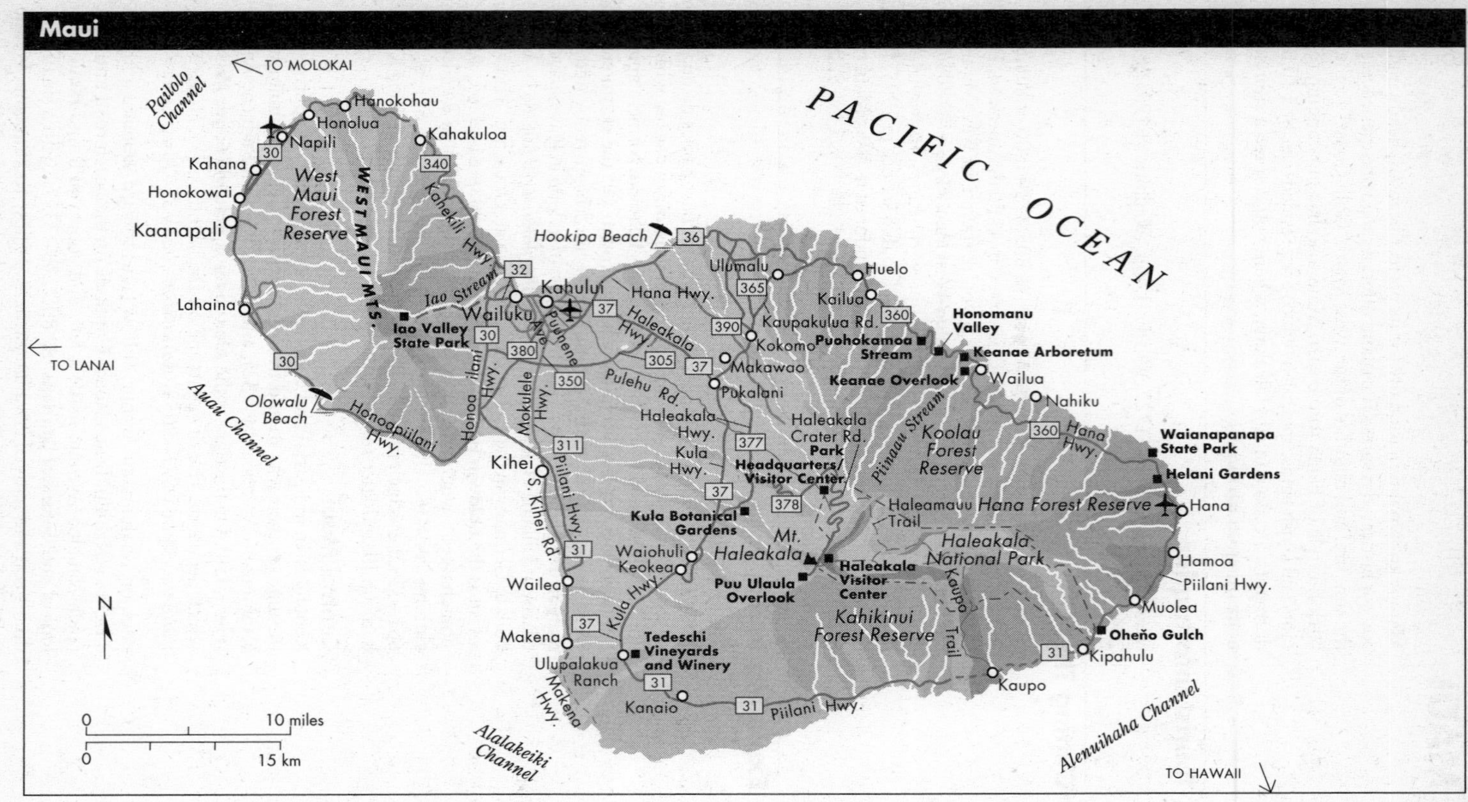
Maui
PACIFIC OCEAN
TO MOLOKAI
Pailolo Channel
Hanokohau
Honolua
Napili
Kahakuloa
Kahana
Honokowai
Kaanapali
Lahaina
West Maui Forest Reserve
WEST MAUI MTS.
Kahekili Hwy.
Iao Stream
Iao Valley State Park
Wailuku
Kahului
Puunene
Hookipa Beach
Hana Hwy.
Haleakala Hwy.
Ulumalu
Huelo
Kailua
Kaupakulua Rd.
Kokomo
Makawao
Pukalani
Pulehu Rd.
Honomanu Valley
Puohokamoa Stream
Keanae Arboretum
Keanae Overlook
Wailua
Nahiku
Piinaau Stream
Koolau Forest Reserve
Haleakala Crater Rd.
Park Headquarters/ Visitor Center
Haleakala Hwy.
Kula Hwy.
Kula Botanical Gardens
Mt. Haleakala
Haleakala Visitor Center
Puu Ulaula Overlook
Haleamauu Trail
Hana Forest Reserve
Haleakala National Park
Kaupo Trail
Kahikinui Forest Reserve
Waianapanapa State Park
Helani Gardens
Hana
Hamoa
Piilani Hwy.
Muolea
Oheño Gulch
Kipahulu
Kaupo
Waiohuli
Keokea
Tedeschi Vineyards and Winery
Ulupalakua Ranch
Kanaio
Makena
Makena Hwy.
Wailea
Kihei
S. Kihei Rd.
Piilani Hwy.
Mokulele Hwy.
Honoa piilani Hwy.
Honoapiilani Hwy.
Olowalu Beach
Auau Channel
TO LANAI
Alalakeiki Channel
Alenuihaha Channel
TO HAWAII
N
0 10 miles
0 15 km
30
340
32
30
380
37
305
350
36
365
390
360
37
377
311
37
378
31
31
37
31
31
360

from 1927. Follow Main Street toward the mountains to reach **Iao Valley State Park,** home of **Iao Needle,** a 1,200-ft rock spire rising from the valley floor.

Haleakala and Upcountry

The western slopes leading up **Mt. Haleakala,** called Upcountry, encompass the fertile land responsible for much of Hawaii's produce and flowers. Starting in Kahului, drive on Haleakala Highway (Hwy. 37) toward Haleakala. At the fork, veer to the left on Hwy. 377. After about 6 mi, make a left onto Haleakala Crater Road. The switchback ascent begins here. At 7,000 ft is **Haleakala National Park Headquarters,** with a gift shop and rest rooms. ☎ *808/572–9306. Park admission charged.*

At **Haleakala Visitor Center,** at about 9,800 ft, a ranger gives lectures on Haleakala geology each afternoon. The road ends at **Puu Ulaula Overlook,** where you'll find a glass-enclosed lookout with a 360-degree view from the summit. Sunrise begins between 5:45 and 7, depending on the time of year. On a clear day you can see the islands of Molokai, Lanai, Kahoolawe, and Hawaii.

Heading down on Hwy. 377, you'll see **Kula Botanical Gardens** (Upper Kula Rd., ☎ 808/878–1715; admission charged), home of bountiful flora. When you join up with Hwy. 37, follow it about 8 mi to **Tedeschi Vineyards and Winery** (Ulupalakua Ranch, Haleakala Hwy., ☎ 808/878–6058) and sample Hawaii's only homegrown wines.

East Maui

The road to Hana is 55 mi of hairpin turns and spectacular scenery. It begins in **Paia** on the north coast and passes **Hookipa Beach,** popular with windsurfers. At mile marker 11, stop at the bridge over **Puohokamoa Stream,** where there are pools, waterfalls, and picnic tables. Another mile takes you to **Kaumahina State Wayside Park,** which also has a picnic area and a lovely overlook to the Keanae Peninsula.

Past **Honomanu Valley,** with its 3,000-ft cliffs and a 1,000-ft waterfall, is the **Keanae Arboretum,** devoted to native plants and trees. Here you can stop and take a fairly rigorous hike. Near mile marker 17 is the **Keanae Overlook,** with views of taro farms and the ocean; it's an excellent spot for photos. As you continue on toward Hana, you'll pass **Waianapanapa State Park** (☎ 808/248–8061), with state-run cabins and picnic areas. Closer to Hana is **Helani Gardens** (☎ 808/248–8274; admission charged), a 60-acre enclave of tropical plants and flowers, such as ginger and bird of paradise, grown by Hana native Howard Cooper.

The small town of **Hana** is just minutes from Helani Gardens. On the hill above town is a cross erected in memory of rancher Paul Fagan, who built the Hotel Hana-Maui and stocked the surrounding pasture with cattle. Once past Hana, the next 10 mi of road are rutted, rocky, and twisting, but a view of the pools at **Ohe'o Gulch** makes the drive worth it.

Shopping

You can have fun browsing through the stores of Front Street in Lahaina or the boutiques in the major hotels. Maui also has several major shopping malls. **Kaahumanu Center** (275 Kaahumanu Ave., Kahului) has nearly 100 shops and restaurants, including Liberty House and the Japanese retailer Shirokiya. Also in Kahului is the **Maui Mall Shopping Center** (corner of Kaahumanu and Puunene Aves.), with 33 stores. The **Lahaina Cannery Shopping Center** (1221 Honoapiilani Hwy., Lahaina), resembling an old pineapple cannery, has some 50 shops, including Dolphin Galleries, which offers sculpture, paintings, and other Maui artwork.

Sports and the Outdoors

Fishing

You can fish year-round here for such catch as tuna, bonefish, Pacific blue marlin, and wahoo. Plenty of fishing boats run out of Lahaina and Maalaea harbors, including ***Finest Kind*** (Lahaina Harbor, Slip 7, ☎ 808/661–0338).

Golf

Kapalua Golf Club (300 Kapalua Dr., Lahaina, ☎ 808/669–8044) has three 18-hole golf courses. The **Wailea Golf Club** (120 Kaukahi St., Wailea, ☎ 808/875–5111) also has three courses.

Sailing

Most companies combine their sailing tours with a meal, snorkeling, or whale watching. Try **Genesis Charters** (Lahaina, ☎ 808/667–5667).

Snorkeling and Scuba Diving

Lahaina has numerous dive shops—including **Dive Maui** (Lahaina Market Place, ☎ 808/667–2080)—which rent equipment and offer diving trips and lessons. Many dive companies offer snorkeling tours as well; the **Ocean Activities Center** (1325 S. Kihei Rd., Kihei, ☎ 808/879–4485) offers an enjoyable trip to the nearby island of Molokini.

Tennis

The finest facilities are at the **Wailea Tennis Club** (131 Wailea Ike Pl., Kihei, ☎ 808/879–1958), often called "Wimbledon West" because of its grass courts.

Windsurfing

Hookipa Bay, 10 mi east of Kahului, is the windsurfing capital of the world. Rent a board or get lessons from **Kaanapali Windsurfing School** (104 Wahikuli Rd., Lahaina, ☎ 808/667–1964).

Beaches

If you start at the northern end of West Maui and work your way down the coast, you'll find the following beaches: **D. T. Fleming Beach,** 1 mi north of Kapalua, is a sandy cove better for sunbathing than swimming in its strong current. **Napili Beach,** a secluded crescent, is right outside the Napili Kai Beach Club. **Kaanapali Beach** is best for people-watching and plenty of action; cruises, windsurfers, and parasails launch from here. Farther south are **Wailea's** five crescent beaches, which stretch for nearly 2 mi with little interruption. South of Wailea are **Big Beach,** a 3,000-ft-long, 100-ft-wide strand, and **Little Beach,** popular for nude sunbathing (officially illegal here).

Dining and Lodging

Maui cuisine consists of more than the poi and pineapple you'll find at a local luau. The island attracts fine chefs who combine unique Hawaiian produce with classic preparations. Some of the best restaurants are in hotels. The island has a large number of luxury hotels and condominiums. West Maui is the center of tourism, while central Maui's choices are limited; East Maui is a mixed bag of rates and comfort. For B&B accommodations contact **Bed & Breakfast Maui-Style** (Box 98, Kihei 96784, ☎ 808/879–7865 or 800/848–5567). For price ranges, see Charts 1 (B) and 2 (B) in On the Road with Fodor's.

East Maui

DINING

Haliimaile General Store. It was a camp store in the 1920s, and now its white, green, and peach tin exterior looks a little out of place in an Upcountry pineapple field. This charmer serves a fine smoked duck with pineapple chutney and dynamite barbecued ribs. *900 Haliimaile Rd., ☎ 808/572–2666. MC, V. $$$*

Casanova Italian Restaurant & Deli. This Upcountry establishment with contemporary decor serves nouvelle Italian food. Try a wood-fired pizza *vulcano,* with grilled eggplant and smoked mozzarella. *1188 Makawao Ave., Makawao, ☎ 808/572–0220. AE, D, MC, V. $$*

★ **Polli's.** Stop by this Upcountry Mexican cantina for tacos, burritos, and enchiladas (vegetarian versions, too). *1202 Makawao Ave., Makawao, ☎ 808/572–7808. AE, MC, V. $*

LODGING

★ **Four Seasons Resort.** Low-key elegance defines this stunning property with refined, open-air public areas and access to one of Maui's best beaches. Nearly all of the rooms have an ocean view and feature elegant marble bathrooms with high ceilings. *3900 Wailea Alanui, Wailea 96753, ☎ 808/874–8000 or 800/334–6284, FAX 808/874–2222. 380 rooms. Facilities: 3 restaurants, bars, pool, tennis courts, golf course, health club, shops. AE, D, DC, MC, V. $$$*

★ **Hotel Hana-Maui.** Surrounded by lush ranch lands, the hotel's buildings have white plaster walls and trellised verandas. Rooms feature bleached-wood floors, overstuffed furniture in natural fabrics, and local art. *Box 9, Hana 96713, ☎ 808/248–8211 or 800/321–4262, FAX 808/248–7264. 96 rooms. Facilities: restaurant, bar, pool, spa, tennis courts, shops. AE, D, DC, MC, V. $$$*

Hana Kai-Maui. This small condominium is the only true beachfront property in Hana. The large, simply furnished units are set on manicured grounds that include a spring-fed swimming pool on one side of the property. *Box 38, Hana 96713, ☎ 808/248–8426 or 800/346–2772, FAX 808/248–7482. 20 units. AE, MC, V. $$*

Aloha Cottages. Two-bedroom units and one studio are sparsely furnished but clean and equipped with kitchens. A special touch is the view of papaya, banana, and avocado trees on the neighboring property. *Hana 96713, ☎ 808/248–8420. 4 cottages. No credit cards. $*

West Maui

DINING

★ **Avalon.** This open-air restaurant combines ethnic influences to create an eclectic cuisine that features such dishes as giant prawns in garlic-and-black-bean sauce. The only dessert, caramel Miranda, is made of fruit and caramel sauce. *Mariner's Alley, 844 Front St., Lahaina, ☎ 808/667–5559. AE, DC, MC, V. $$$*

★ **Gerard's.** This romantic, Victorian-style, indoor-outdoor restaurant is the creation of Gerard Reversade, who serves French dishes, mostly, although the ravioli topped with veal shank is not to be missed. This place has a comfortable ambience, great food, and plenty of stargazing possibilities—it's a celebrity favorite. *Plantation Inn, 174 Lahainaluna Rd., Lahaina, ☎ 808/661–8939. AE, D, DC, MC, V. No lunch. $$$*

Lahaina Coolers. This surf bistro serves unusual dishes, such as Evil Jungle Pasta (chicken and linguine with peanut sauce) and spinach-and-feta quesadilla. *180 Dickenson St., Lahaina, ☎ 808/661–7082. AE, MC, V. $*

LODGING

★ **Kapalua Bay Hotel.** Isolated from the other hotels of West Maui, Kapalua has a California ambience, with exteriors of white and natural wood. The orchid-filled open lobby has a fine view of the ocean, and the rooms are spacious. *1 Bay Dr., Kapalua 96761, ☎ 808/669–5656 or 800/367–8000, FAX 808/669–4694. 194 rooms, 135 condo units. Facilities: 4 restaurants, bars, pool, golf course, tennis courts, shops. AE, D, DC, MC, V. $$$*

★ **Plantation Inn.** This is the kind of place you won't find anywhere else; resembling a renovated Victorian home, the inn is centrally located on a quiet country street in the heart of Lahaina. Its European charm is expressed in wood floors, stained glass, ceiling fans, and brass beds. Downstairs is one of Hawaii's best French restaurants, Gerard's. *174 Lahainaluna Rd., Lahaina 96761, ☎ 808/667–9225 or 800/433–6815, FAX 808/667–9293. 18 rooms. Facilities: restaurant, pool. AE, MC, V. $$*

Pioneer Inn. This plain hostelry retains a flavor of old Lahaina. Downstairs is a boisterous saloon. Rooms in the older section are small and rather dim, with ceiling fans and no air-conditioning—but lots of history; ask about the Spencer Tracy–Katherine Hepburn suite in the newer wing, which is brighter and quieter, with air-conditioning. *658 Wharf St., Lahaina 96761, ☎ 808/661–3636 or 800/457–5457, FAX 808/667–5708. 48 rooms. Facilities: restaurant, bar, shops. AE, DC, MC, V. $*

Nightlife

The best options are in resort areas. **Moose McGillycuddy's** (844 Front St., Lahaina, ☎ 808/667–7758) offers live music Wednesday, Friday, and Saturday night. **Molokini Lounge** (Maui Prince Hotel, Makena Resort, ☎ 808/874–1111) is a pleasant bar with live Hawaiian music and an ocean view. The best luau on Maui is the small, personal, and authentic **Old Lahaina Luau** (505 Front St., Lahaina, ☎ 808/667–1998), which takes place Monday–Saturday 5:30–8:30.

KAUAI

Most of the hotels and attractions that closed due to damage suffered in the wake of Hurricane Iniki in 1992 have reopened, and nature has been busy—and quite effective—repairing and replenishing the island's lush landscape.

Tourist Information

Hawaii Visitors Bureau (3016 Umi St., Suite 207, Lihue 96766, ☎ 808/245–3971) and the **Kauai Visitor Center** (Coconut Plantation Market Place, Waipouli, ☎ 808/822–5113; Kauai Village, Kapaa, ☎ 808/822–7727) are good sources of information.

Getting There

Lihue Airport (☎ 808/246–1400) handles most of Kauai's air traffic; 3 mi east of the county seat of Lihue, it is served by Aloha, Hawaiian, and Mahalo. IslandAir flies to **Princeville Airport** (☎ 808/826–3040), a tiny strip to the north.

Exploring Kauai

A coastal road runs around the rim of Kauai and dead-ends on either side of the rugged 15-mi coast called Na Pali ("the cliffs"). If you're looking for sunshine, head to the southern resort of Poipu; for greener scenery and a wetter climate, try Hanalei and Princeville to the north.

The Road North

From **Wailua Marina** on the east coast, boats depart for **Fern Grotto,** a yawning lava tube with enormous ferns and an 80-ft waterfall. *Smith's Motor Boat Service, 174 Wailua Rd., Kapaa, ☎ 808/822–4111. Admission charged.*

North of here on Hwy. 56 is the former plantation town of **Kilauea.** The **Kilauea Lighthouse** (☎ 808/828–1413), built in 1913, is now part of a wildlife refuge. The **Hanalei Valley Overlook** provides a panorama of more than ½ mi of taro, the staple plant of the Hawaiian diet, plus a 900-acre endangered-waterfowl refuge. **Hanalei** is the site of the **Waioli Mission** (Kuhio Hwy., ☎ 808/245–3202), founded by Christian missionaries in 1837.

To the South and West

In the southern town of **Lihue,** visit the **Kauai Museum** (4428 Rice St., ☎ 808/245–6931; admission charged) to learn about the island's history. Nearby **Kilohana** (3–2087 Kaumualii Hwy., ☎ 808/245–5608), a historic sugar-plantation house dating from 1935, is now a 35-acre visitor attraction with agricultural exhibits, local arts-and-crafts displays, and more. Farther south, Poipu Road (Hwy. 52) runs through the sunny resort of **Poipu** to **Spouting Horn,** a waterspout that shoots up through an ancient lava tube like Old Faithful.

Head west to the sleepy town of **Waimea,** which first welcomed British captain James Cook to the Sandwich Islands in 1778. Drive mauka (toward the mountains) on Waimea Canyon Drive, which makes a steep climb past the spectacular panoramas of **Waimea Canyon.** Created by an ancient fault in the Earth's crust, the canyon measures 3,600 ft deep, 2 mi wide, and 10 mi long. At 4,000 ft the road passes through **Kokee State Park** (☎ 808/335–5871), a 4,345-acre wilderness. The road ends 4 mi above the park at the **Kalalau Lookout.** At 4,120 ft above sea level, it offers the best views on Kauai.

What to See and Do with Children

Smith's Tropical Paradise (174 Wailua Rd., Kapaa, ☎ 808/822–4654; admission charged) is 30 acres of jungle, exotic foliage, tropical birds, and lagoons.

Shopping

In Lihue is **Kukui Grove Center** (3–2600 Kaumualii Hwy.), Kauai's largest mall. East-coast malls are highlighted by **Coconut Plantation Marketplace** (4–484 Kuhio Hwy., Kapaa). **Kauai Village** (4–831 Kuhio Hwy., Kapaa) has 19th-century plantation-style architecture and 25 shops. To the north, **Princeville Center** (5–4280 Kuhio Hwy., Kapaa) has interesting shops, such as Kauai Kite and Hobby Shop.

Sports and the Outdoors

Fishing

For deep-sea fishing, **Sportfishing Kauai** (Koloa, ☎ 808/742–7013) has a 28-ft, six-passenger custom sportfisher.

Golf

Best known are the Makai and Prince courses at **Princeville Resort** (Princeville, ☎ 808/826–3580).

Hiking

Kokee State Park has 45 mi of hiking trails. The **Department of Land and Natural Resources** (Lihue, ☎ 808/241–3444) provides hiking information.

Snorkeling and Scuba Diving

Explore spectacular underwater reefs with **Dive Kauai** (4–976 Kuhio Hwy., Suite 4, Kapaa, ☎ 808/822–0452). **Hanalei Sea Tours** (Box 1437, Hanalei, ☎ 808/826–7254) has a four-hour snorkeling cruise off the Na Pali coast.

Tennis

Princeville Tennis Center (Box 3040, Princeville 96722, ☎ 808/826–9823) has six courts.

Beaches

The waters that hug Kauai are clean, clear, and inviting, but be careful where you go in: The south shore sees higher surf in the summer, while north-shore waters are treacherous in winter.

North Shore

On the winding section of Hwy. 56 west of Hanalei is **Lumahai Beach,** flanked by high mountains and lava rocks. There are no lifeguards here, so swim only in summer. **Hanalei Beach Park** offers views of the Na Pali coast and shaded picnic tables, but swimming here can be treacherous. Near the end of Hwy. 56, **Haena State Park** is good for swimming when the surf is down in summer. Hwy. 56 dead-ends at **Ke'e Beach,** a fine swimming beach in summer.

South and West Shores

Kalapaki Beach, a sheltered bay ideal for water sports, fronts the Marriott. Small to medium-size waves make **Brennecke's Beach** in Poipu a bodysurfer's heaven, and there are showers, rest rooms, and lifeguards. At the end of Hwy. 50W is **Polihale Beach Park,** a long, wide strand flanked by huge cliffs. Swim here only when the surf is small; there are no lifeguards.

Dining and Lodging

On Kauai you can enjoy almost any style of cuisine. Kauai's accommodations range from swanky resorts to bare-bones cabins. For an insider's look at Kauai, book with **Bed & Breakfast Hawaii** (Box 449, Kapaa 96746, ☎ 808/822–7771 or 800/733–1632). For price ranges, see Charts 1 (B) and 2 (B) in On the Road with Fodor's.

East and North Kauai

DINING

La Cascata. Terra-cotta floors and trompe l'oeil paintings give the restaurant the feel of an Italian villa. The tastes of southern Italy are showcased in the grilled Hawaiian swordfish with balsamic vinegar and pancetta. Top it off with a warm sour-cherry tart with vanilla ice cream. *Princeville Hotel, Princeville, ☎ 808/826–2761. Reservations required. Jacket advised. AE, D, DC, MC, V. No lunch. $$$*

★ **A Pacific Cafe.** In this stylishly intimate restaurant, Asian cooking combines with homegrown ingredients. Try the Hawaiian swordfish—with an arugula-pesto crust and wild oyster, mushroom, and scallop sauce—or lamb with a cabernet-hoisin sauce. *Kauai Village Shopping Center, 4–831 Kuhio Hwy., Kapaa,* ☎ *808/822–0013. AE, D, MC, V. No lunch. $$$*

★ **Casa di Amici.** Dine on the porch of this "House of Friends" and choose your own combination of pasta with such sauces as pesto or *salsa di noci* (walnut-cream sauce with Romano cheese and marjoram). *2484 Keneke St. at Lighthouse Rd., Kilauea,* ☎ *808/828–1388. AE, DC, MC, V. No lunch. $$*

Bull Shed. This A-frame restaurant is rustic, with exposed wood, ocean views, and family-style tables. Menu highlights include Alaskan king crab and prime rib. *796 Kuhio Ave., Waipouli,* ☎ *808/822–1655. AE, MC, V. No lunch. $*

LODGING

★ **Princeville Hotel.** This splendid cliff-side property has breathtaking views of Hanalei Bay. Bathrooms have gold-plated fixtures and picture windows that cloud up for privacy at the flick of a switch. *Box 3069, Princeville 96722,* ☎ *808/826–9644 or 800/325–3535,* FAX *808/826–1166. 252 rooms. Facilities: 3 restaurants, 3 lounges, pool, tennis courts, golf course, cinema, shops. AE, D, DC, MC, V. $$$*

Kapaa Sands. Furnishings in this intimate condominium are bungalow style, with rustic wood and ceiling fans. Ask for an oceanfront room with open-air lanai and Pacific views. *380 Papaloa Rd., Kapaa 96746,* ☎ *808/822–4901 or 800/222–4901. 21 units. Facilities: pool. AE, DC, MC, V. $$*

South and West Kauai

DINING

Brennecke's Beach Broiler. At this veteran restaurant with picture windows overlooking the ocean, the chef specializes in mesquite-broiled foods and homemade desserts. *Ho'one Rd., Poipu,* ☎ *808/742–7588. MC, V. $$*

Camp House Grill. Down-home food in a down-home setting is what you'll get at this restaurant on the road to Waimea Canyon: burgers, chicken, ribs, fish, and a host of barbecue specialties. *Kaumualii Hwy. (Hwy. 50), Kalaheo,* ☎ *808/332–9755. MC, V. $*

★ **Green Garden.** In business since 1948, this family-run, no-frills restaurant is brightened by an assortment of hanging and standing plants. Local fare includes breaded mahimahi fillet and passion-fruit chiffon pie. *Hwy. 50, Hanapepe,* ☎ *808/335–5422. AE, DC, MC, V. No dinner Tues. $*

LODGING

★ **Hyatt Regency Kauai.** Low-rise architecture, extensive gardens, and open-air courtyards make this the most Hawaiian Hyatt. Rooms have bamboo and wicker furnishings; two-thirds of the rooms have ocean views. *1571 Poipu Rd., Koloa 96756,* ☎ *808/742–1234;* FAX *808/742–1557. 600 rooms. Facilities: 3 restaurants, 2 lounges, nightclub, 3 pools, health club, 4 tennis courts, golf course, shops. AE, D, DC, MC, V. $$$*

★ **Kauai Marriott Resort.** Formerly the Westin Kauai, this oceanfront property underwent major reconstruction following Hurricane Iniki. The main lobby features an elaborate tropical garden, and the large rooms are decorated in a relaxed, Hawaiian style. *Kalapaki Beach, Lihue 96766,* ☎ *808/245–5050,* FAX *808/245–5049. 355 rooms, 220 1- and 2-bedroom villas. Facilities: restaurants, bars, pools, hot tubs, health club, golf course, tennis courts. AE, DC, MC, V. $$$*

★ **Kokee Lodge.** Twelve mountaintop cabins are surrounded by pine trees and hiking trails. Furnishings are rustic (prices vary according to quality), but each is cozy, with a fireplace and a fully equipped kitchen. *Box 819, Waimea 96796, ☎ 808/335–6061. 12 cabins. Facilities: restaurant, shop. AE, DC, MC, V. $*

Nightlife

Locals enjoy **Kuhio's Nightclub** (Hyatt Regency Kauai, ☎ 808/742–1234), a south shore hot spot. **Legends Nightclub** (Pacific Ocean Plaza, 3501 Rice St., 2nd floor, Nawiliwili, ☎ 808/245–5775) delivers Top 40 tunes in a garden setting. Of Kauai's luaus, **Kauai Coconut Beach Resort Luau** (Coconut Plantation, Kapaa, ☎ 808/822–3455, ext. 651) is regarded by many as the best on the island.

ELSEWHERE IN THE STATE

Molokai

Getting There

Hoolehua Airport (☎ 808/567–6140), a tiny strip just west of central Molokai, is served by Hawaiian Airlines, IslandAir, and Air Molokai.

What to See and Do

With its slow pace and emphasis on Hawaiiana, Molokai drowses in another era. There are no high-rises, no traffic jams, and no stoplights on the 10- by 38-mi island. The fanciest hotels are bungalow style, and there's plenty of undeveloped countryside.

Among interesting sights here are the **Meyer Sugar Mill** (☎ 808/567–6436; admission charged), built in 1878 and reconstructed to teach visitors about sugar's local importance, and **Purdy's Natural Macadamia Nut Farm** (☎ 808/567–6601), a family business where you can learn all about the delectable nuts.

Rustic activities are popular on the island. **Damien Tours** (☎ 808/567–6171) will lead you on a fascinating tour of **Kalaupapa National Historic Park** (Box 222, Molokai 96742, ☎ 808/567–6102). This pretty town, a leper's colony until 1888, is now a National Historic Landmark. The **Molokai Ranch Wildlife Safari** (☎ 808/552–2773) is a tour through a 1,000-acre preserve, home to such animals as the oryx and the eland.

Down Kaluakoi Road, 2 mi beyond Kaluakoi Resort, is **Papohaku Beach,** a 3-mi strip of white-sand glory wide enough for relaxing in privacy.

For more information, including advice on accommodations, contact **Molokai Visitors Association** (Box 960, Kaunakakai 96748, ☎ 808/553–3876 or 800/800–6367) or **Maui Visitors Bureau** (Box 580, Wailuku, Maui 96793, ☎ 808/244–3530).

Lanai

Getting There

Hawaiian Airlines and IslandAir serve this tiny island, whose airport (☎ 808/565–6757) is a 10-minute drive from Lanai City.

What to See and Do

Known for decades as the Pineapple Island after Jim Dole bought it in 1922, Lanai has been renamed Hawaii's Private Island by developer David Murdock, who owns nearly all of its 140 sq mi. Lanai City, the only town on the island, has an 11-room hotel; visitors can also try one of Murdock's two new lavish resorts, geared to upscale guests, or opt for a house rental or B&B experience.

Lanai is for those who are happy to spend a lot of time outdoors, because the island has no commercial attractions other than those offered at the two resorts. Instead, you can visit such sights as the **Garden of the Gods,** where rocks and boulders are scattered across a crimson landscape; spend a leisurely day at **Hulopoe Beach,** where the waters are so clear that you can see fish in hues of turquoise and jade; hike or drive to the top of **Lanaihale,** a 3,370-ft perch from which you can see every inhabited Hawaiian island except Kauai and Niihau; or golf at **Experience at Koele Golf Course** (☎ 808/565–7300). For more information, contact **Destination Lanai** (Box 700, Lanai City 96763, ☎ 808/565–7600).

APPENDIX

STATE-NAME ABBREVIATIONS

The following abbreviations are used for names of states in the United States:

Alabama AL	Nebraska NE
Alaska AK	Nevada NV
Arizona AZ	New Hampshire NH
Arkansas AR	New Jersey NJ
California CA	New Mexico NM
Colorado CO	New York NY
Connecticut CT	North Carolina NC
Delaware DE	North Dakota ND
Florida FL	Ohio OH
Georgia GA	Oklahoma OK
Hawaii HI	Oregon OR
Idaho ID	Pennsylvania PA
Illinois IL	Rhode Island RI
Indiana IN	South Carolina SC
Iowa IA	South Dakota SD
Kansas KS	Tennessee TN
Kentucky KY	Texas TX
Louisiana LA	Utah UT
Maine ME	Vermont VT
Maryland MD	Virgina VA
Massachusetts MA	Washington WA
Michigan MI	West Virginia WV
Minnesota MN	Wisconsin WI
Mississippi MS	Wyoming WY
Missouri MO	District of Columbia D.C.
Montana MT	

TOLL-FREE NUMBERS

Airlines

Air Canada (☎ 800/776–3000)
Alaska (☎ 800/426–0333)
Aloha (☎ 800/367–5250)
American (☎ 800/433–7300)
America West (☎ 800/235–9292)
British Airways (☎ 800/247–9297)
Canadian (☎ 800/426–7000)
Continental (☎ 800/525–0280)
Delta (☎ 800/221–1212)
Hawaiian (☎ 800/367–5320)
IslandAir (☎ 800/323–3345)
MarkAir (☎ 800/627–5247)
Mesa (☎ 800/637–2247)
Northwest (☎ 800/225–2525)
SkyWest (☎ 800/453–9417)
Southwest (☎ 800/435–9792)
TWA (☎ 800/221–2000)
United (☎ 800/241–6522)
USAir (☎ 800/428–4322)

Trains

Amtrak (☎ 800/872–7245)

Buses

Greyhound (☏ 800/231–2222)

Car Rentals

Alamo (☏ 800/327–9633)
Avis (☏ 800/331–1212)
Budget (☏ 800/527–0700)
Courtesy (☏ 800/252–9756)
Dollar (☏ 800/800–4000)
Enterprise (☏ 800/325–8007)
Hertz (☏ 800/654–3131)
National (☏ 800/328–4567)
Rent-A-Wreck (☏ 800/522–5436)
Sears (☏ 800/527–0770)
Thrifty (☏ 800/367–2277)
Ugly Duckling (☏ 800/843–3825)

Hotels

Adam's Mark (☏ 800/444–2326)
Best Western (☏ 800/528–1234)
Clarion (☏ 800/252–7466)
Colony (☏ 800/777–1700)
Comfort (☏ 800/228–5150)
Days Inn (☏ 800/325–2525)
Doubletree (☏ 800/528–0444)
Embassy Suites (☏ 800/362–2779)
Fairfield Inn (☏ 800/228–2800)
Forte (☏ 800/225–5843)
Four Seasons (☏ 800/332–3442)
Guest Quarters Suites (☏ 800/424–2900)
Hilton (☏ 800/445–8667)
Holiday Inn (☏ 800/465–4329)
Howard Johnson (☏ 800/654–4656)
Hyatt & Resorts (☏ 800/233–1234)
Inter-Continental (☏ 800/327–0200)
La Quinta (☏ 800/531–5900)
Marriott (☏ 800/228–9290)
Meridien (☏ 800/543–4300)
Nikko International (☏ 800/645–5687)
Omni (☏ 800/843–6664)
Quality Inn (☏ 800/228–5151)
Radisson (☏ 800/333–3333)
Ramada (☏ 800/228–2828)
Red Lion (☏ 800/547–8010)
Ritz-Carlton (☏ 800/241–3333)
Sheraton (☏ 800/325–3535)
Sleep Inn (☏ 800/221–2222)
Stouffer (☏ 800/468–3571)
Westin Hotels & Resorts (☏ 800/228–3000)
Wyndham Hotels & Resorts (☏ 800/822–4200)

Motels

Budget Hosts Inns (☏ 800/283–4678)
Econo Lodge (☏ 800/553–2666)
Friendship Inns (☏ 800/453–4511)
Motel 6 (☏ 800/437–7486)

Rodeway (☏ 800/228–2000)
Super 8 (☏ 800/848–8888)

State Tourist Information

Alabama (☏ 800/252-2262)
Alaska*
Arkansas (☏ 800/643–8383)
California (☏ 800/862–2543)
Colorado (☏ 800/433–2656)
Connecticut (☏ 800/282–6863)
Delaware (☏ 800/441–8846)
Florida*
Georgia (☏ 800/847–4842)
Hawaii*
Idaho (☏ 800/847–4843)
Illinois (☏ 800/223–0121)
Indiana (☏ 800/289–6646)
Iowa (☏ 800/345–4692)
Kansas (☏ 800/252–6727)
Kentucky (☏ 800/225–8747)
Louisiana (☏ 800/334–8626)
Maine (☏ 800/533–9595)
Maryland (☏ 800/543–1036)
Massachusetts (☏ 800/447–6277)
Michigan (☏ 800/543–2937)
Minnesota (☏ 800/657–3700)
Mississippi (☏ 800/927–6378)
Missouri (☏ 800/877–1234)
Montana (☏ 800/541–1447)
Nebraska (☏ 800/228–4307)
Nevada (☏ 800/237–0774)
New Hampshire (☏ 800/258–3608)
New Jersey (☏ 800/537–7397)
New Mexico (☏ 800/545–2040)
New York (☏ 800/225–5697)
North Carolina (☏ 800/847–4862)
North Dakota (☏ 800/435–5063 or 800/437–2077)
Ohio (☏ 800/282–5393)
Oklahoma (☏ 800/652–6552)
Oregon (☏ 800/547–7842)
Pennsylvania (☏ 800/847–4872)
Rhode Island (☏ 800/556–2484)
South Carolina (☏ 800/346–3634)
South Dakota (☏ 800/732–5682)
Tennessee (☏ 800/836–6200)
Texas (☏ 800/888–8839)
Utah (☏ 800/882–4847)
Vermont (☏ 800/837–6668)
Virginia (☏ 800/847–4882)
Washington (☏ 800/544–1800)
Washington, DC (☏ 800/422–8644)
West Virginia (☏ 800/225–5982)
Wisconsin (☏ 800/432–8747)
Wyoming (☏ 800/225–5996)

*See state sections in the regional chapters above for state tourist office numbers that are not toll-free.

Mileages between Major U.S. Cities

	Abuquerque	Atlanta	Boston	Chicago	Cincinnati	Cleveland	Dallas	Denver	Houston	Kansas City	Los Angeles
Albuquerque	-	1409	2225	1343	1402	1608	666	446	876	818	790
Atlanta	1409	-	1105	703	466	715	791	1404	800	801	2199
Boston	2225	1105	-	1018	861	657	1765	2006	1857	1414	3007
Chicago	1343	703	1018	-	296	365	940	1013	1107	511	2014
Cincinnati	1402	466	861	296	-	249	943	1195	1079	592	2192
Cleveland	1608	715	657	365	249	-	1193	1354	1328	797	2355
Dallas	666	791	1765	940	943	1193	-	825	241	523	1440
Denver	446	1404	2006	1013	1195	1354	825	-	1075	606	1004
Houston	876	800	1857	1107	1079	1328	241	1075	-	764	1545
Kansas City	818	801	1414	511	592	797	523	606	764	-	1610
Los Angeles	790	2199	3007	2014	2192	2355	1440	1004	1545	1610	-
Memphis	1004	401	1309	533	487	736	456	1113	592	474	1798
Miami	2009	695	1524	1388	1149	1251	1342	2088	1215	1485	2759
Minneapolis	1255	1121	1435	417	713	782	962	916	1202	437	917
New Orleans	1178	473	1529	928	818	1067	511	1398	350	842	1894
New York	2002	878	226	814	634	453	1538	1802	1630	1192	2803
Orlando	1770	446	1314	1149	912	1041	1104	1850	976	1247	2521
Philadelphia	1949	779	326	798	581	437	1462	1742	1554	1139	2738
Phoenix	463	1859	2687	1805	1865	2071	1068	832	1173	1280	372
Portland, OR	1411	2599	3179	2126	2370	2466	2125	1241	2366	1796	963
St. Louis	1050	555	1175	293	352	558	647	852	819	249	1840
Salt Lake	646	1876	2396	1403	1647	1743	1290	518	1500	1073	689
San Francisco	1095	2505	3125	2132	2376	2472	1761	1247	1923	1802	381
Seattle	1463	2651	3085	2067	2328	2432	2117	1293	2418	1848	1136
Washington, DC	1875	641	462	733	488	377	1323	1649	1415	1045	2665

Memphis	Miami	Minneapolis	New Orleans	New York	Orlando	Philadelphia	Phoenix	Portland, OR	St. Louis	Salt Lake	San Francisco	Seattle	Washington, D.C.
1008	2009	1255	1178	2002	1770	1949	463	1411	1050	646	1095	1463	1875
401	685	1121	473	878	446	779	1859	2599	555	1876	2505	2651	641
1309	1524	1435	1529	226	1314	326	2687	3119	1175	2396	3125	3085	462
533	1388	417	928	814	1149	798	1805	2126	293	1403	2132	2067	733
487	1149	713	818	634	912	581	1865	2370	352	1647	2376	2328	488
736	1251	782	1067	453	1041	437	2071	2466	558	1743	2472	2432	377
456	1342	962	511	1538	1104	1462	1068	2125	647	1290	1761	2177	1323
1113	2088	916	1398	1802	1850	1742	832	1241	852	518	1247	1293	1649
592	1215	1202	350	1630	976	1554	1173	2366	819	1500	1923	2418	1415
474	1485	437	842	1192	1247	1139	1280	1796	249	1073	1802	1848	1045
1798	2759	917	1894	2803	2521	2738	372	963	1840	689	381	1136	2665
-	1045	848	398	1082	807	1006	1471	2276	286	1553	2104	2328	867
1045	-	1805	887	1298	245	1203	2387	3284	1239	2561	3137	3336	1066
848	1805	-	1243	1231	1567	1215	1718	1737	575	1264	1994	1651	1150
398	887	1243	-	1302	649	1226	1512	2635	681	1802	2272	2687	1087
1082	1298	1231	1302	-	1088	95	2465	2915	952	2192	2921	2881	237
807	245	1567	649	1088	-	994	2149	3046	1061	2322	2899	3098	856
1006	1203	1215	1226	95	994	-	2412	2899	899	2176	2905	2865	142
1471	2387	1718	1512	2465	2149	2412	-	1333	1513	673	750	1489	2337
2276	3284	1737	2635	2915	3046	2899	1333	-	2048	765	634	173	2835
286	1239	575	681	952	1061	899	1513	2048	-	1324	2054	2100	806
1553	2561	1264	1802	2192	2322	2176	673	765	1324	-	735	817	2111
2104	3137	1994	2272	2921	2899	2905	750	634	2054	735	-	807	2841
2328	3336	1651	2687	2881	3098	2865	1489	173	2100	817	807	-	2800
867	1066	1150	1087	237	856	142	2337	2835	806	2111	2841	2800	-

INDEX

A

B

Durham, NC, *398, 399, 401–402*

E

F

I

L

M

O

P

Q

R

S

U

Y

Z

Fodor's Travel Publications

Available at bookstores everywhere, or call 1-800-533-6478, 24 hours a day.

Gold Guides

U.S.

Alaska
Arizona
Boston
California
Cape Cod, Martha's Vineyard, Nantucket
The Carolinas & the Georgia Coast
Chicago
Colorado
Florida
Hawaii
Las Vegas, Reno, Tahoe
Los Angeles
Maine, Vermont, New Hampshire
Maui
Miami & the Keys
New England
New Orleans
New York City
Pacific North Coast
Philadelphia & the Pennsylvania Dutch Country
The Rockies
San Diego
San Francisco
Santa Fe, Taos, Albuquerque
Seattle & Vancouver
The South
U.S. & British Virgin Islands
USA
Virginia & Maryland
Waikiki
Washington, D.C.

Foreign

Australia & New Zealand
Austria
The Bahamas
Bermuda
Budapest
Canada
Cancún, Cozumel, Yucatán Peninsula
Caribbean
China
Costa Rica, Belize, Guatemala
Cuba
The Czech Republic & Slovakia
Eastern Europe
Egypt
Europe
Florence, Tuscany & Umbria
France
Germany
Great Britain
Greece
Hong Kong
India
Ireland
Israel
Italy
Japan
Kenya & Tanzania
Korea
London
Madrid & Barcelona
Mexico
Montréal & Québec City
Moscow, St. Petersburg, Kiev
The Netherlands, Belgium & Luxembourg
New Zealand
Norway
Nova Scotia, New Brunswick, Prince Edward Island
Paris
Portugal
Provence & the Riviera
Scandinavia
Scotland
Singapore
South America
South Pacific
Southeast Asia
Spain
Sweden
Switzerland
Thailand
Tokyo
Toronto
Turkey
Vienna & the Danube

Fodor's Special-Interest Guides

Branson
Caribbean Ports of Call
The Complete Guide to America's National Parks
Condé Nast Traveler Caribbean Resort and Cruise Ship Finder
Cruises and Ports of Call
Fodor's London Companion
France by Train
Halliday's New England Food Explorer
Healthy Escapes
Italy by Train
Kodak Guide to Shooting Great Travel Pictures
Shadow Traffic's New York Shortcuts and Traffic Tips
Sunday in New York
Sunday in San Francisco
Walt Disney World, Universal Studios and Orlando
Walt Disney World for Adults
Where Should We Take the Kids? California
Where Should We Take the Kids? Northeast

Special Series

Affordables

Caribbean

Europe

Florida

France

Germany

Great Britain

Italy

London

Paris

Fodor's Bed & Breakfasts and Country Inns

America's Best B&Bs

California's Best B&Bs

Canada's Great Country Inns

Cottages, B&Bs and Country Inns of England and Wales

The Mid-Atlantic's Best B&Bs

New England's Best B&Bs

The Pacific Northwest's Best B&Bs

The South's Best B&Bs

The Southwest's Best B&Bs

The Upper Great Lakes' Best B&Bs

The Berkeley Guides

California

Central America

Eastern Europe

Europe

France

Germany & Austria

Great Britain & Ireland

Italy

London

Mexico

Pacific Northwest & Alaska

Paris

San Francisco

Compass American Guides

Arizona

Chicago

Colorado

Hawaii

Hollywood

Las Vegas

Maine

Manhattan

Montana

New Mexico

New Orleans

Oregon

San Francisco

Santa Fe

South Carolina

South Dakota

Southwest

Texas

Utah

Virginia

Washington

Wine Country

Wisconsin

Wyoming

Fodor's Español

California

Caribe Occidental

Caribe Oriental

Gran Bretaña

Londres

Mexico

Nueva York

Paris

Fodor's Exploring Guides

Australia

Boston & New England

Britain

California

Caribbean

China

Egypt

Florence & Tuscany

Florida

France

Germany

Ireland

Israel

Italy

Japan

London

Mexico

Moscow & St. Petersburg

New York City

Paris

Prague

Provence

Rome

San Francisco

Scotland

Singapore & Malaysia

Spain

Thailand

Turkey

Venice

Fodor's Flashmaps

Boston

New York

San Francisco

Washington, D.C.

Fodor's Pocket Guides

Acapulco

Atlanta

Barbados

Jamaica

London

New York City

Paris

Prague

Puerto Rico

Rome

San Francisco

Washington, D.C.

Rivages Guides

Bed and Breakfasts of Character and Charm in France

Hotels and Country Inns of Character and Charm in France

Hotels and Country Inns of Character and Charm in Italy

Short Escapes

Country Getaways in Britain

Country Getaways in France

Country Getaways Near New York City

Fodor's Sports

Golf Digest's Best Places to Play

Skiing USA

USA Today The Complete Four Sport Stadium Guide

Fodor's Vacation Planners

Great American Learning Vacations

Great American Sports & Adventure Vacations

Great American Vacations

National Parks and Seashores of the East

National Parks of the West

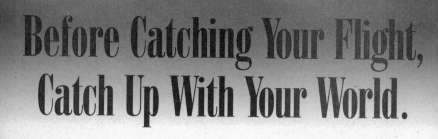

Read each coupon before using. Discounts apply only to the items and terms specified in the offer at participating locations.

For reservations call:
1-800-DAYS INN

- Available at participating properties.
- This coupon cannot be combined with any other special discount offer.
- Limit one coupon per room, per stay.
- Offer expires December 31, 1996.

TASTE PUBLICATIONS INTERNATIONAL

Audio Diversions

Where Books Talk and People Listen.

Audio Diversions offers one of the broadest collections of Literature for Listening currently available. With more than 2,300 titles carefully drawn from among the latest travelbooks and the best in adventure, mystery, biography, business, motivational, inspirational and self help books, Audio Diversions is sure to have what you need to purchase or rent. Rentals come with addressed and stamped packages for easy return. $5.60 for shipping and handling. Call **1-800-628-6145**. Ask for **CLUB 3B**.

TASTE PUBLICATIONS INTERNATIONAL

Valid in the U.S.A. only. Once redeemed, this certificate is void. Certificate subject to Alamo's conditions at the time of rental. Certificate may only be applied toward the basic rate which does not include taxes and other optional items. No refund will be given on any unused portion of the certificate. Certificate is not redeemable for cash. Certificate may not be mechanically reproduced and will not be replaced if expired or lost. Offer not valid: 10/5/95-10/7/95, 11/22/95-11/25/95, 12/14/95-12/30/95, 2/15/96-2/17/96, 4/4/96-4/6/96, 5/23/96-5/25/96, 7/4/96-7/6/96, 7/18/96-8/17/96, 8/29/96-8/31/96, 10/10/96-10/12/96 and 11/27/96-11/29/96.

TASTE PUBLICATIONS INTERNATIONAL

TASTE PUBLICATIONS INTERNATIONAL

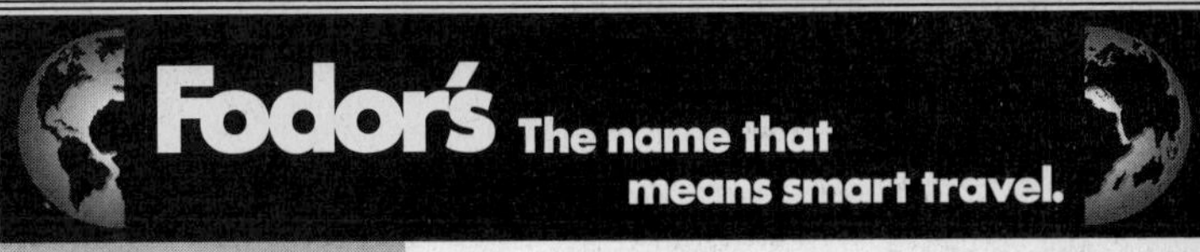

STAY WITH US AND SAVE $$$

Offer expires September 30, 1996

You're invited to stay at any of over 600 Howard Johnson Plazas, Hotels, Park Square Inns, Lodges and HoJo Inns throughout the United States, Canada and Mexico. And if you present this certificate upon check-in, we'll take 10% off the regular room rate for your stay of up to 7 nights. Rates start as low as $29.00 and kids always stay free. So make your reservations today. Call **1-800-I-GO-HOJO** and ask for the 10% TRAVELDEAL discount.

For reservations, call
1-800-I-GO-HOJO
(1-800-446-4656)
or your local travel agent.

FREE CAMPING STAY

Offer expires September 30, 1996

Camp free when you rent a KOA Deal Motor Home from Cruise America. Call **1-800-327-7778** and request a KOA Deal Motor Home rental and learn how to camp free at participating KOA Kampgrounds.

$10.00 OFF A WEEKLY RENTAL!

Offer expires September 30, 1996

You can save an extra $10.00 off Avis weekly rates when you rent any Intermediate through Full Size 4-door car for a week. Just present this coupon at an Avis corporate or participating licensee location in the U.S. It's good through September 30, 1996.

To take advantage of this offer, call your travel consultant, or the Avis Special Promotion reservation number: **1-800-831-8000**. Be sure to mention your Avis Worldwide Discount (AWD) number: **A291813**. Subject to Terms and Conditions on reverse side.

Coupon #MUGD716

ONE HOUR MOTOPHOTO

50% OFF

Offer expires September 30, 1996

One Hour MotoPhoto invites you to enjoy 50% off processing and printing.

Coupon valid only at participating locations. Limit one roll; standard size prints only. Coupon may not be combined with any other coupon or discount.

Remove the coupon you wish to use.

STAY AND SAVE $$$

- Over 600 convenient locations
- Choice of luxurious Plazas, full-service Hotels, classic Lodges, or economical HoJo Inns
- Children under 18 always stay free
- Special discounts for Seniors
- Certificate must be presented upon check-in
- Advance reservations required

For reservations, call

1-800-I-GO-HOJO

or your local travel agent

TASTE PUBLICATIONS INTERNATIONAL

KOA has over 550 locations throughout the U.S. and Canada.

Cruise America and Cruise Canada have over 100 rental centers.

TASTE PUBLICATIONS INTERNATIONAL

Terms and Conditions — Offer valid on an Intermediate (Group C) through a Full Size 4-door (Group E) car for a 5-day rental. Coupon must be surrendered at time of rental; one per rental. May be used in conjunction with Taste Publications rates and discounts. May not be used in conjunction with any other coupon, promotion or offer. Coupon valid at Avis corporate and participating licensee locations in the continental U.S. Offer not available during holiday and other blackout periods. Offer may not be available on all rates at all times. Cars subject to availability. Taxes, local government surcharges, and optional items, such as LDW, additional driver fee and refueling, are extra. Renter must meet Avis age, driver and credit requirements. Minimum age is 25. Offer expires September 30, 1996.

Rental Sales Agent Instructions At Checkout:

- In AWD, enter **A291813**. •In CPN, enter **MUGD716.**
- Complete this information: RA# ____________ Rental Location ____________
- Attach to COUPON tape.

TASTE PUBLICATIONS INTERNATIONAL

ONE HOUR
MOTOPHOTO®

TASTE PUBLICATIONS INTERNATIONAL

Coupons cannot be used in conjunction with other discount offers, for example, special promotional pricing.

Ramada Limiteds, Inns and Plaza Hotels offer you the value and accommodations you expect...And so much more! Over 800 convenient locations. Children under 18 always stay free. Non-smoking and handicap rooms available. For reservations call **1-800-228-2828**.

TASTE PUBLICATIONS INTERNATIONAL

UNITED ARTISTS

A self-addressed stamped envelope must be enclosed to process your order. No refunds or exchanges. Mail order only, not redeemable at box office. Passes have expiration dates, generally one year from purchase.

Name____________________

Address____________________

City__________ State ____ Zip ______

TASTE PUBLICATIONS INTERNATIONAL

Yours for only $19.95 plus $5.95 shipping and handling. Mail check or money order for $25.90 with coupon (IL residents add 8 3/4% sales tax) for each set to:

Joy International
3928 North Rockwell Street, Chicago, IL 60618

Name____________________

Address____________________

City____________________

State__________ Zip __________

003A **109/82** TASTE PUBLICATIONS INTERNATIONAL

Travel Discounters

Minimum ticket price	*Save*
$200.00	$25.00
$250.00	$50.00
$350.00	$75.00
$450.00	$100.00

TASTE PUBLICATIONS INTERNATIONAL

See reverse for order form.

If in doubt, please check with the establishment making the offer.

Life's great at Super 8.™

TASTE PUBLICATIONS INTERNATIONAL

Yours for only $4.99 plus $3.95 shipping and handling.
Mail check or money order for $8.94 with coupon
(IL residents add 8 3/4% sales tax) for each set to:
Joy International
3928 North Rockwell Street, Chicago, IL 60618

Name______________________________

Address____________________________

City_______________________________

State________________ Zip ___________

003A 109/82 TASTE PUBLICATIONS INTERNATIONAL

CPI Photo®
The 1-HR Photo Specialists
Over 600 locations nationwide

Call **1-800-366-3655**
for the location near you.

TASTE PUBLICATIONS INTERNATIONAL

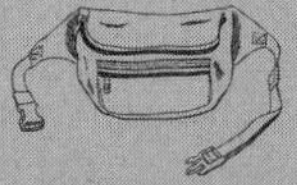

❏ Yes! I want to preserve and protect our National Parks by becoming a National Parks and Conservation Association Member.
❏ I enclose a check for $15.00 for my one-year membership.
❏ Charge my annual dues to my ❏ Visa ❏ MasterCard ❏ Amex

Acct. #: ______________________ Exp. Date: ________

Signature:__________________________

Name: _____________________________

Address: ___________________________

City: ________________ State: ______ Zip: ________

Phone: _____________________________

Please allow 6-8 weeks for delivery of your fanny pack and first issue of National Parks Magazine.

Make checks payable and mail to:
NPCA, 1776 Massachusetts Ave. NW, Washington, DC 20036-1904

TASTE PUBLICATIONS INTERNATIONAL

Fodor's and Taste Publications International cannot be responsible for acts of God, changes of ownership, unforeseen occurrences, closings and the like.

With your 10% **Fodor's Travelers' Discount**, the Choices - and savings - are better. So, call **1-800-4-CHOICE** today!

TASTE PUBLICATIONS INTERNATIONAL

Mail this coupon to:
National Audubon Society
Membership Data Center
P.O. Box 52529, Boulder, CO 80322-2529

Yes! Please enroll me as a 1-year member for $20.00 to the National Audubon Society.

Check one: ____Payment enclosed. ____Bill me later.

Name: ____________________________________

Address: ____________________________________

City: ____________________State: ______Zip: _________

5FDS4

TASTE PUBLICATIONS INTERNATIONAL

The Place
SUBWAY®
Where Fresh is the Taste.™

TASTE PUBLICATIONS INTERNATIONAL

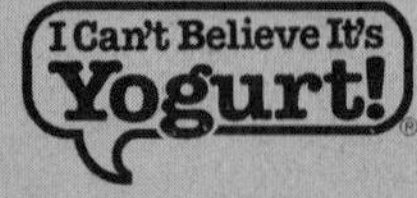

TASTE PUBLICATIONS INTERNATIONAL

Fodor's and Taste Publications will not be responsible if any establishment breaches its contract or refuses to accept coupons; however, Taste Publications will attempt to secure compliance.

We fix transmissions one thank you at a time.

TASTE PUBLICATIONS INTERNATIONAL

All The Difference In The World.™

Please note: Because of high competition in certain markets, occasionally promotional rates will be less than the discounted rate you are quoted. In those cases, it will be to your benefit to reserve at the promotional rate. Discount valid at participating locations only. Discounts apply to Economy through Full-Size cars.

TASTE PUBLICATIONS INTERNATIONAL

TASTE PUBLICATIONS INTERNATIONAL

The name that means smart travel.

SAFE FIT™

$5.00 OFF

Offer expires September 30, 1996

Save $5.00 on SAFE-FIT™ shoulder belt adjuster. Our soft padded SAFE-FIT™ allows any shoulder belt to be positioned comfortably and safely to fit the child who has outgrown the infant seat.

Retails for $15.00. Please enclose a check or money order for $11.95 (includes $1.95 for shipping and handling) with coupon and mail to: P.O. Box 730, Skyland, NC 28776.

CAMPING WORLD®

$5.00 OFF

Offer expires September 30, 1996

The One Accessory Every RV Needs.

With the world's largest selection of RV accessories and supplies, the Camping World catalog is a must for every RV. It's like having a store next door. Shop 24 hours a day, 7 days a week. Call today for a FREE catalog and receive $5.00 off your first order of $25.00 or more.

Call 1-800-845-7875

Mention Code 1A

1058 MC

Hertz

ONE CAR CLASS LEISURE UPGRADE

Offer expires September 30, 1996

Present this coupon at time of rental and receive a One Car Class Leisure Upgrade when you reserve a Compact 4-Door (Class B) through Full Size 2-Door (Class D) car on any Hertz Leisure Daily, Leisure Weekly or Leisure Weekend rates.

For reservations, call Hertz at **1-800-654-2210** and refer to **PC71702**. See reverse for important rental information. Restrictions apply. Advance reservations required.

BUSCH GARDENS.
WILLIAMSBURG, VA.
An Anheuser-Busch Theme Park.

SAVE UP TO $21.00

Valid thru 1996 operating season

Busch Gardens Williamsburg and Water Country USA invite you to enjoy $3.50 off the one-day regular or child's admission price.

For information on operating schedule call **1-800-722-8886**. See reverse for details.

If you encounter any difficulty using these coupons, please call Taste Publications International at (410) 825-3463. They will do their best to rectify the situation to your satisfaction.

SAFE FIT™

TASTE PUBLICATIONS INTERNATIONAL

TASTE PUBLICATIONS INTERNATIONAL

This offer may not be available at some times in locations especially during periods of peak demand. Standard blackout dates apply. This coupon has no cash value, must be surrendered at the time of rental pick-up and may not be used with any other coupon, offer, promotion, or discount. Hertz rate and rental conditions for the renting location apply and the car must be returned to the original renting location. Minimum rental age is 25 and Hertz standard driver qualifications apply. Only one coupon will be honored per rental transaction; taxes and optional items such as refueling are extra. For reservations, call Hertz at **1-800-654-2210** and refer to **PC71702**.

TASTE PUBLICATIONS INTERNATIONAL

BUSCH GARDENS.
WILLIAMSBURG, VA.
An Anheuser-Busch Theme Park.

Present this coupon when purchasing your ticket at any Busch Gardens Williamsburg or Water Country USA General Admission window to receive your discount on the regular one-day admission price. Children two and under are admitted FREE. Admission price includes all regularly scheduled rides, shows and attractions. This coupon has no cash value and cannot be used in conjunction with any other discount. Prices and schedule subject to change without notice. Busch Gardens Williamsburg and Water Country USA have a "no solicitation" policy. Limit six tickets per coupon.

1 2 3 4 5 6

Please circle number of admissions.

PLU# R364 C365

TASTE PUBLICATIONS INTERNATIONAL

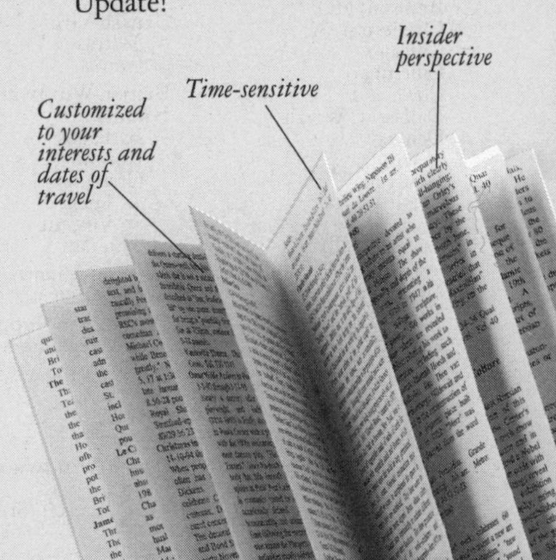

Insider perspective
Time-sensitive
Customized to your interests and dates of travel

DESTINATIONS

Worldview covers more than 160 destinations worldwide. Choose the destination(s) that match your itinerary from the list below:

Europe
- Amsterdam
- Athens
- Barcelona
- Berlin
- Brussels
- Budapest
- Copenhagen
- Dublin
- Edinburgh
- Florence
- Frankfurt
- French Riviera
- Geneva
- Glasgow
- Lausanne
- Lisbon
- London
- Madrid
- Milan
- Moscow
- Munich
- Oslo
- Paris
- Prague
- Provence
- Rome
- Salzburg
- Seville
- St. Petersburg
- Stockholm
- Venice
- Vienna
- Zurich

United States (Mainland)
- Albuquerque
- Atlanta
- Atlantic City
- Baltimore
- Boston
- Branson, MO
- Charleston, SC
- Chicago
- Cincinnati
- Cleveland
- Dallas/Ft. Worth
- Denver
- Detroit
- Houston
- Indianapolis
- Kansas City
- Las Vegas
- Los Angeles
- Memphis
- Miami
- Milwaukee
- Minneapolis/St. Paul
- Nashville
- New Orleans
- New York City
- Orlando
- Palm Springs
- Philadelphia
- Phoenix
- Pittsburgh
- Portland
- Reno/Lake Tahoe
- St. Louis
- Salt Lake City
- San Antonio
- San Diego
- San Francisco
- Santa Fe
- Seattle
- Tampa
- Washington, DC

Alaska
- Alaskan Destinations

Hawaii
- Honolulu
- Island of Hawaii
- Kauai
- Maui

Canada
- Quebec City
- Montreal
- Ottawa
- Toronto
- Vancouver

Bahamas
- Abaco
- Eleuthera/ Harbour Island
- Exuma
- Freeport
- Nassau & Paradise Island

Bermuda
- Bermuda Countryside
- Hamilton

British Leeward Islands
- Anguilla
- Antigua & Barbuda
- St. Kitts & Nevis

British Virgin Islands
- Tortola & Virgin Gorda

British Windward Islands
- Barbados
- Dominica
- Grenada
- St. Lucia
- St. Vincent
- Trinidad & Tobago

Cayman Islands
- The Caymans

Dominican Republic
- Santo Domingo

Dutch Leeward Islands
- Aruba
- Bonaire
- Curacao

Dutch Windward Island
- St. Maarten/St. Martin

French West Indies
- Guadeloupe
- Martinique
- St. Barthelemy

Jamaica
- Kingston
- Montego Bay
- Negril
- Ocho Rios

Puerto Rico
- Ponce
- San Juan

Turks & Caicos
- Grand Turk/ Providenciales

U.S. Virgin Islands
- St. Croix
- St. John
- St. Thomas

Mexico
- Acapulco
- Cancun & Isla Mujeres
- Cozumel
- Guadalajara
- Ixtapa & Zihuatanejo
- Los Cabos
- Mazatlan
- Mexico City
- Monterrey
- Oaxaca
- Puerto Vallarta

South/Central America
- Buenos Aires
- Caracas
- Rio de Janeiro
- San Jose, Costa Rica
- Sao Paulo

Middle East
- Istanbul
- Jerusalem

Australia & New Zealand
- Auckland
- Melbourne
- South Island
- Sydney

China
- Beijing
- Guangzhou
- Shanghai

Japan
- Kyoto
- Nagoya
- Osaka
- Tokyo
- Yokohama

Pacific Rim/Other
- Bali
- Bangkok
- Hong Kong & Macau
- Manila
- Seoul
- Singapore
- Taipei

INTERESTS

For your personalized Travel Update, choose the eight (8) categories you're most interested in from the following list:

1. **Business Services**	Fax & Overnight Mail, Computer Rentals, Protocol, Secretarial, Messenger, Translation Services
Dining	
2. **All-Day Dining**	Breakfast & Brunch, Cafes & Tea Rooms, Late-Night Dining
3. **Local Cuisine**	Every Price Range—from Budget Restaurants to the Special Splurge
4. **European Cuisine**	Continental, French, Italian
5. **Asian Cuisine**	Chinese, Far Eastern, Japanese, Other
6. **Americas Cuisine**	American, Mexican & Latin
7. **Nightlife**	Bars, Dance Clubs, Casinos, Comedy Clubs, Ethnic, Pubs & Beer Halls
8. **Entertainment**	Theater – Comedy, Drama, Musicals, Dance, Ticket Agencies
9. **Music**	Classical, Opera, Traditional & Ethnic, Jazz & Blues, Pop, Rock
10. **Children's Activites**	Events, Attractions
11. **Tours**	Local Tours, Day Trips, Overnight Excursions
12. **Exhibitions, Festivals & Shows**	Antiques & Flower, History & Cultural, Art Exhibitions, Fairs & Craft Shows, Music & Art Festivals
13. **Shopping**	Districts & Malls, Markets, Regional Specialties
14. **Fitness**	Bicycling, Health Clubs, Hiking, Jogging
15. **Recreational Sports**	Boating/Sailing, Fishing, Golf, Skiing, Snorkeling/Scuba, Tennis/Racket
16. **Spectator Sports**	Auto Racing, Baseball, Basketball, Golf, Football, Horse Racing, Ice Hockey, Soccer
17. **Event Highlights**	The best of what's happening during the dates of your trip.
18. **Sightseeing**	Sights, Buildings, Monuments
19. **Museums**	Art, Cultural
20. **Transportation**	Taxis, Car Rentals, Airports, Public Transportation
21. **General Info**	Overview, Holidays, Currency, Tourist Info

Please note that content will vary by season, destination, and length of stay.

Name
Address
City **State** **Country** **ZIP**
Tel # ( ) - **Fax #** ( ) -
Title of this Fodor's guide:
Store and location where guide was purchased:

INDICATE YOUR DESTINATIONS/DATES: You can order up to three (3) destinations from the previous page. Fill in your arrival and departure dates for each destination. **Your Travel Update itinerary (all destinations selected) cannot exceed 30 days from beginning to end.**

		Month / Day		Month / Day
(Sample) **LONDON**	From:	**6 / 21**	To:	**6 / 30**
1	From:	/	To:	/
2	From:	/	To:	/
3	From:	/	To:	/

CHOOSE YOUR INTERESTS: Select up to eight (8) categories from the list of interest categories shown on the previous page and circle the numbers below:
1 2 3 4 5 6 7 8 9 10 11 12 13 14 15 16 17 18 19 20 21

CHOOSE WHEN YOU WANT YOUR TRAVEL UPDATE DELIVERED (Check one):
❑ Please send my Travel Update immediately.
❑ Please hold my order until a few weeks before my trip to include the most up-to-date information.
Completed orders will be sent within 48 hours. Allow 7–10 days for U.S. mail delivery.

ADD UP YOUR ORDER HERE. SPECIAL OFFER FOR FODOR'S PURCHASERS ONLY!

	Suggested Retail Price	Your Price	This Order
First destination ordered	~~$ 9.95~~	$ 7.95	$ 7.95
Second destination (if applicable)	~~$ 6.95~~	$ 4.95	+
Third destination (if applicable)	~~$ 6.95~~	$ 4.95	+

DELIVERY CHARGE (Check one and enter amount below)

	Within U.S. & Canada	Outside U.S. & Canada
First Class Mail	❑ $2.50	❑ $5.00
FAX	❑ $5.00	❑ $10.00
Priority Delivery	❑ $15.00	❑ $27.00

ENTER DELIVERY CHARGE FROM ABOVE: +

TOTAL: $

METHOD OF PAYMENT IN U.S. FUNDS ONLY (Check one):
❑ AmEx ❑ MC ❑ Visa ❑ Discover ❑ Personal Check (U. S. & Canada only)
❑ Money Order/International Money Order

Make check or money order payable to: Fodor's Worldview Travel Update
Credit Card_/_/_/_/_/_/_/_/_/_/_/_/_/_/_/_/_/_/ **Expiration Date:**_/_

Authorized Signature

SEND THIS COMPLETED FORM WITH PAYMENT TO:
Fodor's Worldview Travel Update, 114 Sansome Street, Suite 700, San Francisco, CA 94104

OR CALL OR FAX US 24-HOURS A DAY
Telephone **1-800-799-9609** • Fax **1-800-799-9619** (From within the U.S. & Canada)
(Outside the U.S. & Canada: Telephone 415-616-9988 • Fax 415-616-9989)

(Please have this guide in front of you when you call so we can verify purchase.)
Code: FTG Offer valid until 12/31/97